MOON
HANDBOOKS

WESTERN CANADA

ANDREW HEMPSTEAD

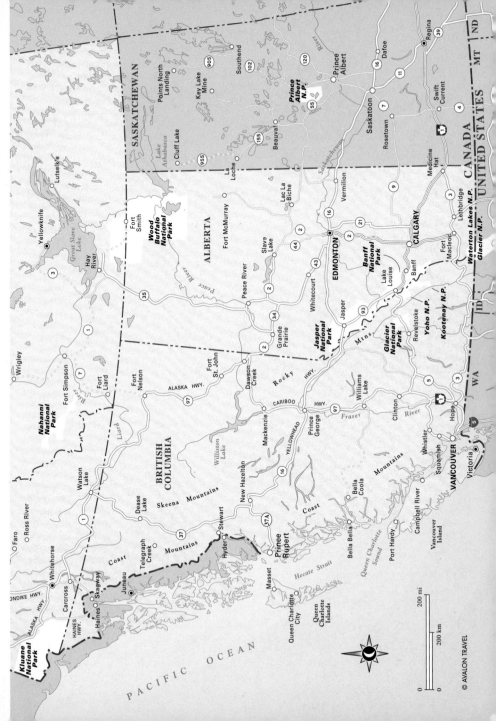

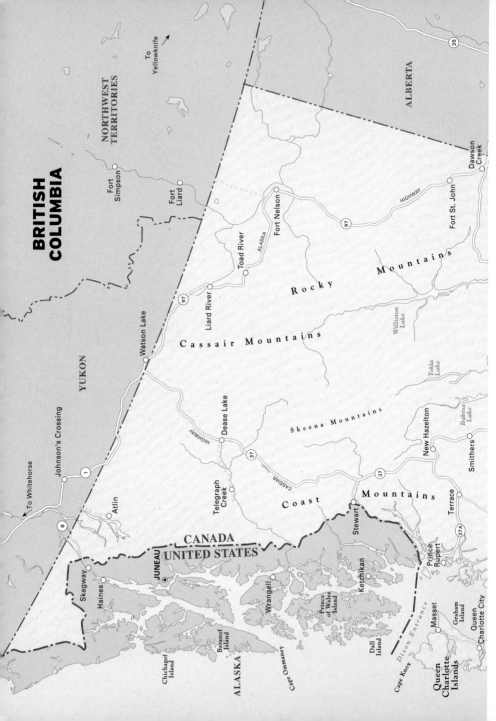

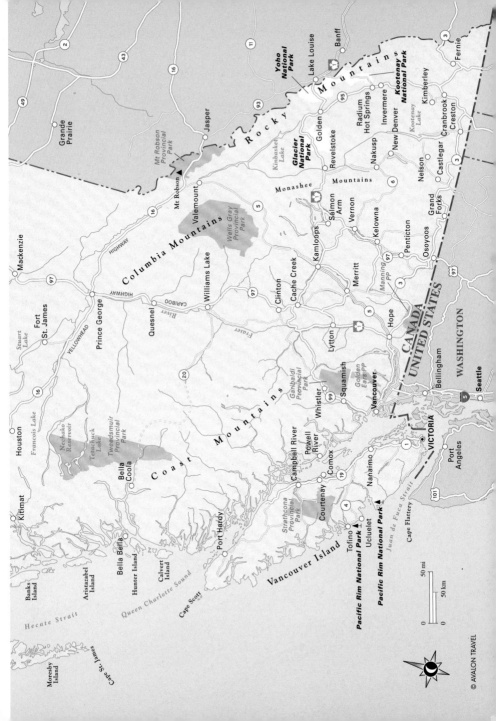

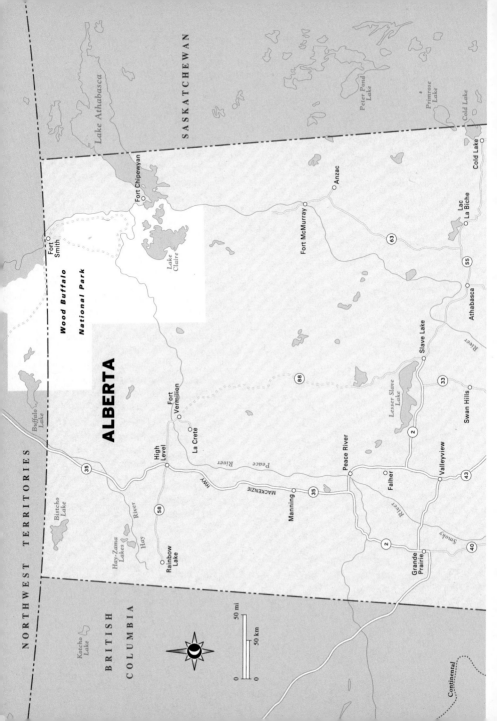

Discover
Western Canada

Comprising two provinces (British Columbia and Alberta) and two territories (Northwest Territories and Yukon Territory), western Canada stretches from the Pacific Ocean to the prairies and north beyond the Arctic Circle. Some landscapes are well known – the old-growth forests of the west coast, the lakes and peaks of the Canadian Rockies, and the tundra of the far north. But there are also many surprises – a desert, orchard-filled valleys, strangely formed badlands, and long stretches of sandy beaches. Best of all, most of this land is unspoiled wilderness, with abundant wildlife and the opportunity for unlimited adventure.

For many visitors, Vancouver, western Canada's largest city, is their first taste of Canada. This vibrant harbor city is a splendid conglomeration of old and new architectural marvels, parks, and gardens. Surprisingly, the region's two largest cities, Vancouver and Calgary, are not the provincial capitals. In British Columbia, this honor goes to stately Victoria, perched at the southeastern tip of Vancouver Island. Meanwhile, seemingly a world away from the ocean, are Calgary and Edmonton, Alberta's two major population centers. Calgary is best known as home to the world-famous Calgary Stampede – a Western wingding of epic proportions – while Edmonton is notable for some of Canada's finest cultural facilities. But most of the western Canada you'll want to see is

found away from the cities, in the surrounding vastness. The protected coastal waterways, the rugged west coast of Vancouver Island, the intriguing Queen Charlotte Islands, the famously scenic Canadian Rockies, and the remote northern latitudes offer experiences to keep even the most jaded jet-setter in awe.

It is difficult to capture the true majesty of western Canada with simple words and pictures. They can't re-create the fragrant smells of a flower-filled alpine meadow, the feel of a fresh sea breeze along a coastal trail, the sense of awe as you watch a grazing grizzly bear, or the adrenaline rush of a bucking bull at the Calgary Stampede. They can't express the thrill of hooking a trophy-size salmon, the solitude of an early-morning mountain hike, or the excitement of white-water rafting. They can't communicate the tranquility of a rustic lakeside cabin or the flavor of a tender cut of Alberta beef. The written word, or even the most appealing images, can't truly convey any of these experiences. You have only one option, and that is to discover the wonders of western Canada firsthand.

Planning Your Trip

▶ WHERE TO GO

Vancouver and Vicinity

Let your mind fill with images of dramatic, snowcapped mountains rising high above a city clinging to the coastline, a downtown core of historic red brick buildings and steel-and-glass skyscrapers, and manicured suburbs fringed by golden sandy beaches and rocky shorelines. These are the magnificent images of Vancouver, British Columbia's largest city. And once you've finished exploring the city, adventures beckon north along the aptly named Sunshine Coast and northeast in the famously classy resort town of Whistler.

Vancouver Island

Victoria, the elegant capital of British Columbia, couldn't be more different than

IF YOU HAVE

ONE WEEKEND: Spend your time in Vancouver and Whistler.

ONE WEEK: Add Vancouver Island and Banff National Park.

TWO WEEKS: Add the Southern Interior and Calgary.

Inner Harbour, Victoria

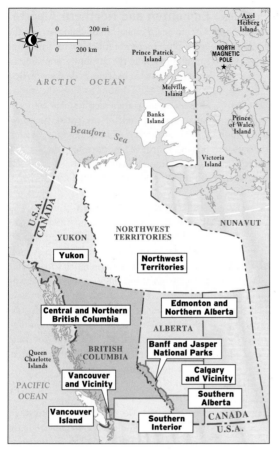

that begins in the gorgeous Okanagan Valley, which is dotted with orchards and wineries. Between the Okanagan and Alberta is a series of brawny mountain ranges. Alpine snowfields feed mighty rivers and massive lakes, creating a recreational playground for anglers, canoeists, and kayakers. As you make your way east from the Kootenay region, the mountains become more dramatic, especially those protected by Yoho National Park.

Central and Northern British Columbia

The central and northern portions of British Columbia are set aside for the adventurous. In the southeast are glaciated mountain ranges, while further west the landscape is dominated by sagebrush-covered hills. To the north is an untamed forested wilderness where opportunities to catch trophy-sized trout are almost

its near neighbor Vancouver. The city projects an intriguing mixture of images—a combination of century-old buildings, ancient totem poles sprouting from shady parks, and exotic restaurants. Beyond the city limits, the rest of Vancouver Island beckons with an array of outdoor experiences that range from hiking the famous West Coast Trail to surfing the waves of Long Beach.

Southern Interior

Cutting a swathe across the southern portion of British Columbia is a diverse region

endless. For a real adventure, jump aboard a ferry at Prince Rupert for the Queen Charlotte Islands, where totem pole villages abandoned by the fearless Haida are slowly being reclaimed by nature.

Calgary and Vicinity

Yahoo! Welcome to cow town, where the Calgary Stampede transforms the city into party central, western style. Before rushing west from Calgary to Banff along the TransCanada Highway, consider detouring through the less-crowded mountains of Kananaskis Country, heading east into Dinosaur Valley, home to the world's most extensive dinosaur fossil beds, or discovering picturesque villages like Markerville.

Southern Alberta

Encompassing a wide swathe of the province south from Calgary, this region has a little of everything, but is compact enough to be a destination in itself. In the west is Waterton Lakes National Park, laced with walking trails. Just an hour's drive from the park and you are surrounded by prairie and attractions like the Remington Carriage Museum and the intriguing history of Head-Smashed-In Buffalo Jump.

Banff and Jasper National Parks

Banff and Jasper: the crown jewels in Canada's national park system and home to the world's most photographed lakes. But what are these parks—originally established as tourist attractions—really like? Lake Louise, Moraine Lake, the Icefields Parkway, and Maligne Lake are just some of the parks' awe-inspiring highlights. Visiting each of these spots is definitely part of the Canadian Rockies experience, but the parks extend well beyond the reach of the regular tour bus crowd.

Edmonton and Northern Alberta

The provincial capital of Edmonton lies near the geographical center of Alberta, with attractions spread throughout the city limits, providing an excuse to leave the confines of downtown. Best known is West Edmonton Mall, the world's largest shopping and entertainment complex. Encompassing half of the entire province, northern Alberta is as much adventure as vacation. It's a forested landscape, punctuated by roads leading to small service towns, historic trading posts, and fish-filled lakes.

Northwest Territories

It's a long drive north from Alberta to the Northwest Territories, but getting there is just the beginning of the adventure. A vacation this far north is not so much about seeing specific sights, but more about simply being here and soaking up the surroundings of one of the world's last great wildernesses. The best places to do this are the national parks of Wood Buffalo and Nahanni, but you can enjoy the surroundings in the extensive territorial park system.

Yukon

Separated from the Northwest Territories by the Mackenzie Mountains and bordered to the west by Alaska, the Yukon is a continuation

camping in Banff National Park

Drumheller, in Dinosaur Valley, east of Calgary

Dawson City, in the Yukon

of surrounding northern wilderness. Many visitors pass through on their way to Alaska, but I encourage you to linger and explore the natural wonders of the national parks and the history of the world's most famous gold rush town, Dawson City. Beyond here, the Dempster Highway leads beyond the Arctic Circle almost to the Arctic Ocean.

▶ WHEN TO GO

Deciding when in the year you'll be visiting western Canada usually depends on your own schedule, but the following thoughts may help you decide the best time to visit.

The high season for travel to western Canada is most definitely summer (July and August). This is the time of year when parks come alive with campers, lakes and streams with anglers, mountains with hikers, woods with wildlife, and roadsides with stalls selling fresh produce. Summer daytime temperatures in Vancouver average a pleasant 23°C (73°F), while hot spots like southern Alberta experience temperatures in the 30s (86–102°F) on many days.

Unless you're governed by a schedule (such as traveling with school-aged children), spring and fall are excellent times to visit western

Canada. While April–June is considered a shoulder season, in many ways the region is at its blooming best in spring, when crowds are at a minimum, the days are long, and lodging rates are reduced.

Fall (mid-September–November) can be a delight, especially September, with its lingering warm temperatures and a noticeable decrease in crowds immediately after the long weekend (at the beginning of the month).

The major cities—Vancouver, Victoria, Calgary, and Edmonton—can be visited year-round, with some outdoor activities—golfing, biking, hiking, and more—possible in the dead of winter on Vancouver Island. Alpine resorts begin opening in December and most have seasons extending through April.

Kicking Horse Mountain Resort, near Golden, in southern British Columbia

▶ BEFORE YOU GO

Passports and Visas

To enter Canada, a passport is required by citizens and permanent residents of the United States. At press time, the U.S. government was developing alternatives to the traditional passport. For further information, see the website http://travel.state.gov/travel. For current entry requirements to Canada, check the Citizenship and Immigration Canada website (www.cic.gc.ca).

All other foreign visitors must have a valid passport and may need a visa or visitors permit depending on their country of residence and the vagaries of international politics. At present, visas are not required for citizens of the United States, British Commonwealth, or Western Europe. The standard entry permit is for six months, and you may be asked to show onward tickets or proof of sufficient funds to last you through your intended stay.

What to Take

You'll find little use for a suit and tie in western Canada. Instead, pack for the outdoors. At the top of your must-bring list should be walking or hiking boots. In summer, temperatures rarely drop below freezing anywhere in the region, so you don't need a down jacket or winter boots. But you should be geared up for a variety of weather conditions, especially at the change of seasons. For dining out, casual dress is accepted at all but the most upscale city and resort restaurants. Don't forget your swimsuit for taking a dip in the waters off Vancouver Island or soaking in a hot tub up at a ski resort.

Winter temperatures vary greatly throughout western Canada. Golfers hitting the links on Vancouver Island in January will undoubtedly be warmly dressed, but they *will* be golfing. In the rest of the region, January brings extremely cold temperatures. For this climate, you should plan to dress in layers, starting with long thermal underwear. If you're traveling from warmer climes, purchasing all the winter necessities once you've arrived is a good idea.

Electrical appliances from the United States work in Canada, but those from other parts of the world will require a current converter (transformer) to bring the voltage down. Many travel-size shavers, hairdryers, and irons have built-in converters.

Explore Western Canada

▶ THE BEST OF WESTERN CANADA

Covering the best of western Canada in two weeks is possible, but it requires some flying to reach the northern territories. If you had three weeks or more, this itinerary could be completed by road. Starting and ending in Vancouver, it requires a rental vehicle for the main portion of the trip, but it has been configured to keep driving to a minimum—around 4,000 kilometers (2,485 miles).

Day 1

Head north from Vancouver airport and loop around Point Grey to the Museum of Anthropology, a wonderful introduction to history of the Pacific Northwest. Duck through the old growth forest behind the museum to get a feel for the city's natural splendor. Check in to your downtown hotel and take a stroll around Canada Place and through Gastown to the Storyeum.

Day 2

Even if you hit the Stanley Park as the sun first rises, you'll find that many locals have beaten you on their morning jog. Catch the ferry to Vancouver Island and you'll be at colorful Butchart Gardens around lunchtime. The rest of the day is spent exploring Victoria's Inner Harbour on foot, including a visit to the Royal British Columbia Museum and Fairmont Empress.

Day 3

Before leaving the capital, take a walk through the lush forests of Goldstream Provincial Park. Drive north and take a whale-watching trip departing the boardwalk village of Tofino. Drive back to Nanaimo, catch the ferry back to Vancouver and drive the Sea to Sky Highway to Whistler.

Canada Place, Vancouver

Day 4

Activities at Whistler can be as energetic as whitewater rafting or as peaceful as riding the Whistler Gondola. Drive to Vernon. Experience the colorful resort village of Silver Star Mountain Resort, go for an afternoon swim in the crystal clear waters of Kalamalka Lake, and spend the night in Kelowna, where the Okanagan Wineries produce some of the country's best wine.

Day 5

Drive to Golden and take the gondola to the top of Kicking Horse Mountain Resort. Continue east into Yoho National Park where the beautiful Emerald Lake beckons. Spend the night in the village of Lake Louise.

Day 6

The best time to see Lake Louise in all her glory is early in the morning. From Lake Louise, it's a short drive to Moraine Lake, where you take to the water in a rented canoe. Continue to Banff via the quietly scenic Bow Valley Parkway. Explore the area around the town of Banff (the path to the top of Tunnel Mountain is a good choice for an easy walk).

Soak up the luxury of the Willow Stream Spa at the Fairmont Banff Springs.

Day 7

Leaving the mountains behind, make time to take in the Olympic legacy that is Canada Olympic Park before heading out to Calgary. If you have some time later in the day, also plan stops at Calgary Tower and the Glenbow Museum.

Day 8

Drive east from Calgary into Dinosaur Valley and Dinosaur Provincial Park. Continue the theme with a visit to the Royal Tyrrell Museum. Stay overnight in Drumheller or begin driving north and stay overnight in Red Deer.

Day 9

Continue north to Edmonton, where the highlights include the Royal Alberta Museum and Fort Edmonton Park. These can easily be seen in a day, but you'll also want to take a break from the official attractions to include a shopping trip to West Edmonton Mall.

Fairmont Banff Springs

BEARS, BISON, AND BELUGAS

Western Canada is renowned for its abundance of wildlife, and luckily for you much of it is accessible to casual observers. But for those who want to make wildlife viewing a focus of their travels, opportunities exist to see grizzly bears, whales, and bison.

BLACK, GRIZZLY, AND KERMODE BEARS

In British Columbia, black bears are very common, and you will most often see them while driving through forested regions such as the **Kootenays**. To view the **kermode,** an extremely rare subspecies of black bear with a white coat, you will need to travel to **Princess Royal Island**. Grizzly Bears are also widespread; **Fish Creek**, near Stewart, is a reliable viewing spot each August, when these magnificent creatures descend from the mountains to feed on salmon.

Black bears are commonly seen in forested regions of the Northwest Territories, and **Kluane National Park**, in the Yukon, is a remote wilderness where backcountry enthusiasts see grizzly bears, moose, caribou, and mountain goats.

Be sure to include bison on your wildlife-viewing adventure.

BISON, BIGHORN SHEEP, MUSK-OX AND CARIBOU

In Alberta, if you want to be *guaranteed* wildlife sightings, plan on spending time at **Elk Island National Park**. This small park east of Edmonton was created to save the bison species.

Bighorn sheep have a reserve set aside especially for them in **Kananaskis Country**, but you may also see sheep driving the roads to Mount Norquay or Lake Minnewanka, or in the south around Waterton Lakes.

In the far north, musk-ox are protected within **Aulavik National Park**. A trip to this park requires the services of a local guide.

Caribou are the most numerous of all northern mammals, migrating across the northern reaches of the continent in massive herds. The largest of these is the **Bluenose herd**, which summers in **Tuktut Nogait National Park**. More accessible is the **Porcupine herd**, which crosses the Dempster Highway each spring when traveling to Alaska's Arctic National Wildlife Refuge from the northern Yukon.

WHALES AND SALMON

Pacific gray whales migrate up and down the coast each spring and fall. Whale-watching trips depart from **Victoria** and **Tofino**, but on the **Queen Charlotte Islands**, you can watch from the comfort of your vehicle as they frolic in a shallow bay near Queen Charlotte City. **Humpback whales** and **orcas** are also sighted on organized whale-watching trips.

To see Arctic Canada's **beluga whales,** you'll need to fly north to Inuvik for a flightseeing trip, where you can see them frolicking in the Bering Sea.

Most people searching for salmon are looking to catch them, but you can watch them migrate up many tidal waterways in late summer, such as the **Capilano River** in Vancouver. North America's largest salmon run takes place every four years (2010, 2014, etc.) through October in the **Adams River**, attracting thousands of spectators to viewing platforms in **Roderick Haig-Brown Provincial Park**.

igloo-shaped church, Inuvik

Day 10

Edmonton is one of the world's largest northern cities, which makes it an ideal jumping-off point for excursions to the Northwest Territories and the Yukon. Begin with the former, by flying into Yellowknife. The sightseeing highlights here are the historic exhibits at the Prince of Wales Northern Heritage Centre and the eclectic streets of Old Town, but you'll also want dine on local game at the Wildcat Café.

Day 11

Fly north to Inuvik. From here it's a short charter flight to end-of-the-world Tuktoyaktuk, a small village where you can dip your toes in the Arctic Ocean. Return to Inuvik for the night.

Day 12

Fly south to Dawson City and spend the day exploring the gold-rush-era buildings of the Dawson Historical Complex National Historic Site. Then head out to the gold fields and try you hand at panning. Take an afternoon flight to Whitehorse, where you can visit the historic paddlesteamer SS Klondike tied up along the river.

Day 13

Return by air to Edmonton and drive west to Jasper National Park. Visit the enchanting Maligne Canyon and take a boat tour on super-scenic Maligne Lake. Spend the night at a cabin accommodation south of town.

Day 14

The drive between Jasper and your starting point, Vancouver, takes the best part of a day. By getting on the road early, there will be enough time to marvel at the magnificent mountain scenery protected by Mount Robson Provincial Park and explore the flower-filled meadows accessed along the Meadows in the Sky Parkway.

▶ WESTWARD BOUND: CALGARY TO VANCOUVER

Truckers make the trip between western Canada's two largest cities in 12 or so hours. Many travelers heading to Vancouver from Alberta also drive the route nonstop, while others overnight along the way. But you're on vacation, so plan on expanding the drive to a weeklong sojourn that will—eventually—get you to Vancouver. This itinerary could be combined with an "open-jaw" air ticket, that is fly into one city and out from another.

Day 1

Westbound from Calgary, you'll pass Canada Olympic Park, a good place to explore before hitting the road proper. In Banff National Park, you'll need to sort the scenic from the *really* scenic. Lake Louise and Moraine Lake are the natural highlights you won't want to miss; both are easily accessible from Lake Louise accommodations.

Day 2

Hopefully, you've followed my lead and made reservations for the bus to Lake O'Hara well in advance. This is one of western Canada's most spectacular hiking destinations. Spend the night at Emerald Lake, which is the perfect place for an evening stroll.

Day 3

Ride the Kicking Horse Mountain Resort gondola, then hit the highway for Glacier National Park. Even from the highway, this park is spectacular, so unless you're a keen hiker or it's getting late in the day, continue to Revelstoke, where the Meadows in the Sky Parkway climbs through Mount Revelstoke National Park. Spend the night at Revelstoke.

Day 4

Drive south from Revelstoke to Nelson. Break up the trip with a short detour to Sandon, British Columbia's only ghost town, and to Kokanee Creek Provincial Park to watch spawning kokanee. You'll find plenty of choices for dinner in Nelson, your overnight stop.

Day 5

Driving through the West Kootenays is a delight, although a roller coaster highway means the trip will take longer than you may imagine. Stop for a swim in Christina Lake en route to an Osoyoos accommodation.

Day 6

Today is an easy day in the southern Okanagan Valley. Visit the Desert Centre before it gets too hot, and then combine tasting sessions at local wineries with beach time down on Osoyoos Lake. Stay overnight at Penticton.

Day 7

Give the direct Coquihalla Highway a miss, and travel down the Fraser River Canyon to Hope. Suburban Vancouver is approaching, so if you feel like stalling the inevitable onslaught of city traffic, take a walk through the Othello–Quintette Tunnels.

the ghost town of Sandon

A WESTERN CANADIAN WINTER

If you enjoy winter sports, you could spend an entire season exploring western Canada. Here are just a few places to enjoy winter recreation, depending on where you're headed.

VANCOUVER

In Vancouver, suit up and head for **Grouse Mountain**, where the ski runs are lit for night skiing and the views back across British Columbia's largest city are breathtaking.

KELOWNA

Upon arrival in Kelowna, spend the afternoon browsing through town or visiting a local winery. Spend the night at **Silver Star Mountain Resort**, a fully self-contained resort, making sure to take a sleigh ride before dinner. The next day, hit the slopes and ski or snowboard the great terrain and enjoy the facilities of an outstanding on-hill village.

ROSSLAND

Experienced skiers looking to indulge in British Columbia's legendary powder will love a visit to Rossland, enjoying the deepest snow this side of a helicopter at **Red Mountain Resort**, a former gold mine and home to some of the area's most challenging lift-served runs.

BANFF

If you head to Banff from Rossland, make sure to stop for a soak at **Radium Hot Springs** along the way. Once in Banff, head out for a few nights at **Sunshine Village.** High above the treeline and accessible only by gondola, here you get to take advantage of the only on-hill accommodations in the mountain parks (the oversized outdoor hot tub is a bonus).

LAKE LOUISE

Join in the postcard view that is Lake Louise by trying ice skating at the rink on the lake in front of the chateau at the **Fairmont Chateau Lake Louise**, which is lit well into the night. You'll want to spend more than a few days here enjoying Canada's second largest alpine resort, but if you're short on time, be sure to at least ride the main chairlift, which takes you high above the tree line for magnificent views in all directions.

WHISTLER

Beautiful snowcapped peaks and crystal clear lakes coupled with a cosmopolitan village right in the middle of it all make Whistler one of Canada's best-known resort towns. **Whistler Blackcomb** is one of North America's best skiing and snowboarding destinations, and is not to be missed.

► TWO WEEKS OF NORTHERN DISCOVERY

Two weeks in the northern regions of western Canada allows the opportunity to travel to many of the places you won't want to miss, but this itinerary by its nature includes a lot of driving, so pad it out with extra days if possible. Alternatively, if you only have a few days, you could fly to Whitehorse and visit the highlights I suggest before flying further north to Inuvik or east to Yellowknife. Like the other itineraries, I assume you have your own vehicle or will be renting one.

Day 1

Drive up Vancouver Island for an afternoon whale-watching trip at Telegraph Cove. Catch the overnight ferry from Port Hardy to Prince Rupert.

Day 2

Connections are usually good for the Queen Charlotte Islands, but make reservations for this and the previous trip in advance to be sure of a spot. The late afternoon is spent on a scenic drive to Naikoon Provincial Park, which is convenient to the many accommodations at Masset.

Day 3

Even if you're not a culture buff, today, which you will spend exploring the abandoned villages of Gwaii Haanas National Park Reserve, will be a highlight of your trip to western Canada. Ferries depart the Queen Charlotte Islands for the mainland in the evening (book a cabin to get a good night's rest onboard).

Day 4

Day 4 is spent driving the Cassiar Highway to Whitehorse. You'll see plenty of wilderness, but also opportunities to see local native culture, including at 'Ksan Historical Village.

Day 5

This morning is spent exploring Whitehorse—walking along the river to the SS *Klondike* and taking a tour of a Dog-Mushing operation. Continue north to Dawson City, where a number of bed-and-breakfasts provide a suitably historic ambience.

Day 6

After a night at one of Dawson City's historical hotels, you'll want to spend as much time as possible wandering around this gold rush town. Many of the most interesting buildings are protected by Dawson Historical Complex National Historic Site, so look for this designation. Stop at the gold fields that made Dawson so famous on the way back to your Whitehorse accommodation.

Day 7

Today is a long driving day to Fort Simpson. Along the way are literally dozens of places

totem in the Yukon

Signpost Forest

you'll be tempted to pull off the road and experience the northern wilderness by dangling a line, searching out wildlife, taking a soak at Liard Hot Springs, or simply enjoying the solitude. The one official attraction along this route is the Signpost Forest.

Day 8

The morning is spent on a flightseeing excursion into Nahanni National Park, where the highlight is seeing Virginia Falls from above. Continue east and north to the territorial capital of Yellowknife for dinner at the Wildcat Café. After dinner, book a tee time to go golfing at Yellowknife Golf Club.

Day 9

Combining visits to the Prince of Wales Northern Heritage Centre and Old Town will give you a good feel for the character of Yellowknife. Take an afternoon flight over the Arctic Circle to Inuvik, where you will stay overnight.

Day 10

It's a short hop by plane from Inuvik to Tuktoyaktuk. Clinging to the edge of the Arctic Ocean, this is the northernmost point of your adventure, so dip your toes in the water for posterity. Most flights include a bus tour of town. Return to Yellowknife for the night.

Day 11

Drive around Great Slave Lake to Wood Buffalo National Park. Dawn and dusk are the perfect times for spotting the park's namesake big game, so keep your eyes peeled in places such as the salt plains. Fort Smith, near the park entrance, is a convenient place to stay the night.

Day 12

It can't be helped. Most of today is spent on the road, driving through the boreal forest of Northern Alberta to William A. Switzer Provincial Park. Fishing, canoeing, or hiking—the choice this evening is yours.

Day 13

Head west through Jasper National Park, detouring to Maligne Lake if the weather is good. Beyond Jasper is Mount Robson Provincial Park, where the highest peak in the Canadian Rockies stands tall. Valemount has a few places to stay, or you can push on to Kamloops for a wider choice of accommodations.

Day 14

Your last day on the road means arriving back in Vancouver. Stall by visiting Wells Gray Provincial Park and going for a canoe paddle, and then visiting Historic Hat Creek Ranch for a final fling of western history.

VANCOUVER AND VICINITY

If you view this gleaming mountain- and sea-dominated city for the first time on a beautiful sunny day, you're bound to fall for it in a big way. After cohosting the 2010 Olympic Winter Games, a worldwide audience was charmed by Vancouver's vibrant, outdoorsy atmosphere. By day, the active visitor can enjoy boating right from downtown, or perhaps venture out to one of the nearby provincial parks for hiking in summer or skiing and snowboarding in winter. More urban-oriented visitors can savor the aromas of just-brewed coffee and freshly baked bread wafting from cosmopolitan sidewalk cafés, join in the bustle at seaside markets, bake on a local beach, or simply relax and do some people-watching in one of the city's tree-shaded squares. By night, Vancouver's myriad fine restaurants, hip nightclubs, and world-class performing arts venues beckon visitors to continue enjoying themselves into the wee hours.

Once you've reluctantly decided to drag yourself away from Vancouver, you'll be confronted by a variety of things to see and do within a day's drive of the city. Although British Columbia is best known for its mountains, the Sunshine Coast, northwest of Vancouver, is a watery playground perfect for swimming, sunbathing on sandy beaches, canoeing and kayaking, beachcombing, scuba diving, boating, and fishing. Spectacular Highway 99, the aptly named Sea to Sky Highway, leads you northeast out of Vancouver along the edge of island-dotted Howe Sound to the resort town of Whistler,

© ANDREW HEMPSTEAD

HIGHLIGHTS

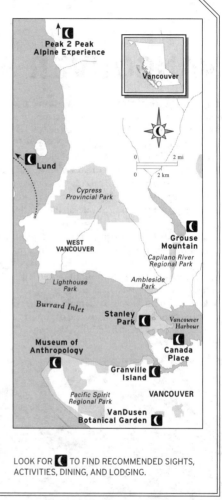

◖ Canada Place: This architectural masterpiece takes pride in its place along the Vancouver waterfront. Its towering white sail-like architecture is a city landmark (page 31).

◖ Granville Island: Interested in the arts? Want to watch wooden boats being built? Do you enjoy browsing through interesting market stalls? You'll find all this and more by catching a ferry to this city island (page 35).

◖ Stanley Park: It will wow you. This massive chunk of downtown has been protected for all time in its forested, old-growth state (page 37).

◖ VanDusen Botanical Garden: Garden lovers will be in their element at this formal garden in the heart of one of Vancouver's most upscale neighborhoods (page 40).

◖ Museum of Anthropology: Inspired by the longhouses of First Nations people, this museum houses a stunning collection of totem poles and related arts and crafts (page 41).

◖ Grouse Mountain: Located on the north side of the city, Grouse Mountain's gondola provides views extending across the city to Mount Baker in Washington state. A wealth of on-mountain activities makes this a good half-day excursion (page 43).

◖ Lund: At the end of the Sunshine Coast, Lund is a delightful fishing village with plenty to see and do (page 74).

◖ Peak 2 Peak Alpine Experience: The resort town of Whistler is worth visiting regardless of the season or your interests. One thing everyone should do is ride the linked Peak 2 Peak gondolas for the views alone (page 78).

LOOK FOR ◖ TO FIND RECOMMENDED SIGHTS, ACTIVITIES, DINING, AND LODGING.

cohost of the 2010 Olympic Winter Games. From Vancouver, two routes head east—you can zip along the TransCanada Highway on the south side of the wide Fraser River or meander along slower Highway 7 on the north side of the river. Both highways take you through the lush, fertile, and obviously agricultural Fraser Valley, converging at Hope.

PLANNING YOUR TIME

Deciding how best to spend your time in Vancouver and the surrounding area is a personal thing—outdoorsy budget travelers will spend their days (and money) in a very different way than a honeymooning couple looking to kick back and relax for a few days. But this is one of the true joys about visiting

Vancouver—there really is something for everyone.

Regardless of whether you have a weekend or a full week scheduled for Vancouver, plan on rising early and heading out to Stanley Park at least once for a walk or ride. Visit the two major museums—Museum of Vancouver and the Museum of Anthropology—-in the mornings. Leave the afternoons for outdoor pursuits that can be active (kayaking on False Creek), educational (Capilano Salmon Hatchery), or breathtaking (Grouse Mountain Skyride).

Once you've finished exploring Vancouver, you'll be faced with a decision—where to next? The second part of this chapter covers the two main options. Your choice is dependent on two main elements: the time of year and your interests. The first option is to jump aboard a ferry for the Sunshine Coast, from where ferries make the link to Vancouver Island (make a detour to delightful Lund en route). Regardless of the season, you'll want to include Whistler in your British Columbia travels. The resort is close enough to Vancouver for a day trip, but it's easy to spend at least a full day exploring the main mountain by gondola, which means that if you want to bike, hike, or golf, you'll need at least two days here. Winter is high season in Whistler; in return for skiing or boarding some of the world's best known slopes, you'll be paying big bucks for accommodations. A third option is heading west into the region covered in the Southern Interior chapter.

HISTORY

In 1792, Captain George Vancouver cruised through the Strait of Georgia, charting Burrard Inlet and claiming the land for Great Britain. In 1808, fur trader/explorer Simon Fraser established a trading post east of today's Vancouver on the river that now bears his name.

The settlement of Vancouver began with the establishment of a brickworks on the south side of Burrard Inlet. Sawmills and related logging and lumber industries followed, and soon several boomtowns were carved out of the wilderness. The first was Granville (now downtown Vancouver), which the original settlers called "Gastown" after one of its earliest residents, notorious saloon owner "Gassy Jack" Deighton.

© ANDREW HEMPSTEAD

Canada Place is a Vancouver icon.

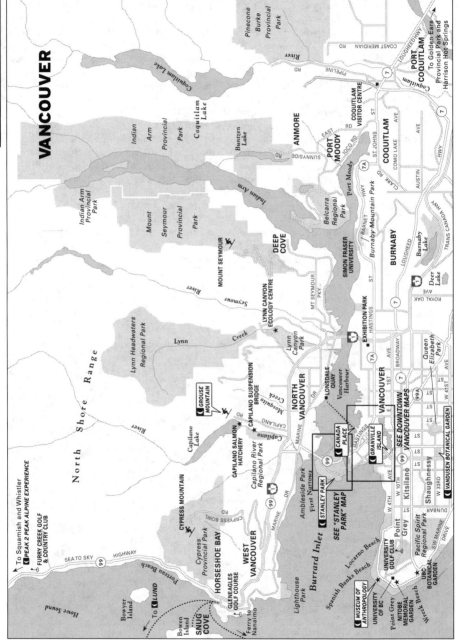

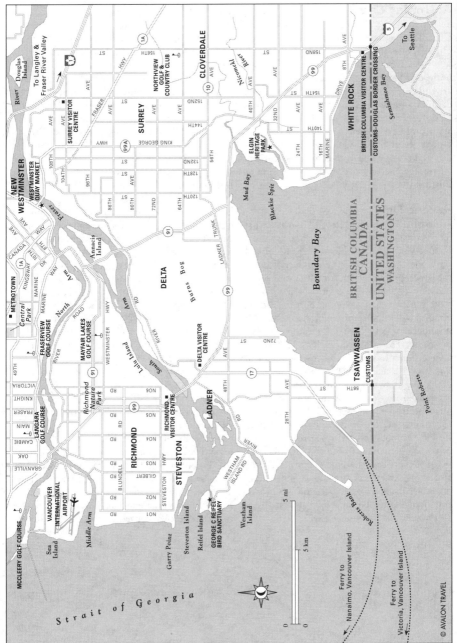

Strait of Georgia

Sea Island

Middle Arm

VANCOUVER INTERNATIONAL AIRPORT

MCCLEERY GOLF COURSE

LANGARA GOLF COURSE

GRANVILLE · OAK · CAMBIE · MAIN · FRASER · KNIGHT · VICTORIA · 49TH

North Arm

FRASERVIEW GOLF COURSE

Central Park

METROTOWN

NEW WESTMINSTER

CANADA WAY · KINGSWAY · 10TH · MARINE · DR

WESTMINSTER QUAY MARKET

Fraser River

1A

91A

Annacis Island

SURREY VISITOR CENTRE

SURREY

FRASER HWY · KING GEORGE HWY 99A

108TH · 104TH · 96TH · 88TH · 80TH · 72ND

132ND ST · 128TH ST · 120TH ST · 144TH · 152ND · 160TH ST · 168TH

96 AVE · 88TH AVE

CLOVERDALE

NORTHVIEW GOLF & COUNTRY CLUB

1A

10

64TH · 56TH · 40TH

Nicomekl River

Serpentine River

91

Richmond Nature Park

RICHMOND

STEVESTON

RICHMOND VISITOR CENTRE

NO6 RD · NO5 RD · NO4 RD · NO3 RD · NO2 RD · NO1 RD · GILBERT RD · BLUNDELL · STEVESTON HWY · WESTMINSTER HWY

99

91

MAYFAIR LAKES GOLF COURSE

Lulu Island

South Arm

Garry Point

Steveston Island

Reifel Island

GEORGE C REIFEL BIRD SANCTUARY

Westham Island

WESTHAM ISLAND RD

LADNER

DELTA

Burns Bog

DELTA VISITOR CENTRE

LADNER TRUNK RD

99

17

48TH · 28TH

56TH ST · 72ND

TSAWWASSEN

CUSTOMS

Point Roberts

Roberts Bank

Boundary Bay

Mud Bay

Blackie Spit

ELGIN HERITAGE PARK

WHITE ROCK

BRITISH COLUMBIA VISITOR CENTRE

CUSTOMS-DOUGLAS BORDER CROSSING

Semiahmoo Bay

32ND · 24TH · 16TH · MARINE DR · 8TH

140TH · 154TH · 158ND

99 · 5

To Seattle

BRITISH COLUMBIA
CANADA
UNITED STATES
WASHINGTON

Douglas Island

To Langley & Fraser River Valley

1A

Ferry to Nanaimo, Vancouver Island

Ferry to Victoria, Vancouver Island

5 mi

5 km

© AVALON TRAVEL

A Growing City

Selected as the western terminus for the Canadian Pacific Railway in 1887, Vancouver suddenly became Canada's transportation gateway to eastern Asia and an important player in the development of international commerce around the Pacific Rim. Over the next three decades, Granville Island and the far reaches of Burrard Inlet sprawled with industry, the West End developed as a residential area, the University of British Columbia grew in stature, and the opening of the Lions Gate Bridge encouraged settlement on the north side of Burrard Inlet.

Recent Times

From what began just 120 years ago as a cluster of ramshackle buildings centered around a saloon, Vancouver has blossomed into one of the world's greatest cities. While the city holds the largest port on North America's west coast, boasting 20 specialized terminals that handle more tonnage than any other port in Canada (around $50 billion worth of goods annually), it is now a lot less reliant on its traditional economic heart for growth. The high-tech industry continues as the fastest-growing sector of Vancouver's economy. Worth $6 billion in 2009, this knowledge-based industry has both revitalized the local economy and created a major shift in government thinking. Tourism contributes more than $5 billion annually to the local economy, with finance, real estate, insurance, and manufacturing also forming large slices of the local economic pie. Vancouver is also North America's third-largest movie-making center (behind Los Angeles and New York), employing up to 50,000 people on as many as 30 productions simultaneously.

ORIENTATION

Vancouver isn't a particularly easy city to find your way around, although an excellent transit system helps immensely. Downtown lies on a spit of land bordered to the north and east by Burrard Inlet, to the west by English Bay, and to the south by False Creek, which almost cuts the city center off from the rest of the city. Due to the foresight of city founders, almost half of the downtown peninsula has been set aside as parkland.

The City of Vancouver officially extends south and west from downtown, between Burrard Inlet and the Fraser River. Here lie the trendy beachside suburb of Kitsilano (known as "Kits" to the locals) and Point Grey, home of the University of British Columbia. To the east, the residential sprawl continues through the suburbs of Burnaby, New Westminster, and Coquitlam, which have a combined population of well over 250,000.

Farther south, the low-lying Fraser River Delta extends all the way to the U.S. border. Between the north and south arms of the river is Richmond, home of Vancouver International Airport. South of the south arm is the mostly industrial area of Delta, as well as Tsawwassen, departure point for ferries to Vancouver Island. Southeast of the Fraser River lie Surrey and the Fraser River Valley towns of Langley, Abbotsford, and Chilliwack—all part of the city sprawl.

Across Burrard Inlet to the north of downtown, North Vancouver is a narrow developed strip backed up to the mountains and connected to the rest of the city by the Lions Gate Bridge. To its west are Horseshoe Bay, departure point for Sunshine Coast and Vancouver Island ferries, and West Vancouver, an upscale suburb.

Sights

As British Columbia's largest city, Vancouver holds an abundance of world-class attractions, as well as many smaller gems that are easy to miss. Whether you're interested in visiting museums or exploring mountain peaks, you will find plenty to do in Vancouver. The hardest part will be working out how best to fit them into your itinerary. Luckily, many attractions are clustered around downtown, with others, such as Granville Island and the city's three major museums, farther out but easily reached by public transportation. Try to arrange your sightseeing schedule around the weather. If the forecast calls for a rainy day, concentrate on the museums, leaving the North Shore and Stanley Park for a sunny day.

DOWNTOWN

Granville Street was Vancouver's first commercial corridor, and if today you stand at its junction with West Georgia Street, you're as close to the "center" of the city as it's possible to be. From this busy intersection, Granville Street extends north toward Burrard Inlet as a pedestrian mall, leading through the central business district (CBD) to Canada Place and the main tourist information center.

Vancouver Lookout

For immediate orientation from downtown, catch the high-speed, stomach-sinking glass elevator up the outside of 40-story **Harbour Centre Tower** (555 W. Hastings St., 604/689-0421, daily 9 A.M.–9 P.M., until 10:30 P.M. in summer, adult $13, senior $11, child $9) to the Vancouver Lookout, an enclosed room 167 meters (550 feet) above street level. The 360-degree views extend all the way to Mount Baker, 140 kilometers (87 miles) to the south. Walk around the circular room to read interpretive panels describing interesting facts about the panorama below and beyond. Keep your receipt and you can return any time during the same day (the top of the tower is a great

place to watch the sun setting over the Strait of Georgia).

◖ Canada Place

The stunning architectural curiosity with the billowing 27-meter-high (88-feet) Teflon-coated fiberglass "sails" on Burrard Inlet—the one that looks as if it might weigh anchor and cruise off into the sunset at any moment—is Canada Place, a symbol of Vancouver and a city icon. Built as the Canada Pavilion for Expo86, this integrated waterfront complex is primarily a convention center and cruise-ship dock. The Vancouver Trade and Convention Centre, which makes up the bulk of the complex, is currently being expanded to triple its size at adjacent Burrard Landing, in a half-billion-dollar expansion project that will change the face of the downtown waterfront. The existing complex at the foot of Burrard Street also houses the luxurious 405-room Pan Pacific Hotel (the glass marvel with domed top), restaurants, shops, and an IMAX theater. Start your self-guided tour at the information booth near the main entrance, then allow at least an hour to wander through the complex. Don't miss walking the exterior promenade—three and a half city blocks long—for splendid views of the harbor, the North Shore, the Coast Mountains, and docked Alaska-bound cruise ships.

Vancouver Art Gallery

Francis Rattenbury, architect of Victoria's Empress Hotel and many other masterpieces, designed Vancouver's imposing neoclassical-revival courthouse, which now houses Vancouver Art Gallery (750 Hornby St., 604/662-4700, daily 10 A.M.–5 P.M., until 9 P.M. on Thurs., adult $19.50, senior $14, child under 12 $7). Initially, the courthouse faced Georgia Street, and although the exterior retains its original 1911 design, the main entrance is now on Robson Street. The gallery's third floor is where you'll find a large collection of works by Canada's preeminent female artist Emily Carr,

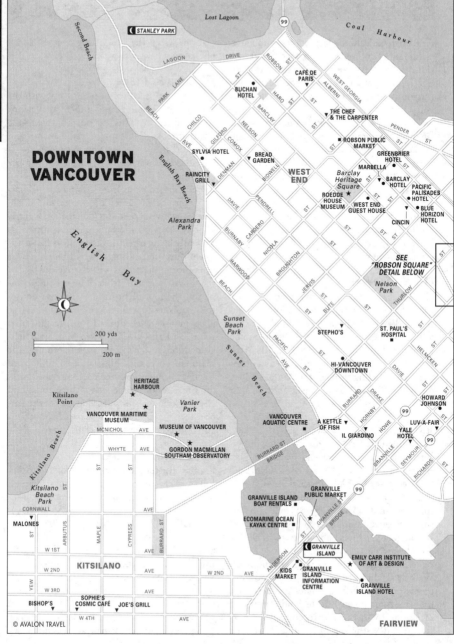

DOWNTOWN VANCOUVER

© AVALON TRAVEL

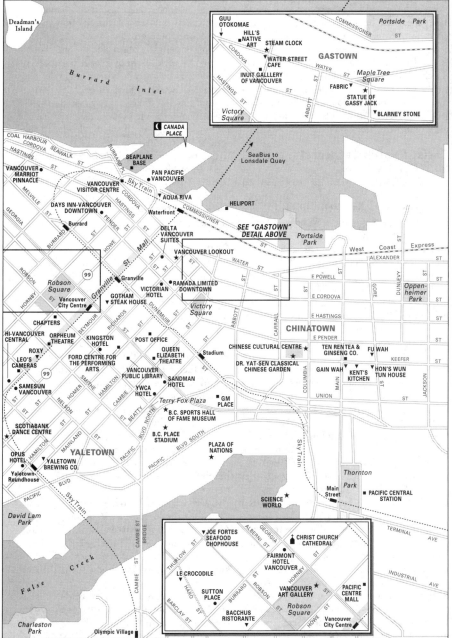

Deadman's Island

Burrard Inlet

GASTOWN

GUU OTOKOMAE
HILL'S NATIVE ART
STEAM CLOCK ★
WATER STREET CAFE
INUIT GALLLERY OF VANCOUVER
FABRIC
STATUE OF GASSY JACK ★
BLARNEY STONE
Maple Tree Square
Portside Park
COMMISSIONER ST
WATER ST
CORDOVA ST
HASTINGS ST
ABBOTT ST
Victory Square

COAL HARBOUR SEAWALK
CORDOVA
HASTINGS
VANCOUVER MARRIOT PINNACLE
MELVILLE
GEORGIA
BURRARD
HOWE
PENDER
HASTINGS ST
SeaBus to Lonsdale Quay
CANADA PLACE
SEAPLANE BASE
PAN PACIFIC VANCOUVER
Sky Train
VANCOUVER VISITOR CENTRE
AQUA RIVA
HELIPORT
DAYS INN-VANCOUVER DOWNTOWN
Burrard
Waterfront
COMMISSIONER
DELTA VANCOUVER SUITES
SEE "GASTOWN" DETAIL ABOVE
Portside Park
West Coast Express
ALEXANDER ST
VANCOUVER LOOKOUT ★
WATER ST
Robson Square
99
Granville
VICTORIAN HOTEL
RAMADA LIMITED DOWNTOWN
E POWELL ST
GORE
DUNLEVY
Oppenheimer Park
Vancouver City Centre
Granville
GOTHAM STEAK HOUSE
DUNSMUIR
Victory Square
E CORDOVA ST
CHAPTERS
HI-VANCOUVER CENTRAL
ORPHEUM THEATRE
KINGSTON HOTEL
POST OFFICE
QUEEN ELIZABETH THEATRE
Stadium
E HASTINGS ST
CHINATOWN
E PENDER
CHINESE CULTURAL CENTRE ★
TEN REN TEA & GINSENG CO.
FU WAH
KEEFER
ROXY
LEO'S CAMERAS
FORD CENTRE FOR THE PERFORMING ARTS
VANCOUVER PUBLIC LIBRARY
SANDMAN HOTEL
DR. YAT-SEN CLASSICAL CHINESE GARDEN
GAIN WAH
KENT'S KITCHEN
HON'S WUN TUN HOUSE
99
SAMESUN VANCOUVER
YWCA HOTEL
Terry Fox Plaza
GM PLACE
COLUMBIA
MAIN
UNION ST
JACKSON
SCOTIABANK DANCE CENTRE
B.C. SPORTS HALL OF FAME MUSEUM ★
B.C. PLACE STADIUM ★
OPUS HOTEL
YALETOWN BREWING CO.
YALETOWN
PLAZA OF NATIONS ★
Yaletown Roundhouse
PACIFIC
BLVD
Thornton Park
David Lam Park
CAMBIE ST BRIDGE
Sky Train
SCIENCE WORLD ★
Main Street
PACIFIC CENTRAL STATION
TERMINAL AVE
INDUSTRIAL AVE
False Creek
Charleston Park
Olympic Village

JOE FORTES SEAFOOD CHOPHOUSE
CHRIST CHURCH CATHEDRAL
ALBERNI ST
GEORGIA
FAIRMONT HOTEL VANCOUVER
LE CROCODILE
THURLOW ST
HARO ST
BURRARD
ROBSON
HORNBY
VANCOUVER ART GALLERY ★
PACIFIC CENTRE MALL
SUTTON PLACE
BARCLAY ST
Robson Square
HOWE ST
BACCHUS RISTORANTE
Vancouver City Centre

along with the works of many other local artists. The gallery also holds pieces by contemporary artists from North America and Europe, as well as an impressive collection of historical art.

Guided tours are available. Kids will enjoy the children's gallery, while adults will appreciate the special-events program, including a lecture series, films, and concerts. The gift shop sells a wide selection of art books, jewelry, and gifts, and the gallery café is always crowded.

Christ Church Cathedral and Vicinity

One block northwest from the art gallery, on the corner of West Georgia and Burrard Streets, is the gracious Christ Church Cathedral. When built in 1895, it was in the heart of a residential area. Over the ensuing century, it has been engulfed by modern developments, and today is Vancouver's oldest church.

Across West Georgia Street from the cathedral is the Hotel Vancouver. Built in 1887, the original hotel on this site featured 200 rooms, half of which had private bathrooms—unheard of in that day. It burned to the ground in 1932 and was replaced by the hotel that stands today, which reflects the heritage of hotels across the country built by the Canadian Pacific Railway with its distinctive chateau-style design topped by a copper roof.

Gastown

"Gassy Jack" Deighton, an English boat pilot, offered locals all the whiskey they could drink in return for helping him build a saloon beside Burrard Inlet in 1867. The town that grew around the saloon was officially named Granville in 1869, but it has always been known as Gastown. The district's tree-lined cobblestone streets and old gas lamps front brightly-painted, restored buildings housing galleries, restaurants, and an abundance of gift and souvenir shops.

Most of the action centers along **Water Street,** which branches east off Cordova Street, an easy five-minute walk from Canada Place. As you first enter Water Street, you're greeted by **The Landing,** a heritage building

that has had its exterior restored to its former glory and its interior transformed into an up-market shopping arcade. Down the hill, at Cambie Street, is a **steam clock**—one of only two in the world. Built by a local clockmaker, it's powered by a steam system originally put in place to heat buildings through an underground pipeline that snakes through downtown. Watch for the burst of steam every 15 minutes, which sets off steam whistles to the tune of Westminster chimes.

Continue east along Water Street to the 1899 **Dominion Hotel** and a string of other buildings built after the Great Fire of 1886. The **Byrnes Block** (2 Water St.) stands on the site of **Deighton House,** Gassy Jack's second and more permanent saloon.

Chinatown

With the second-largest Chinese community in North America and one of the largest outside Asia, Vancouver's Chinatown is an exciting place any time of year. But it's especially lively during a Chinese festival or holiday, when thronging masses follow the ferocious dancing dragon, avoid exploding firecrackers, sample tasty tidbits from outdoor stalls, and pound their feet to the beat of the drums.

Chinatown lies several blocks southeast of Gastown, along East Pender Street between Carrall and Gore Streets. Its commercial center is the block bordered by Main, East Pender, Gore, and Keefer Streets. Stroll through the neighborhood to admire the architecture—right down to the pagoda-roofed telephone booths—or to seek out one of the multitude of restaurants.

Designed primarily to host community programs for the local Chinese population, the **Chinese Cultural Centre** also has a museum (555 Columbia St., 604/687-0282, Tues.–Sun. 11 A.M.–5 P.M., adult $5, senior $3) cataloging the history of Chinese Canadians in Vancouver.

Gardening enthusiasts won't want to miss **Dr. Sun Yat-Sen Classical Chinese Garden** (behind the Cultural Centre at 578 Carrall St., 604/662-3207, summer daily 9:30 A.M.–7 P.M., spring and fall daily 10 A.M.–6 P.M., winter daily 10 A.M.–4:30 P.M., adult $10, senior $9, child $8), which features limestone rockeries, a waterfall and tranquil pools, and beautiful trees and plants hidden away behind tall walls.

To get to Chinatown from downtown, catch bus number 19 or 22 east along Pender Street. Try to avoid East Hastings Street at all times; it's Vancouver's skid row, inhabited by unsavory characters day and night.

FALSE CREEK

False Creek, the narrow tidal inlet that almost cuts downtown off from the rest of the city, has been transformed from an industrial wasteland to an attractive area of waterfront parks and a bona fide tourist attraction. If you walk from downtown, **B.C. Place** (777 Pacific Blvd., 604/669-2300), the world's largest air-supported domed stadium, is a worthwhile stop.

Science World

This impressive, 17-story-high geodesic silver dome (it's best known locally as "the golf ball") sits over the waters of False Creek on the southeast side of the city center (1455 Quebec

the geodesic dome at Science World

© ANDREW HEMPSTEAD

St., 604/443-7440, daily 10 A.M.–5 P.M., adult $18.75, senior and child $13.75, includes admission to one OMNIMAX film). Built for Expo86, this Vancouver landmark is now home to a museum providing exhibitions that "introduce the world of science to the young and the young at heart." The three main galleries explore the basics of physics, natural history, and music through hands-on displays. The audiovisual presentation *Over Canada* is a highlight. An **OMNIMAX theater** (like IMAX) features science-oriented documentaries.

The most enjoyable way to get to Science World is aboard a False Creek Ferry from Granville Island or the Vancouver Aquatic Centre. You could also take the SkyTrain to Main Street Station.

◖ Granville Island

Follow Granville Street southwest through downtown and cross False Creek by bridge or ferry to reach Granville Island. Regarded as one of North America's most successful inner-city, industrial-site redevelopments, the jazzed-up island is *the* place to go on a bright sunny day. Allow at least several hours or an entire afternoon for this hive of activity.

You can spend the better part of a day just walking around the island looking at the marina, the many specialty businesses that reflect the island's maritime heritage, fresh food markets, gift shops, restaurants, and theaters. The highlight is the colorful **Granville Island Public Market** (daily 9 A.M.–7 P.M.), a hub of activity from dawn to dusk and a lot more than a tourist attraction. Inside the market you'll find all kinds of things to eat—fresh fruit and vegetables, seafood from local waters, a wide variety of meats, specialty ingredients, and prepared ready-to-go meals—as well as unique jewelry and crafts, potted plants, and cut flowers.

At the opposite end of the island is the **Emily Carr Institute of Art and Design** (1399 Johnston St., 604/844-3800, daily 8:30 A.M.–11:30 P.M., free). Named for one of Canada's best-known artists, the facility attracts students from across the country to study fine arts,

a sunny day on Granville Island

© ANDREW HEMPSTEAD

applied arts, and media arts. Two galleries are open to the public.

To get to the island by boat, jump aboard one of the small **False Creek Ferries.** The boats run regularly between the island, Vancouver Aquatic Centre at Sunset Beach ($3), and Science World ($5.50). Parking on the island is almost impossible, especially on weekends. If you do find a spot, it'll have a three-hour maximum time limit. For general information on the island and local businesses, visit www.granvilleisland.com.

WEST END

The West End (not to be confused with the West Side, south of downtown, or West Vancouver, on the north side of the harbor) lies west of the Central Business District, between Burrard Street and **English Bay Beach,** the gateway to Stanley Park. Wander down Robson or Denman Streets and you'll soon see the appeal of the urban lifestyle afforded by life in the West End—endless outdoor cafés, a wide range of dining choices, fashionable boutiques, the sandy beaches of English Bay, and, of course, the proximity of Stanley Park.

Robson Street

If you like to shop in trendy boutiques, sample European delicacies, and sip cappuccinos at sidewalk cafés, saunter along this colorful and exciting street linking downtown to the West End. Once the center of a predominantly German neighborhood, Robson Street is also known as "Robsonstrasse." At 1610 Robson (the west end), **Robson Public Market** occupies an impressive atrium-topped building filled with meat, seafood, dairy products, fruits and veggies, nuts, flowers, craft vendors, fresh juice and salad bars, and an international food fair.

Barclay Heritage Square

Most of the West End's turn-of-the-century buildings are long gone, but a precinct of nine homes built between 1890 and 1908 has been saved and is preserved as Barclay Heritage Square, which looks much as it would have when the homes were first built around the turn of the 20th century, right down to the style of the surrounding gardens. The only one of the nine open to the public is **Roedde House** (1415 Barclay St., 604/684-7040). Built in 1893, this Queen Anne Revival-style home is a classic example of Vancouver's early residential architecture. Tours of the house are conducted Tuesday–Saturday noon–4 P.M. and cost adult $5, senior and child $4.

STANLEY PARK

Beautiful Stanley Park is a lush 405-hectare (1,000-acre) tree- and garden-carpeted peninsula jutting out into Burrard Inlet. It is a sight for sore eyes in any weather—an enormous peaceful oasis sandwiched between the city center's skyscrapers and the North Shore at the other end of Lions Gate Bridge. Unlike other famous parks, such as New York's Central Park and London's Royal Park, Stanley Park is a permanent preserve of wilderness in the heart of the city, complete with dense coastal forests and abundant wildlife.

Walk or cycle the 10-kilometer (6.2-mile) **Seawall Promenade** or drive the perimeter via **Stanley Park Drive** to take in beautiful water and city views. Travel along both is one-way in a counterclockwise direction (those on foot can go either way, but if you travel clockwise you'll be going against the flow). For vehicle traffic, the main entrance to Stanley Park is at the beginning of Stanley Park Drive, which veers right from the end of Georgia Street; on foot, follow Denman Street to its north end and you'll find a pathway leading around Coal Harbour into the park. Either way, you'll pass a small information booth where park maps are available. Just before the booth, take Pipeline Road to access **Malkin Bowl,** home to outdoor theater productions; a **rose garden;** and forest-encircled **Beaver Lake.** Pipeline Road rejoins Stanley Park Drive near the Lions Gate Bridge, but by not returning to the park entrance you'll miss most of the following sights.

Vancouver Aquarium

In the forest behind the information booth is Canada's largest aquarium (845 Avison Way, 604/631-2524, daily 9:30 A.M.–7 P.M. in summer, daily 9:30 A.M.–5 P.M. the rest of the year, adult $22, senior $17, child $14). More than 8,000 aquatic animals and 600 species are on display, representing all corners of the planet, from the oceans of the Arctic to the rainforests of the Amazon. Pacific Canada is of particular interest as it contains a wide variety of sea life from the Gulf of Georgia, including the giant fish of the deep, halibut, and playful little sea otters who frolic in the kelp. At the far end of the aquarium, a large pool holding beluga whales—distinctive pure white marine mammals—and sea lions, which can be viewed from above or below ground, represents Arctic Canada.

Seawall Sights

The following sights are listed counterclockwise from the information booth. From this point, Stanley Park Drive and the Seawall Promenade pass the **Royal Vancouver Yacht Club** and then **Deadman's Island,** the burial place of the last of the Coast Salish people.

Stanley Park seawall

© ANDREW HEMPSTEAD

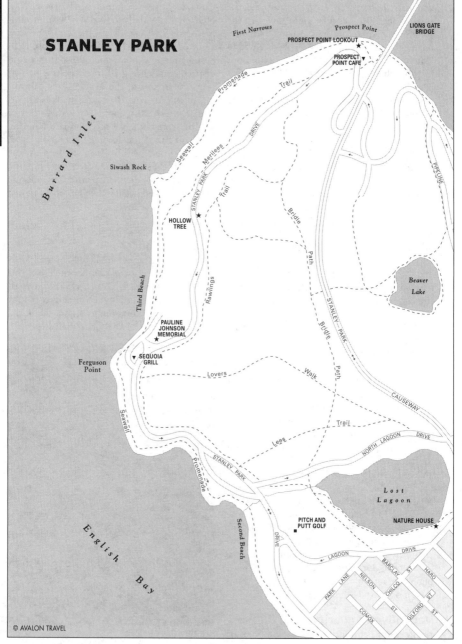

STANLEY PARK

First Narrows

Prospect Point

PROSPECT POINT LOOKOUT ★

LIONS GATE BRIDGE

PROSPECT POINT CAFE ▾

Promenade

Trail

DRIVE

Merilees

STANLEY PARK

Seawall

Siwash Rock

Trail

Bridle

PIPELINE

Path

Burrard Inlet

HOLLOW TREE ★

Rawlings

Beaver Lake

Third Beach

STANLEY PARK

PAULINE JOHNSON MEMORIAL ★

Bridle

Ferguson Point

SEQUOIA GRILL ▾

Lovers

Walk

Path

CAUSEWAY

Seawall

Lees

Trail

NORTH LAGOON DRIVE

Promenade

STANLEY PARK DRIVE

Second Beach

Lost Lagoon

PITCH AND PUTT GOLF ■

NATURE HOUSE ★

DRIVE

LAGOON

DRIVE

English Bay

PARK LANE

NELSON ST

BARCLAY ST

CHILCO ST

HARO ST

GILFORD ST

COMOX

© AVALON TRAVEL

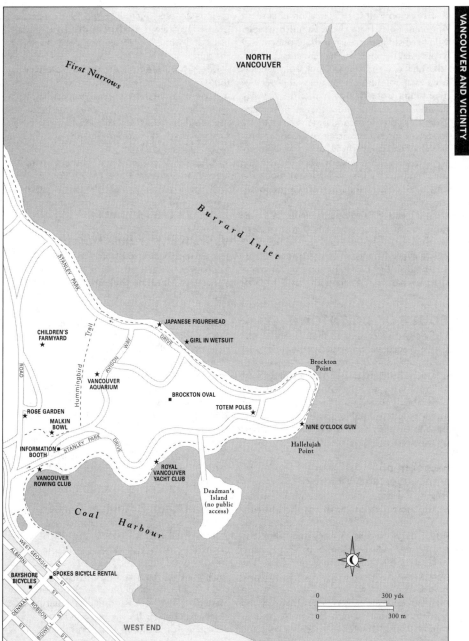

First Narrows

NORTH
VANCOUVER

Burrard Inlet

STANLEY PARK

Trail

Hummingbird

CHILDREN'S
FARMYARD

ROAD

AVISON WAY

DRIVE

★ JAPANESE FIGUREHEAD

★ GIRL IN WETSUIT

Brockton
Point

★ VANCOUVER
AQUARIUM

BROCKTON OVAL

TOTEM POLES ★

ROSE GARDEN

MALKIN
BOWL

STANLEY PARK DRIVE

★ NINE O'CLOCK GUN

Hallelujah
Point

INFORMATION ■
BOOTH

VANCOUVER
ROWING CLUB

ROYAL
VANCOUVER
YACHT CLUB

Deadman's
Island
(no public
access)

Coal Harbour

WEST GEORGIA

ALBERNI

BAYSHORE
BICYCLES

SPOKES BICYCLE RENTAL

ST

ST

DENMAN

ROBSON

ST

BIDWELL

ST

WEST END

0   300 yds

0   300 m

At **Brockton Point** is a collection of authentic totem poles from the Kwagiulth people, who lived along the coast north of present-day Vancouver. Before rounding the actual point itself, you'll pass the **Nine O'Clock Gun,** which is fired each evening at—you guessed it—9 P.M. The **Lions Gate Bridge** marks the halfway point of the seawall and a change in scenery. From this point to Second Beach the views are westward toward the Strait of Georgia. This stretch of pleasant pathway, about two kilometers (1.2 miles) long, is sandwiched between the water and steep cliffs, with **Siwash Rock** the only distinctive landmark. Continuing south, the seawall and Stanley Park Drive converge at the south end of **Third Beach,** a popular swimming and sunbathing spot (and a great place to watch the setting sun). From Second Beach it's only a short distance to busy Denman Street and English Bay Beach, or you can cut across the park past Lost Lagoon and back to Coal Harbour.

SOUTH OF DOWNTOWN

Officially divided into 18 municipalities, the City of Vancouver encompasses the entire peninsula, including the area south of downtown, a largely residential area that extends west to Point Grey and the University of British Columbia. Vancouver's three largest museums and a number of public gardens lie south of downtown. This is the area of the city covered by this section.

Museum of Vancouver and Vicinity

Regional history from Precambrian times to the present comes to life at the Museum of Vancouver (1100 Chestnut St., 604/736-4431, daily 10 A.M.–5 P.M., and Thursday until 9 P.M., closed Mon. Sept.–June, adult $11, senior $9, child $7) in Vanier Park. The West Coast Archaeology and Culture galleries hold ravishing masks, highly-patterned woven blankets, and fine baskets. The Discovery and Settlement gallery details European exploration of British Columbia—both by land and by sea. The Vancouver Stories gallery depicts

various decades, including the 1950s where a shiny 1955 Ford Fairlane is displayed and black and white TVs screen popular shows of the time.

The **H.R. MacMillan Space Centre** (604/738-7827, daily 10 A.M.–5 P.M. in summer, closed Mon. the rest of the year, adult $15, senior and child $10.75), in the same building as the museum, features displays related to planet earth, the surrounding universe, and space exploration.

Adjacent to the museum is the **Gordon MacMillan Southam Observatory** (604/738-7827, by donation), which is open for public stargazing Monday–Friday sunset–midnight when the skies are clear.

Vancouver Maritime Museum

Just a five-minute stroll from the Museum of Vancouver, at the end of Cypress Avenue, is Vancouver Maritime Museum (1905 Ogden Ave., 604/257-8300, daily 10 A.M.–5 P.M. in summer, Tues.–Sat. 10 A.M.–5 P.M. and noon–5 P.M. on Sun. the rest of the year, adult $10, senior and child $7.50). Filled with nautical-themed displays that showcase British Columbia's seafaring legacy, exhibits chronicle everything from the province's first European explorers and their vessels to today's oceangoing adventurers, modern fishing boats, and fancy ships. Beyond the front desk is the historic RCMP vessel, *St. Roch,* which fills the first main room. Now a National Historic Site, the *St. Roch* was the first patrol vessel to successfully negotiate the infamous Northwest Passage.

◖ VanDusen Botanical Garden

Formerly a golf course, this 22-hectare (54-acre) garden (5251 Oak St. at 37th Ave., 604/878-9274, daily 10 A.M.–8 P.M. in summer, 10 A.M.–6 P.M. April and Oct., 10 A.M.–4 P.M. the rest of the year, adult $8.85, senior and child $6.50, discounted in winter), is home to more than 7,500 species from every continent except Antarctica. It's the place to feast your eyes on more than 1,000 varieties of rhododendrons, as well as roses, all kinds of botanical rarities, winter blossoms, an Elizabethan hedge maze, and a children's topiary garden featuring animal shapes. Look for the display board near the front entrance to see what's best for the time of year in which you're visiting. The complex also includes a shop selling cards, perfumes, soaps, potpourri, and all kinds of floral-themed gifts.

Queen Elizabeth Park

Less than two kilometers (1.2 miles) from VanDusen Botanical Garden, this 53-hectare (130-acre) park sits atop 152-meter (500-foot) high **Little Mountain,** the city's highest point, with magnificent views of Vancouver and the Coast Mountains. Highlights include masses of rhododendrons—a vivid spectacle in May and June—formal flower gardens including a rose garden in the park's southwest corner; sunken gardens in the old quarry pits; and **Bloedel Floral Conservatory** (604/257-8570, Mon.–Fri. 9 A.M.–8 P.M. and Sat.–Sun. 10 A.M.–9 P.M. in summer, daily 10 A.M.–5 P.M. the rest of the year, adult $5, senior $3.60, child $2.50), a glass dome enclosing a temperature-controlled, humid tropical jungle. The park's main entrance is by the junction of 33rd Avenue West and Cambie Street.

UNIVERSITY OF BRITISH COLUMBIA

The UBC campus sprawls across **Point Grey,** where it enjoys a spectacular coastal location surrounded by parkland laced with hiking trails. The campus encompasses more than 400 hectares (990 acres) and serves up to 35,000 students at one time.

◖ Museum of Anthropology

Mimicking the post-and-beam structures favored by the Coast Salish, this museum (6393 Northwest Marine Dr., 604/822-5087, daily 10 A.M.–5 P.M. in summer, Tues.–Sun. 11 A.M.–5 P.M. the rest of the year, adult $11, senior and child $9) is home to the world's largest collection of arts and crafts of the Pacific Northwest native peoples. A ramp flanked with sculptures by renowned modern-day carvers leads to the Great Hall, a cavernous 18-meter-high (59-feet) room dominated by towering totem poles collected from along the coast and interspersed with other ancient works. A museum highlight is the collection of works by Haida artist Bill Reid, which includes *The Raven and the First Men.* Carved from a four-ton chunk of yellow cedar, the surrounding seats are a popular spot to sit and simply stare. Other displays include intricate carvings, baskets, ceremonial masks, fabulous jewelry, and European ceramics. The museum holds more than 200,000 artifacts, most of which are stored in uniquely accessible research collections. Instead of being stored in musty boxes out back and available only to anthropologists, the collections are stored in the main museum—in row upon row of glass-enclosed cabinets and in drawers that visitors are encouraged to open. Details of each piece are noted in binders.

University Gardens

Just south of the Museum of Anthropology is the serene **Nitobe Memorial Garden** (604/822-9666, daily 9 A.M.–5 P.M. in summer, adult $6, senior $5, child $2). Spread over one hectare (2.5 acres), this traditional Japanese garden of shrubs and miniatures has two distinct sections: the Stroll Garden, laid out in a form that symbolizes the journey through life, and the Tea Garden, the place to contemplate life from a ceremonial teahouse. Outside of summer, the garden is open limited hours (Mon.–Fri. 11 A.M.–2:30 P.M.), but admission is free.

Also on campus is the delightful **UBC Botanical Garden** (6804 Marine Dr., 604/822-4208, daily 9 A.M.–5 P.M., adult $8, senior and child $6). Set among coastal forest, the 44-hectare (110-acre) site comprises eight themed gardens, including Canada's largest collection of rhododendrons, the British Columbia Native Garden, a display of mountain plants from the world's continents, and medieval healing plants in the Physick Garden. From the Museum of Anthropology, follow Marine Drive south for 2.4 kilometers (1.5 miles) to 16th Avenue.

RICHMOND

The incorporated city of Richmond (population 185,000) sprawls across **Lulu Island** at the mouth of the Fraser River. Most visitors to Vancouver cross the island on their way north from the United States on Highway 99, or to and from the airport or Tsawwassen Ferry Terminal.

Steveston

On Lulu Island's southwestern extremity, the historic fishing village of Steveston is a lively spot worth a visit. In the 1880s it had more than 50 canneries and was the world's largest fishing port. The harbor still holds Canada's largest fleet of commercial fishing boats.

On the harbor front you'll find the **Gulf of Georgia Cannery National Historic Site** (12138 4th Ave., 604/664-9009, daily 10 A.M.–5 P.M. May–Aug., Thurs.–Mon. 10 A.M.–5 P.M. Sept.–mid-Oct., adult $7.80, senior $6.60, child $4), a cannery that operated between 1894 and 1979. Much of the original cannery has been restored. In addition to canning-line exhibits and demonstrations of the various machineries, an audiovisual presentation is offered in the Boiler House Theatre, and the Discovery Area is set aside for children. A short walk from the old cannery is a redeveloped stretch of harbor front where casual visitors and local fishermen mingle at fishing-supply outlets, shops selling packaged seafood products, boutiques, and restaurants. Below the main wharf, fishing boats sell the day's catch—halibut, salmon, crabs, mussels, shrimp, and oysters—to the general public at excellent prices. Naturally, seafood is the specialty at harbor-front restaurants, all of which have outdoor tables. My favorite is **Sockeye City Grill** (3800 Bayview St., 604/275-4347, daily 11 A.M.–9 P.M., $13–27), with tables spread out along the waterfront.

To get to Steveston, take Highway 99 to the Steveston Highway exit, then head west, passing by a magnificent Buddhist temple. The town center is south from the Steveston Highway along the Number 1 Road.

NORTH SHORE

North of downtown lies the incorporated cities of **North Vancouver** and **West Vancouver,** both dramatically sandwiched between the North Shore Range of the Coast Mountains and Burrard Inlet. The North Shore is accessible from downtown via the **Lions Gate Bridge,** but the SeaBus, which runs from Waterfront Station to **Lonsdale Quay** (adults $3.25 each way), offers a more enjoyable alternative to getting caught in bridge traffic. At the lively quay, a small information center (to the right as you come out of the SeaBus terminal) dispenses valuable information, and transit buses depart regularly for all the sights listed below.

Capilano Suspension Bridge

Admission at this major North Shore attraction (604/985-7474, daily 8 A.M.–dusk in summer, 9 A.M.–5 P.M. the rest of the year, adult $30, senior $28, child $19) is a bit steep, but it's one of Vancouver's most popular sights. The first bridge across the Capilano River opened in 1899. Today, several bridges later, a wood-and-wire suspension bridge spans the canyon some 70 fearsome meters (230 feet) above the Capilano River. Allow at least two hours to walk the bridge, step out onto the numerous cantilevered decks, take the Treetops Adventure suspended walkway, and wander along the forested nature trails. Back near the main entrance, native carvers display their skills in the Big House, and you'll find the requisite gift shop and eateries. To get there by car, cross Lions Gate Bridge, turn east onto Marine Drive then immediately north onto Capilano Road, continuing to 3735 Capilano, on your left. By bus, take number 246 north on Georgia Street or hop aboard the SeaBus and take bus number 236 from Lonsdale Quay.

Capilano Salmon Hatchery

This is my favorite North Shore attraction—and not only because it's free. If you've always wanted to know more about the life cycle of salmon, or if you just want some facts to back up your fish stories, visit this hatchery (Capilano Rd., 604/666-1790, daily

8 A.M.–8 P.M. in summer, until dusk the rest of the year) on the Capilano River, upstream from the suspension bridge. Beside the rushing Capilano River and ensconced in cool rainforest, salmon are diverted through a channel and into man-made spawning grounds. The channel is topped by a metal grate in one section and lined with glass windows in another. This allows up-close viewing of the salmon as they fight the current through their July to October run. In addition to the life cycle displays, an exhibit on fly-fishing holds some interesting old tackle.

C Grouse Mountain

Continuing north, Capilano Road becomes Nancy Greene Way and ends at the base of Grouse Mountain, accessed by North America's largest aerial tramway (604/980-9311, adult $38, senior $36, child $23). For a sweeping view of downtown Vancouver, Stanley Park, the Pacific Ocean, and as far south as Mount Baker (Washington), take the almost-vertical eight-minute ride to the summit of this 1,250-meter (4,100-foot) peak. The gondola runs year-round, departing every 15 minutes, 10 A.M.–10 P.M. in summer, shorter hours the rest of the year.   The trip to the top is a lot more than a gondola ride—and it's easy to spend the best part of a day exploring the surrounding area and taking advantage of the attractions included in the price of the ride up. Of the many possible hikes, the one-kilometer (0.6-mile) **Blue Grouse Interpretive Trail** is the easiest and most enjoyable. Another trail leads to a fenced area where wolves and bears are rehabilitated after being orphaned. A trail map is available at the gondola's upper terminal. Other summit activities include a fun but touristy logging show, chairlift rides, a First Nations longhouse with dancing and storytelling, and wide-screen movie presentations of the outdoor wonders of British Columbia and local wildlife. Mountaintop dining facilities are contained in a magnificent log day lodge decorated with stylish West Coast artwork.

To get to the gondola, cross the Lions Gate Bridge from downtown; take the North Vancouver exit, then follow Capilano Road for five kilometers (3.1 miles) up the valley. By public transport, take the SeaBus to Lonsdale Quay, then take bus number 236 to the gondola's lower terminal.

Lynn Canyon Park

On its way to Burrard Inlet, Lynn Creek flows through a deep canyon straddled by this 240-hectare (930-acre) park. Spanning the canyon is the "other" suspension bridge. The one here is half as wide as its more famous counterpart over the Capilano River, but it's a few meters higher and, best of all, it's free. An ancient forest of Douglas fir surrounds the impressive canyon and harbors a number of hiking trails. Be sure to visit **Lynn Canyon Ecology Centre** (3663 Park Rd., 604/990-3755, daily 10 A.M.–5 P.M., free), where displays, models, and free slide shows and films explore plant and animal ecology. Lynn Canyon Park is seven kilometers (4.3 miles) east of the Capilano River. To get there by car, take the Lynn Valley Road exit off Highway 1, east of the Lions Gate Bridge. By public transport, take the SeaBus to Lonsdale Quay, then bus number 228 or 229.

Mount Seymour Provincial Park and Vicinity

Hikers flock to this 3,508-hectare (8,670-acre) park, 20 kilometers (12.4 miles) northeast of downtown. The park lies off Mount Seymour Parkway, which splits east off the TransCanada Highway just north of Burrard Inlet. The long and winding access road to the park climbs steadily through an ancient forest of western hemlock, cedar, and Douglas fir to a small facility area at an elevation of 1,000 meters (3,300 feet). From the parking lot, trails lead to the summit of 1,453-meter (4,770-foot) Mount Seymour; allow one hour for the two-kilometer (one-way) trek.

Cypress Provincial Park

This 3,012-hectare (7,440-acre) park northwest of downtown encompasses a high alpine area in the North Shore Mountains. To get to the park, take the TransCanada Highway 12 kilometers

(7.5 miles) west of Lions Gate Bridge and turn north onto Cypress Bowl Road (Exit 8). Even the park access road up from the TransCanada Highway is worthwhile for the views. At the second switchback, the **Highview Lookout** provides a stunning panorama of the city, with interpretive panels describing the surrounding natural history. There's plenty of hiking in the vicinity—from the main day lodge, well-marked hiking trails radiate out like spokes. One easy trail leads under the Black Chair (to the left as you stand in front of the day lodge) and passes a small alpine lake before ending after 1.3 kilometers (0.8 miles) at a lookout; allow one hour for the round-trip.

Bowen Island

Just a short ferry trip from the mainland, this island (population 3,200) is a world away from the city. **BC Ferries** (604/669-1211) operates a 20-minute service between Horseshoe Bay and the island daily 6 A.M.–9:45 P.M., approximately once an hour. The fare is adult $7.25, child $3.75. The ferry docks at the island's main settlement, aptly named **Snug Cove,** where you'll find all the services of a small town, including bed-and-breakfasts and cafés. There's good swimming at Mannion Bay, near Snug Cove, and **Bowen Island Sea Kayaking** (604/947-9266) rents kayaks (three hours, $45–65) and offers tours (three hours, $65 per person), but the rest of the island is also good to explore. A two-kilometer (1.2-mile) trail leads from Snug Cove to Killarney Lake, where birdlife is prolific and roads lead across to the island's west coast. Island information is available from **Tourism Bowen** (432 Cardena Rd., 604/947-9024, daily 9 A.M.–7 P.M. in summer, www.bowenisland.org).

EAST FROM DOWNTOWN

When you leave Vancouver and head due east, you travel through the most built-up and heavily populated area of British Columbia, skirting modern commercial centers, residential suburbs, and zones of heavy industry. Greater Vancouver extends almost 100 kilometers (62 miles) along the Fraser Valley, through mostly residential areas. The main route east is the TransCanada Highway, which parallels the Fraser River to the south, passing through Burnaby, Langley, and Abbotsford. The original path taken by this highway crosses the Fraser River at New Westminster, the capital of British Columbia for a short period in the 1860s.

Burnaby

Immediately east of downtown, Burnaby was incorporated as a city in 1992 (its population of 240,000 makes it British Columbia's third-largest city), but in reality it's part of Vancouver's suburban sprawl. It extends east from Boundary Road to Coquitlam, while Burrard Inlet lies to the north and riverside New Westminster to the southeast. The TransCanada Highway bisects Burnaby, but access is easiest via the SkyTrain, which makes four stops within the city. Among these stops is **Metrotown,** which is Vancouver's largest shopping mall.

Burnaby Village Museum is a four-hectare (10-acre) open-air museum (604/293-6500, Tues.–Sun. 11 A.M.–4:30 P.M. May–early Sept., closed the rest of the year, adult $12, senior and child $9) in Deer Lake Park, on the south side of the TransCanada Highway. The village is a reconstruction of how a British Columbia town would have looked in the first 20 years of the 1900s, complete with more than 30 shops and houses, heritage-style gardens, a miniature railway, and costumed staff. But the highlight is a historic carousel with more than 30 restored wooden horses. To get there, take Exit 33 south, then turn left onto Canada Way and right onto Deer Lake Avenue, or take the SkyTrain to Metrotown Station and jump aboard bus number 144.

Vicinity of Coquitlam

Coquitlam is a residential area at the head of Burrard Inlet. Immediately north is 38,000-hectare (93,900-acre) **Pinecone Burke Provincial Park,** which extends along the west shoreline of Pitt Lake and as far west as the Boise Valley, scene of a short-lived gold rush in the late 1800s. Much of the park was logged more than 100 years ago, but a few sections of old-growth forest remain, including a 1,000-year-old stand of cedar in the Cedar Spirit Grove. To get to the park from Highway 7, take Coast Meridian Road north to Harper Road, which leads to Munro and Bennett Lakes.

An even bigger tract of wilderness is protected by **Golden Ears Provincial Park,** which encompasses 55,590 hectares (137,000 acres) of the North Shore Mountains east of Coquitlam. To reach the park, follow Highway 7 east from Coquitlam to Maple Ridge, then follow signs north along 232nd Street and 132nd Avenue. The park access road ends at **Alouette Lake,** with fair fishing and lots of nearby hiking. **Lower Falls Trail** is an easy hike that everyone can enjoy. It begins at the end of the road and leads 2.7 kilometers (1.7 miles) to a picturesque waterfall; allow one hour each way.

New Westminster

"New West," as it's best known, is a densely populated residential area 15 kilometers (9.3 miles) southeast of downtown. Its strategic location, where the Fraser River divides, caused it to become a hub of river transportation and a thriving economic center. It was declared the capital of the mainland colony in 1859, then the provincial capital in the years 1866–1868. Only a few historic buildings remain, and the old port area has been totally overtaken by modern developments. The center of the action is **Westminster Quay Market** (810 Quayside Dr., 604/520-3881), along the riverfront and below the old Main Street. Although its hours are very un-market-like (it doesn't open until 9:30 A.M. each day), it holds an interesting selection of fresh produce, take-out food stalls, and specialty shops. Out front is the *Samson V,* built in 1937 and the last remaining paddle wheeler left on the river when it was retired in 1980. It's now open for public inspection (daily noon–5 P.M. June–Aug.); call the local museum at 604/527-4640 for details. Beside the market is the **Fraser River Discovery Centre** (788 Quayside Dr., 604/521-8401, daily 10 A.M.–4 P.M. June–Aug., Wed.–Sat. 10 A.M.–4 P.M. the rest of the year, adult $6, senior and child $5) that describes the river and its importance to the development of New Westminster. Other interpretive boards are spread along the boardwalk in front of the market, as is the unlikely combination of a floating casino, a tugboat-themed playground, and the world's largest tin soldier.

Recreation

BIKING

Stanley Park is a hot spot for cyclists; among its network of bike paths is the popular **Seawall Promenade,** which hugs the coast for 10 kilometers (6.2 miles). Bike travel is in a counterclockwise direction. On the south side of English Bay, a cycle path runs from Vanier Park to Point Grey and the university, passing some of the city's best beaches on the way. On the north side of Burrard Inlet, hard-core mountain bike enthusiasts tackle the rough trails of Cypress Provincial Park and Grouse Mountain. Near the entrance to Stanley Park, where Robson and Denman Streets meet, you'll find a profusion of bike-rental shops. These include **Bayshore Bicycles** (745 Denman St., 604/688-2453) and **Spokes Bicycle Rental** (1798 W. Georgia St., 604/688-5141).

GOLF

One of the best courses open to the public is the **University Golf Club** (5185 University Blvd., Point Grey, 604/224-1818, $70), featuring narrow tree-lined fairways surrounded by mature trees and plays to 6,584 yards. Vancouver Parks and Recreation operates three 18-hole courses on the south side of the city: **McCleery Golf Course** (7188 McDonald St., Southlands, 604/257-8191) has a flat, relatively easy layout with wide fairways; rebuilt in the late 1990s, **Fraserview Golf Course** (7800 Vivian Dr., Fraserview, 604/257-6923) winds its way through a well-established forest; and **Langara Golf Course** (6706 Alberta St. off Cambie St., South Cambie, 604/713-1816) is the most challenging of the three. Greens fees at all three courses are $55–60 during the week and $60–75 on weekends.

Water comes into play on 13 holes of the **Mayfair Lakes & Country Club** (5460 No. 7 Rd., Richmond, 604/276-0505, $85), but its most unique feature is the salmon, which spawn in Mayfair's waterways. Of the many golf courses spread out along the Fraser River Valley, **Meadow Gardens Golf Club** (19675 Meadow Gardens Way, off Hwy. 7, Pitt Meadows, 604/465-5474 or 800/667-6758, $75), on the north side of the river, stands out. The signature 18th hole is a par 5 that comprises island-only landing areas for the drive and the second shot, and then the approach is played to an island green.

BEACHES AND SWIMMING

All of Vancouver's best beaches are along the shoreline of English Bay; 10 have lifeguards on duty 11:30 A.M.–8:45 P.M. through the summer months. Closest to downtown is **English Bay Beach** at the end of Denman Street. Flanked by a narrow strip of parkland and a wide array of cafés and restaurants, this is *the* beach for people watching. From English Bay Beach, the Seawall Promenade leads north to **Second** and **Third Beaches,** both short, secluded stretches of sand. To the south is **Sunset Beach,** most popular with families.

Swimmers take note: Even at the peak of summer, the water here only warms up to about 17°C (63°F), tops. If that doesn't sound very enticing, continue to the south end of Sunset Beach to **Vancouver Aquatic Centre** (1050 Beach Ave., 604/665-3424, adult $5.50, senior $4.20, child $3.30). Inside you'll find a 50-meter heated pool, saunas, whirlpools, and a small weight room.

On the south side of English Bay, **Kitsilano Beach** offers spectacular views back across the bay to downtown and the mountains beyond. Take a dip in the adjacent public pool, which is 137 meters long and was built in 1931. The beach and pool are an easy walk from both Vanier Park and a False Creek Ferries dock.

© ANDREW HEMPSTEAD

the public pool at Kitsilano Beach

VANCOUVER'S BEST HIKING

While Vancouver is not a particularly good city to explore on foot, it does have a number of wonderful urban and wilderness parks where taking a walk is a wonderful way to leave the hustle and bustle of the city behind. Here are a few favorites.

STANLEY PARK

Stanley Park, an urban oasis crisscrossed with hiking trails and encircled by a 10-kilometer (6.2-mile) promenade that hugs the shoreline. The promenade is always busy, especially in late afternoon and on weekends, but you'll find most other trails a lot less used. A good alternative to one long section of the promenade is to ascend the steps immediately north of Lions Gate Bridge to Prospect Point (and maybe stop for a snack at the café), then continue west along the **Merilees Trail,** which follows the top of the cliff band to Third Beach. Along the way, an old lookout point affords excellent views of Siwash Rock and the Strait of Georgia.

PACIFIC SPIRIT REGIONAL PARK AND VICINITY

This 762-hectare (1,880-acre) park out near the university offers 35 kilometers (22 miles) of hiking trails through a forested environment similar to that which greeted the first European settlers over 200 years ago. A good starting point is the Park Centre (604/224-5739), which has a supply of trail maps. The entire park is crisscrossed with trails, so although getting seriously lost is impossible, taking the wrong trail and ending up away from your intended destination is easy. The **Imperial Trail,** starting at the corner of King Edward and 29th Avenues, is a personal favorite. It passes through a forest of red cedar and fir, crosses Salish Creek, then emerges on Southwest Marine Drive, at a monument commemorating the journey of Simon Fraser. From this lofty viewpoint, the view extends across the Strait of Georgia. This trail is 2.8 kilometers (1.7 miles) one-way (allow one hour).

NORTH SHORE

The provincial parks along the North Shore contain outstanding scenery and wildlife, crystal-clear lakes and rivers, and established hiking trails that are generally well maintained and easy to follow.

The westernmost of the city's beaches is also the most infamous. **Wreck Beach** is a nudist hangout, where the unabashed prance around naked and nude dudes sell hot dogs and pop from driftwood concession stands. Swimming here isn't particularly good, but the beach still gets extremely busy. Access to the beach is down a steep trail from Northwest Marine Drive, near the end of University Boulevard (take Trail No. 4, 5, or 6).

CANOEING AND KAYAKING

Granville Island is the center of action for paddlers, and the calm waters of adjacent False Creek make the perfect place to practice your skills. For the widest choice of equipment, head to **Adventure Fitness** (1510 Duranleau St., 604/687-1528) or **Ecomarine Ocean Kayak Centre** (1668 Duranleau St., 604/689-7575).

Both rent single sea kayaks from $36 for two hours or $58 for 24 hours, and double sea kayaks and canoes from $48 for two hours or $72 for 24 hours. Both companies also teach kayaking.

The **Indian Arm** of Burrard Inlet allows for a real wilderness experience, right on the city's back doorstep. This 22-kilometer (13.7-mile) long fjord cuts deeply into the North Shore Range; the only development is at its southern end, where the suburb of Deep Cove provides a takeoff point for the waterway. **Deep Cove Canoe and Kayak Centre** (2156 Banbury Rd., Deep Cove, 604/929-2268) rents canoes and kayaks for $38 for two hours for a single kayak. If you'd prefer to take a tour, contact **Lotus Land Tours** (604/684-4922 or 800/528-3531), which charges $180 per person for a full-day tour, including downtown hotel pickups, a salmon barbecue on an uninhabited island, and instruction.

WINTER RECREATION

While Vancouver is the gateway to world-renowned Whistler and Blackcomb, the city boasts three other alpine resorts on its back doorstep.

Towering above North Vancouver, the slopes of **Grouse Mountain** (Nancy Greene Way, 604/980-9311, www.grousemountain.com) can be seen from many parts of the city, but as you'd expect, on a clear day views from *up there* are much more spectacular. Four chairlifts and a couple of T-bars serve 24 runs and a vertical rise of 365 meters (1,200 feet).

Most runs are lit daily until 10 P.M. and overlook the city of Vancouver, laid out in all its brilliance far below. Facilities at the resort include a snowboard park, a rental shop, a ski and snowboard school, and a couple of dining choices. Lift tickets are adult $58, senior and youth $42, child $31.

Cypress Mountain (Cypress Bowl Road, Exit 8 off Hwy 1, 604/926-5612, www.cypressmountain.com) hosted the freestyle skiing and snowboarding events of the 2010 Olympic Winter Games. It offers about 25 runs across a vertical rise of 534 meters (1,750 feet). Spectacular views take in Howe Sound and Vancouver Island. Lift tickets are adult $52, senior and child $29. Cypress also caters to cross-country skiers and snowshoers, with 16 kilometers (10 miles) of groomed and track-set trails, some of which are lit for night skiing.

With the highest base elevation of Vancouver's three alpine resorts, **Mount Seymour** (604/986-2261, www.mountseymour.com) has snow that is somewhat reliable, but the area's relatively gentle terrain will be of interest only to beginning and intermediate skiers and boarders. Four chairlifts serve 20 runs and a vertical rise of 365 meters (1,200 feet). Daily lift passes are adult $44, senior $32, child $24. You can also rent snowshoes ($16) and tramp along the resort's trail system ($10 for a day pass), but the Friday night guided snowshoe walk ($45) is a real treat—and not only because of the chocolate fondue at the end.

The resort is in Mount Seymour Provincial Park. To get there, head north off the TransCanada Highway 15 kilometers (9.3 miles) east of the Lions Gate Bridge, following the Mount Seymour Parkway to Mount Seymour Road.

SPECTATOR SPORTS

Vancouverites love their sports—not just being involved themselves, but supporting local teams. With a long season and outside activities curtailed by the winter weather, ice hockey—known in Canada simply as "hockey"—draws the biggest crowds, but the city also boasts professional football, baseball, and soccer teams.

Hockey

In 1911 the world's second (and largest) artificial ice rink opened at the north end of Denman Street, complete with seating for 10,000 hockey fans. The local team, then known as the Vancouver Millionaires, played in a small professional league and in 1915 Vancouver won its first and only **Stanley Cup,** the holy grail of professional ice hockey. Joining the National Hockey League (NHL) in 1970, the **Vancouver Canucks** (604/899-7400, www.canucks.com) play out of General Motors Place (across from BC Place Stadium on Griffith Way), which was built for the now defunct Vancouver Grizzlies NBA franchise. The season runs October–April; ticket prices range $45–200.

Football

The **BC Lions** (604/589-7627, www.bclions.com) are Vancouver's Canadian Football League franchise. Home games are played at BC Place Stadium, on the south side of downtown at the corner of Robson and Beatty Streets. The season runs June–November, with most games played in the evening; tickets range $32–84.

TOURS

If you don't have a lot of time to explore Vancouver on your own, or just want an introduction to the city, consider one of the many tours available—it will maximize your time and get you to the highlights with minimum stress.

Trolley and Bus Tours

From a trolley-shaped booth at the top end of Water Street (the main pick-up point), **Vancouver Trolley Company** (604/801-5515 or 888/451-5581) operates an old-fashioned trolley through the streets of downtown Vancouver. The two-hour loop stops at 23 tourist attractions, from Stanley Park in the north to Science World in the south. Trolleys run daily 9 A.M.–4 P.M. April–October, coming by each stop every half hour. Tickets are adult $36, senior $33, child $20.

Gray Line (604/879-3363 or 800/667-0882, www.grayline.ca) offers a large variety of tours. The 3.5-hour Deluxe Grand City Tour, which includes Stanley Park, Chinatown, Gastown, Robson Street, and English Bay, costs adult $65, senior $58, child $42.

Harbor Cruises

From June to September, **Harbour Cruises** (604/688-7246 or 800/663-1500) offers a 75-minute tour of bustling Burrard Inlet on the paddle wheeler MPV *Constitution*. Tours depart from the north foot of Denman Street, up to four times daily April–early October; the cost is adult $25, senior and student $20, child $10. In the evening (7 P.M. June–Sept.), the paddle wheeler heads out into the harbor for a three-hour Sunset Dinner Cruise. The cruise costs adult $75, child $65, which includes dinner.

Entertainment and Events

There's never a dull moment in Vancouver when it comes to nightlife. The city's unofficial entertainment district extends southwest along Granville Street from Granville Street Mall, and south from this strip to False Creek. Cinemas line Granville Street Mall, while beyond the mall are a smattering of nightclubs, with the main concentration of these in Yaletown. Performing arts and concert venues are scattered throughout the city, but the three largest—Ford Centre for the Performing Arts, Queen Elizabeth Centre, and BC Place Stadium—are south of Granville Street along Georgia Street.

For complete listings of all that's happening around the city, pick up the free *Georgia Straight* (www.straight.com). Friday and weekend editions of Vancouver's two daily newspapers, the *Province* or the *Vancouver Sun,* offer comprehensive entertainment listings. **Tickets Tonight** (in the visitor center, 200 Burrard St., 604/684-2787, www.ticketstonight.ca, daily 10 A.M.–6 P.M.) sells half-price tickets the day of major performances.

NIGHTLIFE
Bars

Ever since "Gassy Jack" Deighton set up the city's first liquor outlet (a barrel of whiskey set atop a crude plank "bar") in the area that became known as Gastown, that part of the city has been a favorite drinking spot. The **Steamworks Brewing Co.** (375 Water St., Gastown, 604/689-2739, daily 11:30 A.M.–10 P.M.) is the perfect place to relax with a beer from the in-house brewery. The atmosphere is casual yet stylish, and you'll have great views across Burrard Inlet. At the far end of Gastown, the lively **Blarney Stone** (216 Carrall St., 604/687-4322) frequently resounds with rowdy Irish party bands. The evening crowd here is older and often single.

Yaletown Brewing Co. (1111 Mainland St., 604/681-2739) is the premier drinking hole for the hip population of inner-city Yaletown. Also in Yaletown, the **Opus Bar** (350 Davie St., 604/642-0557) serves up strong cocktails and imported beer in a sizzlingly hip setting off the lobby of the Opus Hotel. At the **Royal Pub** (1025 Granville St., 604/685-5335), join the throngs of young backpackers drinking up nightly specials before retiring to the upstairs hostel.

Nightclubs

Nightclubs change names and reputations with

regularity, so check with the free entertainment newspapers or www.clubvibes.com for the latest hot spots. Best known as "the Fair," **Luv-A-Fair,** (1275 Seymour St., 604/685-3288) is as popular today as when it opened in the late 1980s, especially on Thursday nights, which feature techno tunes.

Appealing to an over-30s crowd is **Skybar** (670 Smithe St., 604/697-9199), a mega-trendy nightspot with drink prices to match. At street level is a martini bar, the second floor is mostly a dance floor, and the complex is topped with a retractable roof that opens a palm-tree studded patio to the elements.

Away from the main entertainment district, Gastown offers a selection of nightclubs, including **Fabric** (66 Water St., 604/683-6695), which has grown to become one of the hottest Vancouver nightspots. Many DJs are imported from London, and although most nights feature the latest techno, hip-hop, and house music from across the Atlantic, the club's appeal has broadened and weeknights occasionally feature soul and jazz. The scene here attracts serious dancers and those who want to be seen dancing.

Live Music

Attracting a huge crowd every night of the week, the classic **Roxy** (932 Granville St., 604/331-7999), presents two house bands playing rock 'n' roll music from all eras to a packed house during the week, and imported bands on weekends. The young, hip crowd, good music, and performance bartenders make this the city's most popular live music venue, so expect a line, especially after 9 P.M. on weekends; cover charges range $5–10. The **Railway Club** (579 Dunsmuir St., 604/681-1625) is a private club where nonmembers are welcome (at a higher cover charge) to listen to acts that range from rock to country.

The **Hot Jazz Society** (2120 Main St., 604/873-4131) presents live jazz on a regular basis; cover charge ranges $7–12. The **Coastal Jazz & Blues Society** (604/872-5200, www.coastaljazz.ca) maintains a listing of all the city's jazz and blues events.

Serious blues lovers should head to the historic **Yale Hotel** (1300 Granville St., 604/681-9253), which has hosted some of the greatest names in the business, including Junior Wells and Stevie Ray Vaughan. The hotel offers plenty of room for everyone, whether you want to get up and dance or shoot pool in the back. Sunday is the only night without live performances, although a jam session starts up around 3 P.M. on Saturday and Sunday afternoons.

THE ARTS
Theater

Vancouver has theaters all over the city—for professional plays, amateur plays, comedy, and "instant" theater. In total, the city boasts 30 professional theater companies and more than 20 regular venues. The **Centre in Vancouver for Performing Arts** (777 Homer St., 604/602-0616, www.centreinvancouver.com) hosts the biggest of musical hits. Matinees prices start at $50, while evening shows range $60–110. A similar facility is the **Chan Centre for the Performing Arts** (6265 Crescent Rd., Point Grey, 604/822-2697), comprising three stages including the 1,400-seat Chan Shun Concert Hall.

The **Arts Club Theatre** (1585 Johnston St., 604/687-1644, www.artsclub.com) always offers excellent theater productions at two Granville Island locations—the **Granville Island Stage** and adjacent **Stanley Industrial Alliance Stage.** Productions range from drama to comedy to improv. Tickets run $24–40; book in advance and pick up your tickets at the door 30 minutes prior to showtime.

One of the great joys of summer in the city is sitting around Malkin Bowl in Stanley Park watching **Theatre Under the Stars** (604/734-1917, www.tuts.ca). Since 1934 these shows have drawn around 1,000 theatergoers nightly, with performances usually musically oriented. The setting itself, an open amphitheater surrounded by towering Douglas fir trees, is as much of an attraction as the performance. The show runs Mon.–Sat. at 7 P.M. June–August. Tickets (adult $34, child $32) go on sale at noon daily from a booth beside the bowl.

Music and Dance

The **Queen Elizabeth Theatre** (630 Hamilton St., 604/665-3050) is the home of **Vancouver Opera** (604/683-0222); tickets begin at $40, rising to $100 for the best seats. The theater also hosts a variety of music recitals and stage performances.

The historic **Orpheum Theatre,** on the corner of Smithe and Seymour Streets, dates to 1927 and houses its original Wurlitzer organ. Now fully restored, the theater provides excellent acoustics for the resident **Vancouver Symphony** (604/684-9100), as well as for concerts by the professional **Vancouver Chamber Choir** (604/738-6822), the amateur **Vancouver Bach Choir** (604/921-8012), and a variety of other musical groups.

Ballet British Columbia (604/732-5003, www.balletbc.com), performs in the Queen Elizabeth Theatre at 630 Hamilton St. throughout its winter season. Tickets range $25–58.

Cinemas

Cinemas are in all the major shopping malls and elsewhere throughout the city. **Cineplex Odeon** (604/434-2463) operates 20 cinemas in Vancouver. Call or check the two daily papers for locations and screenings. Admission to first-run screenings is about $12.

If you're staying at a Robson Street or West End accommodation, head over to **Denman Place Cinema** (corner of Denman and Comox Streets, 604/683-2201) for first- and second-run hits for $4–6. For foreign and Canadian indie films, check out **Pacific Cinematheque** (1131 Howe St., 604/688-8202).

FESTIVALS AND EVENTS

Festivals of some description take place in Vancouver just about every month of the year. Whether it's a celebration of local or international culture, the arts, sporting events, or just a wacky long-time tradition, there's always a reason to party in Vancouver. Many of the most popular festivals are held during summer, the peak visitor season, but the rest of the year is the main season for performances by the city's dance, theater, and music companies, and not-to-be-missed events such as the Christmas Carol Ship Parade. For details and exact dates of the events listed below, contact the numbers or visit the websites given, or visit any local tourist information center.

Tickets for most major events can be booked through **Ticketmaster** (www.ticketmaster.ca).

Spring

The spring event schedule kicks off in a big way the third week of March with the **Vancouver Playhouse International Wine Festival** (604/872-6622, www.playhousewinefest. com). Hosted by various downtown venues, it is one of North America's largest wine festivals, bringing together representatives from more than 150 wineries and 14 countries. Other public events include a variety of nighttime gatherings, such as Bacchanalia, a gala dinner hosted by the Fairmont Vancouver.

The **Vancouver Sun Run** (604/689-9441, www.sunrun.com) is a 10-kilometer (6.2-mile) run (or walk) through the streets of downtown on the third Sunday in April. Attracting more than 45,000 participants, it is Canada's largest (and the world's third largest) such run. For more serious runners, the **Vancouver International Marathon** (604/872-2928, www.bmovanmarathon.ca) takes place two Sundays later.

Summer

Two of summer's most popular cultural events take place from mid-June through late in the season, meaning you can enjoy them at any time through the warmer months. **Bard on the Beach** (604/737-0625, www.bardonthebeach.org, June–Sept.) comprises three favorite Shakespeare plays performed in open-ended tents in Vanier Park, allowing a spectacular backdrop of English Bay, the city skyline, and the mountains beyond. Tickets are well priced at just $24–32 for 1 P.M. and 4 P.M. matinees and from $34 for 7:30 P.M. evening performances. The other event, the **Kitsilano Showboat** (604/734-7332, www.kitsilanoshowboat.com), takes place at nearby Kitsilano

Beach. Amateur variety acts have been taking to this stage since 1935. Performances are Monday, Wednesday, and Friday nights at 7:30 P.M. over a 10-week summer season.

The **Dragon Boat Festival** (604/688-2382, www.dragonboatbc.com) comes to False Creek on the middle weekend in June. In addition to the races, a blessing ceremony and a variety of cultural activities take place in and around the Plaza of Nations.

Late June through early July, Vancouver taps its feet to the beat of the annual **Vancouver International Jazz Festival** (604/872-5200, www.coastaljazz.ca), when more than 1,500 musicians from countries around the world gather to perform traditional and contemporary jazz at 40 venues around the city.

The middle weekend of July, Jericho Beach Park draws lots of folks to the **Vancouver Folk Music Festival** (604/602-9798, www.thefestival.bc.ca). In addition to the wonderful music, the festival features storytelling, dance performances, live theater, and a food fair.

Year after year, Vancouverites await with much anticipation the early August **Celebration of Light** (604/642-6835, www.celebration-of-light.com), the world's largest musical fireworks competition. Each year, three countries compete; each has a night to itself (the last Saturday in July, then the following Wednesday and Saturday), putting on a display that lasts up to an hour from 10:15 P.M.; then on the final night (second Wednesday in August), the three competing countries come together for a grand finale. The fireworks are let off from a barge moored in English Bay, allowing viewing from Stanley Park, Kitsilano Beach, Jericho Beach, and as far away as West Vancouver. Music that accompanies the displays can be heard around the shoreline; if you're away from the action, tune your radio to 101.1 FM for a simulcast.

Summer's busy event schedule winds up at the Pacific National Exhibition Grounds with **The Fair (Pacific National Exhibition)** (604/253-2311, www.pne.bc.ca) in late August. A highlight of this agricultural exposition is the twice-daily RCMP musical ride, a precision drill performed by Canada's famous Mounties.

Fall

Beginning the second week of September, the **Vancouver International Fringe Festival** (604/257-0350, www.vancouverfringe.com) schedules around 500 performances by 100 artists from around the world at indoor and outdoor stages throughout Granville Island.

The **Vancouver International Film Festival** (604/685-0260, www.viff.org) is held late in early October and features more than 300 of the very best movies from around 60 countries at theaters across downtown. In the middle of October, literary types congregate on Granville Island for the **Vancouver International Writers & Readers Festival** (604/681-6330, www.writersfest.bc.ca).

Winter

Through the month of December, VanDusen Botanical Garden is transformed each evening by more than 80,000 lights and seasonal displays such as a nativity scene during the **Festival of Lights** (604/878-9274). Another popular pre-Christmas event is the **Carol Ships Parade of Lights** (604/878-8999, www.carolships.org). For three weeks leading up to Christmas Eve, the waterways of Vancouver come alive with the sounds of the festive season as each night a flotilla of up to 80 boats, each decorated with colorful lights, sails around Burrard Inlet, Port Moody, Deep Cove, and around English Bay to False Creek, while onboard carolers sing the songs of Christmas through sound systems that can clearly be heard along the shoreline.

While most normal folk spend New Year's Day recovering from the previous night's celebrations, up to 2,000 brave souls head down to English Bay Beach and go *swimming*. The information hotline for the **Polar Bear Swim** is 604/732-2304, but all you really need to know is that the water will be *very* cold. The insanity starts at 2:30 P.M.

Shopping

Vancouver has shopping centers, malls, and specialty stores everywhere. Head to Gastown for native arts and crafts, Robson Street for boutique clothing, Granville Street Mall for department stores, Granville Island for everything from ships' chandlery to kids' clothing, Yaletown for the trendy clothes of local designers, the Eastside for army-surplus stores and pawnbrokers, Chinatown for Eastern foods, and the junction of Main Street and E. 49th Avenue for Indian foods.

GASTOWN

Sandwiched between the many cafés, restaurants, and tacky souvenir stores along Water Street are other stores selling Vancouver's best selection of native arts and crafts. One of the largest outlets, **Hill's Native Art** (165 Water St., 604/685-4249) sells $10 T-shirts, towering $12,000 totem poles, and everything in between, including genuine Cowichan sweaters and carved ceremonial masks. Also featuring traditional native art is **Images for a Canadian Heritage** (164 Water St., 604/685-7046). The **Inuit Gallery of Vancouver** (206 Cambie St., 604/688-7323) exhibits the work of Inuit and northwest coast native artists and sculptors. Among the highlights are many soapstone pieces by carvers from Cape Dorset, a remote Inuit village in Arctic Canada.

GRANVILLE ISLAND

Arts and crafts galleries on Granville Island include **Wickaninnish Gallery** (1666 Johnston St., 604/681-1057), which sells stunning native art, jewelry, carvings, weavings, and original paintings; **Gallery of BC Ceramics** (1359 Cartwright St., 604/669-3606), showcasing the work of the province's leading potters and sculptors; and **Forge & Form** (1334 Cartwright St., 604/684-6298), which creates and sells a variety of gold and silver jewelry.

Duranleau Street is home to many maritime-based businesses, adventure-tour operators, and charter operators. The **Quarterdeck** (1660 Duranleau St., 604/683-8232) stocks everything from marine charts to brass shipping bells.

DEPARTMENT STORES, PLAZAS, AND MALLS

Despite looking pretty dowdy these days, **Granville Street Mall** nevertheless forms the heart of the downtown shopping precinct; the two-block stretch of Granville Street is closed to private vehicles, though buses and taxis still

---

SHOPPING IN CHINATOWN

Chinatown evolved more than 100 years ago as a place where Chinese settlers, who mostly lived around the back of False Creek, could shop and eat in an environment they were familiar with. Today, the streets bustle with locals and tourists alike, browsing the many intriguing shops and dining on authentic Chinese cuisine.

The shops sell a mind-boggling array of Chinese goods: wind chimes, soy sauce, teapots, dried mushrooms, delicate paper fans, and much, much more. Along Main Street a number of shops sell ginseng, sold by the Chinese ounce (38 grams or 1.3 U.S. ounces). Cultivated ginseng costs from $12 an ounce, while wild ginseng goes for up to $500 an ounce. In addition to selling the herb, the staff at **Ten Ren Tea and Ginseng Co.** (550 Main St., 604/684-1566) explains ginseng preparation methods to buyers and offers tea tastings, as well. Looking for something to eat? You'll find genuine Cantonese-style cuisine at the east end and tamer Chinese-Canadian dishes at the west end.

pass through. Here you'll find the city's largest department store, **The Bay** (674 Granville St., 604/681-6211), a Canadian chain that evolved from the historic Hudson's Bay Company. Today the store emphasizes Canadian goods, from souvenirs to household appliances. Also on the mall, the **Pacific Centre** features 165 shops, a massive food court, and a three-story-high waterfall.

British Columbia's largest shopping complex, **Metrotown,** houses more than 200 shops. It's on the Kingsway in Burnaby; get there from downtown on the SkyTrain.

OUTDOOR AND CAMPING GEAR
A small stretch of W. Broadway, between Main and Cambie Streets, holds Vancouver's largest concentration of outdoor equipment stores. The largest of these is **Mountain Equipment Co-op** (130 W. Broadway, 604/872-7858, Mon.–Wed. 10 A.M.–7 P.M., Thurs.–Fri. 10 A.M.–9 P.M., Saturday 9 A.M.–6 P.M.). Like the American R.E.I stores, it is a cooperative owned by its members; to make a purchase, you must be a member (a once-only charge of $5). The store holds a massive selection of clothing, climbing and mountaineering equipment, tents, backpacks, sleeping bags, books, and other accessories.

BOOKSTORES
General
In business since the 1950s, **Duthie Books** (2339 W. 4th Ave., Kitsilano, 604/732-5344, Mon.–Fri. 9 A.M.–9 P.M., Sat. 9 A.M.–6 P.M., Sun. 10 A.M.–6 P.M.) is one of the city's few remaining independent bookstores. On Granville Island, search out **Blackberry Books** (1666 Johnston St., 604/685-6188). The Canadian bookstore giant **Chapters/Indigo** has multiple Vancouver stores, including downtown (788 Robson St., 604/682-4066).

Travel
Vancouver has three excellent bookstores specializing in travel-related literature; all are in close proximity to each other in the area between Granville Island and Point Grey. They are: **Wanderlust** (west of Cypress St. at 1929 W. 4th Ave., Kitsilano, 604/739-2182, Mon.–Fri. 10 A.M.–7 P.M., Saturday 10 A.M.–5 P.M., Sunday noon–5 P.M.), **The Travel Bug** (3065 W. Broadway, 604/737-1122, Mon.–Sat. 10 A.M.–6 P.M., Sunday noon–5 P.M.), and **International Travel Maps and Books** (530 W. Broadway, 604/879-3621, Mon.–Fri. 9 A.M.–6 P.M., Saturday 10 A.M.–5 P.M., Sunday noon–5 P.M.).

Accommodations and Camping

Whether you're looking for a luxurious room in a high-rise hotel or a dingy downtown dorm, Vancouver has accommodations to suit all budgets. Downtown hotel room rates fluctuate greatly depending on supply and demand, much more so than bed-and-breakfasts and motels in suburban locations. In Vancouver, demand is highest in summer and on weekdays, so if you're looking to save a few bucks, plan on being in town in the cooler months (May and September are my favorite times in the city), or stay at a business hotel as part of a weekend package. One word of warning: If you plan to have a vehicle, prepare yourself for parking fees up to $30 per day in the downtown area; ask if weekend rates include free parking—they often do.

The following recommendations reflect my favorites in various price categories throughout the city. You won't find every downtown hotel mentioned here, and outside of downtown only convenient and good-value choices are included.

DOWNTOWN
Under $50
As you may imagine, the only downtown accommodations in this price range are backpacker lodges. **HI-Vancouver Downtown** (1114 Burnaby St., 604/684-4565 or 888/203-4302,

www.hihostels.ca) is typical of the new-look facilities operated by Hostelling International, the world's largest and longest-running network of backpacker accommodations. The complex offers a large kitchen, library, game room, free wireless Internet access, a travel agency, bike rentals, bag storage, and a laundry. The dormitories hold a maximum of four beds but are small. For these beds members of Hostelling International pay $31.50, nonmembers $34.50; private rooms range $68–82 s or d.

Housed in the old Royal Hotel, **HI–Vancouver Central** (1025 Granville St., 604/685-5335 or 888/203-8333, www.hihostels.ca) is closer to the nighttime action of the entertainment district and also has its own downstairs bar with nightly drink and food specials. Rates are similar to HI–Vancouver Downtown.

Privately owned backpacker lodges in Vancouver come and go with predictable regularity. A favorite is **Samesun Vancouver** (1018 Granville St., 604/682-8226 or 877/972-6378, www.samesun.com, $30–35 dorms, $70–85 s or d), which is excellent in all respects. The rooms in this old four-story building are small, but each has been tastefully decorated, and the communal lounge and kitchen areas serve guests well. Other facilities include a street-side restaurant, separate TV room, public Internet access or free wireless, and a rooftop patio.

$50-100

Dating to the mid-1990s, the **YWCA** (733 Beatty St., 604/895-5830 or 800/663-1424, www.ywcahotel.com, $68 s, $82–125 d) is popular with female travelers, couples, and families on a budget who don't like the "backpacker scene" at regular hostels. More than 150 rooms are spread over 11 stories. Each room has a telephone, and the private rooms have televisions. Communal facilities include two kitchens, three lounges, and two laundries. Guests also have use of the nearby YWCA Health and Wellness Centre, which houses a pool and gym.

In this price range, you also move into the domain of older hotels—some good, some bad.

Of these, the ◀ **Victorian Hotel** (514 Homer St., 604/681-6369 or 877/681-6369, www.victorianhotel.ca, $99–149 s or d) is one of the best choices. Guest rooms have only basic amenities (many share bathrooms), but they are comfortably furnished and light on the wallet. The central location and complimentary breakfast make this hotel an even better value. Built as a guesthouse in 1898, the rooms are decorated in a regal color scheme, which complements the polished hardwood floors.

Like the Victorian Hotel, the three-story **Kingston Hotel** (757 Richards St., 604/684-9024 or 888/713-3304, www.kingstonhotelvancouver.com) is around 100 years old and has been extensively renovated. Most of the 55 rooms share bathrooms ($75 s, $85 d) but have sinks with running water, while rooms with en suite bathrooms are $125–155 s or d. Amenities include a sauna, laundry, TV rental, and TV lounge with a collection of old-time movies. Room rates include a continental breakfast.

$100-150

Spending $100–150 a night will get you a room in one of the older downtown motels, most of which are southwest toward Granville Island, a 10-minute walk from the central business district. If you're looking for weekend or off-season lodgings, check the websites of the $200-plus recommendations below for rates that fall easily into this price range.

A colorful paint job and bright fabrics can do a lot to reinvent an old hotel, and you won't find a better example than the centrally located ◀ **Howard Johnson Hotel Downtown** (1176 Granville St., 604/688-8701 or 888/654-6336, www.hojovancouver.com, $149–229 s or d). A downstairs restaurant and lounge complete what is all in all a very good deal.

$150-200

Least expensive of the Central Business District hotels is **Vancouver-Days Inn Downtown** (921 W. Pender St., 604/681-4335 or 877/681-4335, www.daysinnvancouver.com, $179 s or d). The 85 rooms are small, and surrounding high-rises block any views. But each room is decorated in bright and breezy pastel colors, has free wireless Internet, and tea- and coffee-makers are provided.

While guest facilities at **Ramada Limited Downtown** (435 W. Pender St., 604/488-1088 or 888/389-5888, www.ramadalimited.org, $189 s or d) are limited compared to other properties in this price category, like the Vancouver–Days Inn, the location is very central. As an old hotel, the 80 rooms are small, but they are well appointed and come with everything from hair dryers to free wireless Internet. Look for the retro neon sign out front.

Sandman Hotels, Inns, and Suites is a western Canadian chain of more than 30 properties, including the flagship **Sandman Hotel Downtown Vancouver** (180 W. Georgia St., 604/681-2211 or 800/726-3626, www.sandman.ca, $159–259 s or d). This hotel features more than 300 rooms, including 87 self-contained suites in the Corporate Tower, an indoor pool, fitness room, lounge, and a 24-hour family restaurant.

$200-250

Granville Island Hotel (1253 Johnston St., 604/683-7373 or 800/663-1840, www.granvilleislandhotel.com, $220 s, $230 d) enjoys a fabulous location on the island of the same name immediately south of downtown. The hotel is designed to attract a young, hip clientele. Contemporary and elegant, the rooms are very spacious and furnished with Persian rugs, marble-floored bathrooms, and modern necessities such as high-speed Internet access. Most also have water views. Other amenities include a fitness center, rooftop whirlpool, sauna, and kayak rentals from the on-site marina. There's also an in-house brewery and excellent restaurant specializing in west coast cuisine.

$250-300

None of the 226 "suites" at **Delta Vancouver Suites,** in the heart of downtown (550 W. Hastings St., 604/689-8188 or 888/890-3222, www.deltahotels.com, $289 s or d) have kitchens, but each is spacious and has a separate

bedroom, comfortable lounge area, and an in-room business center. Other guest amenities include a health club, indoor pool, saunas and whirlpool, and a street-level restaurant open for breakfast, lunch, and dinner. The top three floors are reserved for Signature Club guests, where for a $60–80 premium you'll enjoy the best views, upgraded room amenities, and use of a private lounge where complimentary breakfast and afternoon snacks are served.

$300-400

One block from the city end of Robson Street is the super-luxurious, European-style **C Sutton Place Hotel** (845 Burrard St., 604/682-5511 or 800/961-7555, www.suttonplace.com, from $330 s or d), one of only a handful of properties in North America to get a precious five-diamond rating from the American Automobile Association. Vancouver's most elegant accommodation features 397 rooms furnished with king-size beds, plush bathrobes, ice dispensers, and two phone lines. Le Spa is an in-house spa, fitness, and health facility in the tradition of a luxurious European spa resort.

Drawing a mix of upscale business travelers and international vacationers, **Vancouver Marriott Pinnacle** (1128 W. Hastings St., 604/684-1128 or 800/207-4150, www.marriott.com, $330 s or d) is an excellent choice in the downtown core. The 434 guest rooms feature stylish furniture, elegant bathrooms, a writing desk full of office supplies, two telephones (including a cordless) with voice mail and Internet access, a coffeemaker, ironing facilities, and also an umbrella for Vancouver's occasional rainy days. Guests also enjoy complimentary use of the hotel's health club, which features a 17-meter (60-foot) indoor pool, a hot tub, sauna, and large outdoor patio area.

Regarded as one of Canada's hippest hotels, the **C Opus Hotel** (322 Davie St., Yaletown, 604/642-6787 or 866/642-6787, www.opushotel.com, $389 s or d) fills a very distinct niche in the Vancouver scene—a mega-cool place to stay. This means vibrant colors, striking decor, clean-lined furnishings, 250-count linens, 27-inch TVs, CD players, luxurious bathrooms filled with top-notch bath products, valet-only parking, and upscale dining and drinking off the brightly minimalist lobby. Rooms are decorated in five color themes (chose your favorite when booking online) and come in a variety of configurations, including one daring layout with the bathroom on the floor-to-ceiling-windowed outer wall.

Fairmont Hotel Vancouver (900 W. Georgia St., 604/684-3131 or 800/257-7544, www.fairmont.com, $369 s or d) is a downtown landmark—you can't help but notice the distinctive green copper roof, the gargoyles, and the classic, Gothic château-style architecture of this grand old dame. Facilities include restaurants, a comfortable lounge, an indoor pool, saunas, a weight room, health facilities, 24-hour room service, ample parking, and a large staff to attend to your every whim.

Over $400

For all the modern conveniences along with unbeatable city and harbor views, head for the sparkling **Pan Pacific Hotel Vancouver** (Canada Place, 604/662-8111 or 800/663-1515, www.panpacific.com, $440 s or d), which is generally regarded as one of the world's top 100 hotels. Each of the 503 rooms is spacious, has a luxurious bathroom, and come with extras such as wireless Internet, LCD TV, and plush bathrobes. Upgrades to Pacific Club provide access to a private waterfront lounge. Five Sails, featuring sweeping harbor views, is one of the city's best restaurants.

ROBSON STREET AND THE WEST END
Under $100

A hostel for grownups, the three-story **Buchan Hotel** (1906 Haro St., 604/685-5354 or 800/668-6654, www.buchanhotel.com, $77–139 s or d) is in a quiet residential area one block from Stanley Park. Built as an apartment hotel in 1926, the atmosphere today is friendly, especially in the evening when guests gather in the main lounge. On the downside, the rooms are small and sparsely decorated, and some share bathrooms.

$100-150

Overlooking English Bay, the old-style funky **Sylvia Hotel** (1154 Gilford St., 604/681-9321, www.sylviahotel.com, $129–329 s or d) sports a brick and terra-cotta exterior covered with Virginia creeper. Built in 1912, today it's popular with budget travelers looking for something a little more than a hostel. The less expensive rooms are fairly small.

Built in the 1920s, the European-style **Barclay Hotel** (1348 Robson St., 604/688-8850, www.barclayhotel.com, from $89 s, $109 d) has 80 medium-size rooms, a small lounge, and an intimate restaurant. The rooms are stylish in a slightly old-fashioned way; each holds a comfortable bed, writing desk, couch, and older television. Outside of summer, rates drop to a very reasonable $65–95.

The **Greenbrier Hotel** (1393 Robson St., 604/683-4558 or 888/355-5888, www.greenbrierhotel.com, $149–229 s or d) looks a bit rough on the outside, but each of the 32 units were refurbished for the 2010 Olympic Winter Games, and each has a large living area, full kitchen, and separate bedroom.

$150-200

At the 214-room **Blue Horizon Hotel** (1225 Robson St., 604/688-1411 or 800/663-1333, www.bluehorizonhotel.com, $159–329 s or d), amenities include an indoor lap pool, a fitness room, a sauna, and a variety of services for business travelers. One quirk of the layout is that every room is a corner room, complete with private balcony. To take advantage of this, you should request a room on the upper floors.

$200-250

Built at the turn of the 20th century, the **West End Guest House** (1362 Haro St., 604/681-2889 or 888/546-3327, www.westendguesthouse.com, $140–225 s, $205–225 d including breakfast) has been lovingly refurbished in Victorian-era colors and furnished with stylish antiques to retain its original charm. Each of the eight guest rooms has a brass bed complete with cotton linen and goose-down duvet, an en suite bathroom, a television, and a telephone.

Guests have the use of bikes and can relax either in the comfortable lounge or on the outdoor terrace.

(Pacific Palisades Hotel (1277 Robson St., 604/688-0461 or 800/663-1815, www.pacificpalisadeshotel.com, $235–285 s or d) is touted as being a cross between "South Beach (Miami) and Stanley Park," a fairly apt description of this chic Robson Street accommodation. Interior designers have given the entire hotel a "beachy," ultra-contemporary feel—each of the 233 spacious rooms is decorated with sleek furnishings and a dynamic color scheme. Amenities include a lounge and stylish restaurant, a fitness center, and an 18-meter (59-foot) indoor lap pool.

NORTH SHORE

The best reason to stay on the North Shore is to enjoy the local hospitality at one of the many bed-and-breakfasts, but a number of hotels and motels are also scattered through this part of the city.

$150-200

Perfect as a jumping off point for the ferry trip to the Sunshine Coast or Vancouver Island is the **Horseshoe Bay Motel** (6588 Royal Ave., 604/921-7454, www.horseshoebaymotel.ca, $158–218 s or d), 12 kilometers (7.5 miles) west of the Lions Gate Bridge, tucked below the highway in Horseshoe Bay and right by the BC Ferries terminal. It's within easy walking distance of numerous cafés and restaurants, and the nearby Horseshoe Bay Marina is a pleasant place for an evening stroll. Rooms are clean and comfortable, but you're paying for the location more than anything.

Gracious **(Thistledown House** (3910 Capilano Rd., North Vancouver, 604/986-7173 or 888/633-7173, www.thistle-down.com, $165–295 s or d) has been restored to resemble a country-style inn. Each of the five guest rooms has been tastefully decorated and has its own character, a private bathroom, balcony, and many delightful touches like homemade soap. Rates include a gourmet breakfast served in the dining room and afternoon tea served in the cozy lounge or landscaped gardens, depending on the weather.

Yes, it's a chain motel, but at the **Holiday Inn Express Vancouver North Shore** (1800 Capilano Rd., 604/987-4461 or 800/663-4055, www.holiday-inn.com, $199 s or d) you know exactly what you're paying for—a smartly decorated room with a light breakfast included in the rate of $189 s or d. An outdoor pool is a bonus.

Over $200

If you don't have transportation but don't want to stay downtown, the **Lonsdale Quay Hotel** (123 Carrie Cates Court, North Vancouver, 604/986-6111 or 800/836-6111, www.lonsdalequayhotel.com, $225–295 s or d) is a good choice. It enjoys an absolute waterfront location above lively Lonsdale Quay Market and the SeaBus Terminal, making it just 12 minutes to downtown by water. Each of the 70 rooms is equipped with modern furnishings and free wireless Internet, while amenities include a fitness center, sauna and whirlpool, covered parking, and a restaurant.

KITSILANO, SHAUGHNESSY, AND VICINITY

Hip Kitsilano and old-money Shaughnessy are two of Vancouver's most upscale residential neighborhoods. Accommodations in this part of the city are nearly all bed-and-breakfasts, and the following are my favorites.

Under $50

If you're on a budget and don't need to stay right downtown, **HI-Vancouver Jericho Beach** (1515 Discovery St., Point Grey, 604/224-3208 or 888/203-4303, www.hihostels.ca, May–Sept., dorm bed $25, private room $65 s or d) is a good alternative. The location is fantastic—in a scenic and safe parkland behind Jericho Beach, across English Bay from downtown, and linked to extensive biking and walking trails. Inside the huge white building are separate dorms for men and women, rooms for couples and families, a living area with television, and a kitchen. Additional amenities include a cafeteria, public Internet access, lockers, left-luggage service, and a shuttle to the downtown hostels and rail/bus station. As always, those not members of Hostelling International pay an extra $4 per person per night. To get there, take NW Marine Drive off 4th Avenue W. and turn right down Discovery Street at the arts center.

$100-150

Tucked away near the south end of Pacific Spirit Regional Park is ❰ **Pacific Spirit Guest House** (4080 West 35th Ave., 604/261-6837 or 866/768-6837, www.vanbb.com, $115–125 s, $125–135 d), a well-priced bed-and-breakfast. Choose between the guest room with a king-size bed or one with garden views. All guests are welcome to relax in the lounge and help themselves to tea and coffee, or take advantage of the large collection of books and music in the library. In the morning, a huge, multi-course breakfast will set you up for a day of sightseeing.

On the southern edge of Shaughnessy, **Beautiful B&B** (428 W. 40th Ave., just off Cambie St., 604/327-1102, www.beautifulbandb.bc.ca, $145–255 s or d) is a Colonial-style two-story home on a high point of land where views extend across the city to the North Shore range. Both Queen Elizabeth Park and VanDusen Botanical Garden are within walking distance. The house is decorated with antiques and fresh flowers from the surrounding garden. Two rooms share a bathroom, while the Honeymoon Suite features a fireplace, panoramic views, and a huge en suite bathroom complete with soaker tub.

KINGSWAY

The Kingsway is a main thoroughfare linking downtown to Burnaby. It is lined with a smattering of inexpensive motels—perfect if you want to save a few dollars and like the convenience of being a short bus ride from downtown. Another advantage is that you won't need to worry about parking (or paying for parking). Nearby is a cluster of inexpensive restaurants, the perfect place for a budget-conscious traveler to end the day with a good meal.

$50-100

The least expensive lodging choices in this part of the city are old motels along the Kingsway, the main route between downtown and New Westminster. At the bottom of the price spectrum is the **2400 Motel** (2400 Kingsway, 604/434-2464, $95 s or d), an old roadside-style place with basic rooms, cable TV, and coffee and newspapers offered in the office each morning. It's near Nanaimo Street and within walking distance of the 29th Avenue SkyTrain station.

$100-150

❰ **Pillow Suites** (2859 Manitoba St., Mt. Pleasant, 604/879-8977, www.pillow.net, $125–265 s or d) is a unique lodging three bocks west of the Kingsway and a few hundred meters east of City Hall. The six suites are spread through three adjacent, colorfully painted heritage houses. Each unit is fully self-contained with a kitchen, en suite bathroom, telephone, cable TV, fireplace, and private entrance. Rates range from $125 for the Country Store—formerly a corner store and now filled with brightly painted appliances—to $265 for a complete three-bedroom house that sleeps six comfortably.

$150-200

Holiday Inn Vancouver Centre (711 W. Broadway, 604/879-0511 or 877/660-8550, www.hivancouver.com, $189–249 d) is a two-minute walk to waterfront Charleson Park and then less than one kilometer (0.6 mile) west along False Creek to Granville Island. The hotel itself features 193 rooms spread over 16 floors, an indoor pool complex that opens to an outdoor deck with great views, a lounge, and a restaurant.

RICHMOND

The following Richmond accommodations are good choices for those visitors who arrive late at, or have an early departure from, the international airport. All accommodations detailed in this section offer complimentary airport shuttles.

$100-150

The **Coast Vancouver Airport Hotel** (1041 Southwest Marine Dr., 604/263-1555 or 800/716-6199, www.coasthotels.com, $149 s or d) lies farther from the airport (toward the city) than the rest of the lodgings detailed in this section, but with free airport transfers, free long-term parking, and in-house dining, it is still aimed directly at airport travelers. No surprises with the rooms here—each has modern decor, a work desk, ironing facility, coffeemaker, and free local calls. Other amenities include a fitness center, sports bar, and family restaurant.

Three kilometers (1.9 miles) from the airport, the **Holiday Inn Express Vancouver Airport** (9351 Bridgeport Rd., 604/273-8080 or 877/273-8080, www.holidayinnexpressvancouverairport.com, $149 s or d includes breakfast) is a typical modern, multi-story airport hotel, with large and comfortably furnished rooms.

Over $200

Right at the airport, the **Fairmont Vancouver Airport** (3111 Grant McConachie Way, 604/207-5200 or 866/540-4441, www.fairmont.com, $259 s or d) has 398 guest rooms equipped with remote-controlled everything, right down to the drapes, fog-free bathroom mirrors, and floor-to-ceiling soundproof windows. Other more traditional hotel conveniences include a huge work center, a health club (where swimmers take to the self-adjusted current of a lap pool), and the Spa at the Fairmont massage and treatment facility. Check the website for packages.

CAMPING

You won't find any campgrounds in the city center area, but a limited number dot the suburbs along the major approach routes. Before trekking out to any of them, ring ahead to check for vacancies. Unless otherwise noted, the campgrounds below are open year-round.

North

The closest campground to downtown is

Capilano RV Park (295 Tomahawk Ave., North Vancouver, 604/987-4722, www.capilanorvpark.com, $44–56). To get there from downtown cross Lions Gate Bridge, turn right on Marine Drive, right on Capilano Road, and right again on Welch Street. From Highway 1/99 in West Vancouver exit south on Taylor Way toward the shopping center and turn left over the Capilano River. Amenities include a 13-meter (43-foot) pool, a big hot tub, a TV and games room, and a laundry.

South

Parkcanada (52nd St., Delta, 604/943-5811, www.parkcanada.com, $27.50 tents, $31.50–37.50 hookups) is convenient to the BC Ferries terminal at Tsawwassen, a 30-minute drive south of city center. The campground has a small outdoor pool, but next door is a much larger water park—perfect for the kids. Other amenities include a store with groceries and some RV supplies, laundry, lounge, and free showers. To get there, follow the ferry signs from Highway 99 and turn right off Highway 17 at 52nd Street. Take the first left, and you're there.

Farther south along Highway 99 is **Peace Arch RV Park** (14601 40th Ave., Surrey, 604/594-7009, www.peacearchrvpark.ca, $32.50 tents, $39.50–45.50 hookups), which sprawls over four hectares (10 acres) between White Rock and Delta, 10 kilometers (6.2 miles) from the Douglas Border Crossing (take Exit 10 (King George Highway) north from Highway 99, then the first right, 40th Avenue). The well-tended facilities include a heated pool, playground and mini-golf, game room, coin-operated showers, and a laundry.

East

Adjacent to Burnaby Lake Regional Park, **Burnaby Cariboo RV Park** (8765 Cariboo Place, Burnaby, 604/420-1722 or 800/667-9901, www.bcrvpark.com, $39 tents, $52–59.50 hookups) offers luxurious amenities, including a large indoor heated pool, fitness room, hot tub, sundeck, playground, lounge, barbeque area, grocery store, and laundry facility. The campground offers 217 paved sites, each with full hookups, including 30-amp power, cable TV, telephone, and Internet access. The campground is 17 kilometers (10.6 miles) east of downtown. To get there, take Exit 37 (Gaglardi) from the TransCanada Highway, turn right at the first traffic light, take the first left, then the first right into Cariboo Place. The Production Way SkyTrain station is an eight-minute walk from this campground.

Farther east, **Dogwood Campground & RV Park** (15151 112th Ave., Surrey, 604/583-5585, www.dogwoodcampgrounds.com, $28

unserviced sites, $38 hookups) is 35 kilometers (22 miles) from downtown. It's right beside the TransCanada Highway. To get there from downtown, take Exit 48 and cross back over the highway, turning left onto 154th Street. Eastbound travelers (heading toward the city) should take Exit 50, turn north over the highway and follow 160th Street north to 112th Avenue. Turn left and follow this street to the end. While facilities are basic, they are modern and adequate for most campers' standards, and include a pool and laundry.

Food

With an estimated 2,000 restaurants and hundreds of cafés and coffeehouses, Vancouver is a gastronomical delight. The city is home to more than 60 different cultures, so don't be surprised to find a smorgasbord of ethnic restaurants. The local specialty is west-coast or "fusion" cuisine, which combines fresh Canadian produce, such as local seafood and seasonal game, with Asian flavors and ingredients, usually in a healthy, low-fat way. Vancouver has no tourist-oriented, San Francisco–style Fisherman's Wharf, but however and wherever it's prepared, seafood will always dominate local menus. Pacific salmon, halibut, snapper, shrimp, oysters, clams, crab, and squid are all harvested locally.

DOWNTOWN

Downtown Vancouver has so many good dining options that it is a shame to eat in a food court, but like in cities around the Western world, they are a good place for a fast, reliable, and inexpensive meal. The southwest corner of the Pacific Centre (at Howe and Georgia Streets, diagonally opposite the art gallery) holds a glass-domed food court with many inexpensive food bars and seating indoors and out.

West Coast/Fusion and Seafood

With its prime waterfront location between

Canada Place and Gastown, **◖ Aqua Riva** (200 Granville St., 604/683-5599, Mon.–Fri. 11:30 A.M.–2:30 P.M., daily 5–10 P.M., $15–39) features stunning views across Burrard Inlet to the North Shore range through floor-to-ceiling windows. It's less touristy than you may imagine and well priced for the high standard of food offered. The least expensive way to enjoy the dramatic view is with a pizza baked in a wood-fired oven ($15–16), but dishes such as the grilled salmon are delicious.

At Gastown's busiest intersection, opposite the crowd-drawing steam clock, is **Water Street Cafe** (300 Water St., 604/689-2832, daily 11:30 A.M.–9:30 P.M., $16–33). Unlike dining at most other Gastown eateries, you won't feel like you're in the touristy quarter of Vancouver. White linens, dark blue carpets, and lots of polished woodwork ooze style, while service is professional. Most importantly, the food is well priced and delicious. The wild salmon topped with hazelnuts and a maple butter sauce is a good choice, or go for something lighter, such as the prawn and papaya salad. A good selection of simple pastas provides a break from seafood.

One of Vancouver's finest seafood restaurants is **◖ A Kettle of Fish** (900 Pacific St., 604/682-6661, daily from 5:30 P.M., $18–45), near the Burrard Street Bridge. The casual decor features café-style seating and abundant greenery, while the menu swims with schools of piscatory pleasures. New England clam chowder is one of more than 20 appetizers, while entrées ranging from the simple (fish-and-chips) to the obscenely rich (lobster casserole) make up the main menu. The extensive wine list is especially strong on white wines—the perfect accompaniment for a feast of seafood.

Steak

Steak lovers in the mood for a splurge should consider **Gotham Steakhouse** (615 Seymour St., 604/605-8282, daily from 5 P.M., $29–53). With furnishings of thick leather seats, dark hardwood tables, and plush velvet carpet, the restaurant exudes the atmosphere of a private gentleman's club. If the steak here isn't the best in Vancouver, servings are certainly the most generous, especially the signature dish, a $52.95 porterhouse. Other mains start at $29, with vegetable sides extra, earning the steakhouse awards from city magazines as the "Best Restaurant When Someone Else is Paying."

European

Stepho's (1124 Davie St., 604/683-2555, daily noon–11:30 P.M., $8–14) is one of Vancouver's best-value restaurants. Locals line up here to enjoy the atmosphere of a typical Greek taverna—complete with terra-cotta floors, white stucco walls, arched doorways, blue and white tablecloths, travel posters, and lots of colorful flowering plants. Expect to pay less than $30 for three courses.

Of Vancouver's many Italian restaurants, one of the most popular is **Il Giardino** (1382 Hornby St., 604/669-2422, Mon.–Fri. noon–2:30 P.M. and Mon.–Sat. 6–10:30 P.M., $18–36), in a distinctive yellow Italian-style villa. The light, bright furnishings and enclosed terrace provide the perfect ambience for indulging in the featured Tuscan cuisine.

For Vancouver's finest French cuisine, go to the small, intimate **Le Crocodile** (909 Burrard St., 604/669-4298, Mon.–Fri. 11:30 A.M.–2 P.M., Mon.–Sat. 5:30–10 P.M., $28–42), where a smallish menu relies heavily on traditional French techniques, which shine

through on appetizers (or entrées as they are properly called at Le Crocodile), such as wild mushroom soup with truffle oil or frogs legs sautéed in a chive butter sauce, and mains like pan-seared veal with black truffle–foie gras cream sauce.

Asian

Dining in **Chinatown** offers two distinct options—traditional eateries, where you'll find the locals, and the larger, westernized restaurants that attract non-Chinese and a younger Chinese crowd. A perfect combination of the two is **Kent's Kitchen** (232 Keefer St., 604/669-2237, daily for lunch and dinner, $6–13), a modern café-style restaurant where the service is fast and efficient, the food freshly prepared, and the prices incredibly low. Two specialty dishes, rice, and a can of soda make a meal that costs just $8. Next door to Kent's, **Hon's Wun Tun House** (230 Keefer St., 604/688-0871, daily for lunch and dinner, $7.50–13) is the most lively of five local restaurants started by a Chinese immigrant in the 1970s. It's a large, bright, and modern restaurant that attracts a younger Chinese crowd for mostly westernized Chinese food. Tiny **Gain Wah Restaurant** (218 Keefer St., 604/684-1740, daily for lunch and dinner, $6–11) is typical of the many hundreds of noodle houses found in Hong Kong, and is extremely inexpensive.

Many inexpensive Japanese restaurants are scattered between Granville Street and Gastown. **Guu Otokomae** (375 Water St., 604/685-8682, daily 11:30 A.M.–10:30 P.M.) is a groovy Japanese restaurant with an energetic chef who oversees the needs of mostly young—always loud—patrons. Known in Japan as *izakaya*-style dining, the atmosphere is informal, with a menu that encourages sharing. It's similar to a North American neighborhood pub, but instead of wings and nachos, choices include *harumaki* (spring rolls), *shisoage* (chicken and plum sauce wrapped in thin bread), and *maguro* (tuna with avocado and mango sauce). Expect to pay around $30 per person for dinner.

ROBSON STREET AND THE WEST END

Linking downtown to the West End, Robson Street holds the city's largest concentration of eateries, ranging from Joe Fortes, one of Vancouver's finest seafood restaurants, to the city's Hooters franchise. In addition to a number of fine-dining restaurants, dozens of cafés sprinkle the sidewalks with outdoor tables—perfect for people watching.

Seafood

Half a block off Robson, **€ Joe Fortes Seafood & Chophouse** (777 Thurlow St., 604/669-1940, daily 11 A.M.–11 P.M., $19–46) is named after one of Vancouver's best-loved heroes, a Caribbean-born swimming coach and lifeguard at English Bay. The comfortable interior offers elegant furnishings, bleached-linen tablecloths, a rooftop patio, and an oyster bar where you can relax while waiting for your table. At lunch, the specialty grilled fish goes for $15–20. The dinner menu is slightly more expensive, although there are usually at least a dozen different types of fish offered, most of which are under $30. Eat between 4 and 6 P.M. and pay just $28 for a three-course dinner.

West Coast/Fusion

An innovative menu and views across English Bay make **Raincity Grill** (1193 Denman St., 604/685-7337, Mon.–Fri. 11:30 A.M.–2:30 P.M., daily 5–10 P.M., $17–33) an impressive choice for a meal. The menu changes with the season but always includes seafood and carefully selected local meats, such as free-range chicken from Fraser River Valley farms. Lunch entrées (the salad of scallops and spring vegetables is a particular treat) are $13–19, dinner (such as roasted bison sirloin with organic beets) is more expensive, but also more creative. Sweet treats include a tasty crabapple sorbet ($8.50).

European

The Chef and the Carpenter (1745 Robson St., 604/687-2700, lunch Mon.–Fri., dinner daily from 5 P.M., $19–28) serves up great

---

GETTING A CAFFEINE FIX

One thing that will soon become apparent to first-time visitors is the amount of coffee consumed by the locals. Specialty coffeehouses are everywhere, but nowhere are they as concentrated as along Robson Street.

Starbucks alone has more than 85 Vancouver outlets, including two sitting kitty-corner from each other on Robson Street, along with two others on that same street. **Blenz** is equally well represented throughout the city, with three cafés on Robson Street.

Rather than diving straight into Starbucks, I recommend trying one of the local places. It's only a cup of coffee after all. My pick for coffee and a light snack is the **Bread Garden,** with 20-odd cafés scattered throughout the metropolitan area. One central location is a half block off busy Robson Street at 812 Bute Street (604/688-3213). It's open 24 hours a day and is always busy – so much so that patrons often need to take a number and wait for service. The coffee is great, as are the freshly baked muffins and pastries. Salads and healthy sandwiches are also available.

Gastown's best coffee is roasted at **Smart Mouth Cafe** (131 Water St., 604/569-1480). The café's striking yellow and black interior, daily papers, great coffee, and inexpensive light snacks make this a pleasant escape from touristy Water Street.

---

country-French cuisine in an intimate yet relaxed atmosphere. Portions are large, but save room for the delicious desserts.

Named for a traditional Italian toast, **€ CinCin** (1154 Robson St., 604/688-7338, daily from 5 P.M., $21.50–35.50) is a Mediterranean-style restaurant with a loyal local following. The centerpiece of the dining room is a large open kitchen, with a wood-fired oven and a rotisserie in view of diners. The heated terrace fills up quickly, but is the place to watch the Robson Street action from above. The specialty is traditional pizzas (around $16), but the oven is also used to cook dishes such as AAA cuts of beef. CinCin also does a wicked antipasto ($19.50 per person). This restaurant has been honored by dozens of awards, including for its wine list, featuring more than 300 well-priced choices.

The atmosphere at **Tapastree Restaurant** (1829 Robson St., 604/606-4680, daily 5–10 P.M.) is inviting and cozy, and the service faultless. But it's the food that really shines; the tapas-only menu features choices such as vegetarian antipasto and seared tuna with Chinese mustard, which are mostly $7–15. It's one block along Robson from Denman.

Around the corner, **Café de Paris** (751 Denman St., 604/687-1418, Mon.–Fri. 11:30 A.M.–2 P.M., daily 5:30–10 P.M., $18.50–30) is an intimate yet casual city-style French bistro. Classic French main courses (don't dare call them entrées at this very French restaurant) are under $30, but the daily three-course table d'hôte is the best value at around $40. Wines offered are almost exclusively French.

KITSILANO

The main concentration of restaurants on the south side of False Creek is in Kitsilano, along W. 4th Avenue between Burrard and Vine Streets. This part of the city was the heart of hippiedom 30 years ago, and while most restaurants from that era are long gone, a few remain, and other, newer additions to the local dining scene reflect that period of the city's history.

Casual

Retro-hip **Sophie's Cosmic Café** (2095 W. 4th Ave. at Arbutus St., 604/732-6810, daily 8 A.M.–9:30 P.M., $9–16) typifies the scene, with a definite "cosmic" look, but also provides good value and fast, efficient service. Standard bacon and eggs is $8 and omelets are around $10. The rest of the day, check the blackboard above the food-service window for dishes such as a nut and herb burger ($9). Expect to wait for a table on Sunday morning.

Joe's Grill (2061 W. 4th Ave., 604/736-6588, daily 7 A.M.–10 P.M., $6.50–13), one block east from Sophie's, has survived from the 1960s serving up typical greasy spoon fare at good prices. A breakfast of eggs, bacon, and hash browns is $6; the daily soup-and-sandwich special is just $7; the milkshakes are to die for; and coffee refills are free. In diner tradition, seating is at tables or booths.

Vegetarian

A throwback to the hippie era of the 1960s is **(Naam** (2724 W. 4th Ave. at Stephens St., 604/738-7151, $7–12.50), a particularly good natural-food restaurant in a renovated two-story private residence. Boasting large servings, excellent service, and an easy-going atmosphere that has become legendary, it's open 24 hours a day, every day of the week. Tuscan nachos, chili deluxe, and the Naam salad all shine.

European

Well regarded by both locals and cuisine-savvy travelers, the much-lauded **Bishop's** (2183 W. 4th Ave., 604/738-2025, daily 5:30–10 P.M., $36–39) is very French in all aspects. Owner, and longtime Vancouver restaurateur, John Bishop makes all diners feel special, personally greeting them at the door, escorting them to their table, and then describing the menu and wine list as required. Elegant surroundings, parched-white linen, and soft jazz background music complete the picture. The menu features French classics but changes as seasonal produce, such as scallops and halibut, Fraser River Valley vegetables, and fruits from the Okanagan Valley, become available. Reservations are required.

NORTH SHORE

The pick of spots for breakfast or lunch in suburban Ambleside, west of Lonsdale Quay and the Lions Gate Bridge, is **Savary Island Pie Company** (1533 Marine Dr., 604/926-4021, daily 6 A.M.–7 P.M., lunches $6.50–11.50). Join the line at this super-popular café and order a Caesar salad or a generous slab of chicken potpie, saving room for a cranberry square for dessert.

Seafood

On the north side of Burrard Inlet, **(Salmon**

HOTEL DINING

Generally, hotels have a reputation for ordinary and overpriced restaurants – in existence only for the convenience of guests – but Vancouver is the exception to that rule. Since the first Canadian Pacific Railway passengers arrived at the end of the line to be spoiled by European chefs at the Hotel Vancouver, locals and visitors alike have headed to the city's best hotels to enjoy fine dining in all its glory.

The Wedgewood Hotel's signature dining room, the **Bacchus Ristorante** (845 Hornby St., 604/608-5319, daily for breakfast, lunch, and dinner, $25–45), has the feeling of a romantic European bistro with its dark cherrywood paneling, stone fireplace, and elegant table settings over white linen. The emphasis is on Italian cuisine, but the menu relies heavily on local produce, changing with the seasons – such as pan-seared halibut with a side of scallops topped in a fennel-based sauce, when I last splurged here. Afternoon tea ($29) is served Sat.–Sun. 2–4 P.M.

Fleuri (Sutton Place Hotel, 845 Burrard St., 604/642-2900, $26–39) is in what is generally regarded as one of the world's best hotels. The dinner menu is very serious, with local produce given classic European treatment.

At **900 West** (Fairmont Hotel Vancouver, 900 W. Georgia St., 604/669-9378, daily 6-10 P.M., $28–42), enjoy the atmosphere of a luxurious cruise-ship dining room. The contemporary North American menu is varied, with classic preparations of British Columbia seafood and Alberta beef.

Typifying the new wave in Vancouver's hotel dining scene is **Show Case,** at street level of the Vancouver Marriott Pinnacle (1128 W. Hastings St., 604/639-4040, daily for breakfast, lunch, and dinner, $30–35). Floor-to-ceiling windows and contemporary styling create an environment very different from the elegant old-world feel of Vancouver's other top-end hotel restaurants. Exotic dishes prepared using local seafood and game, are simply and stylishly presented; the tasting menu gives diners the opportunity to experience a variety of dishes, accompanied by matching wines.

House on the Hill (2229 Folkstone Way, West Vancouver, 604/926-3212, Sat.–Sun. 10:30 A.M.–2:30 P.M. and daily 5–10 P.M., $30–37), offers a relaxed atmosphere while providing panoramic views across Burrard Inlet to Stanley Park and the city center from its elevated mountainside location. The cavernous interior is full of northwest coast native arts and crafts—including a dugout canoe suspended over the main dining area. The house specialty of salmon barbecued over an open flame, alder-wood fired grill is also hard to resist. And the price for this signature dish is right at just $30. Or choose a three-course "Uniquely B.C." tasting menu for a reasonable $49. To get there, take the 21st Street exit off Upper Levels Highway to Folkstone Way, turn left on Ski Lift Road.

Information and Services

Before leaving home you should contact **Tourism Vancouver** (604/682-2222, www.tourismvancouver.com). Their website should have everything you need, but you can also request an information package that will come by regular post. Vancouver falls within the Vancouver, Coast, & Mountains Tourism Region (604/739-9011 or 800/667-3306, www.vcmbc.com), one of six such regions throughout the province ("Coast" means the Sunshine Coast and "Mountains" means Whistler and vicinity).

INFORMATION CENTERS
Downtown
The city's main information center is **Vancouver Visitor Centre,** one block from Canada

Place (200 Burrard St., 604/683-2000, daily 8:30 A.M.–6 P.M.). Brochures line the lower level while on the upper level specially trained staff provide free maps, brochures, and public transportation schedules; book sightseeing tours; and make accommodations reservations. Look for public transportation information and timetables to the right as you enter the center.

South

If you approach Vancouver from the south on Highway 5, which becomes Highway 99 in Canada, the first official information center you'll come to is the **British Columbia Visitor Centre @ Peace Arch** (298 Hwy. 99, 800/435-5622, daily 8 A.M.–8 P.M. in summer, daily 9 A.M.–5 P.M. the rest of the year) immediately north of the border and right beside the highway.

Continuing north along Highway 99, **Richmond Visitor Centre** is next to the highway, to the right as you emerge on the north side of the George Massey Tunnel under the Fraser River. Operated by Tourism Richmond (604/271-8280 or 877/247-0777, www.tourism-richmond.com), it's open daily 9:30 A.M.–5 P.M. March–June, daily 9:30 A.M.–5 P.M. July–August, daily 8:30 A.M.–7 P.M. September, and Monday–Friday 10 A.M.–4 P.M. the rest of the year.

LIBRARIES

Vancouver Public Library (350 W. Georgia St., 604/331-3600, Mon.–Thurs. 10 A.M.–9 P.M., Fri.–Sat. 10 A.M.–6 P.M., and Sunday 1–5 P.M. year-round) is a magnificent nine-story facility a few blocks back from the harbor. Its elliptical facade contains a glass-walled promenade rising six stories above a row of stylish indoor shops and cafés. Once inside, you'll soon discover that the city also found enough money to stock the shelves; the library holds more than one million books. To help you find that one book you're searching for, use the self-guided tour brochure available at the information desk.

More than 20 other affiliated libraries are spread across the city. Call 604/331-3600 or visit www.vpl.vancouver.bc.ca for addresses and opening hours. One library branch of particular interest is the **Carnegie Reading Room** (corner of E. Hastings and Main Streets, 604/665-3010, daily 10 A.M.–10 P.M.). It is named for its benefactor, U.S. philanthropist Andrew Carnegie, whose $50,000 donation went a long way toward its 1902 completion as Vancouver's first permanent library.

LAUNDRY

If you have a vehicle, kill two birds with one stone at **Cold Coin Laundry** (3496 West Broadway, 604/737-9642, daily 7 A.M.–10 P.M.), which has laundry facilities, public Internet access ($4 per hour), and better coffee than you may imagine.

EMERGENCY SERVICES

For emergencies, call 911. For medical emergencies, contact the downtown **St. Paul's Hospital** (1081 Burrard St., 604/682-2344), which has an emergency ward open 24 hours a day, seven days a week. Other major hospitals are **Vancouver General Hospital** (899 W. 12th Ave., 604/875-4111) and **Lions Gate Hospital** (231 E. 15th St., 604/988-3131). **Seymour Medical Clinic** (1530 W. 7th Ave., 604/738-2151) is open 24 hours. For emergency dental help, call the **AARM Dental Group** (1128 Hornby St., 604/681-8530). For the **RCMP** (Royal Canadian Mounted Police) call 911 or 604/264-3111.

Getting There and Around

GETTING THERE
By Air
Vancouver International Airport (www.yvr. ca) is on Sea Island, 15 kilometers (9.3 miles) south of Vancouver city center. More than 16 million passengers pass through the terminal annually. The three-story International Terminal and adjacent Domestic Terminal hold coffee shops and restaurants, car-rental agencies, a post office, currency exchanges, newsstands, gift shops, and duty-free shops. Numerous information boards provide a quick airport orientation, and an information booth on Level 3 of the International Terminal offers tourist brochures, bus schedules, and taxi information.

The **Canada Line** (www.translink.ca) is a 16-kilometre (10-mi) stretch of light-rail line linking the airport to downtown Vancouver, with 19 stations en route. The journey between the airport and downtown takes around 30 minutes and costs $6.25. The service runs every 4–10 minutes between 5 A.M. and a little after midnight. A cab from the airport to downtown takes 25 minutes and runs around $45.

By Rail and Bus
The **VIA Rail** (888/842-7245, www.viarail. ca) terminus is **Pacific Central Station** (1150 Station St.), two kilometers (1.2 miles) southeast of downtown. This is also the main **Greyhound** (604/482-8747 or 800/661-8747, www.greyhound.ca) bus depot, with daily service to points throughout western Canada and beyond. Also from here, **Pacific Coach Lines** (604/662-8074 or 800/661-1725, www.pacificcoach.com) runs bus service to Victoria and Whistler, while also picking up for both destinations from Vancouver International Airport.

Pacific Central Station is a $10 cab ride or just a few minutes on the SkyTrain from downtown. Inside you'll find a currency exchange, cash machines, lockers, a newsstand, information boards, and a McDonald's.

GETTING AROUND
TransLink
TransLink (604/953-3333, www.translink. ca) operates an extensive network of buses, trains, and ferries that can get you just about anywhere you want to go within Vancouver. **Buses** run to all corners of the city 5 A.M.–2 A.M. every day of the year. Transfers are valid for 90 minutes of travel in one direction. **SkyTrain** is a computer-operated (no drivers) light-rail transit system that runs along 65 kilometers (40 miles) of track from downtown Vancouver to Vancouver International Airport, through New Westminster, and over the Fraser River to suburban Surrey. The city-center stations are underground but are clearly marked at each street entrance. The double-ended, 400-passenger **SeaBus** scoots across Burrard Inlet every 15–30 minutes, linking downtown Vancouver to North Vancouver in just 12 minutes. The downtown terminus is Waterfront Station, situated beside Canada Place and a five-minute walk from the Vancouver Visitor Centre.

The cost of traveling on any TransLink transportation varies by zones. On weekdays 5:30 A.M.–6:30 P.M. the city is divided into three zones; adult fares range $2.50–4.75 (with a $2.50 surcharge to or from the airport), senior $1.75–3.25, for each sector (Zone 1 encompasses all over downtown and Greater Vancouver; Zone 2 covers all the North Shore, Burnaby, New Westminster, and Richmond; and Zone 3 extends to the limits of the TransLink system). Pay the driver (exact change only) for bus travel or purchase tickets from machines at any SkyTrain station or SeaBus terminal. Request a free transfer from the driver if required. A **DayPass** costs adult $9, senior $7 and allows unlimited travel for one day anywhere on the TransLink system.

Boat
Apart from the SeaBus, the only other scheduled

FERRYING OUT OF TOWN

Vancouver has two ferry terminals, with services heading out of the city to **Vancouver Island** and the **Sunshine Coast.** All ferries are operated by **BC Ferries** (250/386-3431 or 888/223-3779, www.bcferries.com) and reservations (select routes only) can be made online or by phone. In high season (June–Sept.), the ferries run about once an hour, 7 A.M.-10 P.M. The rest of the year they run a little less frequently. Expect a wait in summer, particularly if you have an oversized vehicle (each ferry can accommodate far fewer large vehicles than standard-size cars and trucks).

TSAWWASSEN FERRY TERMINAL

Located 30 kilometers (18.8 miles) south of downtown Vancouver, ferries run from Tsawwassen to the **Southern Gulf Islands; Swartz Bay,** 32 kilometers (20 miles) north of Victoria, Vancouver Island; and to **Nanaimo,** also on Vancouver Island. To get to the terminal from downtown, follow Highway 17 south – in summer this road gets crazy with traffic. Buses also link the ferry terminal with downtown; catch number 601 from downtown.

HORSESHOE BAY TERMINAL

The other ferry route linking the mainland to Vancouver Island runs between Horseshoe Bay and **Nanaimo.** Horseshoe Bay is on the north side of Burrard Inlet, a 20-minute drive northwest of downtown. You don't save any money on this route – the fares are the same – and the wait is often longer. This is also the departure point for ferries to the **Sunshine Coast.**

---

ferry services within the city are on False Creek. Two private companies, **Granville Island Ferries** (604/684-7781) and **Aquabus** (604/689-5858), operate on this narrow waterway. From the main hub of Granville Island, 12- to 20-passenger ferries run every 15 minutes daily 7 A.M.–10 P.M. to the foot of Hornby Street, and under the Burrard Street Bridge to the Aquatic Center (at the south end of Thurlow St.) and Vanier Park (Museum of Vancouver). Every 30–60 minutes both companies also run down the head of False Creek to Stamps Landing, the Plaza of Nations, and Science World. Fares are the same as, and can be used in conjunction with, TransLink buses and trains.

Car Rental

All major car rental companies are represented in Vancouver, and most have check-in desks at the airport. Book through the company's website or toll-free number, but use these numbers to speak with local operators: **Alamo** (604/684-1401), **Avis** (604/606-2869), **Budget** (604/668-7000), **Discount** (604/310-2277), **Dollar** (604/637-1680), **Enterprise** (604/688-5500), **Hertz** (604/606-4711), **National** (604/609-7150), **Rent-a-Wreck** (604/688-0001), and **Thrifty** (604/606-1666).

Taxi

Cabs are easiest to catch outside major hotels or transportation hubs. Trips within downtown usually run around $10. The trip between the airport and downtown is $45. Major companies include **Black Top** (604/683-4567 or 800/494-1111), **Vancouver Taxi** (877/871-1111), and **Yellow Cab** (604/681-1111 or 800/898-8294). A number of wheelchair-accommodating taxicabs are available from Vancouver Taxi. The fares are the same as regular taxis.

Sunshine Coast

The 150-kilometer (93-mile) Sunshine Coast lies along the northeast shore of the Strait of Georgia between Howe Sound in the south and Desolation Sound in the north. This rare bit of sun-drenched Canadian coastline is bordered by countless bays and inlets, broad sandy beaches, quiet lagoons, rugged headlands, provincial parks, and lush fir forests backed by the snowcapped Coast Mountains. Boasting Canada's mildest climate, the Sunshine Coast enjoys moderately warm summers and mild winters. Boaters and kayakers can cruise into a number of beautiful marine parks providing sheltered anchorage and campsites amid some of the most magnificent scenery along the west coast, or anchor at sheltered fishing villages with marinas and all the modern conveniences.

Gibsons Landing

A delightful hillside community of 4,000 a two-minute drive from the ferry dock at Langdale, Gibsons Landing has two sections: the original 100-year-old fishing village around the harbor and a commercial corridor along the highway. Around the harbor, Gower Point Road is a charming strip of seafaring businesses, antique dealers, arty shops, and cafés. Down on the harbor itself is a marina and the pleasant Gibsons Seawalk, a scenic 10-minute meander (lighted at night). **Sunshine Coast Museum** (716 Winn Rd., 604/886-8232, Tues.–Sat 10:30 A.M.–4:30 P.M., donation) features intriguing pioneer and Coast Salish native displays and holds what must be one of the largest seashell collections on the planet (some 25,000).

On the main road, **Cedars Inn Hotel** (895 Gibsons Way, 604/886-3008 or 888/774-7044, www.thecedarsinn.com, $98 s, $104 d) features a heated outdoor pool, sauna, and small exercise room. Gibsons has a surprisingly good selection of eateries, most in the original part of town on a hill above the marina. For home-style cooking at reasonable prices, try **《 Molly's Reach** (647 School Rd., 604/886-9710, breakfast, lunch, and dinner, $11–17), which was originally built as part of the set for *The Beachcombers.* Near the waterfront, **Gibsons Visitor Centre** (417 Marine Dr., 604/886-2374 or 866/222-3806, www.gibsonslandingbc.com, summer daily 9 A.M.–5 P.M.) is a good first stop for Sunshine Coast information.

Roberts Creek

About nine kilometers (5.6 miles) northwest of Gibsons Landing you'll find the small artistic community of Roberts Creek (take the lower road off Highway 101), where arts and crafts appreciators can often snatch up a bargain. In an old-growth forest, **Roberts Creek Provincial Park,** 14 kilometers (8.7 miles) northwest of Gibsons, has hiking trails, waterfalls, a picnic ground, and a pebbly beach. Campsites are $15 per night.

The relaxed atmosphere at **《 Up the Creek Backpacker's B&B** (1261 Roberts Creek Rd., 604/885-0384 or 877/885-8100, www.upthecreek.ca, $25 dorms, $75 s or d) is reason enough to rest your head here overnight. Throw in well-priced beds, modern amenities such as a full kitchen and Internet access, and friendly owners, and you'll want to stay longer. Accommodations are in bright dorms, a private room, or a double cabin, with a self-serve breakfast for extra $5 per person.

Sechelt and Vicinity

The native cultural center and regional service center of Sechelt (population 8,400) perches on the isthmus of the Sechelt Peninsula between the head of Sechelt Inlet and the Strait of Georgia. Logging, fishing, and summer tourism support the town. One of the area's nicest spots is **Porpoise Bay Provincial Park,** four kilometers (2.5 miles) north of Sechelt via East Porpoise Bay Road. The park offers open grassy areas among forests of fir and cedar, and a broad sheltered sandy beach along the

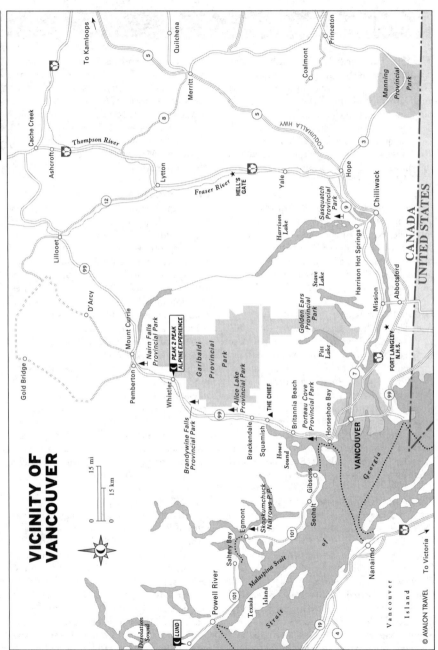

VICINITY OF VANCOUVER

0   15 mi

0   15 km

To Kamloops

Quilchena

Princeton

Coalmont

Manning Provincial Park

Merritt

Cache Creek

Ashcroft

Thompson River

5

8

5

COQUIHALLA HWY

3

Hope

Lytton

12

Fraser River

★ HELL'S GATE

Yale

Chilliwack

CANADA
UNITED STATES

Harrison Lake

Sasquatch Provincial Park

9

Lillooet

99

D'Arcy

Mount Currie

Nairn Falls Provincial Park

Harrison Hot Springs

Stave Lake

Mission

Abbotsford

Gold Bridge

Pemberton

PEAK 2 PEAK ALPINE EXPERIENCE

Garibaldi Provincial Park

Golden Ears Provincial Park

7

FORT LANGLEY N.H.S. ★

Whistler

Alice Lake Provincial Park

Pitt Lake

99

Brackendale

Brandywine Falls Provincial Park

99

Squamish

Britannia Beach

Porteau Cove Provincial Park

Horseshoe Bay

▲ THE CHIEF

Howe Sound

VANCOUVER

Georgia

Egmont

Skookumchuck Narrows P.P.

Gibsons

Sechelt

Saltery Bay

101

Powell River

Malaspina Strait

Texada Island

Nanaimo

19

4

Strait

of

Vancouver Island

To Victoria

LUND

Desolation Sound

© AVALON TRAVEL

St., 604/885-1036, daily 9 A.M.–5 P.M. in summer, shorter hours the rest of the year) is along Highway 101 through town.

SUNSHINE COAST FERRIES

Although the Sunshine Coast is part of the mainland, there is no road access. To reach Powell River, at the end of the road, entails travel with **BC Ferries** (250/386-3431 or 888/223-3779). From Horseshoe Bay, at the west end of Vancouver's north shore, ferries regularly cross Howe Sound to **Langdale.** From there Highway 101 runs up the coast 81 kilometers (50 miles) to **Earls Cove,** where another ferry crosses Jervis Inlet to **Saltery Bay.** These trips take 40 and 50 minutes respectively and run approximately every two hours 6:30 A.M.-11:30 P.M. The cost is adult $11.85, child $5.95, vehicle $39.90, which includes one-way travel on both ferries or round-trip travel on just one ferry. From Saltery Bay, it's 35 kilometers (22 miles) to Powell River, and you can return from there along the same route or loop back on Vancouver Island on the Powell River–Comox ferry (adult $11.80, child $5.90, vehicle $37.50).

Pender Harbour to Earls Cove

Pender Harbour is an orca habitat. These highly intelligent gentle giants, also known as "killer whales," travel in pods of up to 100. Feeding on salmon found year-round in these waters, they grow up to nine meters (29.6 feet) long, weighing as much as eight tons. Keep your eyes on the water and your camera ready to capture their triangular dorsal fins slicing through the waves.

Just before Earls Cove, take the road north to Egmont, then the 3.5-kilometer (2.1-mile) hiking trail along Sechelt Inlet to **Skookumchuck Narrows Provincial Park.** Meaning "turbulent water" in Chinook, Skookumchuck is a narrow, rock-strewn waterway where tidal water roars through four times a day. The resulting rapids and eddies boisterously boil and bubble to create fierce-looking whirlpools—fascinating to see when your feet are firmly planted on terra firma. You'll also see abundant marine creatures in tidal pools. It's a fascinating spot. Take a picnic lunch, pull up a rock, and enjoy the view.

Earls Cove marks the end of this section of Highway 101. From here, BC Ferries offers regular service across Jervis Inlet to Saltery Bay. The 16-kilometer (10-mile) crossing takes 50 minutes.

Saltery Bay and Vicinity

Less than two kilometers (1.2 miles) from the Saltery Bay ferry terminal is 140-hectare (346-acre) **Saltery Bay Provincial Park,** one of the Sunshine Coast's diving hot spots. Waters off the park are accessible from the shore and are full of marine life as well as a bronze mermaid. Camping is $14 per night.

From Saltery Bay, it's 31 kilometers (19.2 miles) of winding road to Powell River. Along the way you'll cross **Lois River,** the outlet for large Lois Lake, and pass a string of coastal communities clinging to the rocky shoreline of Malaspina Strait.

eastern shore of Sechelt Inlet. Hiking trails connect the beach with a day-use area and campground, and a woodland trail meanders along the bank of Angus Creek, where chum and coho salmon spawn in fall. The park is a handy base for kayakers and canoeists exploring Sechelt Inlets Marine Provincial Park. Porpoise Bay and the nearby rivers are also noted for good sportfishing, and oysters and clams are found along the inlet northwest of the park. The 84-site campground ($19) has hot showers.

Out of town to the west, **Rockwater Secret Cove Resort** (5356 Ole's Cove Rd., 604/885-7038 or 877/296-4593, www.rockwatersecret-coveresort.com, $169–279 s or d) is an upscale, absolute waterfront complex overlooking Halfmoon Bay. It has a wonderful restaurant (for the food and view), as well as luxurious accommodations and a variety of water-based activities. **Sechelt Visitor Centre** (5790 Teredo

POWELL RIVER

Situated between Jervis Inlet and Desolation Sound along the edge of Malaspina Strait, Powell River (population 15,500) is almost surrounded by water. It's a thriving center for the region's abundant outdoor recreation opportunities, including salmon fishing (good year-round), trout fishing, scuba diving, sailing, canoeing, kayaking, and hiking. Beyond downtown Powell River (also called Westview) is the original townsite, occupied by an ugly waterfront pulp mill and a number of boarded-up buildings.

Sights

Start your exploration by visiting the excellent **Powell River Historical Museum** across the road from Willingdon Beach (4798 Marine Ave., 604/485-2222, summer daily 9 A.M.–4:30 P.M., the rest of the year Mon.–Fri. 9 A.M.–4:30 P.M., adult $2, child $1), which holds a vast collection of photographs, displays telling the story of this seashore community, native artifacts, and even the shanty home of a hermit who once lived along Powell Lake. Starting across from the museum is the 1.2-kilometer (0.7-mile) **Willingdon Beach Trail,** lined by interpretive boards describing natural features and the uses of old logging machinery scattered along the trail.

North of town is the original townsite, built around a bay that still holds a working pulp and paper mill complex. The *Heritage Walk* brochure (available at the information center) will guide you around the interesting array of buildings that date from 1910 to the 1930s. Many—such as the grand Hotel Rodmay and the imposing Federal Building—have been boarded up for decades.

Recreation

The sheltered Sunshine Coast provides plenty of opportunities for good lake and ocean canoeing or kayaking. One of the best-known local paddles is the **Powell Forest Canoe Route,** a four- to eight-day backcountry trip that requires a few portages, or can be paddled in a single section. **Mitchell Canoe & Kayak**

(8690 Hwy. 101, 604/487-1609, www.canoeingbc.com) rents canoes for $26–33 for one day, or $23–26 per day for five or more days. The company also rents all the necessary accessories and fishing gear, provides free parking, and runs a shuttle service to and from the put-in ($60).

Although **Powell River Sea Kayak** (Malaspina Rd., 604/483-2160 or 866/617-4444, www.bcseakayak.com) outfits for the Powell Forest Canoe Route, kayaks are its specialty. Single and double kayaks for use around local waterways rent for $50–70 for one day, $70–110 for two days, additional days $20–40. Guided two-hour tours are $55, overnight sea-kayaking trips start at $240, and three-hour basic kayaking classes start at $55.

Known as the "Diving Capital of Canada," the Strait of Georgia provides divers with exceptionally clear, relatively warm water and more than 100 exciting dives mapped by local experts. Conditions are particularly excellent in winter, when visibility reaches 30 meters. Expect to see underwater cliffs and abundant marine-life, including sponges, giant octopuses, wolf eels, perch, ling cod, tubeworms, sea anemones, nudibranchs (including intriguing hooded nudibranchs), sea stars, crabs, and tunicates. Diving gear and a list of charter operators are available at **Alpha Dive and Kayak** (7050 Field St., 604/485-6939, www.divepowellriver.com).

Accommodations and Camping

One of the most attractive and relaxing lodgings in Powell River is **⟨ Beacon Bed and Breakfast** (3750 Marine Dr. 604/485-5563 or 800/485-5563, www.beaconbb.com, $109–119 s, $119–129 d), overlooking Malaspina Strait and the peaks of Vancouver Island two kilometers (1.2 miles) south of the ferry terminal. Within the two-story home are two guest rooms, both with ocean views. Facilities include a lounge area overlooking the water, an outdoor hot tub, Internet access, spa services, and in-room luxuries like fluffy robes. Rates include a big breakfast that will set you up for a day of outdoor activities.

The least-expensive motel-like rooms at

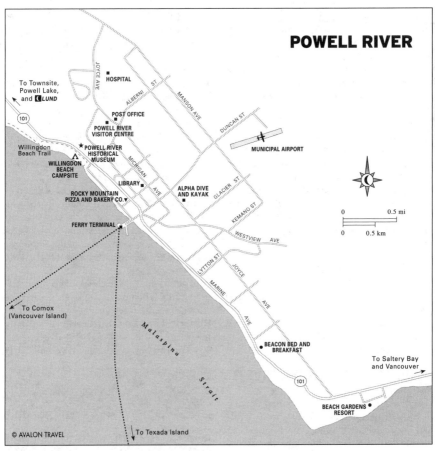

POWELL RIVER

To Townsite,
Powell Lake,
and **C** LUND

HOSPITAL

JOYCE AVE

ALBERNI ST

MANSON AVE

POST OFFICE

DUNCAN ST

POWELL RIVER
VISITOR CENTRE

Willingdon
Beach Trail

★ POWELL RIVER
HISTORICAL
MUSEUM

MUNICIPAL AIRPORT

WILLINGDON
BEACH
CAMPSITE

MICHIGAN

LIBRARY

AVE

ALPHA DIVE
AND KAYAK

GLACIER ST

ROCKY MOUNTAIN
PIZZA AND BAKERY CO. ▼

KEMANO ST

FERRY TERMINAL

WESTVIEW AVE

LYTTON ST

JOYCE

To Comox
(Vancouver Island)

MARINE

AVE

M a l a s p i n a

S t r a i t

BEACON BED AND
BREAKFAST

To Saltery Bay
and Vancouver

101

BEACH GARDENS
RESORT

© AVALON TRAVEL

To Texada Island

0   0.5 mi

0   0.5 km

Beach Gardens Resort (7074 Westminster Ave., 604/485-6267 or 800/663-7070, www.beachgardens.com, $89–189 s or d.), five kilometers (3.1 miles) south of the ferry terminal, are more than made up for by amenities such as an indoor swimming pool, sauna, tennis courts, a fitness room, and a marina with boat rentals and divers' air (it's a great place to meet fellow scuba enthusiasts). The resort's restaurant offers lunchtime buffets and a pub.

Willingdon Beach Campsite (4845 Marine Ave., 604/485-2242, www.willingdonbeach. ca, $18 tent sites, $20–25 hookups) enjoys a great waterfront location one kilometer (0.6

miles) north of the ferry terminal. You'll find sheltered and very popular campsites along the beach, as well as a laundry and washrooms with free hot showers.

Food

Head to **Rocky Mountain Pizza and Bakery Co.** (4471 Marine Ave., 604/485-9111, Mon.–Sat. from 6:30 A.M., Sunday from 8 A.M., pizzas $12–19) for great bakery items, coffee as strong (or as weak) as you like it, and daily newspapers.

At the marina overlooking Powell Lake, north of town, the **Shinglemill** (604/483-2001, daily 11 A.M.–11 P.M., $13.50–27.50) is part pub, part restaurant, with the former spilling out onto a wide deck. The pub menu is wideranging, with the seafood chowder served in a sourdough bread bowl ($7.25) being a good choice. In the restaurant, mains such as salmon baked in a soy-ginger glaze add a little sophistication to the scene.

Information

Powell River Visitor Centre (4871 Joyce Ave., 604/485-4701, www.discoverpowellriver. com, daily 9 A.M.–5 P.M. in summer, weekdays only the rest of the year) is in the Crossorads Village Shopping Centre. **Powell River Public Library** (4411 Michigan Ave., 604/485-4796, Mon.–Sat. 10 A.M.–6 P.M.) is a good place to hang out on a rainy day and to check email.

To Vancouver Island

The ferry terminal in Powell River is at the foot of Duncan St., right downtown. **BC Ferries** (604/485-2943) has regular sailings between Powell River and Comox on Vancouver Island. One-way fares for the 75-minute sailing are adult $11.80, child $5.90, vehicle $37.50.

VICINITY OF POWELL RIVER
C Lund

Twenty-eight kilometers (17.3 miles) north of Powell River, Highway 101 dead-ends on the old wooden wharf of Lund, a tiny fishing village founded in 1889 and named after the Swedish hometown of the first settlers. Lund lies on a secluded harbor backed by the magnificent peaks of the Coast Mountains. Although Lund is best known as the gateway to Desolation Sound, it's worth the trip out just for the relaxed atmosphere and surrounding beauty. Wander around the bustling marina, cruise over to the white sand beaches of Savary Island (604/483-9749, $10 round-trip), and relax with a cold drink on the deck of the Historic Lund Hotel. At the back of the hotel, **Rockfish Kayak** (604/414-9355) rents kayaks for $35–65 per day and leads kayak tours to Okeover Arm (three hours for $65).

One accommodation right in town is the harbor-front **C Historic Lund Hotel** (1436

Hwy. 101, 604/414-0474 or 877/569-3999, www.lundhotel.com, $130–225 s or d). Standard rooms have earthy tones and hardwood floors, with hand-painted murals adding to the charm. Oceanfront rooms are upscale all the way, with handcrafted beds, luxurious bathrooms, and elegant styling throughout. If you're looking for something a little different, choose to stay at **The Dome** (off Baggi Rd., 604/483-9160, www.magicaldome.com, $150 s or d), a five-minute drive from Lund. It's one of the very few places in Canada where you can stay in a geodesic dome—a quirky architectural style that employs dozens of triangular panels to create a rigid spherical structure, creating the most space with the least amount of materials. Inside is a bedroom, loft with second bed, kitchen, lounge area, and wood-burning fireplace. Adjacent is a modern bathhouse, complete with sauna.

In addition to a fine choice of accommodations, Lund is home to a couple of the Sunshine Coast's premier restaurants. The food at **Historic Lund Hotel** (604/414-0474, daily for lunch and dinner, $11–19) is overshadowed by the views, especially if you talk your

© ANDREW HEMPSTEAD

The Historic Lund Hotel has wonderful views.

way to an outside table. The seafood chowder and local oysters are both good starters, followed by halibut and chips as a main and a slab of mud cake for dessert. The ◖ **Laughing Oyster** (Vandermaeden Rd., 604/483-9775, daily noon–9:30 P.M., $19–33) is a hidden gem. Overlooking the water from an elevated setting, diners are seated outside on a deck or inside on tiers that allow everyone to enjoy the view. Starters include oysters prepared in a variety of ways (you can see the restaurant's oyster farm from the deck) and a healthy roasted pecan and blue cheese salad. Mains include a perfectly presented baked halibut dish. The Laughing Oyster is a well-signposted, five-minute drive from Lund.

Desolation Sound

Named by Captain Vancouver in 1792—he was obviously unimpressed—much of this remote waterway is now protected as a marine park. A wilderness-seeker's paradise, the park is totally undeveloped and without road access.

The sheltered waters of **Okeover Arm**—a southern arm of Desolation Sound—are much more accessible, with road access along Malaspina Road, off Highway 101 south of Lund. Forested four-hectare (10-acre) **Okeover Arm Provincial Park** lies on the water; it's a small, rustic park with just a few undeveloped campsites ($12), a pit toilet, and a kayak- and boat-launching ramp, but it's a great spot to camp if you're into canoeing or kayaking.

North of the park **Desolation Resort** (2694 Dawson Rd., 604/483-3592, www.desolationresort.com, mid-Feb.–Sept., $159–339 s or d) offers a wonderful escape at reasonable prices. Accommodations are in freestanding wood chalets set high above the lake edge on stilts. All feature rich-colored wood furnishings, and even the smallest (the bottom half of one unit) has a king-size bed, large deck, kitchen, separate living and dining areas, and a barbecue.

Texada Island

A 35-minute ferry trip from the Powell River ferry terminal, Texada is one of the largest of the gulf islands (50 km/31 mi from north to south and up to 10 km/6.2 mi wide), but the permanent population is only 1,200 and services are limited. From the ferry terminal at Blubber Bay, the island's main road winds south for eight kilometers (five miles) to **Van Anda,** a historic village that once boasted saloons, an opera house, and a hospital. Take a walk along Van Anda's Erickson Beach to appreciate the island's natural beauty. Continuing south, the road leads to Gillies Bay and beyond to **Shelter Point Regional Park,** which has some short but enjoyable hiking trails and a sandy spit that leads to a private high-tide island. At low tide, look for colorful starfish along the shoreline, or try your hand digging for clams. Campsites overlooking the water are $19.

The short hop over to the island from Powell River with **BC Ferries** (604/485-2943) costs adult $7.25, child $3.75, vehicle $17.50 round-trip. Ferries depart about every two hours 8 A.M.–11 P.M.; no reservations taken.

Sea to Sky Highway

The spectacular, aptly-named Sea to Sky Highway (Highway 99) runs 105 kilometers (65 miles) between Horseshoe Bay and Whistler. With the almost-vertical tree-covered **Coast Mountains** to the east and island-dotted **Howe Sound** to the west, this cliff-hugging highway winds precariously through a dramatic glacier-carved landscape.

HORSEHOE BAY TOWARD SQUAMISH
Porteau Cove Provincial Park

On the east shore of Howe Sound, Porteau Cove is best known among the diving populace for its artificial reef of four sunken wrecks, but it also offers good swimming and fishing. In addition, the area's strong winds and lack of waves make for perfect windsurfing conditions. The park has boat-launching and scuba-diving facilities, an ecology information center, picnic tables, and a waterfront campground for tents and RVs. A day pass is $5 per vehicle and camping is $24 per night March–October (free the rest of the year).

Britannia Beach

Small Britannia Beach is worth a stop to visit the **B.C. Museum of Mining** (604/688-8735, daily 9 A.M.–5:30 P.M. mid-May–early October, adult $15, senior and student $12), overlooking Howe Sound. In the early 1930s the Britannia Beach Mine was the British Empire's largest producer of copper, producing more than 600 million kilograms. Today it's not a working mine but a working museum. Ever wondered what it's like to slave away underground? Here's your chance to don a hard hat and raincoat, hop on an electric train, and travel under a mountain without even getting your hands dirty. See fully functional mining equipment along with demonstrations and displays on the techniques of mining. Then take a step into the past in the museum, where hundreds of photos and artifacts tell the story of the mine. Outside of the main mid-May–early October season, the site is open Mon.–Fri. 9 A.M.–4:30 P.M., but no tours are offered. In return, admission is reduced to $5 per person.

SQUAMISH

Squamish (population 15,000), 67 kilometers (42 miles) north of Vancouver and 53 kilometers (33 miles) south of Whistler, enjoys a stunning location at the head of Howe Sound, surrounded by snowcapped mountains.

Sights and Recreation

See around 65 vintage rail cars and engines in a mock working rail yard, complete with a station garden, replica workers' homes, and a restored station at the **West Coast Railway Heritage Park** (Industrial Way, one km from Hwy. 99, 604/898-9336, daily 10 A.M.–5 P.M., adult $12, child $9.50).

At first it may be difficult to see past the industrial scars along Squamish's waterways, but

---

THE "CHIEF"

Towering over Squamish and clearly visible across the highway is the **Stawamus Chief,** one of the world's largest granite monoliths. Rising 762 meters (2,500 feet) from the forest floor, it formed around 100 million years ago when massive forces deep inside the earth forced molten rock through the crust – as it cooled, it hardened and fractured. This created a perfect environment for today's climbers, who are attracted by a great variety of free and aided climbing on almost 1,000 routes.

If you've never climbed or are inexperienced, consider using the services of **Squamish Rock Guides** (604/892-7816, www.squamishrockguides.com) for a variety of courses with equipment supplied; expect to pay around $120 for a one-day introductory course. **Vertical Reality** (37835 2nd Ave., 604/892-8248) offers a full range of climbing equipment and sells local climbing guidebooks.

---

on the west side of downtown a large section of the delta where the Squamish River flows into Howe Sound has escaped development. It comprises tidal flats, forested areas, marshes, and open meadows—and more than 200 species of birds call the area home. Hiking trails lace the area, and there are three main access points: Industrial Road, the end of Winnipeg Street, and the end of Vancouver Street, all of which branch off Cleveland Avenue.

Practicalities

The best place to stay around Squamish is **C Dryden Creek Resorts,** six kilometers (3.7 miles) north of town at Depot Road (604/898-9726 or 877/237-9336, www.drydencreek.com, $89–109 s or d). It's set on six hectares (14 acres) of landscaped parkland with Garibaldi Provincial Park as a backdrop. Each of the six suite-style studios has a cedar ceiling, large skylights, and a fully equipped kitchen with handcrafted cabinets. The resort's campground ($24 unserviced sites, $30 hookups) offers a choice of forested or creek-side sites. Right downtown, **Howe Sound Inn** (37801 Cleveland Ave., 604/892-2603 or 800/919-2537, www.howesound.com, $119 s or d) is a stylish place with 20 modern rooms. Amenities include underground parking, in-room Internet access, a restaurant, and an in-house brewery.

Squamish Visitor Centre (38551 Loggers Lane, 604/815-4994 or 866/333-2010, www.tourismsquamish.com, daily 8 A.M.–6 P.M. in summer, daily 9 A.M.–5 P.M. the rest of the year) is a beautiful glass-and-wood building with a sweeping roofline that reflects the sweeping action of eagles.

NORTH TOWARD WHISTLER
The Eagles of Brackendale

If you're traveling the Sea to Sky Highway in winter, you're probably making a beeline for Whistler, but a stop at Brackendale, just north of Squamish, is well worthwhile. Through the colder months of the year, the river flats behind this sleepy little town are home to a larger concentration of **bald eagles** than anywhere else on the face of the earth. More than 3,000 of these magnificent creatures descend on a stretch of the Squamish River to feed on spawned-out salmon that litter the banks. The birds begin arriving in late October, but numbers reach their peak around Christmastime, and by early February they're gone. The best viewing spot is from the dike that runs along the back of Brackendale. The best place to learn more about these creatures is the **Brackendale Art Gallery** (604/898-3333, www.brackendaleartgallery.

com, daily noon–5 P.M. in Jan., weekends only rest of year), "Eagle Count Headquarters," for slide presentations, talks, and other eagle-related activities. To get there, follow the main Brackendale access road over the railway tracks, take the first right and look for the gallery nestled in the trees on the right.

Alice Lake Provincial Park

Alice Lake, surrounded by a 400-hectare (1,000-acre) park of open grassy areas, dense forests, and impressive snowcapped peaks, is particularly good for canoeing, swimming, and fishing for small rainbow and cutthroat trout. A 1.4-kilometer (0.9-mile) trail encircles the lake, while others lead to three smaller bodies of water; allow 20 minutes for the loop. A campground ($19–24) with showers and picnic tables is open year-round. Park entry is $5 per vehicle for day-trippers.

Brandywine Falls Provincial Park

Stop at this roadside park 45 kilometers (28 miles) north of Squamish and take the short trail to the base of these 66-meter (220-feet) falls. It's the kind of trail that excites all your senses—magnificent frosty peaks high above, dense lush forest on either side, a fast, deep river roaring along on one side, the pungent aroma and cushiness of crushed pine needles beneath your feet. It's most magnificent early in summer. (The falls were named by two railroad surveyors who made a wager on guessing the falls' height, the winner to receive bottles of—you guessed it—brandywine.)

Whistler

As co-host of the Olympic Winter Games, the world's eyes were on Whistler in February 2010—not that this bustling resort town (population 10,000), 120 kilometers (75 miles) north of Vancouver, needed any extra attention. Magnificent snowcapped peaks, dense green forests, transparent lakes, sparkling rivers, and an upscale, cosmopolitan village right

in the middle of it all make Whistler one of Canada's best known and most popular four-season resort towns.

Known intimately among skiers and snowboarders, the town is built around the base of one of North America's finest resorts, **Whistler Blackcomb,** which comprises almost 3,000 hectares (7,400 acres) on two mountains accessed by an ultramodern lift system. A season stretching from November to May doesn't leave much time for summer recreation, but the "off season" is almost equally busy. Among the abundant summertime recreation opportunities are lift-served hiking and glacier skiing and snowboarding; biking through the valley and mountains; water activities on five lakes; horseback riding; golfing on some of the world's best resort courses; and fishing, rafting, and jet-boating on the rivers. The more sedentary summer visitor can simply stay in bustling Whistler Village and enjoy a plethora of outdoor cafés and restaurants.

SUMMER RECREATION
◖ Peak 2 Peak
Alpine Experience

In the few months they aren't covered in snow, the slopes of Whistler and Blackcomb Mountains come alive with locals and tourists alike enjoying hiking, guided naturalist walks, mountain biking, and horseback riding—or just marveling at the mountainscape from the comfort of the lifts. The main lifts on both mountains operate late June through mid-October, with the classic Peak 2 Peak circuit allowing a 4.4-kilometre (2.8-mi) loop incorporating the mountains. A day pass for unlimited lift use is adult $42, senior $35, child $17. A two-day pass is adult $52, senior $45, child $29.

Over 50 kilometers (31 miles) of hiking trails wind around the mountains, including trails through the high alpine to destinations such as beautiful Harmony Lake and the toe of a small glacier. For an adrenaline rush, take the gondola up then ride down on a mountain bike. Die-hard skiers will even find mid-summer skiing and snowboarding (mid-June–late July, adult $54, child $28) on the Horstman Glacier.

Hiking

The easiest way to access the area's most spectacular hiking country is to take a sightseeing lift up Whistler or Blackcomb Mountain. But many other options exist. Walking around

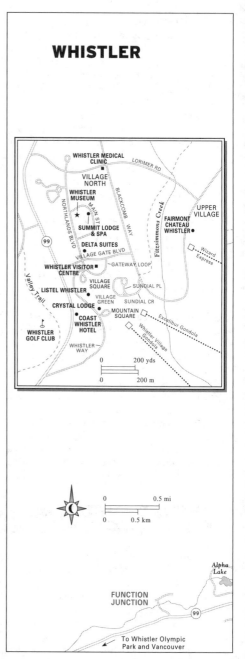

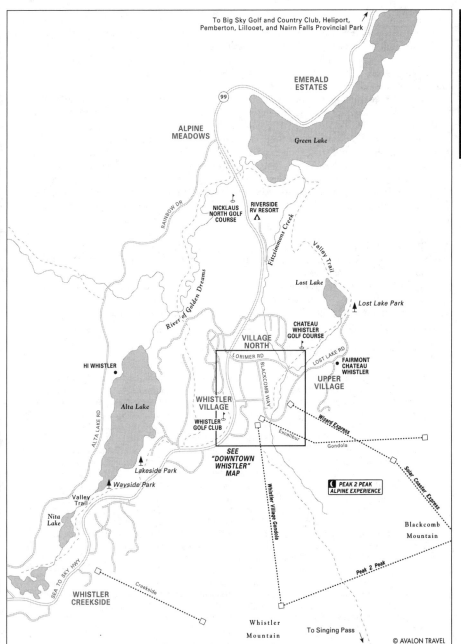

To Big Sky Golf and Country Club, Heliport,
Pemberton, Lillooet, and Nairn Falls Provincial Park

EMERALD
ESTATES

99

ALPINE
MEADOWS

Green Lake

RAINBOW DR

NICKLAUS
NORTH GOLF
COURSE

RIVERSIDE
RV RESORT

Fitzsimmons Creek

Valley Trail

River of Golden Dreams

Lost Lake

Lost Lake Park

CHATEAU
WHISTLER
GOLF COURSE

VILLAGE
NORTH

LORIMER RD

LOST LAKE RD

HI WHISTLER

FAIRMONT
CHATEAU
WHISTLER

BLACKCOMB WAY

UPPER
VILLAGE

Alta Lake

ALTA LAKE RD

WHISTLER
VILLAGE

WHISTLER
GOLF CLUB

Excalibur

Wizard Express

Gondola

SEE
"DOWNTOWN
WHISTLER"
MAP

Lakeside Park

Wayside Park

PEAK 2 PEAK
ALPINE EXPERIENCE

Solar Coaster Express

Valley
Trail

Nita
Lake

Whistler Village Gondola

Blackcomb
Mountain

SEA TO SKY HWY

Peak 2 Peak

Creekside

WHISTLER
CREEKSIDE

Whistler
Mountain

To Singing Pass

© AVALON TRAVEL

Whistler Valley you'll notice signposted trails all over the place. **Valley Trail** is a paved walk/bikeway in summer, a cross-country ski trail in winter. It makes an almost complete tour of the valley, from Whistler Village to Lost and Green Lakes, along the River of Golden Dreams, and past three golf courses to Alta, Nita, and Alpha Lakes, and finally to Highway 99 in the Whistler Creekside area. If you'd rather do a short walk, head for **Lost Lake** via the two-kilometer (1.2-mile) trail from Parking Lot East at the back of Whistler Village, or take the free Whistler Transit System bus from the middle of the village. Once at the beautiful lake, you can saunter along the shore, picnic, or swim.

Mountain Biking

The Whistler Valley is a perfect place to take a mountain bike—you'd need months to ride all the trails here. Many of the locals have abandoned their cars for bikes, which in some cases are worth much more than their cars! You can see them scooting along **Valley Trail,** a paved walk/bikeway that links the entire valley and is the resident bicyclists' freeway. Another popular place for mountain bikers is beautiful **Lost Lake,** two kilometers (1.2 miles) northeast of Whistler Village. On the mountain slopes, **Whistler Mountain Bike Park** (604/904-8134, www.whistlerbike.com, adult $40, child $21) is perfect for adventurous riders to strut their stuff. Using the lifts to access a vertical drop of 1,200 meters (3,900 feet), it features three "Skill Centres," filled with obstacles for varying levels of skill; a Bikercross Course; and a variety of trails to the valley floor. Run the courses by yourself or join a group in a guided descent for $90 including bike rental.

If you didn't bring a bike, not to worry—they're for rent. Rental rates start at around $18 per hour, $40–105 per day. **Backroads Whistler** (604/932-3111, www.backroadswhistler.com) runs a variety of tours, ranging from an easy ride along the valley floor to a hard-core downhill clinic ($95 per person).

A MODERN BOOMTOWN

Although the abundant natural resources of the Whistler Valley had been utilized by native peoples for thousands of years, the history of Whistler as a resort town doesn't really begin until the 1960s, and is associated almost entirely with the development of the ski area. At that time the only development was a bunch of ramshackle summer holiday houses around Alta Lake (which was also the name of the "town," population 300). When the road up from Vancouver was paved in 1964, the first ski lifts were constructed. Early skiers were impressed, and so were investors, who began plans for major base-area facilities. The idea of a European-style ski-in, ski-out village was promoted throughout the 1970s, but it wasn't until 1980 that Whistler Village officially opened. The following year, lift capacity doubled with the opening of an adjacent resort on Blackcomb Mountain. Lift construction continued unabated on both mountains through the 1980s and 1990s, and in 1997 the inevitable happened

and the two mountains came under the control of one company, **Intrawest,** which created the mega-resort of **Whistler Blackcomb.**

Meanwhile, development on the mountains was being overshadowed by construction in the valley below – new base facilities, resort-style golf courses, and upscale accommodations – where the population increased tenfold in 20 years. Through it all, a future cap on development has pushed the cost of living skyward – an empty lot goes for $3.5 million, a family home for $10 million, and a 240-unit development sold out in five hours at an average of $600,000 per condo. And this was *before* Whistler cohosted the 2010 Olympic Winter Games.

The best place to learn the full story of development in the valley is the magnificent new **Whistler Museum** (4333 Main St., 604/932-2019, daily 10 A.M.-4 P.M. July-Aug., Fri.-Sun. 10 A.M.-4 P.M. Sept.-June, adult $5, senior $4, child $3).

This company rents bikes, as do the following: **Sportstop** (4112 Golfers Approach, 604/932-5495), **Whistler Bike Co.** (4205 Whistler Square, 604/938-9511), and **Wild Willies** (4240 Gateway Loop, 604/938-8036).

Water Sports

Sunbathers head to the public beaches along the shores of **Alta Lake.** Wayside Park, at the south end of the lake, has a beach, a canoe launch, an offshore pontoon, a grassy area with picnic tables, and hiking/biking trails. At Lakeside Park, also on Alta Lake, **Whistler Outdoor Experience** (604/932-3389, www.whistleroutdoor.com) rents canoes for $24 an hour or $72 per half day, and kayaks for $20 an hour.

For a little white-water excitement, try river rafting with **Whistler River Adventures** (604/932-3532 or 888/932-3532, www.whistlerriver.com), which provides guided scenic and white-water tours between the end of May and early September. Outings range from an easier float down the Green River for $69 per person to the white-water thrills of a full-day trip on the Elaho and Squamish Rivers for $159.

Golf

Whistler boasts three world-class championship golf courses, each with its own character and charm. The golfing season runs mid-May–October, so in late spring you can ski in the morning and golf in the afternoon. All the courses detailed below have rentals, dining facilities, and off-season/twilight rates. Designed by Arnold Palmer, **Whistler Golf Club** (between Whistler Village and Alta Lake, 604/932-3280 or 800/376-1777, $159) offers large greens and narrow wooded fairways over a challenging 6,676-yard par-72 layout. On the other side of the village, **Chateau Whistler Golf Club** (Blackcomb Way, 604/938-2092 or 888/938-2092, $195) takes advantage of the rugged terrain of Blackcomb Mountain's lower slopes through holes that rise and fall with the lay of the land. The Jack Nicklaus-designed **Nicklaus North** course (just north of Whistler Village, 604/938-9898, $175) is an open layout holding numerous water

hazards. It boasts 360-degree mountain vistas and plays to a challenging 6,900 yards from the back markers.

WINTER RECREATION

No matter what your ability, the skiing at **Whistler Blackcomb,** consistently rated as North America's number-one ski destination, makes for a winter holiday you won't forget in a hurry. The two lift-served mountains, Whistler and Blackcomb, are separated by a steep-sided valley through which Fitzsimmons Creek flows. The lifts of both mountains converge at Whistler Village. Skiing is over almost 3,000 hectares (7,400 acres), comprising more than 200 groomed runs, hundreds of unmarked trails through forested areas, three glaciers, and 12 bowls. Blackcomb and Whistler Mountains are 2,284 meters (7,500 feet) and 2,182 meters (7,160 feet) high respectively. In total, the resort has 34 lifts, including three gondolas, 12 high-speed quad chairlifts, five triples, one double, and 12 surface lifts. Snowboarders are well catered to with four terrain parks and numerous half-pipes. For many, the resort can be overwhelming. Trail maps detail all marked runs but can't convey the vast size of the area. A great way to get to know the mountain is on an orientation tour; these leave throughout the day from various meeting points (ask when and where you buy your ticket) and are free. A lift ticket is adult $91, senior and youth $75, child $45, and those under seven ski/board for free. The resort's website (www.whistlerblackcomb.com) contains everything you'll need to know about the resort and booking winter accommodation packages, or call the general enquires desk (604/932-3434 or 800/766-0449). For accommodation information call Whistler Central Reservations (604/904-7060 or 888/403-4727).

Cross-Country Skiing

The groomed trails at **Whistler Olympic Park** (604/964-2455), built for the 2010 Olympic Winter Games, are open to the public at a cost of $20 for a day pass. Facilities at the venue include rentals ($25–40 per day), a day lodge with restaurant, and lessons; It's located 16 kilometers (10 mi) south of town. Closer to the village, and running in a long loop past Lost Lake and Green Lake is the **Valley Trail,** a paved walk/bikeway in summer that becomes a popular cross-country ski trail in winter; near Lost Lake and on the adjacent Chateau Whistler Golf Course. Most trails are groomed, while some are track set, and a five-kilometer stretch is illuminated for night skiing.

ENTERTAINMENT AND EVENTS
Nightlife

Throughout the year you can usually find live evening entertainment in Whistler Village. The **Garibaldi Lift Co. Bar & Grill** (2320 London Lane, 604/905-2220) features live entertainment most nights—often blues and jazz—and good food at reasonable prices. At **Buffalo Bill's** (Timberline Lodge, 4122 Village Green, 604/932-6613) expect anything from reggae to rock. For more than a decade, **Tommy Africa's** (4216 Gateway Dr., 604/932-6090) has been one of the village's hottest nightspots.

Events

The winter season is packed with ski and snowboard races through mid-April, but the biggest is the **World Ski & Snowboard Festival** (604/938-3399, www.wssf.com). This innovative event brings together the very best winter athletes for the World Skiing Invitational and the World Snowboarding Championship.

Each weekend in May and June and daily through summer, the streets of Whistler come alive with street entertainment such as musicians, jugglers, and comedians. The last weekend of May is the official end of the ski season up on Blackcomb Mountain, with the **Slush Cup** and live music.

Canada Day, July 1, is celebrated with a parade through Whistler Village. **Mountain West Music Fest** (www.mountainwestmusicfest.com)in mid-August offers lots of free entertainment, including outdoor film screenings and street music.

ACCOMMODATIONS AND CAMPING

Whistler's accommodations range from a backpacker lodge to luxury resort hotels. It's just a matter of selecting one to suit your budget and location preference. Skiers may want to be right in Whistler Village or by the gondola base in Whistler Creekside so they can stroll out their door, strap on skis, and jump on a lift.

Winter is most definitely high season, with the week after Christmas and all of February and March a high season within a high season, especially for lodgings. Although winter is peak season, rates quoted below are for summertime.

Under $50

HI-Whistler (5678 Alta Lake Rd., 604/932-5492, www.hihostels.ca) is on the western shore of Alta Lake, boasting magnificent views across the lake to the resort. It's relatively small (just 32 beds), with facilities including a communal kitchen, dining area, and big, cozy living area. Bike and canoe rentals are available. It's understandably popular year-round; members pay $32 per night, nonmembers $36 ($75 and $83 respectively for a twin private room). Check-in is 8–11 A.M. and 4–10 P.M. To get there from the south, take Alta Lake Road to the left off Highway 99 and watch for the small sign on the lake side of the road. **WAVE** transit buses depart Whistler Village and run right past the hostel door.

$100-150

◖ **Crystal Lodge** (4154 Village Green, 604/932-2221 or 800/667-3363, www.crystal-lodge.com, $128–315 s or d) stands out as an excellent value in the heart of the action of Whistler Village. Traditional Rooms are spacious and have a homey feel. The Lodge Wing holds larger suites with balconies. All guests have the use of an outdoor hot tub and heated pool.

$150-200

The modern log cabins at the **Riverside RV Resort** (8018 Mons Rd., 604/905-5533, www.whistlercamping.com, $189 s or d) aren't very spacious, but you're in Whistler, so you'll be spending most of your time hiking, biking, and generally being outdoors anyway. They ooze mountain charm and come complete with a small kitchen and TV/VCR combo. Rates are as low as $129 in fall, but rise well over $200 in winter. An on-site grocery store and café save a trip into town.

On the edge of the village and adjacent to one of the valley's best golf courses is **Coast Whistler Hotel** (4005 Whistler Way, 604/932-2522 or 800/663-5644, www.coastwhistlerhotel.com, $179 s or d). Each of the 194 rooms is simply but stylishly decorated in pastel colors. Facilities include a heated outdoor pool, exercise room, hot tub, restaurant, and bar. Summer rates start at a reasonable $179, but the winter rate of $295 s or d is a little steep considering you're away from the ski lifts.

Centrally located **Delta Whistler Village Suites** (4308 Main St., 604/905-3987 or 888/299-3987, www.deltahotels.com, $195 s or d) combines the conveniences of a full-service hotel with more than 200 kitchen-equipped units—the only such property in Whistler.

$200-250

In the heart of the action, **◖ Listel Whistler** (4121 Village Green, 604/932-1133 or 800/663-5472, www.listelhotel.com, $249 s or d) is a self-contained resort complete with a year-round outdoor pool, outdoor hot tub, and laundry. The in-house Bearfoot Bistro means you don't need to leave for dinner.

Over $250

Summit Lodge & Spa (4359 Main St., 604/932-2778 or 888/913-8811, www.summitlodge.com, $280 s or d) is a luxurious European Alps–style boutique hotel. Each of the 81 units features comfortable furnishings, a slate floor, a fireplace, a balcony, and a small kitchen. Check the website for deeply discounted rates year-round.

Fairmont Chateau Whistler, at the base of Blackcomb Mountain in Upper Village (604/938-8000 or 800/257-7544, www.fairmont.com, from $320 s or d) is Whistler's most luxurious lodging, with its own championship golf course, the Vida Wellness Spa, a health club with the best equipment money can buy, tennis courts, multiple restaurants and lounges, and all the facilities expected of one of the world's best accommodations. The massive lobby is decorated in the style of a rustic lodge, but the rooms couldn't be more different. Each is elegantly furnished and offers great mountain views.

Camping

Enjoying a pleasant location just over two kilometers (1.2 miles) north of the village, **Riverside RV Resort** (8018 Mons Rd., 604/905-5533, www.whistlercamping.com, $35 tents, $57 RVs and trailers) is the only campground within town boundaries. It offers a modern bathroom complex (with in-floor heating), putting course, playground, hot tub, laundry, small general store, and a café (daily from 7 A.M.).

Out of town, the closest campgrounds are in **Brandywine Falls Provincial Park,** 11 kilometers (6.8 miles) south, and **Nairn Falls Provincial Park,** 28 kilometers (17.4 miles) north. Both are open April–November and charge $15 per night.

FOOD

Like the town itself, the dining scene in Whistler is hip, ever-changing, and not particularly cheap. Many small cafés dot the cobbled walkways of Whistler Village, and most bars have reasonably priced pub-fare menus.

For a caffeine fix, **Moguls Coffee House** (4204 Village Square, 604/932-4845, daily from 6:30 A.M.) is as good as any place—it's popular with both locals and visitors, and the outdoor seating catches the morning sun.

Casual

The rustic decor and great Canadian food at **Garibaldi Lift Co. Bar & Grill** (604/905-2220, open daily for lunch and dinner, $12–26) at the base of the Whistler Village gondola makes it a popular après-ski hangout, and by around 8 P.M. everyone's back for dinner. For western-style atmosphere with mountain views, head to the **Longhorn Saloon and Grill** (4290 Mountain Square, 604/932-5999, daily 11 A.M.–11 P.M., $11–31) and share a platter of finger food or order your own cut of prime Alberta beef complete with trimmings for $21–31.

◖ **Citta' Bistro** (4217 Village Stroll, Whistler Village, 604/932-4177, daily 11 A.M.–1 A.M., $15–26) has been around since Whistler first became a hip destination—and it's as popular today as it ever was. If it's a warm evening, try for a table on the patio and order a gourmet pizza for one to go with a locally brewed beer.

Steak

At ◖ **Hy's** (Delta Whistler Village Suites, 4308 Main St., 604/905-5555, daily 5–10 P.M., $25–49), you don't need to ask if the steak is good. Everything on offer is top-notch AAA Alberta beef, including a signature, not-for-the-faint-hearted porterhouse. The scene is upscale, with elegant tables set within rich-colored wood walls.

European

For great Greek food at reasonable prices, **Zeuski's Taverna** (4314 Main St., Town Plaza, Village North, 604/932-6009, daily for lunch and dinner, $15–24) is an excellent choice for souvlaki cooked on the barbecue.

Restaurant entrepreneur Umberto Menghi operates numerous eateries in Vancouver and two restaurants in Whistler Village. Both are reasonably priced with menus influenced by the cuisine of Tuscany. Check out **Il Caminetto** (4242 Village Stroll, 604/932-4442, daily from 5 P.M., $18–35) and **Trattoria** (4417 Sundial Place, 604/932-5858, daily from 5 P.M., $15–31). The former, named for a fireplace that has been replaced by more tables, has a warm, welcoming atmosphere and a long menu of pastas. The latter is less expensive, has a more traditional Tuscan setting and attracts a casual crowd.

After starring in Chef Ramsey's *Hell's Kitchen* during 2009, things have returned to normal at ◖ **Araxi** (4222 Village Square, Whistler Village, 604/932-4540, daily 5–11 P.M., $27.50–36.50),

which consistently wins awards for its traditional Italian menu. Much of the produce is sourced from the Lower Mainland, while the restaurant also boasts an extensive wine list.

INFORMATION AND SERVICES

The **Whistler Visitor Info Centre** is centrally located at 4230 Gateway Drive (604/935-3357, daily 8 A.M.–10 P.M.).

In Whistler Village you'll find a post office, banks, a currency exchange, laundry, supermarket, and liquor store. **Whistler Medical Centre** is at 4380 Lorimer (604/932-3977). Opened in 2008, the **Whistler Public Library** (4329 Main St., 604/935-8433, Mon.–Sat. 11 A.M.–7 P.M., Sun. 11 A.M.–4 P.M.) is a modern facility with an international selection of newspapers and magazines, as well as free public Internet access.

GETTING THERE AND AROUND

The most enjoyable way to reach the resort is aboard the **Whistler Mountaineer** (604/606-8460 or 888/687-7245, www.whistlermountaineer.com), which departs North Vancouver daily May–mid-October for the three-hour trip along Howe Sound. Rates for adult $199, child $109 round-trip, include Vancouver hotel pickups and three hours in the village.

You can also fly in from Vancouver on a floatplane with **Whistler Air** (604/932-6615 or 888/806-2299, www.whistlerair.ca, mid-May–mid-Oct., $169 each way), or catch a **Pacific Coach Lines** (604/662-8074 or 800/661-1725, www.pacificcoach.com) bus from Vancouver International Airport for $52.

Once you're in Whistler, getting around is pretty easy—if you're staying in Whistler Village, everything you need is within easy walking distance. **WAVE** (Whistler and Valley Express, 604/932-4020) operates extensive bus routes throughout the valley daily 6 A.M.–midnight, adult $2, senior and child $1.50. For a cab call **Sea to Sky Taxi** (604/932-3333) or **Whistler Taxi** (604/938-3333). Rental car agencies in Whistler include **Budget** (604/932-1236) and **Thrifty** (604/938-0302).

East from Vancouver

FRASER VALLEY

When you leave Vancouver and head due east, you have a choice of two major routes. The TransCanada Highway, on the south side of the Fraser River, speeds you out of southeast Vancouver through Abbotsford and scenic Chilliwack to Hope. Slower, more picturesque Highway 7 meanders along the north side of the Fraser River to Harrison Hot Springs and crosses over the Fraser River to Hope.

Fort Langley
National Historic Site

This important site (23433 Mavis St., Fort Langley, 604/513-4777, daily 10 A.M.–5 P.M., extended to 9 A.M.–8 P.M. July and Aug., adult $8, senior $6.50, child $4) recreates a Hudson's Bay Company settlement that was part of a network of trading posts across western Canada. Through its formative years, the original fort played a major role in the development of British Columbia. Out of its gates have vamoosed native fur and salmon traders, adventurous explorers who opened up the interior, company traders, and fortune seekers heading for the goldfields of the upper Fraser River. When British Columbia became a crown colony on November 19, 1858, the official proclamation was uttered here in the "big house." Today the restored riverside trading post springs to life as park interpreters in period costumes animate the fort's history. To get there, take Exit 66 from Highway 1 and head north on 232nd Street for five kilometers (3.1 miles).

Kilby Historic Site

Off the beaten track and often missed by those unfamiliar with the area, this historic site (604/796-9576, Thurs.–Mon. 11 A.M.–5 P.M. April.–mid-May, daily 11 A.M.–5 P.M. late May–early Sept., adult $9, senior $8, child $7) lies on the north side of the Fraser River, near the turnoff to Harrison Hot Springs, 40 kilometers (25 miles) east of Mission. The interesting museum/country store, which operated until the early 1970s, is fully stocked with all the old brands and types of goods that were commonplace in the 1920s and 1930s.

Harrison Hot Springs

Of British Columbia's 60 natural hot springs, the closest to Vancouver is **Harrison Hot Springs,** on the north side of the Fraser Valley, 125 kilometers (78 miles) east of downtown. At **Harrison Public Pool** (corner of Harrison Hot Springs Rd. and Esplanade Ave., 604/796-2244, daily 8 A.M.–9 P.M. in summer, daily 9 A.M.–9 P.M. the rest of the year, adult $9, senior and child $6.25), the public is invited to soak away their cares in soothing 38°C (100°F) water. Adjacent **Harrison Lake** has nice beaches and the water is warm enough for swimming. Through town to the north is 1,220-hectare (3,010-acre) **Sasquatch Provincial Park,** named for a tall, hairy, unshaven beast that supposedly inhabits the area. The park extends from a day-use area on the bank of Harrison Lake to picturesque tree-encircled lakes, each with road access, short hiking trails, and picnic areas.

With 337 rooms, lakeside **Harrison Hot Springs Resort & Spa** (100 Esplanade Ave., 604/796-2244 or 800/663-2266, www.harrisonresort.com, $165–320 s or d) is the town's largest accommodation, and it offers guests use of a large indoor and outdoor complex of mineral pools, complete with grassy areas, lots of outdoor furniture, and a café. Within walking distance of the public hot pool and lake is **Glencoe Motel** (259 Hot Springs Rd., 604/796-2574, www.glencoemotel.com, $80 s, $90 d, RV sites $28).

HOPE AND VICINITY

The TransCanada Highway and Highway 7 from Vancouver, the Coquihalla Highway to Kamloops, and Highway 3 from the Okanagan all meet at Hope (population 6,500). Surrounded by magnificent mountains and rivers, with a couple of great wilderness areas only a short drive away, and an abundance of recreational opportunities, Hope is a great place to spend some time.

Sights

To find out more about the history of Hope, visit **Hope Museum** (919 Water Ave., 604/869-7322, daily 9 A.M.–5 P.M. May–June, daily 8 A.M.–8 P.M. July–Aug., by donation), in the same building as the information center. The museum's comprehensive collection of pioneer artifacts is displayed in several recreated settings, including a kitchen, bedroom, parlor, schoolroom, and blacksmith shop. Also don't miss the tree-stump art scattered through town. In Memorial Park, an eagle holding a salmon in its claws (in front of the district office) was carved from a tree with root rot, and it was one of the original tree-stump works of art.

The five **Othello-Quintette Tunnels** through a steep gorge of Coquihalla Canyon were carved out of solid granite by the Kettle Valley Railway, but have been abandoned since the middle of last century. Today a short walk takes you from the **Coquihalla Canyon Provincial Park** parking lot to and through the massive, dark tunnels—a popular tourist attraction. To get to there from downtown, take Wallace Street to 6th Avenue and turn right. Turn left on Kawkawa Lake Road, crossing the Coquihalla River Bridge and railway tracks. At the first intersection take the right branch, Othello Road, and continue until you see a sign to the right (over a rise and easy to miss) pointing to the recreation area. The tunnels are closed November–April.

Practicalities

Hope doesn't offer much hope if you're looking for upscale lodging. Instead you'll find a motley collection of roadside motels. The best value of the downtown options is **Best Continental Motel** (860 Fraser Ave., 604/869-9726, $69–95 s or d), which also has a restaurant. Out on Old Hope–Princeton Way, the much newer **Alpine Motel** (604/869-9931 or 877/869-9931, $75 s, $85 d) offers large, comfortably furnished rooms,

a pool, and a pleasant setting. Along the road up to the tunnels, **Othello Tunnels Campground** (67851 Othello Rd., 604/869-9448, www.othellotunnels.com, $25 unserviced sites, $27 hookups) sits right beside the river. Trees surround some sites, and facilities include hot showers, a covered barbecue area, grocery store, wireless Internet, laundry, and a playground.

Right downtown, the friendly staff at **Hope Visitor Info Centre** (919 Water Ave., 604/869-2021, www.hopebc.ca, daily 9 A.M.–5 P.M., with extended summer hours of 8 A.M.–8 P.M.) can help you decide which of the routes to take out of Hope, but might also convince you to stay in town a little longer.

FRASER RIVER CANYON

From Hope, the old TransCanada Highway runs north along the west bank of the fast-flowing Fraser River. Although the new Coquihalla Highway is a much shorter option for those heading for Kamloops and beyond, the old highway offers many interesting stops and is by far the preferred route for those not in a hurry.

The first worthwhile stop is tiny **Emory Creek Provincial Park,** 15 kilometers (9.3 miles) from Hope. Stopping at this quiet riverside park, it's hard to believe that a little more than 100 years ago it was the site of Emory City, complete with saloons, a brewery, a large sawmill, and all the other businesses of a bustling frontier gold town. The city had virtually disappeared by the 1890s, and today no hint of its short-lived presence remains. Wander along riverside trails, try some fishing, or stay at one of the wooded campsites ($15).

Yale

In 1858 Yale was a flourishing gold-rush town of 20,000, filled with tents, shacks, bars, gambling joints, and shops. But when the gold ran out so did most of the population, and Yale dwindled to the small forestry and service center it has been for 100 years. If you want to find out more about Yale's historic past, the gold rush, the Cariboo Wagon Road, and railway construction, visit **Yale Historic Site** (Douglas

St., 604/863-2324, daily 10 A.M.–5 P.M. May–mid-Oct., adult $5, senior $4.50, child $3), comprising a museum, the 1863 **St. John's Church,** and the chance to try gold panning.

Hell's Gate

At Hell's Gate, the Fraser River powers its way through a narrow, glacially carved, 34-meter-high (111-feet) gorge. When Simon Fraser saw this section of the gorge in 1808 he wrote "we had to travel where no human being should venture—for surely we have encountered the gates of hell," and the name stuck. Today you can cross the canyon aboard the 25-passenger **Hell's Gate Airtram** (604/867-9277, adult $17, senior $15, child $11), which runs daily 10 A.M.–4 P.M. mid-April–mid-October. Across the river you can browse through landscaped gardens, learn more about the fishway and salmon, or even try your hand at gold panning.

North Toward Cache Creek

Another small town with a gold-rush history, **Boston Bar** is today a popular white-water rafting destination for those brave enough to float the Fraser River's roaring rapids. **REO Rafting Adventure Resort** (16 km/10 mi west from Boston Bar, 604/461-7238 or 800/736-7238, www.reorafting.com) offers tent cabins ranging from basic canvas frames ($30 per person) to riverfront tents with peeled log furniture ($170 s or d), or you can stay overnight and take a raft trip, with all meals included, for $209 per person for one night. As the name suggests, the resort is the base for REO Rafting ($145 for a full day on the river), but horseback riding, rock climbing, and guided hiking are also offered.

COQUIHALLA HIGHWAY

The Coquihalla Highway is the most direct link between Vancouver and the interior of British Columbia. It saves at least 90 minutes by cutting 72 kilometers (45 miles) from the trip between Hope and Kamloops.

Merritt

This town of 8,000 in the Nicola Valley, 115 kilometers (71 miles) north of Hope, provides the only services along the Coquihalla Highway. It's also the exit point for those heading east to the Okanagan on the Okanagan Connector. Make your first stop off the highway at **Merritt Visitor Centre,** on a high point east of the highway (250/378-5634, daily 9 A.M.–4 P.M., extended to daily 8 A.M.–6 P.M. in summer). Upstairs in this large log building is an intriguing forestry exhibition, and behind the building is the **Godey Creek Hiking Trail,** which takes you 1.4 kilometers (0.9 miles) one-way to a lookout cabin; allow one hour for the round-trip.

Since the Coquihalla Highway opened, many motels have been built around Merritt, but by far the best choice is one of the originals, the **Quilchena Hotel** (250/378-2611, www.quilchena.com, $79–149 s or d), on Nicola Lake, 20 kilometers (12 miles) east of town on Highway 5A (take Exit 290). Built in 1908 and still part of a working ranch, the property is a destination in itself, with golfing ($20 for nine holes), horseback riding ($45 for a 90-minute trail ride), spa services, swimming, biking (rentals available), canoeing, and fishing. Downstairs in the main hotel building is a saloon (complete with bullet holes in the bar) and a restaurant.

VANCOUVER ISLAND

Vancouver Island, the largest isle along North America's Pacific coast, stretches for more than 450 superb kilometers off the west coast of mainland British Columbia. A magnificent chain of rugged snowcapped mountains, sprinkled with lakes and rivers and pierced by deep inlets, effectively divides the island into two distinct sides: dense, rain-drenched forest and remote surf- and wind-battered shores on the west; and well-populated, sheltered, beach-fringed lowlands on the east. Much of the lush, green island is covered with dense forests of Douglas fir, western red cedar, and hemlock. The climate, stabilized by the Pacific Ocean and warmed by the Japanese current, never really gets too hot or too cold, but be prepared for cloudbursts, especially in winter.

Victoria, the provincial capital, lies at the southern tip of the island and is connected to the much larger city of Vancouver by regular ferry services. Its deeply entrenched British traditions make Victoria unique among North American cities. The rest of the island draws scenery buffs, outdoor adventurers, wildlife watchers, and students of northwest Native American art and culture.

Backpackers head west from Victoria to Port Renfrew, the starting point of the West Coast Trail. Island-hoppers take Highway 17 north up the Saanich Peninsula to Swartz Bay, jump on a ferry, and cruise the scenic Southern Gulf Islands. Other explorers head north up the Island Highway, Highway 1/19, which follows the Strait of Georgia all the way to the island's northern tip. The old highway has mostly been replaced by the Inland Island Highway, but to

© ANDREW HEMPSTEAD

HIGHLIGHTS

◖ Fairmont Empress: You don't need to be a guest at this famous hotel to admire its grandeur. Plan on eating a meal here for the full effect (page 98).

◖ Royal British Columbia Museum: If you only visit one museum on Vancouver Island, make it this one, which tells the story of the province's natural and human history (page 98).

◖ Goldstream Provincial Park: Escape the city in this slice of wilderness, which is laced with hiking trails. If you're visiting in late fall, make a trip to the park to view the spectacle of spawning salmon (page 101).

◖ Butchart Gardens: Even if you have only one day in Victoria, make time to visit Butchart Gardens, one of the world's most delightful gardens (page 101).

◖ Galiano Island: Each of the Southern Gulf Islands has its own charms, but a personal favorite for kayaking is Galiano Island (page 117).

◖ Pacific Rim National Park: Canada isn't renowned for its beaches, but this national park protects some magnificent stretches of sand (page 126).

◖ Telegraph Cove: It's worth the drive to Telegraph Cove just to wander around the postcard-perfect boardwalk village, but you'll also want to take a tour boat in search of orca whales (page 137).

◖ Alert Bay: This tiny village on Cormorant Island is a hotbed of native history. A cultural center and some of the world's tallest totem poles are highlights (page 137).

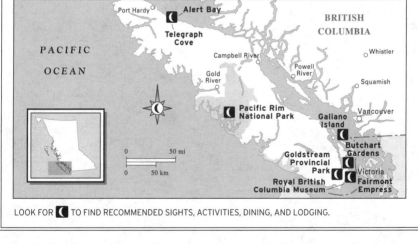

LOOK FOR ◖ TO FIND RECOMMENDED SIGHTS, ACTIVITIES, DINING, AND LODGING.

take in the best the island has to offer, stick to the old route. Along the way you'll pass sandy beaches, resorts, and old logging, mining, and fishing towns that now base their existence to a large degree on tourism.

At Parksville, Highway 4 turns off west and leads through "oooh" and "aaah" mountain scenery to the relatively untamed west coast.

There you'll find picture-perfect fishing villages, driftwood-littered sand for as far as you can see, and Pacific Rim National Park, the only national park on the island. Also on the west coast is Tofino, a base for sea kayaking and whale-watching on Clayoquot Sound. Farther north up Highway 19, at Campbell River, Highway 28 cuts west to Gold River,

VANCOUVER ISLAND

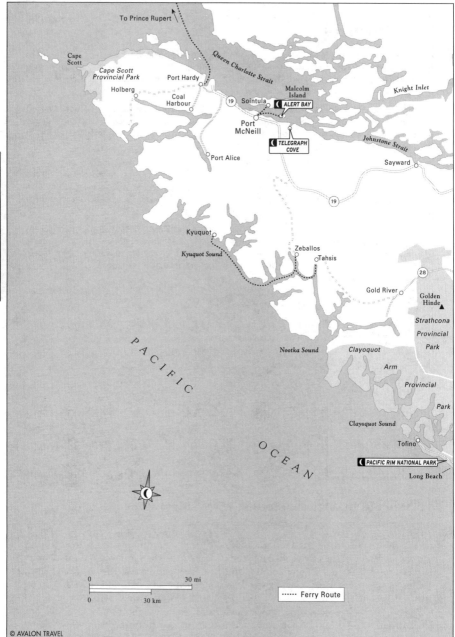

To Prince Rupert

Cape Scott

Cape Scott Provincial Park

Queen Charlotte Strait

Knight Inlet

Holberg

Port Hardy

Coal Harbour

19

Sointula

Malcolm Island

ALERT BAY

Port McNeill

TELEGRAPH COVE

Johnstone Strait

Sayward

Port Alice

19

Kyuquot

Kyuquot Sound

Zeballos

Tahsis

28

Gold River

Golden Hinde

Strathcona Provincial Park

PACIFIC

Nootka Sound

Clayoquot

Arm

Provincial

Park

OCEAN

Clayoquot Sound

Tofino

PACIFIC RIM NATIONAL PARK

Long Beach

0   30 mi
0   30 km

······ Ferry Route

© AVALON TRAVEL

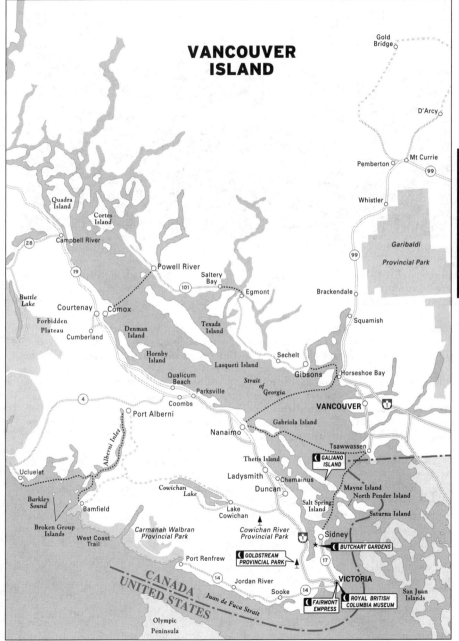

© ANDREW HEMPSTEAD

a beautiful sunset on the west coast of the island

passing through enormous Strathcona Provincial Park.

North of Campbell River lies a surprisingly large area mostly untouched by civilization—in fact, today you can still find maps of the island that fizzle out above Campbell River. Unique Telegraph Cove, a boardwalk village known for its fishing and whale-watching activities, and intriguing Alert Bay on Cormorant Island are highlights north of Campbell River. Finally, the road ends at Port Hardy, the largest community north of Campbell River and the terminus for ferries to Prince Rupert.

PLANNING YOUR TIME

Many visitors to Victoria spend a few nights in the city as part of a longer vacation that includes the rest of Vancouver Island. At an absolute minimum, plan on spending two full days in the capital, preferably overnighting at a character-filled bed-and-breakfast. Regardless of how long you'll be in the city, much of your time will be spent in and around the Inner Harbour, a busy waterway surrounded by the city's top sights and best restaurants. At the top of the must-see list is the Royal British Columbia Museum, which will impress even the biggest museophobes, and the ivy-draped

Fairmont Empress hotel. Victoria's most visited attraction is Butchart Gardens, an absolutely stunning collection of plants that deserves at least half a day of your time. Goldstream Provincial Park and the scenic waterfront drive between downtown and Oak Bay are two outdoor destinations you should figure into your schedule.

Exploring Vancouver Island beyond Victoria requires some advance planning, as well as an idea of where you want to end up. If you have just a day to spare, you can take the oceanside drive west from Victoria or travel north as far as Nanaimo, but to explore the island further you should schedule at least two days and preferably more. The Southern Gulf Islands, linked to Victoria by ferry and floatplane, make a good overnight trip from the capital (for its deserted beaches and unspoiled forests, Galiano Island is my favorite). You should plan on at least two nights out from Victoria to do justice to the west coast town of Tofino and the adjacent Pacific Rim National Park. The island's northern reaches provide a jumping off point for ferry travelers heading to Prince Rupert, but are also worth visiting to take a whale-watching trip from Telegraph Cove and to immerse yourself in native culture at Alert Bay.

Victoria

Many people view Victoria (population 300,000) for the first time from the Inner Harbour, coming in by boat the way people have for almost 150 years; on rounding Laurel Point, Victoria sparkles into view. Ferries, fishing boats, and seaplanes bob in the harbor, with a backdrop of manicured lawns and flower gardens, quiet residential suburbs, and striking inner-city architecture. Despite the pressures that go with city life, easygoing Victorians still find time for a stroll along the waterfront, a round of golf, or a night out at a fine-dining restaurant.

Victoria doesn't have as many official sights as Vancouver, but this isn't a bad thing. Once you've visited "must-sees" like the Royal British Columbia Museum and Butchart Gardens, you can devote you time to outdoor pursuits such as whale-watching, a bike ride through Oak Bay, or something as simple as enjoying a stroll along the beach. You will be confronted with oodles of ways to trim bulging wallets in Victoria. Some commercial attractions are worth every cent, others are routine at best, although the latter may be crowd pleasers with children, which makes them worth considering. Discovering Victoria's roots has been a longtime favorite with visitors, but some locals find the "more English than England" reputation tiring. Yes, there's a tacky side to some traditions, but high tea, double-decker bus tours, and exploring formal gardens remain some of the true joys of Victoria.

HISTORY

In 1792, Captain George Vancouver sailed through the Strait of Georgia, noting and naming Vancouver Island. But this had little effect on the many indigenous communities living along the shoreline. Europeans didn't see and exploit the island's potential for another 50 years, when the Hudson's Bay Company established control over the entire island and the mainland territory of "Columbia."

Fort Victoria

Needing to firmly establish British presence on the continent's northwest coast, the Hudson's Bay Company built Fort Victoria—named after Queen Victoria—on the southern tip of Vancouver Island in 1843. Three years later, the Oregon Treaty fixed the U.S./Canada boundary at the 49th parallel, with the proviso that the section of Vancouver Island lying south of that line would be retained by Canada. To forestall any claims that the United States may have had on the area, the British government went about settling the island. In 1849, the island was gazetted as a Crown colony and leased back to the Hudson's Bay Company. Gradually land around Fort Victoria was opened up by groups of British settlers brought to the island by the company's subsidiary, Puget Sound Agricultural Company. Several large company farms were developed, and Esquimalt Harbour became a major port for British ships.

The Growth of Victoria

In the late 1850s, gold strikes on the mainland's Thompson and Fraser Rivers brought thousands of gold miners into Victoria, the region's only port and source of supplies. Overnight, Victoria became a classic boomtown, but with a distinctly British flavor; most of the company men, early settlers, and military personnel firmly maintained their homeland traditions and celebrations. Even after the gold rush ended, Victoria remained an energetic bastion of military, economic, and political activity, and was officially incorporated as a city in 1862. In 1868, two years after the colonies of Vancouver Island and British Columbia were united, Victoria was made capital. Through the two world wars, Victoria continued to grow. The commencement of ferry service between Tsawwassen and Sidney in 1903 created a small population boom, but Victoria has always lagged well behind Vancouver in the population stake.

INNER HARBOUR SIGHTS

The epicenter of downtown Victoria is the foreshore of the Inner Harbour, which is flanked

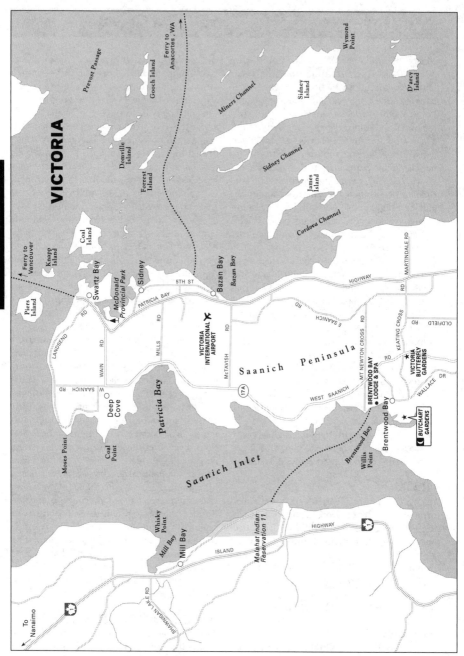

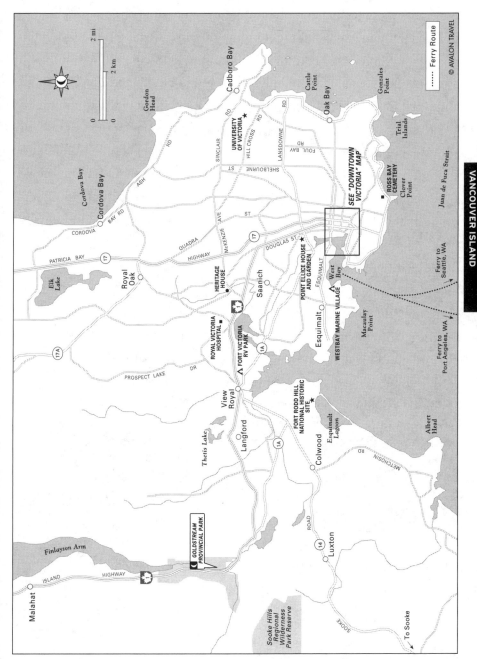

© AVALON TRAVEL

VANCOUVER ISLAND

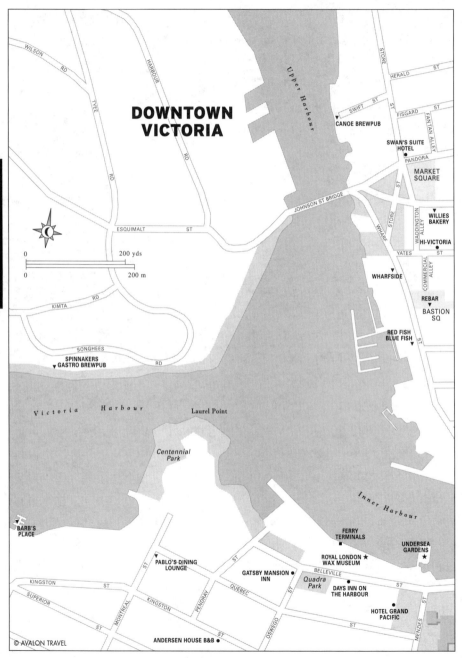

DOWNTOWN VICTORIA

CANOE BREWPUB

SWAN'S SUITE HOTEL

MARKET SQUARE

WILLIES BAKERY

HI-VICTORIA

WHARFSIDE

REBAR

BASTION SQ

RED FISH BLUE FISH

SPINNAKERS GASTRO BREWPUB

Victoria Harbour

Laurel Point

Centennial Park

Inner Harbour

BARB'S PLACE

FERRY TERMINALS

UNDERSEA GARDENS

ROYAL LONDON ★ WAX MUSEUM

PABLO'S DINING LOUNGE

GATSBY MANSION INN

Quadra Park

DAYS INN ON THE HARBOUR

HOTEL GRAND PACIFIC

ANDERSEN HOUSE B&B

0   200 yds

0   200 m

WILSON RD

HARBOUR RD

TYEE RD

ESQUIMALT ST

KIMTA RD

SONGHEES RD

JOHNSON ST BRIDGE

Upper Harbour

STORE ST

HERALD ST

SWIFT ST

FISGARD ST

FAN TAN ALLEY

PANDORA

WHARF ST

STORE ST

WADDINGTON ALLEY

YATES ST

COMMERCIAL ALLEY

KINGSTON ST

SUPERIOR ST

MONTREAL ST

KINGSTON ST

PENDRAY ST

QUEBEC ST

OSWEGO ST

BELLEVILLE ST

MENZIES ST

© AVALON TRAVEL

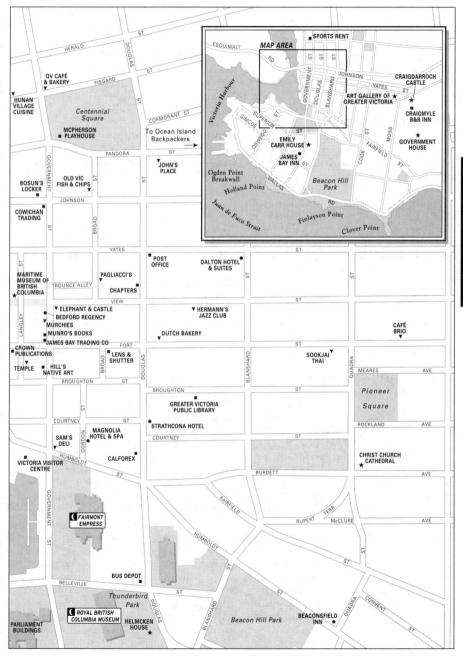

VANCOUVER ISLAND

by the parliament buildings, the city's main museum, and the landmark Fairmont Empress. Government Street leads uphill from the waterfront through a concentration of touristy shops and restaurants, while parallel to the west, Douglas Street is the core street of a smallish Central Business District.

❰ Fairmont Empress

Overlooking the Inner Harbour, the pompous, ivy-covered 1908 Fairmont Empress is Victoria's most recognizable landmark. Its architect was the well-known Francis Rattenbury, who also designed the parliament buildings, the Canadian Pacific Railway steamship terminal (now housing the wax museum), and Crystal Garden. It's worthwhile walking through the hotel lobby to gaze—head back, mouth agape—at the interior razzle-dazzle, and to watch people-watching people partake in traditional afternoon tea. Browse through the conservatory and gift shops, drool over the menus of the various restaurants, see what tours are available, and exchange currency if you're desperate (banks give a better exchange rate). Get a feeling for the hotel's history by joining a tour.

❰ Royal British Columbia Museum

Canada's most-visited museum and easily one of North America's best, the Royal British Columbia Museum (675 Belleville St., 250/356-7226, daily 10 A.M.–5 P.M., adult $15, senior and youth $9.50) is a must-see attraction for even the most jaded museum-goer. Its fine Natural History Gallery displays are extraordinarily true to life, complete with appropriate sounds and smells. Come face-to-face with an ice-age woolly mammoth, stroll through a coastal forest full of deer and tweeting birds, meander along a seashore or tidal marsh, then descend into the Open Ocean Exhibit via submarine—a very real trip not recommended for claustrophobics. The First Peoples Gallery holds a fine collection of artifacts from the island's first human inhabitants, the Nuu-chah-nulth (Nootka). Many of the pieces were collected by Charles Newcombe, who paid the Nuu-chah-nulth for them on

collection sorties in the early 1900s. More modern human history is also explored here in creative ways. Take a tour through time via the time capsules; walk along a turn-of-the-century street; and experience hands-on exhibits on industrialization, the gold rush, and the exploration of British Columbia by land and sea in the Modern History and 20th Century Galleries.

Around the Museum

In front of the museum, the 27-meter (89-foot) high **Netherlands Centennial Carillon** was a gift to the city from British Columbia's Dutch community. The tower's 62 bells range in weight from 8 to 1,500 kilograms (3,300 pounds) and toll at 15-minute intervals daily 7 A.M.–10 P.M.

On the museum's eastern corner, at Belleville and Douglas Streets, lies **Thunderbird Park,** a small green spot chockablock with authentic totem poles intricately carved by northwest coast native peoples. Best of all, it's absolutely free.

Beside Thunderbird Park is **Helmcken House** (10 Elliot St., 250/361-0021, daily 10 A.M.–5 P.M. in summer, daily noon–4 P.M. the rest of the year, adult $5, senior $4, child $3), the oldest house in the province still standing on its original site.

Parliament Buildings

Satisfy your lust for governmental, historic, and architectural knowledge all in one go by taking a free tour of the Parliament buildings (501 Belleville St.), designed by Francis Rattenbury and completed in 1897. On either side of the main entrance stand statues of Sir James Douglas, who chose the location of Victoria, and Sir Matthew Baillie Begbie, who was in charge of law and order during the gold-rush period. Atop the copper-covered dome stands a gilded statue of Captain George Vancouver, the first mariner to circumnavigate Vancouver Island. Walk through the main entrance and into the memorial rotunda, look skyward for a dramatic view of the central dome, then continue upstairs to peer into the legislative chamber, the home of the democratic government of British Columbia. Free guided tours are offered

© ANDREW HEMPSTEAD

Parliament buildings

Local species on display include tasty snapper, enormous sturgeon, schools of salmon, and scary wolf eels. Scuba divers miked for sound make regular appearances at the far end.

OLD TOWN

The oldest section of Victoria lies immediately north of the Inner Harbour between Wharf and Government Streets. Start by walking north from the Inner Harbour along historic Wharf Street, where Hudson's Bay Company furs were loaded onto ships bound for England, gold seekers arrived in search of fortune, and shopkeepers first established businesses. Cross the road to the cobblestone **Bastion Square,** lined with old gas lamps and decorative architecture dating from the 1860s to 1890s.

Maritime Museum of British Columbia

At the top (east) end of Bastion Square, the Maritime Museum of British Columbia (250/385-4222, daily 9:30 A.M.–4:30 P.M., until 6 P.M. in summer, adult $9, senior $6, child $4) traces the history of seafaring exploration, adventure, commercial ventures, and passenger travel through displays of dugout canoes, model ships, Royal Navy charts, figureheads, photographs, naval uniforms, and bells. One room is devoted to exhibits chronicling the circumnavigation of the world, and another holds a theater. The museum also has a nautically oriented gift shop.

SOUTH OF THE INNER HARBOUR
Emily Carr House

In 1871 artist Emily Carr was born in this typical upper-class 1864 Victorian-era home (207 Government St., 250/383-5843, Tues.–Sat. 11 A.M.–4 P.M. May–Sept., adult $6.50, senior and student $5.50, child $4.25). Carr moved to the mainland at an early age, escaping the confines of the capital to draw and write about the British Columbian native peoples and the wilderness in which she lived. She is best remembered today for her painting, a medium she took up in later years.

every 20 minutes 9 A.M.–noon and 1–5 P.M. in summer, less frequently (Mon.–Fri. only) in winter. Tour times differ according to the goings-on inside; for current times, call the tour office at 250/387-3046.

Commercial Attractions

Across the road from the parliament buildings is the **Royal London Wax Museum** (470 Belleville St., 250/388-4461, daily 9 A.M.–5 P.M., until 7:30 P.M. in summer, adult $12, senior $11, child $6). As you enter the grandly ornate building, pay the admission to the cashier on the right. Inside the attraction proper is a series of galleries filled with around 300 wax figures—British Royalty, famous folks such as Mother Teresa and Albert Einstein, Canadian heroes like courageous cancer victim Terry Fox, and Arctic explorers.

On the water beside the wax museum, **Pacific Undersea Gardens** (490 Belleville St., 250/382-5717, daily 9 A.M.–8 P.M. in summer, daily 10 A.M.–5 P.M. the rest of the year, adult $10, senior $9, child $8) of dubious value.

Beacon Hill Park

This large, hilly city park—a lush, sea-edged oasis of grass and flowers—extends from the back of the museum along Douglas Street out to cliffs that offer spectacular views of Juan de Fuca Strait and, on a clear day, the distant Olympic Mountains. Add a handful of rocky points to scramble on and many protected pebble-and-sand beaches and you've found yourself a perfect spot to indulge your senses. The park is within easy walking distance from downtown and can also be reached by bus number 5.

ROCKLAND

This historic part of downtown lies behind the Inner Harbour, east of Douglas Street, and is easily accessible on foot.

Christ Church Cathedral

Christ Church Cathedral (930 Burdett Ave., 250/383-2714) is the seat of the Bishop of the Diocese of British Columbia. Built in 1896 in 13th-century Gothic style, it's one of Canada's largest churches. Self-guided tours are possible Monday–Friday 8:30 A.M.–5 P.M. and Sunday 7:30 A.M.–8:30 P.M. In summer, the cathedral sponsors free choral recitals each Saturday at 4 P.M. The park next to the cathedral is a shady haven to rest weary feet, and the gravestones make fascinating reading.

Art Gallery of Greater Victoria

From Christ Church Cathedral, walk up Rockland Avenue through the historic Rockland district, passing stately mansions and colorful gardens on tree-lined streets. Turn left on Moss Street and you'll come to the 1889 Spencer Mansion and its modern wing, which together make up the Art Gallery of Greater Victoria (1040 Moss St., 250/384-4101, daily 10 A.M.–5 P.M., Thurs. 10 A.M.–9 P.M., closed Mon. outside of summer, adult $12, senior $10, child $2). The gallery contains Canada's finest collection of Japanese art, a range of contemporary art, Emily Carr pieces, and traveling exhibits, as well as a Japanese garden with a Shinto shrine. The Gallery Shop sells art books, reproductions, and handcrafted jewelry, pottery, and glass.

Government House

Continue up Rockland Avenue from the art gallery to reach Government House, the official residence of the lieutenant governor, the queen's representative in British Columbia. The surrounding gardens, including an English-style garden, rose garden, and rhododendron garden, along with green velvet lawns and picture-perfect flower beds, are open to the public throughout the year. On the front side of the property, vegetation has been left in a more natural state, with gravel paths leading to benches that invite pausing to take in the city panorama.

Craigdarroch Castle

A short walk up (east) from the art gallery along Rockland Avenue and left on Joan Crescent brings you to the baronial four-story mansion known as Craigdarroch Castle (1050 Joan Crescent, 250/592-5323, daily 9 A.M.–7 P.M. in summer, daily 10 A.M.–4:30 P.M. the rest of the year, adult $12, senior $11, child $4). The architectural masterpiece was built in 1890 for Robert Dunsmuir, a wealthy industrialist and politician who died just before the building was completed. For all the nitty-gritty, tour the mansion with volunteer guides who really know their Dunsmuir, then admire at your leisure all the polished wood, stained-glass windows, Victorian-era furnishings, and the great city views from upstairs.

WEST OF DOWNTOWN
Point Ellice House and Garden

Built in 1861, this restored mansion (2616 Pleasant St., 250/380-6506, daily 10 A.M.–4 P.M. May–mid-Sept., adult $5, senior $4, child $3) sits amid beautiful gardens along the gorge on Point Ellice, less than two kilometers (1.2 miles) from the Inner Harbour. The best reason to visit is to enjoy a traditional English afternoon tea served 11 A.M.–3 P.M. ($19.95 includes admission). To get there from the Inner Harbour, jump aboard a Victoria Harbour Ferry (10 minutes and $4 each way), or by road take Government or Douglas Street north from downtown, turn left on Bay Street, and turn left again on Pleasant Street.

Fort Rodd Hill
National Historic Site

Clinging to a headland across the harbor entrance from CFB Esquimalt, this picturesque site (603 Fort Rodd Hill Rd., Colwood, 250/478-5849, daily 10 A.M.–5:30 P.M. mid-Feb.–Oct., daily 9 A.M.–4:30 P.M. Nov.–mid-Feb., adult $4, senior $3, child $2.50) comprises **Fort Rodd,** built in 1898 to protect the fleets of ships in the harbor, and **Fisgard Lighthouse,** which dates to 1873. It's an interesting place to explore; audio stations bring the sounds of the past alive, workrooms are furnished as they were at the turn of the century, and the lighthouse has been fully restored and is open to visitors. To get there from downtown, take the Old Island Highway (Gorge Road) and turn left on Belmont Road, then left onto Ocean Boulevard. By bus, take number 50 from downtown, then transfer to number 52.

◖ Goldstream Provincial Park

Lying 20 kilometers (12 miles) from the heart of Victoria, this 390-hectare (960-acre) park straddles Highway 1 northwest of downtown. The park's main natural feature is the **Goldstream River,** which flows north into the Finlayson Arm of Saanich Inlet. Forests of ancient Douglas fir and western red cedar flank the river; orchids flourish in forested glades; and forests of lodgepole pine, western hemlock, and maple thrive at higher elevations. From the picnic area parking lot two kilometers (1.2 miles) north of the campground turnoff, a trail leads 500 meters (0.3 miles) to an interpretation center (250/478-9414, daily 9 A.M.–5 P.M.) where the life cycle of salmon that spawn in the river (Nov.–Dec.) is described. Continue beyond the center for five minutes on foot to reach the head of Finlayson Arm (a great bird-watching spot).

SAANICH PENINSULA

The Saanich Peninsula is the finger of land that extends north from downtown. It boasts Victoria's most famous attraction, Butchart Gardens, as well as Victoria International Airport and the main arrival point for ferries from Tsawwassen.

◖ Butchart Gardens

Carved from an abandoned quarry, these delightful gardens are Victoria's best-known attraction. They're approximately 20 kilometers north of downtown (800 Benvenuto Dr., Brentwood Bay, 250/652-4422, www.butchartgardens.com, adult $30, youth $15, child $3). The gardens are open every day of the year from 9 A.M., closing in summer at 10 P.M. and in winter at 4 P.M., with varying closing hours in other seasons.

The gardens were developed in the early 1900s to beautify an abandoned quarry; the owners creating what has evolved into one of the world's premier private gardens. The gardens now contain more than 5,000 varieties of flowers, and the extensive nurseries test-grow some 35,000 new bulbs and more than 100 new roses every year. Go there in spring, summer, or early autumn to treat your eyes and nose to a marvelous sensual experience. Summer visitors are in for a special treat on Saturday nights (July and August only), when a spectacular fireworks display lights up the garden.

Victoria Butterfly Gardens

In the same vicinity as Butchart Gardens, Victoria Butterfly Gardens (corner of Benvenuto and W. Saanich Roads, 250/652-3822, daily 9 A.M.–5 P.M. summer, daily 10 A.M.–4 P.M. the rest of the year, closed Jan., adult $12, senior $11, child $6.50) offers you the opportunity to view and photograph some of the world's most spectacular butterflies at close range. Thousands of these beautiful creatures—species from around the world—live here, flying freely around the enclosed gardens and feeding on the nectar provided by colorful tropical plants. You'll also be able to get up close and personal with exotic birds such as parrots and cockatoos.

Sidney

The small town of Sidney lies on the east side of the Saanich Peninsula, overlooking the Strait of Georgia. As well as being the departure point for ferries to the San Juan

Islands (Washington), the waterfront area is a pleasant spot to spend a sunny day exploring bustling Port Sidney Marina and the many outdoor cafés. The only official attraction is **Sidney Museum** (9801 Seaport Place at the end of Beacon Ave., 250/656-2140, daily 10 A.M.–4 P.M., donation). The highlight is a display pertaining to whales, which includes skeletons.

RECREATION

All of Vancouver Island is a recreational paradise, but Victorians find plenty to do around their own city. Walking and biking are especially popular, and from the Inner Harbour it's possible to travel on foot or by pedal power all the way along the waterfront to Oak Bay.

Hiking and Biking

If you're feeling energetic—or even if you're not—plan on walking or biking at least a small section of **Marine Drive,** which follows the shoreline of Juan de Fuca Strait from Ogden Point all the way to Oak Bay. The section immediately south of downtown, between Holland Point Park and Ross Bay Cemetery, is extremely popular with early rising locals, who start streaming onto the pedestrian pathway before the sun rises. Out of town, **Goldstream Provincial Park,** beside Highway 1, and **East Sooke Regional Park,** off Highway 14 west of downtown, offer the best hiking opportunities.

You can rent bikes at **Sports Rent,** just north of downtown (1950 Government St., 250/385-7368) from $7–10 per hour or $30–40 per day.

Water Sports

Daily through summer, **Ocean River Sports** (Market Square, 1824 Store St., 250/381-4233 or 800/909-4233, www.oceanriver.com) organizes guided 2.5-hour paddles in the Inner Harbour ($65 pp). They also offer kayaking courses, sell and rent kayaks and other equipment, and offer overnight tours as far away as the Queen Charlotte Islands. **Sports Rent** (1950 Government St., 250/385-7368) rents canoes, kayaks, and a wide range of other outdoor equipment. Expect to pay

about $40 per day and from $160 per week for a canoe or single kayak.

The best beaches are east of downtown. At **Willows Beach,** Oak Bay, most of the summer crowds spend the day sunbathing, although a few hardy individuals brave a swim; water temperature here tops out at around 17°C (63°F). **Elk Lake,** toward the Saanich Peninsula, and **Thetis Lake,** west of downtown along Highway 1, are also popular swimming and sunbathing spots.

ARTS AND ENTERTAINMENT

Victoria has a vibrant performing arts community, with a number of unique events designed especially for the summer crowds. The city lacks the wild nightlife scene of neighboring Vancouver, but a large influx of summer workers keeps the bars crowded and a few nightclubs jumping during the busy season. The city does have more than its fair share of British-style pubs, and you can usually get a good meal along with a pint of lager. The magazine *Monday* (www.mondaymag.com) offers a comprehensive arts and entertainment section.

Nightlife

The **Strathcona Hotel** (919 Douglas St., 250/383-7137) is Victoria's largest entertainment venue, featuring four bars, including one serving a magnificent rooftop patio and the Sticky Wicket, an English bar complete with mahogany paneling. Closer to the Inner Harbour and converted from an old grain warehouse is **Swans Hotel** (506 Pandora St., 250/361-3310), which brews its own beer. A few blocks farther north and right on the water is the **Canoe Brewpub** (450 Swift St., 250/361-1940), housed in an 1894 red-brick building that was at one time home to generators that powered Victoria's street lights. This place is popular with the downtown crowd and has a great deck.

Also offering magnificent water views is **Spinnakers Gastro Brewpub,** across the Inner Harbour from downtown (308 Catherine St., 250/384-6613), which opened in 1984 as Canada's first brewpub. Victoria's many English-style pubs usually feature a wide variety of beers, congenial atmosphere, and inexpensive meals. The closest of these to downtown is the **James Bay Inn** (270 Government St., 250/384-7151). Farther out, **Six Mile House** (494 Island Hwy., 250/478-3121) is a classic Tudor-style English pub that opened its doors over 150 years ago. To get there, head west out of the city along Highway 1 and take the Colwood exit.

Most of Victoria's nightclubs double as live music venues attracting a great variety of acts. **Legends,** in the Strathcona Hotel (919 Douglas St., 250/383-7137), has been a city hot spot for more than 30 years. It comes alive with live rock 'n' roll some nights and a DJ spinning the latest dance tunes on other nights.

Victoria boasts several good jazz venues. The best of these is **Hermann's Jazz Club** (753 View St., 250/388-9166). **Steamers** (570 Yates St., 250/381-4340) draws diverse acts, but generally features jazz and blues on Tuesday and Wednesday night. Contact the **Victoria Jazz Society** (250/388-4423, www.vicjazz.bc.ca) for a schedule of local performances.

Theater and Music

Dating to 1914, the grand old **McPherson Playhouse** (known lovingly as the "Mac" by local theater goers) hosts a variety of performing arts. It's in Centennial Square, at the corner of Pandora Avenue and Government Street. The Mac's sister theater, the **Royal Theatre** (805 Broughton St.) began life as a roadhouse and was used as a movie theater for many years. Today it hosts stage productions and a variety of musical recitals. For schedule information and tickets at both theaters, contact the Royal & McPherson Theatres Society (250/386-6121 or 888/717-6121, www.rmts.bc.ca). Performing arts on a smaller scale can be appreciated in a historic church at the **Belfry Theatre** (1291 Gladstone St., 250/385-6815), which offers live theater Oct.–Apr.; tickets cost $26–35 per person.

Pacific Opera Victoria (250/385-0222, www.pov.bc.ca) performs three productions each year (usually Oct.–Apr.) in the McPherson Playhouse. Tickets run $20–65. The **Victoria Operatic Society** (250/381-1021) presents opera year-round; call for current schedule.

FESTIVALS AND EVENTS
Spring

Officially, of course, February is still winter, but Victorians love the fact that spring arrives early on the west coast—which is the premise behind the **Flower Count,** over the last week in February. While for other Canadians summer is a long way off, locals count the number of blossoms in their own yards, in parks, and along the streets. Totals are tabulated, and gleefully reported across Canada.

The birthday of Queen Victoria (May 24) has been celebrated in Canada since 1834, and is especially relevant to those who call her namesake city home. The Inner Harbour is alive with weekend festivities that culminate in a downtown **Victoria Day Parade** on the holiday Monday. (Although Queen Victoria's actual birthday was May 24, the event is celebrated with a public holiday on the Monday preceding May 25.)

While most visitors associate Victoria with afternoon tea at the Empress, cowboys know Victoria for the **Luxton Pro Rodeo** (250/478-4250), on the third weekend in May. The event features all traditional events as well as mutton-busting for the kids. Access to the Luxton Rodeo Grounds, west of the city toward Sooke, is free, with admission to the rodeo itself costing $12.

Summer

On the first Sunday in August, **Symphony Splash** (250/385-9771, www.symphonysplash.ca) is a feast for the eyes and ears. The local symphony orchestra performs from a barge moored in the Inner Harbour to masses crowded around the shore in this unique musical event that attracts upwards of 40,000 spectators who line the shore or watch from kayaks.

Running 10 days in late August at venues scattered across the city, the **Victoria Fringe Festival** (250/383-2663, www.victoriafringe.com) includes more than 350 acts performing at 6 venues throughout the city, including outside along the harbor foreshore and inside at the Conservatory of Music on Pandora Street. All tickets are under $15.

SHOPPING

Victoria is a shopper's delight. Most shops and all major department stores are generally open Monday–Saturday 9:30 A.M.–5:30 P.M. and stay open for late-night shopping Thursday and Friday nights until 9 P.M. The touristy shops around the Inner Harbour and along Government Street are all open on Sunday. The bottom end of Government Street, behind the Fairmont Empress, is where you'll pick up all those tacky T-shirts and such. Farther up the street are more stylish shops, such as **James Bay Trading Co.** (1102 Government St., 250/388-5477), which specializes in native arts from coastal communities; **Hill's Native Art** (1008 Government St., 250/385-3911), selling a wide range of authentic native souvenirs; and **Cowichan Trading** (1328 Government St., 250/383-0321), featuring Cowichan sweaters.

In Old Town, the colorful, two-story **Market Square** courtyard complex was once the haunt of sailors, sealers, and whalers, who came ashore looking for booze and brothels. It's been jazzed up, and today shops here specialize in everything from kayaks to condoms. Walk out of Market Square on Johnson Street to find camping-supply stores and the interesting **Bosun's Locker** (580 Johnson St., 250/386-1308), in business for over half a century and filled to the brim with nautical knick-knacks.

Bookstores

Don't be put off by the touristy location of **Munro's Books** (1108 Government St., 250/382-2464 or 888/243-2464). It holds a comprehensive collection of fiction and non-fiction titles related to Victoria, the island, and Canada in general. In seaside Oak Bay, **Ivy's Bookshop** (2188 Oak Bay Ave., 250/598-2713) is a friendly little spot with a wide selection that ranges from local literature to current bestsellers.

ACCOMMODATIONS

Finding a room in Victoria can be difficult during the summer months when gaggles of tourists compete for a relative paucity of rooms. If you're after a regular motel room, check the provincial accommodation guide. If you're after something a little more special, you won't go wrong at any of the following places.

Under $50

Budget travelers are well catered to in Victoria, and while the accommodation choices in the capital are more varied than in Vancouver, there is no one backpacker lodge that stands out above the rest.

In the heart of downtown and just a stone's throw from the harbor, **HI-Victoria** (516 Yates St., 250/385-4511 or 888/883-0099, www.hihostels.ca, $30 dorms, $54–70 s or d, discounted for members of Hostelling International) offers separate dorms and bathroom facilities for men and women, as well as two kitchens, a lounge, library, game room, travel services, public Internet terminals, and an informative bulletin board.

Housed in the upper stories of an old commercial building, **Ocean Island Backpackers Inn** (791 Pandora Ave., 250/385-1788 or 888/888-4180, www.oceanisland.com, $25–27 dorms, $47 s, $58–89.50) lies just a couple of blocks from downtown. Guests have use of kitchen facilities, a laundry, and a computer for Internet access. There's also plenty of space to relax, such as a reading room, music room (guitars supplied), television room, and street-level bar open until midnight.

$50-100

In a quiet residential area immediately east of downtown, **Craigmyle B&B Inn** (1037 Craigdarroch Rd., Rockland, 250/595-5411 or 888/595-5411, www.bandbvictoria.com, $65 s, $100–115 d) has been converted from part of the original Craigdarroch Estate (it stands directly in front of the famous castle). This rambling 1913 home is full of character, comfortable furnishings, and lots of original stained-glass windows. Rooms include singles, doubles, and family suites, some share bathrooms, while others have en suite bathrooms. An inviting living room with a TV, a bright sunny dining area, and friendly longtime owners make this a real home away from home.

Another excellent choice at the lower end

of the price spectrum is **Selkirk Guest House** (934 Selkirk Ave., Esquimalt, 250/389-1213 or 800/974-6638, www.selkirkguesthouse.com, $100–135 s or d), on the Gorge Waterway three kilometers (1.9 miles) from the Inner Harbour. While the house has been extensively renovated and offers comfortable accommodations, it's the location that sets this place apart from similarly priced choices. The only thing separating the house from the water is the manicured garden, complete with a hot tub that sits under an old willow tree. Breakfast is an additional $8 per person, but wireless Internet is free.

$100-150

€ Heritage House (3808 Heritage Lane, 250/479-0892 or 877/326-9242, www.heritagehousevictoria.com, $155 s or d), a beautiful 1910 mansion surrounded by trees and gardens, sits in a quiet residential area near Portage Inlet, five kilometers (3.7 miles) northwest of city center. Guests choose from several outstanding rooms, one with a view of Portage Inlet from a private veranda. Enjoy the large communal living room and a cooked breakfast in the elegant dining room.

Dating to 1911 and once home to artist Emily Carr, **James Bay Inn** (270 Government St., 250/384-7151 or 800/836-2649, www.jamesbayinn.com, $125–175 s or d,) is five blocks from the harbor and within easy walking distance of all city sights and Beacon Hill Park. From the outside, the hotel has a clunky, uninspiring look, but a bright and breezy decor and new beds in the simply furnished rooms make it a pleasant place to rest your head. Guests enjoy discounted food and drink at the downstairs restaurant and pub.

Away from the water, but still just one block from Douglas Street, is the 1876 **Dalton Hotel & Suites** (759 Yates St., 250/384-4136 or 888/544-1109, www.daltonhotel.ca, $135–225 s or d), Victoria's oldest hotel. Millions of dollars have been spent restoring the property with stylish wooden beams, brass trim and lamps, ceiling fans, and marble floors reliving the Victorian era.   In the oldest section of downtown, surrounded by the city's best dining and shopping opportunities, is the **Bedford Regency** (1140 Government St., 250/384-6835 or 800/665-6500, www.bedfordregency.com, $139–199 s or d), featuring 40 guest rooms of varying configurations. Stylish, uncluttered art deco furnishings and high ceilings make the standard rooms seem larger than they really are. A better deal are the deluxe rooms and suites, which provide more space and better amenities for only slightly more money.

Just off the main highway between the ferry terminal and downtown, on the road into downtown Sidney, is **€ Cedarwood Inn & Suites** (9522 Lochside Dr., 250/656-5551 or 877/656-5551, www.thecedarwood.ca, $125–145 s or d, cottages $165), highlighted by a colorful garden with outdoor seating overlooking the Strait of Georgia.

$150-200

If you're looking for a modern feel, the centrally located **€ Swans Suite Hotel** (506 Pandora Ave., 250/361-3310 or 800/668-7926, www.swanshotel.com) is an excellent choice. Located above a restaurant/pub complex that was built in the 1880s as a grain storehouse, each of the 30 split-level suites has a loft, full kitchen, dining area, bedroom, and wireless Internet. The furnishings are casual yet elegantly rustic, with west coast artwork adorning the walls and fresh flowers in every room. The rates of $189 for a studio, $249 for a one-bedroom suite, and $329 for a two-bedroom suite are great value. In the off-season all rooms are discounted up to 50 percent.

Just four blocks from the Inner Harbour, the 1905 **€ Beaconsfield Inn** (998 Humboldt St., 250/384-4044 or 888/884-4044, www.beaconsfieldinn.com, $169–299 s or d) is exactly what you may imagine a Victorian bed-and-breakfast should be. Original mahogany floors, high ceilings, classical moldings, imported antiques, and fresh flowers from the garden create an upscale historic charm throughout. After checking in, you'll be invited to join other guests for high tea in the library, then encouraged to return for a glass of sherry before heading out for dinner. As you may expect, breakfast—served in a formal dining room or more casual conservatory—is a grand affair, with multiple courses of hearty fare delivered to your table by your impeccably presented host.

Yes, it's a chain hotel, but **Days Inn on the Harbour** (427 Belleville St., 250/386-3451 or 800/665-3024, www.daysinnvictoria.com, $175 s or d) has a prime waterfront location that will make you feel like you're paying more than you really are.

$200-250

A few blocks back from the Inner Harbour is **Andersen House Bed and Breakfast** (301 Kingston St., 250/388-4565 or 877/264-9988, www.andersenhouse.com, $235–265). Built late last century for a retired sea captain, the house features large high-ceilinged rooms all overlooking gardens that supply the kitchen with a variety of berries and herbs. Each has an en suite bathroom, private entrance, wireless Internet, and CD player (complete with CDs). In the traditions of its original owner,

© ANDREW HEMPSTEAD

Andersen House Bed and Breakfast

the house is decorated with furnishings from around the world, including contemporary paintings.

$250-300

Gatsby Mansion Inn (309 Belleville St., 250/388-9191 or 800/563-9656, www.gatsby-mansion.com, from $255 s, $265 d) has a central position across from the Inner Harbour. Dating to 1897, this magnificent 20-room property has been elegantly restored, with stained-glass windows, a magnificent fireplace, lots of exposed wood, crystal chandeliers under a gabled roof, and antiques decorating every corner. Afternoon tea is served in a comfortable lounge area off the lobby, and the restaurant has a nice veranda.

The ◖ **Magnolia Hotel & Spa** (623 Courtney St., 250/381-0999 or 877/624-6654, www.magnoliahotel.com, $279 s or d) is a European-style boutique hotel just up the hill from the harbor. It features an elegant interior with mahogany-paneled walls, Persian rugs, chandeliers, a gold-leafed ceiling, and fresh flowers throughout public areas. The rooms themselves are each elegantly furnished and feature floor-to-ceiling windows, heritage-style furniture in a contemporary room layout, richly colored fabrics, down duvets, wireless Internet, and coffee-making facilities. Rates include a light breakfast, daily newspaper, passes to a nearby fitness facility, and, unlike most other downtown hotels, free parking.

Possessing a prime waterfront position next to the Parliament Buildings is the **Hotel Grand Pacific** (463 Belleville St., 250/386-0450 or 800/228-5151, www.hotelgrandpacific.com, $260 s or d). Aside from more than 300 rooms, this property is also home to Spa at the Grand, a health club, a variety of restaurants and lounges, and a currency exchange. All rooms are well appointed, spacious, and have small, private balconies.

Over $300

The grand old **Fairmont Empress** (721 Government St., 250/384-8111 or 800/257-7544, www.fairmont.com, from $309 s or d) is

Victoria's best-loved accommodation. Covered in ivy and with only magnificent gardens separating it from the Inner Harbour, it's also in the city's best location. Designed by Francis Rattenbury in 1908, the Empress is one of the original Canadian Pacific Railway hotels. Rooms are offered in 90 different configurations, and like other hotels of the era, most are small, but each is filled with Victorian period furnishings and antiques.

You'll feel like you're a million miles from the city at **Brentwood Bay Lodge & Spa** (849 Verdier Ave., Brentwood Bay, 250/544-2079 or 888/544-2079, www.brentwoodbaylodge. com, $329–549 s or d), an upscale retreat overlooking Saanich Inlet. You can learn to scuba dive, take a water taxi to Butchart Gardens, enjoy the latest spa treatments, or join a kayak tour. The 33 rooms take understated elegance to new heights. Filled with natural light, they feature contemporary west coast styling (lots of polished wood and natural colors), the finest Italian sheets on king-size beds, and private balconies. Modern conveniences such as DVD entertainment systems, wireless Internet, and free calls within North America are a given. Dining options include a wood-fired grill, an upscale restaurant, a coffee bar, and a deli serving up picnic lunches.

CAMPING
West

The closest camping to downtown is at **Westbay Marine Village** (453 Head St., Esquimalt, 250/385-1831, www.westbay.bc.ca, $30–45), across Victoria Harbour from downtown. Facilities at this RV-only campground include full hook-ups and a laundry. It is part of a marina complex comprising floating residences and commercial businesses, such as fishing charter operators and restaurants. Water taxis connect the "village" to downtown.

Fort Victoria RV Park (340 Island Hwy., 250/479-8112, www.fortvictoria.ca, $37) is six kilometers (3.7 miles) northwest of city center on Highway 1A. This campground provides free showers, laundry facilities, and opportunities to join chartered salmon-fishing trips.

Continuing west along Highway 1, take Exit 10, stay in the Colwood Lane, and then take Six Mile Road back under the highway to reach **Thetis Lake Campground** (West Park Lane, 250/478-3845, unserviced sites $26, hookups $30–36), with shaded sites, coin-operated showers, and laundry facilities. It adjoins Thetis Lake Park, which is crisscrossed by hiking trails and has one of the city's favorite swimming and sunbathing spots.

North Along Highway 1

Continuing west from the campgrounds detailed above, Highway 1 curves north through **Goldstream Provincial Park** (19 km/11 mi from downtown, $24) and begins its up-island journey north. The southern end of the park holds 161 well-spaced campsites scattered through an old-growth forest—it's one of the most beautiful settings you could imagine close to a capital city. The campground offers free hot showers but no hookups.

FOOD

While Victoria doesn't have a reputation as a culinary hot spot, for the past decade things have improved greatly with the opening of numerous restaurants serving top-notch cuisine with influences from around the world. Local chefs are big on produce that's organically grown and sourced from island farms. Seafood—halibut, shrimp, mussels, crab, and salmon—also features prominently on many menus.

With a thriving tourist trade centered on the Inner Harbour, chances are you will find something to suit your tastes and budget close at hand—Italian, Mexican, Californian, and even vegan cuisine. Mixed in with a few tourist traps (that advertise everywhere) are a number of excellent harbor-front choices that are as popular with the locals as with visitors. Unlike many cities and aside from a small Chinatown, ethnic restaurants are not confined to particular streets. On the other hand, Fort Street east of Douglas has a proliferation of restaurants that are as trendy as it gets on the island.

You still find great interest in traditional

English fare, including afternoon tea, which is served everywhere from motherly corner cafés to the grand Fairmont Empress. English cooking in general is much maligned, but worth trying. For the full experience, choose kippers and poached eggs for breakfast, a ploughman's lunch (crusty bread, a chunk of cheese, pickled onions), and then roast beef with Yorkshire pudding (a crispy pastry made with drippings and doused with gravy) in the evening.

Cafés and Cheap Eats

While tourists flock to the cafés and restaurants of the Inner Harbour and Government Street, Douglas Street remains the haunt of lunching locals. Reminiscent of days gone by, **John's Place** (723 Pandora Ave., 250/389-0711, Mon.–Fri. 7 A.M.–9 P.M., Sat.–Sun. 8 A.M.–9 P.M., $8–14), just off Douglas Street, serves up excellent value for those in the know. The food is good, the atmosphere casual, and the waitresses actually seem to enjoy working here. It's breakfast, burgers, salads, and sandwiches through the week, but weekend brunch is busiest, when there's nearly always a line spilling onto the street.

In Old Town, **Willies Bakery** (537 Johnson St., 250/381-8414, daily from 7:30 A.M.) is an old-style café offering cakes, pastries, and sodas, with a quiet cobbled courtyard in which to enjoy them. Ignore the dated furnishings at the **Dutch Bakery** (718 Fort St., 250/385-1012, Tues.–Sat. 7:30 A.M.–5:30 P.M.) and tuck into freshly baked goodies and handmade chocolates.

Casual

Right across from the information center, and drawing tourists like a magnet, is **Sam's Deli** (805 Government St., 250/382-8424, daily 7:30 A.M.–6:30 P.M., lunches $6.50–9). Many places nearby have better food, but Sam's boasts a superb location and a casual, cheerful atmosphere that makes it perfect for families. The ploughman's lunch, a staple of English pub dining, costs $9.50, while sandwiches (shrimp and avocado is an in-house feature) range $6.50–9, and salads are all around $7–12.

Touristy **Wharfside Eatery** (1208 Wharf St., 250/360-1808, daily for lunch and dinner, $16–31) is a bustling waterfront complex with a maritime theme and family atmosphere. Behind a small café section and a bar is the main dining room and a two-story deck, where almost every table has a stunning water view. Seafood starters to share include a tasting plate of salmon and mussels steamed in a creamy tomato broth. The lunchtime appetizer menu runs through to the evening menu, which also includes wood-fired pizza ($20–24 for two people), standard seafood dishes, and a delicious prawn and pesto linguini. The cheesecake is heavenly.

Seafood

Victoria's many seafood restaurants come in all forms. Fish-and-chips is a British tradition and is sold as such at **Old Vic Fish & Chips** (1316 Broad St., 250/383-4536, Mon.–Thurs. 11 A.M.–7 P.M., Fri.–Sat. 11 A.M.–8 P.M., $8–11).

Ensconced in a recycled shipping container down by the Inner Harbour, **Red Fish Blue Fish** (1006 Wharf St., 250/298-6877, daily 11:30 A.M.–7 P.M., $9–16.50) does an admirable job of promoting sustainable fisheries. All the seafood served is sourced locally, much of it caught on hand lines by the owners. Order you meal through the porthole and enjoy it outdoors along the waterfront.

Chandlers (1250 Wharf St., 250/385-3474, daily 11:30 A.M.–10 P.M., $18–36) is on the main strip of tourist-catching restaurants along the waterfront, but is generally regarded as Victoria's finest seafood restaurant. Halibut and chips is a popular staple, while salmon comes in variety of ways including grilled with a creamy Dijon glaze.

Away from the tourist-clogged streets of the Inner Harbour is **Barb's Place** (Fisherman's Wharf, at the foot of St. Lawrence St., 250/384-6515, daily 11 A.M.–dusk Mar.–Oct., $10–19), a sea-level eatery on a floating dock. It's not a restaurant as such, but a shack surrounded by outdoor table settings, some protected from the elements by a canvas tent.

The food is as fresh as it gets. Choose cod-and-chips, halibut-and-chips, steamed clams, or splash out on a whole steamed crab. Adding to the charm are surrounding floating houses and seals that hang out waiting for handouts.

Pacific Northwest

Temple (525 Fort St., 250/383-2313, Mon.–Sat. from 4 P.M., $18–32) disregards Victoria's reputation as a bastion of old English culture completely, although you'd never know it from the exterior of the restored heritage building. But step inside and you enter a bright, contemporary room filled with smartly dressed diners relaxing on a lounge, seated at the glass bar, or chatting about sweet nothings in the "confessional room." The menu reflects the ambience, with modern presentations of dishes dominated by organic ingredients sourced from throughout the island.

European

The energetic atmosphere at **(Café Brio** (944 Fort St., 250/383-0009, daily from 5:30 P.M., $15–29) is contagious and the food is as good as anywhere in Victoria. The Mediterranean-inspired dining room is adorned with lively artwork and built around a U-shaped bar, while out front are a handful of tables on an alfresco terrace. A creative menu combines local, seasonal produce with Italian expertise and flair. The handmade charcuterie ($5 each) is always a good choice to begin with, followed by the Tuscan-style fish stew or the Brio Family Meal ($40) designed for sharing.

One of the most popular restaurants in town is **Pagliacci's** (1011 Broad St., 250/386-1662, daily 11:30 A.M.–3 P.M. and 5–10 P.M., $12.50–29), known for hearty Italian food, homemade bread, great desserts, and loads of atmosphere. Small and always busy, the restaurant attracts a lively local crowd, many with children.

Beyond the west end of Belleville Street is **Pablo's Dining Lounge** (225 Quebec St., 250/388-4255, daily from 5 P.M., $18–36), a long-time Victorian favorite. Atmosphere in the Edwardian house is relaxed yet intimate, and the classic European cooking is well prepared

and attractively presented. Everything is good, but the beef tenderloin topped with crabmeat and béarnaise sauce is simply the best.

Vegetarian

(Rebar (50 Bastion Square, 250/361-9223, Mon.–Sat. 8:30 A.M.–9 P.M., Sun. 8:30 A.M.–3:30 P.M., $8–17) is a 1970s-style vegetarian restaurant with a loyal, local following. Dishes such as the almond burger at lunch and Thai tiger prawn curry at dinner are full of flavor and made with only the freshest ingredients. Still hungry? Try the nutty carrot cake. Children are catered to with fun choices such as banana and peanut butter on sunflower seed bread. It's worth stopping by just for juice—vegetable and fruit juices, power tonics, and wheatgrass infusions are made to order for around $5.

Asian

Victoria's small Chinatown surrounds a short, colorful strip of Fisgard Street between Store and Government Streets. The restaurants welcome everyone and generally the menus are filled with all the familiar westernized Chinese choices. Near the top (east) end of Fisgard is **QV Cafe and Bakery** (1701 Government St., 250/384-8831, daily for breakfast, lunch, and dinner, $7.50–16), offering inexpensive western-style breakfasts in the morning and Chinese delicacies the rest of the day. Named for the Chinese province renowned for hot and spicy food, **Hunan Village Cuisine** (546 Fisgard St., 250/382-0661, Mon.–Sat. for lunch and daily for dinner, $9–17) offers simple, well-priced food. Step into the world of British colonialism at the **(Bengal Lounge,** in the Fairmont Empress (721 Government St., 250/389-2727). The curry lunch buffet (daily 11:30 A.M.–2 P.M., $27) and curry dinner buffet (daily 6–9 P.M., $29) come with the three condiments I love to have with curry—shaved coconut, mango chutney, and mixed nuts.

If you've never tried Thai cuisine, you're in for a treat at **Sookjai Thai** (893 Fort St., 250/383-9945, daily 11:30 A.M.–9 P.M., $9–18). The tranquil setting is the perfect place to sample traditional delights such as *Tom Yum Goong,* a prawn and mushroom soup with a hint of tangy citrus, and baked red snapper sprinkled with spices sourced from Thailand. The snapper is the most expensive main, with a number of inspiring vegetarian choices under $10.

INFORMATION AND SERVICES
Information Centers
Tourism Victoria (250/953-2033 or 800/663-3883, www.tourismvictoria.com) runs the bright, modern **Victoria Visitor Info Centre** (812 Wharf St., daily 9 A.M.–5 P.M.), overlooking the Inner Harbour.

Libraries
Greater Victoria Public Library (735 Broughton St., 250/382-7241, Mon.–Sat. 9 A.M.–6 P.M., Sun. 1–5 P.M.) has newspapers from around the world and free Internet access.

Communications
The main **post office** is on the corner of Yates and Douglas Streets. All Victoria's downtown accommodations have in-room Internet access. Those that don't, like the backpacker lodge, have inexpensive Internet booths near the lobby. A good option for travelers on the run is the small café on the lower level of the Hotel Grand Pacific (463 Belleville St., daily 7 A.M.–7 P.M.) where public Internet access is free with a purchase.

Banks
You'll find a currency exchange booth opposite the baggage carousels at Victoria International Airport, but to ensure the best rates, head downtown to one of the major banks, such as the **Bank of Montreal** (1225 Douglas St., 250/405-2090). Private downtown exchange shops include **Custom House Currency Exchange** (815 Wharf St., 250/389-6007) and **FX Connectors Currency Exchange** (1208 Wharf St., 250/380-7888).

Emergency Services
In a medical emergency, call 911 or contact **Victoria General Hospital** (1 Hospital Way, 250/727-4212). For non-urgent cases, a handy

facility is **James Bay Medical Treatment Centre** (230 Menzies St., 250/388-9934). The **Cresta Dental Centre** is at 3170 Tillicum Road at Burnside Street (250/384-7711). **Shopper's Drug Mart** (1222 Douglas St., 250/381-4321) is open daily 7 A.M.–7 P.M.

GETTING THERE
By Air
Vancouver Island's main airport is on the Saanich Peninsula, 20 kilometers (12 miles) north of Victoria's city center. The terminal building houses a lounge, café, and various rental car agencies. The **AKAL Airporter** (250/386-2525 or 877/386-2525, www.victoriaairporter.com) operates buses between the airport and major downtown hotels every 30 minutes for adult $18, child $11 each way. A taxi costs approximately $55 to downtown.

Scheduled flights link the international airports of Vancouver and Victoria, but it's such a short flight (25 minutes from terminal to terminal) that unless you're on a connecting flight, the alternatives are more practical. Smaller airlines, including those with floatplanes and helicopter services, provide a direct link between Victoria's Inner Harbour and the downtown Vancouver waterfront. **Harbour Air** (250/384-2215 or 800/665-0212) charges $125 each way.

By Bus
The main Victoria **bus depot** is behind the Empress Hotel at 700 Douglas Street. **Pacific Coach** (604/662-7575 or 800/661-1725, www.pacificcoach.com) operates bus service between Vancouver's Pacific Central Station and downtown Victoria, via the Tsawwassen–Swartz Bay ferry. In summer the coaches run hourly 6 A.M.–9 P.M. for $43 one-way, $84 round-trip, which includes the ferry fare. The trip takes 3.5 hours. Scheduled bus services on the island is offered by **Greyhound** (604/388-5248) from the same terminal.

By Ferry
From Tsawwassen (Vancouver): Vessels operated by **BC Ferries** (250/386-3431 or 888/223-3779, www.bcferries.com) run regularly across

the Strait of Georgia from Tsawwassen, 30 kilometers (19 miles) south of Vancouver, to the **Swartz Bay Ferry Terminal,** 32 kilometers (20 miles) north of Victoria. Through summer, ferries run hourly 7 A.M.–10 P.M., slightly less frequently the rest of the year. The crossing takes 90 minutes. You can expect a wait in summer; there are limited vehicle reservations available for $15 per booking. Peak fares are adult $13.50, child 5–11 $6.75, vehicle $45.

From Seattle: Clipper Vacations (800/888-2535, www.clippervacations.com) connects Seattle's Pier 69 with Victoria's Inner Harbour up to five times daily. Its turbojet catamaran, the **Victoria Clipper IV,** is North America's fastest passenger ferry, traveling at speeds of up to 45 knots (over 80 kph/50 mph). This speedy vessel makes the crossing in two hours. The cost is adult US$93 one-way, US$155 round-trip.

From Anacortes: Washington State Ferries (206/464-6400, 250/381-1551, or 888/808-7977, www.wsdot.wa.gov/ferries) runs a regular ferry schedule between Anacortes and the San Juan Islands, with the 7:50 A.M. sailing continuing to Sidney, on the Saanich Peninsula 32 kilometers (20 miles) north of Victoria. The return sailing departs Sidney at 11:45 A.M. The one-way fare is adult US$16.40, child US$11.50, vehicle and driver US$66.10. Reservations must be made at least 24 hours in advance.

From Port Angeles: Black Ball Transport (250/386-2202 in Victoria, or 360/457-4491 in Port Angeles, www.cohoferry.com) operates the **MV Coho** across Juan de Fuca Strait between Port Angeles and Victoria's Inner Harbour. It makes four crossings daily in each direction mid-May–mid-October, two crossings daily the rest of the year. Advance reservations are not accepted—phone a day or so before your planned departure for estimated waiting times. The one-way fare is adult US$14.50, child US$7.25, vehicle and driver US$53.

GETTING AROUND

The best way to get to know this compact city is on foot. All the downtown attractions are within a short walk of one another, and the more remote sights are easily reached by road or on the **Victoria Regional Transit System** (250/385-2551, www.busonline.ca). Pick up an *Explore Victoria* brochure at the information center for details of all the major sights, parks, beaches, and shopping areas, and the buses needed to reach them. Per sector bus fare is adult $2.25, senior or child $1.40. Transfers are good for travel in one direction within 90 minutes of purchase. A DayPass, valid for one day's unlimited bus travel, costs adult $7, senior or child $5.

Ferry

The most enjoyable way to get around the city is aboard a **Victoria Harbour Ferry** (250/708-0201). The company's distinctive 12-passenger

---

TOURING VICTORIA

The classic way to see Victoria is from the comfort of a horse-drawn carriage. Throughout the day and into the evening, **Tally-Ho** (250/514-9257) has carriages lined up along Menzies Street at Belleville Street awaiting passengers. A 15-minute tour costs $50, a 30-minute tour is $90, a 45-minute tour costs $115, or take a 60-minute Deluxe Tour for $1705. These prices are per carriage (up to four passengers). Tours run 9 A.M.-midnight and bookings aren't necessary, although there's often a line.

Big red double-decker buses are as much a part of the Victoria tour scene as horse-drawn carriages. These are operated by **Gray Line** (250/388-6539, www.graylinewest.com) from beside the Inner Harbour. There are many tours to choose from, but to get oriented while also learning some city history, take the 90-minute Grand City Drive Tour. It departs from the harbor front every half hour 9:30 A.M.-4 P.M. (adult $25, child $12.50). The most popular of Gray Line's other tours is the one to Butchart Gardens (adult $49, child $16, including admission price).

ferries depart from the Inner Harbour, making 18 stops along 2 routes. One takes in harbor-side docks including Fisherman's Wharf, Ocean Pointe Resort, and Westbay Marine Village, while the other heads up the Gorge Waterway; $4–22.50 per sector, or make the round-trip as a tour for $20–25.

Taxi and Car Rental

Local cab companies include **Blue Bird Cabs** (250/382-4235 or 800/665-7055), **Empress Taxi** (250/381-2222), or **Victoria Taxi** (250/383-7111).

This is the only place in western Canada where some of the rental car business goes to local companies such as **Island Rent-A-Car** (250/384-4881, www.islandrentacar.net). Local contacts for the majors are: **Avis** (250/386-8468), **Budget** (250/953-5300), **Discount** (250/310-2277), **Enterprise** (250/475-6900), **Hertz** (250/952-3765), **National** (250/386-1213), and **Thrifty** (250/383-3659).

Vicinity of Victoria

Two highways lead out of Victoria: Highway 14 heads west and Highway 1 heads north. Highway 14 is a spectacular coastal route that ends in Port Renfrew, the southern terminus of the rugged and remote West Coast Trail. Highway 1 leads north from Victoria to Duncan, Chemainus, and Ladysmith, each with its own particular charm. West of Duncan are massive Cowichan Lake, an inland paradise for anglers and boaters, and Carmanah Walbran Provincial Park, protecting a remote watershed full of ancient Sitka spruce that miraculously escaped logging.

WEST FROM VICTORIA
Sooke

About 34 kilometers (21 miles) from Victoria, Sooke (population 4,800) is best known for a lodge that combines luxurious accommodations with one of Canada's most renowned restaurants. As far as actual local sights go, at **Sooke Region Museum** (2070 Phillips Rd., 250/642-6351, daily 9 A.M.–5 P.M., donation) browse the indoor displays, then wander out back to count all 478 growth rings on the cross-section of a giant spruce tree.

(**Sooke Harbour House** (1528 Whiffen Spit Rd., 250/642-3421 or 800/889-9688, www.sookeharbourhouse.com, $280–625 s or d) combines the elegance of an upscale country-style inn with the atmosphere of an exclusive oceanfront resort. The restaurant attracts discerning diners from throughout the world, but the accommodations offered are equally impressive. The sprawling waterfront property sits on a bluff, with 27 guest rooms spread through immaculately manicured gardens. Each of the rooms reflects a different aspect of life on the west coast, and all have stunning views, a wood-burning fireplace, and deck or patio. Rates include breakfast and a picnic lunch; off-season, these rates are reduced by up to 40 percent. The lodge's restaurant (daily from 5 P.M.) has an ever-changing menu dominated by local seafood, prepared to perfection with vegetables and herbs picked straight from the surrounding garden.

Sooke to Port Renfrew

The first worthwhile stop west of Sooke is **French Beach Provincial Park,** where a short trail winds through a lush forest of Douglas fir and Sitka spruce to a rocky beach. It's a great place for a picnic or a walk—watch for gray whales. Along this stretch of coast, three kilometers (1.9 miles) beyond French Beach, is **Point No Point Resort** (250/646-2020, www.pointnopointresort.com, $190–280 s or d). Enjoying an absolute waterfront location, this lodge has 25 cabins, each with sweeping water views, a full kitchen, and fireplace. Lunch (daily, $7–15) and dinner (Wed.–Sun., $26–34) are available in the lodge restaurant, which overlooks the ocean.

When you emerge at the small logging town of **Jordan River,** take time to take in the smells of the ocean and the surrounding windswept landscape. The town comprises only a few houses, a local logging operation, and a small day use area overlooking one of Canada's best-known surf spots.

Three kilometers west of Jordan River, a 700-meter (0.4-mile) one-way trail leads through Sitka spruce to pebbly **China Beach,** which is strewn with driftwood and backed by a couple of protected picnic sites. Camping (back up by the highway) is $15 per night. The beach and campground are within 1,277-hectare (3,156-acre) **Juan de Fuca Provincial Park,** protecting a coastal strip between Jordan River and Port Renfrew. China Beach is also the beginning of the 47-kilometer (29-mile) **Juan de Fuca Trail,** a coastal hiking route that ends at Port Renfrew.

Port Renfrew

This small seaside community clings to the rugged shoreline of Port San Juan, 104 kilometers (65 miles) from Victoria. An eclectic array of houses leads down the hill to the waterfront. Follow the signs to **Botanical Beach,** a fascinating intertidal pool area where low tide exposes hundreds of species of marine creatures at the foot of scoured-out sandstone cliffs. The three-kilometer (1.9-mile) road to the beach is rough and can be impassable in winter.

VANCOUVER ISLAND

WEST COAST TRAIL

The magnificent West Coast Trail meanders 75 kilometers (47 miles) along Vancouver Island's untamed western shoreline, through **Pacific Rim National Park.** It's one of the world's great hikes – exhilaratingly challenging, incredibly beautiful, and very satisfying. The very quickest hikers can complete the trail in four days, but by allowing six, seven, or eight days you'll have time to fully enjoy the adventure. The trail extends from the mouth of the Gordon River near Port Renfrew to Pachena Bay, near the remote fishing village of Bamfield on Barkley Sound. Along the way you'll wander along beaches, steep cliff tops, and slippery banks; cross rivers by rope, suspension bridge, or ferry; climb down sandstone cliffs by ladder; tread slippery boardwalks, muddy slopes, bogs, and deep gullies; and balance on fallen logs. But for all your efforts you're rewarded with panoramic views of sand and sea, dense lush rainforest, waterfalls cascading into deep pools, all kinds of wildlife – gray whales, eagles, sea lions, seals, and seabirds – and the constant roar and hiss of the Pacific surf pummeling the sand.

The trail can be hiked from either direction – Port Renfrew is the preferred start, as the more demanding terrain is covered first, but you have a better chance of scoring a spot in the daily quota at the other end.

PERMITS, TRANSPORT, AND INFORMATION

The trail is open mid-May–mid-October. For May–September travel, reservations (250/387-1642 or 800/435-5622, $25) are necessary. Ten spots are released each day at 1 P.M. at the registration offices at either end of the trail (expect a 1-2 day wait for your turn to come up). All hikers must obtain a Park Use Permit ($127.50) and take a quick orientation session before heading out. The only other cost is $30 for two river crossings en route; this is collected at the time of your booking.

West Coast Trail Express (250/477-8700 or 888/999-2288, www.trailbus.com) departs Victoria daily for both ends of the trail ($50-70), and also links the two trailheads ($70), the latter perfect for those who drive to either Port Renfrew or Bamfield. The company also rents camping and hiking gear.

The best source of trail information is the **Parks Canada website** (www.pc.gc.ca), which includes an overview of what to expect, instructions on trail-use fees, a list of equipment you should take, and a list of relevant literature. Seasonal park information/registration centers are in Port Renfrew (250/647-5434) and Pachena Bay (250/728-3234).

Accommodations are available at the **Trailhead Resort,** in the heart of town (250/647-5468, www.trailhead-resort.com, $125–250 s or d). It's motel rooms are relatively new, basic but practical, with a balcony out front, or choose to stay in one of two self-contained two-bedroom cabins. On site a store sells camping and fishing gear. Beyond town, at the mouth of the San Juan River, **Port Renfrew Marina and RV Park** (250/647-0002, www.portrenfrewmarina.com, Apr.–Oct., $22) has powered campsites but no showers. This place is primarily a marina complex, with boat charters and fishing gear for sale.

DUNCAN AND VICINITY

Duncan, self-proclaimed "City of Totems," lies at the junction of Highways 1 and 18, about 60 kilometers (37 miles) north of Victoria. Native carvers, many from the local Cowichan band, have created some 80 intricate and colorful totem poles here. Look for them along the main highway near the information center, beside the railway station in the old section of town, and inside local businesses. Two distinctly different native carvings stand side by side behind city hall—a Native American carving and a New Zealand Maori carving.

Sights

Apart from the famous totem poles, Duncan's main attraction is the excellent **Quw'utsun' Cultural Centre** (200 Cowichan Way, 250/746-8119, daily 10 A.M.–5 P.M. May–Sept., daily 10 A.M.–5 P.M. Oct.–Apr., adult $15, senior $12, child $8). Representing the arts, crafts, legends, and traditions of a 3,500-strong Quw'utsun' population spread through the Cowichan Valley, this facility features a long house, carving shed, dance performances, and a gift shop selling Cowichan sweaters. It's also home to the (**Riverwalk Café** (250/746-4370, Tues.–Sat. 11:30 A.M.–3 P.M. June–Sept., lunches $11–16), where you can order mains like salmon and fiddlehead stir-fry.

Another local attraction is the 40-hectare (99-acre) **BC Forest Discovery Centre** (one km/0.6 mi north of town at 2892 Drinkwater

Rd., 250/715-1113, daily 10 A.M.–4 P.M. early Apr.–mid-Oct., until 5 P.M. July–Aug., adult $14, senior $12, child $9). You can catch a ride on an old steam train and puff back in time, through the forest and past a farmstead, a logging camp, and Somenos Lake. Then check out the working sawmill, restored planer mill, blacksmith's shop, and forestry and lumber displays.

Cowichan River

This famous salmon and steelhead fishing river has its source at **Lake Cowichan.** Much of its length is protected by **Cowichan River Provincial Park,** which extends over 750 hectares (1,850 acres) and 20 kilometers (12 miles). There are three access points to the park, including Skutz Falls, where salmon spawn each fall. Camping is $15. The paved road inland dead-ends 32 kilometers (20 miles) from Duncan at Lake Cowichan, a popular spot for canoeing, swimming, and especially fishing—the lake is stocked with kokanee and a variety of trout. Logging roads encircle the lake (75 km/47 mi round-trip) and provide hikers access into the adjacent wilderness, including **Carmanah Walbran Provincial Park.**

Practicalities

(**Sahtlam Lodge and Cabins** (5720 Riverbottom Rd. W, 250/748-7738 or 877/748-7738, www.sahtlamlodge.com, from $550 for three nights) is beside the Cowichan River west of town. Three cabins are spread across the property, and each is equipped with an old-style fireplace, woodstove, and full kitchen. A breakfast basket delivered daily to your cabin is included. On the south side of the river is the turnoff to **Duncan RV Park and Campground** (2950 Boys Rd., 250/748-8511, $20–26), which is one block west of the highway, right beside the river.

Stop at **Duncan Visitor Centre** (381 Trans-Canada Hwy., 250/746-4636 or 888/303-3337, www.duncancc.bc.ca, daily 9 A.M.–6 P.M. summer, Mon.–Sat. 10 A.M.–4 P.M. the rest of the year), on the west side of the highway in Overwaitea Plaza, for the complete rundown on the area.

Southern Gulf Islands

Spread through the Strait of Georgia between mainland British Columbia and Vancouver Island are a group of islands with a mild, almost Mediterranean climate; beautiful scenery; driftwood-strewn beaches; quaint towns; and wide ranging choice of accommodations that combine to make them popular in summer, when laid back locals share their home with flocks of visitors. Still, there's plenty of room to get away from the hustle, with mile after mile of remote coastline and easily reached peaks beckoning to be explored. After kayaking, biking, or hiking, the best way to end the day is at one of the many island restaurants, feasting on salmon and crab brought ashore that morning. Five of the islands—Salt Spring, the Penders, Galiano, Mayne, and Saturna—are populated, and each is linked to the outside world by scheduled ferry service.

SALT SPRING ISLAND

Largest of the Southern Gulf Islands, 180-square-kilometer (70-square-mile) Salt Spring (population 11,000) lies close to Vancouver Island, immediately north of Saanich Inlet. Ferries link the south and north ends of the island to Vancouver Island, and myriad roads converge on the service town of **Ganges.** The island is home to a large number of artisans, along with hobby farmers, retirees, and wealthy Vancouverites who spend their summers at private getaways.

Sights and Recreation

Ask any longtime local and they'll tell you the island's main town, **Ganges,** is over-commercialized. But it's still quaint, and well worth visiting. Set around a protected bay, the original waterfront buildings have undergone a colorful transformation and where once you would have found boat-builders, you can now browse through art galleries, shop for antiques, or dine on innovative cuisine. One of the most eye-catching shops is Jill Louise Campbell Fine Art Gallery.

Near the Fulford Harbour ferry terminal, take Beaver Point Road east to 486-hectare (1,200-acre) **Ruckle Provincial Park.** The access road ends at the rocky headland of Beaver Point, where trails lead north along the coastline, providing great views across to North Pender Island. Along the road north to Ganges, small **Mount Maxwell Provincial Park** protects the slopes of its namesake mountain. A rough unsealed road off Musgrave Road leads to the 588-meter (1,930-foot) summit, from where views extend south across the island to Vancouver Island and east to the other Gulf Islands.

With **Sea Otter Kayaking** (250/537-5678 or 877/537-5678), get up close and personal with local marine and bird life on while exploring the coastline on a guided tour, with a break for a picnic lunch on a remote beach ($115 for six hours).

Practicalities

Maple Ridge Cottages (301 Tripp Rd., 250/537-5977, www.mapleridgecottages.com, $149–199 s or d) is on the banks of St. Mary Lake, a largish body of freshwater that holds a hungry population of bass and trout that can be caught right from the shoreline. For me, the allure of the wooden cottages is the location, but their rustic charm brings back families year after year. Relax on the deck while your catch of the day cooks on the barbecue for the full effect. Free use of canoes and kayaks is a popular bonus. On the north side of the island on St. Mary Lake, **Lakeside Gardens** (250/537-5773, www.lakesidegardensresort.com, Apr.–Nov., $90–145 s or d) offers rustic cabins with shared bathrooms as well as self-contained cottages. You can camp in **Ruckle Provincial Park** ($15), although the camping area is a short walk from the parking lot, making this place unsuitable for RVs.

Head to Ganges and wander around the waterfront for the island's widest choice of dining options. In the heart of the action is the [**Tree House Café** (106 Purvis Lane,

250/537-5379, daily 8 A.M.–10 P.M., $12–17). The "tree" is a plum tree and the "house" is the kitchen. Most people dine outside in the shade of the tree, choosing freshly made dishes such as salmon frittata for breakfast, tuna melt on sourdough at lunch, or Thai chicken curry in the evening.

Salt Spring Island Visitor Info Centre (121 Lower Ganges Rd., 250/537-4223 or 866/216-2936, www.saltspringtourism.com, daily A.M.–5 P.M. in summer, daily 11 A.M.–3 P.M. the rest of the year) is in downtown Ganges, on the main road above the marina.

Getting There

Salt Spring has **BC Ferries** terminals (250/386-3431) with year-round service to two points on Vancouver Island. If you're traveling up from Victoria, the Swartz Bay terminal is the most convenient departure point, with 10–12 departures daily for **Fulford Harbour,** a 20-minute drive south of Ganges. Sailings are even more frequent on the 20-minute run between Crofton, near the Vancouver Island town of Duncan, and **Vesuvius Bay,** at the island's north end. Interisland ferries depart from a third terminal, at **Long Harbour,** east of Ganges. Regardless of the route, the round-trip fare is adult $9.45, child $4.75, vehicle $28.

THE PENDERS

It's just a short hop by ferry from Salt Spring Island to **Otter Bay** on North Pender Island, from where a rickety wooden bridge forms a link to South Pender Island. Between them, the two islands are home to 2,400 people, most of whom live on North Pender. The island has dozens of little beaches to explore, with public roads providing ocean access at more than 20 points. One of the nicest spots is **Hamilton Beach** on Browning Harbour.

Accommodations

The least expensive way to enjoy an overnight stay on North Pender Island is to camp at **Prior Centennial Campground** (mid-May–mid-Oct., $14), a unit of Gulf Islands National Park. Sites are primitive, with no showers or hookups, but the treed location is excellent. The facility is six kilometers (3.7 miles) south of the ferry terminal. The island's premier accommodation is the **Oceanside Inn** (4230 Armadale Rd. five km/3.1 mi from the ferry terminal, 250/629-6691 or 800/601-3284, www.penderisland.com, $169–239 s or d). Each room is elegantly furnished, and a wide balcony takes advantage of the waterfront location. Rates include breakfast in an oceanfront dining room, use of a fitness room, and in-room luxuries such as fluffy bathrobes.

Shopping and Food

The commercial hub of the Penders is the **Driftwood Centre** (Bedwell Harbour Rd.), a city-like shopping mall overlooking cleared pastureland south of the ferry terminal. In addition to gas, groceries, booze, and a bank, you'll find a number of eateries, including a super-busy bakery. For something a little more substantial, move along the mall to the **Pistou Grill** (250/629-3131, Tues.–Sat. 11:30 A.M.–2:30 P.M. and 5:30–8:30 P.M., $13.50–21) for surprisingly innovative cooking that includes seared halibut drizzled with a chardonnay sauce. Also in the mall is **Talisman Books & Gallery** (250/629-6944), stocking an excellent range of local literature and best sellers.

Getting There

Ferries depart the Swartz Bay terminal (250/386-3431) up to seven times a day for North Pender Island. Most sailings are direct (40 minutes), although a couple of the early-ly-morning trips go via Galiano and Mayne Islands (over two hours), so check the timetable carefully before boarding. The round-trip fare is adult $9.45, child $4.75, vehicle $28.

MAYNE ISLAND

Separated from Galiano Island by a narrow channel, Mayne Island is laced with country roads leading to all corners of the island. Village Bay has no village; all commercial facilities are at nearby **Miners Bay,** which got its name during the Cariboo gold rush, when miners used the island as a stopping point.

Island beaches are limited to those at **Oyster Bay,** but visitors can enjoy interesting shoreline walks or take the road to the low summit of **Mount Park** for panoramic views.

Accommodations and Food

The least expensive island accommodation is **Springwater Lodge** (250/539-5521, www.springwaterlodge.com), an old hotel overlooking Active Pass from the west side of Village Bay. Rooms are basic at best and bathrooms are shared, but at just $40 s or d you know what you're getting. Beside the hotel are four well-equipped cabins that go for $95 per night. The inn also has a restaurant open daily for all three meals. Set on four hectares (10 acres) overlooking a protected waterway, less than two kilometers (1.2 miles) south of the ferry terminal, is **◖ Oceanwood Country Inn** (630 Dinner Bay Rd., 250/539-5074, www.oceanwood.com, $179–349 s or d). Paths lead through the very private property, past herb and rose gardens, and down to the water's edge. Within the lodge itself are four communal areas, including a well-stocked library, a comfortable lounge, and a restaurant. Camping at **Mayne Island Eco Camping** (359 Maple Dr., Miners Bay, 250/539-2667, www.mayneisle.com, $12 per person) is pleasant but primitive. Laid out around the back of a short beach, some sites are right on the water while others are spread through the forest. Facilities include outhouses, a (hot) water-fed "tree" shower, and kayak rentals.

No-frills, short order grills are the order of the day at the old **Springwater Lodge** (Village Bay, 250/539-5521, daily for breakfast, lunch, and dinner, $9.50–20). Head to the **Sunny Mayne Bakery & Cafe** (Miners Bay, 250/539-2323, Mon.–Sat. 7 a.m.–5 p.m., Sun. 8 a.m.–4 p.m.) for freshly baked breads, sumptuous cakes and pastries, healthy sandwiches, and the island's best coffee concoctions.

Information

The website www.mayneislandchamber.ca is loaded with useful information, including links to current weather conditions, accommodations, services, and, for those who fall in love with island living, real estate agents. Stock up on reading material at **Miners Bay Books** (478 Village Bay Rd., 250/539-3112).

Getting There

From Swartz Bay, **BC Ferries** (250/386-3431) schedules four sailings daily to Mayne Island; round-trip fare is adult $9.45, child $4.75, vehicle $28.

◖ GALIANO ISLAND

Named for a Spanish explorer who sailed through the Strait of Georgia over 200 years ago, this island is surrounded by beautiful beaches and rocky coves with protected waters that are perfect for kayaking. Combine its natural charms with a well-maintained provincial park, an excellent array of tourist facilities, and 1,000 friendly residents and you come up with one of my favorite places in the province.

Sights and Recreation

Climbing out of Sturdies Bay, roads tempt exploration in all directions. Take Porlier Pass Road to reach **Montague Harbour Provincial Park,** protecting an 89-hectare (210-acre) chunk of coastal forest and a beach of bleached-white broken seashells. You can walk out along the beach and return via a forested trail in around 20 minutes. At the end of the beach are *middens,* manmade piles of empty shells that accumulated over centuries of native feasting. The island is dotted with many less-obvious access points, many of which aren't even signposted. The beach below Active Pass Road is typical; look for power pole numbered 1038 and make your way down the steep trail to a protected cove. Ask at the information center or your accommodation for a full listing of similar spots.

The best way to explore local waterways is with **Galiano Island Kayaking,** based at the marina in Montague Harbour (250/539-2442, www.seakayak.ca). Three-hour guided tours, either early in the morning or at sunset, are $55. Another tour takes in the local marine-life on a six-hour paddle for $85. Those with previous experience can rent a kayak for $58 per day for a single or $80 for a double.

Accommodations and Food

Many of the travelers you'll meet on the ferry trip to Galiano will be staying for a week or more in an island cottage. If this style of vacation sounds ideal, check www.galianoisland.com for a choice of rentals, but do so well before planning your visit because the best ones fill fast. Set on Sturdies Bay waterfront is the **Bellhouse Inn** (29 Farmhouse Rd., 250/539-5667 or 800/970-7464, www.bellhouseinn.com, $155–215 s or d), an 1890s farmhouse that has been taking in travelers since the 1920s. Each of the three guest rooms has water views and the most expensive features a hot tub, private balcony, and fireplace. Rates include a full breakfast and personal touches such as tea or coffee delivered to the room before breakfast.

The campground in **Montague Harbour Provincial Park** (10 km/6.2 mi from the ferry, mid-Apr.–mid-Oct., $15) is one of the best in the Southern Gulf Islands. Sites are set below a towering forest of old growth cedar and fir trees and open to a white shingle beach that is aligned perfectly to watch the setting sun. As with all provincial park campgrounds, facilities are limited to picnic tables, pit toilets, and drinking water.

To immerse yourself in island life, plan on dining at **Galiano Grand Central** (2470 Sturdies Bay Rd., 250/539-9885, Mon.–Thurs. 7 A.M.–2:30 P.M., Fri.–Sat. 7 A.M.–9 P.M., Sun. 7 A.M.–5 P.M., $15–23), which is decorated in lumberjack artifacts and has seating ripped from old buses. Free-range eggs are the prime ingredient in most breakfasts, which are huge. Sandwiches and burgers dominate the lunch menu. In the evening, the blackboard dinner menu reflects whatever is in season. Wireless Internet is free and there is often live music playing in the background on weekends.

Getting There

BC Ferries (250/386-3431) schedules four sailings daily between Swartz Bay and Galiano Island (adult $9.45, child $4.75, vehicle $28 round-trip) as well as a packed schedule of interisland sailings (adult $4.90, child $2.45, vehicle $9).

SATURNA ISLAND

Most remote of the populated Southern Gulf Islands, Saturna protrudes into the heart of Georgia Strait and features a long, rugged northern coastline and more than half its land area within Gulf Islands National Park. It offers a range of accommodations, but other services are limited (no banks or ATMs) and ferries only stop by a couple of times a day.

From the ferry dock at **Lyall Harbour,** the island's main road loops east then south along the coastline for 14 kilometers (8.7 miles), ending at **East Point Regional Park.** Here you can go swimming or simply admire the sweeping views across the border to the San Juans. Before the park, **Winter Cove** is another picturesque diversion.

Practicalities

Most accommodations on Saturna Island are in private-home bed-and-breakfasts. A short walk from where the ferry docks is **Lyall Harbour B&B** (121 E. Point Rd., 250/539-5577 or 877/473-9343, www.lyallharbour.com, $110 s, $140 d). Each of the three guest rooms is spacious and features modern furnishings, a fireplace, and a deck with ocean views. Breakfast is served in a sun-drenched solarium. Overlooking Boot Cove and also within walking distance of the dock, **Saturna Lodge** (130 Payne Rd., 250/539-2254 or 866/539-2254, www.saturna.ca, May–Oct., $119–169 s or d includes breakfast) is a modern accommodation offering six guest rooms, a hot tub, a lounge with fireplace, and extensive gardens. Within the lodge, a small restaurant has a big reputation for seafood and local game and produce. The owners are involved in various projects around the island, including **Saturna Island Vineyards** (8 Quarry Rd., 250/539-5139, daily 11:30 A.M.–4:30 P.M. May–Oct.).

From Swartz Bay, **BC Ferries** (250/386-3431) schedules four sailings daily to Mayne Island (adult $9.45, child $4.75, vehicle $28).

Nanaimo and Vicinity

Nanaimo (na-NYE-mo) sprawls lazily up and down the hilly coastal terrain between sparkling Nanaimo Harbour and Mount Benson, on the east coast of Vancouver Island. With a population of 82,000, it's the island's second-largest city. It's also a vibrant city enjoying a rich history, mild climate, wide range of visitor services, and a direct ferry link to both of Vancouver's ferry terminals.

The Nanaimo Parkway bypasses the city to the west along a 21-kilometer (13-mile) route that branches off the original highway five kilometers (3.1 miles) south of downtown, rejoining it 18 kilometers (11.2 miles) north of downtown.

History

Five native bands lived here (the name Nanaimo is derived from the Salish word *Sney-Ny-Mous,* or "meeting place"), and it was they who innocently showed dull, black rocks to Hudson's Bay Company employees in 1851. For most of the next century, mines in the area exported huge quantities of coal. Eventually, oil-fueled ships replaced the coal burners, and by 1949 most of the mines had closed. Surprisingly, no visible traces of the mining boom remain in Nanaimo, aside from a museum (built on top of the most productive mine) accurately depicting those times, and a sturdy fort (now a museum) built in 1853 in case of a native attack.

SIGHTS

Downtown Nanaimo lies in a wide bowl sloping down to the waterfront, where forward thinking by early town planners has left wide expanses of parkland. Right in front of the Civic Arena is **Swy-A-Lana Lagoon,** a unique tidal lagoon full of interesting marinelife. A promenade leads south from the lagoon to a bustling downtown marina filled with commercial fishing boats and leisure craft. Beside the marina is a distinctive mast-like sculpture that provides foot access to a tiered development with various viewpoints.

Museums

In the city's conference center is **Nanaimo Museum** (100 Museum Way., 250/753-1821, daily 10 A.M.–5 P.M. in summer, Tues.–Sat. 10 A.M.–5 P.M. the rest of the year, adult $2, senior $1.75, child $0.75). Allow at least an hour for wandering through the extensive displays, which focus on life in early Nanaimo and include topics such as local geology, native peoples, and pioneers. Don't miss the impressive native carvings by James Dick. Overlooking the harbor at the junction of Bastion and Front Streets stands **The Bastion** (daily 10 A.M.–3 P.M. June–Aug., donation), a fort built in 1853 by the Hudson's Bay Company to protect employees and their families against an attack by natives. Originally used as a company office, arsenal, and supply house, today the fort houses a small museum. For the benefit of tourists, a group of local university students dressed in appropriate gunnery uniforms fire a cannon over the water from here daily at noon in summer.

Newcastle Island Provincial Marine Park

Newcastle Island is a magnificent chunk of wilderness separated from downtown Nanaimo by a narrow channel. It's mostly forested, ringed by sandstone cliffs and a few short stretches of pebbly beach. Wildlife inhabitants include deer, raccoons, beavers, and more than 50 species of birds. A 7.5-kilometer (4.7-mile) walking trail (allow 2–3 hours) encircles the island, leading to picturesque Kanaka Bay, Mallard Lake, and a lookout offering views east to the snowcapped Coast Mountains.

Camping on the island costs $15, and meals are available in the **Pavilion Bistro** (daily 9 A.M.–7:15 P.M. in summer, Fri.–Sat. nights until 9:15 P.M., $14–23). Ferries (250/754-7893) depart for the island on the hour from Maffeo-Sutton Park daily 10 A.M.–7 P.M. in summer, with extra sailings at 8 P.M. and 9 P.M. on Friday and Saturday. The round-trip fare is adult $8, child $6.

NANAIMO

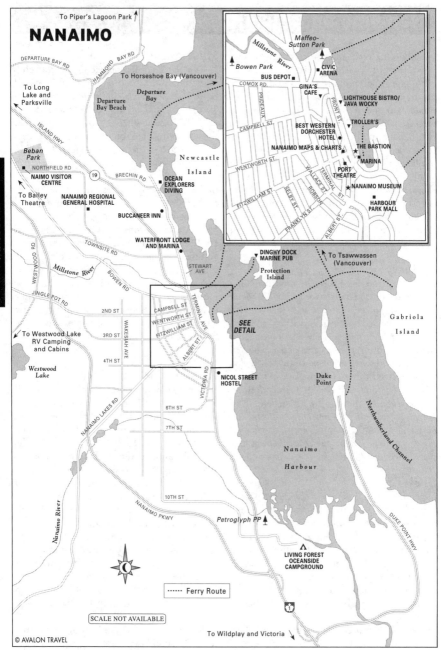

To Piper's Lagoon Park

DEPARTURE BAY RD

HAMMOND BAY RD

To Horseshoe Bay (Vancouver)

To Long
Lake and
Parksville

Departure
Bay Beach

Departure
Bay

ISLAND HWY

Beban
Park

NORTHFIELD RD

Newcastle
Island

NANAIMO VISITOR
CENTRE

BRECHIN RD

OCEAN
EXPLORERS
DIVING

To Bailey
Theatre

NANAIMO REGIONAL
GENERAL HOSPITAL

BUCCANEER INN

WESTWOOD RD

TOWNSITE RD

BOWEN RD

WATERFRONT LODGE
AND MARINA

Millstone River

JINGLE POT RD

STEWART
AVE

DINGHY DOCK
MARINE PUB

To Tsawwassen
(Vancouver)

Protection
Island

To Westwood Lake
RV Camping
and Cabins

2ND ST

WAKESIAH AVE

CAMPBELL ST

TERMINAL AVE

SEE
DETAIL

Gabriola

Island

Westwood
Lake

3RD ST

WENTWORTH ST

FITZWILLIAM ST

4TH ST

ALBERT ST

VICTORIA RD

NICOL STREET
HOSTEL

Duke
Point

NANAIMO LAKES RD

6TH ST

7TH ST

Nanaimo

Harbour

Northumberland Channel

Nanaimo River

10TH ST

NANAIMO PKWY

Petroglyph PP

LIVING FOREST
OCEANSIDE
CAMPGROUND

DUKE POINT HWY

······ Ferry Route

SCALE NOT AVAILABLE

© AVALON TRAVEL

To Wildplay and Victoria

SEE DETAIL

Millstone River

Maffeo-
Sutton Park

Bowen Park

CIVIC
ARENA

BUS DEPOT

COMOX RD

GINA'S
CAFE

PRIDEAUX

FRONT ST

LIGHTHOUSE BISTRO/
JAVA WOCKY

CAMPBELL ST

TROLLER'S

BEST WESTERN
DORCHESTER
HOTEL

THE BASTION

NANAIMO MAPS & CHARTS

MARINA

WENTWORTH ST

WALLACE ST

TERMINAL ST

PORT
THEATRE

NANAIMO MUSEUM

FITZWILLIAM ST

SELBY ST

ROBSON

HARBOUR
PARK MALL

FRANKLYN ST

ALBERT ST

Petroglyph Provincial Park

On the road into downtown Nanaimo from the south, two kilometers (1.2 miles) north of the Nanaimo Parkway intersection, a short trail leads through Petroglyph Provincial Park to ancient petroglyphs (rock carvings). The designs at this park were carved thousands of years ago and are believed to represent human beings, animals, fish, and the rarely depicted sea wolf, a mythical creature part wolf and part killer whale.

Piper's Lagoon Park

Along Hammond Bay Road, north of downtown and beyond Departure Bay, is Piper's Lagoon Park, encompassing an isthmus and a rocky headland that shelter a shallow lagoon. A trail from the parking lot leads to the headland, with views of the mainland across the Strait of Georgia.

RECREATION

A great variety of scuba-dive spots can be accessed from Nanaimo, including a number of vessels that have been sunk especially for diving enthusiast— the HMAS *Cape Breton* and HMAS *Saskatchewan* are both 120-meter (400-foot) long navy destroyer escorts. The much smaller *Rivtow Lion,* a rescue tug, was scuttled in the shallow waters of Departure Bay, making it a popular spot for novice divers. Marinelife is also varied, with divers mixing with harbor seals, anemones, sponges, salmon, and "tame" wolf eels. Near the Departure Bay ferry terminal, **Ocean Explorers Diving** (1090 Stewart Ave., 250/753-2055) is a well-respected operation, offering equipment rentals, charters, guided tours (from $90 per dive including air), and lessons.

WildPlay (13 km/8 mi south of town, 250/716-7874) is home to North America's only bridge-based commercial bungee jump. The cost to jump of the 42-meter-high (138-foot) bridge is $109. At the same facility, other adrenaline rushes can be had by taking the King Swing and climbing through the elevated TreeGo obstacle course.

ENTERTAINMENT AND EVENTS

The impressive 800-seat **Port Theatre** (125 Front St., 250/754-8550) showcases theater productions, musicals, and music performances by a wide range of artists. The **Nanaimo Theatre Group** (250/758-7246) presents live performances at the Port Theatre as well as in the Bailey Theatre (2373 Rosstown Rd.). The best place in Nanaimo for a quiet drink in a relaxing atmosphere is upstairs in the **Lighthouse Pub** (50 Anchor Way, 250/754-3212), built out over the water in front of downtown. This casual pub gets very busy in summer, with nightly drink specials, a pool table, and a good selection of pub food. For a nautical atmosphere, head over to the **Dinghy Dock Marine Pub,** moored at Protection Island (250/753-2373); ferries depart regularly from Nanaimo Boat Basin.

On the fourth Sunday of every July the waters off Nanaimo are filled with bathtubs for the **World Championship Bathtub Race,** the grand finale of the annual **Nanaimo Marine Festival** (250/753-7223, www.bathtubbing. com). Competitors race around a 57-kilometer (36-mile) course in modified bathtubs fitted with 7.5-horsepower outboard motors. The racers are escorted by hundreds of boats of the more regular variety, loaded with people just waiting for the competitors to sink.

ACCOMMODATIONS AND CAMPING
Under $50

A few of Nanaimo's older motels offer rooms under $50 outside of summer, but only **Nicol Street Hostel** (65 Nicol St., 250/753-1188, www.nanaimohostel.com, dorms $22) falls into this price range year-round. In a converted house, this accommodation enjoys a convenient location three blocks from the train station and seven blocks from the bus depot. The hostel operates year-round, providing dormitory-style accommodations as well as campsites, a kitchen, laundry, TV room, and bicycle rentals. Guests can get discounts at many local restaurants and attractions.

$50-100

On an island of overpriced accommodations, the two-story **◖ Buccaneer Inn** (1577 Stewart Ave., 250/753-1246 or 877/282-6337, www.thebuccaneerinn.com, $80–200 s or d) stands out as being excellent value. Bedecked by a nautical-themed mural and colorful baskets of flowers, the motel is surrounded by well-maintained grounds, a sundeck, picnic tables, and a barbecue facility. The rooms themselves are spacious and brightly decorated, and each has a desk, coffee-making facilities, a small fridge, and Internet connections. Friendly owner/operators provide a wealth of information on the local area (as does the motel website).

$100-150

A few blocks toward downtown from the Buccaneer is the **Waterfront Lodge & Marina** (1000 Stewart St., 250/753-7111 or 800/663-2116, www.waterfrontnanaimo.com, from $110 s, $120 d), a four-story waterfront motel facing Newcastle Island that saw a major revamp in early 2010. The rooms are extra large, and each has a kitchen and private balcony.

A bit nicer than you'd expect from the bland exterior, the **Best Western Dorchester Hotel** (70 Church St., 250/754-6835 or 800/661-2449, www.dorchesternanaimo.com, $130–170 s or d) offers water views and a rooftop terrace from a very central location. Rooms in this historic building won't win any design awards, but are relatively modern and many have water views.

Camping

The closest of the commercial campgrounds to downtown is **Westwood Lake RV Camping and Cabins** (380 Westwood Rd., www.westwoodlakecampgrounds.com, 250/753-3922, Unserviced sites are $21, hookups $26–31, cabins $80 s or d, or $90 with linen). Set on the edge of beautiful Westwood Lake, amenities include canoe rentals, a barbecue area, game room, laundry, and hot showers.

Living Forest Oceanside Campground (6 Maki Rd., 250/755-1755, www.campingbc.com, tents $26, hookups $28–39) is set on 20 hectares

(49 acres) of coastal forest at the braided mouth of the Nanaimo River south of downtown. The location is delightful and facilities modern, including a laundry, wireless Internet, general store, game room, and coin showers.

FOOD

If you're wandering along the harbor and looking for a spot to relax with a hot drink, you won't do better than **Javawocky** (90 Front St., 250/753-1688, Mon.–Fri. from 6:15 A.M., Sat.–Sun. from 7 A.M., lunches $4.50–8), overlooking the harbor. It offers all the usual coffee drinks, great milkshakes, inexpensive cakes and pastries, and light lunchtime snacks. Across the promenade from Javawocky is the marina, where you can buy seafood (salmon, halibut, cod, snapper, shrimp, crabs, mussels, and more)—perfect if you're camping or have a motel room with a kitchen. Also at the marina is **Troller's** (104 Front St., 250/741-7994, daily for lunch and dinner in summer, $8–15), with tables and chairs set up around a small takeout counter on one of the arms of the floating dock. As you may expect, the specialty is fish-and-chips. Overlooking the marina, **Lighthouse Bistro** (50 Anchor Way, 250/754-3212, daily 11 A.M.–11 P.M., $8–15.50) is built over the water and has a large heated outdoor deck. The salmon chowder is excellent, served with delicious bread.

Dinghy Dock Pub (250/753-2373, daily 11 A.M.–11 P.M., $12–19) is a floating restaurant moored at nearby Protection Island. Well known for great food and plenty of seagoing atmosphere, the pub also hosts live entertainment on Friday and Saturday nights. To get to the restaurant, take a ferry from Nanaimo Boat Basin. Ferries (250/753-8244) depart hourly 9:10 A.M.–11:10 P.M.

For some of the best Mexican food on the island, head for **Gina's Mexican Cafe,** behind the courthouse (47 Skinner St., 250/753-5411, daily for lunch and dinner, $8–17). The building, a converted residence, is hard to miss—the exterior is painted shades of purple and decorated with a fusion of Mexican and maritime memorabilia.

INFORMATION AND SERVICES

Nanaimo is promoted to the world by **Tourism Nanaimo** (250/756-0106 or 800/663-7337, www.tourismnanaimo.com). The main **Nanaimo Visitor Centre** (2290 Bowen Rd., daily 9 A.M.–6 P.M. in summer, Mon.–Sat. 9 A.M.–5 P.M. the rest of the year) is north of downtown and off the main highway on the grounds of Beban Park.

The main **post office** is on Front Street in the Harbour Park Mall. For emergencies, head to **Nanaimo Regional General Hospital** (1200 Dufferin Cres., 250/754-2141). If you need a pharmacy, go to the centrally located **Pharmasave** (530 5th St., 250/753-8234).

GETTING THERE AND AROUND

BC Ferries (250/386-3431) operates regular services between Vancouver and Nanaimo along two different routes. Ferries leave Vancouver's Tsawwassen terminal up to eight times a day for the two-hour trip to Nanaimo's **Duke Point** terminal, 20 minutes south of downtown. Through downtown, at the north end of Stewart Avenue, is the **Departure Bay** terminal. Ferries from Vancouver's Horseshoe Bay terminal leave up to 11 times a day for Departure Bay. Fares on both routes are the same (adult $13.50, child $6.75, vehicle $45). Limited online reservations are taken ($15 plus ferry fare). **West Coast Air** (604/606-6888 or 800/347-2222) and **Harbour Air** (250/714-0900 or 800/665-0212) fly daily between Vancouver and the seaplane base in downtown Nanaimo for $105 one-way.

From the **Greyhound** depot (corner of Terminal Ave. and Comox Rd., 800/753-4371), buses depart daily for points north and south of Nanaimo and west to Port Alberni and Tofino.

Rental car agencies include **Avis** (250/245-4166), **Budget** (250/754-7368), **Discount** (250/758-5171), **National** (250/758-3509), and **Rent-a-wreck** (250/753-6461).

GABRIOLA ISLAND

Like the Southern Gulf Islands, Gabriola (population 3,500) is partly residential, but also holds large expanses of forest, abundant wildlife, and long stretches of unspoiled coastline. The ferry from Nanaimo docks at Descanso Bay, on the west side of the island. Take Taylor Bay Road north from the ferry terminal to access the island's best beaches, including those within tiny **Gabriola Sands Provincial Park.** Walk out to the park's southern headland to view sandstone cliffs eroded into interesting shapes by eons of wave action. The North and South Roads encircle the island, combining for a 30-kilometer (18.6-mile) loop perfect for a leisurely bike ride. Many scenic spots invite you to pull off—at petroglyphs, secluded bays, and lookouts. **Drumbeg Provincial Park** protects the island's southeast corner, where a short trail through dense forest leads to a secluded bay.

Practicalities

For romantic themed bed-and-breakfast accommodation, **Marina's Hideaway** (943 Canso Dr., 250/247-8854 or 888/208-9850, www.marinashideaway.com, $165 s or d), overlooking Northumberland Channel, is an excellent choice. Each of the three spacious guest rooms in this magnificent waterfront home has a king-size bed, gas fireplace, private entrance, and balcony.

Basic services are available a little over one kilometer (0.6 miles) from the ferry terminal on North Road. There you'll find a café, grocery store, and **Gabriola Island Visitor Centre** (Berry Point Rd., 250/247-9332, www.gabriolaisland.org, daily 10 A.M.–6 P.M. July–early Sept.).

BC Ferries (250/386-3431) schedules 15 sailings daily between the terminal off Front Street in Nanaimo (downtown, across from Harbour Park Mall) and Gabriola Island. The trip takes 20 minutes each way. The peak round-trip fare is adult $8.60, child $4.30, vehicle $20.50.

West Coast

From Nanaimo, it's 35 kilometers (21.7 miles) northwest up Highway 19 to one of Vancouver Island's main highway junctions, where Highway 4 spurs west to Port Alberni and the island's west coast. Follow Highway 4 to its end to reach Pacific Rim National Park, a long, narrow park protecting the wild coastal strip and some magnificent sandy beaches, and Tofino, a picturesque little town that makes the perfect base for sea kayaking, whale-watching, or fishing excursions.

HIGHWAY 4 TOWARD PORT ALBERNI

After turning off Highway 19, make your first stop at **Englishman River Falls Provincial Park,** where the Englishman River cascades down a series of beautiful waterfalls. Within the park you'll find a picnic area, easy hiking trails to both the upper and lower falls, crystal-clear swimming holes, and plenty of unserviced campsites ($19) among tall cedars and lush ferns.

Coombs to Port Alberni

What started just over 30 years ago as a simple produce stand has grown into the **Old Country Market** (250/248-6272, daily 8 A.M.–9 P.M.), the lifeblood of Coombs, along Highway 4A west of Nanaimo. Before moving inside the market building, you'll want to stand out front and look upward, where several goats can be seen contentedly grazing along the roof line, seemingly oblivious to the amused, camera-clicking visitors. Inside is a selection of goodies of epic proportions—a bakery, deli, ice-cream stand, and a wealth of healthy island-grown produce. Behind the main building and in an adjacent property are rows of arty shops selling everything from pottery to jewelry to kites.

Little Qualicum Falls Provincial Park is a 440-hectare (1,100-acre) reserve 10 kilometers (6.2 miles) west of Coombs. The park's main hiking trail leads alongside the Little Qualicum River to a picturesque waterfall. Take your fishing pole along the riverside trail and catch a trout, stop for an exhilarating dip in one of the icy emerald pools, or stay the night in a sheltered riverside campsite ($19).

At the west end of Cameron Lake, Highway 4 dives into one of the last remaining easily-accessible stands of old growth forest in British Columbia. The tallest trees are protected by **MacMillan Provincial Park** (also known as Cathedral Grove). The road through the park is very narrow, so take extra care pulling into the main parking lot. From this point, a 500-meter (0.3-mile) trail leads through a majestic stand of 200- to 800-year-old Douglas firs that rise a neck-straining 70 meters (230 feet) from the forest floor.

PORT ALBERNI AND VICINITY

At the head of the island's longest inlet, Port Alberni is an industrial town of 17,500

Alberni Harbour Quay

© ANDREW HEMPSTEAD

centered around the forestry industry. The town's three mills—lumber, specialty lumber, and pulp and paper—are its main sources of income. But despite this industry, Port Alberni has much to offer, including interesting museums, nearby provincial parks, and a modern marina filled with both charter fishing boats and tour boats, including the famous **MV Lady Rose.**

Sights

Follow the signs from Highway 4 to brightly decorated **Alberni Harbour Quay** (Argyle St.), where you can climb a tower for a great view of the quay, harbor, marina, inlet, and surrounding mountains. Off Argyle Street is Industrial Road, which leads to the **Maritime Discovery Centre** (2750 Harbour Rd., 250/723-6164, daily 10 A.M.–5 P.M., donation). Ensconced in a red and white lighthouse, children will love the hands-on displays that explore the importance of the ocean to the town's history.

Find out more about the origins of the West Coast Trail, see a collection of Nuu-chah-nulth artwork, or tinker with a variety of operating motorized machines from the forestry industry at the **Alberni Valley Museum** (4255 Wallace St., 250/723-2181, Tues.–Sat. 10 A.M.–5 P.M., donation).

Practicalities

Within walking distance of the quay is **Bluebird Motel** (3755 3rd Ave., 250/723-1153 or 888/591-3888, www.bluebirdalberni.ca, $79 s, $89 d), with reliable but unsurprising rooms. Right downtown, at the **Hospitality Inn** (3835 Redford St., 250/723-8111 or 800/723-8111, www.hospitalityinnportalberni.com, $145 s or d), each of the large rooms is air-conditioned and features a comfortable bed and writing desk. **Stamp River Provincial Park** ($19), northwest of Port Alberni, enjoys a beautiful location on the river of the same name. To get there, follow Highway 4 west, and immediately after crossing Kitsuksus Creek take Beaver Creek Road north for 14 kilometers (8.7 miles).

The best place for something to eat is down at Alberni Harbour Quay, where you'll find a

number of small cafes with outdoor seating. At the entrance to the quay is **Blue Door Cafe** (5415 Argyle St., 250/723-8811, daily from 5 A.M.), a small old-style place that's a real locals' hangout. Breakfasts are huge; an omelet with all the trimmings goes for $6–7.50, and bottomless self-serve coffee is an extra buck.

On the rise above town to the east is **Port Alberni Visitor Centre** (2533 Redford St., 250/724-6535 or 866/576-3662, www.avcoc.com, Mon.–Fri. 9 A.M.–5 P.M., Sat.–Sun. 10 A.M.–2 P.M.).

MV *LADY ROSE*

This vintage Scottish coaster (250/723-8313 or 800/663-7192, www.ladyrosemarine.com) has been serving the remote communities of Alberni Inlet and Barkley Sound since 1949 as a supply and passenger service. But because of the spectacular scenery along the route, the cruise is also one of the island's biggest tourist attractions. Depending on the time of year, orcas and gray whales, seals, sea lions, porpoises, river otters, bald eagles, and all sorts of seabirds join you on your trip through magnificent Barkley Sound.

Year-round, the MV *Lady Rose* departs Alberni Harbour Quay Tuesday, Thursday, and Saturday at 8 A.M., reaching Bamfield at 12:30 P.M. After a one-hour layover, she docks back in Port Alberni at 5:30 P.M. In July and August, sailings are also made to Bamfield on Sunday, with a special stop for kayakers in the Broken Group Islands. The round-trip fare is $60 per person. If you want to stay longer in Bamfield, accommodations are available. June–mid-September an extra route is added to the schedule, with the vessel departing Monday, Wednesday, and Friday at 8 A.M. for the Broken Group Islands, arriving at Ucluelet at 12:30 P.M. for a 90-minute layover before returning to Port Alberni around 7 P.M. ($72). The *Lady Rose* also accesses remote Sechart Lodge, where meals are included in the price of $140 s, $215 d per day.

BAMFIELD

One of the island's most remote communities, this tiny fishing village lies along both sides of a narrow inlet on Barkley Sound. Most people arrive here aboard the **MV Lady Rose** from Port Alberni, but the town is also linked to Port Alberni by a rough 100-kilometer (62-mile) logging road. It's well worth the trip out to go fishing, explore the seashore, or just soak up the atmosphere of this picturesque boardwalk village. Bamfield is also the northern terminus of the **West Coast Trail**.

Practicalities

On the boardwalk, but across the channel from the road-side of the village, **Bamfield Lodge** (250/728-3419, www.bamfieldlodge.com, $100–230 s or d) comprises self-contained cabins set among trees and overlooking the water. Rates include boat transfers from across the channel. Part of the lodge is a restaurant with lots of waterside seating, and the owners also operate a charter boat for fishing and wilderness trips.

UCLUELET

A small town of 1,800 on the northern edge of Barkley Sound, Ucluelet (yoo-CLOO-let) has a wonderfully scenic location between the ocean and a protected bay. Like nearby Tofino, the remote town grew as a logging and fishing center, but unlike its neighbor, tourism has been slower to catch on. You can enjoy all the same pursuits as in Tofino—beachcombing, whale-watching, kayaking, and fishing—but in a more low key manner.

Sights and Recreation

Drive through town to reach **He-tin-kis Park,** where a short trail leads through a littoral (coastal) rainforest to a small stretch of rocky beach. The park and beach are part of the **Wild Pacific Trail,** an ambitious project that will eventually wander along the coastline all the way to Pacific Rim National Park. You can take the trail or continue southward by vehicle to reach the end of the road. The lighthouse here is not the world's most photogenic,

but it gets the job done, keeping ships from running ashore along this stretch of particularly treacherous coastline.

Accommodations and Camping

If you're looking at sharing inexpensive accommodations with an outdoorsy crowd, reserve a bed at **Surfs Inn** (1874 Peninsula Rd., 250/726-4426, www.surfsinn.ca, dorms $27, $65–125 s or d). Contained within a restored home along the main road into town, communal facilities include a lounge with wood-burning fireplace, a modern kitchen, wireless Internet, and plenty of space to store bikes and surfboards.

The weathered "eco-industrial" exterior at **Terrace Beach Resort** (1002 Peninsula Rd., 250/726-2901 or 866/726-2901, www.terracebeachresort.ca, $99–349 s or d) is a little deceiving, as the guest rooms feature west coast contemporary styling through very livable units that range from one-bedroom motel rooms to multi-story oceanfront cabins, linked by elevated boardwalks and all enclosed in an old growth forest. Don't be surprised to see actor Jason Priestley wandering through the forest—he and his family own the lodge.

Food

Get your morning caffeine fix along with a chocolate-cluster muffin at **Cynamoka Coffee House** (1536 Peninsula Rd., 250/726-3407, daily 7 A.M.–6 P.M., lunches $6–8). It's through town, up a steep driveway to the right. If you're camping or have access to a barbeque, make a stop at **Oyster Jim's** (2480 Pacific Rim Hwy., 250/726-7350) to pick up fresh oysters that open naturally over hot coals.

◖ PACIFIC RIM NATIONAL PARK

Named for its location on the edge of the Pacific Ocean, this park encompasses a long, narrow strip of coast that has been battered by the sea for eons. The park comprises three "units," each very different in nature and each accessed in different ways. This section of text covers the **Long Beach Unit,** named for an

11-kilometer (6.8-mile) stretch of beach accessed by Highway 4 to Tofino. (To the south, in Barkley Sound, is the Broken Group Islands Unit, while farther south still is the West Coast Trail Unit, named for the famous hiking trail between Port Renfrew and Bamfield)

Flora and Fauna

Like the entire west coast of Vancouver Island, Pacific Rim National Park is dominated by littoral (coastal) rainforest. Closest to the ocean, clinging to the rocky shore, a narrow windswept strip of Sitka spruce is covered by salty water year-round. These forests of spruce are compact and low-growing, forming a natural windbreak for the old-growth forests of western hemlock and western red cedar farther inland. The old-growth forests are strewn with fallen trees and lushly carpeted with mosses, shrubs, and ferns.

The park's largest land mammal is the black bear, some of which occasionally wander down to the beach in search of food. Also present are black-tailed deer, raccoons, otters, and mink. Bald eagles are year-round residents, but it's the migratory birds that arrive in the largest numbers—in spring and fall, thousands of Canada geese, pintails, mallards, and black brants converge on the vast tidal mudflats of Grice Bay, in the north of the park beyond the Tofino golf course.

Long Beach

Ensconced between rocky headlands is more than 11 kilometers (6.8 miles) of hard-packed white sand, covered in twisted driftwood, shells, and the occasional Japanese glass fishing float. Dense rainforest and the high, snowcapped peaks of the Mackenzie Range form a beautiful backdrop, while offshore craggy surf-battered isles are home to myriad marinelife. You can access the beach at many places, but first stop at the **Wickaninnish Interpretive Centre** (250/726-4212, daily 10:30 A.M.–6 P.M. mid-Mar.–mid-Oct.), which overlooks the entire beach from a protected southern cove. This is the place to learn about the natural and human history of both the park

and the ocean through exhibits and spectacular hand-painted murals.

Through summer Long Beach attracts hordes of visitors. Most just wander along the beach soaking up the smells and sounds of the sea, but some brave the cool waters for swimming or surfing. The waves here are reputed to be Canada's best; rent boards and wetsuits in Ucluelet and Tofino. In winter, hikers dress for the harsh elements and walk the surf-pounded beach in search of treasures, admiring the ocean's fury during the many ferocious storms.

Hiking

The most obvious place for a walk is Long Beach, but other options are worth consideration. From the Wickaninnish Centre, an 800-meter (0.5-mile) trail (15 minutes each way) leads south around a windswept headland, passing small coves and Lismer Beach, then descending a boardwalk to pebbly **South Beach.** Back up the hill, the **Wickaninnish Trail** leads 2.5 kilometers (1.6 miles) over to Florencia Bay; allow 50 minutes each way. The beach along the bay can also be accessed by road off the Wickaninnish Centre access road. Continuing northwest toward Tofino, the **Rainforest Trail** traverses an old-growth littoral rainforest in two one-kilometer (0.6-mile) loops (allow 20 minutes for each). Farther north, at the back of the Combers Beach parking lot, is the trailhead for the 1.6-kilometer (one-mile) **Spruce Fringe Loop.** This trail leads along the beach past piles of driftwood and through a forest of Sitka spruce.

Practicalities

You're not charged a fee just to travel straight through the park to Tofino, but if you stop anywhere en route you need to purchase a **National Parks Day Pass** (adult $9, senior $8, child $4, to a maximum of $20 per vehicle) from the information center or fee station.

The park's one official campground (mid-Mar.–mid-Oct., walk-in tent sites $21, unserviced sites $28) fills up *very* fast every day through summer. But it's in a marvelous location behind **Green Point,** a beautiful bluff above the beach. Facilities include drive-in sites, washrooms, picnic tables, an evening interpretive program, and plenty of firewood ($8), but no showers or hookups. Some sites can be reserved through the Parks Canada Campground Reservation Service (877/737-3783, www.pc-camping.ca) for $12 per reservation.

There are no stores or gas stations in the park, but supplies and gas are available in Ucluelet and Tofino. The **Wickaninnish Restaurant** in the Wickaninnish Interpretive Centre (250/726-7706, daily 10:30 A.M.–6 P.M. mid-Mar.–mid-Oct., lunches $16–27) overlooks the wide sweeping bay for which it's named. It's not particularly cheap, but the views are magnificent; and even if you don't indulge in a full meal, it's a great place to sip a coffee while watching the ocean. Sunday brunch is particularly popular. At the junction of Highway 4 and the roads leading north to Tofino or south to Ucluelet is the **Pacific Rim Visitor Centre** (250/726-4600, daily 9 A.M.–7 P.M. in summer, Tues.–Sat. 10 A.M.–4 P.M. the rest of the year).

TOFINO

The bustling fishing village of Tofino sits at the very end of a long narrow peninsula, with winding Highway 4 being the only road access to the outside world. The closest town of any size is Port Alberni, 130 kilometers (81 miles) to the east (allow at least 2.5 hours); Victoria is 340 kilometers (211 miles) distant. Fishing has always been the mainstay of the local economy, but in the last decade Tofino has grown into a vacation hot spot. While the winter population is under 2,000, in summer the population swells to several times that size and the village springs to life—fishing boats pick up supplies and deposit salmon, cod, prawns, crabs, halibut, and other delicacies of the sea, and cruising, whale-watching, and fishing boats, along with seaplanes, do a roaring business introducing visitors to the natural wonders of the west coast.

The town lies on the southern edge of sheltered **Clayoquot Sound,** known worldwide for an ongoing fight by environmentalists to save the world's largest remaining coastal temperate forest. Around 200,000 hectares (494,000 acres) of this old-growth forest remain; a number of parks, including **Clayoquot Arm Provincial Park, Clayoquot Plateau Provincial Park, Hesquiat Peninsula Provincial Park, Flores Island Provincial Park,** and **Maquinna Marine Provincial Park** have resulted from the Clayoquot Sound Land Use Decision. An influx of environmentally-conscious residents over the last two decades has added flavor to one of the west coast's most picturesque and relaxing towns. And due to a large number of aware residents who like Tofino exactly the way it is, it's unlikely that high-rise hotels or fast-food chains will ever spoil this peaceful coastal paradise.

Sights

Tofino is best known for its outdoor recreation, but an interesting diversion is **Tofino Botanical Gardens** (1084 Pacific Rim Hwy., 250/725-1220, daily 8 A.M.–dusk, adult $10, child free), just before town. Developed by knowledgeable locals, it showcases local flora with the emphasis on a fun, educational experience. One garden is devoted to native species you would find in the adjacent national park, another to plants you can eat (but aren't allowed to). This is the only botanical garden I've visited where a colorfully painted camper van from the 1970s is incorporated into a display.

Eagle Aerie Gallery (350 Campbell St., 250/725-3235, daily 9 A.M.–8 P.M. in summer, daily 9:30 A.M.–5:30 P.M. the rest of the year) features the eye-catching paintings, prints, and sculptures of Roy Henry Vickers, a well-known and highly respected Tsimshian artist. You can watch a documentary about the artist, then browse among the artworks—primarily native Canadian designs and outdoor scenes with clean lines and brilliant colors.

Beaches

If you fancy a long walk along a fabulous shell-strewn stretch of white sand, like to sit on craggy rocks watching the waves disintegrate into white spray, or just want a piece of sun all your own to lie in and work on your tan, head for **Chesterman Beach,** just south of Tofino. From that beach, at low tide you can walk all the way out to **Frank Island** to watch the surf pound the exposed side while the tide creeps in and cuts you off from civilization for a few hours. The turnoff (not marked) to Chesterman Beach is Lynn Road, on the right as you leave Tofino.

Surfing

Surfers wanting to hit the water should head south of town to **Live To Surf** (1180 Pacific Rim Hwy., 250/725-4464). The shop rents surfboards for $25 per day and wetsuits for $20, and offers lessons for $75 for two people. The staff will also tell you where the best surf can be found, and if there's no surf, they'll tell you how good it was last week. **Surf Sister** (625 Campbell St., 250/725-4456 or 877/724-7873) is Canada's only all-women surf school.

Whale-Watching

Whale-watching is one of the most popular activities in town, and companies search out whales to watch them cruise up the coast, diving, surfacing, and spouting. Each spring around 20,000 Pacific gray whales migrate between Baja and Alaska, passing through the waters off Tofino between March and May. Most of them continue north, but some stay in local waters through summer. Their feeding grounds are north of Tofino within **Maquinna Marine Park.** On the whale-watching trips, you'll likely spy other marinelife as well; look for sea lions and puffins sunning themselves on offshore rocks, dolphins and harbor seals frolicking in the bays and inlets, and majestic bald eagles gracefully swooping around in the sky or perching in the treetops. Trips depart mid-February–October and generally last 2–3 hours. Expect to pay about $80–90 per person. Most of the whale-watching companies offer a combination trip that includes a soothing soak at **Hotsprings Cove.** For details, contact: **Jamie's** (606 Campbell St., 250/725-3919 or 800/667-9913, www.jamies.com), **Remote Passages** (71 Wharf St., 250/725-3330 or 800/666-9833, www.remotepassages.

com), or the **Whale Centre** (411 Campbell St., 250/725-2132 or 888/474-2288, www.tofino-whalecentre.com).

Sea Kayaking

Exploring the waters around Tofino by sea kayak has become increasingly popular in recent years. **Tofino Sea Kayaking Company** (320 Main St., 250/725-4222, www.tofino-kayaking.com) has designed tours to meet the demand and that suit all levels of experience. Excursions range from a 2.5-hour harbor paddle ($59 per person) to an extended trip to a remote lodge on Vargas Island (three days for $780 per person). The company's experienced staff will also help adventurous, independent paddlers plan an itinerary—many camping areas are within a one-day paddle of Tofino. Single kayak rentals are $52 for one day or $44 per day for two or more days. Double kayaks are $88 and $78, respectively.

Accommodations

Tofino boasts plenty of excellent accommodations, both in town and south along the beach-fringed coastline. But getting a room or campsite in summer can be difficult if you just turn up, so book as far ahead as possible.

Tofino's least expensive accommodation is **Whalers on the Point Guesthouse** (81 West St., 250/725-3443, www.tofinohostel.com, dorm $32, $90–100 s or d). Affiliated with Hostelling International, it is a stylish log structure with a stunning waterfront location, of which the communal lounge area takes full advantage. Other facilities include a modern kitchen, wireless Internet, laundry, large deck with a barbecue, game room, and bike rentals.

Out of town to the south are a number of oceanfront resorts. Of these, **◖ Middle Beach Lodge** (250/725-2900 or 866/725-2900, www.middlebeach.com, $140–400 s or d) does the best job of combining a unique west coast experience with reasonable prices. It comprises two distinct complexes: At the Beach, more intimate and with its own private beach, and At the Headland, with luxurious self-contained chalets built along the top of a rugged headland. A short trail links the two and guests are welcome to wander between them. Outdoor settings are scattered throughout the property.

Cable Cove Inn (201 Main St., 250/725-4236 or 800/663-6449, www.cablecoveinn.com, $225–340 s or d) has a main street address, but you'd never know it sitting on the private deck of your ocean-facing room. It's tucked away in a quiet location overlooking a small cove, yet it's only a two-minute walk from the center of town. Well furnished in a casual yet elegant style, each of the six rooms features a private deck and a fireplace.

You'll find cheaper places to stay in Tofino, but you won't find a lodge like **(Pacific Sands Beach Resort** (Cox Bay, 250/725-3322 or 800/565-2322, www.pacificsands.com, $295–650 s or d), which is perfect for families and outdoorsy types who want to kick back for a few days. Set right on a popular surfing beach eight kilometers (five miles) south of town, guest units come in a variety of configurations, starting with one-bedroom, kitchen-equipped suites. Some of these have a prime beachfront location—ask when booking. The best units are the newest—two-level timber-frame villas equipped with everything from surfboard racks to stainless steel kitchen appliances.

The **(Wickaninnish Inn** (Osprey Lane, Chesterman Beach, 250/725-3100, www.wickinn.com, from $480 s or d) is justifiably regarded as one of the world's great resorts. Just for good measure, the in-house Pointe Restaurant is lauded in a similar manner. Designed to complement the rainforest setting, the exterior post-and-beam construction is big and bold, while the interior oozes west coast elegance. Public areas such as the restaurant, an upscale lounge, a relaxing library, and a downstairs TV room (plasma, of course) make the resort feel like a world unto its self. But it's the guest rooms that will wow you. Spread through two wings, all of the 76 rooms overflow with amenities including fireplaces, oversized soaker tubs, super-comfortable beds, and captivating ocean views through floor-to-ceiling windows.

The Wickaninnish is a five-minute drive south of Tofino, but who cares? You won't want to leave.

Camping

All Tofino's campgrounds are on the beaches south of town, but enjoying the great outdoors comes at a price in this part of the world, with some campsites costing more than $50 a night. Best of the bunch is **Bella Pacifica Campground** (250/725-3400, www.bellapacifica.com, $38–48), which is right on MacKenzie Beach and offers protected tent sites, full hookups, coin-operated showers, and a laundry. Along the same stretch of sand, **Crystal Cove Beach Resort** (250/725-4213, www.crystalcovebeachresort.com, $55) is one of the province's finest campgrounds. Facilities are modern, with personal touches such as complimentary coffee each morning and book exchange.

Food

The **(Common Loaf Bake Shop** (180 1st St., 250/725-3915, daily 8 A.M.–6 P.M.) is a longtime favorite with locals (delicious cinnamon rolls for $1.80); sit outside or upstairs, where you'll have a magnificent view down Tofino's main street and across the sound.

The **Schooner Restaurant** (331 Campbell St., 250/725-3444, daily 9 A.M.–3 P.M. and 5–9:30 P.M., $23–31) has been dishing up well-priced seafood for 50 years. Over time the menu has gotten more creative (think soy-marinated salmon baked on a cedar plank), but old favorites (grilled halibut) still appear. Expect to pay $7–12 for starters and $20–28 for a main.

In an unassuming building near the entrance to town, the **Shelter Restaurant** (601 Campbell St., 250/725-3353, daily from 5:30 P.M., $19–32) brings some big-city pizzazz to tiny Tofino. Inside you'll find an open dining room with imaginative treats such as smoked salmon chowder and macadamia nut-crusted halibut.

South of Tofino, the **(Pointe Restaurant** (Wickaninnish Inn, Osprey Lane, Chesterman

Beach, 250/725-3100, daily for breakfast, lunch, and dinner, $25–42) is quite simply superb in every respect. Built on a rocky headland, the sweeping ocean views from anywhere within the circular dining room are as good as from any restaurant in Canada (ask for a window table when reserving). At breakfast, sparkling wine and orange juice encourage a holiday spirit, or get serious by ordering eggs Benedict with smoked salmon. The lunch and dinner menus highlight seafood and island produce. A good way to start dinner is with the crab bisque or roasted oysters before moving on to the steamed halibut or roasted ling cod. Rounding out a world-class dining experience is the impeccable service and a wine list dominated by Pacific Northwest bottles.

Information and Services

A visit to **Tofino Visitor Centre** (455 Campbell St., 250/725-3414, www.tourismtofino.com, daily 9 A.M.–7 P.M. in summer, daily 9 A.M.–5 P.M. the rest of the year) will ensure you're not bored in this bustling town. **Wildside Booksellers** (320 Main St., 250/725-4222) stocks an excellent selection of natural history and recreation titles.

The **post office**, a **laundry**, and **Tofino General Hospital** (250/725-3212) are all on Campbell Street.

Northern Vancouver Island

Back on the east side of the island, the Inland Island Highway, north of the Highway 4 junction, bypasses a stretch of coast that has developed as a popular holiday area with many beaches, resorts, and waterfront campgrounds.

Approximately halfway up the island is the Comox Valley, a popular year-round destination where you'll find more great beaches and fishing.

North of the Comox Valley, Vancouver Island is mountainous, heavily treed, dotted with lakes, riddled with rivers and waterfalls, and almost completely unsettled. Just one main highway serves the region, passing through the gateway to the north, Campbell River, on its long journey to Port Hardy, terminus for ferries heading north to Prince Rupert.

PARKSVILLE TOWARD COURTENAY
Parksville
Golden sand fringes the coastline between Parksville (population 11,000) and Qualicum Beach. **Parksville Beach** claims "the warmest water in the whole of Canada." When the tide goes out along this stretch of the coast, it leaves a strip of sand up to 1,000 meters (3,300 feet) wide exposed to the sun. When the water returns, voila—sand-heated water. **Rathtrevor Beach Provincial Park,** a 347-hectare (860-acre) chunk of coastline just south of Parksville, protects a long sandy beach, a wooded upland area, nature trails, and bird-watching action that's particularly good in early spring, when seabirds swoop in for an annual herring feast. Plenty of campsites are available, but in summer line up early in the morning to stake your claim (walk-in sites $15, RVs and trailers $24).

Right off Parksville's waterfront downtown strip is **Surfside RV Resort** (200 Corfield St., 250/248-9713, www.surfside.bc.ca, $38–48), packed with families throughout summer. It has all the usual facilities in a prime oceanfront locale (although no surf as the name may suggest).

Qualicum Beach
This beach community (population 7,500) is generally quieter than Parksville, but it shares the same golden sands of Georgia Strait. You can stay on Highway 19 and take the Memorial Avenue exit to reach the heart of the town, but a more scenic option is to continue along the old coastal highway through Parksville. This route is lined with motels, resorts, and RV parks. The attractive downtown area, locally

VANCOUVER ISLAND

known as "The Village," is away from the beach area up Memorial Avenue. If you appreciate high-quality arts and crafts, detour off the main drag at this point and head for the **Old Schoolhouse Arts Centre** (122 Fern Rd. W, 250/752-6133, Mon. noon–4:30 P.M., Tues.–Sat. 10 A.M.–4:30 P.M., free). The gallery occupies a beautifully restored 1912 building, while working artist studios below allow you a chance to see woodcarving, printmaking, pottery, weaving, painting, and fabric art in progress.

Old Dutch Inn (2690 West Island Hwy., 250/752-6914 or 800/661-0199, www.olddutchinn.com, $90–110 s or d) is across the road from the ocean and within walking distance of Qualicum Beach Golf Club. Amenities include an indoor pool, sauna and whirlpool, and a restaurant with lots of outdoor seating. The rooms could be nicer, but the location can't be beat. Give the central campgrounds a miss and continue 16 kilometers (10 miles) northwest from Qualicum Beach to **Qualicum Bay Resort** (5970 West Island Hwy., 250/757-2003 or 800/663-6899, www.resortbc.com, tents $18, hookups $28–32, basic cabins with shared bathrooms $40–55 s or d, motel rooms $85–145 s or d). Separated from the water by a road, this family-oriented resort's facilities include a swimming lake with waterslide, playground, pony rides, game room, ice-cream stand, and restaurant.

Horne Lake Caves

If you can drag yourself away from the beach, consider a half-day detour inland to one of Vancouver Island's most intriguing natural attractions, the Horne Lake Caves. To get there, continue along the old coastal highway for 11 kilometers (6.8 miles) beyond Qualicum Beach and turn off at the Horne Lake Store, following the road for 16 kilometers (10 miles) west to Horne Lake. Two caves are open for exploration without a guide. There's no charge for entering these caves, but you'll need a helmet and light source, which can be rented for $5. Several different guided tours of the more interesting caves are offered. The 90-minute tour

of Riverbend Cave includes a short walk as well as underground exploration and explanation (adult $28, child $22). All caves are open daily 10 A.M.–4 P.M. mid-June–September. A private contractor (250/757-8687, www.hornelake.com) runs the tours using qualified guides. The company also operates the campground ($20–24 per night), has canoes for rent, and organizes a variety of educational programs such as rock climbing and guided nature walks.

COMOX VALLEY

The communities of Courtenay, Cumberland, and Comox lie in the beautiful Comox Valley, nestled between Georgia Strait and high snow-capped mountains to the west. The valley lies almost halfway up the island, 220 kilometers (138 miles) from Victoria, but is also linked to the Sunshine Coast by ferry.

Sights

The valley's largest town and a commercial center for local farming, logging, fishing, and retirement communities, **Courtenay** (population 22,000) extends around the head of Comox Harbour. It's not particularly scenic but has a few interesting sights and plenty of highway accommodations. The main attraction downtown is **Courtenay and District Museum** (207 4th St., 250/334-0686, Mon.–Sat. 10 A.M.–5 P.M., Sun. noon–4 P.M. May–Aug., closed Mon. the rest of the year, donation). The highlight is a full-size replica of an *elasmosaur*. The original—12 meters (39 feet) long and 80 million years old—was found at the nearby Puntledge River. The museum leads tours out to the site daily in July and August and Saturday Apr.–June, on which you have the chance to dig for your very own fossil (adult $25, child $15).

The population of **Comox** is quoted at 12,000, and there's certainly enough room for everyone, but you'd never know it, driving along forested roads that lead to golf courses, retirement communities, and a magnificent stretch of coastline. To reach Comox's small downtown area, take Comox Road eastward after crossing the Courtenay River along Highway 19A. Past the downtown area is a highlight of the valley, **Filberg Heritage Lodge and Park** (Comox Ave. at Filberg Rd., 250/339-2715, daily 8 A.M.). A high hedge hides the property from the outside world, but no admission is charged to wander through the beautifully landscaped grounds that stretch down to Comox Harbour.

Accommodations and Food

The valley's least expensive motels are strung out along the highway (Cliffe Avenue) as you enter Courtenay from the south. The **Anco Motel** (1885 Cliffe Ave., 250/334-2451, www.ancomotelbc.com, $65–75 s, $70–80 d) is typical, with a small outdoor pool as a bonus. Overlooking Gartley Bay south of Courtenay is **Kingfisher Oceanside Resort** (4330 South Island Hwy., 250/338-1323 or 800/663-7929, www.kingfisherspa.com, $185–475 s or d), set around well-manicured gardens and a large heated pool right on the water. The resort also has a spa facility, yoga lounge, a bar with outdoor seating, and a restaurant renowned for its west coast cuisine (and a great Sunday brunch buffet 9:30 A.M.–2 P.M., $25).

An enjoyable place to pitch a tent, **Miracle Beach Provincial Park** ($24) is three kilometers (1.9 miles) off the main highway, 23 kilometers (14.3 miles) north of Courtenay. Highlights include a sandy beach, good swimming and fishing, and nature trails. Look for porpoises and seals at the mouth of Black Creek; orcas in the Strait of Georgia; black-tailed deer, black bear, and raccoons in the park; and seabirds and crabs along the shoreline.

In downtown Courtenay is **Union Street Grill** (477 5th St., 250/897-0081, Mon.–Fri. 11 A.M.–9 P.M., Sat.–Sun. 9 A.M.–9 P.M., $15–26). Come here for well-priced global choices that include a delicious jambalaya and expertly prepared fish from local waters. Save room for a slice of chocolate mocha fudge cake. Also in downtown Courtenay is the **Rose Tea Room** (180 5th St., 250/897-1007, Mon.–Sat. 10 A.M.–7 P.M., afternoon tea $8–12.50), a friendly little place where older locals catch up in a traditional English tearoom setting over simple sandwiches, scones and tea, and

decadent rocky road brownies. Within the waterfront grounds of **Filberg Heritage Lodge** is a small café (Comox Ave. at Filberg Rd., 250/339-2715, Wed.–Mon. 11 A.M.–3 P.M. May–Sept., lunches $7–12), with picnic tables spread out under mature trees. A delightful setting more than makes up for the uninspiring café fare.

Information

Comox Valley Visitor Centre (2040 Cliffe Ave., 250/334-3234, www.comoxvalley-chamber.com, daily 9 A.M.–5 P.M. in summer, Mon.–Fri. 9 A.M.–5 P.M., Sat. 10 A.M.–4 P.M. the rest of the year) is on the main highway leading into Courtenay—look for the totem pole out front.

Ferry to Powell River

BC Ferries (250/386-3431) sails four times daily between Comox and Powell River, saving visitors to northern Vancouver Island from having to backtrack down to Nanaimo or Victoria before returning to the mainland. To get to the terminal, stay on Highway 19 through Courtenay, then take Ryan Road east to Anderton Road. Turn left and follow the signs down Ellenor Road. The regular one-way fare for this 75-minute sailing is adult $11.80, child $5.90, vehicle $37.50.

CAMPBELL RIVER

This scenic resort town of 32,000 stretches along Discovery Passage, 260 kilometers (162 miles) north of Victoria and 235 kilometers (146 miles) southeast of Port Hardy. Views from town—of tree-covered Quadra Island and the magnificent white-topped mountains of mainland British Columbia—are superb, but most visitors come for the salmon fishing.

Sights

The best place to absorb some of the local atmosphere is **Discovery Pier.** The 180-meter (590-foot) long pier is fun to walk on whether you're into fishing or not. Its benches and protected shelters allow proper appreciation of the marina, strait, mountains, and fishing action,

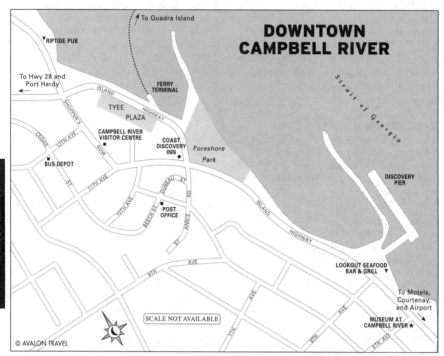

To Quadra Island

DOWNTOWN CAMPBELL RIVER

RIPTIDE PUB

To Hwy 28 and Port Hardy

FERRY TERMINAL

TYEE PLAZA

CAMPBELL RIVER VISITOR CENTRE

COAST DISCOVERY INN

Foreshore Park

BUS DEPOT

POST OFFICE

DISCOVERY PIER

Strait of Georgia

ISLAND HIGHWAY

LOOKOUT SEAFOOD BAR & GRILL

To Motels, Courtenay, and Airport

MUSEUM AT CAMPBELL RIVER ★

SCALE NOT AVAILABLE

© AVALON TRAVEL

even on wet and windy days. May through October is peak season for salmon fishing, but fishing is also good for steelhead (peak season is Jan.–Apr.) and cutthroat trout (Mar.–May). The pier sports built-in rod holders, fish-cleaning stations, shelters for nonanglers, and colorful signs describing the fish you're likely to catch. Anglers cast for salmon (May–Oct.) and the occasional steelhead (Jan.–Apr.), hauling them up in nets on long ropes. When the salmon are running, the pier gets extremely busy, and for good reason—chinook salmon over 14 kilograms (30 pounds) are not uncommon. Rod rentals are available on the pier ($4 per hour, $10 per half-day, $20 per day). Don't forget, you also need a license.

The **Museum at Campbell River** (470 Oceanside Island Hwy., 250/287-3103, daily 10 A.M.–6 P.M. May–Sept., Tues.–Sun. noon–5 P.M. the rest of the year, adult $6, student $4), sits on four hectares (10 acres) overlooking Discovery Passage. First check out the photos and interesting written snippets that provide a look at Campbell River's early beginnings. Then feast your eyes on mystical artifacts, a huge collection of masks, exciting artwork, baskets, woven articles, carved-wood boxes, colorful button blankets, petroglyphs, and totem poles. Finish up in the gift shop, where you can buy stunning native prints, masks, postcards, and other paraphernalia.

Accommodations and Camping

Along the highway south of town only the road separates several motels from Discovery Channel. If you want to save your money for a fishing charter, no worries—book a room at the **Big Rock Motel** (1020 Island Hwy., 250/923-4211 or 877/923-4211, www.bigrockmotel. com, $60 s, $70 d), your average two-story, cinder block motel. Continuing north you'll come to the **Best Western Austrian Chalet** (462 Island Hwy., 250/923-4231 or 800/667-7207, www.bwcampbellriver.com, $99 s, $109 d includes breakfast), with a wide range of facilities including an indoor pool, sauna, barbeque area, and even mini-golf. Right downtown, **Coast Discovery Inn** (975 Shopper's Row, 250/287-7155 or 800/716-6199, www.coasthotels.com, $145 s, $155 d) is a full-service hotel with wireless Internet, a fitness room, restaurant and pub, and a private marina.

The 94-room 🄲 **Painters Lodge** (1625 MacDonald Rd., 250/286-1102 or 800/663-7090, www.painters lodge.com, Mar.–Oct., $219–375 s or d) is one of the better value fishing lodges. It's a grandly presented property that wouldn't look out of place in the English countryside. It's built right on Discovery Passage, with a private marina and every facility a serious angler could ask for. There's also a pool, a restaurant, and free boat shuttles to a sister resort on nearby Quadra Island. Most guests stay as part of a package (for example, $680 for three days, inclusive of flights from Vancouver, accommodation, and fishing trips), or you can build a package that includes guided fishing and water-based nature tours.

Many campgrounds line the highway south of town, and although they're close to the water, the surroundings are generally nothing special. One of the better choices is **Campbell River Fishing Village and RV Park** (260 South Island Hwy., 250/287-3630, www.fishingvillage.bc.ca, $21–25), two kilometers (1.2 miles) south of downtown. As the name suggests, it's set up for anglers, with boat rentals, guided charters, rentals (everything from rods to depth sounders), a tackle shop, and fish-freezing facilities. Other amenities include a playground, laundry, and communal fire pit.

Food

One of the best places to go for a meal is the two-story **Lookout Seafood Bar & Grill** (921 Island Hwy., 250/286-6812, daily 11 A.M.–10 P.M., $9–27), overlooking Discovery Pier and the marina from an absolute waterfront location. The house specialty is, of course, seafood, including a "pail" of clam chowder for $9, fish-and-chips for $11–14, and bouillabaisse for $27. Continuing north along

---

TYEE CLUB

If you're fishing between July 15 and September 15, you may want to try qualifying for Tyee Club membership. This exclusive club, famous among anglers around the world, has been dedicated to upholding the traditional methods of **sportfishing** since 1924. Several rules must be followed in order to become a member: You have to preregister your intent to fish under club rules; troll around the mouth of the Campbell River without using a motor; and use a rod between six and nine feet long, an artificial lure, and a 20-pound-maximum line (not more than 20 pounds pretested breaking weight). Most importantly, you need to land a trophy-size (30 pounds) chinook salmon. The information center supplies a list of charter operators who will fish under these rules, or visit the club website (www.tyeeclub.org).

---

the harbor front is **Riptide Pub** (1340 Island Hwy., 250/830-0044, daily for lunch and dinner, $12.50–22), which is a good place for a full meal, although it doesn't take full advantage of its waterfront location (unless you score a table on the glassed-in patio). The sleek interior is a little nicer than you may imagine while the food is exactly what you'd expect—fresh scallops, oysters, mussels, halibut and salmon.

Information

Park in the large parking lot of **Tyee Plaza** and you're within easy walking distance of the information center and all services. At the front of the parking lot is **Campbell River Visitor Centre** (1235 Shopper's Row, 250/830-0411, Mon.–Sat. 9 A.M.–6 P.M., Sun. 10 A.M.–6 P.M. mid-Apr.–Sept., Mon.–Fri. 9 A.M.–5 P.M., Sat. 10 A.M.–4 P.M. the rest of the year).

QUADRA ISLAND AND VICINITY

A 10-minute ferry ride across Discovery Passage from downtown Campbell River takes you to Quadra Island (population 2,500), which blends beautiful scenery, native culture, and upscale fishing lodges to create a unique and worthwhile detour from your up-island travels. The ferry docks in the south of the island, where most of the population resides. This narrow peninsula widens in the north to an unpopulated area where provincial and marine parks protect a wealth of wildlife. Marinelife around the entire shoreline is widespread; orcas cruise Discovery Passage, and seals and sea lions are commonly spied in surrounding waters.

Sights and Recreation

Learn about the island's long and rich native history at **Nuyumbalees Cultural Centre** (Cape Mudge Village, 250/285-3733, Tues.–Sat. 9 A.M.–5 P.M. May–Sept., adult $15, senior $10, child $5). This excellent facility displays a wide variety of ceremonial dresses used in potlatches, as well as masks and other native artifacts. At the island's southern tip, **Cape Mudge Lighthouse** was built in 1898 to prevent shipwrecks in the wild surging waters around the point. On the east coast is **Heriot Bay,** the name of both a cove and the island's largest community. Narrow Rebecca Spit protects a beach-lined bay from the elements. Roads lead north from Heriot Bay to the island's wild northern reaches, where you can go hiking to the low summit of **Chinese Mountain** (three km/1.9 mi; allow one hour each way), or around **Morte Lake** (five km/3.1 mi; allow 90 minutes for the loop).

Practicalities

The centerpiece of [C] **Tsa-Kwa-Luten Lodge** (250/285-2042 or 800/665-7745, www.capemudgeresort.com, camping $25–30, $145–280 s or d) is the foyer, built by the local Kwagiulth people in the style of a big house (a traditional meeting place) using locally milled woods. Each of the 35 spacious rooms is decorated in northwest native theme, and each has a private balcony with water views. The lodge coordinates fishing charters and cultural activities, and its restaurant specializes in native foods. Another option for campers is the charming

We Wai Kai Campsite (250/285-3111, www.wwkampsite.com), set along a pleasant beach at the head of Heriot Bay. Regular sites are $23, or pay $3 extra for water views.

BC Ferries (250/386-3431) offers services from Campbell River to the island, every hour on the hour 6 A.M.–11 P.M.; round-trip fare is adult $7.90, child $3.95, vehicle $18.50.

Cortes Island

Accessible by ferry from Quadra Island, Cortes Island (pronounced cor-TEZ—it was named by an early Spanish explorer) is a relatively remote place, closer to the mainland than to Vancouver Island. Few visitors venture out here, but those who do are rarely disappointed. Aside from three small villages, the island remains in its natural state. **Manson's Landing Provincial Park** is a beautiful little spot sandwiched between a large tidal lagoon and the forested shoreline of **Hague Lake.** In the south of the island is **Smelt Bay Provincial Park,** another great spot for swimming, beachcombing, and taking in the unique island environment. Camping at Smelt Bay is $15, or park your rig at **Gorge Harbour Marina Resort** (Hunt Rd., Gorge Harbour, 250/935-6433, www.gorgeharbour.com, tent sites $22, hookups $28). This complex also has four guest rooms ($80 s or d for bed-and-breakfast), a small pool, wireless Internet, barbeques, bike and boat rentals, fishing charters, and a restaurant.

The ferry trip between Heriot Bay on Quadra Island and Cortes Island takes 40 minutes. **BC Ferries** (250/386-3431) operates scheduled service between the two islands six times daily, with the first departing Quadra Island at 9 A.M. and the last departing Cortes Island at 5:50 P.M. Peak round-trip fare is adult $9.20, child $4.60, vehicle $21.50.

HIGHWAY 28

Running west from Campbell River, Highway 28 provides access to Strathcona Provincial Park and the west coast. The first place to stop is 1,087-hectare (2,700-acre) **Elk Falls Provincial Park,** six kilometers (3.7 miles) west of Campbell River. Here you can follow beautiful forest trails to waterfalls, go swimming and fishing, and stay the night in the wooded campground (Apr.–Oct., $15).

Strathcona Provincial Park

British Columbia's oldest and Vancouver Island's largest park, Strathcona preserves a vast 250,000-hectare (618,000-acre) inland wilderness, including the island's highest peak, 2,220-meter (7,300-foot) **Golden Hinde.** You'll get a taste of Strathcona's beauty along Highway 28, but to get into the park proper, turn south off Highway 28 halfway between Campbell River and Gold River. This access road hugs the eastern shore of **Buttle Lake,** passing many well-marked nature walks and hiking trails. One of the first is the 10-minute walk to **Lupin Falls,** which are more impressive than the small creek across from the parking lot would suggest. Apart from numerous picnic areas along Buttle Lake, the only facilities within the park are two campgrounds ($15) with unserviced sites only.

◖ TELEGRAPH COVE

Highway 19, covering the 235 kilometers (146 miles) between Campbell River and Port Hardy, traverses relatively untouched wilderness The first of two diversions is the charming village of Telegraph Cove, eight kilometers (five miles) from Port McNeil. Most visitors come to Telegraph Cove to go whale-watching on Johnstone Strait, but the village itself is among the most picturesque on the island. Built around a deep sheltered harbor, it's one of the last existing "boardwalk" communities on the island. Many of the buildings stand on stilts and pilings over the water, linked by a boardwalk. Fewer than 20 people live here year-round, but the population swells enormously during late spring and summer when whale-watching, diving, and fishing charters do a roaring trade, and kayakers arrive to paddle along Johnstone Strait. Walk along the boardwalk, passing cabins, kayak rentals, an art gallery, a small interpretive center, the **Killer Whale Cafe** (late May–mid-Oct.) and a store selling groceries and fishing tackle.

Whale-Watching

Johnstone Strait, offshore from Telegraph Cove, is an unparalleled destination for viewing **orcas** (killer whales) up close and personal. These magnificent, intelligent mammals spend the summer in the waters around Telegraph Cove and are most concentrated in Robson Bight, where they rub on the gravel beaches near the mouth of the Tsitka River.

Stubbs Island Whale Watching (604/928-3185 or 800/665-3066, www.stubbs-island. com, $89 per person) pioneered whale-watching trips in the early 1980s and was involved in the establishment of Robson Bight as an ecological reserve. The company's two boats, *Lukwa* and *Gikumi,* depart Telegraph Cove on 3.5-hour whale-watching cruises daily late May–early October. The experienced crew takes you out to view the whales in their natural habitat and to hear their mysterious and beautiful sounds through a hydrophone (underwater microphone). Both boats are comfortable, with covered areas and bathrooms. Make reservations as far ahead as possible. Dress warmly and don't forget your camera for this experience of a lifetime.

Accommodations and Camping

Many of the buildings on the boardwalk have been converted to guest accommodation and can be rented by the night (reserve well in advance). The quarters range from extremely basic cabins ($110 s or d) to three-bedroom restored houses sleeping up to eight people ($295). About the only thing they have in common is the incredible setting. Finally, a short walk from the village is a campground with wooded sites as well as showers, a laundry, boat launch, and store. Sites are $25–30. For reservations at any of the above options, contact **Telegraph Cove Resorts** (250/928-3131 or 800/200-4665, www.telegraphcoveresort.com).

◖ ALERT BAY

This fascinating village is the only settlement on crescent-shaped Cormorant Island, which lies in Broughton Strait 45 minutes by ferry from Port McNeill. The island's population of 600 is evenly split between natives and nonnatives.

Alert Bay holds plenty of history. Captain Vancouver landed there in the late 1700s, and it's been a supply stop for fur traders and gold miners on their way to Alaska, a place for ships to stock up on water, and home base to an entire fishing fleet. Today the village is one of the region's major fishing and marine service centers, and it has two fish-processing and -packing plants. Half the island is owned by the Kwakiutl, whose powerful art draws visitors to Alert Bay.

Sights

All the island's numerous attractions can be reached on foot or by bicycle. Start by wandering through the village to appreciate the turn-of-the-20th-century waterfront buildings and the colorful totems decorating **Nimpkish Burial Ground.** For an outstanding introduction to the fascinating culture and heritage of the Kwakiutl, don't miss the **U'Mista Cultural Centre** (Front St., 250/974-5403, Mon.–Fri. 9 A.M.–5 P.M., Sat. noon–5 P.M., adult $7, senior $6, child $3). Built to house a ceremonial potlatch collection confiscated by the federal government after a 1921 ban on potlatches, the center contains masks and other Kwakiutl art and artifacts. Take a guided tour through the center, then wander at leisure past the photos and colorful displays to watch two award-winning films produced by the center—one explains the origin and meaning of the potlatch. The center also teaches local children the native language, culture, song, and dance. Also on the north end of the island you'll find the **Indian Big House,** the world's second tallest totem pole (it's 53 meters/174 feet high—the highest is in Victoria), and the historic century-old **Anglican Church.**

Practicalities

The island's least expensive accommodation is **Alert Bay Camping** (250/974-5213, $14–22), overlooking Broughton Strait, with a cook-house and barbecues. On my most recent visit

© ANDREW HEMPSTEAD

Alert Bay is renowned for its totem poles.

to the **Nimpkish Hotel** (318 Fir St., 250/974-2324 or 800/888/646-7547, www.nimpkish-hotel.com, $115–185 s or d), I was surprised to find a completely renovated property with nine beautifully furnished rooms, many with sweeping ocean views and some with luxuries such as jetted tubs and fireplaces. The hotel also has a restaurant, with tables that sprawl outside to a wide waterfront deck.

BC Ferries (250/386-3431) runs to the island from Port McNeill many times daily, with most sailings stopping en route at Malcolm Island. The peak round-trip fare is adult $9.20, child $4.60. You can take a vehicle over for $21.50 round-trip, but there's no real point as everything on the island is reachable on foot.

PORT HARDY

Port Hardy (population 4,600) lies along sheltered Hardy Bay, 235 kilometers (146 miles) north of Campbell River and 495 kilometers (308 miles) north of Victoria. It's the largest community north of Campbell River and the

© ANDREW HEMPSTEAD

Port Hardy is primarily a fishing town.

terminus for ferries sailing the Inside Passage to and from Prince Rupert. The ferry is the main reason most people drive this far north, but Port Hardy is also a good base from which to explore the wild and untamed northern tip of the island or fish for salmon in the sheltered waters of "King Coho Country."

Sights

As you enter the Port Hardy area, take the scenic route to town via Hardy Bay Road. You'll pass several original chainsaw woodcarvings and skirt the edge of peaceful Hardy Bay before entering downtown via Market Street.

One of the most enjoyable things to do in town is to stroll along the seawall to **Tsulquate Park,** where you can appreciate native carvings and do some beachcombing if the tide is out. Many bald eagles reside around the bay, and if you're lucky you'll see them swooping about in the neighborhood. At **Quatse Salmon Stewardship Centre** (Byng Rd., 250/949-9022, daily 8 A.M.–4:30 P.M. May–Sept., adult $5, child $2), the fancy name for a fish hatchery,

you can wander through a gallery realistically depicting typical salmon river habitat and observe incubation and rearing facilities for pink, chum, and coho salmon, as well as steelhead.

Accommodations and Camping

In a town of boring, overpriced motel rooms, **❰ Bear Cove Cottages** (6715 Bear Cove Hwy., 250/949-7939 or 877/949-7939, www.bearcovecottages.ca, mid-Apr.–mid-Oct., $160 s or d) stands out—but as there are only eight of them, you'll need to reserve well in advance. Located right near the ferry terminal, 10 kilometers (6.2 miles) out of town, they sit in a neat row high above the ocean but with stunning water views. Each modern unit comes with a compact but well-designed kitchen, fireplace, a bathroom with jetted tub, and private deck. South of downtown, two hotels overlook Port Hardy's busy harbor from the marina. The **Quarterdeck Inn** (6555 Hardy Bay Rd., 250/902-0455 or 877/902-0459, www.quarterdeckresort.net, $125–150 s or d) offers harbor views from each of its 40 smallish rooms. Facilities include a fitness room, sauna, and laundry. The adjacent **Glen Lyon Inn** (6435 Hardy Bay Rd., 250/949-7115 or 877/949-7115, www.glenlyoninn.com, $135–195 s or d) has older rooms in an original wing and larger and much nicer rooms in a newer addition.

Both of Port Hardy's commercial campgrounds are south of town, halfway around Hardy Bay to the ferry terminal. The pick of the two is **Quatse River Campground** (8400 Byng Rd., 250/949-2395 or 866/949-2395, unserviced sites $20, hookups $25) that is operated in conjunction with the adjacent salmon hatchery. Sites are shaded by a lush old-growth forest and you can fish in the river right off the camping area—then move over to the communal fire pit and recall stories of the one that got away. In the vicinity is **Sunny Sanctuary Campground** (8080 Goodspeed Rd., 250/949-8111 or 866/251-4556, $20–24), also on the Quatse River. Facilities include a nature trail, barbecue shelter, modern bathrooms, firewood and fire rings, and a small store.

Food

Port Hardy doesn't offer a large variety of dining options. Wander around town and you'll soon see what there is. At diner-style **Captain Hardy's** (7145 Market St., 250/949-7133, $7.50–11), the advertised breakfast specials are small and come on plastic plates, but cost only about $5. The rest of the day, it's fish-and-chips and other simple seafood dishes. Dine at the **Oceanside Restaurant,** south of downtown in the Glen Lyon Inn (Hardy Bay Rd., 250/949-3050, daily 6:30 A.M.–9 P.M., $9–18) for the opportunity to see bald eagles feeding right outside the window. The menu is fairly standard, but well priced, with many seafood choices.

Information

Port Hardy Visitor Centre (7250 Market St., 250/949-7622, Mon.–Fri. 8:30 A.M.–6 P.M. and Sat.–Sun. 9 A.M.–5 P.M. mid-May–Aug., Mon.–Fri. 9 A.M.–5 P.M. the rest of the year) is right downtown.

Getting There

Port Hardy Airport, 12 kilometers (7.5 miles) south of town, is served by **Pacific Coastal** (800/663-2872) from Vancouver. It's a spectacular flight, with stunning views of the Coast Mountains for passengers seated on the plane's right side. **Greyhound** (250/949-6300) operates once-daily bus service up the length of the island, scheduled to correspond with ferry departures. The departure of the southbound bus links with ferry arrivals. The journey between Victoria and Port Hardy takes a painful nine hours and costs around $120 one-way. The depot is the North Island Transportation Ltd. ticket office (7210 Market Street).

Continuing North by Ferry

Most people arriving in Port Hardy do so with the intention of continuing north with **BC Ferries** (250/386-3431 or 888/223-3779, www.bcferries.com) to Prince Rupert and beyond. The ferry terminal is at Bear Cove, 10 kilometers (6.2 miles) from downtown Port Hardy. The **Northern Expedition** departs Port Hardy at 7:30 A.M. every second day, arriving in Prince Rupert the same evening at 10:30 P.M. The service runs year-round, but departures are less frequent outside of summer. Peak one-way fare is adult $170, child 5–11 $85, vehicle $390. (These peak-season fares are discounted up to 40 percent outside of summer.) Cabins cost $85–115 for the day.

SOUTHERN INTERIOR

The Southern Interior of British Columbia stretches from the Fraser River Valley in the west to the Canadian Rockies in the east. To the south is the U.S. border and to the north is the TransCanada Highway. Geographically, the region is dominated by a series north-to-south-trending mountain ranges. The valleys are generally populated while the mountains remain forested, wild, and full of wildlife such as bears, elk, deer, and moose.

The region's best-known destination is the Okanagan Valley, which is also closest to Vancouver (around four hours by road). This warm, sunny valley extends 180 kilometers (112 miles) between the U.S.–Canada border in the south and the TransCanada Highway in the north. Lush orchards and vineyards, fertile irrigated croplands, low rolling hills,

and a string of beautiful lakes line the valley floor, where you'll also find 40 golf courses, dozens of commercial attractions, and lots and lots of people—especially in summer. To the east of the Okanagan is the historic city of Nelson, which is surrounded by more dramatic mountains, as well as being within easy reach of lakes, parks, hot springs, and even a ghost town. The highest peaks of the Canadian Rockies form British Columbia's eastern boundary, separating the province from neighboring Alberta. On the British Columbia side of the Canadian Rockies (often called the "BC Rockies") are Kootenay and Yoho National Parks, which may lack the bustling resort towns of their famous Albertan neighbors, Banff and Jasper, but they boast the same magnificent mountain vistas, glacially

HIGHLIGHTS

◖ Desert Centre: You'll forget everything you've heard about Canada, the cold, and igloos when you visit the Desert Centre (page 147).

◖ Okanagan Wineries: Spring and fall are particularly good times for touring valley wineries such as the grand Mission Hill Family Estate (page 155).

◖ Kalamalka Lake: Choosing a favorite Okanagan lake is difficult, but my nod goes to this beauty for its stunning hue, sandy beaches, and warm clear water (page 160).

◖ Silver Star Mountain Resort: It's more than just great skiing and boarding; the gold-rush style buildings and packed summer activity program make this resort a worthwhile destination at any time of year (page 162).

◖ Sandon: In the late 1800s, Sandon was home to more than 5,000 miners. Today, you could fit the entire population in the back of a pick-up truck – not that they'd want to leave western Canada's most authentic ghost town (page 169).

◖ Fort Steele Heritage Town: This living museum brings the gold rush era to life through costumed interpreters and musical theater. You can even try your hand at panning for gold (page 172).

◖ Emerald Lake: One of the famously beautiful lakes of the Canadian Rockies presents ample opportunities to hike, canoe, fish, or simply soak up the mountain scenery (page 186).

◖ Lake O'Hara: In a word – magical. Access is limited by a quota system, so take heed of the reservation information and be prepared for a day of hiking you will always remember (page 186).

◖ Burgess Shale: Visiting this site isn't for everyone – it's a strenuous hike along a restricted access trail – but as one of the world's most important paleontological sites, the trek is a once-in-a-lifetime experience (page 187).

◖ Kicking Horse Mountain Resort: I've ridden all the gondolas in western Canada, and my favorite for unbeatable top-of-the-world views is at this four-season resort near Golden (page 190).

LOOK FOR ◖ TO FIND RECOMMENDED SIGHTS, ACTIVITIES, DINING, AND LODGING.

fed streams and rivers, unlimited hiking opportunities, and abundant wildlife.

Recreational opportunities abound throughout the Southern Interior in all seasons. In summer, vacationers descend on the region for its water-related recreation, which revolves around dozens of lakes, some stretching as far as the eye can see, others notable simply for having warm water. Anglers chase trout, kokanee, and bass while others enjoy canoeing, swimming, or sunbathing on the beaches. Much of the region's higher elevations are protected in rugged parks, including Kootenay and Yoho National Parks, along the Continental Divide. While these natural preserves offer plenty of opportunities for day-trippers, it takes extended backcountry trips to fully experience their beauty. But there are also ample opportunities for hiking in more accessible locales, like along the historic Kettle Valley Railway. In winter, a dozen alpine resorts cater to skiers and snowboarders from around the world, but unlike Whistler and the Banff resorts, the emphasis is on low-key powder days and family fun.

PLANNING YOUR TIME

Regardless of your approach to the Southern Interior, you'll spend time driving Highway 3, which branches east at Hope and continues parallel to the United States border all the way to Alberta. If you are winding your way east from Vancouver to Calgary (Alberta), you could plan to take at least two days to travel via the Southern Interior, but you will need at least three or four days to see all the highlights. Along the way, dozens of roads and highways of varying importance branch north through parallel north–south running valleys. The most direct of these is Highway 97 through the Okanagan Valley, which passes the towns of Osoyoos, Penticton, Kelowna, and Vernon. Passing numerous lakes, orchards, and vineyards, it's a truly spectacular drive. You could plan to spend at least one day in and around each population center, mixing traditional sights such as the Desert Centre at Osoyoos with Okanagan wineries and swimming at Kalamalka Lake.

Like the Okanagan Valley, planning your

© ANDREW HEMPSTEAD

Okanagan Valley orchard

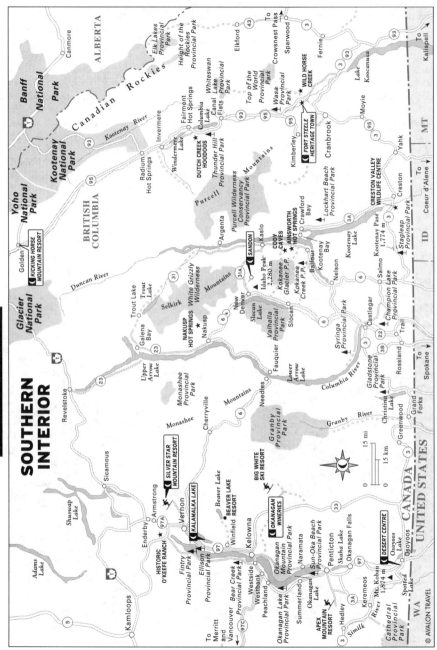

SOUTHERN INTERIOR

time in the Kootenay region is more about your own interests than seeing specific sights. There is historic significance to the main population center of Nelson and the ghost town of Sandon, but you'll also want to allow time for exploring the parks and indulging in water sports. From Nelson, Highway 3 continues its eastward course to the next and easternmost of the Southern Interior's major valleys. The main attractions here are historic parks such as Fort Steele Heritage Town and soothing highlights like Fairmont Hot Springs. Forming the eastern boundary of the Southern Interior are two national parks, Kootenay and Yoho, which are geographically aligned with the famous parks of Alberta, but are within British Columbia. If you've taken three or four days to get this far from Vancouver, plan on another one here, walking around Emerald Lake and taking the gondola at Kicking Horse Mountain Resort. Two of the most special places in the Southern Interior, both within Yoho National Park, require advance planning. Lake O'Hara is only accessible by shuttle bus, while the Burgess Shale can only be visited with a guide.

For many locals, the warm lakes and mountain parks of the Southern Interior are a destinations in themselves, and therefore July through August are by far the busiest months of year. This is when temperatures are at their hottest and the waterways at their busiest. If you're planning to camp, reserve a spot as far in advance as possible. As a general rule, the summer weather will be hot, especially in the Okanagan Valley and along the border, with temperatures cooling off as you climb into the surrounding mountains.

The winter resorts of the Southern Interior are not as well known as Whistler and their counterparts in the Canadian Rockies, but between them they offer something for everyone, from the family atmosphere of Silver Star Mountain Resort to the facilities of Big White to the untracked powder of Red Mountain. If you do decide to visit during the cooler months, you'll find the major attractions open but with shorter hours. Many Okanagan wineries close completely during winter.

One other useful note when planning your time in the Southern Interior: Roads are generally narrow and winding, with mountain passes and ferry crossings slowing down travel time considerably (there are no less than six mountain passes between Hope in the west and Cranbrook in the east).

Vancouver to Penticton

From Vancouver, it's an easy drive through the Fraser River Valley to Hope, from where Highway 3 branches east to Manning Provincial Park and then on to the Okanagan Valley. From Hope, it's 220 kilometers (137 miles) to Penticton, but it's worth the extra time to enter the Okanagan Valley through its southern reaches at Osoyoos.

MANNING PROVINCIAL PARK

This 70,844-hectare (175,100-acre) park in the Cascade Mountains, 64 kilometers (40 miles) east of Hope along Highway 3, stretches down to the Canada–U.S. border. To really appreciate the park, you need to get off the

highway—take in the beautiful bodies of water, drive up to a wonderful stretch of high alpine meadows, or hike through dense subalpine forests.

Sights and Recreation

A summer highlight of the park is driving up to **Cascade Lookout,** a viewpoint offering a magnificent 180-degree panoramic view. Beyond the lookout, the road turns to gravel and continues climbing for nine kilometers, ending at a parking lot surrounded by a rich yellow, orange, and white carpet of wildflowers as far as you can see. Along Highway 3 are some short self-guided nature trails, including a 700-meter

(0.4-mile) walk (20 minutes) through a stand of ancient western red cedars. The trailhead is Sumallo Grove day-use area, 10 kilometers (6.2 miles) east of where Highway 3 enters the park from the west.

At **Manning Park Resort** (250/840-8822, www.manningpark.com), 11 kilometers (6.8 miles) west of Highway 3 along Gibson Pass Road, skiers and snowboarders take advantage of a 437-meter (1,430-foot) vertical rise served by two chairlifts, a T-bar, and a rope tow. Most runs are for intermediate skiers, but novices and experts will also find suitable terrain. Lift tickets are adult $42, senior and child $27. Along with 190 kilometers (118 miles) of wilderness trails, cross-country skiers can enjoy 30 kilometers (18.6 miles) of groomed trails for $15 per day. Cross-country skis rent for $18 per day.

Practicalities

In the heart of the park on Highway 3, **Manning Park Resort** (250/840-8822, www.manning-park.com, $154–349 s or d) is a full-service lodging providing comfortable hotel rooms, cabins, and triplexes, as well as a dining room, self-serve cafeteria, small grocery store, and an open fireside lounge. Other facilities include saunas, indoor pool, TV room, fitness center, tennis courts, coin-operated laundry, and gift shop.

The park's four campgrounds hold a total of 355 sites; in summer, get in early to be assured of snagging one. Each campground provides drinking water and toilets. The most popular is **Lightning Lake** (Gibson Pass Rd., $22), which has showers. The others along Highway 3 have limited facilities and are $15 per site.

The park's **Visitor Information Centre** (250/840-8836, daily 8:30 A.M.–4:30 P.M. in summer, weekdays only the rest of the year.) is one kilometer (0.6 miles) east of Manning Park Resort.

CONTINUING TOWARD THE OKANAGAN VALLEY

From the eastern boundary of Manning Provincial Park, Highway 3 follows the Similkameen River north to Princeton, then turns sharply to the southeast to Osoyoos, at the southern end of the Okanagan Valley, a total distance of 158 kilometers (98 miles).

Princeton

At the confluence of the Similkameen and Tulameen Rivers lies the small friendly ranching town of Princeton (population 3,000). **Princeton and District Museum** (167 Vermilion Ave., 250/295-7588, Mon.–Fri. 1–5 P.M., donation) features pioneer artifacts from Granite City, Chinese and Interior Salish artifacts, and a good fossil display.

On the northeast side of Princeton, the stone-and-concrete ruins of a 1910 cement plant have been incorporated in a unique accommodation complex, ◖ **Princeton Castle Resort** (375 Rainbow Lake Rd., 250/295-7988 or 888/228-8881, www.castleresort.com, camping $30, cabins $165–500 s or d). Surrounding the ruins are cabins and chalets of varying configurations, with the larger chalets taking pride of place along a ridge overlooking a sparkling creek. Beyond the ruins, a road leads up to the resort campground. To get there from Princeton, cross the bridge at the north end of Bridge Street, turn right on Old Hedley Road, cross Highway 5, turn left on Five Mile Road, then continue until the sign to the park leads you right.

Coalmont and Beyond

If you want to see some impressive canyon scenery off the main tourist drag, cross the river at the north end of Princeton's Bridge Street and turn left, heading west toward Coalmont for 18 kilometers (11.2 miles). The attractive 1911 **Coalmont Hotel** (250/295-6066) still serves up beer to thirsty travelers, while quite a number of homes—some with backyards crammed with eclectic collections of rusting mine machinery—line the streets. Travel through Coalmont to reach **Granite City,** site of a gold strike in 1885. After the initial discovery, a 13-saloon gold-rush city sprang to life, quickly becoming the third-largest city in the province. Not much remains of Granite City—a few fallen-down cabins among wild lilac bushes and trees—leaving it to your imagination to re-create the good ol' days.

Cathedral Provincial Park

This remote park protects 33,272 hectares (82,200 acres) of mountainous terrain west of Keremeos. Access along the 21-kilometer (13-mile) road leading into the park is restricted to guests of ◖ **Cathedral Lakes Lodge** (250/226-7560 or 888/255-4453, www.cathedrallakes) or those willing to walk. For this reason, most park visitors stay at the resort, which provides accommodations, meals, use of canoes, a recreation room and hot tub, and transportation to and from the Base Camp, which is accessible by public road. The minimum stay is a two-day package: original cabins and bungalow rooms start at $430 per person, while rooms in the main lodge are $490, inclusive of meals and the shuttle. The lodge also offers the option of a day trip (Fri.–Sun. only) for $150 per person, which includes the shuttle and lunch.

KEREMEOS

As you approach mountain-surrounded Keremeos from the west, the road is lined with lush irrigated orchards and fruit stands, one after another, which is probably what inspired the town's claim to fame as the "Fruit Stand Capital of Canada." Harvest dates are mid-June–mid-July for cherries; mid-July–early August for apricots; mid-July–early September for peaches; mid-August–mid-September for pears; early August–mid-October for apples; early–mid-September for plums; and early September–early October for grapes.

Grist Mill

The town's main historic attraction is the 1877 Grist Mill (250/499-2888, adult $5, child $2.50), where early settlers ground wheat into flour. Costumed interpreters lead tours of the property daily late May–early October, then invite you to try your hand at the many informative and entertaining hands-on displays in the museum and visitor center. A pleasant tearoom overlooks garden plots carefully planted to reflect various eras (the pancake breakfast on summer weekends is a treat). To get there, go through town on the main highway, turn north

© ANDREW HEMPSTEAD

The grist mill in Keremeos has been restored and is still used to grind wheat into flour.

SOUTHERN INTERIOR

on Highway 3A toward Penticton, then right at the Historic Site sign on Upper Bench Road.

OSOYOOS

At the southern end of the Okanagan Valley, this town of 5,000 is nestled on the west shore of **Osoyoos Lake,** Canada's warmest freshwater lake (up to 24°C/75°F in summer). The town also boasts Canada's highest year-round average temperature.

◖ Desert Centre

Away from the valley floor and its many orchards, the landscape is surprisingly arid. In one particular area, a 100-hectare (250-acre) "pocket desert" has the distinction of being Canada's driest spot, receiving less than 300 millimeters (11 inches) of precipitation annually. It is a desert in the truest sense, complete with sand, cacti, prickly pear, sagebrush, lizards, scorpions, rattlesnakes, and other desert dwellers, including 23 invertebrates found nowhere else in the world. Learn more about this unique landscape at the **Desert Centre**

(250/495-2470 or 877/899-0897, summer daily 9:30 A.M.–4:30 P.M., spring and fall daily 10 A.M.–2 P.M., adult $8, senior $7, child $5), a research and interpretive facility, where a boardwalk leads through this very un-Canadian environment. To get there, follow Highway 97 north from Osoyoos, and take 146th Avenue to the west.

Accommodations and Camping

In summer, Osoyoos Lake attracts hordes of water-lovers and sun worshippers, so getting accommodations can be difficult—especially along the prime stretch of lakefront east of downtown along Highway 3. You'll need to book well in advance to get a room during summer at the **C Sandy Beach Motel** (6706 Ponderosa Dr., 250/495-6931 or 866/495-6931, www.sandybeachmotel.com, $169–299 s or d), but you'll be glad you did. Set on a private stretch of sandy beach, the 25-kitchen-equipped units face a grassy courtyard, landscaped with crushed gravel pathways and cacti. Some have one or two separate bedrooms. Along the same stretch but larger and less personal is **Holiday Inn Hotel & Suites** (7906 Main St., 250/495-7223 or 877/660-8550, www.holidayinosoyoos.com, $179 s or d).

Haynes Point Provincial Park (camping $24) protects an extremely narrow low-lying spit that juts into Osoyoos Lake south of downtown. At the far end of the spit is a beautiful campground, with many sites enjoying lakefront settings.

Information

In a parking lot at the corner of Highways 3 and 97 is **Osoyoos Visitor Centre** (9912 Hwy. 3, 250/495-5070, www.destinationosoyoos.com, daily 8 A.M.–6 P.M. in summer, daily 9 A.M.–4 P.M. the rest of the year).

Penticton

One of the Okanagan's three major population centers, Penticton (population 38,000) lies between the north end of Skaha Lake and the south end of Okanagan Lake. The city gets its name from the nomadic Salish natives, in whose tongue Penticton means "Place to Stay Forever." Approaching from the south, you'll see a roadside plaque honoring pioneer Thomas Ellis, who arrived in the valley in 1886, built a great cattle empire, and planted the area's first orchard. Today fruit orchards are everywhere. Penticton's nickname is Peach City; the annual **Peach Festival** celebrates the harvest in mid-August with a week of sailboat races, parades, games, and entertainment. Penticton also participates in the **Okanagan Wine Festival** the first weekend of October, another fruitful event.

SIGHTS AND RECREATION
Downtown

Wander west along the tree-shaded shores of Okanagan Lake to see the **SS *Sicamous*** (1099 Lakeshore Dr. W, 250/492-0403, daily 10 A.M.–4 P.M. mid-Jan–mid-Dec., extended hours 9 A.M.–9 P.M. in summer, adult $5.50, senior $4.50, child $2), a Canadian Pacific Railway sternwheeler that operated on Okanagan Lake from 1914 to 1936. Now resting on the lakeshore, it's easy to spend an hour wandering through the ship, peaking into the purser's office, admiring the furnishings in the grand dining room, and clambering up to the observation deck. The adjacent **rose garden** (free) is worth a stroll to see perfect blooms and manicured lawns, and to read all the stats on the **Okanagan Lake Dam** and flood-control system.

At the opposite end of Lakeshore Drive (to the east) is the **Penticton Art Gallery** (199 Marina Way, 250/493-2928, Tues.–Fri. 10 A.M.–5 P.M., Saturday noon–5 P.M., adult $2, free on weekends), home to locally themed exhibitions.

Penticton Museum (785 Main St., 250/490-2454, Tues.–Sat. 10 A.M.–5 P.M., adult $2.50, child $1) houses an excellent collection

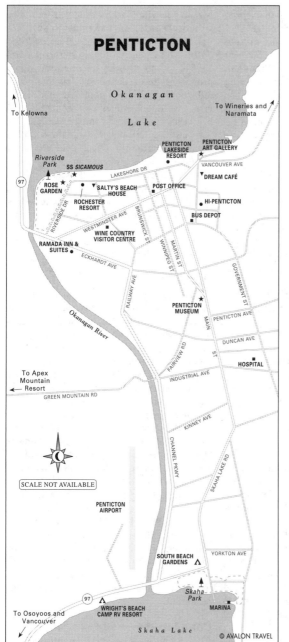

of western Canadian artifacts, covering natural history, local native peoples, the fur-trading days, the gold rush, railways, early Chinese residents, and sternwheelers. It also features an enormous taxidermy section; mining, ranching, and ghost-town artifacts and treasures; and assorted military miscellany.

To Naramata

A 14-kilometer (8.7-mile) secondary road runs northeast out of Penticton, skirting the east side of Okanagan Lake and passing through the small community of **Naramata.** The first of many well-respected wineries along the way is the **Red Rooster Winery** (891 Naramata Rd., 250/492-2424, daily 10 A.M.–6 P.M. Apr.–Oct., daily 11 A.M.–5 P.M. the rest of the year), easily recognized by the mission-style tasting room beside the highway. No tours—instead, enjoy a tasting session of the winery's acclaimed pinot gris and chardonnay wines, then soak up the lake views over a cheese platter or slice of quiche on the verandah. Next up is the aptly named **Hillside Estate** (1350 Naramata Rd., 250/493-6274), with an impressive three-story wooden building holding the main winery. Hillside is known for its pinot noir, but it also produces an unusually dry but fruity riesling. Its wine shop and restaurant are open daily in summer.

Naramata itself is a charming lakeside village, far removed from the commercialism of Penticton. Access to the lake is somewhat limited, although the public beach at Manitou Park is good for swimming.

Continue through Naramata and up into the mountains, where the road fizzles out near the south border of undeveloped **Okanagan Mountain Provincial Park,** still recovering from wildfires that swept through in 2003. The only way to get into this piece of untouched wilderness is to walk or boat over. Hike in for the day for a picnic, some fishing, or to explore the 24 kilometers (15 miles) of trails.

EVENTS

Penticton seems to have festivals, parades, events, or competitions going on throughout the year. The biggest event is the annual **Penticton Peach Festival** (250/487-9709, www.peachfest.com), held on the first weekend of August; it's a tradition going back more than 50 years. Events include peach tasting, the crowning of Miss Penticton, Kiddies Day (the Sunday), a sandcastle competition, fireworks, and nightly entertainment in Gyro Park.

Other annual happenings include the **Spring Wine Festival** (250/861-6654, www.thewinefestivals.com), hosted by many local wineries in late April; the **Ironman Canada** (250/490-8787, www.ironman.ca) triathlon the last Sunday in August; and the **Pentastic Jazz Festival** (www.pentasticjazz.com) the second weekend of September.

ACCOMMODATIONS
In Town

As you'd expect in a resort town, the only accommodation under $50 is in a dormitory. **HI-Penticton** (464 Ellis St., 250/492-3992, www.hihostels.ca, dorm $25–29, $58–96 s or d) occupies a 1950s white stucco residence close to the heart of downtown. Facilities include a kitchen, laundry, bike rentals, and an outdoor barbecue area. Check-in is 8 A.M.–noon and 5–10 P.M.

The least expensive of several lodgings on Lakeshore Drive, close to both the lake and downtown, is the 36-room **Rochester Resort** (970 Lakeshore Dr., 250/493-1128, from $129 s or d). All units have a kitchen and there's a communal barbecue area for guest use. Rooms

here in the winter go for as low as $60. The six-story **Penticton Lakeside Resort** (21 Lakeshore Dr. W, 250/493-8221 or 800/663-9400, www.pentictonlakesideresort.com, $195–275 s or d) is an upscale, downtown property right on the lake. It has more than 200 rooms, an indoor pool overlooking the lake, a whirlpool, saunas, two tennis courts, a bar with a lakeside deck, and a restaurant.

Away from the water, **Ramada Inn & Suites** (1050 Eckhardt Ave. W, 250/492-8926 or 800/665-4966, www.penticton ramada.com, $179 s or d) is a family-friendly, self-contained resort adjacent to an 18-hole golf course. Amenities include an outdoor pool, sprawling courtyard, playground, fitness center, restaurant, and poolside bar. The rooms are decorated in smart color schemes, are air-conditioned, and have no-charge wireless Internet.

Naramata

Located in the village of Naramata, 14 kilometers (8.7 miles) north of Penticton, **Village Motel** (244 Robinson Dr., Naramata, 250/496-5535, www.villagemotel.com) will bring back memories of a bygone era. The nine guest rooms are nicely decorated and open to landscaped gardens and communal barbecue area. Regular rooms are $90 s or d, or pay $145 for a kitchen unit. The motel is within walking distance of the lake.

For the atmosphere of an old-fashioned resort, it's difficult to pass up the **C Naramata Heritage Inn & Spa** (3625 1st St., Naramata, 250/496-6808 or 866/617-1188, www.naramatainn.com, $212–540 s or d includes breakfast). Dating to 1908, the hotel has been completely renovated, yet none of its historic appeal has been lost. The guest rooms have mission-style beds covered with plush duvets, bathrooms with heated floors and claw-foot tubs, and either a balcony or patio. Other amenities include spa services, a wine bar with live jazz on Friday evenings, and a fine-dining restaurant.

Camping

All Penticton's commercial campgrounds are

south of downtown around the north end of Skaha Lake. They're very popular in summer, so make reservations in advance if possible. The least-crowded seems to be **Wright's Beach Camp RV Park** (4200 Skaha Lake Rd., 250/492-7120, www.wrightsbeachcamp.com, unserviced sites $40, hookups $48–53), which is a little bit surprising as it's right on the lake and has a huge playground and an outdoor pool. Across from Sudbury Beach and adjacent to Hwy. 97 is **South Beach Gardens** (3815 Skaha Lake Rd., 250/492-0628, www.southbeachgardens.net, May–Sept., $32–41).

If being by the lake isn't important, choose to stay at **Twin Lakes Golf & RV Resort** (Hwy. 3A, 250/497-8379, www.twinlakesgolfresort.com, Apr.–mid-Oct., $32–37), 19 kilometers (12 miles) southwest of Penticton. The campground is set in the middle of a full-length golf course (greens fees $69, but discounted to $55 for campers), which is surrounded by barren cliffs. Amenities include modern washrooms, free firewood, a restaurant, and a lounge. To get to Twin Lakes, head south from Penticton and turn west off Highway 97 at Kaleden. If you're traveling east from Princeton, turn off Highway 3 at Keremeos.

FOOD

Penticton has a wide variety of restaurants spread along the beach and through downtown. My favorite is the **Ⓒ Dream Café** (74 Front St., 250/490-9012, Wed.–Fri. 11 A.M.–9 P.M., Sat.–Sun. 10 A.M.–9 P.M., $6–19), away from the water but with a dreamy ambience (think eclectic furniture, colorful kites hanging from the ceiling, and soothing background music), friendly staff, and innovative cuisine. The menu takes from throughout Asia: mango roasted chicken, salmon spinach pie, vegetarian Thai curry, rice noodle wraps, and crab cakes with roasted vegetables.

Across the road from the beach along the busy downtown tourist strip is **Salty's Beach House** (1000 Lakeshore Dr., 250/493-5001, daily from 11 A.M., $12–26), with tables inside and out. The menu blends conventional pub

fare with Thai and Caribbean cuisine such as pad Thai and a mango chicken sandwich. The fruity drink menu befits the location.

INFORMATION AND SERVICES

Wine Country Visitor Centre (553 Railway St., 250/493-4055 or 800/663-5052, www.tourismpenticton.com, daily 8 A.M.–7 P.M. in summer, Mon.–Fri. 9 A.M.–6 P.M., Sat.–Sun. 10 A.M.–5 P.M. the rest of the year) is not particularly well signed, but worth stopping at nevertheless. Inside the distinctive adobe style structure is free Internet access, a wine information center, and lots of local literature. From the south, follow the signs north to Kelowna and take Westminster Ave. right off Eckhardt Ave. (Hwy. 97); it's off to the right after a few blocks. Coming into town from the north, cross the canal and take the second road on the left (Westminster Avenue).

Okanagan Books (233 Main St., 250/493-1941) stocks a wide range of local reading as well as all the current bestsellers.

Penticton Regional Hospital is on Carmi Ave. (250/492-4000). The **post office** is on the corner of Winnipeg Street and Nanaimo Avenue.

NORTH OF PENTICTON

Highway 97 links Penticton and Kelowna, running along the west side of Okanagan Lake for the entire 60 kilometers (37 miles). The first worthwhile stop is tiny **Sun-Oka Beach Provincial Park,** a sun-drenched, south-facing park with a sandy beach, paddle boat rentals, and a concession.

Summerland

As you enter picturesque Summerland, nestled between Giants Head Mountain and the lake 16 kilometers (10 miles) north of Penticton, turn west (away from the lake) to reach the **Summerland Sweets** factory (6206 Canyon View Dr., 250/494-0377) to see syrups, jams, and candy being made from fresh and frozen fruit. From Highway 97 take the Dunn Street or Arkell Road exit west, turn right on Gartrell Road, left on Happy Valley Road, right on Hillborn Street, then left on Canyon View Road.

Sumac Ridge Estate (one km/0.6 mi north of Summerland on the lake side of the highway, 250/494-0451) was British Columbia's first estate winery. Today, this well-recognized name appears on a wide variety of red and white wines, including an award-winning cabernet franc and one of the Okanagan's few sparkling wines. Tours and tastings are offered May to mid October two or three times daily., and a bistro is open daily for lunch and dinner year-round.

Continuing Toward Kelowna

On the way to Kelowna you'll pass two entrances to **Okanagan Lake Provincial Park,** a grassy, beach-fringed park popular for boating, swimming, and camping (Apr.–Oct., $24). Ponderosa pines line the shore while exotic trees such as maple and oak shade dozens of picnic tables.

Farther along is the community of **Peachland.** Crammed between a rocky bluff and Okanagan Lake, Peachland was founded in 1808 by Manitoba entrepreneur and newspaperman John Robinson, who came to the Okanagan in search of mining prospects but turned his talents to developing the delicious locally grown dessert peaches. The drive through downtown is a pleasant diversion from Highway 97. On one side is the lake and a long pebbly beach dotted with grassed areas of parkland and supervised swimming areas. On the other is a collection of shops and cafés.

Kelowna

British Columbia's largest city outside the Lower Mainland and Victoria, Kelowna lies on the shores of 170-kilometer (106-mile) long Okanagan Lake, approximately halfway between Penticton in the south and Vernon in the north. The city combines a scenic location among semiarid mountains with an unbeatable climate of long, sunny summers and short, mild winters. The low rolling hills around the city hold lush terraced orchards, and the numerous local vineyards produce some excellent wines. Visitors flock here in summer to enjoy the area's sparkling lakes, sandy beaches, numerous provincial parks, and golfing; in winter they come for great skiing and boarding at nearby Big White Ski Resort.

History

For thousands of years before the arrival of the first Europeans, the nomadic Salish peoples inhabited the Okanagan Valley, hunting (*kelowna* is a Salish word for grizzly bear), gathering, and fishing. Since Father Pandosy planted the first apple trees at his mission in 1859, Kelowna has thrived as the center of the Okanagan fruit, vegetable, and vineyard industry (the valley is

Canada's largest fruit-growing region). In 1960, Kelowna's population stood at 24,000, but as local services improved, the region has become more attractive to older, retired people. In the few years since the millennium, the population has really boomed, and now stands at 115,000, with the number of wineries doubling since the mid-1980s, luxurious resorts being built along the lake, new golf courses opening every year, and exclusive subdivisions carving away land formerly given over to agriculture.

SIGHTS
Downtown

Right downtown, beautiful **City Park** is the largest of Kelowna's many parks. Its 14 hectares (35 acres) hold lots of flowers and large shady trees, expansive lawns, and a long sandy beach. A promenade leads north from the Ogopogo statue past a large marina and a prime waterfront site undergoing redevelopment. Beyond the construction is the **Delta Grand Okanagan Resort** (1310 Water St., 250/763-4500), the Okanagan's most luxurious accommodation. Even if you can't afford a lakefront suite, the resort holds a bar and restaurant with water

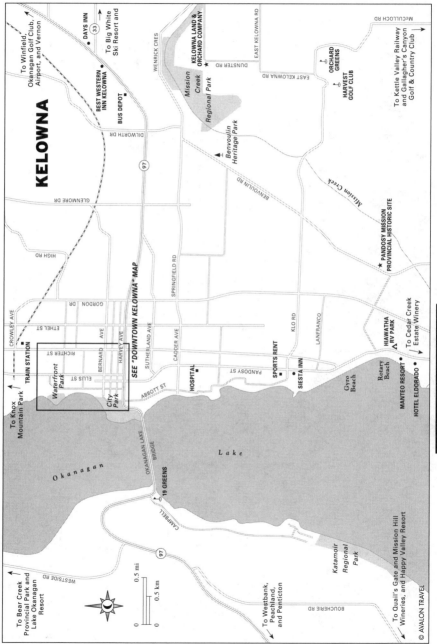

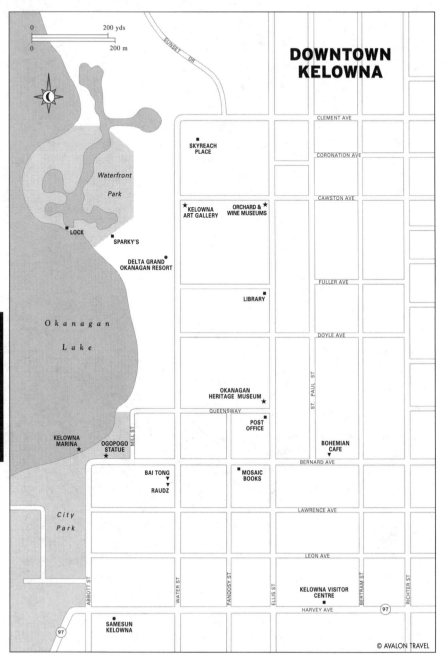

FATHER PANDOSY

The first European to settle in the valley, Father Pandosy, an oblate priest, established a mission on the southern outskirts of present-day downtown Kelowna in 1859. He operated a church, school, and farm here, ministering to natives and whites until his death in 1891. His mission claimed a lot of "firsts" – first white settlement in the Okanagan Valley, first school in the valley, first fruit and vine crops in the valley, and first Roman Catholic mission in the British Columbia interior. Now protected as **Pandosy Mission Provincial Heritage Site** (Benvoulin Rd., daily 8 A.M.–dark, donation), the site remains virtually untouched since Father Pandosy's day, including a chapel and a barn filled with antique farming equipment.

views. Beyond the resort, the promenade crosses a small lock, which allows boaters to travel between the higher water level of an artificial lagoon and the lake itself. Here, you can rent watercraft from **Sparky's** (250/862-2469).

Okanagan Heritage Museum (470 Queensway Ave., 250/763-2417, Mon.–Fri. 10 A.M.–5 P.M. Sat. 10 A.M.–4 P.M., by donation) is opposite the post office; look for the brightly painted totem pole marking the entrance. The museum holds a mishmash of fascinating displays, including horse-drawn carriages; fossils found in the Princeton area; indigenous arts, crafts, clothing, jewelry, beads, and furs; children's books and games; radio equipment; pioneer artifacts; re-creations of an 1861 Kelowna trading post and a Chinese store; and a display of the interior of a Salish winter dwelling. Behind the museum is **Kasugai Gardens,** a quiet retreat from the downtown business district. **Kelowna Art Gallery** (1315 Water St., 250/762-2226, Tues.–Sat. 10 A.M.–5 P.M., Sun. 1–4 P.M., by donation) is a modern facility hosting touring exhibitions and maintaining a permanent collection of contemporary

and historical works by artists from throughout the province.

In an old downtown packinghouse, complete with exposed red-brick walls and hand-hewn wooden beams, the **Orchard Museum** (1304 Ellis St., 250/763-0433, Mon.–Fri. 10 A.M.–5 P.M., Sat. 10 A.M.–4 P.M., donation) tells the story of the local orchard industry through rare photographs, displays, and a hands-on discovery corner. In the same building, the **Wine Museum** (250/868-0441, Mon.–Fri. 10 A.M.–6 P.M., Sat. 10 A.M.–5 P.M., Sun. 11 A.M.–5 P.M., free) has information on local wineries and tours, and sells the finished product.

◖ Okanagan Wineries

Viticulture has been a mainstay of the Okanagan's economy for almost a century, but it has really taken off in the last decade, with local wines exported and winning awards worldwide. Most of the local wineries welcome visitors with tours and tastings year-round (but call ahead outside of summer to check hours). Due to the popularity of visiting the wineries, most now charge a small fee for tasting. **Okanagan Wine Country Tours** (250/868-9463 or 866/689-9463, www.ok-winetours.com) has a variety of tours, including a full day of touring and tasting for $145 per person.

Across Okanagan Lake from Kelowna is **Mission Hill Family Estate** (1730 Mission Hill Rd., Westbank, 250/768-6448), high atop a ridge and surrounded by vineyards with stunning lake views. Mission Hill, British Columbia's most successful winery, encourages visits, with a a 45-meter-high bell tower open for the public to climb. Three different tours ($7–45 per person) depart daily through the summer, each ending with an informal tasting session. At nearby **Quail's Gate Estate Winery** (3303 Boucherie Rd., 250/769-4451) the reserve pinot noir is a signature wine—enjoy a glass or two alfresco at the winery bistro (11 A.M.–4 P.M. and 5 P.M.–dusk May–Oct.).

Back on the main highway, farther south is **Deep Creek Wine Estate** (5355 Trepanier

Bench Rd., Peachland, 250/767-2525, daily 11 A.M.–5 P.M. mid-April–Oct.). The original owner, Walter Hainle, was a pioneer in the development of ice wines, and while this is the style that the vineyard is best known for (produced under the Hainle name), limited quantities of red and white wines are also produced.

Across the lake from the above wineries is the much-heralded **Cedar Creek Estate Winery** (5445 Lakeshore Rd., 250/764-8866), where the vineyards and extensive gardens overlook Okanagan Lake. Tours are offered daily 11 A.M., 1 P.M., and 3 P.M. May to October.

Kettle Valley Railway

The Kettle Valley Railway, which winds around the back of Kelowna, may be protected as a national historic site, but unfortunately nothing could protect the 18 trestle bridges from 2003 wildfires. Plans are in place to have them rebuilt, but until then, opportunities for extended trips along the rail bed are somewhat limited. It's still an interesting spot, and well worth the effort to reach. To get there, take K.L.O. Road to McCulloch Road, turn south (right) and then south (right) again, following Myra Forest Service Road for 8.5 kilometers (5.3 miles). From the parking lot at this point, it's less than one kilometer (0.6 miles) to the first of the burnt trestles.

RECREATION
Golf

Some of Canada's best resort-style golf courses lie in and around Kelowna. These courses, combined with a mild climate and relatively well-priced greens fees, make the Okanagan one of the country's finest golfing destinations. All the courses listed below offer club rentals, power carts (generally around $40), and on-course dining facilities. You also find the rates listed below are discounted in spring and fall.

The **Harvest Golf Club** (2725 K.L.O. Rd., 250/862-3103 or 800/257-8577, greens fee $115), sitting on terraced land southeast of downtown, offers golfers views back across the city and lake. Adjacent to Harvest is **Orchard Greens** (2777 K.L.O. Rd., 250/763-2447,

$22), a fun little nine-hole layout that winds its way through a working apple orchard.

Continue east from the Harvest Golf Club and you'll eventually reach **Gallagher's Canyon Golf & Country Club** (4320 Gallagher's Drive West, 250/861-4240, greens fee $135), one of Canada's finest golf courses. Not particularly long, this immaculately manicured course snakes through a canyon and opens up to fairways lined with mature pine trees. It is a par-72 course that plays to 6,800 yards.

North of town and opposite the airport is **Okanagan Golf Club** (3200 Via Centrale, 250/765-5955), a residential and resort complex featuring 36 of the valley's finest holes. Designed by Jack Nicklaus's company is **The Bear** while **The Quail** features multitiered fairways and large elevations. Greens fees at both are $115, with a discounted twilight rate of $75 for each course.

Skiing and Snowboarding

Big White Ski Resort (250/765-3101 or 800/663-2772, www.bigwhite.com), 57 kilometers (35 miles) east of Kelowna on Highway 33, is one of the Okanagan's three major winter resorts and British Columbia's second largest. Its network of modern lifts, including a gondola and four high-speed quads, opens up over 850 hectares (2,100 acres) of terrain. Lift tickets are adult $72, senior $62, child $38. Adjacent to the main lift-served area is Happy Valley Adventure Centre, a tube park with its own lift. On-mountain facilities in the 9,000-bed base village include rental shops, a ski and snowboard school, accommodations, restaurants and cafés, and a large mall.

NIGHTLIFE

Enjoy a drink overlooking Okanagan Lake in the stylish lounge at the **Hotel Eldorado** (500 Cook Rd., 250/763-7500, daily from 11 A.M.). Right downtown, **Sgt. O'Flaherty's**, in the Royal Anne Hotel (348 Bernard Ave., 250/860-6409) is a friendly pub with bands churning out a variety of music styles nightly from 9 P.M.

At **Lake City Casino** (Grand Okanagan,

1310 Water St., 250/860-9467), don't expect the ritz and glitz of Las Vegas—this is gambling Canadian style, with the action restricted to slot machines, blackjack, roulette, Caribbean stud poker, and mini baccarat, and everyone's ushered out the front door at 2 A.M.

Sunshine Theatre (250/717-5304) puts on three to four plays throughout the summer; pick up a schedule at the information center.

ACCOMMODATIONS AND CAMPING
Under $100

Samesun Kelowna (245 Harvey St., 250/763-9814 or 877/972-6378, www.samesun.com, dorm $32, $74 s or d) is a centrally located, purpose-built backpacker lodge. Inside the distinctive three-story building are 120 beds, many in private rooms (with shared bathrooms), with communal kitchens, bathrooms, a large lounge area, and public Internet access. Out back you'll find a pleasant grassed barbecue area and a beach volleyball court.

$100-150

South of downtown, **Siesta Inn** (3152 Lakeshore Rd., 250/763-5013 or 800/663-4347, www.siestamotorinn.com, $118–168 s or d) offers a beachside atmosphere one block from the water. Rooms open onto a wide balcony overlooking a courtyard and outdoor swimming pool. Many rooms have kitchenettes.

Highway 97 (also known as Harvey Avenue) north of downtown holds many motels tucked between shopping malls, gas stations, and fast-food restaurants. Along this strip is **Days Inn Kelowna** (2469 Hwy. 97 N, 250/868-3297 or 800/329-7466, www.daysinn.com, $129 s or d), with large, modern rooms decorated in Santa Fe style, as well as an outdoor pool and hot tub. As at all Days Inns, rates include a light breakfast.

$150-200

Built in 1926 and moved to its present location in 1989, the 【 **Hotel Eldorado** (500 Cook Rd., south of downtown along Pandosy St., 250/763-7500, www.eldoradokelowna.com,

$189–279 s or d) is a delightful lakeside accommodation offering just 19 rooms, each furnished with antiques and many offering a lake view and private balcony. Hotel facilities include a lakefront café, a restaurant, a lounge, and a marina with boat rentals.

North of downtown, **Best Western Inn Kelowna** (2402 Hwy. 97 N, 250/860-1212 or 888/860-1212, www.bestwesterninnkelowna.com, $169 s or d) is a good choice for those who want the amenities of a full resort but don't want to pay for a waterfront location. Rooms are set around a grassed courtyard, complete with putting greens and an outdoor hot tub. Other facilities include an indoor pool, spa services, fitness room, and a restaurant and pub.

A MOUNTAIN HIDEAWAY

High in the hills northeast of Kelowna, **Beaver Lake Mountain Resort** (250/762-2225, www.beaverlakeresort.com, May-Oct.) is very different from the beachy resort complexes down on the valley floor. Set in a forest, on the edge of a lake famed for rainbow trout fishing, the resort comprises a restaurant, a horseback riding operation (with afternoon pony rides for kids), spa services, and a fishing shop. Boat rentals are well priced at $75 per 24 hours, including gas. Canoes, kayaks, and belly boats are $40 for three hours. Cabins range from tiny "camping cabins" that share bathrooms ($50 s or d) to peeled-log chalets with full kitchens ($160). Cabin number 9 is typical – it's rustic, but enjoys an absolute lakefront setting, a private floating dock, big deck, full kitchen, log fireplace, one bedroom, and a loft – and costs about the same as a room at the Best Western downtown. Make cabin reservations well in advance – locals know a bargain when they see one and book their favorite up to a year in advance. Camping is $25 (no hookups). To get there, head north to Winfield, then 16 kilometers (10 miles) east on Beaver Lake Road.

The rooms are spacious and modern and come filled with niceties such as air-conditioning, bathrobes, hairdryers, Internet access, and free local calls. Rack rates include Continental breakfast, but as always, check the hotel website for deals and packages.

Over $200

Overlooking the same stretch of lake as the Hotel Eldorado is the colorful and modern **◖ Manteo Resort** (3762 Lakeshore Rd., 250/860-1031 or 800/445-5255, www.manteo.com, from $240 s or d). This self-contained complex includes a 78-room hotel and guest and resident facilities such as a private beach, marina with boat rentals, pool complex with a water slide, tennis courts, a small movie theater, a lounge with billiard table, and a barbecue area. Rates start at $240 s or d for a contemporary-styled hotel room ($280 with a water view), but villas that sleep six can be rented for $560 per night. Outside of summer, bed-and-breakfast is around $160 per couple.

The grandest of Kelowna's accommodations is **Delta Grand Okanagan Resort** (1310 Water St., 250/763-4500 or 800/465-4651, www.deltahotels.com, from $289 s or d) is a sprawling lakeside development right downtown and integrated with local walking paths. Along the lake side of the resort is a convoluted lagoon, with its own private lock and watercraft rentals, while farther along are eateries and a bar with outdoor seating. Inside, once past the cavernous lobby, you'll find a fitness center, spa services, restaurants, a lounge bar, and 205 luxuriously appointed rooms.

Lake Okanagan Resort, on the west side of Okanagan Lake, 17 kilometers (10.6 miles) north along Westside Road (250/769-3511 or 800/663-3273, www.lakeokanagan.com, from $205 s or d) sprawls over 100 hectares (250 acres) of absolute waterfront property. It offers tennis courts, a par-3 golf course, swimming pools, a full-service marina, and horseback riding. In the main lodge is a restaurant open daily for dinner, a more casual caf, where dining alfresco is the order of the day, a poolside bar, and an upstairs lounge. The spacious units are each kitchen-equipped and have a private balcony, but are in need of an upgrade.

Camping

The closest campground to downtown is **Hiawatha RV Park** (3787 Lakeshore Rd., 250/861-4837 or 888/784-7275, www.hiawatharvpark.com, tent sites $42, hookups $44–52). It has a separate tenting area, showers, laundry, game room, and playground.

Two provincial parks in the vicinity of Kelowna offer camping. The closest is **Bear Creek Provincial Park** ($24) across the bridge from downtown and then nine kilometers (5.6 miles) north on Westside Road. With 122 sites nestled under cottonwood trees, this park is a world away from the busy nearby commercial campgrounds, but arrive early in the day to ensure a site. Campers also enjoy a short beach and trails that cross back over Westside Road and into desert-like terrain above the lake. **Fintry Provincial Park** ($24) lies 23 kilometers (14.3 miles) farther north along Westside Road in the same beachside setting as Bear Creek, although the campground is less developed. A trail leads from the campground to a deep canyon along Shorts Creek.

FOOD

Downtown Kelowna has a great number of dining choices for everything from a quick coffee to a full meal, but many of the city's finer restaurants are away from the business core, along quiet country roads or at the many golf clubs.

Cafe

Toward the lake, the **Bohemian Cafe** (524 Bernard Ave., 250/862-3517, Wed.–Fri. 7:30 A.M.–2:30 P.M., Sat. 8:30 A.M.–2:30 P.M., Sun. 8:30 A.M.–1 P.M., lunches $6.50–12.50) has a loyal local following for tasty cooked breakfasts and gourmet coffee.

Restaurants

◖ RauDZ (1560 Water St., 250/868-8805, daily from 5 P.M., $13–29), in a restored downtown commercial building features elegant table settings, a martini bar, and comfortable sofas. The menu is typically west coast, but more adventurous than you'd expect this far from Vancouver, with an emphasis on Okanagan produce.

Bai Tong (upstairs at 1530 Water St., 250/763-8638, Mon.–Fri. 11:30 A.M.–2:30 P.M. and 5–10 P.M., $9–16) is a step above your average small-town Asian restaurant. Feast on chicken cooked in a black bean sauce then wrapped in lettuce leaves or stir-fry combos of vegetables and noodles with your choice of meat. You'll find Kelowna's best Japanese food at **Momo Sushi** (377 Bernard Ave., 250/763-1030, Tues.–Sat. for lunch and dinner, Sun. dinner only, $12–17).

INFORMATION AND SERVICES

Kelowna Visitor Centre (544 Harvey Ave., 250/861-1515 or 800/663-4345, www.tourismkelowna.com, daily 9 A.M.–7 P.M. in summer, daily 9 A.M.–5 P.M. the rest of the year) is beside Highway 97 as it passes through the center of the city—watch for the signs. Coming into town from the south on Highway 97, turn left on Richter Street at the traffic light and go back one block. A good map for immediate orientation is posted outside the center; it also incorporates a legend of motels and attractions.

The **post office** is right downtown on Queens-way Avenue. **Kelowna General Hospital** is on the corner of Strathcona Ave. and Pandosy St. (250/862-4000).

Libraries and Bookstores

Mosaic Books (411 Bernard Ave., 250/763-4418 or 800/663-1225, Mon.–Wed. 8 A.M.–6 P.M., Thurs.–Fri. 8 A.M.–9 P.M., Sat. 9 A.M.–6 P.M., Sun. 11 A.M.–5 P.M.) is an independent bookseller that has been serving the valley for over 30 years. As well as an excellent collection of western Canadian titles, it has a wide selection of magazines and an in-house coffee bar. The eye-catching, semicircular building on Ellis St. is **Kelowna Library** (1380 Ellis St., 250/762-2800, Mon. 10 A.M.–5:30 P.M., Tues.–Thurs. 10 A.M.–9 P.M., Fri.–Sat. 10 A.M.–5:30 P.M.).

GETTING THERE AND AROUND

Modern **Kelowna Airport,** the province's third busiest, is 15 kilometers (9.3 miles) north of downtown along Highway 97. It's served by **Air Canada** (250/542-3302) and **WestJet** (800/538-5696), both of which offer daily flights to and from Vancouver, Calgary, and Edmonton. At the airport you'll find car rental outlets, a lounge bar, and a casual café. **Greyhound** (2366 Leckie Rd., 250/860-3835 or 800/661-8747) provides bus service throughout the Okanagan and beyond. Local buses are run by **Kelowna Regional Transit System;** $2 per sector. Get schedule and route information from the downtown terminal (Bernard Ave. at Ellis St., 250/860-8121).

For a taxi, call **Kelowna Cabs** (250/762-2222) or **Checkmate Cabs** (250/861-1111). Another taxi service is offered by **Okanagan Shuttle** (250/766-4280, www.okanaganshuttle.com), which schedules personalized drop-offs at local wineries, golf courses, and the airport.

Rental car agencies include **Avis** (250/491-9500), **Budget** (250/491-7368), **Hertz** (250/765-3822), **National** (250/762-0622), **Rent-a-Wreck** (250/763-6632), and **Thrifty** (250/868-2151). All these companies have vehicles out at the airport, but call in advance to ensure availability, especially in midsummer and during the ski season.

Sports Rent (3000 Pandosy St., 250/861-5699) rents mountain bikes for $9–12 per hour and $25–40 per day.

Vernon and Vicinity

The city of Vernon (population 55,000) lies between Okanagan, Kalamalka, and Swan Lakes, at the north end of the Okanagan Valley, 50 kilometers (31 miles) from Kelowna. The city itself holds little of interest; the surrounding area boasts the main attractions. Among the area highlights are many sandy public beaches; local provincial parks; Silver Star Mountain Resort, a year-round recreation paradise east of the city; and fishing in more than 100 lakes within an hour's drive of the city.

SIGHTS
In Town
Greater Vernon Museum and Archives (3009 32nd Ave., 250/542-3142, Tues.–Sat. 10 A.M.–5 P.M., by donation) holds photos from the early 1900s and a large collection of pioneer and native artifacts. Displays cover natural history, recreation, period clothing, and steamships. In the same vicinity is **Vernon Public Art Gallery** (3228 31st Ave., 250/545-3173, Mon.–Fri. 10 A.M.–5 P.M., Sat. 11 A.M.–4 P.M., by donation), featuring works by local artists as well as touring exhibitions.

Polson Park, off Highway 97 at 25th Avenue, has a Chinese teahouse, a small Japanese garden, and paths along a willow-lined creek, but most people go to stare at the spectacular floral clock—nine meters (30 feet) wide, made up of more than 3,500 plants, and the only one of its kind in western Canada.

Historic O'Keefe Ranch
Established in 1867, the O'Keefe Ranch (250/542-7868, daily 9 A.M.–5 P.M. May–mid-Oct., until 8 P.M. in July and Aug., adult $12, senior $11, youth $10), 13 kilometers (eight miles) north of Vernon toward Kamloops on Highway 9, was one of the Okanagan's first cattle ranches. Today you can tour the opulent, fully furnished O'Keefe Mansion and other noteworthy outbuildings, including a furnished old log house that was the O'Keefes' original home; a working blacksmith's shop; the still-in-

use St. Ann's Church, where services have been held since 1889; a fully stocked general store where you can buy postcards and old-fashioned candy; and the Chinese cook's bunkhouse. If you worked up an appetite in your explorations, visit the **Homestead Restaurant** (daily for lunch and weekends for dinner).

◖ Kalamalka Lake
If you've driven up to Vernon from Kelowna, this was the beautiful lake that Highway 97 paralleled for much of the way. It's known as a "marl" lake because as summer warms the water, the limestone bedrock forms crystals that reflect the sunlight, creating a distinctive aquamarine color that is all the more stunning with surrounding parched hills as a backdrop. The continuously changing emerald and turquoise water and surrounding mountain panorama is best appreciated from **Kal Lake Lookout,** five kilometers back toward Kelowna along Highway 97. Just south of the information center, a steep road winds down to the lakeshore and fine **Kal Beach,** fringed by trees. Parking is across the railway line from the beach (access is under the rail bridge). Also on the beach is a concession and, at the east end, a pub with a huge deck.

Continue beyond the beach for eight kilometers (five miles) to **Kalamalka Lake Provincial Park.** Within this 978-hectare (2,420-acre) park, a 1.5-kilometer (0.9-mile) trail winds down through bunchgrass and ponderosa pines to Turtle Head Point, while other trails lead to a low-lying wetland and lofty viewpoint.

Davison Orchards
Dozens of farms surround Vernon, but one in particular, Davison Orchards (west of downtown off Bella Vista Rd., 250/549-3266, daily 8 A.M.–6 P.M. May–Oct., free) is worth a visit. Set on a sloping hill with views extending across Kalamalka Lake and up the Coldstream Valley, this family-operated business is a hive of tourist activity throughout the warmer

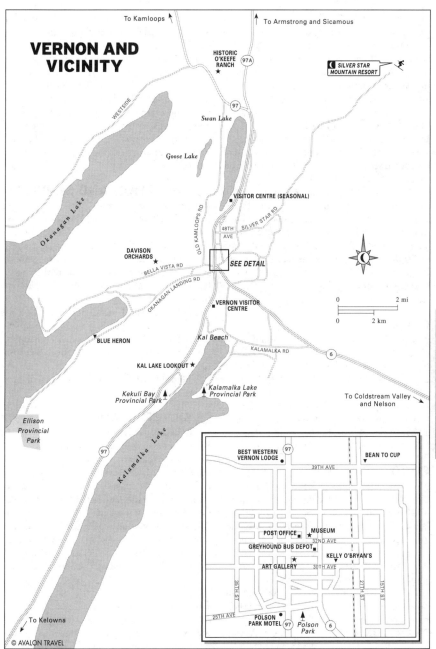

VERNON AND VICINITY

To Kamloops

To Armstrong and Sicamous

HISTORIC O'KEEFE RANCH ★

97A

SILVER STAR MOUNTAIN RESORT

WESTSIDE

97

Swan Lake

Goose Lake

VISITOR CENTRE (SEASONAL)

Okanagan Lake

OLD KAMLOOPS RD

SILVER STAR RD

48TH AVE

DAVISON ORCHARDS ★

BELLA VISTA RD

SEE DETAIL

OKANAGAN LANDING RD

VERNON VISITOR CENTRE

0   2 mi

0   2 km

BLUE HERON

Kal Beach

KALAMALKA RD

6

KAL LAKE LOOKOUT ★

To Coldstream Valley and Nelson

Kekuli Bay Provincial Park

Kalamalka Lake Provincial Park

Ellison Provincial Park

97

Kalamalka Lake

To Kelowna

© AVALON TRAVEL

SOUTHERN INTERIOR

BEST WESTERN VERNON LODGE ●

97

BEAN TO CUP ▼

39TH AVE

POST OFFICE ■   MUSEUM ★

32ND AVE

GREYHOUND BUS DEPOT ■

KELLY O'BRYAN'S ▼

ART GALLERY ★

30TH AVE

35TH ST

27TH ST

15TH ST

25TH AVE

POLSON PARK MOTEL ●

97   Polson Park

6

months. A self-guided walk leads through a garden where everything from cucumbers to cantaloupe is grown, a wagon tour traverses the entire 20-hectare (50-acre) property, and there's a Critter Corral, a café with outside dining, an ice cream stand, and, of course, a fruit and vegetable market.

ACCOMMODATIONS

Downtown and around the outskirts of Vernon are the usual collection of hotels and motels of greatly varying standards. **Polson Park Motel** (3201 24th Ave., 250/549-2231 or 800/480-2231, $70 s, $80 d) is the least expensive of these. Across from Polson Park, the three-story motel has a small outdoor pool and basic rooms. Of a higher standard is **Best Western Vernon Lodge** (3914 32nd St. 250/545-3385 or 800/663-4422, www.bestwesternvernon-lodge.com, $119 s, $129 d), where stylishly decorated rooms overlook an enclosed three-story tropical atrium.

Camping

Two provincial parks within a 15-minute drive of downtown provide campsites. Sixteen kilometers (10 miles) southwest of town on Okanagan Landing Road is **Ellison Provincial Park,** on the east shore of Okanagan Lake ($19), while south along Highway 97 toward Kelowna, **Kekuli Bay Provincial Park** slopes down to a boat launch and pebbly beach on Kalamalka Lake, but it's open to the elements ($24).

FOOD

The best coffee joint is **Bean to Cup** (3903 27th St., 250/503-2222, daily 6 A.M.–midnight, lunches $6.50–10), in a converted residential house. The organic coffee is roasted in-house and a variety of healthy meals are offered. There's also a heated patio and public Internet access.

At **Kelly O'Bryan's** (4215 32nd Ave., 250/549-2112, daily 11 A.M.–midnight, $12–26), tuck in to burgers, steak, seafood, salads, and Irish dishes such as stew and shepherd's pie. For a tropical ambience, try the **BX Creek Bar & Grill** (Best Western Vernon Lodge, 3914 32nd St., 250/545-3385, daily for

lunch and dinner, $10–28). The dining room is set in a garden-filled atrium with a stream flowing through the middle.

The **Blue Heron** (7673 Okanagan Landing Rd., 250/542-5550, daily from 11 A.M., $8–24) is a five-minute drive west of downtown, but well worth the drive. It sits right on Okanagan Lake, and a large deck right on the water is the most popular of the pub's three dining areas. The menu is fairly standard, with lots of dishes to share, but as it's off the tourist path, prices are reasonable.

INFORMATION AND SERVICES

Vernon Visitor Centre (701 Hwy. 97 S, 250/542-1415 or 800/665-0795, www.vernon-tourism.com, daily 8:30 A.M.–6 P.M. in summer,, Mon.–Fri. 8:30 A.M.–4:30 P.M. the rest of the year) is in a spruced up heritage house at the south end of town. If you're driving in from the north, make a stop at the seasonal Info Centre (6326 Hwy. 97 N).

The **Greyhound** bus depot is on the corner of 30th Street and 31st Avenue (250/545-0527). For local bus information and schedules, contact **Vernon Regional Transit System** (250/545-7221).

The **post office** is on the corner of 31st Street and 32nd Avenue.

◖ SILVER STAR MOUNTAIN RESORT

For summer or winter recreation, head up to Silver Star Mountain Resort (250/542-0224 or 800/663-4431, www.skisilverstar.com), a colorful gold-rush-era-style, fully self-contained resort town 22 kilometers (13.6 miles) northeast of Vernon (take 48th Ave. off Hwy. 97). The views of Vernon as you climb the mountain are worth the fairly long, steep drive, and the resort at the top offers great skiing and snowboarding, as well as a variety of summer recreation to suit all ages.

Summer Recreation

Silver Star offers the biggest range of summer recreation of any alpine resort in the interior. Starting at the end of June, a chairlift runs from the village to the top of Silver Star Mountain (1,915 meters/6,280 feet) for terrific views of Vernon and surrounding lakes. Much of the alpine area around the summit is protected by 8,714-hectare (21,500-acre) **Silver Star Provincial Park;** pick up a hiking guide in the village. The summer lift operates daily 10 A.M.–4 P.M. June–September; $18 for one ride, or buy an all-day pass for $34 (the day pass includes access to hiking and biking trails). To learn more about the mountain's natural history, take the naturalist-led three-hour wildflower tour at 1 P.M. Thursday–Sunday; $32 per person, which includes a chairlift ride. Mountain-bike rentals are $18 for one hour, $32 for two hours, and $52 for a full day.

Skiing and Snowboarding

From November through April, skiers and boarders mob Silver Star, coming for great terrain and the facilities of an outstanding on-hill village. The two main faces—Vance Creek, good for beginners, and Putnam Creek, for intermediates and experts—are served by five chairlifts and a couple of T-bars. The resort's 80 runs cover 1,135 hectares (2,800 acres) with a vertical rise of 760 meters (2,490 feet). Lift tickets are adult $71, senior $59, child $36.

Adjacent to the resort is **Sovereign Lake Nordic Club** (250/558-3036), featuring 35 kilometers (22 miles) of groomed and set tracks, while beyond these are 50 kilometers (31 miles) of backcountry trails. A day pass is $15 per person; rentals are available for an additional $20.

Accommodations

The base village contains numerous types of accommodations; book year-round through central reservations (800/663-4431, www. skisilverstar.com) or contact each accommodation directly. The rates quoted below are for summer, which is low season. Through winter, expect to pay double (except at the Silver Star Hostel).

Least expensive is **Silver Star Hostel** (9898 Pinnacles Rd., 250/545-8933 or 877/972-6378, www.samesun.com, $24 dorms, $68 s or d), one of Canada's only ski-in, ski-out backpacker lodges. Facilities include a modern communal kitchen, plenty of table space for dining, and 140 beds in dorms and private rooms.

The **Pinnacles Suite Hotel** (9885 Pinnacles Rd., 250/542-4548 or 800/551-7466, www. pinnacles.com, $99 s or d) has a wide range of rooms to suit all needs and budgets, including many with kitchens. The **Lord Aberdeen Hotel** (139 Main St., 250/542-1992 or 800/553-5885, www.lordaberdeen.com, $85–131 s or d) also offers self-contained suites, with a one-bedroom suite complete with a full kitchen selling for just $115 per night in summer. The most luxurious on-mountain lodging is **Silver Star Club Resort** (off Main St., 250/549-5191 or 800/610-0805, www.silverstarclubresort.com, from $125 s or d), which offers standard hotel rooms and self-contained suites spread through three buildings. Guests enjoy use of all facilities at the nearby National Altitude Training Centre.

West Kootenays

Clustered on the edge of the Monashee Range in the western Kootenays are several communities that seem a world away from the hustle and the bustle of the nearby Okanagan Valley. Grand Forks, Rossland, Trail, and Castlegar all boomed at the turn of the 20th century, when thousands of gold-hungry prospectors descended on the slopes of Red Mountain. Today Red Mountain draws more powderhounds than prospectors, and lakes, rivers, parks, and peaks are the area's main attractions.

GRAND FORKS AND VICINITY

Originally a mining town, Grand Forks (population 4,300) is home to descendants of the Doukhobors, a Russian religious sect who settled here in the early 1900s. Some still speak Russian, which is taught in local schools.

Grand Forks features a mix of impressive historic early-20th-century homes and restored civic buildings.

Accommodations and Camping

In a pleasant setting on the west edge of town, **Pinegrove Motel** (209 Central Ave., 250/442-8203, May–Oct.) offers rooms from $85 s, $95 d (with a huge discount for travelers aged 50 or older). Campers gravitate to the riverside **municipal campground** (mid-May–mid-Oct., $14–20) at the end of 5th Street. Showers and hookups are offered.

Christina Lake

This 19-kilometer (11.8-mile) long lake, 25 kilometers (15.6 miles) east of Grand Forks along Highway 3, is a summer favorite for folks from throughout the West Kootenays, who come for the lake's warm waters and fishing for rainbow trout, bass, and kokanee. The best of many commercial campgrounds at Christina Lake is **Cascade Cove RV Park** (1290 River Rd., 250/447-6662, Apr.–Oct., tenting $24, hookups $28–34). To the north, you sacrifice amenities like hookups and showers for much quieter forested setting at **Texas Creek Campground** (May–Oct., $15), within **Gladstone Provincial Park.**

ROSSLAND

Clinging to the slopes of an extinct volcanic crater deep in the tree-covered Monashee Mountains, Rossland (population 4,000) was once a gold-rush boomtown known as "The Golden City." The precious yellow metal was discovered on Red Mountain 1890, with the town's population peaking seven years later at 7,000. At that time, the city boasted four newspapers, 40 saloons, and daily rail service south to Spokane. By 1929, the mountain had yielded six million tons of ore worth $165 million. Today, tourism supplies the bulk of Rossland's gold.

Sights and Recreation

On the west side of downtown is the **Rossland Museum** (Hwy. 3B and Columbia Ave.,

250/362-7722, daily 9 A.M.–5 P.M. in summer, weekends only noon–4 P.M. the rest of the year, adult $5, senior $4, child $1.50), at the entrance of the Le Roi mine, which catalogs the area's lustrous geological and human history. The museum also holds the western Canada Ski Hall of Fame, which honors such luminaries as Olaus Jeldness—instigator of the local ski craze—and Nancy Greene, a local skier who won a gold medal in the 1968 Olympics. To experience the day-to-day life of the early hard-rock miners, tour **Le Roi Gold Mine,** next to the museum complex. The 45-minute tour includes detailed explanations of how ore is mined, trammed, drilled, and blasted, and tells you how to differentiate igneous, metamorphic, and sedimentary rocks. Museum admission is included in the tour cost of adult $10, senior $8, child $3.

The site of what was once one of the world's richest gold mines is now part of an alpine resort offering some of North America's most challenging lift-served runs. **Red Mountain Resort** (250/362-7384 or 800/663-0105, www.redresort.com) offers skiing and boarding on mountains for all ability levels, but "Red" holds most appeal for experts—and as any local will tell you, the advertised 640 hectares (1,580 acres) of terrain doesn't do justice to the opportunities for skiing in the backcountry. Lift tickets are adult $64, senior $42, child under 12 $32.

Accommodations and Food

The **[Ram's Head Inn** (250/362-9577 or 877/267-4323, www.ramshead.bc.ca, $95–199 s or d), one of Canada's premier small lodges, lies in the woods at the base of Red Mountain. Primarily designed for wintertime, the inn offers 17 ultra comfy guest rooms that ooze mountain magnetism. Factor in a congenial dining room (breakfast only in summer), a game room, sauna, outdoor hot tub, and a spacious communal lounge with luxurious chairs and a large fireplace, and you have the perfect place to spend a couple of nights. Winter packages average around $120–180 per person per night, including lift tickets.

Each morning, locals converge on the **Sunshine Café** (2116 Columbia Ave., 250/362-5099, Mon.–Sat. 7 A.M.–4 P.M., Sun. 8 A.M.–2 P.M., lunches $5–8) for hearty cooked breakfasts from $6. The rest of the day, the café offers a diverse menu including Mexican and Indian dishes. **Goldrush Books and Espresso** (2063 Washington St., 250/362-5333, Mon.–Sat. 7 A.M.–3:30 P.M., Sun. 7 A.M.–1 P.M.) sets a few tables around bookshelves full of local and Canadian literature. On the road up to Red Mountain, **Rock Cut Pub & Restaurant** (250/362-5814, daily from 11 A.M., $9.50–19) is busiest in winter, but open year-round. It offers typical pub fare, smartly presented and well priced. Enjoy the mountain surroundings by eating on the heated deck.

Information

Rossland Visitor Centre (250/362-7722 or 888/448-7444, www.rossland.com, daily 9 A.M.–5 P.M. in summer) is in the museum complex south of downtown.

CASTLEGAR

The area's first nonnative residents, the Doukhobors, arrived in 1908. These pacifist Russian immigrants planted orchards, built sawmills, and even operated a jam factory while living in segregated villages along the valley floor. Many of their descendants still live in the area. Today, mining, transportation, and hydroelectric-power production sustain the local economy and a population of 7,400.

Sights

Castlegar's major attraction is the **Doukhobor Heritage Centre** (east side of the river along Hwy. 3A, 250/365-5327, daily 9 A.M.–6 P.M., adult $8, student $5). Admission includes a guided tour, led by Doukhobor descendants, through the main building and the simply furnished brick dwellings and outbuildings. Along the way you'll see some of the sect's artifacts, including handwoven clothing, crocheted

bedspreads and shawls, a barn full of antique farming implements, and carved wooden spoons and ladles. **Zuckerberg Island,** at the confluence of the Kootenay and Columbia Rivers, is connected to the mainland by a 150-meter (490-foot) suspension bridge. On this tree-covered two-hectare (five-acre) island a short walking trail passes a full-scale model of a *ckukuli* (native winter pit house), as well as a Hiroshima memorial, Russian orthodox chapel house, cemetery, and log house. To get there, turn off Highway 22 at 9th Street, turn left on 7th Avenue, then immediately right.

While you're in a Russian frame of mind, visit **Verigin's Tomb,** the final resting place of Peter Verigin, the spiritual leader who led the Doukhobors to the Kootenays. To get there from the north side of the Kootenay River, head west toward Robson and take Terrace Road to the right. The tomb sits on a high bluff, surrounded by manicured gardens.

Practicalities

The comfortable and reasonably priced **Cozy Pines Motel** (2118 Crestview Cres., 250/365-5613, $70 s, $75 d) offers spotless rooms with kitchenettes and Internet access. Immediately south of the Highway 3 and Highway 22 intersection is the **Sandman Hotel** (1944 Columbia Ave., 250/365-8444 or 800/726-3626, www.sandman.ca, $125 s, $135 d), with an indoor pool and 24-hour restaurant. Campers looking for hookups should head to **Kootenay River Kampground** (651 Rosedale Rd., 250/365-5604 or 877/318-0008, www.kootenayriverrv.com, unserviced sites $15, hookups $20–25), beside the river north of the airport. The setting at **Syringa Provincial Park** ($19), on the banks of Lower Arrow Lake, north out of town toward Nelson then west off Highway 3A, is much nicer, but facilities are limited.

Castlegar Visitor Centre (off Columbia Ave. at 1995 6th Ave., 250/365-6313) is open daily 9 A.M.–6 P.M. in summer, Mon.–Fri. 9 A.M.–5 P.M. the rest of the year.

SOUTHERN INTERIOR

Nelson and Vicinity

The elegant city of Nelson (population 9,800) lies in a picturesque setting on the West Arm of Kootenay Lake, 660 kilometers (410 miles) east of Vancouver. Its relaxed pace, hilly tree-lined streets, and late-19th-century architectural treasures have helped attract an eclectic mix of jaded big-city types, artists, and counterculture seekers. But while the city itself is uniquely charming, the surrounding wilderness of the Selkirk Mountains is Nelson's biggest draw. The area's many lakes provide excellent fishing, sailing, and canoeing, as well as some of British Columbia's best inland beaches.

SIGHTS AND RECREATION

Nelson has 350 designated heritage buildings, more per capita than any other city in western Canada save Victoria. Most can be viewed by walking around the downtown core between Baker and Vernon Streets. Pick up the detailed *Heritage Walking Tour* or *Heritage Motoring Tour* brochures from the information center. The walking-tour brochure includes the 1909

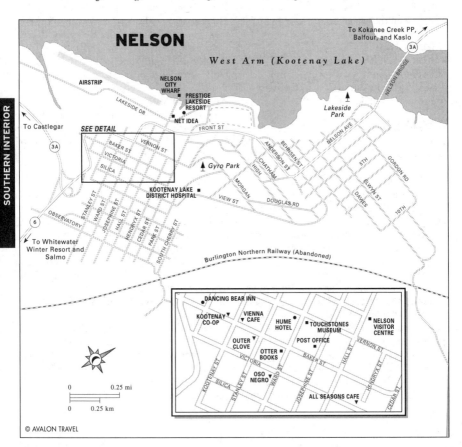

SOUTHERN INTERIOR

NELSON

West Arm (Kootenay Lake)

To Kokanee Creek PP,
Balfour, and Kaslo
3A

NELSON BRIDGE

AIRSTRIP

NELSON CITY WHARF
■ PRESTIGE LAKESIDE RESORT
● NET IDEA

LAKESIDE DR

Lakeside Park

FRONT ST

To Castlegar

SEE DETAIL

3A

BAKER ST
VERNON ST
VICTORIA
SILICA

▲ Gyro Park

BEMSEN ST
ANDERSON ST
CHATHAM
HIGH
NELSON AVE
5TH
GORDON RD
ELWYN ST
DAVIES
10TH

KOOTENAY LAKE DISTRICT HOSPITAL ■
VIEW ST
MORGAN
DOUGLAS RD

To Whitewater Winter Resort and Salmo

6
OBSERVATORY
STANLEY ST
WARD ST
JOSEPHINE ST
HALL ST
HENDRYX ST
CEDAR ST
PARK ST
SOUTH CHERRY ST

Burlington Northern Railway (Abandoned)

0   0.25 mi
0   0.25 km

DANCING BEAR INN ▼

KOOTENAY ▼ CO-OP
VIENNA ▼ CAFE
HUME HOTEL
■ TOUCHSTONES MUSEUM
■ NELSON VISITOR CENTRE

OUTER CLOVE ▼
POST OFFICE
■
VERNON ST

OTTER ■ BOOKS
VICTORIA
BAKER ST
HALL ST
KOOTENAY ST
STANLEY ST
WARD ST
JOSEPHINE ST
HENDRYX ST
CEDAR ST

OSO ▼ NEGRO
SILICA

ALL SEASONS CAFE ▼

© AVALON TRAVEL

NELSON ARTWALK

Organized by the local arts council, Nelson's July–September Artwalk (250/352-2402) highlights the work of up to 100 local artists at venues across the city. Works are displayed citywide at restaurants, hotels, the theater building, art galleries, and even the local pool hall. On the last Friday of every month of the event, receptions are held at each of the venues. The receptions feature live entertainment, refreshments, and the artists themselves on hand to discuss their work. A brochure available at the information center and motels and galleries around town contains biographies of each featured artist, tells where his or her work is displayed, and provides a map showing you the easiest way to get from one venue to the next.

courthouse on Ward Street and the impressive stone-and-brick 1902 city hall on the corner of Ward and Vernon Streets.

Touchstones Museum

Right downtown, Touchstones Museum (502 Vernon St., 250/352-9813, daily 10 A.M.–5 P.M. in summer, Tues.–Sat. noon–4 P.M. the rest of the year, adult $10, senior and child $6) is in a grandly ornate stone building that was originally built in 1902 as a post office. Permanent exhibits concentrate on local history, with displays covering native peoples, explorers, miners, traders, early transportation, Nelson's contribution to World War I, and the Doukhobors (a Russian religious sect that settled in the Kootenays).

Hiking and Biking

The best nearby hiking is in **Kokanee Glacier Provincial Park** (see *New Denver to Nelson* section later in this chapter), but the bed of the Burlington Northern Railway, built in 1893, provides an interesting nine-kilometer trek right on Nelson's back doorstep. Access

the railway from the top end of South Cherry Street. The many old logging and mining roads surrounding the city are great for mountain biking; one favorite is the **Svoboda Bike Trail,** accessed along Elwyn Street beyond the college. For bike rentals and a trail map, head to **Gerick Cycle and Sports** (702 Baker St., 250/354-4622).

Skiing and Snowboarding

Legendary powder and an off-the-beaten-path location makes **Whitewater Winter Resort** (250/354-4944 or 800/666-9420, www.skiwhitewater.com) a hidden gem. The small resort 20 kilometers (12 miles) south of Nelson sits beneath a string of 2,400-meter (7,900-foot) peaks that catch an amazing amount of snow. Three double chairlifts access 18 marked trails (the Summit Chair opens up the best powder-packed slopes). The area's abundant snowfall makes for a long season, but conditions are best in February and March. Whitewater has no on-mountain accommodations—just the lifts and a day lodge with a cafeteria, rental shop, and ski/snowboard school. Lift tickets are adult $57, senior and youth $46.

ACCOMMODATIONS AND CAMPING

Right downtown, the **(Dancing Bear Inn** (171 Baker St., 250/352-7573 or 877/352-7573, www.dancingbearinn.com, dorms $25, $50–56 s or d) offers clean and comfortable accommodations at a very reasonable price. It features a cozy lounge area with a TV, reading material, information on local attractions and restaurants, and a cupboard full of board games. Other facilities include Internet access, kitchen, laundry, and lockers. The dorm-style rooms are spacious, with a maximum of six beds in each. A few doubles and a single room are also available.

The 1898 **Hume Hotel** (422 Vernon St., 250/352-5331 or 877/568-0888, www.humehotel.com, $99–139 s, $109–149 d) is a city landmark. It provides attractive, recently refurbished rooms, some with lake views. Rates include breakfast in the downstairs restaurant.

Down on the lakefront, **Prestige Lakeside Resort** (701 Lakeside Dr., 250/352-7222, www.prestigeinn.com, $189 s or d) features a spa facility, fitness center, swimming pool, private marina, restaurants, and lakeside rooms.

Camping

The best local camping is at lakeside **Kokanee Creek Provincial Park** (20 km/12.5 mi northeast of Nelson on Hwy. 3A, 250/825-4421, $24). Although the large park offers more than 100 sites, it's often full; the beautiful location makes this one of the Kootenays' most popular campgrounds. If the park is full, continue eight kilometers (five miles) farther northeast to Balfour, where you'll find two commercial campgrounds.

FOOD

The counterculture of Nelson is evident at ◖ **Kootenay Co-op** (295 Baker St., 250/354-4077), a grocery store where you can purchase goat's milk ice cream, organic apple juice, hemp toaster waffles, west coast salmon caught by Nisga'a natives, eco-sweet chocolate, and preservative-free bread. If you're looking for lunch on the run, pick up healthy snacks such as sweet curry rolls and vegan carrot cake from the deli counter. Up from the main street, push past the spoiled city kids posing as hippies and duck into **Oso Negro** (604 Ward St., 250/352-7661, Mon.–Sat. 7 A.M.–6 P.M., Sun. 8 A.M.–4 P.M.) for rich coffee roasted in-house. The bagels and other baked goods are also recommended.

Over the last few years, the **Vienna Cafe** (411 Kootenay St., 250/354-4646, Mon.–Fri. 9 A.M.–5:30 P.M., Sat. 9 A.M.–5 P.M.), in Packrat Annie's bookstore, has lost its counterculture vibe, but the food has gotten better. You can't go wrong with a chicken—free range, of course—burger, loaded with feta cheese and green peppers ($8.50). A generous serving of vegetarian five-bean chili will set you back $5, or order a bowl butternut squash soup livened up by a dash of maple syrup for $6. Excellent!

Outer Clove (536 Stanley St., 250/354-1667, Mon.–Sat. 11:30 A.M.–9 P.M., $13–25) is typical of Nelson's better restaurants, appealing to modern tastes but in a relaxed, low-key environment. The emphasis is on garlic (it's even an ingredient in a couple of the desserts), with tapas from $6 (you'd need three for a filling meal) and dinner mains such as Chicken Garlicious.

Tucked into a back alley behind the main street is ◖ **All Seasons Café** (620 Herridge Lane, 250/352-0101, daily for dinner, $22–32), a small yet stylish place with a delightful tree-shaded patio. Dishes such as proscuitto-wrapped beef tenderloin with a side of maple-roasted yams will have you raving, while deserts like chai crème brûlée will have you wishing you had more room.

INFORMATION AND SERVICES

All the information you'll need on Nelson and the Kootenays is available at **Nelson Visitor Centre** (225 Hall St., 250/352-3433, www.discovernelson.com, daily 8:30 A.M.–6 P.M. in summer, Mon.–Fri. 8:30 A.M.–noon the rest of the year). **Otter Books** (398 Baker St., 250/352-3434, Mon.–Sat. 9:30 A.M.–5:30 P.M., Sun. 11 A.M.–4 P.M.) has an excellent selection of books about the Kootenays ranging from ghost town guides to the history of the Kettle River Railway. **Packrat Annie's** (411 Kootenay St., 250/354-4722) sells used books, tapes, and CDs, and offers good people-watching opportunities.

Kootenay Hospital is east of downtown (3 View St., 250/352-3111). The **post office** is at 514 Vernon Street.

SLOCAN VALLEY

The historically rich Slocan Valley, or "Silvery Slocan," nestles snugly between the Slocan and Valhalla Ranges of the Selkirk Mountains. In the 1890s the valley sprang into the limelight when silver was discovered at Sandon. It's much quieter today, offering many picturesque towns and an abundance of outdoor recreation opportunities accessed from Highway 6 northwest of Nelson.

New Denver

This picturesque town of 600 is on Slocan

Lake, opposite Valhalla Provincial Park. Originally called Eldorado and renamed after Denver, Colorado, the town reached its mining peak in the 1890s. Today the main street is lined with funky false-front stores and pioneer-style buildings left over from the prosperous silver days. Visit the **Silvery Slocan Museum** (202 6th Ave., 250/358-2201, daily 10 A.M.–4 P.M. July–Aug., weekends only May and Sept., adult $2, child $1), in a restored bank building, to find out all about New Denver's heyday.

Down on the lake within easy walking distance of the main street, **Sweet Dreams** (702 Eldorado St., 250/358-2415, www.newdenver bc.com, $65–90 s, $80–95 d) is an inviting guesthouse with five large guest rooms, some with shared bathrooms. Rates include a cooked breakfast, and dinner is available with advance notice. Out of New Denver to the south, **C Silverton Resort** (250/358-7157, www.silvertonresort.com, $195–315 s or d) takes advantage of its watery location with self-contained log cabins that are as close to the water as any I've seen in British Columbia. Campers can head to a **municipal campground** (May–Sept., $15–18), on the south side of the town and with full hookups, or **Rosebery Provincial Park** ($14), on Wilson Creek six kilometers (3.7 miles) north of town.

In the local museum, **New Denver Visitor Centre** (202 6th Ave., 250/358-2719, www.slocanlake.com, daily 9 A.M.–5 P.M. July–Aug.) is a friendly little place with lots of ideas that will tempt you to linger longer in the area.

NAKUSP

Forty-eight kilometers (30 miles) northwest of New Denver, Nakusp (population 1,800) was established during the mining-boom years. Today the small town is best known for its hot springs and its stunning location on Upper Arrow Lake at the foot of the Selkirk Mountains. To get to **Nakusp Hot Springs** (250/265-4528, daily 9:30 A.M.–10 P.M. in summer, daily 1–9 P.M. the rest of the year, adult $9, senior and child $8), take Highway 23 north out of town for one kilometer (0.6

miles), then follow the signposted road along Kuskanax Creek for 12 kilometers (7.5 miles).

Practicalities

A nearby resort, with its own private hot springs, is **C Halcyon Hot Springs Village & Spa** (32 km/20 mi north of Nakusp, 250/265-3554 or 888/689-4699, www.halcyon-hotsprings. com, $159–449 s or d). Accommodations are in cabins, cottages (my favorite), chalets, or a luxury family-oriented Lodge Suite. Serviced campsites are $34.50, or $59.50 with hot pool passes. **Nakusp Village Campground** (8th St., 250/265-4019, mid-May–mid-Oct., unserviced sites $22, powered sites $25) has large shaded sites, coin-operated showers, and firewood within walking distance of the beach and the main street.

The place to be seen in Nakusp is the **Broadway Deli Bistro** (408 Broadway St. W, 250/265-3767, daily from 7 A.M.), where you'll find great coffee and a constant stream of muffins coming out of the oven.

Nakusp Visitor Centre (92 6th Ave., 250/265-4234 or 800/909-8819, www.nakusparrowlakes.com, daily 9 A.M.–5 P.M. in summer, Wed.–Sun. 1–5 P.M. the rest of the year) is also a good resource for travelers.

NEW DENVER TO NELSON

Take Highway 31A east from New Denver and you pass the turnoff to the ghost town of Sandon before crossing a low pass and descending to Kaslo, on Kootenay Lake. From Kaslo, Nelson is 70 kilometers (43 miles) to the south, with plenty of spots worth visiting en route.

C Sandon

The original Slocan Valley boomtown, Sandon once was a thriving town of 5,000 people. After the discovery of silver on the slopes of Idaho Peak, Sandon grew quickly and at one time boasted 24 hotels, 23 saloons, banks, general stores, mining brokers' offices, and a newspaper. Its main link to the outside world was the Kaslo & Slocan Railway, built in 1895 to connect Sandon with sternwheeler transportati on Kootenay Lake. The Great Depres

1929 put an end to the heyday, and in 1955 many of the buildings were swept away in spring flooding. Today you can count the population on two hands.

The best place to start a visit to Sandon is the 1900 city hall, where you can pick up the *Sandon Walking Tour Guide.* This brochure details all the original structures—only a fraction of which remain—with a map that makes exploring on foot more enjoyable. Up the creek from city hall are **Sandon Museum** (250/358-7920, summer only) where exhibits bring the old town back to life, and **Silversmith Mine Powerhouse,** which still supplies power to the few remaining residents and retains its title as western Canada's oldest operating hydroelectric plant. On the same side of the creek as the museum an unnamed road leads up to 2,280-meter (7,480-foot) **Idaho Peak.** The road is very rough, passable only in July and August. From the end of the 12-kilometer (7.5-mile) road, a steep one-kilometer (0.6-mile) trail leads to the summit and spectacular 360-degree views of the Kootenays.

Kaslo

Tree-lined streets graced by elegant late-19th-century architecture, and lake and mountain views from almost every street make Kaslo a worthwhile stop. Another of the Kootenays' great boomtowns, Kaslo's population exploded to more than 3,000 after the discovery of silver at Sandon in 1893. Dry-docked by the lakefront is the **SS Moyie,** the last sternwheeler to splash up Kootenay Lake. Built in 1897, the grand old red and white vessel was used for transportation of passengers, freight, and mail right up until its retirement in 1957. Today the ship serves as a museum (324 Front St., 250/353-2525, daily 9:30 A.M.–5 P.M. mid-May–mid-Oct., adult $7, senior $5, child $3), containing a fine collection of photos, antiques, and artifacts of the region.

North of town, the **Lakewood Inn** (Kohle Rd., 250/353-2395, www.lakewoodinn.com, camping $22–28, cabins $100–155) has been taking in guests since the 1920s.

Ainsworth Hot Springs

Overlooking Kootenay Lake from a hillside 40 kilometers (25 miles) north of Nelson, these springs (250/229-4212, 10 A.M.–9:30 P.M. in summer, shorter hours rest of year, adult $10, senior $9, child $8) were discovered in the early 1800s by local natives who found that the hot, odorless water (high in magnesium sulfate, calcium sulfate, and sodium carbonate) helped heal their wounds and ease their aches and pains. Today the springs have been commercialized and include a main outdoor pool, a hot tub, steam bath, and cold plunge pool. The adjacent **Ainsworth Hot Springs Resort** (250/229-4212 or 800/668-1171, www.hotnaturally.com, $138–199 s or d) features exercise and massage rooms, a lounge, and a licensed restaurant overlooking the main pool and beautiful Kootenay Lake.

Cody Caves Provincial Park

High above the hot springs, this cave system is made up of several large chambers totaling 800 meters (2,600 feet) in length. The caves also hold an underground creek that drops over Cody Falls. Experienced spelunkers can explore the caves unguided, but others will want to join a tour with **Hiad Venture Corp.** (250/505-2592). Based at the caves' entrance, this company offers tours daily from 9 A.M. July–August. The one-hour option is $15 per person, but the three-hour tour ($50) is more adventurous and passes formations you won't see on the shorter trip. To get to the caves, turn off Highway 31 just north of Ainsworth Hot Springs, follow a narrow 15-kilometer (9.3-mile) gravel road to a trailhead, then hike 20 minutes.

Kokanee Creek Provincial Park

This 257-hectare (630-acre) park 20 kilometers (12.4 miles) northeast of Nelson features a great beach and one of the Kootenays' most popular campgrounds. Short trails crisscross the park, and kokanee (freshwater salmon) can be viewed in Kokanee Creek at the end of summer (access is from the visitor center). Instead of migrating in from the ocean like their anadromous cousins, kokanee spend their lives in the larger lakes of British Columbia's interior, spawning each summer in the rivers and streams draining into the lakes. The super-popular day-use area runs the length of a one-kilometer (0.6-mile) sandy beach. The large campground's sites have showers, but no hookups, and they fill fast through summer ($24). A visitor center (250/825-4421, daily 9 A.M.–9 P.M. mid-June–mid-Sept.) has displays on local ecosystems, trail reports for Kokanee Glacier Provincial Park, and other useful information.

Kokanee Glacier Provincial Park

Straddling the highest peaks of the Selkirk Mountains, this 32,035-hectare (79,160-acre) mountain wilderness park can be seen from downtown Nelson. The steep and narrow gravel roads into the park are often impassable until late June, and the hiking trails remain snow-covered even later. The park is named for a massive glacier that, along with two other glaciers and 30 lakes, feeds dozens of creeks and rivers flowing west to Slocan Lake and east to Kootenay Lake. The heart of the park is too steep and rugged to be penetrated by roads, so all the best features must be reached on foot. The main access is via an unsealed road that spurs off Highway 3A 20 kilometers (12.4 miles) north of Nelson and follows Kokanee Creek 16 kilometers (10 miles) to **Gibson Lake.** A 2.5-kilometer (1.6-mile) trail circles the lake, but the best hiking is farther afield. From Gibson Lake, it's four kilometers (2.5 miles) uphill to beautiful **Kokanee Lake.**

Nelson to the Rockies

From Nelson, it's 101 kilometers (63 miles), plus a ferry trip, to Creston, then 106 kilometers (66 miles) farther east through the East Kootenays, with the Canadian Rockies rising abruptly from the Columbia Valley to the Continental Divide and the British Columbia–Alberta border to the west. The crossroads of the region is the service center of Cranbrook, from where Highway 3 heads west to Fernie, and Highway 93/95 parallels the Columbia River northward through a region dotted with golf courses, hot springs, and many provincial parks.

Crawford Bay and Vicinity

From Balfour, 21 kilometers (13 miles) northeast of Nelson, the world's longest free ferry ride takes you across Kootenay Lake to Kootenay Bay and the artsy community of Crawford Bay. On the left as you descend the hill is **North Woven Broom** (250/227-9245, daily 9 A.M.–5 P.M. April–mid-Oct.), western Canada's only traditional broom manufacturer. A little farther along is **Kootenay Forge** (daily 9 A.M.–5 P.M. May–mid-Oct., 250/227-9467), a traditional blacksmith shop where you can watch artisans practicing this ancient trade.

Also at Crawford Bay is **Kokanee Springs Golf Resort** (250/227-9226 or 800/979-7999, www.kokaneesprings.com, mid-Apr.–mid-Oct.), one of the province's most picturesque courses. Featuring water views, forested fairways, huge greens, large elevation drops, and colorful flower beds around the tee boxes, it is not only a beautiful place to golf, it's also very challenging. Greens fees are $79, and you can stay at the resort as part of a golfing package (from $149 per person per night).

The pick of local accommodations is ◖ **Wedgwood Manor** (250/227-9233 or 800/862-0022, www.wedgwoodcountryinn.com, April–Oct., $110–150 s or d). Set on 20 beautiful hectares (50 acres) adjacent to the golf course and within walking distance of a beach, this 1910 home offers six heritage-style rooms, each with a private bathroom. Guests can relax in the library or in the extensive gardens.

From Crawford Bay, it's 80 kilometers (50 miles) of lake-hugging road to Creston.

CRESTON

In a wide, fertile valley at the extreme southern end of Kootenay Lake lies Creston, a thriving agricultural center of 5,200. Although the town is south of the Kootenays' most spectacular mountains, the scenery is still impressive; the Selkirk Mountains flank the valley to the west, while the Purcell Mountains do the same to the east.

Sights

Creston Valley Wildlife Management Area,
10 kilometers (6.2 miles) west of Creston (250/428-3259, daily 9 A.M.–5 P.M. May–Aug., Wed.–Sun. 9 A.M.–4 P.M. Apr. and Oct., adult $4, child $2), protects vital resting grounds along the Pacific Flyway, providing a haven for more than 250 species of birds, including a large population of osprey, a flock of the rare Forester's tern, and a nesting colony of western grebe. From the visitors center, hiking trails lead along dikes separating wetlands and ponds. Even along the boardwalk leading into the center you may spy some local residents-turtles that sun themselves on half-submerged logs.

Creston is home to the **Columbia Brewery** (1220 Erickson St., 250/428-1238), producer of British Columbia's popular Kokanee beer. Tours are offered four to six times daily through summer; $2. At the brewery entrance is Kokanee Beer Gear (daily 9 A.M.–4:30 P.M.), a retail shop selling Kokanee souvenirs.

CRANBROOK AND VICINITY

Hub of the eastern Kootenays, Cranbrook (population 20,000) nestles at the base of the Purcell Mountains 106 kilometers (66 miles) east of Creston and provides spectacular views eastward to the Canadian Rockies. The locals are proud of their downtown heritage buildings, which you can view on a self-guided walking tour by picking up the handy *Cranbrook Heritage Tour* brochure from either information center or the railway museum (stop number one on the tour).

Canadian Museum of Rail Travel

Cranbrook's main attraction, this museum is on a side line of the main Canadian Pacific Railway line directly opposite downtown (Van Horne St., 250/489-3918, daily 10 A.M.–6 P.M. Apr.–mid-Oct., Tues.–Sat. 10 A.M.–5 P.M. mid-Oct.–Mar.). Most of the displays are outdoors, spread along three sets of track, including a luxury train (also called "The Millionaires' Train") built for the Canadian Pacific Railway in 1929. Restoration displays, a viewing corridor, a model railway display, a slide show, guided tours of the car interiors, and tea and scones in the Argyle Dining Car are included in the price of the two-hour Deluxe Tour (adult $12, senior $10, child $6.50). You can choose abbreviated tours (from adult $5.25, senior $4.50, child $2.25), but you'll miss the best of the museum.

◖ Fort Steele Heritage Town

At Fort Steele Heritage Town (9851 Hwy. 93, 250/417-6000, daily 9:30 A.M.–6:30 P.M. June–Sept., $5 per person, or pay adult $25, senior and child $15 for two days' admission and all activities), 16 kilometers (10 miles) north of Cranbrook, you'll see more than 60 restored, reconstructed, fully furnished buildings, including log barracks, hotels, a courthouse, jail, museum, dentist's office, ferry office, printing office, and a general store crammed to the rafters with intriguing historical artifacts. In summer, the park staff brings Fort Steele back to life with appropriately costumed working blacksmiths, carpenters, quilters, weavers, bakers, ice-cream makers, and many others. Hop on a stagecoach or a steam train, heckle a street politician, witness a crime and testify at a trial, pan for gold, watch a silent movie, and view operatic performances in the Opera House.

Accommodations and Food

On average, motel prices here are among the lowest in the province, making it a good spot to rest overnight. The flower-basket-adorned **Heritage Estate Motel** (362 Van Horne St., 250/426-3862 or 800/670-1001, $60 s, $75 d) is definitely the best value-for-money choice. The rooms are spacious, and each contains complimentary tea and coffee. I'm not

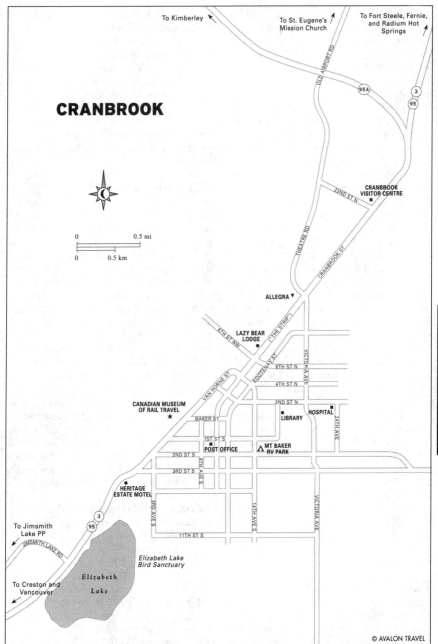

CRANBROOK

To Kimberley

To St. Eugene's
Mission Church

To Fort Steele, Fernie,
and Radium Hot
Springs

0   0.5 mi
0   0.5 km

95A

3
95

OLD AIRPORT RD

22ND ST N

CRANBROOK
VISITOR CENTRE

THEATRE RD

CRANBROOK ST

ALLEGRA

6TH ST NW

(THE STRIP)

LAZY BEAR
LODGE

VAN HORNE ST

KOOTENAY ST

6TH ST N

VICTORIA AVE

4TH ST N

2ND ST N

CANADIAN MUSEUM
OF RAIL TRAVEL

BAKER ST

LIBRARY

HOSPITAL

24TH AVE

1ST ST S

POST OFFICE

MT BAKER
RV PARK

2ND ST S

9TH AVE S

3RD ST S

3RD AVE S

14TH AVE S

VICTORIA AVE

HERITAGE
ESTATE MOTEL

3
95

11TH ST S

To Jimsmith
Lake PP

JIMSMITH LAKE RD

Elizabeth Lake
Bird Sanctuary

To Creston and
Vancouver

*Elizabeth
Lake*

© AVALON TRAVEL

the only one who regards this place as a bargain, so you'll need to book ahead in summer. Continuing north, in the heart of the commercial strip, **Lazy Bear Lodge** (621 Cranbrook St., 250/426-6086 or 888/808-6086, www. lazybear-lodge.ca, $70 s, $75–80 d) is an old roadside motel snazzed up with log trim, beds of bright flowers, and a colorful coat of paint. The rooms remain basic but each has a coffeemaker and wireless Internet, and some have a fridge and microwave. Out front is a small swimming pool for guest use.

One of the area's most attractive campgrounds is in **Jimsmith Lake Provincial Park** (May–Sept., $15), four kilometers (2.5 miles) off the main highway at the southern outskirts of the city. Downtown, **Mt. Baker RV Park** (14th Ave. and 1st St. S, 250/489-0056, www. mountbakerrvpark.com, April–Oct., tents $21, hookups $25–) provides decent city camping.

A few commercial facilities surround the main entrance to Fort Steele, north of town. The largest is **Fort Steele Resort and RV Park** (250/489-4268, www.fortsteele.com, unserviced sites $25, hookups $32–39, log cabin with shared bathroom $79 s or d s or d), which offers a heated outdoor pool, showers, laundry, and a barbecue and cooking facility.

Cranbrook's finest restaurant is **Allegra** (1225 Cranbrook St. N, 250/426-8812, Wed.–Sun. 5–9 P.M., $13.50–27), a friendly little place with casual yet classic European dishes, such as seafood fettuccini and red snapper poached in tomatoes and white wine.

Information
The main **Cranbrook Visitor Centre** (2279 Cranbrook St. N, 250/426-5914 or 800/222-6174, www.cranbrookchamber.com, daily 9 A.M.–5 P.M. in summer, Mon.–Fri. 8:30 A.M.–4:30 P.M. the rest of the year) is at the north entrance to town.

FERNIE AND VICINITY
Fernie (population 5,200) nestles in the Elk Valley 100 kilometers (62 miles) east of Cranbrook on Highway 3. The town itself is a coal-mining and forestry center offering little of visitor interest, but in winter one of British Columbia's great little alpine resorts comes alive nearby. Town center is a couple of blocks south of the highway, holding the usual array of historic buildings and small-town shops. Look for an impressive red-brick courthouse on 4th Avenue and a good bakery on 2nd Avenue. About 12 kilometers (7.5 miles) south of town is 259-hectare (850-acre) **Mount Fernie Provincial Park,** where hiking trails lead along a picturesque creek and to a waterfall.

Fernie Alpine Resort
Fernie Alpine Resort (14 km/8.7 mi south of Fernie, 250/423-4655, www.skifernie.com) is another of British Columbia's legendary winter resorts, boasting massive annual snowfalls, challenging skiing and riding, and uncrowded slopes. The lift-serviced area lies under a massive ridge that catches an incredible nine meters of snow each year, filling a wide open bowl with enough of the white fluffy stuff to please all powderhounds. A few runs are groomed, but the steeper stuff—down open bowls and through trees—is the main attraction. Lift tickets cost adult $76, senior $61, child $25. In July and August, one chairlift operates, opening up hiking and mountain-biking terrain. Hikers pay $16 per ride, or $36 for a day pass. Mountain bikes can be rented at the base village for $40–65. Other summer activities include horseback riding, guided hikes, tennis, and photography courses. Accommodations are available on the hill, and visitors with RVs are offered hookups and shower facilities.

Accommodations and Food
Fernie's range of budget-priced accommodations make the town a great base for budget-conscious travelers.

Fernie's range of inexpensive accommodations makes the town a great base for budget-conscious travelers. Best of the bunch is ◖ **Powder Mountain Lodge** (892 Hwy. 3, 250/423-4492, www.powdermountain-lodge.com; dorms $30, $60–100 s or d). This converted motel has a game room, communal kitchen, loads of parking, a laundry, Internet access, and even an outdoor pool. Accommodations are in dorms and motel rooms, with some of the latter having kitchens and family-friendly layouts. Up at the alpine resort, **Griz Inn** (250/423-9221 or 800/661-0118, www.grizinn.com) offers 45 kitchen-equipped suites, an indoor pool, hot tub, and restaurant. Through summer, room rates start at a reasonable $92 s or d, while a condo unit is $155 for up to four people.

The best bet for campers is **Mount Fernie Provincial Park** (mid-May–Sept.), 12 kilometers (7.5 miles) south of town and four kilometers (2.5 miles) north of the Akamina–Kishinena Provincial Park access road. Facilities are basic, but it's a pleasant setting, and a short trail leads along Lizard Creek to a waterfall. Sites are $16 per night.

You can find a good selection of restaurants scattered through the downtown core, but my best picks are along the highway. Opposite Powder Mountain Lodge, the █ **Curry Bowl** (931 7th Ave., 250/423-2695; Tues.–Sun. 5–10 P.M.) won't win any design awards, but with delicious dishes like mango shrimp curry ($15) and a Vietnamese chicken stir-fry ($13), it really doesn't matter. **Yamagoya** (741 7th Ave., 250/430-0090; daily for lunch and dinner; $12–18) is a stylishly casual dining room that offers top-notch Japanese cuisine at reasonable prices.

Beside the highway, through town to the north, is **Fernie Visitor Centre** (102 Commerce Rd., 250/423-6868, www.fernie-chamber.com, daily 9 A.M.–6 P.M. in summer, Mon.–Fri. 9 A.M.–5 P.M. the rest of the year)

KIMBERLEY

Kimberley (population 7,000), 31 kilometers (19 miles) north of Cranbrook on Highway 95A, is a charming little town, with no commercial strip or fast-food outlets; just streets of old stucco mining cottages with a downtown that's been "Bavarianized." Although named for a famous South African diamond mine, Kimberley boomed as a result of the silver and lead deposits unearthed on nearby North Star Mountain.

Sights

Strolling the **Bavarian Platzl,** you'll feel as though you've just driven into a village high in the Swiss Alps, with only bell-wearing cows and brightly dressed milkmaids missing. This is the focus of downtown—a cheerful, red-brick, pedestrian plaza complete with babbling brook, ornamental bridges, and the "World's Largest Cuckoo Clock" ("Happy Hans" pops out and yodels on the hour). Shops, many German restaurants, and delis line the plaza, selling European specialties. At the far end of the Platzl, **Kimberley Heritage Museum** (250/427-7510, Mon.–Sat. 9 A.M.–4:30 P.M. in summer, Mon.–Sat. 1–4 P.M. the rest of the year, donation) houses mining-history exhibits, a stuffed grizzly bear, a hodgepodge of artifacts, and displays relating to all the locally popular outdoor sports.

Cominco Gardens, also known as Kimberley Gardens, enjoys a hilltop location (4th Ave., 250/427-5160, $3). Originally planted in 1927 to promote a fertilizer developed by Cominco, the one-hectare (2.5-acre) gardens now hold close to 20,000 flowers.

The **Underground Mining Railway** (115 Gerry Sorensen Way, 250/427-0022, adult $15, senior $12, child $7) was constructed from materials salvaged from mining towns around the province. The seven-kilometer (4.3-mile) track climbs a steep-sided valley, crosses a trestle bridge, and stops at particularly impressive mountain viewpoints and the original townsite, before arriving at the **Sullivan Mine Interpretive Centre,** which stands on the site of a massive reclamation project. It runs six times daily through summer.

Recreation

From early December to early April, **Kimberley Alpine Resort** (250/427-4881 or 800/258-7669, www.skikimberley.com) provides great skiing and snowboarding on a wide variety of slopes four kilometers (2.5 miles) west of downtown. Currently there are 67 named runs covering 738 hectares (1,800 acres), with a maximum vertical rise of 750 meters (2,460 feet). Most beginners and intermediates will be content on the well-groomed main slopes, while more experienced skiers and boarders will want to head to the expert terrain served by the Easter Chair. Lift tickets are adult $60, senior $48, child $42. Summer activities include chairlift rides, hiking, mountain biking, and luge rides.

Accommodations and Food

If you plan on golfing or a winter vacation in Kimberley, contact **Kimberley Vacations** (250/427-4877 or 800/667-0871, www.kimberleyreservations.com) for the best package deals. Otherwise contact one of the following choices: If you don't mind being a couple of kilometers out of town, **Travellaire Motel** (toward Marysville at 2660 Warren Ave., 250/427-2252 or 800/477-4499, $58 s, $68 d) provides excellent value. It's only a small place, but is regularly revamped and decked out with new beds and furniture. There's also a barbecue area for guest use. At the base of Kimberley Alpine Resort, **Trickle Creek Lodge** (250/427-5175 or 800/258-7669, www.skikimberley.com, from $149 s or d) is a stunning log and stone structure of 80 spacious guest rooms, each with a kitchen, balcony, and fireplace. Guest facilities include a fitness center and a year-round outdoor heated pool.

Kimberley Riverside Campground (250/427-2929, www.kimberleycampground.com, May–mid-Oct., tenting $21–26, hookups $27–33) is seven kilometers (4.3 miles) south of downtown on Highway 95A, and then three kilometers (1.9 miles) west along St. Mary's River Road. Spread between the road and the river, it's a sprawling complex with an outdoor pool and grocery store.

European gourmet specialties, predominantly German, are available all around town. The **Gasthaus** (in the Platzl, 250/427-4851, daily except Tues. 11:30 A.M.–10 P.M., $8–19>) features German lunches, such as goulash, and German dinner specialties, such as bratwurst, *rheinischer sauerbraten,* Wiener schnitzel, and *kassler rippchen.* Away from the Platzl, **Old Bauernhaus** (280 Norton Ave., 250/427-5133, dinner only, closed Tues., $14–24) features

Bavarian specialties and plenty of atmosphere. It's in a post-and-beam farm building originally constructed about 350 years ago in southern Bavaria. The building was taken apart, shipped to Canada, and painstakingly rebuilt.

Information

For more information on Kimberley and the surrounding area, drop by **Kimberley Visitor Info Centre** (270 Kimberley Ave., 250/427-3666, www.kimberleychamber.com, daily 10 A.M.–6 P.M. in summer, Mon.–Sat. 9 A.M.–5 P.M. the rest of year).

CONTINUING NORTH TOWARD INVERMERE

This stretch of highway passes through a deep valley chock-full of commercial facilities like world-class golf courses, resorts, and hot springs. The low elevation makes for relatively mild winters and an early start to the summer season. And with the Purcell Mountains on one side and the Rockies on the other, the valley certainly doesn't lack for scenery.

Whiteswan Lake Provincial Park

Continuing north, the Rockies close in and the scenery becomes unbelievably beautiful. Twenty-eight kilometers (17.4 miles) north of Skookumchuck, an unsealed logging road takes off east into the mountains, leading to 1,994-hectare (4,930-acre) Whiteswan Lake Provincial Park. The road climbs steadily from the highway, entering Lussier Gorge after 11 kilometers (6.8 miles). Within the gorge, a steep trail leads down to **Lussier Hot Springs.** Two small pools have been constructed to contain the odorless hot (43°C/110°F) water as it bubbles out of the ground and flows into the Lussier River. Within the park itself, the road closely follows the southern shorelines of first **Alces Lake,** then the larger **Whiteswan Lake.** The two lakes attract abundant bird life— loons, grebes, and herons are all common. They also attract anglers, who come for great rainbow trout fishing. Both lakes are stocked and have a daily quota of two fish per person. The park road passes four popular campgrounds.

The sites are $15 per night and fill on a first-come, first-served basis. There are no hookups or showers and reservations aren't taken.

Top of the World Provincial Park

If you thought the scenery around Whiteswan Lake was wild and remote, wait till you see this 8,790-hectare (21,720-acre) wilderness, a rough 52 kilometers (32 miles) from Highway 95 (turn off the Whiteswan Lake access road at Alces Lake). You can't drive into the park, but it's a fairly easy six-kilometer (3.7-mile) hike from the end of the road to picturesque **Fish Lake,** the park's largest body of water. Bring everything you'll need because there are no services within the park. Camping is possible at one of four designated areas for $5 per person, or you can stay in the large cabin nestled in trees beside Fish Lake ($15 per person).

Fairmont Hot Springs

North of Canal Flats, the highway approaches and passes the weirdly shaped **Dutch Creek Hoodoos,** a set of photogenic rock formations carved over time by ice, water, and wind. The highway then quickly reaches these hot springs and surrounding vacation homes, golf courses, and an airstrip long enough to land a Boeing 737. Despite all the commercialism, **Fairmont Hot Springs Resort** (250/345-600, www.fairmonthotspringsresort.com) is still the main attraction. The appeal of the hot springs is simple; unlike most other springs, the hot water bubbling up from underground here contains calcium, not sulfur with its attendant smell. Soaking in the outdoor pools (daily 8 A.M.–10 P.M., adult $10, senior $9, child $8) are a magical experience, especially in the evening. Lazily swim or float around in the large warm pool, dive into the cool pool, or sit 'n' sizzle in the hot pool and watch the setting sun color the steep faces of the Canadian Rockies. The resort also boasts two golf courses, horseback riding, a small alpine resort, a lodge ($164–365 s or d), a RV-only campground ($23–36), and a variety of eateries.

South of the resort is **Spruce Grove Resort** (Hwy. 3, 250/345-6561 or 888/629-4004, www.sprucegroveresort.com, unserviced sites $25–29, hookups $30–34), where campsites are spread through trees and along a quiet eddy in the Columbia River.

INVERMERE AND VICINITY

The next area to lure travelers off Highway 93/95 is **Windermere Lake.** Overlooking the lake, the town of Invermere (population 3,500) is the commercial center of the Columbia Valley. The lake and surrounding wilderness are great spots for recreational activities, and are especially popular among landlocked Albertans. On the approach to town is **Windermere Valley Museum** (622 Third St., 250/342-9769, summer Mon.–Fri. 11 A.M.–4 P.M.), where the entire history of the valley is contained in seven separate buildings. The main street itself (7th Ave.) is lined with restored heritage buildings and streetlights bedecked with hanging baskets overflowing with colorful flowers.

Panorama Mountain Village

Panorama (250/345-6413 or 800/663-2929, www.panoramaresort.com) is a year-round resort village in the Purcell Mountains west of Invermere. Development includes a residential subdivision, a year-round water park, and **Greywolf Golf Course** (greens fee $149) where water comes into play on 14 of the 18 holes. During the warmer months, there are also white-water rafting and inflatable kayak trips down Toby Creek, horseback riding, and, in the village itself, tennis and a swimming pool. It was skiing that first put Panorama on the map, mainly because the resort boasts one of the highest vertical rises in all North America (1,200 m/3,900 ft). Despite the impressive relief, Panorama offers slopes suitable for all levels of expertise (adult $71, child $48).

Practicalities

Invermere holds limited accommodations, but plenty of eateries, grocery stores, and gas stations. On a Saturday morning in downtown Invermere, you'll find all sorts of goodies at the outdoor **market,** which happens right on the main street. Farther down the hill, the **Quality Bakery** (1305 7th Ave., 888/681-9977, Mon.–Sat. 7:30 A.M.–6 P.M., summer daily) lives up to its name with a huge range of ultra-healthy sandwiches and not-so-healthy cakes and pastries. The town's most upscale dining room is **Strand's** (up the hill from the main street at 818 12th St., 250/342-6344; daily 5–9 P.M.; $22–36). It's contained in a restored 1912 heritage house set on landscaped gardens, with diners seated in small, intimate rooms. The immaculately presented seasonal menu often includes delicacies such as trout, salmon, and venison that are served with a wide selection of vegetables.

Back out on the highway, at the south side of the town turn-off, is the **Invermere Visitor Centre** (250/342-2844, www.adventurevalley. com, July–Aug. daily 9 A.M.–5 P.M.).

RADIUM HOT SPRINGS

One of two main western gateways to the Canadian Rockies is the small town of Radium Hot Springs (population 700), which lies at the junction of Highways 93 and 95, 140 kilometers (87 miles) north of Cranbrook and a spectacular two-hour drive through Kootenay National Park from the famous resort town of Banff. Its setting is spectacular; most of town lies on a plateau above the Columbia River, from where the panoramic views take in the Rockies to the east and the Purcell Mountains to the west. As well as providing accommodations and other services for mountain visitors and highway travelers, Radium is a destination in itself for many. Aside from the town's namesake, the area boasts a wildlife-rich wetland, two excellent golf courses, and many other recreational opportunities.

Columbia River Wetland

From its headwaters south of Radium, the Columbia flows northward through a 180-kilometer-long (110-mile-long) wetland to Golden, continuing north for a similar distance before reversing course and flowing south into the United States. The wetland near Radium holds international significance, not only for its size (26,000 hectares/64,250 acres), but also for the sheer concentration of wildlife it supports. More than 100 species of birds live among the sedges, grasses, dogwoods, and black cottonwoods surrounding the convoluted banks of the Columbia. Of special interest are blue herons in large numbers and ospreys in one of the world's highest concentrations. The wetland also lies along the Pacific Flyway, so particularly large numbers of ducks, Canada geese, and other migratory birds gather here in spring and autumn. The northbound spring migration is celebrated with the early May **Wings over the Rockies Bird Festival** (www.wingsovertherockies.org). At any time of year, use the festival website to source the valley's best birding spots.

Recreation

Kootenay River Runners (4983 Hwy. 93, 250/347-9210 or 800/599-4399), offers whitewater rafting trips for adult $69, child $53 for a half-day trip, and adult $97, child $81 full-day. Transportation and wetsuits are provided, and the full-day trip includes lunch. This company also offers a more relaxing evening float through the Columbia River Wetland in large and stable voyageur canoes, which depart daily at 5:30 P.M.; the cost is adult $49, child $35.

Accommodations and Camping

Radium, with a population of just 700, has more than 30 motels, an indication of its importance as a highway stop for overnight travelers. Those that lie along the access road to Kootenay National Park come alive with color through summer as each tries to outdo the others with floral landscaping. When booking any of these accommodations, ask about free passes to the hot pools.

Kootenay Motel (250/347-9490 or 877/908-2020, $60 s, $68 d, $5 extra for a kitchenette) is along Highway 95, up the hill from the junction of Highway 95. Up the hill a little farther, and a little and across the road is **Apple Tree Inn** (Hwy. 93, 250/347-9565 or 800/350-1511, www.appletreeinnbc.com, Apr.–Oct., $80–140 s or d), with a pleasant outdoor barbecue area. Continuing toward the national park entrance there is the **Gables Motel** (5058 Hwy. 93, 250/347-9866 or 877/387-7007, www.gables-motel.ca, from $75 s or d), where each of the 17 smallish rooms has mountain views and is well furnished.

Three kilometers (1.9 miles) south of town, **Radium Resort** (250/347-9311 or 800/667-6444, www.radiumresort.com) is surrounded by an 18-hole golf course and holds a wide variety of facilities, including a health club, indoor pool, restaurant, and lounge. Guest rooms overlook the golf course and are linked to the main lodge building by a covered walkway. Regular motel rooms range $160–190 s or d, while kitchen-equipped condos sleeping up to six people start at $240 per night. Check the website or call for specials (rooms are often sold for around $100, even in the middle of summer). Additionally, golf, ski, and spa packages lower rates considerably, especially before and after summer's peak season.

Prestige Radium Hot Springs (7493 Main St. W, 250/347-2300 or 877/737-8443, www.prestigeinn.com, $170–210 s or d), sits at the town's main intersection. Facilities include a fitness room, indoor pool, gift shop, spa services, an Italian restaurant, and a lounge bar.

Within Kootenay National Park, but accessed from town off Highways 93/95, is **Redstreak Campground** (see *Camping* in the *Kootenay National Park* section). The closest commercial camping is at **Canyon RV Resort,** nestled in its own private valley immediately north of the Highway 93/95 junction (5012 Sinclair Creek Rd., 250/347-9564, www.canyonrv.com, Apr.–Oct., $27–37). Treed sites are spread along both sides of a pleasant creek, and facilities such as showers, laundry, and a playground are provided.

Food

For breakfast, head to **Springs Course** restaurant (Stanley St., 250/347-9311, daily 7 A.M.–9 P.M. Apr.–Oct., $11–24), at the golf course on the west side of the highway. The view from the deck, overlooking the Columbia River and Purcell Mountains, is nothing short of stunning. The food is good and remarkably inexpensive; in the morning, for example, an omelet with three fillings, hash browns, and toast is just $10.

Back in town, **Back Country Jack's** (Main St. W, 250/347-0097, daily 11 A.M.–11 P.M., $8–16) is decorated with real antiques and hard-bench seats in private booths. There's a wide variety of platters to share, including Cowboy Caviar (nachos and baked beans) and a surprisingly good barbecued chicken soup. For a main, the half-chicken, half-ribs, and all the extras for two ($28) is a good deal.

Information

On the east side of the highway, just south of the Highway 93/95 junction, is the **Radium Hot Springs Visitor Info Centre** (7556 Main St. E, 250/347-9331 or 888/347-9331, www.radiumhotsprings.com, daily 9 A.M.–7 P.M. in summer, daily until 5 P.M. the rest of the year). This building is also home to the national park information center.

Kootenay National Park

Shaped like a lightning bolt, this narrow 140,600-hectare (34,700-acre) park lies northeast of Radium Hot Springs and is bordered to the east by Banff National Park (Alberta). Highway 93, extending for 94 kilometers (58 miles) through the park, provides spectacular mountain vistas; and along the route you'll find many short and easy interpretive hikes, scenic viewpoints, hot springs, picnic areas, and roadside interpretive exhibits. The park isn't particularly noted for its day-hiking opportunities, but backpacker destinations such as Kaufmann Lake and the Rockwall rival almost any other area in the Canadian Rockies.

Day-use areas, a gas station and lodge, and three campgrounds are the only roadside services inside the park. The park is open year-round, although you should check road conditions in winter, when avalanche-control work and snowstorms can close Highway 93 for short periods of time.

To Kootenay Valley

Leaving the hot springs, the road parallels Sinclair Creek to tiny **Olive Lake,** which is ringed with bright yellow wildflowers in summer, and **Sinclair Pass.** The highway then descends to the valley floor, passes two riverside picnic areas, and crosses the pretty **Kootenay River** at **Kootenay Crossing.** The highway then climbs a low saddle and descends to the Vermilion River. On the descent, you pass a particularly nice picnic spot at **Wardle Creek.** Across the river, the mountainside is scarred black, the result of a wildfire that devastated over 4,000 hectares (9,900 acres) of forest in the summer of 2001.

Continuing north, the highway passes **Kootenay Park Lodge** (lodging, food, gas, and an official park information) then climbs

Marble Canyon is an easy hike.

through an area affected by a fire that swept through the entire valley in 2003.

Paint Pots and Marble Canyon

A scenic one-kilometer (0.6-mile) trail (20 minutes each way) leads over the Vermilion River to the **Paint Pots,** a unique natural wonder: three circular ponds stained red, orange, and mustard yellow by oxide-bearing springs. The natives collected ochre from around the pools and mixed it with animal fat or fish oil then used it in ceremonial body and rock painting.

Just up the road, be sure to stop and take the enjoyable self-guided trail, one kilometer (0.6 miles) each way, which leads along the ice-carved **Marble Canyon.** The walk takes only about 30 minutes or so, yet as one of several interpretive plaques says, it takes you back over 500 million years.

HIKING

Some 200 kilometers (124 miles) of trails lace Kootenay National Park. Hiking opportunities range from short interpretive walks to

Sinclair Pass marks the entrance to Kootenay National Park.

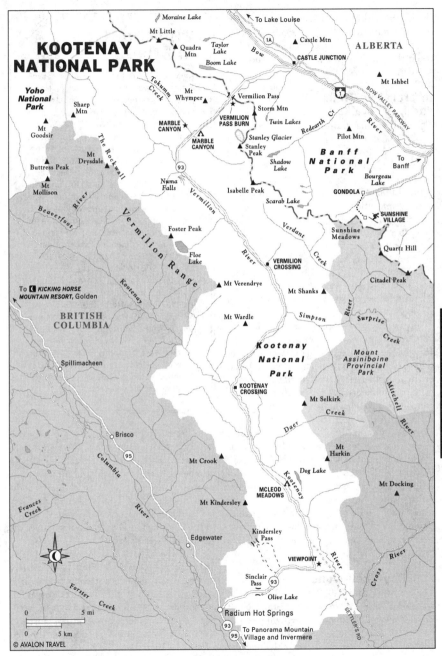

KOOTENAY NATIONAL PARK

Yoho National Park

Moraine Lake
Mt Little
Quadra Mtn
Taylor Lake
Boom Lake
To Lake Louise

Castle Mtn
ALBERTA
CASTLE JUNCTION
Mt Ishbel
BOW VALLEY PARKWAY

Tokumm Creek
Mt Whymper
Vermilion Pass
Storm Mtn
Twin Lakes
Redearth Cr
River

Sharp Mtn
MARBLE CANYON
VERMILION PASS BURN
Stanley Glacier
Pilot Mtn

Mt Goodsir
MARBLE CANYON
Stanley Peak
Banff National Park
To Banff

Buttress Peak
Mt Drysdale
The Rockwall
93
Shadow Lake
Bourgeau Lake
GONDOLA

Mt Mollison
Nuuma Falls
Isabelle Peak
Scarab Lake
SUNSHINE VILLAGE

Beaverfoot
River
Vermilion Range
Vermilion River
Verdant
Sunshine Meadows
Quartz Hill

Foster Peak
VERMILION CROSSING
Creek
Citadel Peak

Floe Lake
Mt Verendrye
Mt Shanks

To **KICKING HORSE MOUNTAIN RESORT**, Golden
Kootenay
Mt Wardle
Simpson
Surprise Creek

BRITISH COLUMBIA
Kootenay National Park
Mount Assiniboine Provincial Park

Spillimacheen
KOOTENAY CROSSING
Mitchell River

Brisco
95
Columbia River
Mt Crook
Daer Creek
Mt Selkirk

Mt Harkin
Mt Docking

Frances Creek
Mt Kindersley
MCLEOD MEADOWS
Dog Lake
Kootenay

Edgewater
Kindersley Pass
VIEWPOINT
River
Cross River

Sinclair Pass
93
Olive Lake
SETTLERS RD

0   5 mi
0   5 km

Radium Hot Springs
93
95
To Panorama Mountain Village and Invermere

© AVALON TRAVEL

challenging treks through remote backcountry. All trails start from Highway 93 on the valley floor, so you'll be facing a strenuous climb to reach the park's high alpine areas, especially those in the south.

Interpretive Trails and Easy Walks

The most popular trails in the park lead to the Paint Pots and through Marble Canyon. At the other end of the park, the area between Redstreak Campground and the hot springs is laced with trails. One particularly scenic loop is the **Juniper Trail** (3.2 km/2 mi, one hour round-trip), which can be picked up just inside the park boundary. Named for the abundance of juniper berries, it provides good valley views with minimal exertion.

From McLeod Meadows Picnic Area, the **Dog Lake Trail** (2.6 km/1.6 mi, 40 minutes one-way) is an easy walk that ends at a small lake hidden from the highway by a forested ridge.

On a sunny day, the trail to **Stanley Glacier** (4.2 km/2.6 mi, 90 minutes one-way) is my favorite in the park. Beginning in the far north of the park, just seven kilometers (4.3 miles) west of the Continental Divide, it climbs steadily for two kilometers (1.2 miles), then levels off and winds through a massive U-shaped glacial valley, with the sheer face of Mount Stanley rising 500 meters (1,640 feet) above the forest to the west. Although the trail officially ends atop a moraine after 4.2 kilometers (2.6 miles), it's worthwhile to continue 1.3 kilometers (0.8 miles) to the tree-topped plateau visible higher up the valley. Surprisingly, once on the plateau, you'll find a gurgling stream, a healthy population of marmots, and incredible views west to Stanley Glacier and north back down the valley.

Full-Day Excursions

The elevation gain (1,050 m/3,445 ft) on the strenuous hike to **Kindersley Summit** (10 km/6.2 mi, four hours one-way) will be a deterrent for many, but views from the summit will make up for the pain endured along the

WHITE-WATER RAFTING

Anyone looking for white-water rafting action will want to run the Kicking Horse River. The rafting season runs late May–mid-September, with river levels at their highest in late June. The Lower Canyon, immediately upstream of Golden, offers the biggest thrills, including a three-kilometer (1.9 mile) stretch of continuous rapids. Upstream of here the river is tamer but still makes for an exciting trip, while even farther upstream, near the western boundary of Yoho National Park, it's more of a float – a good adventure for the more timid visitor. The river is run by a number of companies, most of which offer the option of half-day ($70-90) or full-day ($110-160) trips. The cost varies with inclusions such as transportation from Banff and lunch. Local companies include **Alpine Rafting** (250/344-6778 or 888/599-5299, www.alpinerafting.com), **Wet 'n' Wild Adventures** (250/344-6546 or 800/668-9119, www.wetnwild.bc.ca), **Glacier Raft Company** (250/344-6521, www.glacierraft.com), and **Wild Water Adventures** (403/522-2211 or 888/647-6444, www.wildwater.com).

way. From Highway 93, two kilometers (1.2 miles) west of Sinclair Pass, the trail climbs through a valley, then switchbacks up across a number of avalanche paths and through more forest before emerging at an alpine meadow on Kindersley Pass. This is where the scenery makes the journey worthwhile, with views east to the Continental Divide and north over the Kootenay River Valley.

Of all the lakes in Kootenay National Park, none are as beautiful as **Floe Lake,** which, unfortunately, requires a strenuous day trip to reach (10.4 km/6.5 mi, 3.5 hours one-way, elevation gain 730 m/2,395 ft). From the trailhead eight kilometers (five miles) north of Vermilion Crossing, the trail descends through a forest devastated by a 2003 wildfire, and then parallels Floe Creek almost the entire way. Nestled in a glacial cirque, the lake's aquamarine waters reflect the Rockwall, a sheer limestone wall rising 1,000 meters (3,280 feet) above the far shore. In fall, stands of stunted larch around the lakeshore turn brilliant colors, adding to the incredible beauty.

ACCOMMODATIONS AND CAMPING

The only lodging in the heart of the park is **Kootenay Park Lodge** (403/762-9196, www. kootenayparklodge.com, mid-May–late Sept., $120–185 s or d), a cabin complex at Vermilion Crossing, 65 kilometers (40 miles) from Radium Hot Springs. It consists of a main lodge with restaurant, 10 cabins, and a gift shop. The most basic cabins have a bathroom, small fridge, and coffeemaker, with rates rising to $185 for the newer Verendrye Cabins with a separate bedroom and a fireplace. Utensil and cooking kits are $10 per day.

The well-kept **C Cross River Wilderness Centre** (403/271-3296 or 877/659-7665, www. crossriver.ca; $175 pp including meals) has a real sense of privacy and of being well away from the well-worn tourist path of Highway 93. And they are—tucked in a riverside setting 15 kilometers (9.3 miles) down Settler's Road, which branches off the highway 114 kilometers (71 miles) from Banff and 32 kilometers (20 miles) from Radium Hot Springs. The smart, spacious cabins are equipped with wood-burning fireplaces, log beds draped in down duvets, toilets, and sinks. Showers are located in the main building, along with the lounge, cooking facilities, a dining area, and a deck. As you can imagine, the atmosphere is convivial, with the cabins attracting outdoorsy types who want to enjoy the Canadian Rockies in their natural state—without room service and fine dining. Highly recommended.

C Nipika Mountain Resort (250/342-6516 or 877/647-4525, www.nipika.com; $195 s, $275 d) offers the same wilderness experience as the Cross River Cabins and is in the same vicinity—along Settler's Road, which branches off Highway 93, 114 kilometers (71 miles) from Banff and 32 kilometers (20 miles) from Radium Hot Springs. Sleeping up to eight people, the seven cabins are larger than those at Cross River and have full en suite bathrooms and kitchens with wood-burning stoves. The cabins are modern but were constructed in a very traditional manner—the logs were milled on-site, and construction is dovetail notching. Guests bring their own food and spend their days hiking, fishing, and wildlife watching. In winter, an extensive system of trails is groomed for cross-country skiing.

Camping

The park's largest camping area is **Redstreak Campground** (mid-May–mid-Oct., unserviced sites $27, hookups $35–39) on a narrow plateau in the extreme southwest (vehicle access from Highway 93/95 on the south side of Radium Hot Springs township), which holds 242 sites, showers, and kitchen shelters. In summer, free slideshows and talks are presented by park naturalists five nights a week and typically feature topics such as wolves, bears, the park's human history, or the effects of fire. Trails lead from the campground to the hot springs, town, and a couple of lookouts. A limited number of sites can be reserved through the Parks Canada Campground Reservation Service (877/737-3783, www.pccamping.ca).

The park's two other campgrounds lie to the north of Radium Hot Springs along Highway 93. Both offer fewer facilities (no hookups or

NATIONAL PARK PASSES

Passes are required for entry into Kootenay and Yoho National Parks. Passes are interchangeable between parks – including adjacent Banff and Jasper – and are valid until 4 P.M. the day following purchase. The cost of a **National Parks Day Pass** is adult $10, senior $8.30, child $5. There is a maximum per-vehicle entry fee of double the adult (or senior) rate.

showers). The larger of the two is **McLeod Meadows Campground,** beside the Kootenay River 27 kilometers (16.8 miles) from Radium Hot Springs. Facilities include flush toilets, kitchen shelters, and a fire pit and picnic table at each of the 98 sites. **Marble Canyon,** across the highway from the natural attraction of the same name, offers 61 sites and similar facilities. Both are open late June to early September, and all sites cost $22.

INFORMATION

Kootenay National Park Visitor Centre (250/347-9615; summer daily 9 A.M.–7 P.M., spring and fall daily 9 A.M.–5 P.M.) is outside the park in the town of Radium Hot Springs, at the base of the access road to Redstreak Campground. Here you can collect a free map with hiking trail descriptions, find out about trail closures and campsite availability, get the weather forecast, browse through a gift shop, buy park passes and fishing licenses, and register for overnight backcountry trips.

The other source of park information is at **Kootenay Park Lodge,** at Vermilion Crossing (summer only). It's worth noting that this is the only privately operated official information center in any Canadian national park—a reflection on the folks running this lodge.

Yoho National Park and Vicinity

Yoho, a Cree word of "amazement," is a fitting name for this 131,300-hectare (324,450-acre) national park immediately north of Kootenay National Park and beside Banff National Park to the east. Although it's the smallest of four contiguous parks, its wild and rugged landscape holds spectacular waterfalls, extensive ice fields, a lake to rival those in Banff, and one of the world's most intriguing fossil beds. In addition, you'll find some of the finest hiking in all of Canada on the park's 300-kilometer (186-mile) trail system.

Within the park are four lodges, four campgrounds, and the small railway town of **Field,** where you'll find basic services. The park is open year-round, although road conditions in winter can be treacherous and occasional closures occur on Kicking Horse Pass. The road out to Takakkaw Falls is closed through winter, and it often doesn't reopen until mid-June.

From the park's western edge, Highway 1 follows the Kicking Horse River as it descends to the Columbia River Valley and the town of Golden.

ROAD-ACCESSIBLE SIGHTS

As with all other parks of the Canadian Rockies, you don't need to travel deep into the backcountry to view the most spectacular features—many are visible from the roadside. The sights below are listed from east to west, starting at the park boundary (the Continental Divide).

Spiral Tunnel Viewpoint

The joy that Canadian Pacific Railway president William Van Horne felt upon completion of his transcontinental rail line in 1886 was tempered by massive problems along a stretch of line west of Kicking Horse Pass. "Big Hill" was less than five kilometers (3.1 miles) long, but its gradient was so steep that runaway trains, crashes, and other disasters were common. Nearly a quarter-century after the line opened, railway engineers and builders finally solved the problem. By building two spiral tunnels down through two kilometers (1.2 miles) of solid rock to the valley floor, they lessened the grade dramatically and the terrors came to an end. At this viewpoint along the highway, interpretive displays tell the fascinating story of Big Hill, with distant views to a tunnel entrance.

Yoho Valley

Fed by the Wapta Icefield in the far north of the park, the **Yoho River** flows through this spectacularly narrow valley, dropping more

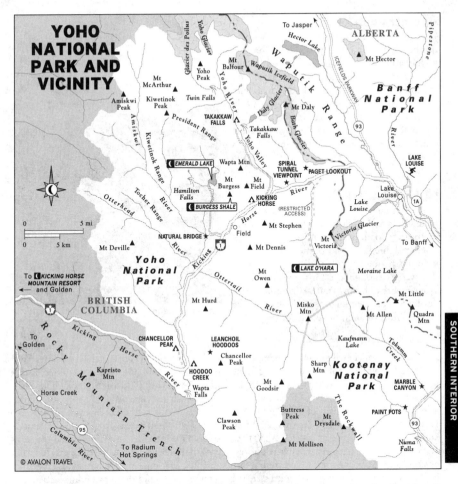

YOHO NATIONAL PARK AND VICINITY

To Jasper

Hector Lake

ALBERTA

Mt Hector

Waputik Range

Glacier des Poilus

Yoho Glacier

Mt Balfour

Waputik Icefield

Mt McArthur

Mt Daly

Banff National Park

Amiskwi Peak

Kiwetinok Peak

Twin Falls

President Range

TAKAKKAW FALLS

Takakkaw Falls

Daly Glacier

Bath Glacier

Amiskwi River

Kiwetinok River

EMERALD LAKE

Wapta Mtn

Yoho Valley

SPIRAL TUNNEL VIEWPOINT

PAGET LOOKOUT

LAKE LOUISE

Otterhead River

Tocher Range

Hamilton Falls

Mt Burgess

Mt Field

BURGESS SHALE

KICKING HORSE

(RESTRICTED ACCESS)

Kicking Horse River

Lake Louise

1A

Mt Deville

NATURAL BRIDGE

Field

Mt Stephen

Victoria Glacier

To Banff

Yoho National Park

Mt Dennis

Mt Victoria

LAKE O'HARA

Moraine Lake

Ottertail River

Mt Owen

To **KICKING HORSE MOUNTAIN RESORT** and Golden

BRITISH COLUMBIA

Mt Hurd

Misko Mtn

Mt Little

Quadra Mtn

Mt Allen

To Golden

Kicking Horse River

CHANCELLOR PEAK

LEANCHOIL HOODOOS

Chancellor Peak

Kaufmann Lake

Tokumm Creek

MARBLE CANYON

Kapristo Mtn

HOODOO CREEK

Wapta Falls

Mt Goodsir

Sharp Mtn

Kootenay National Park

Horse Creek

Rocky Mountain Trench

Clawson Peak

Buttress Peak

Mt Drysdale

PAINT POTS

93

Columbia River

95

To Radium Hot Springs

Mt Mollison

Numa Falls

© AVALON TRAVEL

0   5 mi
0   5 km

Pipestone

ICEFIELDS PARKWAY

93

The Rockwall

than 200 meters (660 feet) in the last kilometer (0.6 miles) before its confluence with the Kicking Horse River. The road leading up the valley passes the park's main campground and climbs a *very* tight series of switchbacks (watch for buses reversing through the middle section). The road ends 14 kilometers (8.7 miles) from the main highway at **Takakkaw Falls,** the most impressive waterfall in the Canadian Rockies. Meaning "wonderful" in the language of the Cree, Takakkaw tumbles 254 meters (830 feet) over a sheer rock wall at the lip of the Yoho Valley, creating a spray bedecked with rainbows.

It can be seen from the parking lot, but it's well worth the easy 10-minute stroll over the Yoho River to appreciate the sight in all its glory.

Natural Bridge

Three kilometers (1.9 miles) west of Field is the turnoff to famous Emerald Lake. On your way out to the lake, you'll first pass another intriguing sight. At Natural Bridge, two kilometers (1.2 miles) down the road, the Kicking Horse River has worn a narrow hole through a limestone wall, creating a bridge. A trail leads to several viewpoints.

◖ Emerald Lake

One of the jewels of the Canadian Rockies, this beautiful lake is surrounded by a forest of Engelmann spruce, as well as many peaks over 3,000 meters (9,800 feet). It's covered in ice most of the year, but comes alive with activity for a few short months in summer when hikers, canoeists, and horseback riders take advantage of the magnificent surroundings. **Emerald Lake Canoe Rentals** (250/343-6000) rents canoes and small boats for $30 per hour, $45 for two hours, or $70 all day.

◖ LAKE O'HARA

Nestled in a high bowl of lush alpine meadows, Lake O'Hara, 11 kilometers (6.8 miles) from the nearest road, is surrounded by dozens of smaller alpine lakes and framed by spectacular peaks permanently mantled in snow. As if that weren't enough, the entire area is webbed by a network of hiking trails. What makes this destination all the more special is that a quota system limits the number of visitors.

© ANDREW HEMPSTEAD

Opabin Plateau

Book the Bus

It's possible to walk to Lake O'Hara, but most visitors take the shuttle bus along a road closed to the public. The departure point is a signed parking lot 15 kilometers (9.3 miles) east of Field and three kilometers (1.9 miles) west of the Continental Divide. Buses for day visitors depart at 8:30 A.M. and 10:30 A.M., returning at 2:30 P.M., 4:30 P.M., and 6:30 P.M. mid-June–early October. The reservation fee is $12 per booking, and the bus fare is $15 per person round-trip. To book a seat, call the dedicated reservations line (250/343-6433). Reservations are taken up to three months in advance, but as numbers are limited, you will need to call *exactly* three months prior to be assured of a seat; even then, you should call as early in the day as possible. All times—bus departures and reservation center hours—are mountain standard time (the same time zone as Banff).

Hiking

The easiest trail is **Lake O'Hara Shoreline** (2.8 km/1.7 mi, 40 minutes), which loops around the picturesque lake, passing a waterfall and

offering myriad perspectives on the surrounding peaks. Many of the region's other hikes lead off the shoreline trail. Of these, the shortest is the **Lake Oesa Trail** (3 km/1.9 mi, one hour one-way), which leads up and into a rocky, water-filled cirque surrounded by talus slopes and 3,000-meter (10,000-foot) peaks. In the adjacent cirque, **Opabin Plateau** (5.9 km/3.7 mi round-trip) can easily be reached in one hour, but it's easy to spend an entire day enjoying the numerous lakes and scrambling around the surrounding slopes. On the edge of the cirque, **Opabin Prospect** is one the most magnificent trail-accessible lookouts in all of western Canada. Other trails lead to **Lake McArthur** (3.5 km/2.2 mi, 80 minutes one-way), a stunning deep-blue body of water edged by colorful alpine meadows, and **Cathedral Basin** (7.5 km/4.7 mi, 2.5 hours one-way), which is a little farther and so receives fewer visitors.

HIKES IN OTHER AREAS OF THE PARK

Emerald Lake

One of the easiest yet most enjoyable walks in

Yoho is the **Emerald Lake Loop** (5.2 km/3.2 mi, 1.5 hours round-trip). The trail encircles the lake and can be hiked in either direction. The best views are from the western shoreline, where a massive avalanche has cleared away the forest of Engelmann spruce. The trail to **Emerald Basin** (4.5 km/2.8 mi, 1.5–2 hours one-way) gains 280 meters (920 feet) of elevation after leaving the lakeshore 1.5 kilometers (0.9 miles) from the parking lot. The most impressive sight awaiting you in the basin is the south wall of the President Range, towering 800 vertical meters (2,625 feet) above. The trail to **Hamilton Falls** (800 m/0.5 mi, 40 minutes one-way) is an easy walk that begins from the Emerald Lake parking lot.

Yoho Valley

The valley for which the park is named lies north of the TransCanada Highway. As well as the sights already discussed, it provides many fine opportunities for serious day-hikers to get off the beaten track. The following day hikes begin from different trailheads near the end of

the Iceline Trail, one of Yoho's finest day hikes

the road up Yoho Valley. In each case, leave your vehicle in the Takakkaw Falls parking lot.

The trail to **Twin Falls** (8 km/5 mi, 2.5 hours one-way) takes over where the road through the Yoho Valley ends, continuing in a northerly direction up the Yoho River to Twin Falls, passing many other waterfalls along the way. At spectacular Twin Falls, water from the Wapta Icefield divides in two before plunging off an 80-meter-high (260-feet-high) cliff.

One of the finest day hikes in all of the Canadian Rockies is the **Iceline Trail** (6.4 km/4 mi, 2.5 hours one-way), which gains a heart-thumping 690 meters (2,260 feet) in elevation. The highlight is a four-kilometer (2.5-mile) traverse of a moraine below Emerald Glacier. Views across the valley improve as the trail climbs to its 2,220-meter (7,283-foot) crest. Many options present themselves along this trail, including continuing on to Twin Falls or backtracking and branching off west to **Yoho Lake.**

◖ Burgess Shale

High on the rocky slopes above Field is a layer of sedimentary rock known as the Burgess Shale, which is famous worldwide, for it has unraveled the mysteries of a major stage of evolution. Encased in the shale, the fossils here are of marine invertebrates around 530 million years old. Generally fossils are the remains of vertebrates, but at this site some freak event—probably a mudslide—suddenly buried thousands of spineless animals (invertebrates), preserving them by keeping out the oxygen that would have decayed their delicate bodies.

Protected by UNESCO as a World Heritage Site, the two research areas are open only to those accompanied by a licensed guide. The **Burgess Shale Geoscience Foundation** (250/343-6006 or 800/343-3006, www.burgess-shale.bc.ca) guides trips to both sites between July and mid-September. The access to **Walcott's Quarry** is along a strenuous 10-kilometer (6.2-mile) trail that gains 760 meters (2,500 feet) in elevation. Trips leave Friday–Monday at 8 A.M. from the trading post at the Field intersection, returning around

6:30 P.M.; $100 per person. Trips to the more easily reached **Mount Stephen Fossil Beds** depart Saturday and Sunday at 8:30 A.M., returning at around 4:30 P.M.; $75 per person. The trail to the Mount Stephen beds gains 520 meters (1,710 feet) of elevation in three kilometers (1.9 miles). The trails to both sites are unrelenting in their elevation gain—you must be fit to hike them. Reservations are a must.

ACCOMMODATIONS AND CAMPING

Marvel at the wonder of Takakkaw Falls from the deck at **HI-Yoho,** also known as Whiskey Jack Hostel (Yoho Valley Rd., 403/760-7580 or 866/762-4122, www.hihostels.ca; mid-June–Sept.; members $23, nonmembers $27). Basic dormitory accommodation is provided for up to 27 guests, who have use of a communal kitchen and showers.

In downtown Field, **Fireweed Hostel** (313 Stephen Ave., 250/343-6999 or 877/343-6999, www.fireweedhostel.com, dorms $40, two-bedroom suite $160) is one of the few private backpacker lodges in the Canadian Rockies—and it's a good one. It's a modern, purpose-built building with solid bunk beds topped by pillow top mattresses, a beautiful lounge with a log fireplace and LCD TV, and a modern well-equipped kitchen.

Also in Field is the simple yet elegant **Kicking Horse Lodge** (100 Centre St., 250/343-6303, www.trufflepigs.com; $165–250 s or d), which offers 14 well-furnished rooms and the highly recommended Truffle Pigs Bistro.

Emerald Lake Lodge (3 km west of Field then 6 km north at the end of the road to Emerald Lake, 250/343-6321 or 800/663-6336, www.crmr.com, from $330 s or d) is a gracious, luxury-class accommodation along the southern shore of one of the Canadian Rockies' most magnificent lakes. Guests lap up the luxury of richly decorated duplex-style units and freestanding cabins. Outfitted in a heritage theme, each has a wood-burning fireplace, private balcony, luxurious bathroom, and comfortable bed topped by a plush duvet. Lodge amenities include a hot tub and sauna,

swimming pool, restaurant, lounge, and lakefront café. Guests can also go horseback riding, or go boating and fishing on Emerald Lake.

Spending a night at **Lake O'Hara Lodge** (250/343-6418, www.lakeohara.com, mid-June–early Oct.) is a special experience, and one that draws familiar faces year after year. Rates of $420 s, $535 d for a room in the main lodge (shared bathrooms) and $760–775 d for a lakeside cabin include all meals, taxes, gratuities, and transportation.

Camping

The park's main camping area is **Kicking Horse Campground** (mid-May–mid-Oct., $28), five kilometers (three miles) northeast of Field along the road to Takakkaw Falls. Facilities include coin showers ($1), flush toilets, and kitchen shelters. Back toward the TransCanada Highway, **Monarch Campground** ($19) offers more-limited facilities and less-private sites. **Hoodoo Creek Campground,** along the TransCanada Highway 23 kilometers (14 miles) southwest of Field, provides 106 private sites among the trees for $21 per vehicle. Amenities include flush toilets, hot water, kitchen shelters, and an interpretive program.

At the end of the road up the Yoho Valley, **Takakkaw Falls Campground** (July–mid-Sept., $19) is designed for tent campers only. Park at the end of the road and load up the carts with your gear for a pleasant 400-meter (0.2-mile) walk along the valley floor. No showers are provided, and the only facilities are pit toilets and picnic tables.

FOOD

In downtown Field, **Truffle Pigs Bistro** (Kicking Horse Lodge, 250/343-6303; daily for lunch and dinner, also breakfast in summer; $17–31) is one of those unexpected finds that makes traveling such a joy. In the evening this place really shines, with dishes as adventurous as smoked Alaskan salmon tiramisu and as simple as an Albertan-raised beef served with baby potatoes and grilled tomato.

Overlooking an arm of Emerald Lake, **Cilantro on the Lake** (250/343-6321, daily

11 A.M.–9 P.M. mid-June–Sept., $25–37) is a casual café featuring magnificent views from tables inside an open-fronted, log chalet–style building or out on the lakefront deck.

INFORMATION

The main source of park information is **Field Visitor Centre** on the TransCanada Highway at Field (250/343-6783, daily 9 A.M.–8 P.M. in summer, daily 9 A.M.–4 P.M. the rest of the year).

GOLDEN

From the western boundary of Yoho National Park, the TransCanada Highway meanders down the beautiful Kicking Horse River Valley to the town of Golden (population 4,800), at the confluence of the Kicking Horse and Columbia Rivers. As well as being a destination in itself, Golden makes a good central base for exploring the region or as an overnight stop on a tour through the Canadian Rockies that takes in the national parks on the western side of the Continental Divide.

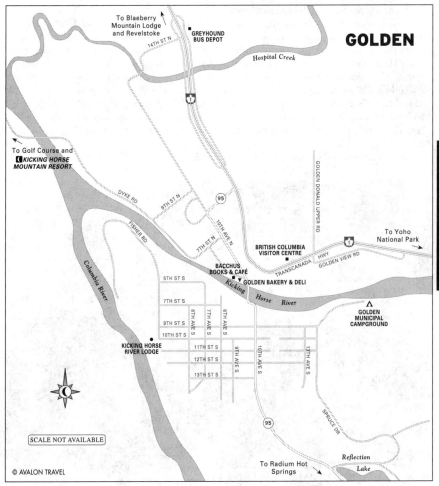

◖ Kicking Horse Mountain Resort

Summer or winter, as you descend into Golden from Yoho National Park, it's easy to make out the ski slopes of Kicking Horse Mountain Resort (250/439-5400 or 866/754-5425, www.kickinghorseresort.com) across the valley. The eight-person gondola transports visitors high into the alpine mid-June–September in just 18 minutes. The 360-degree panorama at the summit is equal to any other accessible point in the Canadian Rockies. Graded hiking trails lead from the upper terminal through a fragile, treeless environment, while mountain bikers revel in a challenging descent in excess of 1,000 meters (3,280 feet). A single gondola ride is adult $31, senior $24, child $13. A better deal is the lunch combo ticket for adult $49, senior $29, child $22. Mountain bikers pay $27 for a single ride while a rent-and-ride package costs $84 for the full day, including a full-suspension bike. The gondola operates through summer daily 10:30 A.M.–5:30 P.M.

While summer is wonderful, it is in wintertime that this resort comes alive. In addition to the gondola, four other lifts transport skiers and boarders to hidden bowls and to a high point of 2,450 meters (8,040 feet), giving the resort North America's second-highest vertical rise (1,260 m/4,135 ft). Lifts operate mid-December–early April and tickets are adult $69, senior $59, child $36. Facilities in the base lodge include rentals, a cafeteria, and a ski school, while the summit restaurant is also open daily for lunch and Friday and Saturday for dinner.

Accommodations and Camping

Kicking Horse River Lodge (801 9th St. N, 250/439-1112 or 877/547-5266, khrl.com; $36 dorm beds, $125–240 s or d) epitomizes the new wave of lodging in the Canadian Rockies. It is a modern, riverfront log building with amenities that include high-speed Internet, a living area with a large-screen TV, and a café with outdoor seating overlooking the Columbia River.

Blaeberry Mountain Lodge (1680 Moberly

the gondola at Kicking Horse Mountain Resort

© ANDREW HEMPSTEAD

School Rd., 250/344-5296, www.blaeberry-mountainlodge.bc.ca, $95–145 s or d) is on a 62-hectare (150-acre) property among total wilderness. Rooms are in the main lodge or self-contained cabins, with plenty of activities available to guests. Blaeberry is nine kilometers (5.6 miles) north of Golden along Highway 1, then seven kilometers (4.3 miles) farther north along Moberly School Road.

Of many new accommodations at the base of Kicking Horse Mountain Resort, **Copper Horse Lodge** (250/344-7644 or 877/544-7644, www.copperhorselodge.com, $180–230 s or d includes breakfast) comes highly recommended. Guest rooms are outfitted in earthy yet stylish color schemes and luxuries such as bathrobes, Internet access, and TV/DVD combos. Other amenities include a restaurant, lounge, and outdoor hot tub.

Through the old part of town and over the Kicking Horse River is **Golden Municipal Campground** (9th St., 250/344-5412, www.goldenmunicipalcampground.com; mid-May–mid-Oct., $20–29). It's a quiet place, strung out along the river and two kilometers (1.2 miles) from downtown along a riverfront walkway. Facilities include picnic shelters, hot coin-operated showers, and 70 sites with fire pits.

Food

At an elevation of 2,347 meters (7,700 feet), the **⊂ Eagle's Eye** is the crowning glory of Kicking Horse Mountain Resort (250/439-5400 or 866/754-5425, daily from 10 A.M.) and is Canada's highest restaurant. Access is by gondola from the resort's base village, 13 kilometers (eight miles) west of downtown Golden. As you'd expect, the views are stunning and are set off by a stylish timber and stonework interior, including a floor-to-ceiling fireplace and a wide wraparound deck protected from the wind by glass paneling. It's open in summer daily for a lunch costing adult $49, senior $42, child $22, which includes the gondola ride. Between 7 and 10 P.M. on Friday evenings, the setting becomes more romantic and the food more adventurous but remains distinctly Canadian. Dinner mains range $25–40 and include such delights

as salmon baked in a saffron-vanilla cream and served with strawberry salsa ($28).

Start your day with the locals at the **Golden Bakery & Deli** (419 9th Ave., 250/344-2928, Mon.–Sat. 6:30 A.M.–6 P.M., $5–8), where the coffee is always fresh and the faces friendly. Baked goodies include breads, pastries, cakes, and meat pies, with inexpensive daily specials displayed on a blackboard in a seated section off to the side of the main counter.

Information

The year-round **British Columbia Visitor Centre** is ensconced in an architecturally striking building beside the highway before it descends into town from the east (111 Golden Upper Donald Rd., 250/344-7125 or 800/622-4653, www.tourismgolden.com, daily 9 A.M.–5 P.M., until 8 P.M. in summer). **Bacchus Books** (409 9th Ave., 250/344-5600; Mon.–Sat. 9 A.M.–5:30 P.M., Sun. 10 A.M.–4 P.M.) has a wide selection of new and used books, with plenty of local reading and detailed maps of the Columbia Valley.

© ANDREW HEMPSTEAD

British Columbia Visitor Centre

SOUTHERN INTERIOR

CENTRAL AND NORTHERN BRITISH COLUMBIA

Ranging from the Canadian Rockies in the east to the Pacific Ocean in the west, and from the TransCanada Highway in the south to the Yukon Territory in the north, the central and northern regions of British Columbia hold a vast array of natural features. These include the massive Fraser River, the lofty peaks of the Cariboo and Coast Mountains, the deeply indented coastal fjords around Bella Coola, and the vast forested landscape of the north. Its mostly forested landscape is broken by two major mountain ranges—the Rockies and the Coast Mountains—and literally thousands of lakes, rivers, and streams. Wildlife is abundant here; the land is home to moose, deer, black and grizzly bears, elk, Dall sheep, and mountain goats.

The most heavily traveled route through central British Columbia is the TransCanada Highway, which for the purposes of this book also forms the region's southern boundary. In the east of the province, the highway bisects Glacier National Park, a small but spectacular park of glaciers and towering peaks. Heading west from the park, the highway passes the heli-skiing hub of Revelstoke and the watery playground of Shuswap Lake before coming to the large population center of Kamloops. From Kamloops, two highways lead north. Highway 5 accesses Wells Gray and Mount Robson Provincial Parks, the former a vast forested wilderness and the latter named for one of the most spectacular mountain peaks in all of Canada. The other route, Highway 97, runs through Cariboo Country, best known for the 1860s gold-rush town of Barkerville,

HIGHLIGHTS

◖ Meadows in the Sky Parkway: Many highway travelers miss Mount Revelstoke National Park, which means you'll probably have this scenic mountain drive to yourself (page 201).

◖ Mount Robson Provincial Park: It's impossible not to be impressed on the drive through this mountainous park, unless of course, clouds are covering the highest peak in the Canadian Rockies (page 210).

◖ Historic Hat Creek Ranch: More than 100 years since the Cariboo Wagon Road bustled with miners heading north in search of their fortune, it's still possible to experience the frontier feeling at this well-preserved ranch (page 212).

◖ Bowron Lake Provincial Park: The main attraction of this lake-filled park is the wilderness canoe circuit, but the park is worth visiting for its scenic locale – and hopefully you'll find time for a quick paddle (page 219).

◖ 'Ksan Historical Village: Learn about native culture at this authentically reconstructed village, where totem poles, longhouses, and Gitxsan arts and crafts are on display (page 227).

◖ Gwaii Haanas National Park Reserve: Traveling to the Queen Charlotte Islands is an adventure in itself, but to *really* get off the beaten track, schedule a trip into this remote park renowned for Haida history (page 242).

◖ Liard River Hot Springs: Reward yourself with a hot soak at this excellent park on the Alaska Highway (page 254).

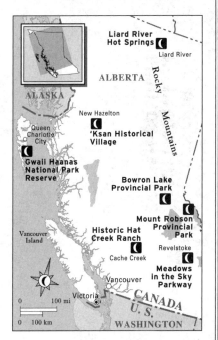

LOOK FOR ◖ TO FIND RECOMMENDED SIGHTS, ACTIVITIES, DINING, AND LODGING.

now completely restored and one of the highlights of a trip north.

Whichever of these two routes you take, you'll finish along the Yellowhead Highway, the gateway to northern British Columbia. The largest city along this route is Prince George, a forestry and service center 780 kilometers (484 miles) north of Vancouver in the heart of a recreational paradise. From Prince George, the Yellowhead Highway runs west to the towns that form jumping-off points for fishing and

boating adventures on surrounding lakes and rivers. The western terminus of the Yellowhead Highway is Prince Rupert, a busy coastal city at the north end of the BC Ferries network, a stop on the Alaska Marine Highway, and gateway to the mystical Queen Charlotte Islands. Two routes head north off the Yellowhead Highway. The Stewart–Cassiar Highway begins west of Prince George and parallels the Coast Mountains, passing the turnoff to the twin towns of Stewart and Hyder and some

CENTRAL AND NORTHERN

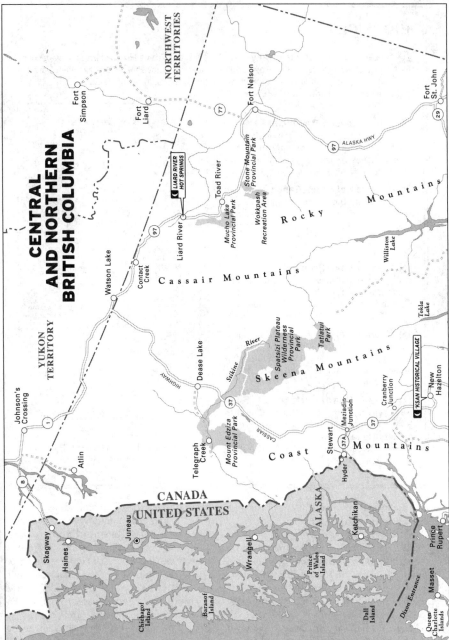

CENTRAL AND NORTHERN BRITISH COLUMBIA

NORTHWEST TERRITORIES

Fort Simpson

Fort Liard

Fort Nelson

77

Fort St. John

29

97 ALASKA HWY

LIARD RIVER HOT SPRINGS

Toad River

Stone Mountain Provincial Park

Mountains

97

Mucho Lake Provincial Park

Wokkpash Recreation Area

Rocky

Liard River

Williston Lake

Watson Lake

Contact Creek

Cassair Mountains

Tokla Lake

YUKON TERRITORY

River

Stikine

Spatsizi Plateau Wilderness Provincial Park

Tatlatui Park

1

Dease Lake

Skeena Mountains

KSAN HISTORICAL VILLAGE

New Hazelton

Johnson's Crossing

HIGHWAY

37

Cranberry Junction

Meziadin Junction

37

8

Atlin

Telegraph Creek

Mount Edziza Provincial Park

CASSIAR

Coast

Stewart

37A

Mountains

CANADA

UNITED STATES

Hyder

ALASKA

Juneau

Ketchikan

Prince Rupert

Skagway

Haines

Wrangell

Prince of Wales Island

Masset

Chichagof Island

Baranof Island

Dall Island

Dixon Entrance

Queen Charlotte Islands

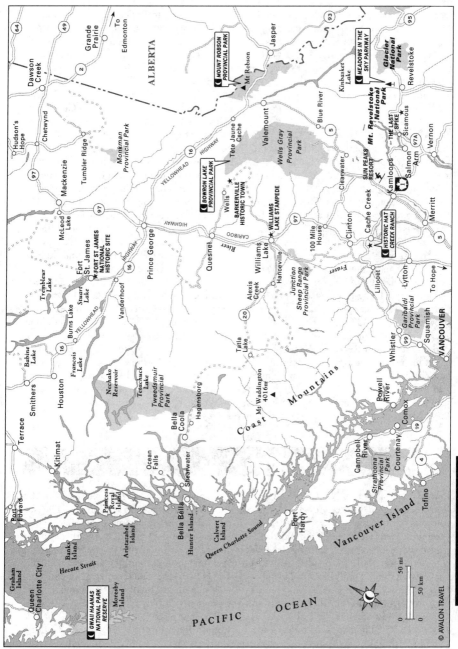

© AVALON TRAVEL

remote provincial parks. It ends at its junction with the other route north—the famous Alaska Highway. Mile Zero of the Alaska Highway is at Dawson Creek, northeast of Prince George. From there the highway winds through kilometer after kilometer of boreal forest, past lakes and mountains to the great northland of the Yukon Territory.

PLANNING YOUR TIME

Planning how to spend your time in central and northern British Columbia has as much to do with integrating the region with the rest of your itinerary as it does trying to work out how to hit all the highlights. The most important thing to remember is that this part of the province is vast—bigger than all the other regions combined, so plan accordingly.

The east–west TransCanada Highway between Banff and Vancouver can easily be traveled in one day, but with two national parks and a string of interesting towns en route, you will want to schedule at least one overnight stop (Revelstoke is a good choice). Even if you're in a hurry, detour along the Meadows in the Sky Parkway in Mount Revelstoke National Park to get high above the alpine. The region's biggest city is Kamloops, from which highways lead in four directions. Hands down, the most scenic is Highway 5 north to Mount Robson Provincial Park, from where the choices are to head northwest to Prince George, gateway to northern British Columbia, or east to Jasper National Park and then south through to Banff. If you drive far enough north along Highway 97 from Kamloops, you'll also reach Prince George. A good way to kick off this long drive north is with a stop at Historic Hat Creek Ranch, where buildings from the Cariboo Gold Rush still stand. Schedule at least two days for the drive west from Prince George to Prince Rupert. To drive the Alaska/Cassiar Highway loop will take at least another four days, including a stop at Liard Hot Springs and a detour to Hyder. Add another three days in the Queen Charlotte Islands for good measure, which should include a day trip to Gwaii Haanas National Park Reserve. One good way to visit the northern portion of the province without retracing your steps is to take the ferry between Prince Rupert and Vancouver Island in one direction.

The summer season in central and northern British Columbia is shorter than elsewhere in the province. For general interest travel, plan a trip during the peak July–August period. June and September are also good for traveling— it's still warm enough to camp out, and as a bonus, you'll miss the worst of the high-summer bug season. Those keen to see grizzly bears in their natural habitat will want to schedule a visit to the Khutzeymateen in June or to Hyder August–September.

Golden to Kamloops

GLACIER NATIONAL PARK

Encompassing 135,000 hectares (333,590 acres) of the Selkirk Mountains west of the Rocky Mountain Trench, this park is a wonderland of jagged snowcapped peaks, extensive ice fields, thundering waterfalls, steep-sided valleys, and fast-flowing rivers. The TransCanada Highway bisects the park, cresting at 1,327-meter (4,550 feet) **Rogers Pass.** From this lofty summit, Golden is 80 kilometers (50 miles) east and Revelstoke is 72 kilometers (45 miles) west.

Those from south of the 49th parallel probably associate the park's name with the American national park in Montana. The two parks share the same name and glaciated environment, but the similarities end there. In the "other" park, buses shuttle tourists here and there and the backcountry is crowded with hikers. Here in the Canadian version, commercialism is almost totally lacking and use of the backcountry is blissfully minimal.

The best place to start a visit to the park is **Rogers Pass Information Centre.** Looking south from the center, you can see the

A RAILWAY AND A ROAD

In a scenario familiar throughout western Canada, the proclamation of Glacier National Park was influenced by the Canadian Pacific Railway's desire to see tourists use its rail line.

For Canadian Pacific Railway engineers, finding a passable train route through the Columbia Mountains proved a formidable challenge. The major obstacle was not the elevation, but the threat of avalanches coupled with narrow valleys and steep approaches. After a route was chosen, workers toiled with picks and shovels for three years, completing the railbed on November 7, 1885. The last spike was driven into the ground at Craigellachie, 100 kilometers (62 miles) to the west of Rogers Pass, and the transcontinental rail line was finally opened. Unfortunately, despite railway engineering ingenuity, frequent and devastating avalanches took their toll, killing more than 200 workers in the first 30 years of operation. Forced to stop the carnage, the Canadian Pacific Railway rerouted the line, tunneling under the actual pass in 1916.

In the 1950s, a team of engineers tackled the same problem that faced those on the railway – this time in an effort to build a highway across the pass. The tunnel approach that had worked for the railway was deemed impractical for a highway, so a new solution to the avalanche danger was required. In 1962 a route over the pass was completed – this time with the addition of concrete snowsheds over sections of the highway. At the same time, the world's largest mobile avalanche-control program was created to stave off danger. Experts constantly monitor weather and snow conditions so they can accurately predict when and where avalanches will occur. Then they close the highway and dislodge potential slides with mobile howitzers, thereby stabilizing the slopes.

Illecillewaet, Asulkan, and Swiss Glaciers. As far as actual "sights" go, driving through the park you'll be surrounded by one of the most awe-inspiring panoramas visible from any Canadian highway. Each roadside viewpoint seems to outdo the last. You can also get out of the car and go hiking to get a better feeling for the park, but most of the trails here entail strenuous climbs.

Through-traffic excepted, permits are required for entry into Glacier National Park; they're available from the Discovery Centre. A one-day permit is adult $8, senior $7, child $4 to a maximum of $20 per vehicle.

The Land

Regardless of whether you approach the park from the east or west, you'll climb over 700 vertical meters (2,300 feet) to reach the summit of Rogers Pass. The pass is not particularly high, but it's impressive. Surrounding peaks, many topping 3,000 meters (9,800 feet), rise dramatically from the pass, with heavy winter snows feeding more than 400 glaciers, some visible from the highway.

Flower lovers will be impressed by the 600 species of flowering plants that have been identified within the park. The best time to see wildflowers in the high meadows and forests is early August, though an amazing profusion of color sweeps through the lower-elevation forests starting in June, and in July the edge of the highway and avalanche paths turn bright yellow with wild lilies. The lower montane forest supports a lush variety of tree species, including mountain hemlock, subalpine fir, Engelmann spruce, western red cedar, and western hemlock.

The rugged terrain and long hard winters in Glacier National Park mean that resident mammals are a tough and hardy bunch. Healthy populations of both black and grizzly bears inhabit the park. The black bears often feed along the roadside in late spring. Grizzlies are less common and tend to remain in the backcountry, but early in the season, lingering snow can keep them at lower elevations; look for them on avalanche slopes.

Hiking

The park's 21 hiking trails cover 140 kilometers

CENTRAL AND NORTHERN

(87 miles) and range from short interpretive walks to long, steep, difficult climbs. Aside from the interpretive trails, most gain a lot of elevation, rewarding hikers with outstanding views. Remember, many of the park's high-elevation trails are covered in snow until well into July.

Two short trails provide an introduction to the park: **Abandoned Rails Interpretive Trail** (one km/0.6 mi, 20 minutes round-trip), which starts to the west of the information center, and the **Meeting of the Waters Trail** (one km/0.6 mi, 25 minutes round-trip), which starts behind Illecillewaet Campground, four kilometers (2.5 miles) south of the information center.

Are you feeling energetic? You'll need to be on the following two hikes, my favorites in the park. Starting from the **Illecillewaet Campground,** the **Avalanche Crest Trail** (4.2 km/2.6 mi, 2.5 hours one-way, elevation gain 800 m/2,632 ft) heads off to the left from the information board, climbing steeply through a subalpine forest for the first three kilometers (1.9 miles), then leveling out and providing stunning views below to Rogers Pass and south to Illecillewaet and Asulkan Glaciers. While elevation on the **Asulkan Valley Trail** (6.5 km/four mi, four hours one-way, elevation gain 930 m/3,059 ft) is similar to others in the steep-sided Illecillewaet River Valley, it is gained over a longer distance, meaning a less strenuous outing. Nevertheless, a full day should be allowed round-trip. From the back of Illecillewaet Campground, the trail follows Asulkan Brook through a valley of dense subalpine forest. Whereas other trails lead to panoramic overlooks, the highlight of this trail's final destination is a view of the immense ice field rising high above you.

Accommodations and Camping

Places to stay within Glacier are limited to one chain motel and two small campgrounds with no hookups. If you're looking for something more, plan on traveling 80 kilometers (50 miles) east to Golden or 72 kilometers (45 miles) west to Revelstoke.

Glacier Park Lodge (250/837-2126 or 888/567-4477, www.glacierparklodge.ca, $145 s, $155 d) lies beside the main information center atop Rogers Pass. It offers 50 midsize rooms with off-season rates under $100. A mostly tour-bus crowd on tight schedules means the heated outdoor pool is usually empty. Within the hotel is a 24-hour café, a restaurant offering reasonably priced buffets through all three meals, and a lounge.

Illecillewaet Campground ($21.50), four kilometers (2.5 miles) south of the information center, is open late June–September. Facilities include cooking shelters, flush toilets, picnic tables, firewood, and an evening interpretive program. Sites are not particularly private, and the surrounding peaks and towering cedar trees mean little sunshine before noon, but the campground is the perfect base for exploring as it's the trailhead for the park's main concentration of hiking trails. Smaller **Loop Brook Campground** (July–Aug., $21.50) is three kilometers (1.9 miles) beyond the Illecillewaet Campground toward Revelstoke, but holds just 20 sites. No reservations are taken.

With just 80 campsites in the entire park and no reservations taken, chances are good that both campgrounds will be full if you arrive late in the afternoon. If that's the case, plan on overnighting 40 kilometers (25 miles) west at **Canyon Hot Springs Resort** (250/837-2420, www.canyonhotsprings.com, May–Sept., tent sites $28, hookups $38, cabins $68 s or d), where you'll find hot springs, showers, a laundry, and a restaurant.

Information

Rogers Pass Discovery Centre (250/837-7500, www.pc.gc.ca, daily 8:30 A.M.–4:30 P.M. May.–mid-June, daily 7:30 A.M.–8 P.M. mid-June–Aug., daily 8:30 A.M.–4:30 P.M. Sept.–Mar.) is beside the highway 1.2 kilometers (0.7 miles) north of the actual pass and resembles the old-fashioned snowsheds that once protected the railroad from avalanches. The center's fascinating displays focus on the park's natural and human history. Videos on various aspects of the park are shown on the television (the viewing area by the fireplace is a great spot to while away time waiting for the clouds to lift), and the center's theater screens documentaries on mountain wildlife and avalanche protection. Staff members provide information on trail conditions and closures, operate a small bookstore, and conduct interpretive programs. The center is also the only place in the park to buy park passes, necessary for those planning any hiking or camping. If you already have a National Parks of Canada Pass, it must be presented for admission to the information center. For road conditions through the park call 250/837-6867.

REVELSTOKE
Revelstoke (population 8,000) lies 72 kilometers (45 miles) west of Rogers Pass at the

confluence of the Illecillewaet River and the mighty Columbia, surrounded by mountains—the Monashees to the west and the Selkirks to the east. The setting couldn't be more spectacular. The town holds a couple of museums, but the main attractions are farther afield, including two massive dams, a national park on the back doorstep, and, in winter, great skiing and snowboarding at Powder Springs.

Downtown
The TransCanada Highway makes a lazy loop around the back of Revelstoke, missing downtown completely. It's well worth the detour to downtown, not just for the best dining and accommodations, but to enjoy the laid-back atmosphere of a small city that has done an excellent job of preserving its heritage. The

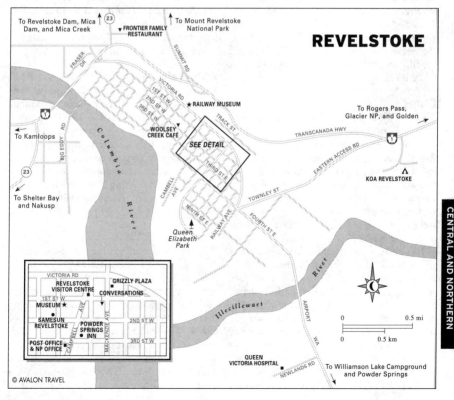

CENTRAL AND NORTHERN

downtown core has been rejuvenated and centers around the appealing, all-brick **Grizzly Plaza.** Pick up the *Heritage Walking & Driving* brochure at the local information center for routes that take in the highlights of downtown's many old buildings.

Museums

Railway buffs shouldn't miss **Revelstoke Railway Museum** (719 Track St., 250/837-6060, daily 9 A.M.–8 P.M. in summer, daily 9 A.M.–5 P.M. spring and fall, Fri.–Tues. 9 A.M.–5 P.M. winter, adult $8, senior $6, child $4), a re-creation of an early Canadian Pacific Railway station. Reflecting the importance of this mode of transportation in Revelstoke's history, the museum centers on a massive 1948 steam locomotive and Business Car No. 4, the ultimate in early rail-travel luxury. **Revelstoke Museum** (corner of Boyle Ave. and 1st St., 250/837-3067, Mon.–Sat. 9 A.M.–6 P.M., Sun. 1–5 P.M. in summer, Mon.–Fri. 1–4:30 P.M. the rest of the year, adult $4, senior $3, child $2) fills two stories of a historic downtown post office building.

Dams

The 1,900-kilometer (1,180-mile) Columbia River, North America's third-longest, is controlled by many dams. Four of these are in British Columbia and two are in the vicinity of Revelstoke. The dams also provide the necessary water for two massive hydroelectric operations. These two generating stations are each capable of producing 1,800 megawatts of electricity—or, combined, 30 percent of the province's needs.

Revelstoke Dam, eight kilometers (five miles) north of the city on Highway 23, was completed in 1985. It's 470 meters (1,540 feet) wide and 175 meters (590 feet) high. The massive reservoir behind the dam stretches over 130 kilometers (81 miles). Nestled in the valley downstream of the dam is the generating station. Exhibits at the two-story **Revelstoke Dam Visitor Centre** (250/814-6697, June–mid-Oct. daily 10 A.M.–5 P.M., adult $6, senior and child $5), above the generating station,

explain the valley's history and the operation and impact of the dams. From the center, a high-speed elevator whisks visitors to the top of the dam for an excellent view.

Upstream of Revelstoke Dam is **Mica Dam,** 140 kilometers (87 miles) via Highway 23 to the north. This dam is much larger—in fact, it's North America's highest earth-filled dam (240 m/790 ft), and stretches 792 meters (2,600 feet) at the crest across the Columbia River Valley.

Skiing and Snowboarding

Revelstoke Mountain Resort (250/814-0087 or 866/373-4754, www.revelstokemountainresort.com), on the lower slopes of Mount Mackenzie, has seen a massive expansion that continues to this day. Currently, an eight person gondola and high-speed lifts open up 1,214 hectares (3,031 acres) of skiing with a vertical rise of 1,713 meters (5,620 feet). The season generally lasts mid-December–early April, and adult lift tickets are adult $74, senior $57, child $26.

Entertainment

In July and August, free entertainment takes place nightly at the **Grizzly Plaza bandshell,** at the bottom end of Mackenzie Avenue. Whether it be comedy or country, crowds of up to a couple of hundred gather, sitting in plastic chairs, snagging a table at a surrounding restaurant, or just standing in the background. For music and dancing of a more formal nature, the young crowd heads for **Big Eddy Pub** (2108 Big Eddy Rd., 250/837-9072).

Accommodations

The best value of all accommodations in town is the **Ⓒ Samesun Revelstoke** (400 2nd St. W, 250/837-4050 or 877/972-6378, www.samesun.com, $24 dorm, $53 s or d), within easy walking distance of downtown. Providing a true home away from home, this heritage house has been fully restored, complete with hardwood floors and comfortable beds with linen. Amenities include kitchen facilities, a laundry, free Internet access, bike rentals, a patio with barbeque, and a game room. The double and twin rooms share bathrooms, but beds are comfortable and linen is supplied.

Downtown, the **Powder Springs Inn** (200 3rd St. W, 250/837-5151 or 800/991-4455, www.powdersprings.ca, $95 s or d) is busiest in winter, making summer rates a relative bargain. Also on the premises are a British-style pub, wireless Internet, spa services, and a hot tub.

Camping

KOA Revelstoke (250/837-2085 or 800/562-3905, www.revelstokekoa.com, unserviced sites $31, hookups $34–44, cabins $65–159 s or d) is off the TransCanada Highway six kilometers (3.7 miles) east of downtown. The well-kept campground offers grassy sites, lots of trees, a swimming pool, propane-filling facilities, a well-stocked store, free hot showers, wireless Internet, laundry facilities, and a main lodge that looks like a Swiss chalet. The fun stuff includes an outdoor pool, canoe rentals, two playgrounds, rock climbing lessons, evening campfires, and daily pancake breakfasts.

Quiet **Williamson Lake Campground** (seven km/4.3 mi south of town on Williamson Lake Rd., 250/837-5512, mid-Apr.–Oct., $18–24.50) lies on the edge of a warm lake perfect for summer swimming. Shaded grassy sites, hot showers, a picnic shelter, and fire pits are all just above the shoreline.

Food

Near the downtown bandshell, **Conversations Coffee House** (205 Mackenzie Ave., 250/837-4772, daily for breakfast and lunch, lunches $6–10) serves up gourmet coffees and light meals in a relaxed atmosphere. Across the road, the **Woolsey Creek Café** (600 2nd St., 250/837-5500, daily for dinner, $12–19), has a warm, friendly atmosphere, but is always full and noisy with locals enjoying a wide range of well-prepared and remarkably inexpensive dishes. I had the Spanish seafood paella, and it was as good as city restaurants where you'd expect to pay double the price.

For hurried highway travelers only, I'll include a spot out on the highway, the **Frontier Family Restaurant** (250/837-5119,

5 A.M.–10 P.M., $9–16), a typical roadside diner with nothing fancy that doesn't need to be.

Information

Revelstoke Visitor Centre (204 Campbell Ave., 250/837-5345, www.seerevelstoke.com) is open daily 8 A.M.–7 P.M. in summer, Mon.–Fri. 8:30 A.M.–4:30 P.M. the rest of the year.

MOUNT REVELSTOKE NATIONAL PARK

Visitors to this 26,000-hectare (64,250-acre) national park on the northern outskirts of Revelstoke can experience a high alpine environment without any strenuous hiking from the enticingly named Meadows in the Sky Parkway. The park protects the highest peaks of the **Clachnacudainn Range,** a northern arm of the Selkirk Mountains. The park's diverse vegetation includes forests of ancient cedar along the Illecillewaet River, subalpine forests of Engelmann spruce and fir on higher slopes, and finally, above the tree line, meadows of low-growing shrubs that come alive with color for a few weeks in midsummer.

Services within the park are limited to picnic areas. Although backcountry camping is allowed in designated areas (permit required, $10 per person per night), no road-accessible campgrounds lie within the park. Revelstoke is home to the park's **administration office** (300 3rd St., 250/837-7500, Mon.–Fri. 8:30 A.M.–4:30 P.M.). As with all Canadian national parks, a permit is required for entry; in this case it applies only to travel on the Meadows in the Sky Parkway. Permits are issued at the park gate, at the lower end of the parkway. A one-day permit is adult $8, senior $7, child $4.

◖ Meadows in the Sky Parkway

This 26-kilometer (16-mile) road one kilometer (0.6 miles) west of the downtown Revelstoke turnoff climbs from the TransCanada Highway to a magnificent alpine meadow high above the tree line. The road is very steep, gaining well over 1,000 meters (3,280 feet) of elevation as it climbs seemingly endless hairpin bends through a subalpine forest of Engelmann spruce, hemlock, and the odd towering cedar. The summit area is snowed in until mid- to late July, depending on how much snow has fallen the previous winter. The public road ends one kilometer (0.6 miles) before the true summit. From this point, you have the option of taking a free shuttle bus (daily 10 A.M.–4:20 P.M., starting as soon as the snow melts off the road) or walk (20 minutes each way) to **Heather Lake.** From this point, the panoramic view takes in the Columbia River Valley and the distant Monashee Mountains, with a variety of hiking trails beckoning further exploration.

Heather Lake is the trailhead for the one-kilometer (0.6-mile) round-trip **Meadows in the Sky Trail,** which features signs explaining the flora of the fragile alpine environment. From the east side of Heather Lake, a nine-kilometer (5.6-mile) trail leads through alpine meadows to the **Jade Lakes.** Along the route, short side trails lead to **Miller** and **Eva Lakes.**

The park's main gate is closed 10 P.M.–7 A.M., prohibiting access.

REVELSTOKE TOWARD SALMON ARM

Continuing west along the TransCanada Highway from Revelstoke, it's 62 kilometers (39 miles) to the next town, Sicamous, then another 42 kilometers (26 miles) to the much larger center of Salmon Arm. The first stop along the way should be intriguing black **Summit Lake,** lying in a heavily forested ravine and fed by a waterfall that plunges over a cliff face high above. Several commercial attractions on this stretch of road compete for your tourist dollar. On the shore of Three Valley Lake is the difficult-to-miss **Three Valley Gap** "ghost" town (250/837-2109, daily 8 A.M.–dusk Apr.–mid-Oct., adult $8, child $4), a rebuilt pioneer community with more than 20 historic buildings moved to the site from around the province. Part of the same complex is **Three Valley Lake Chateau** (250/837-2109 or 888/667-2109, www.3valley.com, early Apr.–early Oct., from $132 s or d), a large motel (200 rooms) overlooking extensive gardens and the lake. Amenities include a café, restaurant, and

indoor pool. Next up is the **Enchanted Forest** (250/837-9477, daily 9 A.M.–sunset in summer, adult $9, child $8), where a trail through towering trees meanders past more than 250 handcrafted figurines to fairyland buildings. **Beardale Castle Miniatureland** (250/836-2268, daily 9 A.M.–6 P.M. May–Sept., adult $8, child $6) takes miniature appreciators through several European towns and a Haida fishing village, into the world of nursery rhymes and fairy tales, and on into the world of trains.

The Last Spike

At **Craigellachie,** signs point off the highway to the Last Spike. It was here on November 7, 1885 that a plain iron spike joined the last two sections of Canadian Pacific's transcontinental rail line, finally connecting Canada from sea to sea. A cairn with a plaque and a piece of railway line marks the spot. **Craigellachie Station** (May–Oct.) is home to a small information center/gift shop selling ice cream.

ADAMS RIVER SOCKEYE

Roderick Haig-Brown Provincial Park, north of Squilax, protects the spawning grounds of North America's largest sockeye salmon run. The runs occur annually, but every four years (2014 is next up) a dominant run brings up to two million fish congregating in the river. They are present for the first three weeks of October, but numbers generally peak in the second week.

These salmon are near the end of their four-year life cycle, having hatched in the same section of the Adams River four years previously. After hatching, they spend up to two years of their life in Shuswap Lake before swimming out to the Pacific Ocean. It is estimated that in conjunction with dominant runs, 15 million Adams River sockeye enter the Pacific, with about 10 million running back toward their birthplace. Just one in five make it the full 500 kilometers (310 miles).

© ANDREW HEMPSTEAD

This train station at Craigellachie marks the place where Canada's transcontinental rail line was completed.

Sicamous

This town of 3,100, 62 kilometers (39 miles) west of Revelstoke, lies on the shore of **Shuswap Lake** and is known as the "Houseboat Capital of Canada." The lake itself is a convoluted body of water with four distinct arms, edged by secluded beaches, rocky coves, 25 marine parks, and more than 1,000 kilometers (620 miles) of shoreline. Houseboating is the number-one activity in these parts, and Sicamous is headquarters to major agencies, including **Blue Water Houseboats** (250/836-2255 or 800/663-4024, www.bluewaterhouseboats.ca) and **Twin Anchors Houseboat Vacations** (250/836-2450 or 800/663-4026, www.twinanchors.com). Rates vary greatly through the May–early October season. Expect to pay around $1,900 for four day's rental in July, with the same boat going for around $1,000 in September.

SALMON ARM

Known as the "Gem of the Shuswap," Salmon Arm (population 17,000) lies along the Salmon Arm of Shuswap Lake, surrounded by lush farmland and forested hills. Legend has it that the name was coined in the days when the rivers here were chockablock with salmon. Farmers used to spear the fish with pitchforks and use them for fertilizer.

Sights

From downtown, follow the Salmon Arm Wharf signs to lakeside **Marine Park,** where picnic tables dot the lawns and colorful flower boxes hang from the lampposts. The attractive **Salmon Arm Wharf,** the largest marina structure in British Columbia's interior, lures you out over the water, past a boat-launching area, a snack bar, and businesses renting motorboats and houseboats.

Two kilometers (1.2 miles) east of Salmon Arm on Highway 97B, **R. J. Haney Heritage Village & Museum** (250/832-5243, daily 10 A.M.–5 P.M. June–early Sept., adult $6) holds the town's main historic attractions. Here you'll find the **Salmon Arm Museum,** which relates the town's earliest days through a slide show, photo albums, and the adjacent **Haney**

CENTRAL AND NORTHERN

House, an early-20th-century farmhouse on beautiful, parklike grounds.

Practicalities

Salmon River Motel and RV Park (one km/0.6 mi west of Salmon Arm, 250/832-3065, $69–89 s or d) offers 10 rooms of a reasonable standard. Out back are a few tree-shaded campsites with hookups ($27). The other option for campers is **Salmon Arm Camping Resort** (Hwy. 97B, 250/832-6489 or 866/979-1659, www.salmonarmcamping.com, mid-May–mid-Oct., camping $31–46, cabins $57–99 s or d) with hot showers, a laundry, wireless Internet, convenience store, miniature golf, and a playground.

Head down through the center of town and over the rail line towards the main wharf to reach **Java Cabana** (680 Marine Dr., 250/832-2329, daily from 7:30 A.M.), a corner coffee house where patrons take full advantage of sunny outdoor table settings. With your coffee, try the Thai salad ($6), then check your email on the public Internet terminals. Right on the lakefront here is the Prestige Inn, home to **Aquatico Bay** (251 Harbourfront Dr., 250/833-5800, daily for breakfast and dinner, $15–39), specializing in steaks and seafood. The restaurant itself is as stylish as dining out gets in Salmon Arm, but if it's a warm evening, you'll want to be outside on the deck.

Salmon Arm Visitor Centre (20 Hudson Ave. NE, 250/832-2230 or 877/725-6667, www.shuswap.bc.ca) is open daily 9 A.M.–6 P.M. in summer, Mon.–Fri. 9 A.M.–5 P.M. the rest of the year.

Kamloops

Kamloops (population 86,000), 110 kilometers (68 miles) west of Salmon Arm and 355 kilometers (220 miles) northeast of Vancouver, is the province's sixth-largest city and a main service center along the TransCanada Highway. The Secwepemc, whose descendents are now known as Shuswap, were the first people to live in this region, basing their lifestyle on hunting and salmon fishing. They knew the area as T'kumlups, meaning "Meeting of the Rivers." Today the local economy revolves around the forest-products industry, copper mining, cattle and sheep ranching, and tourism. The city holds a few interesting sights but is certainly no scenic gem—the surrounding landscape is dominated by barren parched rolling hills. The downtown area, however, lies along the south bank of the Thompson River and is set off by well-irrigated parkland.

SIGHTS
Downtown

Excellent displays at three-story, gold-colored **Kamloops Museum** (207 Seymour St., 250/828-3576, Tues.–Sat. 9:30 A.M.–4:30, adult $3, child $1) cover local native culture, the fur trade (peek in the reconstructed fur trader's cabin), pioneer days, natural history (many stuffed and mounted critters), industry, and transportation. You'll see a furnished turn-of-the-20th-century living area, a stable complete with tack and carriage, a blacksmith shop, paddlewheels, old wall clocks and cameras, and a 15-minute slide presentation on the city's history.

Kamloops Art Gallery (465 Victoria St., 250/377-2400, Mon.–Sat. 10 A.M.–5 P.M., Sun. noon–4 P.M., adult $3, senior $2) features an impressive collection of more than 1,000 works by contemporary artists in all sorts of media—quite a contrast to the museum. The gallery stays open until 9 P.M. on Thursdays, when admission is by donation after 5 P.M.

Secwepemc Museum & Heritage Park

A living-history museum dedicated to the Shuswap tribe, this cultural attraction (250/828-9801, Mon.–Fri. 8:30 A.M.–4:30 P.M., until 8 P.M. in summer, adult $6, senior $4, child $4) offers numerous exhibits focusing

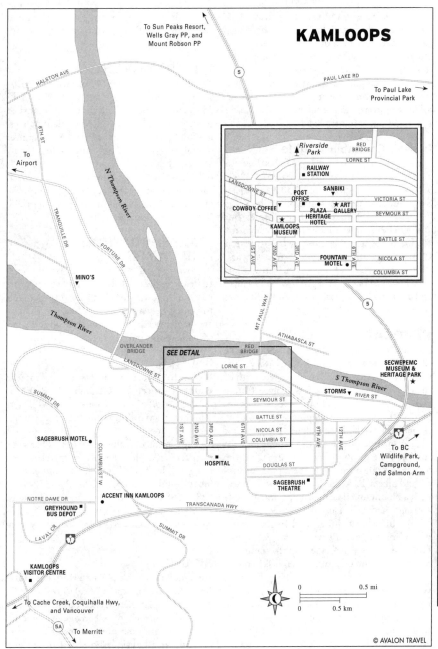

KAMLOOPS

To Sun Peaks Resort,
Wells Gray PP, and
Mount Robson PP

HALSTON AVE

PAUL LAKE RD

To Paul Lake
Provincial Park

6TH ST

To
Airport

N Thompson River

TRANQUILLE DR

FORTUNE DR

MINO'S

Thompson River

OVERLANDER
BRIDGE

LANSDOWNE ST

SUMMIT DR

SAGEBRUSH MOTEL

COLUMBIA ST W

NOTRE DAME DR

GREYHOUND
BUS DEPOT

ACCENT INN KAMLOOPS

LAVAL CR

KAMLOOPS
VISITOR CENTRE

To Cache Creek, Coquihalla Hwy,
and Vancouver

5A

To Merritt

Riverside
Park

RED
BRIDGE

LORNE ST

RAILWAY
STATION

LANSDOWNE ST

POST
OFFICE

SANBIKI

ART
GALLERY

VICTORIA ST

COWBOY COFFEE

PLAZA
HERITAGE
HOTEL

SEYMOUR ST

KAMLOOPS
MUSEUM

BATTLE ST

1ST AVE

2ND AVE

3RD AVE

6TH AVE

NICOLA ST

FOUNTAIN
MOTEL

COLUMBIA ST

MT PAUL WAY

5

ATHABASCA ST

RED
BRIDGE

SEE DETAIL

LORNE ST

SECWEPEMC
MUSEUM &
HERITAGE PARK

S Thompson River

STORMS

RIVER ST

SEYMOUR ST

BATTLE ST

NICOLA ST

COLUMBIA ST

1ST AVE

2ND AVE

3RD AVE

6TH AVE

9TH AVE

12TH AVE

To BC
Wildlife Park,
Campground,
and Salmon Arm

HOSPITAL

DOUGLAS ST

SAGEBRUSH
THEATRE

TRANSCANADA HWY

SUMMIT DR

0   0.5 mi

0   0.5 km

© AVALON TRAVEL

on the Shuswaps' traditions and rich mythology. Among the highlights are an archaeological site dating back 2,000 years, a re-created Shuswap winter village, a salmon-fishing station, a garden filled with native plants for food and medicinal purposes, and a re-creation of a traditional summer shelter. To get to the park, follow Highway 5 north across the Thompson River and take the first right.

British Columbia Wildlife Park

This nonprofit park (9077 Dallas Dr., 16 km/10 mi east of Kamloops, 250/573-3242, 9:30 A.M.–8 P.M. July–Aug., 9:30 A.M.–4 P.M. Sept.–June, adult $10, senior $9, child $7) is primarily a wildlife rehabilitation center, but among the more than 150 furry inhabitants are many species of mammals from western Canada, including a couple of grizzly bears, wolves, cougars, and lynx. Other attractions are a huge visitor center, a glass-walled beehive, and for the kids, a petting zoo and miniature steam train.

RECREATION

In the last decade, **Sun Peaks Resort** (250/578-5474 or 800/807-3257, www.sunpeaksresort.com), a mountain village north of the city along Highway 5 has evolved from a medium-sized local ski hill to a year-round resort, with ongoing development both on the slopes and at the base village, where a golf course spreads out along the valley floor. In summer, the Sunburst Express lift takes the hard work out of reaching the alpine for hikers and bikers. Ride the lift all day for $16 ($32 with a mountain bike). Other activities include golfing a shortish resort-style 18-hole course, tennis, horseback riding, and fishing. High season for the resort is wintertime, when two high-speed lifts whisk skiers up the mountain to runs that include an easy eight-kilometer (five-mile) cruise back to the village. The total vertical rise is 882 meters (2,900 feet) over almost 1,000 hectares (3,300 acres) of terrain. Facilities at the resort include eateries, a rental shop, and the Snow Sports School. Lift tickets are adult $71, senior $56, child $36. On-

mountain accommodations packages are good value—from $80 per person per night including a lift ticket.

ENTERTAINMENT

Two River Junction (814 Lorne St., 250/314-1631, mid-April–mid-Oct., adult $75, child $55 includes dinner) is a dinner and musical revue presented for the entertainment of overnighting passengers on the Rocky Mountaineer (therefore is presented only three or four nights a week), but anyone is welcome to attend. It tells the story of Billy Miner, a U.S. stagecoach robber who, it is claimed, coined the phrase "Hands Up!" and spent the last years of his life in the Kamloops region.

ACCOMMODATIONS AND CAMPING

You won't find quaint or memorable here. Instead, expect reliable motels serving the needs of highway travelers spread throughout the city. On the western approach to the city are many newer motels offering clean and comfortable rooms but no particular bargains.

$50-100

It's nothing to write home about, but the **Fountain Motel** (506 Columbia St., 250/374-4451 or 800/555-1123, $66–78 s or d) offers a higher standard of rooms than the exterior may suggest.

The top end of Columbia Street W has some unspectacular older motels for travelers on a budget. The best of these is the **Sagebrush Motel** (660 Columbia St. W, 250/372-3151, $55 s, $68 d), with 60 air-conditioned rooms, each with a coffee-maker and biggish TVs, as well as an adjacent restaurant open daily from 7 A.M.

$100-150

Right downtown is the **Plaza Heritage Hotel** (405 Victoria St., 250/377-8075 or 877/977-5292, www.plazaheritagehotel.com, $109–245 s or d) first opened in 1928 as one the Interior's finest accommodations. Its restoration and opening as a boutique hotel is more recent.

The 68 rooms feature rich woods, a heritage color scheme, and comfortable beds covered in plush duvets. At street level are the Heritage Restaurant and a stylish lounge bar, and wireless Internet is free throughout.

Just off the highway near the west side access to downtown, **Accent Inn Kamloops** (1325 Columbia St. W, 250/374-8877 or 800/663-0298, www.accentinns.com, $129–159 s or d) offers modern and spacious rooms, with guests having use of an outdoor pool, hot tub, and fitness room. Free email in the lobby and a national paper delivered to your door are unexpected touches. Check the website of this small provincial chain for discounted rates.

Camping
Heading out of Kamloops to the east, 16 kilometers (10 miles) from downtown, **Kamloops RV Park** (9225 Dallas Dr., 250/573-3789, $21–36) offers full hookups, coin-operated showers, a laundry, hot tub, and grocery store, and is next door to the wildlife park.

The city's most scenic campground is at **Paul Lake Provincial Park** (mid-May–mid-Sept., $15), north of Kamloops five kilometers (3.1 miles) on Highway 5, then 17 kilometers (10.5 miles) east on Paul Lake Road. Facilities are basic (no hookups or showers), but the treed setting just a short walk to the beach makes up for it.

FOOD
Kamloops has the usual family-style and fast-food restaurants you'd expect along the highway, as well as some good dining choices in the downtown core. Regarding the latter, **Cowboy Coffee** (229 Victoria St., 250/372-3565, daily from 7 A.M., lunches $5–8) has the best coffee in town, as well as pastries and lunches made daily in-house.

Superb sushi is the draw at (**Sanbiki** (476 Victoria St., 250/377-8857, daily 11:30 A.M.–2:30 P.M. and 5:30–9:30 P.M., $12–21), in a distinctive orange building with a sun-splashed patio out front. The chefs do a great job of sourcing the freshest of ingredients, including—most importantly—seafood. A popular

lunch combo dish is teriyaki chicken, tempura, California roll, salad, and miso soup for $11. Other choices include asparagus *shira-ae,* done in a creamy sesame sauce, hearty rice bowls, and crumbed *panko* prawns.

Kamloops has a couple of decent Greek restaurants, including my favorite, **Mino's** (262 Tranquille Rd., 250/376-2010, daily 11:30 A.M.–10 P.M., $17–30). The setting is fittingly nationalistic and there are no real surprises (think mousaka, souvlaki, lots of lamb, and baklava for dessert), but the food is all well prepared and it's seemingly always busy on weekends.

East of downtown along the river is **Storms** (1502 River St., 250/372-1522, lunch and dinner daily, $17–36), one of Kamloops' best restaurants. The elegant setting includes tables set on an outdoor deck overlooking the river. The menu features classic European and North American dishes, such as a succulent rack of lamb roasted in Dijon mustard and fresh rosemary; or just soak up the river atmosphere with a platter of appetizers.

INFORMATION
Kamloops Visitor Centre (250/372-8000 or 800/662-1994, www.tourismkamloops.com, daily 9 A.M.–6 P.M. in summer, Mon.–Fri. 9 A.M.–5 P.M. the rest of the year) is beside the TransCanada Highway on the western outskirts of town (at Hillside Rd. opposite the Aberdeen Mall).

GETTING THERE AND AROUND
Kamloops Airport is on Airport Road, seven kilometers northwest of city center; follow Tranquille Road through the North Shore until you come to Airport Road on the left. **Air Canada** (888/247-2262) has scheduled flights between Kamloops and Vancouver. The railway station is right downtown at the north end of 3rd Avenue. **VIA Rail** (800/561-8630) runs scheduled service three times weekly west to Vancouver and east to Jasper. **Greyhound** provides daily service to most parts of the province from its Kamloops bus depot (725 Notre Dame

Dr., off Columbia St. W at the west end of town, 250/374-1212).

Local bus transportation (including out to the airport) is provided by **Kamloops Transit System** (250/376-1216); adult fare is $2.50, while a day pass is $6. Taxi companies include **Kami Cabs** (250/374-5151) and **Yellow Cabs** (250/374-3333). For a rental car, call **Budget** (250/376-5423), **Hertz** (250/376-3022), or **National** (250/374-5737).

Kamloops to Jasper

From Kamloops, Highway 5 follows the North Thompson River to Tete Jaune Cache on Highway 16. This stretch of highway is part of the most direct route between Vancouver and Jasper National Park, and is also worthwhile for two excellent provincial parks—**Wells Gray,** a vast wilderness of rivers and mountains, and **Mount Robson,** protecting a spectacular peak that is the highest point in the Canadian Rockies.

Clearwater

The small town of Clearwater (population 1,800), 125 kilometers (78 miles) north of Kamloops, is the gateway to Wells Gray Provincial Park. A few motels, restaurants, gas stations, services, and an information center are on the highway; the rest of the community is off the highway to the south.

Activities at **Dutch Lake Resort & RV Park** (361 Ridge Rd., 250/674-3351 or 888/884-4424, www.dutchlake.com, May–Oct., hook-ups $32–35, cabins $114–249 s or d) revolve around families and the water; the on-site restaurant has a wide patio overlooking the lake.

Housed in a massive log building a few hundred meters along the park access road, the **[C Flower Meadow Bakery** (444 Clearwater Valley Rd., 250/674-3654, Mon.–Fri. 5 A.M.–8 P.M., Sat. 5 A.M.–6 P.M., lunches $6–11) is impossible to miss—and you won't want to either. The breakfast burritos ($6.50) are healthy and huge; the lemon meringues are also super-sized (but probably not as good for you), and the carrot cake will melt in your mouth. There's plenty of room for everyone, with the outdoor seating filling first. On your way out, buy an extra loaf of bread or a stacked sandwich to go for a picnic in the park.

At the turnoff to Wells Gray Provincial Park is **Clearwater Visitor Centre** (250/674-2646, daily 8 A.M.–6 P.M. in summer, weekdays 9 A.M.–5 P.M. the rest of the year).

WELLS GRAY PROVINCIAL PARK

Not as well known as the famous national parks of the Canadian Rockies, Wells Gray is nonetheless well worth the effort to reach. Those who make the long journey are rewarded with snow-clad peaks and extinct volcanoes, amazing waterfalls (so many the park is often referred to as the "Waterfall Park"), flower-filled meadows, and an abundance of wildlife (I counted six bears, five deer, and two moose on my last visit).

The main access road into the 540,000-hectare (1,334,000-acre) park leads north from Clearwater for 37 kilometers (23 miles) to the park boundary. From there it continues 11 kilometers (6.8 miles) to one of the park's highlights, Helmcken Falls, where it turns to gravel and continues another 18 kilometers (11 miles) to its end at Clearwater Lake. Although this access road barely penetrates the park, driving its length is enough to get a taste of the rugged northern reaches. If it's not, you can take a canoe trip or boat tour from the end of the road.

Sights and Hikes

Make your first stop 10 kilometers (6.2 miles) from Clearwater, where a short trail leads through an old-growth forest of cedar and hemlock to a colorful lava canyon where 61-meter-high (200-foot-high) **Spahats Creek Falls** plummets over multicolored bedrock into the Clearwater River. Continuing through the park, take a signposted gravel road to the west to **Green Viewing Tower** atop Green Mountain. The viewpoint provides panoramic views of a volcanic cone and many spectacular, rugged peaks, including snow-covered Garnet Peak, highest in the park. Wells Gray is best known for its waterfalls. The most spectacular of these is incredible **Helmcken Falls,** where the Murtle River cascades in a sparkling, 137-meter-high (450-foot-high) torrent to join the Clearwater River.

Continuing north up the road, a 500-meter (0.3-mile) trail (10 minutes each way) winds through a stand of towering cedar trees to **Bailey's Chute,** a narrow rapids-filled passage. In fall, large numbers of chinook salmon battle the torrent, trying in vain to leap up the chute.

The park access road ends at a boat ramp/ canoe dock beside the southern end of Clearwater Lake, 66 kilometers (41 miles) from the town of Clearwater. To make the most of the lake, you really need to take to the water. Based just before the road ends (take the Clearwater Campground turn-off), **Clearwater Lake Tours** (250/674-2121) offers a couple of options. A four-hour motorboat cruise to Rainbow Falls at the north end of the lake departs daily at 11 A.M. and costs adult $50, senior $38, child $30. For those who would rather propel themselves, a two-hour canoe rental is $25, or pay $40 per day.

Accommodations and Camping

About halfway between Clearwater and Helmcken Falls, **Ⓒ Wells Gray Guest Ranch** (250/674-2792 or 866/467-4346, www.wellsgrayranch.com, May–Oct., camping $20, cabins and lodge rooms $75–180 s or d) is surrounded by grassy meadows full of wildflowers and grazing horses. Activities organized for guests include horseback riding ($45 for a 1.5-hour ride), canoeing, white-water rafting, fishing, and western-style barbeques. Overnight options include well-furnished, kitchen-equipped cabins, ranch house rooms with shared bathrooms and a limited number of campsites. The ranch also has a restaurant and saloon (daily 4 P.M.–midnight).

Each of the three **park campgrounds** along

the access road has drinking water, toilets, and picnic tables; none have hookups or showers. Sites cost $15 per night. If you need a serviced site, stay at tranquil **Wells Gray Golf Resort & RV Park** (35 km/22 mi north of Clearwater, 250/674-0072, May–Oct. $20–27), which has 50 campsites set in the middle of a full-length nine-hole golf course (greens fee $18). Rates include full hookups and use of modern shower facilities.

CONTINUING TOWARD MOUNT ROBSON
Blue River

This picturesque town is the jumping off point for various wilderness adventures in the Cariboo Mountains to the north, Wells Gray Provincial Park to the west, and the northern reaches of the North Thompson River just to the east.

Ⓒ Mike Wiegele's Heli Village (250/673-8381 or 800/661-9170, www.wiegele.com) is designed for the wintertime heli-skiing crowd, but is open year-round. Mike Wiegele was instrumental in the development of "fat boy" skis that helped revolutionize powder skiing by making it easier for everyone. Wintertime visitors enjoy some of the world's most fabulous powder skiing, then kick back each evening at the upscale resort in Blue River. Accommodation is in large two- to six-room log chalets in a private setting beside Lake Eleanor. Amenities include an ultra-modern fitness center, game room, a restaurant overseen by European chefs, and sports shop with bike rentals. In the off-season (Apr.–Nov.), if the resort hasn't been booked by a tour group, the rooms are one of British Columbia's best bargains—$125–225 s or d for a luxurious suite with a full kitchen, log fireplace, and comfortable lounge. **Glacier Mountain Lodge** (250/673-2393 or 877/452-2686, www.glaciermountainlodge.com, $92–229 s or d) is another stylish Blue River accommodation, this one offering 33 well-appointed guest rooms where rates include a continental breakfast buffet and use of a hot tub.

Valemount and Vicinity

Although most highway drivers hurry through

town on their way to Mount Robson Provincial Park, Valemount has plenty to offer those traveling at a slower pace. The town boasts two scenic golf courses, horseback riding at Borderline Ranch (250/566-9161, $150 full day), lots of fishing holes (ask for a brochure at the information center), and mountain scenery all around. If you're passing through mid-August–late September, be sure to visit Swift Creek, below the information center, where chinook salmon spawn after a 1,200-kilometer (745-mile) journey from the Pacific Ocean.

◖ **Mica Mountain Lodge** (Old Tete Jaune Rd., 250/566-9816 or 888/440-6422, www.micamountainlodge.bc.ca, $155–165 s or d) is in a wilderness setting on the northwest side of town. During summer, guests ride horses, canoe, fish, and mountain bike. Come winter, it's cross-country skiing, dog sledding, and snowmobiling that are the major draws. The cabins are charming and practical, with full kitchens, three-piece en suite bathrooms, decks, TVs, and pine log beds.

From the Yellowhead Highway junction 20 kilometers (12 miles) north of Valemount, Prince George is 270 kilometers (168 miles) to the west, and the British Columbia–Alberta border is 76 kilometers (47 miles) east. A worthwhile stop before reaching Mount Robson Provincial Park is **Rearguard Falls,** a one-kilometer hike (20 minutes each way) from the highway. Eight kilometers (five miles) downstream from the falls—some 1,200 kilometers (745 miles) up the Fraser River from the Pacific Ocean—is a spawning ground for Pacific salmon; many of the hardy fish make it all the way to the falls.

◖ MOUNT ROBSON PROVINCIAL PARK

This mountainous park protects 224,866 hectares (555,650 acres) of steep canyons and wide forested valleys; icy lakes, rivers, and streams; and rugged mountain peaks permanently blanketed in snow and ice. Towering over the park's western entrance is magnificent 3,954-meter (12,970-foot) **Mount Robson,** the highest peak in the Canadian Rockies. The elevation differences within the park are as great as anywhere else in the Canadian Rockies, giving rise to a great variety of flora and fauna.

Sights

If you're approaching the park from the west

© ANDREW HEMPSTEAD

Mount Robson is the highest peak in the Canadian Rockies.

along Highway 16, you'll see Mount Robson long before you reach the park boundary, provided the weather is cooperating. It's impossible to confuse this distinctive peak with those that surround it—no wonder it's known as the "Monarch of the Canadian Rockies." Once inside the park boundary, the highway climbs gradually to the main facility area, where you'll find a visitor center, campgrounds, a gas station, and a restaurant. This is as close as you can get to the peak in your vehicle. From the park's only service area, the highway climbs steeply then parallels photogenic **Moose Lake.** Waterfalls on the far side of the lake create a scenic backdrop. Continuing westward, the highway crosses the upper reaches of the Fraser River before passing long and narrow Yellowhead Lake at the foot of 2,458-meter (8,060-foot) **Yellowhead Mountain.** Finally, Highway 16 exits the park at the 1,066-meter (3,500-foot) **Yellowhead Pass,** on the British Columbia–Alberta border 60 kilometers (37.2 miles) east of the visitor center.

Berg Lake Trail

This 19.5-kilometer (12-mile) one-way trail is one of the most popular overnight hikes in western Canada. Beautiful aqua-colored Berg Lake lies below the north face of Mount Robson, which rises 2,400 meters (7,880 feet) directly behind the lake. Glaciers on the mountain's shoulder regularly calve off into the lake, resulting in the icebergs that give the lake its name. Along the route are 75 campsites ($5 per person per night) in seven primitive campgrounds. Bookings for these sites are taken at the visitor center or through BC Parks at 604/689-9025 or 800/689-9025. Book early as the quota fills quickly. From the trailhead two kilometers (1.2 miles) north of the visitor center along a narrow access road, the trail follows the Robson River 4.5 kilometers (2.8 miles) through dense subalpine forest to glacially fed **Kinney Lake.** The first glimpses of Mount Robson comes 17.5 kilometers (10.9 miles) from the trailhead. While the panorama from Berg Lake is stunning, most hikers who have come this far want to spend some time

exploring the area. If the walk in seems too ambitious, **Robson Helimagic** (250/566-4700 or 877/454-4700) makes drop-offs at Robson Pass from Valemount every Monday and Friday; $195 per person (minimum four).

Accommodations and Camping

Mountain River Lodge (four km/2.5 mi west of the visitor center, 250/566-9899 or 888/566-9899, www.mtrobson.com) is in a delightful setting right alongside the Fraser River. The main lodge has four guest rooms, each with a different character, a balcony, and private bathroom. The smallest of the rooms (with a private bathroom down the hall) is $110 s or d while the other three are $135; rates include a cooked breakfast. Self-contained cabins cost $159–179 per night, with breakfast available at an extra charge. One kilometer (0.6 miles) west of Mountain River Lodge is **Mount Robson Lodge** (250/566-4821 or 888/566-4821, www. mountrobsonlodge.com, May–Oct.) with 18 freestanding cabins ($79–129 s or d); the more expensive ones have kitchens, or you can eat at the small coffee shop.

Closest of four park campgrounds to the visitor center (and my favorite!) is **Robson River Campground,** where numerous trails lead down to the river for the classic upstream view of Mt. Robson. It's also only a short walk to the visitor center and a café. Across the highway is the larger **Robson Meadows Campground,** with 125 sites and an outdoor theater that hosts evening interpretive programs through summer. A number of sites at Robson Meadows can be reserved through www.discovercamping.ca. Both campgrounds have flush toilets and showers but no hookups; $19 per site. All facilities are open mid-May–mid-September.

Information

At the park's western entrance, **Mount Robson Visitor Centre** (250/566-9174, daily 8 A.M.–8 P.M. mid-June–mid-Sept., daily 8 A.M.–5 P.M. mid-May–mid-June and mid-Sept.–mid-Oct.) features informative natural-history slide shows, an evening interpretive program, and trail reports updated daily.

Cariboo Country

The wild, sparsely populated Cariboo region extends from Kamloops north to Prince George and west to the Pacific Ocean. Its most dramatic natural features are the mountain ranges rising like bookends to either side. In the west, the **Coast Mountains** run parallel to the coast and rise to a height of 4,016 meters (13,200 feet) at **Mount Waddington,** the highest mountain completely within British Columbia. In the east, the **Cariboo Mountains** harbor numerous alpine lakes, high peaks, and several provincial parks. Between the two ranges flows the **Fraser River,** which is flanked to the west by expansive plateaus home to British Columbia's biggest ranches. This is cowboy country, where horseback holidays and the Williams Lake Stampede are the main visitor draws.

CACHE CREEK

A town born with the fur trade at a spot where traders cached furs and food supplies, Cache Creek was once the largest town between Vancouver, 337 kilometers (200 miles) to the south, and Kamloops, 80 kilometers (50 miles) to the east. But since the new Coquihalla Highway opened, the town is but a shadow of its former self. The surrounding desertlike climate is intriguing; sagebrush and cacti grow on the relatively barren volcanic landscape, and tumbleweeds blow through town.

◖ Historic Hat Creek Ranch

Between 1885 and 1905, the Cariboo Wagon Road bustled with stagecoaches and freight wagons. One of the few sections of the original road still open to the public is at Hat Creek Ranch (Hwy. 97 11 km/6.8 mi north of Cache Creek, 250/457-9722, daily 10 A.M.–6 P.M. mid-May–mid-Oct., until 6 P.M. in July and Aug., adult $9, senior $8, child $6). Many of the original buildings—some dating as far back as 1861—still stand, and visitors can watch the blacksmith at his forge, appreciate a collection of antique farm machinery, enjoy a picnic lunch in the orchard, or take a guided tour of the ranch house. Other facilities include native sweat lodges (similar to a sauna), camping (unserviced sites $10, powered sites $15), cabins (bring your own sleeping bags, $65–85 s or d), and a casual restaurant.

LILLOOET

This historic town of 2,700 was founded as Mile 0 of the 1858 Cariboo Wagon Road—also known as the Gold Rush Trail—which led north to the Barkerville and Wells goldfields. Several towns along the Gold Rush Trail—70 Mile House, 100 Mile House, and 150 Mile House, among them—were named for their distance up the wagon road from Lillooet. With thousands of prospectors passing through in the mid-1800s, Lillooet was the scene of its own gold rush, with a population of 16,000 at one time.

A row of rusty farming relics out front marks **Lillooet Museum** (790 Main St., 250/256-4308, Tues.–Sat. 10 A.M.–4 P.M. mid-May–Oct., daily 9 A.M.–6 P.M. July–Aug., donation). Inside are ore samples and details about the one-time boomtown's mining history and growth. Within the museum is the local visitor info center. After visiting here, saunter along wide Main Street and pretend you're back in the gold-rush era—which won't be hard if you happen to be here in June during **Only in Lillooet Days.** During this weeklong celebration, the town re-creates the Old West with all sorts of entertaining events.

Accommodations and Camping

One block up the hill from the museum, **4 Pines Motel** (108 8th Ave., 250/256-4247 or 800/753-2576, www.4pinesmotel.com, $85 s or d) has 19 simple but comfortable rooms, each with air-conditioning. **Cayoosh Creek Campground** (unserviced sites $16, powered sites $22) is a treed spot near the south end of town, where Cayoosh Creek drains into the much larger Fraser River. Facilities include hot showers and hookups.

CLINTON TO 100 MILE HOUSE
Clinton
The original roadhouse at Clinton, 40 kilometers (25 miles) north of Cache Creek, opened in 1861 at the junction of the original Cariboo Wagon Road and the new route north from Yale. A nearby natural attraction worth seeing is Painted Chasm, in **Chasm Provincial Park,** 16 kilometers (10 miles) north of town, then four kilometers (2.5 miles) east. During the last ice age, glacial meltwater carved a 300-meter (1,000-foot) deep box canyon out of mineral-laden volcanic bedrock. It's quite a spectacle when the sunlight brings out the sparkling reds, yellows, and purples of the minerals.

If experiencing ranch life sounds appealing, it's worth spending at least a couple of days at **Big Bar Guest Ranch** (250/459-2333, www.bigbarranch.com), which offers accommodations in comfortable lodge rooms ($155 pp per day including meals served ranch-style) or tepees ($95 pp including meals), or you can camp for $30. You're free to enjoy the days as you please—try your hand at gold panning, saddle up for a trail ride, herd cattle with the cowboys, cast a line in a local lake, or go for a

ECHO VALLEY RANCH RESORT

You can choose between several guest ranches in Cariboo Country, but none comes close to the luxury offered at Echo Valley Ranch Resort (northwest of Clinton, 250/459-2386 or 800/253-8831, www.evranch.com). Deep in the heart of ranching country, the resort provides the opportunity to immerse yourself in Western culture while indulging in the amenities of an upscale lodge. The emphasis is on horseback riding, with lessons and guided rides scheduled each day, but there are plenty of other things to do, such as a four-wheel-drive excursion into the nearby Fraser River Canyon, watching a falcon trainer at work, and learning about native culture. The centerpiece of the sprawling property is an impressive main lodge, built entirely of glistening spruce logs. Inside is a comfortable lounge area, the communal dining room overlooking an open kitchen, and a downstairs billiards and TV room. Adjacent is an impressive pagoda structure, with full spa services, and the Pavilion, for quiet contemplation.

Rooms in the main lodge are beautifully furnished, and each has a private balcony, while the Honeymoon Cabin sits high above a deep ravine and has a wraparound deck complete with hot tub. Dining is ranch style, at a couple of long tables with plenty of interaction between guests. But the food is anything but chili and beans; the chef, Kim Madsen, used to cook for European royalty.

As you'd expect, staying at Echo Valley isn't cheap (from $300 a person per night in high season), but it's a very special place that my wife and I hold dear memories of from our own honeymoon.

© ANDREW HEMPSTEAD

honeymoon cabin, Echo Valley Ranch Resort

hike. To get to the ranch, turn off the highway nine kilometers (5.6 miles) north of Clinton and head west for 45 kilometers (28 miles). For somewhere to simply rest your head, consider **Cariboo Lodge Resort** (250/459-7992 or 877/459-7992, www.caeiboolodgebc.com, $74 s or d), a huge log structure on Clinton's main street. Although the rooms are motel-like, rates are reasonable and a downstairs restaurant and western-style pub mean you don't have to leave the building after checking in.

North to 100 Mile House
Between 70 Mile House and 100 Mile House are several turnoffs leading to hundreds of lakes, big and small. All information centers in Cariboo Country stock the invaluable *Cariboo-Chilcotin Fishing Guide*. Updated annually, the booklet features essential fishing information (where, when, and with what) for many of the lakes, plus maps, camping spots, and even recipes for the ones that didn't get away.

The most accessible provincial park between Clinton and 100 Mile House is at **Green Lake**, 14 kilometers (8.7 miles) east of Highway 97 (turn off Hwy. 97 16 km/10 mi northeast of 70 Mile House). This large, emerald-colored shallow lake lies along an old Hudson's Bay Company fur-brigade trail; you can see traces of the trail along the lake's shoreline. The park has a shaded lakeside picnic area, a playground, horseshoe pits, relatively warm water for swimming, and a campground ($15, mid-May–Sept.).

Passing through 100 Mile House, it's difficult to miss the **South Cariboo Visitor Centre** (250/395-5353 or 877/511-5353, www.south-caribootourism.com, Mon.–Fri. 8:30 A.M.–4:30 P.M., daily in summer.)—just look for the world's largest cross-country skis out front. At the north end of town, one of the original Cariboo stagecoaches is on display. And bird-watchers might want to detour a couple of kilometers west of town to a wetlands reserve where waterfowl are prolific.

At **150 Mile House**, a side road leads on a 65-kilometer (40-mile) scenic drive (the last 10 km/6.2 mi are unpaved) northeast to **Horsefly**

Lake Provincial Park, protecting a forest of old-growth western red cedar and Douglas fir. You can swim, rent a canoe, or just relax on the pebbly beach. The small campground has sites for $15.

WILLIAMS LAKE
The largest city in the Cariboo region is Williams Lake (population 10,500), an important ranching and forestry center 95 kilometers (59 miles) north of 100 Mile House.

Sights and Recreation
The highlight of the large **Museum of the Cariboo Chilcotin** (113 4th Ave. N, 250/392-7404, Mon.–Sat. 10 A.M.–4 P.M. in summer, Tues.–Sat. 11 A.M.–4 P.M. the rest of the year, adult $2) is the BC Cowboy Hall of Fame and associated rodeo, ranching, and Stampede displays. One of many stores in town selling the painting, pottery, weaving, photography, and jewelry of local artisans is **Station House Gallery,** in the original railway station (1 Mackenzie Ave. N, 250/392-6113). On the eastern outskirts of the city, **Scout Island Nature Centre** (250/398-8532, Mon.–Fri. 9 A.M.–4 P.M., Sun. 1–4 P.M. May–mid-Sept., free) is surrounded by wetlands that serve as a staging area for migratory waterfowl. Colorful displays inside the center catalog the surrounding ecosystem, but the idea is to get out into the wetlands along the easy walking trails.

The region's diverse waterways provide plenty of opportunities for boating. Numerous gently flowing streams and serene lakes make perfect spots for canoe and kayak discovery trips, while the Fraser River provides opportunities for exciting rafting trips down steepwalled canyons, through semi-arid hill country, and past abandoned boom towns. **Chilko River Rafting** (250/267-5258, www.chilkoriver.com) offers a full-day trip down the Chilcotin River for $125 per person.

Williams Lake Stampede
On the first weekend of July, the town comes alive as the best cowboys in the land compete in the Williams Lake Stampede (250/392-

6585, www.williamslakestampede.com), one of Canada's largest rodeos. The whole town dresses up for the occasion; the locals put on Western garb, and the storefronts are decorated accordingly. The highlight of each day's action is the rodeo, when cowboys compete for big bucks in bareback riding, saddle-bronc riding, calf-roping, steer-wrestling, chuck-wagon racing, and the crowd favorite, bull riding. Scheduled around these traditional rodeo events are cow-milking contests, barrel racing, tractor pulls, cattle penning, chariot races, raft races, a parade, barn dances, all-you-can-eat breakfasts and steak-outs, and a host of other decidedly Western-flavored activities.

Accommodations and Camping

The British Columbia accommodation guide details all the usual highway motels in Williams Lake, but for a more memorable overnight experience—longer if you can afford it—plan on spending time east of town at **Eden on Chilko Lake** (604/513-5008 or 877/346-9378, www.adventurewestresorts.com, $395 per person inclusive of meals and activities). Set on a perfect little lake, the resort features a mix of lakefront suites and log cabins, all beautifully furnished and with luxurious bathrooms. The on-site restaurant is notable for its regional cuisine while guests spend the day relaxing, fishing, or involved in activities such as yoga.

Food

Williams Lake lacks outstanding eateries but has no shortage of typical family-style restaurants such as **Boston Pizza** (Coast Fraser Inn, 285 Donald Rd., 250/398-7055, daily for lunch and dinner, $11–19). On the edge of town, **The Laughing Loon** (1730 S. Broadway, 250/398-5666, $12–38) is a neighborhood pub offering a wide-ranging menu of beef, chicken, and pork dishes in a welcoming atmosphere. The building itself is newer, but decor is heritage-style.

Information

Beside the highway on the east side of town is **Williams Lake Visitor Centre** (1148 Broadway, 250/392-5025, www.williamslakechamber.com, daily 8 A.M.–6 P.M. in summer, Mon.–Fri. 9 A.M.–5 P.M. the rest of the year).

HIGHWAY 20

Highway 20, west of Williams Lake, leads 485 kilometers (301 miles) to Bella Coola, the only road-accessible town along the 500 kilometers (310 miles) of coastline between Powell River and Prince Rupert. The highway is paved less than half its length; the rest of the way it's mostly all-weather gravel and can be slow going in spots. But experiencing the vast and varied wilderness of the **Chilcotin Coast** is worthy of as much time as you can afford. And with a ferry at the end of the road providing a link to Port Hardy on Vancouver Island, you'll only need to make the trip one-way.

Williams Lake to Chilko Lake

The road west from Williams Lake meanders through the Fraser River Valley before beginning a steady climb to the **Chilcotin Plateau,** the heart of British Columbia's ranching country. The first worthwhile detour is **Junction Sheep Range Provincial Park,** which lies at the end of a 20-kilometer (12-mile) unpaved road that branches south off Highway 20 at Riske Creek, 47 kilometers (29 miles) west of Williams Lake. The triangular park protects 4,573 hectares (11,300 acres) of mostly semi-arid grasslands between the Fraser and Chilcotin Rivers, home to around 600 bighorn sheep. Back on Highway 20, the first community with services is **Alexis Creek,** 114 kilometers (71 miles) west of Williams Lake.

Continuing toward the coast, Highway 20 narrows and turns to gravel at the small community of Tatla Lake, which is also the turnoff to remote **Ts'il?os Provincial Park.** Pronounced "sigh-loss," Ts'il?os is the native Chilcotin name for the park's highest peak, 3,066-meter (10,060-foot) Mount Tatlow, but its most magnificent feature is 84-kilometer (52-mile) long, glacially fed **Chilko Lake,** which is ringed by the highest peaks of the Coast Mountains. The park is home to a wide variety of wildlife, including grizzly and black bears, bighorn sheep, and, at higher elevations, mountain goats. Fishing in the lake is legendary for rainbow trout (to six pounds).

Continuing West

From Tatla Lake, Highway 20 continues westward, climbing steadily to **Nimpo Lake,** where you'll find more self-contained resorts where the emphasis is on fishing. **Stewart's Lodge** (250/742-3388 or 800/668-4335, www.stewartslodge.com) is one of the larger operations, with cabins on Nimpo Lake, as well as six "outpost" cabins at remote lakes throughout the Chilcotin region. Rates are around $1,000 per person for lodging, meals, and fly-out fishing. From this point, it's 10 kilometers (6.2 miles) west to **Anahim Lake,** where anglers will be tempted to linger at **Anahim Lake Resort** (250/742-3242 or 800/667-7212, www.anahimlakeresort.com, May–Oct., cabins $85–135 s or d, camping $24–30). All but one cabin shares a communal bathroom facility, but they all have a wood stove, fridge, running water, and screened-in verandah.

From Anahim Lake, it's a steady climb of another 30 kilometers (19 miles) to 1,524-meter (5,000-foot) **Heckman Pass** over the Coast Mountains. Continuing west across the pass, you're faced with **The Hill.** This infamous descent from Heckman Pass to the Bella Coola Valley drops nearly the full 1,524 meters (5,000 feet) in less than 10 kilometers (6.2 miles). Be prepared for numerous switchbacks and a gradient as steep as 18 percent.

BELLA COOLA

The urge to see what's at the end of the road brings many travelers over The Hill and down to the small village of Bella Coola, 485 kilometers (301 miles) west of Williams Lake. Here, the Bella Coola River drains into North Bentinck Arm, a gateway to the Inside Passage and the Pacific Ocean.

History

Those with a sense of history will want to visit the spot where Alexander Mackenzie reached the coast, simultaneously becoming the first nonnative to see the area and the first person to cross continental North America. That latter feat earned him a place in history as one of the world's greatest explorers. At **Mackenzie Rock,** in his own words, he "mixed up some vermillion and melted grease and inscribed in large characters on the face of the rock on which we slept last night, this brief memorial: Alexander Mackenzie, from Canada, by Land, the Twenty Second of July, One Thousand Seven Hundred and Ninety Three." To reach the site, you'll need to use the boat charter service offered by **Bella Coola Outfitting** (604/982-0098, www.bcoutfitting.com).

Although the Hudson's Bay Company established a post at Bella Coola in 1869, it wasn't until 1894 that permanent settlement of Bella Coola Valley began in earnest. That year a group of Norwegians arrived and, seeing the fjords and snowcapped peaks, were reminded of home. They settled 15 kilometers (9.3 miles) inland at a spot on the river they named **Hagensborg,** where the many hand-hewn timber buildings still standing are testament to the construction skills of these early settlers. Learn about all this history at the **Bella Coola Valley Museum** (250/799-5767, Wed.–Mon. 9 A.M.–5 P.M. June–Sept., adult $2.50, child $1).

Accommodations and Camping

Between Bella Coola and Hagensborg, the friendly hosts at **Eagle Lodge** (250/799-5587 or 866/799-5587, www.eaglelodgebc.com, June–Oct., $86–190 s or d) will make you feel welcome the moment you step through the front door. Each of eight rooms is configured differently, with the smallest having a twin bed and the largest a two-bedroom suite complete with a kitchen and fireplace. A light breakfast is included, with dinner an extra $32.50 per person, and guests have use of an outdoor hot tub positioned to take full advantage of the rural setting. Right on the river is **Bella Coola Motel** (Clayton St., 250/799-5323, www.bellacoolavalley.com, $90–110 s or d), with clean and comfortable rooms each with a full kitchen and television. Camping here costs $19 per night.

Discovery Coast Passage

BC Ferries (250/386-3431 or 888/223-3779, www.bcferries.com) sailings from Bella Coola open a remote section of the British Columbia coastline that would otherwise be inaccessible. The main route is between Bella Coola and Port Hardy (Vancouver Island). The direct sailing takes 13 hours, or 31 hours with all stops. You will need to study the timetable (on the BC Ferries website) to see which sailing suits your needs. When the ferry does make a stop, it's only for around two hours each time, so if you want to get off, plan on overnighting until the next ferry comes by. Peak one-way fares for the entire trip are adult $170, child 5–11 $85, vehicle $340.

QUESNEL

Back inland, Highway 97 north from Williams Lake takes you to Quesnel. The town (population 9,500) was founded during the Barkerville gold rush of the 1860s. Prospectors traveling north on the Fraser River disembarked at the confluence of the Fraser and Quesnel Rivers, and a town sprang up on the site. Today the town's economy continues to thrive, with Two Mile Flat, east of downtown, North America's most concentrated wood-products manufacturing area.

Sights and Recreation

At **Heritage Corner** (Carson Ave. and Front St.), you can see the Old Fraser Bridge, the remains of the steamer *Enterprise,* a Cornish waterwheel used by gold miners, and the original Hudson's Bay Store. To learn all about Alexander Mackenzie or the gold-rush days, head to **Quesnel Museum** (Highway 97 at Carson Ave., 250/992-9580, daily 9 A.M.–6 P.M. May–Aug., Tues.–Sat. 8:30 A.M.–4:30 P.M. Sept.–Apr., adult $3, child $1.50), which holds almost 30,000 artifacts. The scenic four-kilometer/2.5-mile (allow 75 minutes) **Riverfront Walking Trail** loops around the downtown core, with plaques honoring early residents; start at any point along the river.

Eight kilometers (five miles) west of Quesnel on Baker Drive are the geologically intriguing, glacially eroded hoodoos at **Pinnacles Provincial Park.** The viewpoint is one

kilometer (0.6 miles) from the day use area; allow 40 minutes for the round-trip.

The main event in Quesnel is the **Billy Barker Days** (250/992-1234) celebration, named for the prospector who made the first gold strike in the Cariboo. Over the middle weekend of July, downtown streets are closed to traffic in favor of an outdoor crafts fair, parade, and dancing. Residents casually stroll around town in period costumes from the gold-mining days—men in cowboy hats, women in slinky long dresses with brightly feathered hats. The Quesnel Rodeo is one of some 150 events staged during the festival.

Accommodations and Food

Right downtown is the **Cariboo Hotel** (254 Front St., 250/992-2333 or 800/665-3200, $65 s, $70 d includes a continental breakfast). Built in 1896, this historic inn has nine restored guest rooms with TVs and phones. Three blocks north, the **Travelodge Quesnel** (524 Front St., 250/992-7071 or 800/665-6995, www.travelodgequesnel.com, $85–125) is an older-style place, but the rooms are spacious and it has a small indoor pool, and wireless Internet.

For campers who don't need services, the best bet is to head north 11 kilometers (6.8 miles) to **Ten Mile Lake Provincial Park.** Of the park's two campgrounds, Lakeside is best (Sites 4–9 are closest to the water) and has hot showers and flush toilets ($19). During the week, snagging a spot isn't usually a problem, but on weekends the campground fills with Quesnel locals who come for the swimming, fishing, and canoeing.

A popular coffeehouse is **Granville's** (383 Reid St., 250/992-3667), open daily from 8 A.M. **Savala's Steak House** (240 Reid St., 250/992-9453, daily for lunch and dinner, $12–19) is a solid, small town Greek restaurant. Entrées such as steak, spareribs, pizza, and other Italian dishes include unlimited trips to the salad bar. **Ulysses Restaurant** (122 Barlow Ave., 250/992-6606, daily for lunch and dinner, $12–21) specializes in southern European cuisine. A hearty plate of pasta or souvlaki is around $18.

Information

Quesnel Visitor Centre is beside Lebourdais Park (703 Carson Ave., 250/992-8716 or 800/992-4922, www.northcariboo.com, daily 8 A.M.–8 P.M. in summer, Mon.–Fri. 8:30 A.M.–4:30 P.M. the rest of the year).

EAST FROM QUESNEL

Around 28 kilometers (17.4 miles) east of Quesnel on Highway 26, **Cottonwood House Provincial Historic Park** (250/992-2071, daily 10 A.M.–5 P.M. mid-May–Aug., adult $4.50, senior $3.50, child $2) preserves a roadhouse built in 1864 to serve Barkerville-bound goldseekers. In addition to the old guesthouse, structures at the site include a barn, stable, and other outbuildings. You'll also find an interpretive center and displays of old farming equipment. In summer, carriage rides are a main attraction while the handmade wood products make a good souvenir. Camping beside the Cottonwood River is $12.50–15, and cabins with shared bathrooms are $35 s or d, which includes site admission.

Wells and Vicinity

A few kilometers before reaching Barkerville, Highway 26 passes the village of Wells. Most local businesses hand out historic walking tour brochures of the town, which includes points of interest such as a one-time illegal gambling hall below a barbershop. In the center of the village is the 1933 **◖ Wells Hotel** (2341 Pooley St., 250/994-3427 or 800/860-2299, www.wellshotel.com, $90 s or d), which has been wonderfully restored without losing its historic charm. Lounging in front of the log fireplace, surrounded by historic photos and with polished hardwood floors underfoot is the perfect way to end a day of sightseeing. Or you can relax over dinner at a sidewalk table, and then soak in the rooftop hot tub.

Barkerville

In 1862 Billy Barker struck gold on Williams Creek, 88 kilometers (55 miles) east of Quesnel. One of Canada's major gold rushes followed, as thousands of prospectors streamed in to what soon became known as Barkerville. By the mid-1860s Barkerville's population had peaked at over 10,000. But fortunes began to fade after the turn of the 20th century. In 1916 Barkerville was destroyed by fire. Although the town was quickly rebuilt, the gold played out soon thereafter, and many of the miners lost interest and moved on.

A hundred years after the first strike, the provincial government decided to make the town a heritage site and re-create its boomtown atmosphere. Today, Barkerville (250/994-3332 or 888/994-3332, www.barkerville.ca, mid-May–Sept., adult $13.50, senior $12.25, child $4, plus $2 for an additional day) boasts more than 120 authentically restored buildings. Historic reenactments take place throughout summer, when the town's shops, stores, and restaurants all operate in a century-old time warp. Highlights include the town bakery, which sells some of the most mouthwatering baked goods in the province; stagecoach rides ($9); the chance to try your hand at gold-panning ($7); and the musical comedy performances at the Theatre Royal, presented 2–3 times daily ($15). The Heritage Package (adult $41, senior $37.75, child $25) includes admission and all these extras.

You can spend the night in one of two historic buildings within the town. Inside and out, **King & Kelly Houses Bed and Breakfast** (866/994-0004, www.kellyhouse.ca, $95–125 s or d) fit the heritage theme of Barkerville. Rates include a cooked breakfast that may include delightful apple pancakes topped with real cream. The 1898 **St. George Hotel** (250/994-0008 or 888/246-7690, www.stgeorgehotel.bc.ca, $110–140 s or d includes a cooked breakfast) has been fully restored and offers seven rooms, some of which share bathrooms; all are tastefully furnished with comfortable beds and authentic antiques.

The pick of three BC Parks–operated campgrounds (mid-June–Sept.) along the access road to the historic town is **Lowhee Campground,** ($19) with showers and a playground. **Forest Rose** ($19) also has shower facilities. **Government Hill Campground** ($15) is closest to the historic site, but as all three campgrounds are within walking distance, this is of little consequence. It's also the most rustic, with pit toilets and no showers.

◖ Bowron Lake Provincial Park

Best known for the **Bowron Lake Canoe Circuit,** Bowron Lake Provincial Park encompasses 149,207 hectares (386,700 acres) of magnificent forests, lakes, and rivers in the Cariboo Mountains. To get there, take Highway 26 east of Quesnel toward Barkerville, but just past Wells take a signposted gravel road to the north. The park protects a chain of six major lakes that, roughly, form a diamond-shaped circuit. Campsites, cabins, and cooking shelters are strategically spaced along the way. To circumnavigate the entire 116-kilometer (72-mile) route takes 6–10 days of paddling and requires seven portages, the most difficult being a 2.5-kilometer (1.5-mile) uphill hike at the very start. As well as being proficient in the use of canoes, those attempting the route should be well prepared for backcountry travel and wet weather. Before setting out on the circuit, paddlers must obtain a permit from the BC Parks Registration Centre (daily 7 A.M.–8 P.M. May 15–Sept. 30) at the end of the park access road. Permits cost $60 per person. As a limited number of persons are permitted on the circuit at any given time, you should reserve a spot as far in advance as possible by calling 250/387-1642 or 800/435-5622. The reservation fee is $18 per canoe. A small number of spots are set aside each day for "drop ins," but the sensible course of action is to reserve as far ahead as possible.

Two privately owned lodges near the end of the park access road provide meals and accommodation, and are as popular with those attempting the canoe circuit as with travelers who drive out simply to take in the wilderness setting. Both are right on Bowron Lake and offer a variety of accommodations as well as canoe rentals ($15 per hour, $45 per day), and full outfitting services for those doing the lake circuit. The original 1930s **Bowron Lake Lodge** (250/992-2733 or 800/519-3399, www.bowronlakelodge.com, motel-style rooms $70–125 s or d, campsites $28) burnt down in late 2008, but as the guest rooms were separate, everything is still operational. The resort has both lake and river frontage, including its own private sandy beach. **Beckers Lodge** (250/992-8864 or 800/808-4761, www.beckerslodge.ca, May–early Oct.) has a choice of cabins ($80–220 s or d); my favorite is the family-friendly, peeled-log Betty Wendle Cabin, with an upstairs loft that has water views, a full kitchen, a practical bathroom, separate bedrooms, and solid wooden furnishings throughout. Camping is $20–35.

Prince George

The gateway to northern British Columbia, Prince George (population 71,000) lies roughly at the geographical center of the province, at the confluence of the Fraser and Nechako Rivers. It was here in 1807 that Simon Fraser of the North West Company constructed Fort George, a supply center for trappers and explorers. The railroad reached the area in 1908, spurring growth that lead to a major logging, sawmill, and pulp-mill town. The city has continued from strength to strength, and has grown to become northern British Columbia's economic, social, and cultural center.

SIGHTS

The best place to get a feel for the layout of Prince George is **Connaught Hill,** which affords a panoramic view of the city. To get there from downtown, take Queensway Street south, turn right on Connaught Drive, then right again on Caine Drive. At the summit are grassy tree-shaded lawns, picnic spots, and several well-kept gardens bursting with color in summer. Back down in town, the clearly marked **Heritage River Trail** runs between Cameron Street Bridge and Carrie Jane Gray Park. You can make an 11-kilometer (6.8-mile)

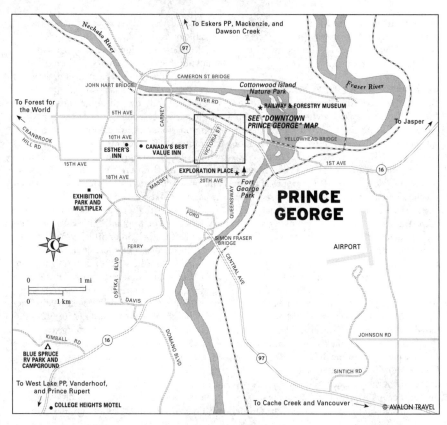

loop of it if you complete the circuit by following Carney Street. Ask for the *Heritage River Trails* pamphlet at the information centers.

Fort George Park

The site where Simon Fraser established Fort George in 1807 is today preserved as 36-hectare (90-acre) riverside Fort George Park. Trails lead through the park along the Fraser River and to the Indian Burial Grounds. The park's indoor highlight is **Exploration Place** (333 Becott Pl., 250/562-1612, daily 10 A.M.–5 P.M. late May–Aug., Wed.–Sun. 10 A.M.–5 P.M. the rest of the year, adult $8.95, senior $6.95, child $5.95). The facility is filled with modern exhibits that go beyond the meaning of a museum in the usual sense.

You'll find a technological dinosaur display, a small IMAX-style theater ($6), high-speed Internet terminals, and many hands-on exhibits. Among the items on display in the History Hall are many stuffed and mounted specimens of wild animals and birds native to British Columbia—including two towering grizzly bears in the foyer—fine crafts of the local Carrier people, an impressive sternwheeler anchor, snowshoes, guns, horrific animal traps and other relics of the fur trade, an old buggy, mock-ups of early business establishments, and a hands-on Science Centre.

Two Rivers Gallery

The architecturally stunning Two Rivers Gallery (725 Civic Plaza, 250/614-7800, Tues.–Sat.

10 A.M.–5 P.M., Sun. noon–5 P.M., adult $5, senior and child $4) is Prince George's major cultural attraction. The large permanent collection is the main draw, but temporary shows that change every four to five weeks are included in the admission fee. It's also a good place to buy high-quality local artwork at a reasonable price. Look for paintings, sculpture, pottery, beadwork, woven and painted silk items, and jewelry.

Prince George Railway and Forestry Museum

The museum (850 River Rd., 250/563-7351, Wed.–Sun. 10 A.M.–6 P.M., adult $6, senior $5, child $3) catalogs Prince George's industrial

history. Take a self-guided tour through some of the antiquated railway cars and buildings, clamber on retired railway equipment, and chug back in time via the black-and-white photo displays and assorted memorabilia. To get there from downtown, take Highway 16 east to the River Road exit (just before the Yellowhead Bridge over the Fraser River) and continue north down River Road one kilometer to the museum.

Cottonwood Island Nature Park

Beyond the railroad museum is the entrance to beautiful 33-hectare (81-acre) Cottonwood Island Nature Park. Beside the Nechako River,

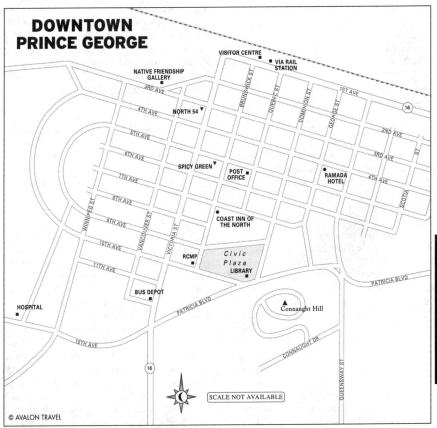

© AVALON TRAVEL

the park's dominant feature is an extensive forest of northern black cottonwood trees. In spring sticky buds cover the cottonwoods, and in summer the air is thick and the ground white with seed-bearing tufts of fluff. You'll see all sorts of birds, and might spy the occasional beaver. The park's trail system is extensive; the short walk between the main parking lot and the river is popular.

ACCOMMODATIONS AND CAMPING

The least expensive place to stay is the **College Heights Motel** (five km/3.1 mi west of downtown along Hwy. 16, 250/964-4708). It has no toll-free number, no website, not even cable TV, but for $45 s, $58 d in high season, what do you expect? It's on the south side of the highway at the top of the rise.

Most Prince George accommodations fall into the $50–100 range, and they are mostly concentrated along the Highway 97 bypass west of downtown. Least expensive of these is **Canada's Best Value Inn** (1630 Central St., 250/563-3671 or 800/663-3290, $79–89 s, $79–109 d), which isn't but has comfortable rooms and a restaurant. The best value along this stretch, with comfortable rooms and a load of extras at a reasonable price, is **Esther's Inn** (1151 Commercial Crescent, 250/562-4131, www.esthersinn.bc.ca, $79–109 s or d). Guest rooms surround a lush tropical atrium packed with palms and philodendrons, waterfalls, Polynesian artifacts, swimming pools, a water slide, and a thatched-roof restaurant. Some rooms have high-speed Internet.

The **Ramada Hotel** (444 George St., 250/563-0055 or 800/830-8833, www.ramadaprincegeorge.com, $140–220 s or d) is an unattractive but distinctive red-brick building in the heart of downtown. Amenities include a restaurant, lounge, pub, pool, sauna and whirlpool, casino, gift shop, and covered parking. Call or check the website, and you should be able to find a room for around $100, even in summer. In the same price category and also centrally located is the 193-room **Coast Inn of the North** (770 Brunswick St., 250/563-0121 or 800/716-6199,

www.coasthotels.com, $155–220 s or d). This full-service hotel has a smallish fitness room, an indoor pool, a sauna, high-speed Internet, and three in-house eateries (including a Japanese restaurant). Like the Ramada, check their website for perpetually discounted rooms.

Camping

Privately operated **Blue Spruce RV Park and Campground** (Kimball Rd., 250/964-7272 or 877/964-7272, Apr.–mid-Oct., unserviced sites $20, hookups $24–30) is five kilometers (3.1 miles) west on Highway 16 from the junction of Highway 97. It's a popular spot, filling up each night during the busy summer months. Each site has a picnic table and a barbecue grate, and the amenities include spotlessly clean heated bathrooms, a coin-operated laundry, a swimming pool, mini-golf, and a playground. The closest provincial park to Prince George is at **Purden Lake** (55 km/34 mi east on Hwy. 16, Apr.–Oct., $15), a picturesque body of water with a small stretch of sandy beach.

FOOD

An excellent place for lunch is **Papaya Grove Restaurant** (Esther's Inn, 1151 Commercial Cres., 250/562-4131). You can choose from among three different seating areas: under a thatched roof, around the pool, or in the bar. All are enclosed within a massive tropical indoor atrium. A set menu is offered, but the buffet is the most popular choice. The daily lunch buffet (11 A.M.–2 P.M.) is around $12, with a different theme each day. Sunday brunch is particularly good; for $17.95 you get all the usual breakfast choices, along with salmon, prawns, roast beef, and a staggering number of desserts. The dinner buffet is $19.95 Sunday–Thursday, $24.95 on Friday and Saturday when prime rib is served.

With a refined atmosphere, well-presented dishes, and adequate service, **North 54** (1493 3rd Ave., 250/564-5400, Mon.–Fri. 11:30 A.M.–2 P.M., Mon.–Sat. 5–9 P.M., $14–35) is one of Prince George's better restaurants. Pastas are mostly under $20, with dishes such as halibut topped with a fruity salsa and roasted rack of lamb capping out at prices similar to big city dining. Also downtown, **Spicy Green** (1215 5th Ave., 250/564-3509, Mon.–Sat. for lunch and dinner, $8–17) is a small Indian restaurant with a long and mostly vegetarian menu. Almost everything is made from scratch, including a delicious shrimp curry.

INFORMATION AND SERVICES

Tourism Prince George (1300 First Ave., 250/562-3700 or 800/668-7646, www.tour-ismpg.com, Mon.–Fri. 8:30 A.M.–5 P.M., with extended summer hours of daily 9 A.M.–8 P.M.) operates an excellent information center right downtown.

Prince George Public Library (887 Dominion St., 250/563-9251, Mon.–Thurs. 10 A.M.–9 P.M., Fri.–Sat. 10 A.M.–5:30 P.M., Sun. 1–5 P.M.) has newspapers and magazines from across North America, public Internet access, and a display of native art and artifacts. **Books & Company** (1685 3rd Ave., 250/563-6637) features a great selection of local and northern British Columbia literature, but what makes it most inviting is the friendly staff, in-house café, and Friday evening jam sessions.

The **post office** is on the corner of 5th Avenue and Quebec Street. **Prince George Regional Hospital** is at 2000 15th Ave. (250/565-2000). The **RCMP** is on the corner of Brunswick and 10th Avenue, behind the library (250/562-3371).

GETTING THERE AND AROUND

The airport is 18 kilometers (11 miles) east of town and is served by connectors for **Air Canada** (888/247-2262) and **WestJet** (800/538-5696). Both these airlines fly daily to Vancouver and other regional centers, as well as Calgary. **VIA Rail** operates transcontinental service from Prince George west to Prince Rupert and east through Jasper and Edmonton to Toronto and beyond. The VIA Rail station is on 1st Avenue between Brunswick and Quebec Streets (250/564-5233). **Greyhound** (1566 12th Ave., 250/564-5454) runs regularly scheduled services from Prince George south to Kamloops and Vancouver (via Williams Lake and Quesnel); west along the Yellowhead Highway to Terrace and Prince Rupert; north to Dawson Creek via Chetwynd; and east along the Yellowhead Highway to Jasper and Edmonton.

Prince George Transit System (250/563-0011, adult $2.25, senior and child $1.75) operates buses throughout the city daily except Sunday. Prince George **handyDART** (250/562-1394) provides door-to-door transportation for disabled passengers unable to use the regular bus service. Car-rental agencies with desks out at the airport are **Budget** (250/963-9669), **Hertz** (250/963-7454), and **National** (250/963-7473).

Prince George to Prince Rupert

From Prince George, Highway 16 (Yellowhead Hwy.) continues westward 726 kilometers (451 miles) to the coastal city of Prince Rupert. It takes a full day to drive the route, but the sensible course of action is to break the journey up with a stop at one of the many inviting towns along the way.

VANDERHOOF AND VICINITY

The first town west of Prince George (65 km/40 mi) is Vanderhoof (population 4,400),

a service center for the Nechako Valley and British Columbia's geographical center (the exact spot is marked by a cairn five kilometers east of town). Vanderhoof grew as a stop on the Grand Trunk Pacific Railway. Today it's a prosperous farming and logging town with the worthwhile **Vanderhoof Heritage Museum** (Hwy. 16, 250/567-2991, daily 10 A.M.–5 P.M., adult $3), consisting of 11 restored heritage buildings, among them a jail, a 1922 schoolhouse, and a restored gambling room.

Practicalities

Right downtown is **North Country Inn** (2575 Burrard Ave., 250/567-3047, $72 s, $84 d), with decent motel-style rooms, some kitchenettes, and in-room Internet access. Part of the complex is Vanderhoof's best restaurant, a rustic log building where breakfasts cost from $7.50 and dinner mains run $15–30 (try the delicious chicken lasagna). **Riverside RV Park & Campground** (250/567-4710, May–Sept., tent sites $18, hookups $21–28) enjoys a pleasant setting beside the Nechako River. Turn north off Highway 16 onto Burrard Avenue and continue through town; the campground is to the west side of Burrard Avenue. Showers and firewood are supplied.

Vanderhoof Visitor Centre (2325 Burrard Ave., 250/567-2124) is open year-round Mon.–Fri. 9 A.M.–5 P.M., with extended summer hours of daily 9 A.M.–6 P.M.

Fort St. James National Historic Site

Fort St. James (population 2,000), 60 kilometers (37 miles) north of Vanderhoof, is home to a sprawling National Historic Site (250/996-7191, daily 9 A.M.–5 P.M. late May–Sept., adult $8, senior $6.50, child $4) protecting the earliest nonnative settlement in northern British Columbia. Established in 1806, Fort St. James was the chief fur-trading post and capital of the large and prosperous district of New Caledonia—the name originally given to the northern part of the province by Simon Fraser. Today the beautifully restored fort forms the centerpiece of a historic park that holds Canada's largest collection of original fur trade buildings. Enter the fort through the Visitor Reception Centre, which has displays on pioneer explorers, fur traders, and the indigenous Carrier people. An audio recording and a map trace the route of the early explorers, and a slide show fills you in on the restoration of the fort's original buildings. In July and August, characters dressed in pioneer garb lurk in the log-constructed general store, the fish cache, the single men's bunkhouse, the main house,

FISH FANTASIES

More than 300 lakes dot the high country between Burns Lake and Houston, with many renowned for fishing. Common species are rainbow, eastern brook, and cutthroat trout, as well as kokanee, chinook salmon, steelhead, and lake char. To even mention all the lakes and their fishing possibilities would take a whole other book. Instead, here are a few places I've had success dangling a line over the years:

Babine Lake, north of Topley, is British Columbia's largest natural lake and is known for its trophy-size rainbow trout as well as steelhead runs in the Babine River. Stay at the well-priced **Babine Lake Resort** (250/692-0363, www.babinelakeresort.com).

Francois Lake, south of Burns Lake, is the place to troll for lake char up to nine kilograms (20 pounds), as well as kokanee and rainbow trout. Stay the night and cook your catch at the lakefront **Birch Bay Resort** (250/699-8484, www.birchbay.ca), where you can choose between camping and cabins.

Morice River, west of Houston (south at the Northwood Pulp Mill sign), combines accessibility and reliability to make it a favorite steelhead fishing spot.

and the veggie garden. You're actively encouraged to get into the spirit of things and play along. Tell them you've just arrived by canoe, want to stay the night in the men's house, and need a good horse and some provision…then see what happens!

The best place to stay in the area is **Stuart Lodge** (Stones Bay Rd., 250/996-7917, www.stuartlodge.ca, $66–72 s, $78–100 d), on the shore of Stuart Lake five kilometers (3.1 miles) west of Fort St. James. The complex's five cottages come with cooking facilities, decks, and TVs. **Paarens Beach Provincial Park** and **Sowchea Bay Provincial Park,** west of Fort St. James, both offer lakeside tent and vehicle camping (May–Sept., $15), swimming, fishing, and lakefront picnic tables.

VANDERHOOF TO SMITHERS

Continuing west from Vanderhoof, the Yellowhead Highway crosses the wide Nechako River, passing the turnoff to **Beaumont Provincial Park,** with a lakeside interpretive trail and a campground (May–Oct., $17 per site).

Fraser Lake

The town of Fraser Lake (population 1,500), 60 kilometers (37 miles) west of Vanderhoof, lies on a chunk of land sloping gently down to its namesake lake. In winter, trumpeter swans settle in at each end of the lake. In summer, a salmon run on the **Stellako River**—a short stretch of water between Fraser and Francois Lakes—draws scores of eager anglers. Overlooking Fraser Lake, **Piper's Glen RV Park** (250/690-7565, www.pipersglenresort.com, May–Sept., camping $18–20, basic cabins $40 s or d) has a grassy lakeshore camping area with full hookups and showers. Guests can rent canoes and motorboats. **Fraser Lake Visitor Centre,** along the highway through town (250/699-8844, daily 8 A.M.–6 P.M. July–Aug.) offers tourism information and a small museum out back.

Burns Lake

The first thing you see when you enter Burns Lake is an enormous chainsaw-carved trout with the inscription "Three Thousand Miles of Fishing!" That pretty much sums up what attracts visitors to the town and surrounding Lakes District. Continue west along the highway through town for about one kilometer until you come to the green-and-white **Heritage Centre** (Hwy. 16, 250/692-3773, daily 1–5 P.M., adult $2) comprising a museum and the local information center. Ask here for a map showing all the heritage buildings around town. For a wonderful view of the area, follow 5th Avenue up the hill out of town, then take the turnoff to **Boer Mountain Forestry Lookout.**

Tweedsmuir Provincial Park

The town of Burns Lake is not only near British Columbia's smallest provincial park

(Deadman's Island in Burns Lake), it also happens to be the northern gateway to the largest: 981,000-hectare (2.42 million-acre) Tweedsmuir Provincial Park. Its northern boundary, formed by **Ootsa** and **Whitesail Lakes,** is accessed along a network of gravel roads south from Burns Lake. Wildlife abounds. If you're in the right place at the right time you can see caribou, mountain goats, moose, black and grizzly bears, mule deer, wolves, smaller mammals such as hoary marmots and wolverines, and many birds. The lakes are filled with fish, including rainbow trout, kokanee, mountain whitefish, and burbot. To get to Ootsa Lake, follow Highway 35 for 16 kilometers (10 miles) south from Burns Lake to Francois Lake, take the free vehicle ferry across Francois Lake, then continue south another 44 kilometers (27 miles) to the settlement of Ootsa Lake. To get *into* the park itself, you'll need a canoe, kayak, motorboat, or chartered floatplane. **Lakes District Air Services** (250/692-3229, www.lakesdistrictair.com) flies charters year-round from a base along Francois Lake Road—on floats in summer and skis in winter. This company also owns fly-in cabins on Tesla and Coles Lakes. The cabins sleep four and come equipped with cooking facilities, hot showers, HF radios, and a couple of small motorboats. A four-day package deal, inclusive of charter flights is $1,450 per person for two people; guests supply food, sleeping bags, and fishing gear.

Houston

Like Burns Lake, Houston's welcoming sign also proudly bears a carved fish—this time a steelhead. Houston calls itself "Steelhead Country," for the only species of trout that migrates to ocean. The forestry town of 4,000 lies at the confluence of the Bulkley and Morice Rivers in the stunning Bulkley Valley, which enjoys the snowcapped Telkwa and Babine Ranges for a backdrop. As in the rest of this region, the local fishing is superb. The best steelhead fishing is in the Morice River—take the highway west toward Smithers, turn left at the Northwood Pulp Mill sign, and continue about 1.6 kilometers

CENTRAL AND NORTHERN

(one mile) to the end. At the dirt road turn right (at the bridge). Both bait fishing and fly-fishing are popular here. **Houston Visitor Centre** (Hwy. 16 at Benson Ave., 250/845-7640, daily 9 A.M.–5 P.M. in summer, weekdays only the rest of the year) is easy to spot—out front is world's largest fly-fishing rod.

Telkwa

As you continue west, the scenery just keeps getting better. You'll pass open fields and rolling, densely forested hills, all the while surrounded by snowcapped mountains peeking tantalizingly out of clouds. The neat little village of Telkwa lies at the confluence of the Bulkley and Telkwa Rivers, almost exactly halfway between Prince George and Prince Rupert. Several species of anadromous fish make spawning runs up the rivers here at various times of year—spring chinook salmon in late June, coho salmon in August, and steelhead between fall and freeze-up. The area also appeals to canoeists, offering stretches of water to suit novices through intermediates. Many of the buildings in the village were put up between 1908 and 1924. The Telkwa Museum Society puts out a *Walking Tour Through Historic Telkwa* brochure, which describes each of the buildings.

On the highway through town, **Two Rivers Lodge** (250/846-6000, www.tworiverslodge.ca, $80–230 s or d) is one of the best places to stay between Prince George and the coast. It offers a beautiful riverside setting and is surrounded by gardens. Options include regular motel rooms, kitchen-equipped suites, and log cabins. Amenities include wireless Internet, barbecues, and communal fire pits. Nearby **Tyhee Lake Provincial Park** has a good swimming beach, picnic facilities, and a campground with hot showers (May–Sept., $22).

SMITHERS AND VICINITY

The Coast Mountains surround the town of Smithers (population 5,800), while the splendid 2,560-meter (8,400-foot) Hudson Bay Mountain towers directly above. It's a vibrant community with some excellent accommodations, fine restaurants, and interesting arts-and-crafts shops. Hiking trails close to town lead to a magnificent glacier, intriguing fossil beds, and a remote recreation area.

Sights

With a mountainous backdrop, it's no surprise that Main Street is jazzed up in a Bavarian theme. Visitors shop here for native crafts and tourist paraphernalia. The grand old 1925 courthouse, at the junction of the Yellowhead Highway and Main Street, is home to **Bulkley Valley Museum** (250/847-5322, daily 9 A.M.–5 P.M. in summer, donation), home to a predictable collection of historic artifacts, highlighted by an interesting collection of black-and-white photos.

Many millions of years ago, the region north of Smithers was a wetland. Over eons, deposited sediments covered and preserved the remains of the plants and animals that died in the water. Around a million years ago, a lava flow covered the entire region. But then during the last ice age, melting ice carved out a canyon that sliced right through the ancient wetlands, exposing the fossil beds. The area is now protected as **Driftwood Canyon Provincial Park.** Most of the fossils here are from plants, but insect and fish fossils have also been uncovered, including some of the world's oldest known trout fossils. A short walk from the road leads to a viewing platform over the east bank of Driftwood Creek, where interpretive panels describe the site's significance. The park is 17 kilometers (10.6 miles) northeast of town; take Highway 16 three kilometers (1.9 miles) east, head north on Old Babine Lake Road, turn left on Telkwa High Road, then right on Driftwood Road.

Accommodations and Camping

Styled on a Bavarian lodge, the 23-room **Stork Nest Inn** (1485 Main St., 250/847-3831, www.storknestinn.com, $85–100 s or d) features comfortable rooms, a cooked breakfast, and airport transfers. The premier accommodation in this region is the **Logpile Lodge** (3105 McCabe Rd., 250/847-5152, www.logpilelodge.com, Mar.–late Dec., $105–155 s or d), north of town (call for directions) and surrounded by a magnificent mountain panorama. Guest rooms on the upper floor have vaulted ceilings while exposed log walls dominate those on the lower floor. All seven rooms have a solid log bed and a private balcony. A big breakfast, cooked to order, will set you up for an activity-filled day (horseback riding, canoeing, fishing, and more) with local operators.

Riverside Park Municipal Campsite (May–Oct., $15–20) is beside the Bulkley River, north of town. It provides shaded sites, a few electrical hook-ups, showers, and a cooking shelter. **Riverside Golf Course** (Hwy. 16 east of town, 250/847-3229, mid-Apr.–mid-Oct., unserviced sites $21, hookups $24–29) has a small campground with nicer facilities.

Food
Mountainside Café (3763 Fourth Ave., 250/847-3455, Mon.–Sat. 11 A.M.–8 P.M., $10–15) is a funky little space with a stylish yet uncomplicated decor. The varied menu includes everything from fish-and-chips to a Thai curry ($14). Expect live music on Thursday evening. At **Schimmel's Bakery** (1172 Main St., 250/847-9044, Tues.–Sat. 5:30 A.M.–5 P.M., lunches $5–8), enjoy a range of delicious cakes and pastries, or try a bowl of homemade soup with a sandwich made to order.

Information
Tourism Smithers (250/847-5072 or 800/542-6673, www.tourismsmithers.com) operates the **Smithers Visitor Centre,** upstairs in the museum building at the corner of Main Street and the Yellowhead Highway (daily 9 A.M.–6 P.M. in summer, Mon.–Fri. 8:30 A.M.–4:30 P.M. the rest of the year). A good source of northern literature is **Mountain Eagle Books** (1237 Main St., 250/847-5245).

Moricetown Canyon
Westbound from Smithers, the first place to stop and stretch your legs is the viewpoint at Moricetown Canyon, where the 500-meter-wide (0.3-mile-wide) Bulkley River funnels and roars its way down through a 15-meter-wide (49-foot-wide) canyon. Salmon desperately hurl themselves up these spectacular rapids in autumn. Below the canyon the river pours into a large pool, one of the best fishing spots in the area. The canyon is part of Moricetown Indian Reserve, which recognizes an area that has been a Carrier village site for more than 5,000 years. Villagers still fish the canyon using traditional spears and nets; look for the locals congregated around the canyon in summer.

NEW HAZELTON AND VICINITY
It's easy to be confused by the three Hazeltons—Hazelton, New Hazelton, and South Hazelton—situated at the most northerly point on the Yellowhead Highway. As usual, the arrival of the Grand Trunk Pacific Railway caused the confusion. The original Hazelton (called Old Town) was established 50 years or so before the railway came. The other two Hazeltons were founded because each of their respective promoters thought he owned a better spot for a new railway town. Today the largest of the three small communities is New Hazelton (population 900), a service center watched over by spectacular Mount Rocher Deboule. At the intersection of Highways 16 and 62, **Hazelton Visitor Centre** (470 9th Ave., 250/842-6071, daily 8 A.M.–5 P.M. mid-June–mid-Sept.) has all the usual literature and holds a display detailing local history within a two-story log building.

'Ksan Historical Village
'Ksan, which means "Between the Banks," is an authentically reconstructed Gitxsan village on the outskirts of Hazelton (250/842-5544, daily 9 A.M.–5 P.M. Apr.–Sept., $2). In the main building is a museum featuring cedar boxes and cedar-bark mats, woven and button blankets, masks, coppers (the most valuable single object a chief possessed), rattles used by shamans, and an art gallery with changing exhibitions. In the adjacent gift shop are the works of on-site artists. Beyond the museum is the main village, which can only be visited as part of a fascinating guided tour (adult $10, senior and student $8.50). Tours leave every

hour on the hour, visiting the burial house, food cache, smokehouse, community houses, and the 'Ksan artists' carving shop and studio. You'll see traditional northwest coast carved interiors, paintings and painted screens, totem poles, and fine examples of native artifacts, arts and crafts, tools and implements, and personal possessions. And you'll learn how the people lived and all about their beliefs and legends.

TERRACE AND VICINITY

Terrace (population 12,500) lies on the Yellowhead Highway, 580 kilometers (360 miles) west of Prince George and 146 kilometers (91 miles) east of Prince Rupert. The city is built on a series of steep terraces along the beautiful Skeena River, the province's second-largest river system, and is completely surrounded by the spectacular Hazelton and Coast Mountains. Fishing is a major draw, with steelhead caught April–May and August–November. Through summer chinook and coho salmon are the main catch.

The main in-town attraction is **Heritage Park** (4113 Sparks St., 250/635-4546, Mon.–Fri. 9:30 A.M.–5:30 P.M. mid-May–June, daily 9:30 A.M.–5:30 P.M. July–Aug., adult $5, senior and child $3), where a one-hour guided tour will take you through an old, beautifully furnished log hotel, a dance hall, a barn, and six authentic log cabins dating from between 1910 and 1955. To get there from downtown, head north up Skeenaview Street.

Nisga'a Memorial Lava Bed Provincial Park

Protecting Canada's youngest lava flow, the fascinating landscape of this 17,683-hectare (43,700-acre) park is unique within the province. The flow is about 18 kilometers (11.2 miles) long and three kilometers (1.9 miles) wide; experts think the molten rock spewed through the earth's crust between 1650 and 1750, killing an estimated 200 natives. You can see all different types of lava, as well as crevasses, spiky pinnacles, sinkholes, craters,

and bright blue pools where underground rivers have risen to the surface. Explore the lava with caution—in some parts the surface may be unstable, and it's very hard on footgear. The only facilities are a day-use area and a couple of short hiking trails. To get to the park, take Highway 16 west out of town for three kilometers (1.9 miles), then head north around the back of the sawmill on Kalum Lake Drive. The park is 78 kilometers (48.5 miles) along this road; watch for logging trucks during the week. The information center in Terrace has an interesting brochure on the lava beds.

Accommodations and Camping

The less expensive motels are strung out along Highway 16 on the eastern and western outskirts of the city. On the east side of town is the **Copper River Motel** (4113 Hwy. 16, 250/635-6124 or 888/652-7222, www.copperrivermotel.com, $75 s, $85 d), set up for anglers, with fishing supplies and guides, 4WD rentals, and free ice. Rooms are clean and have coffee- and tea-making appliances. On the down side are the paper-thin walls. Right downtown is the centrally located **Coast Inn of the West** (4620 Lakelse Ave., 250/638-8141 or 800/716-6199, www.coasthotels.com, $145 s, $155 d), where each of the 60 air-conditioned rooms is decorated in stylish pastel colors. Facilities include a family restaurant and dimly lit lounge.

On Ferry Island in the Skeena River, just over three kilometers east of downtown, **Ferry Island Campground** (250/635-7391, mid-Apr.–mid-Oct., unserviced sites $17, powered sites $21) offers 103 sheltered sites among birch and cottonwood trees, berry bushes, and wildflowers. A few sites have excellent views of the river and mountains, and a hiking trail runs through the woods and around the island. Facilities include picnic tables and shelters, fire grates, firewood, and pit toilets, but no showers.

◖ **Lakelse Lake Provincial Park** (Hwy. 37 16 km/10 mi south of Terrace, $22) is the most developed of the three parks, offering a sandy beach, safe swimming, a hiking trail through an old-growth forest, an interpretive amphitheatre, hot showers, and flush toilets.

Food

One of the most popular places to go for breakfast is the **Northern Motor Inn** (3086 Hwy. 16, 250/635-6375, daily for breakfast, lunch, and dinner, $9–16), near the Chevron gas station just east of Terrace. Large omelets, hash browns, toast, and coffee run around $8–9. Head downtown to **Cafenara** (4716 Lazelle Ave., 250/638-1662, Mon.–Sat. 7 A.M.–9 P.M., Sun. 9 A.M.–4 P.M., lunches $5.50–8) for your daily quota of caffeine in a big-city coffeehouse atmosphere.

For delicious Mexican food, try **Don Diego's** (3212 Kalum St., 250/635-2307, Mon.–Sat. 11 A.M.–9 P.M., Sun. 10 A.M.–2 P.M. and 5–9 P.M., $14–19), where many tables catch the evening sun. It's a small, bright restaurant with lots of plants and Mexican wall hangings. Lunch is $7–12 (the shrimp crepes are superb). It's usually busy, so you may have to wait for a table.

Information

Terrace Visitor Centre (4511 Keith Ave., 250/635-2063 or 800/499-1637, www.kermodeitourism.ca, Mon.–Fri. 8:30 A.M.–8 P.M. and Sat.–Sun. 9 A.M.–8 P.M. in summer, Mon.–Fri. 9 A.M.–5 P.M. the rest of the year) is beside Highway 16 on the east side of town.

For local reading and a good selection of Canadiana, **Misty River Books** (4710 Lakelse Ave., 250/635-4428, Mon.–Thurs. and Sat. 9 A.M.–6 P.M., Fri. 9 A.M.–8 P.M.) should have what you need. If you like to browse rather than buy, visit **Terrace Public Library** (4610 Park Ave., 250/638-8177, Tues.–Sat. noon–3 P.M. and 7–9 P.M., Sun. 1–4 P.M.), which also has free Internet access.

Kitimat

The planned industrial community of Kitimat (population 11,000), at the northern end of Douglas Channel 62 kilometers (39 miles) south of Terrace, was founded by the aluminum giant Alcan (Aluminum Company of Canada) in the 1950s. Described at the time by *National Geographic* as "the most expensive project ever attempted by private industry," construction included one of the world's largest aluminum smelters, a company town to serve the workers, and a massive hydroelectric scheme.

West Toward Prince Rupert

The 147-kilometer (91-mile) stretch of the Yellowhead Highway between Terrace and Prince Rupert rivals any stretch of road in the province for beauty. For almost the entire distance, the highway hugs the north bank of the beautiful Skeena River (*Skeena* is a Gitxsan word for "River of Mist"). On a fine day, views from the road are stunning—snow-dusted mountains, densely forested hillsides, ponds covered in yellow water lilies, and waterfalls like narrow ribbons of silver, snaking down vertical cliffs from the snow high above. In some sections the highway shrinks to two extremely narrow lanes neatly sandwiched between the railway tracks and the river—drive defensively.

Exchamsiks River Provincial Park, on the north side of the highway 50 kilometers (31 miles) west of Terrace, features a grassy picnic area where the deep green Exchamsiks River drains into the much larger Skeena River. Camping is $15 a night. As the highway continues westward, the Skeena widens, eventually becoming a tidal estuary. Sandbars and marshes, exposed at low tide, are a mass of colorful mosses, and wading birds feed in shallow pools. Keep an eye out for bald eagles on the sandbars or perched in the trees above the highway.

CENTRAL AND NORTHERN

Prince Rupert

Prince Rupert (population 15,000), on hilly Kaien Island 726 kilometers (451 miles) west of Prince George, is busy with travelers throughout the summer. The city itself holds an odd but intriguing mixture of cultural icons—totem poles, old English coats of arms and street names, high-rise hotels and civic buildings—all crammed together on the edge of the Pacific Ocean.

SIGHTS AND RECREATION

Plan to spend at least a day in the area, visiting the excellent museum, exploring an old cannery village, or maybe taking a harbor tour. Prince Rupert is also a gateway to the Khutzeymateen Grizzly Bear Sanctuary, but even from town, you're likely to spot bald eagles, seals, and even black bears.

Museum of Northern British Columbia

You can easily spend several hours at this fascinating museum (100 1st Ave. W, 250/624-3207, Mon.–Fri. 9 A.M.–8 P.M. and Sat.–Sun. 9 A.M.–5 P.M. June–Aug., Mon.–Sat. 9 A.M.–5 P.M. the rest of the year, adult $5, child $2), which occupies an imposing post-and-beam building overlooking the harbor. Exhibits trace the history of Prince Rupert from 5,000-year-old Tsimshian settlements through fur-trading days to the founding of the city in 1914 as the western terminus of the Grand Trunk Pacific Railway. Many of the most fascinating displays spotlight the Coast Tsimshian natives—their history, culture, traditions, trade networks, and potlatches. Among the Tsimshian artifacts on display: totem poles, pots, masks, beautiful wooden boxes, blankets, baskets, shiny black argillite carvings, weapons, and petroglyphs. The Monumental Gallery—filled with contemporary art—is worth visiting for the sweeping harbor views alone.

Other Town Sights

Right by the Museum of Northern British Columbia is **Pacific Mariner's Memorial Park,** a grassy area with benches strategically placed for the best ocean views. A statue of a mariner staring out to sea is surrounded by plaques remembering those lost at sea. Also in the park is the *Kazu Maru,* a small fishing boat that drifted across the Pacific from Japan after its owner was lost. It washed up on the Queen Charlotte Islands in 1987, two years after it was reported missing. On the other side of the museum to the memorial park and beside the fire hall is the **Firehall Museum** (200 1st Ave. W, 250/627-1248, Tues.–Sun. 9 A.M.–5 P.M. July–Aug., donation), which features a 1925 REO Speedwagon along with various other firefighting memorabilia. From this museum, continue south along 1st Avenue, then head to the foot of 2nd Street, which ends harborside. Here you'll find the **Kwinitsa Railway Station Museum** (250/624-3207, daily 9 A.M.–noon and 1–5 P.M. in summer), housed in a small railway station—one of only four such remaining buildings that were once part of a chain of 400 identical stations along the Grand Trunk Railway.

North Pacific Cannery

South of Prince Rupert in Port Edward, the North Pacific Cannery (250/628-3538, daily 11 A.M.–5 P.M. May–Sept., adult $12, senior $9, child $6) is the oldest remaining cannery village from over 1,000 similar facilities that were once operating along the west coast of North America. Dating to 1889 and now classified as a national historic site, this living museum is one of the highlights of a visit to Prince Rupert. You can find out everything you've ever wanted to know about fish, the fishing industry, canning—even which fish tastes the best (locals say it's red snapper every time). You're free to stroll at your own pace along the boardwalk through the riverside settlement with its many original buildings, including a church, schoolroom, general store, and living quarters. To get to the village, head out of Prince Rupert on the

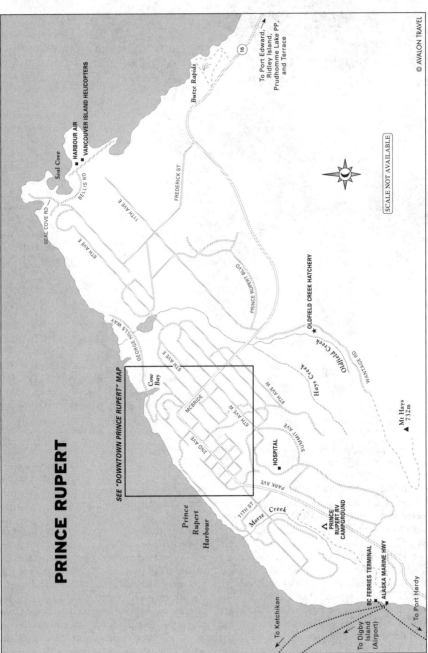

PRINCE RUPERT

CENTRAL AND NORTHERN

© AVALON TRAVEL

SCALE NOT AVAILABLE

Prince Rupert Harbour

Seal Cove

HARBOUR AIR
VANCOUVER ISLAND HELICOPTERS

SEAL COVE RD

BELLIS RD

6TH AVE E

11TH AVE E

FREDERICK ST

GEORGE HILLS WAY

PRINCE RUPERT BLVD

To Port Edward,
Ridley Island,
Prudhomme Lake PP,
and Terrace

Butze Rapids

16

Cow Bay

MCBRIDE

5TH AVE

6TH AVE W

9TH AVE W

2ND AVE

SUMMIT AVE

HOSPITAL

PARK AVE

SEE "DOWNTOWN PRINCE RUPERT" MAP

Hays Creek

Oldfield Creek

OLDFIELD CREEK HATCHERY

WANTAGE RD

Mt Hays
732m

11TH ST

Morse Creek

PRINCE
RUPERT RV
CAMPGROUND

BC FERRIES TERMINAL

ALASKA MARINE HWY

To Ketchikan

To Digby
Island
(Airport)

To Port Hardy

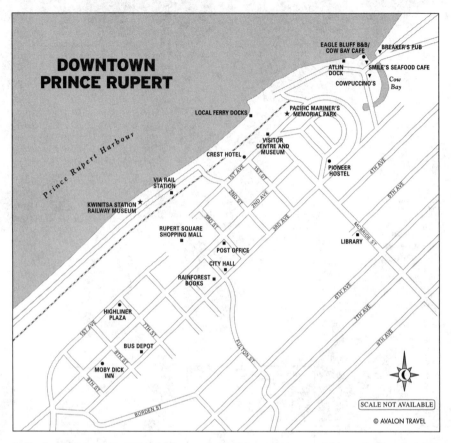

DOWNTOWN PRINCE RUPERT

EAGLE BLUFF B&B/ COW BAY CAFE
BREAKER'S PUB
ATLIN DOCK
SMILE'S SEAFOOD CAFE
COWPUCCINO'S
Cow Bay
LOCAL FERRY DOCKS
PACIFIC MARINER'S MEMORIAL PARK
Prince Rupert Harbour
VISITOR CENTRE AND MUSEUM
CREST HOTEL
PIONEER HOSTEL
4TH AVE
VIA RAIL STATION
5TH AVE
KWINITSA STATION RAILWAY MUSEUM
2ND ST
2ND AVE
3RD AVE
3RD ST
McBRIDE ST
RUPERT SQUARE SHOPPING MALL
POST OFFICE
LIBRARY
CITY HALL
RAINFOREST BOOKS
6TH AVE
8TH AVE
HIGHLINER PLAZA
7TH AVE
1ST AVE
7TH ST
BUS DEPOT
FULTON ST
8TH AVE
8TH ST
MOBY DICK INN
7TH ST
BORDEN ST

SCALE NOT AVAILABLE
© AVALON TRAVEL

Yellowhead Highway and take the first road to the right after leaving Kaien Island.

Touring Local Waterways

Once you're finished with Prince Rupert's land-based attractions, plan on an inexpensive ferry ride, a fishing trip, kayaking, or a grizzly bear–viewing excursion into the Khutzeymateen. **Seashore Charters** (Atlin Terminal, Cow Bay, 250/624-5645 or 800/667-4393, www.seashorecharters.com) is a longtime booking agent representing local charter operators. The most interesting of their tours is to **Laxspa'aws** (Pike Island), where shell middens, petroglyphs, and depressions from prehistoric houses point to human habitation up to 2,000 years ago.

Other options available include yacht trips; day-long cruises looking for eagles, waterfowl, seals, otters, porpoises, and killer whales; and fishing trips for salmon, halibut, or cod, with gear and bait supplied. Expect to pay from $100 per person for a fishing trip.

Jump aboard the small ferries that run around the harbor to communities with no road connections for an inexpensive harbor cruise. Head down to the small docks at the bottom of McBride Street for route and schedule information, or call 250/624-3337. The shortest trip is a 15-minute run to **Dodge Cove** on Digby Island. There's not much to do on the island, but it's a nice cruise there and back, and it costs just $12 round-trip.

The calm waters of Prince Rupert Harbour are perfect for kayaking. Even if you have had no experience in a kayak, **Skeena Kayaking** (Cow Bay, 250/624-8311) will take you on an easy 1.5-hour paddle along the shoreline for $55 per person. A six-hour guided paddle to Tsimshian petroglyphs costs $135, including lunch.

ACCOMMODATIONS AND CAMPING

Prince Rupert's 700 motel rooms fill fast every summer night with travelers waiting for ferries—so book well in advance (if you're traveling onward from Prince Rupert, you should have already made ferry reservations, so you know which nights you'll be in town). Accommodation choices are wide-ranging and although no one property stands out as being good value, all are moderately priced.

Under $50

The distinctive blue and green **Pioneer Hostel** (167 3rd Ave. E, 250/624-2334 or 888/794-9998, www.pioneerhostel.com, dorm beds $25–30, private rooms $60 s or d) is full of

"steadies" in winter, but in summer daily and weekly accommodations are offered. Facilities include simple but clean dorm rooms with shared bathrooms, an outside yard with a barbecue, wireless Internet, a living room with TV, and a small but well-equipped kitchen.

$50-100

My favorite Rupert accommodation is the **Eagle Bluff Bed & Breakfast** (201 Cow Bay Rd., 250/627-4955 or 800/833-1550, $45–60 s, $65–100 d). The house is built out over the water, overlooking the marina and harbor, and lies within easy walking distance of cafés and restaurants. The least expensive rooms share bathrooms and a top floor suite sleeps five. A cooked breakfast—complete with freshly baked muffins—is included.

One of many reasonably priced motels is the **Moby Dick Inn** (935 2nd Ave. W, 250/624-6961 or 800/663-0822, www.mobydickinn. com, $69–89 s, $79–139 d), which is home to the best-priced breakfast restaurant in town. Also in the area is the **Pacific Inn** (909 3rd Ave. W, 250/627-1711 or 888/663-1999, www. pacificinn.bc.ca, $100–175 s or d) with larger

---

THE KHUTZEYMATEEN

Officially protected as a provincial park, the Khutzeymateen is a rugged and remote 44,300-hectare (109,500-acre) tract of wilderness 50 kilometers (31 miles) northeast of Prince Rupert, and is Canada's only grizzly bear sanctuary. To the Tsimshian people, the area was known as the K'tzim-a-Deen, which translates to "The Long Inlet Surrounded by a Steep Valley." To Canadian conservationists the name Khutzeymateen is synonymous with one of their earliest victories – a 1984 decision to set aside an area where grizzly bears would be safe from hunters. The park extends from the upper reaches of Khutzeymateen Inlet to the high peaks of the Kitimat Range, protecting the tidal zone at the head of the inlet where approximately 50 grizzly bears, fresh out of hibernation in May and June, come down to the water's edge to feed

on sedges and grasses. Through summer, the bears remain in the area, feeding in the salmon-rich Khutzeymateen and Kateen Rivers.

Due to the inaccessibility of the region, most visitors arrive on a guided trip. **Prince Rupert Adventure Tours** (250/627-9166 or 800/201-8377, www.adventuretours.net) runs visitors into the area by boat from Prince Rupert for $175 per person, but most of the six-hour trip is spent traveling. Overnight tours are run by **SunChaser Eco-Tours** (250/624-5472, www. sunchistercharters.ca), which offers trips on a live-aboard motor cruiser. Departing from Prince Rupert and taking a half-day to reach the sanctuary, the trips emphasize bear viewing, but time is also spent exploring other aspects of the area's natural and human history; from $1,800 for four days.

rooms. A light breakfast and wireless Internet is included in the rates.

$100-150

The massive building right downtown is the 15-story **Highliner Plaza** (815 1st Ave. W, 250/624-9060 or 800/668-3115, www.highlinerplaza.com, from $129 s or d), where most mid-sized rooms have balconies (request a harbor view for a few bucks extra).

In a prime harborside location, the full-service **Crest Hotel** (222 1st Ave. W, 250/624-6771 or 800/663-8150, www.cresthotel.bc.ca, $157–359 s or d) holds a glass-enclosed waterfront café, a dining room, and a lounge with water views. While rates for the stylishly decorated rooms start at $157, pay from $172 for water views.

Camping

Like the rest of Rupert's accommodations, **Prince Rupert RV Campground** (1750 Park Ave., 250/627-1000, tent sites $21, hookups $32) fills and empties on a daily basis with the arrival and departure of the ferries. If you know when you're arriving in the city, phone ahead to avoid any hassles. The campground is a one-kilometer (0.6-mile) walk from both the city center and ferry terminals. Facilities include hot showers, cooking shelters, a grassy tenting area, pay phones, a mail drop, and visitor information. The other alternative is **Prudhomme Lake Provincial Park** (16 km/10 mi east of downtown, $15).

FOOD

Most of Rupert's larger motels have restaurants, but the place to head for substantial and inexpensive breakfasts is the **Moby Dick Inn** (935 2nd Ave. W, 250/624-6961). You can order anything from a bowl of fruit and a muffin ($4.50) to eggs, bacon, and toast ($6) or steak and eggs ($9.50). It's always crowded, and service can be slow.

East of downtown is **Cow Bay,** originally a fishy-smelling, rough-and-tumble part of town home to a large fishing fleet. The boats are still there, moored in a marina, and a few old buildings still stand. But for the most part, the bay is a changed place. Rowdy dives have been replaced by trendy art and crafts shops, restaurants, and two of the city's best cafés. **Cowpuccino's** (25 Cow Bay Rd., 250/627-1395, daily 7:30 A.M.–10 P.M., lunches $5–8.50) is a great little coffeehouse with freshly brewed coffee, magnificent muffins, delicious desserts, newspapers and magazines to read, and a laid-back atmosphere. Across the way and right on the harbor is **Cow Bay Cafe** (205 Cow Bay Rd., 250/627-1212, Tues.–Sun. 11 A.M.–8 P.M., $8–21), where you can sit at an outside table and take in the smells of the ocean, or stay inside and enjoy the greenery. Good home-cooked meals, including vegetarian dishes, and daily specials start at $8.

Ask a local where to go for good seafood and the answer is invariably **Smile's Seafood Cafe** (113 Cow Bay Rd., 250/624-3072, daily 9 A.M.–10 P.M. July–Aug., daily 11 A.M.–8 P.M. the rest of the year, $12.50–28). This diner-style café, decorated with black-and-white fishing photos and colored-glass floats, has been serving seafood since 1934. It's always busy, mobbed by local fishermen, residents, and visitors no matter what time of day. The extensive menu includes seafood salads and sandwiches, burgers, fish-and-chips, shellfish, and seafood specialties.

INFORMATION AND SERVICES

Prince Rupert Visitor Centre (215 Cow Bay Rd., 250/624-5637 or 800/667-1994, www.tourismprincerupert.com, Mon.–Sat. 9 A.M.–8 P.M. and Sun. 9 A.M.–5 P.M. early June–early Sept., Mon.–Sat. 9 A.M.–5 P.M. the rest of the year) is in a converted fish plant along the Cow Bay waterfront. It's one of the best information centers around, with a knowledgeable staff and lots of printed material on Prince Rupert sights, walking tours, restaurants, services, and ferry schedules.

The **library** is just off McBride Avenue (101 6th Ave., 250/627-1345, Mon.–Thurs.

10 A.M.–9 P.M., Fri. 10 A.M.–5 P.M., Sat.–Sun. 1–5 P.M.). The library has a bank of Internet-connected computers as well as free wireless Internet. If you're looking for books, especially on British Columbia native art or history, spend some time at **Rainforest Books** (251 3rd Ave. W, 250/624-4195, Mon.–Sat. 8:30 A.M.–6 P.M.). This bookstore also stocks a good selection of Queen Charlotte Islands material.

Prince Rupert Regional Hospital is south of downtown at 1305 Summit Avenue (250/624-2171). The **post office** is on 2nd Avenue at 3rd Street. **Laundries** are at 226 7th Street and 745 2nd Avenue W.

GETTING THERE

Prince Rupert Airport (www.ypr.ca) is west of town on Digby Island. It is linked to the city by a ferry that takes buses and foot passengers only—no vehicles. Airlines provide free bus transportation between the airport and downtown, via the ferry, but passengers must pay the ferry fare of $12 per person each way. The pick-up point for Air Canada passengers is the information center; Hawk Air passengers are collected at the Highliner Plaza. The airport is served by **Air Canada** (888/247-2262) and **Hawk Air** (800/487-1216, www.hawkair.ca), both with scheduled flights from Vancouver. **Seal Cove Air Base** lies at the east end of town and serves as the seaplane base for Prince Rupert. To get there, take 5th Avenue east from McBride Street and follow the signs to Seal Cove. The largest operator is **North Pacific Seaplanes** (250/627-1341 or 800/689-4234), which offers a 20-minute flight over the city for $130 per person, an hour-long trip to the Khutzeymateen Valley grizzly bear sanctuary for $310 per person, and a trip to Ketchikan for $550 per person including two hours in that Alaskan town.

Prince Rupert is the western terminus of Canada's transcontinental rail system. To get to the **VIA Rail** station (250/627-7589) take 2nd Street north over the rail line.

TO OR FROM PRINCE RUPERT BY FERRY

Prince Rupert is the northern terminus of the BC Ferries network and the only Canadian stop on the Alaska Marine Highway. The two terminals sit side by side two kilometers (1.2 miles) from downtown.

All ferries are modern vessels with day rooms, sleeping cabins, shower facilities, food service, and plenty of room to sit back and relax. Summer demand means you should book as far in advance as possible if you're transporting a vehicle or would like a cabin.

BC FERRIES

BC Ferries (250/386-3431 or 888/223-3779, www.bcferries.com) offers thrice-weekly (once a week outside summer) service between Port Hardy (Vancouver Island) and Prince Rupert. The 440-kilometer (273-mile) journey takes 15 hours. Sample one-way fares are: adult $125, child 5-11 $62.50, vehicle $410, cabin $75-85.

ALASKA MARINE HIGHWAY

The Alaska Marine Highway (907/465-3941 or 800/642-0066, www.alaska.gov/ferry) operates an extensive network of ferries through southeastern Alaska, with Prince Rupert as a major stop. The first port north from Prince Rupert is Ketchikan (adult US$61, child 5-11 US$30.50, vehicle up to 15 feet US$98), six hours away, with vessels continuing north to Juneau and Skagway (adult US$192, child 5-11 US$94, vehicle up to 15 feet US$374). Renting a cabin for the Prince Rupert-Skagway trip, with for example, an en suite bathroom, costs US$152. Check-in time is three hours ahead of sailing time – it takes up to two hours to go through customs and one hour to load up. Foot passengers must be there one hour ahead of sailing.

From the local **Greyhound** bus depot (112 6th St., 250/624-5090), buses travel east along the Yellowhead Highway to Terrace and Prince George. The run between Prince George and Prince Rupert leaves twice daily. Reservations are not taken—just turn up and buy your ticket on the day you want to go.

GETTING AROUND

Local bus service along four routes is provided by **Prince Rupert Transit System** (2nd Ave. W, 250/624-3343, $1.25–2.50 per sector). The only car-rental agencies in town are **Budget** (250/627-7400) and **National** (250/624-5318). For a cab call **Skeena Taxis** (250/624-2185).

Queen Charlotte Islands

Wild. Quiet. Mysterious. Primordial. Inhabited by the proud and ferocious Haida people for over 10,000 years, the Queen Charlotte Islands spread like a large upside-down triangle approximately 100 kilometers (62 miles) off the northwest coast of mainland British Columbia. Linked to the mainland by scheduled ferry and air services, visitors have the opportunity to immerse themselves in native culture, view the abundant wildlife, explore the rugged coastline, and share a laid-back island camaraderie with the 4,600 permanent residents.

Of the chain's 150 mountainous and densely forested islands and islets, the main ones are **Graham Island** to the north and **Moresby Island** to the south, separated by narrow **Skidegate Channel.** The islands stretch 290 kilometers (180 miles) from north to south and up to 85 kilometers (53 miles) across. Running down the west side of the islands are the Queen Charlotte and San Christoval ranges, which effectively protect the east side from Pacific battering. Nevertheless, the east coast, where most of the population lives, still receives over 1,000 millimeters (39 inches) of rain annually.

Life on the islands is very different from elsewhere in the province. Visitors can expect a friendly reception and adequate services. Motel-style accommodations are available in each town, but bed-and-breakfasts provide a better glimpse of the island lifestyle. Other services are similar to any small town, though choices of fresh fruit and vegetables can be limited. Gasoline is only slightly more expensive than on the mainland, and raging nightlife is nonexistent.

Fauna

Known as the "Canadian Galapagos," the Queen Charlottes are home to an incredible array of fauna—both on land and in the water. The only land mammal indigenous to the islands is the Queen Charlotte otter, a subspecies of the mainland river otter. The world's largest black bears, estimated to number almost 10,000, call the islands home. Though they're a lot heftier than their mainland cousins, they're not a distinct subspecies. Their size comes from a short hibernation and a summerlong salmon feast. Black-tailed deer are common. They were introduced as a meat source and have multiplied many times over. Other land mammals include elk (also introduced), squirrels, beavers, and muskrats.

Stare out to sea to spot killer whales, dolphins, porpoises, harbor seals, sea lions, otters, and tufted puffins. If you visit late April–June, you might spot gray whales feeding in Hecate Strait on their migration from Mexico to Alaska. The most accessible place to whale-watch is along Skidegate Inlet near the museum, where you don't even need to get out of your vehicle.

The antics of tufted puffins keep everyone amused, while serious birders search out cormorants, blue herons, bald eagles, oyster catchers, and guillemots.

The Haida

The Haida people have lived on the Queen Charlottes since time immemorial. Fearless warriors, expert hunters and fishermen, and skilled woodcarvers, they owned slaves and

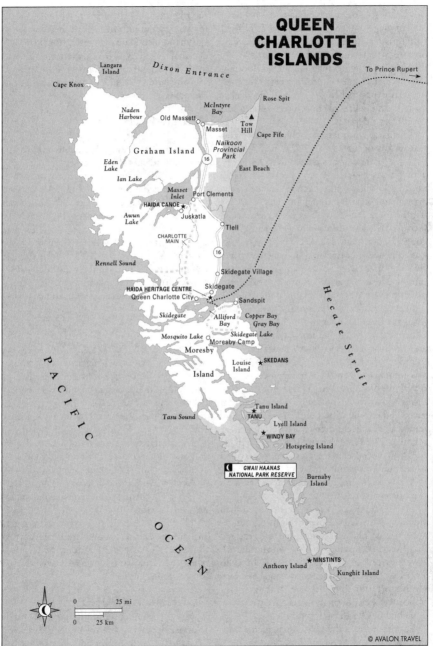

QUEEN CHARLOTTE ISLANDS

To Prince Rupert

Dixon Entrance

Langara Island

Cape Knox

Naden Harbour

Old Massett

McIntyre Bay

Rose Spit

Masset

Tow Hill

Cape Fife

Naikoon Provincial Park

Graham Island

East Beach

Eden Lake

Ian Lake

Masset Inlet

Port Clements

HAIDA CANOE

Awun Lake

Juskatla

Tlell

CHARLOTTE MAIN

Rennell Sound

Skidegate Village

Skidegate

HAIDA HERITAGE CENTRE

Queen Charlotte City

Sandspit

Skidegate

Alliford Bay

Copper Bay

Gray Bay

Mosquito Lake

Moresby Camp

Skidegate Lake

Moresby

Louise Island

SKEDANS

Island

H e c a t e   S t r a i t

P A C I F I C

Tasu Sound

Tanu Island

TANU

Lyell Island

WINDY BAY

Hotspring Island

GWAII HAANAS NATIONAL PARK RESERVE

Burnaby Island

O C E A N

NINSTINTS

Anthony Island

Kunghit Island

0   25 mi

0   25 km

© AVALON TRAVEL

CENTRAL AND NORTHERN

threw lavish potlatches. They had no written language, but they carved records of their tribal history, legends, and important events on totem poles rising up to 104 meters (340 feet) high. Living in villages scattered throughout the islands, they hunted sea otters for their luxuriant furs, fished for halibut and Pacific salmon, and collected chitons, clams, and seaweed from tidepools.

The first contact the Haida had with Europeans occurred in 1774, when Spanish explorer Juan Perez discovered the Charlottes. The islands weren't given a European name until 1787, when British captain George Dixon arrived and began trading with the Haida. He named the islands after his queen, the wife of George III. The Europeans gave the Haida goods, liquor, tools, blankets, and firearms in exchange for sea otter furs; over a 40-year period the otters were hunted almost to extinction. In addition, the traders brought European diseases that ravaged the Haida population.

At the turn of the 19th century, white settlers from the mainland began moving over to the Charlottes to live along the low-lying east coast and the protected shores of Masset Inlet. By the 1830s the traditional lifestyle of the Haida was coming to an end. The governments on the mainland prohibited the Haida from owning slaves and throwing potlatches—an important social and economic part of their culture—and forced all Haida children to attend missionary schools. The Haida abandoned their village sites and moved onto reserves at Skidegate and Masset on Graham Island.

Today totem poles are rising once again on the Queen Charlottes, as a renewed interest in Haida art and culture is compelling skilled elders to pass their knowledge on to younger generations. The first totem pole to be erected in 90 years was put up in 1969 in Masset, followed by one in 1978 at Skidegate. In 1986 a 50-foot dugout canoe, created out of a single huge cedar log, was commissioned for Vancouver's Expo86, and a second canoe was launched in Old Massett.

For many years the Haida struggled alongside the Island Protection Society to preserve their heritage. Their longtime efforts paid off in two major events: In 1981 the best-known of the abandoned Haida villages, **Ninstints,** was declared a UNESCO World Heritage Site, and in 1988 the southern section of the archipelago was proclaimed **Gwaii Haanas National Park Reserve.**

GETTING THERE
Air
The main gateway is Sandspit, where the small air terminal has car rental agencies (book ahead) and an information center, and across the road is the Sandspit Inn. **Air Canada** (888/247-2262) flies daily between Vancouver and Sandspit. The Airporter bus meets all Sandspit flights and transports passengers to Queen Charlotte City for $18. From Prince Rupert's Seal Cove Air Base, **North Pacific Seaplanes** (250/627-1341 or 800/689-4234, www.northpacificseaplanes.com) has scheduled flights to Masset ($160) and Sandspit ($258).

Ferry
In summer, **BC Ferries** (250/386-3431 or 888/223-3779, www.bcferries.com) operates the *Northern Adventure* between Prince Rupert and Skidegate five or six times a week, less frequently the rest of the year. Departure times vary, but most often it's 11 A.M. from Prince Rupert (arriving Skidegate at 5:30 P.M.) and 11 P.M. from Skidegate (arriving Prince Rupert at 6 A.M. or 7:30 A.M.). Peak one-way fares are adult $39, child $19.50, vehicle $140. British Columbia seniors get a discount, as do all travelers outside the peak summer season. Cabins are available for $70–85.

The ferry terminal is five kilometers (3.1 miles) east of Queen Charlotte City at Skidegate. Taxis usually wait at the terminal when the ferry arrives; expect to pay around $15 to get into town.

GETTING AROUND
A ferry connects Graham and Moresby Islands, departing hourly in each direction 7 A.M.–10 P.M.; peak round-trip fare is adult

$7.90, child $3.75, vehicle $18.50. Apart from that, the islands have no public transportation. Handiest for vehicle-less ferry travelers is **Rustic Car Rentals,** based in Queen Charlotte City (250/559-4641). Both **Budget** (250/637-5688) and **National** (250/626-3833) have offices in Sandspit. All companies charge from $45 a day plus $0.20–0.35 a kilometer for the smallest vehicles, with no free daily allowance. Book well ahead.

QUEEN CHARLOTTE CITY

Known to the locals simply as "Charlotte," Queen Charlotte City is spread along the shores of Bearskin Bay, five kilometers (3.1 miles) west of the dock for the mainland ferry. It's not really a city at all—most places that include "city" in their name aren't—but instead a small laid-back fishing village of 950 people. Heritage buildings dating back to the early 1900s (most along the main road) are interspersed with all the services of a small town, with a colorful array of private residences sprawled east and west, overlooking the water and backed by forested wilderness. With a choice of accommodations, it's a good base for exploring the islands.

Accommodations and Camping

Built in 1910, the old Premier Hotel has been totally renovated and now operates as 【 **Premier Creek Lodging** (3rd Ave., 250/559-8415 or 888/322-3388, $35–95 s, $75–95 d), offering beds to suit all budgets. In the main lodge, single "sleeping rooms" with shared facilities cost $35 per person, but definitely worth the extra money are the rooms with private bathrooms, balconies, and harbor views (some with kitchens). Behind the main lodge is the simple **Premier Creek Hostel** (same telephone numbers as the lodge, dorm beds $25). It has two four-bed dorms and one double room, a kitchen, living room, laundry, gas barbecue, and bike rentals.

The least expensive rooms at **Dorothy and Mike's Guest House** (3127 2nd Ave., 250/559-8439, $70–125 s or d) share baths, but my favorite is the Kumdis Room, with an en suite bathroom, and a sliding door opens to a private deck with fantastic views. Common areas include a kitchen, TV room, a large deck area, and a library overflowing with island literature. A hearty cooked breakfast will get you going each morning.

Moonglow Guest House (3611 Highway 33, 250/559-8831, $65 s, $75 d) has just one guest room, but it's a good one, with cooking facilities, a patio with views of Skidegate Inlet, and a private entrance. Behind the property, a trail leads along a creek to a waterfall.

Spruce Point Lodging (609 6th Ave., 250/559-8234, $70 s, $80 d) has a great downtown location with superb water views and offers bed-and-breakfast lodging in simple but comfortable rooms, each with a color TV.

Haydn Turner Park (Apr.–Oct., $12), through town to the west, has toilets, picnic tables, and fire rings for campers, but no showers or hookups.

Food

The place to go for breakfast is **Lam's** (3223 Wharf St., 250/559-4204, Mon.–Sat. 6:30 A.M.–3 P.M., Sun. 8 A.M.–3 P.M., lunches $7–11). All the locals congregate here. In addition to water views, this place has plenty of atmosphere, and the food is good and plentiful for the price (cooked breakfasts from $7), but be prepared to wait for a table. For something more substantial, head to the **Sea Raven Motel** (3301 3rd Ave., 250/559-4423, daily 7 A.M.–2 P.M. and 5–9 P.M., daily for lunch and dinner, $9.50–17). **Howler's Pub and Bistro** (3rd Ave., 250/559-8602, 11 A.M.–10 P.M., $8–21) has a downstairs pub and upstairs dining room. Menus in both are pub-like, but with a surprising number of vegetarian choices and a good selection of desserts.

Information

Down on the waterfront, **Queen Charlotte Visitor Centre** (3220 Wharf St., 250/559-8316, www.qcinfo.ca, daily 10 A.M.–7 P.M. mid-May–mid-Sept.) offers natural history displays, a wide variety of brochures and information on everything that's going on around the islands, and current weather forecasts. For island and north coast literature, head to **Northwest Coast Books** (3205 Oceanview Dr., 250/559-4681). The selection of new and used titles is incredible, with the bookstore wholesaling hard-to-find titles to galleries and museums across North America.

NORTH TO MASSET

From Queen Charlotte City, Graham Island's main road follows the eastern coastline past the ferry terminal and Haida Gwaii Museum to the Haida community of Skidegate Village, from where it's a pleasant 65-kilometer (40-mile) coastal drive to the logging town of **Port Clements** and then 40 kilometers (25 miles) to Masset.

Haida Heritage Centre

While totem poles and other ancient Haida art can be seen in various places around the islands, this museum (250/559-4643, daily 10 A.M.–6 P.M. in summer, Tues.–Sat. 11 A.M.–5 P.M. the rest of the year, adult $12, child $5), on the north side of the Skidegate Landing ferry terminal, allows visitors the opportunity to see a variety of such art in one place. Each of the five traditional longhouses has a theme—the Greeting House, comprising the reception area and a gift shop; the Eating House, a café serving traditional food, the Performing House, which hosts special performances, and two longhouses filled with displays of striking Haida wood and argillite carvings, pioneer artifacts, a beautiful woven blanket, jewelry, historic black-and-white photos, stunning prints by Haida artist Robert Davidson, ancient totems from Tanu and Skedans dating to 1878, the skull of a humpback whale, shells galore, and a collection of stuffed birds.

In the Bill Reid Teaching Centre, the fantastic 15-meter-long canoe *Loo Taas* (which means "Wave Eater") takes center stage. The striking red-and-black vessel was commissioned for Expo86 in Vancouver, after which it was paddled to the Queen Charlottes.

Between late April and early June, migrating **gray whales** rest and feed on shallow gravel bars of Skidegate Inlet in front of the museum on their annual 15,000-kilometer (9,300-mile) odyssey between Mexico and Alaska. Behind the museum a wooden deck overlooking the water is a great vantage point for watching these magnificent creatures, or continue a few hundred yards farther around the bay and search them out from the roadside.

Skidegate Village and Vicinity

Continuing north from the museum you'll soon come to Skidegate Village, a Haida reserve of 700 residents. A weathered totem pole, over 100 years old, still stands here, as well as six newer ones. Facing the beach is a traditional longhouse where local artisans fashion miniature totem poles, argillite ornaments, and jewelry in traditional designs.

From Skidegate, the road follows the shoreline of Hecate Strait, past driftwood-strewn beaches, an attractive old graveyard, and **Balance Rock,** one kilometer (0.6 miles) north of Skidegate Village. A highway sign and turnout mark the start of a short trail down to the rock. Continuing north, the scenery becomes rural, as the road skirts land cleared by early settlers for cattle-grazing; watch for black-tailed deer in this area. Near **Lawn Hill** look for tree stumps that have been carved into the shapes of animals and birds.

Naikoon Provincial Park (Southern End)

Just north of Tlell is the southern tip of Naikoon Provincial Park. While the park's main entrance is farther north out of Masset, visitors exploring the Tlell area will find interesting things to see and do here in the park's south end as well. The main attraction down here is the wreck of the **Pesuta,** a wooden log barge that ran aground in 1928. To get there, park at the picnic area on the north side of the Tlell River and follow the river to its mouth, then walk north along the beach. It's about six kilometers (3.7 miles) each way. Keen hikers may want to attempt the **East Beach Hike,** a 94-kilometer (58-mile) trail that leads all the way north from the Tlell River to Tow Hill via Rose Spit.

Misty Meadows Campground, immediately north of park headquarters, is uncrowded and costs only $15 per site for one of 30 scenic campsites. Facilities include a picnic area and pit toilets.

MASSET AND VICINITY

Originally named Graham City, Masset (population 900) was founded in 1909 just south of a Haida community named Massett. Over time, Massett became known as Old Massett or Haida, and Graham City was incorporated as Masset (with one "t"). The population has decreased since downsizing began on the local Canadian Armed Forces Station, where at one time half the local population lived.

Sights

Bordering Masset to the east is **Delkatla Wildlife Sanctuary,** where you can observe Canada geese, sandhill cranes, trumpeter swans, great blue herons, many varieties of ducks, and other waterfowl resting during migration. Several short walking trails wind through the preserve near town; follow Hodges Avenue west onto Trumpeter Drive and continue alongside the inlet to the trailhead. For better views, drive along Tow Hill Road toward Naikoon Provincial Park, turning left at the sanctuary sign onto Masset Cemetery Road.

If you're in search of Haida treasures, head for the village of **Old Massett,** also known as Haida. It's just a five-minute drive from Masset, west down the coastal road. Go as far as the road takes you and you'll end up at the old blue schoolhouse, now **Ed Jones Haida Museum** (Sat.–Sun. 9 A.M.–5 P.M. in summer, donation). Inside, exhibits include a large collection of fascinating old photographs showing how the villages used to look, Haida art and prints, and some of the original totem poles from around the Queen Charlottes. Outside you'll find a partly completed canoe and a field sprinkled with more totems, these from a more recent era. Across from the museum is a carving shed where artists can be seen working throughout summer.

Accommodations and Food

Several bed-and-breakfasts in Masset provide lodgings and local flavor. Next to the pier, rustic 🄲 **Copper Beech House** (1590 Delkatla Rd., 250/626-5441, www.copperbeechhouse. com, $90 s, $110–140 d) is a New England–style saltbox, decorated with sea treasures and with a beautiful flower garden. Rates include a delicious breakfast prepared by David Phillips, whose enthusiasm for the islands is infectious. Phillips does wonders with local produce—smoking his own seafood and making jams and preserves from locally harvested berries. **Beach Cabins** (14 km/9 mi east of Masset on Tow Hill Rd., 250/626-5472, www.beachcabins. com, $65–90 s or d) comprises cedar-shaked cabins spread through the dense temperate rainforest of Sitka spruce. If you can do without modern conveniences, you'll love this place, but be prepared for outhouses, no electricity, and no phones. **Village of Masset RV Site and Campground** (Tow Hill Rd. two km/1.2 mi north of Masset, $15–22) is opposite the Delkatla Wildlife Sanctuary. The campground features large, fairly private campsites with tables among the trees, and washrooms with coin-operated hot showers.

Naikoon Provincial Park

This wildly spectacular park encompasses some 72,640 hectares (179,500 acres) along the northeast tip of Graham Island. The park's dominant features are its beaches, 97 kilometers (60 miles) of them, bordering Hecate Strait on the east and the turbulent Dixon Entrance on the north. Most of the rest of the park is lowlands, surrounded by stunted lodgepole pine, red and yellow cedar, western hemlock, and Sitka spruce. Wildlife is abundant; black-tailed deer, black bear, marten, river otter, raccoons, red squirrels, beaver, muskrat, small herds of wild cattle, and many species of birds inhabit the park. Dolphins, orcas, porpoises, and seals swim offshore year-round, and northern fur seals and California gray whales migrate north past the park in May and June.

The road east from Masset passes the base of Tow Hill after 26 kilometers (16 miles) and then quickly ends at the southern end of long, sandy **North Beach.** This strip of sand is a beachcomber's delight, as it is strewn with shells, driftwood, and shiny, sea-worn pebbles of every color under the sun. The beach is best known for semiprecious agate, ranging from light yellow in color to almost-translucent, which is found among piles of pebbles that become exposed at low tide starting about three kilometers (1.9 miles) along the beach. At the end of North Beach is **Rose Spit.** Known to the Haida as Naikoon, meaning "Long Nose," this narrow point of land separates the waters of Hecate Strait and Dixon Entrance. From the end of Tow Hill Road, it's about 10 kilometers (6.2 miles) of easy beach walking to the end of the spit; if you allow six hours for the round trip, you'll have enough time to enjoy a picnic lunch among the driftwood along the way.

At **Agate Beach Campground** ($15) near Tow Hill, campsites lie along the back of the beach and offer outstanding views. A shelter and pit toilets are provided, but no showers. In summer you need to nab a spot early in the day—by late afternoon they're all taken.

SANDSPIT AND VICINITY

Across Skidegate Channel from Queen Charlotte City, Sandspit (population 560) is the only community on **Moresby Island.** Home to the islands' main airport and linked to Graham Island by a short ferry trip, the town occupies a low-lying, windswept spit overlooking Shingle Bay. The northern half of Moresby Island is largely given over to logging while the southern half and more than 100 outlying islands fall within Gwaii Haanas National Park Reserve. Those determined to tour the forests in their own vehicle can make an enjoyable loop trip south out of Sandspit. Logging roads lace the forest, leading to beaches strewn with driftwood, streams alive with salmon and steelhead, and beautiful Skidegate and Mosquito Lakes (good trout fishing). Free campgrounds are available at Gray Bay and Mosquito Lake.

Practicalities
Sandspit lacks the appeal of communities on Graham Island, but services are available. **Seaport B&B** (371 Beach Rd., 250/637-5698250/637-2215, www.moresbyexplorers.com, $45 s, $65 d) rents eight basic rooms in three waterfront buildings. Rates include a self-serve breakfast and use of kitchen facilities.

Sandspit Visitor Centre is inside the airport terminal (250/637-5362, daily noon–4 P.M. mid-May–mid-Sept., extended to daily 9 A.M.–5 P.M.in July and August).

◖ GWAII HAANAS NATIONAL PARK RESERVE

World renowned for its ancient Haida villages dotted with totem poles, this park encompasses the southern half of Moresby Island as well as 137 smaller islands in the south of the archipelago—a total of 1,480 hectares (3,660 acres) of land and 1,600 kilometers (1,000 miles) of coastline. It's a remarkable place. Ancient brooding totems and remnants of mighty Haida longhouses stand against a backdrop of lush wilderness—dense trees, thick spongy moss, and rock-strewn beaches with incredibly clear water. Colonies of nesting seabirds and an abundance of marinelife—killer and minke whales, sea lions, tufted puffins—all add to the atmosphere.

Jointly managed by Parks Canada and the Haida nation, the park protects the homeland of seafaring Haida. The Haida inhabited this area for almost 10,000 years, but by the early 1900s, less than 100 years after their first contact with Europeans, their communities were abandoned, the inhabitants having been wiped out by disease or having moved to Old Massett and Skidegate. **Nan Sdins** (Ninstints) on tiny SGaang Gwaii (Anthony Island) near the south end of the park, was once home to around 300 Haida and had been occupied for thousands of years before the arrival of Europeans. Today, a string of weathered totem poles stretch along the shoreline, with the nearby ruins of cedar longhouses slowly being consumed by the surrounding rainforest. Anthony Island was declared a UNESCO World Heritage Site in 1981, just 97 years after the last Haida families had abandoned their remote home. **Gandle K'in** (Hotspring Island), the site of another abandoned village, has the bonus of oceanfront hot pools that held special healing and spiritual qualities to the Haida.

For general park information, click through the links on the Parks Canada website (www.pc.gc.ca). To contact the local park office, call 250/559-8818.

Exploring the Park

The only access to the park is by air or sea. Most visitors arrive as part of a guided tour. The least expensive option is **Moresby Explorers** (250/637-2215 or 800/806-7633, www.moresbyexplorers.com), with a boat trip to Skedans costing $205 per person. An overnight trip with accommodations in a floating cabin is $615, and a four-day excursion to all the park highlights is $1,460. This company also provides kayak rentals and drop-offs for those heading into the park unguided. **Archipelago Ventures** (250/652-4913 or 888/559-8317, www.tourhaidagwaii.com) combines the best of the park into a six-day tour that costs $2,300 per person. The main mode of transportation is a stable 42-foot mothership, with the focus on kayaking, hiking, and soaking

up culture in the abandoned Haida villages. **Ocean Light II Adventures** (604/328-5339, www.oceanlight2.bc.ca) uses the 71-foot *Ocean Light II* for eight days of sailing, visiting all the best-known abandoned Haida villages, exploring the waterways, and searching out land and sea mammals. All meals and accommodations aboard the boat are included in the rate of $3,500 per person. If time is limited, contact **Inland Air** (250/624-2577, www.inlandair.bc.ca) for charter flights departing the wharf in Queen Charlotte City.

Permits

If you aren't visiting the park as part of an organized tour, you need to reserve a permit through Tourism BC (250/387-1642 or 800/435-5622, $15 per booking). A limited number of permits are issued for each day, in addition to six spots that are set aside on a standby basis. These can be claimed at the Queen Charlotte Visitor Info Centre (in Queen Charlotte City) at 8 A.M. on the day of departure. Either way, you must also purchase the permit itself (adult $19.60, senior $16.60, child $9.80 per day) and participate in an orientation session. These are held at the Haida Heritage Centre Monday–Saturday at 9 A.M.

Stewart-Cassiar Highway

An alternative to the Alaska Highway, this route—often referred to simply as "the Cassiar"—spurs north off the Yellowhead Highway 45 kilometers (28 miles) west of New Hazelton and leads north to the Yukon, joining the Alaska Highway just west of Watson Lake. Total length of the trip between the Yellowhead and Alaska Highways is 733 kilometers (455 miles), excluding the 130 kilometers (80 miles) round-trip for the jaunt out to Stewart.

The highway opens up a magnificent area of northern wilderness that in many ways rivals that along the more famous Alaska Highway. The highway is mainly paved, but improved

gravel sections are found on the 80-kilometer (50-mile) stretch north of Meziadin Junction, the 40-kilometer (25-mile) stretch south of Kinaskan Lake, and for around 30 kilometers (19 miles) each side of Dease Lake. Be prepared for washboard conditions on these sections, especially after heavy rain. Dust and mud can also be problematic, and many narrow, one-lane bridges call for extra caution. Gas stations and services can be found along the highway, but it's not a bad idea to fill up with gas wherever and whenever you get the opportunity. And to be on the safe side, take two spare tires, a basic tool kit, a gas can (filled!), and water.

YELLOWHEAD HIGHWAY TO MEZIADIN JUNCTION

Tree-covered hills, dense patches of snow-white daisies, banks of pink-and-white clover and purple lupine, craggy mountains and distant peaks, beautiful lakes covered in yellow water lilies, and lots of logging trucks flying along the road—these are images of the 155 kilometers (96 miles) between the Yellowhead Highway and Meziadin Junction, the turnoff to Stewart.

Kitwanga and Vicinity

This small village just north of the Yellowhead Highway is home to **Kitwanga Fort National Historic Site** (open year-round, free), the first national historic site commemorating native culture in western Canada. The site protects 13-meter (43-foot) high Battle Hill, where 200 years ago a native warrior named Nekt fought off attacks from hostile neighbors. A trail leads from the parking lot down to the flat area around the bottom of the hill, where you can read display panels describing the hill's history.

Continuing north, you're paralleling what was commonly called the Grease Trail, the route coastal natives took to the interior to trade their *oolichan* (tiny oily fish) with other tribes. At the native village of Gitanyow (also called Kitwancool), 23 kilometers (14 miles) from Kitwanga, is the world's greatest remaining concentration of totem poles still in their original location. The oldest, "Hole in the Ice," is approximately 140 years old; some say it's the oldest standing totem pole in the world. It tells the story of a man preventing his people from starving by chopping a hole in the ice and doing a spot of ice fishing.

STEWART (AND HYDER) SIDETRIP

At Meziadin Junction is 335-hectare (830-acre) **Meziadin Lake Provincial Park** (mid-May–late Oct., $15), one of the most picturesque camping spots along the Cassiar, including some sites right on the lakeshore.

From Meziadin Junction, Stewart is 65 kilometers (40 miles) west along a spectacular stretch of highway that crosses the glaciated

Coast Mountains. The first 40 kilometers (25 miles) are all uphill, through thick subalpine forests and past lakes, waterfalls, and a string of glaciers sitting like thick icy slabs atop almost-vertical mountains. Suddenly, and quite unexpectedly, the highway rounds a corner and there in front of you is magnificent, intensely-blue **Bear Glacier.** The glacier tumbles down into small Strohn Lake, where small icebergs float across the surface in the breeze. From Bear Glacier it's downhill all the way to Stewart. Keep an eye out for three mighty waterfalls on the north side of the highway, one after another.

Stewart

The twin towns of Stewart, British Columbia, and Hyder, Alaska, straddle the international boundary at the headwaters of the **Portland Canal,** the world's fourth-longest fjord. Stewart (population 500) enjoys a stunning setting, with snowcapped peaks rising abruptly from the surrounding fjord. After a 1910 gold strike, Stewart's population mushroomed to 10,000. But the boom was short-lived and what's left of the local economy revolves around the lumber industry. To get the lowdown on the town's interesting past, head to **Stewart Historical Society Museum,** in the original city hall (Columbia St. between 6th and 7th Streets, 250/636-2568, daily 10 A.M.–6 P.M. July–Aug., donation). Displays include a tool collection and exhibits on the town's boom-and-bust mining industry.

The premier accommodation is the **Ripley Creek Inn** (250/636-2344, www.ripleycreek-inn.com, $85–105 s, $105–125 d), a funky collection of 33 rooms in historic buildings centrally located to downtown. One is an old hotel, another was once home to a brothel, a third is above the Bitter Creek Cafe. All rooms have modern bathrooms and most are in a contemporary style. Those in the main lodge overlook the estuary and have wireless Internet. Nestled below the towering peaks of the Coast Mountains at the back of town is **Rainey Creek Campground** (8th Ave., 250/636-2537, $15–20).

In an old three-story building on the main street is **Bitter Creek Cafe** (311 5th Ave., 250/636-2166, daily for lunch and dinner, $12–30,), serving great food at reasonable prices. Local halibut is prepared various ways, the beef is shipped in from Alberta, or splurge on the Alaskan king crab legs.

Stewart Visitor Centre overlooks the estuary at the north end of 5th Avenue (250/636-9224 or 888/366-5999, daily 8:30 A.M.–7 P.M. mid-May–Sept.). The staff offers a wealth of local information, including directions out to Salmon Glacier, hiking-trail brochures, and history sheets.

Hyder

Continue through Stewart along the Portland Canal, and next thing you know you've crossed an international border and you're in Hyder, Alaska (population 90)—without all the formalities and checkpoints you'd expect at an international border. The "Friendliest Little Ghost Town in Alaska" is a classic end-of-the-road town, with unpaved roads and a motley assortment of buildings. Local residents send their kids to school in Canada and use the Canadian phone system. Everyone sets their clocks to Pacific Standard Time (except the postmaster, who's on Alaska Time). Prices are quoted in Canadian dollars (except for that same postmaster, who only accepts U.S. currency). Finally, no one ever has to wait for a drink—Hyder has one bar for every 30 residents.

Soak up the historic charm of Hyder by wandering the main street and poking your nose in the few remaining businesses. Join the tradition and tack a bill to the wall of the **Glacier Inn** to ensure that you won't return broke, then toss back a shot of 190-proof, pure grain alcohol in one swallow to qualify for your "I've Been Hyderized" card. At the end of the main drag, head left out to the wharf, where the mountain panorama extends for 360 degrees. Head right and you're on the way to **Fish Creek,** the most accessible place in all of North America to watch bears feasting on salmon (late July–Sept.).

If you want to stay the night in Hyder, choose between basic rooms at the **Sealaska Inn** (250/636-2486, www.sealaskainn.com, $42–79 s or d), set up your tent at the adjacent campground ($15), or pull up your rig into the parking lot up the road ($20–25). If you want to stay forever, marry a local.

The Road to Salmon Glacier

Continuing beyond Hyder, the unpaved road continues up Fish Creek, passing an abandoned mining operation and then the ruins of a covered bridge that provided access to a remote mine up the Texas Creek watershed. From this point the road narrows considerably and becomes increasingly steep (not recommended for RVs), crossing back into Canada and winding through former living quarters for the abandoned gold and mineral ore Premier Mine. The road makes a loop around tailing ponds and continues climbing steeply, with **Salmon Glacier** first coming into view 25 kilometers (15.5 miles) from Hyder. The road parallels the glacier and climbs to a high point after another 10 kilometers (6.2 miles), where the best

© ANDREW HEMPSTEAD

Salmon Glacier

lookout point is. This glacier, fifth largest in North America but also one of the most accessible, is one of British Columbia's most awesome sights, snaking for many kilometers through the highest peaks of the Coast Mountains.

NORTH OF MEZIADIN JUNCTION
Meziadin to Dease Lake

Around 100 kilometers (62 miles) from the junction, **Bell II Lodge** (604/275-4770 or 866/793-2355, www.bell2lodge.com, $124–176 s or d, tent sites $20, RVs and trailers $22–31) comes into view. It's the winter base for Last Frontier Heli-skiing but is a lot more than a spot to spend the night before heading north through the rest of the year. Fishing is the biggest attraction, especially through summer for chinook salmon and late September–early November for steelhead. Also here is a restaurant (daily 7 A.M.–8 P.M.) and a small cafe. The lodge sells all the fishing tackle you'll need and offers a variety of daily guiding services, including heli-fishing.

At the 200-kilometer (124-mile) mark is 1,800-hectare (4,450-acre) **Kinaskan Lake Provincial Park** (camping $15), known for its hungry rainbow trout. In the south of the park, a trail leads one kilometer (0.6 miles) to another reliable fishing hole, **Natadesleen Lake,** then another kilometer (0.6 mile) along an overgrown trail to beautiful, tiered **Cascade Falls.**

The small Tahltan town of **Iskut** has a post office, gas station, and grocery store (open daily 8 A.M.–9 P.M.). Continuing north, the highway runs through the **Stikine River Provincial Park,** a long and narrow 217,000-hectare (536,200-acre) park straddling the Stikine River. The park also links **Spatsizi Plateau Provincial Park** and **Mount Edziza Provincial Park.** The former is British Columbia wilderness at its wildest—656,780 hectares (1.62 million acres) of broad plateaus, stunning glacier-capped peaks, roaring rivers, and fish-filled lakes. Wildlife abounds; grizzly bears, moose, wolves, wolverines, mountain goats, woodland caribou, and more than 100 species of birds are all present, but access is by foot or floatplane only.

Mount Edziza Provincial Park protects a moon-like volcanic landscape, above the tree line and dominated by 2,787-meter (9,140-foot) **Mount Edziza,** an extinct volcano whose glaciated crater is over two kilometers (1.2 miles) wide.

The small community of **Dease Lake,** on the shores of its namesake lake 65 kilometers (40 miles) north of Iskut, provides basic tourist services and a bit more. The best place to eat is the **Boulder Cafe** (250/771-3021, daily 8 A.M.–9 P.M.), where an always-busy waitress will serve you breakfast ($5–9), lunch, or dinner (burgers $8, main dishes from $11) while you admire the old photographs lining the walls.

Telegraph Creek

From Dease Lake an unsealed road leads 119 kilometers (74 miles) west along the Tanzilla River to Telegraph Creek (population 300), which lies on a terraced hill overlooking the Stikine River. The town boasts friendly people, gorgeous scenery, and heritage buildings dating back to the 1860s. Jet boat tours are popular—by the hour or day, upstream through Stikine Grand Canyon Provincial Park or down to Wrangell or Petersburg, Alaska (book through Stikine RiverSong Lodge, 250/235-3196). A 20-kilometer (12.5 miles) road leads west from town to **Glenora,** which had 10,000 residents in its gold-rush heyday. Nowadays, only one or two of the original buildings remain. Originally a Hudson's Bay Company store, the **Stikine RiverSong Lodge** (250/235-3196, www.stikineriversong.com, $65 s, $70 d) has eight guest rooms with shared baths. Use of a kitchen and Internet access incur a small extra charge.

Continuing to the Alaska Highway

As you continue north from the turnoff to Telegraph Creek, the road parallels the east shore of Dease Lake. Good campsites are found by the lake, along with the occasional chunk of jade on the lakeshore—the area has been called the jade capital of the world. From Dease Lake to the Alaska Highway it's clear sailing for 235 kilometers (146 miles) along the northern slopes of the Cassiar Mountains.

The next worthwhile stop is 4,597-hectare (11,360-acre) **Boya Lake Provincial Park,** 150 kilometers (92 miles) north of Dease Lake. White, claylike beaches ring the incredibly clear lake. Walking along the shoreline is worthwhile, or take the short hiking trail that leads to an active beaver pond. The park also has a primitive campground (mid-May–Sept., $15). From Boya Lake, the highway traverses the Liard Plain across the border and into the Yukon. From the border it's another four kilometers (2.5 miles) to the junction of the Alaska Highway, then 21 kilometers (13 miles) east to Watson Lake or 423 kilometers (263 miles) west to Whitehorse.

Prince George to the Alaska Highway

Most travelers use the route north from Prince George to access Mile Zero of the Alaska Highway at Dawson Creek. But this direct route, a distance of 405 kilometers (252 miles), bypasses the region's highlight at **Hudson's Hope,** halfway between Chetwynd and Fort St. John. Whichever route you take, there's plenty to see and do, with interesting provincial parks and towns offering northern hospitality.

TO HUDSON'S HOPE

The first worthwhile stop along Highway 97 is 970-hectare (2,300-acre) **Crooked River Provincial Park,** 80 kilometers (50 miles) north of Prince George. The park's centerpiece is Bear Lake, with a sandy beach, forested picnic area, and good canoeing. At the end of the park access road, a largish campground has well spaced sites (mid-May–Sept., $15), easy access to a beach, pit toilets, drinking water, and a playground.

Carp Lake Provincial Park lies 140 kilometers (87 miles) north of Prince George, then 32 kilometers (20 miles) west (turn off at McLeod Lake) along a sometimes rough unsealed road. The park's epicenter is Carp Lake, a picturesque body renowned for its rainbow trout fishing (although you really need a canoe or motor boat to get out to the best fishing grounds), although you won't catch carp—the lake was named by explorer Simon Fraser, who noted Carrier Indians journeyed to the lake for fish "of the carp kind." The park holds two campgrounds (mid-May–mid-Sept., $15) with facilities limited to pit toilets, picnic tables, and fire rings. The larger of the two, right on Carp Lake, is 15-minute walk to a sandy beach inaccessible by road.

To Powder King Mountain Resort

The forestry town of **Mackenzie** (population 6,200) lies 180 kilometers (112 miles) north of Prince George on the southern arm of massive Williston Lake, North America's largest manmade reservoir. At the town's entrance is the world's largest tree crusher, used during that logging operation. Nearby **Morfee Lake** has swimming off a sandy beach. Take the logging road to the summit of Morfee Hill for lake views. Stay in a regular motel room, some with kitchens, at **Williston Lake Lodge** (Mackenzie Blvd., 250/997-3131 or 888/955-6343, www.willistonlakelodge.com, $73–99 d) or park your rig at **Mackenzie Municipal RV Park** ($16–20) with showers and hookups.

Continuing east toward Chetwynd, the landscape becomes more dramatic as the highway climbs steadily up the western slopes of the Rocky Mountains. Near Pine Pass, **Powder King** (866/769-5464, www.powderking.com) is a remote skiing and boarding destination legendary for its incredible snowfall—over 12 meters (40 feet) annually. One triple chair and two surface lifts serve a vertical rise of 640 meters (2,100 feet) and 600 hectares (1,500 acres). The lifts run Thursday–Sunday only and day tickets are adult $49, senior $37, child $30.

Chetwynd

The touristy highlight of Chetwynd (population 2,800), at the junction of Highways 97 and 29, are the numerous log sculptures carved with chainsaws. **Pinecone Motor Inn** (5224 53rd Ave., 250/788-3311 or 800/663-8082, $90 s, $98 d) has largish rooms with comfortable

TUMBLER RIDGE

Tumbler Ridge, 94 kilometers (58.4 miles) south of Chetwynd, is a modern boomtown that sprang up much the same way gold-rush towns did a hundred years ago. Back in the early 1980s the provincial government struck a deal with several coal companies, agreeing to improve regional infrastructure in return for the companies developing a mine and a township at the site of the rich Northeast Coal Deposits. Tumbler Ridge, now with a population of 2,500, was created virtually overnight. From the start it held all the creature comforts, services, and recreational facilities you'd expect in a long-established town.

The mining operation here is massive. The Quintette Mine moves 120 million tons of earth annually, from which 4.3 million tons of coal are extracted. From the mine, a 13-kilometer (eight-mile) conveyor belt transports raw coal to a processing plant and railhead from where it's shipped to the port city of Prince Rupert. If you're interested in touring the mine (July and Aug. only), contact the **Visitor Centre** (270 Southgate Rd., 250/242-3123, summer 9 A.M.-5 P.M.).

beds. On the east side of town, **Westwind RV Park** (Hwy. 97 N, 250/788-2190, $17–25) has pull-though sites, a laundry, showers, and RV wash. **Chetwynd Visitor Centre** (250/788-1943, www.gochetwynd.com, daily 8:30 A.M.–6:30 P.M. in summer, shorter hours the rest of the year) is in a railway caboose beside the highway through town to the south.

HUDSON'S HOPE

This small town of 1,000 is the only settlement between Chetwynd and Fort St. John. Founded as a fur-trading post in 1805, it is a picturesque spot with two nearby dams attracting the most attention.

Sights

Across from Hudson's Hope Visitor Centre, is **Hudson's Hope Museum** (9510 Beattie Dr.,

250/783-5735, daily 10 A.M.–5:30 P.M. May–Sept., donation), comprising historic buildings such as a trapper's cabin and the log-walled St. Peter's Church moved to the site from throughout the Peace River Valley.

The **W.A.C. Bennett Dam,** seven kilometers (4.3 miles) west of town, is one of the world's largest earth-filled structures. The 183-meter (600-foot) high structure backs up **Williston Lake,** British Columbia's largest lake, which extends more than 300 kilometers (186 miles) along three flooded valleys. At the top of the dam's control building is **Bennett Dam Visitor Centre** (888/333-6667, daily 10 A.M.–6 P.M. May–Sept., free), where displays catalog the construction tasks, a film celebrates the dam's opening, and the uses of electricity are detailed. Guided tours of the dam are scheduled daily 9:30 A.M.–4:30 P.M. through the summer season ($5 per person). The much smaller Peace Canyon Dam is downstream from Bennett Dam, nine kilometers (5.6 miles) south of Hudson's Hope on Highway 29. The visitor center (250/783-9943, daily 8 A.M.–4 P.M. May–Aug., free) focuses on the fascinating natural history, exploration, and pioneers of the area, and the building of the Peace Canyon Project. You can also see the central control system, powerhouse, and switchgear station. Don't miss a trip up to the outside observation deck.

Accommodations and Camping

Neither of the town's accommodations is outstanding, but the **Sportsman Inn** (10501 Beattie Dr., 250/783-5523, $75–145 s or d) has the biggest rooms and an in-house pub and restaurant. The town's three municipal campgrounds each cost $15 per night. Closest to civilization is **King Gething Campground,** on the south end of town, which has flush toilets, coin-operated showers, and plenty of firewood. **Alwin Holland Park,** southeast of town, is more primitive (pit toilets) but is off the main highway and has some nice hiking trails. The third, **Dinosaur Lake Campground,** seven kilometers (4.3 miles) southeast, has pit toilets, firewood, and good fishing and swimming.

Alaska Highway

In the early days, driving the Alaska Highway was notoriously difficult. Travelers returned with tales of endless mud holes and dust, washed-out bridges, flat tires, broken windshields and smashed headlights, wildlife in the road, mosquitoes the size of hummingbirds, and sparse facilities. But they also sported "I drove the Alaska Highway" bumper stickers as though they'd won a prize. Nowadays the route doesn't merit quite the bravado, and is paved the entire way. What hasn't changed is the scenery. You'll still see kilometer after kilometer of unspoiled wilderness, including boreal forests of spruce and aspen, the majestic, snow-dusted peaks of the northern Canadian Rockies, and gorgeous rivers and streams (and you can still buy the stickers).

Although official signage along the Alaska Highway is in kilometers, many services are marked in miles, a legacy of imperial measurement. This only becomes confusing when you consider that highway improvements have shortened the original route. For example, Liard River Hot Springs is still marked as Mile 496, though it's now only 754 kilometers (462 miles) from Dawson Creek.

DAWSON CREEK

Although Dawson Creek (population 11,800) marks the southern end of the Alaska Highway, it's still a long way north—over 400 kilometers (250 miles) northeast of Prince George and 1,200 kilometers (746 miles) north of Vancouver. While the city thrives on its historic location at Mile Zero, it's also an important service center whose economy is more closely tied to neighboring Alberta, a few kilometers to the east, than to British Columbia.

Sights

Upon entering town, make **Northern Alberta Railway Park** on the corner of Highway 2 and the Alaska Highway your first stop. Here you'll find Dawson Creek Visitor Centre, an art gallery, and the **Station Museum** (250/782-9595,

daily 9 A.M.–5 P.M. May–early Sept., Tues.–Sat. 10 A.M.–noon and 1–5 P.M. the rest of the year, adult $5). This marvelous and curious museum, housed in the original 1931 Northern Alberta Railway station, offers exhibits on a wide variety of topics, including construction of the Alaska Highway, the area's railroad history, pioneer life, and local flora and fauna. Among the unusual items on display are a rack of antlers estimated to be several thousand years old, a gas pump from the 1920s, a 1941 Massey-Harris cream separator, and the largest mammoth tusks found in western Canada. In the annex of the towering grain elevator adjacent to the museum is the **Dawson Creek Art Gallery** (250/782-2601, daily 9 A.M.–5 P.M. June–Aug., Tues.–Fri. 10 A.M.–4 P.M. the rest of the year). The elevator itself is fascinating. It was saved from demolition and redesigned with a spiral walkway around the interior walls to make the most of the building's height.

In front of N.A.R. Park is the **Mile Zero Cairn,** the Alaska Highway's official starting point. (The original marker was mowed down by a car in the 1940s.) Despite the cairn's official status, the Mile Zero signpost in the center of 102nd Avenue at 10th Street is more often photographed. It reads "You are now entering the world famous Alaska Highway" and notes the following distances: Fort St. John, 49 miles; Fort Nelson, 300 miles; Whitehorse, 918 miles; and Fairbanks, 1,523 miles.

One kilometers (0.6 miles) west of N.A.R. Park at the Highway 97 split, **Walter Wright Pioneer Village** (250/782-7144, daily 10 A.M.–6 P.M. June–Sept., donation) holds two pioneer churches, a furnished log house, a general store, the Napoleon Loiselle Blacksmith Shop (containing many of his inventions), a trapper's cabin with handmade furniture, and two old schoolhouses.

Accommodations and Camping

Dawson Creek's oldest and most colorful accommodation is the downtown **Alaska Hotel**

DAWSON CREEK

(10209 10th St., 250/782-7998, www.alaska-hotel.com, $55 s or d). Known as the Dew Drop Inn when it first opened in 1928, the hotel has been renovated in a colorful heritage style. Rooms remain basic, with no televisions or phones and shared bathroom facilities. For something a little more modern, you can choose among a number of regular motels spread along the Alaska Highway, such as the **Super 8 Dawson Creek** (1440 Alaska Ave., 250/782-8899 or 800/800-8000, www.super8.com, $129 s or d). Southwest of town, 【 **The Granaries on Bear Mountain** (2106 Ski Hill Rd., 250/782-6302 or 888/782-6304, www.

thegranaries.com, $170–215 s or d) is a wonderful surprise in a part of the province where roadside motels dominate. The guest rooms are ensconced in three circular granaries set around a man-made lake, with a profusion of colorful flowerbeds lining the shoreline. Each granary has been given a complete makeover—a snazzy new conical corrugated metal roof, sliding doors that open to a circular deck facing the lake, and a smart interior decor. Other features include cast iron fireplaces, cooking facilities, jetted tubs, and a breakfast delivered to the door.

Mile Zero RV Park and Campground

(250/782-2590, unserviced sites $21, hookups $34) isn't at Mile Zero of the famous highway—it's about one kilometer (0.6 miles) north from downtown—but it's the pick of Dawson Creek's numerous campgrounds. Sites sit around a large, shaded grassy area, and each one has a picnic table. Facilities include wireless Internet, hot showers, and a laundry. Take Highway 97S west from town to reach **Northern Lights RV Park** (250/782-9433 or 888/414-9433, www.nlrv.com, May–Oct., $20–38.50) which has a mix of RV and tent sites, an RV wash, wireless Internet, free showers, and a laundry.

Information
An almost obligatory stop for travelers heading north on the famous highway is **Dawson Creek**

NORTH TO ALASKA

When the Japanese threatened invasion of North America during World War II, the Alaska Highway was quickly built to link Alaska with the Lower 48. It was the longest military road ever constructed in North America – an unsurpassed road-construction feat stretching 2,288 kilometers (1,421 miles) between Dawson Creek, British Columbia, and Delta Junction, Alaska.

Construction began March 9, 1942, and was completed, incredibly, on November 20 that same year. In less than nine months troops had bulldozed a rough trail snaking like a crooked finger through almost impenetrable muskeg and forest, making literally hundreds of detours around obstacles and constructing 133 bridges. The highway was the major contributing factor to the growth of northern British Columbia in the 1940s. At the height of construction, the region's population boomed. Dawson Creek's population alone rose from 600 to more than 10,000, and Whitehorse replaced Dawson City as a more convenient capital of the Yukon.

Visitor Centre (900 Alaska Ave., 250/782-9595 or 866/645-3022, www.tourismdawsoncreek.com, daily 9 A.M.–5 P.M. May–Aug., Tues.–Sat. 10 A.M.–5 P.M. the rest of the year), in the railway station at N.A.R. Park.

FORT ST. JOHN
As the second-largest community along the Alaska Highway (only Whitehorse, Yukon, is larger), Fort St. John (population 16,000), 72 kilometers (45 miles) northwest of Dawson Creek, is an important service center for local industries, including oil, gas, and coal extraction; forestry; and agriculture. It's one of the province's oldest nonnative settlements—the Beaver and Sekani tribes both occupied the area when European traders arrived in the 1790s—and served as a fur-trading post until 1823. But it wasn't until construction of the Alaska Highway began that Fort St. John really boomed.

Sights
Fort St. John-North Peace Museum (9323 100th St., 250/787-0430, daily 8 A.M.–8 P.M. in summer, Mon.–Sat. 9 A.M.–5 P.M. the rest of the year, adult $5, senior and child $3) is difficult to miss as you drive through town—look for the outside exhibits, including a 40-meter-high (130-foot) **oil derrick.** In the museum local history springs to life with reconstructed historical interiors. A trapper's cabin recalls the original Rocky Mountain fort and fur-trading days, while the pioneer days are commemorated in fully furnished rooms, including a kitchen, bedroom, schoolroom, dentist's office, post office, outpost hospital, and blacksmith's shop. Don't miss the fur press, the birchbark canoe, and the grizzly bear with claws big enough to send shivers up your spine.

Peace River Canyon Lookout provides splendid panoramic views taking in the wide, deep-green Peace River, its rocky canyon walls, and the lush fields along the canyon rim. From the museum head south along 100th Street, crossing the Alaska Highway and continuing along the gravel road, which ends at the edge of the canyon.

Accommodations and Food

With high demand from oil and gas workers, motel rooms here aren't cheap. One of the better motels along the highway is **Blue Belle Motel** (9705 Alaska Hwy., 250/785-2613, $75 s, $85 d), where rooms have such amenities microwaves and coffeemakers, while guests also have use of a barbecue and laundry facility. The six-story **Quality Inn Northern Grand** (9830 100th Ave., 250/787-0521 or 800/663-8313, www.qualityinnnortherngrand.com, $129 s, $139 d) is a modern, full-service hotel with regularly revamped rooms that come with luxuries such as heated bathroom floors. There's also an indoor pool, a fitness room, a lounge, and a family-style restaurant.

Two small provincial parks with campgrounds lie along the shoreline of Charlie Lake, just over six kilometers (3.7 miles) north of town. **Charlie Lake Provincial Park,** at the junction of the Alaska Highway and Highway 29, is mainly a campground ($15 per site), while 312-hectare (770-acre) **Beatton Provincial Park,** on the lake's east shoreline, features beautiful aspen-lined hiking trails, a beach, boating, fishing, swimming, and camping ($15 per site). For more amenities, check in to the **Rotary RV Park,** also beside Charlie Lake (Mile 52, Alaska Hwy., 250/785-1700, unserviced sites $18, hookups $21–28). Amenities include hot showers and a laundry, and it's within walking distance of a general store and Jackfish Dundee's restaurant.

My favorite place to eat in Fort St. John isn't in town, but 6.5 kilometers (four miles) north at Mile 52 of the Alaska Highway. ☪ **Jackfish Dundee's** (250/785-3233, daily 11 A.M.–10 P.M., $12–20) is in a big wooden building that has an inviting atmosphere and lake views. The food is delicious and well priced. Start with calamari with a tangy Thai sauce and choose from mains such as blackened halibut and a juicy slab of Alberta beef. Back in town, grab a city-style coffee and healthy lunch at **Cosmic Grounds** (10430 100th St., 250/261-6648, Mon.–Fri. 7 A.M.–10 P.M., Sat. 8 A.M.–10 P.M., Sun. 10 A.M.–5 P.M., lunch specials around $8).

Information

Fort St. John Visitor Centre (9523 100th St., 250/785-3033, www.cityfsj.com) is open daily 8 A.M.–7 P.M. May–mid-June, daily 8 A.M.–8 P.M. mid-June–mid-Sept., Mon.–Fri. 9 A.M.–5 P.M. the rest of the year.

TO FORT NELSON

The 374-kilometer (232-mile) stretch of the Alaska Highway between Fort St. John and Fort Nelson passes through boreal forest and a landscape that becomes more and more mountainous. It is also provides one of your best chances of spotting wildlife—including moose, bears, deer, elk, and bison—especially if you travel in the cool of the early morning.

From Wonowon, the highway climbs steadily to **Pink Mountain,** at Mile 147. Numerous services perch on the low summit, where snow can fall year-round. On the west side of the highway, **Pink Mountain Campsite** (250/772-5133, $21) provides tent and RV sites. Showers are an extra $3. In typical northern fashion, it also has liquor, a laundry, and gas. A few kilometers beyond the summit is ☪ **Mae's Kitchen** (250/772-3215, Mon.–Sat. 7 A.M.–10 P.M., $8–17), where breakfasts are huge and the pancakes and blueberry muffins are especially good. For lunch, try the house special buffalo burger, complete with fries and salad for $12.

Sikanni Chief to Prophet River

The next services are 30 kilometers (18.6 miles) north of Pink Mountain at **Sikanni River RV Park** (250/772-5400, tents $16, hookups $24, cabins $65 s, $75 d). Twenty kilometers (12.5 miles) north from Sikanni Chief you'll pass the small **Buckinghorse River Wayside Provincial Park.** The river is alive with arctic grayling, providing the perfect meal for campers ($15 per site). From here north, a newer, scenic stretch of the highway runs through **Minaker River Valley** then parallels the **Prophet River,** passing a rustic campground (May–Sept., $12) where a hiking trail leads down to the river.

FORT NELSON

At Mile 300 of the Alaska Highway, 454 kilometers (281 miles) north of Dawson Creek, Fort Nelson (population 4,300) is the largest town between Fort St. John and the Yukon. The earliest of many trading posts was built here in 1800. More than 200 years later, the town continues to be a supply center—now for the surrounding forestry, oil, and gas industries.

Sights

On the west side of the highway at the north end of town, **Fort Nelson Historical Museum** (250/774-3536, daily 8:30 A.M.–7:30 P.M. mid-May–mid-Sept., adult $5, senior and child $3) contains a great collection of Alaska Highway construction items and native and pioneer artifacts. An interesting 30-minute movie, shown throughout the day, uses footage taken during the construction of the highway to effectively convey what a mammoth task the project was. The building is surrounded by machinery and vehicles used during the early days. Around back is a trapper's cabin crammed with antiques. At the end of Mountain View Drive is the **Native Trail,** a four-kilometer (2.5-mile) self-guided interpretive trail that passes two native-style shelters and holds signs describing native foods, local wildlife, and trapping methods. Allow at least one hour round-trip.

Practicalities

Fort Nelson has many hotels and motels spread out along the Alaska Highway. The nicest is **Blue Bell Inn** (4103 50th Ave., 250/774-6961 or 800/663-5267, www.bluebellinn.ca, $95–100), next to the Petro-Canada gas station. The modern two-story lodging has air-conditioned rooms, a laundry, and an adjacent 24-hour restaurant.

Beside the museum is **Westend Campground** (5651 Alaska Hwy., 250/774-2340, Apr.–Oct., $18–27), where you can choose from tent sites in an open area or hookups surrounded by trees. Facilities include coin-operated showers, a laundry, grocery store, RV service bays, and free firewood.

As you enter town from the south, modern **Dan's Neighbourhood Pub** (4204 50th Ave. N, 250/774-3929, daily 11 A.M.–midnight, $11–23) wouldn't look out of place in a big city—and it's always busy.

At Mile 300.5 of the Alaska Highway is **Fort Nelson Visitor Centre** (5430 50th Ave., 250/774-6400, daily 8 A.M.–8 P.M. mid-May–early Sept.).

CONTINUING TO WATSON LAKE

Awaiting the traveler on this 525-kilometer (326-mile) portion of the Alaska Highway are mountain peaks, glacial lakes, mountain streams, provincial parks with some great scenery, and the mighty Liard River.

Soon after leaving Fort Nelson you'll come to a junction with the gravel **Liard Highway,** which runs north 175 kilometers (109 miles) to Fort Liard in the Northwest Territories. From this junction, the Alaska Highway climbs the lower slopes of **Steamboat Mountain,** which, with a certain amount of imagination, resembles an upturned boat.

Summit Lake

This intensely blue lake, 140 kilometers (87 miles) west of Fort Nelson, is a popular stopping point for travelers. It lies at the north end of 25,691-hectare (63,480-acre) **Stone Mountain Provincial Park,** a vast wilderness at the northern reaches of the Rocky Mountains. Named for the predominantly stony nature of mountains that have been folded and faulted by massive forces deep below the Earth's surface, much of the park is above the tree line. For super-fit hikers, the best way to appreciate the landscape is by hiking the 2.6-kilometer (1.6-mile) **Summit Peak Trail,** which ends in a treeless alpine area a strenuous 1,000 vertical meters (3,300 feet) above the trailhead; allow at least two hours each way. The trailhead is on the north side of the highway, across from the campground. Much easier is the 2.5-kilometer (1.5-mile) trail to **Flower Springs Lake,** nestled in alpine peaks south of the highway. Allow one hour each way. The trailhead is three kilometers (1.9 miles) along Microwave Tower Road, which spurs south at the café.

At Summit Lake's eastern end is an exposed campground ($15) with pit toilets and picnic tables.

Muncho Lake Provincial Park

Lying among mountains and forested valleys at the north end of the Rocky Mountains, this 86,079-hectare (212,700-acre) park surrounds stunning **Muncho Lake,** one of the scenic highlights of the Alaska Highway. The magnificent, 12-kilometer-long (7.7-mile-long) body of water is encircled by a dense spruce forest, which gives way to barren rocky slopes at higher elevations. Around three kilometers (1.9 miles) beyond the north end of the lake, natural mineral licks attract Stone sheep and woodland caribou to a roadside quarry. In the vicinity, a hiking trail leads to an escarpment above the Trout River; allow 20 minutes to walk the 1.5-kilometer (0.9-mile) loop.

At around Mile 462 of the Alaska Highway, the small community of Muncho Lake spreads out along the eastern banks of the lake, providing services for park visitors. If you plan to overnight here, try to book ahead; motel rooms and campgrounds all fill up well in advance for July and August. **J & H Wilderness Resort** (250/776-3453), offers simple motel rooms for $84 s or d as well as campsites with clean and modern facilities, including free hot showers, for $22–32. The resort's restaurant (daily 7 A.M.–10 P.M.) dishes up portions with the trucker's appetite in mind. Spread along the lakeshore, **◖ Northern Rockies Lodge** (250/776-3481 or 800/663-5269, www.northernrockieslodge.com, $125 s, $135 d) has a variety of accommodations but a huge common room with a stone fireplace and towering cathedral ceiling brings it all together. Choose from rustic cabins or more comfortable rooms in the main lodge, or park your rig at a lakeside campsite ($38–48). Many guests visit as part of a fishing package, staying in luxurious lakeside

log chalets (around $2,800 per week inclusive of flights from Vancouver, meals, and some activities). Campers who don't need serviced sites have the option of staying at two campgrounds in the provincial park itself, north of the town. Sites at these two campgrounds are all $15 a night, but with only 15 sites in each one, they fill up fast.

◖ Liard River Hot Springs

One of the most wonderful places to stop on the whole highway is this 1,082-hectare (2,670-acre) park, 40 kilometers (25 miles) north of Muncho Lake. Most travelers understandably rush to soak their tired, dusty limbs in the hot pools. But the rest of the park is also worth exploring. Hot gases deep underground force heated ground water upward through a fault in the sedimentary rock. The water fills rock pools constructed by Alaska Highway workers in the 1940s, then overflows into a wide area of marshland. Even in the middle of winter, the water doesn't freeze, creating a microclimate of aquatic plants not normally associated with the northern latitude. Also inhabiting the swamp are many species of small fish plus mammals such as moose, woodland caribou, and black bear, as well as 100 species of birds.

A 500-meter (0.3-mile) boardwalk leads from the main parking lot over warm-water swamps to **Alpha Pool,** where water bubbles up into a long, shallow concrete pool. The pool area, surrounded by decking, has pit toilets and changing rooms. A rough trail leads farther to undeveloped **Beta Pool,** which is cooler, much deeper, and not as busy. Admission to the pools is adult $5, child $3.

At the entrance to the hot springs is a campground (May–mid-Oct., $19) providing toilets and showers. In summer, a percentage of sites can be booked through www.discovercamping.ca. The rest (only 20 sites) are first-come, first-served and are usually filled by noon each day. Gates to the hot springs and campground are locked between 11 P.M. and 6 A.M.

CALGARY AND VICINITY

Calgary's nickname, "Cowtown," is cherished by the city's one million residents, who prefer that romantic vision of their beloved home to the city's more modern identity as a world energy and financial center. The city's rapid growth, from a North West Mounted Police (NWMP) post to a large and vibrant metropolis in little more than 100 years, can be credited largely to the effects of resource development, particularly oil and natural gas. Once run by gentlemen who had made their fortunes in ranching, Calgary is still an important cattle market. But a string of oil-and-gas bonanzas changed everything. The natural resources discovered throughout western Canada brought enormous wealth and growth to the city, turning it into the headquarters for a burgeoning energy industry. Downtown is a massive cluster

of modern steel-and-glass skyscrapers, the legacy of an explosion of wealth in the 1970s, with cranes once again making their appearance as new commercial projects totaling over $1 billion are currently under construction. Set in this futuristic mirage on the prairie are banks, insurance companies, investment companies, and the head offices of hundreds of oil companies. But not forgetting its roots, each July the city sets aside all the material success it's achieved as a boomtown to put on the greatest outdoor show on earth—the Calgary Stampede, a Western extravaganza second to none.

Calgary is centrally located for a number of interesting yet diverse daytrips. While the vast majority of visitors head west, the Red Deer River Valley, east of Calgary, is one of Alberta's

© ANDREW HEMPSTEAD

HIGHLIGHTS

◖ Glenbow Museum: One of Canada's finest private museums, the Glenbow is renowned for its coverage of native history, and the new Mavericks display will captivate even non-museum types (page 262).

◖ Calgary Zoo: Yes, you'll see all the usual suspects (hippos, kangaroos, gorillas), but you'll also find a wide range of Canadian mammals – including some you wouldn't want to meet in the wild (page 267).

◖ Canada Olympic Park: Follow in the footsteps of Eddie the Eagle and the Jamaican bobsled team at the site of the 1988 Olympic Winter Games (page 267).

◖ Calgary Stampede: Few cities are associated as closely with a festival as Calgary is with the Stampede, a 10-day, early-July celebration of everything cowboy (page 274).

◖ Royal Tyrrell Museum: The world's biggest museum devoted entirely to paleontology is *the* place to learn about the importance of Alberta's dinosaur-rich badlands (page 288).

◖ Dinosaur Provincial Park: You can head out to explore the park yourself, but to really make the most of a visit, plan on joining a guided hike or bus tour (page 292).

◖ Kananaskis Country Golf Course: Non-golfers won't be too impressed, but if you do golf and plan on playing just one round in the Calgary area, book a tee time here (page 301).

◖ Highwood Pass: In Peter Lougheed Provincial Park, you'll find the highest road pass in Canada, one of the only places in Canada where you can drive to an area of alpine meadows (page 302).

◖ Lacombe Corn Maze: Get lost in this unique family-operated attraction (page 323).

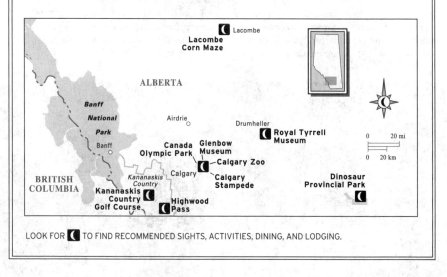

LOOK FOR ◖ TO FIND RECOMMENDED SIGHTS, ACTIVITIES, DINING, AND LODGING.

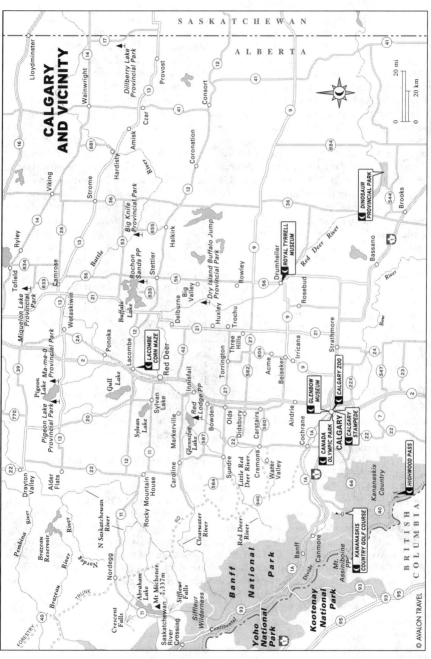

most interesting destinations for one reason: dinosaurs. Here, ancient glacial meltwaters gouged a deep valley into the surrounding rolling prairie, and wind and water have continued the erosion process ever since, all the time uncovering some of the world's premier dinosaur fossil beds. And when you do inevitably turn toward the mountains, there are plenty of reasons to veer from the main highway and explore the southern foothills, which hold some of North America's finest ranching country. Beyond these hills is another reason to delay your arrival in Banff. Known as Kananaskis Country, it is a large tract of mountainous land set aside by the Alberta government as a multiuse recreation area. On the northern edge of Kananaskis Country is the booming mountain town of Canmore, an active outdoor center with a wide array of tourist services. One of the province's busiest roads is Highway 2 through central Alberta between Calgary and Edmonton. This 290-kilometer (180-mile) route takes about three hours to drive straight through, but in the final section of this chapter I'll fill you with ideas for discovering historic towns, exploring scenic parks, and even getting lost (in a corn maze).

PLANNING YOUR TIME

For the vast majority of visitors arriving by air, Calgary International Airport is their first stop in Alberta, and then it's straight off to the mountain national parks of Banff and Jasper. But even with a week in Alberta, it's worth scheduling a day in Calgary—maybe to settle in upon arrival, or to relax the day before flying out—and at least one other to explore the surrounding area. A good first stop to orientate yourself is the top of the Calgary Tower, but attractions such as the Glenbow Museum and Canada Olympic Park should take priority. Another highlight for all ages is the Calgary Zoo, one of the country's best. Attending the Calgary Stampede is a vacation in itself for tens of thousands of visitors each year, but be sure to plan ahead by making accommodation reservations and getting tickets well in advance.

Before charging out in search of dinosaurs,

it is important to understand that the two major attractions, Drumheller's Royal Tyrrell Museum and Dinosaur Provincial Park are separated by a two-hour drive, meaning that if both are visited as a day trip from Calgary, you'll be spending at least five hours on the road. You can include Kananaskis Country and Canmore in your itinerary in a variety of ways, including as a detour between Calgary and Banff, or as a day or overnight trip. Regardless, you won't want to miss the scenery driving over Highwood Pass. Combining the natural attractions of Kananaskis with an afternoon tee time at Kananaskis Country Golf Course would be possible. The route north from Calgary to Edmonton looks straightforward on a map, and the stops you make en route depend mostly on your interests. Those looking for a wilderness experience without the crowds should incorporate the David Thompson Highway into their plan, while those with children will want to stop at the Lacombe Corn Maze.

HISTORY

In addition to being one of Canada's largest cities, Calgary is also one of the youngest; at 140 years old, it has a heritage rather than a history. In 1875 the NWMP established **Fort Calgary** at the confluence of the Bow and Elbow Rivers. It was named after Calgary Bay, a remote Scottish village, with a meaning that is said to translate from Gaelic to "garden on the cove."

The Railway and Ranching

As soon as it was announced that the Canadian Pacific Railway was building its transcontinental railway through Calgary, settlers flooded in. In 1883, a station was built and a townsite was laid out around it. Just nine years after the first train arrived, Calgary acquired city status. In 1886, a fire destroyed most of the town's buildings. City planners decreed that all new structures were to be built of sandstone, which gave the fledgling town a more permanent look. The many sandstone buildings still standing today—the Palliser Hotel, the Hudson's Bay Company store, and the courthouse, for example—are a legacy of this early bylaw.

© ANDREW HEMPSTEAD

Fort Calgary was established in 1875.

An open grazing policy, initiated by the Dominion Government, encouraged ranchers in the United States to drive their cattle from overgrazed lands to the fertile plains around Calgary. Slowly, a ranching industry and local beef market developed. The first large ranch was established west of Calgary, and soon many NWMP retirees, English aristocrats, and wealthy American citizens had invested in nearby land.

Oil

In 1914, the discovery of oil at Turner Valley, a short drive southwest of Calgary, signaled the start of an industry that was the making of modern Calgary. The opening of an oil refinery in 1923 and further major discoveries transformed a medium-sized cow town into a world leader in the petroleum and natural gas industries. Calgary became Canada's fastest-growing city, doubling its population between 1950 and 1975; and today, is still Canada's fastest-growing. The population has increased by more than 25 percent since 1996, with current estimates having the city grow another 25 percent to 1.25 million people in the next decade. Much of the land in and around downtown has been rezoned for multi-family dwellings, with the area south of downtown seeing massive redevelopment and controversial plans in place for the East Village project on the east side of downtown. City limits continue to expand at a phenomenal rate—especially in the northwest, north, and south—with new suburbs, housing estates, and commercial centers extending as far as the eye can see. But Calgary is still a small town at heart, enjoying tremendous civic and public support. Many of the city's self-made millionaires bequeath their money to the city, or, in the case of Glenbow Ranch Provincial Park, deed land for all Calgarians to enjoy. Residents in the thousands are always willing to volunteer their time at events such as the Calgary Stampede. This civic pride makes the city a great place to live and an enjoyable destination for the millions of tourists who visit each year.

ORIENTATION

The TransCanada Highway (Hwy. 1) passes through the city north of downtown and is known as **16th Avenue North** within the city

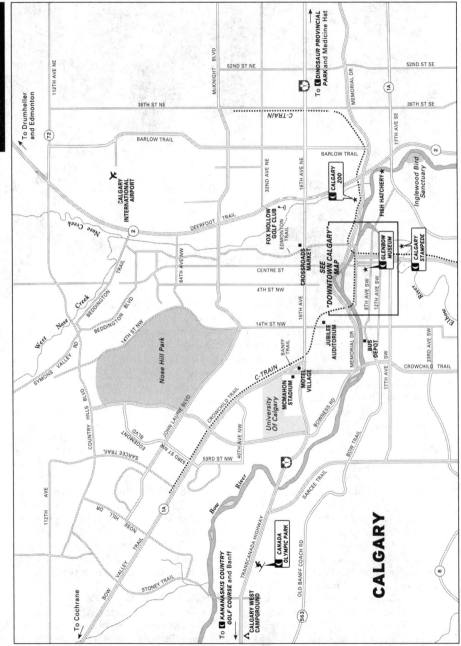

CALGARY

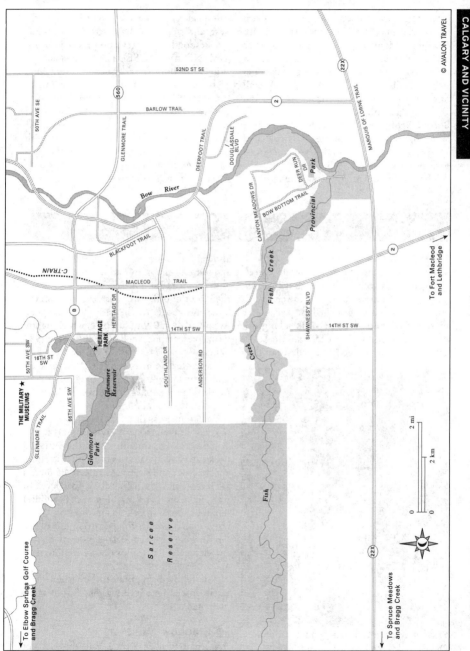

CALGARY AND VICINITY

52ND ST SE

560

BARLOW TRAIL

2

MARQUIS OF LORNE TRAIL

22X

GLENMORE TRAIL

50TH AVE SE

DEERFOOT TRAIL

DOUGLASDALE BLVD

Bow River

DEER RUN DR

Provincial Park

CANYON MEADOWS DR

BOW BOTTOM TRAIL

BLACKFOOT TRAIL

C-TRAIN

Fish Creek

MACLEOD TRAIL

2

To Fort Macleod and Lethbridge

HERITAGE DR

B

SHAWNESSY BLVD

14TH ST SW

HERITAGE PARK

14TH ST SW

50TH AVE SW

16TH ST SW

SOUTHLAND DR

ANDERSON RD

Creek

THE MILITARY MUSEUMS ★

Glenmore Reservoir

66TH AVE SW

GLENMORE TRAIL

Glenmore Park

Sarcee Reserve

Fish

2 mi

2 km

0

0

To Elbow Springs Golf Course and Bragg Creek

To Spruce Meadows and Bragg Creek

22X

limits. Highway 2, Alberta's major north–south highway, is known as **Deerfoot Trail** within city limits. Many major arteries are known as **trails:** The main route south from downtown is **Macleod Trail,** a 12-kilometer (7.5-mile) strip of malls, motels, restaurants, and retail stores. If you enter Calgary from the west and are heading south, a handy bypass to take is **Sarcee Trail,** then **Glenmore Trail,** which joins Highway 2 south of the city. **Crowchild Trail** starts downtown and heads northwest past the university to Cochrane.

The street-numbering system is divided into four quadrants—northwest, northeast, southwest, and southeast. Each street address has a corresponding abbreviation tacked onto it (NW, NE, SW, and SE). The north–south division is the Bow River. The east–west division is at Macleod Trail and north of downtown at **Centre Street.** Streets run north to south and avenues from east to west. Both streets and avenues are numbered progressively from the quadrant divisions (e.g., an address on 58th Ave. SE is the 58th street south of the Bow River, is east of Macleod Trail, and is on a street that runs east to west).

Sights

DOWNTOWN

The downtown core is a mass of modern steel-and-glass high-tech high-rises, but between the skyscrapers are a number of the city's oldest sandstone buildings. The best place to see these is **Stephen Avenue Walk,** along 8th Avenue between 1st Street SE and 3rd Street SW. This bustling, tree-lined pedestrian mall

Stephen Avenue Walk is a pedestrian-only mall.

© ANDREW HEMPSTEAD

also has fountains, benches, cafés, restaurants, and souvenir shops. In summer, the mall is full with shoppers and tourists, and at lunchtime, thousands of office workers descend from the buildings above. At the east end of Stephen Avenue Walk is **Olympic Plaza,** where nightly medal presentations took place during the 1988 Winter Olympic Games. In summer, outdoor concerts are held here, and in winter, the shallow wading pool freezes over and is used as an ice-skating rink. Across 2nd Street SE from the plaza is **City Hall,** built in 1911. It still houses some city offices, although most have moved next door to the modern **Civic Complex.**

Crisscrossing downtown is the **Plus 15** walkway system—a series of interconnecting, enclosed sidewalks elevated at least 4.5 meters (15 feet—hence the name) above road level. In total, 47 bridges and 12 kilometers (7.5 miles) of public walkway link downtown stores, four large malls, hotels, food courts, and office buildings to give pedestrians protection from the elements. All walkways are well marked and wheelchair accessible.

The following sights can be visited separately or seen on a walking tour (in the order presented).

◀ Glenbow Museum

Adjacent to Stephen Avenue Walk, this excellent

CALGARY FOR KIDS

Calgary offers plenty of distractions for children. **Calgary Zoo** and **Heritage Park** (detailed in the main text) mix kid-friendliness with enough of interest to keep grown-ups busy as well. Here are a few other suggestions to keep the young ones occupied.

CREATIVE KIDS MUSEUM/ TELUS WORLD OF SCIENCE

This downtown complex (Mon.-Thurs. 9:30 A.M.-54 P.M., Fri. 9:45 A.M.-5 P.M., the rest of the year Tues Sat.-Sun. 10 A.M.-5 P.M., adult $15, senior $1214.25, child $10) is a wonderful facility chockablock full of interactive exhibits. In the Kids Museum, it's sensory overload in rooms such as Scribble Dee Dee, where young ones hone their painting skills; Sound and Music, with the opportunity to make music; Mindscapes, comprising models of Alberta landscapes that are fully climbable; and Perception, a series of interactive games. In the World of Science section, WOWtown is especially for the under-seven crowd with a working crane model, playground and maze, microscopes, optical illusions, and even a "quiet room." In the **Discovery Dome,** dynamic audiovisuals are projected onto a massive concave screen.

OUT AND ABOUT

Kids will be kids, so plan on taking a break from Calgary's regular attractions and head 10 kilometers (6.2 miles) west of the city limits to **Calaway Park** (TransCanada Hwy., 403/240-3822, Sat.-Sun. 10 A.M.-8 P.M. May-June, daily 10 A.M.-8 P.M. July-Aug., Sat.-Sun. 11 A.M.-6 P.M. Sept.-mid-Oct.), with 27 rides including a double-loop roller coaster. Other attractions include an enormous maze, Western-themed mini-golf, a trout-fishing pond, live entertainment in the Western-style "Showtime Theatre," and many eateries. Admission including most rides is $32 for those aged 7-49, $25 for those aged 3-6 or 50 and over.

The **City of Calgary** (403/268-2489) operates nine outdoor pools (open June-early Sept.) and 12 indoor pools (open year-round). Facilities at each vary. The outdoor pools in **Fish Creek Provincial Park** are among the most popular, while the nearby **Family Leisure Centre** (11150 Bonaventure Dr. SE, 403/278-7542, daily 9 A.M.-9 P.M.) has a lot more to offer than just swimming. Entry of adult $12, child $6 includes use of regular pools as well as a giant indoor water slide, a wave pool, and even a skating rink.

museum (130 9th Ave. SE, 403/268-4100, Mon.–Sat. 9 A.M.–5 P.M., Sun. noon–5 P.M., adult $14, senior $10, child $9) chronicles the entire history of western Canada through three floors of informative exhibits and well-displayed artifacts. The museum's permanent collections of contemporary and Inuit art, as well as special exhibitions from national and international collections, are on the 2nd floor. The 3rd-floor "Niitsitapiisini: Our Way of Life" gallery is the best part of the museum. Developed under the watchful eye of Blackfoot elders, it details the stories and traditions of native peoples through interpretive panels and displays of ceremonial artifacts, jewelry, and a full-size tepee. The Glenbow's renowned library and archives are open Tuesday–Friday 10 A.M.–5 P.M.

Calgary Tower

Cross 9th Avenue from the Glenbow Museum to reach one of the city's most famous landmarks, the Calgary Tower (101 9th Ave., at the corner of Centre St., 403/266-7171, daily 9 A.M.–9 P.M., until 10 P.M. in summer, adult $13, senior $11, child $5). Built in 1968, this 190-meter (620-ft) tower dominated the skyline until 1985, when the nearby Petro-Canada towers went up. Although it's now only Calgary's fourth-tallest building, the ride to the top is a worthwhile introduction to the city. The Observation Terrace affords a bird's-eye view of the Canadian Rockies and the ski-jump towers at Canada Olympic Park to the west; the Olympic Saddledome (in Stampede Park) to the south; and the city below, literally—a glass floor allows visitors to stand right over the

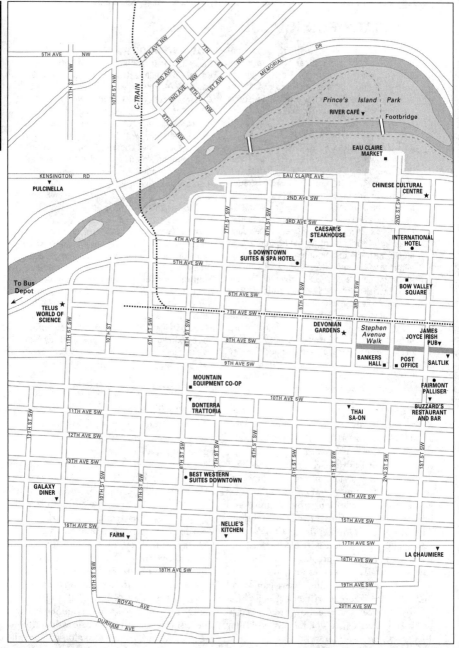

DOWNTOWN CALGARY

6TH AVE NE
5TH AVE NE
4TH AVE NE
3RD AVE NE
2ND AVE NE
1ST AVE NE

DRURY AVE
5TH AVE NE
4TH AVE NE
2ND AVE NE
1ST AVE NE

CENTRE ST
1ST ST NE
2ND ST NE
3RD ST NE
4TH ST
NE
TRAIL
EDMONTON
TRAIL
6TH ST NE
7TH ST NE
7A ST NE
8TH ST NE
9TH ST NE
10TH ST NE
11TH ST NE

MURDOCK RD
MCDOUGALL RD

CENTRE STREET BRIDGE

Bow River

RIVERFRONT AVE

▼ **GOLDEN INN**

▼ **HANG FUNG RESTAURANT**

4TH AVE SE
5TH AVE SE
6TH AVE SE

MEMORIAL DR ••••••••• To **◖CALGARY ZOO** →

St. Patrick's Island

■ **EPCOR CENTRE FOR THE PERFORMING ARTS** ••••

■ **WR CASTELL CENTRAL LIBRARY**

● **HI-CALGARY CITY CENTRE**

★ **HYATT REGENCY**

★ **OLYMPIC PLAZA**

★ **CITY HALL**

Fort Calgary Historic Park

■ **CONVENTION CENTRE**

★ **CALGARY TOWER**

◖ **GLENBOW MUSEUM**

■ **RED ARROW DEPOT**

▼ **DEANE HOUSE**

9TH AVE SE

CENTRE ST
1ST ST SE
3RD ST SE
4TH ST SE
5TH ST SE
6TH ST SE

★ **HOTEL ARTS**

★ **COYOTE'S**

11TH AVE SE
12TH AVE SE
13TH AVE SE
14TH AVE SE

MACLEOD TRAIL
OLYMPIC WAY
5TH ST SE
6TH ST SE

MACDONALD AVE

MAGGIE ST
8TH ST SE
9TH ST SE

17TH AVE SE

Stampede Park

Elbow River

SALISBURY AVE
RAMSAY ST
BURNS AVE

19TH AVE SE

C-TRAIN

To **◖CALGARY STAMPEDE** ↓

0	400 yds
0	400 m

© AVALON TRAVEL

top of 9th Avenue. The tower also houses two restaurants, a snack bar, and a gift shop.

Devonian Gardens

A glass-enclosed elevator rises to the 4th floor of Toronto Dominion Square (8th Ave. and 3rd St. SW, 403/221-4274, daily 9 A.M.–9 P.M., free), where a one-hectare (2.5-acre) indoor garden features 16,000 subtropical plants and 4,000 local plants—138 species in all. Within the gardens are waterfalls, fountains, pools, and bridges. Lunchtime entertainers and art exhibits can often be enjoyed in this serene environment.

Chinatown

At the east end of town on 3rd Avenue is a small Chinatown of approximately 2,000 residents. Chinese immigrants came to Calgary in the 1880s to work on the railroads and stayed to establish food markets, restaurants, and import stores. Chinatown has seen its share of prejudice, from marauding whites gaining revenge for an outbreak of smallpox to bungling city bureaucrats who demanded that the streets be narrow and signs be in Chinese to give the area an authentic look. The **Calgary Chinese Cultural Centre** (197 1st St. SW, 403/262-5071, daily 9 A.M.–9 P.M.) is one of the largest such centers in Canada. It's topped by a grand central dome patterned in the same style as the Temple of Heaven in Beijing. The centerpiece of its intricate tile work is a glistening golden dragon hanging 20 meters (66 ft) above the floor. Head up to the 3rd floor for the best views, passing a mural along the way. At street level is a store selling traditional Chinese medicines and on the lower level is a small museum and gallery (daily 11 A.M.–5 P.M., adult $4, senior and child $2) displaying the cultural history of Calgarians of Chinese descent. One of the museum's most intriguing pieces is the world's oldest known seismograph, which dates to A.D. 132.

West on 1st Avenue

Eau Claire Market at the north end of 3rd Street SW is a colorful indoor market filled with stalls selling fresh fruit from British Columbia, seafood from the Pacific, Alberta beef, bakery items, and exotic imports. Under the same roof are specialty shops, an IMAX and regular theaters, and nine restaurants.

The northern limit of downtown is along the Bow River, where picturesque **Prince's Island Park** is linked to the mainland by a bridge at the end of 3rd Street SW. Jogging paths, tables, and grassy areas are scattered among the trees on this man-made island. To the east is **Centre Street Bridge,** guarded on either side by large (restored) stone lions. For a good view of the city, cross the bridge and follow the trail along the cliff to the west.

Telus World of Science

This complex (701 11th St. SW, 403/268-8300, www.calgaryscience.ca, Mon.–Thurs. 9:45 A.M.–4 P.M., Fri. 9:45 A.M.–5 P.M., Sat.–Sun. 10 A.M.–5 P.M., adult $14.25, child $10, includes admission to the Creative Kids Museum) is kid-oriented, but that's not a bad thing. It's a wonderful facility chockablock with hands-on science exhibits. WOWtown is especially for the under-seven crowd—there's a working crane model, playground and maze, microscopes, optical illusions, and even a "quiet room."

Fort Calgary

In 1875, with the onset of a harsh winter, the newly arrived NWMP built Fort Calgary at the confluence of the Bow and Elbow Rivers in less than six weeks. The original fort is long gone, but after much work, the 16-hectare (40-acre) site has been transformed into a two-part historic park (750 9th Ave. SE, 403/290-1875, daily 9 A.M.–5 P.M., adult $11, senior $10, child $5). Most of the focus is on the interpretive center, housing a replica of 1888 barracks, complete with volunteer RCMP veterans on hand to answer questions. Inside, the lives of Canada's famous "Mounties," the legacy of natives, hardy pioneers, and the wild frontier they tamed are all brought to life through convincingly-costumed interpreters. Beside the barracks is an exact replica of the original fort, built using tools and techniques that are more than 100 years old. History comes alive through a variety of activities and programs, including carpenters at work, a room especially for kids that is filled with games of a bygone era, a museum shop styled on an old Hudson's Bay Company store, and a canteen selling meals that I imagine are more appealing than those the original officers enjoyed.

◖ Calgary Zoo

The Calgary Zoo (1300 Zoo Rd. NE, 403/232-9300, year-round daily 9 A.M.–5 P.M., adult $18, senior $16, child $10) is one of Canada's finest zoos. Unique viewing areas have been designed to allow visitors the best look at the zoo's 1,000-plus animals. For example, in Destination Africa, giraffes tower over a huge glass-walled pool that provides a home to two hippos, with sunken stadium seating allowing visitors a fish-eye view of hippos' often-relaxing day. The second "ecosystem" of Destination Africa is a massive building that re-creates a rainforest, with gorillas and monkeys absolutely everywhere. Other highlights include a section on Australia's nocturnal animals, exotic mammals such as lions and tigers, and conservatories filled with tropical flowers, butterflies, and birds. One of the largest display areas is Canadian Wilds, devoted to the mammals you may or may not see on your travels through Alberta. In the Prehistoric Park section, the world of dinosaurs is brought to life with 27 full-size replicas set amid plantlife and rock formations supposedly similar to those found in Alberta in prehistoric times, but looking more like badlands. Nature Tales is a daily interpretive program that takes in everything from trained elephants strutting their stuff to grizzly-bear feeding.

◖ CANADA OLYMPIC PARK

The 1988 Winter Olympic Games are remembered for many things, but particularly a bobsled team from Jamaica, the antics of English plumber/ski-jumper "Eddie the Eagle," and most of all, for their success. This 95-hectare (235-acre) park (403/247-5452, www.

winsportcanada.ca) on the south side of the TransCanada Highway on the western outskirts of the city is the legacy Calgarians get to enjoy year-round. It was developed especially for the Paralympics and the ski-jumping, luge, bobsled, and freestyle skiing events of the games. Now the park offers activities year-round, including tours of the facilities, luge rides, summer ski-jumping, and sports training camps. In winter, the beginner/intermediate runs are filled with locals who are able to hit the snow as early as November with the help of a complex snowmaking system. Many ski-jumping, bobsled, and luge events of national and international standard are held here throughout winter.

Olympic Hall of Fame

This is North America's largest museum devoted to the Olympic Games (mid-May–Sept. daily 10 A.M.–5 P.M., adult $8, child $5.50). Three floors catalog the entire history of the Winter Olympic Games through more than 1,500 exhibits, interactive video displays, costumes and memorabilia, an athletes timeline, a bobsled and ski-jump simulator, and highlights from the last five Winter Olympic Games held at Albertville (France), Lillehammer (Norway), Nagano (Japan), Salt Lake City (United States), and Turin (Italy), including costumes worn by Jamie Sale and David Pelletier during their infamous silver-then-gold-medal-winning final skate.

Ski-Jumping, Luge, and Bobsled Facilities

Visible from throughout the city are the 70- and 90-meter ski-jump towers, synonymous with the Winter Olympic Games. These two jumps are still used for national and international competitions and training. A glass-enclosed elevator rises to the observation level. The jump complex has three additional jumps of 15, 30, and 50 meters, which are used for junior competitions and training. All but the 90-meter jump have plastic-surfaced landing strips and are used during summer.

At the western end of the park are the luge

and bobsled tracks. A complex refrigeration system keeps the tracks usable even on relatively hot days (up to 28 °C/80 °F). At the bottom of the hill is the Ice House, home to the National Sliding Centre, the world's only year-round facility where athletes can practice their dynamic starts for luge, bobsled, and skeleton. Self-guided tours (mid-May–Sept. daily 10 P.M.–5 P.M.) cost $16 per person.

SOUTH OF DOWNTOWN
The Military Museums

Combining former naval and regiments museums, as well as new galleries devoted to the Canadian Air Force, The Military Museums (4520 Crowchild Trail SW, 403/974-2850, Mon.–Fri. 9 A.M.–5 P.M., Sat.–Sun. 9:30 A.M.–4 P.M., adult $6, senior $4, child $3) opened in 2007 as Canada's largest military museum. Highlights include the history of four regiments—Lord Strathcona's Horse Regiment, Princess Patricia's Canadian Light Infantry, the King's Own Calgary Regiment, and the Calgary Highlanders—and the importance of Canada's navy, which was the Allies' third-largest navy in 1945. On display are three fighter aircraft that flew from the decks of aircraft carriers, as well as uniforms, models, flags, photographs, and a memorial to those who lost their lives in the Korean War.

Heritage Park

This 27-hectare (66-acre) park (1900 Heritage Dr. SW, 403/268-8500, mid-May–Aug. daily 10 A.M.–5 P.M., Sept.–early Oct. Sat.–Sun. only 10 A.M.–5 P.M., Gasoline Alley open year-round daily 9:30 A.M.–5 P.M., adult $20, senior $16, child $15, an extra $12 per person for unlimited rides) is on a peninsula jutting into Glenbow Reservoir southwest of downtown. At the entrance is a cobbled courtyard with shops and the excellent Selkirk Grille Restaurant. In the same building as the restaurant is Gasoline Alley, an indoor exhibit open

year round showcasing the history of vehicles. Behind here, more than 100 buildings and exhibits help re-create an early-20th-century pioneer village. Many of the buildings have been moved to the park from their original locations. Highlights include a Hudson's Bay Company fort, a two-story outhouse, a working blacksmith's shop, an 1896 church, a tepee, and an old schoolhouse with original desks. A boardwalk links stores crammed with antiques, and horse-drawn buggies carry passengers along the streets. You can also ride in authentic passenger cars pulled by a steam locomotive or enjoy a cruise in a paddle wheeler on the reservoir. A traditional bakery sells cakes and pastries, and full meals are served in the Wainwright Hotel. To get there from downtown, take the C-train to Heritage Station and transfer to bus #502 (weekends only).

Fish Creek Provincial Park

At the southern edge of the city, this 1,170-hectare (2,900-acre) park is one of the largest urban parks in North America. The site—much of which was once owned by Patrick Burns—the meat magnate—was officially declared a park in 1975. Three geographical regions meet in the area, giving the park a diversity of habitat. Stands of aspen and spruce predominate, but a mixed-grass prairie, as well as balsam, poplar, and willow, can be found along the floodplains at the east end of the park. The ground is colorfully carpeted with 364 recorded species of wildflowers, and wildlife is abundant. Mule, deer, and ground squirrels are common, and white-tailed deer, coyotes, beavers, and the occasional moose are also present. An interpretive trail begins south of Bow Valley Ranch and leads through a grove of balsam and poplar to a shallow, conglomerate cave. The easiest access to the heart of the park is to turn east on Canyon Meadows Drive from Macleod Trail, then south on Bow River Bottom Trail.

Recreation

The **City of Calgary** (403/268-2489, www.calgary.ca) operates a wide variety of recreational facilities, including swimming pools and golf courses, throughout the city. They also run a variety of excursions, such as canoeing and horseback riding, as well as inexpensive courses ranging from fly-tying to rock-climbing.

WALKING AND BIKING

A good way to get a feel for the city is by walking or biking along the 210 kilometers (130 miles) of paved trails within the city limits. The trail system is concentrated along the Bow River as it winds through the city; other options are limited. Along the riverbank, the trail passes through numerous parks and older neighborhoods to various sights such as Fort Calgary and Inglewood Bird Sanctuary. From Fort Calgary, a trail passes under 9th Avenue SE and follows the Elbow River, crossing it several times before ending at Glenmore Reservoir and Heritage Park. Ask at tourist information centers for a map detailing all trails. The ski slopes at **Canada Olympic Park** (west of downtown along the TransCanada Hwy., 403/247-5452) are the perfect place to hone your downhill mountain-bike skills. Full-suspension-bike rental is $40 for two hours or $60 for a full day, while a day pass for the chairlift is $28.

SWIMMING AND FITNESS CENTERS

The **City of Calgary** (403/268-2489) operates eight outdoor pools (open June through early Sept.) and 12 indoor pools (open year-round). Facilities at each vary. Admission at indoor pools includes the use of the sauna, hot tub, and exercise room. Admission to all pools is adult $6.50–9.80, around half price for seniors and kids.

The **YMCA** (101 3rd St. SW, 403/269-6701, Mon.–Fri. 5:30 A.M.–10 P.M., Sat.–Sun. 7 A.M.–7 P.M., $11.90) is a modern fitness center beside Eau Claire Market at the north end of downtown. All facilities are first-class, including an Olympic-size pool, a weight room, an exercise room, a jogging track, squash courts, a hot tub, and a sauna.

TOURS

Brewster (403/221-8242, www.brewster.ca) runs a Calgary City Sights tour lasting four hours. Included on the itinerary are downtown, various historic buildings, Canada Olympic Park, and Fort Calgary. The tours run June through September and cost adult $53, child $27. Pickups are at most major hotels. Brewster also runs day tours departing Calgary daily to Banff, Lake Louise, and the Columbia Icefield. The latter is a grueling 15-hour trip that departs at 6 A.M. Brewster's downtown office is located on Stephen Avenue Walk at the corner of Centre Street.

AMUSEMENT PARKS

Calaway Park (10 km/6.2 mi west of city limits along the TransCanada Hwy., 403/240-3822, May–June Sat.–Sun. 10 A.M.–7 P.M., July–Aug. daily 10 A.M.–7 P.M., Sept.–mid-Oct. Sat.–Sun. 11 A.M.–6 P.M.) is western Canada's largest outdoor amusement park, with 27 rides including a double-loop roller coaster. Other attractions include an enormous maze, Western-themed mini-golf, a zoo for the kids, a trout-fishing pond, live entertainment in the Western-style "Showtime Theatre," and many eateries. Admission including most rides is $32 for those aged 7–49, $25 for those aged 3–6 and 50 and over.

WINTER RECREATION

When Calgarians talk about going skiing or snowboarding for the day, they are usually referring to the five world-class winter resorts in the Rockies, a one- to two-hour drive to the west. The city's only downhill facilities are at **Canada Olympic Park** (403/247-5452), which has three chairlifts and a T-bar serving a vertical rise of 150 meters (500 ft). Although the slopes aren't extensive, on the plus side are a long season (mid-Nov. to late March), night skiing (week-nights until 9 P.M.), extensive lodge facilities including rentals, and excellent teaching staff. Lift tickets can be purchased on an hourly basis ($28 for four hours) or for a full day ($38). Seniors pay just $16 for a full day on the slopes.

SPECTATOR SPORTS

There's no better way to spend a winter's night in Calgary than by attending a home game of the **Calgary Flames** (403/777-2177, www.calgaryflames.com), the city's National Hockey League franchise. The regular season runs October–April, and home games are usually held in the early evening.

The **Stampeders** (403/289-0205, www.stampeders.com) are Calgary's franchise in the Canadian Football League (CFL), an organization similar to the American NFL. The season runs July–November. Home games are played at the 35,500-seat **McMahon Stadium** (1817 Crowchild Trail NW). From downtown, take the C-train to Banff Trail Station. Tickets range $29–89.

Spruce Meadows

It is somewhat ironic that a city known around the world for its rodeo is also home to the world's premier show-jumping facility, **Spruce Meadows** (Spruce Meadows Way, 403/974-4200, www.sprucemeadows.com). Ever-encroaching residential developments do nothing to take away from the wonderfully refined atmosphere within the white picket fence that surrounds the sprawling 120-hectare (300-acre) site. The facility comprises 6 grassed outdoor rings, 2 indoor arenas, 7 stables holding 700 horse stalls, 90 full-time employees (and many thousands of volunteers), and its own television station that broadcasts to 90 countries.

Spruce Meadows hosts a packed schedule of tournaments that attract the world's best riders and up to 50,000 spectators a day. The four big tournaments are the **National,** the first week of June; **Canada One,** the last week of June; the **North American,** the first week of July; and the **Masters,** the first week of September. The Masters is the world's richest show-jumping tournament, with one million dollars up for grabs on the Sunday afternoon ride-off.

Enjoy the traditions of show-jumping at Spruce Meadows.

General admission is free. Except on the busiest of days, this will get you a prime viewing position at any of the rings. The exception is tournament weekends, when covered reserved seating ($25–35) is the best way to watch the action. To get to Spruce Meadows on tournament weekends, take C-train south to Fish Creek–Lacombe Station, from which bus transfers to the grounds are free. By car, take Macleod Trail south to Highway 22X and turn right toward the mountains along Spruce Meadows Way.

Arts, Entertainment, and Shopping

ffwd (www.ffwdweekly.com) is a free weekly magazine available throughout the city. It lists theater events, cinema screenings, and art displays, and keeps everyone abreast of the local music scene. Tickets to major concerts, performances, and sporting events are available in advance from **Ticketmaster** (403/777-0000, www.ticketmaster.ca).

THE ARTS
Art Galleries
It may put a dent in Calgary's cow town image, but the city does have a remarkable number of galleries displaying and selling work by Albertan and Canadian artisans. Unfortunately, they are not concentrated in any one area, and most require some effort to find. Renowned for its authentic native art, **Micah Gallery** is the exception. It's right downtown on Stephen Avenue Walk (110 8th Ave. SW, 403/245-1340). A cluster of galleries lies along 9th Avenue SE. Most affordable is **Galleria Arts & Crafts** (907 9th Ave. SE., 403/270-3612), with two stories of shelf space stocked with paintings, etchings, metal sculptures, jewelry, and wood carvings. Here also, **The Collectors Gallery** (1332 9th Ave. SE, 403/245-8300) sells the work of prominent 19th- and 20th-century Canadian artists.

Theater
Calgary's Western image belies a cultural diversity that goes further than being able to get a few foreign beers at the local saloon. In fact, the city has 10 professional theater companies, an opera, an orchestra, and a ballet troupe. The main season for performances is September–May.

Alberta Theatre Projects (403/294-7402, www.atplive.com) is a well-established company based in the downtown Epcor Centre for the Performing Arts (220 9th Ave. SE). Usual performances are of contemporary material. Expect to pay under $20 for matinees and up to $66 for the very best evening seats. Also based at the Epcor Centre for the Performing Arts is **Theatre Calgary** (403/294-7440, www.theatrecalgary.com). **Lunchbox Theatre** (115 9th Ave. SE, 403/265-4292, www.lunchboxtheatre.com), in a custom-built theater at the base of the Calgary Tower, runs especially for the lunchtime crowd from September to early May. Adults pay $18, seniors $15 for usually comedic content. For adult-oriented experimental productions, consider a performance by **One Yellow Rabbit** (Epcor Centre for the Performing Arts, 403/264-3224, www.oyr.org).

Music and Dance
Calgary Opera (403/262-7286, www.calgaryopera.com) performs in a restored church (corner 13th Ave. and 7th St. SW) October–April. Tickets range $22–88. The 2,000-seat Jack Singer Concert Hall at the Epcor Centre for the Performing Arts is home to the **Calgary Philharmonic Orchestra** (403/571-0270, www.cpo-live.com), one of Canada's top orchestras. **Alberta Ballet** (403/245-4549, www.albertaballet.com) performs at locations throughout the city.

Cinemas
Many major shopping malls—including Eau Claire Market, closest to downtown—have a **Cineplex** cinema. For information, call the 24-hour film line (403/263-3166) or check the

website (www.cineplex.com). **Uptown Stage & Screen** (610 8th Ave. SW, 403/265-0120, www.theuptown.com) is a restored downtown theater that has a reputation for alternative, art, and foreign films. Over the Bow River from downtown, the 1935 **Plaza Theatre** (1133 Kensington Rd. NW, Kensington, 403/283-2222, www.theplaza.ca) shows everything from mainstream to Hindi.

NIGHTLIFE
Bars and Nightclubs

With a nickname like Cowtown it's not surprising that some of Calgary's hottest nightspots play country music. **Ranchman's** (9615 Macleod Trail SW, 403/253-1100) is *the* place to check out first, especially during Stampede Week. Some of country's hottest stars have played this authentic honky-tonk. Food is served at a bar out front all day, then at 7 P.M. the large dance hall opens with a band keeping the crowd boot-scootin' most nights. The hall is a museum of rodeo memorabilia and photographs, with a chuck wagon hanging from the ceiling. On the south side of the railway tracks from downtown, is hip **Cowboys** (1088 Olympic Way SE, 403/265-0699). The crowd is urban-slick, but when country music plays, the fancy-dancing crowd seems to know every word.

Options for a quiet drink in a refined setting include lounge bars in major downtown hotels. Of these, the **Sandstone Lounge** (Hyatt Regency, 700 Centre St., 403/717-1234) stands out for its central location (off Stephen Avenue Walk), classy surroundings, and extensive drink selection. **Raw Bar** (Hotel Arts, 119 12th Ave. SW, 403/266-4611, daily 11 A.M.–9 P.M.) is as exotic as it gets in Calgary—a cabana-like setting around an outdoor pool. Back on Stephen Avenue Walk, in an old bank building, **James Joyce Irish Pub** (114 8th Ave. SW, 403/262-0708) has Guinness on tap and a menu of traditional British dishes.

If you're looking to dance the night away (without doing it in a line), there's a number of non-country alternatives. Downtown in a grandly restored theater, **The Palace** (218 8th Ave. SW, 403/263-9980) has a large dance floor and big-time lighting and sound systems. **Mercury Lounge** (550 17th Ave. SW, 403/229-0222) attracts a young, hip crowd for its cocktail-bar ambience—the perfect pre-nightclub hangout. For many Mercury patrons, the next stop is **Tequila** (219 17th Ave. SW, 403/209-2215), where a DJ spins house and hip-hop for a young party crowd. Also within walking distance is the **Metropolitan Grill** (880 16th Ave. SW, 403/802-2393), where the over-25 crowd gravitates to the outdoor patio on warm summer nights. Glitzy **Tantra** (355 10th Ave. SW, 403/264-0202) attracts the beautiful, high-end crowd, but remains welcoming.

Jazz and Blues

The days of Buddy Guy and Junior Wells taking to the stage of the venerable King Edward Hotel are just a memory, but a couple of modern venues attract jazz and blues enthusiasts. One of the most popular jazz clubs in town is **Beat Niq** (at the lower level of 811 1st St., 403/263-1650), a New York–style jazz club that welcomes everyone. It's open Thursday–Saturday from 8 P.M. and the cover charge is $12–18.

SHOPPING
Plazas and Malls

The largest shopping center downtown is **Calgary Eaton Centre,** on Stephen Avenue Walk at 4th Street SW. This center is linked to other plazas by the Plus 15 Walkway System. Other downtown shopping complexes are **Eau Claire Market,** at the entrance to Prince's Island Park, where the emphasis is on fresh foods and trendy boutiques; **TD Square,** at 7th Avenue and 2nd Street SW; and **The Bay,** part of Alberta's history with its link to the Hudson's Bay Company. **Uptown 17** is a strip of more than 400 retail shops, restaurants, and galleries along 17th Avenue SW. **Kensington,** across the Bow River from downtown, is an eclectic mix of specialty shops.

Markets

At **Crossroads Market** (1235 26th Ave. SE,

403/291-5208, Fri.–Sun. 9 A.M.–5 P.M.) you'll find rows and rows of local seasonal produce as well as prepared foods like the well-researched Simple Simon Pies. Crossroads is also known for its arts and crafts.

Camping Gear and Western Wear

Mountain Equipment Co-op (830 10th Ave. SW, 403/269-2420) is Calgary's largest camping store. This massive outlet boasts an extensive range of high-quality clothing, climbing and mountaineering equipment (including a climbing wall), tents, sleeping bags, kayaks and canoes, books and maps, and other accessories. The store is a cooperative owned by its members, similar to the American REI stores, except that to purchase anything you must be a member (a once-only $5 charge).

Alberta Boot Co. (614 10th Ave. SW, 403/263-4605), within walking distance of downtown, is Alberta's only Western-boot manufacturer. This outlet shop has thousands of pairs for sale in all shapes and sizes, all made from leather. Boots start at $250 and go all the way up to $1,700 for alligator hide. You'll find **Lammle's Western Wear** outlets in all the major malls and downtown on Stephen Avenue Walk. Another popular Western outfitter is **Riley & McCormick,** also on Stephen Avenue Walk (220 8th Ave. SW, 403/262-1556) and at the airport.

Bookstores

For topographic, city, and wall maps, as well as travel guides and atlases, **Map Town** (400 5th Ave. SW, 403/266-2241 or 877/921-6277, www.maptown.com, Mon.–Fri. 9 A.M.–6 P.M., Sat. 10 A.M.–5 P.M.) should have what you're looking for. Tech-savvy travelers will be impressed by the selection of GPS units and related software, as well as the scanning service, which allows you to have topo maps sent directly to your email inbox.

The suburb of Kensington, immediately northwest of downtown, is home to **Pages** (1135 Kensington Rd. NW, 403/283-6655, Mon.–Sat. 10 A.M.–5:30 P.M., Thurs.–Fri. until 9 P.M., and Sun. noon–5 P.M.), which offers a thoughtful selection of Canadian fiction and nonfiction titles.

Fair's Fair (1609 14th St. SW, 403/245-2778, daily from 10 A.M.) is the biggest of Calgary's secondhand and collector bookstores. Surprise, surprise, it's remarkably well organized, with a solid collection of well-labeled Canadiana filling more than one room. Fair's Fair has another large outlet in Inglewood (907 9th Ave. SE, 403/237-8156). On the north side of downtown, **Aquila Books** (826 16th Ave. NW, 403/282-5832) is a real gem, with one of the world's best collections of antiquarian Canadian Rockies and mountaineering books.

Festivals and Events

SPRING

Calgary International Children's Festival (403/294-7414, www.calgarychildfest.org) is the third week of May. Events include theater, puppetry, and performances by musicians from around the world. It's held in the Epcor Centre for the Performing Arts and Olympic Plaza. Olympic Plaza comes alive with the sights, sounds, and tastes of the Caribbean on the second Saturday of June for **Carifest** (403/774-1300, www.carifestcalgary.ca).

SUMMER

Few cities in the world are associated as closely with an event as Calgary is with the **Calgary Stampede.** For details of the "Greatest Outdoor Show on Earth," held each summer in July, see *Calgary Stampede* later in this section.

Canada Day is celebrated on July 1 in Prince's Island Park, Fort Calgary, the zoo, and Heritage Park. The **Calgary Folk Music Festival** (403/233-0904, www.calgaryfolkfest.

com), during the last weekend of July, is an indoor and outdoor extravaganza of Canadian and international performers that centers on Prince's Island Park. The first full week of August, and also at this downtown riverfront park, is **Afrikadey!** (403/234-9110, www.afrikadey.com), with performances and workshops by African-influenced musicians and artists and screenings of African-themed films.

FALL

In October, **hockey** and **skiing and snowboarding** fever hits the city as the **NHL Calgary Flames** start their season and the first snow flies. Late September through early October sees screenings of movies during the **Calgary International Film Festival** (403/283-1490, www.calgaryfilm.com) at the historic Plaza theater, and at the Globe Theatre and Cineplex at Eau Claire Market. This is followed by **Wordfest** (403/237-9068, www.wordfest.com), where authors talk about their books, workshops are given, and many readings

take place at venues throughout the city and in Banff. As Halloween approaches a good place for kids is Calgary Zoo (403/232-9300, www.calgaryzoo.org), where there are **Boo at the Zoo** celebrations after dark throughout the last week of October.

WINTER

Calgary has joined other major Canadian cities by celebrating New Year's Eve with a **First Night** festival. Although severely curtailed by the weather, Calgarians enjoy the winter with the opening of the theater, ballet, and opera seasons. National and international ski-jumping, luge, and bobsledding events are held at **Canada Olympic Park** November–March.

◖ CALGARY STAMPEDE

Every July since 1912, the city's perennial rough-and-ready cow town image has been thrust to the forefront when a fever known as Stampede hits town. For 10 days, Calgarians let their hair down—business leaders don Stetsons, bankers wear boots, half the town

The Calgary Stampede is western Canada's best-known event.

walks around in too-tight denim outfits, and the rate of serious crime drops. Nine months later, maternity hospitals report a rise in business. For most Calgarians, it is known simply as The Week (always capitalized). The Stampede is many things to many people but is certainly not for the cynic. It is a celebration of the city's past—of endless sunny days when life was broncos, bulls, and steers, of cowboys riding through the streets, and saloons on every corner. But it is not just about the past. It's the cow town image Calgarians cherish, and the frontier image that visitors expect. On downtown streets, everyone is your neighbor. Flapjacks and bacon are served free of charge around the city; normally staid citizens shout "Ya-HOO!" for no particular reason; Indians ride up and down the streets on horseback; and there's drinking and dancing until dawn every night.

The epicenter of the action is **Stampede Park,** immediately south of the city center, where more than 100,000 people converge each day. The nucleus of the Stampede, the park hosts the world's richest outdoor rodeo and the just-as-spectacular chuck wagon races, where professional cowboys from all over the planet compete to share $1.6 million over 10 days. But Stampede Park offers a lot more than a show of cowboy skills. The gigantic midway takes at least a day to get around: a staggering number of attractions, displays, and free entertainment cost only the price of gate admission; and a glittering grandstand show, complete with fireworks, ends each day's shenanigans.

Stampede Parade

Although Stampede Park opens on Thursday evening for **Sneak-a-Peek** (an event that alone attracts approximately 40,000 eager patrons), Stampede Week officially begins Friday morning with a spectacular parade through the streets of downtown Calgary. The approximately 150 parade participants include close to 4,000 people and 700 horses, and the procession takes two hours to pass any one point. It features an amazing array of floats, each cheered by the 250,000 people who line the streets up to 10 deep. The loudest "Ya-HOOs" are usually reserved for Alberta's oldest residents, Stampede royalty, and members of Calgary's professional sports teams; but this is the Stampede, so even politicians and street sweepers elicit enthusiastic cheers.

Rodeo

The pinnacle of any cowboy's career is walking away with the $100,000 winner's check on the last day of competition in the Calgary Stampede. For the first 8 days, 20 of the world's best cowboys and cowgirls compete in 2 pools for the right to ride on the final Sunday. Saturday is a wildcard event. On each of the 10 days, the rodeo starts at 1:30 P.M. Although Stampede Week is about a lot more than the rodeo, everyone loves to watch this event. Cowboys compete in bronc riding, bareback riding, bull riding, calf roping, and steer wrestling, and cowgirls compete in barrel racing. Bull fighting and nonstop chatter from hilarious rodeo clowns all keep the action going between the more traditional rodeo events.

Chuck Wagon Races

The **Rangeland Derby** chuck wagon races feature nine heats each evening starting at 8 P.M. At the end of the week, the top four drivers from the preliminary rounds compete in a $100,000 dash-for-the-cash final. Chuck wagon racing is an exciting sport any time, but at the Stampede the pressure is intense as drivers push themselves to stay in the running. The grandstand in the infield makes steering the chuck wagons through an initial figure eight difficult, heightening the action before they burst onto the track for what is known as the Half Mile of Hell to the finish line. The first team across the finish line does not always win the race; drivers must avoid 34 penalties, ranging from 1 to 10 seconds, which are added to their overall time.

Other Highlights

Agricultural displays are situated in the center of Stampede Park. **Centennial Fair** is an outdoor stage with children's attractions such as duck races and magicians. In the **Agricultural**

Building livestock is displayed, and the World Blacksmith's Competition and horse shows take place next door in the **John Deere Show Ring.**

At the far end of Stampede Park, across the Elbow River, is **Indian Village.** Here, members of the five nations who signed Treaty Seven 100 years ago—the Blackfoot, Blood, Piegan, Sarcee, and Stoney—set up camp for the duration of the Stampede. Each tepee has its own colorful design. Behind the village is a stage where native dance competitions are held.

Once you've paid gate admission, all entertainment (except the rodeo and chuck wagon races) is free. Well-known Canadian performers appear at the outdoor **Coca-Cola Stage** from 11 A.M. to midnight. **Nashville North** is an indoor venue with a bar, live country acts, and a dance floor; open until 2 A.M.

Tickets
Advance tickets for the afternoon rodeos and evening chuck wagon races/grandstand shows go on sale the year before the event (usually sometime in September), with the best seats selling out well in advance. The best views are from the "A" section, closest to the infield yet high enough not to miss all the action. Ticket prices for the first eight days of rodeo competition range $35–75 ($56 for section A). The

evening chuck wagon races/grandstand shows run $42–84 ($72 for section A). Tickets to both the rodeos and chuck wagon races/grandstand shows include admission to Stampede Park. Order tickets by phone (403/269-9822 or 800/661-1767) or online (www.calgarystampede.com).

If you didn't purchase your tickets in advance, you'll need to pay the $14 **general admission** at the gate. Then, once on the grounds, you can purchase "rush seating" tickets for the afternoon's rodeo (adult $15, child $8) or the chuck wagon race/grandstand show (adult $20, child $12). You'll only have access to either an area of the infield with poor views or seats well away from the action.

Information
Check either of Calgary's daily newspapers for a pull-out section with results of the previous day's competition and a schedule of events on the grounds and around town. At Stampede Park, a schedule and maps are available at distinctive **Howdy Folk Chuckwagons** topped with cowboy hats and staffed by friendly volunteers.

For future dates for the Calgary Stampede, contact the Calgary Stampede office at 403/261-0101 or 800/661-1260, www.calgarystampede.com.

Accommodations and Camping

Accommodations in Calgary vary from campgrounds, a hostel, and budget motels to a broad selection of high-quality hotels catering to top-end travelers and business conventions. During Stampede Week, prices are higher than the rest of the year and accommodations are booked months in advance. Rates quoted below are for a double room in summer, but outside of Stampede week.

The bed-and-breakfast scene in Calgary is alive and well. Most are located off the main tourist routes. The **Bed & Breakfast Association of Calgary** (www.bbcalgary.

com) represents around 40 of these homes offering rooms to visitors.

DOWNTOWN
Under $50
Part of the worldwide Hostelling International organization, **HI-Calgary City Centre** (520 7th Avenue SE, 403/670-7580 or 888/762-4122, www.hihostels.ca) is an excellent choice for budget travelers, both for its convenient location and wide variety of facilities. It has 94 beds, most in eight-bed dormitories, but there are a couple of private rooms. Other amenities

include a fully equipped kitchen, laundry facilities, a large common room, Internet kiosks, free wireless Internet, bike rental, an outdoor barbecue, a game room, a snack bar, lockers, and free parking. Members of Hostelling International pay $29.50 for a dorm bed ($33 for nonmembers) or $73–79.50 s or d ($81–87.50 for nonmembers) in the private rooms. It's one block east of the City Hall C-train station.

$50-100

The most central bed-and-breakfast is **Inglewood B&B** (1006 8th Ave. SE, 403/262-6570, www.inglewoodbedandbreakfast.com, $100–165 s or d), named for the historic neighborhood in which it lies. Its location is excellent—close to the river and Stampede Park, as well as a 10-minute stroll from downtown. The three rooms within this modern Victorian-style home each have private bathrooms and rates include a cooked breakfast of your own choosing.

$150-200

A few blocks west of the downtown shopping district, but linked by the C-train, you'll find the 301-room **Sandman Hotel** (888 7th Ave. SW, 403/237-8626 or 800/726-3626, www.sandmanhotels.com, $169–235 s or d). This full-service property features an indoor pool, a family-style restaurant, and large, attractive rooms. Pay under $130 through the website.

Least expensive of the hotels right downtown is the **(5 Downtown Suites & Spa** (618 5th Ave. SW, 403/451-5551 or 888/561-7666, www.5calgary.com, $159–199). Although the 300 rooms are unremarkable, bonuses include full kitchens, free weekend parking, a free business center, spa services, a restaurant and lounge, and a small outdoor pool.

$200-250

(Hotel Arts (119 12th Ave. SW, 403/266-4611 or 800/661-9378, www.hotelarts.ca, $249–436 s or d) is a newish 12-story, 188-room accommodation on the south side of the railway tracks, within easy walking distance of Stampede Park. The rooms are contemporary-slick, with 42-inch LCD flat-screen TVs, cordless phones, high-speed Internet access, luxurious bathrooms, and plush beds with goose-down duvets. Downstairs is a fitness room, an outdoor heated pool surrounded by a beautiful patio, a restaurant, and a lounge.

The **International Hotel of Calgary** (220 4th Ave. SW, 403/265-9600 or 800/661-8627, www.internationalhotel.ca, $239–289 s or d) features 250 spacious one- and two-bedroom suites, an indoor pool, a fitness room, and a restaurant.

$250-300

When I spend the night in Calgary on business I try to stay somewhere different every time (in the name of research). But when it's a special occasion, it's difficult to beat the **(Kensington Riverside Inn** (1126 Memorial Dr. NW, Kensington, 403/228-4442 or 877/313-3733, www.kensingtonriversideinn.com, $299–369 s or d includes breakfast). Why? From the

Kensington Riverside Inn

moment I'm tempted by a homemade cookie from the jar at the reception to the moment I slide between the Egyptian cotton sheets that top ultra-comfortable mattresses, the inn has a captivating atmosphere that is unlike any other city accommodation. Each of the 19 guest rooms has a slightly different feel (from bold contemporary to warmly inviting), but it's in-room niceties such as heated towel racks, or a quiet hour spent in the central living room with evening hors d'oeuvres, that make the inn super special.

Over $300

One block north from the Calgary Tower is the ◖ **Hyatt Regency Calgary** (700 Centre St., 403/717-1234 or 800/492-8804, www.calgary. hyatt.com, $339–429 s or d). Incorporating a historic building along Stephen Avenue Walk in its construction, this 21-story hotel features an indoor swimming pool, a refined lounge, and a renowned restaurant specializing in Canadian cuisine. The hotel's Stillwater Spa is the premier spa facility in Calgary—spend any time here and you'll forget you're in a city

hotel. The up-to-date guest rooms won't take your breath away, but they have a wide range of amenities and luxurious bathrooms.

In the heart of the shopping district, the **Westin Hotel** (320 4th Ave. SW, 403/266-1611 or 888/625-5144, www.westincalgary.com, $419–489 s or d) has a wide range of facilities, including a rooftop indoor swimming pool, a café, the renowned Owl's Nest Restaurant, a lounge, and more than 500 rooms.

Easily Calgary's best-known hotel, the gracious **Fairmont Palliser** (133 9th Ave. SE, 403/263-0520 or 866/540-4477, www.fairmont.com, from $529 s or d) was built in 1914 by the Canadian Pacific Railway for the same clientele as the company's famous properties in Banff and Jasper. The rooms may seem smallish by modern standards, and the hotel lacks certain recreational facilities, but the elegance and character of the grande dame of Calgary accommodations are priceless. The cavernous lobby has original marble columns and staircases, a magnificent chandelier, and solid-brass doors that open onto busy 9th Avenue. As you'd expect, staying at

The Hyatt Regency Calgary rises above downtown.

the Palliser isn't cheap, but it's a luxurious way to enjoy the city.

MACLEOD TRAIL

A string of hotels along Macleod Trail south of downtown picks up highway traffic as it enters the city. Most mid-priced chains are represented, with the following being just a sampling.

$100-150

Most of the chain motels along Macleod Trail fall into this price category. Book in advance or online to pick up rates around $100 a night.

Southernmost of the motels on Macleod Trail is the 34-room **Stetson Village Inn** (10002 Macleod Trail, 403/271-3210 or 888/322-3210, www.stetsoninn.ca, $111 s or d), an older-style place tucked between shopping malls.

The **Best Western Calgary Centre Inn** (3630 Macleod Trail SW, 403/287-3900 or 877/287-3900, www.bwcalgarycentre.com, $149–159 s or d) may be close to the geographical center of the city, but it's not downtown as the name suggests. Each of the rooms is decorated in a bright and breezy color scheme, and comes stocked with amenities such as a hair dryer and coffeemaker. On the premises are an indoor pool and a fitness center.

A few blocks farther south, with a C-train station on its back doorstep, stands **Holiday Inn Macleod Trail** (4206 Macleod Trail SW, 403/287-2700 or 800/661-1889, www.holiday-inn.com, $149 s or d), where the 150 rooms were last renovated in 2009. Facilities here include a large indoor pool, a restaurant, and a lounge.

WEST OF DOWNTOWN
$100-150

Motel Village is Calgary's main concentration of moderately priced motels. The "village" is not an official designation, just a dozen motels bunched together on a single block bordered by 16th Avenue NW, Crowchild Trail, and Banff Trail. From the adjacent Banff Trail station, downtown is a short, safe ride away on

the C-train. Here, the **[(Comfort Inn** (2369 Banff Trail NW, 403/289-2581 or 800/228-5150, www.comfortinncalgary.com, $139–179 s or d includes breakfast) combines a wide range of amenities with reasonable rates to be my pick of Motel Village accommodations. All rooms have a simple yet snazzy contemporary look, along with high-speed Internet, a coffeemaker, a hair dryer, and an ironing facility. Other features include an indoor pool and waterslide complex.

Tucked away on the forested Paskapoo Slopes, beside Canada Olympic Park, **[(Ridge Side Retreat** (430 85th St. SW, 403/288-3415 or 877/344-3400, www.ripleyridge.com, $145–375 s or d includes breakfast) offers guests the choice of accommodations in two rustic cabins—one with a full kitchen, the other with a woodstove and loft—or in spacious, comfortable units such as the City Light Suite, which features panoramic city views from a private sitting room.

$150-200

Directly opposite Canada Olympic Park is the **Four Points by Sheraton Calgary West** (8220 Bow Ridge Crescent NW, 403/288-4441 or 877/288-4441, www.fourpointscalgarywest.com, $169–195 s or d), a real standout for motel accommodations on this side of the city. The 150 rooms are big and bright and each has a balcony (ask for one with a view of Canada Olympic Park). Along with city-hotel luxuries like free wireless Internet and room service, other amenities include an indoor pool and water slide, a fitness center, a day spa, and a restaurant.

Across the road from the Sheraton is **Sandman Hotel & Suites** (125 Bow Ridge Crescent NW, 403/288-6033 or 800/726-3626, www.sandmanhotels.com, $185 s or d). It features spacious modern rooms, an indoor pool, a fitness room, and a 24-hour Denny's restaurant.

NORTHEAST (DOWNTOWN)

Many hotels lie in the northeast section of the city at varying distances from Calgary International

Airport. All of those detailed below have airport shuttles, and most can be contacted directly by courtesy phone from the airport.

$100-150

Check hotel websites listed below for rooms around the $100 mark, or take the easy way out and book your stay at the no-frills **Pointe Inn** (1808 19th St. NE, 403/291-4681 or 800/661-8164, www.pointeinn.com, $100–115 s or d). Facilities include a launderette, a restaurant, and a lounge. Request a nonsmoking room.

$150-200

Holiday Inn Calgary Airport (1250 McKinnon Dr. NE, 403/230-1999 or 800/465-4329, www.holidayinn.com, $160–190 s or d) is a little farther from the airport than the other choices, but since there's a free shuttle that is of little consequence. The smallish indoor pool is the perfect place to refresh yourself after a long flight.

Similarly priced is the **Radisson Hotel Calgary Airport** (2120 16th Ave. NE, 403/291-4666 or 800/395-7046, www.radis-son.com, $160–260 s or d), which features 185 comfortable rooms, an indoor pool, a fitness center, spa services, and a Western-style saloon. Upgrade to a Business Class room ($180) and enjoy better views, an evening turndown service, and breakfast.

Not right at the airport but of a similarly high standard to the Delta Calgary Airport is the **Sheraton Cavalier** (2620 32nd Ave. NE, 403/291-0107 or 866/716-8101, www.sheratoncavalier.com, $180–265 s or d). This full-service hostelry boasts a variety of dining options, a lounge, a fitness room, an indoor water park, and a business center. The 306 rooms are modern, spacious, and equipped with wireless Internet.

Over $200

(Delta Calgary Airport (403/291-2600 or 888/492-8804, www.deltahotels.com, $219 s or d) is the only accommodation right at the airport. The medium-sized rooms come with luxuries like down duvets and plush bathrobes,

each has a writing desk, and most importantly, they are well sound-proofed. Premier Rooms, which are the same size as regular rooms, come with upgraded furnishings for a few bucks extra. Hotel amenities include two restaurants, a lounge, an indoor pool, and a business center.

CAMPING

No camping is available within the Calgary city limits, although campgrounds can be found along all major routes into the city. Shuttle buses run to and from campgrounds into Stampede Park during the Calgary Stampede.

West

The only Calgary campground with an outdoor swimming pool is **(Calgary West Campground** (221 101st St. SW, 403/288-0411 or 888/562-0842, www.calgarycampground.com, mid-Apr.–mid-Oct., unserviced sites $32, hookups $39–43), on a north-facing hill a short way west of Canada Olympic Park. In addition to the pool, modern facilities include showers, a laundry room, a game room, and a grocery store. Around 320 sites are laid out on terraces, so no one misses out on the views.

Calaway Park (10 km/6.2 mi west of city limits, 403/249-7372, www.calawaypark.com, mid-May–Aug., tent sites $24, hookups $29–35) is farther out along the TransCanada Highway. It offers a large, open camping area. Trees are scarce, but on clear days the view of the Canadian Rockies is spectacular.

North

Whispering Spruce Campground (403/226-0097, www.whisperingspruce.com, Apr.–Oct., tent sites $24, hookups $26–28) is on the west side of Highway 2, 10 kilometers (6.2 mi) north of the airport. Facilities include showers, a small grocery store, laundry, a game room, and horseshoe pits.

East

Mountainview Farm Campground, three kilometers (1.9 mi) east of the city limits on the

TransCanada Highway (403/293-6640, www. calgarycamping.com, tent sites $31, hookups $35–40) doesn't have a view of the mountains, but it does have mini-golf and hay rides. The sites are very close together. Facilities include showers, a grocery store, and a laundry room.

Food

Calgary may lack the cultural trappings that Alberta's capital, Edmonton, boasts, but it gives that city a run for its money in the restaurant department. Southwest of downtown, along 17th Avenue and 4th Street, a once-quieter part of the city has been transformed into a focal point for Calgary's restaurant scene, with cuisine to suit all tastes. Familiar North American fast-food restaurants line Macleod Trail south of the city center.

DOWNTOWN
Casual
All of the major high-rise buildings have plazas with inexpensive food courts and cafes—the perfect places for people watching. Local suits all have their own favorite haunts, but only two places really stand out to me as trying that little bit harder to be different and to please at the same time; both are owned by the same company. **Sunterra Village Marché** (Plus 15 Level, TransCanada Tower, 450 1st St. SW, 403/262-8240, Mon.–Fri. 6 A.M.–8 P.M.) is set up to represent a French streetscape, complete with a patisserie, carvery, salad counter, deli, wine bar, and juice joint. **Sunterra Marché** (Plus 15 Level, Bankers Hall, 855 2nd St. SW, 403/269-3610, Mon.–Fri. 6:30 A.M.–6:30 P.M., Sat. 9:30 A.M.–5:30 P.M.) has a much smaller selection, but the same high quality of gourmet-to-go lunches.

At the entrance to Prince's Island Park, **Eau Claire Market** has a large food court and several restaurants. In the food court, you'll find a great seafood outlet, a bakery, Asian-food places such as the Thai **Touch of Ginger** (403/234-8550), and an outlet of the local coffee chain **Good Earth Café** (403/237-8684). Outside the market's western entrance is (**1886 Buffalo Café** (187 Barclay Pde. SW,

403/269-9255, Mon.–Fri. 6 A.M.–3 P.M., weekends 7 A.M.–3 P.M., breakfasts $9–14). Named for the year it was built, this restaurant oozes an authentic Old Calgary ambience. Inexpensive breakfasts attract the most interesting group of diners, but the place is busy all day.

Canadian
Thomsons (112 Stephen Ave. Walk, 403/537-4449, daily 6:30 A.M.–1:30 P.M. and 5–9:30 P.M., $20–36) is in a historic sandstone building cleverly integrated with the modern Hyatt Regency, but it's not aimed at the hotel crowd. First off, the buffet breakfast ($18) is as good as it gets, with omelets made to order and real maple syrup to douse your pancakes. The rest of the day, the menu is dominated by Canadian game and seafood. Maybe start with PEI mussels and bacon in traditional ale, then choose from something as Canadian as grilled arctic char or splurge on the Alberta beef tenderloin.

Walk north from Eau Claire Market to reach the (**River Café** (Prince's Island Park, 403/261-7670, Mon.–Fri. 11 A.M.–11 P.M., Sat. and Sun. 11 A.M.–10 P.M., $24–49), a cozy, rustic dining room that will surprise you with some of Calgary's finest cooking. More of a restaurant than a café, it features extensive use of produce and ingredients sourced from across Canada. Standouts include buffalo, Alberta beef, and salmon dishes, with the latter often incorporating maple syrup. Lunch mains range $17–24 (including a delicious smoked trout flatbread) while weekend brunch ranges $11–19.

Had a bad experience dining in a revolving restaurant? Haven't we all. Hopefully your meal at the **Sky 360** (101 9th Ave. SW, 403/508-5822, daily 11–2 A.M. and 5 A.M.–10 P.M.,

$22–42) atop the Calgary Tower will be memorable for more than the view. A full rotation takes one hour. Expect healthy, modern cooking that uses lots of Canadian produce, with lunchtime sandwiches, such as maple-smoked chicken with apple chutney, for under $20. The

mushroom chowder is a good way to start, before moving on to mains such as a grilled pork chop that swims in a grainy mustard jus.

Seafood

Yes, Calgary is a long way from the ocean, but it nonetheless has a few excellent seafood restaurants. Across the railway tracks from downtown are two of the best: **Cannery Row** (317 10th Ave. SW, 403/269-8889) and, directly upstairs, **McQueens Upstairs** (403/269-4722). Cannery Row is a casual affair, with an open kitchen, an oyster bar, and the ambience of a San Francisco seafood restaurant. Dishes such as grilled swordfish, jambalaya, and blackened snapper are mostly under $20. The menu at McQueens Upstairs is more sophisticated and varied. Dinner entrées start at $21 and rise to over $40 for fresh lobster. Both restaurants are open Monday–Friday for lunch and daily for dinner.

Within the Hyatt Regency building, the sophisticated ambience of **Catch** (100 Stephen Ave. Walk, 403/206-0000, Mon.–Fri. 11:30 A.M.–1:30 P.M., Mon.–Sat. 5:30–9:30 P.M., $34–50) is as big an attraction as the menu of seasonal seafood that is flown in daily from both of Canada's coasts. The main level is an oyster bar, where you can sample a variety of shucked oysters with an extensive choice of drinks, while more formal dining is upstairs in the main room.

Smokehouse

In a city that has traditionally loved its beef, it should be no surprise that a Southern-style smokehouse is popular. One block off Stephen Avenue Walk, ▮ **Palomino** (109 7th Ave. SW, 403/532-1911, Mon.–Sat. for lunch and dinner, $17–24) fits the bill. The biggest change to a building that once held a furniture shop is a massive smoker capable of holding 300 kilograms (750 pounds) of meat at any one time. Forget about that diet and tuck into pork ribs ($17–24), giant Alberta beef ribs ($23), a "Fat Ass Platter" for four ($65), and, as the menu suggests, buy a round of drinks for the kitchen ($20). House wine choices range from "Cheap" to "Decent" and there are drink specials most nights.

GOOD OL' ALBERTA BEEF

Although Alberta isn't renowned for its culinary delights, flavor-filled and tender Alberta beef is a provincial highlight. It's served at most Calgary restaurants, but only a few restaurants specialize in it. The following are my favorites.

Respected **Caesar's Steak House** (512 4th Ave. SW, 403/264-1222, Mon.-Fri. 11 A.M.-midnight, Sat. 4:30 P.M.-midnight, $28-47) has been around for over 30 years – a long time in the restaurant business. The elegant room has a Roman-style decor with dark wood, leather seating, and dim lighting – just what you expect from a steakhouse. Although the menu includes ribs and seafood, it's juicy prime cuts of Alberta beef that this place is known for.

Unlike Caesar's, **Saltlik** (101 8th Ave. SW, 403/537-1160, daily from 11 A.M. for lunch and dinner, $17-31) is anything but traditional. This stylish space filled with contemporary furniture packs in the lunchtime business crowd, but is also a good place for visitors to sample the best cuts of Alberta beef, which is flash-seared at super-high temperatures to seal in the juices.

The food at **Buzzard's Restaurant & Bar** (140 10th Ave., 403/264-6959, Mon.-Fri. 11 A.M.-11 P.M., Sat. 5-11 P.M., $21-26) doesn't come close to competing with the above two steakhouses, but that's not why I've included it. Buzzard's is fun. It's what everyone wants to think Calgary used to be like, but is about as authentic as downtown bankers wearing blue jeans for Stampede. Choices range from bison burgers to elk striploin, and it wouldn't be a complete meal at Buzzard's without sharing a platter of prairie oysters to start.

Asian

Chinatown, along 2nd and 3rd Avenues east of Centre Street, naturally has the best assortment of Chinese restaurants. **Hang Fung Restaurant** (119 3rd Ave. SE, 403/269-4646, daily for lunch and dinner, $7–13), tucked behind a Chinese grocery store of the same name, doesn't try to be anything it's not. Chinese locals come here for simple inexpensive meals, mostly under $10. Just as inexpensive is **Golden Inn Restaurant** (107 2nd Ave. SE, 403/269-2211, daily from 4 P.M., $9–16), which is popular with the local Chinese as well as with professionals, and late-shift workers appreciate its long hours (open until 4 A.M.). The menu features mostly Cantonese-style deep-fried food.

Yuzuki Japanese Restaurant (510 9th Ave. SW, 403/261-7701, weekdays for lunch, daily for dinner, $13–19) is a good downtown eatery where the most expensive lunch item is the assorted sushi for $16, which comes with miso soup. More upscale is **Sushi Hiro** (727 5th Ave. SW, 403/233-0605, Mon.–Fri. 11:30 A.M.–2 P.M., Mon.–Sat. 5–11 P.M., $12–21). If you sit at the oak-and-green-marble sushi counter, you'll be able to ask the chef what's best.

Tucked away across the railway tracks from downtown is ◖ **Thai Sa-On** (351 10th Ave. SW, 403/264-3526, dinner nightly, $11–17), a small space that's big on the tastes of Thailand. The menu offers a great variety of red and green curries, but I tried the red snapper—medium spiced, baked, and served whole—and couldn't have been happier. The prices? For downtown dining, the food is ridiculously inexpensive, with a whole steamed fish with garlic-lime sauce costing just $16.

KENSINGTON

Across the Bow River from downtown lies the trendy suburb of Kensington and **Higher Ground** (1126 Kensington Rd. NW, 403/270-3780, Mon.–Fri. 7 A.M.–10 P.M., Sat 8 A.M.–midnight, Sun. 8 A.M.–11 P.M.), a specialty coffee shop with a few window-front tables and wireless Internet.

The casual, two-story ◖ **Pulcinella** (1147 Kensington Crescent NW, 403/283-1166, Mon.–Sat. 11:30 A.M.–2:30 P.M. and 5–11 P.M., Sun. 4–10 P.M., $12–24) has the most traditional pizza you will find in Canada, right down to an oven constructed of stone imported from the slopes of Mount Vesuvius. Pizzas have perfectly formed crusts and chunky ingredients, many of which have been imported from the mother country.

Sultan's Tent (4 14th St., 403/244-2333, Mon.–Sat. 5–11 P.M., $18–28.50) features swinging lanterns, richly colored tapestries hanging from the walls, piped-in Arabic music, and, most important, delicious Moroccan delicacies. If you're hungry, try the Sultan's Feast ($51), a five-course dinner.

A few blocks toward the city, Kensington's busiest intersection offers a bunch of eateries, including another Italian restaurant, **Osteria de Medici** (201 10th St. NW, 403/283-5553, Mon.–Sat. 11 A.M.–11 P.M., Sun. 4–10 P.M., $17–31). Although still traditional, the atmosphere is more refined and the menu more adventurous than Pulcinella, but service is friendly and prices not as high as they could be.

UPTOWN 17TH AVENUE

The area immediately south of downtown offers a diverse choice of dining options. The major concentrations of restaurants are along 17th Avenue SW as well as south for a couple of blocks along 4th Street. For gourmet coffees, hot chocolate made with locally made Bernard Callebaut chocolate, and exotic teas, join the crowds at **Café Beano** (1613 9th St. SW, 403/229-1232, daily 7 A.M.–11 P.M.).

Breakfast

◖ **Nellie's Kitchen** (738 17th Avenue SW, 403/244-4616, Mon.–Fri. 7:30 A.M.–3:30 P.M., Sat.–Sun. 8:30 A.M.–3:30 P.M., breakfasts $8–11), in the heart of Calgary's trendiest dining strip, is a pleasant surprise. It's a small, outwardly low-key place with a big reputation (so much so that it's now one of five Nellie's restaurants in the city). Service is fast and efficient and, most importantly, the food's great. Breakfasts claim the spotlight—if you're hungry, don't bother with the menu, just order the Belly Buster.

The **Galaxy Diner** (1413 11th St. SW, 403/228-0001, Mon.–Fri. 7 A.M.–3 P.M., Sat.–Sun. 7 A.M.–4 P.M.) is an original 1950s diner where cooked breakfasts start at $7.50, including bottomless coffee and a second serving of hash browns.

Canadian

Typifying the modern wave of slow food is **❰ FARM** (1006 17th Ave. SW, 403/245-2276, daily 11:30 A.M.–2 P.M. and from 5 P.M., $9–21), where the emphasis is on local, seasonal ingredients prepared in simple and tasty ways. Many diners concentrate on the meats and cheeses listed on a large chalkboard hanging on the back wall before moving onto house specialties such as killer BLT salad. The room itself is appealing, with stools along the open kitchen allowing diners to watch their meals being prepared by the friendly kitchen staff.

Formerly a brewpub, **Wildwood Grill** (2417 4th St., 402/228-0100, daily for lunch and dinner, $18–36) has evolved into a respected restaurant serving up a wide selection of Canadian cuisine in a modern mountain setting. Think leek and sweet corn soup or bison carpaccio as starters and grilled medallions of elk loin with spiced chocolate sauce for a main. In the adjacent pub, bring back childhood memories with a meatloaf ($15) that substitutes veal for beef.

European

Few restaurants in the city are as popular as **❰ Chianti** (1438 17th Ave. SW, 403/229-1600, Mon.–Fri. for lunch, daily for dinner, $10–20). More than 20 well-prepared pasta dishes are featured on the menu, and all of the pasta is made daily on the premises. Among many specialties are an antipasto platter and *salmone cappesante,* baked salmon with scallops and mango in a creamy coconut and curry sauce. Most regular pasta entrées are less than $12. The restaurant is dark and noisy in typical

For fresh, innovative cooking, make reservations at FARM.

Italian style. The owner often sings with an accordionist on weekends.

La Chaumiere (139 17th Ave. SW, 403/228-5690, Mon.–Fri. 11:45 A.M.–2:30 P.M. and Mon.–Sat. from 5:45 P.M., dinner reservations required, $26–36.50) occupies an elaborate space east of the main restaurant strip. Generally regarded as one of North America's premier French restaurants, diners here enjoy combinations like lobster bisque and roasted rack of Alberta lamb. The formal service is meticulous.

Information and Services

Information Centers

Tourism Calgary (403/263-8510 or 800/661-1678, www.tourismcalgary.com) promotes the city to the world. The organization also operates two Visitor Information Centres. The one that greets visitors arriving by air is across from Carousel 4 at **Calgary International Airport** (403/735-1234, year-round, daily 6 A.M.–11 P.M.). The other is right downtown, at the base of the **Calgary Tower** (101 9th Ave. SW, 403/750-2362, daily in summer 8 A.M.–8 P.M., the rest of the year Mon.–Fri. 8:30 A.M.–4:30 P.M.).

Libraries

The Calgary Public Library Board's 18 branch libraries are scattered throughout the city. The largest is **W. R. Castell Central Library** (616 Macleod Trail SE, 403/260-2600, www.calgarypubliclibrary.com, Mon.–Thurs. 9 A.M.–8 P.M., Fri. 9 A.M.–5 P.M., Sat. 10 A.M.–5 P.M., Sun. noon–5 P.M.). Four floors of books, magazines, and newspapers from around the world are enough to keep most people busy on a rainy afternoon.

Post and Internet

The downtown post office is at 207 9th Avenue SW. All city libraries provide free Internet access, while all downtown hotels have either wireless or modem Internet access. Alternatively, head to **Hard Disk Cafe** (638 11th Ave. SW, 403/261-5686, daily 7 A.M.–7 P.M.) for some online surfing.

Banks

Calforex, in the Lancaster Building (304 8th Ave. SW, 403/290-0330), exchanges foreign currency and lets you wire international payments. Most major banks carry U.S. currency and can handle basic foreign-exchange transactions.

Photography

I've been trusting my photographic needs to **The Camera Store** (802 11th Ave. SW, 403/234-9935, Mon.–Fri. 8 A.M.–5:30 P.M., Sat. 9 A.M.–5 P.M.) for many years. They have knowledgeable service and sales divisions, with the latter up to speed on the latest digital and video technology.

Laundry

Handy self-service launderettes are **14th Street Coin Laundry** (1211 14th St. SW, 403/541-1636, daily 7 A.M.–11 P.M.), which has washers big enough to handle sleeping bags and blankets, and **Heritage Hill Coin Laundry** (156-8228 MacLeod Trail SE, 403/258-3946).

Emergency Services

For medical emergencies, call 911 or contact **Foothills Hospital** (1403 29th Ave. NW, 403/670-1110) or **Rockyview General Hospital** (7007 14th St. SW, 403/943-3000). Opened in late 2006 across 16th Avenue from Foothills Hospital, the **Alberta Children's Hospital** (2888 Shaganappi Trail NW, 403/955-7211) is difficult to miss with its colorfully modern exterior. For the **Calgary Police,** call 911 in an emergency or 403/266-1234 for non-urgent matters.

Getting There and Around

GETTING THERE

Air

Calgary International Airport (airport code YYC; www.calgaryairport.com) is within the city limits northeast of downtown. It is served by more than a dozen scheduled airlines and used by seven million passengers each year (Canada's fourth-busiest airport). Arrivals is on the lower level, where passengers are greeted by White Hat volunteers who are dressed in traditional Western attire and answer visitors' questions about the airport, transportation, and the city. Across from the baggage carousels is an information desk and a bank of interactive computer terminals linked to hotels and other tourist services. The desks for all major rental-car outlets are across the road.

A cab to downtown runs approximately $40, or take the **Allied Airport Shuttle** (403/299-9555, www.airportshuttlecalgary.com) to major downtown hotels for adult $15, child $10 one-way. This service runs every 30 minutes daily 8 A.M.–midnight.

For details of airlines flying into Calgary, click through the links on the airport website.

Bus

The **Greyhound** bus depot (850 16th St. SW, 403/265-9111 or 800/661-8747, www.greyhound.ca) is two blocks away from the C-train stop ($2 into town), or you can cross the overhead pedestrian bridge at the terminal's southern entrance and catch a transit bus. A cab from the bus depot to downtown runs $12, to HI–Calgary City Centre $15. Greyhound buses connect Calgary daily with Edmonton (3.5 hours), Banff (two hours), Vancouver (15 hours), and all other points within the province.

From their offices near the Calgary Tower, **Red Arrow** (205 9th Ave. SE, 403/531-0350, www.redarrow.ca) shuttles passengers between Calgary and downtown Edmonton, with some services continuing to Fort McMurray in northern Alberta.

GETTING AROUND

Like major cities around the world, locals complain about the road system, but in reality, driving is relatively uncomplicated, especially as new sections of the long-awaited ring road are completed.

Calgary Transit

Calgary Transit (403/262-1000, www.calgarytransit.com) goes just about everywhere in town by combining light-rail lines with extensive bus routes. **C-trains** run along the two rail lines totaling 40 kilometers (25 mi) of track and 36 stations. Both converge on 7th Avenue, running parallel for the entire distance through downtown. One-way bus and rail tickets are adult $2.50, child $1.75—deposit the exact change in the box beside the driver and request a transfer (valid for 90 minutes). A day pass, which is valid for unlimited bus and rail travel, is adult $7.50, child $5.25. The best place for information and schedules is the **Calgary Transit Customer Service Centre** (244 7th Ave. SW, Mon.–Fri. 10 A.M.–5 P.M.).

All C-trains and stations are wheelchair accessible. Low-floor buses are employed on many bus routes; call ahead for a schedule. **Calgary Handi-bus** (403/537-7770, www.calgaryhandibus.com) provides wheelchair-accessible transportation throughout the city.

Taxi

The flag charge for a cab in Calgary is $3.40, and it's around $1.40 for every kilometer. Taxi companies include **Advance** (403/777-1111), **Associated Cabs** (403/299-1111), **Checker/Yellow Cabs** (403/299-9999), and **Mayfair** (403/255-6555).

Car Rental

If you're planning on starting your Alberta travels from Calgary and need a rental car, make reservations as far in advance as possible to secure the best rates. Rentals beginning from the airport incur additional charges, so consider renting from downtown or one of the many hotels that have representatives based in their lobbies.

Rental agencies and their local numbers include: **Avis** (403/269-6166), **Budget** (403/226-1550), **Discount** (403/299-1224), **Economy** (403/291-1640), **Enterprise** (403/263-1273), **Hertz** (403/221-1676), **National** (403/221-1690), **Rent-a-Wreck** (403/287-9703), and **Thrifty** (403/262-4400).

Dinosaur Valley

The most worthwhile non-mountain day trip from Calgary is to Dinosaur Valley, a 90-minute drive from city limits. Centered on the Red Deer River, a 120-kilometer (75-mile) stretch of the river valley is home to some of the world's richest dinosaur fossil beds. Hundreds of specimens from the Cretaceous period have been unearthed, with one spot, Dinosaur Provincial Park, the mother lode for paleontologists. This UNESCO World Heritage Site includes a "graveyard" of more than 300 dinosaurs of 35 species, many of which have been found nowhere else in the world. As a comparison, Utah's Dinosaur National Monument has yielded just 12 species. The valley has more than just dinosaur skeletons, though; paleontologists have unearthed skin impressions, eggshells, dung, and footprints, as well as fossilized insects, fish, amphibians, crocodiles, pterodactyls, and reptiles. And the valley's landforms are as enthralling as the prehistoric artifacts they entomb—spectacular badland formations make for a sight not easily forgotten.

DRUMHELLER

The small city of Drumheller (population 8,000) is set in a spectacular lunar-like landscape in the Red Deer River Valley 138 kilometers (86 miles) northeast of Calgary. Paleontologists from around the globe come to

© ANDREW HEMPSTEAD

Drumheller is renowned for its dinosaur-related attractions.

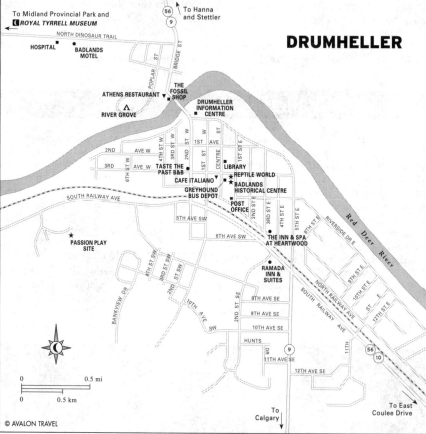

Drumheller and its environs to learn more about the prehistoric animals that roamed the earth millions of years ago. For tourists, the Royal Tyrrell Museum is definitely the highlight of a visit to Drumheller, but there are many other diversions along the valley. Downtown itself is a little rough around the edges, but has been bought to life in recent years with the addition of dinosaur sculptures and murals.

Royal Tyrrell Museum

So many of the world's great museums are simply showcases for natural history, yet nestled in the badlands six kilometers (3.7 mi) northwest

of Drumheller, the Royal Tyrrell Museum (North Dinosaur Trail, 403/823-7707 or 888/440-4240, www.tyrrellmuseum.com, mid-May–Aug. daily 9 A.M.–9 P.M., the rest of the year Tues.–Sun. 10 A.M.–5 P.M., adult $10, senior $8, youth $6, under six free), the world's largest museum devoted entirely to paleontology, is a lot more. It integrates display areas with fieldwork done literally on the doorstep (it lies close by that first "official" discovery), with specimens transported to the museum for research and cataloging. Even for those visitors with little or no interest in dinosaurs, it's easy to spend half a day in the massive complex. The

THE GREAT DINOSAUR RUSH

For generations, natives had regarded the ancient bones that were always common in the valley as belonging to giant buffalo. During early geographical surveys of southern Alberta by George Mercer Dawson, the first official dinosaur discovery was recorded. In 1884, one of Dawson's assistants, Joseph Burr Tyrrell, collected and sent specimen bones to Ottawa for scientific investigation. Their identification initiated the first real dinosaur rush. For the first century of digging, all of the dinosaur bones uncovered were transported to museums around the world for further study. Just more than 100 years after Tyrrell's discovery, a magnificent museum bearing his name opened in the valley. The idea of the museum was promoted by dinosaur hunter Dr. Phil Currie, and since its opening, the dinosaurs have stayed and the tourists have come.

and full-size replicas of dinosaurs are backed by realistic dioramas of their habitat. Another feature is the two-story paleoconservatory, featuring more than 100 species of plants, many of which flourished during the period when dinosaurs roamed the earth. Nearing the end of the tour, the various theories for the cause of the dinosaurs' extinction approximately 64 million years ago are presented. The coming of the ice ages is described in detail, and humanity's appearance on Earth is put into perspective.

The museum is also a major research center; a large window into the main preparation laboratory allows you to view the delicate work of technicians as they clear the rock away from newly unearthed bones.

Other Dinosaur Distractions

Start your downtown Drumheller touring by making your way to the visitor center, at the north end of 2nd Street W and signposted along all approaches. It's impossible to miss—out front is the world's largest dinosaur (403/823-8100, July–Aug. daily 9 A.M.–9 P.M., Sept.–June daily 10 A.M.–5:30 P.M., adult $2, children under five free). An actual *Tyrannosaurus rex* would have been intimidating enough towering over its fellow creatures millions of years ago. But this one is even bigger—at 26 meters (85 feet) high, it is four times as big as the real thing. A flight of stairs leads up to a viewpoint in its open mouth. Also downtown, the **Badlands Historical Centre** (335 1st St. E, 403/823-2593, May–Sept. daily 10 A.M.–6 P.M., adult $5) is a small museum with an interesting display of privately owned and donated prehistoric pieces, most of which have been collected from the Red Deer River Valley.

Along North Dinosaur Trail is **Fossil World** (1381 North Dinosaur Trail, 403/823-4333, summer daily 9:30 A.M.–7 P.M., the rest of the year daily 10 A.M.–5 P.M.) is a modern indoor attraction anchored by a life-size animated Tyrannosaurus rex. The seven-meter-long (21-foot) creature towers above the display room, with eyes that blink, a chest that contracts, and even a wagging tail. A number of interesting fossils are on display and for kids, there's also a

museum holds more than 80,000 specimens, including 50 full-size dinosaur skeletons—the world's largest such display.

The adventure starts as soon as you enter the facility, with a group of life-sized Albertosaurus dinosaurs in a Cretaceous setting to welcome you. Beyond the lobby is a massive, slowly-revolving model of the earth set against a starry night—a perfect introduction to this planet's place in the universe. Beyond the globe, a "timeline" of exhibits covers 3.8 billion years of life on this planet, beginning with early life forms and the development of Charles Darwin's theory of evolution. Before the age of the dinosaurs, the Precambrian and Paleozoic eras saw life on Earth develop at an amazing rate. These periods are cataloged through numerous displays, such as the one of British Columbia's Burgess Shale, where circumstances allowed the fossilization of a community of soft-bodied marine creatures 530 million years ago. But the museum's showpiece is Dinosaur Hall, a vast open area where reconstructed skeletons

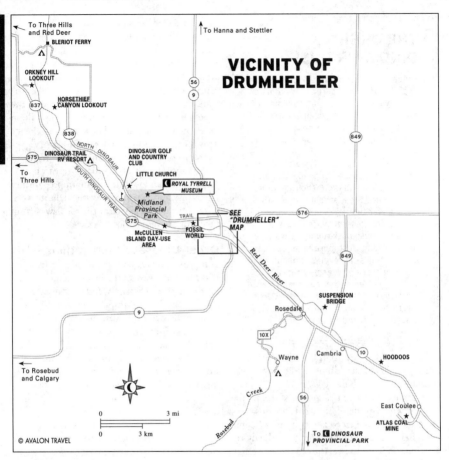

VICINITY OF
DRUMHELLER

climbing wall, dinosaur-themed play area, and the chance to dig for (and keep) a fossil. General admission for everyone aged four or more is $5, or pay $22 for admission and all activities.

Scenic Drives

The **Dinosaur Trail** is a 56-kilometer (35-mile) circular route to the west of Drumheller. From downtown, head out toward the museum, passing **Midland Provincial Park,** where buildings from the coal mining era remain and an island in the Red Deer River is home to a day-use area shaded by willows and cottonwoods. Beyond the Royal Tyrrell Museum, the road climbs steeply

out of the valley onto the prairie benchland. Take the first access road on the left—it doubles back to **Horsethief Canyon Lookout,** where you can catch spectacular views of the badlands and the multicolored walls of the canyons. Slip, slide, or somersault down the embankment here into the mysterious lunar-like landscape, and it's easy to imagine why early explorers were so intrigued by the valley and how easy it was for thieves to hide stolen horses along the coulees in the early 1900s. The halfway point of the trail is the crossing of the Red Deer River on the eight-vehicle **Bleriot Ferry** (8 A.M.–10:40 P.M. Apr.–Nov.), one of the few remaining cable ferries in Alberta. The road continues along the top of the valley to **Orkney Hill Lookout** for more panoramic views across the badlands and the lush valley floor.

The 25-kilometer (15.5-mile) **East Coulee Drive,** southeast from Drumheller, passes three historic coal-mining communities in an area dotted with mine shafts and abandoned buildings. The first town along this route is **Rosedale,** from where a suspension bridge leads across the river to an abandoned mine site. A worthwhile detour from Rosedale is to **Wayne,** an almost–ghost town tucked up a valley alongside Rosebud Creek. It is nine kilometers (5.6 miles) south along Highway 10X, which crosses the creek 11 times. In its heyday early in the 20th century, Wayne had 1,500 residents, most of whom worked in the Rosedeer Mine. By the time the mine closed in 1962, the population had dipped to 250 and then to as low as 15 in the early 1990s, but now the population stands at approximately 30. Many old buildings remain, making it a popular setting for film crews. The oldest operating business in the sleepy hamlet is the 1913 **Rosedeer Hotel** (403/823-9189) and its **Last Chance Saloon,** where the walls are lined with memorabilia from the town's glory days. It opens daily at noon, just in time for a lunchtime buffalo burger. The hotel's back porch overlooking the creek is a great place to sip on a beer and wallow in nostalgia. From Rosedale, Highway 10 continues southeast, passing **hoodoos** to the left. These strangely shaped rock formations along the river valley have been carved by eons of wind and rain. The harder rock on top is more resistant to erosion than the rock beneath it, resulting in the odd, mushroom-shaped pillars. At East Coulee, the **Atlas Coal Mine** (403/823-2220, May–June daily 9:30 A.M.–5:30 P.M., July–Aug. daily 9:30 A.M.–8:30 P.M., Sept.–mid-Oct. daily 10 A.M.–5 P.M., $7, tours $9–12 include admission) protects Canada's only remaining wooden ore-sorting tipple.

Performing Arts

At the hamlet of **Rosebud,** 35 kilometers (22 miles) southwest of Drumheller, students in residence showcase their performance skills at the **Rosebud Theatre** (403/677-2001 or 800/267-7553, www.rosebudtheatre.com). The

fun actually starts across the road from the theater in the restored Mercantile Building, where the actors and actresses serve up a buffet meal. Then everyone heads over to the 220-seat theater for a lively production, always lighthearted and often with a rural theme. Check the website for a schedule.

The **Canadian Badlands Passion Play** (17th Street, 403/823-2001, adult $32, child $15) is a theatrical production of the life of Jesus Christ. The three-hour production is an ambitious affair, with a cast of hundreds in a natural outdoor amphitheater with bench seating for 2,500 set among the badlands. It takes place six times through the month of July.

Accommodations

Despite its popularity as a tourist attraction, Drumheller has a limited number of accommodations. Therefore, unless you're planning a day trip from Calgary, make reservations in advance.

Right on the main thoroughfare through downtown, **Taste the Past B&B** (281 2nd St. W, 403/823-5889, $95 s, $115 d) occupies the 100-year-old home of a coal baron. Guests choose between three simple rooms, but no one chooses to miss the full-cooked breakfast served in the sunny dining room. Period furnishings decorate public areas, including the living room, which is laid out around a fireplace. Outside, the well-tended garden is dotted with fossils.

Within walking distance of downtown is █ **The Inn & Spa at Heartwood** (320 Railway Ave. East, 403/823-6495 or 888/823-6495, www.innsatheartwood.com, $149–309 s or d), a classic country inn that looks a little out of place surrounded by older homes. You can splurge on the Main Turret room with a carriage bed, a fireplace, a jetted tub, and separate sitting area. Or choose one of eight other rooms, all with a cozy Victorian feel thanks to antiques and plush duvets. All rooms have en suites, but only some have televisions and phones. Rates include breakfast.

Ramada Inn & Suites (680 2nd St., 403/823-2028 or 800/272-6232, $149–249 s or d) is at Drumheller's busiest intersection. The 74 rooms are each equipped with a small fridge and a microwave. Rates include a light breakfast and use of the indoor pool, waterslide, fitness room, and hot tub.

Camping

Plenty of choices here, but reservations should still be made as far in advance as possible.

A personal favorite is **(Dinosaur Trail RV Resort** (11 km/7 mi along North Dinosaur Trail, 403/823-9333, www.holidaytrailsresorts.com, May–Sept., $31–48), an oasis of green between the river and the badlands five kilometers (3.1 mi) beyond the Tyrrell Museum. Activities include river floats, fishing, cooling off in the outdoor pool, or exploring the adjacent badlands on foot. Other facilities include horseshoe pits, a playground, a grocery store, and a laundry.

Back toward Drumheller, **River Grove Campground** (25 Poplar St., 403/823-6655, May–Sept., tent sites $25, hookups $29–36) is in a well-treed spot beside the Red Deer River and also offers welcome relief from the heat of the badlands. Serviced sites are semiprivate; tenters have more options and are able to disappear among the trees. The campground offers a nice stretch of sandy beach (by Albertan standards), mini-golf, and an arcade; and town is just a short stroll away.

At the end of the Dinosaur Trail is **Bleriot Ferry Provincial Recreation Area** ($15) with 28 sites, plenty of free firewood, a kitchen shelter, and a small beach on the river.

Food

Like the accommodation scene, finding a restaurant in Drumheller is easy enough; finding a place you'll leave saying "that was a good meal" is a different matter. The cafeteria at the **Royal Tyrell Museum** (North Dinosaur Trail, 403/823-7707, mid-May–Aug. daily 9 A.M.–6 P.M., the rest of the year Tues.–Sun. 10 A.M.–3:30 P.M.) is one of the better spots to enjoy lunch, especially sitting on the patio on a sunny day.

At the Badlands Motel, out toward the museum, **Whif's Flapjack House** (801 N.

Dinosaur Trail, 403/823-7595, 6 A.M.–2 P.M.) serves up a continuous flow of pancakes ($5–8) from when the doors first open each morning.

Downtown, **Café Italiano** (35 3rd Ave. W, 403/823-4443, Mon.–Fri. 7 A.M.–5 P.M., Sat. 9 A.M.–5 P.M., lunches $5–9) pours the best coffee in town. Also on offer are paninis, salads, and homemade desserts.

Athens Restaurant (71 Bridge St. N, 403/823-9400, Mon.–Sat. 4–9 P.M., $16–25) has been around for decades. Although the service is not overly friendly the food is decent. The house specialty is *kleftiko* (spring lamb baked with herbs and spices); have it with the Greek salad for the full effect.

Information and Services

Drumheller Information Centre is in the local chamber of commerce building beside the Red Deer River at the corner of Riverside Drive and 2nd Street W (403/823-8100 or 866/823-3100, www.traveldrumheller.com, daily 9 A.M.–6 P.M., until 9 P.M. Fri. and Sat. in summer). You can't miss it—look for the seven-story *Tyrannosaurus rex* in front.

Drumheller Public Library (224 Centre Street, 403/823-5382, Tues.–Thurs. 11 A.M.–8 P.M., Fri. and Sat. 11 A.M.–5 P.M., Sun. 1–5 P.M.) has public Internet access.

The **post office** is at 96 Railway Avenue E. You can wash your dusty clothes at the **launderette** in the Esso gas station on Highway 9 on the south side of town. It's open until 8 P.M. **Drumheller Hospital** is across the river from downtown at 351 9th St. NW (403/823-6500).

(DINOSAUR PROVINCIAL PARK

Now that you've been through the Royal Tyrrell Museum, you'll want to get out in the field and explore the area where many of the dinosaurs have been unearthed. This region is protected by 7,330-hectare (18,000-acre) Dinosaur Provincial Park, 120 kilometers (75 miles) downstream of Drumheller. It's possible to get there by road from Drumheller—east on

Highway 570 then south on Highway 36—but, from Calgary, the direct route is 200 kilometers (125 miles) east along Highway 1.

Thirty-five species of dinosaurs—from every known family of the Cretaceous period—have been unearthed here, along with the skeletal remains of crocodiles, turtles, fish, lizards, frogs, and flying reptiles. Not only is the diversity of specimens great, but so is the sheer volume; more than 300 museum-quality specimens have been removed and are exhibited in museums around the world. Originally established in 1955 to protect the fossil bone beds, the park's environment is extremely complex and is unique within the surrounding prairie ecosystem. Stands of cottonwoods, a variety of animal life, and, most important, the extensive bone beds, were instrumental in UNESCO's designation of the park as a World Heritage Site in 1979. The Royal Tyrrell Museum operates a field station in the park, where many of the bones are cataloged and stored.

Fieldwork in the Park

Each summer, paleontologists from around the world converge on the park for an intense period of digging that starts in late June and lasts for approximately 10 weeks. The earliest dinosaur hunters simply excavated whole or partial skeletons for museum display. Although the basic excavation methods haven't changed, the types of excavation have. "Bonebeds" of up to one hectare are painstakingly excavated over multiple summers. Access to much of the park is restricted in order to protect the fossil beds. Digging takes place within the restricted areas. Work is often continued from the previous season, or commences on new sites, but

DINOSAURS OF ALBERTA

Dinosaur bones found in the Red Deer River Valley play an important role in the understanding of our prehistoric past. The bones date from the late Cretaceous period, around 70 million years ago, when the area was a low-lying subtropical forest at the mouth of a river flowing into the ocean – and dinosaurs flourished.

Around this time, great quantities of silt and mud were flushed downriver, building up a delta at the edge of the sea. In time, this delta hardened, and the countless layers formed sedimentary rock, trapping the remains of fallen dinosaurs. As the Red Deer River curves through central Alberta, it cuts deeply into the ancient river delta, exposing the layers of sedimentary rock and revealing the once-buried fossil treasures.

The bones of 35 dinosaur species – around 10 percent of all those currently known – have been discovered in Alberta. Like today's living creatures, they are classified in orders, families, and species. Of the two orders of dinosaurs, both have been found in the Red Deer River Valley. The bird-hipped dinosaurs (order Ornithischia) were herbivores, while the lizard-

hipped dinosaurs (order Saurischia) were omnivores and carnivores.

Apart from their sheer bulk, many herbivores lacked any real defenses. Others developed their own protection; the chasmosaurus had a bony frill around its neck, the pachycephalosaurus had a 25-centimeter-thick (10-inch-thick) dome-shaped skull cap fringed with spikes, and the ankylosaurus was an armored dinosaur whose back was covered in spiked plates.

Among the most common herbivores that have been found in the valley are members of the family of duck-billed hadrosaurs. Fossilized eggs of one hadrosaur, the hypacrosaurus, were unearthed still encasing intact embryos. Another common herbivore in the valley was a member of the horned ceratops family; more than 300 specimens of the centrosaurus have been discovered in one "graveyard."

Of the lizard-hipped dinosaurs, the tyrannosaurs were most feared by herbivores. The 15-meter (49-foot) *Tyrannosaurus rex* is most famous among *Homo sapiens*, but the smaller albertosaurus, a remarkably agile carnivore weighing many tons, was the most common tyrannosaur found in the valley.

there's never a lack of bones. New finds are often discovered with little digging, having been exposed by wind and rain since the previous season.

Excavating the bones is an extremely tedious procedure; therefore, only a few sites are worked on at a time, with preference given to particularly important finds such as a new species. Getting the bones out of the ground is only the beginning of a long process that culminates with their scientific analysis and display by experts at museums around the world.

Visitors Center

Your first stop should be the Dinosaur Park Visitor Centre (403/378-4342, Apr.–mid-May daily 9 A.M.–4 P.M., mid-May–Aug. daily 8:30 A.M.–7 P.M., Sept. 9 A.M.–4:30 P.M., the rest of the year weekdays 9 A.M.–4 P.M., adult $3, senior $2.50, child $2), which is a field station associated with the Royal Tyrrell Museum. It offers many interesting displays that provide an overview of the park, its natural history, and the dinosaurs contained within. Complete dinosaur skeletons, a reconstructed 1914 paleontologist field camp, and a dinosaur documentary are highlights.

Interpretive Tours

To make the most of your time in the park, you will want to join one of the park's daily tours. Not only do the guides provide an insight into the area, but some of the tours concentrate on the natural preserve where unguided public access is not allowed. The tours are *very* popular, and this is reflected in the procedure for purchasing tickets. Advance tickets (adult $8, child $4) go on sale May 1 and must be picked up 30 minutes before the departure time. To reserve a seat, click through the Reservations link at www.tpr.alberta.ca/parks/dinosaur or call 403/378-4344. A small percentage of places on each tour are sold the day of as Rush tickets (adult $6.50, child $4.50); be at the visitor center when it opens at 8:30 A.M. to ensure that you get a ticket. Finally, if seats become available through no-shows, you may be able to snag a seat at the last minute. An overview

of the tours follows, or check www.tpr.alberta.ca/parks/dinosaur for a schedule.

The **Badlands Bus Tour** takes you on a two-hour ride around the public loop road with an interpretive guide who will point out the park's landforms and talk about its prehistoric inhabitants. The **Centrosaurus Bone Bed Hike** takes visitors on a 2.5-hour guided hike into a restricted area where more than 300 centrosaurus skeletons have been identified. The **Camel's End Coulee Hike** is an easy 2.5-kilometer (1.5-mi) guided walk to discover the unique flora and fauna of the badlands. Best suited for families with younger children is the **Fossil Safari Hike** to a dig site. Finally, the **Lab Talk** is a 40-minute behind-the-scenes look at the visitor center. This is the only tour that doesn't require reservations; adult $4, child $2.

Documentaries are shown at the visitor center in the evenings, and special events are often staged somewhere in the park. The entire interpretive program operates June–August, with certain tours offered in late May and September.

Exploring the Park on Your Own

Much of the park is protected as a Natural Preserve and is off-limits to unguided visitors. The Natural Preserve protects the bone beds and the valley's fragile environment. It also keeps visitors from becoming disoriented in the uniform landscape and ending up spending the night among the bobcats and rattlesnakes. The area is well marked and should not be entered except on a guided tour. One other important rule: *Surface-collecting and digging for bones anywhere within the park is prohibited.*

You may explore the area bounded by the public loop road and take three short interpretive trails on your own. The **loop road** passes through part of the area where bones were removed during the Great Canadian Dinosaur Rush. By staying within its limits, hikers are prevented from becoming lost, although the classic badlands terrain is still littered with fragments of bones, and the area is large enough to make you feel "lost in time." It's a fantastic place to explore. Of special interest are two dinosaur dig sites excavated earlier this century, one of which contains a still-intact skeleton of a duck-billed hadrosaur.

The **Badlands Trail** is a 1.3-kilometer (0.8-mile) loop that starts just east of the campground and passes into the restricted area. The **Coulee Viewpoint Trail,** which begins behind the Field Station, climbs steadily for 500 meters (1,650 feet) to a high ridge above Little Sandhill Creek. This one-kilometer (0.6-mile) trail takes 20 minutes. It's easy to ignore the nearby floodplains, but the large stands of cottonwoods you'll see were a contributing factor to the park being designated as a UNESCO World Heritage Site. The **Cottonwood Flats Trail** starts 1.4 kilometers (0.9 miles) along the loop road, leading through the trees and into old river channels that lend themselves to good bird-watching. Allow 30 minutes round-trip.

Practicalities

The park's campground is nestled below the badlands beside Little Sandhill Creek. It has 128 sites on 2 loops, pit toilets, a kitchen shelter, and a few powered sites. Unserviced sites cost $20, powered sites $26, and a bundle of firewood is $7. In summer, the campground fills up by early afternoon, so plan ahead by reserving a site (403/378-3700, www.reserve.albertaparks.ca). The only commercial facility within the park is the **Dinosaur Service Centre** (403/378-3777, late May–Aug. daily 10 A.M.–6 P.M.), where you can purchase hot snacks and cold drinks. Within the center are laundry facilities and coin showers, both of which are open 24 hours. No groceries are available in the park.

For information, contact Dinosaur Provincial Park at 403/378-4342, www.tpr.alberta.ca/parks/dinosaur.

BROOKS

The closest mid-sized town to Dinosaur Provincial Park is Brooks (pop. 14,000), 160 kilometers (100 mi) east of Calgary along the TransCanada Highway. Brooks is home to Canada's largest meatpacking plant. The facility employs around 2,500 people, most of them immigrants from places like Sudan and Kenya. This gives Brooks an interesting small-town ethnic diversity unlike anywhere else in Canada.

The 3.2-kilometer-long (two-mile) **Brooks Aqueduct,** seven kilometers (4.3 miles) southeast of town, was completed in 1914 to carry water across a shallow valley to dry prairie on the other side, opening up a massive chunk of otherwise unproductive land to farming. Although now replaced by an earth-filled canal, the impressive structure has been preserved as a National Historic Site and now serves as a monument to those who developed the region.

Also south of town is **Kinbrook Island Provincial Park,** linked to the mainland by a causeway but best known for recreational activities on adjacent Lake Newell, Canada's largest man-made body of water. For visitors, it's swimming, fishing, and boating that draws the summertime crowds. The campground (403/362-2962, unserviced sites $20, powered sites $26) has showers, laundry, firewood sales, and picnic shelters.

West of Calgary

Between the snowcapped peaks of Kananaskis Country and the arid grassland of southern Alberta lies some of North America's best ranching country. From Cochrane in the north, throughout the ranching and farming communities of Okotoks and High River, to the Porcupine Hills northwest of Fort Macleod, these low, rolling hills have been home to many

of western Canada's cowboy heroes and the setting for movies such as the Jackie Chan hit *Shanghai Noon;* the Oscar-winning *Unforgiven,* starring Clint Eastwood; *Legends of the Fall,* starring Brad Pitt; the Kevin Costner western *Open Range;* and most recently the Brad Pitt–driven *The Assassination of Jesse James by the Coward Robert Ford.* Highway 2 follows the eastern flanks of these foothills south from Calgary. Other roads crisscross the region and lead to communities that are rich in heritage, many of which have recently been discovered by artisans and craftspeople who now call them home.

If you have ever dreamed of being a cowboy for a day or a week, this is the place to do it. The area also offers enough museums, teahouses, antique emporiums, and events to keep even the most saddle-sore city slicker busy all summer.

COCHRANE

The foundation of Alberta's cattle industry was laid down here in the 20th century, when Senator Matthew Cochrane established the first of the big leasehold ranches in the province. Today's town of Cochrane, 38 kilometers (24 miles) northwest of downtown Calgary along Highway 1A, has seen its population increase by over 10 percent annually since the mid 1990s, now sitting at over 15,000. Although ranching is still important to the local economy, Cochrane is growing as a "bedroom" suburb of Calgary. The business district, in the older section of town between Highway 1A and the rail line, is a delightful pocket of false-fronted buildings holding cafés, restaurants, and specialty shops.

Sights and Recreation

To prevent the lawlessness that existed across the U.S. West from extending into Canada, the government began granting huge grazing leases across the prairies. One of the original takers was Matthew Cochrane, who established the first real ranch west of Calgary, bringing herds of cattle from Montana to his 76,500-hectare (189,000-acre) holding in 1881. After two harsh winters, he moved his herds south again. A small piece of Cochrane's land holding is now preserved as **Cochrane Ranche Provincial Historic Site.** Almost completely surrounded by development, the 61-hectare (150-acre) site straddles Big Hill Creek one kilometer (0.6 miles) west of downtown along Highway 1A. A short trail leads up to a bluff and Malcolm MacKenzie's *Men of Vision* statue of a rider and his horse looking over the

foothills. An old log cabin by the parking lot is used as an interpretive center (403/932-1193, 9 A.M.–5 P.M. mid-May–Sept.) and picnic tables dot the grounds.

Immerse yourself in the Western lifestyle at **Griffin Valley Ranch** (403/932-7433), one of the few places in Alberta that allows unguided horseback riding. Trails lead through this historic 1,800-hectare (4,500-acre) ranch along creeks, through wooded areas and open meadows, and to high viewpoints where the panorama extends west to the Canadian Rockies. Horse rentals are similarly priced to trail riding (one hour $35, two hours $55, three hours $75); the catch is that at least one member of your party must be a "member" of the ranch (simply sign a waiver and pay the $50 annual fee). To get to the ranch, follow Highway 1A west from Cochrane for 18 kilometers (11 miles), take Highway 40 north, then follow the signs.

Accommodations and Food

You'll find Western-style on a budget at the **Rocky View Hotel** (1st St. and 2nd Ave. W, 403/932-2442, www.rockyviewhotel.com, $55–80 s or d). Rooms are very basic, with shared bathroom facilities and no phones. **Bow River Inn** (Hwy. 22, south of Hwy. 1A, 403/932-7900 or 866/663-3209, www.bowriverinn.com, $89 s or d, kitchenette $129) is a pleasant, reasonably priced motel with a choice of family restaurants within walking distance.

Two kilometers (1.2 miles) south of downtown is **Bow RiversEdge Campground** (900 Griffin Rd., 403/932-4675, www.bowriversedge.com, mid-Apr.–mid-Oct., $35–40), which has a wealth of modern facilities that include Wi-Fi, a playground, and a laundry. **Cochrane Coffee Traders** (114 2nd Ave., 403/932-4395, daily from 7:30 A.M.) is as good as any place to start the day, especially if you snag one of the outdoor tables. Choose from a wide range of specialty coffees and sweet treats, as well as a healthy selection of sandwiches. Back on 1st Street is the two-story wooden-fronted **Rocky View Hotel** (304 1st St. W, 403/932-2442) which houses the **Canyon Rose Restaurant,** a popular all-day dining spot, and the **Stageline Saloon.** Of the many eateries lining Cochrane's downtown 1st Street, the most popular on a hot summer's afternoon is **Mackay's** (403/932-2455), an ice-cream parlor dating to 1948. A blackboard displays up to 50 flavors, but I'm told the favorites are still vanilla, chocolate, and strawberry.

BRAGG CREEK

Bragg Creek is a quiet hamlet nestled in the foothills of the Canadian Rockies, 34 kilometers (21 miles) south of Cochrane. The ideal location and quiet lifestyle have attracted artists and artisans—the town claims to have more painters, potters, sculptors, and weavers than any similarly sized town in Alberta.

Sights

Arriving along Highway 22 from either the north or south, you'll be greeted upon arrival in Bragg Creek by a slightly confusing four-way stop intersection with a treed triangle of land in the middle. Take the option along the north (right) side of the distinctive polished-log Bragg Creek Trading Post II to access the main shopping center, a Western-themed collection of basic town services interspersed with craft shops and cafés. White Avenue, also known as **Heritage Mile** and originally the main commercial strip, has more of the same and leads through an appealing residential area. This road continues southwest to 122-hectare (300-acre) **Bragg Creek Provincial Park,** a day-use area alongside the Elbow River. With a basket of goodies from one of Bragg Creek's many food outlets, leave the main parking lot behind to enjoy a picnic lunch at one of the many riverside picnic tables.

Accommodations and Food

Although lacking motels and campgrounds, Bragg Creek is a popular overnight escape for folks from Calgary. Best of a bunch of bed-and-breakfasts is **High Country House** (call for directions, 403/949-0093, www.high-countryhouse.com, $148–185 s or d), a large, modern house nestled among stands of trees within walking distance of both the river and village. The home has three comfortable guest rooms—two with jetted tubs—a spacious sitting room, and wireless Internet throughout. A healthy cooked or continental breakfast is included in the rates.

Bragg Creek Shopping Centre holds a wide variety of eateries as well as most services, including a gas station, bakery, grocery store, and post office. Around the corner, at the main intersection, is the **Cinnamon Spoon** (Bragg Creek Trading Post II, 403/949-4110, Mon.–Fri. 6 A.M.–5 P.M., Sat.–Sun. 6 A.M.–5 P.M.), with the best coffee in town, as well as pastries, cakes, smoothies, and sandwiches made to order. At the **Steak Pit** (43 White Ave., 403/949-3633, daily from 11:30 A.M., $24–36), the setting is early Canadian, yet elegant. Eating here isn't cheap but *is* comparable to Calgary restaurants. The menu sets out to prove great steaks don't necessitate fancy trimmings, and does so with the best cuts of Alberta beef and great spuds.

Kananaskis Country

During Alberta's oil-and-gas boom of the 1970s, oil revenues collected by the provincial government were channeled into various projects aimed at improving the lifestyle of Albertans. One lasting legacy of the boom is Kananaskis Country (pronounced Can-AN-a-skiss), a sprawling 4,250-square-kilometer (1,640-square-mile) wilderness area west of Calgary that has been developed with an emphasis on providing recreation opportunities for as many people as possible. Although Kananaskis Country lacks the famous lakes and glaciated peaks of Banff and Jasper National Parks, in many ways it rivals them. Wildlife is abundant, and opportunities for observation of larger mammals are superb.

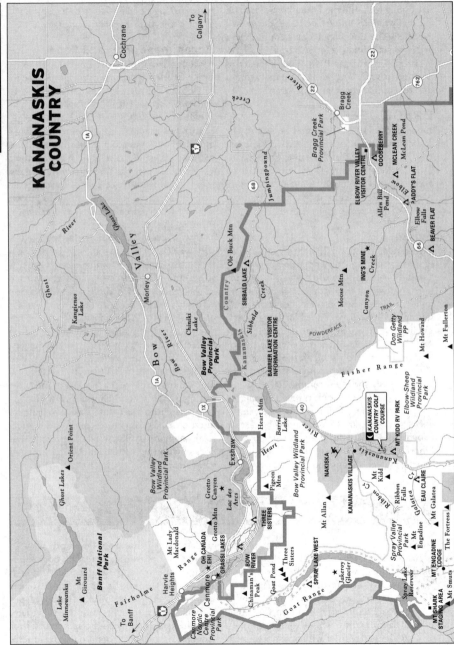

KANANASKIS COUNTRY

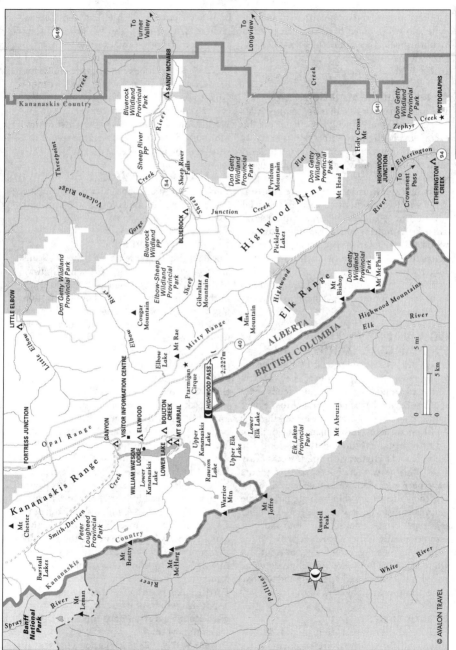

Kananaskis Country

To Turner Valley

To Longview

SANDY MCNABB

549

Bluerock Wildland Provincial Park

Sheep River PP

Sheep River Falls

Don Getty Wildland Provincial Park

541

Don Getty Wildland Provincial Park

Zephyr

PICTOGRAPHS

Creek

Holy Cross Mt

Highwood Mtns

HIGHWOOD JUNCTION

To Crowsnest Pass

Etherington

94

ETHERINGTON CREEK

54

BLUEROCK

Bluerock Wildland PP

Gorge

Pyriform Mountain

Mt Head

Junction Creek

Picklejar Lakes

Elbow-Sheep Wildland Provincial Park

Don Getty Wildland Provincial Park

Mt Bishop

Mt McPhail

Don Getty Wildland Provincial Park

Volcano Ridge

Threepoint

LITTLE ELBOW

Cougar Mountain

Gibraltar Mountain

Sheep

Mt Rae

Misty Range

Mist Mountain

Elk Range

Highwood Mountains

Highwood

Elk

River

River

FORTRESS JUNCTION

Opal Range

Elbow

Elbow Lake

40

2,227m

Ptarmigan Cirque

HIGHWOOD PASS

ALBERTA

BRITISH COLUMBIA

5 mi

5 km

0

0

VISITOR INFORMATION CENTRE

CANYON

ELKWOOD

BOULTON CREEK

MT SARRAIL

Upper Kananaskis Lake

Upper Elk Lake

Lower Elk Lake

Mt Abruzzi

Elk Lakes Provincial Park

WILLIAM WATSON Lodge

LOWER LAKE

Lower Kananaskis Lake

Rawson Lake

Kananaskis Range

Warrior Mtn

Mt Joffre

Russell Peak

Smith-Dorrien

Peter Lougheed Provincial Park

Country

Mt Beatty

Mt McHarg

Pallister

White River

River

Mt Chester

Burstall Lakes

Kananaskis

Mt Leman

River

Spray

Banff National Park

© AVALON TRAVEL

The region has large populations of moose, mule and white-tailed deer, elk, black bears, bighorn sheep, and mountain goats. Wolves, grizzly bears, and cougars are present, too, but are less likely to be seen.

Access and Information

The main access to Kananaskis Country is 80 kilometers (50 miles) west of Calgary off the TransCanada Highway. Other points of access are south from Canmore, at Bragg Creek on the region's east border, or west from Longview in the southeast.

For more information, contact the Tourism, Parks and Recreation office of the provincial government (403/678-5508, www.tpr.alberta.ca/parks). Another good source of information is **Friends of Kananaskis Country** (www.kananaskis.org), a nonprofit organization that advertises educational programs, is involved in a variety of hands-on projects, and promotes Kananaskis Country in partnership with the government.

BOW VALLEY PROVINCIAL PARK

This park, at the north end of Kananaskis Country, sits at the confluence of the Kananaskis and Bow Rivers and extends as far south as Barrier Lake. The entrance to the park is four kilometers (2.5 miles) west of Highway 40 (the main access into Kananaskis Country). To the casual motorist driving along the TransCanada Highway, the park seems fairly small, but more than 300 species of plants have been recorded, and 60 species of birds are known to nest within its boundaries. The abundance of wildflowers, birds, and smaller mammals can be enjoyed along four short interpretive trails. Other popular activities in the park include fishing for a variety of trout and whitefish in the Bow River, bicycling along the paved trail system, and attending interpretive programs presented by park staff.

Practicalities

Facilities at the two park campgrounds, **Willow Rock** and **Bow Valley,** are excellent. They both have showers, flush toilets, and kitchen shelters. Willow Rock also has powered sites and a coin laundry and is open for winter camping. Unserviced sites are $25, powered sites $30. Reservations can be made online for both campgrounds at www.bowvalleycampgrounds.com.

A **visitor information center** (403/673-2163, Mon.–Fri. 8 A.M.–8 P.M. in summer, Mon.–Fri. 8:15 A.M.–4:30 P.M. the rest of the year) is at the park entrance on Highway 1X.

KANANASKIS VALLEY

This is the most developed area of Kananaskis Country, yet summer crowds are minimal compared to Banff.

Sights and Drives

The following sights are along Highway 40 and are detailed from the TransCanada Highway in the north to Peter Lougheed Provincial Park in the south. Your first stop should be **Canoe Meadows,** a large day-use area above the sparkling Kananaskis River. Below the picnic area, white-water enthusiasts use a short stretch of river as a slalom course. Man-made obstacles and gates challenge recreational and racing kayakers, while upstream (around the first bend), the Green Tongue creates a steep wave, allowing kayakers to remain in one spot, spinning and twisting while water rushes past them. South of Canoe Meadows is **Barrier Lake Visitor Information Centre** (403/673-3985, daily 9 A.M.–6 P.M. June–mid-Sept., daily 9 A.M.–4 P.M. the rest of the year). Nestled between Highway 40 and the Kananaskis River, riverside trails lead in both directions, including two kilometers (1.2 miles) downstream to Canoe Meadows. Barrier Lake itself is farther along Highway 40, dominated to the south by the impressive peak of Mount Baldy (2,212 m/7,257 ft). The lake is human-made but still a picture of beauty. From the south end of Barrier Lake, Highway 40 continues south to a spot that will be of particular interest to anglers, **Mount Lorette Ponds,** stocked annually with rainbow trout.

Kananaskis Village lies just off Highway 40

four kilometers (2.5 miles) south of the ponds. The village, the epicenter of action during the 1988 Winter Olympic Games, sits on a high bench below Nakiska—where the downhill events of the games were held—and overlooks a golf course. The village comprises two hotels, restaurants, and other service shops set around a paved courtyard complete with waterfalls and trout-stocked ponds.

From the village, it's 15 kilometers (9.3 miles) farther south to the border of Peter Lougheed Provincial Park. Just beyond the village is **Wedge Pond.** Originally dug as a gravel pit during golf course construction, it is now filled with water and encircled by a one-kilometer (0.6-mile) trail offering fantastic views to towering 2,958-meter (9,700-foot) Mount Kidd.

◖ Kananaskis Country Golf Course

Regularly voted Best Value in North America by *Golf Digest,* this 36-hole layout (403/591-7272 or 877/591-2525, www.kananaskisgolf. com) is bisected by the Kananaskis River and surrounded by magnificent mountain peaks. It comprises two 18-hole courses: **Mount Kidd,** featuring undulating terrain and an island green on the 197-yard fourth hole, and the shorter (which is a relative term—both courses measure over 7,000 yards from the back markers) **Mount Lorette,** where water comes into play on 13 holes. Greens fees are $90 (Albertan residents pay $70) and a cart is an additional $16 per person. Golfers enjoy complimentary valet parking and use of the driving range, as well as a restaurant and bar with awesome mountain views, and a well-stocked golf shop.

Winter Recreation

Nakiska (403/591-7777 or 800/258-7669, www.skinakiska.com) is a state-of-the-art alpine resort built to host the alpine skiing events of the 1988 Winter Olympic Games. Great cruising and fast fall-line skiing on runs cut specially for racing will satisfy the intermediate-to-advanced crowd. The resort has a total of 28 runs and a vertical rise of 735 meters (2,410 feet). Lift tickets are adult $64, senior and youth $54, child $28. Check the website for accommodation packages and transportation schedules from Canmore.

The most accessible of Kananaskis Country's 200 kilometers (124 miles) of cross-country trails are in the Ribbon Creek area. Most heavily used are those radiating from Kananaskis Village and those around the base of Nakiska. Most trails are easy to intermediate, including a five-kilometer (3.1-mile) track up Ribbon Creek. Rentals are available in the Village Trading Post in Kananaskis Village.

Kananaskis Village

Built for the 1988 Winter Olympic Games, Kananaskis Village is home to 412-room **Delta Lodge at Kananaskis** (1 Centennial Road, Kananaskis Village, off of Hwy. 40, 403/591-7711 or 866/432-4322, www.deltahotels.com; from $240 s or d), part of an upscale Canadian hotel chain. It offers three distinct types of rooms in three buildings surrounding a cobbled courtyard. In the main lodge are 251 moderately large Delta rooms, many with mountain views, balconies, and fireplaces. Connected by a covered walkway are 70 Signature Club (a Delta designation) rooms, each boasting elegant Victorian-era charm, a mountain view, a luxurious bathroom complete with bathrobes, oversized beds, and many extras, such as CD players. Guests in this wing also enjoy a private lounge and continental breakfast. Rooms in Mount Kidd Manor combine natural colors with dramatic contemporary styling; some are bedroom lofts with gas fireplaces, kitchenettes, large bathrooms, and sitting rooms. Outdoor seating from various eateries spills into the courtyard and biking and hiking trails radiate out in all directions. All in all, a good place to base yourself for an overnight hotel stay.

The Delta Lodge (403/591-7711) contains three restaurants, a deli, and two bars. For a warm, relaxed atmosphere, head to the **Bighorn Lounge** (daily from 11 A.M.), near the arcade's main entrance. **Obsessions Deli** (daily from 8 A.M.) serves up light snacks, including healthy sandwiches and handmade truffles. Also in the arcade is the **Fireweed Grill** (daily 6 A.M.–10 P.M., $17–31), with a casual Western-style atmosphere, floor-to-ceiling windows, and an adjoining outdoor patio used during summer. **Seasons Steakhouse** (June–Oct. Tues.–Sat. 6–9:30 P.M., $26–39), in the Signature Club wing, is the village's most elegant restaurant.

Other Accommodations and Camping

A magnet for families, the privately owned ◖ **Sundance Lodges** (403/591-7122, www.sundancelodges.com, mid-May–Sept.) is a wonderful option for travelers looking to try camping or who want something a little more adventurous than a regular motel room. Campsites cost $28 per night, with rentals including tents, camp stoves, sleeping bags, and utensil kits available for minimal charge. Next up are the tepees ($57–77), 12 of them, each with colorfully painted canvas walls rising from wooden floors. Inside are mattresses, a heater, and a lantern. Finally, you can stay in one of 18 Trapper Tents ($79 s or d), which are larger but have similar interior fittings and a canvas-covered awning over a picnic table. When you tire of hiking and biking on surrounding trails, return to the lodge for fishing in a man-made pond, horseshoes, badminton, and volleyball. Other amenities include a general store, hot showers, a laundry, and Internet access. Sundance sits beside the Kananaskis River, just off Highway 40, 22 kilometers (13.7 miles) south of the TransCanada Highway.

Mount Kidd RV Park (403/591-7700, www.mountkiddrv.com, unserviced sites $32.50, hookups $41–48, booking fee $8) is a commercial campground along Highway 40 south of Kananaskis Village and the golf course. The campground's showpiece is the Campers Center, containing the main registration area and all the usual bathroom facilities as well as whirlpools, saunas, a wading pool, a game room, a lounge, groceries, a concession area, and a laundry room. Outside are two tennis courts, picnic areas by the river, and many

paved biking and hiking trails. Those who can survive without such luxuries should continue 6.5 kilometers (four miles) south to **Eau Claire Campground** (mid-May–early Sept., $20), operated by Kananaskis Camping (403/591-7226, www.kananaskiscamping.com).

PETER LOUGHEED PROVINCIAL PARK

This park is a southern extension of the Kananaskis Valley and protects the upper watershed of the Kananaskis River. It is contained within a high mountain valley and dominated by two magnificent bodies of water—**Upper** and **Lower Kananaskis Lakes.** The 500-square-kilometer (193-square-mile) wilderness is the second-largest provincial park in Alberta.

Highway 40 is the main route through the park. The most important intersection to make note of is five kilometers (3.1 miles) along Highway 40 from the park's north boundary. At this point, Kananaskis Lakes Road branches off to the west, accessing Upper and Lower Kananaskis Lakes. These two lakes are the center of boating and fishing in the park, and opportunities abound for hiking and camping nearby.

◖ Highwood Pass

In the southeastern corner of the park, Highway 40 climbs to Highwood Pass (2,227 m/7,310 ft), the highest road pass in Canada. On the way up to the pass, a pleasant detour is Valley View Trail, a five-kilometer (3.1-mile) paved road whose route higher up the slopes of the Opal Range allows views across the entire park to the Continental Divide. The pass itself is right at the tree line, one of the most accessible alpine areas in all the Canadian Rockies. Simply step out of your vehicle and follow the interpretive trails through the **Highwood Meadows.** In the vicinity, the **Rock Glacier Trail,** two kilometers (1.2 miles) north of Highwood Pass, leads 150 meters (0.1 miles) to a unique formation of moraine rock.

From the pass, Highway 40 descends into the Highwood/Cataract Creek areas of

Kananaskis Country (Highwood Junction is 35 km/22 mi from the pass). **Note:** The road over the Highwood Pass is in a critical wildlife habitat and is closed December 1–June 15.

Hiking

The park offers a number of interesting interpretive trails and more strenuous hikes. Most trailheads are along Kananaskis Lakes Road, a paved road that leads off Highway 40 to Upper and Lower Kananaskis Lakes. **Rockwall Trail,** from the Visitor Information Centre, and **Marl Lake Trail,** from Elkwood Campground, are wheelchair accessible and barrier-free, respectively. The **Boulton Creek Trail** (4.9 km/three mi, 90 minutes round-trip) is an easy loop that begins from Boulton Bridge, 10 kilometers (6.2 miles) from Highway 40. A booklet, available at the trailhead, corresponds with numbered posts along this interpretive trail.

From the Upper Lake day-use area, at the very end of Kananaskis Lakes Road, the trail to **Rawson Lake** (3.5 km/2.2 mi, 1.5 hours one-way) begins by following the lakeshore for just over one kilometer (0.6-mile). Just beyond the small waterfall it begins an uphill climb (305 m/1,000 ft), ending at a picturesque subalpine lake surrounded by a towering, yet magnificently symmetrical, headwall. The setting of **Elbow Lake** (1.3 km/0.8 mi, 30 minutes one-way) is almost as spectacular as Rawson, but the trail is shorter (and therefore busier). The trailhead is the Elbow Pass day-use area, beside Highway 40, 13 kilometers (eight miles) south of Kananaskis Lakes Road. Continue south along Highway 40 to Highwood Pass (four km/2.5 mi) to the **Ptarmigan Cirque Trail** (5.6 km/3.5 mi, 2 hours round-trip), a steep (elevation gain is 230 m/750 ft) interpretive walk that climbs high into the treeless alpine zone. Along the way you're likely to see numerous small mammals—Columbian ground squirrels, pikas, least chipmunks, and hoary marmots are all common.

Other Recreation

The **Bike Trail** is a 20-kilometer (12.5-mile) paved trail designed especially for bicycles that begins behind the Visitor Information Centre and follows Lower Kananaskis Lake to Mount Sarrail Campground. Many other trails are designated for mountain-biking use; inquire at the Visitor Information Centre (403/591-6344). **Boulton Creek Trading Post** (403/591-7058) rents mountain bikes during summer. Upper and Lower Kananaskis Lakes have fair fishing for a variety of trout and whitefish. A nightly interpretive program takes place in campground amphitheaters throughout the park. Look for schedules posted on bulletin boards, or check with the Visitor Information Centre.

Camping

Within the park are six auto-accessible campgrounds that hold a total of 507 sites. All are on Kananaskis Lakes Road and are linked by bicycle and hiking trails. **Boulton Creek Campground** ($22–34) has coin-operated showers just beyond the registration gate (complete with rack for those who have a bike), flush toilets, a few of the 118 sites with power, and an interpretive amphitheater, and is within walking distance of a restaurant and grocery store. **Elkwood Campground** ($20) is the largest of the park's campgrounds, with 130 sites. It offers showers ($1 for five minutes) along each of four loops, flush toilets, a playground, and an interpretive amphitheater. **Canyon, Lower Lakes,** and **(Interlakes Campgrounds** ($20) are more rustic, with only pit toilets, pump water, and picnic tables (Interlakes has some great water-view sites). **Mt. Sarrail Campground** ($20) is described as a "walk-in" campground for tenters, but some sites are right by the main parking lot. All campgrounds in Peter Lougheed Provincial Park are operated by Kananaskis Camping Inc. (403/591-7226, www.kananaskiscamping.com).

Information and Services

At the excellent Visitor Information Centre (four km/2.5 mi along Kananaskis Lakes Rd. from Hwy. 40, 403/591-6322, summer daily 9 A.M.–7 P.M., the rest of the year Mon.–Fri. 9 A.M.–5 P.M. and weekends 9 A.M.–5 P.M.), exhibits catalog the natural and cultural history of the park through photographs, videos, and hands-on displays. The knowledgeable staff hides hordes of literature under the desk—you have to ask for it. A large lounge area that overlooks the valley to the Opal Range is used mainly in winter by cross-country skiers but is always open for trip planning or relaxing.

Located along Kananaskis Lakes Road, 10 kilometers (6.2 mi) south of Highway 40, **Boulton Creek Trading Post** is the park's only commercial center. It sells groceries, basic camping supplies, fishing tackle and licenses, propane, and firewood. Adjacent is an unremarkable family-style restaurant serving up pasta, burgers, and the like. A cooked breakfast is $10 (although it's not open until 9 A.M.). It also has an ice-cream window and serves coffee.

SPRAY VALLEY PROVINCIAL PARK

The creation of 35,800-hectare (88,460-acre) Spray Valley Provincial Park in 2001 provided the final link in continuous protection between bordering Peter Lougheed Provincial Park in the south and Willmore Wilderness Park beyond the northern reaches of Jasper National Park in the north. The park's dominant feature is **Spray Lake Reservoir,** a 16-kilometer-long (10-mile-long) body of water that provides a variety of recreational opportunities.

The **Smith-Dorrien/Spray Trail** is the only road through the park. This 60-kilometer (37-mile) unpaved (and often dusty) road links Peter Lougheed Provincial Park in the south to Canmore in the north. From the south, the road climbs up the Smith-Dorrien Creek watershed, passing Mud Lake and entering the Spray Valley Provincial Park just south of Mt. Engadine Lodge. Around three kilometers (1.9 miles) farther north is **Buller Pond** (on the west side of the road), from where the distinctive "Matterhorn" peak of Mount Assiniboine can be seen on a clear day. The road then parallels the eastern shoreline of Spray Lake for over 20 kilometers (12.5 miles), passing three lakefront picnic areas. Beyond the north end of Spray Lake, the road passes **Goat Pond** and the Goat Creek trailhead, then descends steeply into the Bow Valley and Canmore.

Accommodations and Camping

Mount Engadine Lodge (403/678-4080, www.mountengadine.com, mid-June–mid-Oct. Jan. weekends, Feb.–March; from $190 s, $390–440 d including meals) is set on a ridge overlooking an open meadow and small creek at the turnoff to the Mount Shark staging area. It comprises luxurious rooms in the main lodge and two cabins set on a ridge overlooking an open meadow and small creek. The main lodge has a dining room, a comfortable lounge area with two stone fireplaces, and a beautiful sundeck holding a hot tub. Breakfast is served buffet-style, lunch can be taken at the lodge or packed for a picnic, and dinner is served in multiple courses of hearty European specialties. Mount Engadine Lodge is 40 kilometers (25 miles) southwest of Canmore, at the turnoff to the Mount Shark staging area.

The park's only campground is **Spray Lake West** (June–Sept., $20), a rustic facility spread out along the western shoreline of Spray Lake. Many of the 50-odd sites are very private, but facilities are limited to picnic tables, fire pits, and pit toilets.

SIBBALD

The Sibbald Creek Trail (Hwy. 68) traverses the rolling foothills of the Sibbald and Jumpingpound Valleys and is accessible from the TransCanada Highway, intersecting Highway 40 south of the Barrier Lake Visitor Information Centre. Fishing is popular in **Sibbald Lake** and **Sibbald Meadows Pond.** A couple of short trails begin at the picnic area at Sibbald Lake, including the 4.4-kilometer (2.7-mile) **Ole Buck Loop,** which climbs a low ridge.

Sibbald Lake Campground offers 134 sites spread around five loops (Loop D comes closest to the lake). Amenities include pit toilets, drinking water, and a nightly interpretive program; $24 per site. For camping information contact Elbow Valley Campgrounds (403/949-3132, www.evcamp.com).

BIGHORN SHEEP

Bighorn sheep are the most distinctive of the hoofed mammals in western Canada. Easily recognized by their impressive horns, they're often seen grazing on grassy mountain slopes or at salt licks beside the road. The color of their coat varies with the season; in summer it's a brownish gray with a cream-colored belly and rump, turning lighter in winter. Males can weigh up to 120 kilograms (265 pounds). Females generally weigh around 80 kilograms (180 pounds). Both sexes possess horns, rather than antlers like moose, elk, and deer. Unlike antlers, horns are not shed each year and can grow to astounding sizes. The horns of rams are larger than those of ewes and curve up to 360 degrees. The spiraled horns of an older ram can measure over one meter (three feet) and weigh as much as 15 kilograms (33 pounds). In fall, during the mating season, a hierarchy is established among these animals for the right to breed ewes. As the males face off against each other to establish dominance, their horns act as both a weapon and a buffer against the head-butting of other rams. The skull structure of the bighorn, rams in particular, has become adapted to these clashes, preventing heavy concussion.

These animals are particularly tolerant of humans and often approach parked vehicles; although they are not dangerous, as with all mammals in the park, you should not approach or feed them.

ELBOW RIVER VALLEY

The main access road into the Elbow River Valley is Highway 66 west from Bragg Creek. It climbs steadily along the Elbow River, passing **McLean Pond** and **Allen Bill Pond** (both are stocked with rainbow trout) and six-meter-high (20-foot-high) **Elbow Falls**, before climbing through an area devastated by wildfire in 1981, then descending to a campground 42 kilometers (26 miles) from Bragg Creek.

Five campgrounds with a combined total of 551 sites lie along the Elbow River Valley. The most developed of the five is **McLean Creek Campground,** 12 kilometers (7.5 miles) west of Bragg Creek. At the campground entrance is the Camper Centre with groceries, coin showers, and firewood ($6 per bundle). Unpowered sites are $25 per night, powered sites $32. For reservations contact Elbow Valley Campgrounds (403/949-3132, www.evcamp.com). The other campgrounds and their distances from Bragg Creek are **Gooseberry** (10 km/6.2 mi), **Paddy's Flat** (20 km/12.4 mi), **Beaver Flat** (30 km/18.6 mi), and, at the very end of the road, **Little Elbow** (50 km/31 mi). Each of these campgrounds has only basic facilities—pit toilets and hand-pumped drinking water—but, still, sites are $24 per night.

SHEEP RIVER VALLEY

The Sheep River Valley lies immediately south of the Elbow River Valley, in an area of rolling foothills between open ranchlands to the east and the high peaks bordering **Elbow-Sheep Wildland Provincial Park** to the west. Access is from the town of Turner Valley (take Sunset Blvd. west from downtown), along Highway 546. The highway passes through **Sheep River Provincial Park** (which protects the wintering ground of bighorn sheep) and **Sheep River Falls,** and ends at a campground 46 kilometers (29 miles) west of Turner Valley.

Along Highway 546, west from Turner Valley, are two campgrounds. **Sandy McNabb Campround** (403/558-2373 or 866/366-2267, www.campingalberta.com, $20), the larger of the two, is a pleasant walk from the river right by the entrance to Kananaskis Country. All sites are filled on a first-come, first-served basis.

HIGHWOOD AND CATARACT CREEK

The Highwood/Cataract Creek areas stretch from Peter Lougheed Provincial Park to the southern border of Kananaskis Country. This is the least developed area in Kananaskis Country. The jagged peaks of the Highwood

Mountains, mostly protected by remote **Don Getty Wildland Provincial Park** are the dominant feature; high alpine meadows among the peaks are home to bighorn sheep, elk, and grizzlies. Lower down, spruce and lodgepole pine forests spread over most of the valley, giving way to grazing lands along the eastern flanks. The main access from the north is along Highway 40, which drops 600 vertical meters (1,970 feet) in the 35 kilometers (22 miles) between **Highwood Pass** and **Highwood Junction.** From the east, Highway 541 west from Longview joins Highway 40 at Highwood Junction.

All three campgrounds in the Highwood/Cataract Creek areas are south of Highwood Junction and are operated by High Country Camping (403/558-2373 or 866/366-2267, www.campingalberta.com).

Canmore

The town of Canmore (12,500) lies in the Bow Valley, 103 kilometers (64 miles) west of Calgary, 28 kilometers (17 miles) southeast of Banff, and on the northern edge of Kananaskis Country. Long perceived as a gateway to the mountain national parks, the town is very much a destination in itself these days. Its ideal mountain location and the freedom it enjoys from the strict development restrictions that apply in the nearby parks have made Canmore the fastest-growing town in Canada, with the population having tripled in the last 20 years. The surrounding mountains provide Canmore's best recreation opportunities. Hiking is excellent on trails that lace the valley and mountainside slopes, with many high viewpoints easily reached. Flowing though town, the Bow River offers great fishing, kayaking, and rafting; golfers flock to three scenic courses; and nearby Mount Yamnuska has become the most developed rock-climbing site in the Canadian Rockies. Canmore also hosted the Nordic events of the 1988 Winter Olympic Games and is the home of the Alpine Club of Canada.

SIGHTS AND RECREATION

Canmore is spread across both sides of the TransCanada Highway, with downtown Canmore occupying an island in the middle of the Bow River. Although development sprawls in all directions, large tracts of forest remain intact, including along the river, where you'll find paths leading beyond built-up areas and into natural areas. The most expansive of these is 32,600-hectare (80,550-acre) **Bow Valley Wildland Provincial Park,** which has been designated in pockets along the valley floor as well as most of the surrounding mountain slopes along both sides of the valley.

Downtown

The downtown core of Canmore, on the southwestern side of the TransCanada Highway, has managed to retain much of its original charm. Many historical buildings line the downtown streets, while other buildings from the coal-mining days are being preserved at their original locations around town. The first building of interest at the east end of the main street is Canmore's original **NWMP post** (609 8th St., 403/678-1955, summer daily 9 A.M.–6 P.M., the rest of the year Mon.–Fri. noon–4 P.M., free), built in 1892. It is one of the few such posts still in its original position, even though at the time of its construction the building was designed as a temporary structure to serve the newly born coal-mining town. The interior is decorated with period furnishings, while out back is a thriving garden filled with the same food crops planted by the post's original inhabitants.

Just off the main street, inside the impressive Civic Centre complex, is **Canmore Museum and Geoscience Centre** (902 7th Ave., 403/678-2462, Mon.–Tues. noon–5 P.M., Wed.–Sun. 10 A.M.–6 P.M., adult $3, senior and child $2). This facility highlights the

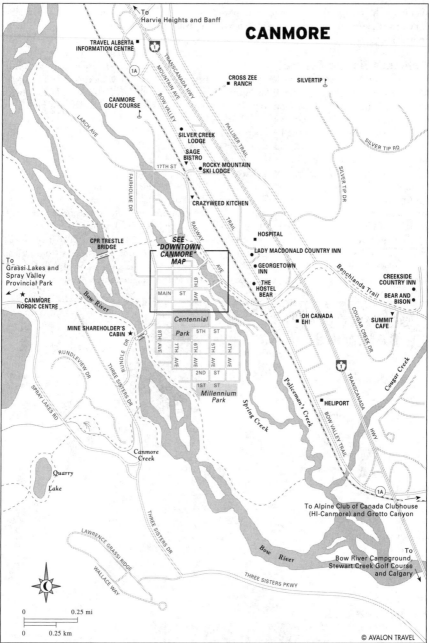

CANMORE

To Harvie Heights and Banff

TRAVEL ALBERTA
INFORMATION CENTRE

1A

TRANSCANADA HWY

MOUNTAIN AVE

BOW VALLEY

CANMORE
GOLF COURSE

LARCH AVE

CROSS ZEE
RANCH

SILVERTIP

SILVER TIP RD

SILVER CREEK
LODGE

SAGE
BISTRO

17TH ST

ROCKY MOUNTAIN
SKI LODGE

PALLISER TRAIL

SILVER TIP DR

FAIRHOLME DR

CRAZYWEED KITCHEN

RAILWAY

CPR TRESTLE
BRIDGE

To
Grassi Lakes and
Spray Valley
Provincial Park

CANMORE
NORDIC CENTRE

Bow River

*SEE
"DOWNTOWN
CANMORE"
MAP*

MAIN ST

6TH AVE

AVE

HOSPITAL

LADY MACDONALD COUNTRY INN

GEORGETOWN
INN

THE
HOSTEL
BEAR

Benchlands Trail

CREEKSIDE
COUNTRY INN

BEAR AND
BISON

COUGAR CREEK DR

SUMMIT
CAFE

MINE SHAREHOLDER'S
CABIN

RUNDLEVIEW DR

THREE SISTERS DR

RUNDLE DR

8TH
AVE

7TH
AVE

*Centennial
Park*

5TH ST

6TH
AVE

5TH
AVE

2ND ST

1ST ST

4TH
AVE

OH CANADA
EH!

*Millennium
Park*

Spring Creek

Policeman's Creek

BOW VALLEY TRAIL

TRANSCANADA HWY

Cougar Creek

HELIPORT

SPRAY LAKES RD

Canmore
Creek

Quarry
Lake

LAWRENCE GRASSI RIDGE

WALLACE WAY

THREE SISTERS DR

1A

To Alpine Club of Canada Clubhouse
(HI-Canmore) and Grotto Canyon

To
Bow River Campground,
Stewart Creek Golf Course
and Calgary

THREE SISTERS PKWY

Bow River

0   0.25 mi

0   0.25 km

© AVALON TRAVEL

region's rich geological history and its importance to the growth of the town and related industries.

Canmore Nordic Centre

This sprawling complex on the outskirts of Canmore was built for the 1988 Winter Olympic Games. The cross-country skiing and biathlon (combined cross-country skiing and rifle shooting) events were held here, and today the center remains a world-class training ground for Canadian athletes in a variety of disciplines. Even in summer, long after the snow has melted, the place is worth a visit. An interpretive trail leads down to and along the west bank of the Bow River to the barely visible remains of Georgetown, a once-bustling coal-mining town. Many other trails lead around the grounds, and it's possible to hike or bike along the Bow River all the way to Banff. **Mountain biking** is extremely popular on 70 kilometers

(43.5 miles) of trails. Bike rentals are available at **Trail Sports** (below the day lodge, 403/678-6764, daily 9 A.M.–6 P.M.), where rates are $15 per hour and $45 per day for a front-suspension bike, $20 and $60, respectively, for a full-suspension bike. Snowmaking guarantees a ski season running December–late March, with rentals and instruction available through Trail Sports.

Hiking

Paved paths around town are suitable for walking and biking. They link Policeman's Creek with the golf course, Nordic center, and Riverview Park on the Bow River. To explore the surrounding wilderness, consider one of the following longer walks.

The historic **Grassi Lakes Trail** (two km/1.2 mi, 40 minutes one-way) begins from just off Spray Lakes Road, one kilometer (0.6 miles) beyond the Nordic center. Around 150 meters

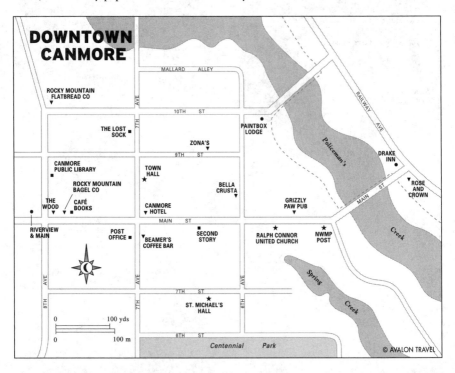

DOWNTOWN CANMORE

© ANDREW HEMPSTEAD

Canmore Nordic Centre

(0.1 miles) from the parking lot, take the left fork. From this point, the trail climbs steadily to stairs cut into a cliff face before leading up to a bridge over Canmore Creek and to the two small lakes. With Chinaman's Peak as a backdrop, these gin-clear, spring-fed lakes are a particularly rewarding destination. Behind the upper lake, an easy scramble up a scree slope leads to four pictographs (native rock paintings) of human figures. They're on the first large boulder in the gorge.

Across the valley, the parking lot at Benchlands Trail and Elk Run Boulevard is the beginning of two trails. One follows **Cougar Creek** into a narrow valley. The first section of trail runs alongside a man-made channel that acts as a conduit for run-off in years of high snowfall (the "creek" is dry all summer). The rough trail then enters a canyon and crosses the creekbed 10 times in the first three kilometers (1.9 miles) to a major fork (allow one hour), which is a fine turnaround point. Where Cougar Creek exits the canyon, look for a faint trail winding up a grassy bank to the left. It leads up **Mount Lady Macdonald** (3.5 km/2.1

mi, 90 minutes one-way), gaining a strenuous 850 meters (2,790 feet) of elevation along the way. The distance given is to a disused helipad below the main summit. It's a steep, unrelenting slog, but views across the Bow Valley are stunning. From this point, the true summit is another 275 vertical meters (900 feet) away, along an extremely narrow ridge that drops away precipitously to the east.

Golf

As with golfing elsewhere in the Canadian Rockies, book all tee times well in advance, but also try to be flexible, because two of Canmore's three courses offer weekday and twilight discounts. **Silvertip** (2000 Silvertip Trail, 403/678-1600 or 877/877-5444, greens fee $175) spreads across a series of wide benches between the valley floor and the lower slopes of Mount Lady Macdonald. The layout is challenging, with the most distinct feature being an elevation change of 200 meters (660 feet) between the lowest and highest points on the course. **Stewart Creek Golf Club** (4100 Stewart Creek Dr., 403/609-6099 or 877/993-

4653, www.stewartcreekgolf.com, $175–195), another newer layout, is made more interesting by hanging greens, greenside exposed rock, and historic mine shafts. **Canmore Golf & Curling Club** (2000 8th Ave., 403/678-4785, $114) is an 18-hole course is an interesting layout, with scenic panoramas and water on some holes.

Horseback Riding

Nestled on a wide bench on the northeastern side of town, **Cross Zee Ranch** (403/678-4171) has been guiding visitors through the valley since the 1950s. From expansive stables, rides pass through thickly wooded areas, along colorful meadows, and to high lookouts. Options include Ranger Ridge and Bone Gully (one hour, $38 per person), Sunny Bench (90 minutes, $52), and the Great Aspens ride (two hours, $68).

ENTERTAINMENT AND EVENTS
Nightlife

Oh Canada Eh! (125 Kananaskis Way, off Bow Valley Trail, 403/609-0004 or 800/773-0004) is a musical dinner show that provides a rip-roaring evening of fun and food in a modern building decorated as a cavernous log cabin. It's unashamedly cheesy, but the parade of costumed Canadian characters—such as lumberjacks, natives, Mounties, and even Anne of Green Gables—will keep you laughing as they sing and dance across the floor. The food is surprisingly good, with Canadian favorites such as Alberta beef, salmon, and maple chocolate cake served buffet-style. Performances are nightly at 6:30 P.M. through summer, and the all-inclusive cost is adult $64, child 6–16 $31.

The Wood (838 8th St., 403/678-3404) has a beer garden that catches the afternoon sun and is especially busy on weekends. At the other end of the main street is the **Drake Inn** (909 Railway Ave., 403/678-5131), with a small outdoor patio and a nonsmoking section with comfortable lounges. Across the road, at the **Rose and Crown** (749 Railway Ave., 403/678-5168), you'll find a beer garden. All these bars have midweek drink specials, and the latter two have a couple of pool tables.

Festivals and Events

Canmore's small-town pride lives on through a busy schedule of festivals and events, which are nearly always accompanied by parades of flag-waving kids, free downtown pancake breakfasts, and an evening shindig somewhere in town.

On the middle weekend of May, it's all about the kids at the **Canmore Children's Festival** (www.canmorechildrensfestival.com), where the fun and frivolity centers on the local high school grounds off 17th Street. Expect lots of music, live theater, story-telling, and educational presentations. **ArtsPeak Arts Festival** (403/678-6436, www.artspeakcanmore.com) is a mid-June celebration hosted at venues throughout town. As the name suggests expect lots of art-oriented festivities, including workshops, displays, and walking tours.

Canada Day is celebrated with a pancake breakfast, parade, various activities in Centennial Park, and 10:30 P.M. fireworks. On the first weekend of August, Canmore hosts a **Folk Music Festival** (www.canmorefolkfestival.com), which starts on Saturday and runs through Monday evening. Canmore Nordic Centre hosts a variety of mountain-biking events each summer, highlighted by a late August stop on the **24 Hours of Adrenalin** tour (www.24hoursofadrenalin.com) in which 1,500 racers complete as many laps as they can in a 24-hour period.

The first Sunday of September is the **Canmore Highland Games** (www.canmorehighlandgames.ca), a day of dancing, eating, and caber tossing, culminating in a spectacular and noisy parade of pipe bands throughout the grounds of Centennial Park. The grand finale is the *ceilidh,* a traditional Scottish celebration involving loud beer-drinking, foot-stomping music, which takes place under a massive tent set up in the park for the occasion. Fall's other major gathering is for the **Festival of the Eagles** (www.eaglewatch.ca), on the middle weekend of October and coinciding with the southbound migration of golden eagles.

ACCOMMODATIONS AND CAMPING

Canmore's population boom has been mirrored by the construction of new hotels and motels. Most of the newer lodgings are on Bow Valley Trail (Hwy. 1A). As with all resort towns in the Canadian Rockies, reservations should be made as far in advance as possible in summer.

Under $50

HI-Canmore (403/678-3200, www.hihostels. ca, dorms $30–36, private rooms $60–81) is an excellent hostel-style accommodation at the base of Grotto Mountain. Affiliated with Hostelling International, the lodge is part of headquarters for the Alpine Club of Canada, the country's national mountaineering organization. In addition to sleeping up to 46 people in seven rooms, it has a kitchen, an excellent library, a laundry room, a bar, a sauna, and a lounge area with a fireplace. To get there from downtown, follow Bow Valley Trail southeast; it's signposted to the left, 500 meters (0.3 mile) after passing under the TransCanada Highway.

Built as a motel, **The Hostel Bear** (1002 Bow Valley Trail, 403/678-1000 or 888/678-1008, www.thehostelbear.com; dorms $32, from $84 s or d) is now a beautiful facility for budget travelers. It features eye-catching timber and river-stone styling outside and an impressive lobby. Amenities include a living area with an LCD TV and fireplace, a large modern kitchen, a laundry, wireless Internet, and comfortable beds for 170 guests, with configurations ranging from 10-bed dorms to private en suite rooms.

$100-150

With around $100 budgeted for a room, it's hard to pass up **Riverview and Main,** centrally located half a block beyond the end of the downtown core (918 8th St., 403/678-9777, www.riverviewandmain.com, $115 s, $135 d). The rooms are decently sized and brightly decorated, and each has access to a deck. The guest lounge centers on a river-stone, wood-burning fireplace. Rates include a selection of hot and cold breakfast items.

Not only can you rent one- and two-bedroom units with full kitchens at **Rocky Mountain Ski Lodge** (1711 Bow Valley Trail, 403/678-5445 or 800/665-6111, www.rockymtnskilodge.com, from $129 s or d), there's plenty of outdoor space for kids to run around, including a small playground. Also on the property is a barbecue and picnic area, a laundry, and wireless Internet. The self-contained suites, some with loft bedrooms, cost from $169.

At the edge of Canmore's downtown core is the **Drake Inn** (909 Railway Ave., 403/678-5131 or 800/461-8730, www.drakeinn.com, from $129 s, $139 d). It offers bright and cheerfully decorated motel rooms. Well worth an extra $10 are Creekside Rooms, featuring private balconies overlooking Policeman's Creek. The adjoining bar opens daily at 7 A.M. for the best-value breakfast in town.

$150-200

Silver Creek Lodge (1818 Mountain Ave., 403/678-4242 or 877/598-4242, www.silvercreekcanmore.ca, $159–289 s or d) provides hotel and suite accommodations within a much larger condominium development. Aside from modern kitchen-equipped rooms, many with mountain views, highlights include the highly recommended Wild Orchid Asian Bistro, spa services, outdoor hot tubs, and underground parking.

Lady Macdonald Country Inn (1201 Bow Valley Trail, 403/678-3665 or 800/567-3919, www.ladymacdonald.com, $160–250 s or d) exudes a welcoming atmosphere and personalized service not experienced in the larger properties. Its 12 rooms are all individually furnished, with the smallest, the Palliser Room, featuring elegant surroundings and a magnificent wrought-iron bed. Rates include a hearty hot breakfast in a country-style breakfast room.

◀ Creekside Country Inn (709 Benchlands Trail, 403/609-5522 or 866/609-5522, www.creeksidecountryinn.com, $159–239 s or d) is a modern mountain-style lodge featuring lots of exposed timber. The 12 rooms are elegant in their simplicity; eight have lofts. Facilities include a lounge with roaring log fire, a small exercise room, a whirlpool, and a steam room. Rates include a gourmet continental breakfast that will set you up for the day.

Named for one of the valley's original coal-mining communities, the ◖ **Georgetown Inn** (1101 Bow Valley Trail, 403/678-3439 or 866/695-5955, www.georgetowninn.ca; $169–230 s or d) is set up as a country inn of times gone by, complete with a pub-style dining room open daily for breakfast, lunch, and dinner. Each of the 20 guest rooms has its own individual charm, with a modern twist on decor that features lots of English antiques. The best value are Victoria Rooms, each with a separate sitting area and electric fireplace ($159).

Over $200

◖ **Bear and Bison** (705 Benchlands Trail, 403/678-2058, www.bearandbisoninn.com, $279–329 s or d) is an elegant lodging with nine guest rooms in three different themes. Each room has a king-size four-poster bed, a jetted tub, a fireplace, and a private balcony or patio. Guests enjoy an inviting library and a private garden complete with an oversized hot tub. Rates include baked goods on arrival, pre-dinner drinks, and a breakfast you will remember for a long time.

Paintbox Lodge (629 10th St., 403/609-0482 or 888/678-6100, www.paintboxlodge.com, $209–289 s or d) has the same upscale charm as the Bear and Bison but enjoys a more central location, just one block from the main street. The lobby itself—exposed hand-hewn timbers, slate tiles, and unique pieces of mountain-themed art—is an eye-catching gem. The upscale mountain decor continues through the eight large guest rooms, each lavishly decorated with muted natural colors and a tasteful selection of heritage artifacts.

Camping

East of Canmore are three government campgrounds operated by **Bow Valley Campgrounds** (403/673-2163, www.bowvalleycampgrounds.com). Each has pit toilets, kitchen shelters, and firewood for sale at $8 per bundle. None have hookups. **Bow River Campground** (open late Apr.–early Sept.) is three kilometers (1.9 miles) east of Canmore at the Three Sisters Parkway overpass; **Three Sisters Campground** (mid-Apr.–Oct.) is accessed from Deadman's Flats, a further four kilometers (2.5 miles) east, but it has a pleasant treed setting; **Lac des Arcs Campground** (late Apr.–mid-Sept.) slopes down to the edge of a large lake of the same name seven kilometers (4.3 miles) farther toward Calgary. Sites are $20–22 and reservations are taken from April 1.

FOOD

The restaurant scene has come a long way in Canmore in the last decade. While you can still get inexpensive bar meals at local pubs, other choices run the gamut, from the lively atmosphere of dining in the front yard of a converted residence to Spanish tapas.

Cafés

The **Rocky Mountain Bagel Company** (830 8th St., 403/678-9978, daily 6:30 A.M.–10 P.M.) is a popular early-morning gathering spot. With a central location, it's always busy but manages to maintain an inviting atmosphere. It's the perfect place to start the day with a good strong coffee and fruit-filled muffin. Down one block, **Beamer's Coffee Bar** (737 7th Ave., 403/609-0111, daily 6:30 A.M.–10 P.M.) is a smaller space with equally good coffee.

Away from downtown, near where Cougar Creek enters Canmore from the Fairholme Range, is the **Summit Café** (1001 Cougar Creek Dr., 403/609-2120, daily 6:30 A.M.–6 P.M.; kitchen closes at 4 P.M.). It features a health-conscious menu including lots of salads, but many people come just to soak up the sun on the outside deck or relax with the daily paper and a cup of coffee.

Pizza

Bella Crusta (702 6th Ave., 403/609-3366, Mon.–Sat. 10 A.M.–6 P.M.) is the purveyor of excellent pizza. Heated slices to go are $6, or pay $14–16 for a family-sized version and heat it yourself on a barbecue as the friendly staff recommends.

Off the top end of Main Street, **Rocky Mountain Flatbread Co.** (838 10th St., 403/609-5508; daily 11:30 A.M.–9:30 P.M., $10–16) is a lovely space of natural tones dominated by a clay wood-fired oven in one corner. The oven is also the main attraction when it comes to the food—gourmet flatbread-style pizzas in the $14–20 range. My advice: Start with a bowl of made-from-scratch chicken noodle soup ($6.50), then move on to the chicken, apple, and cheery tomato pizza (the $16.50 size is enough for two people).

Contemporary Canadian

Canmore has seen many top-notch restaurants open in the last few years, but one of the originals, **Zona's** (710 9th St., 403/609-2000, daily 11 A.M.–2 A.M. but for dinner only outside summer, $13–19), remains popular. The food is great, and so is the restaurant itself—earthy tones, hardwood floors, rustic furniture, bamboo blinds, and kiln-fired clay crockery create an inviting ambience unequaled in Canmore.

The menu takes its roots from around the world, with an emphasis on healthy eating and freshly prepared Canadian produce. Choose from dishes such as lamb shepherd's pie or vegetarian korma. A large deck provides much-needed extra seating in summer.

Crazyweed Kitchen (1600 Railway Ave., 403/609-2530, daily 11:30 A.M.–3 P.M. and from 5 P.M., $18–38) dishes up creative culinary fare that gets rave reviews from even cultured Calgarians. From the busy, open kitchen, all manner of creative dishes are on offer—beef short ribs in curry, steamed Alaskan cod, and gourmet pizzas. Healthy portions are served at tables inside or out. Also notable is the extensive wine list, with glasses from $8 and bottles from $38.

Asian

Wild Orchid Bistro (Silver Creek Lodge, 1818 Mountain Ave., 403/679-2029, daily except Tues. for dinner, call for lunch hours, $15–28) is my favorite Japanese restaurant in the Canadian Rockies. It features all the usual choices, all expertly crafted in the open

© ANDREW HEMPSTEAD

Crazyweed Kitchen is one of Canmore's premier restaurants.

kitchen, as well as many with a Western twist. Perfect presentation, mountain views, and a large deck add to the appeal.

INFORMATION AND SERVICES

The best source of pre-trip information (apart from this book, of course) is **Tourism Canmore** (403/678-1295 or 866/226-6673, www.tourismcanmore.com). A **Travel Alberta Information Centre** (403/678-5277, May–Sept. 8 A.M.–8 P.M., Oct. 9 A.M.–6 P.M.) is just off the TransCanada Highway on the west side of town.

The **Rocky Mountain Outlook** and **Canmore Leader** are both filled with local issues and entertainment listings; both are available free on stands throughout the valley. **Canmore Public Library** (950 8th Ave., 403/678-2468, Mon.–Thurs. 11 A.M.–8 P.M., Fri.–Sun. 11 A.M.–5 P.M.) has free Internet access. At the top end of the main street, **Café Books** (826 Main St., 403/678-0908, Mon.–Sat. 10 A.M.–6 P.M., Sun. 10:30 A.M.–5:30 P.M., later hours in summer) stocks an excellent selection of Canadiana. With a huge collection of used books, **Second Story** (713 8th St., 403/609-2368) hasn't been on the second floor since the weight of the books forced a move downstairs to the basement of the same address.

The post office is on 7th Avenue, beside Rusticana Grocery. **The Lost Sock** laundry (in the small mall on 7th Ave. at 10th St.) is open 24 hours daily and has Internet access. **Canmore Hospital** (403/678-5536) is along Bow Valley Trail. For the **RCMP,** call 403/678-5516.

Central Alberta

The boundaries of this region are defined by Calgary in the south, Edmonton to the north, the Canadian Rockies in the west, and the Saskatchewan border in the east. Although it is a large swathe of the province, in this section I make it manageable for visitors by recommending a variety of routes between Alberta's two largest cities.

CALGARY TO ROCKY MOUNTAIN HOUSE

Highway 22 follows the eastern flanks of the foothills from Cochrane, northwest of Calgary, through a string of small communities to Rocky Mountain House.

Sundre

This town of 2,500, on the banks of the Red Deer River, is the quintessential Albertan town. Surrounded by rolling foothills that are historically tied to the ranching industry, oil and gas now keep the local economy alive. In town, Sundre's **Pioneer Village Museum** (130 Centre St., 403/638-3233, May–Oct. Mon. and Wed.–Sat. 10 A.M.–5 P.M., Sun. 1–5 P.M., Nov.–Apr. Wed.–Sat. 10 A.M.–5 P.M., Sun. 1–4 P.M., adult $10, senior and child $8) displays a large collection of artifacts from early pioneer days, including farm machinery, a blacksmith shop, and an old schoolhouse.

The most appealing of Sundre's four motels is the **Chinook Country Inn** (120 2nd St. SW, 403/638-3300, www.chinookcountryinn. ca, $75 s or d), where the rates include a light breakfast. The town-operated **Greenwood Campground** (403/638-2130, mid-May–late Sept., unserviced sites $20, hookups $25–30), on the west bank of the Red Deer River within walking distance of downtown, has clean facilities that include showers and a covered cooking shelter complete with a wood stove. **Sundre Visitor Information Centre** (403/638-3245, summer daily 10 A.M.–6 P.M.) is on the east bank of the Red Deer River.

Caroline

Named after the daughter of one of the town's earliest settlers, Caroline is the hometown of four-time World Men's Figure Skating champion **Kurt Browning.** His portrait adorns local tourist literature, and the town's Kurt Browning Arena (48th Ave., Mon.–Fri. 8 A.M.–4 P.M.) houses Kurt's Korner, a display of personal memorabilia.

ROCKY MOUNTAIN HOUSE

Best known simply as "Rocky," this town of 6,800 straddles the North Saskatchewan River and is surrounded by gently rolling hills in a transition zone between aspen parkland and mountains. Highway 11 (also known as David Thompson Highway) passes through town on its way east to Red Deer (82 km/51 mi) and west to the northern end of Banff National Park (170 km/106 mi).

Rocky Mountain House National Historic Site

This National Historic Site (seven km/4.3 mi west of Rocky Mountain House on Hwy. 11A, 403/845-2412, mid-May–Aug. daily 10 A.M.–5 P.M., Sept. Mon.–Fri. 10 A.M.–5 P.M.,

adult $4, senior $3.50, child $2) commemorates the important role fur trading played in Canada's history. The first trading post, or fort, was built on the site in 1799. By the 1830s, beaver felt was out of fashion in Europe, and traders turned to buffalo robes. By the 1870s, the fur trade had ended and the last post at Rocky Mountain House closed. Today, the protected areas include the sites of five forts, a buffalo paddock, and a stretch of riverbank where the large voyageur canoes would have come ashore to be loaded with furs bound for Europe. The visitor center is the best place to begin a visit to the site; its interpretive displays detail the history of the forts, the fur trade, and exploration of the West. Two trails lead along the north bank of the river. The longer of the two, a 3.2-kilometer (two-mile) loop, passes the site of the two original forts. Frequent "listening posts" along the trail play a lively recorded commentary on life in the early 1800s. All that remains of the forts are depressions in the ground, but

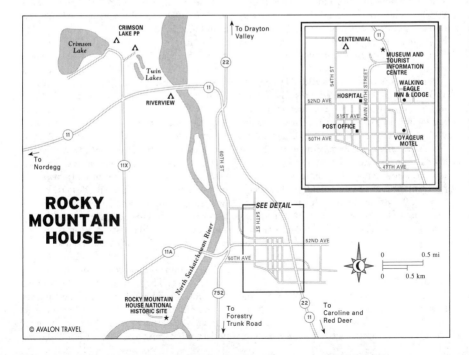

© AVALON TRAVEL

through the commentary and interpretive displays, it is easy to get a good idea of what the forts looked like.

Rocky Mountain House Museum

Rocky Mountain House Museum (5406 48th St., 403/845-2332, July–Aug. daily 9 A.M.–8 P.M., June and Sept. daily 9 A.M.–5 P.M., the rest of the year weekdays only, adult $4, child $1.50) is in the same complex as the information center. Exhibits include an array of pioneer artifacts, including an early Forest Service cabin, a one-room schoolhouse, and an interesting rope-making machine.

Accommodations and Camping

Least expensive of the motels spread out along Highway 11 east of town is the **Voyageur Motel** (403/845-3381 or 888/845-5569, www.voyageurmotel.ca, $60–75 s, $75–90 d), which has large clean rooms with fridge and microwave, or pay an extra $15 for a kitchenette. **Walking Eagle Inn & Lodge** (4819 45th St., 403/845-2804 or 866/845-2131, www.walkingeagle.net, $99–129 s or d), easily recognized by its striking log exterior, has comfortable rooms, a steakhouse restaurant, and a steam room.

Riverview Campground (Hwy. 11, 403/845-4422, unserviced sites $16, hookups $19–26) is the only commercial camping facility in town. The unserviced sites are tucked in among a grove of trees along the North Saskatchewan River. Amenities include a small grocery store, laundry, showers, and free firewood. Another recommended spot is **◖ Crimson Lake Provincial Park** (403/845-2330, $22–28), northwest of town along an access road off Highway 11, where you'll find two campgrounds; sites along the bank of Crimson Lake are mostly powered, whereas those beside Twin Lakes aren't.

Information

Make your first stop in town the tourist information center (54th Ave., 403/845-5450 or 800/565-3793, www.rockychamber.org, late May–Aug. Mon.–Sat. 9 A.M.–7 P.M., Sun.

10 A.M.–6 P.M., the rest of the year Mon.–Fri. 9 A.M.–5 P.M.), beside Highway 11 north of downtown.

DAVID THOMPSON HIGHWAY

The David Thompson Highway (Hwy. 11) climbs slowly from the aspen parkland around Rocky Mountain House westward into the dense forests on the eastern slopes of the Canadian Rockies.

Nordegg

The only community between Rocky and Banff National Park is Nordegg (population 100), 85 kilometers (53 miles) west of Rocky. Established in 1914, Nordegg was a "planned" coal-mining town. The streets were built in a semicircular pattern, centered around the railroad station and shops. Fifty miners' cottages were built, all painted in pastel colors. Gardens were planted, two churches and a hospital were built, and a golf course was developed—miners had never had it better. But the mine closed in early 1955, and by summer it had been abandoned.

The original townsite has mostly disappeared, but remaining mine structures are preserved as a National Historic Site. The Nordegg Historical Society, made up of many former residents, operates the **Nordegg Heritage Centre** (403/721-2625, mid-May–Sept. daily 9 A.M.–5 P.M., free) in a two-story former school building along the main street. Also in this building is the **Miner's Café,** where the soup and sandwich special is $8, and the sandwiches are stacked and delicious. Freshly made fruit pies are an easy choice for dessert. Uphill (within walking distance) from the museum complex is the original townsite, now with only a few buildings still standing. Visitors are free to wander around at their leisure, but ask at the heritage center for a map. Continuing up the hill is the mine infrastructure, much of which still remains. The only access to this section of Nordegg is on a guided tour. These depart twice daily through summer, and are booked through the heritage center. Neither tour goes underground, but the longer version ($8) takes in the briquette processing plants and mine entrances. Call ahead for a schedule.

A good option for budget travelers is **HI-Nordegg** (403/721-2140, www.hihostels.ca, dorms $24–28, $65.50–73.50 s or d), also known as Shunda Creek Hostel. Affiliated with Hostelling International, this huge log chalet in a wilderness setting has a fully equipped kitchen, dining room, fireplace, hot showers, and an outdoor hot tub.

West from Nordegg

Twenty-three kilometers (14 miles) west of Nordegg, an unpaved side road leads eight kilometers (five miles) north to **Crescent Falls,** where there is primitive camping. Back on the highway, the brilliant turquoise water of **Abraham Lake,** one of Alberta's largest reservoirs, comes into view. Don't stop for a photo session just yet, though, because the views improve farther west. **Aurum Lodge** (45 km/28 mi west of Nordegg, 40 km/25 mi east of the Banff National Park, 403/721-2117, www.aurumlodge.com, $149–199 s, $179–229 d, self-contained units $189–249) trades on an eco-friendly stance and wonderfully scenic location overlooking Abraham Lake. Owners Alan and Madeleine Ernst used recycled materials wherever possible during construction, natural light streams into all corners, the kitchen uses a wood-fired stove, and much of the waste is recycled. But don't imagine some backwoods cabin without running water—it's a comfortable and modern lodge. Rooms in the main lodge are simply decorated, but bright and immaculately kept. Cozy self-contained cottages offer a bathroom, kitchen with wood-stove, and lots of privacy. **David Thompson Resort** (403/721-2103 or 888/810-2103, www.davidthompsonresort.com, May–mid-Oct., unserviced sites $21, hookups $31–38, motel rooms and cabins $101 s or d) provides a variety of lodging options. The bathroom facilities were in need of an upgrade at the time of our research trip for this edition, but as a trade off there's a unique open-sided bar that opens for karaoke each night and then again in the morning for a pancake breakfast. Other facilities include a playground with massive slides, Frisbee-golf course, restaurant, and gas station.

At the south end of Abraham Lake, **Kootenay Plains Ecological Reserve** protects a unique area of dry grasslands in the mountains. The climate in this section of the valley is unusually moderate, making it a prime wintering area for elk, mule deer, bighorn sheep, and moose. For thousands of years, the Kootenay peoples would cross the mountains from the Columbia River Valley to hunt these mammals and the bison that were then prolific. Because of the dry microclimate and its associated vegetation, mammals are not abundant in summer.

Two designated wilderness areas near the west end of Highway 11—**White Goat** and **Siffleur**—afford experienced hikers the chance to enjoy the natural beauty and wildlife of the Canadian Rockies away from the crowds associated with the mountain national parks. Both are protected from any activities that could have an impact on the area's fragile ecosystems, including road and trail development. No bridges have been built over the area's many fast-flowing streams, and the few old trails that do exist are not maintained. The only access to these parks is on foot, meaning they are lightly traveled. The main trail into Siffleur Wilderness Area begins from a parking area two kilometers (1.2 miles) south of the Two O'Clock Creek Campground at Kootenay Plains; it's worth mentioning for photogenic **Siffleur Falls,** four kilometers (2.5 miles) from the highway. For more information contact the **Department of Tourism, Parks and Recreation** (403/845-8349, www.albertaparks.ca).

CALGARY TO RED DEER

The original road (Hwy. 2A) between Calgary and Edmonton is now bypassed entirely by Highway 2, a four-lane divided road that makes the trip an easy three-hour drive, with Red Deer marking the midway point.

Carstairs

Carstairs is a small farming, dairy, and ranching

center 67 kilometers (42 miles) north of Calgary. The town's tree-lined streets are dotted with grand old houses, and the grain elevators associated with all prairie towns stand silhouetted against the skyline. The official attractions are outside of town, including **PaSu Farm** (10 km/6.2 mi west of town, 403/337-2800, Tues.–Sat. 10 A.M.–4 P.M., Sun. noon–4 P.M.), a working farm with a dozen breeds of sheep. It also displays a wide variety of sheepskin and wool products, as well as weavings from Africa. The farm's restaurant serves light lunches plus scones, homemade apple pie, and various teas Tuesday–Saturday noon–4 P.M., along with a Sunday lunch (noon–2:30 P.M.). Much of the wool from PaSu Farm is sold to **Custom Woolen Mills** (403/337-2221, Mon.–Fri. 9 A.M.–3 P.M.), on the other side of Carstairs, 20 kilometers (12.5 miles) east on Highway 581 and 4.5 kilometers (2.8 miles) north on Highway 791. At this working museum, the raw wool is processed on clunky-looking machines—some of which date to the 1880s—into wools and yarns ready for knitting (and sale). A self-guided tour is offered.

Olds and Vicinity

Olds is a little more than halfway between Calgary and Red Deer. Surrounded by rich farmland, it's the home of **Olds College** (403/556-8281), which has been a leader in the development of Canadian agriculture for the last 100 years. Visitors are free to wander around the campus, admiring colorful beds of well-tended, prairie-hardy plants. The 600-hectare (1,480-acre) campus is along Highway 2, south of the main street.

Red Lodge Provincial Park protects a forested stretch of the Little Red Deer River 28 kilometers (17.5 miles) northwest of Olds. The park is situated within an ideal habitat for deer and moose. The campground (403/224-2547, mid-Apr.–mid-Oct., $22–28) has a kitchen shelter, coin-operated showers, and firewood, and the river is good for swimming, floating, and fishing.

Torrington

Torrington, on Highway 27, 28 kilometers (17.5 miles) east of Olds, has more gophers than residents. This wouldn't be unusual for a prairie town, except that Torrington's gophers are all stuffed. The **Gopher Hole Museum** (208 1st St., 403/631-3931, June–Sept. daily 10 A.M.–5 P.M., $2.50) is described as "a whimsical portrayal of daily life in our tranquil village." And that it is—approximately 40 dioramas house stuffed gophers in various poses, including gophers in love, gophers playing sports, trailer-court gophers, and even gophers wearing shirts declaring that animal rights activists, who were incensed at the idea of the museum, should "Go stuff themselves." Admission includes a copy of the words to the *Torrington Gopher Call Song*, which wafts through the quiet streets of the village whenever the museum is open.

Dry Island Buffalo Jump

This 1,180-hectare (2,900-acre) park is named for both an isolated mesa in the Red Deer River Valley and the site where natives stampeded bison over a cliff approximately 2,000 years ago. The buffalo jump—a 50-meter (164-foot) drop—is much higher than other jumps in Alberta and is in an ideal location; the approach to the jump is uphill, masking the presence of a cliff until the final few meters. Below the prairie benchland, cliff-like valley walls and banks of sandstone have been carved into strange-looking badlands by wind and water erosion. A great diversity of plantlife grows in the valley; more than 400 species of flowering plants have been recorded. The park is a day-use area only; apart from a picnic area and a few trails, it is undeveloped. Access is along a gravel road east from Highway 21. From the park entrance, at the top of the buffalo jump, the road descends steeply for 200 vertical meters (660 feet) into the valley (it can be extremely slippery after rain) to the bank of the Red Deer River.

Innisfail

Innisfail Historical Village (in the fairgrounds at 42nd St. and 52nd Ave., 403/227-2906, summer Mon.–Sat. 10 A.M.–5 P.M., Sun.

noon–5 P.M., donation) has re-created historic buildings, including a stopping house, a school, a store, a Canadian Pacific Railway (C.P.R.) station, and a blacksmith's shop, on a one-hectare (1.5-acre) site. The Royal Canadian Mounted Police (RCMP) **Police Dog Service Training Centre** (four km/2.5 mi south of town, 403/227-3346, free) is where police dog handlers and their four-legged companions come from across Canada to receive training in obedience, agility, and criminal apprehension. Through summer, public demonstrations are given every Wednesday at 2 P.M. Bookings are not required, but the small grandstand is usually full by start time, so arrive early for the best seats.

Markerville

This town, 16 kilometers (10 miles) west then three kilometers (1.9 miles) north of Innisfail, was originally settled by Icelandic people in the 1880s, who had settled in eastern Canada but after finding the land unproductive continued west. Today, around 100 people—most of

© ANDREW HEMPSTEAD

Markerville is one of Alberta's most attractive towns.

whom trace their heritage back to the original settlers—call Markerville home. It's a pretty village, with smartly painted homes and well-kept gardens. The only official attraction is **Markerville Creamery** (403/728-3006, mid-May–early Sept. Mon.–Sat. 10 A.M.–5:30 P.M., Sun. noon–5:30 P.M.). Between 1902 and the time of its closure in 1972, the creamery won many awards for its fine-quality butters, as you'll learn on a self-guided tour ($2) of the butter-making process. Part of the creamery has been converted to a *kaffistofa* (café) with a choice of Icelandic specialties.

The most famous of the Icelandic immigrants was Stephan A. Stephansson, one of the Western world's most prolific poets. He spent the early part of his life in his homeland, but most of his poetry was written in Canada. Just north of Markerville is his restored 1927 home, the distinctive pink-and-green colored **Stephansson House** (403/728-3929, mid-May–Aug. daily 10 A.M.–6 P.M., adult $3, senior and child $2). Interpretive panels beside the parking lot tell the story of Stephansson and his fellow immigrants, while a short trail leads through a grove of trees to the house itself.

RED DEER

This city of 86,000 (Alberta's third-largest) is on a bend of the Red Deer River, halfway between the cities of Calgary and Edmonton, which are 145 kilometers (90 miles) south and 148 kilometers (92 miles) north, respectively. From the highway, Red Deer seems to be all industrial estates and suburban sprawl, but an extensive park system runs through the city, and many historic buildings have been restored.

The name Red Deer was mentioned on maps by explorer David Thompson in the early 1800s. The Cree name for the river is *Waskasoo* (elk); scholars believe that Thompson translated the word incorrectly, confusing these animals with the red deer of Scotland.

Sights

If you're arriving in Red Deer from either the north or south, stay on Highway 2 until the

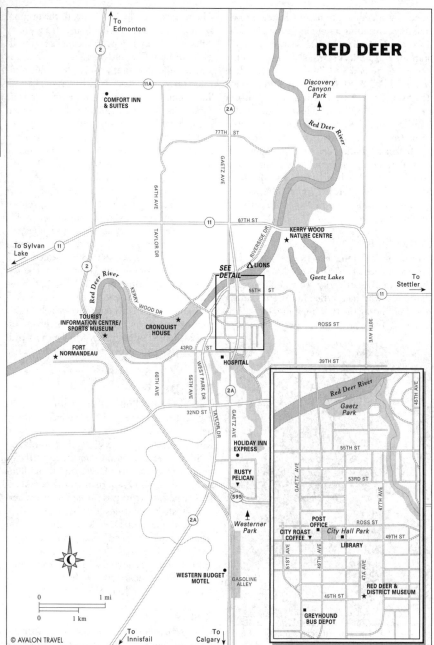

RED DEER

To Edmonton

COMFORT INN & SUITES

Discovery Canyon Park

Red Deer River

77TH ST

GAETZ AVE

64TH AVE

TAYLOR DR

67TH ST

11

KERRY WOOD NATURE CENTRE

To Sylvan Lake

Red Deer River

KERRY WOOD DR

LIONS

RIVERSIDE DR

SEE DETAIL

55TH ST

Gaetz Lakes

To Stettler

TOURIST INFORMATION CENTRE/ SPORTS MUSEUM

CRONQUIST HOUSE

ROSS ST

30TH AVE

FORT NORMANDEAU

43RD ST

39TH ST

HOSPITAL

60TH AVE

55TH AVE

WEST PARK DR

TAYLOR DR

GAETZ AVE

2A

32ND ST

Red Deer River

Gaetz Park

45TH AVE

HOLIDAY INN EXPRESS

55TH ST

RUSTY PELICAN

595

53RD ST

47TH AVE

GAETZ AVE

POST OFFICE

ROSS ST

Westerner Park

CITY ROAST COFFEE

City Hall Park

49TH ST

51ST AVE

LIBRARY

49TH AVE

47A AVE

WESTERN BUDGET MOTEL

GASOLINE ALLEY

45TH ST

RED DEER & DISTRICT MUSEUM

0   1 mi

0   1 km

GREYHOUND BUS DEPOT

To Innisfail

To Calgary

© AVALON TRAVEL

large red-and-white **Red Deer Visitor and Convention Bureau** building comes into view (from the north, take the 32nd St. exit and loop back onto Hwy. 2 northbound). In addition to being a good source of information, it is home to the **Alberta Sports Hall of Fame and Museum** (Hwy. 2, in the same building as the Red Deer Visitor and Convention Bureau, 403/341-8614, summer daily 9 A.M.–6 P.M., the rest of the year daily 10 A.M.–5 P.M., adult $3, child $2). Displays highlight the feats of Albertan sporting heroes such as hockey legend Wayne Gretzky, multiple-time World Figure Skating Champion Kurt Browning, and Red Deer girl Jamie Sale, who, with partner David Pelletier, was belatedly awarded a skating gold medal at the 2002 Winter Olympics after the infamous judging controversy. But it's not all about winter sports—you can also admire the achievements of Albertans like Sharon Wood (the first North American woman to summit Mount Everest) and Jason Zuback (multiple

world long drive golfing champion). From this point, it's possible to walk (or drive via 32nd St.) to **Fort Normandeau** (403/346-2010, mid-May–June daily noon–5 P.M., July–Aug. daily noon–8 P.M., free). This replica is built on the site of a fort constructed in the spring of 1885 in anticipation of the Riel Rebellion—a Métis uprising led by Louis Riel.

The downtown **Red Deer and District Museum** (4525 47A Ave., 403/309-8405, July and Aug. Mon.–Fri. 10 A.M.–5 P.M. and Sat.–Sun. 1–5 P.M., the rest of the year daily noon–5 P.M., donation), which reopened in early 2010 after extensive renovations, tells the story of the area from prehistoric times to the present, with emphasis on the growth and development of the last 100 years. If you have youngsters in tow, head for interactive Children's Zone; if you have a love of the tacky and wacky, search out the display of The World's Most Boring Postcard, a title bestowed on a postcard depicting the museum exterior.

Recreation

Straddling the Red Deer River is 11-kilometer-long (seven-mile-long) **Waskasoo Park.** The park has a 75-kilometer (47-mile) trail system, which is good for walking or biking in summer and cross-country skiing in winter. If you've stopped at the highway-side information center, it's possible to drive through the one-way gate to adjacent **Heritage Ranch** (403/347-4977), where trail rides are $35 per hour.

Continuing downstream, **Kerry Wood Nature Centre** (6300 45th Ave., 403/346-2010, daily 10 A.M.–5 P.M.) has various exhibits and videos on the natural history of the river valley and provides access to a paved walking trail through the adjacent 118-hectare (292-acre) **Gaetz Lakes Sanctuary.** Protected since 1924, this parkland of spruce and poplar interspersed with marshes is home to 128 recorded species of birds and 25 species of mammals.

Children will love **Discovery Canyon Park** (403/343-8311, daily 9 A.M.–8 P.M. in summer), which is all about discovering fun rather than learning. The highlight is a natural stream that has been modified into a

---

A DAY AT THE BEACH

Landlocked Albertans don't have a great deal of choice when it comes to a vacation on the beach, unless they head over the mountains to Invermere, in British Columbia, or jump aboard an airplane. One of the exceptions is **Sylvan Lake,** 22 kilometers (14 miles) west of Red Deer, which has been a popular summer resort since the beginning of the 20th century. It has more than five kilometers (three miles) of sandy beaches, clean warm water, a large marina, and plenty of recreation facilities. Kids will love **Wild Rapids** (Lakeshore Dr., 403/887-3636) and its 11 water slides, heated pool, and sailboard and paddleboat rentals. The beachy stretch of lake is lined with surf-clothing shops, water-sport rentals, casual cafés, kid-friendly accommodations, and even a lighthouse. In the vicinity, Gull, Pigeon, and Miquelon Lakes have pleasant beaches and warm water for swimming.

waterslide, complete with rapids and a big pool at one end. Admission is free and tube rental is $3. To get there, follow 30th Ave, four kilometers (2.5 miles) north of 67th Street.

Accommodations and Camping

Red Deer's location between Alberta's two largest cities makes it a popular location for conventions and conferences, so the city has a lot of hotels. The cheapies are at the south end of the city along "Gasoline Alley." Try **Western Budget Motel** (37468 Hwy. 2 S, 403/358-5755, www.westernbudgetmotel.com, $59–99 s, $79–99 d), on the western side of Gasoline Alley, where the rooms are the best value between Calgary and Edmonton—they are clean, spacious, and relatively modern.

The **Holiday Inn Express** is south of downtown on the northbound side of the road (2803 Gaetz Ave., 403/343-2112 or 877/660-8550, www.hiexpress.com, $119–169 s or d). The rooms are spacious, modern, and well furnished. Breakfast is included in the rates, as is access to an indoor saltwater pool.

While the Western Budget Motel provides excellent value, my pick of the Red Deer accommodations insofar as room quality goes is the (**Comfort Inn & Suites** (6846 66th St., 403/348-0025 or 866/348-0025, www.comfortinnreddeer.com, $140 s or d), just off Highway 2 at the north end of town. Opened in 2005, the spacious rooms are filled with modern conveniences, a light breakfast is included in the rates, and there's an indoor pool with a waterslide. Another reason to stay is this motel's eco-friendly design, which includes a roof covered in solar power panels.

Red Deer has good city camping at the treed **Lions Campground,** on the west side of the river (4759 Riverside Dr., 403/342-8183, May–Sept., unserviced sites $19, powered sites $29). To get there, follow Gaetz Avenue north through town and turn right after crossing the Red Deer River. The campground has showers, full hookups, and a laundry room.

Food

Head to **City Roast Coffee** (4940 Ross St.,

403/347-0893, Mon.–Sat. 7:30 A.M.–6 P.M.) for a caffeine fix in a city-style coffeehouse. Around the corner, a very different type of eatery, the **Jerry Can** (5005 50th Ave., 403/347-9417, open daily for breakfast and lunch), attracts a strange collection of locals who come for the inexpensive meals and to catch up on gossip.

Fast-food and family-style restaurants line 50th (Gaetz) Avenue north and south of downtown, but for Red Deer's most distinguished dining experience plan on eating at the (**Rusty Pelican** (2079 50th Ave., 403/347-1414, daily 11 A.M.–10 P.M., $14–29). Mains range from the semi-exotic (Cajun-style red snapper) to the traditional (prime rib of beef with Yorkshire pudding). A menu filled with seafood starters, a sensibly priced wine list, and melt-in-your-mouth strawberry cheesecake round out this top pick.

Information and Services

The Red Deer Visitor and Convention Bureau operates the excellent tourist information center (403/346-0180 or 800/215-8946, www.tourismreddeer.net, year-round Mon.–Fri. 9 A.M.–5 P.M., Sat.–Sun. 10 A.M.–5 P.M., until 6 P.M. in summer) on Highway 2 between the main north and south entrances to the city. It's on the city side of the highway (if you're arriving from the north, take the 32nd St. exit and loop back onto Hwy. 2 northbound). In addition to providing a load of information, the center has a gift shop, a concession area, and restrooms, and is adjacent to a picnic area.

Red Deer Public Library is an excellent facility housed in a single-story, red-brick building behind City Hall (4818 49th St., 403/346-4576, Mon.–Thurs. 9:30 A.M.–8:30 P.M., Fri.–Sat. 9:30 A.M.–5:30 P.M., Sun. 1:30–5 P.M.).

Getting There

Two scheduled bus services link Red Deer to Calgary and Edmonton. **Greyhound** departs from the depot (4303 Gaetz Ave., 403/343-8866) throughout the day for both cities. **Red Arrow** (403/531-0350 or 800/232-1958, www.

redarrow.ca) offers a more luxurious service, with complimentary beverages and snacks. Their buses depart north of downtown at 5315 54th Street four times daily for Calgary and Edmonton.

LACOMBE

From Red Deer, Highway 2 continues 30 kilometers (19 miles) north to Lacombe, a town of 9,000 that centers on a main street lined with Edwardian-era buildings.

Big-hitting golfers should consider a stop at the nearby **Nursery Golf & Country Club** (Range Rd. 27–0, 403/782-5400, greens fees $42), which is home to Canada's longest golf hole. It's the 11th hole, a par 6 stretching to 782 yards from the back markers. Turn off Highway 2 four kilometers (2.5 miles) north of town.

◖ Lacombe Corn Maze

Only open when the corn reaches a height of six feet, the Lacombe Corn Maze (Hwy. 12, 403/782-4653, late July–Aug. Mon.–Sat. 11 A.M.–9 P.M., Sept.–mid-Oct. Wed.–Fri. 4–8 P.M., Sat. 11 A.M.–8 P.M., adult $9, child

The Lacombe Corn Maze changes design each year.

$7) is a rural highlight of central Alberta, even for adults. Cut in a different design each year, it takes at least an hour to get through, with a "cheat sheet" for those who get truly lost. Also on site is a petting zoo, a tire horse carousel, a corn cannon, a jumping pillow, and miniature train rides to keep the young ones amused for a bit longer.

Practicalities

Between Highway 2 and downtown is a campground and an information center (www.lacombetourism.com), but for motel accommodations, stay on the highway to reach **Wolf Creek Inn** (Hwy. 2, 403/782-4716, $70 s or d). Overlooking a small lake, it's home to 20 simple rooms and has a restaurant that is a popular spot for highway travelers looking to avoid fast-food joints. Access is only from Highway 2 southbound, so if you're heading toward Edmonton, take the second exit and loop back south via the overpass.

HIGHWAY 12 EAST

From Lacombe, it's 70 kilometers (43 miles) west to Stettler on Highway 12. Out of sight to the north is **Buffalo Lake,** a large, shallow body of water surrounded by a hummocky area created by receding ice during the last Ice Age. On the lake's southern shore is ◖ **Ol' MacDonalds Resort** (off Hwy. 835, 403/742-6603, www.olmacdonalds.com, May–Sept., unserviced $25–28, hookups $32–40, cabins $62–150 s or d), a sprawling campground offering over 300 treed sites and an amazing array of things to do. Aside from the beach with shallow, warm water, there's watercraft rentals, evening wagon rides, a petting zoo, indoor mini-golf within a museum, an antique carousel, a café, and bike and buggy rentals.

Stettler

The farming town of Stettler (population 5,800) is home to **Alberta Prairie Railway Excursions** (403/742-2811, www.absteamtrain.com), a tourist train that runs south to the even smaller town of Big Valley. A rollicking good time is had by all, with live music, the occasional train robbery, and a hearty meal served at the turnaround point. Check the website for a schedule; the train runs each weekend May through October (and Thurs. and Fri. in July and Aug.). The fare is adult $85, youth $65, child $35. Stettler also offers the **Town and Country Museum** (6302 44th Ave., 403/742-4534, May–early Sept. daily 10 A.M.–5:30 P.M., adult $3, senior and child $2), a surprisingly large complex comprising over two dozen buildings spread over three hectares (7.5 acres). Highlights include the imposing courthouse, a railway station, and a small farmhouse that provided a home for three generations of the same family.

The nicest of five accommodations in town is **Ramada Inn & Suites** (6711 49th Ave., at the west entrance to town, 403/742-6555 or 888/442-6555, www.ramada.com, $145 s or d), a solid four-story chain hotel that opened in 2007. **Town of Stettler Campground** (6202 44th Ave., 403/742-4411, May–Oct., $14–20) is across the road from a spray park on the west side of town.

Big Knife Provincial Park

Legend has it that Big Knife Creek was named after a fight between two long-standing enemies—one Cree, the other Blackfoot—that resulted in the death of both men. The park's small campground (mid-May–mid-Sept., $18) has limited facilities, but the Battle River flows through the park, making for good swimming and canoeing. To get to the park from Stettler, head east along Highway 12 approximately 40 kilometers (25 miles) to Halkirk, then north on Highway 855 another 20 kilometers (12.5 miles).

Gooseberry Lake Provincial Park

This small park, 14 kilometers (8.7 miles) north of Consort, is on the shore of a tree-encircled lake and is made up of rolling grassland and a series of alkaline ponds. Many birds, including the northern phalarope, use the lake as a staging area along their migratory paths. The campground (403/742-7512, mid-May–mid-Sept., $20–25) is between the lake and a nine-hole golf course and has a kitchen shelter and firewood.

WETASKIWIN

This town, halfway between Red Deer and Edmonton on Highway 2A, is an important wheat-farming and cattle-ranching center of 11,000. In the language of the Cree, Wetaskiwin ("Where Peace was Made") is a reference to nearby hills where a treaty between the Cree and Blackfoot was signed in 1867.

Reynolds-Alberta Museum

This world-class facility, two kilometers (1.2 miles) west of downtown (Hwy. 13, 780/361-1351, daily 10 A.M.–5 P.M., closed Mon. Sept.–May, adult $9, senior $7, child $5), does a wonderful job of cataloging the history of transportation in Alberta, from horse-drawn carriages to luxurious 1950s automobiles. Over 1,000 vehicles have been fully restored, but some, such as a handmade snowmobile, are in their original condition. At the far end of the main room, you can peer into a large hall where the restoration takes place. The transportation displays encircle a large area where traditional farm machinery is on show, from the most basic plow to a massive combine harvester.

Behind the museum lies an airstrip and a large hangar that houses **Canada's Aviation Hall of Fame.** The Hall of Fame recognizes those who have made contributions to the history of aviation and contains several vintage aircraft. Admission is included with a ticket to the Reynolds-Alberta Museum. Hours are also the same. Operating out of the Hall of Fame, **Central Aviation** (780/352-9689) offers a 10-minute flight in an old biplane for $119; weekends only.

Accommodations and Food

Looking for a regular motel room? Try the **Super 8 Motel** (3820 56th St., 780/361-3808 or 800/800-8000, www.super8.com, $109–119 s or d), a newer place that is within walking distance of the museum. Rates include continental breakfast. Opposite the local golf course, **Wetaskiwin Lions RV Campground**

(2.5 km/1.6 mi east of town along Hwy. 13, 780/352-7258, May–Sept., unserviced sites $18, hookups $24–26) has free showers, an Internet kiosk, a laundry room, a cooking shelter, a stocked trout pond, and mini-golf.

Grandma Lee's Bakery (5103 50th Ave., 780/352-7711, Mon.–Sat. 7:30 A.M.–5 P.M.) is enduringly popular with locals for its small-town atmosphere as much as its food. Recommended are the meat pies and tasty pastries. A few doors away, the **Stanley Café** (5015 50th Ave., 780/352-3633, daily noon–8 P.M., $7–11.50) is a plain diner with Westernized Chinese food at low prices. Opposite the information center is **Runway Lunch** (5505 50th Ave., 780/352-3777, Mon.–Fri. 7:30 A.M.–4 P.M., lunches $5.50–8), where the home-style cooking is a welcome respite from the blandness of the fast-food joints lining nearby 56th Street.

Information

At the junction of Highway 2A and 50th Avenue, the local **tourist information center** (4910 55th St., 780/352-8003, year-round Mon.–Fri. 9 A.M.–5 P.M., as well as summer weekends 9 A.M.–3 P.M.) is impossible to miss—just look for the colorful water tower across the road.

CAMROSE AND VICINITY

The population of Camrose, 40 kilometers (25 miles) east of Wetaskiwin, swells the first weekend of August when country music fans descend on the local exhibition grounds for the **Big Valley Jamboree** (780/672-0224 or 888/404-1234, www.bigvalleyjamboree.com), one of North America's largest such gatherings. Daily passes are around $80, and a three-day weekend pass goes for $195; camping is $120 for as long as you can handle the heat, the noise, and the booze (actually, it's not that bad—a great time is had by all).

As a tribute to early Norwegian settlers, a nine-meter (30-foot) scaled-down replica of a Viking longship is on display in the **Bill Fowler Centre** (5402 48th Ave., 780/672-4217, summer Mon.–Fri. 8:30 A.M.–8 P.M. and Sat.–Sun.

9:30 A.M.–5:30 P.M., the rest of the year Mon.–Fri. 8:30 A.M.–4:30 P.M., free). Overlooking Mirror Lake, this building is also home to the local **tourist information center** and the start of a 10-kilometer (6.2-mile) trail system that encircles the lake (2.2 km/1.4 mi) and follows Camrose Creek south to the campground.

Accommodations and Food

Just a couple of blocks from Mirror Lake, the centrally located **Camrose Motel** (6116 48th Ave., 780/672-3364, from $70 s or d) has 20 basic rooms, each with a microwave and a small fridge. The town-operated **Valleyview Campground** (5204 50th Ave., May–Sept., $15–20) has powered sites, showers, a kitchen shelter, and firewood. To get there, follow 53rd Street south from Highway 13 for two kilometers (1.2 miles) and turn left on 39th Avenue.

The friendly, country-style atmosphere is similar at **Camrose Railway Station** (44th St., 780/672-3099, mid-May–Aug. Thurs.–Fri. 1–5 P.M., Sat. 10 A.M.–5 P.M.). It's typical tearoom fare in a restored station. Call ahead for a Saturday schedule—often it's a theme with links to Camrose's past (German, Ukrainian, Native, etc).

Along the highway through town, the **Monte Carlo Restaurant** (4907 48th Ave., Sun.–Mon. 11 A.M.–8 P.M., Tues.–Thurs. 11 A.M.–9 P.M., Fri.–Sat. 11 A.M.–10 P.M., $14–26) is the most popular place in town for a special night out, although the menu isn't particularly creative (think fettuccini alfredo, roast chicken, fish-and-chips, and pork souvlaki).

Miquelon Lake Provincial Park

This 906-hectare (2,240-acre) park, 30 kilometers (19 miles) north of Camrose on Highway 833, is part of the massive 650-square-kilometer (250-square-mile) **Cooking Lake Moraine**, a hummocky, forested region dotted with lakes that extends north to Elk Island National Park. At the end of the last Ice Age, as the sheet of ice that covered much of the continent receded, it occasionally stalled, as it did in this area. Chunks of ice then broke off and melted, depositing glacial till in mounds. Between the mounds are hollows, known as kettles, which have filled with water. The **Knob and Kettle Trail System** starts behind the baseball diamond and is a series of short interconnecting trails through this intriguing landscape. The draw for most visitors is the wide beach fronting a warm and shallow bay. Other amenities include a modern visitor center, a large playground, and an adjacent golf course (780/672-7308). The 🄲 **park campground** (780/672-7274, unserviced sites $22, powered sites $28) has modern washrooms, kitchen shelters, and firewood.

East on Highway 14

From Miquelon Lake Provincial Park it's a short drive north to **Tofield,** from where Highway 14 heads 180 kilometers (112 miles) southeast to Wainwright and then continues east into Saskatchewan. East of Tofield is **Beaverhill Natural Area,** western Canada's only shorebird reserve. The protected area centers on a large, shallow lake where more than 250 bird species have been recorded. **Beaverhill Lake Nature Centre** (403/662-3191, summer Tues.–Sat. 10 A.M.–6 P.M., Sun. 2–4 P.M., free) is an interpretive center with maps of the area and bird checklists. Campers gravitate to **Lindbrook Star Gazer Campground** (51123 Range Rd. 200, 780/662-4439, www.lindbrookstargazer.ca, late May–Sept., $32–37), which has an outdoor swimming pool. To get there from Tofield, head 10 kilometers (6.2 miles) west on Highway 14 then three kilometers (1.9 miles) north on SH 630.

Southeast of **Viking** are two "rib stones," carved with a design resembling bison ribs that have been dated at 1,000 years old. The stones held special significance for generations of Plains Indians, whose lives revolved around the movement of bison herds. They believed that by conducting certain ceremonial rites and by leaving gifts of beads or tobacco around the stones, their luck in hunting would improve. They then gave thanks by leaving more gifts after a successful hunt. The site is not well marked. Fourteen kilometers (8.7 miles) east of Viking on Highway 14 is a historical marker. A little farther east is a gravel road to the south; follow this road two kilometers (1.2 miles) to Highway 615, turn east (left), then take the first gravel road to the south (right) and follow it for 2.5 kilometers (1.5 miles) to a low knoll surrounded by fields. A provincial historic cairn marks the site.

The last town along Highway 14 before Saskatchewan, Wainwright is best known for the military's 400-square-kilometer (154 square miles) **CFB/ASU Wainwright,** a training facility used mostly by reservists. A small head of bison (turn left at the guarded entrance, then right down the fence line for best viewing opportunities) is the only reminder of a national park created in 1908 to protect plains bison. A local restaurant, the 🄲 **Honey Pot Eatery & Pub** (823 2nd Ave., 780/842-4094, Mon.–Sat. 11 A.M.–9:30 P.M., Sun. 11 A.M.–2 P.M., $12–20), is worthy of a mention for the fact that it has been serving up healthy food for much longer than it has been trendy. It's been open since 1979, serving hungry locals and travelers alike dishes as varied as grilled arctic char and elk smothered in saskatoon berries.

Dillberry Lake Provincial Park is on the Alberta/Saskatchewan border, 50 kilometers (31 miles) southeast of Wainwright. The lake is surrounded by sandy beaches and low sand dunes (the biggest dunes are at the southeastern end of the lake), and its clear spring-fed waters are good for swimming. A 200-site campground (780/858-3824, mid-May–mid-Sept., unserviced sites $20, powered sites $26) is behind the park's finest beach and has showers, kitchen shelters, and firewood.

SOUTHERN ALBERTA

Southern Alberta is bordered to the east by Saskatchewan, to the south by Montana in the United States, and to the west by British Columbia. The Alberta–British Columbia border is along the Continental Divide, where the Canadian Rockies rise dramatically from the prairies and are visible from up to 200 kilometers (124 miles) away. From high in these mountains, the Oldman, Crowsnest, Waterton, St. Mary, and Belly Rivers flow east through the rolling foothills and across the shortgrass prairies into the South Saskatchewan River, which eventually drains into Hudson Bay. Among southern Alberta's rivers, only the Milk River is not part of this system; from its headwaters in northern Montana, the river flows north and east across southern Alberta before reentering the United States west of Wild Horse. From there, it joins the Missouri/Mississippi River System, eventually draining into the Gulf of Mexico. All of these rivers have carved deep gorges into the prairies, providing havens for many species of wildlife, including pronghorn, deer, foxes, coyotes, and bobcats.

Southern Alberta reveals plentiful evidence of its history and prehistory. Thousands of years of wind and water erosion have uncovered the world's best-preserved dinosaur eggs near Milk River and have carved mysterious-looking sandstone hoodoos farther downstream at Writing-on-Stone Provincial Park—named for the abundant rock carvings and paintings created there by ancient artists. Head-Smashed-In Buffalo Jump, west of Fort Macleod, was used for at least 5,700 years by native peoples to drive massive herds of buffalo to their deaths.

SOUTHERN ALBERTA

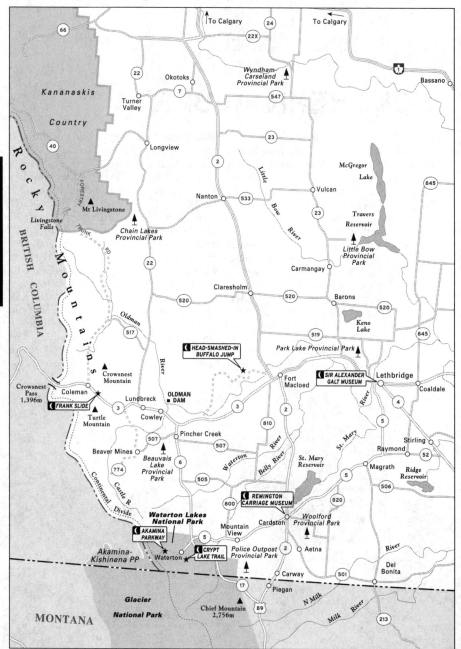

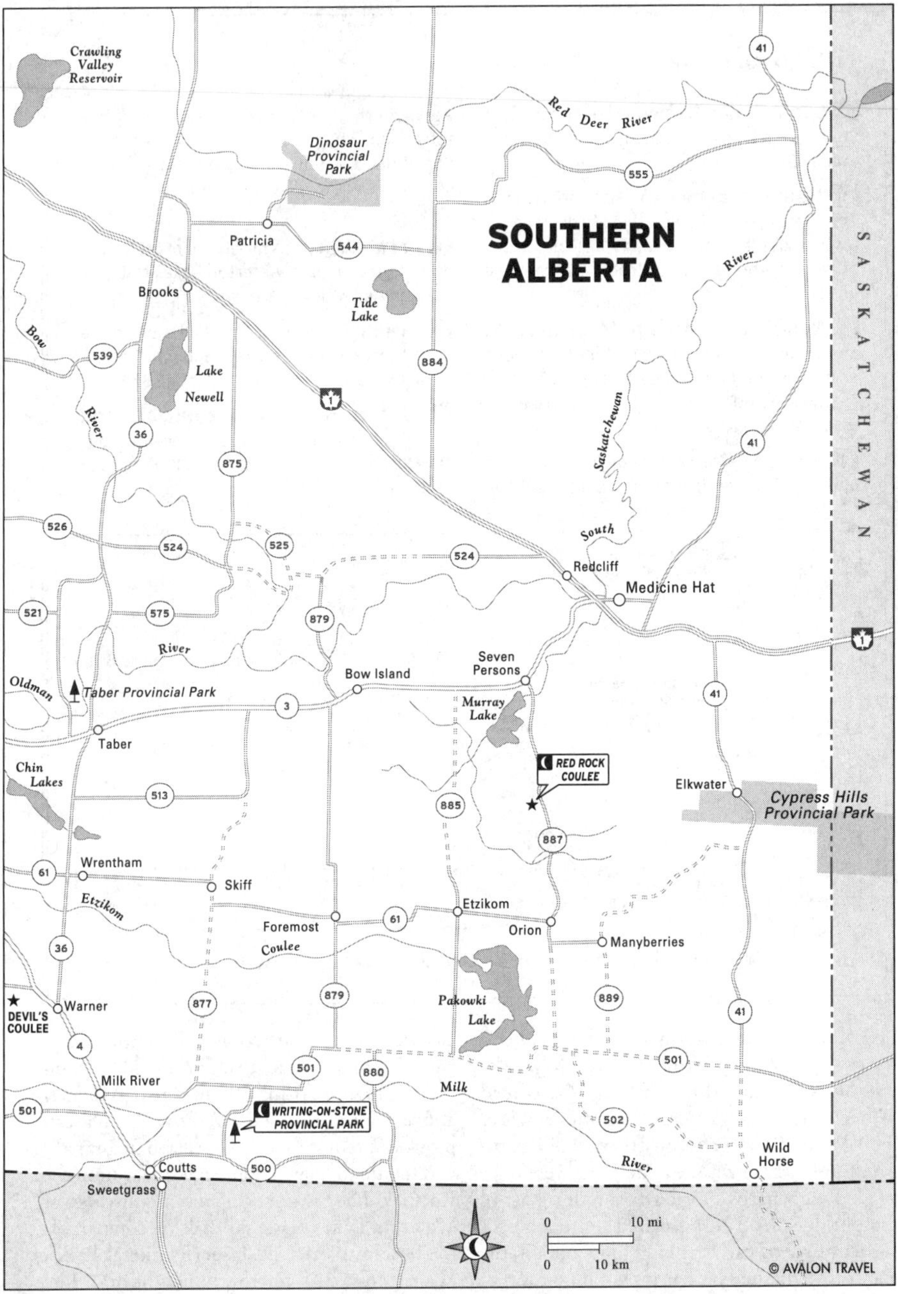

SOUTHERN ALBERTA

Crawling Valley Reservoir

Dinosaur Provincial Park

Red Deer River

Patricia — 544

Brooks — 539

Tide Lake

36 — Lake Newell

875

526 — 524 — 525 — 524 — Redcliff — Medicine Hat

521 — 575 — 879 — South Saskatchewan River

River — Bow Island — Seven Persons

Oldman — Taber Provincial Park — 3 — Murray Lake — RED ROCK COULEE — Elkwater — Cypress Hills Provincial Park

Taber

Chin Lakes — 513 — 885 — 887

61 — Wrentham — Skiff — Etzikom — Orion — Manyberries

Foremost Coulee — 61

36

Pakowki Lake — 889

DEVIL'S COULEE — Warner — 877 — 879

4 — 501 — 880 — Milk — 501 — 502 — Wild Horse

501 — Milk River — WRITING-ON-STONE PROVINCIAL PARK — River

Coutts — 500

Sweetgrass

SASKATCHEWAN

0 10 mi
0 10 km

© AVALON TRAVEL

HIGHLIGHTS

◖ Bar U Ranch National Historic Site: Step back in time at this historic foothills ranch (page 332).

◖ Head-Smashed-In Buffalo Jump: The name may be the first thing to get your attention, but it is the ingenuity of generations of natives who used this ancient site that will amaze you (page 333).

◖ Remington Carriage Museum: With more than 200 beautifully restored carriages on display, this museum will have you yearning for the romanticism of the world before automobiles (page 340).

◖ Akamina Parkway: You'll want to take both scenic drives in Waterton Lakes National

Park, but this one gets the nod as a must-see attraction. Why? Because when you reach the end of the road you can rent a canoe and paddle out onto magnificent Cameron Lake (page 345).

◖ Crypt Lake: This hike is undoubtedly the most spectacular in Waterton Lakes National Park (page 345).

◖ Frank Slide: It is impossible not to be awed by the scope of the rock slide that devastated the town of Frank in 1913 (page 353).

◖ Writing-on-Stone Provincial Park: One of North America's largest concentrations of native rock art is the highlight of this remote prairie park (page 355).

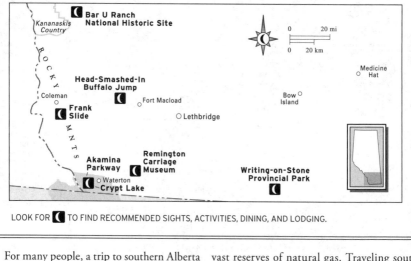

LOOK FOR ◖ TO FIND RECOMMENDED SIGHTS, ACTIVITIES, DINING, AND LODGING.

For many people, a trip to southern Alberta starts in Calgary, from where they take Highway 2 south through Fort Macleod to Alberta's third-largest city, Lethbridge, where Fort Whoop-Up is a reconstruction of a notorious post where whiskey and guns were once traded with natives for buffalo hides. East of Lethbridge, in an area declared "unsuitable for agriculture" by early explorer John Palliser, the city of Medicine Hat has grown up on top of

vast reserves of natural gas. Traveling south from Medicine Hat, the Cypress Hills soon come into view, rising 500 meters (1,640 feet) above the prairies. The tree-covered plateau provides a refuge for many species of mammals, and mountain plants flourish here, far from the Rockies. The breathtaking mountainscapes of Waterton Lakes National Park are comparable to those of Banff and Jasper National Parks, Waterton's two northern neighbors. The

Municipality of Crowsnest Pass comprises several small communities that extend from the ranching center of Pincher Creek west to the British Columbia border. Here you can walk through the foundations of once-thriving communities, tour an underground mine, or climb infamous Turtle Mountain.

PLANNING YOUR TIME

The way to approach your time in southern Alberta depends on the direction of travel. From Calgary, if your vacation is all about the south, it is a 600-kilometer (373-mile) loop on three highways (Hwys. 2, 3, and 1) to hit the major cities of Lethbridge and Medicine Hat. But most of the highlights are away from the main routes, so you would more likely cover 1,000 kilometers (621 miles). Alternatively, if you are approaching from the United States, after crossing the border from Montana you could easily spend two days winding your way north to Calgary and Banff. Regardless, you won't want to miss the Western history of Bar U Ranch National Historic Site, the cultural importance associated with Head-

Smashed-In Buffalo Jump, and the wonderful collection of carriages at the Remington Carriage Museum. Simply because of its out-of-the-way location, you'll want to spend at least one day in Waterton Lakes National Park, exploring the two main roads, including the Akamina Parkway to Cameron Lake. This still allows time to walk some shorter trails. If you're a keen hiker, schedule a trip to magnificent Crypt Lake. The highway west through the Crowsnest Pass makes a loop through the Canadian Rockies possible, or opens up an entire new vacation in the Kootenays region of British Columbia. Either way, you'll drive through the Crowsnest Pass, a low-key yet scenic area rich in coal-mining history—but also with its share of misery, most apparent at the Frank Slide, where a slab of Turtle Mountain destroyed a town in 1913.

Although Writing-On-Stone Provincial Park is relatively remote in relation to the highlights of southern Alberta, and indoor accommodations are nonexistent in and around this park, it is worthwhile for the high concentration of native rock art.

Calgary to Lethbridge

The trip between Calgary and Lethbridge takes about two hours nonstop, but there are many tempting detours in between, including the ranching country southwest of Calgary, the Porcupine Hills west of Claresholm, historic Fort Macleod, and Head-Smashed-In Buffalo Jump, one of the best-preserved sites of its type in North America.

OKOTOKS AND VICINITY

The fast-growing town of Okotoks is in the Sheep River Valley 34 kilometers (21 miles) south of Calgary and just minutes from Highway 2 to the east. It is the largest population base between Calgary and Lethbridge, and many of its 18,000 residents, up from 7,000 just 20 years ago, commute into Calgary to work. Many old buildings still stand and

have been incorporated into a walking tour, with maps available at the tourist information center. Along similar lines is the **Okotoks Art Walk,** which links downtown businesses displaying the works of local artists. Starting point is the **Okotoks Art Gallery** (53 N. Railway St., 403/938-3204, Mon.–Fri. 10 A.M.–5 P.M., Sat.–Sun. noon–5 P.M., donation), through downtown in a restored railway station.

Accommodations and Camping

The best accommodations in town are at **Okotoks Country Inn** (on Hwy. 2A, 403/938-1999 or 877/938-3336, $100 s, $110–130 d), with 40 climate-controlled motel rooms. Rates include a light breakfast. Municipally operated **Sheep River Campground** (99 Woodhaven Dr., 403/938-4282, www.

okotokslionscampground.com, May–Oct., tents $18, hookups $28–35) has a delightful riverside location just a short walk from town off Highway 2A.

Black Diamond

This town of 1,900 on the banks of the Sheep River, west of Okotoks along Highway 7, was named for the coal once mined nearby. Town center is a bustling little strip along Centre Avenue. At the main intersection is the **Black Diamond Hotel** (105 Centre St., 403/933-4656), which has been modernized on the outside, but on the inside retains a classic small-town pub atmosphere that rocks with country music each weekend. **Lions Campground** (access via 5th St. off Centre St., 403/933-5785, May–Oct., unserviced sites $17, powered sites $20–25) is a great little spot by the Sheep River and within easy walking distance of downtown. It has showers, a kitchen shelter, and firewood.

Turner Valley

Linked to Black Diamond by a four-kilometer (2.5-mile) riverside path, Turner Valley (population 2,000) is synonymous with the oil-and-gas industry in Alberta as, Canada's first major crude-oil discovery was made here in 1914. Natural gas has been burned off ever since at an area known as Hell's Half Acre, on the eastern edge of town. Protected as a National Historic Site, the **Turner Valley Gas Plant** is currently closed for reclamation, but head over to **Hell's Half Acre Bridge,** which crosses the Sheep River southeast of downtown, from where gas flares that still burn 24 hours a day can be viewed.

Coyote Moon Café (202 Main St., 403/933-3363, Mon.–Fri. 7:30 A.M.–5 P.M., Sat. and Sun. 9 A.M.–7 P.M., lunches $6–10) is a fantastic little café, always bustling and with wonderful smells coming from the kitchen. Even though this is cowboy country, the coffee choices are city-style all the way. One block south, **Route 40 Soup Co.** (146 Main St., 403/933-7676, Mon.–Tues. 11 A.M.–7 P.M., Wed.–Thurs. 11 A.M.–9 P.M., Fri.–Sat.

11 A.M.–9 P.M., $9) is a real find. The soups are rich, thick, and full of locally sourced produce.

Bar U Ranch National Historic Site

Established in 1882, the Bar U Ranch (31 km/19 mi south of Black Diamond, 403/395-2212 or 800/568-4996, daily 9 A.M.–5 P.M. June–early Oct., adult $7.80, senior $6.60, child $3.90) was one of western Canada's top ranches in the late 1800s. It was a corporate ranch, run by the Northwest Cattle Company and stocked with more than 3,000 cattle driven north from Montana. The company was renowned throughout North America as a leading breeder of Percherons, a type of draft horse that originated in the Perche region of France. Like most of the big ranches in North America, the Bar U was broken up over time. Today a 145-hectare (360-acre) parcel of the original spread has been preserved, and many of the old buildings have been restored. From the visitor center it's a short walk—or wagon ride—to the original ranch buildings, which include a blacksmith's shop and a general store. Ranching skills are also demonstrated. In the **Roadhouse Restaurant,** the menu reflects the food that ranch hands of days gone by would have enjoyed after a long day in the saddle: Buffalo burgers, sourdough breads, hearty soups, and stew are all offered.

HIGH RIVER TO FORT MACLEOD

High River

In the heart of the province's ranching country, 45 kilometers (28 miles) south of Calgary, the town of High River has grown steadily from its beginnings as a fording spot along its namesake. From Highway 2, take 12th Avenue west to the downtown precinct, a compact collection of staid old buildings on the west side of the railway tracks. Housed in a restored Canadian Pacific Railway (C.P.R.) station, the **Museum of the Highwood** (406 1st St. W, 403/652-7156, Mon.–Sat. 10 A.M.–4 P.M., Sun. noon–4 P.M. in summer, $3) is chock-full of

THE BIG ROCK

The name **Okotoks** came from the Blackfoot word *okatak* (rock), probably in reference to the massive boulders seven kilometers (4.3 miles) west of town along Highway 7. Known as *erratics*, they are the largest such geological formations of their type in the world. During the last Ice Age, a sheet of ice up to one kilometer (0.6 miles) thick crept forward from the north. A landslide in what is now Jasper National Park deposited large boulders on top of the ice. The ice continued moving south, carrying the boulders with it. Many thousands of years later, as temperatures warmed and the ice melted, the boulders were deposited far from their source (hence the name "erratic").

displays portraying early Western life. Of particular interest is the exhibit cataloging chuck wagon racing, a sport that has special significance to locals as the area boasts many champions. Better still, if you're visiting on the third weekend of June, plan on attending the **North American Chuckwagon Championships** at the fairgrounds.

Of the three motels in town, the **Super 8** (1601 13th Ave., 403/652-4448 or 866/831-8558, www.super8.com, from $109 s or d) has the newest facilities, including an indoor pool and waterslide. Or camp in **George Lane Memorial Park** (west along 5th Ave. SW, 403/652-2529, www.georgelanecampground.ca, May–Sept., unserviced sites $16, powered sites $25).

Nanton

A couple of attractions make this ranching town 70 kilometers (43 miles) south of Calgary a worthwhile stop. First, beside the southbound lane of Highway 2 is **Nanton Lancaster Society Air Museum** (403/646-2270, daily 9 A.M.–5 P.M. mid-April–mid-Oct., Sat.–Sun. 10 A.M.–4 P.M. mid-Oct.–mid-Apr.), home to one of the few Lancaster bombers still in existence. Second, Nanton is home to a number of

fine antiques shops, mostly on the northbound side of the highway. Also northbound is an early-20th-century schoolhouse that functions as the local **information center** (403/646-5933, daily 9 A.M.–5 P.M. July–Aug.).

The best place to stay in Nanton is the **Ranchland Inn** (on Hwy. 2 northbound at 18th St., 403/646-2933, $70 s, $80 d), offering 27 basic but comfortable rooms. Across the railway tracks east of downtown along 18th Street is **Nanton Campground** (mid-May–Sept., $12), right beside the local 18-hole golf course. Scattered among a grove of trees, the sites have picnic tables, and campers have the use of a covered cooking shelter and showers.

Claresholm

Most people stop at Claresholm (population 3,600), 100 kilometers (62 miles) south of Calgary, just long enough to fill up with gas, grab a burger, and stretch their legs. But it's worth more than a quick stop—allow at least enough time to pop into **Claresholm Museum** (5126 Railway Ave., 403/625-3131, daily 9:30 A.M.–5:30 P.M. mid-May–Sept., donation), in the sandstone Canadian Pacific Railway (C.P.R.) station, and then do a lap of the downtown core and its many historic buildings (those facing Highway 2 are the oldest).

The nicest rooms (by far) are at the **Bluebird Motel** (403/625-3395 or 800/661-4891, www.bluebirdmotel.ab.ca, $78 s, $84–94 d) at the north end of town. All rooms are air-conditioned and feature coffeemakers and large TVs; most also have refrigerators, and the more expensive ones have cooking facilities.

HEAD-SMASHED-IN BUFFALO JUMP

Archaeologists have discovered dozens of buffalo jumps across the North American plains. The largest, oldest, and best preserved is Head-Smashed-In, which is along a weathered sandstone cliff in the Porcupine Hills 14 kilometers (8.7 miles) west of Highway 2, just north of the junction with Highway 3. At the base is a vast graveyard with thousands of years worth of bones from butchered bison piled 10 meters

HEAD-SMASHED-IN WHAT?

The name Head-Smashed-In has no connection to the condition of the bison's heads after tumbling over the cliff. It came from a Blackfoot legend: About 150 years ago, a young hunter wanted to watch the buffalo as they were driven over the steep cliff. He stood under a ledge watching as the stampeding beasts fell in front of him, but the hunt was better than usual, and as the animals piled up, he became wedged between the animals and the cliff. Later his people found him, his skull crushed under the weight of the buffalo – hence the name Head-Smashed-In.

(33 feet) high. The jump represents an exceptionally sophisticated and ingenious hunting technique used by Plains natives at least 5,700 years ago—possibly up to 10,000 years ago—to cunningly outwit thousands of bison, once the largest mammal on the plains. At the time European settlers arrived on the prairies, more than 60 million American bison (also known as buffalo) roamed the plains. The people of the plains depended almost entirely on these prehistoric-looking beasts for their survival. They ate the meat fresh or dried it for pemmican; made tepees, clothing, and moccasins from the hides; and fashioned tools and decorations from the horns. Several methods were used to kill the bison, but by far the most successful method was to drive entire herds over a cliff face. The topography of this region was ideal for such a jump. To the west is a large basin of approximately 40 square kilometers (15 square miles) where bison grazed. They were herded from the basin east along carefully constructed stone cairns (known as drive lines) that led to a precipice where the stampeding bison, with no chance of stopping, plunged to their deaths. Nearby was a campsite where they butchered and processed the meat.

The site has been well preserved. Although a small section of the hill has been excavated, most of it appears today the same as it has for thousands of years. The relative height of the cliff, however, drastically decreased with the buildup of bones. Along with the bones are countless numbers of artifacts such as stone points, knives, and scrapers used to skin the fallen beasts. Metal arrowheads found in the top layer of bones indicate that the jump was used up until the coming of Europeans in the late 1700s. In recognizing the site's cultural and historical importance, UNESCO declared the jump a World Heritage Site in 1981.

Interpretive Centre

As you approach the jump site along Spring Point Road, **Head-Smashed-In Interpretive Centre** (403/553-2731, daily 9 A.M.–6 P.M. in summer, daily 10 A.M.–5 P.M. the rest of the year, adult $9, senior $8, child $5) doesn't become visible until you've parked your car and actually arrived at the entrance. The center—disguised in the natural topography of the landscape—is set into a cliff. A series of ramps and elevators marks the beginning of your tour as you rise to the roof, and from there a trail leads along the cliff top to the jump site. It isn't hard to imagine the sounds and spectacle of thousands of bison stampeding over the rise to the north and tumbling to their deaths below. Back inside you walk down floor by floor, passing displays and films explaining in an interesting and informative way the traditional way of life that existed on the prairies for nearly 10,000 years, as well as the sudden changes that took place when the first European men arrived. Outside the center is another trail that leads along the base of the cliff for a different perspective. Here a large aluminum building covers a recent dig site; the ground is littered with shattered bones. The center also has a gift shop and café selling, of all things, buffalo burgers.

FORT MACLEOD

Southern Alberta's oldest permanent settlement is Fort Macleod (population 3,000), 172 kilometers (107 miles) south of Calgary and 44 kilometers (27 miles) west of Lethbridge.

It was the site of a post established by Colonel James F. Macleod, who had been sent west with orders to curb the whiskey trade. These first troops of the NWMP (North West Mounted Police) eventually put an end to the illicit whiskey trade, and with the help of Métis scout Jerry Potts—who ironically didn't mind a drop of the hard stuff himself—they managed to restore peace between the warring tribes. Potts stayed at Fort Macleod until he died, and is buried in the local cemetery.

Downtown

While nearby Head-Smashed-In Buffalo Jump gets all the attention, the downtown core of Fort Macleod is one of western Canada's finest remaining examples of an early 1900s streetscape. In 1906, a fire destroyed most of the wooden buildings, so a bylaw was passed requiring any new structures to be built of brick or stone. Many buildings along Col. Macleod Boulevard (the main street) function as they did during the town's boom years: The **Queen's Hotel** still has rooms, the **Empress Theatre** (235 Col. Macleod Blvd., 403/553-4404, www.empresstheatre.ab.ca) is the oldest operating theater in the province, and the town office is contained in the only remaining courthouse that dates from Alberta's days as part of the Northwest Territories. The original fort on the Oldman River would have looked much like **The Fort** (219 25th St., 403/553-4703, May Tues.–Fri. daily 9 A.M.–5 P.M., June daily 9 A.M.–5 P.M., July–Aug. daily 9 A.M.–6 P.M., Sept. Wed.–Sun. 10 A.M.–4 P.M., adult $8, senior $7.50, child $5). The museum details the history of the NWMP and the early days of settlement in southern Alberta through buildings reflecting aspects of frontier life, including a chapel, a blacksmith shop, an NWMP building, a law office, and a tepee. In the main arena, riders dress in period costume and perform a scaled-down version of the famous **Mounted Police Musical Ride**—a spectacular display of precision riding—July and August daily at 10 A.M., 11:30 A.M., 2 P.M., and 3:30 P.M.

Practicalities

Motel rooms fill up fast every afternoon in summer, so book ahead or check in early. At the **D.J. Motel** (416 24th St., 403/553-4011, $60 s, $75 d), the 14 rooms are clean and comfortable and each has a small fridge. Barbecues are also supplied. One step up is the **Red Coat Inn** (359 24th St., 403/553-4434 or 800/423-4434, www.redcoatinn.com, $79 s, $85 d, $129 kitchenette), offering air-conditioned rooms and an indoor pool. **Daisy May Campground** (249 Lyndon Rd., 403/553-2455, May–Sept., $25–35) is beside the oldest golf course west of Winnipeg and is within walking distance of downtown. It provides showers, a camp kitchen, a heated pool, laundry facilities, and a game room.

With exposed red brick walls and a polished hardwood floor, the most stylish morning hangout is **Rahn's Bakery & Café** (228 24th St., 403/553-3200, Mon.–Fri. 7 A.M.–5 P.M., Sat. 8 A.M.–2 P.M.). Good coffee and pastries, as well as sandwiches made to order, are all of a high standard.

The **tourist information center** (east end of town on Hwy. 3, 403/553-4955, www.fortmacleod.com) is open daily 9 A.M.–5 P.M. mid-May–August. The Fort gift shop has a large selection of local history and Canadiana books.

SOUTHERN ALBERTA

Lethbridge and Vicinity

An urban oasis on the prairies, this city of rich ethnic origins has come a long way since the 1860s when Fort Whoop-Up, the most notorious whiskey-trading fort in the West, was the main reason folks came to town. Today, Lethbridge (population 85,000) is an important commercial center serving the surrounding ranch and farm country. The city is also a transportation hub, with Highways 3, 4, and 5 converging here. Calgary is 216 kilometers (134 miles) to the north, Medicine Hat 168 kilometers (104 miles) to the east, Waterton Lakes National Park 130 kilometers (81 miles) to the west, and the United States border 105 kilometers (65 miles) to the south.

Native History

This area was the territory of various tribes of the powerful Blackfoot Confederacy. They sheltered from the extreme winters at a site in the Oldman River Valley known to them as *Sikooh-kotoks* (black rocks). The first white traders to the area arrived in the 1850s. Soon after came the whiskey traders who had been forced north by the U.S. Army. Fort Whoop-Up, built on the east bank of the Oldman River, became the most notorious of approximately 50 whiskey posts in southern Alberta. The arrival of whiskey on the plains coincided with a smallpox epidemic and the dislocation of the Cree, who had been forced by the arrival of European settlers into the territory of the Blackfoot, their traditional enemies. These factors combined to create a setting for the last great intertribal battle to be fought in North America. At dawn on October 25, 1870, a party of approximately 800 Cree warriors attacked a band of Blood Blackfoot camping on the west bank of the Oldman River. Unknown to the Cree, a large party of Peigan Blackfoot was camped nearby. Alerted by scouts, the Peigan crossed the river and joined the fray, forcing the Cree back into what is now known as Indian Battle Park. More than 300 Cree and approximately 50 Blackfoot were killed.

SIGHTS

Downtown Lethbridge is relatively compact and parking is easy to come by. It's possible to walk from here to the sights and parks along the valley bottom, but then you're left with an uphill trek back to your vehicle.

Downtown

Considered one of the best small-city museums in the country, the **Sir Alexander Galt Museum** (5th Ave. S off Scenic Dr., 403/320-3898, mid-May–Aug. Mon.–Sat. 10 A.M.–5 P.M., Sun. 1–5 P.M., Sept.–mid-May Mon.–Sat. 10 A.M.–4:30 P.M., Sun. 1–4:30 P.M., adult $5, senior $4, child $3) centers on Discovery Hall, where there is a wealth of interactive displays telling the story of southern Alberta's natural and human history in such an interesting way you won't realize you're actually learning something. The west-facing window provides a view across the valley—in effect a panorama of the city's past.

The **Southern Alberta Art Gallery** (601 3rd Ave. S, 403/327-8770, Tues.–Sat. 10 A.M.–5 P.M., Sun. 1–5 P.M., adult $5, senior $3, child free) has contemporary and historical exhibitions that change throughout the year. The gallery is within **Galt Gardens,** a well-tended park with lots of nice big trees that provide a shaded spot for lunching locals.

Fort Whoop-Up

This was the most notorious whiskey-trading post in the West. The name was coined by someone who had returned to Montana and, when asked how things were going up north, replied, "Oh, they're still whoopin' it up." Trading was simple. Natives pushed buffalo hides through a small opening in the fort wall. In return they were handed a tin cup of whiskey (which was often watered down). The success of the trade led to the formation of the NWMP, who rode west with orders to close down all whiskey-trading forts and end the lawless industry. The Mounties were preceded

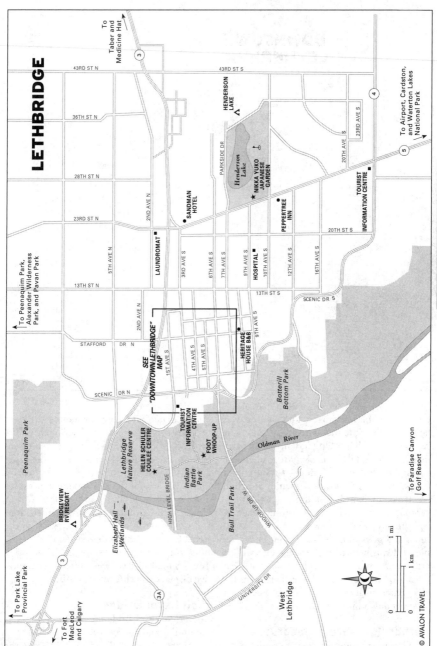

SOUTHERN ALBERTA

LETHBRIDGE

To Taber and
Medicine Hat

To Airport, Cardston,
and Waterton Lakes
National Park

43RD ST N
43RD ST S

HENDERSON
LAKE

36TH ST N

23RD AVE S

28TH N

Henderson
Lake

PARKSIDE DR

NIKKA YUKO
JAPANESE
GARDEN

SANDMAN
HOTEL

PEPPERTREE
INN

20TH ST S

TOURIST
INFORMATION CENTRE

23RD N
2ND AVE N
20TH S

LAUNDROMAT
3RD AVE S
6TH AVE S
7TH AVE S
9TH AVE S
10TH AVE S
12TH AVE S
16TH AVE S

HOSPITAL

5TH AVE N
13TH ST N
13TH ST S

SCENIC DR S

2ND AVE N

SEE
"DOWNTOWN LETHBRIDGE"
MAP

STAFFORD DR W

9TH AVE S

HERITAGE
HOUSE B&B

1ST AVE S
4TH AVE S
5TH AVE S

Botterill
Bottom Park

SCENIC DR N

To Peenaquim Park,
Alexander Wilderness
Park, and Pavan Park

Peenaquim Park

Lethbridge
Nature Reserve

HELEN SCHULER
COULEE CENTRE

TOURIST
INFORMATION
CENTRE

FORT
WHOOP-UP

Indian
Battle
Park

Oldman River

BRIDGEVIEW
RV RESORT

Elizabeth Hall
Wetlands

HIGH LEVEL BRIDGE

Bull Trail Park

WHOOP-UP DR W

To Paradise Canyon
Golf Resort

To Park Lake
Provincial Park

To Fort
MacLeod and Calgary

UNIVERSITY DR

West
Lethbridge

1 mi

1 km

© AVALON TRAVEL

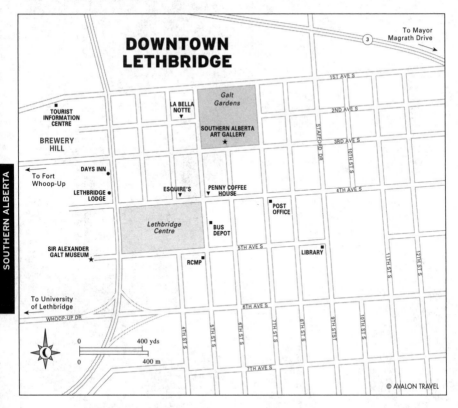

DOWNTOWN LETHBRIDGE

To Mayor
Magrath Drive

TOURIST
INFORMATION
CENTRE

BREWERY
HILL

To Fort
Whoop-Up

DAYS INN

LETHBRIDGE
LODGE

To University
of Lethbridge

WHOOP-UP DR

SIR ALEXANDER
GALT MUSEUM

LA BELLA
NOTTE

Galt
Gardens

SOUTHERN ALBERTA
ART GALLERY

ESQUIRE'S

PENNY COFFEE
HOUSE

Lethbridge
Centre

BUS
DEPOT

POST
OFFICE

LIBRARY

RCMP

1ST AVE S

2ND AVE S

3RD AVE S

4TH AVE S

5TH AVE S

6TH AVE S

7TH AVE S

STAFFORD DR

10TH ST S

11TH ST S

12TH ST S

4TH ST S

5TH ST S

6TH ST S

7TH ST S

8TH ST S

9TH ST S

10TH ST S

0   400 yds

0   400 m

© AVALON TRAVEL

by word of their approach, and the fort was empty by the time they arrived in 1874. The replica Fort Whoop-Up (Indian Battle Park, 403/329-0444, July–Aug. daily 10 A.M.–5 P.M., spring and fall Wed.–Sun. 1–4 P.M., winter Sat.–Sun. 1–4 P.M., adult $7, senior $6, child $5) looks much as it would have in 1869 (except for the soda machine). Costumed staff relive the days when "firewater" was traded for hides and pelts in the Trade Room. A vegetable garden is planted each spring, and visitors are free to climb the corner bastion, which was once used as a lookout. To get there from the city center, turn west onto 3rd Avenue S and follow it down into the coulee.

Lethbridge Nature Reserve

Lethbridge is unique in that it's built on the prairie benchlands and not beside the river that flows so close to town. The largely undisturbed Oldman River Valley has been developed into reserves and parks. One of these, the Lethbridge Nature Reserve, is an 82-hectare (202-acre) area of floodplain and coulees. It's home to the great horned owl—Alberta's provincial bird—porcupines, white-tailed deer, and prairie rattlesnakes. It's also home to the **Helen Schuler Coulee Centre** (403/320-3064, June–Aug. daily 10 A.M.–6 P.M., Sept.–May Tues.–Sun. 1–4 P.M., free), offering interpretive displays and three short trails.

High Level Bridge

The High Level Bridge spans 1.6 kilometers (one mile) and towers 100 meters (330 feet) above the Oldman River Valley—once the longest and highest trestle-construction bridge in the world. It was built by the Canadian Pacific Railway for $1.3 million in 1909, replacing 22 wooden bridges and drastically reducing the length of the line between Lethbridge and Fort Macleod. More than 12,000 tons of steel, 17,000 cubic yards of concrete, and 7,600 gallons of paint were used in its construction. Of the many views of the bridge available along the valley, none is better than standing directly underneath it (walk down from the tourist information center on Brewery Hill).

Nikka Yuko Japanese Garden

This garden (Henderson Lake Park, Mayor Magrath Dr., 403/328-3511, daily 9 A.M.–5 P.M. mid-May–mid-Oct., until 8 P.M. July–Aug., adult $7, senior $5, child $4) was designed as a place to relax and contemplate, with no bright flowers, only green shrubs and gardens of rock and sand. The buildings and bridges were built in Japan under the supervision of a renowned Japanese architect. The main pavilion is of traditional design, housing a *tokonoma*, or tea-ceremony room. Japanese women in traditional dress lead visitors through the gardens and explain the philosophy behind different aspects of the design.

ACCOMMODATIONS AND CAMPING

◀ **Heritage House B&B** (1115 8th Ave. S, 403/328-3824, www.ourheritage.net, $60 s, $80 d) is an excellent alternative to the motels. The 1937 home is considered one of the finest examples of international art deco design in the province. Its two guest rooms are spacious and tastefully decorated, a hearty breakfast is served downstairs in the dining room, and town is only a short walk along the tree-lined streets of Lethbridge's most sought-after suburb.

Out on Mayor Magrath Drive is a string of inexpensive motels, including **Pepper Tree Inn** (1142 Mayor Magrath Dr., 403/328-4436 or 800/708-8638, www.peppertreeinn.ca, $65 s, $80 d including a light breakfast), your run-of-the-mill motel with a small pool in the parking lot out front. Room rates are on the low side

for Lethbridge, but about what they're worth all the same.

The downtown **Days Inn** (100 3rd Ave. S, 403/327-6000 or 800/661-8085, www.ladaysinn.com, from $114 s, $129 d) offers full-on consistency and plenty of amenities at a reasonable price. Rates include continental breakfast, in-room coffee, in-room high-speed Internet, a daily paper, and use of an indoor pool and exercise room.

Lethbridge Lodge (320 Scenic Dr. S, 403/328-1123 or 800/661-1232, www.lethbridgelodge.com, $125–169 s or d) is a modern, full-service hotel with a prime downtown location. The 191 big, bright rooms come in five configurations, including Courtyard Suites with a separate bedroom and living area overlooking an enclosed tropical atrium. Amenities include a restaurant, a lounge, and an indoor pool.

Camping

Henderson Lake Campground (7th Ave. S in Henderson Lake Park, 403/328-5452, www.hendersoncampground.com, tent sites $25, hookups $31–35) has showers, a laundry room, groceries, firewood, and fire rings. The serviced section is little more than a paved parking lot, but tent campers and those with small vans enjoy the privacy afforded by trees at the back of the campground. **Bridgeview RV Resort** (on the west bank of the Oldman River at 910 4th Ave. S, 403/381-2357, www.holidaytrailsresorts.com, tents $28, hookups $43–48) has similar facilities to Henderson Lake Campground, as well as an outdoor heated pool and a restaurant (but the nearby highway can be noisy). Another alternative is **Park Lake Provincial Park** (403/382-4097, mid-May–late Oct., unserviced sites $15, powered sites $21), 17 kilometers (10.5 miles) north of town on Highway 25 then five kilometers northwest.

FOOD

At **Penny Coffee House** (331 5th St. S, 403/320-5282, Mon.–Fri. 7:30 A.M.–9 P.M., Sat. 7:30 A.M.–7 P.M., Sun. 9 A.M.–5 P.M.)

coffee is less than $2, refills are $0.50, and a nice, thick, healthy sandwich with soup is $7.45. Around the corner is another café, **Esquire's** (621 4th Ave. S, 403/380-6747, Mon.–Fri. 7 A.M.–9 P.M., Sat. 9 A.M.–6 P.M., Sun. 9 A.M.–4 P.M., lunches $5–8), with computer and wireless Internet access in a slightly more hip surrounding.

Bontanica (Lethbridge Lodge, 320 Scenic Dr. S, 403/328-1123, daily 7 A.M.–10 P.M., $14–23) is a cool, clean space with lots of healthy choices. The breakfast is especially good and prices all day are surprisingly inexpensive (a dinner buffet Fri.–Sun. is $18). You'll find the city's best dining ambience at **❰ La Bella Notte** (401 2nd Ave. S, 403/331-3319, daily from 11:30 A.M. for lunch and dinner, $14–28). Originally a fire hall, the building has been extensively renovated, including a tiled floor, restored spiral staircase leading to an upstairs lounge, and an earthy heritage color scheme. The menu features lots of Canadian ingredients, with many dishes prepared using traditional Italian techniques.

INFORMATION AND SERVICES

Mayor Magrath Tourist Information Centre (2805 Scenic Dr., 403/320-1222, daily 9 A.M.–8 P.M. in summer, daily 9 A.M.–5 P.M. the rest of the year) is on the south side of the city where Magrath Drive and Scenic Drive meet. **Brewery Gardens Tourist Information Centre** (403/320-1223, daily 9 A.M.–8 P.M. mid-May–Sept., Tues.–Sat. 9 A.M.–5 P.M. Sept. and Oct.) is on the western edge of downtown. The **Chinook Country Tourist Association** (800/661-1222, www.chinookcountry.com) operates both centers.

Lethbridge Public Library (810 5th Ave. S, 403/380-7310, Mon.–Sat. 9:30 A.M.–5:30 P.M., Sun. 1:30–5:30 P.M.) is an excellent facility with a wide range of literature.

The **post office** (704 4th Ave. S) is in a historic stone building. Make a rainy day of it at **Family Coin Laundry** (128 Mayor Magrath Dr. N, daily 7:30 A.M.–8:30 P.M.), one block north of the highway, where there's a lounge, a TV, and free coffee.

GETTING THERE AND AROUND

Buses leave four times daily from the **Greyhound** bus depot (411 5th St. S, 403/327-1551 or 800/661-8747) for Calgary, and twice daily to Medicine Hat and to the United States border at Coutts, where connections to Great Falls and Helena (Montana) can be made.

Lethbridge Transit (403/320-4978) buses run daily, with limited service on Sunday. The main routes radiate from Lethbridge Centre on 4th Avenue S out to the university, Henderson Lake Park, and south along Mayor Magrath Drive. The adult fare is $2.25.

CARDSTON

Cardston is a town of 3,400 at the base of the foothills 76 kilometers (47 miles) southwest of Lethbridge and 35 kilometers (22 miles) north of the United States border. Its rich heritage and a fine carriage museum make it an interesting stop in itself, as well as a good base for exploring Waterton Lakes National Park (a half-hour drive to the west). The town was founded in 1887 by Charles Ora Card of The Church of Jesus Christ of Latter-day Saints (better known as the Mormon Church) after leading 11 families north from Utah in covered wagons. His original log cabin (337 Main St., Mon.–Sat. 11:30 A.M.–5 P.M. July–Aug., donation) still stands.

❰ Remington Carriage Museum

This world-class museum (623 Main St., 403/653-5139, July–Aug. daily 9 A.M.–6 P.M., the rest of the year daily 10 A.M.–5 P.M., adult $9, senior $8, child $5) focusing on the era of horse-drawn transportation boasts North America's largest collection of carriages, buggies, and wagons—around 225 at last count. The main exhibit galleries tell the story of the horse-and-buggy era through a life-size early-20th-century townscape. You can transport yourself through time by watching blacksmiths at work in the carriage factory, listening to deals being made at the carriage dealer, or wandering over to the racetrack, where the rich liked to be seen on their elegant carriages.

Throughout summer, rides are offered on restored and replica carriages (adult $4, child $2.50), and there's a full schedule events in the arena. The center also has a theater, restaurant, and gift shop.

Alberta Temple

While living in simple log cabins, the early Mormon pioneers started planning the construction of the first Mormon temple built outside of the United States. The Cardston Alberta Temple of The Church of Jesus Christ of Latter-day Saints, to give its full name, is a grandly symmetrical marble and granite structure that is visible from just about everywhere in town. Only members of the Mormon faith in good standing may enter the temple itself, but a visitors center (348 3rd Street W, 403/653-1696, 9 A.M.–9 P.M. May–Sept., free) beside the main entrance is open to the public. It depicts the story of the decade-long construction process, with photographs of the stone being hauled in from British Columbia and the massive derrick used to move the blocks into place. It's a friendly little room staffed by church members who are genuinely interested in talking to visitors about their temple.

Entertainment

Carriage House Theatre (353 Main St., 403/653-1000) has a summer program of live theater productions, including musicals, comedy, and special events with a local theme. The performances are held Tuesday–Saturday nights at 7:30 P.M. July–August and cost around $15.

Accommodations and Food

The choices are simple here—good-value motel rooms or camping downtown or in one of the nearby provincial parks. Least expensive of Cardston's motels is the **Flamingo Motel** (848 Main St., 403/653-3952 or 888/806-6835, www.cardstonflamingo.com, $69 s, $79 d), two blocks up the hill from the Remington Carriage Museum. The 38 rooms each have a fridge and microwave while other amenities include a small outdoor pool, barbecue area, and coin laundry. Within walking distance of town is **Lee Creek Campground** (at the end of 7th Ave. W, off Main St., 403/653-3734, May–Sept., unserviced sites $20, hookups $25), an excellent facility with full hookups and showers. East of town, take Highway 505 west from Spring Coulee and you'll quickly reach two campgrounds within **St. Mary's Reservoir Provincial Recreation Area** (mid-May–mid-Oct., $10), with limited facilities, but fronted by sandy beaches and warm water.

◖ **Cobblestone Manor** (173 7th Ave. W, 403/653-2701, summer Mon.–Sat. for breakfast, lunch, and dinner, $16–39) is a unique place to indulge in some fine food. The original structure is a home dating to 1889. In 1913 an eccentric gentleman from Belgium began expanding the building using cobblestones for building blocks. The interior wall panels and ceilings are inlaid with thousands of pieces of hardwood, and the stained-glass bookshelves, Tiffany lights, and antique furniture add to the old-world ambience. The food is not as adventurous as the setting may suggest (think spaghetti and meatballs, Alberta beef, and maple-marinated chicken).

Information

The **tourist information center** (621 Main St., 403/653-3787, daily 8 A.M.–8 P.M. mid-May–Aug.) is in a big open-plan building at the entrance to the carriage museum.

SOUTHERN ALBERTA

Waterton Lakes National Park

Everybody traveling to this rugged 526-square-kilometer (203-square-mile) park does so by choice. It's not on the way to anywhere else or on a major highway, but is tucked away in the extreme southwestern corner of Alberta. The park is bounded to the north and east by the rolling prairies covering southern Alberta; to the south by the U.S. border and Glacier National Park in Montana; and to the west by the Continental Divide, which forms the Alberta–British Columbia border. Botanists have recorded 1,200 species of plants growing within the park's several different vegetation zones, two major flyways pass the park, and although wildlife viewing requires patience the opportunities to see big game are as good as anywhere in western Canada. Bighorn sheep and mule deer make it easy by actually spending time in and around the townsite. The natural mountain splendor, a chain of deep glacial lakes, large and diverse populations of wildlife, and an unbelievable variety of day hikes make this park a gem that shouldn't be missed.

The route to Waterton is almost as scenic as the park itself. From whichever direction you arrive, the transition from prairie to mountains is abrupt, almost devoid of the foothills that characterize other areas along the eastern slopes of the Canadian Rockies. From the park gate, two roads penetrate the mountains to the west. One ends at a large glaciated lake, the other at a spectacular canyon.

You'll often see the park referred to as **Waterton-Glacier International Peace Park.** Although Glacier National Park (Montana) and Waterton are administered separately, there is international cooperation in preserving this pristine mountain wilderness through combined wildlife management, interpretive programs, and search-and-rescue operations. In 1979, UNESCO declared the park a **Biosphere Reserve,** only the second such reserve in Canada. The park gained

Waterton Lakes National Park

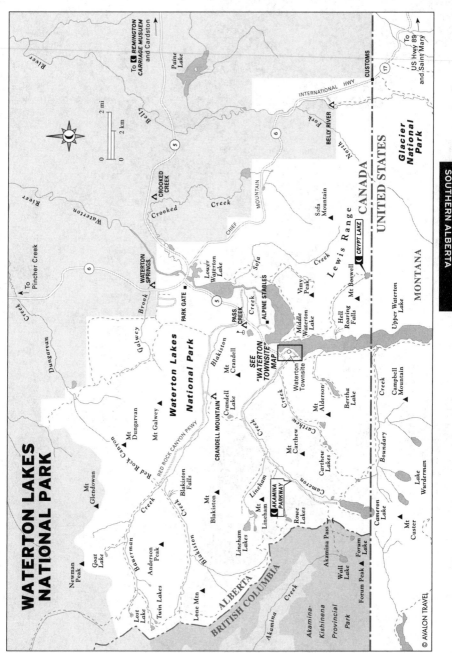

WATERTON LAKES NATIONAL PARK

SOUTHERN ALBERTA

To **C** REMINGTON CARRIAGE MUSUEM and Cardston

To US Hwy 89 and Saint Mary

CUSTOMS

INTERNATIONAL HWY

Paine Lake

Belly River

2 mi

2 km

CROOKED CREEK

Crooked Creek

Creek

CHIEF MOUNTAIN

North Belly River Fork

BELLY RIVER

Sofa Mountain

Lewis Range

CRYPT LAKE

CANADA
UNITED STATES

Glacier National Park

MONTANA

Waterton River

To Pincher Creek

Galwey Brook

WATERTON SPRINGS

PARK GATE

Lower Waterton Lake

Sofa Creek

PASS CREEK

ALPINE STABLES

Blakiston Creek

Mt Crandell

"SEE WATERTON TOWNSITE MAP"

Middle Waterton Lake

Waterton Townsite

Vimy Peak

Mt Boswell

Hell Roaring Falls

Upper Waterton Lake

Dungarvan Creek

Waterton Lakes National Park

Mt Dungarvan

Mt Galwey

Crandell Mountain

CRANDELL MOUNTAIN

Crandell Lake

Cameron Creek

Mt Alderson

Bertha Lake

Campbell Mountain

Mt Glendowan

Red Rock Canyon

RED ROCK CANYON PKWY

Blakiston Falls

Mt Blakiston

Lineham

Lineham Lakes

Mt Lineham

AKAMINA PARKWAY

Rowe Lakes

Mt Carthew

Carthew Creek

Carthew Lakes

Boundary Creek

Lake Wurderman

Newman Peak

Goat Lake

Anderson Peak

Bauerman Creek

Blakiston Creek

Lost Lake

Twin Lakes

Lene Mtn

Akamina Pass

Wall Lake

Forum Lake

Forum Peak

Cameron Lake

Mt Custer

ALBERTA
BRITISH COLUMBIA

Akamina-Kishinena Provincial Park

Akamina Creek

Akamina

© AVALON TRAVEL

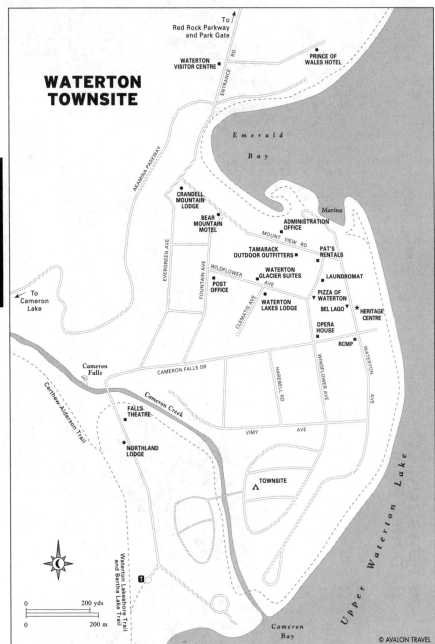

WATERTON TOWNSITE

To Red Rock Parkway and Park Gate

ENTRANCE RD

WATERTON VISITOR CENTRE

PRINCE OF WALES HOTEL

Emerald Bay

AKAMINA PARKWAY

CRANDELL MOUNTAIN LODGE

BEAR MOUNTAIN MOTEL

Marina

ADMINISTRATION OFFICE

MOUNT VIEW RD

TAMARACK OUTDOOR OUTFITTERS

PAT'S RENTALS

EVERGREEN AVE

FOUNTAIN AVE

WILDFLOWER AVE

POST OFFICE

WATERTON GLACIER SUITES

LAUNDROMAT

CLEMATIS AVE

WATERTON LAKES LODGE

PIZZA OF WATERTON

BEL LAGO

HERITAGE CENTRE

To Cameron Lake

OPERA HOUSE

RCMP

WATERTON AVE

Cameron Falls

CAMERON FALLS DR

HAREBELL RD

WINDFLOWER AVE

Carthew-Alderson Trail

Cameron Creek

FALLS THEATRE

VIMY AVE

NORTHLAND LODGE

TOWNSITE

Waterton Lakeshore Trail and Bertha Lake Trail

Upper Waterton Lake

| 0 | 200 yds |
| 0 | 200 m |

Cameron Bay

© AVALON TRAVEL

further recognition in 1995, when, along with Glacier National Park, it was declared a **World Heritage Site** by UNESCO.

Park Entry

All visitors to Waterton Lakes are required to stop at the park entrance and buy a permit. Park entry for one day is adult $8, senior $7, child $4, to a maximum of $20 per vehicle.

SCENIC DRIVES

Both of the following roads lead west off the main park access road.

◖ Akamina Parkway

This road starts in the townsite and switchbacks up into Cameron Creek Valley, making an elevation gain of 400 meters (1,310 feet) before ending after 16 kilometers (10 miles) at Cameron Lake. The viewpoint one kilometer (0.6 miles) from the junction of the park road is on a tight curve, so park off the road. From this lookout, views extend over the entire valley. This section of the road is also a good place to view bighorn sheep. From here to Cameron Lake are a number of picnic areas and stops of interest, including the site of **Oil City,** home of the first producing oil well in western Canada; all that remains are the ill-fated hotel foundations and some depressions in the ground.

Cameron Lake, at the end of the road, is a 2.5-kilometer-long (1.5-mile-long) subalpine lake that reaches depths over 40 meters (130 feet). It lies in a large cirque carved around 11,000 years ago by a receding glacier. Mount Custer at the southern end of the lake is in Montana. To the west (right) of Custer is **Forum Peak** (2,225 m/7,300 ft), whose summit cairn marks the boundaries of Alberta, Montana, and British Columbia. Beside the lakeshore are enclosed information boards and a concession selling light snacks and renting canoes, rowboats, and paddleboats ($30 for the first hour, $25 for additional hours). A narrow trail leads along the lake's west shoreline, ending after two kilometers (1.2 miles, 40 minutes each way).

Red Rock Canyon Parkway

The best roadside wildlife viewing within the park is along this 13-kilometer (eight-mile) road that starts near the golf course and finishes at **Red Rock Canyon.** The transition between rolling prairies and mountains takes place abruptly as you travel up the Blakiston Valley. Black bears (and very occasionally, grizzly bears) can be seen feeding on saskatoon berries along the open slopes to the north. **Mount Blakiston** (2,920 m/9,580 ft), the park's highest summit, is visible from a viewpoint three kilometers (1.9 miles) along the road. The road passes interpretive signs, picnic areas, and Crandell Mountain Campground. At the end of the road is Red Rock Canyon, a water-carved gorge where the bedrock, known as argillite, contains a high concentration of iron. The iron oxidizes and turns red when exposed to air—literally going rusty. A short interpretive trail leads along the canyon.

HIKING

Although the park is relatively small, its trail system is extensive; 224 kilometers (140 miles) of well-maintained trails lead to alpine lakes and lofty summits affording spectacular views. One of the most appealing aspects of hiking in Waterton is that with higher trailheads than other parks in the Canadian Rockies, the treeline (and the best views) is reached quickly.

◖ Crypt Lake

Arguably one of the most spectacular day hikes in Canada is the **Crypt Lake Trail** (8.7 km/5.4 mi, 3–4 hours one-way). Access to the trailhead is aboard the Crypt Lake Shuttle (403/859-2362, $18 round-trip), which departs the Waterton marina daily at 9 A.M. and 10 A.M. for Crypt Landing, returning at 4 P.M. and 5:30 P.M. From Crypt Landing, the trail switchbacks for 2.5 kilometers (1.6 miles) past a series of waterfalls and continues steeply up to a small green lake before reaching a campground. The final ascent to Crypt Lake from the campground causes the most problems, especially for those who suffer from claustrophobia. A ladder on the cliff face leads into a natural tunnel that you must crawl through on your hands and knees. The next part of the trail is along a narrow precipice with a cable for support. The lake at the end of the trail, nestled in a hanging valley, is no disappointment. Its dark green waters are rarely free of floating ice, and the steep walls of the cirque rise more than 500 meters (1,640 feet) above the lake on three sides.

From Town

The trail up to the summit of **Bear's Hump** (1.2 km/0.7 mi, 40 minutes one-way) is one of the most popular short hikes in the park, and although steep, it affords panoramic views of the Waterton Valley. From the back of the visitors center parking lot, the trail switchbacks up the northern flanks of the Bear's Hump, finishing at a rocky ledge high above town.

The trail to **Bertha Lake** (5.8 km/3.6 mi, 2 hours one-way) climbs slowly along Upper Waterton Lake for 1.5 kilometers (0.9 miles), then branches right and moves steadily through a montane forest to Lower Bertha Falls. From here, the trail jogs left, passes through an avalanche slope, and switchbacks steeply to its maximum

elevation on a ridge above the hanging valley in which Bertha Lake lies. The trail gains 460 meters (1,510 feet) of elevation, so you should at least have a mid-level of fitness to attempt it.

Don't let the length of the **Waterton Lakeshore Trail** (14 km/8.7 mi) put you off—it's easy walking the entire way. Most hikers take the Waterton Cruise Company's **MV International** one way ($18, call 403/859-2362) and hike back to town, spending about four hours on the trail.

OTHER RECREATION
Lake Cruise

This is the most popular organized activity in Waterton. From the marina in downtown Waterton townsite, **Waterton Inter-Nation Shoreline Cruise Company** (403/859-2362) runs scheduled cruises across the international boundary to Goat Haunt, Montana, at the southern end of Upper Waterton Lake. The 45-minute trip along the lakeshore passes spectacular mountain scenery and usually wildlife. A half-hour stopover is made at Goat Haunt, which lies in a remote part of Glacier National Park and consists of little more than a dock and

"KOOTENAI" BROWN

John George "Kootenai" Brown was born in England in the 1840s and reputedly was educated at Oxford University. He joined the army and went to India, later continuing to San Francisco. Then, like thousands of others, he headed for the Cariboo goldfields of British Columbia, quickly spending any of the gold he found. After a while he moved on, heading east into Waterton Valley, where his party was attacked by Blackfoot. He was shot in the back with an arrow and pulled it out himself. Brown acquired his nickname through his close association with the Kootenai people, hunting buffalo and wolves with them until they had all but disappeared.

Even though Brown had been toughened by the times, he was a conservationist at heart. After marrying in 1869, he built a cabin by the

Waterton Lakes and became the valley's first permanent resident. Soon he started promoting the beauty of the area to the people of Fort Macleod. One of his friends, local rancher F. W. Godsal, began lobbying the federal government to establish a reserve. In 1895, an area was set aside as a Forest Reserve, with Brown as its first warden. In 1911, the area was declared a national park, and Brown, age 71, was appointed its superintendent. He continued to push for an expansion of park boundaries until his final retirement at age 75. He died a few years later. His grave along the main access road to the townsite is a fitting resting place for one of Alberta's most celebrated mountain men. His Waterton cabin is preserved at Kootenai Brown Pioneer Village in nearby Pincher Creek.

© ANDREW HEMPSTEAD

Take a cruise on Upper Waterton Lake.

interpretive displays. You can return on the same boat or go hiking and return later in the day. A popular option is to take an early boat trip and walk back to town on the **Waterton Lakeshore Trail,** which takes about four hours. Departures are twice daily May–June and September–early October and four times daily in July and August (first departure at 9 A.M.). Remember, you are crossing into another country on this cruise, so correct documentation is required, including for U.S. citizens (no different from crossing into the United States at a regular border crossing). Tickets cost $34 round-trip, $20 one-way (children are half price), and you'll need to book ahead in summer.

Horseback Riding

Just off the main park access road before town is **Alpine Stables** (403/859-2462), which offers hour-long trail rides (starting on the hour 9 A.M.–5 P.M.) for $35. Two-hour rides cost $60 and pass through prime wildlife-viewing habitat. The three-hour ride, costing $80, takes in the bison paddock, while eight hours in the

saddle opens up possibilities such as a climb to the summit of Vimy Peak for $145.

Interpretive Programs

Interpretive programs begin in late June and run through to the first weekend of September. The subject matter changes from year to year, but you can rely on interesting, interactive topics that mix learning with fun. Presentations at the **Falls Theatre** (in town, across the road from Cameron Falls) and at **Crandell Theatre** (Crandell Campground) usually begin nightly at 8 P.M., with guest speakers appearing at the Falls Theatre Saturday night. Ask at the Waterton Visitor Centre (403/859-5133) for a printed schedule.

ACCOMMODATIONS AND CAMPING

Waterton has a limited number of accommodations. Most start opening in May and by mid-October are closed, with only the backpacker lodge, Kilmorey Lodge, Crandell Mountain Lodge, and Waterton Glacier Suites open year-round. All accommodations are within the townsite, so walking to the marina and shops isn't a problem.

Under $50

◖ HI-Waterton Alpine Centre (101 Clematis Dr., 403/859-2150 or 888/985-6343, www.watertonlakeslodge.com, dorm beds $32–40, family rooms $105) is in a wing of Waterton Lakes Lodge, one of the village's premier accommodations. Just 21 beds are spread through six rooms, with a maximum of four beds in any one room. Amenities include a small lounge area, shared kitchen, and washrooms.

$50-100

One block from the main street, the **Bear Mountain Motel** (208 Mount View Rd., 403/859-2366, www.bearmountainmotel.com, mid-May–Sept., $80 s, $85 d, kitchenettes from $95) is an older park-at-your-door 34-unit motel with basic furnishings and no phones.

Also in this price bracket is **Northland Lodge** (Evergreen Ave., 403/859-2353, www.northlandlodgecanada.com, early May–early Oct., $89–125), a rambling old home backing onto wilderness but just a short walk from both Cameron Falls and the main street. It features nine guest rooms, a lounge with a TV and fireplace, and a deck. Rates include tea, coffee, and muffins in the morning.

$100-150

◖ Crandell Mountain Lodge (Mount View Rd., 403/859-2288 or 866/859-2288, www.crandellmountainlodge.com, $140–220 s or d), a centrally located country-style inn. Each of the 17 rooms has a private bath and is beautifully finished with country-style furnishings (no phones). Two rooms are wheelchair-accessible. Rates are reduced around 30 percent mid-September–May.

$150-200

Waterton Glacier Suites (Windflower Ave., 403/859-2004 or 866/621-3330, www.watertonsuites.com) is open year-round and provides excellent value. Each of the 26 units features stylish, modern decor that hints at Western, as well as air-conditioning, a fridge, and microwave. Two-bedroom suites are $169 s or d, units with a jetted tub and fireplace are $225, and spacious loft units are $259. Off-season rates range $135–175.

Over $200

Modern **Waterton Lakes Lodge** (corner of Windflower Ave. and Cameron Falls Rd., 403/859-2151 or 866/985-6343, www.watertonlakeslodge.com, Apr.–Oct., $185–245 s or d) is on a 1.5-hectare (3.7-acre) site in the heart of town. All 80 rooms are large and modern, and each has mountain-themed decor and mountain views. In-room amenities include air-conditioning, a TV/VCR combination, Internet access, and a coffeemaker. The complex also holds the Waterton Health Club (free entry for guests), a restaurant, and a lounge with big screen TVs.

Waterton's best-known landmark is the **Prince of Wales Hotel** (403/236-3400 or 406/892-2525, www.glacierparkinc.com, mid-May–mid-Sept., $265–345 s or d), a seven-story gabled structure built in 1927 on a hill overlooking Upper Waterton Lake. The best place to appreciate the grandeur and location (even if you're not a guest) is by standing in the lobby area and gazing out across the lake and up into the exposed timber-frame ceiling. Off the lobby you'll find a restaurant, lounge, and gift shop. The opulence and history of this hotel are unequaled in Waterton, but don't expect the facilities of a similarly priced city hostelry: Rooms have no television, and Value Rooms on the upper floors have no elevator access.

Park Campgrounds

The park's three campgrounds hold a total of 391 campsites. The most popular camping spot—thanks to a central location and top-notch amenities—is the **Townsite Campground** (mid-Apr.–mid-Oct., tent sites $23, unserviced sites $28, hookups $39), within walking distance of the lake, trailheads, restaurants, and shops. The campground also offers showers and kitchen shelters. Reservations are taken for a percentage of sites through the

Parks Canada Campground Reservation Service (877/737-3783, www.pccamping.ca). The 129 sites at **Crandell Campground** (mid-May–early Sept., $21.50), 10 kilometers (6.2 miles) from the townsite on Red Rock Canyon Parkway, are sprinkled through a lightly forested area of the valley bottom. This campground has flush toilets and kitchen shelters but no hookups. Pleasant Crandell Lake is an easy 2.4-kilometer (1.5-mile) walk from the southwest corner of the campground.

Belly River Campground (mid-May–early Sept., $15), 26 kilometers (16 miles) from the townsite along Chief Mountain International Highway, is the smallest (24 sites) and most primitive of the park's developed campgrounds. Located beside a shallow, slow moving body of water, facilities are limited to pit toilets, a kitchen shelter, and drinking water.

Commercial Campgrounds

You're a little way from the action at the commercial campgrounds outside the park, but the wider range of facilities (especially if you have a young family) and the peace of mind of being able to reserve a site with hookups make them a viable alternative. Closest is **Waterton Springs Campground** (three km/1.9 mi north of the park gate on Hwy. 6, 403/859-2247 or 866/859-2247, www.watertonspringscamping.com, late May–Sept., tents $18, hookups $23–29).

Family fun is the order of the day at the **Great Canadian Barn Dance Campground** (Wynder Rd., Hill Spring, 403/626-3407 or 866/626-3407, www.gcbd.com, May–Oct., $22–37), a converted farm lying 40 minutes along rural roads from the park. As the name suggests, the action revolves around a weekend barn dance, held in an authentic barn. To get there from Waterton, head 18 kilometers (11 miles) east on Highway 5, 21 kilometers (13 miles) north on Highway 800, and then 1.6 kilometers (one mile) east on Highway 505 to Wynder Road.

FOOD

When it's time to eat, the park offers everything from meals to fit the most austere budget to fine dining. Unless you're planning a meal at the Prince of Wales, the dress code in park restaurants is casual.

Waterton Bagel & Coffee Co. (in the theater building on the corner of Windflower Ave. and Cameron Falls Dr., 403/859-2211, daily 7 A.M.–9:30 P.M.) brews up the best coffee in town.

Pizza of Waterton (305 Windflower Ave., 403/859-2660, Mon.–Fri. 5–10 P.M., Sat.–Sun. noon–10 P.M.) dishes up the best—okay, the only—pizza in town. It's actually pretty good, piled high with toppings of your choice. A 12-inch (good for two) costs $21, beer is $5, and there's a choice of wines for less than $25 per bottle. Eat in, at the picnic tables out front, or take your order back to your campsite.

Bel Lago (113 Waterton Ave., 403/859-0003, daily 11 A.M.–10 P.M., $18–32), with as many tables outside as in and live music on weekend nights, offers satisfying pastas and Italian specialties.

High tea is a tradition at the landmark **Prince of Wales Hotel** (403/859-2231), but it's an overpriced one. Sure, it's tasty and memorable—think finger sandwiches, pastries and cakes, tea, coffee, and other beverages served up on white linen at tables with the best view in town—but as any self-respecting Brit will tell you, it's more of an *afternoon* tea rather than the more substantial *high* tea. It's served in the lobby daily 2–5 P.M. and costs $34 per person. The big windows at the hotel's **Royal Stewart Dining Room** (breakfast 6:30–10 A.M., lunch 11:30 A.M.–2 P.M., dinner 5–9:30 P.M., $23–34) allow you to gaze down along Upper Waterton Lake while soaking up an old-world elegance unequaled in the park. A simple breakfast buffet every morning ($18 per person) is worth attending for the views alone.

INFORMATION

On the main access road, the **Waterton Visitor Centre** (403/859-5133, daily 9 A.M.–8 P.M. June–Aug., daily 9 A.M.–5 P.M. May and early Sept.) provides general information on the park, sells fishing licenses, and issues Wilderness Use Permits. Outside of summer, head to the park administration office (Mount View Rd., 403/859-2224, Mon.–Fri. 8 A.M.–4 P.M.), which offers the same services as the visitor center. For online information, visit the websites of Parks Canada (www.pc.gc. ca) or the chamber of commerce (www.watertonchamber.com).

Tamarack Outdoor Outfitters (Mount View Rd., 403/859-2378, daily 8 A.M.–8 P.M.) has a section devoted to books, with field and recreation guides dominating. The **Waterton Natural History Association,** based in the Waterton Heritage Centre (117 Waterton Ave., 403/859-2624, 10 A.M.–5 P.M. May–Sept., until 8 P.M. July and Aug.), stocks every book ever written about the park.

SHOPPING AND SERVICES

The numerous tourist-oriented gift shops along Waterton Avenue are worth browsing through when the weather isn't cooperating. **Tamarack Outdoor Outfitters** (Mount View Rd., 403/859-2378, daily 8 A.M.–8 P.M.) is a five-generation family business that stocks a little of everything. Here you'll find a good range of outdoor clothing and equipment, fishing tackle, books, a currency exchange, and picnic supplies. Waterton has no banks, but travelers checks are accepted at most businesses, and **ATMs** are scattered throughout town. The **post office** is beside the fire station on Fountain Avenue and there's a **laundry** on Windflower Avenue.

GETTING THERE AND AROUND

The closest that **Greyhound** buses come to the park is Pincher Creek, 50 kilometers (31 miles) away. From the depot (1015 Hewetson St., 403/627-2716), a cab to the park (call **Crystal Taxi,** 403/627-4262) will run around $70 each way.

Tamarack Outdoor Outfitters (Mount View Rd., 403/859-2378, www.watertonvisitorservices. com) operates hiker shuttle services to various trailheads within the park. **Pat's** (Mount View Rd., 403/859-2266) rents mountain bikes for $9.50 for the first hour then $7 per hour thereafter to a maximum of $40 per day. Motorized scooters are $31 per hour or $120 per day.

Crowsnest Pass

The municipality of Crowsnest Pass is along Highway 3 between Pincher Creek and the Continental Divide in the southwestern corner of the province. It encompasses a handful of once-bustling coal-mining communities, including Bellevue, Hillcrest, Frank, Blairmore, and Coleman. Many topographic features in the area are named "Crowsnest," including a river, a mountain, and the actual pass (1,396 m/4,580 ft) on the Continental Divide. From Pincher Creek, it's 62 kilometers (39 miles) to the pass. The area is worth exploring for its natural beauty and recreation opportunities alone; the Crowsnest River reputedly offers some of Canada's best trout fishing. But a trip through this area wouldn't be complete without visiting the historic towns and mines along the route.

PINCHER CREEK AND VICINITY

The town, in a shallow valley 211 kilometers (131 miles) south of Calgary, is surrounded by some of the country's best cattle land and is reputed to be the windiest spot in Alberta. The NWMP established a horse farm at what is now known as Pincher Creek in 1876. They found that oats and hay, the horses' main source of sustenance, grew much better here in the foothills than at their newly built post at Fort Macleod. The story goes that a member of the detachment found a pair of pincers near the river—lost many years earlier by prospectors from Montana—and the name stuck. Word of this fertile agricultural land quickly spread, and soon the entire area was settled.

Town Sights

In addition to providing a home for the local information center, **Pioneer Place,** a large log structure across the river from Main Street, is the gateway to **Kootenai Brown Pioneer Village** (1037 Bev McLachlin Dr., 403/627-3684, daily 10 A.M.–6 P.M. June–Aug., Mon.–Fri. 10 A.M.–4:30 P.M. Sept.–May, adult $5, senior $4). Within the park are numerous historic buildings moved to the site. Highlights include the cabin of legendary mountain man Kootenai Brown, a sprawling 1894 ranch house, a blacksmith workshop, Doukhobor barn, a sod hut, and a NWMP barn dating to 1878. All of the buildings are open for viewing, each restored to period settings.

Around Pincher Creek

Completed in 1991, the **Oldman River Dam,** north of Pincher Creek below the confluence of the Crowsnest, Castle, and Oldman Rivers, is a 25-kilometer-long (15.5-mile-long) reservoir held back by one of Alberta's highest dam walls (76 m/250 ft); Highway 785, which branches north from Highway 3 three kilometers (1.9 miles) east of the Pincher Creek turnoff, crosses the wall and allows access to the base of the spillway, where there's camping, excellent fishing for rainbow trout, and a specially built kayaking course. The reservoir above is also a popular recreation spot for boating and fishing.

Deep in the foothills 20 kilometers (12.5 miles) southwest of Pincher Creek, **Beauvais Lake Provincial Park** holds an 18-kilometer network of hiking trails, including a short walk to a beaver pond. The lake is also good for boating and is stocked annually with rainbow and brown trout. The main campground (403/382-4097, $15–21), at the lake's western end, is fairly primitive (pit toilets, no showers), but a few powered sites were added in 2007. If you're tent camping, continue beyond the summer cabins to a group of roadside walk-in sites.

Accommodations and Food

Pincher Creek's older motels are spread along a four-block strip of Highway 6 east of downtown, including a real cheapie—the **Blue Mountain Motel** (981 Main St., 403/627-5335,

$65 s, $75 d). South of town off Highway 6 (call for directions) is **Valley Blue Ranch** (403/627-2382, www.valleyblueranch.com, $90 s, $120 d including breakfast), which is primarily in business as a cattle ranch, but opens the door of its modern ranch house to visitors throughout the year. The two guest rooms have a bright, country-style ambience, while the main living area and breakfast room have sweeping views across the rolling foothills.

Memorial Campground (May–Oct., tents $15, powered sites $20–25) is in a residential area on Wentworth Avenue, just off Highway 6, and linked to Kootenai Brown Pioneer Village via a riverside trail. Rates include the use of showers and an unlimited supply of firewood. Much nicer if you don't need hookups is **Cottonwood Campground** (May–early Sept., $15–21), 500 meters (0.3 miles) downstream of the Oldman River Dam, 10 kilometers (6.2 miles) northeast of town. The 82 sites are spread throughout stands of towering cottonwood trees and all have easy river access.

The **Swiss Alpine Restaurant** (988 Main St. at Waterton Ave., 403/627-5079, Tues.–Sat. 11 A.M.–10 P.M., $15–22) is a longtime favorite with locals and savvy travelers in the know. The lounge displays lots of taxidermy and a Western-style atmosphere, and the dining area has good food, including Alberta beef and lamb, delicious salads (the Alpine salad is especially good), and traditional Swiss dishes such as fondue.

You'll pass **Twin Butte General Store** (Hwy. 6 24 km/15 mi south of Pincher Creek, 403/627-4035, daily 10 A.M.–8 P.M., $9–21) on the drive to Waterton Lakes, but it's also worth a detour for lunch or dinner. Stuck in the middle of what is seemingly nowhere, the store has a small restaurant attached to one side. The specialty is simple Mexican dishes, all inexpensive and served with a smile.

Information

Pincher Creek Tourist Information Centre (1037 Bev McLachlin Dr., 403/627-5855 or 888/298-5855, www.pinchercreek.ca, daily 10 A.M.–6 P.M. June–Aug., Mon.–Fri. 10 A.M.–4:30 P.M. Sept.–May) is in Pioneer Place, an impressive log building across the river from downtown.

PINCHER CREEK TO LEITCH COLLIERIES

The first worthwhile stop as Highway 3 begins its westward climb to the Crowsnest Pass from Pincher Creek is **Lundbreck Falls** (signposted from the highway), where the Crowsnest River plunges 12 meters (40 feet) into the canyon below. Below the falls is **Lundbreck Falls Recreation Area** (May–Oct., unserviced sites $12, powered sites $17), where 65 campsites are spread out along two loops, one right by the river.

From the falls, Highway 3 passes the junction of Highway 22, which heads north to Kananaskis Country and Calgary. The next community west on Highway 3 is **Burmis**, which is well known for the **Burmis Tree**, a photogenic limber pine beside the north side of the highway.

Leitch Collieries

At the beginning of the 20th century, Leitch Collieries was the largest mining and coking operation in Crowsnest Pass, and in 1915 it became the first operation to cease production. Now it's a series of picturesque ruins with one of the most informative interpretive exhibits in the area. A trail runs through the mine ruins and around the surrounding area. The site is open year-round, with guided tours running in summer daily at 11 A.M. and 2 P.M.

BELLEVUE

Entering Bellevue from the east is the tiny **Wayside Chapel**, which seats eight people. Recorded sermons are held throughout summer, and the doors are always open. The main reason to stop in the town itself is for a **Bellevue Underground Mine Tour** (21814 28th Ave., 403/564-4700, adult $10, senior $9, child $8). The tour is as realistic as possible without actually making you shovel dirt. The mine is cold, dark, and damp. Before entering you are given a hard hat and a headlamp, which you can attach to your hat or carry by hand. The guides carry blankets for those visitors who get cold—the average temperature in the mine is 7°C (45°F). The tour runs every

The Burmis Tree is the jewel of Burmis.

© ANDREW HEMPSTEAD

half hour 10 A.M.–5:30 P.M. mid-May–August. To get to the mine, follow the signs down the hill from the top end of 213th Street.

FRANK

Frank is probably the most famous (or infamous) town in the Crowsnest Pass area. In 1901, two Americans acquired mineral rights to the area directly below Turtle Mountain. Within months, their company, the Canadian-American Coal and Coke Company, had established a mine and laid out the townsite of Frank. The mine, when operational, became the first to sell coal in the pass and continued to thrive along with the town of Frank, whose population swelled to 600.

The original townsite of Frank is now an industrial park. To get to it, cross the rail line at 150th Street (just west of the turnoff for the interpretive center). Take the first left and look for a rusty fire hydrant to the right. This landmark, which once stood on Dominion Avenue, Frank's main street, is all that remains of the ill-fated town. This road then continues across Gold Creek and into the slide area.

◖ Frank Slide

It was before dawn early on April 29, 1903. Everything in town was quiet, and the night shift was hard at work deep inside Turtle Mountain. Then, without warning, a gigantic chunk of the north face of the mountain sheared off, thundering into the valley below and burying part of Frank. It was the world's most destructive rockslide, burying 68 of the town's residents. (Amazingly, none of the 20 working coal miners were killed. After being trapped for 14 hours, they dug themselves out.) Looking at the north face of Turtle Mountain will give you an idea of the slide, but the full extent doesn't become apparent until you actually drive through the slide area or view the fan of limestone boulders that spread more than three kilometers (1.9 miles) from the base of the mountain and more than two kilometers (1.2 miles) to the east and west. Today, Turtle Mountain is monitored daily with some of the world's most advanced seismographic

equipment but has shown no sign of moving since.

Frank Slide Interpretive Centre (403/562-7388, July–Aug. daily 9 A.M.–6 P.M., the rest of the year daily 10 A.M.–5 P.M., adult $9, senior $8, child $5), on a slight rise at the northern edge of the slide area, is an excellent place to learn more about the history of the valley, its settlers, and its tragedies. The audiovisual presentation *In the Mountain's Shadow* is a particularly moving account of the terrible working and social conditions in the valley. A 1.5-kilometer (0.9-mile) self-guided trail leads down into the slide. Better still, scramble up the slope behind the parking lot and walk along the ridge for a view of the entire slide area.

BLAIRMORE

With a population of 4,900, Blairmore is the largest of the Crowsnest Pass communities. Most of Blairmore's historic red-brick buildings can be viewed along Main Street (20th Ave.). The most impressive is the three-story 1912 **Cosmopolitan Hotel,** where an ever-obliging publican had his liquor license revoked many times for serving thirsty miners after-hours. The annual **Rum Runner Days** on the second weekend of July is a rip-roaring celebration of the town's seedy past. It kicks off with a pancake breakfast and parade on Saturday, followed by a barbecue and music in Bandstand Park. The weekend culminates with live music on the local ski hill.

Accommodations and Food

The historic **Cosmopolitan Hotel** (13001 20th Ave., 403/562-7321, $65 s, $75–95 d) has 16 guest rooms. They're still basic, and some share bathrooms, but the price is right. Continuing west along the main street is the **Highwood Motel** (11373 20th Ave., 403/562-8888 or 888/562-8881, $65 s, $80 d), which has a restaurant and pub on the premises. **Lost Lemon Campground** (11001 19th Ave., 403/562-2932, www.lostlemon.com, Apr.–Oct., tents $22, hookups $27–32) is a private facility across the railway tracks at the west end of town. It has showers, an outdoor swimming pool, a hot tub, a playground, and a laundry room, and is situated right beside the Crowsnest River, making it the perfect overnight stop for anglers.

The best place for a meal is **❰ Stone's Throw Cafe** (13047 20th Ave., 403/562-2230, Mon.–Sat. 7 A.M.–5 P.M., Sun. 10 A.M.–4 P.M., lunches $5.50–8) in a restored heritage building across main street from the gazebo. Everything is made fresh, including breakfast wraps, delicious pita melts, soup & sandwich deals, and fruit smoothies. The coffee is the best in the pass; or you can choose from one of the many teas. Wireless Internet is another plus.

COLEMAN AND VICINITY

Westernmost of the Crowsnest Pass communities is Coleman, 15 kilometers (nine miles) from the British Columbia border. The town expanded rapidly at the end of the 19th century and by 1904 it had two hotels, two churches, and several stores along Main Street. When the Coleman Colliery closed in 1983, many of the town's miners joined the ranks of the unemployed, some found work in the British Columbia mines, and others packed up their belongings and left the pass completely. Many buildings along the main street remain boarded up. In a former high school building, the **Crowsnest Museum** (7701 19th Ave., 403/563-5434, summer Tues.–Sun. 8 A.M.–5 P.M., the rest of the year Mon.–Fri. 10 A.M.–noon and 1–5 P.M., adult $7, senior $5, child $4) offers two floors crammed full of exhibits and artifacts from throughout the region. The adjacent schoolyard has displays of farming, mining, and firefighting equipment. Across the street is the *Coleman Journal* **building.** The *Coleman Journal* was a Pulitzer Prize–winning weekly newspaper that was published until 1970. After extensive restoration, the building has been opened to the public. Interpretive panels explain the slow process of early newspaper publishing. It's open the same hours as the museum.

Accommodations and Food

On the north side of the highway three kilometers (1.9 miles) west of Coleman is **Crowsnest Mountain Resort** (4210 21st Ave., 403/562-

7993, www.albertaresort.com, $110 s, $135 d), a combination of five modern chalets, restaurant, and real estate development. Each chalet has a simple yet practical layout, kitchenette, full bath, covered porch with barbecue, and in-floor heating.

While most of downtown Coleman's businesses have relocated to the highway, **Chris's Restaurant** (7802 17th Ave., 403/563-3093, Mon.–Fri. 6 A.M.–10 P.M., Sat.–Sun. 8 A.M.–8 P.M., $3.50–9) manages to hang on. Choose from hamburgers, cheeseburgers, bacon burgers, and loaded burgers. The menu might be limited, but the burgers are good and start at just $3.50. Up on the highway is **Cinnamon Bear Bakery** (8342 20th Ave., 403/562-2443, Mon.–Sat. 7:30 A.M.–5:30 P.M., $5.50–9), a sweet-smelling café where coffee is less than $2, a double iced chai is just $3.50, and a made-to-order soup and sandwich combo is $8.50.

Continuing West Along Highway 3

Atlas Road spurs north three kilometers (1.9 miles) west of Coleman leading to **Allison Creek Trout Brood Station** (403/563-3385, Wed.–Sun. 10 A.M.–noon and 1–3 P.M. July–Aug.), where you can take a self-guided tour to learn how brown, brook, and rainbow trout are raised to provide eggs for trout hatcheries around the province. From the hatchery, Allison Creek Road spurs left to **Allison/Chinook Recreation Area,** with a network of forested hiking trails concentrated around Chinook Lake. The lake itself is a pretty body of water, with **Crowsnest Mountain** forming an imposing backdrop. It takes around 30 minutes to walk around the lake (a little longer if you stop to marvel at the osprey). The park also has a largish campground (403/563-5395, www.rocky-mountaincamping.ca, May–mid-Oct., $15) with limited facilities.

Back on Highway 3, the **Travel Alberta Information Centre** (403/563-3888, 10 A.M.–6 P.M. mid-May–mid-June and 9 A.M.–6 P.M. mid-June–Aug.) has a spectacular view of Crowsnest Mountain.

Lethbridge to Medicine Hat

SOUTH FROM LETHBRIDGE ON HIGHWAY 4

From Lethbridge, it's a fast 105 kilometers (65 miles) to the Coutts–Sweetgrass border crossing, which leads into Montana. Hopefully you're not planning on leaving Alberta just yet, because along the way are two out-of-the-way attractions well worth your attention.

The dominant feature of the prairie landscape south of Lethbridge is the **Milk River.** This waterway is unique among western Canada's river systems in that it is the only one that flows south to the Missouri River, eventually draining into the Gulf of Mexico.

Devil's Coulee

On May 14, 1987, Wendy Slobada, an amateur paleontologist, was exploring the coulees near her family's ranch outside of Milk River when she discovered some fossilized eggshells. The find sent waves of excitement around the scientific world, and the site became known as **Devil's Coulee Dinosaur Egg Site,** one of the most exciting fossil discoveries ever made. What she had found were clutches of eggs that had been laid by hadrosaurs approximately 75 million years ago. Each prehistoric egg was about 20 centimeters (eight inches) long and contained the perfectly formed bones of embryonic dinosaurs. No other find in the entire world has taught scientists more about this part of the dinosaur's life cycle.

Devil's Coulee Dinosaur Heritage Museum (403/642-2118, www.devilscoulee.com, daily 9 A.M.–5 P.M. late May–Aug.) is in the village of Warner, on Highway 4, 66 kilometers (41 miles) southeast of Lethbridge. It is only a small facility, but a display reconstructs the site. Tours to the site of the find leave from the museum weekends in June and daily 10 A.M. and 1 P.M. July–August. Tour cost is $18 per person and advance reservations are required.

◖ Writing-on-Stone Provincial Park

This park, off Highway 501 43 kilometers (27 miles) east of the town of Milk River, has the largest concentrations of petroglyphs and pictographs found in North America. But that's only one of the reasons to venture out into this remote part of the province: A warm river for swimming, great canoeing, intriguing rock formations, and abundant wildlife round out one of Alberta's premier non-mountain parks. The park protects a stretch of the Milk River that has cut a deep valley into the rolling shortgrass prairie. Soft sandstone and shale cliffs are capped with harder, iron-rich sediments. Years of wind and water erosion have carved out the softer, lower rock, leaving mushroom-shaped pinnacles and columns called **hoodoos.**

Writing-On-Stone was a place of great spiritual importance to generations of natives, a place for contact with the supernatural. They attempted to interpret previous carvings and paintings, added their own artwork to the rock, and left gifts of tobacco and beads as a way of communicating with the spirits of the dead. Much of the cliff art remains visible today, providing clues to the region's early inhabitants. Artifacts excavated from below the cliffs suggest that the area had been inhabited for at least 3,000 years, but any rock art of that age would have been destroyed by erosion long ago. Of the carvings visible today, the earliest are thought to be the work of the Shoshoni, created approximately 700 years ago. During the 1730s, the Shoshoni were driven into the mountains by the Blackfoot. The valley's strange rock formations led the Blackfoot to believe that the area was a magical place—a place to be respected and feared—and that existing carvings were created by the spirits. The Blackfoot added their own artistry to the rocks, and many of the Blackfoot carvings are panels that tell a story. The **Hoodoo Interpretive Trail** is a two-kilometer (1.2-mile) hike along the cliffs, with numbered posts that correspond to a trail brochure available from the information center. Along the way are some examples

© ANDREW HEMPSTEAD

hoodoos above the campground at Writing-on-Stone Provincial Park

of petroglyphs and pictographs (including the famous battle scene) that have been ravaged by time and vandals.

Before descending to the river, stop at the hilltop **Interpretive Centre** (403/647-2364, mid-May–early Sept. daily 9 A.M.–7 P.M.), with floor-to-ceiling windows allowing sweeping views across the hoodoos and river. The park has an excellent campground (reserve online at www.reserve.albertaparks.ca, unserviced sites $20, powered sites $26) with 67 sites (only seven with power) nestled below the hoodoos in a stand of cottonwood trees. A riverside trail loops along the edge of the campground, continuing upstream to the most spectacular hoodoos. Although the campground is open year-round, firewood ($10 per bundle) and facilities such as showers are only available May–early September.

HIGHWAY 3 EAST FROM LETHBRIDGE
Coaldale

The first town east of Lethbridge on Highway 3 is Coaldale, with a population of 7,200. The main reason to leave the highway here is to visit the **Alberta Birds of Prey Centre** (north of Highway 3 at 20th St., then left on 16th Ave., 403/345-4262, daily 9:30 A.M.–5 P.M. mid-May–mid-Sept., $8.50, senior $7.50, child $5.50). The aim of this off-the-beaten-path center is to ensure the survival of birds of prey such as hawks, falcons, eagles, burrowing owls, and great horned owls, Alberta's provincial bird. Many of the birds are brought to the center injured or as young chicks. They are nurtured at the center until they are strong enough to be released back into the wild. The Natural History Centre features the works of various wildlife artists and has displays cataloging human fascination with birds of prey through thousands of years. Integrated with this main building is an aviary where you can view birds that are recovering from injury and where tame birds fly free (well, kind of, anyway). Entry includes an invitation to watch "flying programs" (daily at 10 A.M., 12:30 P.M., 2 P.M., and 3:30 P.M.) and the opportunity to be photographed with a falcon.

Taber

Taber, 51 kilometers (32 miles) east of Lethbridge, is most famous for its deliciously sweet **Taber corn.** Long hot days and cool nights bring out a sweetness that isn't found in regular corn. August and early September is the best time to look for corn vendors along the road. Or find corn, along with other fresh local produce, each Thursday at the farmers market in the Taber Agriplex. On the last weekend of August, when the corn has ripened, the town's **Cornfest** celebration takes place, with a pancake breakfast, a midway, hot-air-balloon flights, a classic-car show, and, of course, plenty of corn to taste.

Calgary to Medicine Hat

The TransCanada Highway heads out of Calgary in a southeasterly direction. It passes through Bassano and then Brooks, gateway to Dinosaur Provincial Park, before reaching Medicine Hat after 300 kilometers (186 miles).

STRATHMORE AND VICINITY

From Calgary, the TransCanada Highway parallels the Bow River (although it's never in sight) 100 kilometers (62 miles) to Bassano. The only town along the way is Strathmore, home to the early August **Strathmore Heritage Days** (403/934-5811, www.strathmorerodeo. com), which includes one of Canada's largest rodeos, chuck wagon races, and country music performers. These traditional rodeo goings-on are often overshadowed by the Saturday-night Running of the Bulls, where local adrenaline junkies pay $100 to get chased around the main rodeo ring by about 30 bloodthirsty bulls. It's actually a lot tamer than the Pamplona version, and a little different in that participants must be sober.

Wyndham-Carseland Provincial Park

Visit this 178-hectare (440-acre) park for the fishing and bird-watching. Rainbow and brown trout, up to 60 centimeters (24 inches) long, are caught in the Bow River where it flows through the park; the best fishing is in the deeper main channel. Also within the park is a large population of white pelicans, as well as prairie falcons, Canada geese, kingfishers, and great blue herons. A 200-site campground (May–Oct., $20) is spread out along the south side of the river. The park is about 30 kilometers (19 miles) south of Strathmore via Highway 24 or 817.

BASSANO

Bassano is on the TransCanada Highway midway between Calgary and Medicine Hat. It's a thriving agricultural town of 1,200 people.

Bassano Dam

The biggest local attraction is this dam, nine kilometers (5.6 miles) south of Highway 1. To get there, follow the signs through town, along the rail line, and through the fields (if you cross a single-lane bridge, you're on the right road). The dam combines a 2.3-kilometer (1.4-mile) earthen embankment with a spillway at a sharp bend in the Bow River. Water is diverted from behind the spillway into a 4,500-kilometer (2,800-mile) system of gravity-fed canals supplying water to the 100,000-hectare (250,000-acre) **Eastern Irrigation District,** land that would otherwise be agriculturally worthless. Built by the Canadian Pacific Railway between 1910 and 1914, the dam was known as the most important structure of its type in the world because of its great length and unique foundations.

BROOKS

Brooks (population 14,000) is in the heart of Alberta's extensive irrigated farmlands, 160 kilometers (100 miles) east of Calgary along the TransCanada Highway. The town began as a railway stop in the 1880s, thriving when

SOUTHERN ALBERTA

RED ROCK COULEE

South of **Seven Persons**, the last community on Highway 3 before Medicine Hat, is a small area of badlands on a gentle rise in the surrounding plains. The bedrock here is relatively close to the surface, and wind and water erosion have cut through the topsoil to expose it. In some places, the erosion has extended into the bedrock itself, revealing varicolored strata laid down millions of years ago. This strange landscape is dotted with red boulder-shaped concretions measuring up to 2.5 meters (eight feet) across. These intriguing rock formations formed under the surface of a prehistoric sea,

when sand, calcite, and iron oxide collected on a nucleus of shells, bones, and corals. They became part of the bedrock as layers of sediment were laid down, but as erosion took its course, the surrounding bedrock disappeared and the concretions emerged. The formations here are believed to be the largest of their type in the world. To get there, follow Highway 887 south from Seven Persons for 23 kilometers (14 miles). Where the road curves sharply to the east (left), continue straight ahead uphill on an unsealed road and park at the lone picnic table. The boulders are laid out below and to the south.

© ANDREW HEMPSTEAD

the Canadian Pacific Railway completed the irrigation system centered on Bassano Dam. Today, the oil and gas industry is important to the local economy, but it's Canada's largest meat-packing plant, on the west side of town, that gets most of the attention. The facility employs around 2,500 people, most of them immigrants from places like Sudan and Kenya. This gives Brooks an interesting small town ethnic diversity unlike anywhere else in

Canada. For visitors, Brooks offers all tourist services and is a good base for exploring Dinosaur Provincial Park.

Sights

Until the 1970s, **Brooks Aqueduct,** seven kilometers (4.3 miles) southeast of town, carried water across a shallow valley to dry prairie on the other side, opening up a massive chunk of otherwise unproductive land to farming. At the time of its completion in 1914, the 3.2-kilometer (two-mile) aqueduct was the longest concrete structure of its type in the world and had been designed and built using unique engineering principles. Although now replaced by an earth-filled canal, the impressive structure has been preserved as a National Historic Site and serves as a monument to those who developed the region. Admission to the small interpretive center (403/362-4451, 10 A.M.–6 P.M. mid-May–Aug.) is free.

Brooks and District Museum (Sutherland Dr., 403/362-5073, late May–early Sept. daily 9 A.M.–5 P.M. donation) catalogs the area's past from the era of dinosaurs to the heady days of a short-lived oil boom. Curious gardeners won't want to miss the **Crop Diversification Centre** (two km/1.2 mi east of town, 403/362-3391), where research is done on greenhouse crops, various fruits, ornamental flowers, vegetables, oil seeds, and weed control.

This 48-hectare (120-acre) park 13 kilometers (eight miles) south of Brooks is an island in **Lake Newell.** A causeway across wetlands links the park to the mainland, with a trail looping around the area. Lake Newell, Canada's largest manmade body of water, was developed as a constant source of water for Eastern Irrigation District farmland. For visitors, it's swimming, fishing, and boating that draws the summertime crowds. The lake is home to northern pike, walleye, and whitefish, the latter two of which have been stocked in years gone by. The campground (403/362-2962, unserviced sites $20, powered sites $26) has showers, laundry, firewood sales, and picnic shelters. The adjacent beach has a playground and concession.

Accommodations and Food

The best of a bunch of cheap motels along 2nd Street W (off the westernmost access to town) is **Tel-Star Motor Inn** (813 2nd St. W, 403/362-3466 or 800/260-6211, $75 s, $79 d). Each air-conditioned room has a microwave and fridge. **Travelodge Brooks** (1240 Cassils Rd., 403/362-8000 or 800/578-7878, www.travelodge.com, $125 s or d) is a reliable choice. **Kiwanis Campground** (Cassils Rd. by eastern access, 403/362-5073, $20–30) has a few pull-though powered sites and a handy highway location, but better options exist out of town. Halfway between Brooks and Tilley is **Tillebrook Provincial Park** (403/362-4525, mid-Apr.–Oct., tenting $20, hookups $26), one of several campgrounds built along the TransCanada Highway during that road's construction.

Medicine Hat and Vicinity

The prosperous industrial city of Medicine Hat (population 61,000) sits on some of western Canada's most extensive natural-gas fields, 168 kilometers (104 miles) east of Lethbridge and 40 kilometers (25 miles) west of the Saskatchewan border. Known as "The Hat" to locals, the city straddles the South Saskatchewan River along which many areas are protected as parkland. The city also holds interesting attractions such as the remains of Canada's once-thriving pottery industry and an archeological site regarded as one of the most extensive and richest finds from the late-prehistoric period of native history. Travelers keeping an eye on their spending will also appreciate Medicine Hat—it's home to some of western Canada's cheapest motels and consistently has Canada's cheapest gas prices.

The Name "Medicine Hat"

Many tales describe how the name Medicine Hat evolved. One of the most popular legends tells the story of the Cree chief who led his people to the cliffs above the South Saskatchewan River. Here, the Great Serpent told him that he must sacrifice his wife to the river in exchange for a *saamis* (medicine hat). This would give him magical powers and allow him to defeat the Blackfoot when they attacked later that night. Another story tells of how the Blackfoot

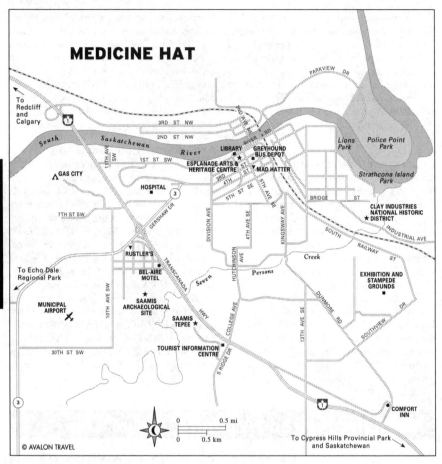

MEDICINE HAT

were forced into the waters of the South Saskatchewan River by the Cree, who then fired an arrow into the heart of the Blackfoot medicine man. As he slowly sank below the water's surface, his hat was swept away into the hands of the Cree. The Blackfoot saw this as a terrible omen and retreated.

SIGHTS AND RECREATION
Saamis Tepee

Since it's the location of Medicine Hat's main information center, it makes sense that you stay on the TransCanada Highway (approaching from either direction) and take the signposted exit (South Ridge Drive) to the Saamis Tepee. Besides, standing more than 20 stories high beside the TransCanada Highway, with a base diameter of 50 meters (160 feet) and made entirely of steel (it weighs 1,000 tons), this is one sight you don't need detailed directions to find. Originally erected during the 1988 Calgary Winter Olympic Games to commemorate the cultural roles played by natives in the history of North America, it has since been moved to its present site. It overlooks Seven Persons Creek Coulee, an archaeological site used in late prehistoric times as a native camp where buffalo were dried and processed. A self-guided interpretive trail, beginning at the tepee, leads to a bluff and into the valley where the camp was located.

Downtown

Many early-20th-century buildings located in the downtown area are still in active use, including private homes, churches, and businesses. The availability of local clay led to thriving brick-manufacturing plants here during the late 1800s; many original buildings still stand in mute testimony to the quality of the bricks. But the main attraction is more modern. The **Esplanade Arts & Heritage Centre** (401 1st St. SE, 403/502-8580, Mon.–Fri. 10 A.M.–5 P.M., Sat. and Sun. noon–5 P.M., adult $4, child $3, free for everyone on Thurs.) combines a museum, art gallery, gift shop, theater, and archives. The museum portion holds a permanent collection of exhibits explaining the history of the natives that once inhabited the plains, the growth of the city, and the

important role played by ranching and farming in southeastern Alberta, the NWMP, and the arrival of the railway. Local, provincial, and nationally acclaimed artists have their work displayed in art gallery, although the center is best known for hosting national and international exhibitions.

Clay Industries
National Historic District

Nearby clay deposits led to a large pottery and brick industry that thrived from the late 1880s to World War II. The clay was mass-produced into high-quality china at various factories on the north side of the railway line east of downtown. It is this area that is now protected as a historic district. For the first 50 years of last century, **Medalta** was a household name in Canada. Their china, popular in homes and used exclusively by Canadian Pacific Railway-owned hotels, is now prized by collectors. Since closing in 1954, fire, wind, and rain have taken their toll on the buildings, which have been declared a National Historical Site. Part of the

Esplanade Arts & Heritage Centre

Medalta site has been restored and operates as a museum (713 Medalta Ave. SE, 403/526-2777, mid-May–early Sept. daily 9:30 A.M.–5 P.M., the rest of the year Tues.–Sat. 10 A.M.–4 P.M., adult $10, senior and child $8), displaying the history of the clay and pottery industries in Medicine Hat and has some fine examples of the now highly prized Medalta pieces. The original kilns are open for inspection and there is a gift shop filled with pottery. Admission includes a walking tour.

Medicine Hat Exhibition and Stampede

An annual extravaganza since 1887, this event (403/527-1234, www.mhstampede.com) has grown to become Alberta's second-richest rodeo (behind the Calgary Stampede), guaranteeing knuckle-clenching, bronc-riding, foot-stompin' fun through the last week of July. Various events are held throughout the city, culminating with the weekend rodeo and chuck-wagon races. The stampede also features many exhibitors displaying their wares, as well as a midway, a Pioneer Village, a trade show, and lots of free entertainment. A top country act is the Saturday night feature.

ACCOMMODATIONS

Medicine Hat has some of Alberta's cheapest motel rooms. Most of the cheapies are bunched together along the downtown side of the TransCanada Highway around Gershaw Drive, including the **Bel-Aire Motel** (633 14th St. SW, 403/527-4421, $55 s, $60 d). The 12 rooms are cooled by noisy air-conditioners and each has a small fridge.

Rising from an area of strip malls beside the TransCanada Highway, the **Comfort Inn** (2317 TransCanada Hwy., 403/504-1700 or 800/228-5150, www.choicehotels.ca, $95–145 s or d) is easily recognized by its modern lines and burgundy-and-yellow color scheme. The sharp design is carried through into the 100 guest rooms, each of which comes loaded with amenities. Other features are an indoor pool, a business center, high-speed Internet throughout, and a fitness room. Local calls

and a big continental breakfast are included in the rates.

Camping

Gas City Campground (580 1st St., SE, 403/528-8158, May–Oct., unserviced sites $20, hookups $33–38) is on the edge of town, has nearly 100 sites, and is far enough away from the highway to be relatively quiet. From the back of the campground, a trail heads along the river and into town. At night, this is a good spot to view the illumination of Medicine Hat's industrial core. Good hot showers, laundry facilities, groceries, and full hookups make this the place to try first. To get there, turn off the highway at 7th Street SW and follow the signs down 11th Avenue.

FOOD

Mad Hatter (513 3rd St. SE, 403/529-2344, Mon.–Fri. 7 A.M.–5:30 P.M., Sat. 8 A.M.–5:30 P.M., Sun. 10 A.M.–5 P.M., lunches $5.50–7.50) is a funky little space with a friendly, small-town ambience. Coffee beans are roasted in-house and the light meals are all made fresh daily

If you're staying in one of the cheap highway motels, saving money is obviously important to you. If that's the case, you'll want to head to **Rustler's** (901 8th St. SW, 403/526-8004, daily 8 A.M.–10 P.M., $13–20.50) for a meal. It's one of the city's oldest eating establishments and, because of its history (see the menu for the amusing tale), a real Wild West atmosphere prevails. Seating is out back in the tavern or in a restaurant section, where a glass tabletop reveals a poker game complete with gun and bloodstained playing cards. The place is popular all day, but breakfast is especially crowded. Large portions of eggs, bacon, and hash browns begin at $5, omelets at $5.50. For the rest of the day, it's hard to beat the beef. Last time through I enjoyed the Alberta rib eye with roasted potatoes and vegetables.

INFORMATION

To get to the **tourist information center** (8 Gehring Rd. SE, 403/527-6422 or 800/481-

2822, www.tourismmedicinehat.com, daily 8 A.M.–7 P.M. mid-June–Aug., Mon.–Fri. 9 A.M.–5 P.M., Sat. 10 A.M.–3 P.M. the rest of the year), take the Southridge Drive exit from the TransCanada Highway just east of the big tepee.

Downtown, **Medicine Hat Public Library** (414 1st St. SE, 403/502-8527, Mon.–Thurs. 10 A.M.–9 P.M., Fri. and Sat. 10 A.M.–5:30 P.M., Sun. 1–5:30 P.M.) overlooks the river and has free Internet.

CYPRESS HILLS PROVINCIAL PARK

Covering an area of 200 square kilometers (77 square miles), Cypress Hills occupies a small section of an upland plateau that extends well into Saskatchewan, with the entire area protected as Cypress Hills Provincial Park. The hills rise as high as 500 meters (1,640 feet) above the surrounding grasslands, and at their top elevation (1,466 m/4,800 ft, the same as the town Banff), they are the highest point between the Canadian Rockies and Labrador. The French word for lodgepole pine is *cyprés,* which led to the hills being named Les Montagnes de Cyprés, and thus Cypress Hills, when in fact cypress trees have never grown in the park.

The park is 70 kilometers (43 miles) southeast of Medicine Hat along Highway 41. It offers good hiking, fishing, or just plain relaxing and is popular as a place to escape the high summer temperatures of the prairies. The only commercial facilities are in the townsite of **Elkwater,** which sits in a natural amphitheater overlooking **Elkwater Lake.** The facilities are limited (no bank, one restaurant, one motel, one gas station), so come prepared.

Flora and Fauna

The park supports more than 400 recorded plant species in four ecological zones: **prairie, parkland, foothills,** and **boreal forest.** The best way to view the flora of the park is on foot; many trails pass through two or three zones in the space of an hour's walking. Sixteen species of orchid are found in the park—some are very

common, whereas others, such as the sparrow's egg lady's slipper, are exceedingly rare.

The unique environment of the hills provides a favorable habitat for 37 species of mammals, 400 species of birds, and a few turtles. Big game was once common throughout the hills, but in 1926 the last remaining large mammal—a wolf—was shot. Soon thereafter, elk were reintroduced to the park and now number more than 200. Moose, never before present in the park, were introduced in the 1950s and now number about 60.

Exploring the Park

To access the center of the park, take Reesor Lake Road east from Highway 41, passing a herd of cattle and a viewpoint with spectacular vistas of the transition from grassland to forest. The road then descends steeply to **Reesor Lake,** which has a campground, a picnic area, a short hiking trail to a viewpoint, and excellent fishing for rainbow trout. Bull Trail Road off Reesor Lake Road leads to **Spruce Coulee** and a reservoir stocked with eastern brook and rainbow trout. Most of the trails are easy to moderate, following the shores of Elkwater Lake (wheelchair accessible) and climbing out of the townsite into open fields and mixed forests. **Spruce Coulee Trail** (eight km/five mi) is the longest hike. It starts behind the rodeo grounds and leads through woodland and past a few beaver ponds before reaching Spruce Coulee.

Just east of the marina, **Elkwater Boat & Bike Rentals** (403/893-3835) rents mountain bikes ($6 per hour, $30 per day), canoes ($8 per hour, $40 per day), and motorboats ($22 per hour). Golfers have been walking the rolling fairways of **Elkwater Park Golf Club** (403/893-2167, $28) since 1937. It's on the park's southern edge.

Accommodations and Food

Within the townsite, **C Elkwater Lake Lodge** (401 4th St., 403/893-3811 or 888/893-3811, www.elkwaterlakelodge.com, $135–200 s, $115–160 d) features spacious air-conditioned, kitchen-equipped standard rooms, fireplace rooms, condos with 1–3 bedrooms, and rustic cabins with kitchens. Amenities include an indoor saltwater pool, a hot tub, a library filled with local literature, and landscaped gardens with an outdoor rock fireplace. Also on site is **Buglers,** an inviting restaurant open daily for breakfast, lunch, and dinner. The dinner menu covers all bases, with mains ranging $16–28 and delicious cheesecake for $6.

Within the park are more than 500 campsites in 12 campgrounds. The main camping season is mid-May–mid-September although some campgrounds remain open year-round with limited facilities. Closest to Elkwater are **Beaver Creek Campground** ($34), with full hookups, and **Elkwater Campground** ($22–34) with unserviced and hookups. Both have showers. **Reesor Lake Campground** ($22, no showers or hookups) at the eastern end of the park is much quieter—listen for bugling elk in the fall. Reservations for some campgrounds are taken (call 403/893-3835 or 403/893-3782 Mon.–Fri. only).

Information

Cypress Hills Visitor Centre (403/893-3833, mid-May–Sept. daily 9 A.M.–7 P.M., Oct.–mid-May Thurs.–Sun. 9 A.M.–4 P.M.) overlooks Elkwater Lake, a short walk from the townsite campgrounds. Audiovisual programs explain the natural history and archaeological and historical resources of the park, and a nightly interpretive program operates during July and August.

BANFF AND JASPER NATIONAL PARKS

The Canadian Rockies are protected by a string of parks and wilderness reserves, but none are as scenic or well-known as Banff and Jasper National Parks. Encompassing some of the world's most magnificent mountain scenery, snowcapped peaks form a spectacular backdrop for glacial lakes, fast-flowing rivers, endless forests, and three famous resort towns, Banff, Lake Louise, and Jasper.

The 6,641 square kilometers (2,564 square miles) protected by Banff National Park and the 10,900 square kilometers (4,208 square miles) protected by Jasper is only one component of a complex geological and natural area consisting of four adjacent national parks that together have been declared a World Heritage Site by UNESCO (the others are Kootenay and Yoho to the west in British Columbia). The parks' vast wilderness is home to deer, moose, elk, mountain goats, bighorn sheep, black and grizzly bears, wolves, and cougars. Many of these species are commonly sighted from the highway, others forage within the towns, and some remain deep in the backcountry. The human species is concentrated in the picture-postcard town of Banff, located near Banff National Park's southeast gate, 128 kilometers (80 miles) west of Calgary. Northwest of Banff, along the TransCanada Highway, is Lake Louise, regarded as one of the seven natural wonders of the world, rivaled for sheer beauty only by Moraine Lake, just down the road. Just north of Lake Louise, the Icefields Parkway begins its spectacular course alongside the Continental Divide to Jasper National Park and natural wonders such as the Columbia

© ANDREW HEMPSTEAD

HIGHLIGHTS

◖ **Fairmont Banff Springs:** You don't need to book a room here to enjoy the many wonders of one of the world's great mountain resorts – join a guided tour, enjoy a meal, or simply wander through the grand public areas (page 378).

◖ **Sunshine Meadows:** No public road access makes this delightful alpine destination a prime spot for hikers looking to escape the crowds (page 382).

◖ **Lake Louise:** Famous Lake Louise has hypnotized visitors with her beauty for more than 100 years. Rent a canoe from the boathouse for the ultimate lake experience (page 399).

◖ **Moraine Lake:** If anywhere in the Canadian Rockies qualified as a double must-see, it would be this deep-blue body of water surrounded by glaciated peaks. Escape the lakeside crowd by hiking into Larch Valley (page 399).

◖ **Bow Lake:** Although you can soak up this lake's beauty from the Icefields Parkway, a walk along its northern shoreline early in the morning is a sure way to make the most of this scenic gem (page 407).

◖ **Peyto Lake:** Another one of Banff's famous lakes. The main difference is the perspective from which it is viewed – a lookout high above its shoreline (page 407).

◖ **Columbia Icefield:** Don't miss this glacial area at the southern end of Jasper National Park. Take the Ice Explorer tour to get a close-up view of this natural wonder (page 408).

◖ **Mount Edith Cavell:** Although this distinctive peak is visible from various points within Jasper National Park, no vantage point is as memorable as that from its base, reached by a walking trail from the end of a winding access road (page 416).

◖ **Maligne Lake:** The most famous body of water in Jasper National Park, and for good reason – it's simply stunning. Take a tour boat to Spirit Island or hike the Lake Trail (Mary Schäffer Loop) along the lake's eastern shore (page 417).

LOOK FOR ◖ TO FIND RECOMMENDED SIGHTS, ACTIVITIES, DINING, AND LODGING.

Icefield. Continuing north, the town of Jasper is a smaller, less commercial version of Banff.

One of the Canadian Rockies' greatest draws is the accessibility of its natural wonders. Most highlights are close to the road system. For more adventurous travelers, an excellent system of hiking trails leads to alpine lakes, along glacial valleys, and to spectacular viewpoints where crowds are scarce and human impact has been minimal. Also popular within the parks is fishing, boating, downhill skiing, golfing, horseback riding, and white-water rafting. Summer in the park is busy. In fact, the parks receive nearly half of their four million annual visitors in just two months—July and August. The rest of the year, crowds are minimal. In winter, four world-class alpine resorts—Ski Norquay, Sunshine Village, Lake Louise, and Marmot Basin—crank up their lifts. Since it's low-season, hotel rates are reasonable. And if you tire of downhill skiing or snowboarding, you can try cross-country skiing, ice-skating, or snowshoeing; take a sleigh ride; soak in a hot spring; or go heli-skiing across the mountains in British Columbia.

Park Entry

Permits are required for entry into Banff and Jasper National Parks. A **National Parks Day Pass** is adult $9.80, senior $8.30, child $4.90 to a maximum of $20 per vehicle. It is interchangeable between parks and is valid until 4 P.M. the day following its purchase. If you'll be traveling in the parks extensively, consider an annual **National Parks of Canada Pass,** good for entry into national parks across Canada, for adult $53, senior $45, child $27, to a maximum of $107 per vehicle. Passes can be bought at all park entrances, park information centers, and at campground kiosks. For more information, check online at the Parks Canada website (www.pc.gc.ca).

PLANNING YOUR TIME

If you are planning to visit western Canada, it is almost inevitable that your itinerary will include the Canadian Rockies, both for the many and varied outdoor attractions and for the central location between Vancouver and Calgary. The two main national parks can be anything you want them to be, depending on the time of year you visit and what your interests are. The main population centers are the towns of Banff and Jasper, both with all the services of large towns, as well as landmark accommodations like the Fairmont Banff Springs and Fairmont Jasper Park Lodge. North of the town of Banff is Lake Louise, an iconic body of water rivaled in beauty only by its immediate neighbor, Moraine Lake. Both are accessible by road, but to combine beauty with wilderness, you'll need to strap on hiking boots are visit places like Sunshine Meadows or Larch Valley.

For the trip between Banff and Jasper, plan on spending a full day on the Icefields Parkway, including stops at Bow and Peyto Lakes and an Ice Explorer excursion at Columbia Icefield. If your time in Jasper is limited, Maligne Lake should be atop your list of priorities. Of all the hikes in Jasper, none are more scenic than the hike to Cavell Meadows.

BANFF AND JASPER

© ANDREW HEMPSTEAD

Lake Louise

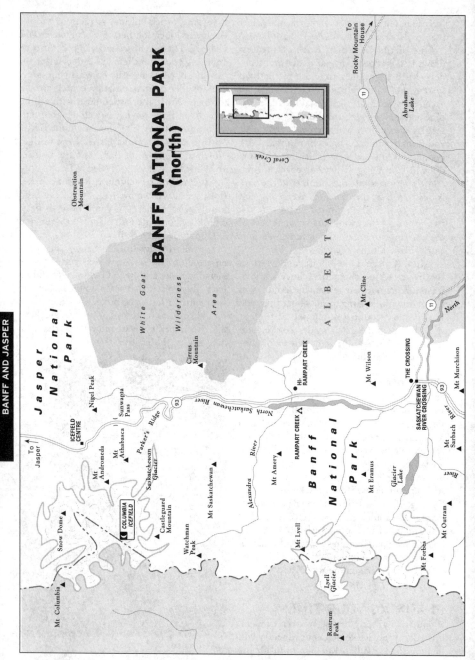

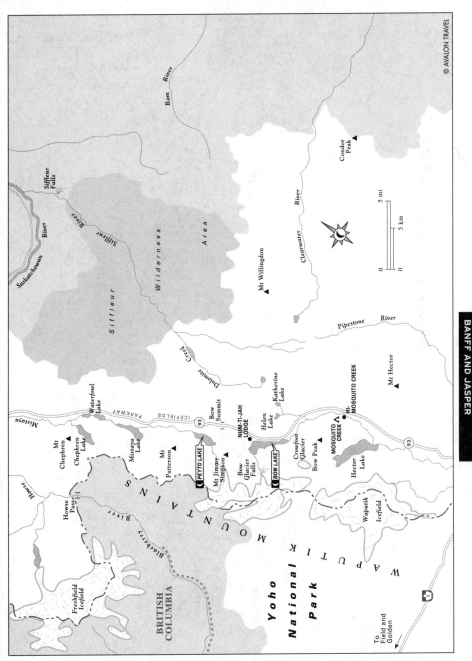

© AVALON TRAVEL

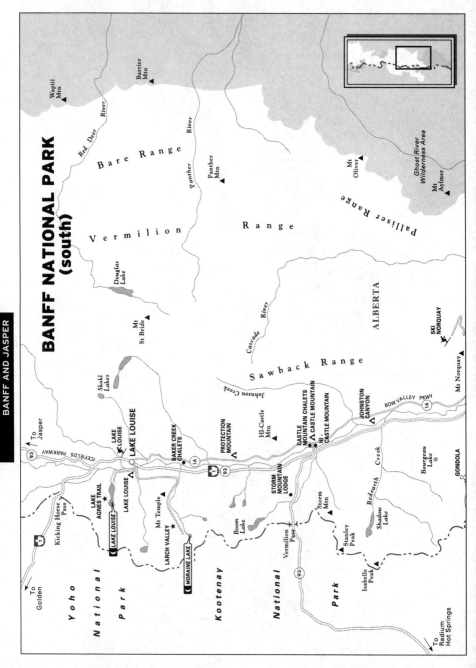

BANFF NATIONAL PARK (south)

Wapiti Mtn ▲

Barrier Mtn ▲

Red Deer River

Bare Range

Panther River

Ghost River Wilderness Area

Mt Oliver ▲

Panther Mtn ▲

Mt Aylmer ▲

Palliser Range

Vermilion   Range

Douglas Lake

ALBERTA

Cascade River

Mt St Bride ▲

SKI NORQUAY

Skoki Lakes

Sawback Range

Mt Norquay ▲

Johnson Creek

To Jasper

ICEFIELDS PARKWAY

LAKE LOUISE

LAKE LOUISE

BAKER CREEK CHALETS

PROTECTION MOUNTAIN

HI-Castle Mtn

CASTLE MOUNTAIN CHALETS

▲ CASTLE MOUNTAIN

HI-CASTLE MOUNTAIN

JOHNSTON CANYON

BOW VALLEY PKWY

1A

93

LAKE AGNES TRAIL

LAKE LOUISE ◄

LAKE LOUISE ▲

Mt Temple ★

LARCH VALLEY

MORAINE LAKE ◄

STORM MOUNTAIN LODGE

93

Storm Mtn ▲

Bourgeau Lake

GONDOLA

To Golden

Kicking Horse Pass

Boom Lake

Vermilion Pass

Stanley Peak ▲

Redearth Creek

Shadow Lake

Yoho   National   Park

Kootenay   National   Park

Isabelle Peak ▲

To Radium Hot Springs

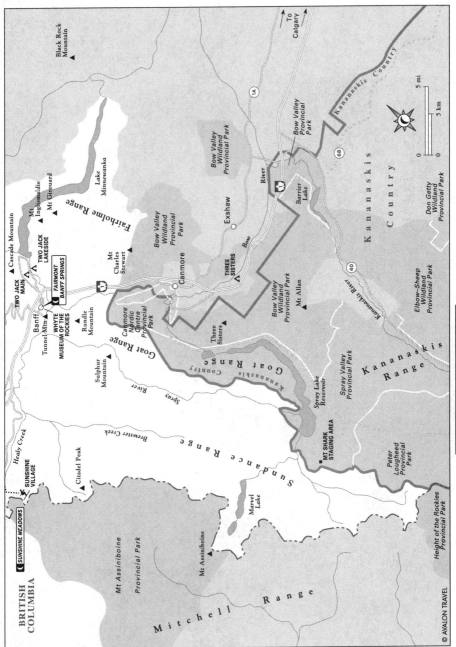

BANFF AND JASPER

© AVALON TRAVEL

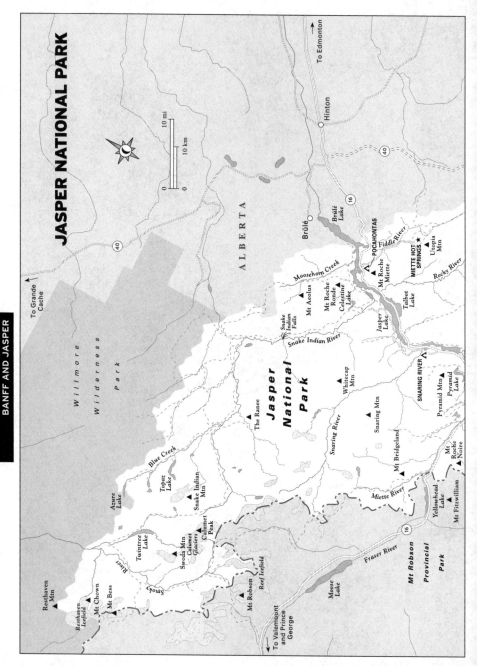

JASPER NATIONAL PARK

To Grande Cache

Willmore Wilderness Park

ALBERTA

To Edmonton

Hinton

40

Brûlé

Brûlé Lake

16

POCAHONTAS

Fiddle River

Mt Roche Miette

MIETTE HOT SPRINGS

Utopia Mtn

Rocky River

Moosehorn Creek

Mt Aeolus

Mt Roche Ronde

Celestine Lake

Snake Indian Falls

Snake Indian River

Jasper Lake

Talbot Lake

The Ranee

Jasper National Park

Whitecap Mtn

Snaring River

Snaring Mtn

SNARING RIVER

Pyramid Mtn

Pyramid Lake

Blue Creek

Topaz Lake

Snake Indian Mtn

Azure Lake

Mt Bridgeland

Mt Roche Noire

Miette River

16

Yellowhead Lake

Mt Fitzwilliam

Twintree Lake

Swoda Mtn

Calumet Glaciers

Calumet Peak

Smoky River

Mt Robson Provincial Park

Fraser River

Resthaven Mtn

Resthaven Icefield

Mt Chown

Mt Bess

Reef Icefield

Mt Robson

Moose Lake

To Valemount and Prince George

10 mi

10 km

0

0

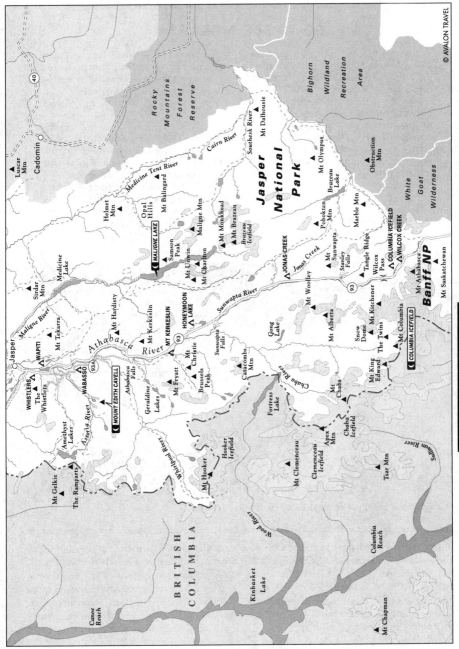

© AVALON TRAVEL

WHERE CAN I GO TO SEE A BEAR?

This commonly asked question doesn't have an exact answer, but the exhilaration of seeing one of these magnificent creatures in its natural habitat is unforgettable.

From the road, you're most likely to see black bears, which range in color from jet black to cinnamon brown. They are often sighted along the **Bow Valley Parkway** at dawn or late in the afternoon, most commonly in spring. Farther north, watch for black bears along the **Icefields Parkway,** especially in the vicinity of **Cirrus Mountain.**

Grizzly bears spend most of the year in remote valleys, often on south-facing slopes. During late spring, they are occasionally seen in the area of **Bow Pass.** In recent years, a grizzly has taken up residence in the **Bow Valley** between the town of Banff and Lake Minnewanka. The one place I can guarantee you'll see a grizzly is the **Lake Louise Visitor Centre.** She's stuffed (literally), but gives you a good idea just how big these magnificent creatures are.

The chance of encountering a bear face-to-face in the backcountry is remote. To lessen chances even further, several simple precautions should be taken. Never hike alone or at dusk, always make lots of noise when passing through heavy vegetation, keep a clean camp, and read the pamphlets available at all park visitors centers. If you're in a vehicle and spot a bear, stay there. Visitors centers in Banff and Lake Louise compile lists of all recent bear sightings.

© ANDREW HEMPSTEAD

From the road, you're most likely to see black bears.

In compiling this chapter, I assumed you enjoy the outdoors—hiking, fishing, watching wildlife, and the like—but maybe not with a backpack full of provisions strapped to your back. Keeping this in mind, I'd recommend spending at least four days in the two parks—one each in **Banff, Lake Louise,** and **Jasper,** with the fourth spent along the Icefields Parkway.

Unless you're a die-hard skier or snowboarder, summer is definitely the best time of year to visit. The months of July and August are the busiest, with crowds decreasing exponentially in the weeks before and after these two months. June and September are wonderful times to visit the park. Aside from the crowd factor, in June wildflowers start blooming and wildlife is abundant. September sees temperatures ripe for hiking, and the turning colors are at their peak. In either month, discounted accommodations are a welcome bonus. In May and the stretch of October through November, the park is at its quietest. The park's three alpine resorts begin opening in December and remain in operation until April or May. While skiing and boarding are the big wintertime draw, plan on expanding your experience by joining a sleigh ride, trying snowshoeing, or heading out ice fishing.

Town of Banff

Many visitors to the national park don't realize that the town of Banff is a bustling commercial center with 8,000 permanent residents. The town's location is magnificent. It is spread out along the Bow River, extending to the lower slopes of Sulphur Mountain to the south and Tunnel Mountain to the east. In one direction is the towering face of Mount Rundle, and in the other, framed by the buildings along Banff Avenue, is Cascade Mountain. Hotels and motels line the north end of Banff Avenue, and a profusion of shops, boutiques, cafés, and restaurants hugs the south end. Also at the south end, just over the Bow River, is the Park Administration Building. Here the road forks—to the right is the historic Cave and Basin Hot Springs, to the left The Fairmont Banff Springs and Banff Gondola. Some people are happy walking along the crowded streets or shopping in a truly unique setting, but visitors who are more interested in some peace and quiet can easily slip into pristine wilderness just a five-minute walk from town.

HISTORY

On November 8, 1883, three young railway workers—Franklin McCabe and William and Thomas McCardell—went prospecting for gold on their day off. After crossing the Bow River by raft, they came across a warm stream and traced it to its source at a small log-choked basin of warm water that had a distinct smell of sulphur. Nearby, they detected the source of the foul smell coming from a hole in the ground. Nervously, one of the three men lowered himself into the hole and came across a subterranean pool of aqua-green warm water.

The three men had not found gold, but something just as precious—a hot mineral spring that in time would attract wealthy customers from around the world. Word of the discovery soon got out, and the government encouraged visitors to the Cave and Basin as an ongoing source of revenue to support the new railway.

A small reserve was established around the springs on November 25, 1885, and two years later the reserve was expanded and renamed **Rocky Mountains Park.** It was primarily a business enterprise centered around the unique springs and catering to wealthy patrons of the railway. The Banff Springs Hotel, the world's largest hotel at the time, opened in 1888. Enterprising locals soon realized the area's potential and began opening restaurants and offering guided hunting and boating trips. By 1900, the bustling community of Banff had eight hotels and had became Canada's best-known tourist resort, attracting visitors from around the world.

Changing Attitudes

At the turn of the 20th century, Canada had an abundance of wilderness; it certainly didn't need a park to preserve it. The only goal of Rocky Mountains Park was to generate income for the government and the Canadian Pacific Railway (C.P.R.). In 1902, the park boundary was again expanded to include 11,440 square kilometers (4,420 square miles) of the Canadian Rockies. This dramatic expansion meant that the park became not just a tourist resort but also home to existing coal-mining and logging operations and hydroelectric dams. Government officials saw no

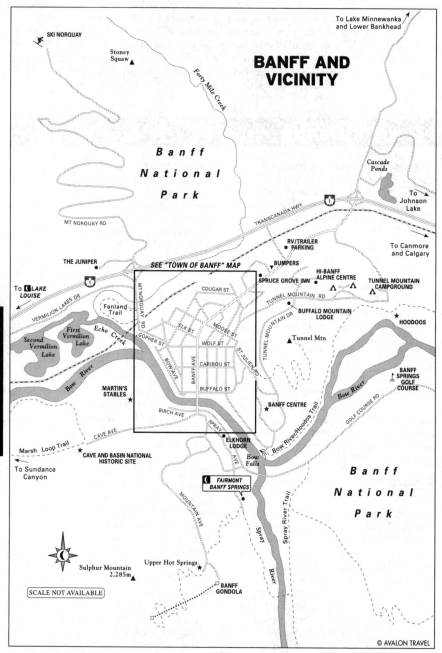

To Lake Minnewanka
and Lower Bankhead

**BANFF AND
VICINITY**

SKI NORQUAY

Stoney
Squaw ▲

Forty Mile Creek

B a n f f

N a t i o n a l

P a r k

Cascade
Ponds

To
Johnson
Lake

TRANSCANADA HWY

MT NORQUAY RD

RV/TRAILER
PARKING

To Canmore
and Calgary

THE JUNIPER

SEE "TOWN OF BANFF" MAP

BUMPERS

HI-BANFF
ALPINE CENTRE

TUNNEL MOUNTAIN
CAMPGROUND

To **LAKE
LOUISE**

COUGAR ST

SPRUCE GROVE INN

VERMILION LAKES DR

MT NORQUAY RD

Fenland
Trail

Echo Creek

First
Vermilion
Lake

Second
Vermilion
Lake

ELK ST

MOOSE ST

TUNNEL MOUNTAIN RD

BUFFALO MOUNTAIN
LODGE

HOODOOS

GOPHER ST

WOLF ST

TUNNEL MOUNTAIN DR

● Tunnel Mtn

Bow River

BOW AVE

BANFF AVE

CARIBOU ST

ST JULIEN RD

BANFF
SPRINGS
GOLF
COURSE

MARTIN'S
STABLES

BUFFALO ST

Bow River

GOLF COURSE RD

BIRCH AVE

BANFF CENTRE

Bow River/Hoodoo Trail

CAVE AVE

SPRAY AVE

ELKHORN
LODGE

Marsh Loop Trail

CAVE AND BASIN NATIONAL
HISTORIC SITE

Bow
Falls

To Sundance
Canyon

B a n f f

**FAIRMONT
BANFF SPRINGS**

MOUNTAIN AVE

N a t i o n a l

P a r k

Spray River Trail

Spray

River

Sulphur Mountain
2,285m ▲

Upper Hot Springs ★

**BANFF
GONDOLA**

SCALE NOT AVAILABLE

© AVALON TRAVEL

conflict of interest, actually stating that the coal mine and township at **Bankhead** added to the park's many attractions. As attitudes began to change, the government set up a Dominion Parks Branch, whose first commissioner, J. B. Hawkins, believed that land set aside for parks should be used for recreation and education. Gradually, resource industries were phased out. Hawkins's work culminated in the National Parks Act of 1930, which in turn led Rocky Mountains Park to be renamed Banff National Park.

Development and the Future

For the first century of its existence, the town of Banff was run as a service center for park visitors by the Canadian Parks Service in Ottawa—a government department with plenty of economic resources but little idea about how to handle the day-to-day running of a midsized town. Any inconvenience this arrangement caused park residents was offset by cheap rent and subsidized services. In June 1988, Banff's residents voted to sever this tie, and on January 1, 1990, Banff officially became an incorporated town, no different than any other in Alberta (except that Parks Canada controls environmental protection within town limits).

SIGHTS AND DRIVES
Banff Park Museum

Although displays of stuffed animals are not usually associated with national parks, the Banff Park Museum (93 Banff Ave., 403/762-1558, May–Sept. daily 10 A.M.–6 P.M., the rest of the year daily 1–5 P.M.; adult $4, senior $3.50, child $3) provides an insight into the park's early history. Visitors during the Victorian era were eager to see the park's animals without actually having to venture into the woods. A lack of roads and scarcity of large game resulting from hunting meant that the best places to see animals, stuffed or otherwise, were the game paddock, the zoo, and this museum, which was built in 1903. Staff lead a guided tour through the facility Monday–Friday at 3 P.M. and Saturday–Sunday at

2:30 P.M. The museum also has a Discovery Room, where touching the displays is encouraged, and a reading room is stocked with books on the park.

Whyte Museum of the Canadian Rockies

This downtown museum (111 Bear St., 403/762-2291, daily 10 A.M.–5 P.M., adult $7, child free) houses the world's premier collection of Canadian Rockies literature and art. Included in the archives are more than 4,000 volumes, oral tapes of early pioneers and outfitters, antique postcards, old cameras, manuscripts, and a large photography collection. The highlight is the photography of Byron Harmon, whose black-and-white studies of mountain geography have shown people around the world the beauty of the Canadian Rockies. On the grounds are several heritage homes formerly occupied by local pioneers, including Bill Peyto, and a backcountry cabin used by wardens.

The Whyte Museum hosts town walking tours through summer. The most popular of these is the **Historic Banff Walk,** which departs from the museum daily at 2:30 P.M., taking around 90 minutes to traverse the historic parts of downtown; $8 per person. The **Heritage Homes Tour** allows an opportunity for visitors to take a closer look at the historic residences located in the trees behind the museum, including that of Peter and Catharine Whyte. This tour departs in summer daily at 11 A.M. and 2:30 P.M. and also costs $8 per person. Around 40 minutes is spent visiting the home of a prominent Banff family on the **Luxton Home & Garden Tour.** Departures are summer only, daily at 1 P.M.; $8.

Cascade Gardens

Across the river from downtown, Cascade Gardens offers a commanding view along Banff Avenue and of Cascade Mountain. The gardens are immaculately manicured, making for enjoyable strolling on a sunny day. The stone edifice in the center of the garden is the **Park Administration Building** (101 Mountain Ave.), which dates to 1936. It replaced a private spa and hospital operated by one of the park's earliest entrepreneurs, Dr. R. G. Brett. Known as Brett's Sanatorium, the original 1886 structure was built to accommodate guests drawn to Banff by the claimed healing qualities of the hot springs' water.

Buffalo Nations Luxton Museum

Looking like a stockade, this museum (1 Birch Ave., 403/762-2388, summer daily 11 A.M.–6 P.M., the rest of the year 1–5 P.M.; adult $8, senior $6, child $2.50) overlooks the Bow River across from Central Park. It is dedicated to the heritage of the natives who once inhabited the Canadian Rockies and adjacent prairies. It contains an elaborately decorated tepee, hunting equipment, arrowheads dating back 4,000 years, stuffed animals, original artwork, peace pipes, and traditional clothing. The adjacent Indian Trading Post is one of Banff's better gift shops and worth a browse.

Cave and Basin National Historic Site

At the end of Cave Avenue, this historic site (403/762-1566, summer daily 9 A.M.–6 P.M., the rest of the year Mon.–Fri. 11 A.M.–4 P.M., Sat.–Sun. 9:30 A.M.–5 P.M.; adult $4, senior $3.50, child $2.50) is the birthplace of Banff National Park and of the Canadian National Parks system. After its discovery in 1883—lounging in the hot water was considered a real luxury in the Wild West—bathhouses were installed, and bathers paid $0.10 for a swim. The pools were eventually lined with concrete, and additions were built onto the original structures. Ironically, the soothing minerals in the water that had attracted millions of people to bathe here eventually caused the pools' demise. The minerals, combined with chlorine, produced sediments that ate away at the concrete structure until the pools were deemed unsafe in 1993. Although the pools are now closed for swimming, a narrow tunnel winds into the dimly lit cave, and short trails lead from the center to the cave entrance and through a unique environment created by the hot water from the springs.

Banff Gondola

The easiest way to get high above town without breaking a sweat is on this gondola (Mountain Ave., 403/762-2523, 7:30 A.M.–9 P.M. in summer, shorter hours the rest of the year, closed for two weeks in Jan., adult $28, child $13.50). The modern four-person cars rise 700 meters (2,300 feet) in eight minutes to the summit of 2,285-meter (7,500-foot) **Sulphur Mountain.** From the observation deck at the upper terminal, the breathtaking view includes the town, Bow Valley, Cascade Mountain, Lake Minnewanka, and the Fairholme Range. Bighorn sheep often hang around below the upper terminal. The short **Vista Trail** leads along a ridge to a restored weather observatory; back in the upper terminal there are three restaurants and a gift shop.

◖ Fairmont Banff Springs

On a terrace above a bend in the Bow River is one of the grandest and most famous mountain-resort hotels in the world. "The Springs" has grown with the town and is an integral part of local history. Built by the Canadian Pacific Railway, it opened in 1888 and was, at the time, the world's largest hotel. Overnight, the quiet community of Banff became a destination resort for wealthy guests from around the world, and the hotel soon became one of North America's most popular accommodations. Every room was booked every day during the short summer seasons. Guest numbers reached 22,000 in 1911, and construction of a new hotel, designed by Walter Painter, began that year. The original design—an 11-story tower joining two wings in a baronial style—was reminiscent of a Scottish castle mixed with a French country chateau.

Don't let the hotel's opulence keep you from spending time here. Wander through on your own, admiring the 5,000 pieces of furniture and antiques (most of those in public areas are reproductions), paintings, prints, tapestries, and rugs. Take in the medieval atmosphere of Mount Stephen Hall with its lime flagstone floor, enormous windows, and large oak beams; take advantage of the luxurious spa facility; or relax in one of 12 eateries or four lounges.

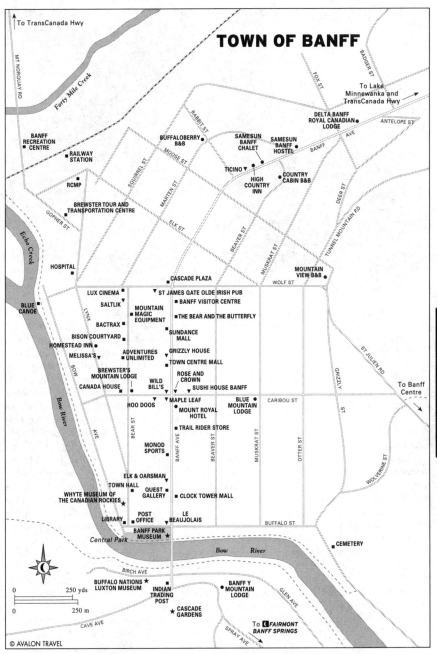

TOWN OF BANFF

To TransCanada Hwy

MT NORQUAY RD

Forty Mile Creek

BADGER ST

FOX ST

To Lake Minnewanka and TransCanada Hwy

RABBIT ST

ANTELOPE ST

DELTA BANFF ROYAL CANADIAN LODGE

BANFF RECREATION CENTRE

RAILWAY STATION

MOOSE ST

SQUIRREL ST

BUFFALOBERRY B&B

SAMESUN BANFF CHALET

SAMESUN BANFF HOSTEL

BANFF AVE

RCMP

TICINO ▼

HIGH COUNTRY INN

COUNTRY CABIN B&B

DEER ST

BREWSTER TOUR AND TRANSPORTATION CENTRE

MARTEN ST

ELK ST

BEAVER ST

TUNNEL MOUNTAIN RD

GOPHER ST

Echo Creek

HOSPITAL

MUSKRAT ST

MOUNTAIN VIEW B&B

WOLF ST

BLUE CANOE

CASCADE PLAZA

LUX CINEMA

SALTLIK

LYNX

ST JAMES GATE OLDE IRISH PUB

BANFF VISITOR CENTRE

THE BEAR AND THE BUTTERFLY

MOUNTAIN MAGIC EQUIPMENT

BACTRAX

BISON COURTYARD

HOMESTEAD INN

MELISSA'S

SUNDANCE MALL

ADVENTURES UNLIMITED

GRIZZLY HOUSE

TOWN CENTRE MALL

ST JULIEN RD

To Banff Centre

BREWSTER'S MOUNTAIN LODGE

CANADA HOUSE

WILD BILL'S

ROSE AND CROWN

SUSHI HOUSE BANFF

GRIZZLY ST

BON AVE

Bow River

HOO DOOS

MAPLE LEAF

MOUNT ROYAL HOTEL

BLUE MOUNTAIN LODGE

CARIBOU ST

BEAR ST

TRAIL RIDER STORE

BANFF AVE

BEAVER ST

MUSKRAT ST

OTTER ST

WOLVERINE ST

MONOD SPORTS

ELK & OARSMAN

TOWN HALL

QUEST GALLERY

CLOCK TOWER MALL

WHYTE MUSEUM OF THE CANADIAN ROCKIES ★

LIBRARY

POST OFFICE

LE BEAUJOLAIS

BUFFALO ST

BANFF PARK MUSEUM ★

Central Park

CEMETERY

Bow River

BIRCH AVE

BUFFALO NATIONS LUXTON MUSEUM ★

INDIAN TRADING POST

BANFF Y MOUNTAIN LODGE

GLEN AVE

0   250 yds

0   250 m

CASCADE GARDENS ★

To ◖ FAIRMONT BANFF SPRINGS

CAVE AVE

SPRAY AVE

© AVALON TRAVEL

The Fairmont Banff Springs is one of the world's greatest mountain resorts.

© ANDREW HEMPSTEAD

The hotel is a 15-minute walk southeast of town, either along Spray Avenue or via the trail along the south bank of the Bow River. **Banff Transit** buses leave Banff Avenue for the Springs twice an hour ($2). Alternatively, horse-drawn buggies take passengers from the Trail Rider Store (132 Banff Ave., 403/762-4551) to the Springs for about $90 for two passengers.

Bow Falls

Small but spectacular Bow Falls is below the Fairmont Banff Springs, only a short walk from downtown. The waterfall is the result of a dramatic change in the course of the Bow River brought about by glaciation. At one time the river flowed north of Tunnel Mountain and out of the mountains via the valley of Lake Minnewanka. As the glaciers retreated, they left terminal moraines, forming natural dams and changing the course of the river. Eventually the backed-up water found an outlet here between Tunnel Mountain and the northwest ridge of Mount Rundle. The falls are most spectacular in late spring when runoff from the winter snows fills every river and stream in the Bow Valley watershed.

Vermilion Lakes

This series of shallow lakes forms an expansive montane wetland supporting a variety of mammals and 238 species of birds. Vermilion Lakes Drive, paralleling the TransCanada Highway immediately west of Banff, provides the easiest access to the area. The level of **First Vermilion Lake** was once controlled by a dam. Since its removal, the level of the lake has dropped. This is the beginning of a long process that will eventually see the area evolve into a floodplain forest such as is found along the Fenland Trail. **Second** and **Third Vermilion Lakes** have higher water levels that are controlled naturally by beaver dams. Near First Vermilion Lake is an active osprey nest. The entire area is excellent for wildlife viewing, especially in winter when it provides habitat for elk, coyote, and the occasional wolf.

Mount Norquay Road

One of the best views of town accessible by vehicle is on this road, which switchbacks steeply to the base of Ski Norquay, the local hangout for skiers and boarders. On the way up are several lookouts, including one near the top where bighorn sheep often graze.

Lake Minnewanka

Lake Minnewanka Road begins where Banff Avenue ends at the northeast end of town. After passing under the TransCanada Highway, **Cascade Falls** is obvious off to the left beyond the airstrip. In winter, these falls freeze and you'll often see ice climbers slowly making their way up the narrow thread of frozen water. Continuing straight ahead at the first intersection, the next turnout along this road is at **Lower Bankhead,** where a short interpretive trail leads through the remains of a century-old coal-mining town.

Lake Minnewanka (meaning "Lake of the Water Spirit"), the largest body of water in Banff National Park, is surrounded on three sides by an imposing mountain backdrop. Even if you don't feel up to an energetic hike, it's worth going for a short walk along the lakeshore. **Minnewanka Lake Cruise** (403/762-3473) has a 90-minute cruise to the far reaches of the lake, passing the Devil's Gap formation. It departs from the dock 3–5 times daily (first sailing is 10:30 A.M.) mid-May–end of September and costs adult $44, child $19. The lake is great for fishing (lake trout to 15 kg/33 lb) and is the only one in the park where motorboats are allowed; Lake Minnewanka Boat Tours rents aluminum boats with small outboard engines and represents local fishing guides.

Bow Valley Parkway

Two roads link Banff to Lake Louise. The TransCanada Highway is the quicker route, more popular with through traffic. The other is the more scenic 51-kilometer (32-mile) Bow Valley Parkway, which branches off the TransCanada Highway five kilometers (3.1 miles) west of Banff. Between March and late June, the southern end of the parkway (as far north as Johnston Canyon) is closed daily 6 P.M.–9 A.M. for the protection of wildlife.

As you enter the parkway, you pass the quiet, creek-side **Fireside** picnic area, where an interpretive display describes how the Bow Valley was formed. **Muleshoe** wetland consists of oxbow lakes that were formed when the Bow River changed its course and abandoned its meanders for a more direct path.

Johnston Creek drops over a series of spectacular waterfalls within **Johnston Canyon.** The canyon is not nearly as deep as Maligne Canyon in Jasper National Park—30 meters (100 feet) at its deepest, compared to 50 meters (165 feet) at Maligne—but the catwalk that leads to the lower falls has been built through the depths of the canyon rather than along its lip, making it seem just as spectacular. The lower falls are one kilometer (0.6 mile) from the highway, while the equally spectacular upper falls are another 1.6 kilometers (one mile) upstream. Beyond this point are the **Ink Pots,** mineral springs whose sediments reflect sunlight, producing a brilliant aqua color. While in the canyon, look for nesting great gray owls and black swifts.

At the west end of **Moose Meadows,** a small plaque marks the site of **Silver City.** At its peak this boomtown had a population of 2,000, making it bigger than Calgary at the time. During its heady days, five mines were operating, extracting not silver but ore rich in copper and lead.

Continuing toward Lake Louise from Moose Meadows, the aptly named **Castle Mountain** comes into view. One of the park's most recognizable peaks, the mountain consists of very old rock (approximately 500 million years old) sitting atop much younger rock (a mere 200 million years old). This unusual situation occurred as the mountains were forced upward by pressure below the earth's surface, thrusting the older rock up and over the younger rock in places.

The road skirts the base of the mountain, passes Castle Mountain Village (which has gas, food, and accommodations), and climbs a small hill to **Storm Mountain Viewpoint,** which provides more stunning views and a picnic area.

HIKING

Although many landmarks can be seen from the roadside, to really experience the park's personality, you'll need to go for a hike. One of the best things about Banff's approximately 80 hiking trails is the variety. From short interpretive walks originating in town to easy hikes rewarded by spectacular vistas to myriad overnight backcountry opportunities, Banff's trails offer something for everyone. Before attempting any hikes, however, you should visit the **Banff Visitor Centre** (224 Banff Ave., 403/762-1550), where staff can advise you on the condition of trails and closures, and a small gift store sells hiking books, including the recommended *Canadian Rockies Trail Guide.*

From Town

Fenland Trail (two km/1.2 mi, 30 minutes) is a nice easy walk that will give you a taste of the Bow Valley ecosystem. From the Forty Mile Creek Picnic Area, along Mount Norquay Road just beyond the rail crossing, the trail dives headfirst into a transitional area between wetland and floodplain forest. This fen environment is prime habitat for many species of birds. The work of beavers can be seen along the trail, and elk are here during winter.

The trail to the top of **Tunnel Mountain** (2.3 km/1.4 mi, 30–60 minutes one-way) gains 300 meters (990 feet) of elevation from St. Julien Road, 350 meters (0.2 miles) south of Wolf Street. It ascends the mountain's western flank through a forest of lodgepole pine, switchbacking past some viewpoints before reaching a ridge just below the summit. Here the trail turns northward, climbing through a forest of Douglas fir to the summit (which is partially treed, preventing 360-degree views).

Sundance Canyon (4.4 km/2.7 mi, 90 minutes one-way) is a wonderful walk, especially on a sunny afternoon, as much of the trail is along an open riverbank. The trail begins at the Cave and Basin National Historic Site and follows a paved path for the first three kilometers (1.9 miles), then enters the forest and ends at a shaded picnic area from which the 2.4-kilometer (1.5-mile) Sundance Loop begins.

From a viewpoint famous for the Fairmont Banff Springs outlook, the **Bow River/Hoodoos Trail** (4.8 km/three mi, 90 minutes one-way) passes under the sheer east face of Tunnel Mountain and follows the river into a meadow where deer and elk often graze. The trail ends at hoodoos, strange limestone-and-gravel columns jutting mysteriously out of the forest. An alternative to returning the same way is to catch the **Banff Transit** bus from Tunnel Mountain Campgrounds. It leaves every half hour ($1).

Sunshine Meadows

Sunshine Meadows, straddling the Continental Divide, is a unique and beautiful region of the Canadian Rockies. It's best known as home to Sunshine Village, a self-contained alpine resort accessible only by gondola from the valley floor. But for a few short months each summer, the area is clear of snow and becomes a wonderland for hiking. Large amounts of precipitation create a lush cover of vegetation—more than 300 species of wildflowers alone have been recorded here. The most popular destination is **Rock Isle Lake,** an easy 2.5-kilometer (1.6-mile) jaunt from the upper village that crosses the Continental Divide while gaining only 100 meters (330 feet) of elevation. From the lakeside viewing platform, a variety of options present themselves, including a loop around Larix Lake and a traverse along Standish Ridge.

It's possible to walk the six-kilometer (3.7-mile) restricted-access road up to the meadows, but a more practical alternative is to take the Sunshine Meadows Shuttle along a road closed to public traffic. This service is operated by **White Mountain Adventures** (403/762-7889 or 800/408-0005, www.sunshinemeadows-banff.com). Through a June–September season, buses depart Banff (daily at 8:30 A.M., adult $55, child $30 round-trip) and the Sunshine Village parking lot (daily on the hour 9 A.M.–5 P.M., adult $15, child $15 round-trip).

Between Banff and Lake Louise

The easiest hike between Banff and Lake Louise is along Johnston Canyon, but there are also some more challenging options. The following three are my favorites.

Cory Pass (5.8 km/3.6 mi, 2.5 hours one-way) is a long, hard slog from the Fireside Picnic Area (the elevation gain is 920 m/3,020 ft), but once at the objective, a wild, windy, desolate area surrounded by jagged peaks, the view of dogtoothed Mount Louis is worth every bit of energy expended.

Rockbound Lake is a delightful little body of water tucked behind Castle Mountain. The trail (8.4 km/5.2 mi, 2.5 hours one-way) itself is unremarkable, but crowds are minimal and the lake is surrounded by impressive peaks. The trail begins at Castle Mountain Junction, 30 kilometers (18.6 miles) west of Banff.

From a signed parking lot along the TransCanada Highway three kilometers (1.9 miles) west of Sunshine Village Junction, the trail to **Bourgeau Lake** gains 730 meters (2,400 feet) over 7.6 kilometers (4.7 miles). Hikers are rewarded with the spectacle of a small subalpine lake nestled at the base of an impressive limestone amphitheater. Allow 2.5 hours each way.

OTHER RECREATION
Mountain Biking

Whether you have your own bike or you rent one from the many bicycle shops in town, cycling in the park is for everyone. Loop roads through the golf course and past Lake Minnewanka are popular, as is the Bow Valley Parkway, while Mount Norquay Road is a steep grunt favored by local riders for the exercise. Several routes into the backcountry have been designated as mountain bike trails. These include Sundance (3.7 km/2.3 mi one-way), Rundle Riverside to Canmore (15 km/9.3 mi one-way), and Spray River Loop (via Goat Creek, 48 km/30 mi round-trip). **Abominable** (229 Wolf St., 403/762-5065), **Bactrax** (225 Bear St., 403/762-8177), **Banff Adventures Unlimited** (211 Bear St., 403/762-4554), and **Banff Springs Ski & Mountain Sports** (Fairmont Banff Springs, 405 Spray Ave., 403/762-5333), rent front- and full-suspension mountain bikes for $8–15 per hour and $35–60 per day. Rates include a helmet, lock, and biking map.

Horseback Riding
Warner Guiding & Outfitting (www.

horseback.com) offers a great variety of trips. Their main office is downtown in the Trail Rider Store (132 Banff Ave., 403/762-4551), although trips depart from either **Martin's Stables** (403/762-2832), behind the recreation grounds on Birch Avenue, or **Banff Springs Corral** (403/762-2848), along Spray Avenue. From Martin's Stables, the one-hour trip departs daily 9 A.M.–6 P.M. and takes in a pleasant circuit around the Marsh Loop ($40). A two-hour trip around the Sundance Loop ($72) departs four times daily. Other longer trips include the three-hour Mountain Morning Breakfast Ride, featuring a hearty breakfast along the trail (departs 9 A.M., $102); and the Evening Steak Fry, a three-hour ride with a suitably western steak and baked bean dinner along the trail (departs 5 P.M., $102).

Rafting and Canoeing
Rocky Mountain Raft Tours (403/762-3632) offers one-hour (adult $42, child $21) float trips down the Bow River, beginning just below Bow Falls and ending along the golf course loop road. No rapids are involved, so you'll stay dry. On a quiet stretch of the Bow River, at the north end of Wolf Street, **Blue Canoe** (403/762-3632 or 403/760-5007, daily 9 A.M.–9 P.M. May–Sept.) rents canoes for use on the river from where it's an easy paddle upstream to the Vermilion Lakes and Forty Mile Creek; $30 one hour, $45 two hours, or $60 for a full day of paddling.

Golf
Spread out along the Bow River below Mount Rundle is the **Banff Springs Golf Course** (403/762-6801), considered one of the world's most scenic. Not only is the course breathtakingly beautiful, but it's also challenging for all levels of golfer. Pick up a copy of the book *The World's Greatest Golf Holes,* and you'll see a picture of the fourth hole on the Rundle Nine. It's a par 3, over Devil's Cauldron 70 meters (230 feet) below, to a small green backed by the sheer face of Mount Rundle rising vertically more than 1,000 meters (3,280 feet) above the putting surface. Another unique feature of the course is

the abundance of wildlife—there's always the chance of seeing elk feeding on the fairways, or coyotes, deer, or black bears scurrying across in front of you as you putt. Greens fees (including cart and driving range privileges) are $220, discounted to $125 in May and late September–early October. The Tunnel 9 offers the same spectacular challenges as the main course but lacks the history; nine holes cost $80, depending on the season. At the clubhouse are a pro shop with club rentals ($50–65), putting greens, a driving range, two chipping greens, and a restaurant with a stunning wrap-around deck.

Tours

Brewster (403/762-6767 or 877/791-5500, www.brewster.ca) is the dominant tour company in the area. The three-hour Discover Banff bus tour takes in downtown Banff, Tunnel Mountain Drive, the hoodoos, the Cave and Basin, and Banff Gondola (gondola fare included). This tour runs in summer only and departs from the bus depot daily at 8:30 A.M.; call for hotel pick-up times. Adult fare is $78, children half price. Brewster also runs several other tours. A four-hour tour to Lake Louise departs select Banff hotels daily ($65). In winter, this tour departs Tuesday and Friday mornings, runs five hours, and includes Banff sights. During summer, the company also offers tours from Banff to Lake Minnewanka ($64, includes two-hour boat cruise), and Columbia Icefield ($149).

Discover Banff Tours (Sundance Mall, 215 Banff Ave., 403/760-5007 or 877/565-9372, www.banfftours.com) is a smaller company, with smaller buses and more personalized service. Its tour routes are similar to Brewster's: A three-hour Discover Banff tour visits Lake Minnewanka, the Cave and Basin, the Fairmont Banff Springs, and the hoodoos for adult $52, child $32; a full-day trip to the Columbia Icefield is adult $154, child $79; and a two-hour Evening Wildlife Safari is adult $42, child $25. This company offers a good selection of other tours throughout the year, including a wintertime "Icewalk" in frozen Johnston Canyon (adult $66, child $40).

THE BREWSTER BOYS

Few guides in Banff were as well known as Jim and Bill Brewster. In 1892, aged 10 and 12 respectively, they were hired by the Banff Springs Hotel to take guests to local landmarks. As their reputation as guides grew, they built a thriving business. By 1900, they had their own livery and outfitting company, and soon expanded operations to Lake Louise. Other early business interests of the Brewsters included a trading post, the original Mt. Royal Hotel, the first ski lodge in the Sunshine Meadows, and the hotel at the Columbia Icefield.

Today, a legacy of the boys' savvy, **Brewster,** a transportation and tour company, has grown to become an integral part of many tourists' stays. The company operates some of the world's most advanced sightseeing vehicles, including a fleet of Ice Explorers, on Athabasca Glacier.

Spas and Hot Springs

The luxurious **Willow Stream** spa (Fairmont Banff Springs, 403/762-2211, daily 6 A.M.–10 P.M.) is the place to pamper yourself. The epicenter of the facility is a circular mineral pool capped by a high glass-topped ceiling and ringed by floor-to-ceiling windows on one side and on the other by hot tubs fed by cascading waterfalls of varying temperatures. Other features include outdoor saltwater hot tubs, private solariums, steam rooms, luxurious bathrooms, a café featuring light meals, and separate male and female lounges complete with fireplaces and complimentary drinks and snacks. Numerous other services are offered, including facials, body wraps, massage therapy, salon services, and hydrotherapy. Entry to Willow Stream is included in some package rates for guests at the hotel. Admission is $80 per day, which includes the use of a locker and spa attire, with almost 100 services available at additional cost (most of these include general admission, so, for example, you can spend the day at Willow Stream and receive a one-hour massage for $185).

The **Upper Hot Springs** (Mountain Ave., 403/762-1515, 10 A.M.–10 P.M., $7.50) were developed in 1901 as an alternative to those at the Cave and Basin, and are still run by Parks Canada. Most folks come for a relaxing soak, but massages are available for an additional charge.

WINTER RECREATION

Of Alberta's five major alpine resorts, three are in Banff National Park. Apart from an abundance of snow, the resorts have something else in common—spectacular views—which alone are worth the price of a lift ticket. If skiing and snowboarding aren't your thing, you'll still always find something to do: cross-country skiing, ice-skating, snowshoeing, or just relaxing. Crowds are nonexistent, and hotels reduce rates by up to 70 percent (except Christmas holidays), which is reason enough to venture into the mountains. Lift and lodging packages begin at $100 per person.

Ski Norquay

Visible from town, the steep eastern slopes of Mount Norquay are home to a small resort (403/762-4421, www.banffnorquay.com) with a big reputation. Since Canada's first chairlift was installed in 1948, the resort has had an experts-only reputation, mainly because of terrain serviced by the North American Chair (including the famous double-black-diamond Upper Lone Pine run); but out of sight from the valley floor is a variety of intermediate terrain that has made the resort a favorite with shredders and cruisers alike. Lift tickets are adult $65, youth and senior $55, child $25. Hourly passes provide some flexibility (two hours $30, three hours $40, etc). A few runs are lit for night skiing and boarding on Friday evening; adult $28, senior $26, child $15. A shuttle bus makes pickups from Banff hotels for the short, six-kilometer (3.7-mile) ride up to the resort ($8).

Sunshine Village

The skiing and boarding at Sunshine (403/762-

6500 or 877/542-2633, www.skibanff.com) has lots going for it—over six meters (20 feet) of snow annually (no need for snowmaking up here), wide-open bowls, a season stretching for nearly 200 days, and the park's only slope-side accommodations. A gondola whisks guests six kilometers (3.7 miles) from the valley floor to an alpine village and eight high-speed quads (including the world's fastest) serving everything from beginner slopes to some of Canada's steepest lift-served runs, including the infamous Delirium Dive. The total vertical rise is 1,070 meters (3,510 feet) and the longest run (down to the lower parking lot) is eight kilometers (five miles). Day passes are adult $78, senior $64, youth $58, child $31, and those younger than 6 ride free. Two days of lift access and one night's lodging at slope-side Sunshine Inn cost $220 per person in high season—an excellent deal. The inn has a restaurant, lounge, game room, and large outdoor hot tub.

Rentals and Sales

Each resort has ski and snowboard rental and sales facilities, but getting your gear down in town is often easier. **Abominable Ski & Sportswear** (229 Banff Ave., 403/762-2905) and **Monod Sports** (129 Banff Ave., 403/762-4571) have been synonymous with Banff and the ski industry for decades, and while the **Rude Boys Snowboard Shop** (downstairs in the Sundance Mall, 215 Banff Ave., 403/762-8480) has only been around since the 1980s, it is *the* snowboarder hangout.

Cross-Country Skiing

No better way of experiencing the park's winter delights exists than skiing through the landscape on cross-country skis. Many summer hiking trails are groomed for winter travel. The most popular areas are Johnson Lake, Golf Course Road, Spray River, and Sundance Canyon. Weather forecasts (403/762-2088) and avalanche hazard reports (403/762-1460) are posted at both information centers. Rental packages are available from **Banff Springs Ski & Mountain Sports** (Fairmont Banff Springs, 405 Spray Ave., 403/762-5333), **Snow Tips**

(225 Bear St., 403/762-8177) and **Mountain Magic Equipment** (224 Bear St., 403/762-2591). Expect to pay $30–60 per day.

Ice Skating and Sleigh Rides

Rinks are located on the **Bow River** along Bow Street, and on the golf course side of the **Fairmont Banff Springs.** The latter rink is lit after dark and a raging fire is built beside it—the perfect place to enjoy a hot chocolate. Early in the season (check conditions first), skating is possible on **Vermilion Lakes** and **Johnson Lake.** Rent skates from **Banff Springs Ski & Mountain Sports** (Fairmont Banff Springs, 405 Spray Ave., 403/762-5333) for $7 per hour.

Warner Guiding and Outfitting (403/762-4551) offers sleigh rides on the frozen Bow River throughout winter ($25 per person).

NIGHTLIFE

Like resort towns around the world, Banff has a deserved reputation as a party town, especially among seasonal workers, the après-ski crowd, and young Calgarians. Crowds seem to spread out, with no particular bar being more popular than another or being a place where you can mingle with fellow travelers. Given the location and vacation vibe, drink prices are as high as you may expect, with attitude thrown in for free.

Bars

Wild Bill's (upstairs at 201 Banff Ave., 403/762-0333) is named for Banff guide Bill Peyto and is truly legendary. Bands play most nights; as a general rule, expect alternative music or underground country early in the week and better-known rock or pop Thursday–Sunday. Across the road, the **Maple Leaf** (137 Banff Ave., 403/760-7680) has a stylish downstairs space set aside as a bar. The **Elk & Oarsman** (119 Banff Ave., 403/762-4616) serves up beer and more in a clean, casual atmosphere that is as friendly as it gets in Banff. Across the road from Wild Bill's is the **Rose and Crown** (202 Banff Ave., 403/762-2121), serving British beers and hearty pub fare. It also features a rooftop patio and rock-and-roll bands a few nights a week, but there's not much room for

dancing. Also down the main drag is **Tommy's** (120 Banff Ave., 403/762-8888), a perennial favorite for young seasonal workers, and those who once were but now consider themselves as locals.

Away from busy Banff Avenue is **Melissa's** (218 Lynx St., 403/762-5776), which is a long-time favorite drinking hole for locals. It has a small outdoor patio, a long evening happy hour, a pool table, and multiple TVs. From "Mel's," cut down Bear Street to reach █ **The Bison Restaurant and Lounge** (Bison Courtyard, Bear St., 403/762-5550), where prices are reasonable. Add funky surroundings and a sunny courtyard to the mix and you have an excellent choice for a drink and meal. **Saltlik** (221 Bear St., 403/762-2467), best known as an upscale (and upstairs) steakhouse. At street level, the lounge opens to a street-side patio. Around the corner, the **St. James Gate Olde Irish Pub** (207 Wolf St., 403/762-9355) is a large Irish-style bar with a reputation for excellent British-style meals and occasional appearances by Celtic bands.

Nightclubs

Banff has two nightclubs. Cavernous **Aurora** (downstairs in the Clock Tower Mall at 110 Banff Ave., 403/760-5300) was formerly an infamous gathering place known as Silver City, but renovations in the late 1990s added some class to Banff's clubbing scene. It's respectable early in the evening but becomes one obnoxiously loud, overpriced, smoky pickup joint after midnight. The other option is **Hoo Doos** (at 137 Banff Ave. but enter from Caribou St., 403/762-8434), a stylish setup with similar city-like surroundings.

FESTIVALS AND EVENTS
Spring

Most of the major spring events take place at local alpine resorts, including a variety of snowboard competitions that are great fun for spectators. One long-running spring event is the **Slush Cup,** which takes place at Sunshine Village in late May. Events include kamikaze skiers and boarders who attempt to jump an ice-cold pit of water. While winter enthusiasts are at higher elevations, swooshing down the slopes of some of North America's latest-closing resorts, late spring sees the Banff Springs golf course open for the season.

During the second week of June, the **Banff Television Festival** (403/678-9260, www. banfftvfest.com) attracts the world's best television directors, producers, writers, and even actors for meetings, workshops, and awards, with many show screenings open to the public.

Summer

Summer is a time of hiking and camping, so festivals are few and far between. The main event is the **Banff Arts Festival** (403/762-6214 or 800/413-8368, www.banffcentre.ca), a three-week (mid-July–early Aug.) extravaganza presented by professional artists studying at the Banff Centre. They perform dance, drama, opera, and jazz for the public at locations around town.

On July 1, Banff celebrates **Canada Day** with a pancake breakfast, a parade down Banff Avenue, and an afternoon of fun and frivolity in Central Park that includes live music.

Each summer the national park staff presents an extensive **Park Interpretive Program** at locations in town and throughout the park, including downstairs in the visitors center daily at 8:30 P.M. All programs are free and include guided hikes, nature tours, slide shows, campfire talks, and lectures. For details, consult *The Mountain Guide* available at the Banff Visitor Centre (403/762-1550), or look for postings on campground bulletin boards.

Fall

Fall is the park's quietest season, but busiest in terms of festivals and events. First of the fall events, on the last Saturday in September, **Melissa's Road Race** (www.melissasroadrace.ca) attracts more than 2,000 runners (the race sells out months in advance) in 10- and 22-kilometer races. The **International Banff Springs Wine and Food Festival** is hosted by the Fairmont Banff Springs at the end of

October. To encourage tourism during the quietest time of the year, **Winterstart** (Nov.–mid-Dec.) features cheap lodging and a host of fun events. This coincides with the opening of lifts at the park's three winter resorts beginning in mid-November.

One of the year's biggest events is the **Banff Mountain Film Festival** (Banff Centre, 403/762-6675 or 800/413-8368, www. banffcentre.ca), held on the first weekend of November. Mountain-adventure filmmakers from around the world submit films to be judged by a select committee. Films are then shown throughout the weekend to an enthusiastic crowd of thousands. Exhibits and seminars are also presented, and top climbers and mountaineers from around the world are invited as guest speakers. Tickets for daytime shows start at $45 (for up to 10 films). Night shows are from $38, and all-weekend passes cost around $180. Starting in the days leading up to the film festival, then running in conjunction with it, is the **Banff Mountain Book Festival,** which showcases the work of publishers, writers, and photographers whose work revolves around the world's great mountain ranges.

Winter

By mid-December lifts are operating at all local winter resorts. **Santa Claus** makes an appearance on Banff Avenue at noon on the last Saturday in November; if you miss him there, he usually goes skiing at each of the local resorts on Christmas Day. Events at the resorts continue throughout the long winter season, among them **World Cup Downhill** skiing at Lake Louise in late November. **Banff/Lake Louise Winter Festival** is a 10-day celebration at the end of January that has been a part of Banff's history since 1917. Look for ice sculpting on the frozen lake in front of the Chateau Lake Louise, the Lake Louise Loppet, barn dancing, and the Town Party, which takes place in the Fairmont Banff Springs.

SHOPPING
Canadiana and Clothing

Few companies in the world were as responsible

for the development of a country as was the **Hudson's Bay Company** (HBC) in Canada. Founded in 1670, the HBC established trading posts throughout western Canada, many of which attracted settlers, forming the nucleus for towns and cities that survive today, including Alberta's capital, Edmonton. HBC stores continue their traditional role of providing a wide range of goods, in towns big and small across the country. In Banff, the HBC store is at 125 Banff Avenue (403/762-5525).

Another Canadian store, this one famous for its fleeces, sweaters, leather goods, and as supplier to the Canadian Olympic teams, is **Roots** (227 Banff Ave., 403/762-9434). For belts, buckles, and boots, check out the **Trail Rider Store** (132 Banff Ave., 403/762-4551). **Rude Boys** (215 Banff Ave., 403/762-8480) is a snowboard and skate shop downstairs in the Sundance Mall, but don't expect to find anything suitable for your grandparents.

Camping and Outdoor Gear

Inexpensive camping equipment and supplies can be found in **Home Hardware** (221 Bear St., 403/762-2080) and in the low-ceilinged downstairs section of the **Hudson's Bay Company** (125 Banff Ave., 403/762-5525). More specialized needs are catered to at **Mountain Magic Equipment** (224 Bear St., 403/762-2591). The store stocks a large range of top-quality outdoor and survival gear (including climbing equipment) and rents tents ($20 per day), sleeping bags ($12), backpacks ($10), and boots ($10). Mountain Magic Equipment also sells and repairs all types of bikes.

Two of the best spots to shop for outdoor apparel are locally owned **Abominable Ski & Sportswear** (229 Banff Ave., 403/762-2905) and **Monod Sports** (129 Banff Ave., 403/762-4571).

Gifts and Galleries

Banff's numerous galleries display the work of mostly Canadian artists. **Canada House Gallery** (201 Bear St., 403/762-3757) features a wide selection of Canadian landscape and wildlife works and native art. The **Quest** Gallery (105 Banff Ave., 403/762-2722) offers a diverse range of affordable Canadian paintings and crafts, as well as more exotic pieces such as mammoth tusks from prehistoric times and Inuit carvings from Nunavut. Across the Bow River from downtown, browse through native arts and crafts at the **Indian Trading Post** (1 Birch Ave., 403/762-2456).

ACCOMMODATIONS

Banff has a few accommodations right downtown, but most are strung out along Banff Avenue, an easy walk from the shopping and dining precinct. Nearby Tunnel Mountain is also home to a cluster of accommodations. This section also includes three excellent options between Banff and Lake Louise.

Finding a room in Banff in summer is nearly as hard as trying to justify its price. By late afternoon just about every room and campsite in the park will be occupied, and basic hotel rooms begin at around $150. Fortunately, many alternatives are available, including backpacker lodges, bed-and-breakfast rooms in private homes, and cabins, which are cost-effective for families or small groups. Wherever you decide to stay, it is vital to book well ahead during summer and the Christmas holidays. The park's off-season is October–May, and hotels offer huge rate reductions during this period.

All rates quoted below are for a standard room in the high season (June–early Sept.).

Under $50

◖ HI-Banff Alpine Centre (801 Hidden Ridge Way, 403/762-4123 or 866/762-4122, www.hihostels.ca) is just off Tunnel Mountain Road three kilometers (1.9 miles) from downtown. This large, modern hostel sleeps 216 in small two-, four-, and six-bed dormitory rooms as well as four-bed cabins. The large lounge area has a fireplace, and other amenities include a recreation room, public Internet access, bike and ski/snowboard workshop, large kitchen, self-service café/bar, and laundry. In summer, members of Hostelling International pay $33 per person per night (nonmembers $37) for a dorm bed or $83 s or d ($88 for nonmembers) in a private room. The hostel is open all day, but check-in isn't until midday. To get there from town, ride the Banff Transit bus ($2), which passes the hostel twice an hour during summer.

Facilities at **Banff Y Mountain Lodge** (102 Spray Ave., 403/762-3560 or 800/813-4138, www.ymountainlodge.com, dorm $33, $88 s, $99 d) include the casual Sundance Bistro (7 A.M.–10 P.M.), a laundry facility, and a communal area where the centerpiece is a massive stone fireplace with writing desks and shelves stocked with books scattered throughout.

Along the main strip of accommodations and a five-minute walk to downtown is **Samesun Banff Chalet** (433 Banff Ave., 403/762-4499 or 877/972-6378, www.samesun.com; dorm $35, private $149 s or d). As converted motel rooms, each small dormitory has its own bathroom. Guest amenities include a lounge, wireless Internet, free continental breakfast, and underground parking. Slightly further from downtown, **Samesun Banff Hostel** (449 Banff Ave., 403/762-5521, www.samesun.com; dorm $33, private from $89 s or d) has older rooms, but is set around a pleasant courtyard.

Thirty-two kilometers (20 miles) from Banff along the Bow Valley Parkway, **HI-Castle Mountain** (403/760-7580 or 866/762-4122, www.hihostels.ca, $23–27) is near several interesting hikes and across the road from a general store with basic supplies. This hostel sleeps 28 in two dorms and has a kitchen, octagonal common room with wood-burning fireplace, hot showers, and bike rentals. Check-in is 5–10 P.M.

$50-100

Accommodations in this price range are limited to private rooms at the three backpacker lodges (above) and at a few bed-and-breakfasts. The best value of these is **Mountain View B&B** (347 Grizzly St., 403/760-9353, www.mountainviewbanff.ca, May–Sept., $95–130 s or d), on a quiet residential street three blocks from the heart of downtown. The two guest rooms are simply furnished, each with a double bed,

TV, sink, and bar fridge. They share a bathroom and a common area that includes basic cooking facilities (microwave, toaster, kettle) and opens to a private deck. Off-street parking and a light breakfast round out this excellent choice.

$100-150

Blue Mountain Lodge (137 Muskrat St., 403/762-5134, www.bluemtnlodge.com, $105–109 s, $129–179 d) is a rambling, older-style lodge with 10 guest rooms, each with a private bath, TV, and telephone. The Trapper's Cabin room is the most expensive, but the gabled ceiling, walls decorated with snowshoes and bearskin, and an electric fireplace create a funky, mountain feel. All guests have use of shared kitchen facilities, a lounge, and Internet access while enjoying an expansive cold buffet breakfast to set you up for a day of hiking.

The eight guest rooms at the **Elkhorn Lodge** (124 Spray Ave., 403/762-2299 or 877/818-8488, www.elkhornbanff.ca, from $135 s or d) are nothing special, but travelers on a budget who aren't fans of bed-and-breakfasts will find this older lodge suitable. The four small sleeping rooms—each with a bathroom, TV, and coffeemaker—are $135 s or d, while larger rooms with fridges are $195–265. Rates include a light breakfast. It's halfway up the hill to the Fairmont Banff Springs.

The wilderness setting at **Johnston Canyon Resort** (403/762-2971 or 888/378-1720, www.johnstoncanyon.com, mid-May–early Oct., $149–314 s or d), 26 kilometers (16 miles) west of Banff, is unequalled by any of the other choices in this price range. The rustic cabins are older, and some have kitchenettes. On the grounds are tennis courts, a barbecue area, and a general store. Basic two-person duplex cabins are $149, two-person cabins with a gas fireplace and sitting area are $189, and they go up in price all the way to $314 for a Classic Bungalow complete with two bedrooms, cooking facilities, and heritage-style furnishings.

$150-200

Some of Banff's private residences have cabins

for rent. One of the reasons that **⟨ Country Cabin Bed & Breakfast** (419 Beaver St., 403/762-3591, www.banffmountaincountry. com/cabin, $150 s or d) is the best of these is the quiet location off busy Banff Avenue but still within easy walking distance of downtown. The log cabin has a separate bedroom, a full bathroom with log and tile features surrounding a jetted tub, and a living area equipped with a fold-out futon and a TV/VCR combo. If you don't feel like dining downtown, you can cook up a storm on the barbecue supplied.

Spruce Grove Inn (545 Banff Ave., 403/762-3301 or 800/879-1991, www.banffsprucegroveinn.com; $165–275 s or d) is a modern mountain-style lodge and relatively good value at $185 s or d (upgrade to a king bed for $200 s or d or a Loft Suite that sleeps four for $225).

Toward downtown from the Spruce Grove is the **High Country Inn** (419 Banff Ave., 403/762-2236 or 800/293-5142, www.banffhighcountryinn.com, from $175 s or d), which has a heated indoor pool, spacious hot tubs, a cedar-lined sauna, and the ever-popular Ticino Swiss/Italian restaurant. All rooms are adequately furnished with comfortable beds and an earthy color scheme.

Constructed by the Canadian Pacific Railway in 1922, **⟨ Storm Mountain Lodge** (Hwy. 93, 403/762-4155, www.stormmountainlodge. com, early Dec.–mid-Oct., $169–289 s or d) is at Vermilion Pass, a 25-minute drive from Banff or Lake Louise (head west from the Castle Mountain interchange). Each cabin has its original log walls along with a log bed, covered deck, a wood-burning fireplace, and bathroom with claw-foot tub. They don't have phones or TVs, so there's little to distract you from the wilderness experience. Off-season deals include a breakfast and dinner package (mid-Apr.–mid-June) from $225 d. The lodge restaurant is one of my favorite places to eat in the park.

$200-250

Stylish **⟨ Brewster's Mountain Lodge** (208 Caribou St., 403/762-2900 or 888/762-2900, www.brewstermountainlodge.com, $220–280

s or d) features an eye-catching log exterior with an equally impressive lobby. The Western theme is continued in the 77 upstairs rooms. Superior rooms feature two queen-size beds or one king-size bed, deluxe rooms offer a private balcony, and loft suites have hot tubs. All rates include breakfast, and if you don't feel like dining out you can order room service from noon onward.

The 134-room **Banff Ptarmigan Inn** (337 Banff Ave., 403/762-2207 or 800/661-8310, www.bestofbanff.com, $245 s or d) is a slick, full-service hotel with 134 tastefully decorated rooms, down comforters on all beds, a restaurant, heated underground parking, wireless Internet, and a variety of facilities to soothe sore muscles, including a spa, whirlpool, and sauna.

Hidden Ridge Resort (Tunnel Mountain Rd., 403/762-3544 or 800/661-1372, www. bestofbanff.com, $220–540 s or d) sits on a forested hillside away from the main buzz of traffic. Choose from modern condo-style units or much larger Premier King Jacuzzi Suites. All units have wood-burning fireplaces and balconies or patios. In the center of the complex is a barbecue area and hot tub.

$250-300

At Castle Junction, 32 kilometers (20 miles) northwest of Banff, is **Castle Mountain Chalets** (403/762-3868 or 877/762-2281, www.decorehotels.com, $255–335 s or d). Set on 1.5 hectares (four acres), this resort is home to a collection of magnificent log chalets. Each has high ceilings, beautifully handcrafted log interiors, at least two beds, a stone fireplace, a full kitchen with dishwasher, a bathroom with hot tub, and satellite TV. Part of the complex is a grocery store, barbecue area, and the only gas station between Banff and Lake Louise.

Continuing along the Bow Valley Parkway toward Lake Louise is **⟨ Baker Creek Chalets** (403/522-3761, www.bakercreek. com, $290–365 s or d), 40 kilometers (25 miles) northwest of Banff. Each of the log chalets has a kitchenette, loft, fireplace, and outside deck (complete with cute woodcarvings of

© ANDREW HEMPSTEAD

Baker Creek Chalets

bears climbing over the railings). The Trapper's Cabin is a huge space with a log bed, antler chandelier, wood-burning fireplace, double-jetted tub, and cooking facilities. A lodge wing has eight luxurious suites, each with richly accented log work, a deck, a microwave and fridge, and a deluxe bathroom. The restaurant here is highly recommended.

The best rooms along Banff's motel strip are at **Delta Banff Royal Canadian Lodge** (459 Banff Ave., 403/762-3307 or 888/778-5050, www.deltahotels.com, from $290 s or d). It features 99 luxuriously appointed rooms, heated underground parking, a lounge, a dining room where upscale Canadian specialties are the highlight, a large spa/pool complex, and a landscaped courtyard.

Over $300

Bed-and-breakfast connoisseurs will fall in love with **Buffaloberry B&B** (417 Marten St., 403/762-3750, www.buffaloberry.com; $325 s or d), a purpose-built lodging within walking distance of downtown. The home itself is a beautiful timber and stone structure, while inside, guests soak up mountain-style luxury in the vaulted living area which comes complete with a stone fireplace, super comfortable couches, and a library of local books. The spacious rooms come with niceties such as pillow-top mattresses, TV/DVD combos, heated bathroom floors, and bathrobes.

At **Buffalo Mountain Lodge,** a 15-minute walk from town on Tunnel Mountain Road (at Tunnel Mountain Dr., 403/762-2400 or 800/661-1367, www.crmr.com, $319 s or d), you'll notice the impressive timber-frame construction as well as the hand-hewn construction of the lobby, with its vaulted ceiling and eye-catching fieldstone fireplace. The 108 rooms, chalets, and bungalows all have fireplaces, balconies, large bathrooms, and comfortable beds topped by feather-filled duvets; many have kitchens. And you won't need to go to town to eat—one of Banff's best restaurants, Cilantro Mountain Café, is adjacent to the main lodge.

The **Fairmont Banff Springs** (403/762-2211 or 800/257-7544, www.fairmont.com, from $439 s or d) is one of the world's great mountain resort hotels. The rooms have recently been modernized—think Internet access and air-conditioning—although many date to the 1920s, and as is common in older establishments, these accommodations are small (Fairmont rooms are 14.4 square meters/155 square feet). But room size is only a minor consideration when staying in this historic gem. With 12 eateries, four lounges, a luxurious spa facility, a huge indoor pool, elegant public spaces, a 27-hole golf course, tennis courts, horseback riding, and enough twisting, turning hallways, boardwalks, towers, and shops to warrant a detailed map, you'll not be wanting to spend much time in your room. Most summer visitors stay as part of a package—the place to find these is on the Fairmont website (www.fairmont.com).

CAMPING

Within Banff National Park, 13 campgrounds hold more than 2,000 sites. Although the town of Banff has five of these facilities with more than 1,500 sites in its immediate vicinity, all fill by early afternoon. The three largest campgrounds are strung out over 1.5 kilometers (0.9 mile) along Tunnel Mountain Road, with the nearest sites 2.5 kilometers (1.6 miles) from town. A percentage of sites at Tunnel Mountain Campground can be reserved through the **Parks Canada Campground Reservation Service** (877/737-3783, www.pccamping.ca), and it's strongly recommended that you do reserve if you require power hookups. Although plenty of sites are available for those without reservations, they fill fast each day (especially in July and August). The official checkout time is 11 A.M., so plan on arriving at your campground of choice earlier than this in the day to ensure getting a site.

Near the Town of Banff

Closest to town is **Tunnel Mountain Campground,** which is three campgrounds rolled into one. The location is a lightly treed ridge east of downtown, with views north to Cascade Mountain and south to Mount Rundle. From town, follow Tunnel Mountain Road east, to beyond the Douglas Fir Resort (which is within walking distance for groceries, booze, and laundry). If you're coming in off the TransCanada Highway from the east, bypass town completely by turning left onto Tunnel Mountain Road at the Banff Rocky Mountain Resort. Approaching from this direction, the first campground you pass is the park's largest, with 622 well-spaced, relatively private sites ($28), each with a fire ring and picnic table. Other amenities include drinking water, hot showers, and kitchen shelters. This campground has no hookups. It is open mid-May–early September. Less than one kilometer (0.6 mile) farther along Tunnel Mountain Road toward town is a signed turnoff ("Hookups") that leads to a registration booth for two more campgrounds. Unless you have a reservation, you'll be asked whether you require an electrical hookup ($32) or a site with power, water, and sewer ($38), then sent off into the corresponding campground. The power-only

section (closest to town) stays open year-round, the other mid-May–September. Both have hot showers but little privacy between sites.

Along Lake Minnewanka Road northeast of town are two campgrounds offering fewer services than the others, but with sites that offer more privacy. The pick of the two is **◖ Two Jack Lakeside Campground** (June–mid-Sept., $32), with 80 sites tucked into trees at the south end of Two Jack Lake, an extension of Lake Minnewanka. Amenities include hot showers, kitchen shelters, drinking water, and flush toilets. It's just over six kilometers (3.7 miles) from the TransCanada Highway underpass. The much larger **Two Jack Main Campground** (mid-June–mid-Sept., $22) is a short distance farther along the road, with 381 sites spread throughout a lightly forested valley. It offers the same amenities as Two Jack Lakeside, sans showers.

Bow Valley Parkway

Along Bow Valley Parkway between the town of Banff and Lake Louise are three campgrounds. Closest to Banff is **Johnston Canyon Campground** (early June–mid-Sept., $28 per site), between the road and the rail line 26 kilometers (16 miles) west of Banff. It is the largest of the three campgrounds, with 140 sites, and has hot showers but no hookups. Almost directly opposite is Johnston Canyon Resort, with groceries and a restaurant, and the beginning of a trail to the park's best-known waterfalls.

Continuing eight kilometers (five miles) toward Lake Louise, **Castle Mountain Campground** (early June–early Sept., $22 per site) is also within walking distance of a grocery store (no restaurant), but it has just 44 sites and no showers. Services are limited to flush toilets, drinking water, and kitchen shelters.

Protection Mountain Campground (July–Aug., $22 per site), another 14 kilometers (8.7 miles) west and just over 20 kilometers (12.5 miles) from Lake Louise, opens as demand dictates, usually by late June. It offers 89 sites, along with flush toilets, drinking water, and stove-equipped kitchen shelters.

FOOD

From lobster to linguini, alligator to à la carte, and fajitas to fudge, anyone who spends time in Banff will find something that suits his or her taste and budget. In July and August, the most popular restaurants don't take reservations and you can expect to wait for a table.

Cafés

Banff's lone bakery is  **Wild Flour** (Bison Courtyard, 211 Bear St., 403/760-5074; daily 7 A.M.–6 P.M.), and it's a good one (albeit a little pricey). Organic ingredients are used whenever possible, and everything is freshly baked daily. The result is an array of healthy breads, mouthwatering cakes and pastries, and delicious meat pies. Eat inside or out. On the same street, the **Cake Company** (220 Bear St., 403/762-8642) serves great coffee and delicious pastries, muffins, and cakes baked daily on the premises. **Evelyn's Coffee Bar** (201 Banff Ave., Banff Ave., 403/762-0352) has good coffee and huge sandwiches. The few outside tables—on the busiest stretch of the busiest street in town—are perfect for people watching.

Steak

Even though **Bumper's** (603 Banff Ave., 403/762-2622, 4:30–10 P.M., $18–34) is away from the center of Banff, it's worth leaving the shopping strip and heading out to this popular steak house. Large cuts of Alberta beef, an informal atmosphere, efficient service, and reasonable prices keep people coming back. Favorite choices are the slabs of Roast Prime Rib of Beef, in four sizes of cuts and cooked to order.

Banff's most fashionable steak house is **Saltlik** (221 Bear St., 403/762-2467, daily from 11 A.M., $21–39). It's big and bold and the perfect choice for serious carnivores with cash to spare. The concrete and steel split-level interior is complemented with modish wood furnishings. Facing the street, glass doors fold back to a terrace for warm-weather dining. The specialty is AAA Alberta beef, finished with grain feeding to enhance the flavor, then flash-seared at 650°C (1,200°F) to seal in the juices, and served with a side platter of seasonal vegetables. Entrées are priced comparable to those at a city steak house, but the cost creeps up as you add side dishes.

Evelyn's Coffee Bar is one of Banff's favorite cafés.

BANFF AND JASPER

© ANDREW HEMPSTEAD

Canadian

Occupying the prime position on one of Banff's busiest corners is the **Maple Leaf** (137 Banff Ave., 403/760-7680, daily 11 A.M.–11 P.M., $21–37). Take in the dramatic Canadian-themed decor—exposed river stone, polished log work, a two-story interior rock wall, and a moose head (tucked around the corner from the street-level lounge). Some upstairs tables surround a busy area by the bar and kitchen, so try to talk your way into the back corner. The cooking uses modern styles with an abundance of Canadian game and produce. The lunch menu has an Atlantic salmon burger, along with lots of lighter salads and stir-fries. Some of Canada's finest ingredients appear on the dinner menu: herb and citrus-crusted halibut and bison tenderloin are standouts.

The Bison Restaurant and Lounge (Bison Courtyard, Bear St., 403/762-5550) is a two-story eatery featuring a casual lounge (daily for lunch and dinner; $10–28) downstairs and a more formal and expensive upstairs restaurant (daily for dinner; $26–45). The most sought-after tables at the downstairs lounge are outside in the courtyard, while inside is furniture ranging from painted tree stumps to a long bar. The chefs do an excellent job of sourcing top-notch local ingredients to create a delicious Caesar salad ($10), bison chili (also $10), and gourmet sandwiches ($13–17). Upstairs, in the main restaurant, the interesting decor sees chic-industrial blending with mountain-rustic. Tables are inside or out at this upstairs dining room, and almost all have a view of the open kitchen. The food is solidly Canadian, with a menu that takes advantage of wild game, seafood, and Alberta beef. Also of note is the wine list, which again is extremely well priced, compared to other Banff restaurants.

European

If you are staying up on Tunnel Mountain—or even if you're not—**Cilantro Mountain Café** (Buffalo Mountain Lodge, 403/760-3008, daily 11 A.M.–11 P.M. in summer, Wed.–Sun. 5–10 P.M. the rest of the year, closed mid-Sept.–mid-Dec., $15–28) is an excellent choice

for a casual, well-priced meal. You can choose to dine inside the cozy log cabin that holds the main restaurant and open kitchen, or out on the patio. Starters are dominated by seafood options, but the flatbread, baked to order and delivered with choice of dips, is a good choice to share. The thin-crust, wood-fired pizza for one is the highlight; a small but varied selection of other mains change as seasonal produce becomes available.

Even if you've tried exotic meats, you probably haven't had them in a restaurant like the **❰ Grizzly House** (207 Banff Ave., 403/762-4055, daily 11:30 A.M.–midnight, $18–32), which provides Banff's most unusual dining experience. The decor is, to say the least, eclectic (many say eccentric)—think lots of twisted woods, a motorbike hanging from the ceiling, a melted telephone on the wall. Each table has a phone for across-table conversation, or you can put a call through to your server, the bar, a cab, diners in the private booth, or even those who spend too long in the bathroom. The food is equally unique and the service as professional as anywhere in town. The menu hasn't changed in decades, and this doesn't displease anyone. Most dining revolves around traditional Swiss fondues, but with nontraditional dipping meats such as rattlesnake, alligator, shark, ostrich, scallops, elk, and wild boar.

Ticino (High Country Inn, 415 Banff Ave., 403/762-3848, daily 5–10 P.M., $15–38) is a park institution that reflects the heritage of park's early mountain guides, with solid timber furnishings, lots of peeled and polished log work, and old wooden skis, huge cowbells, and an alpenhorn decorating the walls. It's named for the southern province of Switzerland, where the cuisine has a distinctive Italian influence. The Swiss chef is best known for a creamy wild mushroom soup, unique to the region; his beef and cheese fondues; juicy cuts of Alberta beef; and veal dishes. Save room for one of Ticino's sinfully rich desserts. Also of note is the professional service.

You'll think you've swapped continents when you step into **❰ Le Beaujolais** (212 Buffalo St. 403/762-2712, daily from 6 P.M.,

$26–38), a Canadian leader in French cuisine. With crisp white linens, old-style stately decor, and immaculate service, this elegant room has been one of Banff's most popular fine-dining restaurants for 20 years. Its second-floor location ensures great views of Banff, especially from window tables. The dishes feature mainly Canadian produce, prepared and served with a traditional French flair. Entrées begin at $26, but the extent of your final tab depends on whether you choose à la carte items or one of the three- to six-course table d'hôte menus—and also on how much wine you consume. Nationalism shows through in the 10,000-bottle cellar, with lots of reds from the Bordeaux and Burgundy regions of France.

The town's most acclaimed restaurant, the **(** **Banffshire Club** (Fairmont Banff Springs, Banff Ave., 403/662-6860, Tues.–Sat. 6–10 P.M., $28–45), is a bastion of elegance seating just 76 diners. Extravagantly rich wood furnishings, perfectly presented table settings, muted lighting, and kilted staff create an atmosphere as far removed from the surrounding wilderness as is imaginable. Reservations and a jacket are required.

Asian

At the back of the Clock Tower Mall, **Pad Thai** (110 Banff Ave., 403/762-4911, lunch and dinner daily, $9–15) is a real find. The namesake dish is $10.50, curries are all around the same price, and delicious spring rolls are $4.50. You can eat in or take out.

A couple of doors off Banff Avenue, **Sushi House Banff** (304 Caribou St., 403/762-2971, daily for lunch and dinner, $3–6 per plate) is a tiny space with a dozen stools set around a moving miniature railway that has diners picking sushi and other delicacies from a train as it circles the chef, loading the carriages as quickly as they empty.

Out of Town

Juniper Bistro (The Juniper, Norquay Rd., 403/763-6205, daily 7 A.M.–9:30 P.M., $25–37) is well worth searching out for both Canadian cuisine and unparalleled views across town to Mount Rundle and the Spray Valley. The stylish interior may be inviting, but in warmer weather, you'll want to be outside on the patio, where the panorama is most spectacular. The menu blends traditional tastes with Canadian produce.

(**The Bistro** (Baker Creek Chalets, 40 km/24.7 mi northwest of town along the Bow Valley Pkwy., 403/522-2182, Sat.–Sun. 7 A.M.–2 P.M., Mon.–Fri. noon–2 P.M. and daily 5–9:30 P.M.; $18–34) is a small dining room that characterizes the term "mountain hideaway." The menu isn't extensive, but dishes feature lots of Canadian game and produce, with favorites like beer-braised bison short ribs and cedar-planked salmon.

The food at **(** **Storm Mountain Lodge** (Hwy. 93, 403/762-4155, May–mid-Oct. daily 7:30–10:30 P.M. and 5–9 P.M., early Dec.–Apr. Fri.–Sun. 5–9 P.M., $24–36) is excellent, but it's the ambience you'll remember long after leaving—an intoxicating blend of historic appeal and rustic mountain charm. The chef uses mostly organic produce with seasonally available game and seafood—bison, venison, wild salmon, and the like—to create tasty and interesting dishes well suited to the I-must-be-in-the-Canadian-wilderness surroundings. Storm Mountain Lodge is a 25-minute drive northwest from Banff; take the TransCanada Highway toward Lake Louise and head west at the Castle Mountain interchange.

INFORMATION

The best place to make your first stop upon arrival in town is the **Banff Visitor Centre** (224 Banff Ave., daily 8 A.M.–8 P.M. mid-June–Aug., daily 8 A.M.–6 P.M. mid-May–mid-June and Sept., daily 9 A.M.–5 P.M. the rest of the year). On the right-hand side is a desk staffed by **Parks Canada** employees. They will answer all of your queries regarding Banff's natural wonders and advise you of trail closures. Across the floor is a desk for **Banff Lake Louise Tourism Bureau** (403/762-8421, www.banfflakelouise.com), representing businesses and commercial establishments in the park. Here you can find out about accommodations and restaurants and have any other questions answered.

To answer the most frequently asked question, the restrooms are downstairs.

Books and Bookstores

Banff Public Library (opposite Central Park at 101 Bear St., 403/762-2661, Mon.–Thurs. 10 A.M.–8 P.M., Fri. 10 A.M.–6 P.M., Sat. 11 A.M.–6 P.M., and Sun. 1–5 P.M.) boasts an extensive collection of nonfiction books, many about the park and its environs, which makes it an excellent rainy-day hangout. Internet access is free, but book ahead.

The **Bear and the Butterfly** (214 Banff Ave., 403/762-8911; summer daily 9:30 A.M.–9:30 P.M., shorter hours the rest of the year), operated by the nonprofit Friends of Banff organization, holds a thoughtful selection of nature and recreation books. They also have a smaller store within the Banff Visitor Centre (224 Banff Ave., 403/762-8918). The **Whyte Museum Bookstore** (111 Bear St., 403/762-2291; daily 10 A.M.–5 P.M.) specializes in regional natural and human history.

SERVICES

The **post office** (Mon.–Fri. 9 A.M.–5:30 P.M.) is on the corner of Buffalo and Bear Streets opposite Central Park. **Freya's Currency Exchange** is in the Clock Tower Mall (108 Banff Ave., 403/762-4652).

All the major hotels have guest Internet access of some kind or another, and the library has free access. You can also head downstairs to the **Cyberweb Internet Cafe** (Sundance Mall, 215 Banff Ave., 403/762-9226, daily 9 A.M.–midnight).

The only downtown laundry is **Cascade Coin Laundry,** on the lower level of the Cascade Plaza (daily 7:30 A.M.–10 P.M. **Chalet Coin Laundry** is on Tunnel Mountain Road at the Douglas Fir Resort, within walking distance of all Tunnel Mountain accommodations (daily 8 A.M.–10 P.M.).

Mineral Springs Hospital (301 Lynx St., 403/762-2222) has 24-hour emergency service. **Rexall Drug Store,** on the lower level of the Cascade Plaza (317 Banff Ave., 403/762-2245), is open daily until 9 P.M.

GETTING THERE

Calgary International Airport, 128 kilometers (80 miles) east, is the closest airport to Banff National Park. **Brewster** (403/762-6767 or 800/661-1152, www.brewster.ca) is one of many companies offering shuttles between the airport and Banff National Park. Its service leaves the airport twice daily, stopping at Banff then continuing to Lake Louise. Calgary to Banff is adult $52, child $26. This shuttle delivers guests to all major Banff hotels as well as the park's main bus terminal, the **Brewster Tour and Transportation Centre,** a five-minute walk from downtown Banff at 100 Gopher Street. Offering door-to-door service for around the same price is **Banff Airporter** (403/762-3330 or 888/449-2901, www.banffairporter.com); adjacent desks at the airport's Arrivals level take bookings, but reserve a seat by booking over the phone or online in advance.

Greyhound (403/762-1092 or 800/661-8747, www.greyhound.ca) offers scheduled service from the Calgary bus depot at 877 Greyhound Way SW, five times daily to the Banff Railway Station and Samson Mall, Lake Louise. Greyhound buses leave Vancouver from the depot at 1150 Station Street, three times daily for the scenic 14-hour ride to the park.

GETTING AROUND

Banff Transit (403/760-8294) operates bus service along two routes through the town of Banff: one from the Fairmont Banff Springs to the RV and trailer parking area at the north end of Banff Avenue, the other from the Fairmont Banff Springs to the Tunnel Mountain Campgrounds. Buses run twice an hour 7 A.M.–midnight mid-May–September. The two routes are merged as one October–December, with buses running hourly noon–midnight. No local buses run the rest of the year. Travel costs $2 per sector.

Cabs around Banff are reasonably priced—flag drop is $5, then it's around $2 per kilometer. Transfers from the Banff bus depot to Tunnel Mountain accommodations will run around $10, same to the Fairmont Banff Springs, more after midnight. Contact **Banff Taxi** (403/762-4444).

Plan on renting a vehicle before you reach the park. In addition to high pricing for walk-in customers, the main catch is that no local companies offer unlimited mileage. The most you'll get is a free 150 kilometers, and then expect to pay $0.25 per kilometer. Agencies and their local contact numbers are **Avis** (Cascade Plaza, 317 Banff Ave., 403/762-3222), **Budget** (Brewster's Mountain Lodge, 208 Caribou St., 403/762-4565), **Hertz** (Fairmont Banff Springs, Spray Ave., 403/762-2027), and **National** (corner of Lynx and Caribou streets, 403/762-2688). Reservations for vehicles in Banff should be made well in advance, especially in July and August.

Lake Louise and Vicinity

As the first flush of morning sun hits Victoria Glacier, and the impossibly steep northern face of Mount Victoria is reflected in the sparkling emerald-green waters of Lake Louise, you'll understand why this lake is regarded as one of the world's seven natural wonders. Overlooking the lake is one of the world's most photographed hotels, Chateau Lake Louise. Apart from simply viewing the lake, the area has plenty to keep you busy. Some of the park's best hiking, canoeing, and horseback riding are nearby. And only a short distance away is Moraine Lake, not as famous as Lake Louise but rivaling it in beauty.

Lake Louise is 56 kilometers (35 miles) northwest of Banff along the TransCanada Highway, or a little bit farther if you take the quieter Bow Valley Parkway. The hamlet of Lake Louise, composed of a small mall, hotels, and restaurants, is located in the Bow Valley, just west of the TransCanada Highway. The lake is 200 vertical meters (660 feet) above the valley floor, along a winding four-kilometer (2.5-mile) road. Across the valley is Canada's second-largest ski area, Lake Louise, a world-class facility renowned for its diverse terrain, abundant snow, and breathtaking views.

Fairmont Chateau Lake Louise is one of the world's most photographed hotels.

BANFF AND JASPER

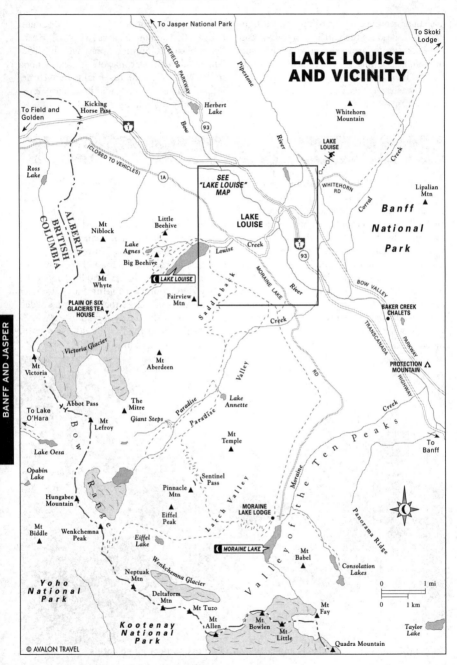

LAKE LOUISE AND VICINITY

© AVALON TRAVEL

◖ Lake Louise

In summer, around 10,000 visitors a day make the journey from the Bow Valley floor up to Lake Louise. By noon the tiered parking lot is often full. From the parking lot, a paved trail leads in front of the Fairmont Chateau Lake Louise to the lake's eastern shore. The lake is 2.4 kilometers (1.5 miles) long, 500 meters (1,640 feet) wide, and up to 90 meters (295 feet) deep. Its cold waters reach a maximum temperature of 4°C (39°F) in August. The snow-covered peak at the back of the lake is **Mount Victoria** (3,459 m/11,350 ft), which sits on the Continental Divide.

Fairmont Chateau Lake Louise is a tourist attraction in itself. Built by the Canadian Pacific Railway to take the pressure off the popular Fairmont Banff Springs, the chateau has seen many changes in the last 100 years, yet it remains one of the world's great mountain resorts. No one minds the hordes of camera-toting tourists who traipse through each day—and there's really no way to avoid them. The immaculately manicured gardens between the chateau and the lake make an interesting foreground for the millions of Lake Louise photographs taken each year. Aside from soaking up the view, hiking is one of the few activities you don't have to pay for. At the lakeshore boathouse, canoes can be rented for $50 per hour, or you can take a trail ride from **Lake Louise Stables** (403/522-3511) for $72 for two hours.

◖ Moraine Lake

Although less than half the size of Lake Louise,

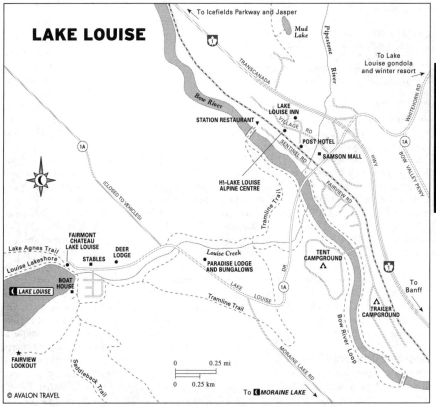

LAKE LOUISE

To Icefields Parkway and Jasper

BANFF AND JASPER

© AVALON TRAVEL

LAKE OF LITTLE FISHES

During the summer of 1882, Tom Wilson, an outfitter, was camped near the confluence of the Bow and Pipestone Rivers when he heard the distant rumblings of an avalanche. He questioned Stoney Indian guides and was told the noises originated from the "Lake of Little Fishes." The following day, Wilson, led by a native guide, hiked to the lake to investigate. He became the first white man to lay eyes on what he named Emerald Lake. Two years later, the name was changed to Lake Louise, honoring Princess Louise Caroline Alberta, daughter of Queen Victoria. In 1890, a modest two-bedroom wooden hotel replaced a crude cabin that had been built on the shore of the lake, as word of its beauty spread. After many additions, a disastrous fire, and the addition of a concrete wing in 1925, the chateau of today took shape, with the most recent addition being a conference center in early 2004.

Moraine Lake is just as spectacular and worthy of just as much film. It is located up a winding road 13 kilometers (eight miles) off Lake Louise Drive. Its rugged setting, nestled in the Valley of the Ten Peaks among the towering mountains of the main ranges, has provided inspiration for millions of people from around the world since Walter Wilcox became the first white man to reach its shore in 1899. Wilcox's subsequent writings—such as "no scene has given me an equal impression of inspiring solitude and rugged grandeur"—guaranteed the lake's future popularity. The lake often remains frozen until June, and the access road is closed all winter. A trail leads along the lake's northern shore, and canoes can be rented for $30 per half hour from the lakeside concession.

Sightseeing Gondola

During summer, the main ski lift at Lake Louise Mountain Resort (403/522-3555) whisks visitors to Whitehorn Lodge in either open chairs or enclosed gondola cars. The view from the top—across the Bow Valley, Lake Louise, and the Continental Divide—is among the most spectacular in the Canadian Rockies. Short trails lead through the forests, across open meadows, and, for the energetic, to the summit of Mount Whitehorn, more than 600 vertical meters (1,970 vertical feet) above. Visitors are free to walk these trails, but it pays to join a guided walk ($5) if you'd like to learn about the surrounding environment. The lift operates May–September daily 9 A.M.–4 P.M., with extended summer hours of 8:30 A.M.–6 P.M., adult $26, child $13. Ride-and-dine packages are an excellent deal. Pay an extra $3 per person and have a buffet breakfast (8–11 A.M.) included with the gondola ride or $7 extra for the buffet lunch (11:30 A.M.–2:30 P.M.).

HIKING

The variety of hiking opportunities in the vicinity of Lake Louise and Moraine Lake is surely equal to any area on the face of the earth. The region's potential for outdoor recreation was first realized in the late 1800s, and it soon became the center of hiking activity in the Canadian Rockies. This popularity continues today; trails here are among the most heavily used in the park. Hiking is best early or late in the short summer season. Head out early in the morning to miss the strollers, high heels, dogs, and bear-bells that you'll surely encounter during the busiest periods.

The two main trailheads are at Fairmont Chateau Lake Louise and Moraine Lake. Two trails lead from the village to the chateau (a pleasant alternative to driving the steep and very busy Lake Louise Drive). Shortest is the 2.7-kilometer/1.7-mile **Louise Creek Trail.** It begins on the downstream side of the point where Lake Louise Drive crosses the Bow River, crosses Louise Creek three times, and ends at the Lake Louise parking lot. The other trail, **Tramline,** is 4.5 kilometers (2.8 miles) longer but not as steep. It begins behind the railway station and follows the route of a narrow-gauge railway that once transported guests from the Canadian Pacific Railway line to Fairmont Chateau Lake Louise.

Lake Louise

Drive four kilometers (2.5 miles) from the TransCanada Highway up to Lake Louise to access the following trails. Probably the busiest trail in all of the Canadian Rockies is the **Louise Lakeshore Trail** (two km/1.2 mi, 30 minutes one-way), which follows the north shore of Lake Louise to the west end of the lake. Here numerous braided glacial streams empty their silt-filled waters into Lake Louise. Along the trail's length are benches to sit and ponder what English mountaineer James Outram once described as "a gem of composition and of coloring...perhaps unrivalled anywhere." Continue beyond the end of the lake to reach **Plain of the Six Glaciers** (5.3 km/3.3 mi, two hours), which is a little more strenuous (370-m/1,215-ft elevation gain), where you can reward yourself with a snack from the teahouse.

The trail to **Lake Agnes** (3.6 km/2.2 mi, 90 minutes one-way) is a short, steep ascent to another teahouse (homemade soups, healthy sandwiches, and hot drinks); this one picturesquely sited on the edge of an alpine lake. From the teahouse, a one-kilometer (0.6-mile) trail leads to **Little Beehive** and impressive views of the Bow Valley. Another trail leads around the northern shore of Lake Agnes, climbing to the **Big Beehive,** a total of five kilometers (3.1 miles) from the chateau. This is a great place to admire the uniquely colored waters of Lake Louise directly below.

Paradise Valley

This aptly named valley lies between Lake Louise and Moraine Lake; access is from Moraine Lake Road, 3.5 kilometers (2.2 miles) from Lake Louise Drive. You can hike as far up the valley as you like, but the most popular loop is 18 kilometers (11.2 miles), which will take around six hours, sans stops. The trail crosses Paradise Creek numerous times in the first five kilometers (3.1 miles), then divides, following either side of the valley to form a loop. **Lake Annette** is 700 meters (0.4 miles) along the left fork. It's a typical subalpine lake in a unique setting—nestled against the near-

vertical 1,200-meter (3,940-foot) north face of snow- and ice-capped **Mount Temple.** Those continuing farther will be rewarded with views across the valley and a series of waterfalls known as the **Giant Steps.**

Moraine Lake

Before heading off into the hills, make sure you savor the beauty of Moraine Lake from two spots—from the top of the high rock pile at the lake's outlet and from along the paved lakeshore trail. Now you're ready to tackle one of the many surrounding trails, such as to **Larch Valley** (2.9 km/1.8 mi, 60 minutes one-way), which gains 400 meters (1,300 feet) of elevation from just beyond the canoe dock. In fall, when the larch trees have turned a magnificent gold and the sun is shining, few spots in the Canadian Rockies can match the beauty of this valley. But don't expect to find much solitude (and don't be too disappointed if trail restrictions are in place due to wildlife movement). Although the most popular time for visiting the valley is fall, it's a worthy destination all summer, when the open meadows are filled with colorful wildflowers. The trail to **Eiffel Lake** branches off the Larch Valley Trail after 2.4 kilometers (1.5 miles), by which time most of the elevation gain has already been made. The lake itself soon comes into view. It's small, and looks even smaller in its rugged and desolate setting, surrounded by the famed Valley of the Ten Peaks. Total trail length from the parking lot is 5.6 kilometers (3.5 miles); allow two hours each way.

WINTER RECREATION

Lake Louise is an immense winter playground offering one of the world's premier alpine resorts, unlimited cross-country skiing, ice-skating, and sleigh rides.

Lake Louise Mountain Resort

Canada's answer to U.S. mega-resorts such as Vail and Killington is Lake Louise (403/522-3555 or 877/253-6888, www.skilouise.com), which opens in November and operates until mid-May. The nation's second-largest winter resort (behind only Whistler/Blackcomb) comprises 1,700 hectares (4,200 acres) of gentle trails, mogul fields, long cruising runs, steep chutes, and vast bowls filled with famous Rocky Mountain powder. The resort is made up of four distinct faces and eight lifts, including western Canada's only six-passenger chairlift. Resort statistics are impressive: a 990-meter (3,250-foot) vertical rise, 1,700 hectares (4,200 acres) of patrolled terrain, and more than 100 named runs. The four back bowls are each as big as many midsize resorts and are all well above the treeline. Lift tickets are $79 per day adult, $65 senior, $54 youth, and $23 children younger than 12. Free shuttle buses run regularly from Lake Louise accommodations to the hill. From Banff you pay $15 round-trip for transportation to Lake Louise. For information on packages and multi-day tickets that cover all three park resorts, go to www.skibig3.com.

Cross-Country Skiing

The most popular cross-country skiing areas are on Lake Louise, along Moraine Lake Road, and in Skoki Valley at the back of the Lake Louise ski area. For details and helpful trail classifications, pick up a copy of *Cross-Country Skiing–Nordic Trails in Banff National Park*, from the Lake Louise Visitor Centre.

Ice Skating and Sleigh Rides

Of all the skating rinks in Canada, the one on frozen Lake Louise, in front of the Chateau, is surely the most spectacular. Spotlights allow skating after dark, and on special occasions hot chocolate is served. Skates are available in the chateau at **Monod Sports** (403/522-3837, $12 for two hours).

Brewster Lake Louise Sleigh Rides (403/522-3511) offers rides in traditional horse-drawn sleighs along the shores of Lake Louise beginning from in front of the chateau. Although blankets are supplied, you should still bundle up. The one-hour ride is adult $28, child $14. Reservations are necessary. The rides are scheduled hourly from 11 A.M. on weekends, from 3 P.M. weekdays.

ACCOMMODATIONS AND CAMPING

In summer, accommodations at Lake Louise are even harder to come by than in Banff, so it's essential to make reservations well in advance. Any rooms not taken by early afternoon will be the expensive ones.

Under $50

With beds for $100 less than anyplace else in the village, the 164-bed **HI-Lake Louise Alpine Centre** (Village Rd., 403/522-2200 or 866/762-4122, www.hihostels.ca) is understandably popular. Of log construction, with large windows and high vaulted ceilings, the lodge is home to a funky café, a library of mountain literature, wireless Internet, a laundry, and a game room. Members of Hostelling International pay $38 per person per night (nonmembers $42) for a dorm bed or $109 s or d ($119 for nonmembers) in a private room. The hostel is open year-round, with check-in after 3 P.M. In summer and on weekends during the winter season, advance bookings (up to six months) are essential.

$150-200

Historic **Deer Lodge** (403/410-7417 or 800/661-1595, www.crmr.com, $175–275 s or d) began life in 1921 as a teahouse, with rooms added in 1925. Facilities include a rooftop hot tub with glacier views, game room, restaurant (breakfast and dinner), and bar. The least expensive rooms are small and don't have phones. Rooms in the $200–250 range are considerably larger, or pay $275 for a heritage-themed Tower Room. Deer Lodge is along Lake Louise Drive, up the hill from the village, and just a five-minute walk from the lake itself.

$200-250

An excellent option for families and those looking for old-fashioned mountain charm is **Paradise Lodge and Bungalows** (403/522-3595, www.paradiselodge.com, mid-May–early Oct., $215–345 s or d). This family-operated lodge provides excellent value in a wonderfully tranquil setting. Spread around well-manicured gardens are 21 attractive cabins in four configurations. Each has a rustic yet warm and inviting interior, with comfortable beds, a separate sitting area, and a recently renovated bathroom. The smallest cabins have a small fridge, microwave, and coffeemaker, while the larger ones have full kitchens and separate bedrooms. Instead of television, children are kept happy with a playground that includes a sandbox and jungle gym. Twenty-four luxury suites, each with a fireplace, TV, one or two bedrooms, and fabulous mountain views, start at $290. To get there from the valley floor, follow Lake Louise Drive toward the Fairmont Chateau Lake Louise for three kilometers (1.9 miles); the lake itself is just one kilometer (0.6 mile) farther up the hill.

Aside from the chateau, the **Lake Louise Inn** (210 Village Rd., 403/522-3791 or 800/661-9237, www.lakelouiseinn.com, from $220 s or d) is the village's largest lodging, with more than 200 units spread throughout five buildings. Across from the lobby, in the main lodge, is a gift shop and an activities desk, and beyond that is a pizzeria, a restaurant, a bar, and a large indoor pool. Most rates booked online include breakfast.

Over $250

The European-style ☪ **Post Hotel** (403/522-3989 or 800/661-1586, www.posthotel.com, $345–455 s or d) is one of only a handful of Canadian lodges that have been accepted into the prestigious Relaix & Châteaux organization. Bordered to the east and south by the Pipestone River, it is as elegant, in a modern, woodsy way, as any other mountain accommodation. Many rooms have whirlpools and fireplaces, while some have kitchens. Other facilities include the upscale Temple Mountain Spa, an indoor pool, a steam room, and a library. The hotel has 17 different room types, with 26 different rates depending on the view.

The famously fabulous **Fairmont Chateau Lake Louise** (403/522-3511 or 800/257-7544, www.fairmont.com, from $659 s or d), a historic 500-room hotel on the shore of Lake Louise, has views equal to any mountain resort in the world. But all this historic charm and mountain scenery comes at a price. During

© ANDREW HEMPSTEAD

The Post Hotel is an elegant, European-style hotel.

the summer season (late June–mid-Oct.), the rack rate for rooms *without* a lake view is $659 s or d, while those with a view are $829. Rooms on the Fairmont Gold Floor come with a private concierge and upgraded everything for a little over $1,000. As at the company's sister property in Banff, most guests book a room as part of a package, either online at www.fairmont.com or through a travel agent, and end up paying closer to $400 for a room in peak summer season.

Backcountry Accommodations

If you're prepared to lace up your hiking boots for a true mountain experience, consider spending time at **(Skoki Lodge** (403/256-8473 or 800/258-7669 www.skoki.com, mid-June–mid-Oct. and mid-Dec.–mid-Apr., from $194 pp), north of the Lake Louise ski resort and far from the nearest road. Getting there requires an 11-kilometer (6.8-mile) hike or ski, depending on the season. The lodge is an excellent base for exploring nearby valleys and mountains. It dates to 1931, when it operated as a lodge for local Banff skiers, and is now a National Historic Site. Today it comprises a main lodge, sleeping cabins, and a wood-fired sauna. Accommodations are rustic—propane heat but no electricity—but comfortable, with mostly twin bedrooms in the main lodge and cabins that sleep up to five. Rates include three meals daily, including a picnic lunch that guests build from a buffet-style layout before heading out hiking or skiing.

Camping

Exit the TransCanada Highway at the Lake Louise interchange, 56 kilometers (35 miles) northwest of Banff, and take the first left beyond Samson Mall and under the railway bridge to reach **Lake Louise Campground,** within easy walking distance of the village. The campground is divided into two sections by the Bow River, but linked by the Bow River Loop hiking trail that leads into the village along either side of the Bow River. Individual sites throughout are close together, but some privacy and shade are provided by towering lodgepole

pines. Just under 200 serviced (powered) sites are grouped together at the end of the road. In addition to hookups, this section has showers and flush toilets ($38). Across the river are 216 unserviced sites, each with a fire ring and picnic table. Other amenities include kitchen shelters and a modern bathroom complex complete with hot showers ($34). A dump station is near the entrance to the campground ($8 per use). An interpretive program runs nightly at 9 P.M. (except Tuesday) throughout summer in the outdoor theater. Sites can be booked in advance by contacting the **Parks Canada Campground Reservation Service** (877/737-3783, www.pccamping.ca). The many sites available on a first-come, first-served basis fill fast in July and August, so plan on arriving early in the afternoon to ensure a spot. The serviced section of this campground is open year-round, the unserviced section mid-May–September.

FOOD

A competing guidebook encourages readers to "eat at your hotel." Not only is this unhelpful, it's misleading—the village of Lake Louise may exist only to serve travelers, but there are good dining options serving all budgets.

Breakfast

If you don't feel like a cooked breakfast, start your day off at **(Laggan's Mountain Bakery** (Samson Mall, 403/552-2017, daily 6 A.M.–8 P.M.), *the* place to hang out with a coffee and a freshly baked breakfast croissant, pastry, cake, or muffin. The chocolate brownie is delicious (order two slices to avoid having to line up twice).

Across the TransCanada Highway, the **Lodge of the Ten Peaks,** at the base of Lake Louise Mountain Resort (403/522-3555), is open daily 7:30–10:30 A.M. in summer for a large and varied breakfast buffet that costs a super-reasonable adult $13. An even better deal is to purchase a breakfast/gondola ride combo for $29 (the gondola ride alone is $26). The buffet lunch (11:30 A.M.–2:30 P.M.) is $19, or $33 with the gondola ride.

If you made the effort to rise early and

experienced the early-morning tranquility of Moraine Lake, the perfect place to sit back and watch the tour bus crowds pour in is from the dining room of **Moraine Lake Lodge** (403/522-3733, daily from 7:30 A.M. June–Sept.). Staying overnight at the lodge may be an extravagant splurge, but breakfast isn't. A simple, well-presented continental buffet is $15, while the hot version is a reasonable $18.50.

European

In 1987, the ◖ **Post Hotel** was expanded to include a luxurious new wing. The original log building was renovated as a rustic, timbered dining room (403/522-3989, daily 11:30 A.M.–2 P.M. and 5–9:30 P.M., $31–44) linked to the rest of the hotel by an intimate lounge. Although the dining room isn't cheap, it's a favorite of locals and visitors alike. The chef specializes in European cuisine, preparing several Swiss dishes (such as veal *zurichois*) to make owner George Schwarz feel less homesick. But he's also renowned for his presentation of Alberta beef, Pacific salmon, and Peking duck. The 32,000-bottle cellar is one of the finest in Canada. Reservations are essential for dinner.

Canadian Contemporary

One hundred years ago visitors departing trains at Laggan Station were keen to get to the Chateau Lake Louise as quickly as possible to begin their adventure. Today, guests from the chateau, other hotels, and even people from as far away as Banff are returning to dine in the Lake Louise Railway Station Restaurant (200 Sentinel Rd., 403/522-2600, $16–34), which combines a dining room in the actual station (daily 11:30 A.M.–9 P.M.) with two restored dining cars (summer Fri.–Sat. 6–9 P.M. in summer). Although the menu is not extensive, it puts an emphasis on creating imaginative dishes with a combination of Canadian produce and Asian ingredients. Lighter lunches include a Caesar salad topped with roasted garlic dressing—perfect for those planning an afternoon hike. In the evening, expect starters

such as pear and prosciutto bruschetta and entrées such as a memorable pan-seared salmon smothered in roasted corn salsa.

Fairmont Chateau Lake Louise

Within this famous lakeside hotel is a choice of eateries and an ice-cream shop. For all chateau dining reservations, call 403/522-1817. The **Poppy Brasserie** has obscured lake views and is the most casual place for a meal. Breakfasts (daily 7–11:30 A.M.) are offered buffet-style ($28 per person), a little expensive for light eaters. Lunch and dinner (daily 11:30 A.M.–8:30 P.M., $18.50–32) are à la carte. The **Walliser Stube** (daily 6–9 P.M.) is an elegant two-story wine bar decorated with rich wood paneling and solid oak furniture. It offers a simple menu of German dishes from $21, as well as cheese fondue. The **Lakeview Lounge** (daily noon–9 P.M.) is along floor-to-ceiling windows with magnificent lake views. Choose this dining area for afternoon tea (daily noon–4 P.M., reservations required, $31 per person, or $39 with a glass of champagne).

The **Fairview Dining Room** (daily 6–9 P.M., $31–37) has a lot more than just a fair view. As the chateau's signature dining room, it enjoys the best views and offers the most elegant setting. The menu combines Canadian produce with classic European cooking styles.

INFORMATION AND SERVICES

Lake Louise Visitor Centre (403/522-3833, daily 8 A.M.–8 P.M. mid-June–Aug., daily 8 A.M.–6 P.M. mid-May–mid-June and Sept., daily 9 A.M.–4 P.M. the rest of the year) is beside Samson Mall on Village Road. This excellent Parks Canada facility has interpretive displays, slide and video displays, and staff on hand to answer questions, recommend hikes suited to your ability, and issue camping passes to those heading out into the backcountry. Look for the stuffed (literally) female grizzly and read her fascinating, but sad, story.

A small postal outlet in Samson Mall also serves as a bus depot and car rental agency. Although Lake Louise has no banks, there's a currency exchange in the Fairmont Chateau

Lake Louise and a cash machine in the grocery store. The mall also holds a busy laundry (daily 8 A.M.–8 P.M. in summer, shorter hours the rest of the year) and **Pipestone Photo** (403/522-3617, daily 9 A.M.–7 P.M.).

GETTING THERE AND AROUND

Brewster (403/762-6767 or 800/661-1152, www.brewster.ca) and **Banff Airporter** (403/762-3330 or 888/449-2901, www.banffairporter.com) each offer at least a couple of shuttles per day that continue beyond Banff to Lake Louise from Calgary International Airport. Both charge around the same amount—$70 each way, with a slight round-trip discount. **Greyhound** (403/522-3870) leaves the Calgary bus depot (877 Greyhound Way SW) five times daily for Lake Louise. From Vancouver, it's a 13-hour ride to Lake Louise aboard the Greyhound bus.

The only car-rental agency in the village is **National** (403/522-3870); you'd be better off picking up a vehicle at Calgary International Airport. **Lake Louise Taxi & Tours** (Samson Mall, 403/522-2020) charges $3 for flag drop, then $1.85 per kilometer. From the mall to Fairmont Chateau Lake Louise runs around $15, to Moraine Lake $35, and to Banff $165. **Wilson Mountain Sports** (Samson Mall, 403/522-3636) has mountain bikes for rent from $15 per hour or $45 per day (includes a helmet, bike lock, and water bottle). They also rent camping, climbing, and fishing gear.

Icefields Parkway

Completed in 1939, the 230-kilometer (143-mile) Icefields Parkway between Lake Louise and Jasper is one of the most scenic, exciting, and inspiring mountain roads ever built. From Lake Louise, it parallels the Continental Divide, following in the shadow of the highest, most rugged mountains in the Canadian Rockies. The route can be driven in three hours, but you'll want to spend at least one day, and probably more, stopping at each of the viewpoints, hiking the trails, watching the abundant wildlife, and just generally enjoying one of the world's most magnificent landscapes. Although the road is steep and winding in places, it has a wide shoulder, making it ideal for an extended bike trip. Allow seven days to pedal north from Banff to Jasper, staying at hostels or camping along the route. This is the preferable direction to travel by bike because the elevation at the town of Jasper is more than 500 meters (1,640 feet) lower than either Banff or Lake Louise.

The parkway remains open year-round, although winter brings with it some special considerations. The road is often closed for short periods for avalanche control, so check road conditions in Banff or Lake Louise before setting out. And fill up with gas, because no services are available mid-October–April.

SIGHTS

The Icefields Parkway forks right from the TransCanada Highway just north of Lake Louise. The impressive scenery begins immediately. Just three kilometers from the junction is **Herbert Lake,** the perfect place for early-morning or evening photography when the **Waputik Range** and distinctively shaped **Mount Temple** are reflected in its waters.

The panorama at **Hector Lake Viewpoint** is partially obscured by trees, but the emerald-green waters nestled below a massive wall of limestone form a breathtaking scene. **Bow Peak,** seen looking northward along the highway, is only 2,868 meters (9,400 feet) high but is completely detached from the Waputik Range, making it a popular destination for mountain climbers. As you leave this viewpoint, look across the northeast end of Hector Lake for glimpses of **Mount Balfour** (3,246 m/10,650 ft) on the distant skyline.

Crowfoot Glacier

The aptly named Crowfoot Glacier can best be appreciated from north of Bow Lake. From the viewpoint, 17 kilometers (10.6 miles) north of Hector Lake, it is easy to see how this and other glaciers are formed. It sits on a wide ledge near the top of Crowfoot Mountain, from where its glacial "claws" cling to the mountain's steep slopes. The retreat of this glacier has been dramatic. Only 50 years ago, two of the claws extended to the base of the lower cliff.

◖ Bow Lake

The sparkling, translucent waters of Bow Lake are among the most beautiful that can be seen from the Icefields Parkway. The lake was created when moraines, left behind by retreating glaciers, dammed subsequent meltwater. On still days, the water reflects the snowy peaks, their sheer cliffs, and the scree slopes that run into the lake. You don't need to take a photography class to take good pictures here! At the southeast end of the lake is a day-use area with waterfront picnic tables. At the upper end of the lake is Num-Ti-Jah Lodge and the trailhead for a walk to Bow Glacier Falls.

The road leaves Bow Lake and climbs to **Bow Summit.** Looking back, the true color of Bow Lake becomes apparent, and the Crowfoot Glacier reveals its unique shape. At an elevation of 2,069 meters (6,790 feet), this pass is one of the highest points crossed by a public road in Canada. It is also the beginning of the Bow River—the one you camped beside at Lake Louise, photographed flowing through the town of Banff, and strolled along in downtown Calgary.

◖ Peyto Lake

From the parking lot at Bow Summit, a short, paved trail leads to one of the most breathtaking views you could ever imagine. Far below the viewpoint is Peyto Lake, an impossibly intense green-colored lake whose hues change according to the season. Before heavy melting of nearby glaciers begins (June–early July), the lake is dark blue. As summer progresses,

Peyto Lake

© ANDREW HEMPSTEAD

BANFF AND JASPER

meltwater flows across a delta and into the lake. This water is laden with fine particles of ground-rock debris known as "rock flour," which remains suspended in the water. The mineral content of the rock flour is not responsible for the lake's unique color; rather, it's created by the particles reflecting the blue-green sector of the light spectrum. Therefore, as the amount of suspended rock flour changes, so does the color of the lake.

To Saskatchewan River Crossing

From Bow Pass, the parkway descends to a viewpoint directly across the Mistaya River from **Mount Patterson** and the **Snowbird Glacier,** clinging precariously to the mountain's steep northeast face. **Mistaya Lake** is a three-kilometer-long (1.9-mile-long) body of water that sits at the bottom of the valley between the road and the divide, but it can't be seen from the parkway. The best place to view this panorama is from the **Howse Peak Viewpoint** at Upper Waterfowl Lake. From here, the high ridge that forms the Continental Divide is easily distinguishable. Numerous trails lead around the swampy shores of **Upper** and **Lower Waterfowl Lakes,** providing one of the park's best opportunities to view moose, which feed on the abundant aquatic vegetation that grows in Upper Waterfowl Lake.

From a parking lot 14 kilometers (8.7 miles) northeast of Waterfowl Lake Campground, a short trail descends into the montane forest to **Mistaya Canyon.** Here, the effects of erosion can be appreciated as the Mistaya River leaves the floor of Mistaya Valley, plunging through a narrow-walled canyon into the North Saskatchewan Valley. The area is scarred with potholes where boulders have been whirled around by the action of fast-flowing water, carving deep depressions into the softer limestone bedrock below.

Saskatchewan River Crossing to Sunwapta Pass

On the north side of the North Saskatchewan River, the Icefields Parkway follows the base of **Mount Wilson.** A pullout just past Rampart Creek Campground has good views of Mount Amery to the west and Mounts Sarbach, Cheph-ren, and Murchison to the south. Beyond here is the **Weeping Wall,** a long cliff of gray limestone where a series of waterfalls tumbles more than 100 meters (330 feet) down the steep slopes of **Cirrus Mountain.** In winter, this wall of water freezes, becoming a popular spot for ice climbers to test their skills. Before ascending to Sunwapta Pass, the road makes a sweeping curve over an alluvial plain of the North Saskatchewan River. Halfway up the pass is a viewpoint well worth stopping for. From here, views extend down the valley to the slopes of Mount Saskatchewan and, on the other side of the parkway, Cirrus Mountain. Another viewpoint, farther up the road, has the added attraction of **Panther Falls** across the valley.

A cairn at **Sunwapta Pass** (2,023 m/6,640 ft) marks the boundary between Banff and Jasper National Parks. It also marks the divide between the North Saskatchewan and Sunwapta Rivers, whose waters drain into the Atlantic and Arctic Oceans, respectively.

C Columbia Icefield

The largest and most accessible of 17 glacial areas along the Icefields Parkway is 325-square-kilometer (125-square-mile) Columbia Icefield, 132 kilometers (82 miles) north from Lake Louise and 105 kilometers (65 miles) south from Jasper. It's a remnant of the last major glaciation that covered most of Canada 20,000 years ago, and it has survived because of its elevation at 1,900–2,800 meters (6,230–9,190 feet) above sea level, cold temperatures, and heavy snowfalls. From the main body of the ice cap, which sits astride the Continental Divide, six glaciers creep down three main valleys. Of these, **Athabasca Glacier** is the most accessible and can be seen from the Icefields Parkway; it is one of the world's few glaciers that you can drive right up to.

The magnificent **Icefield Centre** is nestled at the base of Mount Wilcox, overlooking the Athabasca Glacier. It is a staging point for tours onto the glacier, but also has the **Glacier Gallery,** a display area detailing all aspects of the frozen world, including the story of glacier formation and movement. Back on the main floor of the center you'll find a Parks Canada information desk (780/852-6288), a tour ticketing desk, restrooms, and a large gift shop. Upstairs you'll find a variety of uninspired eateries. (For northbound travelers, my advice is to pick up lunch at Laggan's Mountain Bakery in Lake Louise.) The entire Icefield Centre closes down for the winter in mid-October, reopening the following year in mid-April. During summer, the complex (including display area) is open daily 9 A.M.–11 P.M., with reduced hours outside of July and August.

Across from the Icefield Centre, an unpaved road leads down through piles of till left by the retreating Athabasca Glacier to a parking area beside Sunwapta Lake. Like all glaciers, the broken surface of the Athabasca is especially hazardous because snow bridges can hide its deep crevasses.

The safest way to experience the glacier firsthand is aboard an Ice Explorer, a specially developed vehicle with balloon tires that can travel over the crevassed surface. A 90-minute

© ANDREW HEMPSTEAD

Taking an Ice Explorer is the safest way to experience the Athabasca Glacier.

tour includes informative commentary and time spent walking on a section of the glacier that has been checked for crevasses. Tours operate 9 A.M.–5 P.M. mid-April–mid-October (try to plan your tour for before 10 A.M. or after 3 P.M. to miss the tour-bus crowd) and cost adult $47, child $23. No reservations are taken; instead head to the ticketing office on the main level of the Icefield Centre. For tour information, contact **Brewster** (403/762-6700, www. explorerockies.com).

Columbia Icefield to Jasper

Sunwapta Lake, at the toe of the Athabasca Glacier, is the source of the **Sunwapta River,** which the Icefields Parkway follows for 48 kilometers (30 miles) to Sunwapta Falls. Eight kilometers (five miles) north from the Icefield Centre, the road descends to a viewpoint for **Stutfield Glacier.** Six kilometers (3.7 miles) farther down the road is **Tangle Ridge,** a grayish-brown wall of limestone over which Beauty Creek cascades. At this point the Icefields Parkway runs alongside the Sunwapta River, following its braided course through the

Endless Range, the eastern wall of a classic glacier-carved valley. Another 41 kilometers (25 miles) along the road a 500-meter (0.3-mile) spur at Sunwapta Falls Resort leads to **Sunwapta Falls.** Here the Sunwapta River changes direction sharply and drops into a deep canyon. The best viewpoint is from the bridge across the river, but it's also worth following the path on the parking lot–side of the river downstream along the rim of the canyon.

After following the Athabasca River for 17 kilometers (11 miles), the road ascends to **Goat Lookout,** with picnic tables offering panoramic river views. Below the lookout is a steep bank of exposed glacially ground material containing natural deposits of salt. The local mountain goats spend most of their time on the steep slopes of Mount Kerkeslin, to the northeast, but occasionally cross the road and can be seen searching for the salt licks along the riverbank, trying to replenish lost nutrients.

Nine kilometers (5.6 miles) beyond Goat Lookout and 32 kilometers (20 miles) south of Jasper, the Icefields Parkway divides when an old stretch of highway (Hwy. 93A) crosses the

Athabasca River and continues along its west side for 25 kilometers (15.5 miles) before rejoining the parkway seven kilometers (4.3 miles) south of the town. At the southern end of this loop the Athabasca River is forced through a narrow gorge and over a cliff into a cauldron of roaring water called **Athabasca Falls.**

HIKING

The following trails along the Icefields Parkway are listed south to north.

Banff National Park

The trail to **Bow Glacier Falls** (3.4 km/2.1 mi, one hour one-way) gains minimal elevation, making it enjoyable for everyone. It begins by skirting one of the most beautiful lakes in the Canadian Rockies before ending at a narrow but spectacular waterfall. The trailhead is at Num-Ti-Jah Lodge, 36 kilometers (22.3 miles) northwest from the TransCanada Highway. Another 20 kilometers (12 miles) farther is Waterfowl Lakes Campground, the starting point of a trail to **Chephren Lake** (four km/2.5 mi, 60–90 minutes one-way). A minimal output of energy (the elevation gain is just 100 m/330 ft) is amply rewarded—the lake is a beauty and crowds are minimal.

Take advantage of a high point along the Icefields Parkway, four kilometers (2.5 miles) south of Sunwapta Pass, to climb even higher, to **Parker's Ridge** (2.4 km/1.5 mi, one hour one-way). This trail climbs through a fragile alpine environment to the summit of a ridge from where the panorama extends across two-kilometer-wide (1.2-mile-wide) Saskatchewan Glacier to Castleguard Mountain.

Jasper National Park

The trail to **Wilcox Pass** (four km/2.5 mi, 90 minutes one-way), beginning from the Wilcox Creek Campground, three kilometers (1.9 miles) south of the Icefield Centre, is moderately strenuous. On the plus side, the elevation gain (340 m/1,115 ft) allows panoramic views of the valley, Columbia Icefield, and surrounding peaks, with the flower-filled alpine meadows only adding to the appeal.

Continue along Highway 93A one kilometer (0.6 miles) beyond Athabasca Falls and take the 5.5-kilometer (3.4-mile) Geraldine Fire Road to access the trail to **Geraldine Lakes** (five km/3.1 mi, 2 hours one-way). The first of four lakes is an easy two-kilometer (1.2-mile) walk. From the back of the lake, the trail climbs steeply past a scenic 100-meter-high (330-foot-high) waterfall, and traverses some rough terrain where the trail becomes indistinct; follow the cairns. At the end of the valley is another waterfall. The trail climbs east of the waterfall to a ridge above the second of the lakes, five kilometers (3.1 miles) from the trailhead. Two other lakes, accessible only by bush bashing, are located farther up the valley.

ACCOMMODATIONS AND FOOD

Four lodges and four hostels lie along the Icefields Parkway. A number of other accommodations and Jasper's main campgrounds are also along the parkway, but within close proximity to the town of Jasper.

Note that the main dining options are restaurants and cafés operated by the following resorts and hotels.

Under $50

Facilities at the four hostels along the Icefields Parkway are limited, and beds should be reserved (403/670-7580 or 866/762-4122, www.hihostels.ca) as far in advance as possible. Southernmost is **HI-Mosquito Creek** (June–Mar., members $23, nonmembers $27), 24 kilometers (15 miles) from Lake Louise, which offers accommodations for 32 in four- and six-bed cabins. Facilities include a kitchen, wood-heated sauna, and a large common room with fireplace. Although the hostel has no showers, guests are permitted to use those at the nearby Lake Louise Alpine Centre.

HI-Rampart Creek (May–Mar., members $23, nonmembers $27), another 64 kilometers (40 miles) along the parkway, is nestled below the snowcapped peak of Mount Wilson, with views across the North Saskatchewan River to even higher peaks along the Continental

Divide. Like Mosquito Creek, it's near good hiking and has a kitchen and sauna. Its four cabins have a total of 24 bunk beds.

HI-Beauty Creek (May–Sept., members $23, nonmembers $27), 17 kilometers (10.5 miles) north of Columbia Icefield and 144 kilometers (90 miles) north from Lake Louise, is nestled in a small stand of Douglas fir between the Icefields Parkway and the Sunwapta River. Each of its separate 12-bed male and female cabins has a woodstove and propane lighting. A third building holds a kitchen and dining area. There are no flush toilets or showers.

Farther north is the equally rustic **HI-Athabasca Falls** (closed Tues. Oct.–April and all of Nov., members $23, nonmembers $27), 32 kilometers (20 miles) south of the town Jasper and 198 kilometers (123 miles) north from Lake Louise. It is larger than the one at Beauty Creek and has electricity. Athabasca Falls is only a few minutes' walk away.

$50-150

The Crossing (403/761-7000, www.thecrossingresort.com, mid-Mar.–mid-Oct., $159–209 s or d) is a large complex 87 kilometers (54 miles) north of Lake Louise and 45 kilometers (28 miles) south of Columbia Icefield. The motel rooms offer a decent combination of size and value,and most have views west to the Continental Divide. In addition to overnight rooms, The Crossing has the only gas between Lake Louise and Jasper, a self-serve cafeteria, a restaurant, a pub with a cook-your-own-steak grill, and a supersized gift shop.

$150-200

Historic **Sunwapta Falls Resort** (780/852-4852 or 888/828-5777, www.sunwapta.com, May–mid-Oct., $199–395 s or d) is 55 kilometers (34 miles) south of the town of Jasper and within walking distance of the picturesque waterfall for which it is named. It features 52 motel-like units, with either two queen beds or one queen bed and a fireplace; some have balconies. In the main lodge is a lunchtime self-serve restaurant popular with passing travelers. In the evening this same room is transformed into a

restaurant featuring simply prepared Canadian game and seafood in the $21–29 range and a delectable wild berry crumble for $7.50.

The **Glacier View Inn** (780/852-6550 or 877/423-7433, www.brewster.ca, May–Sept., $250–265 s or d), the top story of Columbia Icefield Centre, lies in a stunning location overlooking the Columbia Icefield, 132 kilometers (82 miles) north of Lake Louise and 105 kilometers (65 miles) south of the town of Jasper. It features 29 standard rooms, 17 of which have glacier views, and three larger, more luxurious corner rooms. All units have satellite TV and phones. Because of the remote location, dining options are limited to the in-house café and restaurant. The **Glacier Dining Room** opens daily at 7 A.M. for a breakfast buffet, reopening 6–9:30 P.M. for dinner. On the same level is a cafeteria-style café and a snack bar.

Over $200

Pioneer guide and outfitter Jimmy Simpson built **C Simpson's Num-Ti-Jah Lodge** (403/522-2167, www.num-ti-jah.com, from $320 s or d), on the north shore of Bow Lake, 40 kilometers (25 miles) north of Lake Louise, as a base for his outfitting operation in 1920. In those days, the route north from Lake Louise was nothing more than a horse trail. With a rustic mountain ambience that has changed little since Simpson's passing, an overnight stay at Num-Ti-Jah is a memorable experience. Just don't expect the conveniences of a regular motel. Under the distinctively red, steep-pitched roof of the main lodge are 25 rooms, some of which share bathrooms, and there's not a TV or phone in sight. Downstairs, guests soak up the warmth of a roaring log fire while mingling in a comfortable library filled with historic mountain literature. A dining room lined with historic memorabilia is open for breakfast and dinner.

CAMPING

Beyond Lake Louise, the first camping along the Icefields Parkway is at **Mosquito Creek Campground** (year-round, $21), 24 kilometers (15 miles) from the TransCanada Highway.

Don't be perturbed by the name, though; the bugs here are no worse than anywhere else. The 32 sites are nestled in the forest, with a tumbling creek separating the campground from a hostel. Each site has a picnic table and fire ring, while other amenities include pump water, pit toilets, and a kitchen shelter with an old-fashioned woodstove.

◖ **Waterfowl Lake Campground** (late June–mid-Sept., $27) is 33 kilometers (20 miles) north along the Icefields Parkway from Mosquito Creek. It features 116 sites between Upper and Lower Waterfowl Lakes, with a few sites in view of the lower lake. Facilities include pump water, flush toilets, and kitchen shelters with wood-burning stoves. Rise early to watch the first rays of sun hit Mount Chephren from the shoreline of the lower lake, then plan on hiking the four-kilometer (2.5-mile) trail to Chephren Lake—you'll be first on the trail and back in time for a late breakfast.

Continuing toward Jasper, the Icefields Parkway passes The Crossing, a good place to gas up and buy last-minute groceries before reaching **Rampart Creek Campground** (late June–early Sept., $21), 31 kilometers (19 miles) beyond Waterfowl Lake and 88 kilometers (55 miles) from Lake Louise. With just 50 sites, this campground fills early. Amenities include kitchen shelters, pit toilets, and pump water.

Over Sunwapta Pass and within Jasper National Park, **Wilcox Creek** and **Columbia Icefield Campgrounds** are within two kilometers (1.2 miles) of each other just south of the Columbia Icefield, around 125 kilometers (78 miles) north of Lake Louise, and just over 100 kilometers (62 miles) south of the town of Jasper. Both are primitive facilities with pit toilets, cooking shelters, and fire rings; all sites are $16. Smallish sites at Columbia Icefield Campground are set in a stunted subalpine forest of aspen and spruce, with views extending across to the Athabasca Glacier. Immediately to the south, Wilcox Creek offers larger sites, better suited to RVs and trailers, but with no hookups. Continuing north is **Jonas Creek** and then **Honeymoon Lake** and **Mt. Kerkeslin Campgrounds.** All cost $16 per night and have only primitive facilities.

Town of Jasper

At the top end of the Icefields Parkway, 280 kilometers (174 miles) north of Banff and a 3.5-hour drive west of the provincial capital, Edmonton, the town of Jasper is the service center of the park. For you the visitor, Jasper is the wonderfully underrated counterpart to its neighbor, Banff. Jasper has just half the population of Banff, but it's also less commercialized and its streets are a lot quieter. Part of the town's charm is its location at the confluence of the Athabasca and Miette Rivers, surrounded by the rugged, snowcapped peaks of Jasper National Park.

Connaught Drive, the town's main street, parallels the rail line as it curves through town. Along here, you'll find the park information center, the bus depot, the rail terminal, restaurants, motels, and a series of parking lots. Behind Connaught Drive is Patricia Street (one-way northbound), which has more restaurants and services and leads to more hotels and motels on Geikie Street. Behind this main commercial core are rows of neat houses—much less pretentious than those in Banff—and all the facilities of a regular town, including a library, a school, a swimming pool, and a hospital.

HISTORY

A trading post in the valley that served for many years as a supply depot for fur traders was run by a clerk named Jasper Hawes. In time, the settlement became known as Jasper's House. In 1907 the federal government officially declared the boundaries of Jasper Forest Park and bought all the land within it, except for one homestead owned by Lewis Swift. (This parcel remained privately owned until 1962,

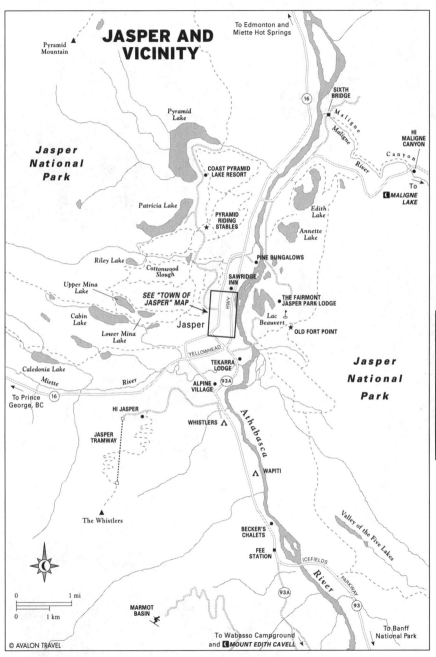

JASPER AND VICINITY

Pyramid Mountain

To Edmonton and Miette Hot Springs

Jasper National Park

Pyramid Lake

SIXTH BRIDGE

16

Maligne

Maligne River

Canyon

HI MALIGNE CANYON

COAST PYRAMID LAKE RESORT

Patricia Lake

PYRAMID RIDING STABLES

Edith Lake

Annette Lake

To MALIGNE LAKE

Riley Lake

Cottonwood Slough

PINE BUNGALOWS

Upper Mina Lake

SAWRIDGE INN

SEE "TOWN OF JASPER" MAP

THE FAIRMONT JASPER PARK LODGE

Cabin Lake

HWY

Lac Beauvert

Jasper

Lower Mina Lake

OLD FORT POINT

Caledonia Lake

YELLOWHEAD

Jasper National Park

Miette

River

TEKARRA LODGE

16

To Prince George, BC

93A

ALPINE VILLAGE

HI JASPER

Athabasca

JASPER TRAMWAY

WHISTLERS

WAPITI

The Whistlers

Valley of the Five Lakes

BECKER'S CHALETS

FEE STATION

ICEFIELDS

0   1 mi

0   1 km

93A

River

PARKWAY

93

MARMOT BASIN

To Wabasso Campground and MOUNT EDITH CAVELL

To Banff National Park

© AVALON TRAVEL

BANFF AND JASPER

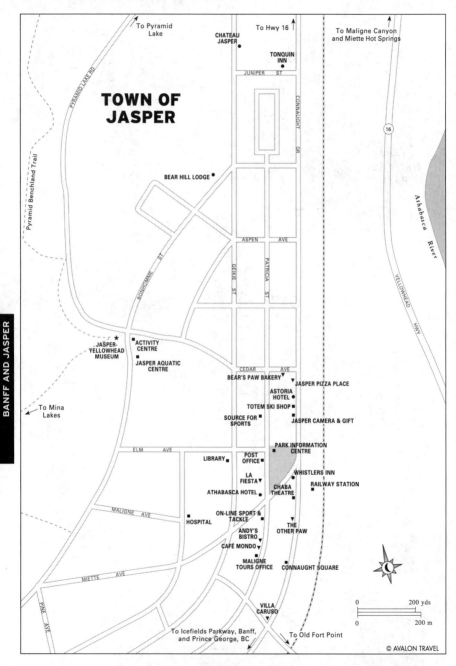

To Pyramid Lake

To Hwy 16

To Maligne Canyon and Miette Hot Springs

CHATEAU JASPER

TONQUIN INN

JUNIPER ST

CONNAUGHT DR

16

PYRAMID LAKE RD

TOWN OF JASPER

Pyramid Benchland Trail

BEAR HILL LODGE

Athabasca River

ASPEN AVE

GEIKIE ST

PATRICIA ST

BONHOMME ST

YELLOWHEAD HWY

JASPER-YELLOWHEAD MUSEUM

ACTIVITY CENTRE

JASPER AQUATIC CENTRE

To Mina Lakes

CEDAR AVE

BEAR'S PAW BAKERY

JASPER PIZZA PLACE

ASTORIA HOTEL

TOTEM SKI SHOP

SOURCE FOR SPORTS

JASPER CAMERA & GIFT

PARK INFORMATION CENTRE

ELM AVE

LIBRARY

POST OFFICE

LA FIESTA

WHISTLERS INN

RAILWAY STATION

ATHABASCA HOTEL

CHABA THEATRE

MALIGNE AVE

HOSPITAL

ON-LINE SPORT & TACKLE

THE OTHER PAW

ANDY'S BISTRO

CAFÉ MONDO

MIETTE AVE

MALIGNE TOURS OFFICE

CONNAUGHT SQUARE

PINE AVE

VILLA CARUSO

0   200 yds

0   200 m

To Icefields Parkway, Banff, and Prince George, BC

To Old Fort Point

© AVALON TRAVEL

BANFF AND JASPER

long after the stubborn Mr. Swift had passed away.) When the Grand Trunk Pacific Railway was completed in 1911, visitors flocked into the remote mountain park settlement, and its future was ensured. The first accommodation for tourists was 10 tents on the shore of Lac Beauvert, which became known as Jasper Park Camp. In 1921, the tents were replaced by the original Jasper Park Lodge. By the summer of 1928, a road was completed from Edmonton, and a golf course was built.

Incorporation

Although the infrastructure of the town began developing in the 1960s, it was run from Ottawa by Parks Canada until 2002. In that year, Jasper was incorporated as a "town," with locally elected residents serving as mayor and council members. Decisions made by the council must still balance the needs of living in a national park, but also represent locals who call the park home. On the surface, obvious visible changes of this autonomy are a new emergency services building, a new wastewater treatment plant, and improvements to an ever-increasing downtown parking problem. One thing hasn't changed, and that's the basic premise of the town's existence: More than 50 percent of Jasper's 5,200 residents work in the hospitality industry, serving the needs of two million visitors annually.

SIGHTS AND DRIVES

With all the things to do and see in the park, it's amazing how many people hang out in town. July and August are especially busy; much-needed improvements to the parking situation have had little impact on the traffic—try for a parking spot in the lot along the railway line. The best way to avoid the problem is to avoid town during the middle of the day. The park information center, on Connaught Drive, is the only real reason to be in town. The shaded park in front of the center is a good place for people watching.

Museums

At the back of town is the excellent **Jasper-**

Yellowhead Museum and Archives (400 Pyramid Lake Rd., 780/852-3013; mid-June– Sept. daily 10 A.M.–9 P.M., the rest of the year Thurs.–Sun. 10 A.M.–5 P.M.; adult $5, senior and child $4), as unstuffy as any museum could possibly be. The main gallery features colorful, modern picture boards with exhibits that take visitors along a timeline of Jasper's human history through the fur trade, the coming of the railway, and the creation of the park.

The Den (corner of Connaught Dr. and Miette Ave., 780/852-3361, daily 9 A.M.–10 P.M., $3), in the darkened bowels of the Whistlers Inn, is a throwback to a bygone era, when displays of stuffed animals were considered the best way to extol the wonders of nature. "See animals in their natural setting" cries museum advertising, but the shrubbery looks suspiciously like fake Christmas trees and the bull elk seems to be screaming "Get me out of here!"

Patricia and Pyramid Lakes

A winding road heads through the hills at the back of town to these two picturesque lakes, formed when glacial moraines dammed shallow valleys. The first, to the left, is Patricia; the second, farther along the road, is Pyramid, backed by **Pyramid Mountain** (2,765 m/9,072 ft). Both lakes are popular spots for picnicking, fishing, boating, and swimming (Pyramid only). Boat rentals are available at **Pyramid Lake Boat Rentals** (780/852-4900). Canoes, rowboats, paddleboats, and kayaks are $35 for the first hour and $25 for each additional hour. Motorboats are $55 per hour. The road continues around the lake to a footbridge, which leads to an island popular with picnickers.

Jasper Tramway

This gondola (780/852-3093, summer daily 9 A.M.–8 P.M., shorter hours Apr.–June and Sept.–mid-Oct., closed the rest of the year, adult $28, child 5–14 $14) climbs more than 1,000 vertical meters (3,280 feet) up the steep north face of **The Whistlers,** named for the hoary marmots that live on the summit. The tramway operates two 30-passenger cars that take seven minutes to reach the upper terminal, during which time the conductor gives a lecture about the mountain and its environment. From the upper terminal, a 1.4-kilometer (0.9-mile) trail leads to the 2,470-meter (8,104-foot) true summit. On a clear day you can see Mount Robson (3,954 m/12,970 ft)—the highest peak in the Canadian Rockies—to the northwest. Free two-hour guided hikes leave the upper terminal for the true summit daily at 10 A.M., 11 A.M., 2 P.M., and 3 P.M. You should allow two hours on top and, on a clear summer's day, two more hours in line at the bottom. The tramway is three kilometers (1.9 miles) south of town on Highway 93 (Icefields Parkway) and then a similar distance up Whistlers Road.

🄲 Mount Edith Cavell

The original Icefields Parkway (Hwy. 93A), which followed the southeast bank of the Athabasca River, has been bypassed by a more direct route on the other side of the river. Along the original route, known also as the Athabasca Parkway, a 14.5-kilometer (nine-mile) road winds its way up to a parking area below the northeast face of 3,363-meter (11,033-foot) Mount Edith Cavell, the park's most distinctive peak. It can be seen from many vantage points in the park, including the town and the gold course, but none is more impressive than directly below it. On this face, **Angel Glacier** lies in a saddle on the mountain's lower slopes. From the parking area, the **Path of the Glacier Trail** (one hour round-trip) traverses moraines deposited by the receding Angel Glacier and leads to some great viewpoints.

Edith and Annette Lakes

These two lakes along the road to Jasper Park Lodge—across the Athabasca River from town—are perfect for a picnic, a swim, or a pleasant walk. They are remnants of a much larger lake that once covered the entire valley floor. The lakes are relatively shallow; therefore, the sun warms the water to a bearable temperature. In fact, they have the warmest waters of any lakes in the park. The 2.5-

kilometer (1.6-mile) **Lee Foundation Trail** encircles Lake Annette and is wheelchair accessible. Both lakes have day-use areas with beaches and picnic areas.

Maligne Canyon

This unique geological feature has been eroded out of the easily dissolved limestone bedrock by the fast-flowing Maligne River. Surface water here is augmented by underground springs; thus, it seems that more water flows out of the canyon than into it. At the top of the canyon, opposite the teahouse, are large potholes in the riverbed. These potholes are created when rocks and pebbles become trapped in what begins as a shallow depression, and under the force of the rushing water the rocks carve jug-shaped hollows into the soft bedrock.

To get here, head northeast from town and turn right onto Maligne Lake Road. The canyon access road veers left 11 kilometers (6.8 miles) from Jasper. An interpretive trail winds down from the parking lot, crossing the canyon six times. The most spectacular sections of the canyon can be seen from the first two bridges,

© ANDREW HEMPSTEAD

Maligne Canyon

© ANDREW HEMPSTEAD

Maligne Lake

at the upper end of the trail. To avoid the crowds at the upper end of the canyon, an alternative would be to park at Sixth Bridge, near the confluence of the Maligne and Athabasca Rivers, and walk *up* the canyon.

Medicine Lake

From the canyon, Maligne Lake Road climbs to Medicine Lake, which does a disappearing act each year. The water level fluctuates because of an underground drainage system known as karst. At the northwest end of the lake, where the outlet should be, the riverbed is often dry. In fall, when runoff from the mountains is minimal, the water level drops, and by November the lake has almost completely dried up. Early Indians believed that spirits were responsible for the phenomenon, hence the name.

◖ Maligne Lake

Continue beyond Medicine Lake to reach Maligne Lake (48 km/30 mi from Jasper), the largest glacier-fed lake in the Canadian Rockies and second largest in the world. Activities are plentiful, but other than taking in the spectacular vistas, the only thing you won't need your wallet for is hiking one of the numerous trails in the area. The most popular tourist activity at the lake is a 90-minute narrated cruise on a glass-enclosed boat up the lake to oft-photographed **Spirit Island.** Cruises leave every hour on the hour 10 A.M.–5 P.M. in summer, with fewer sailings in May and September (adult $55, child $27.50). Many time slots are booked in blocks by tour companies, so reservations are suggested. Canoes and kayaks can be rented at the Boat House, a provincial historic site dating to 1929, for $30 per hour or $89 per day. Double sea kayaks go for $35 per hour and $107 per day. The lake also has excellent trout fishing, a gift shop, and a café. **Maligne Lake Shuttle** runs out to the lake 3–4 times daily mid-May–late September. The first shuttle leaves for the lake each morning at 8:30 A.M. ($40 round-trip). All commercial operations to and around the lake are operated by **Maligne Tours** (616 Patricia St., 780/852-3370 or 866/625-4463, www.malignelake.com), based in downtown Jasper.

BANFF AND JASPER

Miette Hot Springs

From Jasper, it's 50 kilometers (31 miles) to the park's eastern boundary along Highway 16, following the Athabasca River the entire way. A side road 43 kilometers (27 miles) from town leads 18 kilometers (11 miles) to the warmest springs in the Canadian Rockies (780/866-3939, mid-May–mid-Oct. 10:30 A.M.–9 P.M., extended to 8:30 A.M.–10:30 P.M. in summer, adult $6.25, senior and child $5.25). In 1910, a packhorse trail was built up the valley and the government constructed a bathhouse. The original hand-hewn log structure was replaced in the 1930s with pools that remained in use until new facilities were built in 1985. Water that flows into the pools is artificially cooled from 54°C (128°F) to a soothing 39°C (100°F). A newer addition to the complex is a cool plunge pool.

HIKING

The 1,200 kilometers (745 miles) of hiking trails in Jasper are significantly different from those in the other mountain national parks. The park has an extensive system of interconnecting backcountry trails that, for experienced hikers, can provide a wilderness adventure rivaled by few areas on the face of the earth. I'll leave descriptions of these longer trails to experts Brian Patton and Bart Robinson, authors of *The Canadian Rockies Trail Guide* (sold at the Park Information Centre and other retailers through the park) and concentrate on the most popular hikes.

Before setting off on any hike, whatever the length, go to the **Park Information Centre** in downtown Jasper for trail maps, trail conditions, and trail closures.

Around Town

Numerous official and unofficial hiking trails weave across the benchland immediately west of the town of Jasper, many branching out from beside the museum. To get a taste of this accessible section of the park, plan on taking the **Pyramid Benchland Trail** (seven km/4.3 mi, 5 hours round-trip), which climbs onto the bench before emerging at a bluff overlooking the Athabasca River Valley. In the vicinity, two kilometers (1.2 miles) along Pyramid Lake Road, the **Patricia Lake Circle** (five km/3.1 mi, 90 minutes round-trip) doesn't actually encircle Patricia Lake, but instead just passes along a portion of its southern shoreline, with good chances of spying beaver in the adjacent Cottonwood Slough.

Feeling energetic? Continue to the end of Pyramid Lake Road and lace up for the trail to **The Palisade** (11 km/6.8 mi, four hours one-way), gaining 850 meters (2,790 feet) of elevation along the way.

Near Mount Edith Cavell

Cavell Road begins 13 kilometers (eight miles) south from town along Highway 93A and ends after 14.5 kilometers (nine miles) at the trailhead for the **Cavell Meadows Trail** (four km/2.5 mi, 1.5 hours one-way)—one of most scenic in the park. The trail starts out following the paved Path of the Glacier Loop, then branches left, climbing steadily through a subalpine forest of Engelmann spruce and then stunted subalpine fir to emerge facing the northeast face of Mount Edith Cavell and Angel Glacier. The view of the glacier from this point is nothing less than awesome, as the ice spills out of a cirque, clinging to a 300-meter-high (980 feet) cliff face. The trail continues to higher viewpoints and an alpine meadow that, by mid-July, is filled with wildflowers.

The trail into the **Tonquin Valley** is one of the overnight treks that I'd said earlier was beyond the scope of this book, but this one is just too good to pass up. The easiest of two approaches begins opposite the hostel on Cavell Road and follows the **Astoria River** (19 km/11.8 mi, 6–7 hours one-way) for much of the way. Amethyst Lakes and the 1,000-meter (3,280-foot) cliffs of the Ramparts first come into view after 13 kilometers (eight miles). At the 17-kilometer (10.5-mile) mark the trail divides. To the left it climbs into Eremite Valley, where there's a campground. The right fork continues following Astoria River to Tonquin Valley, Amethyst Lakes, and a choice of four campgrounds and two lodges.

Maligne Lake Area

Hikes in the vicinity of Maligne Lake, 48 kilometers (30 miles) from the town of Jasper, provides many opportunities to view the lake and explore its environs. To get there, take Highway 16 east for four kilometers (2.5 miles) from town and turn south on Maligne Lake Road.

The **Lake Trail (Mary Schäffer Loop)** (3.2 km/two mi, one hour round-trip) is the easiest local trail, but also offers the most spectacular views. From the boat house, follow the lakeshore through an open area of lakeside tables to a point known as **Schäffer Viewpoint,** named for the first white person to see the valley. Across the lake are the aptly named Bald Hills, the Maligne Range, and to the southwest, the distinctive twin peaks of Mount Unwin and Mount Charlton. After dragging yourself away from the spectacular panorama, continue along a shallow bay before following the trail into a forest of spruce and subalpine fir, then looping back to the middle parking lot.

The loop trail through the **Opal Hills** (8.2 km/5.1 mi, three hours round-trip) begins from the upper parking lot, climbing a total of 455 meters (1,500 feet) to the high alpine meadows.

The **Bald Hills Trail** (5.2 km/3.2 mi, two hours one-way) gains 495 meters (1,620 feet) along an old fire road that leads to the site of a fire lookout. The 360-degree view takes in the jade-green waters of Maligne Lake, the Queen Elizabeth Ranges, and the twin peaks of Mount Unwin and Mount Charlton. The trail begins from the picnic area at the very end of Maligne Lake Road.

OTHER RECREATION

A number of booking agents represent the many recreation-tour operators in Jasper. The **Jasper Adventure Centre** (Chaba Theatre, 604 Connaught Dr., 780/852-5595, www.jasperadventurecentre.com) takes bookings for all the activities below, as well as for accommodations and transportation to various points in the park and beyond. **Maligne Tours** (616 Patricia St., 780/852-3370, www.malignelake.com) operates all activities in the Maligne Lake area, including the famous lake cruise.

Mountain Biking

In addition to the paved roads, many designated unpaved bicycle trails radiate from the town. One of the most popular is the Athabasca River Trail, which begins at Old Fort Point and follows the river to a point below Maligne Canyon. Cyclists are particularly prone to sudden bear encounters; make noises when passing through heavily wooded areas. The brochure *Mountain Biking Trail Guide* lists designated trails and is available from the information center and all local sport shops. Rental outlets include **Source for Sports** (406 Patricia St., 780/852-3654), **Freewheel Cycle** (618 Patricia St., 780/852-3898), **Vicious Cycle** (630 Connaught Dr., 780/852-1111), and the **Activity Centre** at Jasper Park Lodge (780/852-5708). Expect to pay $8–12 per hour or $28–50 for any 24-hour period, which includes a helmet and lock.

Horseback Riding

On the benchlands immediately behind the town of Jasper is **Pyramid Riding Stables** (Pyramid Lake Rd., 780/852-7433). The stables offer one-, two-, and three-hour guided rides for $45, $70, and $95, respectively. The one-hour trip follows a ridge high above town, providing excellent views of the Athabasca River Valley. **Skyline Trail Rides** (The Fairmont Jasper Park Lodge, 780/852-4215) offers a one-hour guided ride around Lake Annette ($39 per person) and a two-hour ride along the Valleyview Trail ($60 per person). Both companies operate mid-April–October.

Overnight pack trips consist of 4–6 hours of riding per day, with a few nights spent at a remote mountain lodge where you can hike, boat, fish, or ride. Rates start at $180 per person per day for meals, accommodation, and a horse, of course. For details, contact **Skyline Trail Rides** (780/852-4215 or 888/852-7787, www.skylinetrail.com) or **Tonquin Valley Adventures** (780/852-1188, www.tonquinadventures.com).

White-Water Rafting

On the **Athabasca River,** the Mile 5 Run is an easy two-hour float that appeals to all ages. Farther upstream, some operators offer a trip that begins from below Athabasca Falls, on a stretch of the river that passes through a narrow canyon; this run takes three hours. The boulder-strewn rapids of the **Sunwapta River** offers more thrills and spills—these trips are for the more adventurous and last 3–4 hours. Most companies offer a choice of rivers and provide transportation to and from downtown hotels. Expect to pay $60–70 for trips on the Athabasca and from $80 for the Sunwapta. The following companies offers tours with downtown pickups: **Maligne Rafting Adventures** (780/852-3370 or 866/625-4463), **Raven Adventures** (780/852-4292 or 866/496-7238), **Rocky Mountain River Guides** (780/852-3777 or 866/952-3777), and **White Water Rafting** (780/852-7238 or 800/557-7238). **Jasper Raft Tours** (780/852-2665 or 888/553-5628) specialize in family-friendly trips, floating a 16-kilometer (10-mile) stretch of the Athabasca River in large, stable inflatable rafts; adult $55, child $20.

Fishing

Fishing in the many alpine lakes—for rainbow, brook, Dolly Varden, cutthroat, and lake trout, as well as pike and whitefish—is excellent. Many outfitters offer guided fishing trips. Whether you fish with a guide or by yourself, you'll need a national park fishing license ($10 per day, $35 per year), available from the park information center. Guided fishing trips on the lake are offered from the Boat House by **Maligne Tours** (780/852-3370); half-day $180 per person for two people, full-day $225 per person for two.

Source for Sports (406 Patricia St., 780/852-3654) and **Online Sport & Tackle** (600 Patricia St., 780/852-3630) sell and rent fishing tackle and also have canoe and boat rentals.

Tours

Brewster (780/852-3332) offers a four-hour

GLORIOUS GOLF

Even if your game's not on, it's difficult not to enjoy walking the fairways of **The Fairmont Jasper Park Lodge Golf Course** (780/852-6090), consistently ranked as one of the top 10 courses in Canada. Designed by renowned golf-course architect Stanley Thompson, the course opened in 1925 after 200 workers had spent an entire year clearing trees and laying out the holes to Thompson's design.

The 18-hole, 6,670-yard course takes in the contours of the Athabasca River Valley and hugs the banks of turquoise-colored Lac Beauvert for a memorable three-hole stretch. It's a true test of accuracy; and with holes named The Maze, The Bad Baby, and The Bay, you'll need lots of balls. Greens fees for 18 holes vary with the season: $225 mid-June–September, $160 mid-May–mid-June, and $125 in early May and from October 1 through closing (usually mid-October). A power cart is $40 per round. Golfing after 5 P.M. is $110 with a cart – a great deal during the long days of June and July. Other amenities include a driving range, club rentals ($50-60), a café, a restaurant, and a well-stocked pro shop.

Discover Jasper tour taking in Patricia and Pyramid Lakes, Maligne Canyon, and Jasper Tramway (ride not included in fare). It departs daily at 8:30 A.M. April–October from the railway station ($52). **Maligne Tours** (616 Patricia St., 780/852-3370, www.malignelake. com) schedules a variety of tours, including a six-hour trip to Maligne Lake ($95, includes cruise). **Jasper Adventure Centre,** in the Chaba Theatre (604 Connaught Dr., 780/852-5595, www.jasperadventurecentre. com) operates several well-priced tours, including the following: Mount Edith Cavell (departs 2 P.M., three hours, $65), Maligne Valley (departs 9:30 A.M., five hours, $95, including boat tour), and Miette Hot Springs (departs 6 P.M., four hours, $72). Similarly priced tours take in historical sites and local wildlife.

WINTER RECREATION

Winter is certainly a quiet time in the park, but that doesn't mean there's a lack of things to do. Marmot Basin offers world-class alpine skiing; many snow-covered hiking trails are groomed for cross-country skiing; portions of Lac Beauvert and Pyramid Lake are cleared for ice-skating; horse-drawn sleighs travel around town; and Maligne Canyon is transformed into a magical, frozen world. Hotels reduce rates by 40–70 percent through winter and many offer lodging and lift tickets for less than $100 per person.

Marmot Basin

The terrain at Marmot Basin (780/852-3816 or 800/363-3078, www.skimarmot.com) is highly underrated, with the most adventurous skiers and boarders spending their day in Charlie's Basin, a massive powder-filled bowl. Marmot Basin has seven lifts servicing 600 hectares (1,500 acres) of terrain and a vertical rise of 900 meters (2,940 feet). The longest run is 5.6 kilometers (3.5 miles). Marmot doesn't get the crowds of the three resorts in Banff National Park, so lift lines are uncommon. The season runs early December–late April. Lift tickets are adult $72, senior and child $58. Rentals are available at the resort or in town at **Totem Ski Shop** (408 Connaught Dr., 780/852-3078).

Cross-Country Skiing

For many, traveling Jasper's hiking trails on skis is just as exhilarating as on foot. An extensive network of 300 kilometers (185 miles) of summer hiking trails is designated for skiers, with around 100 kilometers (62 miles) groomed. The four main areas of trails are along Pyramid Lake Road, around Maligne Lake, in the Athabasca Falls area, and at Whistlers Campground. A booklet available at the park information center details each trail and its difficulty. Weather forecasts and avalanche-hazard reports are posted here also.

Rental packages are available from **Source for Sports** (406 Patricia St., 780/852-3654), the rental shop at **The Fairmont Jasper Park Lodge** (780/852-3433), and **Totem Ski Shop**

(408 Connaught Dr., 780/852-3078), offering rentals, repairs, and sales.

Maligne Canyon

By late December, the torrent that is the Maligne River has frozen solid. Where it cascades down through Maligne Canyon the river is temporarily stalled for the winter, creating remarkable formations through the deep limestone canyon. **Jasper Adventure Centre** (306 Connaught Dr., 780/852-5595) offers exciting three-hour guided tours into the depths of the canyon throughout winter daily at 9 A.M., 1 P.M., and 6 P.M. (adult $55, child $25).

ENTERTAINMENT AND EVENTS
Nightlife

The most popular nightspot in town for younger travelers is the **Atha-B,** in the Athabasca Hotel (510 Patricia St., 780/852-3386), where bands play some nights. It gets pretty rowdy with all the seasonal workers, but it's still enjoyable; there's a minimal cover charge. This hotel also has a large lounge and a bar with a pool table and a popular 5–7 P.M. happy hour. **Pete's Club** (upstairs at 614 Patricia St., 780/852-6262) has a jam on Tuesday night and bands playing Friday–Sunday. The music varies—it could be blues, rock, or Celtic. Right downtown, the **Whistle Stop Pub,** in the Whistlers Inn (105 Miette Ave., 780/852-3361), has a great atmosphere with a classic wooden bar and memorabilia everywhere. **Downstream Bar** (620 Connaught Dr., 780/852-9449) has live music Friday and Saturday.

You don't need to be a guest of Jasper's finest hotel, the The Fairmont Jasper Park Lodge (780/852-3301), to enjoy the ambience of its three lounges: the **Emerald Lounge** has comfortable indoor seating and a long outdoor terrace overlooking Lac Beauvert; **Tent City** is a sports-style bar with a relaxed atmosphere and two pool tables; while **Palisade's** is a winter-only bar attracting the après-ski crowd each evening.

Festivals and Events

Canada Day (July 1) celebrations begin with a pancake breakfast and progress to a flag-raising ceremony (in front of the information center) and a parade along Connaught Drive. Live entertainment and a fireworks display end the day. The **Jasper Heritage Rodeo** (www.jasperheritagerodeo.com), on the second weekend of August, dates from 1926 and attracts pro cowboys from across Canada. Apart from the traditional rodeo events, the fun includes a mechanical bull, a children's rodeo, a casino, pancake breakfasts, the ever-popular stick-pony parade, and the crowning of Miss Rodeo Jasper. Most of the action takes place in the arena at the Jasper Activity Centre, behind town on Pyramid Lake Road.

On the other side of the calendar, winter is not totally partyless—**Jasper in January** is a two-week celebration that includes fireworks, special evenings at local restaurants, a chili cook-off, discounted lift tickets at Marmot Basin, and all the activities associated with winter.

ACCOMMODATIONS

In summer, accommodations here are expensive. All of the regular motels are within walking distance of town and most have restaurants. Luckily, alternatives to staying in $200-plus hotel rooms do exist. The best alternatives are the lodges scattered around the edge of town. Open in summer only, each offers a rustic yet distinct style of accommodation in keeping with the theme of staying in a national park. Additionally, many private residences have rooms for rent in summer; three hostels are close to town; and there's always camping in the good ol' outdoors.

Under $50

On the road to the Jasper Tramway, seven kilometers (4.3 miles) south from town off the Icefields Parkway, is **HI-Jasper** (780/852-3215 or 877/852-0781, www.hihostels.ca), which has 84 beds, a large kitchen, a common room, showers, laundry, public Internet access, an outdoor barbecue area, and mountain-bike rentals. Members of Hostelling International pay $26, nonmembers $30. Private rooms are $63 and $71 s or d respectively. Private rooms are $60 and $70 s or d respectively. In the summer months this hostel fills up every night. The front desk is open daily noon–midnight.

HI-Maligne Canyon (June–Sept., members $23, nonmembers $27) is on Maligne Lake Road, beside the Maligne River and a short walk from the canyon. Although rustic, it lies in a beautiful setting. The 24 dorm beds are in two cabins; other amenities include electricity, a kitchen, and a dining area.

(HI-Mount Edith Cavell (mid-June–mid-Oct., members $23, nonmembers $27) offers a million-dollar view for the price of a dorm bed. It's 13 kilometers (eight miles) up Cavell Road off Highway 93A, and because of the remote location there's usually a spare bed. Opposite the hostel are trailheads for hiking in the Tonquin Valley, and it's just a short walk to the base of Mount Edith Cavell. The hostel is rustic (no showers and only pit toilets) but has a kitchen, dining area, and outdoor wood sauna. Check-in is 5–11 P.M.

$100-150

If you're simply looking for somewhere to rest your head, consider Jasper's least expensive hotel rooms at the downtown **Athabasca Hotel** (510 Patricia St., 780/852-3386 or 877/542-8422, www.athabascahotel.com, from $105 s or d), which dates to 1928. The cheapest of its 61 rooms share bathrooms and are above a noisy bar, but the price is right. This hotel also has more expensive rooms, each with a vaguely Victorian decor and private bathrooms ($149–179 s or d).

$150-200

(Becker's Chalets (780/852-3779, www.beckerschalets.com, May–mid-Oct., $160–250 s or d) is spread along a picturesque bend on the Athabasca River six kilometers (3.7 miles) south of town. Moderately priced chalets, each with kitchenette, gas fireplace, and double bed ($145, or $175 for those on the riverfront), are an excellent deal. Becker's also boasts one of the park's finest restaurants.

PRIVATE HOME ACCOMMODATIONS

At last count, Jasper had more than 100 residential homes offering accommodations. Often they supply nothing more than a room with a bed, but the price is right – $50-100 s or d. Use of a bathroom may be shared with other guests or the family; few have kitchens and only a few supply light breakfast. In most cases, don't expect too much with the lower-priced choices. The positive side, apart from the price, is that your hosts are usually knowledgeable locals and downtown is only a short walk away. For a full listing that includes the facilities at each approved property, check the Jasper Home Accommodation Association website (www. stayinjasper.com). The Park Information Centre has a board listing private-home accommodations with rooms available for the upcoming night.

With a variety of cabin layouts and a central location, **Bear Hill Lodge** (100 Bonhomme St., 780/852-3209, www.bearhilllodge.com, mid-Apr.–mid-Oct., $189–225 s or d) makes a great base camp for travelers who want the cabin experience within walking distance of downtown. The original cabins are basic, but each has a TV, bathroom, gas fireplace, and coffee-making facilities. Also offered are larger rooms with wood-burning fireplaces.

A short distance south along Highway 93A from downtown, at the junction of the Icefields Parkway three kilometers (1.9 miles) south of town, is **Alpine Village** (780/852-3285, www. alpinevillagejasper.com, late Apr.–mid-Oct., $190–320 s or d). This resort is laid out across well-manicured lawns, and all buildings are surrounded by colorful gardens of geraniums and petunias. After a day exploring the park, guests can soak away their cares in the outdoor hot pool or kick back on a row of Adirondack chairs scattered along the Athabasca River. The older sleeping cabins have been renovated, while the Deluxe Bedroom Suites, which opened in 2009, feature open plans, stone fireplaces, luxurious bathrooms, and decks with private forested views.

$200-250

The lure of ◖ **Tekarra Lodge** (Hwy. 93A, 1.6 km/one mi south from downtown, 780/852-3058 or 888/962-2522, www.tekarralodge. com, mid-May–early Oct., $210–290 s or d) is its historic log cabins and forest above the confluence of the Miette and Athabasca Rivers. Each cabin has been totally modernized yet retains a cozy charm, with comfortable beds, fully equipped kitchenettes, wood-burning fireplaces, and smallish but adequate bathrooms. The spacious Athabasca Cabins are well-suited for small families. An on-site restaurant is open for breakfast (7:30–11 A.M.) and dinner (5–11 P.M.).

This is the price range that most downtown Jasper hotel rooms fall within. Right downtown is the **Astoria Hotel** (404 Connaught Dr., 780/852-3351 or 800/661-7343, www.astoria-hotel.com; $207–215 s or d). This European-style lodging was built in 1924 and has been kept in the same family ever since. Rooms are brightly furnished and each has a fridge, TV, and VCR. Outside of summer, these same rooms cost from $120. Note that there is no elevator in this four-story hotel. Similarly priced are the **Tonquin Inn** (100 Juniper St., 780/852-4987 or 800/661-1315, www.tonquininn.com, from $211–398 s or d), with an outdoor hot tub, laundry facilities, a steakhouse restaurant, and a sunny lounge bar; and **Maligne Lodge** (900 Connaught Ave., 780/852-3143 or 800/661-1315, www.malignelodge.com, $204–271 s or d). These places are worth considering outside of summer, when the cabin accommodations are closed and rates are discounted substantially.

It's impossible to miss the sprawling grounds of **Coast Pyramid Lake Resort** (780/852-4900 or 888/962-2522, www.coasthotels.com; late April–late Oct.; $225–325 s or d), across the road from Pyramid Lake. Plenty of water-based activities and rentals, a fitness center, and a large barbecue area make the resort a good choice for families.

$250-350

At **Château Jasper** (96 Geikie St., 780/852-5644 or 800/661-1315, www.chateaujasper.com, $298 s or d), guest rooms are spacious and elegantly finished with maple furnishings and low ceilings that give them a cozy feel. Bathrooms are particularly well equipped, with guests also enjoying the use of plush bathrobes. The in-house dining room, Silverwater Grill, combines a café that pours some of Jasper's finest coffee with a bistro-style restaurant.

Over $350

◖ **The Fairmont Jasper Park Lodge** (780/852-3301 or 800/257-7544, www.fairmont.com, from $398 s or d) lies along the shore of Lac Beauvert (meaning "beautiful green lake" in French), across the Athabasca River from downtown. As the park's original resort and its most famous, it covers a sprawling property with plenty of activities. The best known of these is the golf course, but guests also enjoy walking trails, horseback riding, canoeing, tennis, and swimming in an outdoor heated pool that remains open year-round. The main lodge features stone floors, carved wooden pillars, and a high ceiling. This building contains multiple restaurants and lounges, an activity booking desk, a fitness room, a game room, and Jasper's only covered shopping arcade. The 446 rooms vary in configuration and are spread out over the expansive property. All have coffeemakers, TV, telephones, and Internet access. The least expensive Fairmont Rooms are smallish, hold two twin beds, and offer limited views. Also away from the lake are larger Deluxe Rooms; each has a patio or balcony. Junior Suites have a distinct country charm, and each has either a sitting room and balcony or patio with lake views. Moving up to the more expensive options, Lakeview Suites overlook Lac Beauvert and are backed by the 18th fairway of the golf course. Each features a patio or balcony, fireplace, and two TVs. For a super-splurge, consider the cabins (starting from $800). Most guests don't pay the summer rack rates quoted here. The cost of lodging is usually included in one of the plethora of packages offered (click on the "Package Finder" link on the Fairmont website for all the options). Outside of summer, The Fairmont Jasper Park Lodge becomes a real bargain, with rooms with lake views (remember it'll be frozen in winter) for less than $200.

CAMPING

Campgrounds in Jasper begin opening in mid-June, and all but Wapiti are closed by mid-October. All campsites have a picnic table and fire ring, with a fire permit costing $8 (includes firewood). A percentage of sites in the most popular campgrounds can be reserved through the Parks Canada Campground Reservation Service (877/737-3783, www.pccamping.ca) for a nominal fee. If you're traveling in July or August, know which dates you'll be in Jasper, and require hookups, it is strongly advised to take advantage of this service.

Near the Town of Jasper

Whistlers Campground, at the base of Whistlers Road, three kilometers (1.9 miles) south of town, has 781 sites, making it the largest campground in the Canadian Rockies. It is divided into four sections; prices vary with the services available—walk-in sites $22.50, unserviced sites $27.40, powered sites $32.30, full hookups $38.20. Each section has showers. Whistlers is open May–mid-October.

Two kilometers (1.2 miles) farther south along the Icefields Parkway is **Wapiti Campground,** which offers 366 sites and has showers; unserviced sites $27.40, powered sites $32.30. This is the park's only campground open year-round, with serviced winter camping $20 per night.

Sites at **Wabasso Campground,** along Highway 93A approximately 16 kilometers (10 miles) south of town, are set among stands of spruce and aspen; $21.50 per night.

East Along Highway 16

East of town, off Highway 16, are two smaller, more primitive campgrounds. **Snaring River Campground,** 17 kilometers (11 miles) from Jasper on Celestine Lake Road, is $15.70

(overflow camping is $10); **Pocahontas Campground,** 45 kilometers (28 miles) northeast, is $21.50. Both are open mid-May–early September.

FOOD

It's easy to get a good, or even great, meal in Jasper. Connaught Drive and Patricia Street are lined with cafés and restaurants. Considering that this is a national park, menus are reasonably well priced. You should expect hearty fare, with lots of beef, game, and a surprising selection of seafood.

Coffeehouses and Cafés

You'll smell the wonderful aroma of freshly baked bread even before entering █ **Bear's Paw Bakery** (4 Cedar Ave., 780/852-3233, daily 6 A.M.–6 P.M.). The European-style breads are perfect for a picnic lunch, but not as tempting as the cakes and pastries. Operated by the same owners, **The Other Paw** (610 Connaught Dr., 780/852-2253; daily 7 A.M.–6 P.M.) has a slightly more contemporary feel, but more of the same great baked goods, as well as delicious salads.

In Jasper Marketplace, with a couple of tables spilling onto the sidewalk, **Café Mondo** (616 Patricia St., 780/852-9676; daily 8 A.M.–8 P.M., until 9 P.M. in summer) is a popular hangout for locals each morning, but where this place shines is the pizza by the slice and freshly made salads through the day.

In the railway station is **Trains & Lattes** (607 Connaught Dr., 780/852-7444; daily 6 A.M.–7 P.M.), a small espresso bar.

Nutter's (622 Patricia St., 780/852-5844) is another good pre-hiking stop, with a wide choice of goodies in bulk bins.

Casual

Pizza lovers congregate at **Jasper Pizza Place** (402 Connaught Dr., 780/852-3225, $14–26). It's a large and noisy restaurant with bright furnishings, a concrete floor, exposed heating ducts, and walls lined with photos from Jasper's earliest days. One half is self-serve, the other table service, and upstairs is a rooftop patio. Regular thick-crust pizzas are available from 11 A.M. but it's not until 5 P.M., when the wood-fired oven begins producing thin-

© ANDREW HEMPSTEAD

Bear's Paw Bakery

crust pizzas with adventurous toppings, that this place really shines.

On the same side of town as Jasper Pizza Place is one of Jasper's oldest restaurants, **Papa George's** (Astoria Hotel, 406 Connaught Dr., 780/852-3351, daily 7 A.M.–10 P.M., $12–19), which has been dishing up hearty fare to park visitors since 1925. The setting is old-fashioned, with east-facing windows taking in the panorama of distant mountain peaks.

Canadian

One of Jasper's best restaurants, **❰ Becker's Gourmet Restaurant** (780/852-3535, May–mid-Oct. daily 8–11 A.M. and 5:30–9 P.M.; $19.50–34) is six kilometers (3.7 miles) out of town to the south along the Icefields Parkway, but well worth the short drive. From this cozy dining room where the atmosphere is intimate, or from the adjacent enclosed conservatory, the views of Mount Kerkeslin and the Athabasca River are inspiring. This restaurant is a throwback to days gone by, with an ever-changing menu of seasonal game and produce that includes a daily wild game special. A menu staple is the baked rack of lamb smothered with apricot glaze. The breakfast buffet costs $16.

Back toward town from Becker's, on Highway 93A, is the dining room of historic **Tekarra Lodge** (780/852-4624, 8–11 A.M. and 5:30–10 P.M. May–Sept., $20–32). The setting may be mountain-style rustic, but the cooking appeals to modern preferences with combinations like banana-crusted chicken breast with sweet mango curry sauce.

Steak

❰ Villa Caruso (640 Connaught Dr., 780/852-3920, daily 11 A.M.–midnight, $19.50–37) is a steakhouse with a modern mountain vibe. The upstairs location—request a balcony table if the weather's warm—allows great views across the valley. The menu features a wide variety of Alberta beef dishes, including a massive 16-ounce T-bone. But there's a lot more than steak on offer, including chicken, seafood, and pasta dishes.

Prime Rib Village (Tonquin Inn, 100

Juniper St., 780/852-4966, daily from 5 P.M., $27–36) has been a long-time Jasper favorite. Charbroiled steaks and hearty servings of prime rib cost are the main draw, but the prime rib sandwich, with a plate-load of extras, will fill any carnivorous cravings for a few dollars less. This restaurant also offers a surprisingly good selection of seafood.

European

❰ Andy's Bistro (606 Patricia St., 780/852-4559, daily 5–9:30 P.M., $24–43) is an elegantly casual eatery offering a wide range of uncomplicated dishes using Canadian game and produce prepared with Swiss-influenced cooking styles. Start with a plate piled high with Prince Edward Island steamed mussels, then choose between dishes such as lobster-stuffed chicken breast or cheese fondue for two. Andy's has an extensive cellar of wines but no official wine list. Instead, diners are encouraged to choose from red wines set along the bar and white wines from the fridge. Also notable at Andy's is the staff, who seem experienced and knowledgeable.

Miss Italia Ristorante (610 Patricia St., 780/852-4002, daily for breakfast, lunch, and dinner, $15–21), upstairs in the Patricia Centre Mall, features bright and breezy interior decor with tables also set on a narrow terrace bedecked in pots of colorful flowers. Cooked breakfasts (from 8 A.M.) are $6–10. The rest of the day, pastas made fresh daily average $15, a baked filet of Atlantic salmon is $17, and souvlaki with a side of salad and pita bread is just $18. Check out the daily specials before ordering—they are taken from the regular menu but discounted a couple of bucks and come with soup or salad. Along the same strip is **Something Else Restaurant** (621 Patricia St., 780/852-3850, daily 11 A.M.–11 P.M., $15–18.50), where the specialty is generous portions of Greek food in a casual setting.

Directly behind the park information center, **La Fiesta** (504 Patricia St., 780/852-0404, daily noon–11 P.M., $19–29) is a small eatery where the Mediterranean meets Mexico. It offers a tapas-style menu of Mexican dishes, as well as adventurous delights such as pork kebabs served with a fig and pine nut relish and mussels steamed in a tequila broth. This is also the best place in town for a martini.

The Fairmont Jasper Park Lodge

Jasper's premier accommodation, across the river from downtown, offers a choice of casual or elegant dining in a variety of restaurants and lounges. Opposite the reception area is a dedicated dining reservation desk, staffed daily 11 A.M.–8 P.M. in summer, or call 780/852-6052. Reservations are required for the Edith Cavell and Moose's Nook dining rooms.

Downstairs in the shopping arcade, **Meadows Restaurant** is a casual room open for a breakfast buffet (daily 6–11:30 A.M., $24–30) and then in the evening for dinner (summer Wed.–Sun 6–9 P.M.). The turnover of food is quick, meaning everything remains fresh. Request a table away from the buffet for a quieter dining experience.

The **Emerald Lounge** (daily 11:30 A.M.–10 P.M., $18–36) takes pride of place in the expansive lobby of the main building. Table settings of various configurations are spread throughout the room while also sprawling out and along a terrace, from where views over picturesque Lac Beauvert to distant mountains are uninterrupted. Both lunch and dinner menus feature imaginative modern Canadian cuisine, but with dinner (from 5:30 P.M.) being decidedly more expensive. At lunch, salads can be made into a full meal by adding extras such as smoked salmon and slices of chicken breast, or stick to mains such as bison burger.

The elegantly rustic **Ⓒ Moose's Nook Northern Grill** (daily 6–9 P.M., $28–42) is a good place to enjoy traditional Canadian fare, such as grilled wild boar chops, whiskey-flamed arctic char, or a chargrilled Albertan rib eye steak. Be sure to leave room for dessert—the chestnut-crusted cheesecake smothered in maple syrup is incredible.

The **Edith Cavell** (daily 6–9 P.M., $49) is the finest fine-dining restaurant in Jasper. Its dark oak walls contrast with the white linens and large, bright windows overlooking Lac Beauvert

and the mountains beyond. Even though the restaurant has changed little over time, its overly pretentious atmosphere has softened and service has become more comfortable. Still, this is seriously cultured dining, unequaled in Jasper. With an emphasis on local produce and Canadian game and seafood, the classic cuisine is served with a French flair. Dress code is "business casual": no T-shirts or jeans; a jacket and tie are "recommended but not required."

INFORMATION

The residence of Jasper's first superintendent, a beautiful old stone building dating to 1913, is now used by Parks Canada as the park information center. It's right downtown (Connaught Dr., 780/852-6176, www.pc.gc.ca, summer daily 8:30 A.M.–7 P.M., the rest of the year daily 9 A.M.–4 P.M.). The staff provides general information on the park and can direct you to hikes in the immediate vicinity. Also within the building is the **Parks Canada Trail Office** (780/852-6177), which handles questions for those going into the backcountry and issues the relevant passes. **Jasper Tourism and Commerce** (780/852-3858, www.jasper-canadianrockies.com) also has a desk in the building, and the friendly staff never seem to tire of explaining that all the rooms in town are full. As well as providing general information on the town, they have a large collection of brochures on activities, shopping, and restaurants. Beside the main Parks Canada desk is the **Friends of Jasper National Park** outlet selling topographic maps, books, and local publications. Look for notices posted out front with the day's interpretive programs.

Jasper's weekly newspaper, **The Booster,** is available throughout town on Wednesday. As well as newsworthy stories, it includes a list of upcoming events and trail reports.

The official Town of Jasper website (www.jasper-alberta.com), with lists of current events, weather conditions, and loads of helpful links, is also worth checking out.

Jasper National Park Radio is on the AM band at 1490. For weather conditions in the park, call 780/852-6176.

Libraries and Bookstores

Housed in Jasper's original Royal Canadian Mounted Police detachment building, small **Jasper Municipal Library** (500 Robson St., 780/852-3652, Mon.–Thurs. 10 A.M.–8 P.M., Fri.–Sat. 10 A.M.–5 P.M.) holds just about everything ever written about the park.

Head to the **Friends of Jasper** store (780/852-4767) in the park information center or the **museum** for a good selection of books on the park's natural and human history. A larger selection of literature, including lots of western Canadiana, can be found at **Jasper Camera and Gift** (412 Connaught Dr., 780/852-3165, daily 9 A.M.–10 P.M.).

SERVICES

The **post office** (502 Patricia St.) is behind the park information center. **More Than Mail** (620 Connaught Dr., 780/852-3151, daily 9 A.M.–10 P.M.) offers a wide range of communication services, including regular post, public Internet access, fax and copying facilities, a work area for laptops, international calling, and currency exchange. Other places with Internet access are **Digital Den** (upstairs at 610 Patricia St., 780/852-9765, daily 9 A.M.–10 P.M.) and **Jasper Municipal Library** (Elm Ave., 780/852-3652, Mon.–Thurs. 10 A.M.–8 P.M., Fri.–Sat. 10 A.M.–5 P.M.).

The two **laundries** on Patricia Street are open 6 A.M.–11 P.M. and offer **showers** that cost $2 (in quarters) for 10 minutes.

The **hospital** is at 518 Robson St. (780/852-3344). For the **RCMP,** call 780/852-4848.

GETTING THERE

Getting to Jasper by public transportation is easy, although the closest airport handling domestic and international flights is in Edmonton, 360 kilometers (224 miles) to the east. Jasper is on the transcontinental **VIA** (800/561-8630, www.viarail.ca) rail route, with trains running each way three times weekly. The railway station is central to town at 607 Connaught Drive. Lockers are available for $1 per day. Car-rental agencies and a café are here, too.

The railway station also serves as a bus depot. **Greyhound** buses (780/852-332 or 800/661-8747) depart Jasper for all points in Canada (except Banff), including Vancouver (three times daily, 12–13 hours), Edmonton (five times daily, 4.5 hours), and Prince Rupert (once daily, 18 hours). The main carrier up the Icefields Parkway from Calgary and Banff is **Brewster** (780/852-3332 or 866/606-6700, www.brewster.ca). This company operates a shuttle between Calgary International Airport daily May–mid-Oct. ($134 each way).

GETTING AROUND

The **Maligne Lake Shuttle** (780/852-3370) runs out to Maligne Lake 3–4 times daily mid-May–September ($40 round-trip) from its depot (616 Patricia St.). Stops are made at Maligne Canyon and HI–Maligne Canyon. Other pick-up points include the Jasper Inn and Jasper Park Lodge.

Rental cars start at $60 per day with 150 free kilometers. The following companies have agencies, and their local numbers are: **Avis** (780/852-3970), **Budget** (780/852-3222), **Hertz** (780/852-3888), and **National** (780/852-1117).

Cabs in town are not cheap. Most drivers will take you on a private sightseeing tour or to trailheads if requested; try **Jasper Taxi** (780/852-3600).

EDMONTON AND NORTHERN ALBERTA

Edmonton, Alberta's capital, sits in the center of the province and is a gateway to the vast forests of northern Alberta. It's a vibrant cultural center, but its reputation as a boomtown may be its defining characteristic. The proud city saw not one, but three major booms in the 20th century and is once again experiencing exponential growth. Its population has mushroomed to more than 740,000 (1,000,000 if the surrounding area is included), making it the sixth-largest city in Canada. Although Calgary is the administrative and business center of the province's billion-dollar petroleum industry, Edmonton is the technological, service, and supply center.

The North Saskatchewan River Valley winding through the city has been largely preserved as a 27-kilometer (17-mile) greenbelt—the largest urban park system in Canada. Rather than the hodgepodge of slums and streets you might expect in a boomtown, the modern city of Edmonton has been extremely well designed and well built, with an eye toward the future. The downtown area sits on a spectacular bluff overlooking the river-valley park system. Silhouetted against the deep-blue sky, a cluster of modern glass-and-steel high-rises makes a dynamic contrast to the historic granite Alberta Legislature Building and the lush valley floor below. But the city's biggest attraction is the ultimate shopping experience of West Edmonton Mall, the world's largest shopping and amusement complex.

Edmonton is a natural gateway to northern Alberta, extending from Highway 16 north to the 60th parallel. This is a sparsely populated

© ANDREW HEMPSTEAD

HIGHLIGHTS

((Muttart Conservatory: Four glass pyramids make up this interesting attraction. It's especially fun to visit the greenhouses in winter, when you can feel the humidity of the jungle pyramid while snow covers the outside grounds (page 441).

((Fort Edmonton Park: Immerse yourself in the past at this sprawling riverside attraction, where costumed interpreters add to the historic atmosphere (page 441).

((Royal Alberta Museum: Exhibits in this, one of Canada's premier museums, cover Alberta's one billion years of natural and human history (page 442).

((Old Strathcona: Edmonton's best-preserved historical district centers on Whyte Avenue, a continuous strip of trendy boutiques, funky cafés, and interesting bookstores (page 443).

((West Edmonton Mall: Simply put, there is no place like it in Canada. The world's largest shopping and indoor amusement complex truly does have something for everyone (page 443).

((Elk Island National Park: Nowhere else in the province offers the wildlife-viewing opportunities of this small park. Sightings of elk, moose, and bison are (almost) guaranteed (page 461).

((Métis Crossing: This, Canada's largest Métis cultural center, spreads across a riverfront site important for its historical links to native peoples and fur traders (page 464).

((Syncrude and Suncor Plant Tours: With more oil reserves than the rest of the world combined, it's no surprise that Fort McMurray is booming. The best way to take it all in is on one of these bus tours (page 469).

((William A. Switzer Provincial Park: Dotted with fish-filled lakes and home to abundant big game, this park is a great place for outdoor enthusiasts to pitch a tent for a night or two (page 479).

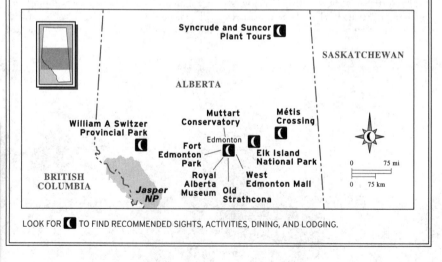

LOOK FOR ((TO FIND RECOMMENDED SIGHTS, ACTIVITIES, DINING, AND LODGING.

land of unspoiled wilderness, home to deer, moose, coyotes, foxes, lynx, black bears, and the elusive Swan Hills grizzly bear. For the most part, it is heavily forested, part of the boreal forest eco-region that sweeps around the Northern Hemisphere, broken only by the Atlantic and Pacific Oceans. Only a few species of trees are adapted to the long, cold winters and short summer growing seasons characteristic of these northern latitudes. Conifers such as white spruce, black spruce, jack pine, fir, and larch are the most common. This vast expanse of land is relatively flat, the only exceptions being the Swan Hills—which rise to 1,200 meters (3,900 feet)—and, farther north, the Birch and Caribou Mountains. The Athabasca and Peace river systems are the region's largest waterways. Carrying water from hundreds of tributaries, they merge in the far northeastern corner of the province and flow north into the Arctic Ocean. A third major watercourse, the North Saskatchewan River, flows east from the Continental Divide, crossing northern Alberta on its way to Hudson Bay. Alberta's earliest explorers arrived along these rivers, opening up the Canadian West to the trappers, missionaries, and settlers who followed.

PLANNING YOUR TIME

The region covered in this chapter centers on Alberta's capital, but also includes the entire northern half of the province. You could zip through Edmonton's highlights in a single day, but that somewhat defeats the purpose of a break from an otherwise outdoorsy destination. Instead, plan to spend at least one night in Edmonton, spoiling yourself at an upscale accommodation (the Union Bank Inn if a central location is important, The Varscona for a boutique splurge, or the Fantasyland Hotel if you have kids) and dining at one of the city's many fine restaurants. Regardless of your interests, West Edmonton Mall is the one attraction you won't want to miss. Even if shopping malls are not your idea of a vacation, the sheer excess of it all is an unforgettable eye-opener. In order of importance, plan on also visiting the Royal Alberta Museum, Fort Edmonton Park, and Muttart Conservatory.

The vast region north of Edmonton is a destination that can be included on an itinerary that continues north to the Northwest Territories or as a stand-alone vacation with the focus on outdoor activities such as canoeing, fishing, camping, or bird-watching. Specific highlights are often separated by a full day's drive. The exception to this is Elk Island National Park, close enough to Edmonton to make it part of a trip to that city. On a three-day loop from the capital, you could include this park, plus cultural highlights such as Métis Crossing and any one of a dozen provincial parks (with great canoeing and abundant wildlife, William A. Switzer Provincial Park is a personal favorite). Fort McMurray is the center of world attention for its oil sands, and although it's a long drive (or a short flight), a visit could be compared to spending time in a boomtown of a century ago, like Dawson City. But don't trek north without reservations for accommodation and a Syncrude or Suncor plant tour.

HISTORY

For at least 3,000 years, natives came to the river valley where Edmonton now stands, searching for quartzite to make stone tools. They had no knowledge of—or use for—the vast underground resources that would eventually cause a city to rise from the wilderness.

The First 100 Years

European fur traders, canoeing along the North Saskatchewan River, found the area where Edmonton now stands to be one of the richest fur-bearing areas on the continent. Large populations of beavers and muskrats lived in the surrounding spruce, poplar, and aspen forest. In 1795 a fort was established on the site of the present Legislature Building grounds. It was an ideal location for trading—Cree and Assiniboine could trade beaver, otter, and marten pelts in safety, without encroaching on the territory of fierce Plains Indians, such as the Blackfoot, yet the fort was far enough south to be within range of the Blackfoot, who came north with buffalo meat and other natural resources. After 100 years, the fur trade ended

NORTHERN ALBERTA

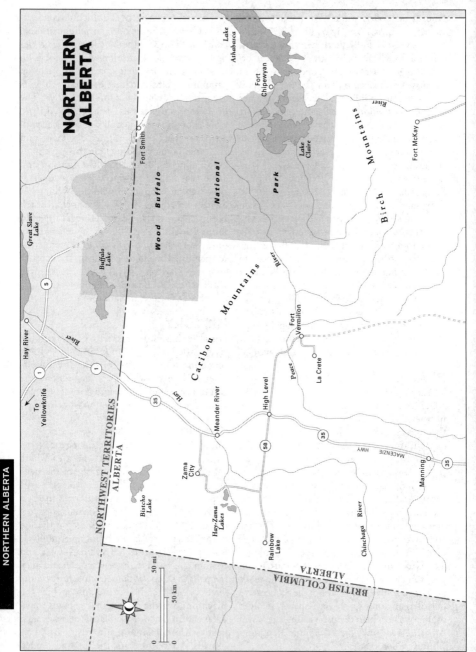

NORTHERN ALBERTA

NORTHERN ALBERTA

Lake Athabasca

Fort Chipewyan

Fort Smith

Great Slave Lake

Buffalo Lake

Wood   Buffalo   National   Park

Lake Claire

Birch   Mountains

River

Fort McKay

Hay River

River

5

1

To Yellowknife

1

35

Hay

Meander River

Caribou   Mountains

River

Fort Vermilion

High Level

Peace

La Crete

58

35

MACKENZIE   HWY

Manning

35

NORTHWEST TERRITORIES

ALBERTA

Zama City

Hay-Zama Lakes

Bistcho Lake

Rainbow Lake

Chinchaga   River

BRITISH COLUMBIA

ALBERTA

50 mi

50 km

0

0

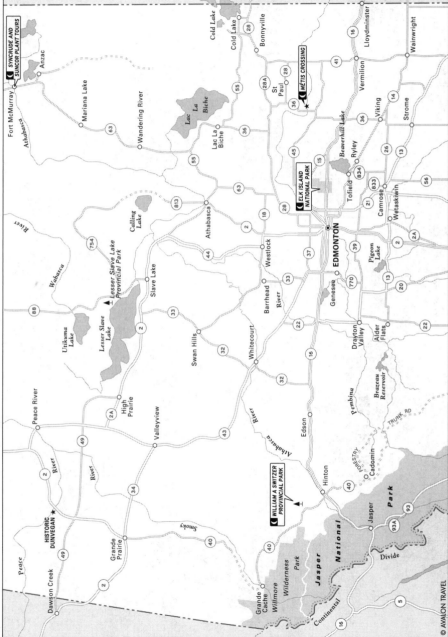

© AVALON TRAVEL

EDMONTON

To Fort Saskatchewan

To Lloydminster

To Fort McMurray

To Athabasca and Slave Lake

ALBERTA RAILWAY MUSEUM

North Saskatchewan River

MANNING DR

50TH ST

66TH ST

153RD AVE

82ND ST

112TH AVE

LA BOHEME

WAYNE GRETZKY DR

REXALL PLACE

NORTHLANDS

COMMONWEALTH STADIUM

EDMONTON CITY CENTRE AIRPORT

HOSPITAL

137TH AVE

167TH AVE

VIA RAIL STATION

ALBERTA AVIATION MUSEUM

111TH AVE

107TH AVE

142ND

TELUS WORLD OF SCIENCE

156TH ST

118TH

YELLOWHEAD HWY

170TH ST

ST ALBERT TRAIL

Sturgeon River

FATHER LACOMBE CHAPEL

ST VITAL AVE

ST ALBERT PLACE

LOIS HOLE CENTENNIAL PROVINCIAL PARK

SIR WINSTON CHURCHILL AVE

184TH ST

Big Lake

215TH ST

AVE

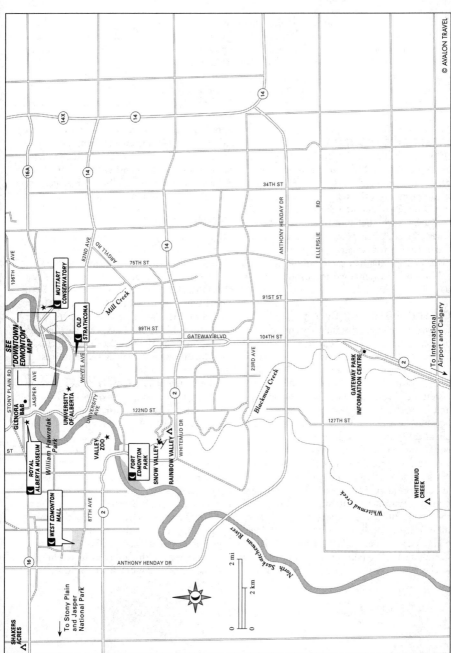

NORTHERN ALBERTA

abruptly as European fashions evolved. Many of the posts throughout the west were abandoned, but Edmonton continued to be an important stop on the route north. Goods were taken overland from Edmonton to Athabasca Landing, where they were transferred to barges or steamers and taken north on the Athabasca River.

Selecting the Capital

When the province of Alberta was inaugurated on September 1, 1905, the decision about a capital did not come easily. The Alberta Act made Edmonton the temporary capital, but it had plenty of competition, especially from Calgarians, who believed their city to be the financial and transportation center of the province. Heated debates on the subject took place in the Canadian capital of Ottawa, but Edmonton has remained the capital to this day.

Oil and a Growing City

Fur was Edmonton's first industry and coal was its second (the last of 150 operations closed in 1970), but Edmonton's future lay in oil. Since the discovery of "black gold" in 1947 at nearby Leduc, Edmonton has been one of Canada's fastest-growing cities. The building of pipelines and refineries created many jobs, and the city became the center of western Canada's petrochemical industry. As demand continued to rise, hundreds of wildcat wells were drilled around Edmonton. Farmers' fields were filled with derricks, valves, and oil tanks, and by 1956, more than 3,000 producing wells were pumping within 100 kilometers (62 miles) of the city. A 20-square-kilometer (eight-square-mile) area east of the city was filled with huge oil tanks, refineries, and petrochemical plants. Changes were also taking place within the city as the wealth of the oil boom began to take

hold. Restaurants improved and cultural life flourished. The city's businesses were jazzed up, and the expanding business community began moving into the glass-and-steel skyscrapers that form the city skyline today.

Currently experiencing the trickle down effects of another oil boom, planned developments in the surrounding service area total approximately $40 billion this decade, with Edmonton benefiting directly from spin-off infrastructure. A great deal of this development is associated with the **oil sands** of northern Alberta, with a new pipeline and processing facilities being built in the city.

ORIENTATION

Highway 2 from Calgary enters Edmonton from the south and divides just north of Gateway Park Tourist Information Centre. At that point, it becomes known as **Gateway Boulevard** (also known as **103rd St.**). Southbound, it's **Calgary Trail (104th St.)**. From the south, you can get to West Edmonton Mall and Highway 16 West by taking **Anthony Henday Drive,** which crosses the North Saskatchewan River southwest of downtown.

The **Yellowhead Highway** passes through the city east to west, north of downtown. To get downtown from the east, take 97th Street. From downtown, Jasper Avenue changes to Stony Plain Road as it heads west, eventually joining Highway 16 at the city's western limits.

Avenues run east to west, numbered from 1st Avenue in the south. Streets run north to south, numbered from 1st Street in the east. Even-numbered addresses are on the north sides of the avenues and west sides of the streets. The center of the city is crossed by both 101st Street and 101st Avenue, the latter having retained its original name of **Jasper Avenue.**

Sights

DOWNTOWN AND VICINITY

The downtown core, on the northern side of the North Saskatchewan River, is fairly compact and is within walking distance of many hotels. **Jasper Avenue** (101st Ave.) is downtown's main thoroughfare, lined with restaurants and shops. At the east end of Jasper Avenue is the **Shaw Conference Centre,** a glass-and-steel building that appears to cling to the wall of the river valley. On 102nd Street is the 36-story ManuLife Place, Edmonton's tallest building. A few blocks east is the **Arts District,** comprising the provincial government buildings, including the futuristic city hall, and an array of performing-arts centers. (The streets immediately east of 97th Street are a skid row with sleazy bars and suspicious-looking characters—not the place to linger at night.)

Throughout all of the development, several historic buildings managed to survive. Many can be seen along **Heritage Trail,** a route taken by early fur traders that linked the old town to Fort Edmonton. Today the trail begins at the Shaw Conference Centre, at the corner of Jasper Avenue and 97th Street, and ends at the legislature grounds. The path is easy to follow—the sidewalk is paved with red bricks and lined with period benches, replica lampposts, and old-fashioned street signs.

Arts District

This complex, in the heart of downtown, occupies six square blocks and is one of the city's showcases. Within its limits are the Stanley A. Milner Library, the Edmonton Art Gallery, Sir Winston Churchill Square, City Hall, the Law Courts Building, the Shaw Conference Centre, and the performing-arts community's pride and joy, the magnificent Citadel Theatre and adjacent Winspear Centre.

Opened in early 2010, the futuristic **Edmonton Art Gallery of Alberta** (northeast of Sir Winston Churchill Square on 99th St., 780/427-6223, Mon.–Wed. and Fri.

10:30 A.M.–5 P.M., Thurs. 10:30 A.M.–8 P.M., and Sat.–Sun. 11 A.M.–5 P.M., adult $10, senior $7, child $5) is an impressive 7,900-square-meter (85,000-square-foot) facility fronted by giant swirling steel curves representing the northern lights. The gallery houses an extensive collection of 4,000 modern Canadian paintings, as well as historical and contemporary art in all forms of media. Various traveling exhibitions are presented throughout the year. The exhibit From Sea to Sea: The Development of Canadian Art, catalogs the entire history of the country's art through well-designed displays. The gallery also offers a theater, gift shop, and café.

Chinatown

An elaborate gateway designed by a master architect from China welcomes visitors to where Edmonton's small Chinatown *used* to be. The gate spans 102nd Avenue at 97th Street; eight steel columns, painted the traditional Chinese color of red, support it. Stretched across the center of the arch's roof is a row of ornamental tiles featuring two dragons, the symbol of power in China. The 11,000 tiles used in the gate were each handcrafted and glazed in China. In the last few years, Chinatown has moved up the road a few blocks. The archway now leads into an area of cheap boardinghouses and deserted parking lots but forms a colorful break from the pawnshops of 97th Street.

Fairmont Hotel Macdonald

This hotel (10065 100th St.) overlooking the river valley has long been regarded as Edmonton's premier luxury accommodation. For many years, it was the social center of the city. It was built in 1915 by the Grand Trunk Railway in the same chateau style used for many of the Canadian Pacific hotels across the country. After it closed in 1983, plans to tear it down were aborted; $28 million was spent on refurbishing it and the hotel reopened, as grand and elegant as ever. The main lobby has been

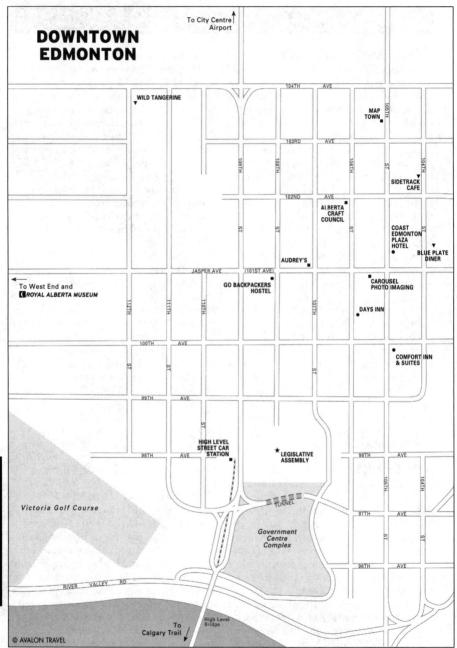

DOWNTOWN EDMONTON

To City Centre Airport

104TH AVE

WILD TANGERINE

MAP TOWN

103RD AVE

SIDETRACK CAFE

102ND AVE

ALBERTA CRAFT COUNCIL

COAST EDMONTON PLAZA HOTEL

BLUE PLATE DINER

AUDREY'S

JASPER AVE (101ST AVE)

To West End and ROYAL ALBERTA MUSEUM

GO BACKPACKERS HOSTEL

CAROUSEL PHOTO IMAGING

DAYS INN

100TH AVE

COMFORT INN & SUITES

99TH AVE

HIGH LEVEL STREET CAR STATION

LEGISLATIVE ASSEMBLY

98TH AVE

TUNNEL

Victoria Golf Course

Government Centre Complex

97TH AVE

96TH AVE

RIVER VALLEY RD

To Calgary Trail

High Level Bridge

© AVALON TRAVEL

NORTHERN ALBERTA

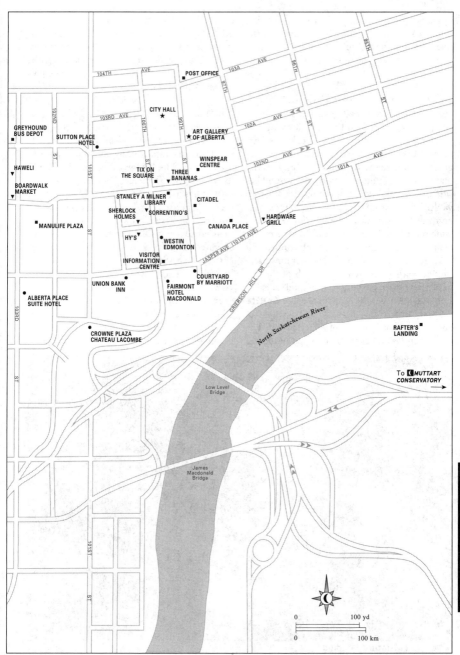

104TH AVE

POST OFFICE

103RD AVE

GREYHOUND BUS DEPOT

CITY HALL

103A AVE

SUTTON PLACE HOTEL

102A AVE

ART GALLERY OF ALBERTA

102ND AVE

HAWELI

WINSPEAR CENTRE

101A AVE

BOARDWALK MARKET

TIX ON THE SQUARE

THREE BANANAS

STANLEY A MILNER LIBRARY

CITADEL

MANULIFE PLAZA

SHERLOCK HOLMES

SORRENTINO'S

HARDWARE GRILL

CANADA PLACE

HY'S

WESTIN EDMONTON

JASPER AVE (101ST AVE)

VISITOR INFORMATION CENTRE

UNION BANK INN

COURTYARD BY MARRIOTT

FAIRMONT HOTEL MACDONALD

GRIERSON HILL DR

ALBERTA PLACE SUITE HOTEL

CROWNE PLAZA CHATEAU LACOMBE

North Saskatchewan River

RAFTER'S LANDING

To **(MUTTART CONSERVATORY**

Low Level Bridge

James Macdonald Bridge

0   100 yd

0   100 km

NORTHERN ALBERTA

totally restored and opens to the Confederation Lounge and The Library, a bar overlooking the river that has the feel of an Edwardian gentleman's club. Ask at the reception desk for a map of the hotel.

Alberta Legislature Building

Home of the provincial government, this elegant Edwardian building overlooking the North Saskatchewan River Valley is surrounded by 24 hectares (59 acres) of formal gardens and manicured lawns. It officially opened in 1912 and, for many years, stood beside the original Fort Edmonton. Its 16-story vaulted dome is one of Edmonton's most recognizable landmarks. The interior features a wide marble staircase that leads from the spacious rotunda in the lobby to the chamber, and is surrounded by stained-glass windows and bronze statues. Immediately north of the legislature building, beyond the fountains, is the **Legislative Assembly Interpretive Centre** (10820 98th Ave., 780/427-7362), which recounts the development of Alberta's political history and serves as the starting point for free tours of the Legislature Building. Between mid-May and October, tours depart daily on the hour in the morning from 9 A.M. and every 30 minutes in the afternoon weekdays until 5 P.M., the rest of the year hourly weekdays 9 A.M.–4 P.M. and weekends noon–4 P.M.

High Level Bridge

This bridge crosses the North Saskatchewan River at the bottom end of 109th Street. It was built in 1913, linking the new capital to Strathcona. The bridge is 775 meters (2,500 feet) long and 53 meters (180 feet) above the river. It has been used as a tramway, a railway, a sidewalk, and a roadway. A streetcar crosses the bridge from beside the Grandin LRT Station to as far south as Old Strathcona. The service operates mid-May to August 15 at 45 minutes past the hour Sunday–Friday 11 A.M.–4 P.M., Saturday 9 A.M.–4 P.M., and costs just $4 one-way.

In 1980, the **Great Divide Waterfall** was added to the bridge. When turned on, a curtain of water higher than Niagara Falls cascades down along the entire length of the bridge. It

Alberta Legislature Building

© ANDREW HEMPSTEAD

NORTHERN ALBERTA

usually operates during special events such as Capital Ex, Canada Day, and Sundays of long weekends in summer.

◖ Muttart Conservatory

Nestled in the valley on the south side of the North Saskatchewan River are four large pyramid-shaped greenhouses that make up the Muttart Conservatory (9626 96A St. off 98th Ave., 780/442-5311, Mon.–Fri. 9:30 A.M.–5:30 P.M., Sat. and Sun. 11 A.M.–5:30 P.M., adult $9.75, senior $7.25, child $5). Three of the greenhouses contain the flora of specific climates. In the arid pyramid are cacti and other hardy plants found in desert-like conditions. The tropical pyramid holds a humid jungle, one of North America's largest orchid collections, and colorful and raucous exotic birds, who live among the palms. The temperate pyramid features plant species from four continents, none of which would grow naturally in Edmonton's harsh environment. The contents of the fourth pyramid change with the season but always feature colorful floral displays such as red, white, and yellow poinsettias at Christmastime. Take bus number 85 or 86 south along 100th Street to get to the conservatory.

John Walter Museum

This historic site (10627 93rd Ave., 780/496-4852, Sun. 1–4 P.M. Feb.–Dec., donation), near the Kinsmen Sports Centre, consists of three houses—dating from 1875, 1884, and 1900—that were built by John Walter, who operated a ferry service for travelers to cross the river. Walter also opened a carriage works, a lumber mill, and a coalmine, and at one time even built a steamship. Today, each of the three houses feature exhibits corresponding to the period of its construction and depicting the growth of Edmonton and the importance of the North Saskatchewan River. On Sunday afternoons, the buildings are open with bread-making demonstrations, old-fashioned games, or some other related activity scheduled. The grounds are pleasant to walk through at any time.

Rutherford House

This elegant Edwardian mansion (11153 Saskatchewan Dr., 780/422-2697, daily 9 A.M.–5 P.M. in summer, Tues.–Sun. noon–5 P.M. the rest of the year) was built in 1911 for Alexander C. Rutherford, Alberta's first premier. The Rutherford family lived in this house for 30 years. The covered sun porch operates as a tearoom in summer (Tues.–Sun. 11:30 A.M.–4 P.M.), serving lunch ($8–11) and afternoon tea ($7–22), using historical recipes from 1915 or earlier. It's on the University of Alberta campus.

◖ Fort Edmonton Park

An authentic reconstruction of the early trading post from which Edmonton grew is only a small part of this exciting attraction (off Whitemud Dr. near Fox Dr., 780/496-8787, Mon.–Fri. 10 A.M.–4 P.M., Sat. and Sun. 10 A.M.–6 P.M. May and June, daily 10 A.M.–6 P.M. July and Aug., 10 A.M.–4 P.M. Sept., adult $13.50, senior $10.25, child $6.75), Canada's largest historic park. From the entrance, a 1919 steam locomotive takes you through the park to the Hudson's Bay Company Fort, which has been built much as the original fort would have looked like in 1846—right down to the methods of carpentry used in its construction. Step outside the fort and walk forward in time to 1885 Street, recreating downtown Edmonton between 1871 and 1891, when the West was opened up to settlers. The street is lined with wooden-facad shops such as a bakery, a boat builder, a blacksmith, and a trading post. As you continue down the road, you round a corner and are on 1905 Street, in the time period 1892–1914, when the railway had arrived and Edmonton was proclaimed provincial capital. **Reed's Tea Room,** near the far end of the street, serves English teas and scones noon–4 P.M. in a traditional atmosphere. By this time, you're nearly on 1920 Street, representing the years 1914–1929—a period of social changes when the business community was developing and the city's industrial base was expanding. Stop by Bill's Confectionary (noon–4 P.M.) for a soda or sundae, hitch a lift aboard the streetcar, or plan an overnight stay at the Hotel Selkirk to round out the roaring '20s experience.

What really makes this park come alive are the costumed interpreters, immersed in life as it was in the Edmonton of days gone by—preparing cakes and pastries for sale at the bakery, tending to carefully re-created vegetable plots, making butter beside the farmhouse, giving piano lessons to interested passersbys, or just getting together for a friendly game of horseshoes.

John Janzen Nature Centre

Beside Fort Edmonton Park (use the same parking lot) is John Janzen Nature Centre (780/496-2939, Mon.–Fri. 9 A.M.–4 P.M. year-round, longer hours and weekends in summer, adult $2, senior and child ($1.65), which has hands-on exhibits, displays of local flora and fauna (both dead and alive), and a four-kilometer (2.5-mile) self-guided interpretive trail that leads through the river valley and loops back to the center. In one room, various natural environments have been simulated with displays of frogs, fish, snakes, salamanders, and a working beehive made from glass. Throughout the year, special events are held, films are shown, and Sunday nature walks are conducted.

Valley Zoo

Across the river from Fort Edmonton Park is the city zoo (end of Buena Vista Rd., off 142nd St., 780/496-6911, May–Aug. 9:30 A.M.–6 P.M., the rest of the year daily 9:30 A.M.–4 P.M., adult $9.75, senior $7.25, child $5), which holds approximately 350 animals, representing all seven continents. It is designed mainly for kids, with a petting zoo, camel and pony rides, paddleboats, a miniature train, and cut-out storybook characters. To get there by bus, take number 12 west along 102nd Avenue to Buena Vista Road and walk 1.6 kilometers (one mile) down to the park. On summer Sundays, bus number 200 leaves on the hour from the University Transit Centre and goes right to the zoo.

◖ Royal Alberta Museum

The provincial museum (12845 102nd Ave., 780/453-9100, daily 9 A.M.–5 P.M., adult $10,

senior $8, child $5) overlooks the river valley west of downtown in the historic neighborhood of Glenora. Exhibits catalog one billion years of natural and human history. The highlight is most definitely the **Wild Alberta Gallery,** where a water setting and the province's four natural regions—mountain, prairie, parkland, and boreal forest—are re-created with incredible accuracy. Lifelike dioramas are only part of the appeal. Much of the exhibit encourages visitor interaction to solve the mystery of what is Alberta's most dangerous mammal, to touch the teeth of a grizzly bear, or soak up the sound of a bull moose calling the female members of his species. Elsewhere in the museum, the Natural History Gallery explains the forces that have shaped Alberta's land, describes the dinosaurs of the Cretaceous period and mammals of the Ice Age (such as the woolly mammoth), and displays a large collection of rocks and gems. Another section, the Syncrude Gallery of Aboriginal Culture, details Alberta's indigenous peoples—from their arrival 11,000 years ago to the way in which their traditions live on today—through thousands of artifacts, Aboriginal interpreters, and audiovisual presentations.

In front of the museum is **Government House** (780/427-2281, tours Sun. 11 A.M.–4:30 P.M. in summer, free), an impressive three-story sandstone structure built in 1913 for Alberta's lieutenant governor, who would entertain guests in the lavish reception rooms or in the surrounding gardens. The building was later used as a hospital, and then restored to its former glory in the 1970s.

Telus World of Science

This multipurpose complex in Coronation Park (11211 142nd St., 780/452-9100, daily 10 A.M.–5 P.M., until 9 P.M. in summer, adult $14, senior $12, child $9.50) is one of Edmonton's major attractions and most recognizable landmarks. Displays are spread over three levels and six galleries, including a look into the future of communications, the chance to solve a crime along Mystery Avenue, a ham radio station hooked up to similar stations around the world, a weather display that includes an audiovisual of the deadly tornado that hit Edmonton in the summer of 1987, a tribute to Royal Canadian Mounted Police (RCMP), a theater where laser light shows are presented daily noon–7 P.M., a chance to learn about the environment in Green's House, a learning room especially for younger kids, and an interactive gallery where you are encouraged to try sports such as wheelchair racing. Also in the building, an **IMAX Theatre** presents spectacular video productions—seemingly always of an interesting nature—adult $14, senior $12, child $9.50 for the theater only; $22.50, $19, and $15.25, respectively, for admission to one IMAX feature and the other displays.

◖ OLD STRATHCONA

When the Calgary and Edmonton Railway Company completed a rail line between the province's two largest cities, it decided to end it south of the North Saskatchewan River and establish a townsite there, rather than build a bridge and end the line in Edmonton. The town was named Strathcona, and it grew to a population of 7,500 before merging with Edmonton in 1912. Because of an early fire-prevention bylaw, buildings were built of brick. Today many still remain, looking much as they did at the turn of the 20th century. Old Strathcona is Edmonton's best-preserved historical district. In addition to the historical buildings, the area has been refurbished with brick sidewalks and replica lampposts.

The best way to get to Old Strathcona from downtown is aboard the **High Level Street Car** (780/437-7721), which runs from the west side of the Alberta Legislature Building to the 104th Street and 85th Avenue intersection on Old Strathcona. It departs downtown mid-May to August 15 at 45 minutes past the hour Sunday–Friday 11 A.M.–4 P.M., and Saturday 9 A.M.–4 P.M. in summer only, $4 one-way. From the station, wander south to bustling Whyte Avenue.

Sights

The commercial core of Old Strathcona is centered along Whyte (82nd) Avenue west of the rail line. More than 75 residential houses built before 1926 are scattered to the north and west of Whyte Avenue. Across from the rail line is the **Strathcona Hotel** (corner of 103rd St. and Whyte Ave.), one of the few wood-framed buildings surviving from the pre-1900 period. Before Strathcona had permanent churches, congregations worshiped in the hotel, and during Prohibition it was used as a women's college. The two blocks east of the hotel are lined with cafés and restaurants, used bookstores, and many interesting shops. In a converted bus garage one block north is the **Old Strathcona Farmer's Market** (10310 83rd Ave., 780/439-1844, Sat. 8 A.M.–3 P.M. year-round), with plenty of fresh produce, crafts, and homemade goodies for sale. Within walking distance of Whyte Avenue are several small museums

Many of the historic buildings have plaques at street level, but the brochures *A Walk Through Old Strathcona* and *Historical Walking and Driving Tour: Strathcona* make a stroll much more interesting. For more information on the district, contact the **Old Strathcona Foundation** (780/433-5866, www.oldstrathconafoundation.ca).

◖ WEST EDMONTON MALL

Feel like a trip to the beach to do some sunbathing and surfing? Would you like to play a round of golf? How about launching from the world's only indoor bungee jump? Do you like eating at Parisian cafés? Does watching a National Hockey League team in training seem like a good way to spend the afternoon? Do the kids like sea lion shows? And at the end of the day, would you like to sink into a hot tub, surrounded by a lush tropical forest? All of these activities are possible under one roof at West Edmonton Mall, the largest shopping and indoor amusement complex in the whole world. Calgary may have the greatest *outdoor* show on earth, but Edmonton has what can surely be billed as the greatest *indoor* show on earth, a place that is visited by 22 million people annually. Much more than an oversized shopping mall, Edmonton's top tourist attraction is a

WEST EDMONTON MALL

90TH AVE

PARKING

MAIN LEVEL

MINI GOLF

BOURBON STREET

GUEST SERVICES

178TH ST

Deep Sea Adventure

ICE PALACE

INFORMATION BOOTH

FANTASYLAND HOTEL

World Waterpark

GALAXYLAND AMUSEMENT PARK

SEARS

170TH ST

THE BAY

PARKING

TRANSIT STATION

PARKING

ZELLERS

87TH AVE

SCALE NOT AVAILABLE

© AVALON TRAVEL

shop-and-play four-season wonderland, where many visitors check into the 355-room luxury Fantasyland Hotel, stay a weekend, and never set foot outside the mall's 58 entrances.

Mall Attractions

Galaxyland Amusement Park (adult $31.95, families $84.95, senior or those under four feet $24.95) is the world's largest indoor amusement park, with 25 rides, including Mindbender—a 14-story, triple-loop roller coaster (the world's largest indoor roller coaster)—and Space Shot, a 13-story, heart-pounding free fall. Off to one side, Galaxy Kids Playpark offers the younger generation the same thrills and spills in a colorful, fun-loving atmosphere. Admission to the Playpark is free, but the rides cost money.

In the two-hectare (five-acre) **World Waterpark** (adult $31.95, families $84.95, senior or those under four feet $24.95) you

almost feel as though you're at the beach: The temperature is a balmy 30°C (85°F), and a long, sandy beach (with special nonslip sand), tropical palms, colorful cabanas, a beach bar, and waves crashing on the shore all simulate the real thing. The computerized wave pool holds 12.3 million liters (2.7 million gallons) of water and is programmed by computer to eject "sets" of waves at regular intervals. Behind the beach are 22 water slides that rise to a height of 26 meters (85 feet). The World Waterpark also has the world's only indoor bungee jump, **Center for Gravity** (780/489-4339, $75), three whirlpools, and a volleyball court.

At the same end of the mall as World Waterpark is the world's largest indoor lake. Here, you can gawk at the area along its entire 122-meter (400-foot) length from either the main or second floor of the mall. The most dominant feature of the lagoon is a full-size

WEST EDMONTON MALL TRIVIA

WEST EDMONTON MALL IS:

- the world's largest shopping and amusement complex, encompassing 483,000 square meters (5.3 million square ft) – that's equivalent to 115 football fields

WEST EDMONTON MALL HAS:

- over 800 stores

- over 100 eateries

- 58 entrances

- 21 movie screens

- 325,000 light bulbs

- five postal codes

- the world's largest parking lot (parking for 20,000 vehicles)

- the world's largest indoor amusement park

- the world's largest water park, covering two hectares (five acres) and containing 12.3 million liters (2.7 million gallons) of water

- the world's largest indoor lake (122 m/400 ft long)

- the world's tallest indoor bungee jump

WEST EDMONTON MALL:

- cost over one billion dollars to construct

- employs 23,500 people

- uses the same amount of power as a city of 50,000

- attracts 22 million people a year (over 60,000 per day)

replica of Christopher Columbus's flagship, the *Santa Maria*. You can jump aboard a bumper boat ($4 for five minutes); descend into the depths of the **Sea Life Caverns** ($5.95 per person) to view sharks, penguins, and a variety of colorful fish; or take a scuba-diving course.

Other major attractions in the mall include **Professor WEM's Adventure Golf** (adult $10, senior and child $7); and, smack in the middle of the mall, the **Ice Palace** (adult $8, senior or child $6, skate rental $4), an NHL-size skating rink. Three themed streets, **Europa Boulevard, Chinatown,** and the glitzy New Orleans–style **Bourbon Street** feature some of the mall's 100 restaurants and eateries.

Hours and Other Practicalities

Shopping hours vary seasonally but are generally Monday–Saturday 10 A.M.–9 P.M. and Sunday noon–6 P.M. Hours of the various attractions and restaurants vary. Many restaurants stay open later, and the nightclubs stay open to the early hours of the morning.

Mall maps color-code each of four phases to make finding your way around easier (shops and attractions use a phase number as part of their address). The information center is on the main level near the Ice Palace; the tech-savvy can download a Mobile Mall Map to their mobile devices. When your legs tire, scooter rentals are available near the information booth; $6 for the first hour, $4 for each additional hour.

For more information, contact West Edmonton Mall at 780/444-5200, www.west-edmontonmall.com. The mall is on 170th Street, between 87th and 90th Avenues. Parking is usually not a problem, but finding your car again can be, so remember which of the 58 entrances you parked near (a parking lot along 90th Ave. at 175th St. is designated for RVs). From downtown, take bus number 100.

DEVON
Devonian Botanic Garden

These gardens (780/987-3054, July–Aug. Mon.–Wed. 10 A.M.–6 P.M., Thurs.–Sun. 10 A.M.–8 P.M., May and Sept. daily 10 A.M.–5 P.M., adult $13, senior $8.50, child

$5), developed by the University of Alberta, are southwest of the city and five kilometers (3.1 miles) north of the small town of Devon. The highlight is the **Kurimoto Japanese Garden,** one of the world's northernmost authentic Japanese gardens. The various natural elements are complemented by an ornamental gate, an arched bridge, and decorative lanterns. Other features are the large Alpine Garden, with examples of plants from mountainous regions; the Herb Garden, where, in August, the aroma is almost overpowering; the Peony Collection, which is at its most colorful in July; a greenhouse filled with plants unique to the Southern Hemisphere; and the Native People's Garden, which is surrounded by water and showcases plants used by the native people of Alberta.

ST. ALBERT

The city of St. Albert (population 59,000)—northwest of Edmonton along the St. Albert Trail—is one of Alberta's oldest settlements but has today become part of Edmonton's sprawl. Albert Lacombe, a pioneering western Canadian priest, built a mansion overlooking the Sturgeon River in 1861, when Fort Edmonton was only a small trading post. A sawmill and gristmill were constructed, and by 1870, St. Albert was the largest agricultural community west of Winnipeg.

Sights

Father Lacombe's first log chapel, the **Father Lacombe Chapel** (west of Hwy. 2 on St. Vital Ave., 780/459-7663, daily 10 A.M.–6 P.M. mid-May–Aug., adult $2, senior and child $1.50), was built in 1861. In front of the chapel, a cast-iron statue of Father Lacombe that was made in France overlooks the city. The imposing building beside the chapel is **Vital Grandin Centre,** built in 1887 as a hospital. Down in the river valley is **St. Albert Place**

FATHER ALBERT LACOMBE

Dressed in a tattered black robe and brandishing a cross, Father Albert Lacombe, known to natives as "the man with the good heart," dedicated his life to those with native blood. His reputation extended to every corner of the province – he was a spokesman for the Church, an effective influence on government policies, and, most importantly, he had a hand in just about every advance in the often-tense relationship between warring tribes and white men.

Father Lacombe originally came to what is now Alberta in 1852 to serve the Métis and natives who had moved to Fort Edmonton, later founding a mission at what is now St. Albert. He traveled widely, instigating Canada's first industrial school for natives, mediating a dispute between the railway company and angry leaders of the Blackfoot over rights to build a rail line through a reserve, and he wrote the first Cree dictionary. The trust he built up with native leaders was great; during one rebellion of the Blackfoot Confederacy, it is claimed that his influence prevented the slaughter of every white man on the prairies.

FATHER LACOMBE, O.M.I.

A MISSIONARY   UN MISSIONNAIRE
& PIONEER   & PIONNIER
OF THE NORTHWEST. DU NORD-OUEST.

© ANDREW HEMPSTEAD

on St. Anne Street, a contoured brick building designed by Douglas Cardinal. Inside is the **Musée Heritage Museum** (780/459-1528, Tues.–Sat. 10 A.M.–5 P.M., Sun. 1–5 P.M., donation), with displays telling the story of St. Albert's history and the people who made it happen. From the museum, walk along the river (three km/1.9 mi) or drive (take Sir Winston Churchill Ave. to Riel Dr.) to **Lois Hole Centennial Provincial Park,** protecting Big Lake and surrounding wetlands. Here, bird-watchers have the chance to see some 40 species of water and wading birds, including trumpeter swans.

Recreation

River Valley Park System

One of the first things you'll notice about Edmonton is its large amount of parkland. The city has more land set aside for parks, per capita, than any other city in Canada. Most parks interconnect along the banks of the North Saskatchewan River and in adjoining ravines, encompassing 7,400 hectares (18,300 acres) and comprising the largest stretch of urban parkland in North America. Within these parks are picnic areas, swimming pools, historic sites, golf courses, and many kilometers of walking and biking trails. One of the larger individual parks is **William Hawrelak Park,** west of the university along Groat Road. A one-way road loops through the park, circling a lake with paddleboats and fishing, passing many quiet picnic areas and an outdoor amphitheater that hosts a wide range of summer events.

The River Valley Park System provides ample opportunity for cross-country skiing. More than 75 kilometers (47 miles) of trails are groomed from December to early March. The most popular areas are in William Hawrelak Park, up Mill Creek Ravine, and through Capilano Park. The **Kinsmen Sports Centre** (780/944-7400) has cross-country ski rentals; $12 for two hours, or $18 per day, including boots and poles.

Swimming and Fitness Centers

It's often crowded, it's commercial, and it's not cheap, but Edmonton's ultimate swimming, sliding, and sunbathing experience awaits at **World Waterpark** in the West Edmonton Mall (170th St. and 87th Ave., 780/444-5200, adult $31.95, families $84.95, senior or those under four feet $24.95).

Edmonton's outdoor swimming season lasts approximately three months beginning at the end of May. Of the five outdoor pools owned by the city, the one in **Queen Elizabeth Park** is in a particularly picturesque location among poplar trees and with a view of the city skyline over the river; access is from 90th Avenue. Another pool, close to the city center, is in **Mill Creek Park,** north of Whyte Avenue (82nd Ave.) on 95A Street. Admission to all outdoor pools is $4. When the weather gets cooler, or to take advantage of more facilities, head to one of the city's many indoor pools, where admission includes the use of saunas, a hot tub, weight rooms, and water slides. The largest of these is **Kinsmen Sports Centre** (9100 Walterdale Hill, 780/944-7400), on the south side of the North Saskatchewan River. Admission of adult $8, senior $6, child $4, includes use of the pools, fitness center, sauna, and jogging track, all of which were given a thorough upgrade in early 2007. For information on all city-operated pools, call 780/496-7946.

Golf

Canada's oldest municipal course is the **Victoria Golf Course** (west of the Legislature Building along River Road, 780/496-4710, $38–46), which is still owned and operated by the city. This 18-hole course is only a little more than 6,000 yards in length but is made challenging by narrow fairways and smallish greens.

As a keen golfer, I can highly recommend the

HOCKEY: CANADA'S UNOFFICIAL NATIONAL SPORT

Ask most people – even Canadians – what the national sport of Canada is and they'll say "ice hockey" (simply "hockey" to Canadians), or you'll get a wacky answer like "dog-mushing." Although both answers are wrong (lacrosse is the official national sport), don't try telling that to the fans of the **Edmonton Oilers** (780/414-4625 or 866/414-4625, www.edmontonoilers.com), or to fans in Calgary and Vancouver, also home to franchises that compete in the National Hockey League for the Stanley Cup.

During the 1980s, when Wayne Gretzky was leading the Oilers, the Cup resided almost permanently in Edmonton, "City of Champions." Since 1988, when Gretzky was sold to the L.A. Kings, the team has met with mixed success, although they did reach the Stanley Cup final in 2006. Home games are played September–April in Rexall Place. From downtown, the easiest way to get there is by LRT to the Coliseum station. Tickets cost from $60 and go all the way up to $225 for rink-side seats.

following courses that have opened in the last decade: 7,330-yard **RedTail Landing** (Hwy. 2 by the airport, 780/890-7888, $95), a links-style layout with well-placed bunkers and multiple

water hazards; **The Ranch** (52516 Range Rd., Spruce Grove, 780/470-4700, $75), featuring a water-lined trio of finishing holes; and **Northern Bear** (Township Rd. 510, 780/922-2327, $95), designed by Jack Nicklaus.

Tours

If you are pressed for time, or even if you're not, a guided tour of Edmonton may be a good idea. The big tour companies bypass Edmonton, leaving a variety of small operators to offer personalized service and flexible schedules. As you'd expect from a former museum guide, Cameron Malcolm of **Out an' About Tours** (780/909-8687, www.outanabouttours. com) emphasizes the heritage and culture of Edmonton and Old Strathcona on his half-day Alberta Past & Present Tour ($65), with the option to add a visit to Fort Edmonton Park ($65). Wayne Millar of **Watchable Wildlife** (780/405-4880, www.birdsandbackcountry. com) leads visitors through regional parks. Wayne's forte is the areas east of Edmonton, including Elk Island National Park and the Cooking Lake Moraine (three-hour evening tour is $79).

The **Edmonton Queen** (Rafter's Landing, 9734 98th Ave., 780/424-2628) is a 52-meter (170-foot) paddle wheeler that departs across from Muttart Conservatory for cruises along the North Saskatchewan River. One-hour cruises depart Friday–Sunday at noon and 3 P.M. ($18, child under 11 $12, lunch extra), evening cruises depart at 7:30 P.M. (adult $48, child under 11 $22, including dinner).

Arts, Entertainment, and Shopping

For details on theater events throughout the city, a listing of art galleries, what's going on where in the music scene, cinema screenings, and a full listing of festivals and events, pick up a free copy of **See Magazine** (www. seemagazine.com) or **Vue Weekly** (www. vueweekly.com). Both are published every Thursday and are available all around town,

with all the same information presented on the respective websites. Tickets to most major performances are available from **Tix on the Square** (Sir Winston Churchill Square, 9930 102nd Ave., 780/420-1757, www.tixonthesquare.ca, Mon.–Fri. 9:30 A.M.–6 P.M., Sat. 9:30 A.M.–4 P.M.), a non-profit outlet operated by the local arts council.

NIGHTLIFE
Bars and Nightclubs

The **Sidetrack Cafe** (10238 104th St., 780/421-1326) is central to downtown, serves excellent food, and presents live entertainment nightly from 9 P.M. Shows change dramatically—one night it might be stand-up comedians, the next a blues band, then jazz the following night—and the only thing you can rely on is that it will be busy. Monday is usually comedy night and Sunday variety night. Cover charges vary; $4–10 is normal. Downtown, the **Sherlock Holmes** (10012 101A Ave., 780/426-7784) serves a large selection of British and Irish ales and is the place to go on St. Patrick's Day (March 17). The rest of the year, drinkers are encouraged to join in nightly sing-alongs with the pianist. Sherlock Holmes also has locations in Old Strathcona (10341 82nd Ave., 780/433-9676) and along West Edmonton Mall's Bourbon Street (780/444-1752). Old Strathcona is also home to **O'Byrne's Irish Pub** (10616 82nd Ave., 780/414-6766), where Celtic bands often play. The **Stonehouse Pub,** a few blocks west of downtown (11012 Jasper Ave., 780/420-0448), attracts an older crowd, with classic rock and roll pumping from the jukebox. It has an outdoor patio, plenty of pool tables, big-screen TVs, and nightly drink specials. **Confederation Lounge** (Fairmont Hotel Macdonald, 10065 100th St., 780/424-5181) oozes old-time style while **Bellamy's** (Crowne Plaza Chateau Lacombe, 10111 Bellamy Hill, 780/428-6611) is a quiet space with river views.

Cook County Saloon (8010 Gateway Blvd., 780/432-2665) is consistently voted Canada's Best Country Nightclub by the Canadian Country Music Association. Its mellow honky-tonk ambience draws crowds, and Canadian and international performers play here. Free two-step lessons are offered on select weeknights, and on Friday and Saturday nights the action really cranks up with live entertainment and a DJ spinning country Top 40 discs. On these two nights, the cover is $8 after 8 P.M. Beyond West Edmonton Mall is **Cowboys** (10102 180th St., 780/481-8739), with a Western theme but attracting a young, frat-like crowd with theme nights, popular promotions, white-hatted and scantily clad shooter girls, and a huge dance floor.

Jazz and Comedy

The Edmonton Jazz Society is a volunteer-run organization that manages the **Yardbird Suite** (11 Tommy Banks Way., 780/432-0428, www.yardbirdsuite.com). Live jazz fills the air nightly 10 P.M.–2 A.M. September–June. Admission is $5–24. The **Full Moon Folk Club** (www.fmfc.org) sponsors visiting performers at a variety of venues, including St. Basil's Cultural Centre (10819 71st St.); tickets are well priced at approximately $15.

At **Yuk Yuk's Komedy Kabaret** (Century Casino, 13103 Fort Rd. NW, 780/481-9857, www.yukyuks.com), show times vary, but generally, Wednesday is amateur night, and the pros hit the stage Thursday–Saturday. Tickets are $5–19.

PERFORMING ARTS

Edmonton's 14 theater companies present productions at various locations all year long. For most companies, September–May is the main season. The **Citadel** (9828 101A Ave., 780/425-1820 or 888/425-1820, www.citadeltheatre.com) is Canada's largest theater facility, taking up an entire downtown block. From the outside, it looks like a gigantic greenhouse; one entire side is glass, enclosing a magnificent indoor garden complete with a walking paths and benches. The complex houses five theaters: The Maclab Theatre showcases the work of teens and children; the intimate Rice Theatre features mainly experimental and innovative productions; Zeidler Hall hosts films, lectures, and children's theater; Tucker Amphitheatre presents concerts and recitals across a pond and surrounded by tropical greenery, and often puts on small lunchtime stage productions; and Shoctor Theatre is the main stage for the Citadel's long-running subscription program ($28–65 per production).

For slightly more adventurous productions and occasional international imports, see what's

NORTHERN ALBERTA

going on at the **Northern Light Theatre** (11516 103rd St., 780/471-1586, www.northernlighttheatre.com, $20). Edmonton's oldest theater is the **Walterdale Playhouse** (10322 83rd Ave., 780/439-2845, www.walterdaleplayhouse.com, from $8), in the heart of Old Strathcona, which presents historical and humorous material through an October–June season in a 1910 fire hall.

In the heart of the Arts District is the magnificent **Winspear Centre** (corner of 99th St. and 102nd Ave., www.winspearcentre.com), a venue renowned as an acoustic wonder that is also capable of producing high-quality amplified sound. It is home to the **Edmonton Symphony Orchestra** (780/428-1414 or 800/563-1108, www.edmontonsymphony.com, $29–48) and attracts a wide variety of national and international musical acts, ranging from choirs to classical performers. Both the **Edmonton Opera** (780/429-1000, www.edmontonopera.com) and the **Alberta Ballet** (780/428-6839, www.albertaballet.com) perform at the Jubilee Auditorium in the University of Alberta (11455 87th Avenue).

SHOPPING

Naturally, any talk of a shopping trip to Edmonton includes **West Edmonton Mall** (at 87th Ave. and 170th St.), the world's largest shopping and amusement complex; the mall is covered under **Sights,** earlier in this chapter. Downtown's major shopping centers are **City Centre** and **ManuLife Place,** while on the southern outskirts, **South Edmonton Common** (corner Gateway Blvd and 23rd Ave.) provides a home for 35 big-box stores.

Camping Gear and Western Wear

Downtown, **Uniglobe Geo Travel** (10237 109th St., 780/424-8310) stocks a wide range of travel clothing and accessories, and also operates as a travel agency. **Mountain Equipment Co-op,** a Canadian outdoor equipment cooperative similar to R.E.I. in the United States, is west of the Royal Alberta Museum (12328 102nd Ave., 780/488-6614). Across the railway tracks from Old Strathcona is **Track 'n'**

Trail (10148 82nd Ave., 780/432-1707), which carries a wide variety of cross-country skiing, camping, and climbing gear.

Alberta's largest supplier of western wear is **Lammle's,** with five outlets through the city, including one in West Edmonton Mall (Phase I, 780/444-7877). High-quality boots are also sold by **Diablo Boots** (3440 Gateway Blvd., 780/435-2592).

Art Galleries

Scattered throughout the city are commercial art galleries, many of which exhibit and sell Canadian and native art. Eight galleries within six blocks of each other and the corner of Jasper Avenue and 124th Street have formed the **Gallery Walk Association of Edmonton** (www.gallery-walk.com). All are worth visiting, but the **Bearclaw Gallery** (10403 124th St., 780/482-1204) is of special note for those searching out the unique art of the First Nations. Tucked in among the shoe shops and souvenir stands in West Edmonton Mall is **Northern Images** (780/444-1995), also with a good collection of native and northern arts and crafts. Finally, headquarters for the **Alberta Craft Council** is the Edmonton store (10186 106th St., 780/488-6611).

Bookstores

Of the independent bookstores, **Audrey's** (10702 Jasper Ave., 780/423-3487, Mon.–Fri. 9 A.M.–9 P.M., Sat. 9:30 A.M.–5:30 P.M., Sun. noon–5 P.M.) has the city's largest collection of travel guides, western Canadiana, and general travel writing on two vast floors. **Map Town** (10344 105th St., 780/429-2600, Mon.–Fri. 9 A.M.–5:30 P.M., Sat. 10 A.M.–5 P.M.) stocks the provincial 1:50,000 and 1:250,000 topographical map series along with city maps, world maps, Alberta wall maps, travel guides, field guides, atlases, and a huge selection of specialty maps.

Old Strathcona is an excellent place for browsing through used bookstores. **Wee Book Inn** (10310 82nd Ave., 780/432-7230) is the largest and stocks more recent titles and a large collection of magazines. **Alhambra Books**

(10115 81st Ave., 780/439-4195) specializes in Canadiana and has an extensive collection of Albertan material, including pamphlets and newspapers. **Athabasca Books** (8228 105th St., 780/431-1776) stocks mostly history and literature books. Old Strathcona has only two new-book stores. They are **Greenwood's** (7925 104th St., 780/439-2005), which stocks a lot of everything, and **Chapters** (10504 82nd Ave., 780/435-1290).

Festivals and Events

Spring

The **International Children's Festival** (780/459-1542, www.childfest.com) takes place the weekend closest to June 1 in the Arden Theatre, St. Albert. Acts from around the world include theater, music, dance, storytelling, and puppetry.

The Works: Art & Design Festival (780/426-2122, www.theworks.ab.ca) features art exhibitions on the streets, in parks, and in art galleries through Old Strathcona for two weeks from late June.

During the last week of June through early July, the **Edmonton International Jazz Festival** (780/990-0222, www.edmontonjazz. com) is held at various indoor and outdoor venues, including the renowned Yardbird Suite. Many foreign performers make appearances.

Summer

For 10 days in early July, downtown's Winston Churchill Square comes alive during the **Edmonton International Street Performers Festival** (780/425-5162, www. edmontonstreetfest.com), with almost 1,000 performances by magicians, comics, jugglers, musicians, and mimes.

The 10-day **Capital Ex** (780/471-7210, www.capitalex.ca) beginning on the third Thursday of each July, kicks off with a massive parade through downtown. Much of the activity is centered on Northlands (7300 116th St.), featuring a midway, casino, free music concerts, gold-panning, the Alberta Tattoo, the RCMP musical ride, thoroughbred racing, the Global Connections pavilion featuring an international marketplace, and a trade show of upscale arts and crafts. This is the city's biggest annual event, attracting approximately 800,000 visitors, so be prepared for big crowds everywhere. Running in conjunction with Capital Ex is **Taste of Edmonton** (Sir Winston Churchill Square, 780/423-2822, www.eventsedmonton. ca), where visitors can sample signature dishes from Edmonton's wide range of restaurants.

Fifty outdoor ethnic pavilions at Hawrelak Park are just a small part of the **Heritage Festival** (780/488-3378, www.heritage-festival.com), which is held on the August Long Weekend as a celebration of the city's multicultural roots. Visitors to the festival have the opportunity to experience international singing and dancing, arts-and-crafts displays, costumes, and cuisine from more than 60 cultures.

During the **Edmonton Folk Music Festival** (780/429-1999, www.edmontonfolkfest. org), held on the second weekend of August, Gallagher Park comes alive with the sound of blues, jazz, country, Celtic, traditional, and bluegrass music. Tickets are $55 per day, although advance weekend passes are better value for keen folkies.

Quickly becoming one of the city's most popular events is the **Fringe Theatre Festival** (780/448-9000, www.fringetheatreadventures. ca), a 10-day extravaganza that begins on the second Thursday in August. It is held throughout Old Strathcona, in parks, on the streets, in parking garages, and in the area's historic restored theaters. With more than 1,000 performances and a crowd of half a million looking on, the festival has become North America's largest alternative-theater event, attracting artists from around the world. Tickets are generally inexpensive.

Symphony under the Sky (780/428-1414, www.edmontonsymphony.com), held on the weekend closest to August 31, is the last gasp in Edmonton's busy summer festival schedule. Led by the Edmonton Symphony Orchestra, this five-day extravaganza of classical music takes place in William Hawrelak Park.

Fall and Winter

Farmfair International (780/471-7210, www. farmfairinternational.com) showcases some of North America's best livestock through sales and auctions, but exhibits, a trade show, the judging of Miss Rodeo Canada, and thousands of farm animals draw in casual visitors. The fair takes place at Northlands the second week of November. That same week, Rexall Place hosts the **Canadian Finals Rodeo** (780/471-7210, www.canadianfinalsrodeo.com). This $500,000 event is the culmination of the year's work for Canada's top 10 money-earning cowboys and cowgirls in seven traditional rodeo events. The action takes place Wednesday–Sunday at 7 P.M. and Sunday at 1 P.M.

Accommodations and Camping

Nearly all of Edmonton's best hotels are located downtown. Other concentrations of motels can be found along Gateway Boulevard (Hwy. 2 from the south) and scattered along Stony Plain Road in the west. The towns of Leduc and Nisku have several motels close to Edmonton International Airport. Other options include bed-and-breakfasts, two backpacker lodges, and camping (just five minutes from downtown, or in campgrounds west, east, or south of the city).

DOWNTOWN

All but two of the following accommodations (Glenora B&B Inn and La Boheme are the exceptions) are within walking distance of each other within the downtown core. As with city hotels around the world, parking is extra ($15–25), but may be included with weekend rates.

Under $50

Housed in one of the few older downtown hotels to escape the wrecking ball is **Go Backpackers Hostel** (10815 Jasper Ave., 780/423-4146 or 877/646-7835, www.gohostels.ca, dorm beds $25–28, $70–80 d), a few blocks from the heart of the city and surrounded by cafés, restaurants, and pubs. The hostelry has a total of 184 beds in eight- and four-bed dorms, and a few private twin and double rooms. Facilities include two lounges, a communal kitchen, and public Internet access in the lobby.

$50-100

Between downtown and the Royal Alberta Museum, **Glenora B&B Inn** (12327 102nd Ave., 780/488-6766 or 877/453-6672, www. glenorabnb.com, $70–155 s, $90–175 d) is a short walk from the galleries of 124th Street. The building that houses this bed-and-breakfast was built as a commercial enterprise in 1912 and has been completely renovated with the guest rooms above a guest parlor and street-level restaurant where a full breakfast is served (included in rates). Even the least expensive rooms have an en suite bathroom, or pay extra for a Medium Suite, with basic cooking facilities.

$100-150

Sure, it's a chain hotel, but **Comfort Inn Edmonton** (10425 100th Ave., 780/423-5611 or 888/384-6835, www.comfortinnedmonton. com, $110–150 s or d) is a good choice. The 108 rooms are sensibly furnished for both leisure and business travelers. Parking, local calls, and in-room coffee are complimentary.

The **Days Inn** (10041 106th St., 780/423-1925 or 800/329-7466, www.daysinn.com, from $119 s or d) is another solid choice in the same neighborhood. Parking and wireless Internet are included. The in-house restaurant is open 6:30 A.M.–9 P.M. and a lounge stays open until midnight.

No, it's not downtown, but it's close. **La Boheme** (6427 112th Ave., 780/474-5693, www.laboheme.ca, $125 s, $155 d) is in the historic Gibbard building, which originally held Edmonton's first luxury apartments. Today, the La Boheme restaurant downstairs is one of the city's best, and six upstairs rooms have been graciously refurnished and are run as a bed-and-breakfast. The building is certainly charming, right down to its creaky floors. Each of the simply furnished rooms has a separate sleeping area. Rates include a continental breakfast.

If you plan to be in the city for a few days and want to cook your own meals, suite hotels (also called apartment hotels) offer a good value. **Alberta Place Suite Hotel** (10049 103rd St., 780/423-1565 or 800/661-3982, www.alberta-place.com, $112–179 s or d) is one of the best choices. The 84 suites are large, and each has a well-equipped kitchen. Continental breakfast and daily papers are complimentary, a Hertz agent is on-site (discounted rentals for guests), and Jasper Avenue is only half a block away.

$150-200

If you're looking for accommodations in this price category, it's very hard to do better than the ((**Union Bank Inn** (10053 Jasper Ave., 780/423-3600 or 888/423-3601, www.union-bankinn.com, $199–349 s or d) for value, charm, and location. The inn is in a restored 1911 bank building in the heart of the city. The owners have transformed the historic building into a luxurious boutique hotel, featuring a fireplace, down comforters, and bathrobes in each of 34 tastefully decorated rooms spread through two themed wings (heritage and contemporary). Rates include a cooked breakfast, a wine-and-cheese tray presented to guests each evening, and free parking between 3 P.M. and 9 A.M.

Centrally located on the corner of Jasper Avenue and 99th Street, the ((**Courtyard by Marriott** (1 Thornton Court, 780/423-9999 or 866/441-7591, www.marriott.com, $169 s or d) is a modern and unpretentious hotel with magnificent views across the river valley. The 177 rooms that fill with natural light (or none at all if you close the heavy curtains) have plenty of space and big, modern bathrooms. Downstairs is a bistro with tables that spill onto a magnificent riverside patio.

The lobby of the **Coast Edmonton Plaza Hotel** (10155 105th St., 780/423-4811 or 800/716-6199, www.coasthotels.com, $169–189 s or d) has a distinct alpine feel, yet the rest of the property is nothing but city-style. Handsome rooms come with niceties—such as robes—that make you believe you're paying more than you are. You can pay more, for a Superior Room, and it will be money well spent. Facilities include an indoor pool, an exercise room, laundry service, a lounge, and a restaurant.

The 24-story **Crowne Plaza Chateau Lacombe** (10111 Bellamy Hill, 780/428-6611 or 800/661-8801, www.chateaulacombe.com, $129–229 s or d) sits on Bellamy Hill, and its unusual cylindrical design distinguishes it against the skyline. The Chateau Lacombe features a fitness center, gift shop, a bar with river views, and a revolving restaurant that actually has decent food.

Over $200

The **Fairmont Hotel Macdonald** (10065 100th St., 780/424-5181 or 800/441-1414, www.fairmont.com, from $229 s or d) is an Edmonton landmark that was originally part of the Canadian Pacific hotel chain (along with the Palliser Hotel in Calgary and the Banff Springs Hotel in Banff), but is now part of the Fairmont Hotels and Resorts chain. The 198 guest rooms come in several configurations (many are on the small side). A subtle air of old-world European elegance extends throughout the rooms and public areas such as the upscale restaurant and the beautiful lounge overlooking the river valley.

Joined to the pedway system and very central, but still affording great river views, is the 20-story **Westin Edmonton** (10135 100th St., 780/426-3636 or 800/228-3000, www.thewestinedmonton.com, $249–329 s or d). The 416 rooms are large, luxurious, and come with all the comforts of home. Weekend package deals are almost half price. Hotel facilities include a large indoor pool and a fitness center. The in-house eatery, Pradera, is a stylish space that spills into the cavernous lobby.

It's upscale all the way at the **Sutton Place Hotel** (10235 101st St., 780/428-7111 or

866/378-8866, www.suttonplace.com, $319–459 s or d), in the financial district and linked to other buildings by the pedway system. In each of the 313 elegantly furnished rooms, you'll find marble tabletops, walnut furniture, brass trimmings, a large work area, and a bay window. Other hotel facilities include an indoor pool, an exercise room, a lounge, and a restaurant notable for its well-priced breakfast buffet ($18) and flavor-filled menu of local specialties.

SOUTH OF DOWNTOWN

Gateway Boulevard, an extension of Highway 2 as it enters the city from the south, offers a few cheap roadside motels just beyond Gateway Park, and is then dotted with chain hotels all the way to Old Strathcona. Remember when looking at addresses along this strip that Gateway Boulevard is Highway 2 northbound and Calgary Trail is Highway 2 southbound.

Under $50

HI-Edmonton (10647 81st Ave., Old Strathcona, 780/988-6836 or 877/866/762-4122, www.hihostels.ca, dorms $28–35.50, $89 s, $99 d) is within walking distance of the hippest Edmonton neighborhood. The building may seem a little clinical at first, but that feeling goes away when you begin to take advantage of the facilities offered. The lounge area is spacious and comfortable, and there's a quiet and private backyard, plenty of space in the kitchen, and off-street parking. Throughout summer, various trips and barbecues are put on, and a desk is set up in the lounge to take bookings for local sights and recreation. Most rooms are two-bed dorms, but there are a few rooms with six beds. Check-in is after 3 P.M. From the Greyhound bus depot, walk two blocks east to 101st Street and catch the number 4, 6, 7, or 9 bus south. Get off at 82nd Avenue, then walk two blocks east and one south, and you're there.

$50-100

At the southern city limits, **Chateau Motel** (1414 Calgary Trail SW, 780/988-6661, $60–69 s, $69–89 d) has easy access to the airport and each room has a microwave and fridge. The smallest single rooms are very small, but all are clean and comfortable.

$100-150

As you drive north along Gateway Boulevard, it's impossible to miss the 11-story, pastel-colored **Delta Edmonton South** (4404 Gateway Blvd., 780/434-6415 or 800/268-1133, www.deltahotels.com, $189 s or d) towering over the major intersection with Whitemud Drive. Guests are offered a wide variety of facilities and services, including an indoor pool, restaurant, lounge, airport shuttle, and valet parking.

Adjacent to the Delta is the **Radisson Hotel Edmonton South** (4440 Gateway Blvd., 780/437-6010 or 888/333-3333, www.radisson.com, from $169 s or d), another 200-room-plus, full-service hotel centered on a greenery-filled atrium.

Over $150

One of the city's finest accommodations is **C The Varscona,** situated in the heart of Old Strathcona (8208 106th St., 780/434-6111 or 866/465-8150, www.varscona.com, from $180 s or d). The Varscona experience combines the personalized atmosphere of a boutique hotel with all the amenities you'd expect of an upscale chain. The 89 guest rooms are spacious and elegantly furnished in one of three pleasing styles. They all have king beds, large bathrooms, and niceties such as bathrobes and gourmet in-room coffee. Casual Murrieta's is the Varscona's contribution to Old Strathcona's vibrant dining scene, while O'Byrne's Irish Pub, also located in the hotel, is the place to relax with a pint. Parking, a light breakfast, daily newspaper, and an evening wine-and-cheese-tasting session are all included in the rates.

Look no further than the **C Hotel Selkirk** (780/496-7227 or 877/496-7227, www.hotelselkirk.com, mid-May–Aug., $185–235 s or d) for a unique overnight experience with a historic twist. The original Hotel Selkirk along Jasper Avenue burned down in 1962, but the historic property has been re-created in minute detail in Fort Edmonton Park, off Whitemud

Drive southwest of downtown. The guest rooms have a cozy, Victorian feel but enjoy modern conveniences such as air-conditioning and Internet connections. Meal and accommodation packages are inclusive of breakfast and dinner in the downstairs Johnson's Café. Drinks in the Mahogany Room, at a replica of Canada's longest bar, are extra.

WEST EDMONTON
$50-100

The three-story **West Harvest Inn** (17803 Stony Plain Rd., 780/484-8000 or 888/882-9378, www.westharvest.ca, $99 s or d) has 160 well-appointed air-conditioned rooms and a shuttle to West Edmonton Mall.

$100-150

The pick within a cluster of choices along Stony Plain Road, a five-minute drive from the mall, is the **Sandman Hotel West Edmonton** (17635 Stony Plain Rd., 780/483-1385 or 800/726-3626, www.sandman.ca, $139–169 s or d). The rooms are handsomely appointed in sharp tones and comfortable furnishings. The central atrium holds a pool and restaurant—a pleasant respite from the busy road out front.

Over $200

West Edmonton Mall Inn (17504 90th Ave., 780/444-9378 or 800/737-3783, www.westedmontonmall.com, $169 s, $189 d) lies across the road from its namesake. It features 88 well-appointed rooms, each with two comfortable beds, a coffeemaker, and a Sony PlayStation. Check the website for packages that include mall activities.

Within West Edmonton Mall is the 355-room **₵ Fantasyland Hotel** (17700 87th Ave., 780/444-3000 or 800/737-3783, www.fantasylandhotel.com, $249–449 s or d), famous for elaborately themed rooms that are way over the top. The hotel has over 100 themed rooms, as well as more than 200 regular rooms and a few extremely spacious Executive Suites with jetted tubs, and three restaurants. But it's the themed rooms that this hotel is known for. No catching a cab back to your hotel after a day of shopping here—just ride the elevator to the room of your wildest fantasy. The choice is yours—Hollywood, Roman, Polynesian, Victorian, African, Arabian, Igloo, Waterpark, Western, Canadian Rail, or Truck (where you can slumber in the bed of a real pickup truck). Each theme is carried out in minute detail. The Polynesian room fantasy, for example, begins as you walk along a hallway lined with murals depicting a tropical beach, floored with grass matting. You'll walk through a grove of palm trees before reaching your room. In the colorful room, an enormous hot tub is nestled in a rocky grotto, and the bed is shaped like a warrior's catamaran, with a sail as the headboard.

CAMPING
South

The best camping within the city limits is at the **Rainbow Valley Campground** (13204 45th Ave., 780/434-5531 or 888/434-3991, www.rainbow-valley.com, mid-Apr.–mid-Oct., tent sites $26, powered sites $30). The location is excellent and, as far as city camping goes, the setting is pleasant. Facilities include free showers, a laundry room, a barbecue grill, a playground, and a cooking shelter. In summer, all sites are full by noon, so reserve ahead by credit card. To get there, turn south off Whitemud Drive at 119th Street, then take the first right and follow it into the valley.

If you're coming into the city from the south, take Ellerslie Road west from Highway 2 to access **Whitemud Creek Golf and RV Resort** (3428 156th St., 780/988-6800, www.whitemudcreek.com, $45). The 125 fully serviced sites are bunched together in the middle of a full-length, nine-hole golf course ($35), which is adjacent to a pleasant little creek. Facilities include a stocked trout pond, modern washrooms, a laundry room, and a clubhouse restaurant. To get there, follow Ellerslie Road three kilometers (1.9 miles) west from Highway 2, then take 127th Street for three kilometers (1.9 miles) south, then 40th Avenue west for a similar distance.

West

Continue west from West Edmonton Mall to **Shakers Acres** (21530 103rd Ave., 780/447-3564 or 877/447-3924, www.shakersacresrvpark. com, $31–38), on the north side of Stony Plain Road.

Farther out, in Spruce Grove, is the **Glowing Embers Travel Centre** (26309 Hwy. 16, 780/962-8100 or 877/785-7275, www.glowingembersrvpark.com, Apr.–Oct., $38–45). All facilities are modern, and although tents are allowed, they may look out of place among the satellite-toting RVs. Facilities include a recreation hall, a grocery store, wireless Internet, a restaurant (breakfast and lunch only), an RV wash, a laundry, and service bays with licensed technicians on hand.

East
Half Moon Lake Resort (21524 Hwy. 520, 780/922-3045, www.halfmoonlakeresort. ca, tents $35, hookups $38–42) is on the shore of a shallow lake, 30 kilometers (19 miles) from Edmonton. It has a large area set aside especially for tents, but the emphasis is mainly on activities such as fishing, swimming, canoeing, boating, and horseback riding. To get there from downtown, head east on 82nd Avenue to Highway 21, three kilometers (1.9 miles) east of Sherwood Park, then south to Highway 520, then 10 kilometers (6.2 miles) east.

Food

Eating out in Edmonton used to be identified with the aroma of good ol' Alberta beef wafting from the city's many restaurants, but things are changing. Today, 2,000 restaurants offer a balance of international cuisine and local favorites in all price brackets. From the legendary home-style cooking of Barb and Ernie's to the historic elegance of Madison's Grill, there's something to suit everyone's taste and budget.

DOWNTOWN
Cafés and Cheap Eats
Looking north to City Hall, **(Three Bananas** (9918 102nd Ave., 780/428-2200, Mon.–Fri. 8 A.M.–7 P.M., Sat. 10 A.M.–7 P.M., Sun. 11 A.M.–5 P.M., lunches $4.50–12) is a bright, inspiring space in the heart of downtown. The menu features the usual array of coffee concoctions, single serve pizzas, and grilled paninis, all made to order.

In an inconspicuous spot on the west side of downtown **Blue Plate Diner** (10145 104th St., 780/429-0740, Mon.–Fri. 11 A.M.–10 P.M., Sat.–Sun. 9 A.M.–10 P.M., $12–18) is a welcoming place, with simple furnishings and a thoughtful menu of dishes made fresh each day. Vegetarian choices include a lentil and nut loaf doused with miso gravy.

Pub Dining
Surrounded by the city's highest high-rises is the **Sherlock Holmes** (10012 101A Ave., 780/426-7784, Mon.–Sat. from 11:30 A.M., $12–16), a charming English-style pub with a shingled roof, whitewashed walls with black trim, and a white picket fence surrounding it. At lunchtime, it is packed with the office crowd. Try traditional British dishes such as bangers and mash, meatloaf, and steak and mushroom pie, washed down with a pint of Newcastle ale or Guinness stout. Still hungry? The bread and butter pudding ($8) is a delicious way to end your meal.

In the West End, **Sidetrack Cafe** (10238 104th St., 780/421-1326, Mon.–Fri. from 7 A.M., weekends from 9 A.M., $9–14) has been a music hot spot for more than two decades, but it also has a reputation for excellent food. Big, hearty breakfasts cost $4–7.50. Soups, salads, burgers, sandwiches, pizza, and world fare are all on the menu. The soup-and-sandwich lunch deal includes a bottomless bowl of soup. Dinners (5–10 P.M.) are mostly pub staples.

Canadian
The area along 97th Street has always been Edmonton's own little skid row, but this is changing. Now, it's home to the **(Hardware Grill** (9698 Jasper Ave., 780/423-0969,

Mon.–Fri. 11:30 A.M.–1:30 P.M. and Mon.–Sat. from 5 P.M., $30–49), one of the city's finest restaurants. Located at the street level of an early 1900s red-brick building (once a hardware store), the white linen and silver table settings contrast starkly with the restored interior. The menu features dishes using a wide variety of seasonal Canadian produce, including pork, lamb, beef, venison, and salmon, all well prepared and delightfully presented.

At **C Madison's Grill** (10053 Jasper Ave., 780/401-2222, daily for breakfast and dinner, weekdays only for lunch, $28–40), the official-looking architecture of this former bank remains, with contemporary styling balancing columns and ornate ceiling. The kitchen features the best in Canadian ingredients, with the Alaskan king crab lasagna a real treat. The lunchtime pan-seared calamari salad keeps up the seafood theme. Good food coupled with impeccable service makes Madison's the perfect place for a splurge.

In general, revolving restaurants are renowned for bad food as much as great views. But **La Ronde** (10111 Bellamy Hill, 780/420-8366, daily 5:30–10:30 P.M., Sun. 10:30 A.M.–2 P.M. for brunch, $28–39), atop the Crowne Plaza Chateau Lacombe, is an exception. The Canadian-inspired menu features delicacies such as maple-glazed arctic char, grilled bison rib eye, and east coast lobster, or enjoy a three-course table d'hôte for $53.

European

Among the dozens of Italian restaurants in the city, one of the most popular is **Sorrentino's** (10162 100th St., 780/424-7500, Mon.–Fri. 11:30 A.M.–10 P.M., Sat. 5–10 P.M., $15–31). The decor is stylish, with a great old-world Italian charm. The food is simple and satisfying. Begin with prawns sautéed in a gorgonzola cream reduction, then move onto a traditionally rich pasta dish, or something lighter such as Greek-style lamb medallions.

As you descend the stairs to **The Creperie** below the Boardwalk Market (10220 103rd St., 780/420-6656, Tues.–Fri. for lunch, daily for dinner, $20–26), a great smell, wafting from somewhere in the depths of this historic building, hits you in the face. It takes a minute for your eyes to adjust to the softly lit dining area, but once you do, its inviting French provincial atmosphere is apparent. As you've probably guessed, crepes are the specialty. Choose from fillings as varied as the Canadian-influenced Crepe Pacific ($20), filled with shrimp, salmon, and asparagus, to the classic chocolate crepe ($8) for dessert.

The **Harvest Room,** in the Fairmont Hotel Macdonald (10065 100th St., 780/429-6424, daily for breakfast, lunch, and dinner, $28–45), has the look of a cruise-ship dining room of yesteryear, but remains remarkably unstuffy. The food itself blends Canadian specialties, sourced locally where possible, with European influences and a very comprehensive wine list. Royal (high) Tea is served each summer afternoon at 3 P.M. (reservations recommended); $33 per person includes a hotel tour.

Asian

On the west side of downtown, **Wild Tangerine** (10383 112th St., 780/429-3131, Mon.–Fri. 11:30 A.M.–10 P.M. and Sat. 5–11:30 P.M., $13–26) boasts imaginative cooking in a casual, color-filled room. Many dishes have their origins in Asia, but have been given a modern makeover with local produce as a base (think grilled salmon dusted with lemon tea or mussels boiled open in red curry). Save room for the chocolate brownie covered in orange marmalade and cream cheese.

My favorite East Indian restaurant in Edmonton is **Haweli** (10220 103rd St., 780/421-8100, daily for lunch and dinner, $14–22), which has an enchantingly simple ambience, complete with silk curtains separating some tables and soothing background music.

OLD STRATHCONA

This historic suburb south of downtown offers Edmonton's largest concentration of cafés and restaurants. There's a great variety of choices, and because it's a popular late-night hangout, many eateries are open to the wee hours.

Cafés

Block 1912 (10361 82nd Ave., 780/433-6575, Mon.–Sat. 9 A.M.–10 P.M., Sun. 10 A.M.–10 P.M., lunches $5.50–8.50) offers a great variety of hot drinks, cakes, pastries, and healthy full meals in an inviting atmosphere, which includes several comfortable lounges. Newspapers from around the world are available. Brightly lit **Muddy Waters** (8211 111th St., 780/433-4390, Mon.–Fri. 10:30 A.M.–midnight, Sat. noon–1 A.M., Sun. 4–11 P.M.) is a popular coffeehouse with students from the nearby university who really know their coffee and like to study into the night.

Mexican and Cajun

Julio's Barrio Mexican Restaurant (10450 Whyte Ave., 780/431-0774, daily until midnight, $11–19) is a huge restaurant decorated with earthy colors and Southwestern-style furniture and has a true Mexican ambience. The menu is appealing but limited. If you just want a light snack, try the warm corn chips with jack cheese and freshly made salsa ($7.25); for something more substantial, consider the fajitas, presented in a cast iron pan. This place doesn't get really busy until after 9 P.M.

Da-de-o (10548 Whyte Ave., 780/433-0930, Mon.–Tues. and Thurs.–Sat. 11:30 A.M.–11 P.M., Sun. noon–10 P.M., $9–18) is styled on a 1950s diner in New Orleans. The menu features Cajun cuisine, including po'boys—Southern-style sandwiches using French bread and fillings such as blackened catfish and tequila salsa ($11)—as well as catfish salad, Southern fried chicken, jambalaya, and inexpensive dishes like barbecue beans and rice ($8) that have appeal to the money-watching university crowd. When the hip, evening crowd arrives, service can be blasé at best.

Chinese

West of Old Strathcona, toward the University of Alberta, is **Mandarin Restaurant** (11044 82nd Ave., 780/433-8494, Mon.–Fri 11:30 A.M.–2:30 P.M. and daily for dinner from 4:30 P.M., $9–18), consistently voted as having the best Chinese food in the city, but you'd never know by looking at it. It's informal, noisy, family-style dining, and the walls are plastered with sporting memorabilia donated by diners. Most dishes are from northern China, which is known for traditionally hot food, but enough Cantonese dishes are offered to please all tastes.

Fine Dining

A few blocks east of the railway tracks, in a renovated shop, is one of Edmonton's most popular restaurants, the **Unheardof** (9602 82nd Ave., 780/432-0480, Tues.–Sun. from 5:30 P.M., $35–45). The main dining room is filled with antiques, and the tables are set with starched-white linen and silver cutlery. The menu changes weekly, featuring fresh game such as venison tenderloin, homemade chutneys, and relishes during fall, and chicken and beef dishes the rest of the year. Although it's most obviously an upscale restaurant, the service is comfortable, but most importantly, the food is absolutely mouthwatering. Reservations are essential.

Information and Services

Information Centers

The most central source of tourist information is the downtown office of **Edmonton Tourism** (9990 Jasper Ave., 780/426-4715 or 800/463-4667, www.edmonton.com, Mon.–Fri. 7 A.M.–7 P.M.), opposite the Fairmont Hotel Macdonald. If you're driving up to Edmonton from the south along Highway 2, move over to the left lane as you enter the city in preparation for a stop at Edmonton Tourism's **Gateway Park Visitor Information Centre** information center (780/496-8400, Mon.–Fri. 8:30 A.M.–4:30 P.M. and Sat.–Sun. 9 A.M.–5 P.M.). Within this complex, you'll find interpretive displays on the oil industry, stands filled with brochures, and direct-dial phones

NORTHERN ALBERTA

for Edmonton accommodations. On the arrivals level of the **Edmonton International Airport** is another information center year-round Mon.–Fri. 8 A.M.–midnight, Sat.–Sun. 9 A.M.–midnight).

Libraries

Edmonton Public Library (www.epl.ca) has 16 libraries spread throughout the city. The largest is the **Stanley A. Milner Library** (7 Sir Winston Churchill Square, 780/496-7000, Mon.–Fri. 9 A.M.–9 P.M., Sat. 9 A.M.–6 P.M., Sun. 1–5 P.M.). This large, two-story facility, connected to the downtown core by pedways, is a great place to spend a rainy afternoon. It carries newspapers, magazines, and phone books from all corners of the globe, as well as rows and rows of western Canadiana. Throughout the week, author readings take place on the main level.

Communications

The main **post office** is downtown at 9808 103A Avenue. All downtown hotels have in-room Internet access, while most others have wireless Internet or an Internet booth in the lobby. Public Internet access is free at all city libraries, or you can pay approximately $5 for 30 minutes downtown at the **Bohemia Cyber Café** (11812 Jasper Ave., 780/429-3442,

Mon.–Fri. 10 A.M.–1 A.M., Sat. 11 A.M.–1 A.M., Sun. 11 A.M.–midnight).

Banks

Main branches of most banks in the downtown area will handle common foreign-currency exchange transactions, as will **Currencies International** (780/484-3868) beside the Fantasyland Hotel lobby in West Edmonton Mall.

Laundry

On the west side of the city is **LaPerle Homestyle Laundry** (9756 182nd St., 780/483-9200), which is handy to the hotels in the area and has large washers and dryers for sleeping bags.

Emergency Services

For medical emergencies, call 911 or one of the following hospitals: **Grey Nuns Community Hospital** (corner of 34th Ave. and 66th St., 780/735-7000); **Northeast Community Health Centre** (14007 50th St., 780/472-5000); **Royal Alexandra Hospital** (10240 Kingsway Ave., 780/735-4111); **University of Alberta Hospital** (8440 112th St., 780/407-8822). For the **Edmonton Police Service,** call 780/423-4567.

Getting There and Around

Getting There

Edmonton International Airport (www.fly-eia.com) is beside Highway 2, 29 kilometers (18 miles) south of the city center. On the **arrivals** level is a small information center (year-round Mon.–Fri. 8 A.M.–midnight, Sat.–Sun. 9 A.M.–midnight). Also at the airport are car-rental desks, hotel courtesy phones, a restaurant, and a currency exchange. **Sky Shuttle** (780/465-8515 or 888/438-2342, www.edmontonsky-shuttle.com) departs the airport for downtown hotels every 20 minutes (every 30 minutes on weekends) on three different routes. One-way to downtown is $15, round-trip $30; check in

at the counter beside the information center. The cab fare to downtown is set at $50 one-way.

The **VIA Rail station** is a small, modern building beyond the west end of the City Centre Airport northwest of downtown (12360 121st St., 800/561-8630, www.viarail.ca, 8 A.M.–3:30 P.M.). A Hertz rental outlet is open for arriving and departing trains, but reservations are necessary. Trains leave Vancouver (1150 Station St.) and Prince Rupert three times weekly for the 23.5-hour trip to Edmonton (via Jasper), continuing on the Canadian route to the eastern provinces.

The **Greyhound** bus depot (10324 103rd St., 780/420-2400 or 800/661-8747, www.greyhound.ca, Mon.–Sat. 5:30 A.M.–midnight, Sun. 10 A.M.–6 P.M.) is within walking distance of downtown. Within the depot is a fast-food eatery, a convenience store, a cash machine, and large lockers ($2). Buses leave daily for all points in Canada, including Calgary (3.5 hours), Jasper (4.5 hours), and Vancouver (15–17 hours). **Red Arrow** (780/424-3339, www.redarrow.ca) buses leave Edmonton 5–7 times daily for Red Deer and Calgary and once daily for Fort McMurray. The downtown office and pick-up point is off to one side of the Holiday Inn Express (10014 104th Street).

Getting Around

While reaching Edmonton's most popular attractions is easy using public transit, the road system and clear signage makes driving relatively simple also. Major highways from the east, west, and south converge on downtown, with bypasses such as Whitemud Dr. (for those traveling from the south to West Edmonton Mall) making avoiding downtown easy.

Combining buses and light rail transit (LRT), the **Edmonton Transit System** (780/496-1611, www.edmonton.ca) links downtown to all parts of the city and most tourist attractions. The LRT has 13 stops (Canada's smallest subway system) running east–west along Jasper Avenue (101st Ave.), northeast as far as Clareville and south to Century Park. The LRT runs underground through the city center, connecting with many pedways. Travel between Grandin and Churchill is free Monday–Friday 9 A.M.–3 P.M. and Saturday 9 A.M.–6 P.M. Transit fare anywhere within the city is adult $2.50 per person; transfers are available upon boarding and can be used for additional travel in any direction within 90 minutes. Day passes are $7.50. For more information and passes, go to the **Customer Services Outlet** (Churchill LRT Station, 99th St., 780/496-1622, Mon.–Fri. 8:30 A.M.–4:30 P.M.).

A great way to travel between downtown and Old Strathcona is on the **High Level Street Car** (780/437-7721, $4 one way). Trains and trams originally traveled this historic route over the High Level Bridge, but today a restored street car makes the journey from the west side of the Alberta Legislature Building to Old Strathcona between mid-May and August every 30 minutes daily 11 A.M.–4 P.M.

The standard flag charge for cabs is $3.29 plus approximately $1.85 per kilometer, but most companies have flat rates for major destinations within the city. Major companies are **Checker Cabs** (780/484-8888), **Alberta Co-op Taxi Line** (780/425-2525), **Prestige Cabs** (780/462-4444), and **Yellow Cab** (780/462-3456).

Car rental agencies and their local numbers are: **Avis** (780/448-0066), **Budget** (780/448-2000), **Discount** (780/448-3888), **Enterprise** (780/440-4550), **Hertz** (780/415-5283), **National** (780/422-6097), **Rent-a-Wreck** (780/986-3335), and **Thrifty** (780/890-4555).

Lakeland

Highway 16, east from Edmonton, follows the southern flanks of a region containing hundreds of lakes formed at the end of the last Ice Age by a retreating sheet of ice nearly one kilometer (0.6 miles) thick. History buffs appreciate the legacies of early white settlers that dot the landscape here—restored fur-trading posts, missions, and the Ukrainian Village near Vegreville. Other visitors are attracted by the region's vast areas of unspoiled wilderness, including seven provincial parks. Anglers will feel right at home among the area's countless lakes, and wildlife-watchers are drawn to Elk Island National Park, which rivals Tanzania's Serengeti Plain for the population densities of its animal inhabitants.

NORTHERN ALBERTA

◖ ELK ISLAND NATIONAL PARK

Heading east from Edmonton on Highway 16, you'll reach Elk Island National Park in well under an hour. This small, fenced, 194-square-kilometer (75-square-mile) park preserves a remnant of the aspen parkland that once covered the entire northern flank of the prairie. It's also one of the best spots in Alberta for wildlife-watching; with approximately 3,000 large mammals, the park has one of the highest concentrations of big game in the world. Set aside in 1906 to protect a herd of elk now numbering around 1,600, the park also provides a home for moose, two species of bison, white-tailed and mule deer, coyotes, beavers, muskrats, mink, and porcupines. The many lakes and wetland areas in the park serve as nesting sites for waterfowl, and approximately 230 species of birds have been observed here.

Park entry for one day is adult $7.90, senior $6.90, child $3.90 to a maximum of $20 per vehicle; if you've purchased an annual pass, you'll be waved straight through the fee station (but stop to pick up park information anyway).

Recreation

Twelve hiking trails, ranging in length from 1.4–18.5 kilometers (0.9–11.5 miles), cover all areas of the park and provide excellent opportunities to view wildlife. A park information sheet details each one. Make sure to carry water with you, though, because surface water in the park is not suitable for drinking. The paved **Shoreline Trail** (three km/1.9 mi one-way) follows the shore of Astotin Lake from the golf course parking lot. The **Lakeview Trail** (3.3 km/two mi round-trip) begins from the northern end of the recreation area and provides good views of the lake. Hike this trail in the evening for a chance to see beavers. The only trail on the south side of Highway 16 is the **Wood Bison Trail** (18.6 km/11.5 mi round-trip), which has an interpretive display at the trailhead. In winter, the trails provide excellent cross-country skiing and snowshoeing.

The day-use area at **Astotin Lake,** 14 kilometers (8.7 miles) north of Highway 16, is the center of much activity. There's a pleasant beach and picnic area; canoes, rowboats, and small sailboats can be rented; and the rolling

THE BISON OF ELK ISLAND

Two species of bison inhabit Elk Island National Park, and to prevent interbreeding, they are separated. All bison on the north side of Highway 16 are **plains bison,** whereas those on the south side are **wood bison.** Wood bison are darker in color, larger (an average bull weighs 840 kg/1,850 lbs), and have long, straight hair covering the forehead. Plains bison are smaller, have shorter legs, a larger head, and frizzy hair. In summer they grow distinctive capes of woolly hair that cover their front legs, head, and shoulders.

Before the late 1700s, 60 million plains bison lived on the North American plains. In less than a century, humanity brought these shaggy beasts to the brink of extinction. By 1880, incredibly, only a few hundred plains bison remained. A small herd, the ancestors of today's herd, was corralled at what was then

Elk Island Reserve. A small part of the herd is kept in a large enclosure just north of the Park Information Centre, while the rest roam freely through the north section of the park. Today they number approximately 630 within the park.

The wood bison was thought to be extinct for many years – a victim of hunting, severe winters, and interbreeding with its close relative, the plains bison. In 1957, a herd of 200 was discovered in the remote northwestern corner of Wood Buffalo National Park. Some were captured and transported to Elk Island National Park, ensuring the survival of the species. Today it's the purest herd in the world and is used as breeding stock for several captive herds throughout North America. To view the herd of 400, look south from Highway 16 or hike the Wood Bison Trail.

fairways of adjacent **Elk Island Golf Course** (780/998-3161, $36) provide an interesting diversion for golfers.

Practicalities

Sandy Beach Campground, on the north side of the Astotin Lake day-use area, is the only overnight facility within the park. It has fire pits, picnic tables, flush toilets, and showers; $26 per night plus $9 for a firewood permit. If you're traveling in the peak of summer (especially on weekends), it is strongly recommended to use the **Parks Canada Campground**

Reservation Service (877/737-3783, www. pccamping.ca) for a nonrefundable $11 reservation fee. A concession selling fast food and basic camping supplies operates May–October at Astotin Lake, and the golf course (780/998-3161) has a casual restaurant.

The **Park Information Centre** (780/992-5790, weekends only May and June, daily 10 A.M.–6 P.M. July and Aug.) is less than one kilometer (0.6 miles) north of Highway 16 on the Elk Island Parkway. For online information, click through the links on the Parks Canada website (www.pc.gc.ca).

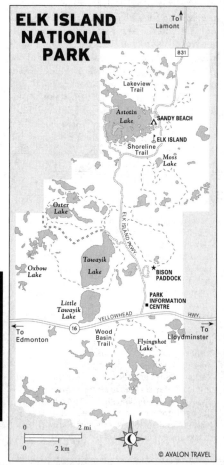

ELK ISLAND NATIONAL PARK

EAST ALONG THE YELLOWHEAD HIGHWAY

South of Elk Island National Park is the 97-square-kilometer (34-square-mile) **Cooking Lake-Blackfoot Recreation Area,** part of the massive Cooking Lake Moraine, formed during the last Ice Age as the retreating sheet of ice stalled for a time, leaving mounds and hollows that have since filled with water. Large natural areas of wetland and forest provide habitat for abundant wildlife, including moose, elk, white-tailed deer, coyotes, beavers, and more than 200 species of birds. Much of the well-posted trail system is for hikers only, but some parts are open to horses and mountain bikes. The **Blackfoot Staging Area,** off Highway 16, is the trailhead for a good selection of short hiking trails.

Ukrainian Cultural Heritage Village

This heritage village (50 km/31 mi east of Edmonton, 780/662-3640, daily 10 A.M.–6 P.M. late May–Aug., Sat.–Sun. 10 A.M.–6 P.M. Sept., adult $8, senior $7, child $4) is a realistic replica of a Ukrainian settlement, common in the rural areas of east-central Alberta at the turn of the 20th century. The first—and largest—Ukrainian settlement in Canada was located in this region. Driven from their homeland in Eastern Europe, Ukrainians fled to the Canadian prairies where, for many years, they dressed and worked in the ways of the Old World. These traditions are kept alive with costumed guides and a lively program of cultural events.

The world's largest *pysanka* – a Ukrainian Easter egg – is on the edge of Vegreville.

© ANDREW HEMPSTEAD

Vegreville

Although first settled by French farmers from Kansas, this town of 5,300 is best known for its Ukrainian heritage. Today Vegreville's biggest attraction is the world's largest **pysanka,** a giant, traditionally decorated Ukrainian Easter egg at the east end of town. It measures eight meters (26 feet) in length, weighs 2,270 kilograms (5,000 lbs), and can turn in the wind like a giant weathervane.

Vegreville celebrates its multicultural past on the Canada Day (July 1) weekend with the **Ukrainian Pysanka Folk Festival.**

Vermilion

Many downtown buildings here date to the 1919–1920 period after a fire destroyed the original main street (50th Avenue) in 1918. Made of locally fired brick, many have plaques detailing their history. Pick up a walking-tour brochure at the information center (daily 10 A.M.–6 P.M. in summer) by the entrance to town. In a 1928 school building, **Vermilion Heritage Museum** (50th Ave. at 53rd St.,

780/853-6211, daily 1–5 P.M. mid-June–Aug., donation) features an extensive photographic collection and native artifacts.

Lloydminster

North America has several twin cities that straddle borders (such as Minneapolis and St. Paul), but Lloydminster is the only one that has a single corporate body in two provinces (or states, depending on the case). Approximately 60 percent of the city's 22,000 residents live on the Alberta side, separated from their Saskatchewan neighbors by the main street.

Barr Colony Heritage Cultural Centre (4515 44th St., 306/825-5655, daily 10 A.M.–8 P.M. July–Aug., Wed.–Sun. 1–5 P.M. the rest of the year, adult $6.75, child $4.75) houses the Richard Larsen Museum featuring a collection of artifacts and antiques used by early settlers. Also here: the Imhoff Art Gallery, which contains more than 200 works of early-1900s artist Count Berthold Von Imhoff; a room dedicated to describing oil sands technology; and a number of historic building dotting the courtyard.

Although it looks decidedly un-tropical from outside, kids will love the **Tropical Inn** (5621 44th St., 780/825-7000 or 800/219-5244, www.tropicalinns.com, $105–155 s or d) for its indoor waterslide and pool complex. The 165 guest rooms are surprisingly appealing, with nice extras such as dry-cleaning and high-speed Internet rounding out a good choice for overnight accommodations. **Weaver Park Campsite** (behind the Barr Colony Centre, 306/825-3726, unserviced sites $15, hookups $20–25) has showers and a grocery store. Much nicer is **Rolling Green Fairways** (780/875-4653, www.lloydminstergolf.com, $28–30), two kilometers (1.2 miles) west of the city on Highway 16, then one kilometer (0.6 miles) north. Amenities include showers, a laundry room, free firewood, and, as the name suggests, an adjacent golf course.

Local visitors centers include the provincially operated **Travel Alberta Information Centre** (one km/0.6 mi east of town, daily 9 A.M.–6 P.M. mid-May–mid-June, daily 8 A.M.–6 P.M. in summer) and the **Saskatchewan Visitor Reception Centre** (beside the Barr Colony Centre, 306/825-8690, spring daily 9 A.M.–5 P.M., summer daily 8 A.M.–8 P.M.), mainly a source of information for those heading east.

EDMONTON TO COLD LAKE

Highway 28 leaves Edmonton heading north through the suburbs. After a series of 90-degree turns—first one way, then the other, then back again—it comes to the village of **Waskatenau,** where it straightens out to pursue an easterly direction heading toward Cold Lake.

Long Lake Provincial Park

During the last Ice Age, the low-lying area occupied by this 764-hectare (1,890-acre) park was part of a deep glacial meltwater channel that has now filled with water. Today it's surrounded by boreal forest, although aspens predominate in the park because of fires over the years. Anglers chase northern pike, perch, and walleye. Right on the lake is a 220-site **campground** (780/576-3959, Apr.–Oct., unserviced sites $20, powered sites $26), with flush toilets, showers, a grocery store, and canoe rentals. To get there from Highway 28, head north from Waskatenau on Highway 831 for 48 kilometers (30 miles).

◖ Métis Crossing

At the junction of Highway 855 and Victoria Trail, 10 kilometers (6.2 miles) south of Smoky Lake, Métis Crossing (780/656-2229, daily 11 A.M.–6 P.M. mid-May–Aug., adult $5, senior and child $3) is the country's largest cultural center dedicated to the Métis, the descendants of those born as the result of relationships between French traders and native Cree women. George McDougall established a mission on the site in 1862 and within a decade it was surrounded by a bustling Métis community, who used the riverfront setting as a hub for trade. The restoration project is still in its infancy (the first phase opened in late 2006), but already there are plenty of things to do and see, including a restored barn containing the story

STILL WAITING...

St. Paul, 210 kilometers (130 miles) northeast of Edmonton, has spent many thousands of dollars developing an attraction that hasn't had a single official visitor in more than 30 years. And the skeptics doubt it ever will.

You guessed it (or maybe you didn't): St. Paul has the world's only **UFO landing pad** – a raised platform forlornly waiting for a visitor from outer space. Beside the pad, the **Tourist Information Centre** (50th Ave. at 53rd St., 780/645-6800, summer daily 9 A.M.–5 P.M.) has interesting displays including photos of "real" UFOs as well as descriptions of some famous hoaxes. The building is a raised, UFO-shaped circular structure; if approaching from outer space, look for the green flashing light on top.

of the people's role in the fur trade and how a distinct culture emerged. A craft store, playground, and campground are also on site.

Victoria Settlement

Victoria Settlement (7 km/4.3 mi east of Hwy. 855, 780/656-2333, daily 10 A.M.–6 P.M. mid-May–Aug., adult $3, senior $2, child $1.50) is the perfect compliment to Métis Crossing. In 1864, the Hudson's Bay Company established a fur-trading post at the site. The post closed in 1897 and was abandoned until the early 1900s, when groups of Ukrainian settlers moved to the area. When the railway bypassed the settlement in 1918, businesses moved north to Smoky Lake, and the area was abandoned once again. Head to the 1906 Methodist church for a slideshow about the settlement or wander past the clerk's 1864 log cabin to the river and the graves of the founder's three daughters. Picnic tables are set among broad maple trees, which were planted during the fur-trading days.

Fort George and Buckingham House

The site of these two fur-trading posts on the

north bank of the North Saskatchewan River has been designated a Provincial Historical Site (13 km/eight mi east of Elk Point, 780/724-2611, daily 10 A.M.–6 P.M. mid-May–Aug., adult $3, senior $2, child $1.50). In 1792, soon after the North West Company had established Fort George, the Hudson's Bay Company followed suit a few hundred steps away with Buckingham House. Both posts were abandoned in the early 1800s and have long since been destroyed; depressions in the ground, piles of stone, and indistinct pathways are all that remain. Above the site is an interpretive center with audio and visual presentations explaining the rivalry between the two companies and the history of the forts. Interpretive trails lead from the center down to the river.

Whitney Lakes Provincial Park

Four lakes are protected by this 1,490-hectare (3,680-acre) park on Highway 646. The fishing is excellent in all lakes but Borden. Because the park is in a transition zone, plant, mammal, and bird species are diverse. A mixed forest of aspen, white spruce, balsam poplar, and jack pine grows on the uplands, whereas black spruce and tamarack grow in lower, wetter areas. Beavers are common—look for their ponds on the north side of Laurier Lake. Other resident mammals include porcupines, white-tailed deer, coyotes, and, during berry season, black bears. Birds are abundant, especially waterfowl and shorebirds. A 1.5-kilometer (0.9-mile) interpretive trail starts at the day-use area at the northeast corner of Ross Lake. Fishing is best for northern pike, perch, and pickerel. Within the park are two campgrounds totaling more than 200 sites. **Ross Lake Campground** has 149 powered sites on six short loops around the south and eastern shore of the lake. Coin-operated showers are located between loops A and B. Whitney Lakes Campground is smaller and has no showers but does have power hookups. A trail along the shore links both campgrounds. Sites are $15–21 and no reservations are taken. Both are open May to mid-October.

Glendon

Twenty-five kilometers (15.5 miles) farther east is a turnoff to Glendon. This village's claim to fame takes the cake, or actually, the *pyrogy*— it has the **world's largest pyrogy.** This important part of the Ukrainian diet (something like boiled potato- or onion-filled ravioli) can be sampled next to Pyrogy Park (free camping) in the Pyrogy Park Cafe, opposite the Pyrogy Motel (780/635-3002; from $65 s or d) on Pyrogy Drive.

Bonnyville

This agricultural center (population 5,500) is on the north shore of **Jessie Lake,** where more than 300 species of waterfowl and shorebirds have been recorded. Spring and fall are the best viewing times, although many species are present year-round, nesting in the marshes and aspen parkland surrounding the lake. Numerous viewing platforms, linked by the **Wetlands Nature Trail,** are scattered along Lakeshore Drive and Highway 41.

West of town between Highways 28A and 660 is **Moose Lake Provincial Park.** Access to the lake is possible from many directions, but the 736-hectare (1,820-acre) provincial park is on the lake's north shore. Ground squirrels and coyotes are common, and black bears occasionally wander through. The park's namesake, however—moose—are long gone. The lakeshore is a good place to explore, with trails leading either way from the day-use area to good sandy beaches. Another trail leads to the tip of Deadman's Point and to a bog that is home to many species of birds. The small campground (mid-May–mid-Sept., unserviced sites $15, powered sites $21) has 59 sites on two loops, both of which have access to the beach.

COLD LAKE

At the end of Highway 28, a little less than 300 kilometers (186 miles) northeast of Edmonton, is Cold Lake (population 12,500), the collective name for three distinct communities. The area you'll want to visit is Cold Lake North, on the south shore of Alberta's seventh-largest lake. Although the military has been present in this area for more than half a century, it is the **Cold Lake Oil Sands** that hold the key to the region's economic future. The heavy oil found north of

Cold Lake is similar to that of the Athabasca Oil Sands at Fort McMurray, but the extraction process is different. The oil-rich sands lie in a 50-meter-thick (160-feet-thick) underground reservoir, making surface mining impractical. Instead, steam is pumped into the reservoir, thinning out the tar-like bitumen, which is then pumped to the surface and piped to Edmonton.

Sights and Recreation

The lake itself is massive—approximately 22 kilometers (13.6 miles) wide, 27 kilometers (13.6 miles) long, and reaches depths of 100 meters (330 feet). The 250-berth **marina** (at the end of the main street) provides a home for **Cap'n Ronn Charters** (780/812-8895), which offers varying packages in a modern seven-meter (23-foot) boat. Charters are from $80 per hour for up to four people, but it's least expensive for a full day of guided fishing ($525).

Cold Lake Provincial Park spreads over 5,855 hectares (14,470 acres) of an isthmus east of town along 16th Avenue. Although the beaches are much nicer on the northwestern shore of the lake, fishing is excellent here, and the park offers many interesting places to explore. The park's dominant feature is **Hall's Lagoon,** on the northwest side of the isthmus. The lagoon is very shallow, and thick vegetation lines its banks. This is the best place for viewing birdlife, with an observation platform and identification boards set up for birders. Within the park are many short hiking trails, most radiating from the campground and day-use area. The campground (May–Oct., unserviced sites $18, powered sites $24) has coin-operated showers, firewood, a beach, and a summer interpretive programs.

Accommodations

Within walking distance of the marina is the **Dockside Inn** (1002 8th Ave., 780/639-3030 or 877/639-3038; $75 s, $85 d), with tolerable air-conditioned rooms, an Internet kiosk, and a Laundromat. Much nicer is the **Lakeland Inn** (5411 55th St., 708/594-3311 or 877/594-3311; $120 s, $138 d), where each of the 121 rooms has wireless Internet, comfortable beds, and air

conditioning. Dining options include a café, lounge, and restaurant.

Information

Housed in a two-story building on the highway through Cold Lake South is **Cold Lake Information Centre** (780/594-4497 or 800/840-6140, www.coldlake.com, May–Aug. Mon.–Fri. 9 A.M.–9 P.M., Sat.–Sun. 10 A.M.–6 P.M.).

LAC LA BICHE AND VICINITY

The historic town of Lac La Biche (population 2,600) is located on the southern flanks of the boreal forest, 225 kilometers (140 miles) northeast of Edmonton. The town itself has little of interest, but nearby you'll find a restored mission, two interesting provincial parks, many excellent fishing lakes, and a gravel road that may or may not get you to Fort McMurray.

The town lies on a divide that separates the Athabasca River System, which drains into the Arctic Ocean, from the Churchill River System, which drains into Hudson Bay. The historic Portage La Biche, across this strip of land, was a vital link in the transcontinental route taken by the early fur traders. Voyageurs would paddle up the Beaver River from the east to Beaver Lake and portage the five kilometers (3.1 miles) to Lac La Biche, from where passage could be made to the rich fur-trapping regions along the Athabasca River. In 1798, David Thompson built Red Deer Lake House for the North West Company at the southeast end of the lake. Soon after, Peter Fidler built Greenwich House nearby for the Hudson's Bay Company. By the early 1820s, this northern route across the continent was virtually abandoned for a shorter route along the North Saskatchewan River via Edmonton House. The mission is the best place to learn about the town's colorful past, but you can also get a taste at lakeside **McArthur Place** (Churchill Dr., 780/623-4323), which is a replica of the Lac La Biche Inn that once stood on the same site. Now functioning primarily as the town office, it also holds an information center, historic displays, and a stuffed cougar. Out front, a paved walking trail leads along the shoreline to a statue of explorer extraordinaire David Thompson.

Lac La Biche Mission

The mission was established beside the Hudson's Bay Company post in 1853 and was moved to its present site, 11 kilometers (6.8 miles) northwest of Lac La Biche, in 1855. It became a base for priests who had missions along the Athabasca, Peace, and Mackenzie Rivers and was used as a supply depot for voyageurs still using the northern trade route. The parish expanded, adding a sawmill, a gristmill, a printing press, and a boat-building yard. Today, the original buildings still stand, and services take place each Sunday in the church. A free, guided tour takes one hour, or you can wander around the buildings yourself (780/623-3274, daily 10 A.M.–5 P.M. mid-May–early Sept., adult $5, senior $4.25, child $3.50).

Local Parks

Located on the largest of nine islands in Lac La Biche, **Sir Winston Churchill Provincial Park** is linked to the mainland by a 2.5-kilometer (1.6-mile) causeway. The trees on the island are much larger than those found on the mainland, a result of little disturbance from people and no major fires in more than 300 years. A loop road around the island passes through a lush, old-growth coniferous forest, with walking trails leading to sandy beaches (the best are on the northeast side of the island), marshes rich with birdlife, and a bird-viewing platform where a mounted telescope lets you watch white pelicans and double-crested cormorants resting on a gravel bar. A **campground** (780/623-4144, May–mid-Oct., $23–26) with showers and a few powered sites is on the south side of the island. Access is from Highway 881.

Encompassing 60,000 hectares (148,000 acres) of boreal forest mostly in its natural state, as well as 11 major lakes, **Lakeland Provincial Park** and an adjacent recreation area are a wildlife-watcher's paradise. Deer, moose, beavers, red foxes, lynx, coyotes, a few wolves and black bears, and more than 200 species of birds can be spotted in the area. A colony of great blue herons, Alberta's largest wading bird, lives at **Pinehurst Lake**, 27 kilometers (17 miles) off Highway 55. Campgrounds are located at **Pinehurst, Ironwood, Seibert,** and **Touchwood Lakes.** Each site has pit toilets and kitchen shelters, and firewood is available for sale; $13–18 per night.

Accommodations and Camping

La Biche Inn (101st Ave., 780/623-4427 or 888/884-8886, $65 s, $75 d) has a restaurant and a nightclub where the disc jockey sits in a big rig. The closest campgrounds are east and north of town in the two provincial parks. **Fish'N Friends** (three km/1.9 mi east and a similar distance south off Highway 36, 780/623-9222, www.fish-nfriends.com, mid-May–Oct., $22–25) is a full-service RV park with a large marina, boat rentals, a general store stocked with fishing tackle, and barbecues, perfecting for cooking up freshly caught walleye.

Fort McMurray

It's a long drive north to reach Fort McMurray, 450 kilometers (280 miles) north of Edmonton, but it's far from a dead-end town. This city is a modern-day boomtown that revolves around the **Athabasca Oil Sands,** the world's greatest known deposit of oil. The city is awash with money—and workers spending it—but on a larger scale, the financial impact on the province and country is mind-blowing. So if you're not a construction worker or oilman, why should you make the long trek north? Actual "sights" are oil sands–related (tours through the mining operations are very popular), but nowhere in the world has so much economic development ever been concentrated in one place, which makes simply being there an interesting study in socioeconomics.

NORTHERN ALBERTA

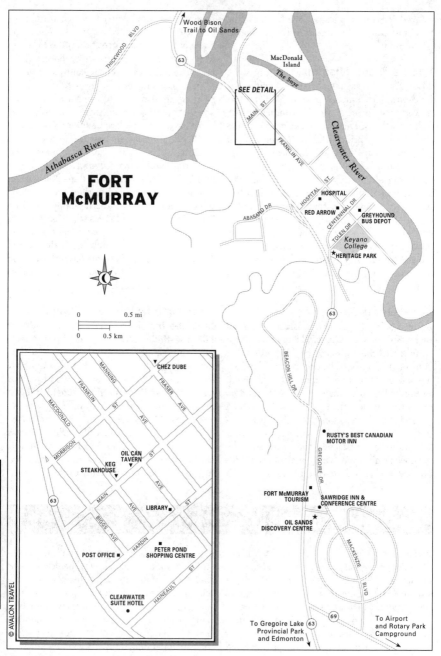

FORT McMURRAY

Wood Bison Trail to Oil Sands

THICKWOOD BLVD

63

Athabasca River

MacDonald Island

The Snye

SEE DETAIL

MAIN ST

FRANKLIN AVE

Clearwater River

HOSPITAL ST

HOSPITAL

RED ARROW

CENTENNIAL DR

ABASAND DR

TOLEN DR

GREYHOUND BUS DEPOT

Keyano College

★ HERITAGE PARK

63

BEACON HILL DR

RUSTY'S BEST CANADIAN MOTOR INN

GREGOIRE DR

FORT McMURRAY TOURISM

SAWRIDGE INN & CONFERENCE CENTRE

OIL SANDS DISCOVERY CENTRE ★

MACKENZIE BLVD

To Gregoire Lake 63 Provincial Park and Edmonton

69

To Airport and Rotary Park Campground

0   0.5 mi
0   0.5 km

Detail inset:

CHEZ DUBE ▼

MANNING ST

FRANKLIN AVE

FRASER AVE

MACDONALD

MORRISON

63

OIL CAN TAVERN ▼

KEG STEAKHOUSE ▼

MAIN AVE

ST

ST

LIBRARY ■

BIGGS AVE

HARDIN ST

POST OFFICE ■

PETER POND SHOPPING CENTRE ■

HAINEAULT ST

CLEARWATER SUITE HOTEL ●

© ANDREW HEMPSTEAD

oil sands tour, Fort McMurray

SIGHTS AND RECREATION
Oil Sands Discovery Centre

For an insight into the history, geology, and technology of the Athabasca Oil Sands mining process, head to this large interpretive center (515 Mackenzie Blvd., 780/743-7167, daily 9 A.M.–5 P.M. mid-May–Aug., Tues.–Sun. 10 A.M.–4 P.M. the rest of the year, adult $6, senior $5, child $4). Start your visit by watching *Quest for Energy,* a multimedia, big-screen presentation about the industry that has grown around the resource. The center houses an interesting collection of machinery and has interactive displays, hands-on exhibits, and interpretive presentations. Outside is the Industrial Equipment Garden, where an older-style bucket-wheel excavator and other machinery are displayed. To be moved to this site, the excavator had to be disassembled, with some sections requiring a 144-wheel, 45-meter-long (150-foot-long) trailer for the 45-kilometer (28-mile) trip from the mine.

◖ Syncrude and Suncor Plant Tours

Touring the oil sands plants is the best way to experience the operation firsthand. The scope of the developments is overwhelming, while the size of the machinery is almost inconceivable. Two companies—Syncrude and Suncor—are involved in tour programs offered through Fort McMurray Tourism (780/791-4336 or 800/565-3947, www.fortmcmurraytourism.com). Tours of the Syncrude site depart every Saturday at 9 A.M. in June, Wednesday–Saturday at 9 A.M. July–August, and Friday–Saturday at 9 A.M. in September. The Suncor tour departs Sunday–Monday at 1 P.M. in June and Sunday–Tuesday at 1 P.M. July–August. Regardless of which tour you choose, the itinerary is similar. Departing from the Oil Sands Discovery Program, they involve a bus ride north with stops at Wood Bison Trail Gateway and the Giants of Mining display, and then a tour of either the Syncrude or Suncor sites, with time set aside to get out of the bus at a lookout point. The round-trip takes around four hours. Tour cost is adult $30, senior and youth $25, which includes entry to the Discovery Centre and to Heritage Park. Children under 12 are not permitted and a security check is made before departure (have a photo ID ready). To join a tour you *must* make

ATHABASCA OIL SANDS

The numbers that oil types throw around when talking of the Athabasca Oil Sands are impossible to comprehend – 315 billion barrels of recoverable oil (more than present in all of Saudi Arabia) from a 1.6 trillion-barrel reserve (only 800 billion barrels of conventional crude oil are known to remain on this entire planet) just means *lots* to most people. Still, that's a lot of oil and the math is easy – it will take 100 years to extract just 20 percent of the recoverable oil.

The oil is not conventional oil but a heavy oil, commonly called bitumen. Extracting and processing it to produce a lighter, more useful oil is expensive. Of the many crucial differences between conventional oil reserves and the heavy, tar-like oil sands of Fort McMurray, none is more important than the associated costs. Operating costs for extracting and processing the oil sands' bitumen currently run at around $15 per barrel, compared to Middle East crude, which can be pumped out of the ground for just $1 a barrel. Benefits include no exploration costs for oil sands and that the processing plants are connected to the insatiable U.S. market by pipelines. Still, with improvements in technology, world supplies of conventional crude slowly being depleted, and oil prices fluctuating dramatically, the oil sands of Fort McMurray are the focus of big oil companies with *big* money – some $100 billion worth of planned development is underway to complement existing infrastructure.

THE PROCESS

The sands are mined in two different ways – deposits close to the surface are strip-mined, while the oil deeper down is extracted in situ (using steam injection). In the case of surface deposits, the size of the machinery used to scrape off the surface layer of muskeg and excavate the oil sands below it is mind-boggling. Extracting oil sands that lie deep below the earth's surface is very costly. A simplified explanation of the process is that the fields are tapped by parallel wells. Steam is injected in one, loosening then liquefying and separating the oil from the sand. A second, lower well, extracts the resulting oil. Once on the surface, it must be chemically altered to produce a lighter, more useful oil.

---

advance reservations. The tourism office has put together some accommodation/tour packages that are an excellent deal—around $180 per person for two nights' accommodation and a tour.

Wood Bison Trail

Driving north from the city on Highway 63 gives you a chance to view the mining operations (albeit at a distance), plus make a few interesting stops. Up to 40,000 vehicles a day traverse this route, including 400 buses filled with workers, so be prepared for a lot of traffic, especially during shift changes.

Make your first stop 27 kilometers (17 miles) north of Fort McMurray at the **Wood Bison Trail Gateway,** where there is an impressive wood bison sculpture made from oil sands. Also on display is a 100-million-year-old cypress tree found fossilized in the oil sands. This pullout is also the starting point for the **Matcheetawin Discovery Trails,** two interpretive loops over a reclaimed mine now covered in a mixed forest of aspen and spruce. The longer of the two passes a lookout over the Syncrude development. Continuing north three kilometers (1.9 miles) is a turn to the left that climbs to a viewpoint over a herd of 300 bison. The road then parallels a reclamation pond to the **Giants of Mining** exhibit, comprising some of the original machinery used in oil sands development. This is the beginning of the Syncrude spread, and as the road loops around the pond, you begin to get a feel for the scope of the operation. Around 55 kilometers (34 miles) from Fort McMurray, the road forks. To the left is Fort McKay, and to the right Highway 63 crosses the Athabasca River and continues 10 kilometers (6.2 miles) to a dock. Here, supplies such as petroleum and building materials are loaded onto barges and transported downstream (north) to remote communities such as Fort Chipewyan.

This is the end of the summer road. Between December and March, a winter road is built over the frozen muskeg and river 225 kilometers (140 miles) to Fort Chipewyan and up the Slave River to Fort Smith in the Northwest Territories.

Gregoire Lake Provincial Park

Southeast of the city 29 kilometers (18 miles) is Gregoire Lake, the only accessible lake in the Fort McMurray area. The 690-hectare (1,700-acre) park on the lake's west shore is a typical boreal forest of mixed woods and black spruce bogs. Many species of waterfowl nest on the lake, and mammals such as moose and black bears are relatively common. Some short hiking trails wind through the park, and canoes are rented in the day-use area, which also has a sandy beach and playground.

ACCOMMODATIONS AND CAMPING

High demand dictates that there are no bargains in Fort McMurray, and in fact, just getting a room can be difficult. Therefore, if you're planning to stay indoors, it's imperative that you book your Fort McMurray accommodations as far in advance as possible. Check with Fort McMurray Tourism (780/791-4336 or 800/565-3947, www.fortmcmurraytourism.com) for accommodation/tour package deals.

$50-100

Rusty's Best Canadian Motor Inn (385 Gregoire Dr., 780/791-4646, www.bestcdn.com, $84 s, $94 d) is one of a bunch of properties four kilometers (2.5 miles) south of downtown near the visitors center. All rooms have a fridge and some have kitchens, or you can dine in the hotel restaurant or lounge.

$150-200

An excellent alternative to the hotel options is ◖ **Chez Dube** (10102 Fraser Ave., 780/790-2367 or 800/565-0757, www.chezdube.com,

$175 s, $190 d), a turreted 14-room bed-and-breakfast surrounded by a well-tended garden that includes colorful flowerpots hanging from the verandah. The rooms each have a pastel color scheme, comfortable beds, en suite bathroom, Wi-Fi Internet, and television. Rates include a full breakfast and use of a games room. It backs onto the riverfront park and is only a few blocks from the main street.

Over $200

Fort McMurray's largest accommodation, with 190 rooms, is the **Sawridge Inn and Conference Centre** (530 Mackenzie Blvd., 780/791-7900 or 800/661-6567, www.sawridge.com, $219–249 s or d), which underwent a major revamp in 2003. Rooms have all the standard amenities business travelers demand, including wireless Internet. The city's best breakfast (included in the rate) is served each morning in the downstairs restaurant and a lounge is spread around an indoor pool complex.

◖ **Clearwater Suite Hotel** (4 Haineault St., 780/799-7676 or 877/799-7676, www.clearwaterfortmcmurray.com, $259–299 s or d) is aimed at long term stays, but is the nicest choice right downtown. Guest rooms are modern and come with 32-inch TVs, free Internet access, a washer/dryer combo, a kitchen, and free breakfast. It's well worth the few extra dollars for a King Suite.

Camping

Rotary Park Campground (Hwy. 69, 780/790-1581, $20) offers showers, cooking facilities, and powered sites, and is open year-round. The park is signposted but easy to miss; turn east along Highway 69 and look for the entrance to the left.

Further from town is the forested campground at **Gregoire Lake Provincial Park** (19 km/12 mi south on Hwy. 63 then 10 km/6.2 mi east on Hwy. 881, 780/334-2111, unserviced sites $20, powered sites $23), which has 140 fairly private sites, 60 with power hookups. Amenities include showers, firewood, and watercraft rentals.

FOOD

Even though the average wage in Fort McMurray is twice the national average, it doesn't mean the locals have fancy tastes. In fact, the city lacks any really good restaurants at all, with all the business going to fast-food restaurants and family-oriented chains, the best of which is the **Keg Steakhouse** (Nomad Inn, 10006 MacDonald Ave., 780/791-4770, Mon.–Sat. 11 A.M.–midnight, Sun. 4–11 P.M., $18–28), known for fine cuts of Alberta beef. For breakfast, it's hard to resist recommending the **(Hearthstone Grill** (Sawridge Inn, 530 Mackenzie Blvd., 780/791-7900, daily from 6:30 A.M., $15–31), which has a surprisingly good buffet at an even better price—just $12 including coffee. Adding to the appeal is an open dining space that is stylish and welcoming.

INFORMATION AND SERVICES

Fort McMurray Tourism (780/791-4336 or 800/565-3947, www.fortmcmurraytourism. com) does an excellent job of promoting the city to the world. They operate an information center south of downtown (Mon.–Fri. 8 A.M.–5 P.M. and Sat.–Sun. 9 A.M.–5 P.M. June–Aug., Mon.–Fri. 8:30 A.M.–4:30 P.M. Sept.–May), just north of the Oil Sands Discovery Centre. In addition to having a wealth of information on the city, the organization represents many northern fly-in fishing lodges and offers overnight accommodation packages.

The **post office** is at 9521 Franklin Avenue. **Fort Laundromat** (Plaza I on Franklin Ave.) is open daily 9 A.M.–9 P.M. **Fort McMurray Public Library** is housed in a large, rust-colored building (9907 Franklin Avenue, 780/743-7800, Mon. 5–9 P.M., Tues.–Wed. 10 A.M.–5 P.M., Thurs. 1–9 P.M., Fri.–Sat. 10 A.M.–5 P.M., Sun. 1–5 P.M.). It has free Internet access, or you can pay a few bucks an

hour at **Frogz** (8706 Franklin Ave., 780/743-3839, Tues.–Sun. 3–10 P.M.).

For emergencies, contact **Fort McMurray Regional Hospital** (7 Hospital Street, 780/791-6161) or the **RCMP** (780/799-8888).

GETTING THERE AND AROUND

It's a long 450-kilometer (280-mile) drive up to Fort McMurray on a highway that is regarded as one of the most dangerous in the province (mostly due to the high volume of traffic), and so many people prefer to fly. The **airport** is nine kilometers (5.6 miles) south, then six kilometers (3.7 miles) east of downtown. **Air Canada** (888/247-2262, www.air-canada.com), **Westjet** (800/538-5696, www. westjet.com), and **Air Mikisew** (780/743-8218 or 888/268-7112, www.airmikisew.com) fly daily between Edmonton and Fort McMurray, with Air Mikisew departing from the centrally located Edmonton City Centre Airport. A cab to downtown is $35. **Greyhound** (8220 Manning Avenue, 780/791-3664) has services three times daily to Edmonton. **Red Arrow** (8217 Franklin Ave., 800/232-1958) offers a more luxurious service than Greyhound, with fewer stops, more legroom, and free coffee and snacks. Either way, it's a five-hour trip to Edmonton.

Wood Buffalo Transit (780/743-4157) is a local transit service to outlying suburbs and the Oil Sands Discovery Centre. Buses run seven days a week and travel costs $1.75 per sector; seniors ride free. Cab companies include **Access Taxi** (780/799-3333), **Sun Taxi** (780/743-5050), and **United Class Cabs** (780/743-1234). The following car rentals are available in town, and all have airport counters: **Avis** (780/743-4773), **Budget** (780/743-8215), **Hertz** (780/743-4047), and **National** (780/743-6393).

North-Central Alberta

From downtown Edmonton, Highway 2 (called the St. Albert Trail in the vicinity of Edmonton) heads north into a once-forested land, along the **Athabasca Landing Trail,** a historic portage route used by natives and then traders and explorers that linked the North Saskatchewan and Athabasca river systems.

ATHABASCA

At the end of the Athabasca Landing Trail, 147 kilometers (91 miles) north of Edmonton, is the town of Athabasca (population 2,300), on a hill that slopes gently to the river. Although the Hudson's Bay Company buildings have long since disappeared, many later buildings from the days of the stern-wheelers remain, including the 1912 railway station and a 1913 brick schoolhouse. From town, walk through **Muskeg**

Creek Park (good berry-picking in late summer) and you'll emerge at **Athabasca University** (780/675-6111, www.athabascau.ca). This facility has a full-time staff of 1,200, a choice of 700 programs at all levels including graduate, a library with 100,000 books, an extensive art collection, and an annual budget exceeding $110 million—but there's not a single student in sight. That's because it's a correspondence university, one of the largest in North America and open to students regardless of their geographical location or previous academic levels.

Practicalities

Several motels are on Highway 2 south of town, including **Athabasca Hillside Motel** (4804 46th Ave., 780/675-5111 or 888/675-8900, www.athabascahillsidemotel.net, $65–90 s,

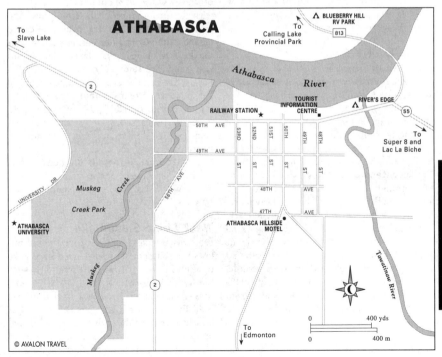

© AVALON TRAVEL

$75–95 d), with kitchenettes in each of the 17 rooms. Much nicer is the **Super 8** (4820 Wood Heights Rd., 780/675-8888 or 800/800-8000, www.super8.com, $109 s or d), through town to the east. It's a larger, modern hotel with spacious rooms, a business center, free breakfast, and an adjacent A&W restaurant. **River's Edge Campground** (50th Ave., May–Aug., unserviced sites $15, powered sites $20) sits on the edge of downtown where the Tawatinaw River drains into the much wider Athabasca River. Amenities are limited to a small bathroom complex with coin showers. Most RVers head north across the river to **Blueberry Hill RV Park** (Hwy. 813, 780/675-3733 or 800/859-9452, www.blueberryhillrvpark.ca, May–Oct., tenting $22, hookups $29), which has pull-through sites, modern washrooms, a laundry, a playground, and free firewood. It's also adjacent to an excellent golf course.

The **tourist information center** (50th Avenue, 780/675-9297, daily 10 A.M.–8 P.M. late May–early Sept.) is in an orange CN caboose along the riverfront.

SLAVE LAKE

The town of Slave Lake (population 6,700) is on the southeastern shore of **Lesser Slave Lake,** 110 kilometers (68 miles) west of Athabasca and 250 kilometers (155 miles) northwest of Edmonton. Once an important staging point for steamboat freight and passengers, the town today is a popular base for anglers and the jumping off point for Highway 88 (**Bicentennial Highway**), which winds its way through uninhabited wilderness to High Level. The first section of this highway passes through **Lesser Slave Lake Provincial Park,** which protects long sandy beaches, unique sand dunes, and wetland and boreal forest habitats supporting diverse wildlife. At the north end of the park, a steep eight-kilometer (five-mile) road leads to the plateau-like summit of 1,030-meter (3,380-foot) Marten Mountain, from where views extend across the lake.

Fishing

Lesser Slave Lake (1,150 sq km/440 sq mi)

is the largest lake in Alberta accessible by road and has some of the province's best fishing, with northern pike to nine kilograms (19.8 pounds), walleye to four kilograms (8.8 pounds), whitefish to 2.5 kilograms (5.5 pounds), and yellow perch to one kilogram (2.2 pounds)—enough to make any self-respecting fisherman quit his job, pack the rod and reel, and head north. The most productive fishing is done from out in the middle of the lake. Ask at the information center for a list of local fishing guides, who rent boats from $25 per hour, $60 half-day, or $120 full-day.

Practicalities

The **Highway Motor Inn,** on Highway 2 by the tourist information center (600 14th Ave. SW, 780/849-2400 or 888/848-2400, $65 s, $75 d) has basic rooms, or upgrade to those at the **Sawridge Inn and Conference Centre** (1200 Main St. S, 780/849-4101 or 800/661-6657, www.sawridge.com, $119 s, $129 d), with the amenities of a full-service hotel and in-house dining options that include the casual **Hearthstone Grille.** The business class rooms are decidedly bigger than the standard rooms and come with Internet access and bathrobes for just $10 extra. Lesser Slave Lake Provincial Park's **Marten River Campground** (6 km/3.7 mi north of town, 780/849-7100, May–Oct., unserviced sites $20, powered sites $26) has coin-operated showers, a beach, and a summer interpretive program.

The **tourist information center** (off Highway 2, west of Main Street, 780/849-4611, www.slavelake.com) is open daily 10 A.M.–7 P.M. May–August.

West Along Slave Lake

From Slave Lake, Highway 2 westbound follows the southern shore of Lesser Slave Lake to High Prairie. At **Kinuso,** a small **museum** (780/775-3774, Mon.–Fri. 10 A.M.–4 P.M. May–Aug.) centers around a stuffed grizzly bear that stands over 2.5 meters (eight feet). A little farther along the highway, a nine-kilometer (5.6-mile) gravel road leads north to Lesser Slave Lake and **Spruce Point Park** (780/775-

2117, www.sprucepointpark.ca, mid-May to mid-Sept., $21–28) that bustles with families and fisherman throughout summer. From the main camping area, a wide grassy area leads down to a lakefront beach and a marina with boat and canoe rentals and a fish-cleaning shed. Other park amenities include a general store (stocked with lots of fishing tackle), horseshoe pits, hiking trails, and showers.

Grouard (population 400), near the west end of Lesser Slave Lake, grew up around the St. Bernard Mission. On the grounds of Northern Lakes College, the **Native Cultural Arts Museum** (780/751-3306, May–Sept. Tues.–Fri. 10 A.M.–4 P.M., Sat. 10 A.M.–6 P.M., donation) is dedicated to promoting a better understanding of North American native cultures through exhibition of native arts and crafts as well as the outdoor re-creation of a native village.

At **Hilliard's Bay Provincial Park,** 13 kilometers (eight miles) east of Grouard on the northwest shore of Lesser Slave Lake, the **Boreal Forest Interpretive Trail** meanders through a forest habitat that includes gnarled paper birches. The park campground (780/849-7124, May–early Oct., unserviced sites $20, powered sites $26) has showers, kitchen shelters, and firewood.

McLennan

Known as the Bird Capital of Canada, this town of 1,000 is on **Kimiwan Lake** at the confluence of three major bird migration paths—the Mississippi, Pacific, and Central. An estimated 27,000 shorebirds and 250,000 waterfowl reside or pass through here; more than 200 different species are sighted annually. An excellent interpretive center (780/324-2004, May–Sept. daily 10 A.M.–7 P.M.) overlooking the lake has a display on migration patterns, computers loaded with information on local species, checklists, and binoculars for loan. From the center, a boardwalk leads through a wetland area to a gazebo and a bird blind. Panels along the boardwalk provide pictures and descriptions of commonly sighted species.

HIGHWAY 18 WEST

Seventy-three kilometers (45 miles) north of Edmonton on Highway 2, Highway 18 heads west through some of Canada's most productive mixed farming land. Major crops include wheat, barley, oats, canola, and hay. Livestock operations include cattle, hogs, poultry, dairy cows, and sheep; the area is home to several large feedlots and Alberta's two largest livestock auctions. At the junction of Highways 2 and 18, a gravel road leads north to **Nilsson Bros. Inc.** (780/348-5893, www.nbinc.com), Canada's largest cattle auction market. Live auctions are held in summer every Tuesday morning. Buyers are from throughout North America, but anyone is welcome to attend. The auctioneer is lightning fast—Alberta's best beef cattle are sold hundreds at a time by gross weight. The facility is open every day; ask to have a look around. The staff restaurant, open for an hour at lunchtime, serves hearty meat-and-potato meals for a reasonable price. Just don't ask for lamb.

Barrhead and Vicinity

Continuing west on Highway 18 takes you to Barrhead, an agriculture and lumber town of 4,200 located 1.5 hours northwest of Edmonton. **Barrhead Centennial Museum** (along Highway 33 at 57th Avenue, 780/674-5203, Tues.–Sat. 10 A.M.–5 P.M. and Sun. 1–5 P.M. mid-May–Aug., adult $2), with displays depicting the town's agricultural past, is north of downtown. The town's symbol is the great blue heron; you can see a model of one at the top end of 50th Street, or head out to **Thunder Lake Provincial Park** 21 kilometers (13 miles) west of town on Highway 18 for the chance to see a real one.

HIGHWAY 43 WEST

This major route connects Edmonton with Grande Prairie, a total distance of 460 kilometers (286 miles). A few towns and parks provide an opportunity to break up the journey.

Whitecourt

Whitecourt (population 9,000) sits at the

confluence of the Athabasca, McLeod, and Sakwatamau Rivers on Highway 43, 177 kilometers (110 miles) northwest of Edmonton and 341 kilometers (212 miles) southeast of Grande Prairie. To learn about the importance of local logging enterprises, visit the **Forest Interpretive Centre** (on the south side of town, 780/778-2214, Mon.–Fri. 9 A.M.–6 P.M. year-round, with extended hours daily 9 A.M.–6 P.M. in July and Aug., free). Displays re-create forest environment and a logging camp, and a series of hands-on, interactive exhibits describe every aspect of the industry. The center also holds the town's information center (780/778-5363).

Most of Whitecourt's dozen motels are on Highway 43 as it enters town from the southeast. The best of these, **Green Gables Inn** (3527 Caxton St., 780/778-4537 or 888/779-4537, www.greengablesinn.ca, $104 s, $109 d) has wireless Internet, an exercise room, and a restaurant (where guests enjoy complimentary breakfast). **Lions Club Campground** (mid-Apr.–mid-Oct., tent sites $20, RVs $24–28) at the south end of the service strip, is set in a heavily forested area and has a laundry and showers.

Carson-Pegasus Provincial Park

This 1,178-hectare (2,900-acre) park is on the southern edge of the Swan Hills, 30 kilometers (19 miles) north of Whitecourt. Because of its location in a transition zone, it contains forest typical of both the foothills (lodgepole pine and spruce) and the boreal forest (aspen, poplar, birch, and fir). More than 40 species of mammals have been recorded here, including deer, moose, and black bear. The epicenter of the park is McLeod Lake, where the fishing is excellent for rainbow trout (stocked annually) and the day-use area offers canoe, rowboat, and motorboat rentals, and a sandy beach. The campground (780/778-2664, www.carsonpegasus.com, $22–28, firewood $7) has flush toilets, showers, kitchen shelters, and an interpretive theater.

Whitecourt to Grande Prairie

Continuing west through Valleyview, **Sturgeon Lake** is known for its excellent northern pike, perch, and walleye fishing and two interesting provincial parks. **Williamson Provincial Park** may be only 17 hectares (42 acres) but it has a sandy beach, good swimming, and a campground (May–mid-Sept., $20–25). Protecting a much larger chunk of forested lakeshore is 3,100-hectare (7,660-acre) **Young's Point Provincial Park.** Here you'll find good bird-watching for forest birds and waterfowl, and productive fishing among the dense aquatic growth close to the shore. Hiking trails begin at the day-use area and lead along the lake and to an active beaver pond. The campground (unserviced sites $20, powered sites $26) has flush toilets, showers, and is near a sandy beach.

West of Edmonton

From the provincial capital, the Yellowhead Highway (Hwy. 16) heads west through a region of aspen parkland and scattered lakes to the Canadian Rockies foothills and the border of Jasper National Park. The region's other main thoroughfare, Highway 40, spurs north off the Yellowhead Highway to Grande Cache and Willmore Wilderness Park. An area of frenzied oil activity during the early 1970s, the region west of Edmonton is the center for a large petroleum industry, as well as for farming, coal mining, forestry, and the production of electricity. The major towns are Edson and Hinton, both on the Yellowhead Highway.

FROM EDMONTON TOWARD HINTON

Long after leaving Edmonton's city limits, the Yellowhead Highway is lined with motels, industrial parks, and housing estates. The towns of Spruce Grove and Stony Plain flash by, and farming begins to dominate the landscape.

Wabamun and Nearby Lakes

Wabamun is the name of a town, a lake, and a provincial park 32 kilometers (20 miles) west of Stony Plain. The skyline around Wabamun Lake is dominated by high-voltage power lines coming from the three coal-fired generating plants that supply more than two-thirds of Alberta's electrical requirements. **Wabamun Lake Provincial Park** is on sparkling blue Moonlight Bay at the lake's eastern end. The fishing is good for northern pike (especially in fall); a beach is the perfect spot for a swim; and the hiking trail is a good spot for wild-life viewing. The park campground (780/892-2702, mid-May–early Oct., unserviced sites $20, powered sites $26) has almost 300 sites, but because of its proximity to Edmonton, is very busy on weekends. Amenities include coin-operated showers, firewood, kitchen shelters, and a concession.

Pembina River Provincial Park

The Pembina River Valley is the first true wilderness area west of Edmonton. White spruce and aspen blanket the park and provide a habitat for many mammals, including beavers, mule deer, white-tailed deer, and moose. Fishing in the river is particularly good for northern pike and walleye, and those who don't fish might appreciate the deep swimming hole behind a weir, or the hiking trails in the northern part of the park. On the eastern side of the river, the **campground** (780/727-3643, mid-May–Oct., unserviced sites $20, powered sites $26) has flush toilets, kitchen shelters, showers, an interpretive program, and firewood.

Edson

Edson is a mid-sized town of 8,100, 199 kilometers (124 miles) west of Edmonton.

Most motels are along the main highway through town—locally known as 2nd Avenue (heading east) and 4th Avenue (heading west). The **Sundowner Inn** (5150 2nd Ave., 780/723-5591 or 877/723-5591, $99 s, $109 d) has the basics and a few bonuses too—an indoor pool and a recreation room with a fireplace and pool table. **Lions Park Campground** (east end of town, 780/723-3169, May–Sept., unserviced sites $18, powered sites $21) has 48 treed sites far enough from the highway to be relatively quiet. Facilities include extra hot (and fast) showers and plenty of free firewood, which is just as well because you need a bonfire to cook anything on the oversized fire rings.

HINTON

On the south bank of the Athabasca River and surrounded by total wilderness, this town of 9,500, 287 kilometers (178 miles) west of Edmonton, makes an ideal base for a couple of days' exploration. It's also only 75 kilometers (47 miles) from Jasper—but before speeding off to the famous mountain parks, take time out to explore Hinton's immediate vicinity. In town, don't be put off by the unappealing location of the **Natural Resource Interpretive Park,** behind the Canadian Tire store on the west side of town—much of the park is out of sight in the valley below. Up top you'll find a lookout, a 154-ton dump truck, and panels describing local industry, while a trail leads down to a

Natural Resource Interpretive Park, Hinton

NORTHERN ALBERTA

small arboretum and through an area of wetlands. On the campus of the **Hinton Training Centre** (1176 Switzer Dr., 780/865-8200, Mon.–Fri. 8:30 A.M.–4:30 P.M.) there is a small museum dedicated to the history of forestry, including a display on wildfire management. Adjacent is a 1922 ranger cabin. The museum is also the starting point for the **Interpretive Nature Trail**—a 1.6-kilometer (one-mile) path that winds around the perimeter of the school, passing various forest environments, Edna the erratic (a huge boulder carried far from its source during the last Ice Age), and a viewpoint with magnificent views of the Athabasca River Valley and Canadian Rockies.

Accommodations and Food

I recommend giving the regular motels a miss and staying out of town at one of the following two accommodations. Halfway between Hinton and Jasper, ■ **Overlander Mountain Lodge** (780/866-2330 or 877/866-2330, www.overlandermountainlodge.com, $159–219 s or d) has an inviting wilderness setting and energetic hosts with plenty of suggestions to keep you busy through the day. Choose from regular guest rooms in various styles, cozy cabins, or a large, three-bedroom log chalet. Mountain charm continues through to the dining room, where Canadian specialties anchor a seasonal menu.

■ **Black Cat Guest Ranch** (780/865-3084 or 800/859-6840, www.blackcatguestranch.ca, $115 s or d) is another nearby mountain retreat. All of the rooms have private baths and mountain views. Horseback riding is available during the day, and in the evening, guests can relax in the large living room or hot tub. A meal package is adult $46, child $33. To get to the ranch, take Highway 40 north for six kilometers (3.7 miles), turn left to Brûlé and continue for 11 kilometers (6.8 miles), then turn right and follow the signs.

Apart from the fast-food restaurants that line the highway from one end of town to the other, Hinton has little to offer the hungry traveler. The **Husky Restaurant,** as usual, serves filling meals at good prices; it's open 24

SUNDANCE PROVINCIAL PARK

As an alternative to continuing west along Highway 16 from Edson to Hinton, consider the **Emerson Creek Road,** which links the two towns along an unpaved route north of the main highway. It also provides access to 3,712-hectare (9,170-acre) Sundance Provincial Park, protecting a variety of interesting geological features and the picturesque Emerson Lakes. A 5.7-kilometer (3.5-mile) trail winds around the lakes to an old trapper's cabin and past some active beaver dams; allow 90 minutes to complete the entire loop. The lakes are stocked with brook trout and Sundance Creek with rainbow and brown trout. A small campground (May–Sept., $12) at the lakes has sites with no services but free firewood.

A good map of local logging roads is required to ensure you stay on the right route. These are available at the information centers in both Edson and Hinton.

---

hours. If gas-station dining isn't your style, try **Tokyo Sushi** (Black Bear Inn, 571 Gregg Ave., 780/865-2120, $8–16), a modern, family–style restaurant with good value Japanese food.

Information

The **tourist information center** (Gregg Ave., 780/865-2777, daily 8:30 A.M.–6 P.M. in summer, weekdays 9 A.M.–4 P.M. the rest of the year) is on the south side of the highway surrounded by gardens in the middle of the commercial strip. It's impossible to miss. Most of the best this region has to offer lies outside of Hinton, and in this regard, the staff does a wonderful job of supplying information on hiking, fishing, and canoeing opportunities that would otherwise be easy to miss.

HIGHWAY 40 TO GRANDE PRAIRIE

Take divided Highway 16 west out of Hinton and, before you know it, Highway 40 spurs north, passing the following sights, reaching Grande Cache after 142 kilometers (88 miles). From this remote mountain town, it's another 181 kilometers (112 miles) to Grande Prairie along a mostly unpaved road.

William A. Switzer Provincial Park

This 2,688-hectare (6,640-acre) park, 26 kilometers (16 miles) northwest of Hinton on Highway 40, encompasses a series of shallow lakes linked by Jarvis Creek. Most of the park is heavily forested and home to elk, moose, and deer. The lakes are excellent for canoeing, birdwatching, and wildlife viewing, but fishing is considered average. Highway 40 divides the park roughly in two, with many access points. From the south, the first road loops around the west side of Jarvis Lake, passing a pleasant picnic area and camping before rejoining Highway 40. At the north end of Jarvis Lake is Kelley's Bathtub day-use area, where a short trail leads to a bird blind. The main **campground** is on **Gregg Lake.** It offers 164 sites, coin-operated showers, kitchen shelters, an interpretive theater, and winter camping; unserviced sites $20, powered sites $26. In the same vicinity are **Graveyard/Halfway** and **Cache Campgrounds,** where sites range $17–20 per night. In the south of the park is **Jarvis Lake Campground** ($20). For more information on the park, call 780/865-5600; for campsite reservations, call 780/865-5152.

On to Grande Cache

From William A. Switzer Provincial Park, it is 118 kilometers (73 miles) to Grande Cache. A 32-kilometer (20-mile) gravel spur to **Rock Lake-Solomon Creek Wildland Provincial Park,** 15 kilometers (9.3 miles) north of Switzer park, makes a tempting detour. Although the park extends from Willmore Wilderness Park in the north to Brûlé Lake in the south, most of it is remote, untracked wilderness. The only facilities are at Rock Lake itself (camping $20). From Rock Lake Road, Highway 40 continues to climb steadily, crossing Pinto Creek and Berland River (small campground),

then follows Muskeg River for a short while. Continuing north, the road then passes **Pierre Grey Lakes,** a string of five lakes protected as a provincial recreation area. The lakes lie in a beautiful spot, with prolific birdlife and waters stocked annually with rainbow trout. From the boat launch, a rough trail leads 1.6 kilometers (one mile) along the lakeshore to the site of a trading post. Camping is $17 per night.

Grande Cache

Grande Cache is a remote coal-mining town of 3,700, 450 kilometers (280 miles) west of Edmonton and 182 kilometers (113 miles) south of Grande Prairie. The surrounding wilderness is totally undeveloped, offering endless opportunities for hiking, canoeing, kayaking, fishing, and horseback riding.

Grande Cache Tourism and Interpretive Centre (780/827-3300 or 888/827-3790, daily 9 A.M.–6 P.M. in summer, Mon.–Sat. 9 A.M.–5 P.M.the rest of the year) is outstanding, not just considering the size of the town that it represents, but for the wealth of information contained within it. It's easy to spend at least one hour in the two-story complex, with displays that include information about the human history of the region, the local industry, taxidermy, tree identification, and Willmore Wilderness Park. Other features include an information desk, a gift shop, and a large deck from where views extend across the Smoky River Valley to the highest peaks of the Canadian Rockies.

In recent years, Grande Cache has placed itself on the calendar of extreme, ultra-marathoners the world over as host of the early August **Canadian Death Race** (www.canadiandeathrace.com). The foot race takes place along a super-demanding 125-kilometer (78-mile) course, which summits three peaks.

On the highway through town is the **Big Horn Motor Inn** (780/827-3744 or 888/880-2444, www.bighorninn.com, $90 s, $100 d). If you're looking for something a little more adventurous, consider a stay at **Sheep Creek Back Country Lodge & Cabins** (780/831-1087 or 877/945-3786, www.sheepcreek.net, mid-June–mid-Sept., $95–110 s or d), which is accessed by a short walking trail and a suspension bridge from 24 kilometers (15 miles) north of town. It attracts an eclectic array of guests—anglers, hunters, mountain bikers—but everyone is welcome. Each rustic cabin has a simple kitchen, bedroom, deck, chemical toilet, and gravity-fed shower. A communal fridge/freezer is located in the main building. Guests bring their own food and towels. **Marv Moore Campground** (Shand Ave., 780/827-2404, mid-May–mid-Oct., unserviced sites $20, powered sites $25) has semiprivate, well-shaded sites and showers, kitchen shelters, a laundry, and firewood.

Willmore Wilderness Park

This 460,000-hectare (1,137,000-acre) northern extension of Jasper National Park lies south and west of Grande Cache, and is divided roughly in half by the Smoky River. The park is accessible only on foot, horseback, or, in winter, on skis. It is totally undeveloped—the trails that do exist are not maintained and are mostly those once used by trappers. The diverse wildlife is one of the park's main attractions; white-tailed and mule deer, mountain goats, bighorn sheep, moose, elk, caribou, and black bears are all common. The park is also home to wolves, cougars, and grizzly bears.

The easiest way to access the park is from **Sulphur Gates Provincial Recreation Area,** six kilometers (3.7 miles) north of Grande Cache on Highway 40 and then a similar distance along a gravel road to the west. Those not planning a trip into the park can still enjoy the cliffs at **Sulphur Gates,** which rise above the confluence of the Sulphur and Smoky Rivers. The color difference between the glacial-fed Smoky River and spring-fed Sulphur River is apparent as they merge. Anyone planning an extended trip into the park should be aware that no services are available, most trails are unmarked, and certain areas are heavily used by horse-packers. Get a taste of the park with **Taste of Wilderness Tours** (780/827-4250, www.tasteofwilderness.ab.ca), which offers day and overnight hikes within the park.

More information is available by visiting www.wilmorewildernesspark.com, which represents local outfitters.

Grande Prairie and the Northwest

From its source in the interior of British Columbia, the **Peace River** has carved a majestic swath across the northwestern corner of Alberta's boreal forest. Explorers, trappers, settlers, and missionaries traveled upstream and established trading posts along the fertile valley and surrounding plains. The posts at Fort Vermilion and Dunvegan have slipped into oblivion and are now designated as historical sites, while the region's largest city, Grande Prairie, has gone from strength to strength as a regional center. As the name suggests, Grande Prairie (population 51,000) is surrounded by plains. Grasslands are something of an anomaly at such northern latitude. To the south and west are heavily forested mountains, and to the north and east are boreal forests and wetlands. But the grasslands here, *la grande prairie,* provided the stimulus for growth in the region. Edmonton is 460 kilometers (286 miles) to the southeast, while Dawson Creek (British Columbia) and Mile Zero of the Alaska Highway are 135 kilometers (84 miles) to the northwest.

SIGHTS AND RECREATION

Although malls, motels, restaurants, and other services are spread out along Highway 2 west and north of town, the center of the city has managed to retain much of its original charm. A short walk west of downtown on 100th Avenue is **Bear Creek,** along which most of Grande Prairie's sights lie.

Muskoseepi Park

Muskoseepi (bear creek in the Cree language) is a 405-hectare (1,000-acre) park that preserves

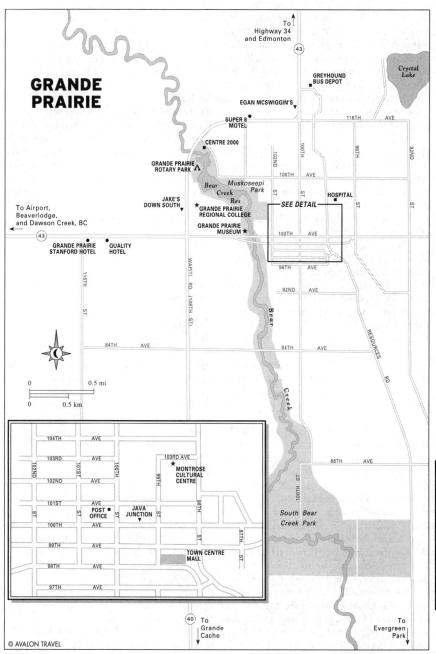

GRANDE PRAIRIE

To
Highway 34
and Edmonton

(43)

Crystal
Lake

GREYHOUND
BUS DEPOT

EGAN MCSWIGGIN'S

SUPER 8
MOTEL

116TH   AVE

CENTRE 2000

102ND

100TH

96TH

92ND

ST

ST

ST

ST

108TH   AVE

GRANDE PRAIRIE
ROTARY PARK

Bear
Creek
Res

Muskoseepi
Park

SEE DETAIL

HOSPITAL

To Airport,
Beaverlodge,
and Dawson Creek, BC

JAKE'S
DOWN SOUTH

GRANDE PRAIRIE
REGIONAL COLLEGE

GRANDE PRAIRIE
MUSEUM

100TH   AVE

(43)

GRANDE PRAIRIE
STANFORD HOTEL

QUALITY
HOTEL

96TH   AVE

116TH

ST

WAPITI   RD. (108TH ST.)

Bear

92ND   AVE

84TH   AVE

84TH   AVE

Creek

RESOURCES   RD.

0   0.5 mi

0   0.5 km

68TH   AVE

100TH   ST

South Bear
Creek Park

104TH   AVE

103RD   AVE

102ND

101ST

100TH

ST

103RD AVE

99TH

MONTROSE
CULTURAL
CENTRE

102ND   AVE

101ST   AVE

POST
OFFICE

JAVA
JUNCTION

98TH

ST

100TH   AVE

99TH   AVE

97TH

ST

98TH   AVE

TOWN CENTRE
MALL

97TH   AVE

(40) To
Grande
Cache

To
Evergreen
Park

© AVALON TRAVEL

a wide swathe of land through the heart of the city. At the north end of the park is **Bear Creek Reservoir,** the focal point of the park. Here you'll find an interpretive pavilion, a heated outdoor pool, tennis courts, mini-golf, and canoe rentals ($10 per hour). At the magnificent open-plan **Centre 2000,** Grande Prairie's main information center, a stairway leads up to the **Northern Lights Lookout.** From Centre 2000, 40 kilometers (25 miles) of hiking and biking trails follow both sides of Bear Creek to the city's outer edge. Overlooking the reservoir (access from the Hwy. 2 bypass) is **Grande Prairie Regional College.** Designed by renowned architect Douglas Cardinal, the flowing curves of this brick building are the city's most distinctive landmark.

A 20-minute walk south through the park leads to **Grande Prairie Museum** (780/532-5482, Mon.–Fri. 8:30 A.M.–4:30 P.M., Sat. 10 A.M.–4:30 P.M., Sun. noon–4:30 P.M., adult $5, senior $4, child $3). If you're driving, access is east along 102nd Avenue from downtown. Indoor displays include the Heritage Discovery Centre, which catalogues the area's early development through interactive exhibit, a natural history display, and dinosaur bones from a nearby dig site. Historic buildings outside include a church, a schoolhouse, a blacksmith shop, and a fire station.

Saskatoon Island Provincial Park

For thousands of years, natives have come to this area to collect, as the name suggests, saskatoon berries. The "Island" part of the name dates to the 1920s, when much of what is now protected was an island; today the park is an isthmus between Little and Saskatoon Lakes. Sweet, purple-colored saskatoon berries are still abundant and cover nearly one-third of the 102-hectare (250-acre) park. Late July and August are the best times for berry picking, although park rangers don't encourage the activity. This park is also one of the few places in Canada where trumpeter swans can be viewed during the spring nesting season. The campground (780/538-5350, May–Sept., unserviced sites $20, powered sites $26)

has showers, groceries, a food concession, and mini-golf, and is beside a beach. The park is 20 kilometers (12.5 miles) west of Grande Prairie on Highway 2, then three kilometers (1.9 miles) north.

Events

Evergreen Park, south of downtown, hosts many of the city's larger events, including a farmers market each Saturday during summer, horse racing, demolition derbies, and fall harvest festivals. The weekend closest to May 31 is **Grande Prairie Stompede** (780/532-4646, www.gpstompede.com), a gathering of North America's best cowboys and chuck wagon drivers. The regional fair, with a livestock show, chuck wagon races, and a midway, is the last weekend of July. For further information on these events, call the park administration (780/532-3279). Muskoseepi Park hosts **National Aboriginal Day** on the fourth weekend of June.

ACCOMMODATIONS AND CAMPING

Motels are west and north of downtown along Highway 2. **Grande Prairie Stanford Hotel** (11401 100th Ave., 780/539-5678 or 800/661-8160, www.grandeprairiestanfordhotel.com, $130 s, $135 d) is a 204-room complex, with mid-sized guest rooms, a fitness room, an outdoor hot tub, a restaurant, and a bar. The **Quality Hotel** (11201 100th Ave., 780/539-6000 or 800/661-7954, www.choicehotels.ca, $135 s or d) stands out not only for its sleek exterior, but inside for modern, well-designed rooms with all the amenities. A fitness center, business center, restaurant, and lounge are on site. Rates include local calls, a light breakfast, and an airport shuttle. Don't expect any surprises at the **Super 8 Motel** (10050 116th Ave., 780/532-8288 or 800/800-8000, www.super8.com, $139 s or d)—just the usual high standard of reliable rooms, an indoor pool and waterslide, a laundry facility, and a free continental breakfast.

Grande Prairie Rotary Park (along the Highway 2 bypass, 780/532-1137, May–Sept., tents $20, RVs and trailers $28–35) overlooks Bear Creek and is just across from Centre 2000. It has showers and a laundry room but few trees; no reservations taken.

FOOD
The dining scene in Grande Prairie is unremarkable at best.

Jake's Down South (10702 108th St., 780/532-5667, daily 11 A.M.–10 P.M., $15–27) doesn't look like much from the outside, but the Southern-style food is as good as you're likely to come across in Grande Prairie. Think jambalaya and blackened catfish. Across the road, the Grande Prairie Regional College has a cafeteria that bustles with students (and locals looking for a cheap meal) throughout the school year. **Delmonica's** (Grande Prairie Stanford Hotel, 11401 100th Ave., 780/539-5678; daily for breakfast, lunch, and dinner) is one of many hotel dining rooms with a lunchtime buffet.

INFORMATION
Overlooking Bear Creek Reservoir, **Centre 2000** (off the Hwy. 2 bypass at 11330 106th St., 780/539-7688, www.gptourism.ca, daily 9 A.M.–7 P.M. May–Sept., daily 8:30 A.M.–4:30 P.M. the rest of the year) houses the local tourist information center. One desk is staffed by Travel Alberta employees, while an adjacent space is dedicated to supplying local information. Part of the Montrose Cultural Centre, **Grande Prairie Public Library** (9839 103rd Ave., 780/532-3580, Mon.–Thurs. 10 A.M.–9 P.M., Fri.–Sat. 10 A.M.–6 P.M., and Sun. 2–5 P.M.) is an excellent facility with wireless Internet access, as well as regular modem-connected computers.

NORTH FROM GRANDE PRAIRIE
Sexsmith
North of Grande Prairie, the small town of Sexsmith is a pleasant place to stop, with most businesses fronted by early 1900s–style facades. One block off the main street is the **Sexsmith Blacksmith Shop** (780/568-3668,

Mon.–Fri. 9:30 A.M.–4:30 P.M. and Sat.–Sun. 10 A.M.–4 P.M. June–early Sept., donation), a working museum restored to its original 1916 condition. Inside the log structure are more than 10,000 artifacts, including caches of moonshine, which were hidden in the log walls to prevent detection by the North West Mounted Police (NWMP).

West from Rycroft
One of the picturesque spots in this region is protected as **Moonshine Lake Provincial Park.** More than 100 species of birds and, in winter, high concentrations of moose call this 1,080-hectare (2,670-acre) park home. Some people claim that the lake is named for the moon's reflection on its still water, although it more likely came from a fellow who sold moonshine to travelers en route to Dawson Creek. Year-round **campsites** (unserviced sites $20, powered sites $25, no reservations taken) are scattered among stands of aspen, poplar, and white spruce. Amenities include showers, flush toilets, kitchen shelters, a concession, and firewood.

Dunvegan
As Highway 2 descends into the Peace River Valley from the south, it crosses Alberta's longest suspension bridge at Dunvegan—a point that was the site of many trading posts and a mission. On the north side of the river is the **Visitor Reception Centre** (780/835-7150, mid-May–early Sept. daily 10 A.M.–6 P.M., adult $3, senior $2, child $1.50), featuring displays that tell the story of Dunvegan and its role in the early history of northern Alberta. On the riverbank are the restored church and rectory of the St. Charles Roman Catholic Mission, circa 1885 (look for the gnarled maple tree, planted by early missionaries, behind the mission site). A gravel road leads under the bridge to the site of the original settlement, **Fort Dunvegan,** which was built as a trading post for the North West Company in 1805, and was in use until 1918. Nothing but depressions in the ground remain from the original settlement, but set back from the road is a

NORTHERN ALBERTA

white Hudson's Bay Company factor's house. Adjacent to these historic sites is **Dunvegan Provincial Park** (780/538-5350, Apr.–Oct., powered sites $26), a 67-site campground.

Peace River

Many historic buildings line the main street (100th St.) of this bustling northern town of 6,200. By the river is **Peace River Museum** (10302 99th St., 780/624-4261, Mon.–Sat. 10:30 A.M.–4 P.M., adult $3), with displays of native clothing, the fur trade, early explorers, and the development of the town. Two spots near downtown afford excellent views of the Peace River and the valley through which it flows. To access the closest, take 100th Avenue under Highway 2 and follow this winding road to its end, or alternatively, take 101st Street south to 107th Avenue, which links up with Judah Hill Road. This road passes **Sagitawa Lookout,** from where you can see the town, the valley, and the confluence of the Peace and Smoky Rivers.

The least expensive rooms in town are at the **Western Budget Motel** (7701 100th Ave., 780/624-3445, www.westernbudgetmotel.com, $89 s, $99 d). It may be across the river from downtown, but the rooms are comfortable and there's an on-site restaurant. **Lions Club Park** (on the west side of the river, 780/624-2120, Apr.–Oct., unserviced sites $20, hookups $25–30) has well-shaded campsites, showers, and a laundry room.

The **Mighty Peace Tourist Association** is based out of an old railway station at the top end of 100th Street (780/338-2364 or 800/215-4535, www.mightypeace.com, daily 10 A.M.–6 P.M. June–Sept.).

MACKENZIE HIGHWAY

Named for 18th-century explorer Alexander Mackenzie, this route, also known as Highway 35, extends from Grimshaw, 24 kilometers (15 miles) west of Peace River, for 473 kilometers (294 miles) north to the Northwest Territories. It passes through a vast, empty land dominated by the Peace River and a seemingly endless forest of spruce, poplar, and jack pine.

Grimshaw

Make a point of stopping at the local **information center** (daily 9 A.M.–5 P.M. June–Sept.) in a blue rail car at the main intersection. It's stocked with brochures for onward travel and staffed by friendly locals who seem genuinely interested in your travels.

Lac Cardinal

North of Grimshaw, on the eastern shore of Lac Cardinal, is **Queen Elizabeth Provincial Park.** The lake is very shallow, and no streams flow from it. This creates an ideal habitat for many species of waterfowl. Beavers, moose, and black bears are also present. The park **campground** (780/624-6486, mid-May–mid-Oct., unserviced sites $20, powered sites $26) has pit toilets, firewood, and kitchen shelters. Immediately south of the park is **Lac Cardinal Pioneer Village Museum** (780/332-2030, daily 11 A.M.–5 P.M. May–Sept.), featuring a large outdoor collection of memorabilia from the Peace River region.

Manning

As the highway descends into the picturesque Notikewin Valley, it passes through Manning (population 1,200). At the south end of town, one kilometer (0.6 miles) east on Highway 691, is the excellent **Battle River Pioneer Museum** (780/836-2374, daily 1 A.M.–6 P.M. May–Sept., from 10 A.M. July–Aug., donation), which has a large collection of antique wrenches, taxidermy (including a rare albino moose), carriages and buggies, farm machinery, a birch necklace carved out of a single piece of wood, and a collection of prehistoric arrowheads—ask to see the one embedded in a whalebone.

Manning Motor Inn (780/836-2801, $109 s, $119 d) is at the south end of town and has a restaurant. **Town of Manning Campground** (May–Sept., $20) is immediately west of the tourist information center in a shaded spot beside the Notikewin River. The campground is small (nine sites), but has powered sites. It is also possible to camp at the golf course, north of town (780/836-2176, May–Sept., $20), which offers powered sites and a clubhouse restaurant. The **Old Hospital Gallery & Museum** (780/836-3606, Mon.–Sat. 10 A.M.–5 P.M. May–Sept.) combines historic displays related to the building with an art gallery and the local information center.

A Short Detour

North of Paddle Prairie, an unpaved road (Hwy. 697) leads east to the Peace River and Tomkin's Landing and one of only eight ferry crossings in the province (operates daily 24 hours in summer). Continuing east, **La Crete** (population 2,300) has grown into an agricultural center on the northern fringe of the continent's arable land. Most residents are Mennonites who moved to the region in the 1930s. They are from a traditional Protestant sect originating in Holland, whose members settled in remote regions throughout the world and established self-sufficient agricultural lifestyles, in hopes of being left to practice their faith in peace. On the streets and in the local restaurants, you'll hear their language, *Plattdeutsch* (Low German), which is spoken by Mennonites throughout the world.

Fort Vermilion

This town of 780, on the south bank of the Peace River, 40 kilometers (25 miles) north of La Crete and 77 kilometers (48 miles) east of High Level, was established as a trading post in 1788. Many old buildings and cabins, in varying states of disrepair, still stand. Pick up a *Fort Vermilion Heritage Guide* from the **Fort Vermilion Heritage Centre** (780/927-4603, Mon.–Thurs. 9 A.M.–9 P.M., Fri.–Sat. 9 A.M.–5 P.M., Sun. 1–9 P.M. June–Aug.) to help identify the many historical sites in town. The **Mary Batt & Son General Store** was constructed from logs removed from the 1897 Hudson's Bay Company post.

Across from the river, the **Sheridan Lawrence Inn** (4901 River Rd., 780/927-4400, $82 s, $89 d) is the only place to stay in town. It offers 16 rooms and a small restaurant open daily from 7 A.M., with a Canadian and Chinese menu.

High Level

Named for its location on a divide between the Peace and Hay River watersheds, High Level (population 4,100), 279 kilometers (173 miles) north of Grimshaw, is the last town before the Alberta/Northwest Territories border. It is a major service center for a region rich in natural resources. Grain elevators, serving agricultural communities to the east, are the northernmost in the world. Northeast of High Level are the **Caribou Mountains,** which rise to a forested plateau 800 meters (2,600 feet) above the Peace River. The most accessible part of the forest is **Hutch Lake,** 32 kilometers (20 miles) north of town. The lake is surrounded by aspen and poplar and is the source of the **Meander River.** The dominant feature here is **Watt Mountain** (780 m/2,600 ft), which you can see to the northwest of High Level. From Hutch Lake, a service road leads 10 kilometers (6.2 miles) to a lookout and 21 kilometers (13 miles) to a fire tower on the summit. The recreation area at the north end of the lake has a large picnic area, an interpretive trail, and camping. Maps are available at the tourist information center.

The only worthwhile sight in town is **Mackenzie Crossroads Museum** (at the south entrance to town, 780/926-2470, Mon.–Sat. 9 A.M.–7 P.M. May–Sept., Mon.–Fri. 9 A.M.–5 P.M. the rest of the year, adult $2, student $1). Located in the tourist information center building, the museum is themed on a northern trading post, with interesting displays telling the human history of northern Alberta. In another room, the industries upon which High Level was built are described through photographs and interpretive boards. A three-dimensional map of northwestern Alberta gives a great perspective of this inaccessible part of the province.

Motel prices in High Level are just a warm-up for those over the border in the Northwest Territories, so don't be surprised at $80 rooms that you'd prefer to pay $40 for. One of the least expensive is **Our Place Motel** (10402 97th St., 780/926-2556 or 866/926-3631, $79 s, $89 d), with an adjacent restaurant and wireless Internet throughout.

NORTHWEST TERRITORIES

One of three Canadian territories (the Yukon and Nunavut are the other two), the Northwest Territories is a vast wilderness of uncompromising nature. Stretching from the 60th parallel across the Arctic Circle and into the High Arctic, it takes in some of the world's biggest and deepest lakes, the massive Mackenzie River, and treeless tundra that seemingly extends forever. Although the Northwest Territories is vast, many of the highlights are accessible by air or road, including one route leading north through Northern Alberta from Grimshaw. Whether it's your first time or your 40th, crossing the 60th parallel into the Northwest Territories marks the beginning of a new adventure. And for road travelers, the adventure starts in the most accessible section of the territories,

along the Waterfalls Route through a vast expanse of stunted boreal forest broken only by two of North America's largest rivers, the Slave and Mackenzie. To the north lies Great Slave Lake, named for the Slavey Dene who have trapped and fished along its southern shores for thousands of years. This vast inland freshwater sea is the world's 10th-largest lake. The region's main communities are Hay River, on the south shore of Great Slave Lake; and Fort Smith, the gateway to Wood Buffalo National Park, the second-largest national park in the world. Paved and improved gravel roads link the two towns and continue around the west and north sides of Great Slave Lake to the city of Yellowknife, known as the "Diamond Capital of North America." From this point, it's air travel only north to

© ANDREW HEMPSTEAD

HIGHLIGHTS

🌙 **Wood Buffalo National Park:** A visit to the world's second largest national park requires time and patience, but visitors will be rewarded with the sight of the world's largest free-roaming herd of bison (page 494).

🌙 **Prince of Wales Northern Heritage Centre:** Yellowknife's premier attraction lays out the entire natural and human history of the territory in a modern, inviting lakefront setting (page 497).

🌙 **Yellowknife's Old Town:** Park your car and explore one of western Canada's most eccentric neighborhoods on foot, taking time out for a meal at the utterly unique Wildcat Cafe (page 499).

🌙 **Golfing Under the Midnight Sun:** There's no such thing as twilight rates at the Yellowknife Golf Club, where it's possible to tee off day and night in late June and early July (page 500).

🌙 **Nahanni National Park:** A day trip by floatplane is fine, but a guided trip down the South Nahanni River is what draws most visitors to this remote and mountainous park (page 505).

🌙 **Tuktoyaktuk:** If you're the type that needs to see what's at the end of the road, you won't want to miss "Tuk," a tiny village perched on the edge of the Arctic Ocean, but made accessible for all with day trips from Inuvik (page 513).

LOOK FOR 🌙 TO FIND RECOMMENDED SIGHTS, ACTIVITIES, DINING, AND LODGING.

two of the world's 10 largest lakes, one of the world's longest rivers, a waterfall twice the height of Niagara Falls, one UNESCO World Heritage Site, three more national parks, and an amazing abundance of wildlife. Hiking the Canol Road, canoeing the South Nahanni River, fishing for trophy-size lake trout in Great Bear Lake, and watching beluga whales frolic in the Beaufort Sea are just the highlights.

PLANNING YOUR TIME

Heading to the Northwest Territories is not to be taken lightly. You will need to plan ahead, especially if you have a specific activity in mind, such as joining a guided rafting trip through Nahanni National Park, which requires booking well in advance and making the relevant transportation bookings. Those driving north from Alberta should allow at least one week in the Northwest Territories. This is enough

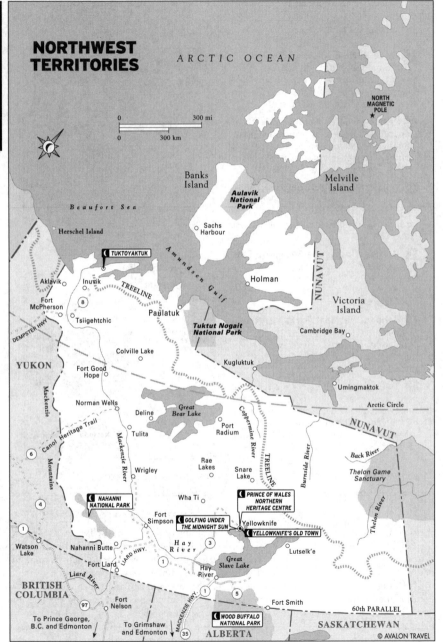

NORTHWEST TERRITORIES

ARCTIC OCEAN

NORTH MAGNETIC POLE ★

0 — 300 mi
0 — 300 km

Banks Island

Aulavik National Park

Melville Island

Beaufort Sea

Sachs Harbour

Herschel Island

Holman

TUKTOYAKTUK

Amundsen Gulf

NUNAVUT

Aklavik

Inuvik

TREELINE

Victoria Island

Fort McPherson

Tsiigehtchic

Paulatuk

Cambridge Bay

DEMPSTER HWY.

Tuktut Nogait National Park

YUKON

Colville Lake

Kugluktuk

Fort Good Hope

Arctic Circle

Norman Wells

Deline

Great Bear Lake

NUNAVUT

Coppermine River

Canol Heritage Trail

Tulita

Port Radium

Back River

6

Mackenzie River

Rae Lakes

TREELINE

Burnside River

Thelon Game Sanctuary

Mountains

Wrigley

Snare Lake

4

Wha Ti

NAHANNI NATIONAL PARK

PRINCE OF WALES NORTHERN HERITAGE CENTRE

Thelon River

1

Fort Simpson

GOLFING UNDER THE MIDNIGHT SUN

Yellowknife

Watson Lake

YELLOWKNIFE'S OLD TOWN

Nahanni Butte

Hay River

3

Lutselk'e

LIARD HWY.

Fort Liard

1

Great Slave Lake

BRITISH COLUMBIA

Liard River

Hay River

60th PARALLEL

97

Fort Nelson

1

5

Fort Smith

MACKENZIE HWY.

To Prince George, B.C. and Edmonton

To Grimshaw and Edmonton

35

WOOD BUFFALO NATIONAL PARK

SASKATCHEWAN

ALBERTA

© AVALON TRAVEL

time to see the abundant natural wonders of Wood Buffalo National Park before heading to the capital of Yellowknife, where two days is enough time to see the Prince of Wales Northern Heritage Centre, wander through Old Town, try your hand at fishing, and go paddling in one of the many surrounding lakes. If it's late June, golfing under the midnight sun is a once-in-a-lifetime experience, but the local links is worth hitting at any time of the summer. Backtracking from the capital, head west to Fort Simpson for a flightseeing day trip into Nahanni National Park. Exiting the Northwest Territories at Fort Liard will set you up for another week's worth of adventures in northern British Columbia and the Yukon.

If you're keen to travel above the Arctic Circle, it is possible to combine a driving tour to Yellowknife with a flight to Inuvik. The town itself is interesting, but it's the prospect of experiencing a sun that never sets (in late June) or seeing—or swimming in, for the brave—the Arctic Ocean on a side trip to Tuktoyaktuk that brings most visitors this far north. The ideal scenario would be to book a three-night stay, flying up from Yellowknife (or Calgary or Edmonton) to Inuvik, with one full day to explore town and another to visit "Tuk." Travelers with reliable vehicles can also reach Inuvik by road through the Yukon. Allow at least four days for the round-trip from Dawson City.

Waterfalls Route

Named for the many waterfalls in the accessible south-central portion of the Northwest Territories, this region is reached by road from northern Alberta and provides the gateway to Yellowknife. The largest population center is Hay River, on the southern shore of Great Slave Lake.

60TH PARALLEL TO HAY RIVER

The wood-and-stone structure marking the 60th parallel is a welcome sight after the long drive north through northern Alberta up the Mackenzie Highway. North of the border, the highway number changes from 35 to 1, and the road follows the Hay River 118 kilometers (73 miles) to Great Slave Lake. This stretch is known as the **Waterfalls Route,** for the impressive falls along the way.

Just beyond the border is the **60th Parallel Visitors Centre** (867/875-5570, mid-May–mid-Sept. daily 8:30 A.M.–8:30 P.M.), well worth a stop just to have a chat with the friendly hosts. The center offers maps and brochures, camping permits, fishing licenses, and displays of local arts and crafts. And the coffeepot is always on, accompanied by freshly made scones, if you're lucky. Behind the center is the **60th Parallel Campground** (mid-May–mid-Sept., unserviced sites $15), a small facility beside the Hay River.

Twin Falls Gorge Territorial Park

North of the border, the Hay River has carved a deep gorge into the limestone bedrock. Punctuating the river's flow are two dramatic waterfalls that formed a major barrier for early river travelers, forcing a portage along the west bank. Encompassing both falls, and equally impressive, is Twin Falls Gorge Territorial Park. From the first day-use area, a short trail leads to a viewing platform overlooking **Alexandra Falls,** where the peat-colored Hay River tumbles 34 meters (112 feet). **Louise Falls,** three kilometers (1.9 miles) downstream, is not as high, but its intriguing steps make it just as interesting. **Louise Falls Campground** (mid-May–mid-Sept., unserviced sites $17) has water, pit toilets, and bug-proof cooking shelters.

HAY RIVER

This town of 3,600 lies 118 kilometers (73 miles) north of the border, 1,070 kilometers

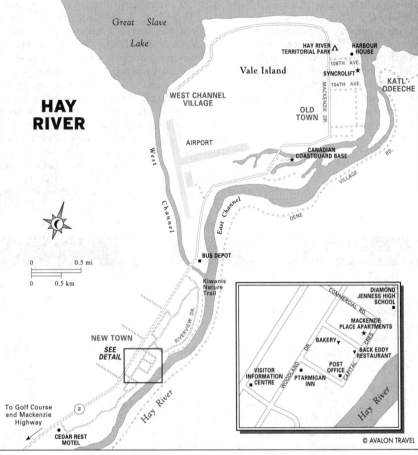

© AVALON TRAVEL

(665 miles) north of Edmonton and 500 kilometers (310 miles) from the territorial capital of Yellowknife. Hay River is a vital transportation link for waterborne freight bound for communities along the Mackenzie River and throughout the western and central Arctic.

Within the town limits, several distinct communities surround the delta, which was formed where the Hay River flows into Great Slave Lake. Most modern development, including motels, restaurants, and government offices, is located in **New Town,** on the west bank of the Hay River. A bridge links New Town to **Vale Island,** where the airport, campground, and excellent beaches are located. Also on the island are the communities of **Old Town,** which was partially destroyed by flooding in 1963, and **West Channel Village,** which grew around the commercial fishing industry. Across the mouth of Hay River is Katl'odeeche (Hay River Dene Reserve), the only native reserve in the Northwest Territories.

Sights

To get oriented, head to the manager's office (2nd floor) at the 17-story **Mackenzie Place**

Apartment Building. Ask for a key and ride the claustrophobia-inducing elevator to the roof, where panoramic views of the Great Slave Lake, Hay River, and the boreal forest extend to the horizon. The **Diamond Jenness Secondary School** (Riverview Dr.) was named for a famed Northern anthropologist and is undoubtedly the town's most unusual structure. It was designed by Douglas Cardinal, an Albertan architect whose distinctive work is found throughout that province. Its curved walls alone would have made it a Northern landmark, but the choice of color for the entire exterior was left to the students—and they chose purple! (It's known to locals as the "Purple People Eater.") Behind the school, the **Kiwanis Nature Trail** leads along the west bank of the Hay River (look for fossils) to various signposted points of interest, then across Highway 2 and along the West Channel to Great Slave Lake.

The boarded-up shop fronts, dusty streets, and empty houses of **Vale Island** belie the activity that still takes place along the waterfront. The large **Canadian Coast Guard Base** is responsible for all search-and-rescue operations in the western Arctic. And the facilities of the **Northern Transportation Company Ltd.** (NTCL), a large shipping concern, include shipyards, a dry dock, freight-storage areas, and a syncrolift—a hydraulic device that removes vessels from the water for easy maintenance (it's one of only four in Canada; it can be seen to the right along 106th Ave.).

From Old Town, Mackenzie Drive—the island's main thoroughfare—continues past a popular swimming beach and a radio observatory before it dead-ends in **West Channel Village,** a once-prosperous fishing community.

Recreation

The beaches of Vale Island are very popular during summer, even if the water may be a little cold for most southerners. The best beach is within **Hay River Territorial Park** at the end of 106th Avenue, although those farther around the island are quieter. Anglers will find plentiful northern pike and pickerel in the Hay River.

Hay River Golf Club (13 km/eight mi south

© ANDREW HEMPSTEAD

The Diamond Jenness Secondary School is a local landmark.

of town, 867/874-6290) is the finest course in the territory. It has nine holes with grassed fairways, artificial greens, a driving range, and a superbly crafted log clubhouse (well worth a look, even for non-golfers). A round of golf (18 holes) is $40. The course also has a driving range, and club rentals are available.

Accommodations and Camping

The seven-room **Harbour House Bed and Breakfast** (106th St., 867/874-2233, www. greenwayrealty.ca, $80 s, $90 d) is an excellent choice for accommodations in Hay River. Across from Vale Island's best beach, the setting is wonderful and the mood casual. Rates include a full breakfast.

A couple of kilometers (1.2 miles) south from downtown is **Cedar Rest Motel** (938 Mackenzie Hwy., 867/874-3732, $95 s, $105 d), a place that looks half finished, with a massive gravel parking lot out front broken by a gas station. At the centrally located **Ptarmigan Inn** (867/874-6781 or 800/661-0842, www.ptarmiganinn.com, $134–179 s or d), rooms are air-conditioned and have high-speed Internet access.

Hay River Territorial Park (867/874-3772, Vale Island, mid-May–mid-Sept., $17–21) is a short walk from the beach and seven kilometers (4.3 miles) from downtown. The 35 sites are private, a few have power, and all have picnic tables and fire rings.

Food

Beside Northern, **Hay River Bakery** (867/874-2322, Mon.–Fri. 8 A.M.–6 P.M.) has a wide variety of cakes and pastries and is a good place for an inexpensive lunch.

Keys Dining Room (Ptarmigan Inn, 867/874-6781, Mon.–Sat. 7 A.M.–9 P.M., Sun. 8 A.M.–9 P.M., $16–29) is your typical hotel restaurant, with something for everyone (think stir-fries, pastas, beef), as well as locally caught whitefish. Worth the effort to find is **Back Eddy Restaurant** (6 Courtoreille St., 867/874-6680, Mon.–Fri. 11 A.M.–2 P.M. and 5–9 P.M., Sat. 11 A.M.–10 P.M., $15–27), above Rings Drug Store on Capital Crescent. Meals are served in the lounge or, for families, in a separate dining area. The menu features pickerel and whitefish fresh from the lake.

Information

Hay River Visitor Information Centre (73 Woodland Dr., 867/874-3180, www.hayriver. com, mid-May–mid-Sept. daily 9 A.M.–9 P.M.) is at the south entrance to town. It has bundles of brochures and books, and, almost as importantly, the coffeepot is always on. **Hay River Centennial Library** (75 Woodland Dr., 867/874-6486, Mon.–Thurs. 10 A.M.–5 P.M., Fri.–Sun. 1–5 P.M.) has free wireless Internet.

Getting There

Hay River Airport is on Vale Island, a $15 cab ride from town. During freeze-up and breakup of the Mackenzie River, road traffic through to Yellowknife is blocked, and Hay River Airport becomes the center of frenzied activity; freight and passengers arriving by road from the south transfer to planes for the short hop over Great Slave Lake. **First Air** (800/267-1247, www. firstair.ca) flies once or twice daily between Hay River and Yellowknife.

The bus depot is at the south end of Vale Island. **Greyhound** departs daily for Edmonton (16 hours). Connecting with the Greyhound services is **Frontier Coachlines** (867/873-4892), using the same depot.

HAY RIVER TO FORT SMITH

The 270-kilometer (168 miles) road linking Hay River to Fort Smith (Hwy. 5) is paved for the first 60 kilometers (37 miles) then turns to improved gravel. No services are available along this route. A gravel road to the north, 49 kilometers (30 miles) from Highway 2, leads two kilometers (1.2 miles) to **Polar Lake.** The lake is stocked with rainbow trout and has good bird-watching around the shoreline.

Another 11 kilometers (6.8 miles) beyond the Polar Lake turn-off, the highway divides: The right fork continues to Fort Smith, the left to Fort Resolution.

Fort Resolution

This historic community of 470 is in a forested

PINE POINT: A MODERN GHOST TOWN

In 1951 the mining giant Cominco began extracting lead and zinc from an open-pit mine east of Hay River at a site known as Pine Point. With production on the increase, a town was built, at one time boasting more than 2,000 residents. Low lead and zinc prices, coupled with rising operational costs, forced Cominco to close the mine in 1988. One of the lease conditions was that Cominco was to restore the land to its original condition when it left. As a result, the whole town – a school, a hospital, a supermarket, and hundreds of houses – had to be moved. After standing empty for a few years, the buildings were moved to various locations throughout the north. Today all that remains are tailing piles from the mine, paved streets, sidewalks, and a golf course with a rough that makes the U.S. Open look tame.

area on the shore of Great Slave Lake around 170 kilometers (106 miles) east of Hay River. The original fort, built by the North West Company in 1786, was to the east, on the Slave River Delta. When the post was moved, a Chipewyan Dene settlement grew around it, and in 1852 Roman Catholic missionaries arrived, building a school and a hospital. A road connecting the town to Pine Point was completed in the 1960s, and today the mainly Chipewyan and Métis population relies on trapping and a sawmill operation as its economic base.

Continuing to Fort Smith on Highway 5

From the Fort Smith/Fort Resolution junction, 60 kilometers (33 miles) east of Hay River, it's another 210 kilometers (130 miles) southeast to Fort Smith. After an hour of smooth sailing, the road enters **Wood Buffalo National Park,** the largest national park in North America. Five kilometers (3.1 miles) beyond the park entrance sign is the **Angus Fire Tower.** Behind the tower is one of many sinkholes found in the northern reaches of the park. This example of karst topography occurs when underground caves collapse, creating a craterlike depression. This one is 26 meters (85 feet) deep and 40 meters (130 feet) across. The next worthwhile stop is at **Nyarling River,** 14 kilometers (8.7 miles) farther east. The dried-up riverbed is actually the path of an underground river, hence the name *Nyarling* (underground, in the Slavey language).

As the highway continues east, it enters an area where the Precambrian Shield is exposed, making for a rocky landscape where stunted trees cling to shallow depressions that have filled with soil. To the north, an access road leads to several small waterfalls in **Little Buffalo Falls Territorial Park** and a campground (mid-May–mid-Sept., $17) with pit toilets, a kitchen shelter, and firewood.

FORT SMITH

Until 1967, this town of 2,300 was the territorial capital. It still functions as an administrative center for various governmental offices and is the educational center for the Northwest Territories. The town was established because of formidable rapids on the Slave River, a vital link for all travelers heading north. In 1872, the Hudson's Bay Company opened a post, later known as Fort Fitzgerald, at the southern end of the rapids. Two years later, the company established a fort near the northern end of the portage route, at Fort Smith.

Sights

Most people who venture to Fort Smith do so to visit Wood Buffalo National Park, but there are a couple of interesting sights within town limits.

In the 1920s, when Fort Smith was the capital of the Northwest Territories, administrative duties fell to the local bishop, whose house and gardens are now part of **Fort Smith Mission Historic Park** (corner of Mercredi Ave. and Breynat St., 867/874-6702, free). Declared a

Territorial Historic Park in 1991, it's an ongoing restoration project; at this stage, interpretive signs explain the various buildings, and gardens are planted for each summer. The fort-shaped **Northern Life Museum** (110 King St., 867/872-2859, daily 1–5 P.M. June–Aug., free) houses many artifacts collected by early missionaries, including dog-mushing equipment, Inuit carvings, and the first printing press in the north. Along the riverfront on Marine Drive is the **Slave River Lookout.** Use the spotting scope here to search out white pelicans nesting on rocks scattered through the river.

Accommodations and Camping
Thebacha Bed & Breakfast (53 Portage Ave., 867/872-2060, www.taigatour.com, $80 s, $100 d) offers four guest rooms, breakfast, and the use of a kitchen in a centrally located residence. For motel accommodations, consider **Pelican Rapids Inn** (152 McDougal Rd., 867/872-2789, $140 s or d), with 31 basic but spacious rooms.

The only campground close to town is the **Queen Elizabeth Territorial Park,** four kilometers (2.5 miles) west toward the airport; turn north on Teepee Trail Road. Sites cost $17 per night and are spread out and private, with pit toilets and cooking shelters. Showers and flush toilets are available in the warden's compound.

◖ WOOD BUFFALO NATIONAL PARK
From Fort Smith, Highway 5 continues through town and loops back south into Alberta (just beyond town limits). The border is also the northern boundary of Wood Buffalo National Park, the second largest national park in the world (the largest is in Greenland). Throughout this 45,000-square-kilometer (17,400-square-mile) chunk of boreal forest, boreal plains, shallow lakes, and bogs flow two major rivers—the Peace and Athabasca. These drain into **Lake Claire,** forming one of the world's largest freshwater deltas. The Peace-Athabasca Delta is a mass of confusing channels, shallow lakes, and sedge

Salt Plains at Wood Buffalo National Park

© ANDREW HEMPSTEAD

WHOOPING CRANES

Through a successful captive-breeding program, the whooping crane, *Grus americana*, has become a symbol of human efforts to protect endangered species in North America. Whoopers, as they are commonly called, have never been prolific. They stand 1.3 meters (four feet), have a wingspan of 2.4 meters (eight feet), and are pure white with long black legs. (They are often confused with the slightly smaller, reddish-brown sandhill crane, which is common in the park.) Their naturally low reproduction rate, coupled with severe degradation of their habitat, caused their numbers to dip to as low as 21 in 1954 – a single flock nested in Wood Buffalo National Park. Today, the population of the highly publicized and heavily studied flock has increased to more than 350, more than half the number that remain worldwide (most of the others are in captivity). The birds nest in a remote area of marshes and bogs in the northern reaches of Wood Buffalo far from human contact, migrating south to the Texas coast each fall.

meadows, surrounded by a wetland that is a prime wintering range for bison, rich in waterfowl, and home to beavers, muskrats, moose, lynx, wolves, and black bears. From the delta, the Slave River, which forms the park's eastern boundary, flows north into Great Slave Lake.

Probably best known for being the last natural nesting habitat of the rare whooping crane, the park is also home to the world's largest free-roaming herd of bison. It has extensive salt plains and North America's finest example of gypsum karst topography—a phenomenon created by underground water activity. For all of these reasons, and as an intact example of the boreal forest that once circled the entire Northern Hemisphere, the park was declared a UNESCO World Heritage Site in December 1983.

Sights

The expansive **Salt Plains** in the northeast of the park are one of Wood Buffalo's dominant natural features. Underground water flows through deposits of salt left behind by an ancient saltwater ocean, emerging in the form of salt springs. Large white mounds form at their source, and where the water has evaporated the ground is covered in a fine layer of salt. The best place to view this phenomenon is from the **Salt Plains Overlook**, 35 kilometers (22 miles) west of Fort Smith, then 11 kilometers (6.8 miles) south on Parson's Lake Road. The panoramic view of the plains is spectacular from this spot, but it's worth taking the one-kilometer (0.6-mile) trail to the bottom of the hill.

In the same vicinity, a bedrock of **gypsum karst** underlies much of the park. Gypsum is a soft, white rock that slowly dissolves in water. Underground water here has created large cavities beneath this fragile mantle. This type of terrain is known as karst, and this area is the best example of karst terrain in North America. As the bedrock continues to dissolve, the underground caves enlarge, eventually collapsing under their own weight, forming large depressions known as **sinkholes.** The thousands of sinkholes here vary in size from three meters (10 feet) to 100 meters (330 feet) across. The most accessible large sinkhole is behind the Angus Fire Tower, 150 kilometers (93 miles) west of Fort Smith.

The **Peace-Athabasca Delta** is in a remote part of this remote park and is rarely visited. Getting to the delta requires some planning because no roads access the area. The most popular visitor destination on the delta is **Sweetgrass Station,** located 12 kilometers (7.5 miles) south of the Peace River. The site is on the edge of a vast meadow that extends around the north and west shore of Lake Claire, providing a summer range for most of the park's bison. A cabin with bunks and a woodstove is available for visitors to the area at no charge, although reservations at the park information center are required. The cabin is an excellent base for exploring the meadows around Lake Claire and viewing the abundant wildlife. From Fort Smith, **Northwestern Air** (867/872-2216, www.nwal.ca), charges around $500 each way to fly two people and their gear between Fort Smith and Sweetgrass Station.

Practicalities

The **Visitor Reception Centre** (126 McDougal Rd., Fort Smith, 867/872-7900, Mon.–Fri. 9 A.M.–5 P.M. plus summer weekends 1–5 P.M.) offers trail information, a short slideshow, and an exhibit room. Another park office (780/697-3662), open similar hours, is in Fort Chipewyan.

Within the park itself, the only developed facilities are at **Pine Lake,** 60 kilometers (37 miles) south of Fort Smith. The lake has a campground ($15.70 per night) with pit toilets, covered kitchen shelters, and firewood ($6.80 per bundle). On a spit of land jutting into the lake beyond the campground is a picnic area with bug-proof shelters. The park staff presents a summer interpretive program at various locations; check the schedule at the park information center or on the campground notice board.

HAY RIVER TO YELLOWKNIFE

Yellowknife, on the north shore of the Great Slave Lake, is a long 480-kilometer (300-mile) haul from Hay River, through a monotonous boreal forest of spruce, poplar, and jack pine.

Note: Twice a year, for a few days or up to three weeks (at breakup and freeze-up, respectively, of the Mackenzie River), the road to Yellowknife is not passable (call 800/661-0750 or check online at www.gov.nt.ca for current conditions). In summer, the free ferry operates daily 6 A.M.–midnight, while in winter an ice road is constructed across the river.

Lady Evelyn Falls Territorial Park

From Enterprise, south of Hay River, Highway 1 heads northwest, coming to Lady Evelyn Falls Territorial Park after 53 kilometers (33 miles). The namesake falls, where the wide **Kakisa River** cascades off a 15-meter (50-

foot) escarpment, are easily accessible from the highway, seven kilometers (4.3 miles) down a gravel road. A short trail leads from the day-use area down to a platform overlooking the falls. The falls are part of a territorial park that has a **campground** (mid-May–mid-Sept., $17) with pit toilets, bug-proof cooking shelters, and firewood.

Fort Providence

The highway forks 85 kilometers (53 miles) from Enterprise: To the left, Highway 1 continues west to Fort Simpson, and to the right, Highway 3 heads north toward Yellowknife. Highway 3 crosses the Mackenzie River via a ferry, 24 kilometers (15 miles) from the junction. Across the river and just up the highway, a spur road leads eight kilometers (five miles) to the Slavey Dene community of Fort Providence (population 600), perched high above the river on its steep northern bank. On the riverfront through town, markers honor the roles played in the region's history by Alexander Mackenzie and the Church.

Rae-Edzo

Rae-Edzo, 214 kilometers (133 miles) north of Fort Providence, is the largest Dene community in the Northwest Territories, with a population of 1,500 Dogrib Dene. They settled around a Hudson's Bay Company post as early as 1852. In the 1960s, the government began developing a new townsite, Edzo, closer to the highway. The school at Rae was closed, and a new one opened at Edzo. Today, most of the people continue living at Rae, where the water access is better for fishing and hunting, whereas the government buildings are up on the highway at Edzo. The 10-kilometer (6.2-mile) side trip to Rae is worth taking. The resilient community is perched on a rocky outcrop jutting into **Marian Lake.** The main road through town leads to a small island, where the rocky beaches are littered with boats, fishing nets, and dogs tied up waiting for snow. Apart from the snowmobiles, the village looks much as it did 100 years ago.

Yellowknife

Built on dreams, perseverance, and the ingenuity of a small group of pioneers who came in search of gold, the territorial capital of Yellowknife has grown into a modern urban center of 16,000. Its frontier-town flavor and independent spirit distinguish it from all other Canadian cities. It's the northernmost city in Canada, the *only* city in the Northwest Territories, and the only predominantly non-native community in the territories. Located on the North Arm of the Great Slave Lake, the city clings precariously to the ancient, glacial-scarred rock of the Canadian Shield. Edmonton is 1,530 kilometers (950 miles) south by road, 965 kilometers (600 miles) by air. The Arctic Circle is 440 kilometers (273 miles) north.

At first, Yellowknife looks little different from other small Canadian cities, but unique contrasts soon become apparent. Some residents write computer programs for a living, whereas others prepare caribou hides; architect-designed houses are scattered among squatters' log cabins; and the roads are seemingly always under repair, a legacy of permafrost. To the Dene, Yellowknife is known as *Som bak'e* (Place of Money).

History

Samuel Hearne dubbed the local Dene natives the Yellowknife for the copper knives they used. Miners on their way to the Klondike were the first to discover gold in the area, but they didn't rush in to stake claims because of the area's remote location and the difficulty of extracting the mineral from the hard bedrock. But as airplanes began opening up the north, the area became more attractive to gold seekers. Hundreds of claims were staked between 1934 and 1936, and a boomtown sprang up along the shore of Yellowknife Bay. After the war, growth continued, and soon the original townsite around the bay was at full capacity. A new town, just up the hill, was surveyed, and by 1947 the city center of today began taking shape. In 1967, a road was completed to the outside and the city came to rely less on air travel. The city was named the

territorial capital the same year. The last gold mine closed in 2004, but this coincided with the beginning of a diamond rush. Although these precious gems lie in the Canadian shield hundreds of kilometers north of Yellowknife, the city is the center of resource development, as well as services such as cutting and polishing, giving claim to the title "Diamond Capital of North America."

SIGHTS
◖ Prince of Wales Northern Heritage Centre

The entire history of the Northwest Territories is cataloged at this modern facility (4750 48th St., 867/873-7551, June–Aug. daily 10:30 A.M.–5:30 P.M., the rest of the year Mon.–Fri. 10:30 A.M.–5 P.M. and Sat.–Sun. noon–5 P.M., free), within walking distance of downtown and on the shore of Frame Lake. The Feature II Gallery displays a collection of Dene, Métis, and Inuit artifacts, while the Land Speaks Gallery catalogs the arrival of European explorers, miners, and missionaries and their impact on the environment. Meanwhile, the Aviation Gallery presents a realistic display of a bush pilot and his plane, and features a wall of fame for the pilots who helped open up the north. Also here is a live hookup to the traffic controllers at Yellowknife Airport. A library stocks 6,000 historical and fiction books on the north.

Legislative Assembly of the Northwest Territories

This building on the shore of Frame Lake is the heart of territorial politics. Opened in 1993, it was designed to blend in with the surrounding landscape and made use of Northern materials. Through the front doors of a massive glass-walled facade is the Great Hall, topped by skylights and lined with the artwork of Angus Cockney. The building's centerpiece is the circular Chamber, in which the members of the legislative assembly sit facing the Speaker. Behind the Speaker stretches a massive zinc-

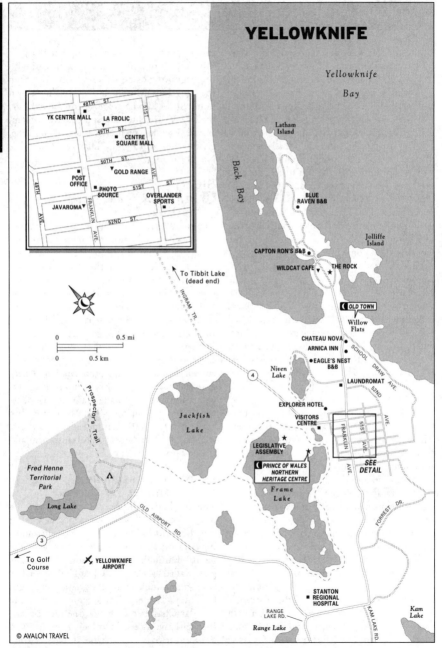

YELLOWKNIFE

Yellowknife Bay

Latham Island

Back Bay

BLUE RAVEN B&B

Jolliffe Island

CAPTON RON'S B&B

WILDCAT CAFE   THE ROCK

OLD TOWN

Willow Flats

To Tibbit Lake
(dead end)

INGRAM TR.

CHATEAU NOVA
ARNICA INN
EAGLE'S NEST B&B

SCHOOL DRAW AVE.

Niven Lake

LAUNDROMAT

52ND

0   0.5 mi
0   0.5 km

4

EXPLORER HOTEL

VISITORS CENTRE

FRANKLIN AVE.

51ST AVE.

Jackfish Lake

LEGISLATIVE ASSEMBLY

PRINCE OF WALES NORTHERN HERITAGE CENTRE

SEE DETAIL

Prospector's Trail

Fred Henne Territorial Park

Frame Lake

Long Lake

FORREST DR.

3

OLD AIRPORT RD.

To Golf Course

YELLOWKNIFE AIRPORT

STANTON REGIONAL HOSPITAL

KAM LAKE RD.

RANGE LAKE RD.

Range Lake

Kam Lake

Detail inset

48TH ST.

YK CENTRE MALL   LA FROLIC

49TH ST.

51ST

CENTRE SQUARE MALL

50TH ST.

50TH AVE.

POST OFFICE

GOLD RANGE

51ST ST.

PHOTO SOURCE

OVERLANDER SPORTS

48TH AVE.

FRANKLIN AVE.

JAVAROMA

52ND ST.

plated mural of a Northern landscape. The building is open Mon.–Fri. 7 A.M.–6 P.M., Sat.–Sun. 10 A.M.–6 P.M. Free one-hour tours (867/669-2300) are offered June to August Mon.–Fri. at 10:30 A.M., 1:30 P.M., and 3:30 P.M. and Sunday at 1:30 P.M., the rest of the year weekdays only at 10:30 A.M. Outside you'll find Capital Area Park and a Ceremonial Circle comprising flags that represent each of the territories' 33 communities.

◖ Old Town

From the city center, Franklin Avenue (50th Ave.) descends a long, dusty hill to Yellowknife's Old Town. In the 1930s, the first log and frame buildings were erected at this site. Along the narrow streets, Quonset huts, original settlers' homes, converted buses, old boats, and tin shanties look incongruous in a Canadian capital city. Some of the most unusual housing is in **Willow Flats,** east of Franklin Avenue. **Ragged Ass Road,** named for a mine claim, has the most unusual houses, many posting signs telling the story of the building. Farther north along Franklin Avenue is an area known simply as **The Rock,** for the huge chunk of Canadian Shield that towers above the surrounding landscape. At the top of The Rock is the **Pilot's Monument,** dedicated to the bush pilots who opened up the north. At the corner of Pilots Lane and Wiley Road is **Weaver & Devore,** an old-time general store selling just about everything. Many of their larger orders have to be flown in to buyers scattered throughout the north. East of The Rock, in Yellowknife Bay, is **Jolliffe Island,** once a fuel depot but now a residential area. The homes are reached by boat or canoe in summer and by road in winter. At the north end of The Rock, a causeway, built in 1948, connects **Latham Island** to the mainland. At the south end of the island are floatplane bases, where the constant buzz of small planes taking off and landing symbolizes the north.

Ingraham Trail

Apart from Highway 3 from the south, the Ingraham Trail (Hwy. 4 East) is the only route out of the city. It then crosses the Yellowknife River and passes **Prosperous, Pontoon,** and **Prelude Lakes,** each with day-use areas and great for fishing, boating, and swimming. Continuing east, the road parallels the Cameron River within **Hidden Lake Territorial Park,** 48 kilometers (30 miles) from Yellowknife. Trails lead down to the riverbank, and waterfalls dot the park. The road ends at **Tibbit Lake,** 71 kilometers (44 miles) from Yellowknife.

Fred Henne Territorial Park

Forest-encircled **Long Lake,** opposite Yellowknife Airport, is used by visitors mainly for the excellent camping facilities, but it's also a good example of the wilderness surrounding the city. The four-kilometer (2.5-mile) round-trip **Prospector's Trail,** which begins from the campground, is a good way to experience the unique landscape. You can hike to the park from the city center along the trails around **Frame Lake.**

RECREATION
Fishing and Canoeing

The brochures of many fishing-charter operators fill the Northern Frontier Regional Visitors Centre, but Greg Robertson at **Bluefish Services** (867/873-4818, www.bluefishservices.ca) offers the widest range of fishing opportunities, including fishing for arctic grayling from local river banks, chasing northern pike out on North Arm, and trawling the deepest parts of Great Slave Lake for massive lake trout. A four-hour trip, which includes fishing, sightseeing, and a fish fry, is $110 per person. For serious anglers, full-day fishing costs $235. **Enodah Wilderness Travel** (867/873-4334, www.enodah.com) has a lodge on Trout Rock, a small island 30 kilometers (19 miles) west of Yellowknife that was once the site of a Dogrib community. A day trip including guided fishing and access by floatplane is $520 per person, and three-day fishing trips are $1,685 per person.

Overlander Sports (4909 50th St., 867/873-2474, closed Sun.) rents canoes and kayaks for $45 per day, which allows enough time to explore nearby Jolliffe Island and its surrounding waters. For those interested in longer trips, weekly rates are $200.

◖ Golfing Under the Midnight Sun

For a unique Northern experience, consider playing 18 holes at **Yellowknife Golf Club** (west of town along Hwy. 3, 867/873-4326, May–Sept.), where the "greens" are artificial grass, and to combat rock and gravel fairways, each shot must be hit from a small mat that players carry around the course. Greens fee is $36 and mat rental is $5, and you can tee off day and night in late June and early July. Aside from the unique playing conditions, facilities are similar to those at any regular golf course: a pro shop with rentals ($21), a driving range, a restaurant, and a beer cart, of course. Also look in the clubhouse for some great photos of the course's early days.

NIGHTLIFE

Entertainment at the **Gold Range Hotel** (5010 50th St., 867/873-4441), best known as the "Strange Range," is like no other in the country. Don't be put off by the unusual characters, hundreds of empty beer glasses, and bouncers with legs like tree trunks; it isn't as rowdy as it seems. If you like to mix with the locals, this is the place to do it, and you may help them claim the title for highest beer sales per capita in Canada; so far they run only second. For something a little more subdued, plan on relaxing at the **Trapline Lounge** in the Explorer Hotel (4825 49th Ave., 867/873-3531).

FESTIVALS AND EVENTS

The week closest to the longest day of the year (June 21) is the **Sumer Solstice Festival** (www.solsticefestival.ca), featuring street entertainment, celebrations of native culture, and the Canadian North Midnight Classic (this event is popular with visitors, so make reservations in advance (867/873-4326, www.yellowknifegolf. com). **Folk on the Rocks** (867/920-7806, www. folkontherocks.com), held during the middle weekend of July, takes place on the shore of Long Lake and attracts Northern and Southern performers of folk, reggae, and Inuit music. A weekend ticket is $100. On the other side of the calendar, the **Caribou Carnival** (www.cariboucarnival.net) began more than 50 years ago among locals as a test of outdoor skills. It still tests the locals, who compete in a variety of themed events, but there's also a children's tent, native displays, live music, pancake breakfasts, and delicacies such as caribou cake for visitors to try. The action takes place throughout the city on the last weekend in March.

ACCOMMODATIONS AND CAMPING
$50-100

The only accommodations with rooms for less than $100 are bed-and-breakfasts. Ask at the Visitors Centre for a current list of B&Bs, or contact **Captain Ron's** (8 Lessard Dr., 867/873-3746, $85 s, $95 d), overlooking the floatplane base. It has four guest rooms, a sundeck, a library, and a guest lounge.

$100-200

◖ **Eagle's Nest B&B** (222 Niven Dr., 867/920-2688, www.ykeaglesnest.ca, $100 s, $110 d) is a modern home in a new housing estate, and a 10-minute walk from both downtown and Old Town. Three of the four smallish guest rooms share a bathroom, but all have a clean, modern outlook, with hardwood floors and comfortable beds. Amenities include a living room, business center, den, private balconies, and a kitchen open for guest use. Rates include a light breakfast.

Yellowknife's least expensive motel is the **Arnica Inn** (4115 Franklin Ave., 867/873-8511, www.arnicainn.ca, $149–169 s or d), halfway between downtown and Old Town. Rooms are in reasonable shape and come with wireless Internet. The small in-house café is inexpensive and open daily for breakfast and lunch.

Chateau Nova (4401 50th Ave., 867/873-9700 or 877/839-1236, www.chateaunova. com, $179–219 s or d) is the rather grand name of a newish hotel a few blocks from downtown on the way to Old Town. Rooms are modern and come with niceties such as bathrobes and a writing desk. Other amenities include free airport shuttles, a small fitness room with a big hot tub, a business center with Internet access, spa services, and a restaurant with the best pizza in town.

$200-250

With 187 rooms, the **《 Explorer Hotel** (4825 49th Ave., 867/873-3531 or 800/661-0892, www. explorerhotel.ca, $220–232 s or d) is Yellowknife's largest accommodation. It also has the nicest rooms, with modern conveniences such as coffeemakers, hairdryers, and free wireless Internet, as well as big city extras such as room service and free airport shuttles. It also has a restaurant, lounge, fitness room, and gift shop.

Camping

The city's only campground is at **Fred Henne Territorial Park** (867/920-2472, $17–21), across from the airport and a one-hour walk from downtown. Amenities include bug-proof cooking shelters, woodstoves, showers, and some powered sites. Along the Ingraham Trail, at Reid Lake, and at Prelude Lake Territorial Parks are primitive campgrounds. All three are open mid-May–mid-September and online reservations can be made at www.campingnwt.ca.

FOOD

Yellowknife has a decent selection of restaurants, as well as all the usual fast-food choices, and city-style coffee at places like **Javaroma** (5201 50th Ave., 867/669-0725). Head to **Northern Fancy Meats** (314 Woolgar Ave., 867/873-8767, Mon.–Sat. 9 A.M.–6 P.M.) for Northern game meat and in-house sausages and jerky.

Downtown

Of the many hotel dining rooms, none is better than **Traders Grill** (Explorer Hotel, 4825 49th Ave., 867/873-3531, Mon.–Fri 7 A.M.–9 P.M., Sat.–Sun. 8 A.M.–9 P.M., $22–38), a stylish space with professional service and a wide-ranging menu that includes a few local seafood choices (crumbed turbot, seafood chowder, and baked arctic char). Cooked breakfasts top out at $15 for eggs Benedict made with smoked arctic char.

Le Frolic (5019 49th St., 867/669-9852, $17–35) is the downstairs half of a French restaurant combo (L'Heritage, upstairs, is more formal and expensive) that presents game like arctic char, musk ox, and caribou with French flair. With the bison burger at $17, you don't need to spend a fortune, but the wild-game fondue (deer, caribou, and bison) with seasoned game broth is hard to pass up.

Old Town

Head down the hill from the city center to enjoy Northern cuisine and typically hospitable Northern atmosphere at any of the following restaurants. The **《 Wildcat Café** (3904 Wiley Rd., 867/873-8850, June–Aug. Mon.–Sat. 7:30 A.M.–9 P.M. and Sun. 10 A.M.–9 P.M., $19–28) has been famous since it was opened by Willy Wiley and Smoky Stout in 1937, becoming the first place in Yellowknife to sell ice cream. The café closed its doors in 1959 but reopened with some remodeling in 1977. The distinctive Northern feel hasn't been lost—log walls, wooden tables, a sloping floor, and a congenial atmosphere are part of the charm. It only has a few tables and is perpetually full, so chances are you'll end up sharing a table. The blackboard menu changes daily but features dishes such as lake trout, whitefish, and musk ox.

INFORMATION

The **Northern Frontier Regional Visitors Centre** (4807 49th St., 867/873-4262 or 877/881-4261, www.northernfrontier.com, June–Aug. daily 8:30 A.M.–6 P.M., the rest of the year Mon.–Fri. 8:30 A.M.–5:30 P.M., Sat.–Sun. noon–4 P.M.) overlooks Frame Lake. It's stocked with brochures on everything you'll need to know about Yellowknife, historic photographs, and interesting displays.

Libraries and Bookstores

On the second floor of Centre Square Mall is

Yellowknife Public Library (5022 49th St., 867/920-5642, Mon.–Thurs. 10 A.M.–9 P.M., Fri.–Sat. 10 A.M.–6 P.M.). Although small, it has newspapers from throughout Canada, lots of literature on the north, and public Internet access. **Yellowknife Book Cellar** (Panda II Mall, 867/920-2220, www.yellowknifebooks. com) has a wide selection of Northern and Canadian literature. In addition to walk-in customers, they serve Northerners looking for specialty titles and outsiders looking for local literature.

SERVICES

The post office is at 4902 50th Street. Public Internet access is free at the library or head to **Frostbyte Café** (5110 50th Ave., 867/669-8840). Wash clothes at the **Arctic Laundromat** (4310 Franklin Ave., daily 8:30 A.M.–11 P.M.). **Yellowknife Foto Source** (5005 Franklin Ave., 867/873-2196) entered the digital age as quickly as any Southern photo shop. Stop by for parts, service, or to download digital files to print.

Stanton Regional Hospital (867/920-4111) is on Old Airport Road at Range Lake Road. For the **RCMP,** call 867/669-5100.

GETTING THERE

Yellowknife Airport, five kilometers (3.1 miles) west of the city along Highway 3, is the hub of air travel in the Northwest Territories.

It's open daily 24 hours, has an inexpensive café (5:30 A.M.–10 P.M.), a bar, lockers, and rental car desks. **First Air** (867/669-8500 or 800/267-1247) uses Yellowknife as its western hub, with flights arriving and departing daily from Edmonton, Inuvik, and many Nunavut communities. Other airlines flying in and out of the capital include **Canadian North** (867/873-4484 or 800/661-1505), and **Northwestern Air** (867/872-2216 or 877/872-2216).

Frontier Coachlines (113 Kamlake Rd., 867/873-4892) offers bus service five times weekly from Hay River to Yellowknife, with connections from there to Greyhound's other Canadian services.

GETTING AROUND

Yellowknife Transit (867/873-4693, adult $2.50, senior and child $1.50 per sector) operates along three routes, including out to the campground and airport, Monday–Friday and with a limited Saturday service. Cab companies are **City Cab** (867/873-4444) and **Sunshine Taxi** (867/873-4414). Rental-car agencies include **Budget** (867/920-9209), **Hertz** (867/766-3838), and **National** (867/873-3424). Rates start at $60 per day and $360 per week for a small car. Generally no mileage allowance is given on daily rentals, but you get 250 kilometers included with weekly rentals.

Nahanni Country and the Mackenzie Valley

The Dene word for "spirit," Nahanni Country extends west from where the main highway north to Yellowknife crosses the Mackenzie River to the utter wilderness of the Mackenzie Mountains. The two main towns of Fort Simpson and Fort Liard are jumping-off points for the real adventure—rafting down the South Nahanni River through Nahanni National Park.

WEST TO FORT SIMPSON

From the Yellowknife junction, the Mackenzie Highway continues west through a typical

northern boreal forest, reaching the largest town in the region, Fort Simpson, after 268 kilometers (166 miles). The road is unpaved but well maintained.

Sambaa Deh Falls Territorial Park

Approximately 136 kilometers (84 miles) from the turn-off at Highway 3, the Mackenzie Highway reaches Sambaa Deh Falls on the Trout River. The falls are directly downstream from the road bridge and are easily accessible from the day-use area, on the other side of the road. Here, the river is forced through a narrow gorge, exploding into the deep pond below. A one-kilometer (0.6-mile) trail upstream leads to a fossil-filled limestone outcrop. The park has camping (showers, bug-proof cooking shelters, and well-maintained sites for $17 per night) and a **Visitors Centre** (daily 8 A.M.–8 P.M. mid-May–mid-Sept.) with a fossil display and TV room where nature videos are shown.

FORT SIMPSON

Best known as an access point for Nahanni National Park, the town of Fort Simpson (population 1,200) is at the confluence of two major rivers—the Liard and Mackenzie—with ferry crossing (daily 8 A.M.–11:45 P.M. late May–late Oct., free) required to reach town from the Mackenzie Highway. Throughout summer, the town is a hive of activity, with a constant buzz of floatplanes taking off to remote fly-in fishing lakes and hunt camps, groups of Gore-Tex–clad adventurers from around the world checking their equipment before heading off for the adventure of a lifetime down the South Nahanni River, and the occasional canoe-load of paddlers stopping in on their way to the Arctic Ocean.

Sights and Recreation

The main street through Fort Simpson is typical of Northern towns, with all the usual services, a couple of motels, and lots of modular buildings. The most interesting sights are one block east on Mackenzie Drive, running alongside the Mackenzie River. This was the main street before the highway was completed and businesses moved closer to it. At the south end, a beached stern-wheeler on the riverbank soon comes into view. Built in 1920, this boat was one of many that plied the Mackenzie River. Also here is a small monument noting the importance of the river in the town's history. Across the road is **Fort Simpson Heritage Park,** the site of the original Hudson's Bay Company post (the only original building remaining is the company's outhouse). Here you find a restored home used for various cultural

ALBERT FAILLE

Each spring from 1916–1961, Albert Faille left Fort Simpson by scow in a feverish, determined quest for the elusive Nahanni gold. Some said it was sheer lunacy, others a waste of time. But his relentless obsession and exploits against insurmountable odds created the Faille legend, which has become synonymous with the Nahanni.

Of Swiss descent, Faille was born in Minnesota. He was one of the earliest men to tackle the river alone, and at the time, the first to winter there in seven years. He built a cabin at the mouth of the Flat River, but it was at Murder Creek, upstream from the cabin, that Faille believed his fortune in gold lay. At times he'd be given up for dead, and rumors and tales would begin to unfold – but then he would turn up at Fort Simpson for supplies. He spent most winters in a small cabin that still stands today, overlooking the Mackenzie River in Fort Simpson. He died there in 1974. His scows still lie out front, ready for breakup and another attempt for the elusive key to finding gold. His final trip is documented by a 1961 National Film Board production that can be seen in the Fort Simpson and Blackstone visitors centers.

gatherings. Continuing farther along the river, you pass plaques noting the historic importance of various structures, including the cabin of Nahanni legend **Albert Faille,** who wintered here between his gold-seeking trips. Peering through the windows and marveling at the wooden scows laying in the yard gives you some insight into the life of this amazing man, particularly if you've watched the National Film Board documentary about him shown at the Visitors Centre.

Many local lakes have great fishing for northern pike, pickerel, lake trout, and arctic grayling, but are only accessible by air. **Simpson Air** (867/695-2505, www.simpsonair.ca) flies to Little Doctor Lake, where they operate a lodge, as well as **McGill Lake** and **Mustard Lake.**

Accommodations and Food

Along the road into town is ☾ **Bannockland B&B** (867/695-3337, $155–175 s or d). Rates for the five rooms include a cooked breakfast and airport transfers. Rooms in both of Fort Simpson's hotels are little more than basic and both charge from $120 s, $140 d. They are the **Maroda Motel** (867/695-2602), where some rooms have kitchenettes, and the **Nahanni Inn** (867/695-2201), which has a coffee shop (open daily at 8 A.M.) and dining room.

On the road to the Papal Grounds is **Fort Simpson Territorial Park** (mid-May–mid-Sept., $17), where 32 sites (four with power hookups) provide ample privacy. Showers and a large supply of firewood are available.

Information and Services

At the south entrance to town is the excellent **Fort Simpson Visitor Centre** (867/695-3182, www.fortsimpson.com, mid-May–mid-Sept. daily 9 A.M.–8 P.M.), which contains a re-creation of the original Hudson's Bay Company post and some interesting historical displays. Don't miss the 1961 National Film Board documentary on Nahanni legend Albert Faille, which is shown, along with others, in the theater. Diagonally opposite the Visitors Centre is the **Tourist Service Centre,** with coin showers, a car wash, and a laundry. The library (Antoine Dr.) has public Internet access.

LIARD HIGHWAY

From the Mackenzie Highway, southeast of Fort Simpson, to Fort Nelson (British Columbia) is 394 kilometers (245 miles) of relatively straight road through a boreal forest of spruce, aspen, and poplar. Wildlife along this route is abundant; chances are you'll see moose and black bears, especially at dawn and dusk. The only services are at Fort Liard.

Blackstone Territorial Park

A little more than 100 kilometers (62 miles) from the Mackenzie Highway, where the Blackstone River drains into the Liard River, a small territorial park has been established at a site known as **Blackstone Landing.** Inside the park visitors center (daily 8 A.M.–8 P.M. mid-May–mid-Sept.) are some interesting displays on the area's history and a good selection of locally made documentaries to watch. The center is the starting point for a short trail that leads to a trapper's cabin. The park's campground ($21) has flush toilets, showers, and two bugproof, woodstove-equipped cooking shelters. Black bears are common, so keep your food securely stored.

FORT LIARD

Best known as the "Tropics of the North" for its warm microclimate (many locals maintain vegetable gardens), this town of 400 is set among a lush forest of poplar and birch on the banks of the Liard River. The area has been settled since 1807, when the North West Company established where the Petitot River drains into the Liard. Until the 1960s, most of the Dene inhabitants spent winter away from Fort Liard, and modern development didn't begin until the highway opened to Fort Nelson. Traditional lifestyles are still important to residents, nearly all of whom spend time trapping, hunting, fishing, and making clothing and crafts.

Birchbark Baskets

The women of Fort Liard are famous for these baskets, made for storing food, collecting berries, carrying supplies, or even boiling water. Birch is abundant in the area and has a remarkably pliable nature, ideal for bending and sewing. The bark contains a natural wax, making it not only rot-resistant but also waterproof. Baskets are still made in the long, tedious process handed down from generation to generation. They are sewn together with specially prepared roots and decorated with porcupine quills. Available from the small gift store on Fort Liard's main street (or in Fort Simpson and Hay River), they make a wonderfully authentic Northern souvenir.

Practicalities

The small but well-maintained **Hay Lake**

Campground has pit toilets, firewood, and drinking water. It's along the Fort Liard access road. Accommodations above the **Liard Valley General Store** (867/770-4441, $125 s, $150 d) sleep 24 in 12 basic rooms. Back out on the highway is the only gas station (7 A.M.–11 P.M.) between Fort Simpson and Fort Nelson.

◀ NAHANNI NATIONAL PARK

One of the most spectacular, wildest, and purest stretches of white water in the world is the **South Nahanni River.** Protecting a 300-kilometer (186-mile) stretch of this remote river is 4,766-square-kilometer (1,234-square-mile) Nahanni National Park. This roadless park is a vast wilderness inhabited only by bears, mountain goats, Dall sheep, caribou, moose, and wolves.

Accessible only by air, the best way to really experience the park is on a raft or canoe trip down the South Nahanni River, but many visitors just fly in for the day. However you decide to visit the park, the adventure will remain with you for the rest of your life. But with names on the map like Headless Creek, Deadmen Valley, Hell's Gate, Funeral Range, Devils Kitchen, Broken Skull River, and Death Canyon, you'd better tell someone where you're going before heading out.

History

Slavey Dene, who lived on the lowlands along the Mackenzie and Liard Rivers, feared a mysterious group of natives living high in the Mackenzie Mountains, calling them the *Nahanni* (People Who Live Far Away). The first white men to travel up the South Nahanni River were fur trappers and missionaries, followed by men lured by tales of gold. In 1905, Willie and Frank McLeod began prospecting tributaries of the Flat River in search of an elusive mother lode. Three years later, their headless bodies were discovered at the mouth of what is now known as Headless Creek; for many years thereafter, the entire valley was called Deadmen Valley. Very quickly, stories of gold mines, murder, lush tropical valleys, and a tribe of Indians dominated by a white woman became rampant. These stories did nothing but lure other prospecting adventurers to the valley—Jorgenson, Shebbach, Field, Faille, Sibbeston, Kraus, and Patterson. Many died mysteriously: Jorgenson's skeleton was found outside his cabin, his precious rifle gone; Shebbach died of starvation at the mouth of Caribou Creek; the body of Phil Powers was discovered in his burned-out cabin; Angus Hall just plain disappeared.

The Land

The headwaters of the **South Nahanni River** are high in **Mackenzie Mountains,** which form the remote border between the Northwest Territories and the Yukon. Flowing in a roughly southeasterly direction for 540 kilometers (336 miles) it drains into the Liard River, a major tributary of the Mackenzie River. The South Nahanni, cut deeply into the mountains, is known as an "antecedent;" that is, it preceded the mountains. It once meandered through a wide-open plain. As uplift in the earth's surface occurred, the river cut down through the rising rock strata and created the deep, meandering canyons present today.

The starting point for many river trips and the destination of most day trippers is **Virginia Falls;** at 92 meters (300 feet) they are twice as high as Niagara Falls. Over many thousands of years, erosion has forced the falls upstream, creating a canyon system with walls over one kilometer (0.6 miles) high immediately downstream of the falls.

Running the South Nahanni with an Outfitter

For most people, whether experienced or first-time canoeists, the advantages of a trip down the South Nahanni River with a licensed outfitter far outweigh the disadvantages.

The two outfitters I recommend are **Nahanni River Adventures** (867/668-3180 or 800/297-6927, www.nahanni.com) and **Nahanni Wilderness Adventures** (403/678-3374 or 888/897-5223, www.nahanniwild. com). Each offers trips of varying lengths—8–12 days from Virginia Falls, two weeks from

Rabbitkettle Lake, or up to three weeks from Moose Ponds. Crafts used are rafts, two-person canoes, or longer voyageur-type canoes. Trips start at $3,900 for an eight-day float. The best way to get a feeling for which trip suits your needs and interests is by talking to the outfitters (they all love "their" river, so getting them to talk is no problem). Guided trips operate mid-June–early September, and many dates fill up fast. The staging area for both outfitters is the north end of the old airstrip in downtown Fort Simpson.

Your Own White-Water Expedition

Experienced white-water enthusiasts planning their own trip down the Nahanni have four main components to organize: permits and fees, transportation into the park, transportation down the river, and supplies. The best place to start planning your trip is the Parks Canada website (www.pc.gc.ca/nahanni), where you can download reservation forms and pay the park use fee ($147.20 per person). Only 12 non-guided visitors are allowed to start down the river each day, so reservations are an absolute necessity. Most expeditions begin with a floatplane trip to Virginia Falls and end outside of the park, where the Liard River flows alongside the Liard Highway. The charter cost from Fort Simpson to Virginia Falls for two people, one canoe, and 500 pounds of gear, is around $1,200. This is just an example—if there are four of you, you would travel in a bigger plane (a Beaver) and the cost would run around $2,000. For detailed quotes contact **Simpson Air** (867/695-2505, www.simpsonair. ca) or **Wolverine Air** (867/695-2263, www.wolverineair.com). These are the same two companies used by commercial guides, so they're flying into the park all the time. A few years ago, I picked up a guy who'd just come down the river and was hitchhiking back to Watson Lake from Blackstone Landing. He'd started at Moose Ponds, which is closer to Watson Lake (Yukon) than any Northwest Territories community; therefore chartering a plane from Watson Lake costs less, but it seemed an inconvenient way to save a couple hundred bucks. If

you need a canoe or other equipment, contact the floatplane companies or the commercial outfitters for rentals.

Flightseeing

Calling a flightseeing trip into Nahanni "awe-inspiring" doesn't do it justice—it is simply one of the most memorable flights I have ever taken. Getting into the park for just the day is problematic but well worth the effort and cost. Typically, charter operators use a floatplane to fly from Fort Simpson to Virginia Falls, with up to two hours spent at the falls, enough time to walk the 1.3-kilometer (0.8-mile) portage to the base of the falls. If you have three or more people in your group, there are no problems; just call each operator for the best quote (or get the staff at Fort Simpson Visitor Centre to do it for you) and expect to pay around $500 per person for a four- to five-hour trip. Groups of less than three have the choice of chartering an entire plane (from approximately $1,400) or waiting around for other interested parties to turn up. Each of the air charter companies can tailor flights to suit your needs. By waiting around until the plane is full, or by booking in advance, you have a better chance of keeping the cost down. Fort Simpson operators are the following: **Simpson Air** (867/695-2505) or **Wolverine Air** (867/695-2263).

Information

The outfitters on the river are experts in their own right and can answer many of your questions long before you arrive. For specific information on the park, check the website (www.pc.gc.ca/nahanni) or contact **Park Headquarters** in Fort Simpson (867/695-3151). The **Fort Simpson Visitor Centre** (867/695-3182, mid-May–mid-Sept. 9 A.M.–8 P.M.) has park displays as well as relevant videos and books for visitor use.

TOWNS ALONG THE MACKENZIE RIVER

In 1789, Alexander Mackenzie became the first European to travel the river that now bears his name. After his reports of rich fur resources reached the outside, the North West Company established fur-trading posts along the river. The Dene, who were originally nomadic, settled at the trading posts, forming small communities that still exist today. The only road into the region begins at Fort Simpson and extends north to Wrigley.

Wrigley

The road between Fort Simpson and Wrigley traverses thick boreal forest, breaking only for a short ferry trip at **Ndulee** (daily 9–11 A.M. and 2–8 P.M.), 84 kilometers (52 miles) out of Fort Simpson.

Most of the community's 160 residents are Slavey Dene who live a semi-traditional lifestyle. Across the Yukon River from the village is **Roche qui-Trempe-à -L'eau** (The Rock that Plunges into the Water), an isolated hill that has been eroded away by the river on one side, creating a sheer cliff that drops 400 meters (1,300 feet) into the water below.

The **Petanea Hotel** (867/581-3102, www.wrigleyhotel.com) is in a modular building that holds five guest rooms. Rates are $240 per person per day with three meals. The hotel also has a small coffee shop and a dining room that opens in the evening. Enquire here about boat rentals and tours.

Norman Wells

Oil is the lifeblood of Norman Wells (population 800), which lies along the Mackenzie River halfway between Fort Simpson and Inuvik. Unlike other settlements along the Mackenzie River, Norman Wells did not originate as a trading post but owes its existence to oil. Imperial Oil produces 10 million barrels annually from field tapped by over 150 wells (the company's largest source of conventional crude oil), shipping to market by pipeline. The infrastructure is unique in that it comprises man-made islands in the middle of the Mackenzie River, directly offshore from town, allowing oil extraction to continue throughout breakup and freeze-up of the river.

The center of town, a 20-minute walk from the airport, is a semicircle of semipermanent buildings around a dusty parking lot. Here you'll find the **Yamouri Inn** (867/587-2744, $130 s, $140 d), which has rooms, a dimly lit cocktail lounge, a coffee shop, and a restaurant. Closer to the airport is the **Mackenzie Valley Hotel** (867/587-2511, www.mackenzievalleyhotel.com, $130 s, $160 d). The 34 rooms are cheerfully painted and each comes with a TV and phone.

Norman Wells has an impressive three-story airport complete with an observation deck and revolving baggage claim—not bad for a town of 800 people. It is a one-kilometer (0.6-mile) walk into town. **North-Wright Airways** (867/587-2333, www.north-wrightairways.com) has daily flights from Yellowknife to Norman Wells, as well as from Norman Wells to all Mackenzie River communities.

Canol Heritage Trail

The large U.S. military force present in Alaska during World War II needed oil to fuel aircraft and ships, which were in place for expected Japanese attacks. The strategically located Norman Wells oil fields were chosen as a source of crude oil, with little regard for the engineering feat needed to build a pipeline over the Mackenzie Mountains. To this day, it remains one of the largest projects ever undertaken in northern Canada. More than $300 million was spent between 1942 and 1945, employing 30,000 people who laid 2,650 kilometers (1,650 miles) of four- and six-inch pipeline and built a road over some of North America's most isolated and impenetrable mountain ranges. It was abandoned less than a year after completion. Today, the roadbed remains—strewn with structures, trucks, and equipment used in the project's construction—and is considered by many to be one of the world's great wilderness hikes. It follows the original route for 372 kilometers (231 miles), from the Mackenzie River across from Norman Wells to the Yukon border. Following the road causes little problem, but the logistics of getting to the beginning of the trail, arranging food drops, crossing rivers (most bridges have been washed out), and returning to Norman

Wells require much planning. Rick Muyres of **Mountain River Outfitters** (867/587-2697, www.mountainriver.nt.ca) can provide transportation and logistical support.

Tulita

This small Slavey Dene community (population 300) is south of Norman Wells, where the Great Bear River drains into the Mackenzie River. This strategic location has made it a transportation hub since the days of Sir John Franklin. An Anglican church, built of squared logs and dating to the 1860s, sits on the riverbank, beside the Hudson's Bay Company post. Many houses have colorful tepees in their yards, which are used for drying and smoking fish, standing in stark contrast to a modern school building.

The **Two Rivers Hotel** (867/588-3320, $169 s, $219 d) has eight rooms with single and double beds, all with a shared bathroom and kitchen. Meals can also be arranged in the dining room. If you're interested in a boat trip chasing arctic grayling in the Great Bear River or to the **Smoking Hills,** where an exposed seam of coal burns permanently, make enquires at the hotel.

Great Bear Lake

East of the Mackenzie River, Great Bear Lake is one of the world's best freshwater fishing lakes, and it has the records to prove it. This lake holds world records for *all* line classes of lake trout and arctic grayling; the overall world record trout weighed in at a whopping 32.5 kilograms (72 pounds) and measured more than one meter (three feet). The lake also holds world records for most classes of arctic grayling, including the overall record.

Around the lake are small fishing lodges offering all-inclusive packages, including Great Bear Lake Lodge operated by **Plummer's Arctic Lodges** (204/774-5775 or 800/665-0240, www.canadianarcticfishing.com). Accommodations, all meals, guides, professionally equipped boats, and round-trip air charters from Winnipeg or Edmonton are included in the package; US$4,600 for seven days.

Formerly known as Fort Franklin, **Déline** (meaning "flowing water") is the only community on the lake. In 1825, Sir John Franklin wintered at the trading post here before setting off on one of his many expeditions in search of the Northwest Passage. Today, the Slavey Dene of Déline live a traditional lifestyle, trapping, fishing, and making crafts including moccasins for which they are well known. The tepee-shaped church is worth visiting, and the hike along the shore of Great Bear Lake offers rewarding vistas and passes several historic sites. Right in town, **Grey Goose Lodge** (867/589-5500, www.greygooselodge.ca, $185 pp including breakfast) is a modern accommodation with 12 guest rooms, canoe and motorboat rentals, and fishing charters.

Fort Good Hope

Overlooking the Mackenzie River and flanked by boreal forest, this Slavey Dene community of 550 is on the east bank of the Mackenzie River, 190 kilometers (118 miles) downstream of Norman Wells and just south of the Arctic Circle. A trading post was established here in 1805 by the North West Company, but the oldest building in town is the 1860 **Our Lady of Good Hope Church,** which has been declared a National Historic Site. The church's interior, decorated in ornate panels and friezes painted by an early missionary, Father Emile Petitot, depicts aspects of his travels and life in the north.

One of the highlights of a trip to Fort Good Hope is visiting **The Ramparts,** where 200-meter-high (660-foot) cliffs force the Mackenzie River through a 500-meter-wide (1,640-foot) canyon. Although the cliffs continue for many kilometers, the most spectacular section is upstream of town and can be reached on foot or by boat. Arrange boat rentals and tours through the **Ramparts Hotel** (867/598-2500, $165 pp). Overlooking the river, this hotel has a restaurant with a simple menu (entrées $21–32).

Colville Lake

This community of 50 North Slavey Dene,

just north of the Arctic Circle on the southeast shore of Colville Lake, was established in 1962 when a Roman Catholic mission was built. It is the territories' only community built entirely from logs. The largest building is the church, which supports a bell weighing 454 kilograms (1,000 pounds). The mission was built by Father Bern Will Brown, who has now left the church and is one of the north's most respected artists. His paintings, which depict the lifestyle of Northerners, are in demand across North America. Brown is also the host at **Colville Lake Lodge** (867/709-2500), which combines log cabin accommodation with excellent fishing for lake trout, arctic grayling, northern pike, whitefish, and inconnu, with a small museum highlighting life in the north. The lodge also has an art gallery, boat and canoe rentals, and common kitchen facilities.

Western Arctic

The northwestern corner of the Northwest Territories, where the Mackenzie River drains into the Arctic Ocean, is linked to the outside world by the Dempster Highway, the continent's northernmost public road. The region, which is entirely above the Arctic Circle, encompasses the Mackenzie River valley and the vast barrens flanking the Arctic Ocean.

INUVIK

You must see Inuvik (population 3,300) with your own eyes to believe it, and then you may still doubt what you see: brightly painted houses on stilts, a monstrous church shaped like an igloo, metal tunnels snaking through town, and a main street where businesses have names such as Eskimo Inn, 60 Below Construction, and Polar TV. Inuvik (Place of Man, in Inuvialuktun) is obviously a planned community, transformed from some architect's drafting board into full-blown reality high above the Arctic Circle. All aspects have been scientifically planned, right down to the foundations—all structures sit on piles of rock, ensuring stability in the permafrost and preventing heat from turning the ground into sludge.

Inuvik marks the end of the Dempster Highway, as far north as you can drive on a public road in North America, which is reason enough for many visitors to make the trek to town. If you come up from Calgary, you will have driven 3,560 kilometers (2,210 miles), from Seattle 4,030 kilometers (2,500 miles), from Los Angeles 6,100 kilometers (3,790 miles), or from New York 7,600 kilometers (4,720 miles).

Sights

It's easy to spend a whole day walking around town, checking out the unique considerations involved in living above the Arctic Circle. *Utilidors,* for example, snake around town, linking businesses and houses and passing right through the middle of the schoolyard. These conduits contain water, heat, and sewerage pipelines and are raised above the ground to prevent problems associated with permafrost. Inuvik's most famous landmark is **Our Lady of Victory Church,** commonly known as the **Igloo Church** (174 Mackenzie Rd., 867/777-2236) for its distinctive shape. The church, on Mackenzie Road, is not always open; ask at the rectory for permission to enter. The interior is decorated with a series of paintings by Inuvialuit artist Mona Thrasher, depicting various religious scenes. A few blocks to the east is the **Aurora Research Institute** (191 Mackenzie Rd., 867/777-3298, Mon.–Fri. 9 A.M.–5 P.M.), one of three support facilities for scientific projects throughout the Northwest Territories. West along Mackenzie Road is **Ingamo Hall,** a three-story structure built with more than 1,000 logs. The best views of the delta are, naturally, from the air, but the next best thing is to climb the 20-meter (66-foot)

© ANDREW HEMPSTEAD

Our Lady of Victory Church, commonly known as the Igloo Church

observation tower in **Jak Territorial Park,** six kilometers (3.7 miles) south of downtown.

Tours

It seems that everyone who visits Inuvik takes at least one tour, whether it's around town, on the delta, or to an outlying community. **Arctic Nature Tours** (beside the igloo church on Mackenzie Rd., 867/777-3300, www.arctic-naturetours.com) offers an extensive variety of tours June–early September; those that require flying include transportation from town out to the airport. The town tour ($45) lasts approximately two hours, taking in all the sights. Another popular excursion is Mackenzie Delta Legends Tour to the camp of an Inuvialuit elder ($160), where tea and bannock is served. In addition to Tuktoyaktuk tours, the company has trips to remote **Herschel Island,** located in the Beaufort Sea. The island was a major whaling station during the early 1900s, but today only ruins remain. This trip is especially good for bird-watchers because more than 70 avian species have been recorded on the island. The

flight to the island passes **Ivvavik National Park** in the northern Yukon, providing opportunities to see musk oxen, caribou, and grizzly bears. A two-hour stay on the island costs $425 per person, including the 90-minute (one-way) flight. Overnight stays begin at $805 per person.

Festivals and Events

Summer Solstice in June is celebrated by **Midnight Madness,** although because the sun doesn't set for a month, the actual date of the festival is of little importance. Celebrations on the weekend closest to the solstice (June 21) include traditional music and dancing and a feast of lobster imported from the east coast for the occasion. The **Great Northern Arts Festival** (www.gnaf.org), held during the third week of July, features carving demonstrations, musical performances such as Inuit drumming, displays, and sales of Northern art.

Accommodations and Camping

A few locals run bed-and-breakfasts, which are

relatively inexpensive and a friendly alternative to the impersonal hotels. Accommodations at the centrally located **☾ Polar B&B** (75 Mackenzie Rd., 867/777-2198, $105 s, $115 d) are comfortable, with a shared bathroom, kitchen, laundry, and lounge with television. Rates include a self-serve breakfast. One block farther down the hill is **Robertson's B&B** (41 Mackenzie Rd., 867/777-3111, June–Sept., $90 s, $100 d). This place has a large deck with great view of the delta. The two guest rooms share a single bathroom, but the price is right.

Inuvik's two downtown motels are owned by the Mackenzie Delta Hotel Group (www.mackenziedeltahotel.com), a native co-operative. Each has a coffee shop, a restaurant, and basic rooms with private baths. They are the uninspiring **Eskimo Inn** (133 Mackenzie Rd., 867/777-2801, $119–149 s, $129–159 d), with some rooms designated as nonsmoking, and the **Mackenzie Hotel** (185 Mackenzie Rd., 867/777-2861, $189 s, $204 d), with air-conditioning and in-room Internet access. On the way to the airport and the pick of the town's

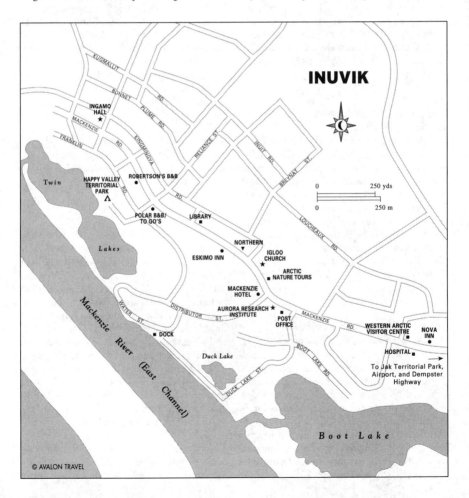

INUVIK

© AVALON TRAVEL

motels for room quality, is the **Nova Inn** (288 Mackenzie Rd., 867/777-2647 or 866/374-6682, www.novainninuvik.com, from $89 s, $129 d), which offers 42 comfortable rooms, each with Internet access, work desk, coffeemaker, and a fridge.

Happy Valley Territorial Park (867/777-3652, June–Aug., unserviced sites $18, powered sites $21) is on a bluff overlooking the delta, yet one block from the main street. It has 20 private, unserviced sites and a gravel parking area for RVs and trailers that need power. Amenities include flush toilets, showers, and firewood. Outside of town toward the airport is the **Jak Territorial Park** (June–Aug., unserviced sites $18, powered sites $21), with similar facilities, as well as an observation tower with river views.

Food

The thing to do this far north is to sample local fare such as musk ox, caribou, and arctic char. The least expensive way to do this is at **(To Go's** (71 Mackenzie Rd., 867/777-3030), which has a few tables and a take-out menu. Caribou burgers and musk ox burgers ($8.50) are the same price as regular hamburgers but cheaper than mushroom burgers. Pizza starts at $16; extras such as musk ox are $3.50, and the Northern Pizza—with the works—is $25.

Tonimoes (Mackenzie Hotel, 185 Mackenzie Rd., 867/777-2861, Tues.–Sat. 6–10 P.M., Sunday for brunch) serves a good selection of Northern cuisine (starting at $17.95 for a caribou burger).

Information and Services

The **Western Arctic Visitor Centre** (867/777-4727, www.inuvik.ca, daily 9 A.M.–8 P.M. mid-May–mid-Sept.) is at the entrance to town, a 10-minute walk from downtown. This modern facility features displays on the people of the north, details on each of the western Arctic communities, and all the usual tour information. Out back, a trail leads through a re-creation of an Inuvialuit whaling camp and a Gwich'in fishing camp. **Inuvik Centennial Library** (100 Mackenzie Rd., 867/777-

8620, Mon.–Thurs. 10 A.M.–9 P.M., Fri. 10 A.M.–6 P.M., Sat.–Sun. 1–5 P.M.) has a fairly extensive collection of Northern books and literature, as well as free public Internet access.

The **post office** is at 817 Mackenzie Road. **Inuvik Regional Hospital** (867/777-8000) is at the east end of town.

Getting There and Around

Mike Zubko Airport, 12 kilometers (7.5 miles) south of town, is the hub of air transport in the western Arctic. A cab between the airport and downtown is $35 for one or two passengers. From Calgary and Edmonton, **First Air** (867/669-8500 or 800/267-1247) and **Canadian North** (867/873-4484 or 800/661-1505) fly to Inuvik via Yellowknife. Heading north, sit on the left side of the plane for views of the Mackenzie Mountains. The local airline, with scheduled flights to communities throughout the western Arctic, is **Aklak Air** (867/777-3777, www.aklakair.ca).

For a cab, call **United Taxi** (867/777-5050). The cabs don't have meters because fares are set: $10 anywhere around town, $45 to the airport, and $460 to Tuktoyaktuk on the winter road.

AKLAVIK

Theoretically, this community in the middle of the Mackenzie Delta was abandoned more than 35 years ago when the government built Inuvik, but don't tell that to the 700 Dene and Inuvialuit who call Aklavik, 58 kilometers (36 miles) to the west, home. Wooden sidewalks, a legacy of Aklavik's one-time importance, link the original Hudson's Bay Company post and a mission church (now a small museum) to newer structures, built before the big move east was announced. Many large houses still stand, testimony to the fortunes made by prosperous traders in days gone by. Trails lead in all directions from town, inviting the curious to explore this small delta island.

Tours

Most people arrive in Aklavik as part of a tour from Inuvik with **Arctic Nature Tours**

(867/777-3300). On clear days, the 20-minute flight is awe-inspiring. For independent travelers, this company will arrange flights and advise on accommodation in the town's only hotel, or contact **Aklak Air** (867/777-3777, www.aklakair.ca).

◖ TUKTOYAKTUK

Most travelers, not satisfied with driving to the end of the road, hop aboard a small plane in Inuvik for the flight along the Mackenzie Delta to Tuktoyaktuk, a small community perched precariously on an exposed gravel strip on the Beaufort Sea. Although it would be a harsh and unforgiving place to live, a visit to "Tuk," as it is sensibly known, is a delightful eye-opener. The community is spread out around **Tuktoyaktuk Harbour** and has spilled over to the gravel beach, where meter-high (three-foot) waves whipped up by cold Arctic winds roll in off the Beaufort Sea and thunder up against the shore. The most dominant natural features of the landscape are **pingos,** massive mounds of ice forced upward by the action of permafrost. The mounds look like mini-volcanoes protruding from the otherwise flat environs. The ice is camouflaged by a natural covering of tundra growth, making the pingos all the more mysterious. Approximately 1,400 pingos dot the coastal plain around Tuk, one of the world's densest concentrations of these geological wonders peculiar to the north.

Sights

Most visitors see Tuk from the inside of a transporter van driven by accommodating locals who never tire of the same hackneyed questions about living at the end of the earth. The bus stops at **Our Lady of Lourdes,** once part of a fleet of vessels that plied the Arctic delivering supplies to isolated communities. Here also are two mission churches built in the late 1930s. A stop is also made at the Arctic Ocean, where you are encouraged to dip your toes in the water or go for a swim if you really want to impress the folks back home. (Tuk is actually on the Beaufort Sea, an arm of the Arctic Ocean, but who's telling?) For a few extra bucks, you are given some time to explore on

your own, including walking along the beach, climbing a nearby pingo, and checking out the well-equipped ocean port.

Practicalities

Tuk is the most popular flightseeing destination from Inuvik, and a variety of trips are offered from Inuvik. Trips start at $305, which includes the return flight (worth the price alone) and a tour of the town. The flight into Tuk is breathtaking—the pilots fly at low altitudes for the best possible views. For those who wish to spend longer in Tuk (there are enough things to do to hold your interest for at least one day), extended tours visit the community's unique cool room and include lunch with an Inuvialuit family, for $385 per person. For tour details, contact **Arctic Nature Tours** (867/777-3300). Scheduled flights are operated by **Aklak Air** (867/777-3777); accommodations are at the 18-room **Hotel Tuk Inn** (867/977-2381, $165–225 s or d).

PAULATUK

Meaning "Place of the Coal" in the local language, Paulatuk, 400 kilometers (250 miles) east of Inuvik, is a small community of 190 Inuvialuit, most of whom live a traditional lifestyle of hunting, trapping, and fishing. A Roman Catholic mission and trading post, established in 1935, attracted Inuvialuit families from camps along the Arctic coast. Their descendants continue living off the abundant natural resources. To the northeast are the **Smoking Hills,** seams of coal, rich with sulfide, that were ignited centuries ago and still burn today, filling the immediate area with distinctively shaped clouds of smoke. Sprawling across Parry Peninsula, to the east of Paulatuk, is **Tuktut Nogait National Park,** the major staging area for the 125,000-strong **bluenose caribou herd,** which migrates across the north.

Practicalities

The only accommodation in town is the **Paulatuk Visitor Centre Hotel** (867/580-3051, $185 pp), with 10 rooms that share bathrooms and a small kitchen. The only scheduled flights to Paulatuk are with **Aklak Air** (867/777-3777, www.aklakair.ca) from Inuvik. This company also does plane charters into the nearby park; or contact the Paulatuk Community Corporation (867/580-3601) for boat access.

BANKS ISLAND

Banks Island is one of the best places in the world for viewing musk oxen. Approximately 60,000 (half the world's population and the largest concentration) of these shaggy beasts call the island's **Aulavik National Park** home. Separated from the mainland by **Amundsen Gulf,** Banks is the most westerly island in the Canadian Arctic archipelago. Throughout the barren, low, rolling hills that characterize this island flow some major rivers, including the **Thomsen,** the northernmost navigable river in Canada.

Sachs Harbour (Ikaahuk)

The only permanent settlement on Banks Island is Sachs Harbour (population 150), at the foot of a low bluff along the southwest coast, 520 kilometers (323 miles) northeast of Inuvik. The town has no restaurants, only a small co-op grocery store (closed Sun.). **Aklak Air** (867/777-3777) has a twice-weekly scheduled flight to Sachs Harbour from Inuvik.

ULUKHAKTOK

Most of **Victoria Island,** separated by the Prince of Wales Strait from Banks Island,

falls within Nunavut. The exception is the island's western corner, including Diamond Jenness Peninsula, where the community of Ulukhaktok (population 360) lies. Formerly known as Holman, homes here sit behind a gravel beach at the end of horseshoe-shaped Queens Bay and are surrounded by steep bluffs that rise as high as 200 meters (660 feet). The village was founded around a Hudson's Bay Company post in 1939. Inuit that moved to the post were taught printmaking by a missionary, Reverend Henri Tardi, and to this day printmaking is a major source of income for the community. Ulukhaktok also has a golf course, the northernmost in the world. Playing a round of golf here is really something to tell the folks back at the country club; for the record, the course is at a latitude of 70'44' North. In mid-July, the course hosts the **Billy Joss Open** (867/396-3080), attracting entrants from as far away as the United States.

Practicalities

Ulukhaktok's only hotel is the **Arctic Char Inn** (867/396-3501, www.arcticcharinn.com, $219 pp includes meals). Scheduled flights into Ulukhaktok are three times weekly from Yellowknife with **First Air** (867/396-3063). **Whitney & Smith** (403/678-3052, www.legendaryex.com) is a highly respected adventure tour company that includes at least one canoeing trip annually down the Thomsen River.

YUKON

The Yukon sits like a great upside-down wedge—bordered by Alaska, British Columbia, Northwest Territories, and the Arctic Ocean—at the north corner of western Canada. Wilderness and history enriched by the Klondike gold rush combine to create a unique destination, very different from the rest of the country, but easily accessible by plane or by the Alaska Highway. The massive St. Elias Mountains pass through the territory's southwest corner, while the rest of the Yukon is a huge expanse of rolling hills, long narrow lakes, and boreal forests that give way to rolling tundra north of the Arctic Circle. Through the heart of it all flows the Yukon River. Wildlife is present in amazing numbers: 300,000 caribou, 50,000 moose, 22,000 Dall and Stone sheep, 10,000 black bears, 7,000 grizzlies, 4,500 wolves, and 2,000 mountain goats.

The territorial human population is just 31,000, almost 75 percent of them living in the capital, Whitehorse. One of the world's largest northern cities, this bustling city is filled with gold rush history, but is also a great place to soak up city luxuries before heading into the wilderness. In addition to modern hotels, Whitehorse boats a couple of golf courses, great biking and canoeing, good food, and an unexpected surprise, simply divine coffee roasted within city limits. From the capital, the Alaska Highway draws many road warriors farther west, passing by the magnificent wilderness of Kluane National Park before jogging north to Alaska. The Klondike Highway runs 536 kilometers (333 miles) from Whitehorse to Dawson City, site of the world's most frenzied gold rush. The

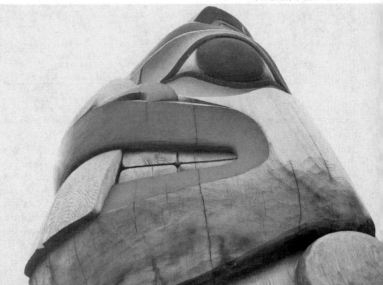

HIGHLIGHTS

◖ Signpost Forest: The first attraction north of the border is a little bit corny, but with an interesting history and thousands of town signs to look at, it's a good place to stretch your legs (page 519).

◖ SS *Klondike*: Step aboard one of the grandest stern-wheelers ever to ply the waters of the Yukon River (page 524).

◖ Dog-Mushing: A summertime visit to the kennels of Frank Turner will give you a taste of what winter brings. And if you are visiting in winter, there's the opportunity to try the pastime yourself (page 527).

◖ Kluane National Park: This park may border the Alaska Highway, but plan on hiking or canoeing to soak up this northern wilderness in all of its raw beauty (page 532).

◖ Dawson City Museum: This museum should be the starting point of a walking tour through the infamous mining town – worth the price of admission for the mining-history displays alone (page 538).

◖ Dawson Historical Complex National Historic Site: A walk through Dawson City leads past all of Dawson's most important and distinctive historic buildings, now protected as a National Historic Site (page 539).

◖ The Gold Fields: Once you've seen Dawson City, get out into the actual gold fields – and even try your hand at panning for gold (page 539).

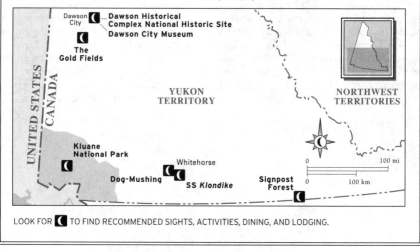

LOOK FOR ◖ TO FIND RECOMMENDED SIGHTS, ACTIVITIES, DINING, AND LODGING.

trip north from Whitehorse along the Yukon River follows the same route taken by thousands of stampeders in the late 1890s, except instead of riverboats it's RVs and rental cars filled with modern-day travelers in search of adventure. Parks Canada and the Klondike Visitors Association (KVA) have been doing an outstanding job bringing the color of life back to Dawson City. Many ramshackle buildings have been spruced up with brightly painted facades and informative window displays, and most of the commercial hotels, gift shops, restaurants, beauty parlors, bed-and-breakfasts, and other businesses have followed suit. Thankfully, much of the semi–ghost town flavor remains.

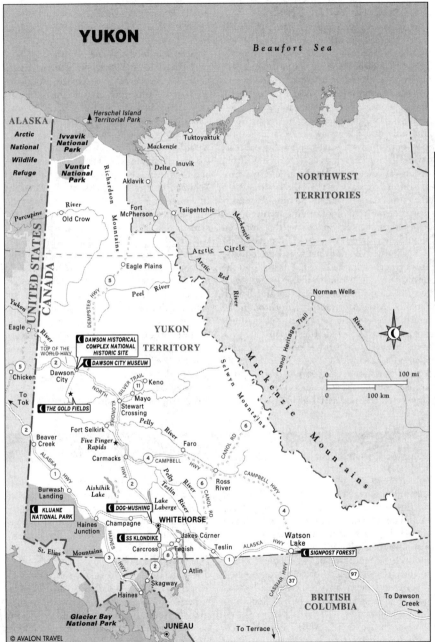

YUKON

YUKON

Beaufort Sea

ALASKA

Arctic

National

Wildlife

Refuge

Herschel Island
Territorial Park

*Ivvavik
National
Park*

*Vuntut
National
Park*

Tuktoyaktuk

Mackenzie

Delta

Inuvik

NORTHWEST

TERRITORIES

Aklavik

Richardson

River

Old Crow

Fort
McPherson

Tsiigehtchic

Mackenzie

Porcupine

Mountains

Arctic Circle

UNITED STATES

CANADA

Yukon

River

Eagle Plains

Arctic

Red

River

Mackenzie

Norman Wells

Peel   River

Canol Heritage Trail

River

DEMPSTER HWY.

YUKON

5

Eagle

TOP OF THE
WORLD HWY.

TERRITORY

Selwyn

Mountains

Chicken

5

2

DAWSON HISTORICAL
COMPLEX NATIONAL
HISTORIC SITE

DAWSON CITY MUSEUM

100 mi

0

100 km

To Tok

2

Dawson
City

SILVER TRAIL

11 Keno

Mackenzie

Mountains

THE GOLD FIELDS

NORTH

KLONDIKE

Mayo

Stewart
Crossing

CANOL RD.

6

Beaver
Creek

Fort Selkirk

Pelly   River

Faro

Five Finger
Rapids

HWY.

Carmacks

2

4

CAMPBELL

HWY.

CAMPBELL HWY.

Aishihik
Lake

Pelly

Teslin

River

River

6

Ross
River

CANOL RD.

Burwash
Landing

ALASKA

1

HWY.

KLUANE
NATIONAL PARK

DOG-MUSHING

Lake
Laberge

4

St. Elias

Haines
Junction

Champagne

WHITEHORSE

HAINES

SS KLONDIKE

Jakes Corner

Watson
Lake

3

HWY.

Carcross

8

Tagish

Teslin

ALASKA

HWY.

1

SIGNPOST FOREST

Mountains

2

Atlin

CASSIAR HWY.

37

97

To Dawson
Creek

Skagway

**BRITISH
COLUMBIA**

*Glacier Bay
National Park*

JUNEAU

To Terrace

© AVALON TRAVEL

PLANNING YOUR TIME

The Yukon is a destination in itself, with some excellent packages offered by the local airline, Air North (867/668-2228, www.flyairnorth.com), that include airfares from the southern gateways of Vancouver, Edmonton, and Calgary, as well as accommodations and the option of traveling one-way in a rented campervan.

If you want to get a taste of the far north and only have a few days, these deals are the best option. For those driving, allow at least two full, long days to reach Watson Lake from either Vancouver or Edmonton. Add in a minimum of five days in the Yukon along with the return day and you have a nine-day excursion. For the amount of driving involved, this isn't a very practical option and therefore you should allow at least two weeks from the southern gateways. You don't necessarily need to use this extra time in the Yukon, but it allows the opportunity to break up highway time with leisurely stops in northern or central British Columbia, or to include a loop through the southern Northwest Territories. But the most popular way to include the Yukon in a two-week itinerary is to travel one-way by ferry down Alaska's Inside Passage. You can use BC Ferries (www.bcferries.com) to travel up the British Columbia coast as far as Prince Rupert, from where the Alaska Marine Highway System

(www.dot.state.ak.us/amhs) delivers travelers as far north as Skagway and Haines, both an hour's drive from the Yukon.

Why should you travel all this way? Sure there are official "sights," but the purpose of your trip should be primarily to experience wilderness in its most pristine form, in officially designated areas such as Kluane National Park—canoeing across a lake at dawn, soaking in hot springs, or viewing the abundant wildlife. That said, almost everyone makes a stop at the Signpost Forest in Watson Lake, and then spends a day exploring the history of Whitehorse at attractions like the SS *Klondike*. In winter, dog-mushing is becoming big tourism business, but even in summer, visiting the kennels of a racer like Frank Turner will give you a taste of this exiting sport.

From Whitehorse, it's an easy day's drive north to Dawson City, where you should plan to spend at least two days. Dawson City Museum encapsulates the history of this infamous mining town in one building, but to experience the real Dawson, you want to spend the rest of the day on foot visiting the Dawson Historical Complex National Historic Site and a half-day exploring the nearby Gold Fields, where at least one company offers the chance to try gold-panning, and where you can even stay overnight in a traditional wall tent.

The Southeast

The **Alaska Highway** (Alcan) crosses into the Yukon some 1,000 kilometers (620 miles) northwest of Dawson Creek, then ducks back in and out of British Columbia a couple more times before crossing into the Yukon again and reaching the highway town of Watson Lake. From this point, travelers either continue east to the territorial capital or complete the loop through northern British Columbia by taking the Cassiar Highway (Hwy. 37) south to Meziadin Junction.

Over the years, the Alaska Highway has been shortened by straightening some sections

and cutting out big bends completely. Mileage posts in British Columbia have been replaced to reflect these new distances, but those on the Yukon side haven't—so you'll see a 40-kilometer (25-mile) discrepancy beyond the border.

WATSON LAKE

This is the first town in Yukon Territory for all drivers heading north from British Columbia. Even though it's not pretty, it's a welcome sight after the several hundred kilometers on the Cassiar Highway or the all-day ride from Fort Nelson on the Alaska Highway.

Originally inhabited by Kaska Indians, Watson Lake (the town) was created to serve one of a string of airfields constructed across northern Canada in 1940, and its existence was ensured when the Alcan was routed through to service the airfield. Today Watson Lake functions as the hub of a large area of southern Yukon, southwestern Northwest Territories, and northern British Columbia. With a population of 1,500, it's the third largest town in the territory.

◖ Signpost Forest

The famous Signpost Forest originated in 1942 by a G.I. working on the highway who, when given the task of repainting the road's directional sign, added the direction and mileage to his hometown of Danville, Illinois. Since then, more than 40,000 other signs have been added to the collection with town signs, license plates, posters, pie tins, gold-panning pans, mufflers, driftwood, even flywheels stating where the contributor is from and who he/she is. You can put up your addition personally or take it inside to the adjacent **Watson Lake Visitor**

Information Centre (corner of Alaska Hwy. and Robert Campbell Hwy., 867/536-7469, early May–late Sept. daily 10 A.M.–6 P.M., July–Aug. daily 8 A.M.–8 P.M.) and have them put it up for you. In the center, you'll get a history lesson on the Signpost Forest, as well as the engineering feat that is the Alaska Highway through photos, displays, dioramas, and a three-projector audiovisual presentation.

Other Sights

Across from the information center, the **Northern Lights Centre** (867/536-7827, May–Sept.) is dedicated to the enthralling *aurora borealis,* also known as the northern lights. The highlight is a planetarium-type theater that shows a stunning one-hour presentation of northern lights footage shot in the Yukon. It runs several times daily from 1 P.M. to 8:30 P.M. The center also has a live feed to the Hubble telescope and a SciDome space show.

Take Eighth Street north a few blocks up from the Alaska Highway to **Wye Lake,** where a trail encircle the lake, complete with a boardwalk platform from which to view migrating

YUKON

© ANDREW HEMPSTEAD

You can add your own hometown to the Signpost Forest.

shorebirds and resident grebes. If you're traveling with kids, make a stop five kilometers (3.7 miles) south of town at **Lucky Lake** (June–Aug.), a day-use recreation area complete with a waterslide that will land them into the surprisingly warm lake.

Accommodations and Camping

Coming into Watson Lake from the road, you'll be tired and hungry, guaranteed. Half a dozen motels, several campgrounds, and a handful of restaurants are there to serve. **Cedar Lodge Motel** (Mile 633 Alaska Hwy., 867/536-7406, www.cedarlodge.yk.net, $85 s or d) has standard motel rooms with phones and cable TV. The hands-on owners have also developed suites in a building they moved from an abandoned mining town (from $95 s or d). Also in town is the more modern **Big Horn Hotel** (Mile 633 Alaska Hwy., 867/536-2020) with attractively appointed rooms, including kitchen suites, starting at $125 s or d.

Nugget City (867/536-2307 or 888/536-2307, www.nuggetcity.com, May–Oct.) is a large tourist complex 20 kilometers (12 miles) west of Watson Lake (just past the Cassiar turn-off). The least expensive wooden cabins ($125–210 s or d) are spotlessly clean and come with a deck and satellite TV. Even taking into consideration the nondescript interiors, they are a good value. Fancier suites come with jetted tubs and covered decks. Tent sites are $22 and large pull-through hookup sites come with power, water, and satellite TV hookups for $38–50. The on-site restaurant has a good selection of Northern foods and a nice deck.

Other camping options are **Downtown RV Park** (right in the middle of town, 867/536-2646, $32–32) with full hookups and showers, and **Watson Lake Public Campground,** which is three kilometers (1.9 miles) off the highway at Kilometer 1,025 and has no services for $17 per night.

Food

Both the **Belvedere** (867/536-7712) and **Watson Lake Hotels** (867/536-7781) have coffee shops and dining rooms open from 6 A.M.

Both also have bars, the latter decorated with Northern memorabilia.

Wolf it Down Restaurant (Nugget City, 20 km/12 mi west of town, 867/536-2307, May–Oct. daily 6:30 A.M.–9:30 P.M.) is a touristy place with decent food, including Northern specialties like bison burgers, and an in-house bakery.

WATSON LAKE TO WHITEHORSE

It's 454 kilometers (282 miles) from Watson Lake to Whitehorse. A pullout at Kilometer 1,163 marks the **Continental Divide** between rivers that drain (via the Mackenzie system) into the Arctic Ocean and those that empty (via the Yukon) into the Pacific.

◖ Dawson Peaks Resort & RV Park (Km 1,232, 867/390-2244 or 866/402-2244, www.dawsonpeaks.ca, mid-May–mid-Sept.) stands out above other lodges between Watson Lake and Teslin for both location and services. Right on Teslin Lake, it features treed tent sites ($14), RV sites ($16–27), motel rooms ($79 s or d), and basic lakeside cabins ($104–109 s or d). The restaurant not only has good food (entrées $12–19, delicious rhubarb pie $4 per slice), it has table settings on a wonderful deck overlooking the lake. Owners David Hett and Carolyn Allen will make you feel welcome, tempting you to make your stop more than a simple overnight stay with canoe rentals ($24 for a half-day) and motorboat rentals ($35 per hour); guided fishing for trout, pike, and inconnu ($75 per hour); and land and river tours (from $60 per hour).

Teslin

Just over halfway between Watson Lake and Whitehorse, Teslin (Km 1,293) is reached after crossing the impressive Nisutlin Bay Bridge (longest on the Alaska Hwy.). Its mostly Tlingit population live a traditional lifestyle: hunting, fishing, trapping, carving, and sewing. The **George Johnston Museum** (867/390-2550, daily 9 A.M.–7 P.M. in summer, $3) has displays on native culture, Yukon frontier artifacts, and one-of-a-kind photographs taken 1910–1940 by Johnston, a Tlingit hunter and trapper.

Teslin has the aforementioned **Dawson Peaks Resort & RV Park,** as well as the in-town **Yukon Motel** (867/390-2443, www.yukonmotel.com, motel rooms $85 s, $95 d, camping $27), which is on the lake and has boat rentals, gas, a restaurant, and a room filled with wildlife dioramas. Another camping option is **Teslin Lake Campground** ($14), through town at Kilometer 1,307.

Teslin to Whitehorse

It's 183 kilometers (114 miles) between Teslin and Whitehorse with the Alaska Highway closely paralleling Teslin Lake for the first 40 kilometers (25 miles) or so. At the lake's northern outlet is **Johnson's Crossing** (Km 1,346, 867/390-2607, May–Sept., campsites $22–32), which has the usual Alaska Highway set-up—campground (some sites with electricity), gas, groceries, a restaurant (delicious cinnamon buns), and showers.

At Kilometer 1,413, halfway between Jake's Corner and Whitehorse, is █ **Inn on the Lake** (867/660-5253, www.exceptionalplaces.com, $229–249 s or d), the most upscale lodging along the entire Alaska Highway. The main lodge is a peeled-log building with a living room, library, solarium, and spiffy dining room with a vaulted ceiling. Each of 15 guest rooms and cottages is decorated with stylish furnishings and has a comfortable bed, quality linens, wireless Internet, and a well-appointed bathroom. Rates include breakfast and the use of canoes and kayaks.

ATLIN

The small community of Atlin lies 100 kilometers (62 miles) south of Jake's Corner, back over the border in British Columbia. It is British Columbia's northernmost and westernmost settlement. Although isolated from the rest of British Columbia, it is one of the province's most picturesque communities. The glaciated peaks of the Coast Mountains form a stunning backdrop for the town, which is on a gently sloping hill overlooking beautiful 140-kilometer-long (85-mile-long) **Atlin Lake.**

Atlin was a boomtown with more than 8,000 people during the 1898 Klondike gold rush, when gold was discovered in nearby Pine Creek. Today they're still finding some color hereabouts, but the town's population has dwindled to about 400.

The highlight of Atlin is the surrounding scenery. Wandering along the lakeshore you'll have outrageous views of sparkling peaks, glaciers, waterfalls, and mountain streams. Tied up on the lake in front of town is the **SS *Tarahne*,** a 1916 steamer that has been restored.

Sights

Atlin Historical Museum (3rd St. and Trainor St., 250/651-7522, June–early Sept. daily 9 A.M.–5:50 P.M., adult $3), housed in a 1902 schoolhouse, lets you relive the excitement of the gold rush. Scattered through town are many historic buildings and artifacts pretty much untouched from the gold-rush era.

South of Atlin along Warm Springs Road are various lakes, camping areas, and, at the end of the road, **warm springs.** The springs bubble out of the ground at a pleasant 29°C (84°F) into shallow pools surrounded by flower-filled meadows.

Practicalities

Holding a prime downtown, lakefront location is the **Atlin Inn** (1st St., 250/651-7546 or 800/682-8546, from $135 s or d) which comprises 18 motel rooms and a string of kitchen-equipped cottages. It also has a restaurant open daily at 7 A.M. and a lounge with a great patio.

For primitive camping, the first of four spots through Atlin to the south is **Pine Creek Campground** ($8), with pit toilets and firewood (no drinking water).

CARCROSS AND VICINITY

Rather than drive straight through to Whitehorse, many travelers hang a left at Jake's Corner to Carcross (a contraction of "caribou crossing"), on Highway 2 between Skagway (Alaska) and Whitehorse. This picturesque village of 400 sits at the north end of Lake Bennett, which forms the headwaters of the Yukon River. It was an important stopping point for miners during the Klondike gold rush and today is chock-a-block with buildings from that era.

Sights

Make your first stop the **Carcross Visitor Information Centre** (867/821-4431, early May–late Sept. daily 10 A.M.–6 P.M., July–Aug. daily 8 A.M.–8 P.M.), housed in a railway station that served passengers along the White Pass & Yukon Route (WP&YR). It contains not only brochures from all over the Yukon, but also fine historical exhibits. WP&YR trains crossed the original "swing bridge" in town, built to allow the riverboats to pass; walk across the bridge for a look back. A footbridge is just north of this. In the old Carcross **cemetery,** two kilometers (1.2 miles) away, rest such stampede-starting notables as Skookum Jim, Tagish Charlie, and Kate Carmack.

Accommodations and Food

The standout lodging is on Spirit Lake, a 10-minute drive north of Carcross toward Whitehorse. At **Spirit Lake Wilderness Resort** (867/821-4337 or 866/739-8566, www.spiritlakeyukon.com) the lakeside cabins ($75 s or d) are my pick for the views and rustic charm, although they don't have electricity or running water (shared shower facilities). Other choices are cottages ($65 s or d) and motel rooms ($99 s or d) that lack the atmosphere but are more comfortable. Tent sites are $25 and hookups $30–35. Activities include canoeing and horseback riding and there's an on-site restaurant.

 Wheaton River Wilderness Retreat (867/668-2997, www.wheatonriver.net, $125 s or d) is truly in the wilderness, 22 kilometers (13.7 miles) along Annie Lake Road, which branches off Highway 2 north of Spirit Lake. Accommodation is offered for up to four people in a riverfront cabin constructed with timber milled onsite by the owners. The interior is spacious, airy, and modern, with wooden furniture carved by the owners. Breaskfast is $10 per person, and other meals are also available; or you can cook up a feast yourself on the wood stove or barbecue.

Whitehorse

Whitehorse is a friendly oasis in the heart of an unforgiving land. With 25,000 residents, Whitehorse is the largest city in northern Canada and is home to almost 75 percent of the Yukon's total population. It squats on the western bank of the Yukon, hemmed in by high bluffs that create something of a wind tunnel along the river. To the east, the bare rounded hulk of Grey Mountain (1,494 m/4,900 ft) fills the horizon. Whitehorse has its share of gold-rush history and nostalgia, but is not dominated by it; as the capital of Yukon Territory for the past half-century, this small city has a brash, modern frontier energy all its own. It's easy to slip into Whitehorse's strong stream of hustle and bustle, which seems to keep pace with the powerful Yukon itself. Yet the town also has a warm, homespun vitality to it, like huddling around the fire on a cold Northern night.

History

The name Whitehorse was given to the treacherous rapids encountered by stampeders, who likened them to the flowing manes of Appaloosas. An entry in an early edition of the *Klondike Nugget* described the scene:

Many men who ran these dangerous waters had never handled a boat in their lives until they stopped at Lake Bennett to figure out which end of their oar went into the water.... The boats filed into that tremendous first section of the canyon, dodged the whirlpool in the middle, rushed down the second section of the canyon, tossed

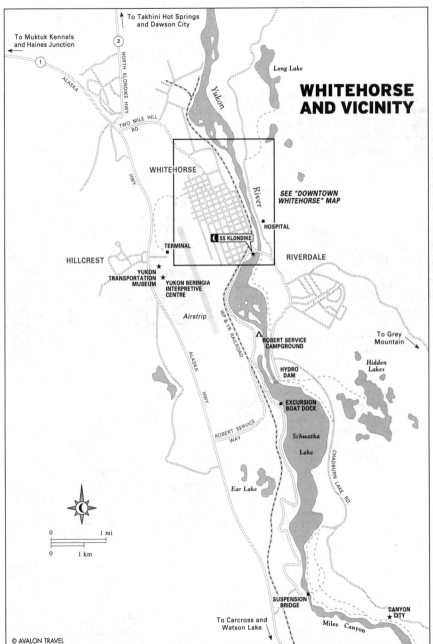

WHITEHORSE AND VICINITY

To Takhini Hot Springs and Dawson City

To Muktuk Kennels and Haines Junction

2

1

ALASKA

NORTH KLONDIKE HWY.

TWO MILE HILL RD.

Long Lake

Yukon

WHITEHORSE

River

SEE "DOWNTOWN WHITEHORSE" MAP

HOSPITAL

TERMINAL

SS KLONDIKE

HILLCREST

RIVERDALE

YUKON TRANSPORTATION MUSEUM

YUKON BERINGIA INTERPRETIVE CENTRE

HWY.

Airstrip

WP & YR RAILROAD

To Grey Mountain

ROBERT SERVICE CAMPGROUND

Hidden Lakes

ALASKA HWY.

HYDRO DAM

EXCURSION BOAT DOCK

Schwatka Lake

ROBERT SERVICE WAY

CHADBURN LAKE RD.

Ear Lake

0   1 mi

0   1 km

SUSPENSION BRIDGE

CANYON CITY

To Carcross and Watson Lake

Miles Canyon

YUKON

© AVALON TRAVEL

around for a while in the seething water of the rapids, made that stupendous turn into White Horse, as with rapidly accelerating speed they plunged into the final chaos of angry water...

A few men drowned; many managed to hang onto their lives but lost their boats and grub-stakes. Regulations were put in place that allowed only expert handlers to pilot the rapids. Undoubtedly, this saved countless lives and supplies in the more than 7,000 boats that passed through in the first, crazy rush to the Klondike. Soon after, an eight-kilometer (five-mile) horse-drawn tramway was built around the rapids to the present site of Whitehorse, where goods were reloaded into boats to complete the journey to Dawson City. A tent city sprang up at the tramway's lower end, and Whitehorse was born.

The town's role as a transportation hub began in 1900, when the WP&YR reached Whitehorse, finally connecting Skagway (Alaska) to the Yukon. At Whitehorse, passengers and freight transferred to riverboats for the trip down the Yukon River to Dawson City. In 1942–1943 this role grew substantially, as did Whitehorse along with it, during the construction of the Alaska Highway. In 1953, Whitehorse eclipsed declining Dawson in population and importance and became the territorial seat of government. Whitehorse today thrives on highway traffic, territorial administrative duties, and its function as a supply center for Yukon mines.

SIGHTS

In addition to providing big city comforts before folks head into the wilderness, Whitehorse has enough attractions to keep you busy for at least two full days. Many of these are within walking distance of downtown and most accommodations. One natural attraction that is well worth extra time is the Yukon River. An ongoing rejuvenation program is beautifying the riverfront along downtown, with **Shipyards Park,** at the north end of downtown, a sign of what will come in the future.

Shipyards features a wide-open green space, picnic tables, viewing platform, and stage.

◖ SS *Klondike*

Start your visit to Whitehorse with a tour of this National Historic Site—the largest stern-wheeler ever to ply the waters of the Yukon, the SS *Klondike,* which is dry-docked along 2nd Avenue at the south end of town (867/667-3910, mid-May–mid-Sept. daily 9:30 A.M.–5 P.M., $6.05 per person for the tour). Launched in 1929 and rebuilt after it sank in 1936, the *Klondike* made 15 round-trips a season, requiring one and a half days and 40 cords of wood for the downstream trip to Dawson, four and a half days and 120 cords back to Whitehorse. The *Klondike* is beautifully and authentically restored, right down to the 1937 *Life* magazines and the food stains on the waiters' white coats. Bridges erected along the road to Dawson in the mid-1950s blocked the steamer's passage and she has sat in the same spot since her last run in 1955. The best way to learn about the vessel and her colorful history is by joining a tour that runs every 30 minutes, proceeding from the boiler, freight, and engine deck, up to the dining room and first-class cabins, and finally up to the bridge.

MacBride Museum

North of the visitors center and across the road from the river is the excellent MacBride Museum (1124 1st Ave. at Wood St., 867/667-2709, summer daily 9:30 A.M.–5:30 P.M., the rest of the year Tues.–Sat. noon–4 P.M., adult $8, senior $7, child $4.50). The main building is a sod-roofed log cabin filled with historical items, including stuffed Yukon wildlife and hundreds of gold-rush photographs. Surrounding it are other buildings and equipment: the old government telegraph office, engine No. 51 from the WP&YR, Sam McGee's cabin, and even a one-ton copper nugget.

Yukon Beringia Interpretive Centre

Named for the landmass that once linked Asia

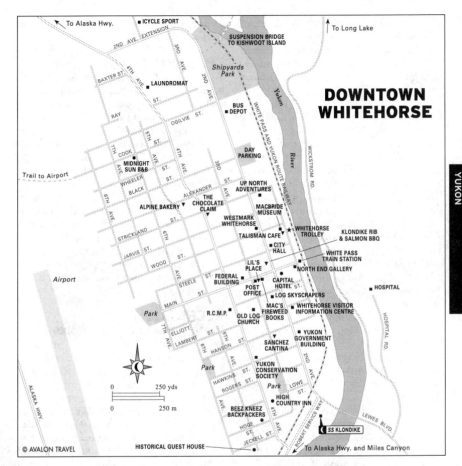

DOWNTOWN WHITEHORSE

To Alaska Hwy.
■ ICYCLE SPORT
2ND. AVE. EXTENSION
SUSPENSION BRIDGE TO KISHWOOT ISLAND
To Long Lake
Shipyards Park
BAXTER ST.
4TH AVE.
3RD AVE.
2ND. AVE.
Yukon River
WICKSTROM RD.
RAY
■ LAUNDROMAT
ST.
OGILVIE ST.
■ BUS DEPOT
WHITE PASS AND YUKON ROUTE RAILWAY

YUKON

Trail to Airport
5TH AVE.
7TH
COOK
MIDNIGHT SUN B&B
WHEELER ST.
BLACK
4TH AVE.
ST.
3RD
ST.
DAY PARKING
UP NORTH ADVENTURES
8TH AVE.
ALPINE BAKERY ▼
THE CHOCOLATE CLAIM ▼
ALEXANDER
ST.
MACBRIDE MUSEUM
WESTMARK WHITEHORSE
STRICKLAND
6TH
ST.
TALISMAN CAFE ▼
★ WHITEHORSE TROLLEY
KLONDIKE RIB & SALMON BBQ
JARVIS ST.
WOOD ST.
■ CITY HALL
WHITE PASS TRAIN STATION
Airport
AVE.
STEELE ST.
LIL'S PLACE
FEDERAL BUILDING
NORTH END GALLERY
Park
MAIN ST.
POST OFFICE
CAPITAL HOTEL ST.
LOG SKYSCRAPERS
■ HOSPITAL
R.C.M.P.
OLD LOG CHURCH
MAC'S FIREWEED BOOKS
WHITEHORSE VISITOR INFORMATION CENTRE
7TH AVE.
ELLIOTT ST.
LAMBERT ST.
HANSON ST.
SANCHEZ CANTINA
YUKON GOVERNMENT BUILDING
HOSPITAL RD.
Park
HAWKINS ST.
ROGERS ST.
YUKON CONSERVATION SOCIETY
2ND. AVE.
LOWE ST.
Park
ALASKA HWY.
0   250 yds
0   250 m
BEEZ KNEEZ BACKPACKERS
HIGH COUNTRY INN
HOGE ST.
4TH AVE.
ROBERT SERVICE WAY
LEWES BLVD.
© AVALON TRAVEL
HISTORICAL GUEST HOUSE
JECKELL ST.
SS KLONDIKE
To Alaska Hwy. and Miles Canyon

and North America, this dramatic multimedia center (Alaska Hwy., 867/667-8855 May–Sept. daily 9 A.M.–6 P.M., the rest of the year Sun. 1–5 P.M., adult $7.50, senior $6.50, child $5) out by the airport contains life-size exhibits of animals from the last Ice Age, including a spectacular 12,000-year-old, four-meter-tall (12-foot) woolly mammoth skeleton. Visitors will learn about the prehistoric animals that once roamed the north through exhibits, computer kiosks, dioramas, and a fascinating 30-minute film. A reconstruction of a 24,000-year-old archaeological site is also here, plus a gift shop and café.

Yukon Transportation Museum

Located next to the Beringia Interpretive Centre, this is one of the finest museums in the north (30 Electra Cres., 867/668-4792, mid-May–Aug. daily 10 A.M.–6 P.M., adult $6, senior $5, child $3). You could easily spend a few hours examining the many excellent displays and watching the long historical videos. Here's just a sample: Look up to view *Queen of the Yukon,* the first commercial aircraft in the territory, hanging from the ceiling; take the Golden Stairs up to the second floor, where murals and artifacts re-create the gold rush from Skagway to Dawson; sit in Lake Annie, a WP&YR railcar, and watch the 30-minute video while the model train circles the track; and check out the Alcan room with a fascinating video on the highway's construction. Out front is a DC-3 that acts as the world's largest weathervane.

Schwatka Lake and Miles Canyon

Cross the bridge beside the *Klondike* and take Lewis Boulevard south or walk along the riverside trail south 4.5 kilometers (2.8 miles) toward the **Whitehorse Dam** that created Schwatka Lake, tamed the once-feared White Horse Rapids, and now provides electricity for the city. The world's longest wooden **fishway** (366 m/1,200 ft) allows fish to get around the dam and up to their spawning grounds upriver. Three underwater windows inside the fishway building (867/633-5965, June–early Sept. daily 8:30 A.M.–8:30 P.M.) give you a good look at the chinook (king) salmon (late July–early Sept. is best).

From the dam, continue south on Chadburn Lake Road to the head of the lake where the Yukon River flows through spectacular Miles Canyon. A path along the canyon leads to the distinctive **Lowe Suspension Bridge** (1923), the first bridge across the Yukon—the views are superb.

Continue two kilometers (1.2 miles) beyond the bridge, staying on the east side, to reach the site of **Canyon City,** which slipped into oblivion after the opening of the railway in 1900 put an end to river travel above Whitehorse.

As an alternative to accessing these sights by road, consider walking. It's 10 kilometers (6.2 miles) round-trip from downtown, with the option of crossing the suspension bridge and returning along the west bank of the river, or jumping aboard a city transit bus (hourly along South Access Rd.) to get back to town. Another way to see the lake and surrounding sights is with **Yukon River Cruises** (867/668-4716, adult $30, child $15) aboard the MV *Schwatka,* a tour boat that departs daily at 2 P.M. June–early September (plus 6 P.M. in mid-July to mid-Aug.) for two-hour cruises. The departure point is along Miles Canyon Road one

kilometer (0.6 miles) south of downtown on the *west* side of the dam.

Takhini Hot Springs

These odorless (no sulfur) hot springs (867/456-8000, mid-May–mid-June daily noon–10 P.M., mid-June–mid-Sept. daily 8 A.M.–10 P.M.) bubble out of the ground at 36°C (96°F) north of Whitehorse. They have been developed and are as popular with locals as they are with visitors. All-day access is adult $8, senior $6.50, child $5.75. The attached café has some of the best chicken soup north of Vancouver. The hot springs campground costs $16.50 for tents and $25–35 for RVs and trailers (this is a good place to spend the night, take an early dip, then hit the road to Dawson). Get to Takhini by driving 18 kilometers (11.2 miles) north from Whitehorse toward Dawson City, then take the 10-kilometer (6.2-mile) side road to the west (it's well signposted).

RECREATION
Historical and Nature Walks

Whitehorse is small enough that you can cover downtown by foot. A pleasant paved **walkway** follows the Yukon River from the SS *Klondike* to the north end of town.

To learn more about local history, take a volunteer-led 45-minute historical walking tour (June–Aug. Mon.–Sat. at 9 A.M., 11 A.M., 1 P.M., and 3 P.M.) of downtown Whitehorse buildings offered by the **Yukon Historical & Museums Association.** It leaves from Donnenworth House (3126 3rd Ave., 867/667-4704). If the tour times don't fit into your plans, stop by the Donnenworth House, pick up the walking tour book, and take a self-guided tour.

The **Yukon Conservation Society** (302 Hawkins St., 867/668-5678, Mon.–Fri. 10 A.M.–4 P.M.) leads a variety of hikes, from two to six hours, several times a day in July and early August. One of the most interesting is a two-hour trip to Miles Canyon; or if the family is with you, the kids may enjoy joining the association's Kid Ed-Ventures program for a morning. The hikes are free; bring bug spray,

FLOATING THE YUKON

Every year hardy souls re-create the 742-kilometer (464-mile) route taken by stampeders heading to the Klondike goldfields by floating the Yukon River from Whitehorse. The most authentic way to travel is by canoe, which takes 12-15 days. While this is a trip for experienced wilderness travelers only, two Whitehorse companies make organization easy by providing rentals and transfers. Both companies also offer the option of floating the river as part of a guided tour.

Kanoe People (867/668-4899, www.kanoepeople.com) has been around the longest (since 1974), and rents canoes for $30 per day or $180 per week. They specialize in one-way rentals to Carmacks or Dawson and guided tours, such as a seven-day river trip with meals and accommodations for $2,000. **Up North Adventures** (103 Strickland St., 867/667-7035, www.upnorth.yk.ca) also offers canoe rentals (as well as bike and kayak rentals) with a local drop-off and pick-up service perfect for a single day on the river. For example, pay $65 per person for a full-day rental and return transportation from Lake Laberge. Their 17-day Whitehorse to Dawson float is $2,280 per person.

wear sturdy boots, and have a lunch for the longer excursions. You can also buy self-guided trail booklets at the society's office and set out on your own.

◀ Dog-Mushing

Also known as dog-sledding, sled-dogging, or simply mushing, what was once a form of transportation has grown into a major winter pastime, both as a recreational activity and as a competitive sport. One of the legends of the mushing world is Frank Turner, who owns and operates **Muktuk Kennels** (west of Whitehorse toward Haines Jct., 867/668-3647, www.muktuk.com), which is a place of work for Turner and his team of handlers, but also a bona fide

tourist attraction. Through summer, visitors are invited to take a look around for $15, but much more informative is the three-hour tour of the kennels daily at 1 P.M. for $35, or $75 with a dinner of Northern delicacies. In fall (Sept.–Nov.), you can join a training run with the dogs aboard an ATV ($85). As you'd expect, it is in winter that the action really cranks up, with options that range from a full-day mushing trip ($185–265 pp) to attending a weeklong Rookie Ranch ($2,270).

Biking and Golf

Whitehorse is relatively flat, making biking easy and fun. Rent mountain bikes from **Up North Adventures** (103 Strickland St., 867/667-7035). If you're interested in joining up with some locals, drop by **Icycle Sport** (9002 Quartz Rd., 867/668-7559) and ask about evening group rides after the shop closes at 6 P.M.

Along the Alaska Highway south of the city is **Meadow Lakes Golf Resort** (867/668-4653), a short nine-hole course kept in excellent condition through the summer golfing season. As with the course in Yellowknife, one of the unique features is tee times as late as 10:30 P.M. in late June and early July.

SHOPPING

A number of fine galleries are scattered around town. The Northern Fibres Guild produces a free booklet that describes local artists with illustrations of their work; it's available at the Visitor Information Centre. Well worth a visit are the **North End Gallery** (118 1st Ave., 867/393-3590) and the **Midnight Sun Gallery** (205 Main St., 867/668-4350), the latter featuring the brightly colored, Northern-themed paintings of Ted Harrison.

Across from the information center, **Folknits** (3123 3rd Ave., 867/456-4192) sells spinning fiber and finished knitwear made from *quviuq,* the fine underhair of the musk ox. Look for the log cabin with two moose on the roof.

Bookstores

Mac's Fireweed Books (203 Main St.,

867/668-6104, www.yukonbooks.com) is the biggest and most complete bookstore in the Yukon, with a large selection of local- and general-interest books, children's books, and magazines. It's open daily until midnight in the summer. If you can't find what you're looking for using the in-store searchable database at **Well-Read Books** (4137 4th Ave., 867/393-2987, www.wellreadbooks.yk.net), the knowledgeable staff will lead you in the right direction when it comes to looking through their used book collection.

ENTERTAINMENT AND EVENTS

Frantic Follies is one of many vaudeville revues along the route north to Alaska that is styled on the stage shows that entertained stampeders back in the days of the Klondike gold rush. The Follies are performed nightly at the Westmark Whitehorse (201 Wood St., 867/668-2042, May–mid-Sept. nightly at 8:30 P.M., adult $24, child $10).

Whitehorse has no lack of rowdy bars and none are as popular as **"The Cap"** (in the Capital Hotel, 103 Main St., 867/667-2565)—although renovated it's still music central for Whitehorse, with rock bands seven nights a week. **Yukon Brewing Company** (102 Copper Rd., 867/668-4183) is the only brewery in the territory. Free tours (with samples) are offered daily at 2 P.M. and a gift shop is open daily 11 A.M.–6 P.M. These brews are available throughout Canada, but they are also available on tap throughout Whitehorse.

Festivals and Events

One of the Yukon's biggest events is the **Yukon Quest** (867/668-4711, www.yukonquest.com) a 1,600-kilometer (1,000-mile) dog-mushing race between Whitehorse and Fairbanks held each February. As the race is winding down, Whitehorse spins into action with the **Frostbite Music Festival** (www.frostbitefest.ca), featuring an eclectic mix of concerts, dances, and workshops highlighting Canada's thriving independent music industry.

The summer solstice (June 21) is celebrated with a **Midnight Sun Golf Tournament** at Mountainview Golf Course (867/633-6020). The **Yukon International Storytelling Festival** (www.storytelling.yk.net) attracts storytellers from around the world who combine their words with music and dance. The venue is the **Yukon Arts Centre** (300 College Dr., 867/667-8574), which hosts events year-round.

ACCOMMODATIONS AND CAMPING

Whitehorse has a surprising number of motels and hotels for its size: 23, accounting for more than 900 rooms. The competition, of course, works to the traveler's advantage, and some of the digs are actually affordable.

Under $50

Beez Kneez Bakpakers (408 Hoge St., 867/456-2333, www.bzkneez.com, dorm $25, $60 s or d) has dorm beds, private rooms with two single beds, and a cabin that sleeps two. Other amenities include a living room, a communal kitchen, laundry facilities, free use of bikes, and Internet access.

$50-100

❰ Historical Guest House (5128 5th Ave., 867/668-3907, www.yukongold.com, $85–110 s, $95–110 d) is a comfortable downtown home that was built in 1907 and has been extensively restored, exposing much of the original hand-hewn log work. Each of the two upstairs guest rooms has its own bathroom, while the basement holds a self-contained suite. Other amenities include a communal kitchen and living area, and out back is a garden and barbecue. Rates include a light, self-serve breakfast. The owners live next door.

If you're planning on traveling as far north as Whitehorse, you're more adventurous than most travelers, so why not do something really unique and stay on a ranch with 100 mushing dogs? You can at **Muktuk Adventures** (west of Whitehorse toward Haines Jct., 867/668-3647, www.muktuk.com, $85–95 s or d including breakfast), on the property of mushing legend

Frank Turner. Accommodation choices are wooden cabins or a room in the main lodge. Dinner is provided at an extra charge. The property is right on the Takhini River and in addition to tours of the facility, there are canoe rentals, hiking, and trail riding.

$100-150

For modern, comfortable bed-and-breakfast accommodations within walking distance of downtown restaurants and shops, make reservations at **Midnight Sun B&B** (6188 6th Ave., 867/667-2255 or 866/284-4448, www.midnightsunbb.com, $119 s, $135–140 d). Four of the five guest rooms are en suite, and one has a private bathroom down the hall. Each room also has a TV, phone, and Internet access. Guests have use of a lounge and kitchen.

Sundog Retreat (off the Klondike Hwy., 867/633-4183, www.sundogretreat.com, $130–200 per cabin) comprises six cabins spread over 60 hectares (160 acres) on a lightly treed property north of downtown (see the website for a map). Each cabin has a kitchen and one or two bedrooms; some have decks and all are very private.

$150-200

My choice for downtown hotel accommodation is the **High Country Inn** (4051 4th Ave., 867/667-4471 or 800/554-4471, www.highcountryinn.yk.ca, $169–259 s or d), a large and well-appointed hostelry with a variety of accommodations, starting at $169 s or d for standard rooms, and going all the way up to $269 for the Presidential Suite. The hotel has a fitness room, a business center with Internet access, and its own airport shuttle. Downstairs is a bistro-style restaurant and a lounge with a large patio.

Camping

The prime choice for tenters (no RVs allowed) is ◖ **Robert Service Campground** (South Access Rd., 867/668-3721, www.robertservicecampground.com, mid-May–Sept., $18), a two-kilometer (1.2-mile) drive or 20-minute walk south of town along the Millennium

Trail. It has a small store and café, showers, and free firewood. Government-run **Wolf Creek Campground** ($14), 11 kilometers (6.8 miles) south of Whitehorse along the Alaska Highway, has campsites for tents and RVs (but no hookups), a nature trail, water, outhouses, and cooking shelters.

Near the south entrance to town, **Hi Country RV Park** (91357 Alaska Hwy., 867/667-7445 or 877/458-3806, www.hicountryrvyukon.com, tents $16, hookups $25–33) is one of a half-dozen private campgrounds spread along the Alaska Highway within a five-minute drive of downtown. It has 130 sites spread among the trees, modern shower facilities, a laundry, RV wash, dump station, wireless Internet, and convenience store. Farther south, **Pioneer RV Park** (91091 Alaska Hwy., 867/668-5944, www.pioneer-rv-park.com, May–Sept., tents $15, hookups $22–28) has a similar setting as well as an on-site mechanic, discounted fuel for guests, and wireless Internet access.

FOOD
Cafes and Other Cheap Eats

Even though chains such as Starbucks have made an appearance in Whitehorse, go beyond what you know and search out **Midnight Sun Coffee Roaster** (9002 Quartz Rd., 867/668-7559, Mon.–Sat. 8 A.M.–5 P.M.), with coffee that is as good as you'll find anywhere. It comes with locally inspired monikers like Sam McGee's Black. Also well worth a visit is **The Chocolate Claim** (305 Strickland St., 867/667-2202, Mon.–Fri. 7:30 A.M.–6 P.M., Sat 8:30 A.M.–6 P.M., lunches $6.50–9), an arty space with handmade chocolates, freshly baked sunflower bread, sandwiches, savory soups, and cappuccino.

In a two-story log building just off 4th Avenue on the north side of downtown, ◖ **Alpine Bakery** (411 Alexander St., 867/668-6871, Mon.–Sat. 8 A.M.–6 P.M.) bakes wholesome European-style breads with organic ingredients, but they aren't cheap. A specialty is Expedition Bread, which stays edible for up to a month. The bakery is also part deli.

Lil's Place (209 Main St., 867/668-3545,

daily 7 A.M.–9 P.M., $5.50–12) is set up as a 1950s diner complete with vinyl booths, a jukebox, gumball machines, and a menu of burgers and shakes.

Canadian

Right downtown, dining at **C Bistro on Fourth** (High Country Inn, 4051 4th Ave., 867/667-4471, 7 A.M.–9:30 P.M., $15–31) combines Northern favorites with a clean, comfortable atmosphere and reasonable prices. The best choices focus on classic dishes with a Northern twist, such as a caribou burger. Most steak and seafood mains, including choices such as pork ribs barbecued on the heated deck, are under $30.

Housed in Whitehorse's oldest commercial building, the **Klondike Rib & Salmon BBQ** (2116 2nd Ave., 867/667-7554, mid-May–Sept. daily for dinner, $14–29) has a family-friendly atmosphere of long tables covered with checked tablecloths and a finger-lickin' menu. The house specialty is barbecued ribs, but you'll also find steaks, Caesar salad, smoked salmon, halibut fish-and-chips, miner's soup with caribou sausage, and bumbleberry pie. It's busy, noisy, fun, and tasty. Close by, the **Talisman Café** (River View Hotel, 102 Wood St., 867/667-7801, Mon.–Sat. 7 A.M.–8 P.M., Sun 6 A.M.–4 P.M.) is very different. The atmosphere is heady and the food runs the entire spectrum—from bannock and jam ($3) at breakfast to couscous salad ($7) and a Mediterranean platter ($18) in the evening.

Mexican

Sanchez Cantina (211 Hanson St., 867/668-5858, Mon.–Sat. 11:30 A.M.–2:30 P.M. and 5–9:30 P.M., $10–16.50) is a casual, quiet place with familiar Mexican favorites. Sides of salsa and guacamole are made in-house and are delicious.

INFORMATION

Whitehorse Visitor Information Centre (corner 2nd Ave. and Lambert St., 867/667-3084, early May–late Sept. daily 10 A.M.–6 P.M. extended to daily 8 A.M.–8 P.M. July–Aug., the rest of the year Mon.–Fri. 8:30 A.M.–5 P.M., Sat. 10 A.M.–2 P.M.) promotes both Whitehorse and the Yukon. The **City of Whitehorse** website (www.whitehorse.ca) is a handy pre-trip reference.

The excellent **Whitehorse Public Library** (2071 2nd Ave., 867/667-5239, Mon.–Fri. 10 A.M.–9 P.M., Sat. 10 A.M.–6 P.M., Sun. 1–9 P.M.) is directly across from the visitors center. It has a good selection of Northern literature, newspapers from around the world, and public Internet access.

GETTING THERE

The airport is right above town on the bluff. You can't miss the "world's largest weathervane"—the restored DC-3 (mounted on a moveable pedestal) that points its nose into the wind. From downtown, get to the airport by going north along 4th Avenue to the Alaska Highway and take a left, or go south out 2nd Avenue and turn right. Most hotels provide a shuttle, or you can catch a cab for around $14 to downtown. From its Whitehorse hub, local carrier **Air North** (800/661-0407, www.flyairnorth.com) has flights to and from the southern gateways of Edmonton, Calgary, and Vancouver, as well as onward flights to Dawson City and Inuvik. **Air Canada** (888/247-2262) has service to Whitehorse from both Vancouver and Calgary. **First Air** (800/267-1247, www.firstair.ca) has scheduled service between Whitehorse and Yellowknife (NWT) three times a week.

Whitehorse Bus Depot (2191 2nd Ave. behind Qwanlin Mall, 867/668-2223) is the northern terminus for **Greyhound**. In summer, one bus a day (departs 1 P.M.) heads south along the Alaska Highway. The only bus service that continues west from Whitehorse to Alaska is **Alaska Direct Bus Line** (867/668-4833 or 800/770-6652, www.alaskadirectbusline.com, mid-May–Sept.), to Anchorage (US$220) and Fairbanks (US$190). **Alaska/Yukon Trails** (800/770-7275, www.alaskashuttle.com) charges US$149 each way for the shuttle trip between Whitehorse and Dawson City, with onward travel to Fairbanks (Alaska) an option.

GETTING AROUND

Whitehorse Transit (867/668-7433, Mon.– Sat. 6 A.M.–7 P.M., Fri. to 10 P.M., $2.50) operates a citywide public bus service. Pick up a schedule at the visitor centre or from the drivers. All routes begin and end beside Canadian Tire, opposite Qwanlin Mall.

Local taxi companies are **5th Avenue Taxi** (867/667-4111), **Whitehorse Taxi** (867/393-6543), and **Yellow Cab** (867/668-4811).

All major car-rental companies are represented at the airport. If you're planning on renting a vehicle in Whitehorse, check mileage allowances. Unlike elsewhere in Canada, companies do not include unlimited travel.

For example, **National** charges $70 a day and $420 a week for their smallest vehicles, with a maximum of 200 free kilometers (93 miles) per day.

Whitehorse is a popular starting point for European travelers who want to explore the Yukon and Alaska in a campervan, so you'll find plenty of choices. Plan on spending around $1,200 per week for a truck and camper, or $1,800 per week for a 24-foot motor home, both with 100 kilometers (62 miles) free per day. Local rental companies include **CanaDream** (867/668-3610, www.canadream.com) and **Fraserway** (867/668-3438 or 800/806-1976, www.fraserway.com).

YUKON

Whitehorse to Beaver Creek

Before leaving Whitehorse, you need to decide whether to take the Alaska Highway straight through to Alaska or continue north to Dawson City and then continue along the Top of the World Highway, which loops back down to the Alaska Highway at Tok (Alaska). The latter option adds less than 200 kilometers (120 miles) to the distance between Whitehorse and Tok, while taking in Dawson City, a must-stop on any Northern itinerary. The entire loop, beginning and ending at Whitehorse, is 1,480 kilometers (920 miles).

This section covers the direct route to Alaska, along the Alaska Highway to Beaver Creek. The total distance to the border is 460 kilometers (187 miles). Haines Junction is the only town of any consequence en route, beyond which the highway parallels Kluane National Park.

Whitehorse to Haines Junction

It's an easy 160-kilometer (100-mile) drive to Haines Junction from the capital. The scenery doesn't really become memorable until the highway closes in on Haines Junction, when the Kluane Icefield Ranges and the foothills of the St. Elias Mountains start to dominate the view; when it's clear, Mount Hubbard

(4,577 m/15,000 ft) looms high and white straight ahead.

A worthwhile stop is Kilometer 1,604, 21 kilometers (13 miles) east of Haines Junction. Here a log bridge dating to the early 1900s has been rebuilt. Walk out onto it to compare the log action with the steel-supported highway bridge.

Government campgrounds between Whitehorse and Haines Junction are located at Kilometer 1,543; Kilometer 1,602; and Kilometer 1,628.

HAINES JUNCTION

Established in 1942 as a base camp for Alaska Highway construction, this town of 800 is the largest between Whitehorse and Tok and is the gateway to Kluane National Park, the most accessible of the Yukon's three national parks. It's also the first town north of Haines (Alaska), and so sees a lot of traffic from the ferry passing through.

Sights

At the village square near the intersection of the Alaska and Haines Highways, a grotesque sculpture of mountains, mammals, and humans has been placed. Ironically, it's part of a Yukon beautification program. It looks more like a misshapen cupcake with really ugly icing. Here you can also read the signboards describing the history and attractions of the Haines Junction area and sign your name in the gigantic guest book. Just up the road toward Whitehorse is **Our Lady of the Way Church,** built in 1954 by a Catholic priest who converted an old Quonset hut by adding a wooden front, a shrine on top, and a steeple with bell in back.

Accommodations and Camping

Haines has a bunch of motels to choose from (listed in the territorial tourism guide), along with the following three choices.

Paddle Wheel Adventures (867/634-2683, www.paddlewheeladventures.com) rents modern Quonset-style huts, each with a cooking facilities and a private bathroom, for a reasonable $60 per night. Primarily outfitters, they also rent canoes and bikes and lead guided raft and fishing tours.

The Cabin (27 km/16.8 mi south of Haines Jct. on Hwy. 3, 867/634-2626, www.thecabinyukon.com, $85 s, $95 d) comprises five rustic cabins, each with a kitchenette and deck with views extending over Kluane National Park.

The **Raven Hotel** (867/634-2500, www. ravenhotelyukon.com, May–Sept., $120 s, $135 d including breakfast) offers the 12 nicest motel rooms in town, a restaurant with lots of local specialties, and an art gallery/gift shop. You can't miss it; the Raven looks like a modular mansion, right in the middle of town.

Right downtown, **Kluane RV Kampground** (867/634-2709, www.kluanerv.ca, tents $18, hookups $24–30) separates tenters from RVers but offers lots of services for both. For in-town camping, the tent sites are pleasant, with lots of trees, and barbecues and firewood supplied. The sites with hookups come with cable TV and Internet access, but don't have much privacy. Other amenities include a shower block, laundry, car and RV wash, grocery store, and gas.

Food

Village Bakery (867/634-2867, May–Sept.) is a popular hangout, with delicious muffins, strudels, doughnuts, and cheese sticks, as well as breads, sourdough sandwiches (try the smoked salmon, which is smoked on-site), soups, quiches, sourdough pizzas, lasagna, meat pies, and whatever else the good cooks feel like creating. On Friday at 6:30 P.M. there's a salmon barbecue ($17) and live music on the deck.

Several of the hotels also serve meals, including—most notably—the **Raven Hotel** (867/634-2500, May–Sept. daily 5:30–10 P.M., $18–31). The menu here changes daily, but the choices are always varied and thoughtful. Considering the remote location, the owners do a great job of sourcing fresh produce to go with lots of local game and seafood. Views of the snowcapped peaks of Kluane National Park are a bonus.

Information

Haines Junction Visitor Information Centre (867/634-2345, early May–late Sept. daily 10 A.M.–6 P.M., July–Aug. daily 8 A.M.–8 P.M.) is a provincially operated facility on the highway through town.

◖ KLUANE NATIONAL PARK

The lofty ice-capped mountains of southwest Yukon, overflowing with glaciers and flanked by lower ranges rich in wildlife, have been set aside as 21,980-square-kilometer (8,490-square-mile) Kluane (Kloo-AH-nee) National Park. Although the Alaska and Haines Highways, which run along the fringe of the park, make it accessible, Kluane is a wilderness hardly touched by human hands; once you leave the highways you'll see few other people. No roads run into the park itself, so to experience the true magnificence of this wilderness you must embark on an overnight hike or take a flightseeing trip.

The Land

The St. Elias Range, running from Alaska through the Yukon to British Columbia, is the highest mountain range in North America and the second-highest coastal range in the world (only the Andes are higher). **Mount Logan,** at 6,050 meters (19,850 feet), is the highest peak in Canada. The ranges you see from the Alaska Highway are impressive enough, but only through gaps can you glimpse the fantastic Icefield Ranges lying directly behind. These peaks are surrounded by a gigantic ice field plateau 2,500–3,000 meters (8,200–9,800 feet) high, the largest non-polar ice field in the world, occupying a little more than half the park. Radiating out from the ice field like spokes on a wheel are valley glaciers up to 60 kilometers (37 miles) long, some very active. Such is the importance of this area that—together with Wrangell–Saint Elias and Glacier Bay National Parks in Alaska, and Tatshenshini-Alsek Provincial Park in British Columbia—Kluane has been declared a World Heritage Site by UNESCO.

Although more than half of Kluane is ice, rock, and snow, the remainder includes habitat that holds large populations of wildlife. Some 4,000 Dall sheep—one of the world's largest populations—reside on the high open hillsides northwest of Kaskawulsh Glacier and elsewhere in the park. Many can be seen from the highway in the vicinity of Sheep Mountain. Kluane also has significant numbers of moose, caribou, mountain goats, and grizzly bears.

Flightseeing

Flightseeing over the park is available from the Haines Junction Airport. The one-hour flight affords a spectacular view of Mount Logan plus several glaciers and is highly recommended if you happen to be there on a clear day. Contact **Sifton Air** (867/634-2916). Prices with **Trans North Helicopters** (867/634-2242) start at $180 per person for a 30-minute glacier tour. Trans North is based beyond Haines Junction around Kilometer 1,698.

Tours

If you're not comfortable exploring the backcountry without a local guide, consider using **Kluane Ecotours** (867/634-2600, www.kluaneco.com), which offers day and overnight trips on foot and in kayaks and canoes, including a paddling/hiking combo to King's Throne.

Practicalities

Easily accessible 27 kilometers (17 miles) south of Haines Junction and within Kluane National Park is **Kathleen Lake Campground** (867/634-7250, mid-May–mid-Sept., $16), with 39 sites between the highway and the lake. Amenities are limited to firewood ($9 for a fire permit), drinking water, and pit toilets, but it's a delightful spot that is a popular launching spot for kayaks and canoes. It also has a short interpretive trail and is the starting point for a five-kilometer (3.1-mile) trek up to the King's Throne, so named for its sweeping views across the park; allow five hours round-trip.

In Haines Junction, the **Kluane Visitor Reception Centre** (867/634-2293, www.pc.gc.ca, mid-May–mid-Sept. daily 9 A.M.–5 P.M.) has a relief map of the park and an excellent 20-minute sight-and-sound slide show presented every half hour. On the Alaska Highway 72 kilometers (45 miles) north of Haines Junction, **Tachal Dhal Visitor Centre** (867/734-7250, mid-May–mid-Sept. daily 9 A.M.–4 P.M.) has a spotting scope to look for Dall sheep on nearby Sheep Mountain (late Aug.–mid June is the best time of year for sheep-spotting).

HAINES JUNCTION TO BEAVER CREEK

For most of the 300 kilometers (186 miles) to Beaver Creek, the Alaska Highway parallels Kluane National Park or Kluane Wildlife Sanctuary—a comparatively well-populated, civilized, and stunningly scenic stretch of the road. Along the way are three government campgrounds (Km 1,725; Km 1,853; and Km 1,913), three little settlements, and a dozen lodges.

At **Soldier's Summit,** one kilometer (0.6 miles) north of the Tachal Dhal Visitor Information Centre, a sign commemorates the official opening of the Alcan on November 20, 1942, a mere eight months after construction began; an interpretive trail from the parking area leads up to the site of the dedication ceremony.

Destruction Bay

This tiny town at Kilometer 1,743 was named when the original road-construction camp was destroyed by a windstorm in 1942. Destruction Bay has a gas station, the 32-room **Talbot Arm Motel** (867/841-4461, $90 s, $105 d), a cafeteria and dining room, an RV park, showers, general store, and gift shop.

Burwash Landing

On Kluane Lake, 127 kilometers (79 miles) northwest of Haines Junction, is Burwash Landing, population 90. The fine **Kluane Museum of Natural History** (867/841-5561, mid-May–mid-Sept. daily 9 A.M.–6:30 P.M., adult $5, child $4) includes a wildlife exhibit, native artifacts, a large model of the area, a theater where a wildlife video is shown, and some interesting fossils. Also take a gander at **Our Lady of the Rosary Church,** a log structure built in 1944.

Burwash Landing Resort (867/841-4441) has hotel rooms from $95 s or d, a restaurant, lounge, RV park, and boat rentals. The cafeteria is huge, there's a fine dining room, and the bar gets raucous most nights—check out the back wallpapered with money. You can boat and fish in the lake from here; guides are available.

BEAVER CREEK

The last place with facilities in the Yukon, Beaver Creek is a tiny town (population 110) with a big travel-based economy.

Accommodations and Food

On the west side of town, the **1202 Motor Inn** (867/862-7600 or 800/764-7601 in Alaska or 800/661-0540 in western Canada, www.1202motorinn.ca, $85–175 s or d, RV sites $28) has motel rooms in an older wing, more modern units, large kitchen-equipped suites, and parking for RVs. The complex also has a rustic log dining room, a lounge, public

Internet access, and gas (which will be cheaper on the U.S. side of the border). It's also open year-round. The biggest place in town is the **Westmark Inn Beaver Creek** (867/862-7501 or 800/544-0970, www.westmarkhotels.com, mid-May–mid-Sept., $99 s or d), with 174 tiny, nondescript rooms aimed at the escorted-tour crowd.

The Westmark hosts performances of **Rendezvous Dinner Theatre,** a lighthearted musical theatre nightly in the summer. It costs $55 for dinner and the show or $25 for the show alone.

Information

Beaver Creek Visitor Information Centre (867/862-7321, early May–late Sept. daily 10 A.M.–6 P.M., July–Aug. daily 8 A.M.–8 P.M.) is operated by the Yukon government as an information resource for travelers entering the territory from Alaska.

Onward to Alaska

The Canada–U.S. border is 32 kilometers (20 miles) west of Beaver Creek and the **U.S. Customs post** is another one kilometer (0.6 miles) west. Heading into Alaska, be sure to turn your watches back one hour to Alaska Standard Time. Traveling in the opposite direction, **Canadian Customs** is well inside Canada, just three kilometers (1.9 miles) northwest of Beaver Creek. Both posts are open 24 hours a day year-round, and you'll need a passport regardless of your citizenship or which direction you're headed.

If you're reading this before leaving home, begin planning your Alaska travels by contacting the **Alaska Travel Industry Association** (907/465-2017, www.travelalaska.com) and requesting an information package. The best guidebook out there is Don Pitcher's *Moon Alaska* (Avalon Travel Publishing). In Whitehorse, you'll find copies at Mac's Fireweed Books.

Whitehorse to Dawson City

It's 536 kilometers (333 miles) north from Whitehorse to Dawson City. Allow six or seven hours non-stop, or stretch the trip out to a full day or two by stopping at the places detailed below.

Lake Laberge

Lake Laberge, 62 kilometers (38.5 miles) from Whitehorse, is famous primarily as the site of the burning of the corpse in Robert Service's immortal poem "Cremation of Sam McGee." The excellent trout fishing here has also been well-known since stampeder days, when the fish were barged to Dawson by the ton. You can also continue 22 kilometers (14 miles) north to **Fox Lake Campground,** with summertime swimming.

Carmacks

A little more than 180 kilometers (120 miles) from Whitehorse, the river town of Carmacks (population 420) is named for George Washington Carmack, credited with the Bonanza Creek strike that triggered the famous Klondike gold rush.

Get the lay of town by driving down Three Gold Road (at the Carmacks Hotel) to the Yukon River. A two-kilometer (1.2 miles) **boardwalk** runs along the river from here to a park, complete with a gazebo. There are benches, viewing platforms, and interpretive signs along the way. **Tage Cho Hudan Interpretive Centre** (867/863-5830) exhibits archaeological displays and a diorama of a mammoth snare, plus interpretive trails and a gift shop. Find it at the second driveway north of the bridge.

Hotel Carmacks (867/863-5221, www.hotelcarmacks.com, from $95 s or d) rents modern rooms and cabins in a building behind the main complex. Here you'll find a large lounge sporting a couple of pool tables and an interesting brass railing along the bar, perfect for bellying up to. Part of its restaurant occupies the old Carmacks roadhouse, built in 1903 and the only remaining roadhouse of the 16 that once operated between Whitehorse and Dawson.

Five Finger Rapids

North of Carmacks 25 kilometers (15.5 miles) is a pullout overlooking Five Finger Rapids, where four rock towers here choke the river, dividing it into five channels through which the current rips. At **Five Finger Rapids Recreation Site** a wooden platform overlooks the river, and stairs lead down to the river. Allow an hour or so for the round-trip to the river—a nice little walk to break up the drive.

Pelly Crossing

In another 108 kilometers (67 miles) you come to Pelly Crossing, roughly halfway between Whitehorse and Dawson. Downtown, interpretive panels describe the town and its native population, who moved upstream from remote Fort Selkirk after the Klondike Highway was completed in the 1950s.

Silver Trail

The first settlement north of Pelly River is **Stewart Crossing,** the site of an 1883 trading post and the last gas stop before Dawson City, another 181 kilometers (112 miles) north.

At this point, the Silver Trail (Hwy. 11) branches northeast through a heavily mined area of silver deposits. Two small towns and loads of history make a detour worthwhile.

Mayo (population 400), above a wide bend of the Stewart River, was once a bustling silver-mining center, with the ore transported out of the wilderness by stern-wheeler, eventually reaching smelters in San Francisco. Stop by the two-story **Binet House** (304 Second Ave., 867/996-2926, May–Sept. daily 10 A.M.–6 P.M.) for a rundown of the Mayo District, including historical photos; displays on the geology, minerals, flora, and fauna of the area; and silver samples. The **Bedrock Motel** (north side of town, 867/996-2290, www.

YUKON

bedrockmotel.com, $95 s or d) is a modern wooden lodge with 12 clean, comfortable guest rooms, as well as RV parking ($25). Amenities include a laundry and canoe rentals.

From Mayo, it's eight kilometers (five miles) of paved road and then 51 kilometers (32 miles) on hard-packed gravel to **Keno City,** passing **Elsa,** the site of a silver mine that closed as recently as 1989, along the way. Once a booming silver town, Keno's population has dwindled to just 20. Its long and colorful history is cataloged at the **Keno City Mining Museum** (867/995-3103, June–early Sept. daily 10 A.M.–6 P.M., donation asked for admission), fittingly housed in a 1920s saloon. The adjacent cabin has an interesting collection of locally collected fossils.

On the south side of town, **Keno City Cabins** (867/995-2829, $85–105 d)—there's only two of them—are well-equipped, with cooking done on a woodstove.

Dawson City

Of all the towns in Canada, Dawson City (not to be confused with Dawson Creek, British Columbia) has the widest fame and the wildest past. Although the Klondike gold rush was short lived, tourists have rediscovered Dawson's charms in a big way. Many historic buildings have been given cheerful coats of paint, others have very effectively been left to the ravages of Mother Nature. Walking tours are the best way to take in the history, but you can also listen to Robert Service recitals at the cabin this famous poet once called home, try your hand at panning for gold, or gamble the night away at an old-time casino.

The year-round population is around 1,400, but this almost doubles in summer. It's a long way north, some 536 kilometers (333 miles) from Whitehorse, but 60,000 visitors make the trek annually to this delightful salmagundi of colorful historic facades and abandoned buildings, tiny old cabins and huge new ones, rusted old stern-wheelers and touristy casinos.

HISTORY

The Klondike gold fields cover an area of 2,000 square kilometers (770 square miles) southeast of Dawson. It was in 1896 that a Nova Scotian prospector, Robert Henderson, discovered the first gold—about 20 cents' worth per pan—in a creek he went ahead and named Gold-Bottom Creek. He spent the rest of the summer working the creek, while passing news of his find to fellow prospectors who were in the area. One such man was George "Siwash" Washington Carmack, who with partners Tagish Charlie and Skookum Jim struck gold in extraordinary quantities—$3–4 a pan—on nearby Rabbit Creek (soon to be renamed Bonanza). They staked three claims before word began to spread. By fall most of the richest ground had been claimed.

Gold Fever

News of the strike reached the outside world a year later, when a score of prospectors, so loaded down with gold that they couldn't handle it themselves, disembarked in San Francisco and Seattle. The spectacle triggered mass insanity across the continent, immediately launching a rush the likes of which the world had rarely seen before and has not seen since. Clerks, salesmen, streetcar conductors, doctors, preachers, generals (even the mayor of Seattle) simply dropped what they were doing and started off "for the Klondike." City dwellers, factory workers, and men who had never climbed a mountain, handled a boat, or even worn a backpack were outfitted in San Francisco, Seattle, Vancouver, and Edmonton, and set out on an incredible journey through an uncharted wilderness with Dawson—a thousand miles from anywhere—as the imagined grand prize.

Out of an estimated 100,000 "stampeders" that started out, 35,000 made it to Dawson.

Meanwhile, the first few hundred lucky

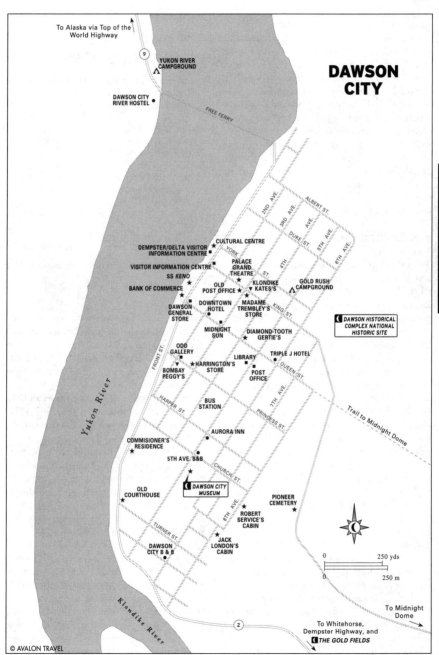

DAWSON CITY

To Alaska via Top of the World Highway

9

YUKON RIVER CAMPGROUND

DAWSON CITY RIVER HOSTEL

FREE FERRY

YUKON

2ND AVE.
3RD AVE.
ALBERT ST.
AVE.
DUKE ST.
5TH AVE.
6TH AVE.
4TH

CULTURAL CENTRE

DEMPSTER/DELTA VISITOR INFORMATION CENTRE

YORK ST.

PALACE GRAND THEATRE

VISITOR INFORMATION CENTRE

SS KENO

KLONDIKE KATE'S'S

OLD POST OFFICE

GOLD RUSH CAMPGROUND

BANK OF COMMERCE

DOWNTOWN HOTEL

MADAME TREMBLEY'S STORE

KING ST.

DAWSON GENERAL STORE

DAWSON HISTORICAL COMPLEX NATIONAL HISTORIC SITE

MIDNIGHT SUN

DIAMOND-TOOTH GERTIE'S

ODD GALLERY

FRONT ST.

LIBRARY

TRIPLE J HOTEL

HARRINGTON'S STORE

POST OFFICE

QUEEN ST.

BOMBAY PEGGY'S

HARPER ST.

BUS STATION

7TH AVE.

PRINCESS ST.

Trail to Midnight Dome

AURORA INN

COMMISIONER'S RESIDENCE

5TH AVE. B&B

CHURCH ST.

DAWSON CITY MUSEUM

OLD COURTHOUSE

PIONEER CEMETERY

8TH AVE.

ROBERT SERVICE'S CABIN

TURNER ST.

JACK LONDON'S CABIN

DAWSON CITY B & B

Yukon River

Klondike River

2

To Midnight Dome

To Whitehorse, Dempster Highway, and THE GOLD FIELDS

0   250 yds
0   250 m

© AVALON TRAVEL

stampeders to actually reach Dawson before the rivers froze that winter (1897) found the town in such a panic over food that people were actually fleeing for their lives. At the same time tens of thousands of stampeders were heading toward Dawson along a variety of routes, including over the **Chilkoot Pass** and down the Yukon River. Most hopefuls were caught unprepared in the bitter grip of the seven-month Arctic winter, and many froze to death or died of scurvy, starvation, exhaustion, heartbreak, suicide, or murder. And when the breakup in 1898 finally allowed the remaining hordes to pour into Dawson the next spring, every worthwhile claim had already been staked.

Heyday and Pay Dirt

That next year, from summer 1898 to summer 1899, was a unique moment in history. As people and supplies started deluging Dawson, all the hundreds of thousands in gold, worthless previously for lack of anything to buy, were spent with a feverish abandon. The richest stampeders established the saloons, dance halls, gambling houses, trading companies, even steamship lines and banks—much easier ways to get the gold than mining it. The casinos and hotels were as opulent as any in Paris. The dance-hall girls charged $5 in gold per minute for dancing (extra for slow dances), the bartenders put stickum on their fingers to poke a little dust during transactions, and the janitors who panned the sawdust on the barroom floors were known to wash out $50 nightly. Dawson burned with an intensity born of pure lust, the highlight of the lives of every single person who braved the trails and experienced it.

In 1899, most of Dawson burned to the ground, and at the same time, word filtered in that gold had been discovered on the beaches of Nome, and just as the Klondike strike had emptied surrounding boomtowns, Nome emptied Dawson. By the summer of 1899, as the last bedraggled and tattered stampeders limped into Dawson two years after setting out, the 12-month golden age of Dawson was done. The city's heyday was as brief as its reputation was beefy, and Dawson quickly declined

---

PARKS AND PARTNER'S PASS

The best way to enjoy all of Dawson's historic attractions at a reasonable price is by purchasing a Parks and Partner's Pass ($30.90 per person), which includes admission for one day to 11 local attractions as well as a guided walking tour. Passes are also available to any three attractions ($13.70) or any five attractions ($22). They can be purchased from the Visitor Reception Centre. For more information, go to www.pc.gc.ca and click through to the links for the Dawson Historical Complex National Historic Site.

---

into another small town on the banks of the Yukon.

SIGHTS

Dawson's plentiful free or inexpensive attractions can keep you happily busy for several days. The compact downtown area mixes dirt streets and crumbling wooden storefronts with faux gold rush–era buildings and bustling tourist businesses.

Start your exploration at the **Dawson City Visitor Information Centre** (867/993-5274, early May–late Sept. daily 10 A.M.–6 P.M., July–Aug. daily 8 A.M.–8 P.M.), right in the thick of things at Front and King Streets. Outstanding one-hour, historically loaded **walking tours** of the town core leave from the visitors center several times a day; a schedule is posted at the center.

◖ Dawson City Museum

If possible, before you do anything else in town, try to visit this excellent and extensive museum (595 5th Ave., 867/993-5291, daily 10 A.M.–6 P.M. mid-May–early Sept., adult $9, senior and child $7), housed within the imposing 1901 Administration Building. The south and north galleries present an enormous amount of history, from fossils and flora and fauna through northern Athabascan lifestyles up to the gold rush and the subsequent developments. The museum has a wealth of material to draw from and it's all nicely presented. The mining-history displays alone, from hand mining to dredges, are worth the price of admission; also check out the display on law and order during the gold rush. The "visible storage area" houses about one-fifth of the museum's collection of 30,000 artifacts.

SS *Keno*

The restored riverboat SS *Keno,* built in 1922 in Whitehorse, is beached on Front Street. It was used to transport ore from the mining area around Mayo down to the confluence of the Yukon, from where larger riverboats transported it upriver to Whitehorse and the railhead. The *Keno* sailed under its own steam to its resting place here in 1960 but wasn't restored until 40 years later. Tour cost is adult $7.50, senior $6.50, child $4.50.

◖ Dawson Historical Complex National Historic Site

The most historically important buildings dotted around Dawson City are protected as a National Historic Site. Combine these with the most picturesque ruins of permafrost, gravity, and neglect that have purposely been left alone and you can plan on spending the best part of a day wandering around town. The following buildings are open mid-May–mid-September, with a variety interpretive programs offered at each.

On King Street, up a block from the visitors center, is the **Palace Grand Theatre,** built in 1899 from wood salvaged off stern-wheelers by "Arizona Charlie" Meadows, the most famous bartender/gunslinger on the Trail of '98. At the time, the Grand was one of the most luxuriously appointed theaters in the west, hosting everything from Wild West shows to opera. The original horseshoe balcony, private box seats, and lavish interior have been lovingly restored. Take a tour daily at 2 P.M. (adult $7.50, senior, $6.50, child $4.50).

The beautifully restored **Commissioner's Residence** on Front Street near Church Street was the official residence of the Commissioner of the Yukon 1900–1916. Tours (adult $7.50, senior $6.50, child $4.50) of the mansion and gardens are given daily by costumed interpreters.

In the vicinity of the theater are many buildings with historic window displays. Walk three blocks south down 3rd Avenue (at Harper St.) to take a snap of the terribly slanted, oft-photographed **Strait's Auction House.**

Robert Service Cabin

Stroll three blocks uphill from the museum to 8th Avenue (at Hanson St.) to see the log cabin that Robert Service called home 1909–1912. Service, who never took shovel nor pan to earth nor water, wound up as a troubadour–bank teller in Dawson and made his fame and fortune unexpectedly while living here, penning such classic prose poems as "The Cremation of Sam McGee" and "The Shooting of Dan McGrew." No one has lived in this cabin since Service left Dawson a celebrity in 1912, and people have been making pilgrimages to it ever since. The cabin is open daily 9 A.M.–5 P.M. in the summer, and Charlie Davis does recitations of Service's best-known poems at 3 P.M. for adult $7.50, senior $6.50, child $4.50.

Midnight Dome

This 885-meter (2,900-foot) hill provides a 360-degree view of the area. The Yukon River stretches out in both directions and Dawson is right below you, to the west the Top of the World Highway winds away to Alaska, and to the south you look directly up Bonanza Creek, past the wavy tailings and hillsides pitted by hydraulic monitors that still bring pay dirt down for sluicing. The sign on top identifies all the topographic features. If you're driving, take King Street through downtown from Front Street and follow the signs; it's seven kilometers (4.3 miles) to the top. A steep hiking trail begins at the end of Queen Street (ask at the visitors center for a trail map).

◖ The Gold Fields

For a close-up look at where the Klondike

© NATALIA BRATSLAVSKY / ISTOCKPHOTO.COM

the historic facades of Dawson City

gold frenzy took place, head two kilometers (1.2 miles) back out of town and take Bonanza Creek Road south.

The highlight of the drive is a visit to **Dredge No. 4,** the largest wooden-hulled gold dredge in North America. Built in 1912, this massive machine scooped pay dirt from the creek beds right up until 1966. Tours are offered May–August and cost adult $7.50, senior $5.50, child $4.50 (or are included in the Parks and Partner's Pass).

The Klondike Visitors Association owns **Claim 6** on the famous Bonanza Creek. You can pan for gold free of charge mid-May–mid-September. Buy a pan from any one of many shops in Dawson or rent one from the RV park at the Bonanza Creek Road turn-off. Downstream a ways, **Claim 33** (867/993-5303) is a commercial panning operation where you pay a small fee to pan for guaranteed "color." Hope I'm not giving away any secrets, but it's spiked. Still, it's good fun and a way to practice your technique.

A monument at **Discovery Claim,** 16 kilometers (10 miles) south from the main highway,

marks the spot where George Carmack made the strike in 1896 that set the rush into motion.

The road continues beyond the monument to the confluence of Bonanza and Eldorado Creeks, site of the gold-rush town of Grand Forks, and then splits. The left fork is part of a 100-kilometer (62-mile) loop through some seriously isolated country before rejoining the Klondike Highway near the airport.

ENTERTAINMENT

Canada's first legal casino, **Diamond Tooth Gerties** (4th and Queen, 867/993-5575, early May–mid-Sept. Sun.–Wed. 7 P.M.–2 A.M. and Thurs.–Sat. 2 P.M.–2 A.M.), was named for a Dawson dance-hall queen with a diamond between her two front teeth. Though casinos were as common as sluice boxes and saloons at the height of the Dawson madness, gambling in the Yukon (and throughout Canada) wasn't formally legalized until 1971, the year this place opened. Games include slot machines, blackjack, poker, sic bo, and roulette, with odds

ONLY IN THE NORTH . . .

Dawson's most infamous nightcap can be "enjoyed" at the **Downtown Hotel** (Queen St. and 2nd Ave., 867/993-5346). It all began in 1973 when "Captain" Dick Stevenson was searching though an abandoned cabin and he came across a pickle jar that held a toe that had been severed by an ax. Inspiration (if it could be called that) struck, and the toe landed in a drink. The original toe is long gone – it was swallowed by an overzealous patron – but at last check, the bar in the Downtown Hotel had eight toes to choose from, all looking ghastly at best. They're preserved in salt, and came from donations by folks who lost them in accidents or because of frostbite. It's pretty gross, but amazingly popular – 2,000 or so folks become members of the **Sourtoe Cocktail Club** annually. Sourtoe cocktails are $5 (you can put the toe in any drink). The bartenders make sure the toe touches your lip to receive an official certificate showing your prowess in stupid bar tricks.

that decidedly favor the house. Drinks are not free, even if you're dropping major-league cash. This sure isn't Vegas! The 30-minute floorshow of Geritol oldies and cancan kicks is presented nightly at 8:30 P.M., 10:30 P.M., and midnight. Cover charge is $10.

Gerties is run by the Klondike Visitors Association as a money-maker to restore and promote Dawson City. Take a look around town and you'll see how much money they make at Gerties (or how much the tourists lose)—around $1 million annually. I'm not saying that you won't come out in front, but just approach this joint with the attitude that you're making a donation. And why not? It's for a very good cause.

SHOPPING

The Klondike Institute of Art and Culture operates the **Odd Gallery** (2nd Ave. and Princess

St., 867/993-5005), which hosts exhibits of art by Yukoners. This association also organizes the mid-August **Yukon Riverside Arts Festival** beside the Yukon River as it flows past downtown. **Art's Gallery** (3rd Ave. and King St., 867/993-6967) sells excellent hand-blown art glass, scrimshaw, pottery, batiks, and baskets woven from birch, cedar, or spruce root.

The most interesting of touristy Dawson's many gift shops is the **Gold Claim** (3rd Ave. and Princess St., 867/993-6387) operated by Stuart Schmidt, whose grandfather was one of the original Klondikers. Schmidt uses gold he's mined himself to make hand-forged jewelry. **Fortymile Gold Placers** (3rd Ave. and York St., 867/993-5690) is in the business of selling and buying claims, but also sells raw gold out of its offices.

ACCOMMODATIONS AND CAMPING

Check the **Klondike Visitors Association** website (www.dawsoncity.ca) for a complete list of local lodgings. If you arrive in Dawson without reservations, be sure to check out the lodging notebook in the Visitor Information Centre; often hotels, motels, and bed-and-breakfasts will advertise special rates for the night here.

Under $50

◖ **Dawson City River Hostel** (867/993-6823, www.yukonhostels.com, mid-May–Sept.) is Canada's northernmost hostel. Located on the west side of the Yukon, it's a quick ferry ride from Dawson. A back-to-the-land spirit infuses this friendly place where dorm-style lodging in cabins is $18 for members of Hostelling International (nonmembers $22), private rooms are $46 s or d, and tent spaces cost $14 s, $23 d. The hostel doesn't have electricity (and therefore it's cash only), but does have a cooking area with woodstove, canoe and mountain bike rentals, a communal cabin, plus the funkiest bathhouse going.

$50-100

The cheapest place right downtown is the

shockingly pink **Westminster Hotel** (975 3rd Ave., 867/993-5463, www.thewestminsterhotel-1898.com), where basic rooms with shared bath go for $45–55 s, $55–65 d. The Westminster is definitely not for everyone and it helps to be a heavy sleeper, as the downstairs bar gets noisy Friday–Saturday when the country house band gets going.

If you really want to immerse yourself in the gold-mining culture of Dawson, consider staying at a camp set up by **Eureka Gold Panning Adventures** (867/633-6519, www.eurekagoldpanning.com) beyond Bonanza Creek Road along Hunker Creek. Morris and Sandy George supply wall tents, cooking facilities, wood-burning heaters, and solar showers. You supply sleeping bags and food. Rates are $60 s, $75 d, but most visitors stay as part of a package, such as $100 per person for one night accommodation and two full days of gold-panning. Round-trip transportation from Dawson, if required, is $60 for one person, $85 for two.

$100-150

In addition to having great breakfasts, **Klondike Kate's** (3rd and King, 867/993-6527, www.klondikekates.ca, Apr.–Sept., $100–140 s, $120–160 d) has 15 spacious wood cabins, each with a bathroom, cable TV, free Internet, and a phone.

Next to the museum, **5th Avenue B&B** (867/993-5941 or 866/631-5237, www.5thavebandb.com, $95–125 s, $105–135 d) may have an uninspiring name but the aquamarine exterior is impossible to miss. It features seven comfortable guest rooms with shared or private baths and a large sitting area. Rates include all-you-can-eat continental breakfast.

Across from Diamond Tooth Gertie's is the **Triple J Hotel** (5th and Queen, 867/993-5323 or 800/764-3555, www.triplejhotel.com, mid-May–mid-Sept.), a gold rush–era–looking hotel that, beyond the facade, is a modern complex of motel rooms ($132 s, $142 d), hotel rooms ($132 s, $142 d), and cabins ($142 s, $152 d).

Fun and funky on the outside, the rooms at

the **Downtown Hotel** (Queen at 2nd, 867/993-5346 or 867/993-5346, www.downtownhotel.ca, $118 s, $133 d) are somewhat clinical. Still, it's close to everything and the on-site bar has a rocking nighttime atmosphere.

Over $150

On the outskirts of town and less than a block from the Klondike River, **Dawson City B&B** (451 Craig St., 867/993-5649, www.dawsonbb.com, $165 s or d) is a neat two-story home with a pleasing blue and white exterior. Rates include a cooked breakfast, bikes, fishing poles, and airport transfers.

The **Aurora Inn** (5th Ave., 867/993-6860, www.aurorainn.ca, $149 s, $169–199 d) is a modern wooden lodging with a distinctive yellow facade. The rooms are bright and spacious, with simple furnishings and practical bathrooms.

Bombay Peggy's Inn & Pub (2nd at Princess, 867/993-6969, www.bombaypeggys.com, $169–189 s, $179–199 d) is named for the former madam of a brothel that once operated in the building. Not only has it been totally renovated, it was moved from its original location. Most rooms are decorated in bold Victorian colors, with hardwood floors and lavish bathrooms with antique tubs. You don't have to abandon modern comforts for the sake of atmosphere—there's also high-speed Internet. Rates include a light breakfast. About the only reminders of the building's previous use are a racy cocktail list in the downstairs lounge and the phone number. It's also one of the few Dawson lodgings open year-round.

Camping

Yukon River Campground (across the river from town, mid-May–mid-Sept., $15) is convenient but lacks amenities (drinking water, pit toilets, and firewood only). The free ferry from town runs 24 hours daily. Walk downstream from the campground to reach three rusting riverboats that are slowly disintegrating where they were beached many years ago.

RVers can circle their rigs right downtown

at the **Goldrush Campground** (5th and York, 867/993-5247, www.goldrushcampground. com, mid-May–mid-Sept., unserviced sites $19, hookups $31.50–38.50). Amenities include coin showers, a laundry, and wireless Internet throughout. South of town, **Bonanza Gold RV Park** (867/993-6789 or 888/993-6789, www.bonanzagold.ca, tents $10, hookups $23–39) has modern facilities, but tents are not permitted.

FOOD

Dawson is great for eating out; check the menu book at the Visitor Information Centre to see which places look inviting.

Riverwest Bistro Restaurant (Front St., 867/993-6339, daily from 7:30 A.M.) has good coffee plus a deli with the best sandwiches in town, and a delightful selection of baked goods.

The breakfast special at ◖ **Klondike Kate's** (3rd Ave. and King St., 867/993-6527, April–Sept. daily 6:30 A.M.–11 P.M., $14–24) isn't as legendary as the restaurant's namesake was during the gold rush, but it's still mighty popular. Bacon and eggs with baked beans and home fries will set you back $9. Pancakes and omelets are similarly priced. At lunch, salads and gourmet sandwiches are all under $15, while at dinner, plan on starting with prawns in ouzo ($11), and go on to pan-seared arctic char ($23). This place has a warm ambience and Dawson's nicest patio.

Groceries

Dawson City General Store (540 Front St., 867/993-5813, daily 8 A.M.–9 P.M.) has a bakery and groceries, but your best bet for fresh meat and deli items is the **Bonanza Market** (2nd and Princess, 867/993-6567, Mon.–Sat. 9 A.M.–7 P.M.).

INFORMATION

The centrally located **Dawson City Visitor Information Centre** (Front St. and King St., 867/993-5274, early May–late Sept. daily 10 A.M.–6 P.M., July–Aug. daily 8 A.M.–8 P.M.) is extremely well organized and prepared for the most common questions from the hordes of hopefuls that are, after all, Dawson's legacy. It stocks books of menus, hotel rates, and gift shops; schedules of tours; hours of attractions; and much, much more. Additionally, the **Klondike Visitors Association** (867/993-5575 or 877/465-3006, www.dawsoncity.ca) has a website filled with useful information.

The library is at 5th and Queen in the same building as the public school (remove your shoes before entering). **Maximillian's Gold Rush Emporium** (Front St., 867/993-5486) has a great selection of northern literature. One of the most unique souvenirs you can get in Dawson is an authentic **placer map** showing all the gold fields and claims. They are available along with topo maps at the **mining recorder's office** (5th Ave. between Queen St. and Princess St.).

GETTING THERE

Dawson is accessible from the south via the year-round **North Klondike Highway** (536 km/333 mi from Whitehorse), with westward connections to Alaska over the seasonal **Top of the World Highway** (280 km/174 mi to Tok, Alaska).

Dawson's airport is 17 kilometers (10.6 miles) east of town. **Air North** (867/668-2228) links Dawson with Inuvik and Whitehorse, with direct connections south to Vancouver, Calgary, and Edmonton from the capital. Taxis and a shuttle bus meet all flights.

Alaska/Yukon Trails (888/600-6001, www. alaskashuttle.com) has a thrice-weekly summer bus service connecting Dawson City with Whitehorse ($149) and Fairbanks (US$169).

CONTINUING WEST TO ALASKA

If you arrived in Dawson City by road from Whitehorse, you have the option of returning the way you came or continuing to Alaska along the Top of the World Highway. If you arrived in town by public transportation, your options are a little more varied—fly or bus it out in either direction or catch the *Yukon Queen* to Eagle.

DEMPSTER HIGHWAY

Dawson is the jumping off point for the 741-kilometer (460-mile) Dempster Highway that leads across the **Arctic Circle** to **Inuvik** in the Northwest Territories. Unpaved all the way, it traverses endless tundra and snowcapped mountain ranges; it crosses the migration path of the Porcupine caribou herd; and, in winter, you can drive clear through to the **Arctic Ocean** on the frozen Mackenzie River. But it's also one of the most remote public roads in North America, one for which you must be prepared with a full gas tank and spare tires. You also need to turn around at the end and return to Dawson along the same route.

DRIVING THE DEMPSTER

Request information packages from either of the territorial tourism bureaus before leaving home, then make a stop at the **Dempster/ Delta Visitor Information Centre** (Front St.,

Dawson City, 867/993-6167, mid-May–mid-Sept. daily 9 A.M.–8 P.M.). The ferry crossing of the Peel River operates mid-June–October. For a schedule and general highway conditions call 800/661-0750 or go online to www.dot. gov.nt.ca.

Numerous campgrounds and three lodges dot the route. A good spot to spend the night before hitting the highway is **Klondike River Lodge** (867/993-6892), east of Dawson at the start of the highway. Tent sites are $12, hookups $28, and motel rooms $135 s or d. They also have gas pumps and a small restaurant. The **Arctic Circle** is reached at Kilometer 403 (Mile 250) and the Yukon/Northwest Territories border at Kilometer 471 (Mile 293). **Fort McPherson,** 550 kilometers (342 miles) from Dawson, is a Gwich'in Dene village of 800 with a visitors center and other highway services.

Top of the World Highway

Heading west toward Alaska, the Top of the World Highway crosses the Yukon River at the edge of Dawson. A free **ferry,** with room for up to eight regular-sized vehicles, crosses the Yukon River mid-May–mid-September, on demand 24 hours a day (except Wed. 5–7 A.M.). It's a fun ride even if you're not heading up the Top of the World Highway.

From the west bank of the Yukon, the highway climbs out of Dawson into the alpine tundra of the lower White Mountains, with vast vistas in which you can see the road running along the ridge tops in the distance. Civilization along the highway, however, is nonexistent until you reach **Poker Creek,**

Alaska at Kilometer 106 (Mile 66). With a population of two, this is the northernmost border station in the United States. It's open for as long as the Dawson car ferry operates (usually mid-May–mid-Sept.), daily 9 A.M.–9 P.M. After crossing into Alaska, you must also turn your watch *back* one hour to Alaska Time (which means if you're traveling to Dawson from Alaska, the border station is open daily 8 A.M.–8 P.M.).

Note: The Dawson ferry can get heavily backed up in mid-summer, with delays of up to two hours at the busiest times (7–11 A.M. and 4–7 P.M.). Don't head off too late in the day if you intend to make the border crossing before it closes.

BACKGROUND

The Land

Western Canada can be described in one word—vast. The two provinces and two territories have a total land area of 3,440,000 square kilometers (1,327,000 square miles), approximately half the size of the continental United States. The Northwest Territories alone is double the size of Texas, yet has a population of just 43,000. British Columbia is Canada's third largest province (behind only Ontario and Quebec). Covering 948,596 square kilometers (366,300 square miles), it's four times larger than Great Britain, 2.5 times the size of Japan, larger than all U.S. states except Alaska, and larger than California, Oregon, and Washington combined.

Western Canada is a mostly arbitrary designation for Canada's western regions. This book covers the two western provinces—**British Columbia** and **Alberta**—and two territories—the **Northwest Territories** and the **Yukon.**

Mountains

Mountainous terrain dominates western Canada, a continuation of the same geology that runs along the entire western margin of the United States. The mountain ranges run in a north–south direction, and are separated by a series of parallel valleys. In northern regions, the ranges are lower, wider, and less

© ANDREW HEMPSTEAD

well defined; they rise to vast plateaus, then give way to endless rolling hills, and eventually to endless arctic tundra and the Canadian Shield.

The steep **Coast Mountains,** an unbroken chain extending for 1,500 kilometers (930 miles), rise abruptly from the Pacific Ocean and form a stunning backdrop to the seaside city of Vancouver and a winter playground for skiers and snowboarders at Whistler/Blackcomb alpine resort. Their high point, and the highest peak entirely within British Columbia, is 4,016-meter (13,200-foot) **Mount Waddington.** A northern extension of the Coast Mountains is the **St. Elias Range,** which pass through the southwestern corner of the Yukon. These remote mountains include 6,050-meter (19,800-foot) **Mount Logan,** Canada's highest peak. East of the Coast Mountains are the **Columbia Mountains,** the collective name for the **Cariboo, Monashee, Selkirk,** and **Purcell Ranges.** These ranges rise to their highest points in the south, where they're separated by deep valleys and long lakes. To the east of these ranges are the **Canadian Rockies,** reaching a high point at the summit of 3,954-meter (13,000-foot) **Mount Robson.** Creating a natural border between the provinces of British Columbia and Alberta, the Rockies north of the 49th parallel don't rise to the heights they do in the United States, but the national parks of Banff, Jasper, Kootenay, and Yoho combine to create one of the most magnificent and famous travel destinations on the face of this planet.

Waterways

Western Canada has around 50,000 named lakes, rivers, and streams that lie in dozens of drainage basins separated from each other by **divides,** simply high points of land. The most important of these is the **Continental Divide,** atop the Rocky Mountains and the dividing line between British Columbia and Alberta. From this point all rivers flow either west to

AURORA BOREALIS

Seeing the aurora borealis, or **northern lights,** is an emotional experience for some, spiritual for others, and without exception is unforgettable – an exhibition of color that dances across the sky like a kaleidoscope.

Auroral light is created through a complex process – a spontaneous phenomenon with no pattern and no "season" – that starts with the sun and finishes within the Earth's atmosphere. Essentially a huge atomic-fusion reactor, the sun emits the heat and light that keep us alive, and also emits ions that are thrust through space at high speeds. When these electrically charged particles reach the Earth's rarefied upper atmosphere – about 180 kilometers (112 miles) above the surface – they are captured by the Earth's magnetic field and accelerated toward the poles. Along the way they collide with the atoms and molecules of the gases in the atmosphere, which in turn become temporarily charged, or ionized. This absorbed energy is then released by the ionized gases, often in the form of light. The color of the light varies depending on the gas: Nitrogen atoms produce a violet and sometimes red color, oxygen produces green or, at higher altitudes, orange.

Because the magnetic field is more intense near the north and south magnetic poles, the lights are best seen at high latitudes. In northern latitudes the light show takes place up to 160 nights annually, with the best displays north of the 60th parallel. They generally start as a faint glow on the northeastern horizon after the sun has set, improving as the sky becomes darker.

the Pacific Ocean or east to the Atlantic and north to the Arctic Oceans.

British Columbia's largest watershed is drained by the **Fraser River.** With its headwaters at the Continental Divide in Mount Robson Provincial Park, this mighty river drains almost 25 percent of the province on its 1,368-kilometer (850-mile) journey to the Pacific Ocean at Vancouver. The Fraser is not the province's longest river, though. That title belongs to the **Columbia River,** which follows a convoluted course through southeastern British Columbia before crossing the U.S. border and draining into the Pacific Ocean in Oregon, 2,000 kilometers (1,240 miles) from its source.

Central and most of southern Alberta are drained by the **Saskatchewan River System,** which eventually flows into Hudson Bay and the Atlantic Ocean. Its two notable tributaries are the **North Saskatchewan River,** originating from the Columbia Icefield, and the **Red Deer River,** which flows through "Dinosaur Valley."

The **Peace River,** the only river system to cut across the Canadian Rockies, flows in a northeasterly direction from British Columbia and through northern Alberta to the Mackenzie River System (10th longest in the world), whose waters flow through the Northwest Territories to the Arctic Ocean. Also in the north is the famous **Yukon River.** Although its headwaters are high in the Coast Mountains, it heads north then west on a convoluted course to the Bering Sea.

CLIMATE

The sheer size of western Canada makes for different climates and radically varying temperatures, which rise or fall with changes in elevation, latitude, slope aspect, and distance from the ocean. The coastline of British Columbia boasts the mildest climate of all Canada, but this comes with one drawback—it rains a lot. The two main cities,

Vancouver and Victoria, lie within this zone. As prevailing moisture-laden westerlies blow across British Columbia, the cold heights of interior mountain ranges wring them dry, producing drier, hotter summer temperatures and sunnier skies the farther east you travel. The same is true in winter, except the temperature range is reversed—winter temperatures in Calgary are lower than in the interior of British Columbia and significantly lower than in Vancouver. In winter, the dry winds blasting down the eastern slopes of the Canadian Rockies can raise temperatures on the prairies by up to 40°C (72°F) in 24 hours. Called **chinooks,** these desiccating air currents are a phenomenon unique to Alberta.

Northern Latitudes

In general, the human species live in the middle latitudes and is accustomed to the particular set of natural phenomena common to those latitudes—the sun rises in the east each morning and sets in the west each evening; night follows day; vegetation is lush; and water most often occurs as a liquid. But in the Far North, these comfortable patterns don't exist. In winter, the sun doesn't rise for days (or, in the high arctic, even months), whereas in summer, it circles endlessly around the horizon. And for more than half the year, lakes, rivers, and the ocean aren't free-flowing water but solid ice. The region's climate is harsh, but the image of the Canadian North being a land of eternal ice and snow is a misconception. During the summer months, late May–September, the weather can be quite pleasant.

Much of the north is covered by **permafrost**—ground with an average annual temperature below freezing. In much of the mainland, the topsoil melts each summer. This is known as an *active layer* of permafrost. But farther north and in the Arctic Archipelago, the ground remains continuously frozen in a layer 2–500 meters (6–1,640 feet) deep, which is called *continuous permafrost.*

Flora

Western Canada can be divided into four major geographical areas: the Pacific coast, the mountainous interior, the plains of Alberta, and the arctic. Within each of these four main areas are distinct vegetation zones, the boundaries of which are determined by factors such as precipitation, latitude, and altitude.

COASTAL
Temperate Rainforest

Coastal regions that receive more than 1,000 millimeters (40 inches) of rain annually are dominated by temperate rainforest—predominantly evergreens. Just 0.02 percent of the world's land area is temperate rainforest and a full 25 percent of this amount is located in British Columbia. Coastal forest is mostly **hemlock, western red cedar, Sitka spruce,** and, in drier coastal areas, **Douglas fir.** The Queen Charlottes' rainforest is thickly covered in spongy, pale green moss, which

grows alongside coastal Douglas fir. In the region's subalpine areas you'll find **mountain hemlock.**

INTERIOR MOUNTAINS

With vast elevation changes, naturally the flora is diverse, ranging from the cacti of Canada's only desert in the Okanagan Valley to the equally hardy flowering plants that cling to glaciated peaks, coming alive with color for a few short weeks of summer.

Montane

The montane forest holds the greatest diversity of life of any vegetation zone and is prime winter habitat for larger mammals. But this is also where most development occurs and therefore the habitat is often much changed from its natural state.

In the southern portion of interior British Columbia, valleys are cloaked in montane

© ANDREW HEMPSTEAD

The Southern Gulf Islands have a temperate climate, which supports a number of evergreens.

forest to an elevation of about 1,500 meters (4,900 feet). Drier and south-facing areas support a mixture of Douglas fir and **ponderosa pine** in the south-central region. Farther east in the Canadian Rockies, **aspen, balsam poplar,** and **white spruce** thrive. **Englemann spruce** take hold at higher elevations and to the north. **Lodgepole pine** is common throughout. The first species to appear after fire, its seed cones are sealed by a resin that is melted only at high temperatures. When fire races through the forest, the resin melts and the cones release their seeds. Large tracts of **fescue** grassland are common in the very driest areas.

Subalpine

Subalpine forests occur where temperatures are lower and precipitation higher than in the montane. In the Canadian Rockies, this is generally 1,500–2,200 meters (4,900–7,200 feet) above sea level. In the southern interior of British Columbia, it begins (and ends) at higher elevations. The upper limit of the subalpine zone is the treeline. The climax species are Engelmann spruce and **subalpine fir,** although as in the montane, extensive forests of lodgepole pine occur in areas that have been scorched by fire in the last 100 years. At higher elevations, stands of **larch** are seen. Larches are deciduous conifers. Unlike other evergreens, their needles turn a burnt-orange color each fall, producing a magnificent display for photographers.

Alpine

The alpine zone extends from the treeline to mountain summits. The upper limit of tree growth south of the 60th parallel varies between 1,800 and 2,400 meters (5,900–7,900 feet) above sea level, dropping progressively to the north until it meets the treeless tundra of the Northwest Territories. Vegetation at these high altitudes occurs only where soil has been deposited. Large areas of alpine meadows burst with color for a short period each summer as **lupines, mountain avens, alpine forget-me-nots, avalanche lily, moss campion,** and a variety of **heathers** bloom.

THE PLAINS

East of the Canadian Rockies, the mountains dramatically give way to seemingly endless plains. Although the average elevation is 1,000 meters (3,300 feet) above sea level, the land is incredibly flat; in the southeast corner of Alberta, the Cypress Hills rise 500 meters (1,600 feet) above the surrounding land, yet are the highest point between the Canadian Rockies and Labrador, 5,000 kilometers (3,100 miles) distant. While it certainly isn't obvious at first, the plains are made up of the following three vegetation zones.

Prairie

Southern Alberta is dominated by prairie, the warmest and driest of Canada's ecological zones. The land is flat, open grassland, with trees supported only where water flows. Along most waterways, **cottonwood,** aspen, and poplar provide welcome shade for larger mammals (including *Homo sapiens*) while **willows** clog riverbanks. Water from these rivers is pumped up from the valley floors and diverted by canals across the prairies, making widespread agriculture possible. Native grasses such as rough fescue and **grama** survive without a helping hand. Amid the seemingly desolate landscape, colorful flowers such as the **wild rose** can be found.

Aspen Parkland

Unique to Canada, this area is a transition zone between the prairie grassland to the south and the boreal forest to the north. As the name suggests, trembling aspen (named for light, flattened leaves that "tremble" in even the slightest wind) is the climax species, but much of this zone has been given over to agriculture. Best known for it mammal populations, Elk Island National Park is one of the few remaining areas of this unique habitat.

Boreal Forest

Technically, the boreal forest, cutting a wide swath across western Canada, is part of the "plains." Encompassing almost half of Alberta and continuing into northern British Columbia and the two territories, the landscape is certainly flat. But it's also heavily treed. Only a few species of trees are able to adapt at these northern latitudes. In the southern part of the boreal forest, aspen and balsam poplar dominate. Farther north, conifers such as white spruce, lodgepole pine, and **balsam fir** are more common, with **jack pine** growing on dry ridges, and **tamarack** also present. The entire forest is interspersed with lakes, bogs, and sloughs, where black spruce and larch are the dominant species. In drier, upland areas the lush undergrowth is home to **raspberries, saskatoons, and buffalo berries.** To the north, where drainage is generally poor, the ground cover is made up of dense mats of peat.

THE TREELINE AND BEYOND

The treeline is a convoluted line that designates the northernmost extent of tree growth. It occurs below the 60th parallel in Eastern Canada, crossing the Arctic Circle some 500 kilometers (300 miles) north of Yellowknife before running along the top of the continent and into Alaska. It varies in latitude due to elevation—as a generalization it begins farther north as latitude descends. The treeline is not a line of trees as the name might suggest, but a transition in vegetation types (sometimes called *taiga*) that may be up to 100 kilometers (62 miles) wide. Where trees do grow in this transition, they are predominantly evergreens of the boreal forest, and because of little precipitation and a short growing season (70–80 frost-free days annually), are almost always stunted. Black spruce, white spruce, jack pine (the most northerly of the pines), and aspen are the most common trees found here. **White birch** is the only deciduous tree able to withstand the region's climate.

Tundra

Above the treeline, in an area of continuous permafrost, is the arctic biome—the tundra. Here a unique selection of vegetation has successfully adapted to the region's extreme seasonal changes of temperature and sunlight, as well as its lack of precipitation (less than

the Sahara Desert). Where water and wind have deposited soil, usually in depressions or along the banks of rivers, the vegetation is more varied. Almost all plants are perennials, able to spring to life quickly after a winter of hibernation. Brightly colored flowers such as **yellow arctic poppies, purple saxifrage, pink rhododendrons,** and **white heather** carpet entire landscapes during the short summer. **Willows** are one of the few woody plants to survive on the otherwise treeless tundra; they're found across the Arctic mainland along with **ground birch** and **Labrador tea.** Other areas are almost completely devoid of soil, supporting little more than arctic ferns, lichens, and mosses. Low temperatures here restrict bacterial action, and as a result, the soil is lacking in the nitrogen necessary for plant growth. Occasional oases of lush vegetation mark spots where the soil received a nitrogen boost—as from a rotting animal carcass or the detritus of an ancient Inuit campsite.

ENVIRONMENTAL ISSUES

Humans have been exploiting western Canada's abundant natural resources for 10,000 years. Indigenous people hunting bison obviously had little effect on ecological integrity, but over time, the eradication of the species by white settlers and the clearing of land for agriculture did. Today, it is minimizing the effects of logging operations and the fossil fuel industry, global warming, and development within national parks that are hot-button environmental issues in the region.

Forestry

The issue of forestry management in western Canada is very complex, and beyond the scope of a guidebook. In British Columbia, where a couple of mega-companies control an industry worth $17 billion annually to the local economy, many forestry decisions have as much to do with politics as they do with good management of the natural resource. The most talked about issue is **clear-cutting,** where entire forests are stripped down to bare earth, with the practice in old-growth forests especially contentious. The effect of this type of logging goes

GREENPEACE

During the late 1960s, Vancouver became a gathering point for the hippie movement, the Haight-Ashbury of the north. Members of this genre moved into the older houses of Kitsilano's 4th Avenue, turning them into havens that spilled into the nearby waterfront parks. A small group began expressing their dismay at U.S. government testing of nuclear weapons in the waters off the Alaskan coastline. Convinced that they could do something about it, the group chartered a small ship and, amid much publicity, sailed north for the test site. The year was 1971, the ship was named *Greenpeace*, and the rest, as they say, is history.

Greenpeace is now headquartered in Amsterdam but active worldwide in the fight to make governments and big business environmentally responsible for the planet. On the local front, Greenpeace continues the fight to save the old-growth forests of Clayquot Sound, stop mining of Alberta's tar sands, promote renewable energy, and stop whaling in the Pacific.

annually to the British Columbia economy, but that's just a drop in the ocean compared to neighboring Alberta. But along with all the money comes a number of environmental issues, none more talked about than the reduction of greenhouse gas emissions, which are absorbed by the air, and as a result contribute to global warming. Government and industry work together closely to reduce emissions, mostly through modern technologies. Traditional techniques such as using sulfur from sour gas wells to make fertilizer are being joined by radical new ideas. Of these, one of the most interesting is the capture of carbon dioxide at its industrial source, from where the emission is compressed and then injected under the ground into depleted oil and gas reservoirs.

The use of alternative, non-polluting "green power" is increasing exponentially. Almost 90 percent of power used by Alberta government facilities comes from renewable sources such as the sun and wind, and interest-free loans are offered for municipalities to become energy efficient. As elsewhere in the world, it is usually only when the ecology of somewhere special is threatened that the public hears about it. Development of an open pit mine at northern Alberta's McClelland Lake Wetlands, once considered for UNESCO World Heritage Site classification, is one such issue.

National Parks

Environmental issues within Canada's national parks are an ongoing hot topic, with the mountain parks of western Canada the center of most debate. On the surface, the commercialism within national parks seems to work against the mandate for their existence, but because they have grown from what were originally money-making exercises, the situation is unique. It is also important to remember that 100 years ago the parks were home to logging and mining operations and that wardens were directed to "exterminate all those animals which prey upon others." It wasn't *that* long ago that park lakes were stocked with nonnative fish for the pleasure of anglers, and still

beyond just the removal of ancient trees; often salmon-bearing streams are affected. Clayquot Sound is synonymous with environmentalists' fight against the logging industry. The sound is home to the world's largest remaining coastal temperate forest. Environmentally friendly options are practiced, with companies such as the Eco-Lumber Co-op selling wood that is certified as being from responsibly managed forests.

You see the extent of logging through British Columbia when you arrive, but visit Google Maps (http://maps.google.com) and click on the Satellite link. Then zoom into British Columbia—northern Vancouver Island is a good example—to see just how extensive the clear-cut logging is.

Oil and Gas Industry

The oil and gas industry is worth $6 billion

today wildlife is "managed" to some degree by relocating troublesome bears and moving elk away from population centers.

The **town of Banff,** the largest urban center in any national park in the world, is center of much debate about development within Canada's national park system. The town does have a good reason for its existence—serving the needs of up to 50,000 visitors daily. Along with obvious amenities such as accommodations and restaurants come needs such as a sewage plant, municipal infrastructure, schools, a hospital, and all the businesses you would expect to find in a mid-sized town. But you can also park in a multistory car park, go to Starbucks, get a tattoo, buy a bearskin rug, and sleep in a chain motel (obviously I'm not recommending this as an itinerary)—all within a national park. Many visitors only see the commercialism along Banff Avenue, but balancing human-use issues with the protection of the mountain ecosystem is behind

decisions such as capping future development, closing the Banff airstrip and buffalo paddock, and restricting the use of mountain bikes on some local trails. Farther afield, the need to protect wildlife has lead to speed restrictions and closures on roads passing through critical habitat, access to some areas of the backcountry has been curtailed, ski resorts only offer limited summer activities, and in some cases, such as in Kootenay National Park, accommodations in wildlife corridors have been expropriated.

Contacts

For more information on any of these issues, contact the following local environmental organizations: **Canadian Parks and Wilderness Society** (www.cpaws.org), **Greenpeace** (www.greenpeace.ca), **Society Promoting Environmental Conservation** (www.spec.bc.ca), and **Valhalla Wilderness Society** (www.vws.org).

Fauna

Western Canada is one of the best places in the world for wildlife-watching. Thanks to a diverse topography that provides a wide variety of habitat, large mammals are abundant, including elk, moose, bighorn sheep, and bears, all of which are widespread and easily viewed throughout the region. Species diversity in the Northwest Territories and northern Yukon is relatively low compared to other parts of the world. Species concentrations here, however, are enormous, including some of the world's largest populations of caribou, musk oxen, polar bears, whales, and seabirds.

BEARS

Three species of bears are present in western Canada, but only two—black bears and grizzlies—are widespread and abundant. The two can be differentiated by size and shape. Grizzlies are larger than black bears and have a

flatter, dish-shaped face and a distinctive hump of muscle behind the neck. *Color is not a reliable way to tell them apart:* Black bears are not always black. They can be brown or cinnamon, causing them to be confused with the brown grizzly.

Black Bears

If you spot a bear feeding beside the road, chances are it's a black bear. These mammals are widespread throughout all forested areas of western Canada, with an estimated population of 150,000 throughout the region. Their weight varies considerably, but males average 150 kilograms (330 pounds) and females 100 kilograms (220 pounds). Their diet is omnivorous, consisting primarily of grasses and berries, but supplemented by small mammals. They are not true hibernators, but in winter they can sleep for up to a month at a time before changing position.

THE ELUSIVE KERMODE

Little-known outside British Columbia is the Kermode (kerr-MO-dee), an elusive subspecies of black bear inhabiting only the vast tract of wilderness north of Terrace, British Columbia, and uninhabited Princess Royal Island, off the nearby coast.

First studied by Francis Kermode, director of the provincial museum at the turn of the 20th century, the bear was originally thought to be a distinct species. It's slightly larger than other black bears, has a different jaw structure, and, although its color varies, some individuals are pure white. These white bears are not albinos, merely the lightest-colored members of the species.

The Tsimshian called the Kermode "spirit bear" and often rendered it in human form in their artwork. Once close to extinction, the Kermode is now fully protected.

Grizzly Bears

Grizzlies (called brown bears along the British Columbia coast), second largest of eight recognized species of bears (only polar bears are larger), have disappeared from most of North America but are widespread throughout western Canada, numbering around 12,000. Grizzlies are only occasionally seen by casual observers; most sightings occur in alpine and subalpine zones, although sightings at lower elevations are not unusual, especially when snow falls early or late. During fall along the British Columbia coast, salmon runs draw bears to local river systems, almost guaranteeing sightings at a few accessible spots. The bears' color ranges from light brown to almost black, with dark tan being the most common. On average, males weigh 200–350 kilograms (440–770 pounds), with those along the coast often weighing a lot more. Apart from the salmon feasting, grizzlies eat small and medium-size mammals and berries in fall. Like black bears, they sleep through most of the winter.

© ANDREW HEMPSTEAD

There are an estimated 12,000 grizzly bears in western Canada.

Polar Bears

Evolved from the grizzly bear 250,000–400,000 years ago, polar bears weigh up to 600 kilograms (1,300 pounds) and measure 3.5 meters (11.5 feet) from head to tail. Their most distinctive feature is a pure white coat, but they also have long bodies with large necks. The bears' scientific name, *Ursus maritimus* (maritime bear), aptly refers to their habitat, which is the permanent pack ice of the Arctic Ocean east to Hudson Bay. Polar bears are at home in the sea and have been known to swim hundreds of kilometers.

THE DEER FAMILY
Mule Deer and White-Tailed Deer

These deer are similar in size and appearance. Their color varies with the season but is generally light brown in summer, turning dirty-gray in winter. Though both species are considerably smaller than elk, the mule deer is a little stockier than the white-tailed deer. The mule deer has a white rump, a white tail with a dark tip, and large mule-like ears. It inhabits open forests along valley floors. The white-tailed deer's tail is dark on top, but when the animal runs, it holds its tail erect, revealing an all-white underside. White-tails frequent thickets along rivers, lakes, and highways. They are especially prevalent on Vancouver Island. **Sitka deer,** a subspecies, inhabit the Queen Charlotte Islands.

Moose

The giant of the deer family is the moose, an awkward-looking mammal that appears to have been designed by a cartoonist. It has the largest antlers of any animal in the world, stands up to 1.8 meters (6 feet) at the shoulder, and weighs up to 500 kilograms (1,100 pounds). Its body is dark brown, and it has a prominent nose, long spindly legs, small eyes, big ears, and an odd flap of skin called a bell dangling beneath its chin. Apart from all that, it's good-looking. Each spring the bull begins to grow palm-shaped antlers that by August will be fully grown. Moose are solitary animals preferring marshy areas and weedy lakes.

They are most common in northern British Columbia, often seen by travelers along the Alaska Highway, but also make their home throughout the Canadian Rockies. Although they may appear docile, moose will attack humans if they feel threatened.

Elk

The elk (also known as wapiti) has a tan body with a dark-brown neck, dark-brown legs, and a white rump. This second-largest member of the deer family weighs 250–450 kilograms (550–1,000 pounds) and stands 1.5 meters (5 feet) at the shoulder. Beginning each spring, stags grow an impressive set of antlers, covered in what is known as velvet. The velvet contains nutrients that stimulate antler growth. By fall, the antlers have reached their full size and the velvet is shed. Rutting season takes place between September and October; listen for the shrill bugles of the stags serenading the females. Elk are common in the Canadian Rockies, where large herds make a home in and around the towns of Banff and Jasper, often nonchalantly wandering along streets and feeding on tasty plants in residential gardens.

Caribou

Native people named the animal *caribou* (hoof scraper) for the way it feeds in winter, scraping away snow with its hooves to search out food. The species seems ungainly, but has adapted superbly to life in the harsh northern climates. Standing approximately 1.5 meters (5 feet) tall at the shoulder, Caribou are smaller than elk and have a dark-brown coat with creamy patches on the neck and rump. Like the elk, they breed in fall, with the males gathering a harem. Above the treeline, they congregate each fall for a migration west to the boreal forest. As many as 400,000 of the animals may band together into a single herd. Each spring the process is reversed as they head east to summer calving grounds, high above the Arctic Circle. Small populations of **woodland caribou** inhabit the Yukon, northern British Columbia, and remote corners of the Canadian Rockies.

Male elk grow antlers, which are covered in "velvet."

OTHER LARGE MAMMALS
Bighorn Sheep

Bighorn sheep (also called Dall Sheep or Rocky Mountain sheep) are easy to recognize—if you spy an animal with spiraled horns that curve up 360 degrees, it's a bighorn. They spend summers grazing on open slopes or along roadsides, often attracted by natural salt deposits, such as along the Alaska Highway and in Jasper National Park east of the town.

Mountain Goats

The remarkable rock-climbing ability of these nimble-footed creatures allows them to live on rocky ledges or near-vertical slopes, safe from predators. They also frequent the alpine meadows and open forests of the Canadian Rockies, where they congregate around natural licks of salt. The goats stand one meter (3.2 feet) at the shoulder and weigh 40–530 kilograms (140–290 pounds). Both sexes possess a peculiar beard, or rather, goatee. The goats shed their thick coats each summer, making them look ragged, but by fall they've regrown a fine, new white woolen coat.

Pronghorn

Found roaming the prairie grasslands of southeastern Alberta, the pronghorn, often called antelope, is one of the fastest animals in the New World, capable of sustained speeds up to 80 kilometers (50 miles) per hour. Other remarkable attributes also ensure its survival, including incredible hearing and eyesight, and the ability to go without water for long periods of time.

Musk Oxen

These shaggy beasts, hunted to near extinction by the turn of the 20th century, are now restricted to the high Arctic. Banks Island is home to around 65,000 musk oxen, over half the world's total population. The image of them in a defensive circle, protecting their young from predators or the cold, is an endearing symbol of the North. Known to the Inuit as *oomingmak,* meaning "bearded one," they are covered with an underlayer of short, fine wool and a topcoat of shaggy hair up to 60 centimeters (24 inches) long. This gives the animals their characteristic prehistoric appearance and helps protect them from frequent blizzards and winter temperatures that in some areas average –30°C (–22°F).

WILD DOGS AND CATS
Wolves

Now inhabiting only the mountains and boreal forests, the wolf was once the target of a relentless extermination campaign. They weigh up to 60 kilograms (132 pounds), stand up to one meter (3.2 feet) high at the shoulder, and resemble large huskies or German shepherds. Their color ranges from snow white to brown or black. Unlike other predators, they are complex and intriguing animals that adhere to a hierarchical social order and are capable of expressing happiness, humor, and loneliness. British Columbia's vast wilderness is home to an estimated 8,000 wolves. Ironically, the one region that has a declining population is the national parks of the Canadian Rockies.

Coyotes

The coyote is often mistaken for a wolf, though in fact it is much smaller, weighing only up to 15 kilograms (33 pounds). It has a pointed nose and long bushy tail. Its coloring is a mottled mix of brown and gray, with lighter-colored legs and belly. The coyote is a skillful and crafty hunter, preying mainly on rodents. Their eerie concerts of yips and howls can be heard across much of western Canada and they are often seen patrolling the edges of highways and crossing open meadows in low-lying valleys.

Foxes

The smallest of the North American wild canids is the **swift fox,** which had been eradicated from the Canadian prairies by 1928 but was reintroduced to the southeastern corner of Alberta in 1983. Today, a small population continues to thrive in this dry and desolate landscape, but the species is still considered endangered. The **red fox** is slightly larger than the swift fox and is common throughout Alberta and southern latitudes of the Northwest Territories and the Yukon.

Cougars

Rarely encountered by casual hikers, cougars (known in other parts of North America as mountain lions, pumas, or catamounts) measure up to 1.5 meters (5 feet) long. The average male weighs 75 kilograms (165 pounds) and the female 55 kilograms (120 pounds). The fur generally ranges in color from light brown to a reddish-tinged gray, but occasionally black cougars are reported. Cougars are versatile hunters whose acute vision takes in a peripheral span in excess of 200 degrees. The cougar is a solitary animal with distinct territorial boundaries. Although this limits its population density, there are more cougars than ever as the animal expands its traditional range. The cougar population of Vancouver Island is the densest of anywhere in North America, and the species is present as far east as the eastern slopes of the Canadian Rockies.

Lynx

The elusive lynx is identifiable by its pointy black ear tufts and an oversized tabby-cat appearance. The animal has broad, padded paws that distribute its weight, allowing it to float on the surface of snow. It weighs up to 10 kilograms (22 pounds), but appears much larger because of its coat of long, thick fur. The lynx, uncommon but widespread throughout the region, is a solitary creature that prefers the cover of subalpine forests, feeding mostly at night on snowshoe hares and other small mammals.

SMALL MAMMALS
Beavers

One of the animal kingdom's most industrious mammals is the beaver. Growing to a length of 50 centimeters (20 inches) and tipping the scales at around 20 kilograms (44 pounds), it has a flat, rudder-like tail and webbed back feet that enable it to swim at speeds up to 10 kilometers (6 miles) per hour. The exploration of western Canada can be directly attributed to the beaver, whose pelt was in high demand in fashion-conscious Europe in the early 1800s. The beaver was never entirely wiped out, and today the animals can be found in almost any forested valley with flowing water. Beavers build their dam walls and lodges of twigs, branches, sticks of felled trees, and mud.

Squirrels

Several species of squirrel are common in western Canada. The **golden-mantled ground squirrel,** found in rocky outcrops of subalpine and alpine regions, has black stripes along its sides and looks like an oversized chipmunk. Most common is the **Columbian ground squirrel,** which lives in burrows, often in open grassland. It is recognizable by its reddish legs, face, and underside, and a flecked, grayish back. The bushy-tailed **red squirrel,** the bold chatterbox of the forest, leaves telltale shelled cones at the base of conifers. The lightly colored **Richardson's ground squirrel,** which chirps and flicks its thin tail when it senses danger, is found across much of western Canada; on the prairie, it is often misidentified as a gopher. Another species, the nocturnal **northern flying fox,** glides through the montane forests of mountain valleys but is rarely seen.

Hoary Marmots

High in the mountains, above the treeline, hoary marmots are often seen sunning themselves on boulders in rocky areas or meadows. They are stocky creatures, weighing around four kilograms (9 pounds). When danger approaches, these large rodents emit a shrill whistle to warn their colony. Marmots are only active for a few months each summer, spending up to nine months a year in hibernation.

Porcupines

This small, squat animal is easily recognized by its thick coat of quills. It eats roots and leaves but is also known as being destructive around wooden buildings and vehicle tires. Porcupines are common and widespread throughout all forested areas, but they're hard to spy because they feed most often at night.

Other Rodents

Widespread throughout western Canada, **muskrats** make their home in the waterways and wetlands of all low-lying valleys. They are agile swimmers, able to stay submerged for up

© ANDREW HEMPSTEAD

The golden-mantled ground squirrel is found in rocky outcrops of subalpine and alpine regions.

to 12 minutes. They grow to a length of 35 centimeters (18 inches), but the best form of identification is the tail, which is black, flat, and scaly. Closely related to muskrats are **voles,** which are often mistaken for mice. They inhabit grassy areas of most valley floors.

Hares and Pikas

Varying hares are commonly referred to as snowshoe hares because their thickly-furred, wide-set hind feet mimic snowshoes. Unlike rabbits, which maintain a brown coat year-round, snowshoe hares turn white in winter, providing camouflage in the snowy climes they inhabit. The small, gray-colored **pika,** or rock rabbit, lives among the rubble and boulders of scree slopes above the treeline, a neighbor of the larger marmot.

Weasels

Many of the world's 70 weasel species can be found in the western regions of Canada, including the **wolverine,** largest of the weasels worldwide, weighing up to 20 kilograms (44 pounds). Known to natives as *carcajou* (evil one), the wolverine is extremely powerful, cunning, and cautious. This solitary creature inhabits forests of the subalpine and lower alpine regions, feeding on any available meat, from small rodents to the carcasses of larger mammals.

The **fisher** has the same habitat as the wolverine, but is much smaller, reaching just five kilograms (11 pounds) in weight and growing up to 60 centimeters (24 inches) in length. Smaller still is the **marten.** Three subspecies of the **American badger** inhabit western Canada. A larger member of the weasel family, this creature is uncommon, naturally secretive, and also nocturnal, so sightings are extremely rare.

River otters have round heads, short, thick necks, webbed feet, long facial whiskers, and grow longer than one meter. They are widespread but not common throughout the northern half of Alberta. **Minks,** at home in or out of water, are smaller than otters and feed on muskrats, mice, voles, and fish.

As well as being home to the largest member of the weasel family, Canada holds the smallest—the **least weasel** (the world's smallest carnivore), which grows to a length of just 20 centimeters (8 inches) and weighs a maximum of 60 grams (2 ounces).

SEA MAMMALS
Whales

Once nearly extinct, today an estimated 20,000 **gray whales** swim the length of the British Columbia coast twice annually between Baja Mexico and the Bering Sea. The spring migration (Mar.–Apr.) is close to the shore, with whales stopping to rest and feed in places such as Clayoquot Sound and the Queen Charlotte Islands.

Orcas (also known as "killer whales") are actually the largest member of the dolphin family. Adult males can reach 10 meters (33 feet) in length and up to 10 tons in weight, but their most distinctive feature is a dorsal fin that protrudes more than 1.5 meters (5 feet) from the back.

Belugas—also called "white whales" for their coloring—are common off the Arctic coast. They winter in the Bering Sea and off the west coast of Greenland and migrate to estuarine areas such as the Mackenzie Delta in the western Arctic for summer calving season.

Seals

Five types of seals inhabit western Canadian waters. The most abundant, smallest, and most important to the Inuit are the **ringed seals,** whose name refers to the cream-colored circular markings on their backs. The largest are the **bearded seals,** which weigh up to 250 kilograms (550 pounds), and have facial whiskers resembling a beard.

FISH
Salmon

Five species of salmon are native to the tidal waters of British Columbia. Largest is the **chinook** (known as "king salmon" in the United States), which grows to 30 kilograms (66 pounds) in local waters. Averaging 2–3 kilograms (4.4–6.6 pounds), **sockeye salmon**

IT'S A SALMON'S LIFE

The five species of Pacific salmon are *anadromous*, meaning they live in both freshwater and saltwater at different stages. The life cycle of these creatures is truly amazing. Hatching from small eggs in freshwater often hundreds of miles upriver from the ocean, the fry find their way to the ocean, undergoing massive internal changes along the way that allow them to survive in saltwater. Depending on the species, they then spend 2-6 years in the open water. After reaching maturity, they begin the epic journey back to their birthplace, to the patch of gravel on the same river from which they emerged. Their navigation system has evolved over a million years, using, it is believed, a sensory system that combines measurements of sunlight, the earth's magnetic field, and atmospheric pressure to find their home river. Once the salmon are in range of their home river, scent takes over, returning them to the exact spot where they were born. Once the salmon reach freshwater they stop eating. Unlike other species of fish (including Atlantic salmon), Pacific salmon die immediately after spawning; hence the importance of returning to their birthplace, a spot the salmon instinctively know gives them the best opportunity for their one chance to reproduce successfully.

(red salmon) are the most streamlined of the Pacific salmon. When ready to spawn, the body of the sockeye turns bright red and the head dark green. **Chum salmon** (dog salmon) are very similar in appearance to sockeye, and their bodies also change dramatically when spawning. Bright, silver-colored **coho salmon** (silver salmon) average 1.5–3 kilograms (3.3–6.6 pounds). Smallest are **pink salmon,** which rarely weigh more than four kilograms (nine pounds). Their most dominant feature is a tail covered in large oval spots.

Kokanee are a freshwater salmon native to major lakes and rivers of the southern interior. They are directly related to sockeye salmon, spawning in the same freshwater range, and look similar in all aspects but size—kokanee rarely grow to more than 30 centimeters (12 inches) in length.

Trout

Trout are part of the same fish family as salmon but, with one or two exceptions, live in freshwater their entire lives. Interestingly, the trout of western Canada are more closely related to Atlantic salmon than to any of the species of Pacific salmon detailed above. The predominant species is the **rainbow trout,** common in lakes and rivers throughout the region. Many subspecies exist, such as the **steelhead,** an ocean-going rainbow trout that inhabits rivers flowing into the Pacific Ocean.

Other trout species present include the **bull trout,** which struggles to survive through high levels of fishing and a low reproductive cycle. Throughout the mid-1900s, this truly native Canadian trout was perceived as a predator of more favored introduced species, and was mostly removed. **Cutthroat trout,** found in high-elevation lakes, are named for a bright red dash of color that runs from below the mouth almost to the gills. Colorful **brook trout** are native to eastern Canada, but are now widespread throughout lakes and streams on the Alberta side of the Continental Divide. The **brown trout** was introduced from Europe in 1924 and is now found in the Bow and Red Deer watersheds of Alberta. The **lake trout,** which grows to 20 kilograms (44 pounds), is native to large, deep lakes of the western provinces.

Other Freshwater Species

The **whitefish,** a light gray fish, is native to lower-elevation lakes and rivers across British Columbia and Alberta. Inhabiting northern waters are **arctic grayling** and **Dolly Varden** (named for a colorful character in a Charles Dickens story). **Walleye** (also called "pickerel") grow to 4.5 kilograms (10 pounds) and are common in sandy-bottomed areas of lakes in northeastern British Columbia and northern Alberta. The monster freshwater fish of western Canada is the **sturgeon,** growing to more than 100 kilograms (220 pounds) in size and living for upwards of 100 years. The biggest of this species inhabit the Fraser River.

BIRDS

Bird-watching is popular throughout western Canada, thanks to the approximately 500 resident bird species and the millions of migratory birds that follow the Central and Pacific Flyways each year. All it takes is a pair of binoculars, a good book detailing species, and patience.

Raptors

A wide variety of raptors are present in western Canada—some call the region home year-round, while others pass through during annual spring and fall migrations. British Columbia is home to a quarter of the world's **bald eagles. Golden eagles** migrate across the regions, heading north in spring to Alaska and crossing back over in fall en route to Midwest wintering grounds. **Ospreys** spend summers across western Canada, nesting high up in large dead trees, on telephone poles, or on rocky outcrops, but always overlooking water. They feed on fish, hovering up to 50 meters (160 feet) above water, watching for movement, then diving into the water, thrusting their legs forward and collecting prey in their talons.

Falcons have adapted to the prairies and northern treeless landscapes. Most widespread is the **prairie falcon,** whose territory extends from the prairies to the foothills. Other falcons present include the **American kestrel,** which is commonly seen perched on fence posts and power poles throughout the prairies; the **merlin,** which tends to nest close to populated areas; and the rare **peregrine falcon,** which has been clocked at speeds of up to 290 kilometers (180 miles) per hour when diving for prey.

Hawks have adapted to hunting in wooded areas by developing short, rounded wings and long tails. The rust-colored **ferruginous hawk,** the largest hawk in North America, inhabits the treed areas of the prairies. The **marsh hawk** is widespread through the prairies and parkland, and as the name suggests, lives around areas of wetland. Farther north, the **red-tailed hawk** resides in the aspen parkland and southern extent of boreal forest.

Distinct from all previously listed species are a group of raptors that hunt at night. Best known as **owls,** these birds are rarely seen because of their nocturnal habits but are widespread throughout forested areas of the mountains. Most common is the **great horned owl,** identified by its prominent "horns," which are actually tufts of feathers.

Shorebirds, Seabirds, and Waterfowl

Nationalistic in name, the **Canada goose** is one of the most common and distinctive

Blue herons are found along the Pacific coast.

THE CANADA GOOSE

Each spring and fall the skies of western Canada come alive with the honking of the Canada goose, a remarkable bird whose migratory path takes it clear across the North American continent. Each spring, family units migrate north to the same nesting site, year after year. These are spread throughout Canada, from remote wetlands of northern Alberta to desolate islands in the Arctic Ocean.

Groups of families migrate together in flocks, the size of the flock varying according to the region, subspecies, and season. Preparation for long flights includes hours of preening and wing flexing. Once in the air they navigate by the sun, moon, and stars, often becoming disoriented in fog or heavy cloud cover. They are intensely aware of air pressure and humidity. In spring Canada geese hitch a ride north on the strong winds produced by low-pressure systems rolling up from the southwest. In fall they take advantage of Arctic fronts that roar south. If weather conditions aren't right, the geese will rest for a while, usually in farmers' fields (taking advantage of freshly sown crops). The V formation for which the geese are famous serves a very specific purpose: Each bird positions itself behind and slightly to the side of the bird immediately ahead, in this way every goose in the flock has a clear view, and all but the leader benefit from the slipstream of the birds ahead.

© ANDREW HEMPSTEAD

Canada goose

---

birds of western Canada. In the same family, **trumpeter swans, whistling swans,** and the endangered **whooping crane** are also present. In the duck family, **mallards** are present everywhere and **pintails** can often be seen feeding on grain in farmers' fields. The **wood duck** is much less common; identified by a distinctive crest, it can be spied around wetlands. Other widespread waterfowl species include **loons, grebes,** and three species of **teal.** Shorebirds present along the Pacific coast include **plovers, sandpipers, dowitchers, turnstones, gulls, terns,** and **herons.** Many shorebirds migrate vast distances through western Canada to nesting grounds in the Northwest Territories and Alaska, including the **arctic tern,** which makes an annual journey from Antarctica.

History

THE EARLIEST INHABITANTS

Approximately 15,000 years ago, at the end of the last Ice Age, human beings began migrating from northeast Asia across the Bering Strait, which was then dry land. At this time, the northern latitudes of North America were covered by an ice cap, forcing these people to travel south down the west coast before fanning out across the ice-free southern latitudes. As the ice cap receded northward, the people drifted north also, perhaps only a few kilometers in an entire generation, and began crossing the 49th parallel about 12,000 years ago. By the time the ice cap had receded from all but the Far North and the highest mountain peaks, a number of distinct cultures had formed.

The Northwest Coast

Around 12,000 years ago, Canada's west coast had become ice-free, and humans settled along its entire length. Over time they had broken into distinct linguistic groups, including the Coast Salish, Kwagiulth, Tsimshian, Gitksan, Nisga'a, Haida, and Tlingit; but all these peoples relied on two things: cedar and salmon. Their lifestyle was very different from that of the stereotypical North American indigenous people—they had no bison to depend on, they didn't ride horses, nor did they live in tepees—but they developed a unique and intriguing culture that remains in place in small pockets along the west coast. These coastal bands lived comfortably off the land and the sea, hunting deer, beaver, bear, and sea otters; fishing for salmon, cod, and halibut; and harvesting edible kelp.

West coast native society emphasized the material wealth of each chief and his tribe, displayed to others during special events called "potlatches." The potlatch ceremonies marked important moments in tribal society, such as marriages, puberty celebrations, deaths, or totem-pole raisings. The wealth of a tribe became obvious when the chief gave away enormous quantities of gifts to his guests—the nobler the guest, the better the gift. The potlatch exchange was accompanied by much feasting, speech-making, dancing, and entertainment, all of which could last many days. Stories performed by hosts garbed in elaborate costumes and masks educated, entertained, and affirmed each clan's historical continuity.

The Interior Salish

Moving north with the receding ice cap around 10,000 years ago, the Salish spread out across most of southwestern and interior British Columbia. After spending summers in the mountains hunting and gathering, they would move to lower elevations to harvest their most precious natural resource—salmon. At narrow canyons along the Fraser River and its tributaries, the Salish put their fishing skills to the test, netting, trapping, and spearing salmon as the fish traveled upstream to spawn. Much of the catch was preserved by drying or roasting, then pounded into a powder known as "pemmican" for later use or to be traded. The Salish wintered in earth-covered log structures known as "pit houses." Depressions left by these ancient structures can still be seen in places such as Keatley Creek, alongside the Fraser River.

Those who settled along the upper reaches of the Columbia River became known as the Shuswap. They spent summers in the mountains hunting caribou and sheep, put their fishing skills to the test each fall, then wintered in pit houses along the Columbia River Valley; they were the only Salish who crossed the Rockies to hunt buffalo on the plains. Within the Salish Nation, three other distinct tribes have been identified: the Lillooet, the Thompson (Nlaka'pamux), and the Okanagan.

The Kootenay

The Kootenay (other common spellings include Kootenai, Kootenae, and Kutenai) were once hunters of buffalo on the great American plains, but were pushed westward by fierce enemies. Like the Salish did farther west, they then moved north with the receding ice cap. They crossed the 49th parallel around 10,000 years ago, settling in the Columbia River Valley, along the western edge of the Canadian Rockies. Also like the Salish, they were hunters and gatherers and came to rely on salmon. The Kootenay were generally friendly, mixing freely with the Salish and treating the earliest explorers (including David Thompson) with respect. They regularly traveled east over the Rockies to hunt—to the wildlife-rich Kootenay Plains or farther south to the Great Plains in search of bison.

Blackfoot

The Blackfoot Confederacy was a group of traditional prairie dwellers and was the most warlike and feared of all native groups in Canada. Linguistically linked to the Algonkians, they were the stereotypical Indian depicted in story and film, bedecked in costumes and headdresses and mounted on horses. (This perception is somewhat skewed, however, because the horse was only introduced to North America by the Spanish in the mid-1600s and appeared north of the 49th parallel in the mid-1700s.) Before the arrival of Europeans, the Blackfoot Confederacy ruled the southern half of Alberta and comprised of three allied bands, which hunted and camped together, intermarried, shared customs, and spoke dialects of the Algonkian language. They were the **Blackfoot** (best known today as **Siksika**), who lived along the North Saskatchewan River; the **Blood,** along the Red Deer River; and the **Peigan,** along the Bow River.

The **Sarcee** are also considered part of the Blackfoot Nation but are of Athabascan linguistic stock. This small tribe divided from the subarctic Beaver in the mid-1800s and integrated themselves with the Blackfoot in customs, lifestyle, and marriage but retained their original tongue.

Assiniboine

Around 1650, the mighty Sioux nation began splintering, with many thousands moving north into present-day Canada. Though these immigrants called themselves Nakoda meaning "people," other tribes called them Assiniboine, meaning the "people who cook with stones." Europeans translated Assiniboine as Stone People, or Stoney for short. Slowly, generation after generation, smaller groups pushed westward along the Saskatchewan River system, allying themselves with the Cree but keeping their own identity, and pushing through the Blackfoot territory of the plains to reach the foothills approximately 200 years ago. They split into bands, moving north and south along the foothills and penetrating the wide valleys where hunting was productive. They evolved a very different lifestyle from that of the Plains Indians. Moving with the seasons, they lived in small family-like groups, diversifying their skills, becoming excellent hunters of mountain animals and gathering berries in fall, and becoming less dependent on buffalo. They were a steadfast yet friendly people.

Cree

Before the arrival of Europeans, the Cree had inhabited most of eastern Canada for thousands of years. As the European fur traders pushed westward from Hudson Bay, the Cree followed, displacing enemies and adapting to new environments. By 1800, the Cree had moved as far west as the Peace River and to the northern slopes of the Rocky Mountains. They lived mostly in the forests fringing the prairies, acting as a middleman between Europeans and local natives, searching out furs and trading buffalo hides obtained from plains natives for European goods. Although not related, the Cree and Assiniboine freely mixed together, camping, hunting, and fighting as a group.

The Athabascans

Athabascan (often spelled Athapaskan) is the most widely spread of all North American linguistic groups, extending from the Rio Grande to Alaska. It is believed that Athabascan-speaking people followed the receding ice cap and settled in forested areas throughout the subarctic approximately 7,000 years ago.

Athabascans led a simple, nomadic life and were generally friendly toward each other and neighboring tribes. Although culturally diverse, the nature of this tribe's lifestyle left few archaeological remains; therefore, they are the least known of the natives who once lived in western Canada. The largest division of the Athabascans was the Carrier group. They lived throughout the northern reaches of the Fraser River basin and along the Skeena River watershed. The Carrier, along with Athabascan tribes that lived farther north (including the Chilcotin, Tahltan, and Inland Tlingit), adopted many traits of their coastal neighbors, such as potlatch ceremonies and raising totem poles. One Athabascan group inhabiting northern Alberta was the Beaver, who were forced westward, up the Peace River watershed, by the warlike Cree (the name Peace River originated after the two groups eventually made peace). Across the subcontinental divide to the north, the Mackenzie River watershed was the traditional home of another distinct Athabascan band, known today as the Dene (DEN-ay). Like the Beaver, they were nomadic hunters and gatherers but also relied heavily on fishing.

Inuit

A second group of people crossed the Bering land bridge much later than the first—approximately 10,000 years ago—and settled in Alaska. Eventually, people from this group would migrate across the Arctic coast in two major waves. The first wave occurred approximately 4,000 years ago when the people known as the **Dorset culture** began to move east. They lived in skin tents in summer and snow houses—previously unknown in Alaska—in winter. The second eastward migration, that of the **Thule culture,** occurred approximately 1,000 years ago and picked up elements of the Dorset culture, such as snow houses and intricate carvings, as it progressed. The Thule lived in semipermanent villages and specialized in hunting sea mammals. The Thule are ancestors of the Inuit.

Métis

The exact definition of Métis varies across Canada, but the term originated in the 1700s to describe those born of a mixed racial heritage as the result of relationships between French traders and native Cree women. The Métis played an invaluable role in the fur trade because they were able to perform traditional tasks and were bilingual. By the early 1800s, a distinct Métis culture developed, mostly along major trading routes. As the fur trade ended and the great buffalo herds disappeared, many Métis found themselves drawn toward the familiarity of their own people and settled along Central Canada's Red River. Government threats to take their land along the Red River led to the 1869 Riel Rebellion and the 1885 North West Rebellion, after which the displaced Métis drifted back westward to the boreal forests, eking out food by hunting, trapping, and fishing. They were a people stuck between two cultures; they were excluded from treaties signed by full-blooded natives but were not a part of mainstream Canadian society.

EUROPEAN EXPLORATION AND COLONIZATION
By Sea

It was only a little more than 200 years ago that the first European explorers began to chart the northwest corner of North America. In 1774, the ship of Mexican Juan Perez was the first vessel to explore the coastline and trade with the natives. He was quickly followed by Spaniard Don Juan Francisco de la Bodega y Quadra, who took possession of the coast of Alaska for Spain. England's Captain James Cook arrived in 1778 to spend some time at Nootka, becoming the first nonnative to actually come ashore. Cook received a number of luxuriantly soft sea otter furs, which he later sold at a huge profit in China. This news spawned a fur-trading rush that began in 1785 and continued for 25 years. In 1789, Bodega y Quadra established a settlement at Nootka, but after ongoing problems with the British (who also claimed the area), he gave it up. In 1792, Captain George Vancouver, who had been the navigator on Cook's 1778 expedition, returned

HISTORICAL BOUNDARIES OF WESTERN CANADA

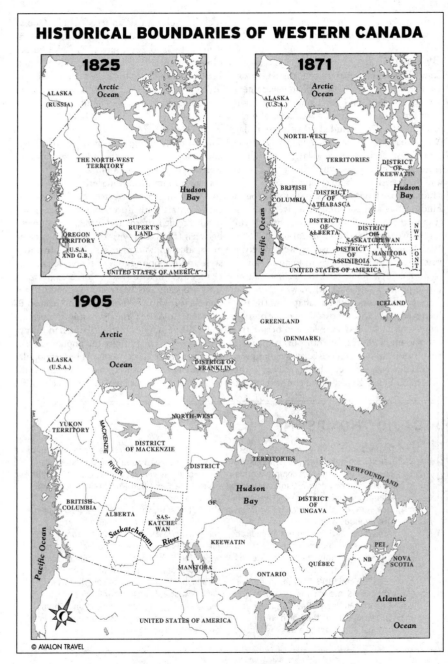

1825

ALASKA (RUSSIA)
Arctic Ocean
THE NORTH-WEST TERRITORY
Hudson Bay
OREGON TERRITORY (U.S.A. AND G.B.)
RUPERT'S LAND
UNITED STATES OF AMERICA

1871

ALASKA (U.S.A.)
Arctic Ocean
NORTH-WEST
TERRITORIES
DISTRICT OF KEEWATIN
Hudson Bay
Pacific Ocean
BRITISH COLUMBIA
DISTRICT OF ATHABASCA
DISTRICT OF ALBERTA
DISTRICT OF SASKATCHEWAN
DISTRICT OF ASSINIBOIA
MANITOBA
N.W.T.
ONT.
UNITED STATES OF AMERICA

1905

ALASKA (U.S.A.)
Arctic Ocean
ICELAND
GREENLAND (DENMARK)
DISTRICT OF FRANKLIN
YUKON TERRITORY
MACKENZIE RIVER
DISTRICT OF MACKENZIE
NORTH-WEST
DISTRICT
TERRITORIES
NEWFOUNDLAND
Hudson Bay
BRITISH COLUMBIA
ALBERTA
SASKATCHEWAN
Saskatchewan River
OF
DISTRICT OF UNGAVA
KEEWATIN
PEI
NB
NOVA SCOTIA
Pacific Ocean
MANITOBA
QUÉBEC
ONTARIO
Atlantic Ocean
UNITED STATES OF AMERICA

© AVALON TRAVEL

to the area and sailed into Burrard Inlet, claiming the land for Great Britain.

By Land

Some 100 years before Europeans began exploring the west coast, the British government granted the Hudson's Bay Company the right to govern Rupert's Land, a vast area of western Canada that included all of present-day Manitoba, Saskatchewan, Alberta, and the Northwest Territories. The land was rich in fur-bearing mammals, which both the British and the French sought to exploit for profit. The Hudson's Bay Company first built forts around Hudson Bay and encouraged natives to bring furs to the posts. Soon, however, French fur traders working for the Montreal-based North West Company began traveling west to secure furs, forcing their British rivals to do the same.

Both companies began establishing trading posts, often beside each other, which created a rivalry that continued unabated until they merged in 1821. Most posts were made of solid log construction and were located beside rivers, the main routes for transportation. The first European to reach the coast overland was Alexander Mackenzie, who traveled via the Peace and Fraser Rivers—you can still see the rock in the Dean Channel (off Bella Coola) where he inscribed "Alexander Mackenzie from Canada by land 22nd July 1793." Not far behind came other explorers, including Simon Fraser, who followed the Fraser River to the sea in 1808, and David Thompson, who followed the Columbia River to its mouth in 1811.

The Native Response

The fur trade brought prosperity to the indigenous society, which was organized around wealth, possessions, and potlatches. The traders had no interest in interfering with the natives and, in general, treated them fairly. This early contact with Europeans resulted in expanded trade patterns and increased commerce between tribes. But with the Europeans came guns, alcohol, and diseases. And native lifestyle and the boundaries of the various tribes changed dramatically as commerce between the Europeans and locals caused tribes to abandon their traditional homesites and instead to cluster around the forts for trading and protection. While natives of the plains had always slaughtered many buffalo, the population had remained relatively constant. As beaver populations dwindled, however, traders turned to buffalo hides. Within 10 years, the once-prolific

DAVID THOMPSON

David Thompson, one of Canada's greatest explorers, was a quiet, courageous, and energetic man who drafted the first comprehensive and accurate map of western Canada. He arrived in Canada from England as a 14-year-old apprentice clerk for the Hudson's Bay Company. With an inquisitive nature and a talent for wilderness navigation, he quickly acquired the skills of surveying and mapmaking. Natives called him Koo-koo-sint, which translates as The Man Who Looks at Stars.

Between 1786 and 1808, Thompson led four major expeditions into what is now Alberta – the first for the Hudson's Bay Company and the last three for its rival, the North West Company. The most important one was the fourth,

1806-1808, during which he discovered the Athabasca Pass through the Continental Divide. For many years, this was the main route across the Canadian Rockies to the Pacific Ocean.

In 1813 Thompson began work on a master map covering the entire territory controlled by the North West Company. The map was four meters (13 feet) long and two meters (6 feet) wide, detailing more than 1.5 million square miles. On completion it was hung out of public view in the council hall of a company fort in the east. It was years later, after his death in 1857, that the map was "discovered" and Thompson became recognized as one of the world's greatest land geographers.

herds were practically eradicated. Without their traditional food source, the indigenous plains people were weakened and left more susceptible to diseases such as smallpox and scarlet fever.

Keen to confirm British sovereignty, the British government began colonizing Vancouver Island. Leaving the island in the hands of the Hudson's Bay Company, chief factor James Douglas began "purchasing" land from the natives. He made treaties with the tribes in which the land became the "entire property of the white people forever." Out on the prairies, the now-famous North West Mounted Police had established posts to try to curb the whiskey trade and restore peace. Facing no other choice, the chief of all plains chiefs, Crowfoot, of the powerful Blackfoot Confederacy, signed the first major treaty in 1877, with others following. Relegated to reserves, which consisted of land set aside by the government for specific native bands, the native lifestyle was changed dramatically, and forever. Their self-sufficiency taken away, the tribes were forced to accept what they were given.

BOOMING TIMES

The discovery of gold along the Fraser River in 1858 led to western Canada's first population explosion. At the time only Vancouver Island was part of the British Empire. Realizing that enormous wealth could be buried on the mainland, and with U.S. miners arriving in Victoria by the shipload, the British government quickly responded by creating a mainland colony. At first it was named New Caledonia, but because there was a French territory of the same name, Queen Victoria was asked to change the name, which she did, using "Columbia," which appeared on local maps, and adding "British," just to make sure the United States knew who owned the territory.

The Dominion of Canada

By 1867, some of the eastern provinces were tiring of British rule, and a movement was abuzz to push for Canadian independence. The British government, wary of losing Canada as

it had lost the United States, passed legislation establishing the Dominion of Canada, which British Columbia was invited to join in 1871. It joined, with one important condition: that it be connected to the rest of the country by railway. At that time, the North-West Territories—comprising all of western Canada except British Columbia—was a foreign land to those in eastern Canada: Life was primitive and lawless, and no post had more than a couple dozen residents. But in an effort to solidify the dominion, the government bought the North-West Territories back from the Hudson's Bay Company in 1869.

This region had been divided into districts. One of these, the Yukon, was separated in 1898, the same year the greatest gold rush the world had ever seen was playing out near Dawson City. Thus it was only sensible to declare that boomtown the capital of the Yukon (it was changed to Whitehorse in 1953). Two other districts, Alberta and Saskatchewan, were admitted as provinces of the Canadian Confederation in 1905.

The Coming of the Railway

Scorned in the east as being unnecessary and uneconomical, the rail line reached Winnipeg in 1879, and Calgary then Banff in 1883, before the final spike was driven on November 7, 1885. The completion of a transcontinental railway did more than fulfill a government promise, it changed the face of the west. A northern route through Edmonton to Prince Rupert was completed by the Grand Trunk Railway in 1914, roads were built, industries—including logging, mining, farming, fishing, and tourism—started to develop, and settlers began pouring in to surveyed land offered at $10 per quarter section (160 acres). Vancouver, at the terminus of the railway, also got a huge boost, as overnight it became a transportation hub for the entire Pacific Rim.

Alberta's Black Gold

Fifty years after the Klondike gold rush, Alberta had a gold rush of its own, except it wasn't shiny nuggets that created the excitement, it was black

NUNAVUT

On April 1, 1999, the map of Canada was redrawn when the Northwest Territories was divided up and Canada's third territory, Nunavut, was born. Nunavut, meaning "Our Land," encompasses the Keewatin, Arctic coast, and Baffin regions – more than two million square kilometers – and is home to 29,500 people, of whom 25,000 are Inuit. While native groups around the world dragged issues of land claims through courts, held demonstrations, and, in parts of Canada, took up arms, the Inuit led a low-profile 15-year campaign that on July 9, 1993, culminated in the passage in Canadian Parliament of the historic bill creating Nunavut.

But Nunavut was a lot more than the world's largest land claim, it was an enormous step for the Inuit. Now they assume responsibility for a chunk of land four times the size of Texas. Although Nunavut was a victory for the Inuit, it hasn't automatically solved the many social problems experienced in the region – unemployment is three times the national average and and the cost of living is twice the national average. Only 21 kilometers of government-maintained roads cross the region, and only 5 percent of its population has completed high school. Nevertheless, after 100 years, the Inuit once again have control of their land.

The capital of the territory is **Iqaluit**. The working language of the government (www.gov.nu.ca) is **Inuktitut**. Tourism is a thriving business in Nunavut. If you're contemplating a trip, start by contacting **Nunavut Tourism** (867/979-6551 or 866/686-2888, www.nunavuttourism.com).

---

gold—oil. When Leduc Oil Well No. 1, south of Edmonton, began belching black rings of smoke in February 1947, Alberta had hit the jackpot and a new economy for all of Canada had begun. Capitalists poured billions of dollars into Alberta as every valley, hill, and flat was surveyed, and soon farmers' fields throughout the province were littered with beam pumps bobbing up and down. By 1954, eight major fields had been proven to contain eight billion barrels of recoverable crude oil. Calgary became the financial and administrative headquarters of the industry, while Edmonton—at the center of many of the fields—became the technological, service, and supply center. In less than a decade, the province's population doubled to more than one million.

THE NEW MILLENNIUM

Vancouver, Calgary, and Edmonton have embraced the information-technology boom, diversifying the resource-based economy of both provinces. Nonrenewable resources are still the backbone of western Canada's economy, however.

Since Martin Frobisher took 1,000 tons of fool's gold from the Canadian Arctic back to England in 1576, natural resources have always played a vital role in the exploration and economy of Canada. It looks like this will continue well into the future—the oil sands of northern Alberta hold the world's largest deposit of oil, in the last decade the Northwest Territories has become one of the world's largest diamond producers, and the potential of vast reserves of natural gas off the British Columbia coast are just being realized.

With a growing, relatively young, and well-educated population; a strong economy; and staggering resources still available in the ground, the future remains bright for Canada's western provinces.

Economy and Government

ECONOMY
The economy of western Canada has always been closely tied to the land—based first on the fur trade, followed by fishing and forestry in British Columbia and agriculture and oil in Alberta. The two western provinces account for one third of Canada's economic output. As a result of its vast natural resources, Alberta leads the way with a GDP of $260 billion.

Energy
Alberta lies above an immense basin of porous rock containing abundant deposits of oil, natural gas, and coal. The **oil** in Alberta occurs in three forms: crude oil, heavy oil, and oil sands. Most is refined for use as gasoline for cars, diesel for trucks, and heating fuel for homes. As technology improves and prices prove extraction to be economically viable, the oil sands of northern Alberta are playing an increasingly important role in meeting world energy demands. The Athabasca Oil Sands, near Fort McMurray, are the world's largest such deposit, with an estimated 175 billion barrels of recoverable oil.

Natural gas was first discovered in southeast Alberta in 1883, but it wasn't seen as a viable source of energy until 1900. Canada has always had more gas than it can use (currently, proven reserves stand at two trillion cubic feet), and 70 percent is exported via pipelines to other provinces and the United States. Gas is mostly used for home heating but is also a source material for the petrochemical industry.

Western Canada's first **coal** mine began operations on Vancouver Island in the 1850s, followed by numerous others across British Columbia and Alberta. Coal was first used to heat homes and provide fuel for steam locomotives, but oil took over those duties in the early 1950s. The industry was revived in the 1960s with the advent of coal-fired electric power plants. This market has since broadened, and today coal is British Columbia's most important mineral export, worth $1 billion annually. Alberta mines more coal, but the value is less.

Minerals
British Columbia is a mineral-rich province, and historically mining has been an important part of the economy. Today, the province is home to 26 major mines and three mineral processing plants that produce $3.6 billion worth of exports. In the Northwest Territories, mining has always been a mainstay of the economy. Currently, eight mines produce $1 billion worth of minerals annually, principally zinc, gold, and diamonds. The latter is particularly high profile, with the territories' four mines responsible for 10 percent of the total value of diamonds extracted worldwide. The website www.certifiedarcticdiamond.com is filled with interesting information on the local industry.

Forestry
Almost two thirds of British Columbia—some 60 million hectares (148 million acres)—is forested, primarily in coniferous softwood (fir, hemlock, spruce, and pine). These forests provide about half Canada's marketable wood and about 25 percent of the North American inventory. Along the coast the hemlock species is dominant; in the interior are forests of spruce and lodgepole pine. Douglas fir, balsam, and western red cedar are the other most valuable commercial trees. The provincial government owns 94 percent of the forestland, private companies own 5 percent, and the national government owns the remaining 1 percent. Private companies log much of the provincially owned forest under license from the government. Around 75 million cubic meters of lumber are harvested annually, generating $10 billion in exports (more than all other industries combined). Although over half of Alberta is forested, the industry constitutes a tiny percentage of the total economic output, mainly because of the slow regrowth rate of northern forests.

Agriculture
Although oil and gas form the backbone of

Alberta's economy, farms and ranches still dominate the landscape. More than 20 million hectares (49.2 million acres) are used for agriculture, half of which is cultivated—a back-breaking job that was started when the first homesteaders moved west. Alberta produces about 20 percent of Canada's total agricultural output, directly employing 50,000 people in the process. The largest portion of the province's $4.5 billion annual farm income comes from cattle ($1.4 billion). Alberta has four million head of beef cattle—just under half of Canada's total—as well as 140,000 dairy cows. The largest crop is wheat, used mainly for bread and pasta. Barley, used for feeding livestock and making beer, accounts for more than $500 million in annual revenues.

The agricultural facts and figures from British Columbia are very different for a single reason—only 4 percent of this mountainous province is arable, and of this, just 25 percent of the land is regarded as prime for agriculture. Nevertheless, agriculture is an important part of the provincial economy: 19,000 farms growing 200 different crops contribute $1.5 billion annually to the economic pie. The most valuable sector of the industry is dairy farming, with 72,000 dairy cows contributing around $350 million to the provincial economy. The best land for dairy cattle is found in the lower Fraser Valley. Almost all of British Columbia's fruit crops are grown in the Okanagan Valley; apples are the best-known produce, but a burgeoning viticulture industry produces grapes in more than 150 vineyards. The province holds around 600,000 beef cattle, including 20,000 run on Canada's largest ranch, the 200,000-hectare (494,000-acre) Douglas Lake Ranch.

Fishing

Commercial fishing, one of British Columbia's principal industries, is worth $500 million annually and comes almost entirely from species that inhabit tidal waters. The province has 6,000 registered fishing boats and 600 fish farms. The industry concentrates on salmon (60 percent of total fishing revenues come from six species of salmon): Boats harvest the five species indigenous to the Pacific Ocean, and the aquaculture industry revolves around Atlantic salmon, which is more suited to farming. Other species harvested include herring, halibut, cod, sole, and a variety of shellfish, such as crabs. Canned and fresh fish are exported to markets all over the world—the province is considered the most productive fishing region in Canada. Japan is the largest export market, followed by Europe and the United States.

Tourism

Tourism is the second most important industry to the economies of each jurisdiction in western Canada, but it is the largest employer, employing over 200,000 people in British Columbia and Alberta combined. This segment continues to grow, as more and more people become aware of western Canada's outstanding scenery; its numerous national, provincial, historic, and regional parks; and the bountiful outdoor recreation activities available year-round. British Columbia reports 48 million annual "visitor nights" (the number of visitors multiplied by the number of nights they stayed within British Columbia), while Alberta comes up with a figure of 20 million (a figure that counts every visitor only once, but includes intraprovincial travel). The largest number of visitors comes from other provinces. Both provinces report more than 1,000,000 visitors from the United States, while the United Kingdom, Japan, Germany, and Australia also contribute significant numbers. Tourism British Columbia promotes Canada's westernmost province to the world, while Travel Alberta, a branch of the government's Department of Economic Development, markets that province. North of the 60th parallel, NWT Arctic Tourism and Tour Yukon are the government departments responsible for marketing the two territories.

GOVERNMENT

Canada is part of the British Commonwealth, but the monarchy and the elected government of Great Britain have no control over Canada's political affairs. The British monarchy is represented in Canada by a governor general. The country's constitution is based on five important acts of British Parliament, the most recent being the Canada Act of 1982. That act gave Canada the power to amend its constitution, provided for recognition of the nation's multicultural heritage, and strengthened provincial ownership of natural resources, the latter being especially important for Alberta.

The Canadian government operates through three main agencies: the Parliament (made up of the Senate and the House of Commons), which makes the laws; the Executive (Cabinet), which applies the laws; and the Judiciary, which interprets the laws. The leader of the political party voted into power by Canadian citizens becomes the head of government, known as the prime minister. The prime minister then chooses a cabinet of ministers from members of his or her party. Each minister is responsible for the administration of a department. Although elected for a five-year term, the prime minister may call an election at any time.

At a provincial level, the monarchy is represented by a lieutenant governor. Like the governor general, the position is mainly ceremonial.

British Columbia

Under the lieutenant governor are members of the Legislative Assembly (MLAs). Assembly members are elected for a period of up to five years, though an election for a new assembly can be called at any time by the lieutenant governor or on the advice of the premier. In the Legislative Assembly are the premier, the cabinet ministers and backbenchers, the leader of the official opposition, other parties, and independent members. The laws of British Columbia are administered by the cabinet, premier, and lieutenant governor; they are interpreted by a judiciary made up of the Supreme Court of British Columbia, Court of Appeal, and County or Provincial Courts.

The current ruling party is Gordon Campbell's Liberal Party, which swept to power in April 2001. Provincial politics in British Columbia have traditionally been a two-party struggle. For information on the provincial government, its ministries, and current issues, visit www.gov.bc.ca.

Alberta

The members of the Alberta Legislature are elected on a party system in the same way as those in British Columbia. The leader of the party in power, known as the premier, oversees the running of 18 departments. With so much control over the province's natural resources and, in turn, Alberta's future, many premiers have enjoyed a particularly high profile. One such premier, Peter Lougheed, initiated the Heritage Savings Trust Fund, which collects billions of dollars in oil royalties for the people of Alberta. Initiated in 1976, the fund changed direction in the mid-1990s, steering toward long-term financial returns as opposed to specific projects. Now, the Alberta Heritage Fund holds monies for programs and services, but most of the fund's $14.5 billion is invested. The Progressive Conservative Party is currently in power. Other parties include the New Democratic Party, the Liberal Party, and Alberta Alliance. The website of the Alberta government is www.alberta.ca.

Northwest Territories and the Yukon Territory

North of the 60th parallel are three territories (the third is Nunavut). Simply put, these three Northern jurisdictions lack the population to qualify as provinces, and therefore fall under the constitutional control of the federal government. Fully elected assemblies give the territories a degree of independence, but there are no political parties. Instead, a single member of each electoral district is voted to the legislative assembly. Members of the assembly then elect a premier and cabinet ministers. At the top of the territorial ladder is a commissioner, who performs a role similar to the lieutenant governor's. For information on the Northwest Territories government go to www.gov.nt.ca; the website of the Yukon government is www. gov.yk.ca.

The People

For thousands of years before the arrival of Europeans to western Canada, several distinct indigenous peoples had lived off the land's abundant natural resources. With the coming of Europeans, however, the native groups were overrun and reduced in numbers.

NATIVES

As natives signed treaties, giving up traditional lands and settling on reserves (known as "reservations" in the United States), their lifestyles changed forever. They were no longer free to settle where they chose, they no longer hunted or fought, and their medicine men could do nothing to stop the spread of diseases brought by Europeans. The first Indian Act, drafted in 1876, attempted to prepare natives for "European" society, but it only ended up isolating them further.

Natives who are registered as members of a band are known as "status" Indians; that is, they have the right to use designated reserve lands and have access to federal funding. Originally, the Indian Act sought to assimilate natives by removing their "status" when they were considered ready to assimilate, such as when they earned a university degree, or in the case of native women, when they married a nonnative man. The Indian Act has been rewritten many times, including as recently as 1985, when many antiquated sections were repealed. The most important recent change was that natives didn't have to surrender their status to become a Canadian citizen and, therefore, vote and own property. As a direct result of these changes, many natives who had lost their status, or in fact never had it, have been reclaiming it over the last 30 years. Therefore, the population of status Indians has grown considerably in recent years. Today, 130,000 status Indians live in British Columbia and 85,000 in Alberta.

In the Northwest Territories, roughly half the population is of native descent. The Dene and Métis peoples are along the Mackenzie River Basin and the Inuit live above the treeline and along the Arctic coast.

NONNATIVES

When British Columbia joined the confederation to become a Canadian province in 1871, its population was only 36,000, and 27,000 of the residents were natives. A decade later, a Dominion census in 1881 recorded only 18,072 nonnatives in what would later become the province of Alberta. Calgary's nonnative population was recorded at just 75. With the completion of the Canadian Pacific Railway in 1885, Europeans came in droves—drawn first by game and arable land, then by mining, and later by the oil-and-gas boom of Alberta. People of many diverse cultures moved west, forming a melting pot of traditions. As early as 1921, 30 different languages were noted in Alberta alone, in addition to the many distinct languages of the natives.

Today 4.2 million people live in British Columbia and 3.2 million in Alberta. The two territories barely register a blip on the population meter, with 38,000 residents in the Northwest Territories and 31,000 in the Yukon. British Columbia holds 12 percent of Canada's total population, while Alberta has a little over 10 percent. Alberta is Canada's fastest growing province, with an annual population growth of 3 percent, double the national average. British Columbia is Canada's second fastest growing province. Around 60 percent of total population growth is attributed to westward migration across the country. Retirees make up a large percentage of these new arrivals, as do young professionals, to a lesser extent.

In British Columbia, the population is concentrated in the southwest, namely in Vancouver, on the south end of Vancouver Island, and in the Okanagan Valley. These three areas make up less than 1 percent of the province, but contain 80 percent of the population. Alberta's population is also concentrated in the cities; Calgary and Edmonton hold well over half the province's total population.

Around 40 percent of western Canadians are of British origin, followed by 30 percent of other European lineage, mostly French and German. To really get the British feeling, just spend some time in Victoria—a city that has retained its original English customs and traditions from days gone by. While the native peoples of western Canada have in many ways adopted the technology and the lifestyle of Europeans and their descendents, they still remain a distinct group, contributing to, and enriching the culture of, the province. Asians have made up a significant percentage of the population since the mid-1800s, when they arrived to work on the railway and then in search of gold.

CULTURE
Religion
While the importance of religion in western Canada's history is undeniable, Canadians in general are less religious today than they were 50 or even 30 years ago. Also skewing the numbers somewhat is the fact that, as elsewhere in western society, many Canadians identify themselves with a specific religion, but do not attend services.

Christianity is the dominant faith in western Canada, with 70 percent of the population identifying themselves with this faith. Around 30 percent are not aligned with any specific religion, while the remaining 5 percent are mostly Eastern faiths such as Islam. Roman Catholicism is the Christian denomination of choice for almost one in five British Columbians and one in four Albertans. The other major Christian denominations represented are Anglican and the United Church of Canada, with numbers of Presbyterian, Lutheran, and Baptist present but slowly declining. The Church of Jesus Christ of Latter-Day Saints is well represented in southwestern Alberta, especially in Cardston, which was settled by Mormons from Utah in 1887. Today, Mormonism is the religion of choice for around 75 percent of this town's population.

Mirroring the rest of Canada, the number of evangelicals—those in organizations like the Pentecostal Assemblies, but also within existing denominations—is on the rise. The vast majority of Muslims, Buddhists, Hindus, and Sikhs live in the major cities, most notably Vancouver. This city is home to half of Canada's 260,000 Sikhs, as well as 85,000 Buddhists and 56,000 Muslims. The number of Eastern religion adherents throughout western Canada has doubled in the last decade, mostly through immigration.

Language
English is the official language of both provinces and territories, and the first language of the vast majority of its residents. On a national level, Canada has two official languages—English and French. All communication from the federal government is in both languages, which becomes most apparent in national parks, where by law all signage and literature must be in both languages, and you will be greeted by parks' staff with "Hello, Bonjour." The Official Languages Act has many other components you will experience in everyday travel, including the requirement that Air Canada provide bilingual service and that most consumer goods sold within Canada have labeling in both English and French (exceptions include such things as books and items like jars of jam sold at fruit stands). French speakers (around 25 percent of the population) are concentrated in Quebec, but you'll experience pockets of Francophone culture in towns established by French fur traders, including St. Paul and La Crete (both in northern Alberta).

Arts and Crafts
The arts and crafts of Canada's indigenous people are available throughout western Canada. It tends to fall into one of two categories: "arts" such as woodcarving and painting, argillite carving, jade- and silverwork, and totem restoration (all generally attended to by the men); and "handicrafts" such as basketry, weaving, beadwork, skinwork, sewing, and knitting (generally created by women). Today, all of

these arts and crafts contribute significant income to First Nations communities.

Painting and woodcarving are probably the most recognized art forms of Pacific Northwest natives. Along the Pacific coast—in museums and people's homes, outdoors, and of course in all the shops—you can see brightly colored carved totems, canoes, paddles, fantastic masks, and ceremonial rattles, feast dishes, bowls, and spoons. Fabulous designs, many featuring animals or legends, are also painstakingly painted in bright primary colors on paper.

Basketry comes in a variety of styles and materials. Watch for decorative cedar-root (fairly rare) and cedar-bark baskets, still made on the west coast of Vancouver Island; spruce-root baskets from the Queen Charlotte Islands; and beautiful, functional, birch-bark baskets from Fort Liard (NWT). In Alberta, jewelry, beaded moccasins, baskets, and leatherwork such as headdresses are favorite souvenirs. And all outdoorspersons should consider forking out for a heavy, water-resistant, raw sheep's-wool sweater; they're generally white or gray with a black design, and much in demand because they're warm, good in the rain, rugged, and last a lifetime. One of the best places to get your hands on one is the Cowichan Valley (Vancouver Island).

Carved argillite (black slate) miniature totem poles, brooches, ashtrays, and other small items, highly decorated with geometric and animal designs, are created exclusively by the Haida on the Queen Charlotte Islands (Northern British Columbia).

ESSENTIALS

Getting There

BY AIR

Vancouver International Airport (YVR) is the gateway to Canada from around the Pacific Rim. Regularly scheduled service to and from Vancouver is offered by major airlines throughout the world. Victoria may be the capital of British Columbia, but it falls a distant second when it comes to international flights; the only destinations served from its international airport are major Canadian cities and Seattle. Calgary and Edmonton have international airports served by major airlines from throughout the world.

Many flights from the south are routed through Vancouver or Calgary before continuing to Edmonton, giving you a choice of final destinations for little or no price difference. Getting to Yellowknife or Whitehorse generally requires a plane change in Vancouver, Calgary, or Edmonton. Flights to these northern destinations, as well as smaller centers throughout the region, are usually made by local airlines that have code-share agreements with Air Canada, so you should have no trouble booking flights and making connections to even the most out-of-the-way place.

Air Canada

Canada's national carrier is Air Canada

(514/393-3333 or 888/247-2262, www.air-canada.ca). It offers direct flights to Vancouver from the following North American cities: Whitehorse, Calgary, Edmonton, Winnipeg, Toronto, Ottawa, Montreal, Halifax, Boston, Chicago, Dallas, Denver, Honolulu, Los Angeles, New York (JFK), Portland, San Francisco, Seattle, Spokane, and Washington, D.C. Air Canada also offers direct flights to Calgary from all major Canadian cities, as well as from Los Angeles, San Francisco, Las Vegas, Denver, Phoenix, Houston, Chicago, Washington, D.C., Dallas/Fort Worth, New York, and Orlando. Direct flights to Edmonton originate in all major Canadian cities west of Montreal, while flights from the U.S. cities noted above are routed through Vancouver or Calgary.

From Europe, Air Canada flies directly from London and Frankfurt to Calgary and Vancouver, and from other major European cities via Toronto. From the South Pacific, Air Canada operates flights from Sydney and, in alliance with Air New Zealand, from Auckland directly to Vancouver. Asian cities served by direct Air Canada flights to Vancouver include Beijing, Nagoya, Osaka, Seoul, Shanghai, Taipei, and Tokyo. Air Canada's flights originating in the South American cities of Buenos Aires, Sao Paulo, Lima, and Bogotá are routed through Toronto, where you'll need to change planes for your western destination.

WestJet

Similar in concept to Southwest Airlines, WestJet (604/606-5525 or 800/538-5696, www.westjet.com) has daily flights to and from the following Canadian cities: Victoria, Vancouver, Calgary, Edmonton, Regina, Saskatoon, Winnipeg, Thunder Bay, Hamilton, Toronto, Ottawa, Montreal, Halifax, and as far east as St. John's, Newfoundland.

U.S. Airlines

Air Canada offers most flights into western Canada from the United States, but Vancouver, Calgary, and Edmonton are also served by the following U.S. carriers: **Alaska**

Airlines (800/252-7522, www.alaksaair.com) from Anchorage and Los Angeles; **American Airlines** (800/433-7300, www.aa.com) from Chicago and Dallas; **Continental Airlines** (800/231-0856, www.continental.com) from its Houston hub and New York (Newark); **Delta** (800/221-1212, www.delta.com) with summer-only flights from Atlanta and Salt Lake City; **Frontier Airlines** (800/432-1359, www.frontierairlines.com) from Denver; **Harmony Airways** (866/868-6789, www.harmonyairways.com) from Honolulu, Kahului, and Los Angeles; **Horizon Air** (800/547-9308, www.horizonair.com) from Seattle; **Northwest Airlines** (800/225-2525, www.nwa.com) from Detroit, Memphis, and Minneapolis; and finally, **United Airlines** (800/241-6522, www.united.com) from Chicago, Denver, San Francisco, and Seattle.

Other International Airlines

British Airlines (800/247-9297, www.britishairlines.com) flies daily between London and Vancouver. **KLM** (604/278-3485, www.klm.nl) flies nonstop to Calgary and Vancouver from Amsterdam, and **Lufthansa** (800/563-5954, www.lufthansa.de) from Frankfurt.

Qantas (800/227-4500, www.qantas.com.au) flies from Sydney to Vancouver, while flights originating in Melbourne and Brisbane are routed through Los Angeles. **Air New Zealand** (800/663-5494, www.airnewzealand.com) operates in alliance with Air Canada, with a change of airline in Honolulu or Los Angeles. This airline makes flights throughout the South Pacific, including Nandi (Fiji). **Air Pacific** (800/227-4446, www.airpacific.com) flies from points throughout the Pacific to Honolulu and then on to Vancouver.

BY RAIL

This form of transportation, which opened up the West to settlers, began to fade with the advent of efficient air services. Today, however, improved service, a refitting of carriages, a competitive pricing structure, and the luxurious privately operated Rocky Mountaineer have helped trains regain popularity in western

Canada. Scheduled services along the original transcontinental line through Calgary and Banff ended in 1991, but continue along a northern route.

VIA Rail

The *Canadian* runs between Toronto and Vancouver via Edmonton and Jasper three days a week in either direction and provides two classes of travel: Economy, which features lots of leg room, reclining seats, reading lights, pillows and blankets, and a Skyline Car complete with bar service; and Silver and Blue, which is more luxurious, featuring a variety of sleeping-room configurations, daytime seating, a domed lounge and dining car reserved exclusively for passengers in this class, shower kits for all passengers, and all meals.

If you're traveling to Alberta from the eastern provinces, the least expensive way to travel is on a **Canrailpass,** which allows unlimited travel anywhere on the VIA Rail system for 12 days within any given 30-day period. During high season (June 1–Oct. 15) the pass is adult $923, senior (over 60) and child $831, with extra days (up to three are allowed) $79 and $71 respectively. The rest of the year the fare is adult $576, senior and child $518, with extra days $49 and $44, respectively.

On regular fares, discounts of 25–40 percent apply to travel in all classes October–June. Those over 60 and under 18, as well as students under 25, receive an additional 10 percent discount that can be combined with other seasonal fares. Check for advance-purchase restrictions on all discount tickets.

BY BUS

Greyhound (403/260-0877 or 800/661-8747, www.greyhound.ca) serves areas throughout Canada. From the east, buses depart Toronto daily for Vancouver via two different routes—one through Calgary, the other through Edmonton. From Vancouver, the main routes are north through Prince George to Whitehorse, west along the TransCanada Highway to Banff and Calgary, and a more northern route to Jasper and Edmonton.

Travel by Greyhound is simple—just roll up at the depot and buy a ticket. No reservations are necessary. Greyhound bus depots in all cities and towns are centrally located and linked to other public transportation (or, at the very least, cabs meet all arrivals). Always check for any promotional fares available at the time of your travel. Regular-fare tickets are valid for one year and allow unlimited stopovers between paid destinations.

When calling for ticket information, ask about any special deals. Other discounts apply to regular-fare tickets bought 7, 14 days, and 21 days in advance, to travelers 65 and over, and to 2 people traveling together. Greyhound's **Discovery Pass,** valid for unlimited travel throughout North America, is sold in periods of 7 days ($199), 15 days ($299), 30 days ($399), and 60 days ($499). Passes can be bought 14 or more days in advance online, 7 or more days in advance from any Canadian bus depot, or up to the day of departure from U.S. depots.

BY FERRY

One of the most pleasurable ways to get your first view of Canada is from sea level. Many scheduled ferry services cross from Washington State to Victoria (Vancouver Island), but no ferries run to Vancouver from south of the border.

From Washington State

The **Victoria Clipper** (206/448-5000 or 800/888-2535, www.victoriaclipper.com) is a fast passenger-only service connecting Seattle's Pier 69 with Victoria. From farther north, at Anacortes, **Washington State Ferries** (250/381-1551, www.wsdot.wa.gov/ferries) runs a once-daily passenger and vehicle service to Sidney, 30 kilometers (18.6 miles) north of Victoria. If you're traveling up the east coast of Washington State to Vancouver Island and want to bypass the built-up corridor between Tacoma and the international border, consider heading out to Port Angeles on the Olympic Peninsula, where the **MV Coho** (360/457-4491, www.cohoferry.com) departs for a twice daily crossing to Victoria.

BY CAR OR RV

Most visitors to western Canada travel in their own vehicle, or rent one upon arrival. Driver's licenses from all countries are valid in Canada for up to three months. You should also obtain a one-year **International Driving Permit** before leaving home if the license from you home country is in a language other than English. Inexpensive and available from most motoring organizations, they allow you to drive in Canada (in conjunction with your regular license), without taking a test, for up to three months. You should also carry car registration papers or rental contracts. Proof of insurance must also be carried, and you must wear seat belts. All highway signs in Canada give distances in **kilometers** and speeds in **kilometers per hour** (kph). The speed limit on most major highways is 100 kph (62 mph).

Insurance

If entering Canada from the United States in your own vehicle, check that your insurance covers travel in Canada. U.S. motorists are advised to obtain a Canadian Non-Resident Inter-Provincial Motor Vehicle Liability Insurance Card, available through U.S. insurance companies, which is accepted as evidence of financial responsibility in Canada.

When renting a vehicle in Canada you have the option of purchasing a Loss Damage Waiver, along with other types of insurance, such as for your personal effects. Before leaving home, find out if you're already covered. Many people are—through gold credit cards, higher levels of motoring association membership, or home insurance (in the case of personal effects)—and additional coverage may be unnecessary.

Crossing into Canada by Land

Ports of Entry (border crossings) are spread at regular intervals along the entire U.S./Canada border. The main port of entry into British Columbia is **Peace Arch,** south of Vancouver. **Coutts/Sweetgrass,** north of Great Falls, Montana, along Highway 14, is the main crossing into Alberta. Both posts are open 24 hours daily.

Getting Around

BY AIR

Air Canada Jazz, a connector airline for Air Canada, offers scheduled flights to all cities and many larger towns within British Columbia and Alberta. Flights are booked through Air Canada (514/369-1386 or 888/247-2262, www.aircanada.com). **Pacific Coastal Airlines** (604/273-8666 or 800/663-2872, www.pacific-coastal.com) flies to towns on Vancouver Island, along the Sunshine Coast, and as far north as the Queen Charlotte Islands from Vancouver and Victoria. **Harbour Air** (604/274-1277 or 800/665-0212, www.harbour-air.com) links Vancouver, Victoria, and Nanaimo with scheduled seaplane service. **Hawk Air** (250/635-4295 or 800/487-1216, www.hawkair.net) flies throughout northern British Columbia from Vancouver. **Central Mountain Air** (250/877-5000 or 888/865-8585, www.flycma.com) serves towns throughout both British Columbia and Alberta, but the only direct link between the two is a daily Edmonton–Fort St. John flight.

The main northern carrier is **First Air** (613/254-6200 or 800/267-1247, www.firstair.ca), which flies as far south as Edmonton, as well as to Inuvik and Whitehorse, and throughout Nunavut from Yellowknife. With flights from Calgary and Edmonton, **Canadian North** (867/873-4484 or 800/661-1505, www.canadiannorth.com) links all the major northern centers with daily flights, and flies as far south as Calgary and Ottawa. Meanwhile, **Northwestern Air** (867/872-2216 or 877/872-2216, www.nwal.ca) flies to Yellowknife via Hay River and Fort Smith from Edmonton. Finally, **Air**

North (867/668-2228 or 800/661-0407, www.flyairnorth.com) flies to Whitehorse and throughout the Yukon from Vancouver, Calgary, and Edmonton.

BY RAIL

The only scheduled rail service in western Canada is along the transcontinental line from Vancouver to Jasper and Edmonton. The other option is the privately operated Rocky Mountaineer.

Rocky Mountaineer

Rocky Mountaineer Vacations (604/606-2245 or 800/665-7245, www.rockymountaineer. com) operates a summer-only luxurious rail trip through the interior of British Columbia between Vancouver and Banff or Jasper. A third route links Whistler and Vancouver via the Cariboo region of central British Columbia. Travel is during daylight hours only so you don't miss anything. Trains depart in either direction in the morning (every second or third day), overnighting at Kamloops or Quesnel. One-way travel in RedLeaf Service, which includes light meals, nonalcoholic drinks, and Kamloops accommodations, costs $859 per person d from Vancouver to either Banff or Jasper and $959 from Vancouver to Calgary. GoldLeaf Service is the ultimate in luxury. Passengers ride in a two-story glass-domed car, eat in a separate dining area, and stay in Kamloops's most luxurious accommodations. GoldLeaf costs $1,739 per person from Vancouver to Banff or Jasper and $1889 to Calgary

The same company also operates the **Whistler Mountaineer** (604/606-2245 or 800/665-7245, www.whistlermountaineer. com, May–mid-Oct.) between Vancouver and Whistler. The fare for a round-trip is adult $199 or $249, depending on the class of travel.

BY BUS

Greyhound (800/661-8747, www.greyhound. ca) bus routes radiate from all major cities including Vancouver, Victoria, Calgary, and Edmonton. Northern terminuses of

Greyhound service are Hay River (Northwest Territories) and Whitehorse (Yukon). Getting to Vancouver Island is easy with **Pacific Coach Lines** (604/662-8074 or 800/661-1725, www. pacificcoach.com), which provides bus service between Victoria and both Vancouver city center and Vancouver International Airport. In Alberta, **Brewster** (403/221-8242, www. brewster.ca) provides coach service between Calgary and Banff and Jasper National Parks, while **Red Arrow** (780/424-3339 or 800/232-1958, www.redarrow.ca) connects Calgary, Edmonton, and the oil sands city of Fort McMurray.

BY FERRY

Many interior lakes and rivers are crossed by ferries owned and operated by the government. Of course, no service is available between freeze-up and breakup, but the rest of year, expect daily service from 6 A.M. until at least 10 P.M. Some of the ferries are small, capable of carrying just two vehicles, while others can transport up to 50. Passage is free on all these ferries, including the 45-minute sailing across Kootenay Lake between Balfour and Kootenay Bay (Southern Interior)—the world's longest free ferry trip.

BC Ferries

Government-owned BC Ferries (250/386-3431 or 888/223-3779, www.bcferries.com) serves 46 ports with a fleet of 40 vessels. All fares listed for "vehicles" in this book cover vehicles up to 20 feet long and under seven feet high (or under six feet, eight inches high on a few routes). Larger vehicles such as RVs pay more. Also note that prices listed for all types of vehicles are in addition to the passenger price; the vehicle's driver is not included in the vehicle fare.

Vancouver has two major ferry terminals. From Tsawwassen, south of downtown, ferries run regularly across the Strait of Georgia to the Vancouver Island centers of Swartz Bay (north of Victoria) and Nanaimo. From Horseshoe Bay, west of downtown Vancouver, ferries ply the strait to Nanaimo. Also from Horseshoe Bay,

© CAPRICORNIS/123RF.COM

ferry in Horseshoe Bay near Vancouver

ferries run across Howe Sound to Langdale, gateway to the Sunshine Coast. From Powell River, at the north end of the Sunshine Coast, ferries depart for Comox (Vancouver Island), making it possible to visit both Vancouver Island and the Sunshine Coast without returning to Vancouver. BC Ferries also provides regular services from Vancouver Island to populated islands in the Strait of Georgia.

From Port Hardy at the northern tip of Vancouver Island, a ferry runs north up the coast to Prince Rupert. From the end of May through September the ferry goes every other day, October–April once a week, and during May twice a week. The trip takes 15 hours and links up with the Alaska Marine Highway. Also from Prince Rupert, ferries run out to the Queen Charlotte Islands. These longer sailings require reservations, which should be made as far in advance as possible.

CAR AND RV RENTAL

All major car-rental agencies have outlets at Vancouver, Victoria, Calgary, and Edmonton International Airports as well as at smaller airports like Kelowna, Yellowknife, and Whitehorse. To ensure that a vehicle is available for you when you arrive, book in advance, especially during the busy June–September period.

In summer, expect to pay around $60 per day for an Economy or Compact car, $75 for an Intermediate, $85–100 for a Full Size, and over $100 for an SUV. Between late September and mid-June all vehicles are heavily discounted, with smaller vehicles available from $40 per day and $210 per week. Most major agencies offer unlimited mileage, but not for rentals originating in Banff or Jasper National Parks, or in northern destinations like Yellowknife and Whitehorse. In all cases, insurance costs from $20 per day and is compulsory unless covered by a personal policy or on your credit card. Charges apply if you need to drop off the car at an agency other than the rental location. All agencies provide free pickup and drop-off at major city hotels.

Vehicles can be booked through parent companies in the United States or elsewhere using the Web or toll-free numbers. **Discount** (403/299-1202 or 800/263-2355, www.discountcar.com) is a Canadian company with 200 rental outlets across the country. Their vehicles are kept in service a little longer than the other majors, but they provide excellent rates—even through summer—especially if booked in advance. Other companies include **Avis** (800/974-0808, www.avis.ca), **Budget** (800/268-8900, www.budget.com), **Discount** (800/263-2355, www.discountcar.com), **Dollar** (800/800-4000, www.dollar.com), **Enterprise** (800/325-8007, www.enterprise.com), **Hertz** (800/263-0600, www.hertz.ca), **National** (800/227-7368, www.nationalcar.com), **Rent-a-Wreck** (800/327-0116, www.rentawreck.ca), and **Thrifty** (800/847-4389, www.thrifty.com).

RV Rental
Camper vans, RVs, and travel trailers are a great way to get around western Canada without having to worry about accommodations each night. The downside is cost. The smallest vans, capable of sleeping two people, start at $150 per day with 100 free kilometers (62 miles) per day. Extra charges include insurance, a preparation fee (usually around $50 per rental), a linen/cutlery charge (around $60 per person per trip), and taxes. Major agencies, with rental outlets in Vancouver and Calgary, include **Cruise Canada** (403/291-4963 or 800/671-8042, or in the U.S. 800/327-7778, www.cruisecanada.com), **CanaDream** (403/291-1000 or 800/461-7368, www.canadream.com), **Fraserway** (604/527-1102 or 877/747-7947, www.fraserway.com), and **Go West** (403/240-1814 or 800/661-8813, www.go-west.com). In most cases, a drop-off fee of $400 applies to drop-offs made in Vancouver from rentals originating in Calgary, or vice versa. Whitehorse is a mini-hub for RV rentals, with CanadaDream, Fraserway, and locally owned **Klondike RV Rentals** (867/456-2729, www.yukonrecreation.com) represented. The former two often have package deals with minimal drop-fees in Vancouver. At the end of the summer season (early September), look for some great online bargains all around.

Visas and Officialdom

ENTRY FOR U.S. CITIZENS
Citizens and permanent residents of the United States are required to carry a passport for both entry to Canada and for re-entry to the United States. For further information, see the website http://travel.state.gov/travel. For current entry requirements to Canada, check the Citizenship and Immigration Canada website (www.cic.gc.ca).

ENTRY FOR OTHER FOREIGN VISITORS
All other foreign visitors entering Canada must have a valid passport and may need a visitor permit or Temporary Resident Visa depending on their country of residence and the vagaries of international politics. At present, visas are not required for citizens of the United States, British Commonwealth, or Western Europe. The standard entry permit is for six months, and you may be asked to show onward tickets or proof of sufficient funds to last you through your intended stay. Extensions are available from the Citizenship and Immigration Canada office in Calgary. This department's website (www.cic.gc.ca) is the best source for the latest entry requirements.

CLEARING CUSTOMS
You can take the following into Canada duty-free: reasonable quantities of clothes and personal effects, 50 cigars and 200 cigarettes, 200 grams of tobacco, 1.14 liters of spirits or wine, food for personal use, and gas (normal tank capacity). Pets from the United States can generally be brought into Canada, with certain caveats. Dogs and cats must be more than three months old and have a rabies certificate showing date of vaccination. Birds can be brought in only if they have not been

mixing with other birds, and parrots need an export permit because they're on the endangered species list.

Handguns, automatic and semiautomatic weapons, and sawn-off rifles and shotguns are not allowed into Canada. Visitors with firearms must declare them at the border; restricted weapons will be held by Customs and can be picked up on exit from the country. Those not declared will be seized and charges may be laid. It is illegal to possess any firearm in a national park unless it is dismantled or carried in an enclosed case. Up to 5,000 rounds of ammunition may be imported but should be declared on entry.

If you've been in Canada more than 48 hours, on reentering the United States, you can bring back up to US$400 worth of household and personal items, excluding alcohol and tobacco, duty-free. If you've been in Canada fewer than 48 hours, you may bring in only up to US$200 worth of such items duty-free.

For further information on all customs regulations contact **Canada Border Services Agency** (204/983-3500 or 800/461-9999, www.cbsa-asfc.gc.ca).

Recreation

The great outdoors: Western Canada certainly has plenty of it. With spectacular scenery around every bend, millions of hectares of parkland, and an abundance of wildlife, the region is an outdoorsperson's fantasy come true. Hiking, fishing, golfing, canoeing, kayaking, white-water rafting, scuba diving, downhill and cross-country skiing—it's all here.

HIKING

Just about everywhere you go in western Canada you'll find good hiking opportunities, from short walks in urban parks to backcountry treks through untamed wilderness. Best of all, it's free.

In British Columbia the regional parks surrounding Vancouver have a wide variety of trails, while over on Vancouver Island the challenging **West Coast Trail** is renowned for its coastal scenery. Many provincial parks scattered through the province—Garibaldi, Manning, Kokanee Glacier, and more—hold a range of hikes, but always with mountain scenery as a backdrop. The national parks of the Canadian Rockies hold the greatest concentration of hiking trails. Here you can find anything from short interpretive trails with little elevation gain to strenuous slogs up high alpine passes. Some trails are accessible from downtown Banff, while others require some advance planning, like those around Lake O'Hara (Yoho National Park), which are on a quota system.

Heli-hiking is an out-of-the-ordinary way to experience the high alpine without making the elevation gain on foot. The day starts with a helicopter ride into the mountains, where short, guided hikes are offered and a picnic lunch is served. Whistler, Valemount, and Canmore are bases for heli-hiking operations.

CYCLING AND MOUNTAIN BIKING

Cycling is a great way to explore western Canada. The casual pace allows riders time to stop and appreciate the scenery, wildlife, and flowers that can easily be overlooked at high speeds. Some of the most popular areas for road cycling trips are the **Southern Gulf Islands** (quiet, laid-back, loads of sunshine, rural scenery, and lots of artists), **Vancouver Island** (following the Strait of Georgia past lazy beaches and bustling resort towns), and the **Canadian Rockies** (endless mountain scenery). One of the most challenging and scenic on-road routes is the **Icefields Parkway** between Lake Louise and Jasper, which has several well-placed hostels along its length.

Bike rentals are available in all cities and resort towns. Expect to pay $5–10 per hour and $25–30 per day for a regular town bike and from $15 per hour and $45 per day for a full-suspension mountain bike.

Cycle Tours

Backroads (510/527-1555 or 800/462-2848, www.backroads.com) offers cycling tours around the Southern Gulf Islands (Vancouver Island) and through the Canadian Rockies. These excursions are designed to suit all levels of fitness and all budgets. An average of six hours is spent cycling each day, but the less ambitious always have the option of riding in the support van. The cost for a six-day trip, inclusive of luxurious accommodations, is US$3,500. A local company with a long-standing track record is **Backroads Whistler** (604/923-3111, www.backroadswhistler.com), with tours through the Whistler Valley and beyond.

HORSEBACK RIDING

Horses are a traditional means of transportation in the Canadian West; many of the roads began as horse trails. Through the foothills

© ANDREW HEMPSTEAD

horseback riding in the Canadian Rockies

of Alberta, ranches still dominate the landscape, and at places like **Griffin Valley Ranch** (near Calgary), unguided riding is permitted. Within the national parks of the Canadian Rockies, horse travel is restricted to certain areas, but trail riding is a popular way to enjoy the scenery. Overnight pack-trips present another option in these mountains. On these, expect to ride for up to six hours per day, with nights spent at a remote mountain lodge or a tent camp, usually in a scenic location where you can hike, fish, or ride farther. Rates range $150–240 per person per day, which includes the riding, accommodations, and food.

Guest ranches, where accommodations and meals are included in nightly packages, include ultra-luxurious **Echo Valley Ranch & Spa** (250/459-2386 or 800/253-8831, www.evranch.com) in the Cariboo (Central British Columbia), **Boundary Ranch,** in Kananaskis Country (403/591-7171 or 877/591-7177, www.boundaryranch.com), and **Black Cat Guest Ranch,** near Hinton in Northern Alberta (780/865-3084 or 800/859-6840, www.blackcatguestranch.ca). Expect to pay from $140 per person per day for accommodations, meals, and trail riding.

FISHING
Freshwater

Fishing is productive in literally thousands of rivers and lakes across western Canada. Hundreds of lakes are stocked at least annually. Rainbow trout are to western Canada what bass are to the eastern United States—a great fighting fish. They are found in lakes and rivers throughout the west and are the most common of the stocked fish because they're easy to raise and can adapt to various conditions. You can catch them on artificial flies, small spinners, or spoons.

One particular type of rainbow trout, the large anadromous steelhead, is renowned as a fighting fish. They are caught along the Pacific Coast in northern rivers such as the Skeena. The largest species of trout is the lake trout. The largest "lakies" generally come from northern lakes, including Cold Lake

WILDLIFE AND YOU

The abundance of wildlife in western Canada is one of the region's biggest attractions. To help preserve this unique resource, use common sense.

- **Do not feed the animals.** Many animals may seem tame, but feeding them endangers yourself, the animal, and other visitors, as animals become aggressive when looking for handouts.

- **Store food safely.** When camping, keep food in your vehicle or out of reach of animals. Just leaving it in a cooler isn't good enough.

- **Keep your distance.** Although it's tempting to get close to animals for a better look or photograph, it disturbs the animal and, in many cases, can be dangerous.

- **Drive carefully.** The most common cause of premature death for larger mammals is being hit by vehicles.

catch with anglers, mostly because they taste so good. The largest northern pike (up to 17 kg/38 lbs) inhabit northern lakes and rivers. Jigging with a large lure around the weedy extremes of large lakes gives the angler the best chance of hooking one of these monsters. Perch, at the other end of the size scale from pike, but inhabiting the same shallow waters, are a fun, easy-to-catch fish—if you see kids fishing off a pier, chances are they're after perch. Arctic grayling, easily identified by a large dorsal fin, are common in cool clear lakes and streams throughout the far north of Alberta. These delicious-tasting fish are most often taken on dry flies, but their soft mouths make keeping them hooked somewhat of a challenge.

The Northwest Territories is a legendary destination for serious anglers. Inland lakes and rivers are the domain of trophy-size lake trout, arctic grayling, walleye, and northern pike (jackfish). Great Bear Lake holds world records in *every* class of lake trout and arctic grayling (including a 34.5-kilogram/76-pound lake trout). The arctic char, caught in rivers, lakes, and the open ocean of the Arctic coast and Arctic archipelago, is famous both as a fighting fish and as an acclaimed Northern delicacy.

Freshwater Licenses

British Columbia licenses: Prices vary according to your age and place of residence. British Columbia residents pay $36 for a freshwater adult license, good for one year. All other Canadians pay $20 for a one-day license, $36 for an eight-day license, or $55 for a one-year license. Nonresidents of Canada pay $20, $50, and $80, respectively. For more information visit www.fishing.gov.bc.ca.

Alberta licenses: Alberta has an automated licensing system, with licenses sold in sporting stores, gas stations, and so forth. To use the system, a **Wildlife Identification Number** (WIN) card is needed. These cards are sold by all license vendors and cost $8 (valid for five years). An annual license for Canadian residents age 16 and older is $26; for nonresidents it is $71, $48 for a five-day license, or $27 for a single day. The *Alberta Guide to Sportfishing*

(Northern Alberta). A more central spot is Lake Minnewanka (Banff National Park). Both these lakes have boat rentals and guides. Fishing for cutthroat, which inhabit the highest mountain lakes, requires using the lightest of tackle because the water is generally very clear. Brook trout are found in rivers and lakes throughout the Canadian Rockies. Brown trout are widespread: Most often caught on dry flies, they are difficult to hook onto.

Kokanee rarely grow to more than one kilogram (2.2 pounds), but this freshwater salmon is an excellent sport fish inhabiting lakes of interior British Columbia. Feeding near the surface and caught on wet or dry artificial flies, they taste great, especially when smoked. Walleye (also called pickerel) grow to 4.5 kilograms (10 pounds) and are common in sandy-bottomed areas of lakes throughout the prairies and northern British Columbia. They are a popular

Regulations, which outlines all of the open seasons and bag limits, is available from outlets selling licenses, as well as online at www.my-wildalberta.com.

Northwest Territories licenses: In the NWT, a three-day license costs $15 for Canadians, $30 for nonresidents. A season license is $20 or $40, respectively. To download a *Northwest Territories Sport Fishing Guide* go to the website of Environment and Natural Resources (www.enr.gov.nt.ca).

Yukon licenses: The Department of Environment website (http://environmentyukon.gov.yk.ca) is the best source for Yukon license information. Canadians pay $15 for six days, or $25 to fish for the entire season. Nonresidents of Canada pay $10 and $35 respectively.

NATIONAL PARK PASSES

Passes are required for entry into most of western Canada's national parks (the exception is Wood Buffalo). The cost of a **National Parks Day Pass** is adult $7.90-9.80, senior $6.90-7.75, and child $3.90-4.90, depending on the park. There is a maximum per-vehicle entry fee of double the adult (or senior for vehicles carrying only seniors) rate. Passes are interchangeable between parks and are valid until 4 P.M. the day following purchase.

An annual **National Parks of Canada Pass,** good for entry into all Canadian national parks for one year from the date of purchase, is adult $53, senior $45, child $27, to a maximum of $107 per vehicle. The annual **Discovery Package** includes entry into all parks as well as Parks Canada-managed National Historic Sites for $85, senior $73, child $42, to a maximum of $166 per vehicle.

Passes can be purchased at park gates, at all park information centers, and at campground fee stations. For more information, check the Parks Canada website (www.pc.gc.ca).

National park licenses: Fishing in national parks requires a separate license, which is available from park offices and some sport shops; $10 for a one-day license, $35 for an annual license.

Tidal

The tidal waters of British Columbia hold some of the world's best fishing—Port Alberni, Tofino, Campbell River, and Port Hardy, all on Vancouver Island, are popular bases. The five species of Pacific salmon are most highly prized by anglers. The chinook (king) salmon in particular is the trophy fish of choice. They commonly weigh over 10 kilograms (22 pounds) and are occasionally caught at over 20 kilograms (44 pounds). Other salmon present are coho (silver), pink (humpback), sockeye (red), and chum (dog). Other species sought by recreational anglers include halibut, lingcod, rockfish, cod, perch, and snapper.

A tidal-water sportfishing license for Canadian residents, good for one year from March 31, costs $22.05 ($11.55 for those 65 and over); for nonresidents of Canada, the same license costs $106.05, or pay $7.35 for a single-day license, $19.95 for three days, or $32.55 for five days. A salmon conservation stamp is an additional $6.30. Licenses are available from sporting stores, gas stations, marinas, and charter operators. For further information contact **Fisheries and Oceans Canada** (604/666-0566, www.pac.dfo-mpo.gc.ca).

The **Sport Fishing Institute of British Columbia** (604/270-3439, www.sportfishing.bc.ca) produces a free annual magazine, *Sport Fishing,* that lists charter operators and fishing lodges, and details license requirements.

CANOEING AND KAYAKING

Canoes are a traditional form of transportation throughout western Canada. You can rent one at many of the more popular lakes, but if you bring your own you can slip into any body of water whenever you please, taking advantage of an unparalleled opportunity for admiring scenery and viewing wildlife from water level. One of the most popular backcountry canoe routes is in Bowron Lake

Canoeing is fun for all ages.

Provincial Park (Central British Columbia), where a 117-kilometer (73-mile) circuit leads through a chain of lakes in the Cariboo Mountains. **Paddle Canada** (613/547-3196 or 888/252-6292, www.paddlingcanada.com) represents qualified guides and can recommend canoe routes.

Anywhere suitable for canoeing is also prime kayaking territory, although most keen kayakers look for white-water excitement. The best wilderness kayaking experiences are in the interior of British Columbia and the Canadian Rockies.

The British Columbia coastline is great for sea kayaking, and rentals are available in most coastal communities. The Southern Gulf Islands (Vancouver Island) are ideal for kayakers of all experience levels, while destinations such as Desolation Sound (vicinity of Vancouver), the Broken Group Islands (Vancouver Island), and the Queen Charlotte Islands (northern British Columbia) are the domain of experienced paddlers.

Most outfits offering kayak rentals also provide lessons and often tours. One such Vancouver operation is the **Ecomarine Ocean Kayak Centre** (604/689-7575, www.ecomarine.com). Tofino, on Vancouver Island's west coast, is a popular base for sea kayakers. Here, **Tofino Sea Kayaking Company** (250/725-4222 or 800/863-4664, www.tofino-kayaking.com) rents kayaks and leads tours through local waterways.

WHITE-WATER RAFTING

The best and easiest way to experience a white-water rafting trip is on a half- or full-day trip with a qualified guide. In the vicinity of Vancouver, the Green, Fraser, Nahatlatch, and Thompson Rivers are run commercially. In the Canadian Rockies, the Kicking Horse, Sunwapta, and Kananaskis Rivers provide the thrills. Expect to pay $90–140 for a full day's excitement, transfers, and lunch.

For those with some experience in both river *and* wilderness travel, there are some excellent opportunities for extended river trips. Close to Vancouver, the classic of these run

© ANDREW HEMPSTEAD

the Chilko, Chilcotin, then Fraser Rivers and lasts up to two weeks. In the far north of the province, the Tatshenshini and Alsek Rivers are popular destinations, while in the Northwest Territories the legendary South Nahanni River is at the top of many people's to-do list.

BOATING

British Columbia's 25,000 kilometers (15,535 miles) of coastline, in particular the sheltered, island-dotted Strait of Georgia between Vancouver Island and the mainland, is a boater's paradise. Along it are sheltered coves, sandy beaches, beautiful marine parks, and facilities specifically designed for boaters—many accessible only by water. One of the most beautiful marine parks is Desolation Sound, north of Powell River (vicinity of Vancouver).

SCUBA DIVING

Some of the world's most varied and spectacular cold-water diving lies off the coast of British Columbia. Diving is best in winter, when you can expect up to 40 meters (130 feet) of visibility. The diverse marinelife includes sponges, anemones, soft corals, rockfish (china, vermilion, and canary), rock scallops, and cukes. Plenty of shipwrecks also dot the underwater terrain. *Diver* magazine is a good source of local information; its scuba directory lists retail stores, resorts, charter boats, and other services. The most popular dive sites are off the Gulf Islands, Nanaimo, Campbell River, and Powell River (the scuba diving capital of Canada). Many of the coastal communities along Vancouver Island and the Sunshine Coast have dive shops with gear rentals and air tanks, and many can put you in touch with charter dive boats and guides. Being landlocked, Alberta is not renowned for scuba diving. A few interesting opportunities do exist, however, including the flooded townsite of Minnewanka Landing in Banff National Park.

GOLF

With beautiful scenery, long sunny days, and more than 500 courses, western Canada is an ideal spot for golfers. Some of the world's best-known golf courses are in western Canada, along with hundreds you've probably never heard of, including a few in the Northwest Territories and the Yukon with artificial grass greens. Municipal courses offer the lowest greens fees, generally $10–25, but the semi-private, private, and resort courses usually boast the most spectacular locations. At these courses, greens fees can be more than $200. At all but the smallest municipal courses, club rentals, power carts, and lessons are available; and at all but the most exclusive city courses, nonmembers are welcomed with open arms.

SKIING AND SNOWBOARDING

Most of the developed winter recreation areas are in the southern half of British Columbia and in the Canadian Rockies. Whether you're a total beginner or an advanced daredevil, you'll find slopes to suit. The price of lift tickets is generally reasonable, and at the smaller, lesser-known resorts, you don't have to spend half your day lining up for the lifts. Generally resorts are open December–April. The best known of the British Columbian resorts is **Whistler/Blackcomb** (vicinity of Vancouver), but others scattered through the southern interior provide world-class skiing and snowboarding on just-as-challenging slopes. The best of these include **Big White Ski Resort, Silver Star Mountain Resort, Red Mountain, Whitewater, Fernie Alpine Resort,** and **Panorama Resort** (southern British Columbia); and **Sun Peaks Resort** (central and northern British Columbia). Banff National Park is home to Canada's second largest resort, **Lake Louise,** as well as **Sunshine Village** and **Ski Norquay. Nakiska** (vicinity of Calgary) was developed for the 1988 Olympic Winter Games.

Heli- and Sno-Cat Skiing and Snowboarding

Alternatives to resorts are also available. If you're an intermediate or advanced skier or snowboarder, you can go heli-skiing and heli-boarding in the mind-boggling scenery

ALPINE CLUB OF CANADA

The Alpine Club of Canada (ACC), like similar clubs in the United States and Great Britain, is a non-profit mountaineering organization whose objectives include the encouragement of mountaineering through educational programs, the exploration and study of alpine and glacial regions, and the preservation of mountain flora and fauna.

The club was formed in 1906, mainly through the tireless campaign of its first president, Arthur Wheeler. A list of early members will be familiar to all Canadian mountaineers – Bill Peyto, Tom Wilson, Byron Harmon, Mary Schäffer. Today the club membership includes 3,000 alpinists from throughout Canada.

The club's ongoing projects include operating the Canadian Alpine Centre (Lake Louise Hostel), maintaining a system of 20 huts throughout the backcountry of the Canadian Rockies, and publishing the annual *Canadian Alpine Journal* – the country's only record of mountaineering accomplishments. A reference library of the club's history is kept at the Whyte Museum of the Canadian Rockies in Banff.

For further information and membership details, contact club headquarters in Canmore, Alberta (403/678-3200, www.alpineclubofcanada.ca).

and deep, untracked powder of the Coast and Chilcotin Ranges, the central Cariboo Mountains, and the Bugaboos. The world's largest heli-ski operation is **CMH Heli-skiing** (403/762-7100 or 800/661-0252, www.cmhski.com), which includes almost limitless terrain over five mountain ranges accessed from 11 lodges. **Mike Wiegele Helicopter Skiing** (250/673-8381 or 800/661-9170, www.wiegele.com) offers heli-skiing and heli-boarding in the Monashee and Cariboo Mountains from a luxurious lodge at Blue River.

Another, less-expensive alternative is to hook up with one of the many Sno-Cat operations in the province. Sno-Cats are tracked, all-terrain vehicles (similar to snow groomers but capable of carrying passengers) that can transport skiers and snowboarders up through the snow to virgin slopes in high-country wilderness. British Columbia has been a world leader in this type of skiing, and many operators are scattered through the province. **Revelstoke Mountain Resort** (250/837-2188, www.discoverrevelstoke.com) offers the best of both worlds—this alpine resort in central British Columbia offers lift accessed skiing and boarding, plus cat- and heli-skiing. Thanks to its location amid some of the continent's most consistent powder snow, **Island Lake Lodge** (near Fernie, 250/423-3700 or 888/422-8754, www.islandlakelodge.com) has gained a reputation for both its Sno-Cat skiing and boarding and its luxurious lodgings.

Accommodations

The good news is that western Canada has a wide range of accommodations to suit all budgets. The very best options are detailed through the book, while this section broadly describes various accommodation types, as well as some hints on saving money along the way.

Tourism offices in Alberta (**Travel Alberta,** 780/427-4321 or 800/252-3782, www.travelalberta.com) and British Columbia (**Tourism**

British Columbia, 250/387-1642 or 800/435-5622, www.hellobc.com) produce annual accommodation guides that include hotels, motels, lodges, and bed-and-breakfasts, with prices included. The same departments in the Northwest Territories (**Northwest Territories Tourism,** 867/873-7200 or 800/661-0788, www.spectacularnwt.com) and the Yukon (**Tourism Yukon,** 403/667-5340 or 800/661-

0494, www.travelyukon.com) include lodgings in their general travel guides. Each of the above departments will send out these guides for free, or you can download them from their websites.

All rates quoted in this handbook are for the cheapest category of rooms during the most expensive time period (summer). Accommodation prices in Whistler and the national parks of the Canadian Rockies are slashed by as much as 70 percent in shoulder seasons, while in major cities weekend rates are discounted up to 50 percent. To all rates quoted, you must add the 5 percent goods and services tax (GST) and either an 8 percent provincial room tax (British Columbia) or a 4 percent tourism marketing levy (Alberta).

HOTELS AND MOTELS

Hotels and motels of some sort exist in just about every town through western Canada. Check your favorite chain—most are represented, as are locals such as upscale **Delta Hotels and Resorts** (www.deltahotels.com) and **Fairmont Hotels and Resorts** (www.fairmont.com), and the mid-priced **Sandman** (www.sandmanhotels.com).

Ubiquitous park-at-your-door, single-story road motels are located in almost every town and on the outskirts of all major cities. In most cases, rooms are fine, but check before paying, just to make sure. Most motels have a few rooms with kitchenettes, but these fill fast. In the smaller towns, expect to pay $50–80 s, $60–90 d.

Most major towns and all cities have larger hotels, each of which typically has a restaurant, café, lounge, and pool. At these establishments, expect to pay from $70 s, $80 d for a basic room. Downtown hotels in Vancouver, Victoria, Calgary, and Edmonton begin at $120 s or d. A good deal can be suites or executive suites, with kitchenettes and one or two bedrooms for little more than a regular room.

Finding inexpensive lodging in resort areas is difficult in summer. By late afternoon the only rooms left are in the more expensive categories, and by nightfall all of these rooms are booked,

too. Hotel rooms in Whistler and Banff begin around $160.

BED-AND-BREAKFASTS

Bed-and-breakfast accommodations are found throughout western Canada. Staying at this type of accommodation is a great way to meet the locals. They're usually private residences, with up to four guest rooms, and as the name suggests, breakfast is included. Rates fluctuate enormously. In Vancouver and Banff, for example, they start at $80 s, $90 d and go up to more than $200. Guests can expect hearty home cooking, a peaceful atmosphere, personal service, knowledgeable hosts, and conversation with fellow travelers. On the downside, facilities and the amount of privacy afforded can vary greatly. This uncertainty as to what to expect upon arrival can be off-putting for many people, especially sharing a bathroom with other guests—which is a common and accepted practice in European bed-and-breakfasts. If having a bathroom to yourself is important to you, clarify with the bed-and-breakfast operator when reserving. Here is one interpretation of terms:

En suite: Refers to a bathroom that is private, inside, and attached to the sleeping unit (literally "in suite").

Private: A bathroom that is for the sole use of a particular sleeping unit but may be outside of the room.

Shared or semiprivate: Bathrooms that are used in common by more than one room. No more than two guest rooms should share a single bathroom.

These descriptions are courtesy of the **British Columbia Bed & Breakfast Innkeepers Guild** (www.bcsbestbnbs.com), which represents more than 140 bed-and-breakfasts. The association maintains a useful website with simple descriptions and a color photo of each property, with availability shown for many bed-and-breakfasts. In the world of the Internet, **Bed and Breakfast Online** (www.bbcanada.com) is an old-timer, having been online since 1995. You can't make bookings through this company, but links are provided and an ingenious search engine helps you find the accommodation that best fits your needs.

BACKPACKER LODGES

Options for budget travelers in western Canada range from a tree house on Salt Spring Island (Vancouver Island) to a luxurious log lodge at Lake Louise (Banff National Park). **Hostelling International** (formerly the Youth Hostel Association) has undergone a radical change in direction and now appeals to all ages, with a limited number of privately run "hostels" providing other options. Either way, staying in what have universally become known as "backpacker" lodges is an enjoyable and inexpensive way to travel. Generally, you need to provide your own sleeping bag or linen, but most hostels supply extra bedding (if needed) at no charge. Accommodations are in bunk beds (2–10 in each room) or double rooms that share bathrooms. Each also offers a communal kitchen, lounge area, and laundry facilities, while most have Internet access, bike rentals, and organized tours.

Hostelling International-Canada (613/237-7884, www.hihostels.ca) operates 30 hostels across British Columbia and Alberta (none in the NWT or Yukon). High-season rates for members are $17–38 per night, nonmembers $21–42; single and double rooms are more expensive. Whenever you can, make reservations in advance, especially in summer. The easiest way to do this from outside Canada is through Hostelling International's main website (www.hihostels.com).

If you plan to travel extensively using hostels, join Hostelling International before you leave home (otherwise it's $4 extra per night). In Canada, an annual membership for **HI-Canada** (613/237-7884, www.hihostels.ca) is $35. In the United States, membership of **HI-USA** (301/495-1240, www.hiayh.org) is US$28. Other contact addresses include: **YHA England and Wales** (0870/770-8868, www.yha.org.uk), **YHA Australia** (02/9261-1111, www.yha.com), and **YHA New Zealand** (03/379-9970 or 0800/278-299, www.yha.

co.nz). For other countries, click through the links provided at www.hihostels.com.

The privately owned **SameSun Backpacker Lodges** (877/972-6378, www.samesun.com) comprises eight backpacker lodges spread across the two provinces, but you'll find a private lodge in Edmonton and another in Dawson City.

CAMPING AND RV PARKS

Almost every town in western Canada has at least one campground—picnic tables, cook shelters, showers, and powered hookups are standard amenities. Often those campgrounds in smaller towns are a bargain—it's not uncommon to pay less than $20 for a site with hookups and hot showers. In resort towns, camping isn't such a bargain, with most sites in the $30–40 range and a few places charging more than $40 per night (the campground in Whistler tops out at $57). If you're planning a summer trip to Vancouver, Vancouver Island, the Sunshine Coast, Whistler, the Okanagan Valley, Calgary (especially during Stampede), or Edmonton, you should try to book in advance.

Camping facilities in national parks are excellent; most parks have at least one campground with hot showers and hookups. A percentage of sites in most national park campgrounds can be reserved through the **Parks Canada Campground Reservation Service** (450/505-8302 or 877/737-3783, www.pccamping.ca) for a nonrefundable $11 reservation fee. If you're traveling in the height of summer and require electrical hookups, this booking system is highly recommended. The remaining campsites in the national parks operate on a first-come, first-served basis and often fill by midday in July and August.

In British Columbia, you can reserve a spot at the 60 most popular provincial parks by calling **Discover Camping** (604/689-9025 or 800/689-9025, www.discovercamping.ca). Reservations are taken between March 15 and September 15 for dates up to three months in advance. The reservation fee is $6.42 per night, to a maximum of $19.26, and is in addition to applicable camping fees. Reservations for provincial parks in Alberta are made directly with each campground. Contact numbers are given where relevant throughout the travel chapters of this book. In the Northwest Territories, you'll find 21 territorial parks with campgrounds. Three of these, all within the vicinity of Yellowknife, accept bookings through the website www.campingnwt.ca. The reservation fee is $10 per booking.

Campground Terms

Campground operators use a variety of terms to describe the services offered and in this book I have tried to be as consistent as possible. Beginning with an easy one—an **RV** is any type of recreational vehicle, including a fifth-wheeler, motorcoach, campervan, camping trailer, or tent trailer. A **serviced site** is a campsite that offers the individual unit access to power, water, sewer, cable TV, the Internet, or a combination of any of these five services. A site with one or more of these services is known as a **hookup.** Sites with a combination of power, water, and sewer are known as **full hookups.** In this book, if a campground offers power as the only service, the sites are referred to as **powered.** The difference between a **tent site** and an **unserviced site** (one with no hookups) is that RVs are permitted on the later. "Unserviced" does not mean the campground itself lacks facilities such as bathrooms. The term **dry camping** is sometimes used to describe a campsite with no hookups. **Boondocking** can also mean camping without hookups, but more often means simply camping for free in an undesignated area. Finally, a **pull-through** campsite means you can pull right though, with no need to back in or out.

Also, many of the more popular campgrounds, including all provincial parks, charge a **reservation fee** of up to $8 per reservation. This is *not* a deposit, but rather an additional charge.

Backcountry Camping

Backcountry camping in the national parks and Kananaskis Country is $10 per person per night, while a season pass ($70) is valid for unlimited national park backcountry travel and camping for 12 months from its purchase date. Before heading out, you must register at the respective park information center (regardless of whether you have an annual pass) and pick up a Backcountry Permit (for those without an annual pass, this costs the nightly camping fee multiplied by the number of nights you'll be in the backcountry). Many popular backcountry campgrounds take reservations up to three months in advance. The reservation fee is $10 per party per trip. Most campgrounds in the backcountry have pit toilets, and some have bear bins for secure food storage. Fires are discouraged, so bring a stove.

Food and Drink

Canada is not world-renowned for its culinary delights, but the western region does have two specialties. **West coast** cuisine (also called fusion cooking), means an abundance of local seafood (halibut, salmon, crab) and fresh produce prepared with an Asian influence, and is currently the flavor of the month in British Columbia. **Alberta beef,** the staple of that province, is delicious and served in most restaurants. **Game meats,** such as elk and bison, as well as caribou and musk ox, are also widely available farther north. Otherwise, Canadian food is similar to American food—in general, bland and not very interesting.

If you're RVing it or camping, eating cheaply in western Canada is easy. The large grocery chains—**Safeway, Sobeys, Superstore,** and **Overwaitea**—generally have the least expensive groceries, with prices slightly higher than in the United States. In most I.G.A. stores, you'll find an excellent bakery. If you're barbecuing, know that most urban campgrounds discourage open fires, and provincial and national parks charge up to $8 for a small bundle of firewood.

For a three-course meal in a family-style restaurant, including a steak dish, expect to pay $35–45 per person—double that in the better eateries. Vancouver, Victoria, Edmonton, Calgary, and Banff have an astonishing array of ethnic restaurants (Banff, a town of 8,000, has more than 100 restaurants). Inexpensive options are **Husky** restaurants, located in gas stations of the same name along all major routes; **Boston Pizza,** a chain of Canadian family-style restaurants; and **Tim Hortons,** best known for coffee and donuts.

Wine

British Columbian wine is highly regarded, having won awards throughout the world. The province is one of the few places in the world capable of producing ice wines, made by a process in which the grapes aren't harvested until after the first frost; the frost splits the skins and the fermentation process begins with the grapes still on the vine. These concentrated juices from classic varietals such as riesling and Gew ürztraminer create a super-sweet wine. Ice wine is generally marketed in a distinctively narrow 375-ml bottle and promoted as a dessert wine. The largest concentration of vineyards is in the Okanagan Valley, with more than 40 wineries ranging from large-scale commercial operations to small plots of grapes grown on hobby farms. Expect to pay $15–35 for a bottle of locally produced wine.

Beer

Vancouver, Victoria, Calgary, and Edmonton each have specialty brewers that brew boutique

---

WINES OF BRITISH COLUMBIA

Wines from the Okanagan Valley receive acclaim worldwide, although this success is only recent. In fact, it was doubted that quality grapes could be grown north of the 49th parallel until the late 1980s, when most of the original vines were ripped out and replaced with classic European varietals. The valley's climate – long summer days and cool nights – produces small grapes with higher than usual sugar content, creating intensely flavored and aromatic wines. A wide variety of red and white wine grapes are planted, with the reds thriving in the warmer south end of the valley, where merlot, cabernet franc, and pinot noir grapes produce the best local wines. The entire winemaking process in the Okanagan has been one of experimentation, and along the way more unusual varietals such as ehrenfelser and auxerrois have been grown with success, making tasting local wines all the more interesting.

---

beers for sale in the immediate area. Alberta's largest homegrown brewery is **Big Rock** in Calgary. With one of North America's most modern breweries, Big Rock is unique in that it uses all natural ingredients and doesn't pasteurize the finished product; this shortens the shelf life, but a great deal more of the natural flavor is retained. **Kokanee,** brewed in Creston and widely available throughout western Canada, is a fine-tasting beer that should be taken on all camping trips. All the popular Canadian and American beers are available at bars and liquor stores.

Conduct and Customs

As with jurisdictions across North America, the provincial governments of both British Columbia and Alberta struggle with spending and debt issues. Thanks to an abundance of natural resources, though, the standard of living in both provinces is the envy of Canada Although Alberta has been led by a conservative government for seemingly forever, lifestyles in the main urban areas and resort towns are more liberal leaning. The political scene in British Columbia is similar, although the province has been governed by many different parties over the last two decades.

Liquor Laws

Liquor laws in Canada are enacted on a provincial level, with Alberta having the most relaxed version. The minimum age for alcohol consumption in Alberta is 18 (it's 19 in British Columbia, the NWT, and Yukon). Additionally, the liquor industry in Alberta is privatized. This means that there are a lot more liquor stores with less restrictions (open seven days, can sell cold beer, and more). In an interesting twist, liquor stores in the Northwest Territories are operated by the government, but locally brewed beer can be sold in convenience stores.

Like the rest of North America, driving in western Canada under the influence of alcohol or drugs is a criminal offence. Those convicted of driving with a blood alcohol concentration above 0.8 face big fines and an automatic one-year license suspension. Second convictions (even if the first was out of province) lead to a three-year suspension. Note that in both British Columbia and Alberta drivers below the limit can be charged with impaired driving. Alberta operates a Checkstop program, which gives the RCMP the power to stop drivers at random and test for alcohol. It is also illegal to have an open container of alcohol in a vehicle or in public places.

Smoking

Smoking is banned in virtually all public places across Canada. Most provinces have enacted province-wide bans on smoking in public places, including British Columbia and Alberta.

Tipping

Gratuities are not usually added to the bill. In restaurants and bars, around 15 percent of the total amount is expected. But you should tip according to how good (or bad) the service was, as low as 10 percent or up to and over 20 percent for exceptional service. The exception to this rule is groups of eight or more, when it is standard for restaurants to add 15–20 percent as a gratuity. Tips are sometimes added to tour packages, so check this in advance, but you can also tip guides on stand-alone tours. Tips are also given to bartenders, taxi drivers, bellmen, and hairdressers.

Tips for Travelers

EMPLOYMENT AND STUDY

The resort towns of Whistler and Banff are especially popular with young workers from across Canada and beyond. Aside from Help Wanted ads in local papers, a good place to start looking for work is the Whistler Chamber of Commerce (click on Employment Resources at www.whistlerchamber.com) and, in Banff, the **Job Resource Centre** (www.jobresourcecentre.com).

International visitors wishing to work or study in Canada must obtain authorization *before* entering the country. Authorization to work will only be granted if no qualified Canadians are available for the work in question. Applications for work and study are available from all Canadian embassies and must be submitted with a nonrefundable processing fee. The Canadian government has a reciprocal agreement with Australia for a limited number of **holiday work visas** to be issued each year. Australian citizens aged 30 and under are eligible; contact your nearest Canadian embassy or consulate. For general information on immigrating to Canada contact **Citizenship and Immigration Canada** (www.cic.gc.ca).

VISITORS WITH DISABILITIES

A lack of mobility should not deter you from traveling to western Canada, but you should definitely do some research before leaving home.

If you haven't traveled extensively, start by doing some research at the website of the **Access-Able Travel Source** (www.accessable.com), where you will find databases of specialist travel agencies and lodgings in western Canada that cater to travelers with disabilities. **Flying Wheels Travel** (507/451-5005, www.flyingwheelstravel.com) caters solely to the needs of travelers with disabilities. The **Society for Accessible Travel and Hospitality** (212/447-7284, www.sath.org) supplies information on tour operators, vehicle rentals, specific destinations, and companion services. For frequent travelers, the annual membership fee (adult US$45, senior US$30) is well worthwhile. **Emerging Horizons** (www.emerginghorizons.com) is a U.S. quarterly magazine dedicated to travelers with special needs.

Access to Travel (800/465-7735, www.accesstotravel.gc.ca) is an initiative of the Canadian government that includes information on travel within and between Canadian cities, including Calgary and Edmonton. The website also has a lot of general travel information for those with disabilities. The **Canadian National Institute for the Blind** (800/563-2642, www.cnib.ca) offers a wide range of services from its Vancouver (604/431-2121) and Edmonton (780/488-4871) offices. Finally, the **Canadian Paraplegic Association** (613/723-1033 or 877/324-3611, www.canparaplegic.org), with chapter offices in Vancouver and Calgary, is another good source of information.

TRAVELING WITH CHILDREN

Regardless of whether you're traveling with either toddlers or teens, you will come upon decisions affecting everything from where you stay to your choice of activities. Luckily for you, western Canada is very family-friendly, with a variety of indoor and outdoor attractions aimed specifically at the younger generation.

Admission and tour prices for children are included throughout the destination chapters of this book. As a general rule, these reduced prices are for children aged 6–16 years. For two adults and two or more children, always ask about family tickets. Children under 6 nearly always get in free. Most hotels and motels will happily accommodate children, but always try to reserve your room in advance and let the reservations desk know the ages of your kids. Often, children stay free in major hotels, and in the case of some major chains—such as Holiday Inn—eat free also. Generally, bed-and-breakfasts aren't suitable for children, and in some cases don't accept kids at all. Ask ahead.

As a general rule when it comes to traveling with children, let them help you plan the trip, looking at websites and reading up on the province together. To make your vacation more enjoyable if you'll be spending a lot of time on the road, rent a minivan (all major rental agencies have a supply). Don't forget to bring along favorite toys and games from home—whatever you think will keep your kids entertained when the joys of sightseeing wear off.

The websites of **Tourism British Columbia** (www.hellobc.com) and **Travel Alberta** (www.travelalberta.com) have sections devoted to children's activities. Another handy source of information is **Kid Friendly** (604/926-0061, www.kidfriendlycanada.com), a non-profit organization that has compiled an online database of, you guessed it, kid-friendly attractions, lodgings, and restaurants throughout Canadian provinces, including British Columbia. The website even has room for your children to write about their vacation. Another useful online tool is **Traveling Internationally with Your Kids** (www.travelwithyourkids.com).

Health and Safety

Compared to other parts of the world, Canada is a relatively safe place to visit. Vaccinations are required only if coming from an endemic area. That said, wherever you are traveling, carry a medical kit that includes bandages, insect repellent, sunscreen, antiseptic, antibiotics, and water-purification tablets. Good first-aid kits are available at most camping shops. Health care in Canada is mostly dealt with at a provincial level.

Taking out a travel-insurance policy is a sensible precaution because hospital and medical charges start at around $1,000 per day. Copies of prescriptions should be brought to Canada for any medicines already prescribed.

Giardia

Giardiasis, also known as beaver fever, is a real concern for those heading into the backcountry. It's caused by an intestinal parasite, *Giardia lamblia,* that lives in lakes, rivers, and streams. Once ingested, its effects, although not instantaneous, can be dramatic; severe diarrhea, cramps, and nausea are the most common symptoms. Preventive measures should always be taken, including boiling all water for at least 10 minutes, treating all water with iodine, or filtering all water using a filter with a pore size small enough to block the *giardia* cysts.

Winter Travel

Travel through western Canada during winter months should not be undertaken lightly. Before setting out in a vehicle, check antifreeze levels, and always carry a spare tire and blankets or sleeping bags. **Frostbite** is a potential hazard, especially when cold temperatures are combined with high winds (a combination known as **windchill**). Most often, frostbite leaves a numbing, bruised sensation, and the skin turns white. Exposed areas of skin, especially the nose and ears, are most susceptible.

Hypothermia occurs when the body fails to produce heat as fast as it loses it. It can strike at any time of the year but is more common during cooler months. Cold weather, combined with hunger, fatigue, and dampness, creates a recipe for disaster. Symptoms are not always apparent to the victim. The early signs are numbness, shivering, slurring of words, dizzy spells, and, in extreme cases, violent behavior, unconsciousness, and even death. The best way to dress for the cold is in layers, including a waterproof outer layer. Most importantly, wear headgear. The best treatment is to get the victim out of the cold, replace wet clothing with dry, slowly give him or her hot liquids and sugary foods, and place the victim in a sleeping bag. Warming too quickly can lead to heart attacks.

Information and Services

MONEY

As in the United States, Canadian currency is based on dollars and cents. Coins come in denominations of $0.01, $0.05, $0.10, and $0.25, and $1 and $2. The one-dollar coin is the gold-colored "loonie," named for the bird featured on it. The unique two-dollar coin, introduced in 1996, is silver with a gold-colored insert. Notes come in $5, $10, $20, $50, and $100 denominations.

All prices quoted in this book are in Canadian dollars unless otherwise noted. American dollars are accepted at many tourist areas, but the exchange rate is more favorable at banks. Currency other than U.S. dollars can be exchanged at most banks, airport money-changing facilities, and foreign exchange brokers in Vancouver, Victoria, Whistler, Calgary, Banff, Jasper, and Edmonton. Traveler's checks are the safest way to carry money, but a fee is often charged to cash them if they're in a currency other than Canadian dollars. All major credit and charge cards are honored at Canadian banks, gas stations, and most commercial establishments. Automatic teller machines (ATMs) can be found in almost every town.

Costs

The cost of living is lower in western Canada than the eastern provinces and is generally similar to the United States. By planning ahead, having a tent or joining Hostelling International, and being prepared to cook your own meals, it is possible to get by on less than $100 per person per day. Gasoline is sold in liters (3.78 liters equals one U.S. gallon). As of the writing of this edition, gas was from $1 per liter for regular unleaded. In remote areas, such as along the Icefields Parkway (Banff and Jasper National Parks) and in the two territories, the price is higher, up to $1.50 per liter.

Taxes

Canada imposes a 5 percent **goods and services tax (GST)** on most consumer purchases. Purchases in British Columbia incur a 12 percent **harmonized sales tax** onto most purchases, which includes the GST. So when you are looking at the price of anything, remember that the final cost you pay will include an additional 12 percent in taxes. Alberta is the only province that doesn't impose a provincial sales tax. Alberta does have a 4 percent tourism tax on any accommodation with four or more rooms.

COMMUNICATIONS
Postal Services

All **mail** posted in Canada must have Canadian postage stamps attached. First-class letters and postcards are $0.54 to destinations within Canada, $0.98 to the United States, and $1.65 to all other destinations. Post offices are open Monday–Friday only. The website of **Canada Post** is www.canadapost.ca.

Telephone

Except for local calls, all numbers must be dialed with the area code, including long-distance calls from within the same area code. The country code for Canada is 1, the same as the United States. Public phones accept $0.05 $0.10, and $0.25 coins. Local calls from payphones are usually $0.35–0.50 and most long-distance calls cost at least $2.50 for the first minute from public phones. Pre-paid **phone cards,** which are available from gas stations and drug and grocery stores, provide considerable savings for those using public phones. They come in $5–50 amounts.

Internet

It will probably surprise no one that public Internet access is available across western Canada. Most hotels either have wireless or modem access (for a small charge), or a communal business center. Beyond your accommodation, the best place to try for access is local libraries, where more often than not, you only need to show some identification to use a computer. Internet booths can also be found in airports, cafés, and some shopping malls.

MAPS AND TOURIST INFORMATION
Maps

Driving maps are available at bookstores, gas stations, and gift shops throughout western Canada. In Vancouver, pick up maps at these specialty bookstores: **International Travel Maps and Books** (530 W. Broadway, 604/879-3621, www.itmb.com), **The Travel Bug** (3065 W. Broadway, 604/737-1122, www.travelbug-books.ca), or **Wanderlust** (1929 W. 4th Ave., Kitsilano, 604/739-2182, www.wanderlustore. com). In Calgary and Edmonton, contact **Map Town** (Calgary: 400 5th Ave. SW, 403/266-2241, www.maptown.com; Edmonton: 10344 105th St., 780/429-2600, www.mapamia. com). By request, all these retailers can send out a catalog of maps designed specifically for hiking (topographical maps), camping (road/access maps), fishing (hydrographic charts of more than 100 lakes), and canoeing (river details such as gradients). They also supply wall maps, thematic maps, historic maps, and aerial photography. **Gem Trek** (www.gemtrek.com) produces some of the best and most useful maps you're ever likely to find. They specialize in the Canadian Rockies, and the maps are available throughout the region. **Map Art** (905/436-2525, www.mapart.com) produces a variety of maps for the region, including an annual atlas for both British Columbia and Alberta.

Tourist Offices

Begin planning your trip by contacting a government tourist office: **Tourism British Columbia** (250/387-1642 or 800/435-5622, www.hellobc.com), **Travel Alberta** (780/427-4321 or 800/252-3782, www.travelalberta. com), **Northwest Territories Tourism** (867/873-7200 or 800/661-0788, www. spectacularnwt.com), and **Tourism Yukon** (867/667-3084 or 800/661-0494 or 800/661-0494, www.travelyukon.com). Their literature and maps can be downloaded from their websites or ordered by phone. Major cities have multiple tourist information centers, and at least one open year-round. Each town of any size in western Canada has its own information center. Hours vary, but most are open daily in July and August. When these are closed, head to the local chamber of commerce for information. Most chamber offices are open Monday–Friday year-round.

WEIGHTS AND MEASURES

Like every country in the world except the United States, Liberia, and Myanmar, Canada is on the metric system (see the "Metric System" chart at the back of this book), although many people talk about distance in miles and supermarket prices are advertised by ounces and pounds.

Electricity

Electrical voltage is 120 volts, the same as in the United States.

RESOURCES

Suggested Reading

NATURAL HISTORY

The Atlas of Breeding Birds of Alberta. Edmonton: Federation of Alberta Naturalists, 1992. Comprehensive study of all birds that breed in Alberta, with easy-to-read distribution maps, details on nesting and other behavioral patterns, and color plates.

Aulenback, Kevin. *Identification Guide to the Fossil Plants of the Horseshoe Canyon Formation of Drumheller, Alberta*. Edmonton: University of Alberta Press, 2009. While there are many books about the dinosaurs of Alberta, this is the only one in print devoted to the plants that existed during the dinosaur era.

Baldwin, John. *Mountain Madness: Exploring British Columbia's Ultimate Wilderness*. Vancouver: Harbour Publishing, 1999. Filled with stunning photography, this coffee table book is a worthwhile purchase for climbers or anyone interested in the natural landscapes of the Coast Mountains.

Cannings, Richard. *British Columbia: Natural History*. Vancouver: Douglas & McIntyre, 2004. The natural history of the province divided into 10 chapters, from the earliest origins of the land to problems faced in the new millennium. It includes lots of color photos, diagrams, and maps.

Folkens, Peter. *Marine Mammals of British Columbia and the Pacific Northwest*. Vancouver: Harbour Publishing, 2001. In a waterproof, fold-away format, this booklet provides vital identification tips and habitat maps for 50 marine mammals, including all species of whales present in local waters.

Foster, John E., Dick Harrison, and I. S. MacLaren, eds. *Buffalo*. Edmonton: University of Alberta Press, 1992. A series of essays by noted historians and experts in the field of the American bison, addressing their disappearance from the prairies and the development of buffalo jumps. One essay deals with Wood Buffalo National Park.

Gadd, Ben. *Handbook of the Canadian Rockies*. Jasper: Corax Press, 2009. The latest edition of this classic guide is in color, and although bulky for backpackers it's a must-read for anyone interested in the natural history of the Canadian Rockies.

Gill, Ian. *Haida Gwaii: Journeys through the Queen Charlotte Islands*. Vancouver: Raincoast Publishing, 1997. A personal and touching view of the Queen Charlottes complemented by the stunning color photography of David Nunuk.

Haig Brown, Roderick. *Return to the River*. Vancouver: Douglas & McIntyre, 1997. Although fictional, this story of the life of one salmon and its struggle through life is based on fact, and is a classic read for both anglers and naturalists. It was originally published in 1946 but has recently been reprinted and is available at most bookstores.

Herrero, Stephen. *Bear Attacks: Their Causes and Avoidances.* Toronto: McClelland & Stewart, 2003. Through a series of gruesome stories, this book catalogs the stormy relationship between people and bruins, provides hints on avoiding attacks, and tells what to do in case you're attacked.

Jones, Karen. *Wolf Mountains.* Calgary: University of Calgary Press, 2002. Explores the history of wolves in the Canadian Rockies, with emphasis on the often controversial relationship between man and wolf.

Marty, Sid. *The Black Grizzly of Whiskey Creek.* Toronto: McClelland & Stewart, 2008. True story of a grizzly bear that went on a terrifying rampage near the town of Banff.

Musiani, Marco. *A New Era for Wolves and People.* Calgary: University of Calgary Press, 2009. A detailed analysis of the relationship between wolves and people in both North America and Europe. All contributors are wolf experts; includes stunning images.

Patterson, W. S. *The Physics of Glaciers.* Toronto: Pergamon Press, 1969. A highly technical look at all aspects of glaciation: why glaciers form, how they flow, and their effect on the environment.

Rezendes, Paul. *Tracking and the Art of Seeing.* Charlotte, Virginia: Camden House Publishing, 1992. This is one of the best of many books dedicated to tracking the North American mammals. It begins with a short essay on the relationship of humans with nature.

Sharp, Robert P. *Living Ice: Understanding Glaciers and Glaciation.* Cambridge, England: Cambridge University Press, 1988. A detailed but highly readable book on the formation, types, and results of glaciers.

Whitaker, John. *National Audubon Society Field Guide to North American Mammals.* New York: Random House, 1997. One of a series of field guides produced by the National Audubon Society, this one details mammals through color plates and detailed descriptions of characteristics, habitat, and range.

HUMAN HISTORY

Allen, D. *Totem Poles of the Northwest.* Surrey, British Columbia: Hancock House Publishers Ltd., 1977. Describes the importance of totem poles to native culture and totem pole sites and their history.

Bone, Robert. *The Geography of the Canadian North.* Toronto: Oxford University Press, 1992. An in-depth look at the role Canada's north has played and will play in the management of world resources, and the impact of self-government on the region.

Brado, Edward. *Cattle Kingdom: Early Ranching in Alberta.* Victoria: Heritage House, 2009. Details the colorful story of early ranchers, from the days of trading posts through to modern day cowboys and the Calgary Stampede.

Burton, Pierre. *Klondike: The Last Great Gold Rush, 1896–1899.* The Klondike gold rush is brought to life by Canada's preeminent historian/writer in this book that has been reprinted many times, most recently by Random House in 2001.

Duff, Wilson. *The Indian History of British Columbia: The Impact of the White Man.* Victoria: University of British Columbia Press, 1997. In this book Duff deals with the issues faced by natives in the last 150 years but also gives a good overview of their general history.

Engler, Bruno. *Bruno Engler Photography.* Calgary: Rocky Mountain Books, 2002. Swiss-born Engler spent 60 years exploring and photographing the Canadian Rockies. This impressive hardcover book showcases over 150 of his most timeless images.

Hewitt, Steve. *Riding to the Rescue.* Toronto: University of Toronto Press, 2006. This book examines the influence of Royal Canadian Mounted Police from WWI to the late 1930s, when they morphed from iconic horsemen to a modern police force.

Jenness, Diamond. *The Indians of Canada.* Toronto: University of Toronto Press, 1977. Originally published in 1932, this is the classic study of natives in Canada, although Jenness's conclusion, that they were facing certain extinction by "the end of this century," is obviously outdated.

Lavallee, Omer. *Van Horne's Road.* Montreal: Railfare Enterprises, 1974. William Van Horne was instrumental in the construction of Canada's first transcontinental railway. This is the story of his dream, and the boomtowns that sprung up along the route. Lavallee devotes an entire chapter to telling the story of the railway's push over the Canadian Rockies.

Mallory, Enid. *Robert Service: Under the Spell of the Yukon.* Vancouver: Heritage House, 2006. Follows the life of Robert Service, best known for poems such as "The Cremation of Sam McGee," from the time he stepped off a ship in Vancouver to his wildly successful change in careers in Dawson City.

McMillan, Alan D. *Native Peoples and Cultures of Canada.* Vancouver: Douglas & McIntyre, 1995. A comprehensive look at the archaeology, anthropology, and ethnography of the native peoples of Canada. The last chapters delve into the problems facing these people today.

Murray, Tom. *Canadian Pacific Railway.* Osceola, Wisconsin: Voyageur Press, 2006. Railway buffs are spoilt for choice when it comes to reading about the history of Canada's

transcontinental railway, but this large format book stands apart for its presentation of historic images and coverage of the railway industry today.

Nikiforuk, Andrew. *Tar Sands: Dirty Oil and the Future of a Continent.* Vancouver: Greystone Books, 2008. From this book's subtitle, it's easy to tell that this is a critical look at the industry for which Alberta is best known.

Reksten, Terry. *Rattenbury.* Winlaw, British Columbia: Sono Nis Press, 1998. The biography of Francis Rattenbury, British Columbia's preeminent architect at the beginning of the 20th century. The histories of his most famous Victoria and Vancouver buildings are given, and the final chapter looks at his infamous murder at the hands of his wife's young lover.

Schäffer, Mary T. S. *A Hunter of Peace.* Banff: Whyte Museum of the Canadian Rockies, 1980. This book was first published in 1911 by G. P. Putnam & Sons, New York, under the name *Old Indian Trails of the Canadian Rockies.* Tales recount the exploration of the Rockies during the turn of the century. Many of the author's photographs appear throughout.

Scott, Chic. *Pushing the Limits.* Calgary: Rocky Mountain Books, 2000. A chronological history of mountaineering in Canada, with special emphasis on many largely unknown climbers and their feats, as well as the story of Swiss guides in Canada and a short section on ice climbing.

Turner, Dick. *Nahanni.* Surrey, British Columbia: Hancock House, 1975. One of the north's most celebrated authors recounts stories of early life in the north and particularly on the South Nahanni River.

Twigger, Robert. *Voyageur: Across the Rocky Mountains in a Birchbark Canoe.* London: Weidenfeld, 2006. This is the rollicking tale of author Twigger's adventures building a canoe and crossing the Canadian Rockies on a diet of porridge, fish, and whisky—exactly as Alexander Mackenzie had 200 years previously.

Woodman, David C. *Unravelling the Franklin Mystery.* Montreal: McGill-Queen's University Press, 1991. Many volumes have been written on the ill-fated Franklin Expedition. This one, using Inuit recollections, is among the best.

RECREATION

Christie, Jack. *52 Best Day Trips from Vancouver.* Vancouver: Douglas & McIntyre, 2007. Although the organization of this book is sometimes difficult to follow, it is the most comprehensive guide available to all recreational opportunities in the vicinity of Vancouver, especially the provincial parks. Jack Christie is a prolific author who also writes *Best Weekend Getaways from Vancouver* and *The Whistler Book* (both published by Douglas & McIntyre, Vancouver).

Corbett, Bill. *Best of Alberta: Day Trips from Calgary.* Vancouver: Whitecap Books, 2006. Multiple books have been written about the things to do and see in Banff, which this book covers, along with dozens of ideas for daytripping south and north of the famous park and all within a two-hour drive of Calgary.

Gadd, Ben. *The Canadian Hiker's and Backpacker's Handbook.* Vancouver: Whitecap Books, 2008. Whether you're interested in learning the basics or are a seasoned traveler, this is the best book for reading up on your backcountry and hiking skills.

Gersh-Young, Marjorie. *Hot Springs and Hot Pools of the Northwest.* Santa Cruz: Aqua Thermal Access, 2008. Details the most popular hot springs including those in British Columbia, including both commercial and undeveloped sites. A short history, directions, and practicalities are given for each one.

Mitchell, Barry. *Alberta's Trout Highway.* Red Deer: Nomad Creek Books, 2001. "Alberta's Trout Highway" is the Forestry Trunk Road (Hwy. 40), which runs the length of Alberta's foothills. Entertaining and useful descriptions of Mitchell's favorite fishing holes are accompanied by maps and plenty of background information.

Patton, Brian, and Bart Robinson. *Canadian Rockies Trail Guide.* Banff: Summerthought Publishing, 2007. Now in its eighth edition, this is the ultimate authority for hiking in the Canadian Rockies. It covers 230 trails and 3,400 kilometers (2,100 miles) in the mountain national parks as well as in surrounding provincial parks. A full page is devoted to each trail, making it the most comprehensive hiking book available.

OTHER GUIDEBOOKS AND MAPS

Andrews, D. Larraine. *The Cowboy Trail.* Edmonton: Blue Couch Books, 2006. This book explores the route north through the Alberta foothills from the U.S. border in the south to Highway 16 in the north. Includes detailed information on everything from ranch vacations to toponymy.

Backroad Mapbooks. Vancouver: Mussio Ventures. This western Canada atlas series is perfect for outdoor enthusiasts, with detailed maps, and highlights such as campgrounds, fishing spots, and swimming holes. www.backroadmapbooks.com.

Gem Trek Publishing. Victoria, British Columbia. This company produces tear-proof maps for all regions of the Canadian Rockies. Relief shading clearly and concisely shows elevation, and all hiking trails have been plotted using GPS. On the back of each map are descriptions of attractions and hikes, along with general practical and educational information. www.gemtrek.com.

MapArt. Driving maps for all of Canada, including provinces and cities. Maps are published as old-fashioned fold-out versions, as well as laminated and in atlas form. www. mapart.com.

The Milepost. Bellevue, Washington: Vernon Publications. This annual publication is a must-have for those traveling through western Canada and Alaska. The maps and logged highway descriptions are incredibly detailed. Most northern bookstores stock *The Milepost,* or you can order it by calling 800/726-4707 or visiting the website www.milepost.com.

Patton, Brian. *Parkways of the Canadian Rockies* Banff: Summerthought Publishing, 2008. A comprehensive map and driving guide to Canadian Rockies' highways. Includes color photography and details of many short hikes.

MAGAZINES

Beautiful British Columbia. Victoria. This quarterly magazine depicts the beauty of the province through stunning color photography and informative prose. It's available by subscription (www.bcmag.ca).

The Canadian Alpine Journal. Canmore, Alberta. Annual magazine of the Alpine Club of Canada with articles from its members and climbers from around the world. www. alpineclubofcanada.ca.

Canadian Geographic. Ottawa: Royal Canadian Geographical Society. Bimonthly publication pertaining to Canada's natural and human histories and resources. www.canadiangeographic.ca.

Explore. Calgary. Bimonthly publication of adventure travel throughout Canada. www. explore-mag.com.

Nature Canada. Ottawa, Ontario. Quarterly magazine of the Canadian Nature Federation. www.cnf.ca.

Up Here. Yellowknife. Magazine of life in Canada's North. Eight issues annually. www. uphere.ca.

Western Living. Vancouver, British Columbia. Lifestyle magazine for western Canada. Includes travel, history, homes, and cooking. www.westernliving.ca.

FREE CATALOGS

Accommodations. Tourism British Columbia. Updated annually, this free booklet is available at information centers throughout British Columbia or by calling 250/387-1642 or 800/435-5622, or online at www.hellobc. com.

Alberta Accommodation Guide. Lists all hotel, motel, and other lodging in the province. Available through Travel Alberta (780/427-4321 or 800/252-3782, www.travelalberta. com) or from local information centers. The online version is at www.explorealberta. com.

Alberta Campground Guide. Alberta Hotel & Lodging Association. Lists all campgrounds in the province. Available through Travel Alberta (780/427-4321 or 800/252-3782, www. travelalberta.com) or from local information centers. The online version is at www.explorealberta.com.

Tour Book: Western Canada and Alaska. Booklet available to members of the Canadian or American Automobile Association.

Internet Resources

TRAVEL PLANNING

Canadian Tourism Commission
www.canadatourism.com
Official tourism website for all of Canada.

Tourism British Columbia
www.hellobc.com
Learn more about the province, plan your travels, and order tourism literature.

Travel Alberta
www.travelalberta.com
Learn more about the province, plan your travels, and order tourism literature. This official tourism site also has up-to-date event calendars, tips for traveling with children, and an extensive library of images.

PARKS

Parks Canada
www.pc.gc.ca
Official website of the agency that manages Canada's national parks and national historic sites. Website has information on each of western Canada's national parks (fees, camping, and wildlife) and national historic sites.

Parks Canada Campground Reservation Service
www.pccamping.ca
Online reservation service for national park campgrounds.

GOVERNMENT

Citizenship and Immigration Canada
www.cic.gc.ca
Check this government website for anything related to entry into Canada.

Environment Canada
www.weatheroffice.gc.ca
Five-day forecasts from across Canada, including almost 300 locations through western Canada. Includes weather archives such as seasonal trends and snowfall history.

Government of Canada
www.gc.ca
The official website of the Canadian government.

CONSERVATION

Biosphere Institute of the Bow Valley
www.biosphereinstitute.org
Canmore-based organization mandated to gather and circulate information on management of the Bow River watershed. Online references includes studies, publications, and human-use guidelines for the region.

Bow Valley Wildsmart
www.wildsmart.ca
This non-profit organization has put together a wealth of information on how to stay safe in the Bow Valley watershed, including reported wildlife sightings.

Canadian Parks and Wilderness Society
www.cpaws.org
Non-profit organization that is instrumental in highlighting conservation issues throughout Canada. The link to the Calgary chapter provides local information and a schedule of guided walks.

Yellowstone to Yukon Conservation Initiative
www.y2y.net
Network of 800 groups working on conservation issues along the Canadian Rockies from the United States north to the Yukon.

Yukon Conservation Society
www.yukonconservation.org
This Whitehorse-based organization is active in a variety of natural resource issues, but also offers public programs of hikes and lectures.

TRANSPORTATION AND TOURS

Air Canada
www.aircanada.ca

Canada's national airline.

Brewster
www.brewster.ca

Banff-based operator offering day trips, airport shuttles, and package tours throughout western Canada.

Rocky Mountaineer Vacations
www.rockymountaineer.com

Luxurious rail service to and from Vancouver to Banff and Jasper, including via Whistler.

VIA Rail
www.viarail.ca

Passenger rail service across Canada.

PUBLISHERS

Gem Trek
www.gemtrek.com

You can pick up basic park maps free from local information centers, but this company produces much more detailed maps covering all the most popular regions of the Canadian Rockies.

Heritage House
www.heritagehouse.ca

With more than 700 non-fiction books in print, this large Vancouver publisher is known for its historical and recreation titles covering all of western Canada.

Lone Pine
www.lonepinepublishing.com

Respected for its field guides, this company has books on almost every natural history subject pertinent to western Canada.

Rocky Mountain Books
www.rmbooks.com

Check out the catalog of this Calgary publisher and you'll surely be impressed by the list of outdoor recreation guides.

Summerthought Publishing
www.summerthought.com

If you plan on doing lots of hiking, you'll want a copy of the authoritative *Canadian Rockies Trail Guide* by this Banff publisher.

Index

W

List of Maps